T0338991

METTERNICH

Metternich

STRATEGIST AND VISIONARY

Wolfram Siemann

Translated by Daniel Steuer

THE BELKNAP PRESS OF
HARVARD UNIVERSITY PRESS
Cambridge, Massachusetts
London, England

First Harvard University Press paperback edition, 2023
First printing

Originally published in German as *Metternich: Stratege und Visionär, eine Biografie,* by Wolfram Siemann, revised edition, 2017, © Verlag C. H. Beck oHG, München 2016

The translation of this work was funded by Geisteswissenschaften International—Translation Funding for Humanities and Social Sciences from Germany, a joint initiative of the Fritz Thyssen Foundation, the German Federal Foreign Office, the collecting society VG WORT, and the Börsenverein des Deutschen Buchhandels (German Publishers and Booksellers Association).

Library of Congress Cataloging-in-Publication Data
Names: Siemann, Wolfram, author. | Steuer, Daniel, translator.
Title: Metternich : strategist and visionary / Wolfram Siemann ; translated by Daniel Steuer.
Other titles: Metternich. English
Description: Cambridge, Massachusetts : The Belknap Press of Harvard University Press, 2019. |
    "Originally published in German as Metternich: Stratege und Visionär, eine Biografie,
    by Wolfram Siemann, revised edition, 2017, (c) Verlag C. H. Beck oHG, München 2016."—Title
    page verso | Includes bibliographical references and index.
Identifiers: LCCN 2019005672 | ISBN 9780674743922 (cloth : alk. paper) | ISBN 9780674292185 (pbk.)
Subjects: LCSH: Metternich, Clemens Wenzel Lothar, Fürst von, 1773–1859. | Statesmen—Austria—
    Biography. | Diplomats—Austria—Biography. | Austria—History—1789–1900. | Europe—Politics
    and government—1789–1900.
Classification: LCC DB80.8.M57 S5313 2019 | DDC 940.27092 [B]—dc23
LC record available at https://lccn.loc.gov/2019005672

Frontispiece: Portrait of Metternich by François Gérard (1810; copy)

CONTENTS

A NOTE ON THE FRONTISPIECE

It has not been possible to trace the history of the oil painting by the French painter François Gérard (1770–1837) in the usual catalogues of art history or by other means. This is not surprising, given that there is apparently only one privately owned original and one copy, which is kept at Königswart Castle. The painting is often dated in relation to reproductions, in particular an engraving in the portrait collection at the Austrian National Library that was made by the Viennese copperplate engraver David Weiß (1775–1846) on the basis of the oil painting. The original is sometimes dated between 1808 and 1809 (see, e.g., Husslein-Arco, *Europa in Wien;* illustration of the suspected original on p. 166, dated 1809 on pp. 165 and 167). This date, however, cannot be correct, because the painting shows Metternich with the collar of the Order of the Golden Fleece, which the emperor did not bestow on Metternich until March 10, 1810 (the document is dated March 15, 1810). Napoleon's much sought-after court painter created portraits of the emperor and his family, of rulers, statesmen, and generals and their wives, but rarely of envoys in Paris, which is what Metternich was until 1809. In 1810, Metternich returned to the court in Paris on the occasion of Marie Louise and Napoleon's wedding—this time as minister of foreign affairs and as a celebrated escort of the bride. He stayed from March 28 to September 24, 1810. According to the former curator, Miloš Řiha, the painting at Königswart Castle is marked "Copy of 1810." It was therefore Gérard who produced the original portrait of the thirty-seven-year-old Metternich as well as the copy in the summer of 1810 in Paris.

TRANSLATOR'S NOTE

The story of the publication of Metternich's posthumous papers, including their subsequent translation into English, is not an altogether happy one. The present biography is mostly based on archival sources (that is, the original texts), but the eight volumes edited by Metternich's son Richard between 1880 and 1884 often differ from these. The five-volume English edition of the *Memoirs of Prince Metternich*, in turn, represents a selection from the German edition (only part of which, incidentally, is a memoir in the conventional sense, while the remainder consists of letters, memoranda, and various other documents). And this English translation is not completely free of error—even, at times, error that turns the proper meaning into its opposite.

In light of this, the translation of Metternich's own words, in case of doubt, follows the authoritative quoted version, based on the archival sources, while citations in the notes are given to both the German and English published versions, as few readers will have the privilege of being able to consult the original sources. Where the existing English translation has had to be corrected, this is indicated by "transl. modified" in cases involving light editing, and "transl. amended" in cases in which the text has had to be changed substantially.

At the time of Metternich's career as a diplomat and politician, French was the official language of diplomacy, and many of his communications were, accordingly, written in French. Occasionally, where the French original captures a particular nuance that might otherwise be lost, it was included in the German edition of this book, and in such cases the French has also been included in this translation.

German titles, names of institutions, and terms have been retained, or added in brackets, where no good English equivalent exists, or where a specific meaning is attached to a term. A case in point is the seemingly innocuous word *Ruhe*. Following the Prussian defeat at Jena / Auerstedt, the Prussian governor of Berlin published an appeal containing the phrase "Ruhe ist die erste Bürger-pflicht," or "the foremost duty of the citizen is to remain calm." This became proverbial, and the term *Ruhe* therefore acquired a very specific semantic penumbra. Because one of the central themes of this book is Metternich's aim of creating and maintaining peace, *Friede* must be clearly distinguished from *Ruhe,* which implies the maintenance of social order.

Explanatory notes by the translator have been added where an English-speaking audience might be less familiar with a name or event than would a German-speaking audience. Some notes have also been added concerning information on the texts involved. All such notes have been kept to a minimum.

All emphases are in the original, unless otherwise indicated.

PREFACE TO THE ENGLISH-LANGUAGE EDITION

Clemens von Metternich, the state chancellor of the old Habsburg monarchy, has given his name to an entire era: the "age of Metternich." The picture that history has so far formed of this man has been a highly ambivalent one. His opponents past and present have cast him as a villain and evil character, and historians of a nationalistic bent—with his best-known biographer, Heinrich von Srbik, setting the tone for that group—have judged him to be a cunning, womanizing, effeminate, and cosmopolitan enemy of the German nation, and even of the very notion of nationality. In the history of international relations, by contrast, where questions of war and peace are of paramount importance, the view of him has always been a different one, and this is especially the case in the Anglophone world. The former U.S. secretary of state Henry Kissinger was one of the most famous proponents of an alternative view, which, in 1954, he put forward in the still widely read book *A World Restored: Metternich, Castlereagh, and the Problems of Peace.* Kissinger highlighted one of Metternich's most important insights, namely that lasting peace can only be secured through an international balance of power based on a shared legal order. This biography places this insight at the center of its narrative, arguing that Metternich's long-term master plan was to secure a peace based on solidarity and consensus. Looking at the world today, it is obvious that for this reason Metternich is to be considered not only a major historical figure but also someone whose principles may still be of considerable importance. As this positive perspective on Metternich is associated in particular with the Anglophone world, I had always hoped that my biography might also become available to an English-speaking audience.

There is a second, hitherto unacknowledged, reason for Anglophone readers, in particular, to be interested in Metternich. On one occasion, in private conversation with Dorothea von Lieven, the wife of the Russian ambassador in London, Metternich, who was of course a German from the Rhineland, said, "Austria is my moral fatherland." But he immediately added: "If I were not what I am, I would like to be an Englishman. If I could be neither the one nor the other I would rather be nothing at all." This biography shows in detail, for the first time, that from an early age and throughout his life Metternich was an admirer of the English political system, which he considered to be the best in the world, albeit a system not yet realizable under the social and political conditions that prevailed in the continental Europe of his time. He was strongly influenced by Edmund Burke and also by his personal experiences of the British parliament, whose sittings he attended while staying in London. To him, this system represented what he called a "historically evolved constitutionalism" and embodied the ideal of a pragmatic, rather than doctrinal or ideological, conservatism. Metternich retained a life-long enthusiasm for all things English, including parliamentary government, Burke's *Reflections on the Revolution in France,* and English society in general. In his later years, he even discovered the writings of Alexis de Tocqueville and—to the great surprise of an American visitor of his—developed a solid understanding of the peculiarities of American democracy.

This book is the first biography of Metternich to be thoroughly based on archival material. For the first time, the family archives in Prague, which include Metternich's extensive personal papers, his library at Königswart Castle, and the documents of the Rhenish Johannisberg archive were systematically consulted. Starting work on the documents in the family archive made me feel as though I was Howard Carter discovering the tomb of Tutankhamun. These previously unknown documents provided a view of another Metternich, of Metternich the "strategist and visionary" and, as I have mentioned, of Metternich the Anglophile—aspects of the man that had gone unnoticed.

Readers are likely to discover similarities between Metternich's time and our own. That was not my intention at the outset. I did not want to push the issue of Metternich's contemporary relevance in order to make him appear more important. In my eyes, he is not a "hero," and in any case this is not how historians should approach their subjects. Historians should attempt to leave the moral prejudices of their own times behind and try to understand the mentality and intellectual attitudes of the past, in this case a past more than two hundred years away. My aim was to reconstruct Metternich's intentions, achievements, and failures; I wanted to demonstrate the incongruence between what he wanted and what he was able to do. But, astonishingly, Metternich nevertheless ended up coming across as a surprisingly "modern" figure, and not only because of his views on war and peace. To us who live in an age in which terrorists massacre innocent bystanders in the name of a higher cause, the unprovoked killing of the writer August von Kotzebue by the student Carl Ludwig Sand—also in the name of some higher ideal—appears just as reprehensible as it did to most people at the time. The countermeasures taken in response to Kotzebue's murder and other violent incidents may be compared to the activities of modern intelligence services and the other state institutions responsible for safeguarding constitutions. The Holy Roman Empire and the Habsburg monarchy were not kinds of nation-states, nor were they "failed" nation-states; they were historically evolved legal orders that are best understood as composite monarchies and multinational orders. Much like the European Union today, they tried to find a solution to the problem of how to guarantee harmony and unity between different nationalities in a way that advances the common interests of all. In the case of the Swiss confederation we may consider this experiment to be a successful one; in the case of the EU, the outcome is yet to be determined.

This book tells about a fictional journey into the past, and, as a kind of travel guide, the author often has occasion to stop and pause. He would be content if, in the end, those following him on this tour of Metternich's "life in seven stages" came to know an important figure of world history a little better and formed their own judgment on that figure's successes and failures. If he also succeeded in opening up a new and broader perspective on the major transitional period that took place in Europe and across the Atlantic between the time of the French Revolution and the dawn of nation-states after the revolutions of 1848, then the book's subtitle—"strategist and visionary"—would be truly justified.

METTERNICH

INTRODUCTION

A LIFE IN SEVEN STAGES

Before writing the major biography you hold in your hands, I published a rough sketch of Metternich's life in the form of a slim monograph which appeared in 2010. It may therefore be appropriate to say a few words about the difference between the two texts. It would, of course, have been impermissible simply to retell the story of this important statesman in an expanded version that retained the same style. A short sketch tempts an author to present the results in advance and to give a picture of the protagonist's personality and character in the beginning, when the reader should, in fact, gradually become familiar with them in the course of the narrative. The larger canvas of a full biography permits the biographer to take a different approach, and it affords greater freedom. It allows the author to adopt a different role—as it were, that of a knowledgeable companion and travel guide, one who takes a curious reader on a journey through the past. Thus, together we shall immerse ourselves in historical epochs and landscapes that have long since become alien to us. And the life we will be concerned with on our travels covers more historical epochs than most other statesmen have been able to experience—let alone to help shape, over the course of some fifty years, and then comment upon in retrospect.

If we leave aside the origins of the Metternich family, which go back to the Middle Ages, we shall be traversing seven past landscapes, separated by six historical transition points that mark alterations in the political system. Together, they led Metternich and his contemporaries from the age of the ancien régime right up to the beginnings of modernity in the nineteenth century. The remainder of this introduction is a short travel brochure, indicating what the reader who wants to go with us on this journey through these seven epochs can expect to see. We may define a historical experience as being of an epochal nature if it engraved the collective memory of its contemporaries with such force that, throughout their lifetimes, it did not let go of them and kept resurfacing in their conversations, recollections, and interpretations. For each of our seven epochal experiences, our brochure will also briefly indicate the perspectives from which they were perceived at the extreme ends of the political spectrum.

1. The first of Metternich's seven epochs lasted from his early childhood to the formative years of his youth (1773–1788). He was a sensitive observer, and during those years he witnessed the splendor and apocalyptic atmosphere of the ancien régime, as well as the intellectual fascination of the Enlightenment sweeping through aristocratic and bourgeois circles. The years between 1766 and 1777, in particular, saw the formation of a coherent generation, which would go on to provide Europe with its leading intellectual, political, and military figures. It was for this generation, which we shall later have occasion to characterize more precisely, that the historiographical labels "Generation Metternich" (for those born around 1773) and, seen from the opposite end of the political spectrum, so to speak, "Generation Bonaparte" (beginning in 1769) were coined.[1] All its members were embedded within the old cosmopolitan Europe of enlightened erudition as it could be found, in a more reserved style, in the busy metropolis of London, in fiery style in the seething intellectual hotbed that was Paris, and in a more measured and engaged style of laborious elaboration on the pulpits and in the offices of many German university and residential towns, where the attempt was made to combine the tradition of German public law, which reached back hundreds of years, with the challenges of enlightened rationality.

2. This old cosmopolitan Europe disintegrated under the onslaught of a dual crisis. When the Atlantic revolutions captured the old Continent in the form of the French Revolution in 1789, they drew in the young Metternich and his family as they steamrolled over the Rhineland, the Austrian Netherlands, and the United Provinces. In a first war (1792–1797), a coalition of German, Dutch, Spanish, British, Italian, and Russian troops tried to fend off the new age that was dawning. While some of his contemporaries still harbored timid hopes for a reform of the old "German freedom," others believed that they would not be able to break the resistance of the old powers without terror.

3. In the almost twenty-five years from 1792 to 1815, which saw an almost un-interrupted world war raging (and, given what scholars have established about these years, it is no exaggeration to say this), Metternich experienced this new kind of clash between nations and empires, first as an envoy, then as the foreign minister of the Austrian monarchy. Napoleon, the alleged "world soul on horseback," in Hegel's words,[2] put his stamp on this conflict. For some he was the "man of the century," for others an example of the worst kind of military despot. It was an epoch which confused those living through it, not least the peoples that were subjected to foreign rule: it produced bloody wars of unprecedented proportions at the same time as it promised freedom and moral progress for mankind. The Napoleonic myth seemed to embody this Janus-faced nature almost perfectly. What war actually meant, what it brought about, and how one might use it in new ways for the purpose of progress and in order to ruthlessly destroy one's enemies—these were among the questions which occupied the Metternich generation.

4. The following epoch comprises the years 1815 to 1830. It saw what Paul Schroeder called the "construction of the nineteenth-century system" of European states, which remained in place between the Vienna Congress of 1814–1815 and the European revolutions of 1848–1849. This system functioned as a large and effective mechanism for the prevention of wars and revolutions, and within it Metternich acted as the "coachman of Europe," to go by the not entirely accurate epithet he was given. He himself believed that the fragile European structure could only, at best, be patched up and given a series of makeshift repairs that might, perhaps, succeed in avoiding another great European war. Such a war, he believed, would be more devastating than any of the previous ones. To his enemies, this was the politics of Metternich's "restoration."

5. In 1830, this new war, so feared by Metternich, seemed to be in the cards. Starting out from Paris, the July Revolution spread to most of the European Continent, especially to its southern parts. From then on, people's expectations oscillated between two poles. On the one hand, there were hopes for a "spring of nations," which, however, could be brought about only by a large uprising, or perhaps by a massive war waged by an alliance of the enslaved peoples. This outcome was propagated by the "Young Germany," the "Young" Poland, Italy, or Hungary. On the other hand, there was the constant fear of a renewed outbreak of an uncontrollable terror which might entail the collapse of all civilization.

6. The sixth epochal experience emerged out of the European revolutions of 1848–1849. For some, these signaled a move toward unified nation-states with free and democratic Constitutions. For others, Metternich among them, the

revolutions meant the beginning of a time in exile and represented an unresolved crisis within the process of modernization. It was this crisis which fueled the growth of nationalism in the first place and thus destroyed the relations between the old states of Europe.

7. The seventh epoch, finally, comprised the mastery of the revolutions, the "reaction," and—in the case of the Habsburg Monarchy—a long-overdue bureaucratic modernization in the form of neo-absolutism. Metternich, as his first major biographer, Heinrich von Srbik, wrote, observed all this "from his box seat." Nevertheless, he continued to pull strings in the background (to an extent that has fully been appreciated only recently), and his advice continued to be in demand among political insiders. This period extended beyond the collapse of the "Vienna system" in the course of the Crimean War (1853–1856) and reached up to the first battles between the emerging nation-states. From 1859 onward, the Habsburg Monarchy was involuntarily drawn into these first wars between the emerging nation-states. Metternich, who died in 1859, saw his legacy, if there was a legacy, ultimately gambled away.

Thus, in Metternich's life seven decisive experiences, each of which constitutes an epoch, follow on from one another: the Enlightenment, the French Revolution, the permanent existential threat of a war, the reconstruction of Europe ("restoration"), the "spring of nations," the revolutionary crisis within the process of modernization, and the conflicts between nations that led to the formation of nation-states. In another historical age, each of these epochs would have sufficed to fill the life of a whole generation—in our case, all seven of them were experienced by one individual. How did this shape him? Metternich, at one and the same time a descendant of a storied family of counts and an enlightened free spirit, saw old orders perish, including—almost—that of his own aristocratic house, the Metternichs. Before his eyes, new orders emerged, and he helped in building them. This forced him to live through the times of changing discourses that marked the path from the old European ("feudal") society of estates to a market-based capitalism. He was born as a member of the nobility of the Holy Roman Empire, a nobility that depended upon the peasantry, and from this, as the owner of an ironworks with a workforce of 400, he grew into the role of a manufacturer in the early industrial era.

Earlier biographies of Metternich, without exception, assume an almost static core to his personality. They do not consider the possibility that the decisive and system-toppling experiences he underwent might also have left their traces and transformations in his life. From the earliest days of his youth up until his old age, Metternich was a *Homo scribens,* an intellectual, whom many, including his main biographer, Heinrich von Srbik, erroneously pegged as a rigid doctrinal thinker. But as an intellectual, Metternich used his ongoing writing as a way of constantly assuring himself of his motivations and his goals. He was an avid reader, too, even on his weeks-long travels by coach through Europe. He read newspapers and books, and liked historical and fictional texts; and, if it could not be helped, he even read his opponents' pamphlets. Most of all, he looked at documents and memoranda. Wherever he was, he wrote letters to members of his family, to friends, companions, and, of course, with particular frankness, to his great mistresses, Wilhemine von Sagan and Dorothea von Lieven. Aphorisms, memoranda, and correspondence line the path of his life. As he was incapable of throwing away anything he felt to be of importance, his posthumous papers (the "Acta Clementina" in Prague), which he himself arranged, and the archive of the Metternich family, which has survived completely intact, are inexhaustible sources of information for anyone seeking an understanding of this easily misunderstood character.

Our travel guide will take care to lead his party step-by-step out of the depths of time and progressively forward. Along the way, he wants to make visible the important and formative moments—the primordial events—which would reappear as key triggers in the context of later conflicts, crises, and constellations. Only these events—the origins of later déjà-vu experiences, as it were—render his actions and judgments intelligible. From this perspective, perhaps, the fundamental concepts associated with what Reinhart Koselleck has called the "saddle period" between the eighteenth and nineteenth centuries—concepts such as "right," "revolution," "reform," "nation," "civilization," "representation," the "people," and "popular sovereignty"—will appear in a new light. However, attempting to understand everything the way that Metternich did does not mean having to think that all of his views were justified. This biography is not an apologia. There is, today, no good reason for taking such a course. But it is the privilege of a historian writing today that he or she may try to derive what Metternich silently thought, what he implicitly meant but often did not make explicit, from the background of his earlier experiences. Maybe this is what it means to do "justice" to a historical figure.

A rich and methodologically fruitful debate in the wake of so-called postmodernism has given rise to doubts about the very possibility of historical narration, and it has raised the question of whether biography as a genre of historiography—that is, as the coherent description of a life according to the model of Goethe's Wilhelm Meister novels—is not simply an "illusion," as Pierre Bourdieu suggested. Granted, the days of the old educational novel and the historical certainties associated with that genre are over. Indeed, they have been dead for a long time, at least since Johann Gustav Droysen's *Outline of the Principle of History,* in which he wrote: "The data for historical investigation are not past things, for these have disappeared, but things which are still present here and now, whether recollections of what was done, or remnants of things that have existed and of events that have occurred."[3] Put differently: the past as such, or an entire past life, cannot be "reconstructed"; the gaps and contingencies of the surviving fragments do not permit this. But it is still possible, nevertheless, to confront the available evidence relating to a past life with justified questions about it. And if in the course of doing so new, meaningful contexts arise which not only let the "picture" of history and its characters move in black and white, producing at best varying shades of grey, but make this picture "colorful,"[4] then the present book—and your travel guide—will have succeeded in one important point.

METTERNICH'S BIOGRAPHERS ACROSS THE GENERATIONS

Like many other important statesmen, Metternich began to think about his posthumous image early in his life. From 1820 onward, he made notes from memory that were to serve as building blocks for his autobiography. He was acutely aware of the role played by someone writing his memoirs, and included in his manuscripts only what concerned his own person and was useful in filling the gaps left by the official correspondence.[5] The genuine scholarship of the historian, in his eyes, consisted in the fact that the researcher was admitted access to the imperial archives, "and, drawing from this double source, they will more easily appreciate the great epoch during which destiny had laid upon me the difficult task of playing an active part on the world's stage."[6] Only historians, he believed, were able to judge the deeds and aims of statesmen impartially and justly. As he held such a high opinion of historians, he sharply distinguished between the judgments of his contemporaries and those of historians. For him, only the latter mattered. In 1829, in further autobiographical notes, he remarked that "the historian is not yet born who will describe the numerous events of the first decades of the nineteenth century. Contemporaries cannot reasonably do more than collect materials for those who, in a subsequent period, will be called upon to write the true history of the past with that calmness and impartiality which are always wanting to those who have taken an active part in the events."[7]

Metternich was also keenly aware of the polarizing effect his personality had on his contemporaries. After all, they—as he himself wrote—had coined the misnomer the "Metternich system" in order to criticize him. In this context, too, he trusted in the historians' methodically different way of proceeding: "The archives of all countries contain ample proof of what I wanted and promoted, as well as of what I did not want and therefore fought against. The verdict, which will have to come from an impartial history, will decide on the worth of the former and the worthlessness of the latter element."[8]

One of his visitors at Schloss Johannisberg, the Prussian politician Joseph Maria von Radowitz, a supporter of the so-called lesser German solution [*kleindeutsche Lösung*][9] under Prussia's leadership, even offered his services as Metternich's impartial biographer. Metternich, Radowitz said, would not be able to find a spirit closer to his own.[10] Radowitz thoroughly misjudged Metternich, who, as was his habit, politely kept his distance. In fact, he considered Radowitz to be an "eccentric mind"; he called him a "diabolus rotae"—that is, a prejudiced advocatus diaboli who proceeds from false premises and only wants to provoke. Radowitz, he wrote, is "one of those spirits who do not stop halfway, and who numb themselves and strive to numb others, with the richness of their ideas and words." In short: Metternich considered him to be the prototype of a passionate, and certainly not impartial, contemporary.[11]

Metternich's opinion of the historians of coming generations was, however, overly optimistic. They argued and quarreled over him with an intensity that, in this epoch, is only matched by their arguments over the case of Napoleon. Between 1836 and 2015, around thirty biographies of Metternich have been published, covering all periods of his life. We may roughly distinguish five generations and changing perspectives.

First, there are his contemporaries, who are actually not well suited to writing the history of this time. During the same phase, the first editions of memoirs, collected writings, and documents pertaining to Metternich's contemporaries appeared, and he was able to study them intensely. He delved into them, red pen in hand, marked up the texts, and then copied with his quill passages that seemed important to him. Thus he would study, for instance, the memoirs of Napoleon on St. Helena (the famous *Mémorial de Sainte-Hélène,* dictated to Emmanuel de Las Cases), the writings of Friedrich Gentz, or a biography of Freiherr vom Stein,[12] and even the comprehensive history of the time of the Revolution by Adolphe Thiers, who had taken the trouble to visit and question Metternich for a firsthand account of the events. The great extent to which Metternich's judgment regarding the partiality of contemporaries applied to the early biographers was demonstrated very clearly by two individuals who had originally belonged to his inner circle. Wilhelm Binder, a professor of philology and history at the high school [*Gymnasium*] in Biel, Switzerland, was the first to produce a biography of Metternich. Published in 1836, it may safely be filed under the heading "hero worship." The critical voice was provided by Josef von Hormayr, a court historian and a former director of the Haus-, Hof-, und Staatsarchiv in Vienna. As the leader of an "alpine revolution" that had been planned in 1813, Metternich had had him imprisoned (we shall return to this in more detail). As a result, Hormayr had become his unrelenting enemy. He left Austria, and ended up working for the state of Bavaria. In 1848, his desire for revenge inspired him to write a pamphlet under the title *Kaiser Franz und Metternich,* which portrays Metternich as a cold schemer, an absolutist, and a repressor of any kind of intellectual progress, as frivolous, superficial, and lacking character. Hormayr constructed the blueprint for the scathing picture of Metternich, which would go on to dominate historical interpretations of him, particularly those originating from the states of the "lesser Germany."

This raft of interpretation prefigures the *second generation* of biography, after 1866 and thus a few years after Metternich's death, in which debates were fueled and kept alight by a division among commentators: on the one hand there was the view from the perspective of the "lesser Germany" and the Reich, and on the other from the perspective of the "greater Germany" and Habsburg. This fundamental divide meant that the understanding of Metternich was relentlessly and exclusively informed by the "German question." What had been initiated by Hormayr was developed into a storm of propagandistic criticism by Heinrich von Treitschke, the Saxon who had turned into a Prussian. Although his *History of Germany in the Nineteenth Century* was no biography in the narrow sense, it did more than any other work to influence the image of Metternich, as it was a staple of any educated bourgeois household's bookshelf. The professor of history—someone who, as a historian, should, according to Metternich, have written *sine ira et studio* [without harboring prejudices and without passion]—recognized in the chancellor a traitor of the German nation, a diplomatic plotter, an "adroit" man, someone "devoid of ideas," someone endowed with "calculating cunning" and "good-natured and smiling mendacity," a corrupt man, a dishonest man, or, to use Srbik's later label: a "non-German."[13] The first volume of this raging book was published in Berlin in 1879. Only a year later, the son of the chancellor, Prince Richard von Metternich, published the first volume of the "Posthumous Papers," containing material from the family archive and the Haus-, Hof- und Staatsarchiv in Vienna. He wanted to stem the swelling tide of dismissive criticism.

From among the academic historians, it was Viktor Bibl—originally "deutschnational,"[14] but later fully committed to National Socialism—who carried Treitschke's picture of Metternich into the interwar years following 1918, in large part through a pamphlet whose subtitle referred to Metternich as the "demon of Austria," and in which Bibl undertook to settle scores with that demon. Bibl laid the main blame for the decline of the Habsburg Empire at the feet of Prince Metternich, schemer and liar, and declared that—given the criticism leveled by other historians against his radical and anti-European interpretation of Metternich—it was to his, Bibl's, "satisfaction and honor to find himself in the dock together with Heinrich Treitschke."[15]

The focus of the *third generation* of the interwar years was determined by the experience of the Great War. Here we find Srbik, whose attitude to Metternich was ambivalent, and whom we shall have to look at separately later, and Constantin de Grunwald, who was much admired by Srbik and who defended Metternich against various criticisms in a biography first published in 1938. On the basis of fresh sources, he argued that the great diplomat Metternich recognized early on the threat faced by European civilization.[16] And in 1933 the Englishman Algernon Cecil had already given the Anglo-Saxon audience the first serious biography of the chancellor in the English language. Cecil glorified Metternich as a great European and savior, in contrast to the totalitarian, revolutionary terrorism at the time and—in a contemporary reference—Hitler.[17]

The *fourth generation* suffered the shock of the Second World War and the catastrophe of the Holocaust. As a result, historians born during the interwar years were inclined to view Metternich even more as a European, as a peacemaker and master of international diplomacy. These historians, we may say, inherited the experience of the Great War from their parents' generation and added to it their own experience of the Second World War. For instance, Alan Warwick Palmer (born 1926) saw Metternich as the "Councillor of Europe"; his fellow Englishman Desmond Seward (born 1935) subtitled his book on Metternich "The First European." We may also think of the Frenchman Charles Zorgbibe (born 1935), who depicted Metternich as "le séducteur diplomate," a seducer in the field of diplomacy.[18] Then there is the American Paul W. Schroeder (born 1927), who made groundbreaking contributions to the reevaluation of Metternich's diplomacy.[19] Finally, and importantly, there is Henry Kissinger, the American politician and political scientist, originally born in Fürth in 1923, in whose masterful doctoral thesis one can detect the experience of both world wars and at the same time a sense of the new threat to humanity posed by the possibility of nuclear war. The programmatic subtitle of his thesis alone gave an entirely new meaning to the term "restoration": "A World Restored: Metternich, Castlereagh and the Problem of Peace."[20] Even though these historians (with the exception of Palmer and Zorgbibe) were not really biographers, they deserve our attention as examples of the international reorientation in the way Metternich was perceived. And so does the Austrian Helmut Rumpler (born 1935), who took the chancellor's policies regarding different national identities more seriously than anyone had before, and regarded him, as a politician of the Habsburg Monarchy, as influencing European politics far beyond the issue of the "lesser" versus the "greater" Germany.[21]

Apart from the works of professional historians, there is a plethora of more or less popular descriptions of his life written by diplomats, members of the military, journalists, and other amateur historians, all of whom were fascinated by one aspect or another of Metternich. In part due to the sometimes large circulations of these works, they often contributed significantly to the spread and reinforcement of existing clichés. And that was the case from the very start. Beginning with the year of the chancellor's death, we have the works of a member of the Prussian Parliament and liberal journalist;[22] an Austrian secondary school teacher and member of the Ministry for Education;[23] an English colonel;[24] an Austrian major interested in cultural history;[25] a spirit merchant at Sandeman and captain in the British army;[26] a journalistic writer and president of the Austrian PEN-Club;[27] a French ambassador to Luxemburg;[28] a Swiss diplomat;[29] a French general and high commissioner in Austria;[30] a dramaturg, author, and actor;[31] a main editor at Deutsche Welle;[32] a journalist of the British yellow press and best-selling author;[33] an author and member of the Gruppe 47;[34] and a medical doctor, retrained as a historian and a founding member of Opus Dei.[35] Metternich, it seems, is a medium through which any author may reach a market and at the same attempt some education of the masses. As a concrete example, let us take a quick look at Bernd Schremmer, a teacher and freelance writer from Brandenburg, whose book *Kavalier und Kanzler* [Cavalier and chancellor] serves up almost every conceivable cliché regarding Metternich: It calls him an absolutist and a repressor, an obstinate man living a life of self-deception, and an anti-democrat whose lasting achievement was having inadvertently helped the progress of democracy through his resistance to it.[36]

Almost all of the biographies mentioned here share one feature: they all draw on the same sources, especially on the posthumous papers of Metternich and other authors, which are not always reliably edited, and, in terms of secondary literature, in particular on Srbik as the one proper and undisputed source and canonical authority. From this material, they construct their individual pictures of Metternich, without ever examining their judgments and evaluations against the authentic sources that exist in the archives. We may therefore conclude that since Srbik's work, which is based on archival research, no independent biography of Metternich has appeared.

THE RISKS AND LIMITATIONS OF SRBIK'S BIOGRAPHY OF METTERNICH

Srbik's work, published in 1925, stands out from all other existing biographies in terms of its scholarship, erudition, and use of archival documents. It is rightly seen as the achievement of a lifetime. Srbik's name seems—not only in professional circles—to be intimately linked to that of Metternich, and consequently information taken from his work is simply treated as authoritative, even if more recent research has clearly falsified it.

Let me illustrate this with an example. A luxuriously edited volume that was recently published on the occasion of the 200th anniversary of the Vienna Congress[37] contains a brief biographical sketch of Metternich's life with the very apt title "Das Leben eines Geradlinigen" [The life of an upstanding character]. In it, the author touches upon Metternich's time as an ambassador in Paris and in this context avers that Metternich is guilty of fundamental misinterpretations of the political situation in 1809. With his reports from Paris and his support for a people's war, he is said to have, "to a large extent," brought about Austria's decision to go to war. This thesis has long since been refuted (namely, since 1968) by painstaking research drawing on documents in the Prague and Vienna archives.[38] The author adopts this discredited judgment from Srbik, whose evaluations are not based on a consultation of the relevant sources because these are, as he put it, "practically endless." Srbik turned Metternich "into one of the main initiators of the glorious, unhappy war of 1809."[39] The more recent author, however, is unaware that this view has been undermined by later research and follows Srbik's opinion because he considers it to be "still . . . unsurpassed."[40]

However, not all details are in need of correction. What renders Srbik's work highly problematic from the perspective of what we know today is its overall design, its basic ideological texture, which is directly transposed onto the interpretation of its subject matter.

Anyone who approaches Srbik's take on the life and politics of Metternich faces a two-volume mountain of 1,431 pages, and hardly anyone has read every single line of it. As I intend to visit sources that Srbik consciously avoided or did not have access to, it seems appropriate at this point to mention the risks encountered when consulting Srbik's oeuvre of 1925. And just to avoid any misunderstanding: the distance between now and then is far too great, in every respect, to indulge in any "pleasure in murdering the grandfathers," as Thomas Nipperdey put it in his plea for a denationalization of the writing of history. This plea, however, is as relevant now as it ever was.[41]

Biological Racism

Given Srbik's reputation, it may seem shocking to suggest that biological racism is the ground on which his biography rests, but it cannot be pushed to one side, because it is the factor that fundamentally determines his evaluation of Metternich. Here and in what follows, I shall quote at length from the author in order to forestall any accusation that I illegitimately, or even maliciously, charge him with these false assumptions.

Srbik's key thesis in his search for the "ideas in the system" of Metternich is this: "The primary concept for Metternich is that of race" (vol. 1, p. 389). This thesis is altogether unfounded.[42] If one is looking for Metternich's key concepts, then they are the "law," as he understands it, then "nationality," and, most importantly, "society." The latter he understood in the modern sense of a "collective singular."[43] This alone is enough to place Metternich in a different system of coordinates than those assumed by Srbik. Srbik's key thesis is not an isolated slip. Expanding on it, he writes: "He saw the urge of the German tribes, states, and landscapes toward segregation as an immutable racial property and thus deeply rooted in German nature and history" (vol. 1, p. 406). The concern with "spiritual specificity" and the "character of large peoples" that Srbik recognizes in Metternich, he unites with the generic concept of "race" into which, he alleges, Europe disintegrated in the nineteenth century (vol. 1, p. 355). As Srbik's judgment on the Treaties of Tilsit of 1807 shows, there is a systematic aspect to this nomenclature: "The Roman and Slavonic cultures agreed in order to dominate and divide the earth, and in order to oppress Germany and England" (vol. 1, p. 114).

Pursuing his peoples-based critique of civilization, Srbik juxtaposes the old state—a rule-governed, rational union that works to achieve common purposes—with a new state that he sees as a "blood-filled natural body" (vol. 1, p. 374). In this, he anticipates the national socialist idea of the body of a people. His definition of the real political task, which Metternich in his eyes failed to achieve, is "to guarantee the leadership of the German political body" (vol. 2, p. 391). In the "European character of the Austrian state" (vol. 1, p. 198) he saw precisely the opposite of this. Just like Oswald Spengler—one of his sources—he turns peoples and cultures into "organisms with an individual soul."[44]

Srbik raises the question of the "division between race, people, and nation" (vol. 1, p. 406). The "German people," he writes, "is a structure of Germanic tribes" who live in a "community of blood" (vol. 2, p. 391). Passages that sometimes sound like quotations from historical sources actually express Srbik's very own convictions, convictions he explicitly confirmed once again in 1951 when he argued for "an evaluation of racial ideology that is as impartial as possible,"[45] still pleading, even at that point, for a properly understood "German racial theory."[46]

Nationalism as a Weapon

The consequences of Srbik's racial approach for his picture of Metternich are obvious. They consist of a series of negative judgments in places where a historian would rather expect explanations and historical contextualization. Thus, he says about Metternich: "The moral and spiritual energies of the people which, if awakened, are truly the greatest means of rescue, remained internally alien to him" (vol. 1, p. 124). Srbik constructs an integrated and unhistorical concept of a "people" and uses it as a basis for making deductions, where Metternich uses the term "nationality," which must be understood differently. Against this standard of a "people," Srbik concludes that Metternich's nature lacked "the gift of heroism which provides the capacity for the highest achievement" because "he did not realize the political value of national cultural treasures, of an autonomous national state, and the transformation of a monarchical army into an army of the people." Srbik thinks Metternich lacks insight into the "unity of state and people, state and culture" (vol. 1, p. 127).

Because "nation and state were alien concepts" to his way of thinking, Metternich is said "originally" to have had "only minor and vague ideas about a community of the German people as a state and culture" (vol. 1, p. 85). During the years 1813–1815, "the feeling for a national German state as a point of reference" was alien to him (vol. 1, p. 180), and he harbored "a coldness toward the national will" (vol. 1, p. 197). Srbik denies that Metternich possessed any "patriotic feeling" (vol. 1, p. 125), and even where Metternich declares, to Napoleon, that he takes himself to be a German, Srbik objects: "His Germanness was altogether of the unrealistic and universal kind that we find at the end of the previous century" (vol. 1, p. 407). He ultimately labels Metternich "un-German": he detects in him a "European frame of mind [*Gesinnung*] which is, viewed from today's perspective, non-national," and which "internally bound him to the character of Austria as a non-national state" (vol. 1, p. 193). And he concludes: "There was no place in Metternich's mind or heart open to the high values of a national German Reich or federal state" (vol. 1, p. 378). Srbik makes this claim despite the fact that Metternich spoke of the German Confederation as "Germany" and as the "fatherland." Thus, he condemns the core idea of a federalism that Metternich pursued because the chancellor "was a representative of the federalist idea, which is, indeed, appropriate for Austria. This federalism he wanted to build on the basis, not of national entities, but of the historical-legal bodies of countries, and he did not want to let it go further than the legal-administrative sphere" (vol. 2, p. 189).

Where Is the Will to Create a German Cultural Imperialism?

Metternich distanced himself repeatedly and very explicitly from any "Germanizing" [*Germanisieren*] in the vein of Joseph II, and he pleaded for equality between the nationalities throughout the Austrian monarchy. Srbik blames him for this because he finds lacking in Metternich the sort of domestic German cultural imperialism that he considers appropriate: "It is right that the German nationality enjoys priority over the many others who fill the space of the state, because the ruling dynasty originally belonged to it, and because it is the true element of civilization in this enormous union of peoples. By virtue of its cultural superiority it is therefore called to take the leadership within the state" (vol. 1, p. 431).

Srbik's fundamental position leads him to regard Metternich's policies, which are basically defensive—that is, aimed at preserving peace with the outside—from the very outset as wrong. This is also the reason for Srbik's judgment that the chancellor fails to achieve his alleged task in eastern and southeastern Europe during the revolution of 1848–1849—when "the German soul was most deeply wounded" (vol. 2, p. 372). Regarding the time of the Revolution, Srbik speaks of the danger that Austria's "German people of the leader [*deutsches Führervolk*] will be pushed back, weighed down, by the alien nations within the multilingual state until they become a minority, no longer capable of fulfilling the task of permeating a natural space with predominantly German culture." He sees "the German-Austrian peculiarity as a people facing the danger of Slavonification" and pleads for "the expansion of German material and spiritual influence, and German influence in terms of power politics further east" in Europe (vol. 2, p. 373). In these matters Srbik is driven by the conviction that "from the very beginning, the pan-Slavic idea, with the fundamental ingratitude of the national instinct, turned against Germanness [*Deutschtum*] as the bringer of culture" (vol. 2, p. 188). All this shows clearly how Srbik imposes an interpretive framework on Metternich's ideas of the state, law, federalism, and nationality that can only result in condemnation but not in historical explanation. In Srbik's eyes, Metternich's fault was that he did not want to conquer eastern Europe for the Germans.

The Theory of the Master Race and the Political Myth of the Führer

Of crucial importance to a biography is the question of whether the biographer makes a particular view of human nature his norm. A historian committed to academic standards, in particular, must be as self-critical and cautious as possible regarding this question. But the opposite applies in the case of Srbik, who puts forward his ideal dogmatically and insists that Metternich conform to it. There are characters who, for Srbik, are models to be followed: Mazarin, Richelieu, Stein, Napoleon, and, in particular, Prince Felix zu Schwarzenberg, who emerged as the Austrian prime minister out of the revolutionary era in 1848. Srbik's canonical values lead him to make judgments such as the following: Metternich "always lacked the highest virtues: political passion, untiring energy, original creative powers" (vol. 1, p. 316); he was "not a strong personality, not a Richelieu and not a Mazarin" (vol. 1, p. 319). Napoleon, by contrast, possesses "the power of the personality that conquers the world" and a "titan's will to rule" (vol. 1, p. 347). Regarding 1848, Srbik remarks that "the time lacked a great individual who could have created a new world order"; Metternich "lacked the Promethean spark of truly creative power in his politics" (vol. 1, p. 229). "He was never a man of the great, decisive, creative deed" (vol. 1, p. 113).

In Schwarzenberg, Srbik saw embodied the opposite of all that: He was a "man of deeds," "a creative spirit, absolutist in all of his nature, but capable also of entering into a pact with constitutionalism, the bourgeoisie, and the masses if it was in the interest of his great idea of the state; a bold and cold-blooded calculator when it came to power relations and fleeting constellations, one who played a virtuoso game of chess with other states without consideration given to legitimacy or tradition . . . ; a political master type [*Herrennatur*] and a warrior" (vol. 2, p. 391). Srbik glorifies in Schwarzenberg a "man of an iron will" with a "talent for political leadership [*Führergabe*]" (vol. 2, p. 450). Unlike Metternich, "Schwarzenberg pushed the German question toward a solution" (vol. 2, p. 392).

It is important to highlight Srbik's ideology of a master race because it is anchored in a framework that declares the western European type of legal thought, with its emphasis on international law and constitutionalism, to be outdated. The consequence for Srbik's biography of Metternich is that the protagonist appears to be a statesman from a bygone era, someone who wanted to lead Austria to greater unity, but on the basis of international law and the founding documents of the German Confederation (vol. 2, p. 391). Srbik ranks the irrationality of the deed above the rationality of political actions: "The nature of a leading statesman . . . can never be exhausted by a political theory. . . . The selfish moment, the will to power, and the ambition to act effectively can never be subtracted from his actions" (vol. 1, pp. 414–15). Metternich lacked "the vigorous drive of life in his own chest," something that would have enabled him, as it once did Frederick the Great, "to act heroically and boldly, and to practice Machiavellian politics," rather than to apply, as he did, "the petty and petty-minded means of statecraft" (vol. 1, p. 415).

Srbik's view of Metternich's mediating policies in mid-1813, which were decisive for achieving victory in the Napoleonic Wars, is of a piece with these judgments: "This policy does not shine under any heroic light, but shows a cold heart and a deviousness that exceeds even that of Hardenberg; hate and greatness of the soul were unknown to it" (vol. 1, p. 149). It is of little help that, following this unequivocal condemnation, Srbik contradicts himself by presenting this policy as without alternative: "In its masterful deliberateness, it was probably the only one suitable to set the half-wrecked boat of Austria afloat again, and at the same time to serve the narrower interests of the state as well as the old community of states, while yet not putting all the eggs in one basket." For all that, his judgment remains unchanged: "His policies were meant to remain informed by soberness and a passionless lack of imagination" (vol. 1, p. 164). Metternich's reservations regarding Blücher's risky individual initiatives, which led to many a lost battle, should not be "rated too highly in ethical terms," Srbik thinks (vol. 1, p. 167).

If we are to put Srbik's picture of Metternich's character in its proper place, it would help to have a quotation that sums up this picture in full. He writes:

> Metternich, however, was not one of the truly great who imposed their personal peculiarities and the individuality of their life on an age, thereby giving that age a new form . . . He was no deep and forceful thinker, and he was not endowed with a concentrated energy that acts with an iron and ruthless will. Metternich did not possess a great instinct for power; according to his whole nature he was not a man of deeds; he shied away from decisive opposition and from battle on a grand scale . . . because the graceful and softly passive [*Weichempfängliche*] outweighed manly daring from the very beginning. (vol. 1, p. 257)

The fact that Srbik's source for this characterization is none other than Hormayr, who hated Metternich, speaks for itself.

If we take all of Srbik's characterizations together, what emerges is the ideology of a master race and the myth of the Führer as Srbik found these ideas, preformed, in intellectual history, in particular in Nietzsche. Of the member of the master race, he speaks straightforwardly: He is the one who defies "convention and morality . . . with his master morality of the stronger, the new overman, who, wholly dedicated to life in this world, lives heroically according to his own laws. He is the leader of a noble selection of individuals, who must be obeyed by those with the nature of a slave; the will to power heads the list of his table of values; the overman is above the law, he is someone who dares, a warrior and victor amidst humans that are akin to predatory animals."[47] Another inspiration for Srbik's emphasis on the emotions, in the face of which a rational politician like Metternich can only fail, was Nietzsche's pupil Oswald Spengler.[48] In Srbik, the norm takes precedence over historical reality, and thus he ignores Metternich's limited room for political maneuver. Srbik also does not consider the extent to which the emperor and other parts of the court, especially the treasury [*Hofkammer*], were bound to limit the activities of the "man of deeds" in any case.

Misleading Personal Memoirs

Srbik's picture of Metternich is not only affected by his ideological prejudices. At times, an excessive use of personal memoirs also clouds his vision. Srbik admits in his introduction that "a systematic sifting through the sheer endless collections at the Haus-, Hof- und Staatsarchiv in Vienna and the masses of documents and letters at the Metternich's family archive in Plaß by a single person . . . was inconceivable" (vol. 1, p. xii). He made use of unpublished archival documents at random, and thus disappointed Metternich's hope that future historians would not depend on the opinions, rumors, and moods of his contemporaries but would research the actions and sequences of events as they are recorded in official documents. What insights are offered by, for example, Metternich's "reports" to the emperor between 1809 and 1848, held in the Vienna archive, if one goes through them systematically—in particular up to the death of Emperor Franz I in 1835—rather than picking reports randomly from a period of just three years? Only then does one get an impression of Metternich's ongoing work at his writing desk in the chancellery and gain a distance from the subjective impressions of his contemporaries. And only then is it possible to fathom which and how many problems and questions landed on his desk during his time in office.

Personal sources of the kind Srbik prefers can, of course, also be valuable, but they bear risks because it is not clear to what extent the subjective impressions they convey contain valid points. How reliable can a judgment of Metternich's character and personality be when it comes from the perspective of someone as bitter as Hormayr? Srbik frequently falls prey to the judgment of his witnesses or—even worse—emphasizes in them that which corresponds to his framework of norms. If, on a particular day, Friedrich Gentz notices a momentary "inclination toward inertia" in Metternich, is this enough reason to portray him as temporarily oblivious to his duties, as fickle, and as preferring to pursue his "individual urge for pleasure" rather than stick to a fixed timetable (vo. 1, p. 255)? With such a conclusion, Srbik once more reinforces the cliché of the pleasure-seeking courtier, someone superficial, vain, careless (vol. 1, p. 143), and possessed of a grotesque sense of superiority (vol. 1, p. 270). But how could such a character leave behind a body of documents in the archives of Vienna and Plaß that is so large that Srbik must capitulate in front of, in his words, "sheer endless collections"?

Contradictions in Srbik's Portrayal of Metternich

Even if we leave aside all the objections raised so far, any reader of Srbik's work seeking to do justice to his achievement faces a difficult task. Beyond his axioms, he presents many fitting characterizations that flatly contradict his ideological superstructure. On the one hand, Metternich is said to have seen "the nineteenth-century tendencies toward nations and freedom simply as destructive forces" (vol. 2, p. 312); on the other, he is said to have acted so that "the state can become more stable by treating national differences with care," because he demanded "the promotion of the spiritual and material development of the nationalities" (vol. 2, p. 184).

When it comes to diminishing Metternich's intellectual qualities, Srbik never holds back: "He never realized the extent to which the principles he taught were doctrinal" (vol. 1, p. 322). On the other hand, he claims: "He is an empiricist, but above pure empiricism he employs a constructive theory which integrates the real" (vol. 1, p. 306). "He was a 'philosopher' in the sense of his time; with a theistic orientation, and he was an admirer of human reason as capable of recognizing eternal truths, even those that lie in a very remote distance" (vol. 1; p. 307).

On the one hand, Srbik presents Metternich as a reactionary and as a politician who belonged to "patriarchal and estates-based absolutism" pursuing political stability (vol. 2, p. 446), as a representative of "pure monarchy" (vol. 2, p. 303). But on the other, Srbik claims that, between 1842 and 1844, he wanted to reorganize the entire administration of the state, that he planned a large-scale program of restructuring (vol. 2, p. 198), and that in the case of Hungary he "expressed a decisive willingness to engage in positive and fruitful cooperation" (vol. 2, p. 200).

This and other contradictions in Srbik's biography cannot be resolved. They indicate either that the manuscript is a combination of different stages of work on the project or that, in particular cases, the author succumbed to the predominant impressions conveyed by certain sources. At least he did not succeed in subordinating the wealth of observation and information fully to the dictates of his norms—this is fortunate, one might think, because at least his apodictic, and contradictory, condemnations relativize each other. Readers of Srbik should, however, arm themselves with a generous amount of skepticism in order to decide which judgments they consider correct and want to accept. In that sense, because of its ambivalent evaluations and its omissions, this biography, which has for a long time been taken to be canonical, does indeed come to be something of a bible: it is possible to read both a "good" and a "bad" Metternich into it.

All in all, the time has come for a biographer to do justice to a changed contemporary world—something every author must face, in any case. And such a world always provides us with new perspectives on a previous life. Today, the contemporary world is no longer that of the two world wars but of a *fifth generation* after 1945—namely, the generation of those who experienced the world-historical shift of 1989–1990. This shift, no less than the previous wars, determines the experience of a generation of historians—after all, it continues to be momentous for Europe as well as for the "German question." Among the themes that exercised the generation born after 1945 is not only that of *Metternich and Austria: An Evaluation,*[49] but also the wider issue of—as I would put it—"Metternich and Europe Revisited." It is a promising sign that the Italian historian Luigi Mascilli Migliorini (born in 1952) recently published the first Metternich biography to come from his country in which the chancellor appears as the "architect of Europe" and not as an enemy of Italy.[50]

I

ORIGINS

Family Ties and the Rise of the Metternichs

"Why just the Metternichs?" you might ask yourself if you looked at family trees showing the hundreds of aristocratic families that have died out since the Middle Ages. Why have they survived and others not? As early as 1751, Johann Gottfried Biedermann, the pastor of the Prince of Brandenburg-Kulmbach, published such a genealogy—a "genealogical register" [*Geschlechts-Register*]. Tracing the lines of ancestors from the Middle Ages feels like taking a walk across a large aristocratic cemetery in which scores of dynastic branches found their final resting place, whether they belonged to the lower rural aristocracy or had ascended to become barons and imperial counts. Most of the lateral lines of the Metternich family—the zu Burscheids, zu Niederbergs, zu Chursdorffs, zu Rodendorffs, and Müllenarcks—had met the same fate. But the most important line had survived: the zu Winneburg und Beilsteins. Biedermann judged the importance of these gentlemen, the Barons and Counts Metternich, as follows: "This is one of the largest and most noble houses of counts and barons in all of Germany." At that point, it had produced three electoral archbishops—a feat matched only by the Schönborns. And the most famous of its offspring had not yet entered this world![1] Into this dynastic bedrock he would be born.

Could it be that the survival of the Metternich family offers one of the keys to understanding the unique path our protagonist took through life? So far, it has not been asked with enough insistence what his venerable descent might have meant for Metternich, or what emanated from it. It offered him what a parvenu like Bonaparte craved: an old family, reaching back over generations, which gave him the self-confidence that comes with an autonomous life resting on rights and on "land and people"—a large estate and the immediate power to rule, embedded within a vast network of near and distant relatives spread across the whole of the old German empire. The glorious and resounding name of a dynasty alone lent an aura to its members. However much the bourgeois critique of the aristocracy might finally have sunk in, following the Revolution of 1789, when Metternich and Napoleon faced each other at the famous Dresden meeting in 1813, an awareness that one of them was an upstart—in his memoirs, Metternich would describe him as a "parvenu"[2]—and the other a dignitary steeped in tradition would have played a role beyond whatever words were exchanged, and despite the fact that one called himself "emperor" where the other was a mere "state minister." This all makes it worthwhile to engage with that old aristocratic—old European—world and intellectual universe, for later we will be able to judge whether, and to what extent, Metternich really should be seen as simply a representative of the ancien régime—of "restoration" and regression—or whether he was instead someone who overcame the stance of an unqualified adherence to the traditions of the old German empire.[3]

With the benefit of historical hindsight, we can recognize three fundamental elements on which rested the enduring success of the Metternichs over centuries. And these can be given three short labels: "emperor," "Church," and "strength of the family." "Emperor" stands for their allegiance to power; "Church" for their embeddedness within the network of the imperial Catholic Church, which benefited their careers; and "strength of the family," finally, for their regular production of numerous descendants—always including a son and heir—as well as the sustained energy with which they preserved and increased the family fortune.

Let us imagine the rise through aristocratic ranks as a walk through a five-story *palais*.[4] The *ground floor* is occupied by the patent nobility, court nobility, and the nobility of office; they do not bear any further of the marks of the highborn. (In mediaeval times, these would have been the ministry officials and ordinary knights.) Those who have the right to call themselves lords, who have acquired an ancestral seat—a castle—either in some feud or because it has been bestowed upon them as a reward for their services, and who now, as Wilhelm Heinrich Riehl put it, rule over "land and people," have successfully progressed to live on the *first floor*. (Aristocratic credentials and rule could be permanently established only on the basis of landed property.) The *second floor* is reserved for the barons with their privileges—which they call their "liberties"—for instance, the right to a seat and vote on the country's assemblies of the estates.

Another flight of stairs brings us to the *third floor,* where we find the *counts,* who, like little monarchs, rule over, judge, and protect their subjects. (They enjoyed imperial immediacy and had access to the Imperial Diet of the Holy Roman Empire, where they had also established their own Curia.) The *highest floor,* the *bel étage,* finally, belongs exclusively to the princes. (They were considered to be the most important estate in the Imperial Diet, and their voices were heard first, before the others were allowed to speak.) The higher we ascend in this *palais,* the fewer are the residents on each floor—and the greater the energy required to move in. Tenacity and perseverance over many generations are required to make the ascent.

THE MINISTERIAL METTERNICHS

In the following sections we shall follow the Metternichs up the five flights of stairs in our imaginary *palais.* Those living in early modern times would have arranged the aristocracy in the form of a "Ständetreppe," with steps representing the estates. The ascent up these steps will help us answer the question "Why did the Metternichs succeed, and not others?" The oldest traces of the family are, indeed, to be found on the *ground floor,* where members of the family are thought to have acted as bailiffs for the Merovingians or the Pepin Carolingians in the area of the old Colonia Agrippina and the Colonia Trevirensis (today Cologne and Trier). Beginning in 1166, we find chamberlains of the Church in Cologne mentioned in official documents; they were members of the von Hemberg family in Hemmerich near Bonn and belonged to the class of service gentry. Three black scallops formed part of their coat of arms. One branch of this family built a moated castle[5] at the foot of Hemmerich Castle in a place called "Metternich," and from then on they called themselves the "Lords of Metternich." They retained the three scallops in their coat of arms, thus conspicuously demonstrating their link with the zu Hembergs. As late as 1813, the later Austrian chancellor integrated the three scallops into his newly created princely emblem.

The name "Metternich" suggests that the place on the road from Deutz to Trier, later the location of a chain village formed during Roman colonization, was originally a Celtic settlement. The idea that the Metternichs were of Roman lineage might therefore actually contain a grain of truth. The place still exists. Those who want experience the beginnings of the House of Metternich firsthand will find it between Bonn and Euskirchen on the fertile loess soil along the extensive valley of the river Swist, between the border of the Lordship of Tomberg in the south, and the place where the Swist flows into the Erft in the north.

The Metternich coat of arms in 1707.

THE LORDS OF KÖNIGSWART

The "first representative of the scallop lineage,"[6] which documents from the early fourteenth century show to be a Lord Metternich, is a certain Sybgin (or Sibido)—a vassal and knight of the archdiocese of Cologne. He is the oldest ancestor of the lineage of Metternichs from which an uninterrupted line can

Family Tree of the Metternichs from Its Beginnings
to Clemens of Metternich

1. Sibido (Sybgin) von Metternich, Lord of <u>Metternich</u>
(the one with the three scallops in his coat of arms) (ca. 1325–ca. 1382)
∞ Frau von Dünstekoven

|

2. Johann I, Lord of <u>Metternich</u> (1340–1449)
∞ 1375 Anna von Binsfeld

|

3. Johann II, Lord of <u>Sommersberg</u> († after 1465) /
Otto II, Lord of <u>Metternich</u> (Niederberg lineage)
∞ 1424 Agnes Rumschöttel v. Fritzdorff of Sommersberg (*1405)

|

4. Karl II, Lord of <u>Sommersberg</u> and <u>Zievel</u> (1425–1496) / *Ludwig (Brohl lineage)*
∞ 1456 Lady Sybilla (Belgine) Beisselin von Gymnich (*1430)

|

5. Edmund, Lord of <u>Vettelhoven</u> and <u>Sommersberg</u> (1475–1540) /
Dieter Lord Zievel (distribution of estates 1516, Zievel-Burscheid lineage)
∞ 1495 Lady Amalia Kolff von Vettelhoven

|

6. Johann, Lord of <u>Vettelhoven</u>, bailiff in <u>Sinzig</u> (1500–1575) /
Dietrich (Sommersberg / Chursdorf lineage)
∞ 1547 Lady Katharina von der Leyen (1528–1567)

|

7. Lothar (Archbishop of Trier: 1599–1623) / **Johann Dietrich,** Lord of <u>Sinzingen</u> (1553–1625)
Bernhard Lord <u>Vettelhoven</u>
∞ 1579 Lady Anna Frey von Dehren (*1560)

|

8. Wilhelm (from 1635 Baron) of <u>Metternich-Winneburg and Beilstein</u> (1590–1655) /
Brothers: Lothar (†1663), Carl (†1636), Emmerich (†1653), Johann Reinhard (†1638)
∞ 1619 Lady Anna Elenora Broemserin von Rüdesheim (1600–1660)

|

9. Karl Heinrich (Archbishop of Mainz: 1679) / **Philipp Emmerich** (from 1679 Count)
von <u>Metternich-Winneburg and Beilstein</u> (1628–1698)
∞ 1652 Maria Elisabeth Magdalena Baroness Waldpotin von Bassenheim (1630–1685)
Lothar Friedrich Lord Metternich-Burscheid (Archbishop of Mainz: 1673–1675)

|

10. Franz Ferdinand, Count <u>Metternich-Winneburg and Beilstein</u> (1660–1719)
∞ 1683 Elenore Juliana Countess von Leinigen Westerburg (1667–1742)

|

11. Philipp Adolph, Count <u>Metternich-Winneburg and Beilstein</u> (1686–1739)
∞ 1707 Lady Maria Franziska Schenckin von Schmidtberg (1685–1723)
|

12. Johann Hugo Franz, Count <u>Metternich-Winneburg and Beilstein</u> (1710–1750)
∞ 1745 Clara Louisia Elisabeth Baroness Kesselstadt (1726–1746)
|

13. Franz Georg, Count <u>Metternich-Winneburg and Beilstein</u>
(from 1803 Prince Ochsenhausen) (1746–1818)
∞ 1771 Maria Beatrix Aloysia Baroness Kageneck (1754–1828)
|

14. Clemens Wenzeslaus Lothar, Count (from 1813 Prince)
<u>Metternich-Winneburg and Beilstein,</u> (from 1818) Duke of Portella (1773–1859)
∞ 9.27.1795 Eleonore von Kaunitz (10.1.1775–3.19.1825)
∞ 11.5.1827 Lady Maria Antonia Leykam (8.15.1806–1.17.1829)
∞ 1.30.1831 Lady Melanie Maria Antonia Zichy-Ferraris von Zichy und Vásonykeö
(1.18.1805–3.3.1854)

Note: * indicates date of birth; † indicates date of death; ∞ indicates marriage. Bold type indicates the thirteen members of the family leading in direct line to Clemens von Metternich. Underlining marks changes in the family's ancestral seat, until it permanently became Winneburg and Beilstein. Italics mark a new side lineage of the family. Boxes indicate the three archbishops in the family who played a crucial role in the rise of the Metternichs. Taken from the Metternich family archive, NA Prague RAM Krt. 1, 1687, Krt. 58, 3211 and Krt. 200, 1983, and combined with the information in Broemser, *Zur Geschichte der Familien Metternich,* which is backed up by absolutely reliable documentary evidence.

---

be drawn that leads, after fourteen generations, up to the protagonist of our story. Sybgin, the first ancestor, entered the *first floor,* that of the *noble lords,* who from now on not only sported their own coat of arms but also had their own ancestral home.

What happened next was typical of the lordships of the lower nobility. Alfons von Klinkowström, the Metternichs' archivist, who wrote a short legal history of the family in 1882, complained about "the many divisions of the family into numerous branches and sub-branches," into "multiply split lineages."[7] The distribution of estates, gains through marriage, lineages coming to an end, and at times even the use of military means—all of these brought about changes in the House of Metternich. Changing ancestral homes give us some insight into the struggles for survival and the battles to stay on top that took place, as well as showing us where the family was centered. Before continuity was established more firmly with the Barons of Winneburg and Beilstein, the ancestral home shifted over seven generations from Metternich (Niederberg lineage), to Sommersberg (Chursdorff lineage), to Zievel (Burscheid lineage), and to Vettelhoven.[8] All of these castles, some of which still exist as ruins, are situated within a triangle between Düren, Bonn, and Münstereifel. All of the minor branch lines of the family died out, with the exception of the Lordship of Winneburg and Beilstein.

In the seventh generation, the son and heir Johann Dietrich (1553–1625) found himself without a real ancestral home. Apart from some manorial estates acquired through marriage, he only had those in Sinzig at his disposal, where he was bailiff. The paternal inheritance of the Lordship of Vettelhoven had gone to his older brother. At the same time, Johann Dietrich had taken the position of a counselor of the Electorate of Trier. But in this seventh generation, in which, due to the division of estates, the House of Metternich had reached its lowest point, it also started its ascent, putting an end to this ruinous process of ongoing division. This was achieved by the common efforts of the two brothers: Lothar, the older one, managed to profit from the two pillars of empire and church by being unanimously elected archbishop and prince elector by the chapter of the Cathedral of Trier in 1599; Johann Dietrich, the younger one, contributed the third element by producing twelve children, of which nine were male—but he no longer possessed an ancestral home. The boys gave the archbishop, their uncle, ample opportunity to support his nephews by providing them with church offices, newly acquired estates, and enfeoffments. And the brothers shared a sense of determination and persistence. Both considered the acquisition of a permanent ancestral home to be the most urgent task facing the family.

Königswart

The foundation for a new ancestral home was laid with the purchase of the dominion of Königswart (Kynžvart). If there were a logic operating in history, it would be only fitting that today the place with the most historical significance for the Metternich family lies in the Czech Republic: in Bohemia, which was then a crown land of the Habsburg Empire. There, a modern time traveler would find a splendidly restored palace, and if she entered the former princely estate and made her way through the various rooms, she might find herself with the feeling that the old chancellor had just left them. Almost 150 years before his birth, the purchase of the dominion provided his family with a material basis for existence until 1945. Such a reliable material basis had never existed in the family before, and the task was to secure and increase it. When Metternich acted as master of the works for the palace between 1828 and 1833, he called on the help of Pietro Nobili, the director of the Vienna Academy of the Fine Arts and court architect who has never properly been appreciated by art historians.[9] Nobili transformed the estate, which had originally been designed as a Renais-

The palace at Königswart after its renovation in 1833.

sance fortress and then turned into a Baroque building at the end of the seventeenth century, into a classic Renaissance palace. In stylistic and historical terms, then, Metternich restored his family's ancestral home to be as it was in its early heyday. Such an architectural gesture toward the beginnings of his family's ascendancy can hardly have been accidental.

The circumstances surrounding the purchase reveal an unprecedented feat of strength by the family, a feat that again clearly displays all three elements of the Metternichs' success: the purchase depended on support from the imperial church, the backing of the emperor, and the tenacity of the family.

On April 10, 1630, Johann Reinhard, a member of the eighth generation of Metternichs, along with four of his brothers purchased the palace in the presence of an Appellationsrat.[10] He signed the deed at the exact spot where, in 1618, the famous Defenestration of Prague marked the beginning of the Thirty Years War.[11] And when a year later, in 1631, the Bohemian deputies refused to support the election of Ferdinand II as Holy Roman Emperor at the assembly in Frankfurt, and the election threatened to fall through, it was Prince Elector Lothar of Trier who took the side of the Habsburg candidate and helped to push through his election. The House of Habsburg never forgot this, and they referred to it in all of the documents relating to the elevation of members of the Metternich family to higher social ranks. Even before his intervention, Lothar had been actively involved in the formation of the so-called Catholic League in 1609, a countermovement to the Protestant Union, and in the royal elections of 1612 he had supported the Habsburg candidate, Emperor Matthias.[12]

The purchase of Königswart required a major effort. The five sons of Johann Dietrich—Johann having died at this point—had to raise 66,114 Rhenish guilders to buy it. We cannot here go into every little detail regarding the sources of this money. But a little hint at one of them may be illuminating, as it shows how faithfulness to the emperor actually paid off in this instance: In 1629 one of the brothers, Wilhelm, received a pension of 14,624 guilders from the Spanish court of the Habsburgs for his military services.[13] It is also worth looking at the offices the brothers held between them in 1630, which are listed in the deed, as they demonstrate the effects of sinecures accumulated over twenty-four years by their powerful uncle, Prince Elector Lothar. Listed as buyers were:

• Johann Reinhard von Metternich of Streichenberg, dean of the Cathedral of Mainz, administrator (governor) of the abbey of Halberstadt, *thesauriarius* (administrator of goods and assets) and canon at Magdeburg, provost at Frankfurt, Roman imperial counselor, electoral privy councillor, and president of the privy council at Mainz.

• Carl von Metternich, chor bishop of Trier, canon of Augsburg and Eichstätt, provost of the imperial Freistift Aachen[14] (this is the same Carl whose gravestone, designed by Matthias Rauchmüller and renowned among art historians, can still be admired in the Liebfrauenkirche in Trier).[15]

• Emmerich von Metternich, canon at Trier, Paderborn, and Verden, and colonel appointed to the Bavarian cure—this demonstrates that it was possible to switch between clerical and military offices.

• Wilhelm von Metternich, Lord of Berburg, Knight of the Order of St. Jacob, Roman imperial counselor and chamberlain, counselor of the Trier cure, bailiff at Mayen, Monreal, and Kaisersesch. And

• Lothar von Metternich, Lord of Differdingen and Hackenbeck, counselor of the imperial cure of Trier and bailiff of Montabaur.

The deed played an important foundational role for the family in various ways: It showed the emperor's gratitude toward the Metternichs for their loyalty during the great wars of religion, for they had fought for him not only diplomatically, like Lothar, but also militarily. At the same time, the emperor punished the previous owners of the now-united lordships: "Due to serious wrongdoing," the holder Hanns Sebastian von Zedlitz, he wrote, had forfeited his rights to the palace and marketplace of Königswart, including all villages and "gardens." The same applied to Hannß Bärthlmes Schirntinger, "due to the wrongdoings committed in the very harmful rebellion against the imperial majesty." Both estates were to be confiscated "as punishment following condemnation." This is how the emperor punished the revolting Protestants in Bohemia. This was the precise reason the Metternichs had the opportunity to move their economic existence and the center of their lives to Bohemia. This was not to say that they might not later, on official business, reside in Koblenz; yet Königswart remained the secure place in the background—and a welcome source of income. Indeed, following expulsion from their lands on the west bank of the Rhine in 1794, Königswart was a lifeline for the family—not only as a safe haven, but also as an economic resource, without which the young Count Clemens could never have married the niece of the powerful Prince of Kaunitz, the state chancellor of the Habsburg court.

The economic gain for the five brothers should also not be underestimated. Königswart was a lordship with so-called *Meierhöfe*,[16] with sheep farms, agricultural fields, cattle, meadows, agricultural buildings and equipment, orchards and vegetable gardens, pastures, waters, and lucrative small industries, with a brewery, a malthouse, and mills. All this yielded rent (taxes) that the local "subjects" had to pay.

The nobility of this lordship lived in the world of feudal rights and privileges that the delegates at the National Assembly in Frankfurt's Paulskirche were still raging against in 1848–1849. It was this economic reality, based on the rule of the landed gentry, that the state chancellor, for his part, was responsible for bringing to an end, in favor of a market-oriented agrarian capitalism.

The Metternich brothers acquired a free hereditary property for themselves and their descendants. The lordship was entirely free of all the feudal dependencies that would have pertained to their previous possessions. Their ownership was entered into the Bohemian registry, and the previous owners were removed. With this, the Metternichs became naturalized Bohemians (*Inkolat*)[17] and acquired *Standschaft*—the right, exclusive to the nobility, to be represented at state assemblies. The Lordship of Königswart embodied, within its confines, all the traits of the feudal order in which a noble lord ruled over his subjects on the basis of his own right and authority, not just as a subsidiary of an imperial or ecclesiastical office. This is not to say that a lord might not have such a subsidiary function—in fact, it was wise for a lord to have such a role, for it allowed the house to prosper. But the lord was "sovereign." The enduring aim of the Metternichs was to bolster this sovereignty, and in this endeavor they could call upon the strength of the family, which we have already seen in action above. Something more, however, was needed in order to open the door leading to the second floor, where the barons lived.

THE BARONS OF WINNEBURG AND BEILSTEIN

Before the most prominent member of the Metternichs strode upon the stage of Habsburg, imperial, and European politics, what significance did the family have for the emperors? No other evidence reveals more about the answer to this question than the documents certifying the elevation of the family to the social ranks of barons, counts, and princes. In these papers, the emperors concentrated solely on this one family, and the Imperial Chancellery conscientiously used the vast archival memory of the imperial house in order to justify the elevations. The document on the Metternichs' promotion to baronage, dated October 28, 1635, marks the beginning of the imperial attention they enjoyed.[18] It was the result of a specific constellation of factors: the hitherto unappreciated importance of the Metternichs within the network of conflicts of the Thirty Years War against the background of the rivalry between the House of Habsburg and France. The document emphasizes this importance, referring to, among other things, the election of the emperor in 1619, in which Prince Elector Lothar von Metternich had helped to hinder the Protestant opponent of the reformed church, Friedrich V of the Palatinate. But it focused to an even greater extent on praising the political and military achievements of the Metternichs during the "very harmful and most hostile rebellions" in the kingdom of Bohemia, and on how the Metternich brothers had shown heroic courage and fearless bravery in the face of "our enemies" in the "rebellions that subsequently spread to and fro throughout the Holy Empire and the bloody wars that followed in their wake."

The document's references to such dramatic contemporary events show that the elevation to the rank of baron was reserved for the most faithful and courageous of the emperor's followers. The document emphasized especially the brothers' military achievements, and in particular those of Carl, who used all his strength against the "*recent,* highly dangerous French incursion" into the electorate of Trier, and recaptured it. Prince Elector Philipp von Sötern, the successor to Lothar von Metternich, had broadened an originally regional conflict with the chapter of the cathedral (and not least with the Metternichs who belonged to it) and with the estates into a conflict of international proportions. Around the time that the Holy Roman Emperor was about to put an end to the fateful war with the Peace of Prague, in 1635, the archbishop of Trier asked the French king for help, and on August 20, 1632, French troops occupied Trier. That act constituted a case of high treason. The archbishop declared the brothers Carl and Emmerich von Metternich, who had fled to Luxembourg and the protection of Habsburg Spain, deprived of all secular and clerical offices and sinecures and set out to have them arrested. As one of the successors in the chapter of the cathedral, he even wanted to appoint the French cardinal Richelieu. The "recent recapturing" of Trier mentioned in the document refers to March 26, 1635, when Habsburg-Spanish troops, accompanied by Carl von Metternich, conquered Trier in a surprise attack, and his brother Emmerich, threatened with an imperial ban himself, personally arrested the archbishop and exiled him.[19] The arrest of Philipp von Sötern caused a major stir within the empire, and an even stronger one in France, where it was felt to be an extreme provocation, given that France had taken the prince elector under its protection. King Louis XIII declared war on Spain and on the emperor, even though Emperor Ferdinand II had already made peace with some of the empire's principalities in Prague.

The Metternichs were thus at the very heart of events, and they sided with the emperor when the Thirty Years War expanded into an unprecedented European struggle over power that would last for another thirteen years. The document is a token of an allegiance to the emperor that was unshakable even in the face of death and that was crucial at a turning point in the history of the House of Habsburg. It is for this reason that Emperor Ferdinand II made the five brothers barons. They had reached the second floor of the aristocratic *palais,* and the document explicitly declared that it honored "the ancient noble, magnificent and knightly family of the von Metternichs, which stretches back hundreds of years." In more concrete terms this meant:

- The emperor's chancellery from then on listed the Metternichs as "highborn" [*Wohlgeboren*].

- More importantly: they received the right ("prerogative") to be represented in imperial and other assemblies, chivalrous games, "beneficia," and cathedral chapters. Thus, in addition to the noble right to a voice, they now gained membership of the noble estate beyond Bohemia in the empire at large (although they did not yet have a formal seat in the Imperial Diet).

- They could receive income from baronial fiefs and secondary fiefs [*Afterlehen*], a fact that would soon become relevant.

- And they could acquire or build new ancestral homes or palaces within the Habsburg realms; fortify towns, ancestral homes, or palaces in their possession; and assume further noble names to be added to their existing titles, seals, and undertakings.

Winneburg and Beilstein

By linking the privilege of "receiving baronial fiefs and secondary fiefs" with the rank of baron, the document of the Imperial Chancellery took into consideration the contemporary interests of the Metternichs, who at the time were competing over the acquisition of the shires of Winneburg and Beilstein at the Mosel. In this context, too, the confessional nature of the Thirty Years War created new frontiers and excellent opportunities for material redistribution. Enter one of the Metternich brothers, Emmerich, the imperial constable in chief [*Generalwachtmeister*].[20] In 1635 he led imperial troops in the conquest of Beilstein Castle, driving out the Swedish occupiers. At the same time, he learned that the owners of the castle, the Lords of Winneburg and Beilstein, had joined "the Swedish as the enemies of the empire or of His Majesty the Emperor" and thus committed a crime against the crown. Both shires were fiefdoms belonging to Cologne. Emmerich therefore asked the archbishop of Cologne to confer the now-vacant fiefdoms upon him and his brothers, and the archbishop provided the requested deed of enfeoffment on July 30, 1635.[21]

But because both shires, as fiefdoms, were also associated with the electorate of Trier, Emmerich requested the enfeoffment from the cathedral chapter of Trier as well. There is an irony here: at the time, the cathedral chapter was administering Trier on behalf of the emperor because it had lost the prince elector, Philipp von Sötern, who had been spectacularly arrested and imprisoned—by Emmerich. The latter now received a document giving him an entitlement to the enfeoffment until a legally appointed prince elector could sign the official deeds. On February 7, 1652, von Sötern died, and soon afterward his successor and the emperor confirmed that the imperial dominium of Winneburg and Beilstein did not have any legal heirs, but that the Barons of Metternich were "legal *possessores*." The imperial decree of March 28, 1654, gave them the right to take the names of the lordships that had now definitively been given to them.[22] From then on, their title was "Barons of Metternich, Winneburg and Beilstein." The adjunct "Winneburg and Beilstein" remained part of the name right up to the last representative of the family line, Princess Tatiana (died July 26, 2006), although the "Beilstein" part was later neglected.

The state chancellor showed how important this part of his family's history was to him when, in 1832, he repurchased Winneburg, now a ruin, in order "to acquire the castle for my family again, whose name it has retained despite all the changes that have taken place, and will retain in the future."[23] He did not do this to gain any advantage; he donated the income from the gardens and meadows "to be distributed among the poor" of the district. He even detailed the process of how this should be done: the income was to be established by

The ruin of Beilstein Castle, aquatint by Carl Bodmer (around 1835).

auctioning the yields within the parish and then putting the money into a re-lief fund for the poor.[24]

Metternich also made public his renewed claim to ownership. In his iron-works in Königswart, he had the family's coat of arms cast in iron, and he mounted them on the main tower of the ruin during a public ceremony under the aegis of the county's chief councillor on October 14, 1834. A representative of the hospital that profited from the Metternichs' contributions to the relief fund infused the event with the sort of romantic adoration for castles that was characteristic of the times when they declared "how this venerable ruin of the old Winneburg Castle, through the ages, has reminded us of the old splendor and glory of the princely dynasty, so highly praised for many centuries and throughout all of Germany, and belonging to us, the people of the Rhine, and how we therefore always like to be at the site of this sublime monument of times gone by in order to indulge in the greatness of the past and to form a strong vision for the future out of it." On this occasion, the imperial nobility, Habsburg, and Germany appear to have been a historical unity. After general cheers for "the returned noble compatriot, the great and much-celebrated statesman, Prince Metternich-Winneburg," a further toast invoked the patriotic spirit of the Lesser Germany at a celebration otherwise harmonious and merry with wine: "To the good of Prussia and all German states, which helped through their concerted actions to liberate the Rhineland from foreign domination!"[25] This formulation makes clear the competing national myths at play: on the one

The ruin of Winneburg Castle near Cochem, aquatint by Carl Bodmer
(around 1835).

side Habsburg, represented by Prince Metternich, on the other Prussia, sym-
bolized by the Hohenzollern. Nevertheless, the state chancellor, we may assume,
filed the article on the celebration with a feeling of satisfaction.

THE COUNTS AS MEMBERS OF THE IMPERIAL DIET

The simple fact of owning the lordships could not satisfy the Barons of Metternich, Winneburg and Beilstein. The lordships promised more because these
noble estates were listed in the Imperial Register—the register of those lord-

ships that were associated with a seat in the Imperial Diet. Their owners were entitled to this seat, but also had to demonstrate that they were worthy of it in terms of social rank. With the lordship came the title of count. This elevation of the Metternichs to the *third floor,* to *"Counts* of Metternich-Winneburg and Beilstein, Lords of Königswart,"[26] was also accompanied by certain favorable circumstances. A family member who was a prince elector and archbishop orchestrated the promotion from the background, just as Lothar had. That was Karl Heinrich, the oldest son of Wilhelm, one of the five brothers who had been made barons.[27] The family's elevation by Emperor Leopold I, on March 20, 1679, fell during the short period of Karl Heinrich's term as archbishop, between his election on January 9 and his death on September 26, 1679.

In the eyes of the Habsburg dynasty, the Metternichs had been able to increase their "moral capital" significantly in the time after 1635. The document of 1679 is official evidence of the importance which the House of Metternich by then held for the Habsburgs, providing a *narratio* that lists the names of all those Metternichs who had fought for the emperor, along with their specific achievements. The list begins with Archbishop Lothar, followed by Lothar's brother, the privy councillor of the electorate of Trier, Johann Dietrich, and his five sons, then the archbishop of Mainz, Karl Heinrich, and the imperial quartermaster [*Feldzeugmeister*] and burgrave of Eger, Philipp Emmerich, who was the second son of Wilhelm, one of the purchasers of Königswart. The document does not fail to emphasize that the quartermaster, despite having lost a leg after being hit by a cannonball in battle, continued his military service "with heroic composure" following his recovery. To write the extensive history of the Metternich family that forms the background to this list would be a task of its own. Here we need only take note of how broad and unfailing was this family's support for the emperor: at five imperial elections in the 1600s, at Imperial Diets, in colleges of prince electors, in cathedral chapters, and in archdioceses. After 1648 there were 137 canons that came from the Metternich family.[28] They helped the emperor in dealing with sensitive diplomatic affairs and negotiations, not least in the battle against the Protestants, with the rebellious Bohemian estates, and with the hostile Turks. All this, however, justified the Metternichs' elevation in rank only because "the whole lineage remained in the one and only true Catholic Church, never left it, and thus none [of its members] ever served another but our old house of German and Spanish descent." If you wanted to serve the emperor, you had to be Catholic. The qualities of the Metternichs as rulers were further enhanced by their elevation to the rank of counts: they now had the privilege to mint; were members of the Westphalian college of counts in the Imperial Diet; had access to all cathedral chapters (which secured the livelihoods of their descendants); had the authority to give fiefdoms to aristocratic knights; and were able to express all this publicly by taking the "title, predicate and word of honor 'Hochwohlgeboren.'"

The Indivisibility of the Family Fortune

The experiences of earlier centuries had shown the Metternichs that acquired wealth can disappear quickly through inheritance and the division of estates. What allowed the family to establish and maintain their noble status as a unified dynastic family, securing their wealth and thus the material basis of their existence, was a certain legal construct of inheritance and property law that is characteristic of old Europe. This was the entail [*Fideikommiss*], a contract that in effect transformed the family's assets into a trust that was administered by the head of the family but was not at his disposal. In the case of the Metternichs, it was the generation of Archbishop Lothar and his brother Johann Dietrich that showed that they had recognized the problem and that they were determined to erect barriers to the dissolution of the acquired wealth.

It was Lothar who developed a strategy to this end. On December 19, 1620, he created a family foundation and dedicated it to the "blood sons from marriage and the male marital lines descending from them." This was done "out of benevolent affection, as implanted by nature, for those related by blood," for "our family [*Stamm*] and name."[29] From this we can see that the particular "strength" of the family is not a retrospect invention by the historian; those of its members who played a central role, such as Lothar, consciously created and realized this strength as part of their plans for the family. Lothar's plan, in particular, demanded that the family be God-fearing, practice the skills proper to members of the nobility, visit foreign nations, learn languages, and be educated for a clerical or secular professional career. He also planned for assistance in cases of misfortune. It was imperative that those benefiting from the trust "had to be obliged to follow the ancient Catholic Roman religion, to be led to it and remain bound to it." Whoever dissented from it, by, for instance, becoming a Lutheran—"which God in his mercy may prevent from happening"—or did not study, or lacked proper obedience to the family and relatives, would lose his stipend. Those who did not marry according to the "old knightly" rules (i.e., in a way that befitted their social status) were also excluded from the trust.

But in his will of November 27, 1621, Lothar went even further, committing his heirs to deepen further the unity of the family.[30] He was thinking of all five of his nephews, who would later buy Königswart, but he excluded the three who held clerical offices (Johann Reinhard, Emmerich, and Carl) as heirs, and made the two in secular positions, Wilhelm and Lothar, the sole heirs of the estates he had acquired with "private money." This inheritance was to be

First page of the imperial document (August 20, 1756), signed by
Franz I, which sets out the rules for tutelage within the Metternich
entail.

"indivisible" [*unentgänzt*]: in the case of the death of one of them, possession
of his half of the inheritance would automatically pass to the other.

This arrangement avoided the emergence of a critical situation when the five
brothers later bought Königswart, ruling out the three brothers in clerical offices as heirs. On May 8, 1644, Lothar and Wilhelm agreed to a family contract
whose preamble shows that they had fully adopted their uncle's (the archbishop's) program of consolidating the family's position.[31] It is surprising to see
how passionately they felt about the fateful division of estates, which had for

Imperial seal of Joseph II on the document of March 3, 1768, which
assigned early privilege of age ("venia aetatis") to Franz Georg.

many centuries simply been accepted, declaring that "through good honest
brotherly unity and lasting alliances families and houses rise and are preserved,
while harmful misunderstandings, dismemberment of the inheritance and estates cannot sustain them, but necessarily lead to their demise." They explicitly
refer to Lothar, whose deeds, they say, "may lead to the steady rise of the Metternich family, our line, and continually guarantee the preservation of future
generations." "The rise and preservation of our house": this was the brothers'
maxim. From then on, the division of the ancestral homes of the Metternichs,
by marriage, inheritance, or attachments, was no longer permitted—whether
those homes were in Bohemia or in other parts of the empire—and newly
acquired possessions immediately became part of the family's estate.

This contract, a "family alliance" [*Stammesvereinigung*] in perpetuity, turned out to be a stroke of luck; by 1697 the entire family estate was in the hands of Philipp Emmerich, the son of Wilhelm, who formulated the definite entail. This reaffirmed all previous contracts, but this time was backed up by an edict of Emperor Leopold that put the estate of the Metternich family under the direct protection of the emperor.[32]

As it turned out, this would save the House of Metternich when, half a century later, it was staring into the abyss. When Johann Hugo, the grandfather of our protagonist, died on May 24, 1750, his son and heir (and Clemens Metternich's father), Franz Georg (born March 9, 1746), was only just four years old (his two younger brothers both died before 1753). Such was the tremendous protection that Emperor Franz I offered the Metternichs that he personally vetted and approved Franz Georg's new legal guardian. As when the family was promoted to a higher social rank, the relevant document—unusually ornate and delicately sealed—goes through all the achievements of the "ancient" family of the Metternichs, once more testifying to the high standing of the family in the eyes of the Habsburg dynasty.[33]

When the twenty-two-year-old Franz Georg desired to receive the privileges of maturity before reaching the age of majority—that is, before his twenty-fourth birthday—so that he could head the family entail, this also had to be thoroughly examined by the emperor, by that point Joseph II, taking into account the worthiness of the family and the special circumstances. He declared his consent on March 3, 1768, in a document no less magnificent than that appointing the guardian.[34] In 1770 Metternich's father reconfigured the foundation of the family in a new family contract.[35] The circumstances of the times, however, brought catastrophes for the family: they were forced to flee from their estates in the Rhineland (1794), the estate in Württemberg that they received in compensation was confiscated (1809), and the House finally faced complete bankruptcy. Despite all the reluctance of someone holding on to tradition, in 1815 Franz Georg was forced to yield and prematurely hand over the role of head of the entail to his son, Clemens. We shall look at this in more detail later.

THE HIGHEST FLOOR: THE PRINCES IN THE BEL ÉTAGE

But before all this occurred, Franz Georg did all he could to compensate for the period of weakness that had befallen the House of Metternich during the times of legal guardianship. In this, his success was not due to profit drawn from his lordships—he was incompetent in financial matters, and the revolutionary circumstances of the times made it difficult to achieve such gains. But he was able to use the moral capital of his family and the means at the disposal of the ancient meritocratic nobility: those of various services to the emperor. Thus was the family finally elevated to *princely status* on June 30, 1803.[36] As the Lordships of Winneburg and Beilstein had entered into French possession, the Metternichs needed a new lordship. Kaiser Franz II turned the secularized former imperial abbey Ochsenhausen in Wurttemerg into a principality for the Metternichs, "in order to leave the memory of their merits for posterity and thereby encourage others to follow their example." As this promotion demonstrates, many of the historical achievements we have already touched upon stayed in the imperial memory. The document, once again, provides a long list of them.

The honors and achievements of Franz Georg, as the one who was actually honored, were the result of thirty years of services to the emperor. Anyone who had persevered over such a long stretch of time, and in all kinds of offices, cannot possibly have fit Srbik's judgment of him as "without any special talents or deep knowledge" and "of a comparatively narrow intellectual horizon, without an independent will or capacity for autonomous action . . . , without lively ambition of his own"—in short, a mediocre "failure."[37] Quite to the contrary, the emperor had every reason to attest publicly to the "expertise, diligence, sagacity and efficiency" Franz Georg had shown during "critical events." Which political engagements did he stress? From 1773, Franz Georg had been a Habsburg diplomat, as their ambassador first at the Imperial Circle of the Upper Rhine, then at the Imperial Circle of the Lower Rhine and Westphalia. He acted as the emperor's representative at elections of the imperial church. He appeased the protests against the politics of Joseph II, protests that culminated in the unrest in the county of Liege; in other words, he brought to an end the Belgian revolution of 1790 in the Austrian Netherlands—which, of course, was in the interest of the Habsburgs. The same year, he acted as the electoral envoy for the Bohemian electorate at the election of Emperor Leopold II. In 1791 he developed a successful cooperative politics with the estates as the imperial and royal minister of the Austrian Netherlands (i.e., as the quasi-head of government) in Brussels. Finally, in 1797 he attended the Congress of Rastatt as the authorized representative of the emperor, as his "plenipotentiary." Thus, in the course of his life he was part of all the institutions that formed the complex structure of the Holy Roman Empire.[38]

Franz Georg was awarded numerous honors during these three decades. He was an Imperial Royal Chamberlain [*kaiserlich-königlicher wirklicher Kämmerer*], an Imperial Royal Privy Councillor, and a Knight of the Golden Fleece, and carried the Grand Cross of the Royal Hungarian Order of St. Stephen. These honors are a reflection of the symbolic and political rituals that research into the early modern period has now documented, after such forms had been neglected for a long time. We now better understand the "emperor's old cloth," which cloaked, as Barbara Stollberg-Rilinger put it, the "constitutional history and symbolic language of the Holy Roman Empire." In the document, the storied history of the Metternich family even serves to adumbrate the life of the eldest son, Clemens, who was an authorized minister (envoy) at the Prussian Court in Berlin at the time.

Franz Georg was mocked for his elevation to the rank of Prince of Ochsenhausen, even by Archduke Johann.[39] But those who were familiar with the Holy Roman Empire had to acknowledge the logic of this step. The Metternichs were members of the Imperial Diet, and this membership was inseparable from possession of a county within the empire. Loss of the latter automatically meant loss of the former. In order to give them back this important political quality, it was necessary to equip them with an adequate self-governed dominion. And Ochsenhausen Abbey, which had been just that prior to its secularization, fit the bill. It was by no means an "insufficient compensation" for the possession the Metternichs had lost west of the Rhine.[40] Indeed, it was more than sufficient. And Franz Georg, who had been involved in the negotiations, had made sure that this would be the case. Ochsenhausen was far larger and generated more income than Winneburg and Beilstein. It was this fact alone that made it possible, "according to the Constitution of the German Reich and the descendancy," to turn it into a principality, and to legitimize the elevation of the Metternichs to the rank of imperial princes.

The emperor, however, did not grant the princely honor in an altogether selfless manner. Franz Georg had to pay 31,612 guilders in cash to the tax office at the chancellery of the Imperial Court.[41] The need to pay this sum contributed significantly to the threat of bankruptcy the Metternichs faced. We shall return to this. It should not be forgotten, in all this, that Franz Georg himself, on May 26, 1803, sent a personal request to the emperor to be elevated to the rank of prince. His motivation for doing so, he said, was nothing but the wish, as the head of the family, to plan for the future and to take care of his descendants. He believed that as a prince he would be immune from the deprivations of rights that were already threatened for the counts.[42] Just one day after his promotion, and even before he was due at an audience with the emperor in order to thank him for it, the new Prince of Ochsenhausen passed a decree for the administration of his principality and used this opportunity to say how important it was "that such an honor bestowed upon a family that had dedicated itself over centuries to the German fatherland in the rank of clerical, electoral, and princely titles now also received imperial confirmation by being awarded a seat and vote in the Council of Princes."[43] Franz Georg was still completely absorbed in the tradition of the Holy Roman Empire and of his own house. And the congratulatory epistles that flooded in from all corners of the empire seemed to confirm him in his view of the world.[44]

By now the Metternichs had reached the top floor of our aristocratic *palais*. They possessed an individual vote (a so-called *Virilstimme*), and not just a collective vote *(Kurialstimme),*[45] at the Imperial Diet; they were members of the Imperial Council of Princes (which always made the decisions before the other estates in the Imperial Diet had their say); and, by becoming a prince, Franz Georg helped to restore the Catholic majority in the Imperial Council. But only three years later, the foundation on which the Metternich family stood was fatally fractured. Suddenly the Holy Roman Empire was nothing but a historical relic (if we leave aside certain continuities that extended into the nineteenth century). This must have been a personal tragedy for the Metternichs, the last of the aristocratic climbers. Whatever they did, they always came too late, and they ultimately failed. But did this mean that the family tradition, so bound up with the Holy Roman Empire, had also become obsolete?

For Clemens von Metternich, at least, there was to be an elevation beyond prince. To begin with, he remained a count, as only the head of the entail was a prince—Clemens's father, Franz Georg. This changed following victory in the Battle of Leipzig. A prince without a realm? The way Clemens von Metternich became a prince differed dramatically from the sorts of promotions we have seen so far. There was no document, no ornate seal, and the only reference made was to his father. But instead there was an extraordinary justification and personal statement by the emperor, who declared the honored person the savior of the state. Franz I, who thought ritual forms important and, in principle, was hostile to change, made the honoring of his state minister a public political matter. The handwritten letter from the emperor, dated October 20, 1813, which Metternich kept in his private archive, was published two weeks later, in full, on the front page of the *Wiener Zeitung*:

Dear Count Metternich!
The wise direction of the department I have entrusted to you during these difficult times has made it a beacon of success at one of the most decisive moments for the fate of the world. I therefore feel inclined to show you my appreciation in public by extending the princely honor, which your house already enjoys according to the right of primogeniture, not only to you but to all of your descendants in direct line from both sexes. With this decree, I also wish to keep the example of your father and the services you have rendered me and the state alive in the memory of your future de-

scendants, and to encourage them to act in the same way for the best of the monarchy.[46]

The emperor also exempted his commendable statesman from the state tax [*Kameral-Taxe*] on account of "his outstanding services to the state and the person of His Highest Majesty."[47] And in 1816, following the successful Vienna Congress, he gave Clemens von Metternich the dominion and castle Johannisberg in the Rheingau as a further sign of his appreciation.

How much the new honor meant to him and to his family Metternich revealed in 1814, in the midst of war, while pursuing Napoleon in France. In Langres, he developed initial ideas for a new princely coat of arms for his family,[48] and from Chaumont, where the allies formed their alliance against Napoleon, he asked the emperor to approve the design, which the emperor immediately did, "with great pleasure."[49] This final coat of arms, which has remained unchanged ever since, symbolically incorporated all the stages of the rise of the erstwhile Lords of Metternich: the heart-shaped inescutcheons stood for their beginnings; the black scallops were taken from the family coat of arms; and placed above the coat of arms was the final destination, the princely crown. The two areas with steplike diagonal bars and the crosses represent the Lordship of Winneburg, and the two areas decorated with bugles and ribbons refer to the Lordship of Beilstein. The ox head symbolizes the new Principality of Ochsenhausen.[50] Metternich explicitly wanted to add a motto, "after the fashion of the English Order of the Garter."

Being familiar with Metternich's noble ancestry [*reichsherrliche Herkunft*], with the perseverance of his family in their ascent, and with his understanding of the legal character of the Holy Roman Empire gives us a sense of what he meant with his motto "Strength in Law" [*Kraft im Recht*].[51] Against this background, one can also understand his later reaction to the stigma that was attached to the "Metternich system": he rejected it as an "illogical confusion of concepts." What took place, he said, was "the toppling of the old historical order of affairs in the empire."

The following demonstrates the position Metternich adopted during these times of radical change. It is evidence of the profundity of the state chancellor's insight that, in 1820, he came to a realistic conclusion regarding the ambivalence of his place between two historical epochs: "My life has fallen at a hateful time. I have come into the world either too early or too late. Now, I do not feel comfortable; earlier, I should have enjoyed the time; later, I should have helped to build it up again; today I have to give my life to prop up the moldering edifice. I should have been born in 1900, and I should have had the twentieth

The Great Princely Coat of Arms of the Metternich family, bearing the
motto "Kraft im Recht" [Strength in Law], 1814.

century before me."[52] While his father mourned the old times, he felt as if he
had fallen out of time. This, however, was no reason for him to doubt the
deeper significance and lasting legitimacy of his motto, which had grown out
of the old Holy Roman Empire. As his last documented words, uttered a little
more than two weeks before his death, reveal, in abiding by this motto, he felt
like a "rocher d'ordre": a rock of order.[53] Whether the "order" he stood for was
at all times the same will, with any luck, become visible in the course of our
progress through the history of this truly remarkable and memorable life.

2

METTERNICH'S GENERATION

Ancien Régime and Enlightenment, 1773–1792

PARENTAL HOME, CHILDHOOD, AND EDUCATION

Birth in Koblenz

Metternich was very aware of his ancestry. At the very beginning of his "Auto-biographical Memoirs," he declares: "Brought up in my father's house with loving care, I grew up under the influences of the position in which I was born—the public station of my father in the Imperial service, the French social life, and the moral laxity which characterized the smaller German States, before the storm burst forth which was soon afterwards to annihilate them."[1] Thus, even at fifty-three, Metternich[2] still recalled his childhood and, indeed, managed even then to paint a clear picture of the most important forces that determined his childhood and youth.

Metternich was born on May 15, 1773, in the family home in Koblenz and—as the birth certificate, written in Latin, tells us—christened Clemens Wenceslaus Lotharius Nepomucenus.[3] It was customary for those nobles with a sense of tradition to express something of their family's history through the many names given to their firstborn son. The fact that Clemens's father, Franz Georg, felt compelled in this way to honor the deeds of Lothar, the first prince elector of the family, is a sign of the gratitude the family felt toward this ancestor. Likewise, he considered it appropriate to pay respect to his former superior, the archbishop of Trier and prince elector Clemens Wenzeslaus of Saxony. Metternich would later repeatedly boast about having had him as his godfather—even though he was in fact represented by Franz Ludwig von Kesselstadt at the christening ceremony (a fact about which he kept a studied silence).

As a reliable protector of the house, the imperial church also acted favorably toward the young Clemens. When, in 1775, a prebend became available at the cathedral chapter of the archdiocese of Trier through the death of the previous recipient, Franz Georg did not hesitate to apply on behalf of his son—who was no more than two at the time. This cost him 500 reichstaler in fees. Even for an imperial count, the success of such an application could not be taken for granted, as it depended on a very detailed examination of whether his genealogy and noble standing were appropriate.[4] For this, he had to "demonstrate his descent from knights and members of cathedral chapters," a process then called Aufschwörung.[5] In the case of Franz Georg, it required fourteen documents of proof and certification: all the "arbor genealogiae"—that is, the family tree—plus the genealogical table from both the paternal and the maternal side of the family. Franz Georg explicitly referred to his descent from six generations of counts,[6] although usually only four were required. In this context, he had to compensate for the slight handicap that his wife, Beatrix, had become a countess only in 1770, shortly before their wedding, but the prestige of the Metternich family was supposed to offset that. Franz Georg listed four arguments: his family held a seat and had a vote at the Westphalian college of counts, where they were "superior [to the other counts] according to rank and order, as evidenced by the state calendars"; by marriage, they were related to the imperial houses of Anhalt, Nassau, Waldeck, and Lippe; according to documentary evidence they descended from the "ancient dynasties of Braunshorn [Beilstein] and Winneburg, whereof the coat of arms are still retained"; and, finally, Franz Georg pointed to his achievements as the head of the Catholic section in the Westphalian college of counts. This would surely impress the noble counts, who, in the cathedral chapters along the Rhine, had always managed to keep important positions to themselves. In 1777 Franz Georg succeeded in securing another prebend at the cathedral chapter of Mainz. These prebends would come in very handy later, when the two brothers, Clemens and Joseph, pursued their studies. In this way, the family's noble ancestry and the father's position in serving the emperor had a very real influence on Clemens's day-to-day life.

But why was Clemens born in Koblenz, in the Metternicher Hof at the Münzplatz, and not at Königswart? His more recent forefathers had shifted the center of gravity of their lives back to the Rhineland, lured by electoral ambitions and imperial positions—and thus it was, too, with Franz Georg.

The long list of functions that Metternich's father had fulfilled, first in the service of the Trier electorate, and then later in the service of the emperor,

The birthplace: Metternicher Hof in Koblenz (1674).

suggest a picture of an honorable politician. It is reported that toward the end of 1785, Emperor Joseph II said of him: "I think he is the best we have in the empire," because the others "are not up to these people" [i.e., imperial dignitaries who were not well disposed toward the emperor].[7] When Clemens was born, Franz Georg—then only twenty-eight—was already Count of Winneburg and Beilstein, Lord of Königswart, Spurkenburg, Naunheim, Reinhardstein, and Pousseur, hereditary archchamberlain of Mainz, imperial chamberlain, privy minister of the Trier electorate [*kurfürstlich Trierer geheimer Konferenzminister*], and vice-chamberlain [*Vize-Oberhofmarschall*].[8] Later, numerous offices were added to this list, among them in particular that of the imperial envoy to the electoral courts in Mainz, Trier, and Cologne. And even as late as 1810, Franz Georg still enjoyed the trust of the emperor to such a degree that the latter officially made him state minister in Vienna, standing in as foreign secretary for his own son, Clemens, during Clemens's long absence at Napoleon's court.

The Parental Home: Childhood, Youth, Educational Principles

As a rule, children of noble households in Metternich's time still experienced their parents as ideal representatives of their social rank: distanced and committed to the tasks of administration, representation, and estate-specific forms of sociability. The devotion, love, and attention his parents showed to Clemens are therefore all the more surprising. As a six-year-old, he was taken to Strasbourg to be vaccinated against smallpox.[9] At twelve he was encouraged by his father to develop a practice of diligent letter writing. Franz Georg praised the way his son used these letters to worry over his parents' health, but advised him—in a fatherly way—to avoid the repetition of thoughts and expressions and also to write in large script, lest the writing become illegible. And he expressed his hopes that Clemens would one day write things worth reading. From early on, the father included cuttings from newspapers in his letters and told his son to file them; he wrote lovingly about Clemens's mother and said he was happiest only when being with his family, signing his letters "your faithful father and friend."[10] This idea of the father as a friend and partner indicates an enlightened, bourgeois attitude and must have bolstered the sensitive adolescent's self-confidence. Immediately after Franz Georg's death, Metternich's drafts for an obituary reveal that the talk of a "fatherly friend" had not been empty: "His heart was German, simple and pure [*deutsch-bieder und rein*]. No tempest of the times could reduce his devotion to his fatherland and to the old and venerable empire; loyal and enlightened as a servant of the state, he was at the same time the best father and the most reliable friend."[11]

His mother, Beatrix, quite simply doted on her firstborn, and from early on she let the young man in on all of her political ideas—and her strategies for marrying off her daughter, Pauline. An uninterrupted correspondence, especially during his studies, provided Clemens with a motherly care that does not show any signs of that distance one might expect from the nobility. The mother frequently ended her letters with formulations like this: "My dear and excellent Clemens, you are my friend, my confidant, I cannot express how happy I feel to have you as my child."[12]

Franz Georg was an enlightened servant of the state. At no point in that revolutionary age, which led up to the times of the restoration, did he change his ways, something for which he was repeatedly criticized by the courtly ranks. For the young Clemens, his father's character had happy consequences: "At seventeen I was my own man. My father granted me complete freedom after he had established how little I was inclined to commit foolish acts, or even to consider them."[13] This is how the state chancellor would later describe the educa-

Metternich's father, Franz Georg von Metternich (unknown artist).

tional style in his parental home. Franz Georg had done a lot to foster this self-confidence in his son, as a condition for a strong-willed, fundamental trust in himself. In the final version of his memoirs, Metternich omitted to mention that his father took him along on highly political business when he was still a child and offered him ample opportunities to develop his social skills. As early as possible, he began to prepare him for a diplomatic career, and even for that of a statesman. In 1780 Franz Georg took seven-year-old Clemens with him to Cologne and Münster, where, as imperial commissioner on the personal orders of Emperor Joseph II, Franz Georg helped to secure the election of Habsburg archbishop Maximilian, a brother of the emperor, as coadjutor. (Coadjutors were adjuncts to bishops and were often seen as their preordained successors.) Joseph II relied on the "loyalty, skill, and experience" that Franz Georg had shown when dealing with such matters before, by which he meant that Franz Georg had the ability to make the cathedral chapter feel as though it were

Metternich's mother, Beatrix, née von Kageneck (unknown artist).

making a free choice while in fact preventing the election of anyone other than the emperor's chosen candidate.

On that occasion the young Clemens experienced firsthand how successfully his father conducted his political business. And his father would surely not have hesitated to show him the exuberant thank-you letter from Maria Theresia that he received following Maximilian's election.[14] This journey was not an isolated incident. In 1786 the father took Clemens, now thirteen, with him on trips as imperial commissioner to elections of coadjutants in Hildesheim and Paderborn. In June of the same year, Clemens also went to Königswart for the first time, and here, too, he witnessed how greatly politics influenced the family. When, upon the death of Frederick the Great, his father had to leave Königswart immediately and return to his duties as ambassador, this was another indication that he was the Austrian emperors' most trusted servant in the empire.

The Tutor Johann Friedrich Simon

In Metternich's times, the people who saw to the upbringing of noble offspring were not parents but wet nurses, nannies, governesses, and—in the case of sons—private tutors, so-called Hofmeister. The sons' tutors pursued the ideal of the educated courtier and gallant chevalier. Manners ("conduite"), the arts (especially music), languages, riding, fencing, and dancing were all part of the educational program for boys. In addition, there was a rich curriculum in history, state science [*Staatskunde*], genealogy, and cameralism.[15] The relationship between the father and his first son was determined early on by the latter's future role as heir.

Franz Georg's choice of tutor for his two sons, Clemens and his younger brother, Joseph, shows us how carefully he thought about their education. The choice fell on Johann Friedrich Simon, the perfect embodiment of the new educational ideas of the time. Simon was born in Alsace and was originally a Protestant theologian, but he had given up his studies in favor of modern pedagogics, which he learned with Johann Bernhard Basedow at his "Philanthropinum" in Dessau, seen as the mecca of enlightened education and as a "nursery of humanity." Basedow, the master, was critical of the old teaching methods of mechanical learning and cramming; he taught that it was important to learn in a playful way, through independent activity and experience. He promoted in particular the teaching of living languages, including one's native tongue, in addition to the classical ones. His disciple Simon was especially impressed by this latter point. Following the principle "docendo discitur"—learning by teaching—he became a tutor himself after his return to Alsace. He started a progressive "educational institution for Protestant women of rank," which, however, was not a success and was forced to close.[16] Thus, in 1783 he settled on being a schoolteacher in Neuwied, about ten kilometers northwest of Koblenz.

What might have motivated a Catholic imperial count to invite this Protestant educator into his house to act as tutor to his sons? Both men, obviously, were sympathetic to the Enlightenment, which, without being explicitly political, expressed itself in three principles: they understood religion as a predominantly moral and not a dogmatic institution; they believed barriers between the estates were to be overcome in the form of secret societies; and they held cosmopolitan ideals that they cultivated together in the appropriate social circles. In 1785, for instance, Franz Georg became a member of the Masonic Lodge "Karoline zu den drei Pfauen" in Neuwied, a group to which Simon also belonged; both were also members of the Illuminati.[17] Franz Georg was serious about the Enlightenment as the appropriate form of thinking and living for his

times, and also for his own house, and Simon had the requisite progressive ped-
agogy, eloquence, and passion for "the German fatherland." Educational capa-
bility was the decisive factor in choosing a tutor. The great importance Franz
Georg attached to linguistic abilities, and in particular near-native competence
in another language, is revealed by a warning he gave Clemens: "For a German
it is always particularly necessary, not only to speak and write his mother
tongue, but to do so with that excellence which corresponds with a thorough
education, and a perfection of language which will raise him above the crowd.
Much reading and writing acts on the powers of the mind, and in order to prac-
tise these, I shall continue my correspondence with you, dear Clemens, and
your brother in German, whilst you can carry it on in French with your
mother."[18] In 1786 Simon began teaching the young Clemens at home, having
gathered his courage on January 11 and written "humbly" to the imperial count.
As the professor and director of the Hochfürstlich-Privilegierte Erziehungs-
anstalt [Princely educational institution] in Neuwied, Simon, the quintessen-
tial educationalist, suggested to Franz Georg introducing a new method of
teaching languages he had developed at schools in Trier and Koblenz. At the
same time, he presented the principles for an educationally inspired reform of
German grammar and linguistics that he called an "attempt at a generally understandable German grammar for all of the German youth, independent of
rank or gender."[19] More precisely, he recommended that the "higher ranks"—
that is, the nobility—who must also learn foreign languages should not begin
to do so before they had "become familiar to some degree with the spirit of
their mother tongue." At the moment, "the German youth cannot learn its
mother tongue without having first been chased through the purgatory of
Latin." Simon thus presented himself as an original thinker and so as an excellent candidate to be Clemens's tutor. Simon's erudition, Franz Georg thought,
would rub off on his son. The bible of French Enlightenment, Diderot's *Encyclopédie,* was part of Simon's private library.[20]

Simon influenced Metternich's religious mentality in a very particular way.
He did not deny his theological training, but he guided his pupil to an understanding of God that was based not on church dogma but on the history of
religion. Fully in line with the spirit of the Enlightenment, he spoke of God as
"l'Être Suprème," the Supreme Being.[21] He taught that the Bible had to be understood as a historical piece of writing that had sometimes had to be corrected, partly because of mistakes in the translation, and partly because we now
had a better understanding of "human nature." Adam and Eve's fall in Genesis, he suggested, gave God the opportunity to impose an educational program
on humans. The first humans had been like overgrown children who "first had
to acquire their knowledge through experience and reflection," and God had

been like a wise father who taught them. It was not original sin that led Adam and Eve astray, but a lack of experience. But it was below God's dignity to mock the humans who had done wrong out of ignorance. Simon considered God to be "le premier Chef et Directeur de toute la nature" [the highest master and director of all of nature]. He thought the true spirit of Christianity was reconcilable with rational philosophy; it was about filling the heart with brotherly love. It would be physically and morally impossible to love a God whose highest pleasure was to see humans act against all pleasurable feelings ("sentiments agréable")—feelings he himself had planted in them in the first place—and then to ask them to do penance for them. Throughout all theological matters, Simon taught one particular method: to look for historical origins, and in this way to discover the intellectually satisfying truth, a truth that was simple and comforting for all human beings if only they tried to think and feel. He did not derive this truth from unchanging holy scripture, but from the correct historical reading of it.[22]

Simon saw experience—the knowledge of things that frees one from prejudice—as truly promoting enlightenment. World history was actually a big educational project: the expulsion from paradise and the painful conquest and cultivation of the earth has taught human beings how to recognize God's influence on the growing and becoming of nature. The experience of working the fields was complemented by reflection: "Experience and thinking are the only major forces which form the human mind."[23]

Exposure to such an enthusiastic and original character had a dramatic effect on the receptive, intelligent, and youthful Metternich, but not in the sense of an immediate "influence"—rather, it provided Metternich with a set of instructions for becoming an independent critical mind, including in religious matters. The mind was not to be directed by ecclesiastical dogma or orthodox belief in the scriptures but by the empirically based omnipotence of reason—something Simon also thought was expressed in the order of creation. This practical theism, which saw God's hand in nature but posited reason as the highest judge in all questions of action and evaluation and took Jesus to have been an exemplary human being, created that free space for independent thinking that Metternich occupied throughout his life. Early on, his educator confirmed him in his need to adopt a fundamentally critical and rational attitude and thus to establish a distance between himself and the surrounding world.

It was this distance that Metternich later invoked when he looked back and asked why he never allowed himself to be taken in by the pathos of the French Revolution. "[I was] its close observer, and subsequently became its adversary; and so I have ever remained without having been once drawn into its whirlpool.

I have known more than enough people whose characters had not sufficient strength to resist the luring illusions of innovations and theories which my own understanding and conscience discarded as not fit to pass before the court of reason and of legitimate right [*des guten Rechts*]."[24] His old tutor, Hofmeister Simon—who was very likely someone he had in mind when he spoke of those who had been "lured" by illusions—had, in his appeals to the critical use of reason, provided him with the very critical capacity that allowed him, in 1789, to distance himself from his teacher when the latter "plunged himself headlong into the torrent of the Revolution."[25] Metternich also called him his "Jacobin teacher," and said he had witnessed his "errors."[26] He did not develop any hateful feelings for him—indeed, he never developed such feelings toward those who thought differently—but rather looked on him as an object of study; his motto was "to study the enemy and know my way about his camp."[27] He would later take the same stance toward Napoleon. Of Simon and another "Jacobin" he declared: "I must do both these men the justice to state that they never attempted to influence my opinions."[28] Here, too, Metternich showed, very early on, a trait that stayed with him until old age. In the course of sorting his archive, he happened upon Simon's letters. He did not deny the importance that Simon undoubtedly had had for him, but he rather calmly observed that, given what became of Simon, the letters were now of "psychological interest."[29]

The Tutor Abbé Ludwig Bertrand Höhn

The young Clemens had a second tutor, as a spiritual corrective to Simon, so to speak: the Abbé Ludwig Bertrand Höhn. He had succeeded an older brother of his order to the position of Hofmeister after that brother's death in 1782. Bertrand taught Clemens "classics" (i.e., classical antiquity, including the Greek and Latin languages) and—together with Simon—the classical humanist subjects.[30] When Clemens later studied at Strasbourg, the Abbé Bertrand remained a reliable point of reference for him, while Simon drifted off into revolutionary circles. In his choice of Clemens's spiritual educators, the father was as cautious and consciously undogmatic as he was in his choice of Simon: both (Bertrand's predecessor and Bertrand himself) were members of the Piarist Order, who were active in education and in schools, in particular in the Habsburg Monarchy.[31] The order originated in Trastevere, a poor quarter of Rome, and hence took as its mission caring for the socially marginalized and attending to the pressing problems of everyday life, as well as reform of the church.

In Metternich's judgment, the Abbé Bertrand was "a calm and educated man," and when, at the age of nineteen, Metternich decided that he had reached a point where he no longer needed an educator, he remarked about him: "My tutor had become my friend and counselor."[32] Indeed, over the years the teacher–pupil relationship had developed into a relationship of trust and friendship. A letter Metternich wrote—under extremely trying circumstances, namely immediately before the Battle of Leipzig, on October 3, 1813, from the headquarters in Teplitz—shows us as much. The concerned abbé had been following events from neighboring Tajax (Djákovice) in southern Moravia, where he was working. Despite all the pressing problems he was facing, Metternich responded to Bertrand's anxious letter, not with a few glib phrases, but with exceptional seriousness and openness, as was only appropriate for his former teacher. He explained his political convictions to him in a way that made his actions intelligible as part of a larger mission, and he conveyed the interconnection between rational action and divine plan taught to him by Simon. We cannot expect God's help without acting ourselves, he said:

> I have begun a great work; I have slowly advanced. All our powers had to be concentrated, and we had to wait for the right moment. We had to have *moral* right on our side in order to be able *materially* to make this right prevail. Heaven has blessed our undertaking; *heaven helps us because we help ourselves,* and in a short time it will be with French tyranny as with the cedar of Lebanon. . . . That I shall complete this work, if God gives me the health and time to do so, you may rest assured.[33]

Metternich concludes with the words: "Fare thee well, dear Abbé, and keep your friendship for me." One addresses someone in such terms only if one feels personally grateful and committed to him.

STUDIES IN STRASBOURG AND MAINZ: FORMATION OF A POLITICAL AND HISTORICAL VIEW OF THE WORLD

For a biographer it is as tempting as it is necessary to consider the question of the extent to which early influences play a role in the later thought and actions of the protagonist, and in this regard the years of university study are always of particular interest. In his memoirs, Metternich provides some clues, but a lot is only hinted at and can be deciphered only against the backdrop of his correspondence, the judgments he expresses in official documents, and the aperçus we find in his posthumous papers. Such a systematic and chronological reading, following the progress of his education, has not been undertaken before, and we will attempt to fill this gap in what follows. The key moments for an understanding of Metternich's later political and historical perspective are to be found in the years 1788 to 1794. He himself would have agreed with this claim, although with hindsight, in 1818, he put it with even more certainty: "At seventeen—leaving aside experience—I was what I am today, exactly what I am today, with the same mistakes, the same virtues."[34]

In April 1788, Metternich (born May 15, 1773) was only just fifteen years of age when he departed for Strasbourg with his two tutors in order to take up his studies.[35] By age seventeen, halfway through 1790, he had completed these studies. But this by no means meant that his development was now "complete," as he later claimed. There followed his studies at Mainz, the imperial coronations of 1790 and 1792, his time in Brussels, and his stay in England. These events had such a lasting influence on him that one can only call his development "complete" in August 1794. In that month, in his second major pamphlet, he set out his political worldview. The fundamental experiences of his studies, the Revolution, war, and the decline of the empire all fall within the period of the six years between 1788 and 1794.

Metternich at the University

Franz Georg sent his two sons to study in Strasbourg. The costs involved, no doubt, were a burden to him. The financial support of the prebend from the cathedral chapter in Mainz, which in 1783 had passed from Clemens to his younger brother, Joseph, at least secured the latter's upkeep, and was therefore a welcome help. This "stipend" was paid as a "biennium," every two years, and yielded "the not insignificant revenue" of 700 to 800 guilders per year. The sum was calculated from the natural produce in the dominions of the church, which varied according to the harvest and market prices. The recipient agreed to a "code of conduct which every domicellar or canon of Mainz who wants to go and study, upon arrival, had to follow."[36] Under the terms of the prebend, Strasbourg was a possible university destination because it could be reached from Mainz within twenty-four hours, and it was thus perfectly possible to be supported beyond the two years.

Clemens, by contrast, had to negotiate his finances directly with his father. Every quarter, he reported to his "dear papa" how he had spent his days, but most of all how, given the restricted means, he was trying to lead an extremely frugal life. This he demonstrated with tabular surveys in order, say, to get approval for a theater subscription so that he could while away the dreary winter days by watching comedies.

Both tutors provided the father with exact accounts of the progress made by the two sons. From mid-June 1788, Simon reported regularly on the studies of his disciples. He taught them to swim; accompanied them to their classes and lectures; arranged social gatherings with twelve young aristocrats who attended the same course on natural history; and made experimental physics part of the curriculum. The young Count Clemens, he wrote, has developed "si gai, beau et aimable" [joyfully, beautifully, and pleasantly].[37] The Abbé Bertrand also wrote regularly to Franz Georg and tried to justify the expenses incurred. On May 13, 1789, he provided a summary of the situation of his two disciples. They lived, he wrote, "dans le grande [*sic*] monde" [in high society] and, by virtue of their birth, knowledge, and age, were already part of the local aristocracy. Wherever they appeared, they drew people's attention, and people sought them out to invite them to picnics, concerts, and balls.[38]

In return, Franz Georg regularly provided the two tutors with instructions, of a kind we would expect from him by now: he urged his sons to learn languages, in particular English, and thus guided the young Metternich to "a language which constantly requires large investments of time and practice," as the abbé replied. Fortunately, he wrote, Clemens's language teacher had spent almost twelve years in London and, even according to the judgment of Englishmen, spoke the language very well.

When writing to Franz Georg, Bertrand was cautious in his judgments of Clemens's behavior: he had very suddenly lost all his silliness, and he, the abbé, wished that Clemens would demonstrate a more steady and determined character, but this weakness could be put down more to his age than to his heart. A little later, on December 30, 1790, Franz Georg wrote to Clemens, who had just moved from Strasbourg to the University in Mainz together with his brother. Both were still under the care of the Abbé Bertrand, who enjoyed the absolute trust of the family. With the characteristics of student life in mind, the father told Clemens the two brothers should "refrain from all offensiveness toward others" and dedicate themselves solely to the actual purpose of their stay—namely, to serve the higher sciences and "to gain the respect and affection of others through decent behavior and common politeness." Bertrand had already sent the father very good study certificates: "Now you must seek to preserve this initial good reputation you have earned, because everything depends on this. . . . And generally I recommend to you to take care of your health meticulously, as man's happiness depends on it."[39] In the same letter, Franz Georg let his firstborn know that his appointment to the Netherlands had been decided and would soon be announced publicly.

Studies in Strasbourg with Christoph Wilhelm Koch

In its heyday during the ancien régime, the Protestant University of Strasbourg was like a "revolving door between France and Germany."[40] It was the leading university in France, just as it was—next to Göttingen—the leading university in the German-speaking cultural space. Eberhard Weis brilliantly describes the "special spirit of this city," which united "German and French culture, the gothic and the rococo, Catholicism and Protestantism, absolute monarchy and the self-administration granted to the former imperial city, aristocracy and a wealthy, self-confident bourgeoisie, the arts and the sciences."[41] This atmosphere allowed for the emergence of a cosmopolitan spirit that influenced the elite up to the age of nationalism. In Metternich's judgment, the university "enjoyed great fame, and was much frequented by Germans, who went there on account of the facilities it offered for acquiring the German and French languages."[42]

Beginning in 1772, the lectures of Christoph Wilhelm Koch, who taught state law and history, in particular earned the university a reputation as a "diplomatic school." Koch taught Goethe; Montgelas, the most famous of the Bavarian reformers of the state; Constant, the propagandist for constitutional liberalism; Michel Gaudin, Napoleon's finance minister; Prince Andrej Rasumowsky, who later was the Russian ambassador in Vienna and delegate of the tsar at the Vienna Congress; and our Metternich, who was in Strasbourg between April 1788 and July 1790.

The precocious Metternich, listening to Koch at the age of fifteen to seventeen, owed important elements of his later political view of the world to this teacher. This we know without having to resort to biographical speculation because their ideas correspond so closely, and so often, that their similarities surpass what might be accounted for by a nebulous "spirit of the age." We can find the analogies to Metternich's later thinking *in nuce* in Koch's three-volume *Gemählde der Revolutionen in Europa seit dem Umsturze des Römischen Kaiserthums im Occident bis auf unsere Zeiten* [Depiction of the revolutions in Europe from the end of Roman occidental imperialism to our times], which is the summary of his lifelong research. A copy of this work can still be found in Metternich's library in Königswart. It displays an attitude toward dealing with history that the later state chancellor showed on a daily basis. Let us take a look at the essential features of this attitude.

History, Koch says, is "a kind of philosophy." It accumulates experiences and teaches by way of example "how one should comport oneself in all situations of private and public life." History does not teach contents or facts but how to use historical knowledge. It teaches a method of thinking and for ordering experience. Koch introduces his work by formulating principles that we find in an almost identical form in Metternich. His numerous reflections on politics and the motives for human actions are based on the following assumption as their philosophical base:

> There are certain principles and rules of behavior that are eternally true because they correspond to the unchanging nature of how things are. If

we study history, we collect these principles, and in this way we can form a system of morality [*Sittenlehre*] and politics for ourselves. . . . Especially those who dedicate themselves to the study of politics, or are destined to become directors of public affairs, will discover in history the motivating forces of governments, their mistakes and qualities, their strengths and weaknesses. In this, they will find the origins and development of empires, the principles which led to their rise, and also the causes that prepared their downfall.[43]

Koch's perspective on history is not about progress in a naive Enlightenment sense. Instead, history is a neutral tool for analysis. A politician, Koch holds, must look at history scientifically, establish its systematic and regular features, and search for causal connections. If we consider his approach from today's perspective, but translate his concepts into modern methodology, then we get a politically minded social scientist, a Max Weber, who looks to history not for norms but for ideal types, in order to capture the complex empirical reality and "to organize it intellectually." This is in no way an illegitimate way of modernizing Koch and Metternich. History, the Strasbourg teacher says, is a sequence of progressions as well as of delusions, of enlightenment and superstition, and neither the delusions nor the superstitions ever end. The reflecting mind tries to recognize the traces of what is regular in this empirical chaos, in order to plan the future according to a purpose: "History is better than any prescription for healing us from the confusions caused by our self-love and from national partiality. Whoever is familiar only with his *own* country will easily imagine that the government, the customs and concepts, or the ideas held in *that* corner of the planet where *he* lives are the only rational ones. Self-love, so natural to the human being, feeds this prejudice and lets him undervalue other nations."[44] Metternich would later experience in political practice how difficult it was to bring the twelve different nationalities of the Habsburg Monarchy into harmony. And he recognized that the blindness and self-love of the national idea can justify political terrorism. In Koch he found the theoretical armor that, in the long term, made him a cosmopolitan who put peace and political rationality above the national interests of states, those interests that increasingly pushed to the foreground in the long nineteenth century.

For Koch, history was a scientific method, not a scholarly collection of facts and sources. Those who studied with him were made to understand the value of sources, of the critique of sources, and the need to support historical claims with sources. One might be led to think that Koch was a pupil of Ranke when he demands that one "examine the mind and character" of every historiographer "and also the circumstances under which they wrote"; "impartiality" he took to be "an essential trait for the historiographer," who needs to leave behind the prejudices of his nation, his sect, or social rank.[45] And, finally, the historiographer must also take note of the auxiliary disciplines: geography, genealogy, and chronology. History, he writes, is a sequence of periods that follow each other in "revolutions," and beginning from its primordial base in antiquity it is a European history, or—even more precisely—a global history, because North America, the Spanish colonies, Canada, East India, and not least the Ottoman Empire also form part of its horizon.

Koch taught history as a study of states and their wars, and he saw the fundamental problem of history as creating and preserving peace. What Metternich later faced on a daily basis as his political task, Koch's "diplomatic school" presented to him as a theoretical problem. Here he learned that the history of the European states after the Peace of Westphalia in 1648 was about maintaining the balance between the major powers. The politics pursued by Louis XIV, he was told, gave France "a dominance" and "made it so frightful that all the political machinery was directed against France."[46] Metternich's idea of European power politics, however, went beyond the idea of a mechanical structure inherent in the relations between the states. He posited that international politics had to be subjected to ethical norms, to a modern international law of a kind that had not previously existed. This principle leads us to the second academic teacher who was important for Metternich. And thus we move on to Mainz, where Clemens and his brother arrived in mid-October 1790, now accompanied by only one of their Hofmeisters, Abbé Bertrand.

Studies in Mainz with Niklas Vogt

The two brothers spent two years in Mainz,[47] before departing for Brussels at the beginning of September 1792. The period was framed by two imperial coronations in nearby Frankfurt. Mainz was a Catholic university that once had been extremely backward, but a reform in 1784, following the suspension of the Jesuit Order in 1773 and the beginning of the reign of the penultimate electoral prince, Friedrich Karl von Erthal (1774–1802), had changed this. The reform had been acknowledged throughout the empire for its enlightened impulses.[48] In the context of this reform, the discipline of history acquired a new and independent profile and developed into an "indispensable fundamental science."[49]

Niklas Vogt, appointed professor of universal history in the newly founded historical statistical faculty, contributed substantially to this development. His lively delivery made him popular with the students. In 1790, of the 300 students of Mainz, 91 could be found at his lectures.[50] Vogt introduced a new style of interacting with his students. As a convinced Kantian, he preached that enlightenment spreads through "publicity," something that put him at odds with the freemasons and illuminati. To that end, he invited all of his pupils, regardless of social rank, and also the female students, to the salons in his house. The young Metternich attended his lectures on German imperial history and was one of Vogt's favorite students, and later admitted "how many helpful resources I was later to draw on from his lectures." It was at these lectures that he learned— in a fashion even more pronounced and pervasive than Koch's—to use history as a guiding discipline.

Vogt possessed a special educational talent. When he embarked on a new chapter in one of his lectures, he began by asking questions that at once caught the attention of his listeners: "How did the common citizens deprive themselves of their freedom?"; "How did bishops and abbots become sovereigns?"; "How did a great woman save the Austrian monarchy and thus the Constitution of the German empire?"; "How did Germany help to bring about the French Revolution?"[51] While in Mainz, Metternich internalized this way of providing answers by circling around historical questions, thus relating history to the present and further consolidating the basis of one's judgments. In 1801 he presented a masterpiece along these lines in the form of his draft instructions for the embassy in Dresden.

Vogt soon came to appreciate the young count as an alert listener, and he discussed fundamental problems of "historical critique" in personal conversations with him. He recognized Metternich's peculiar personality, which united three traits: a capacity for quick absorption, a talent for critical observation, and an inclination to identify principles in the seemingly obvious. This led Vogt to give Metternich a piece of advice that may appear prophetic, and that Metternich would return to many times. It would be wrong to assume that Metternich returned to it for narcissistic self-reflection; rather, the quotation is an example of Vogt's educational and emphatic fervor (for which there is plenty of other evidence) in his dealings with his student, whom he knew was meant to embark on a diplomatic career. He told him:

> Your intellect and your heart are on the right road; persevere therein also in practical life, the lessons of History will guide you. Your career, however long it may be, will not enable you to see the end of the conflagration which is destroying the great neighbouring kingdom. If you do not wish to expose yourself to reproaches, never leave the straight path. You will see many so-called great men pass by you with swift strides; let them pass, but do not deviate from your path. You will catch up with them, and be it only because your path and theirs will cross when they retreat![52]

What Metternich discreetly omits is the fact that his revered teacher had temporarily become a fervent admirer of Napoleon, only to later become bitterly disappointed by him.

What Vogt had to say about the peculiarity of the Constitution of the German empire left a lasting impression on Metternich because it related to the foundations of his own family. Vogt taught that it was a mixed Constitution: "Fortunately for Europe, this important country [Germany] is divided into several states which are, however, united into one main state, so that it is fair to say that the balance in Europe is concentrated in Germany, and that its laws are at the same time an important part of international law."[53] The "division into several smaller states" saved Europe from facing a monarch who "would inevitably be in a position of dominance and consequently . . . would find it easy to found, by himself, a universal monarchy." In other words, the mixed federal Constitution of the Holy Roman Empire, sitting at the center of the Continent, protected the other European states against a German despotism. Vogt had elaborated this fundamental idea in 1787 in the first volume of his *Über die Europäische Republik* [On the European republic], titled *Politisches Sistem* [Political system]. The motto was taken from Montesquieu *(The Spirit of the Laws),* an author Vogt recommended rather gushingly. The motto expressed the idea that the competing powers had to be forced into a common balanced "concert."[54]

Vogt transferred this principle of the division of power onto all human societies, all of which he saw as formed by attractive and repulsive forces. A balance needed to be found between cosmopolitanism, patriotism, and egotism: this was the only way to tame the egotistical drives of nature, whether in families, villages, cities, fiefdoms, or religious communities; in social estates, provinces, states, or the European republic; or even at the level of a "global citizenship" [*Weltbürgerschaft*]. Vogt was well aware of all the deficiencies of the empire's mixed Constitution; nevertheless, he saw it as guaranteeing the freedom and legal security of the lesser powers. For him, the main principle of the great European law was this: "Every community, every province, every country should be allowed to have its own laws and institutions as it sees fit, as long as they are not in obvious contradiction to the common good." The sole purpose of higher laws was to impede the "harmful excesses" of subordinate laws.[55] These views demonstrate that for those living in the late eighteenth century, cosmopolitanism, patriotism, and nationalism were by no means mutually exclusive.[56]

In Vogt's views the young Metternich found justification for what, later on, his father in dealing with the Belgian estates, and he himself in dealing with the Bohemian and Hungarian estates, would take to heart: respect for the historically given statutes. At the same time, he learned to despise absolutist inclinations like those of Emperor Joseph II. The constitutional principles, as taught by Vogt, stayed with Metternich in particular because of their comparison with related "constitutional" states in Europe, such as England, the Dutch states represented in the States General, or the Swiss confederation: "Among all European states, none remained as faithful to the original German Constitution, and thus to its freedom, as England. The English Constitution shows us what a wonderful edifice of bourgeois freedom lay dormant in our Old Gothic Europe."[57] As Vogt's presentation of the English Constitution followed Montesquieu, quoting him over whole pages, Metternich became familiar with the French author as well.[58] Then, Vogt would go on to contrast the English Constitution with the German: "Of all European states, the German empire has the most peculiar Constitution. If we look at its form, we must call Germany a limited aristocratic monarchy. But if we consider the actual connections within this Gothic edifice, then it turns out to be an association of sovereign princes, headed by two powerful Houses, Austria and Brandenburg, at the center of which [empire] we find concentrated the balance of all of Europe."[59] When, before the Vienna Congress, Metternich pondered the question of how Europe should be reconstituted, he had this idea of a "composite state" in mind. He spoke of "reconstruction," not "restoration," and he referred to the peculiarity of the Habsburg Empire, which, like the later German Confederation, was a successor to the Holy Roman Empire. The following passage shows clearly the great extent to which his ideas depended on Vogt's: "The Empire of Austria, without being a federal state, had yet the advantage and the disadvantage of a federal Constitution. If the head of the house was in the modern sense of the word absolute, this notion was restricted in its sovereign power, according to the different Constitutions of the several countries whose crowns he united on his own head."[60] Vogt taught Metternich a philosophy of history that encouraged him not to feel that he was at the mercy of anonymous forces that could not be challenged. As in the case of Koch, the curriculum included references to the teachings of the Greek and Romans, as this is where European historical accounts began. The classical doctrine of the ancients according to which the ideal mixed Constitution will always threaten to degenerate was adopted by thinkers in the eighteenth century. Constitutional systems were constructed in line with a sequence that was believed to be based on a law: as soon as degeneration sets in, monarchy turns to despotism or tyranny; aristocracy into oligarchy; and democracy into demagogy. Vogt also taught his students this classical doctrine of state forms.[61] According to Montesquieu, a mixed Constitution created "the power to halt power," and it had to be sought in order to avoid the endless circle of tyranny and demagogy.

This historical pattern was also later used by Metternich to produce a plausible explanation for the sequence of events in the French Revolution. The French aristocracy wanted to break the power of the monarchy and tame it by establishing a balance of power among the king, Louis XVI, the nobility, and the people. This plan failed because the "democratic" people removed the monarchy and inaugurated the republic, which developed in the form of the reign of terror. And the reign of terror, in turn, unleashed the forces that called for a new tyrant (Napoleon). The task now was to tame the power of this tyrant by "reconstructing" a mixed constitutional order in Europe, in Germany, and in the Habsburg Empire. The revolution of 1848, finally, seemed to set the whole cycle of 1789 in motion again.

It is always difficult to provide undeniable proof of a teacher's "influence" on his or her pupils. As a rule, one has to make do with plausible analogs in the intellectual makeup of the latter. In addition, there may be hints in pupils' statements. Metternich, for instance, mentions Vogt explicitly in his memoirs, and even calls him his "friend," an honor he bestowed on only a few people. This, however, does not make him an unconditional devotee. Some of the views Vogt later developed—his romanticizing return to Germanic history, the religious coloring of his philosophy of history—were not shared by the more rational Metternich. But the model of the empire as a nested grid of states corresponded well with his aristocratic experience and his experience of the empire's legal framework; it formulated concisely what he had hitherto only intuitively perceived.

Vogt died in 1836—he was by then a senator in Frankfurt—and Metternich fulfilled his teacher's dying wishes. Vogt wanted to be as close as possible to his famous disciple and to be buried at Johannisberg. His funeral took place on May 21. His grave can still be found today at the external wall of the chapel of Johannisberg Castle. In August 1838 the state chancellor had a commemorative plaque of black marble installed inside the chapel. This was destroyed during the Second World War but later restored. Metternich's inscription, in shining golden letters, says: "This is the place of rest chosen by Niklas Vogt—born in Mainz on 6 December 1756 / died in Frankfurt on 19 May 1836—this gravestone is dedicated to the faithful defender of the old law, the enthusiastic friend of the German fatherland, the ardent promoter of the history of his homeland, by his friend and grateful pupil Prince C. W. L. Metternich."[62] This was a public confession that was also noted by the press at the time.

All of the principles that Metternich learned from Koch and Vogt come together in a "confession" made by him in his memoirs, written in old age. Metternich dates the beginning of his active political career to the year 1801, and he gives an honest summary that "candidly state[s] the principles on which the actions of my political life have been based."[63] This passage does not portray Metternich as the great man of the "restoration," but as a politician of the Enlightenment who belonged to a generation of cosmopolitans. It is striking to see how the views he had acquired in the course of his studies stood the test of time as guidelines that he had followed in his political practice. Metternich's attitude toward politics is particularly characteristic and at the same time surprisingly modern: it is that of a soberly analyzing scientist. "Politics is the science of the vital interests of states at the highest level."[64] Acknowledging what he took from his teachers, he writes that it is "modern history" that teaches him, that provides the medium in which meanings form, and thus allows for the categorization and evaluation of events.

The task, Metternich writes, is to reconcile the special interests of a state with the general interest, because only the general interest can guarantee the existence of the states. Metternich's confession is born of an awareness that he lives in the "modern age," and in this context he advocates an international law that seeks to establish a system of balance that encapsulates and transcends the individual interests of states. Politics, for him, possessed a moral core which contained Kant's categorical imperative (here expressed in biblical language). It was inevitable that this core would be resisted by all politicians who were interested only in the mechanics of power and in a raison d'état, as well as by universal rulers of the Napoleonic type. It is well worth presenting this fundamental confession verbatim, for it also shows how modern Metternich's language was:

> That which characterizes the modern world, and essentially distinguishes it from the ancient, is the tendency of nations to draw near to each other, and in some fashion to enter into a social league. . . . In the ancient world, policy isolated itself entirely. . . . The law of retaliation set up eternal barriers and founded eternal enmities between the societies of men. . . . Modern history, on the other hand, exhibits the principle of the solidarity of nations and of the balance of power, and furnishes the spectacle of the combined endeavors of several states against any temporary predominance of a particular state in order to impede the further extension of the influence of that state's power, and to force it to return to the common law. The establishment of international relations upon the basis of reciprocity, under the guarantee of respect for acquired rights, and the conscientious observance of the given word, constitutes, at the present day, the essence of politics, of which diplomacy is only the daily application. Between politics and diplomacy there exists, in my opinion, the same difference as between science and art.[65]

Vogt had confronted Metternich with a theoretically advanced vision for a political order. This vision ended in a "European League of Nations," which Vogt also called "the European Republic."[66] For him, the European empires and nations formed a "great system of peoples, driven by the spirit of the same customs and politics" and should be "united into a common republic." The free and independent nations should be united by a common bond, resulting in "all of Europe being organized as a formal republic." The fundamental maxim of such an entity would be that no European state should be allowed to become so powerful that it could not be resisted. This, for Vogt, is the "balance of power."[67] This idea of a "league of nations" for Europe was, as we shall see, also adopted by Metternich and made part of his political repertoire.

The formative influences to which Metternich was exposed during his university studies at the end of the ancient régime were thus part of the horizon of the European Enlightenment. They turned Metternich into a representative of a generation that saw itself as part of a European community. Next to learned scholars, the nobility was to uphold this perspective because it was the last one to be nationalized. "Generation Metternich" took to heart the values we have presented here. Born around 1770, its members all subscribed to the idea of the old European legal order, which they understood, not as a feudal, repressive system, but as an order in which the less powerful also had rights. Within the context of the literature on the late stages of the *Ius publicum Imperii*, the empire's public law, they are also described as belonging to "generation Pütter."[68] It would be worthwhile asking whether "Generation Bonaparte," which we mentioned in the Introduction, is related to Generation Metternich not only temporally but intellectually (although they would hardly have been aware of this). When Metternich, in an important conversation with Napoleon, set aside his position as an Austrian minister and looked for some common basis with his interlocutor, he called himself—in front of his greatest opponent—a "cosmopolitan."[69] Later the minister would also share this European, or even universal, outlook with British colleagues of a kindred spirit, whose opinions had formed under similar generational conditions—among them politicians like Wellington and Castlereagh. Metternich practiced his supposedly "restorative" politics after 1815 on the basis of shared experiences of the Revolution, and its rejection, as well as common European norms. It is easily forgotten that it was driven by a cosmopolitan attitude.[70]

3

A DOUBLE CRISIS

Empire and Revolution, 1789–1801

At the end of the eighteenth century, central Europe experienced an unprecedented "clash of cultures." The old Holy Roman Empire sat at the center of the Continent like an old solid rock. It had evolved historically and was complicated and hierarchical. This empire was challenged by a vision of rationality, centralization, and emancipation that derived from the Enlightenment and found its violent expression in the attack of the French Revolution against the so-called ancien régime. The young Metternich grew up in the context of both of these worlds.

The imperial elections following the death of Emperor Joseph II on February 20, 1790, which had been foreseen, and the entirely unexpected death, on March 1, 1792, of Emperor Leopold II, whose reign had been associated with great hope for the future, meant that the Holy Roman Empire was tested twice in quick succession. Imperial coronations required an enormous investment in terms of money, personnel, ceremonial decorum, and legal process. It was therefore a clear sign of the often-doubted vitality and agency of this complex structure of states that it came to grips with these difficult challenges within a short period of time. In the judgment of the public, by contrast, a view has prevailed that is closer to the statement made by Karl Heinrich Lang, the son of a Swabian priest, on the occasion of the coronation in 1790. He called the ceremony a "picture of the ice-cold and rigid old German imperial Constitution which has become infantile, . . . as a carnival performance of an imperial coronation that flaunts its torn costumes."[1] Lang, and many others after him, did not understand the centuries-old and still desired political function performed by this staging. "The totality of the symbols, gestures, rituals, and processes in which the order of the empire was tangibly embodied" achieved something that every society needs: it produced what Barbara Stollberg-Rilinger called the "spell of a collective fiction" that equips an institutional order with a visible meaning.[2]

It was previously not known which function had been allocated to the young Metternich at the imperial elections—which culminated in coronations in Frankfurt Cathedral—or how his involvement was made possible at all. As a long-standing servant of the empire's rulers, his father, Franz Georg, was appointed as one of the three so-called electoral envoys [*Wahlgesandter*] that Bohemia had to send to the elections. The first of these envoys (Prince Esterházy) acted as the Bohemian Prince elector. Franz Georg was Esterházy's deputy, but at the same time the head of the Catholic Rhenish and Westphalian imperial counts. This latter role he could forsake and leave to his son, who thus became the representative of the imperial counts from this region at the imperial coronation. Thus, Imperial Count Metternich officially took part in both coronations (at seventeen and nineteen years old), which left lasting impressions upon him, not least because participation was an enormous honor for someone from his rank and at his age.

Against the backdrop of the French Revolution, Metternich experienced the imperial coronation on September 30, 1790, and—to an even greater extent—the one on July 14, 1792, as another world. For him, the latter was "one of the most sublime and at the same time splendid spectacles the world has ever seen. Everything, down to the most trifling details, spoke to the mind and heart."[3] Or to put it into more modern terms: everything created political meaning in a symbolic and sensual way. Metternich was sober enough in his analysis not only to see the "force of tradition," the splendor and glory, but also to ask the anxious question of whether the Revolution must not sooner or later set this old edifice alight. He considered the empire a centuries-old "protective power against a movement whose origin must be sought for long before the outbreak of 1789."[4] Metternich, who had studied in Strasbourg and Mainz, saw in Frankfurt, the old center of the empire, a "defensive power" against the first stirrings of Jacobinism. It was to him a place "where human grandeur was united with a noble national spirit." In his understanding, in this empire it was possible to be a patriotic German—this he concluded from its Constitution. At the same time, he saw that it "was already in a condition of evident decay." He counted among those who were responsible for this the French emigrants who joined the ceremony in 1792.

It was also not previously known what, precisely, Metternich experienced or from what vantage point he experienced it. And yet it is important to know which aspects of the empire's symbolic language he witnessed directly and how he was involved in the proceedings.[5] According to protocol, only a select few of the nobility were allowed actively to take part in the ceremony. That Clemens played a role in it confirmed to him and the public at large that he was a member of the higher echelons of the imperial counts.

In 1790 Metternich experienced the events as follows: during the coronation of the emperor, the counts were in the care of the imperial quartermaster, whose task it was to organize the ceremony down to the smallest detail. At eight o'clock, the counts had to assemble in the antechamber of the imperial quarters. At eleven o'clock, the imperial Kammerfourier, who was responsible for the imperial accommodation, called them in. The Kammerfourier would later organize and oversee the catering at the banquet, where the counts would serve the food. In a strict order, the counts joined the procession by foot to the cathedral, "in rich gallant dress." Here, Beatrix's efforts in negotiating by correspondence a splendid Maltese uniform for her son paid off very well. Inside the church, the counts took their places immediately behind the imperial princes on draped seats, from where they witnessed the ceremonial coronation, with all its rituals and regalia, up close.

The act of the coronation was not only a spectacle but also a constitutional act. The emperor first had to take an oath in front of all the empire's representatives present that he would respect and preserve the empire's law and justice, keep the peace of the church, and listen to the advice of the princes, the empire, and those faithful to it. The subsequent promotions in social rank, performed by accolades, were part of the ceremony. In 1790 the recipients included a chamberlain from Zweibrücken, Baron Montgelas, and Maximilian Count Metternich zur Gracht, a member from a side branch of Clemens's family.[6]

The congregation then left the church—again, strictly in order of rank—and, accompanied by bells ringing and cannon firing, proceeded to the Römer,[7] where the prince electors had to perform their hereditary roles of imperial chamberlain [*Reichserbkämmerer*], imperial chief supervisor of banquets [*Reicherbtruchsess*], imperial cupbearer [*Reichserbschenk*], and imperial marshal [*Reichserbmarschall*].[8] At the banquet, the imperial counts performed their "imperial dish-carrying duties." In prescribed sequence, with their hats held under their arms, they had to serve the food, led by the imperial marshal, holding a baton. The thirty-six imperial counts served in four groups, according to their rank. In addition, the ruling lords had priority over the nonruling. Among those serving at the ceremony, Clemens held the twenty-fifth place.

After each course, the counts had some time to gather around the throne, where the crowned emperor sat underneath a baldachin. After the coronation banquet, the archbishop of Mainz spoke the benediction, and the emperor retreated to the imperial quarters "to resounding cheers and shouts of 'viva!'"[9]

What to us today appears curious, even odd, can be understood from a contemporary perspective as a way of staging, in a symbolic and visceral manner, the empire's Constitution and its structure, order of social ranks, and origins. To those familiar with imperial law, every detail of the ceremony, the imperial insignia, and robes signified a part of the empire's history from the times of Charlemagne and the Golden Bull, even if some elements acquired their semblance of authenticity only in retrospect. Here, Metternich experienced a reality that he would later describe as "the old historical order in the empire," which the French Revolution had abolished. Ironically, soon afterward it was the self-proclaimed successor to Charlemagne, Napoleon, who would copy the hereditary imperial offices in an almost bizarre fashion in his emperorship, as Metternich would witness in person in Paris. Here, by contrast, he experienced the original. This was the law that he had in mind: decentralized, with a complex structure, balanced, based on merit, and integrated into a composite state system that was not at all conducive to wars of aggression (of the kind for which the later nation-states mobilized their resources) but capable of defending itself against outside aggression. The Turkish Wars were still very much part of living memory.

In his second role (in addition to his being an electoral envoy) as head of the Westphalian College of Counts, Franz Georg demonstrated the self-confidence that comes from being close to the center of power within a well-ordered system. This impressed his son. Franz Georg and further representatives, one for each of the three other colleges of counts, had the honor and right to congratulate the emperor as members of a special deputation. In two coaches, each drawn by six horses, they entered the yard where the imperial court had its quarters and were led to the newly elected emperor by the chief imperial chamberlain [Oberstkämmerer]. Franz Georg was permitted to congratulate him in a personal address in which he assured him "that the estate of the imperial counts will make it their pleasant duty to prove to Your Imperial Majesty, known by everyone as a just and generous head of the Roman Empire, their deepest loyalty as well as their infinite willingness to serve the welfare of the House of Your Serene Highness on every occasion."[10] One should not be deceived by this rhetoric of submission: this was actually an oath of obeisance by a representative of an estate that, at the same time, confirmed the members of that estate as independent rulers.

In Metternich's memory, the celebrations in 1792 culminated in another public appearance. Prince Esterházy, the first electoral envoy of the Bohemian electorate and a colleague of his father, had invited some distinguished guests to his palace in Frankfurt. In front of the building he had erected a wooden house covered with a fine canvas, much to the astonishment and delight of his guests. He had draped the windowsills of the ground floor with portraits of the emperors from Charlemagne onward. From there, the guests, to the sound of drums and trumpets, climbed stairs with Doric columns to the first floor, where they headed toward a portrait of the new emperor, which was framed by a sparkling illumination. The emperor, the princes, the whole court—including the young imperial count—admired this "temple of fire." Esterházy had charged Clemens with "the direction of the banquet," and he "opened the ball with the young Princess of Mecklenburg," who was no more than sixteen years of age at the time and who later became Queen of Prussia. Through his mother, the two families were already in close contact. With this banquet, the ancien régime celebrated itself in all its richness. And as the Vienna Congress of 1815 would later show, it was not the last one of its kind.

1789: THE RUPTURE OF THE FRENCH REVOLUTION

Metternich interpreted the French Revolution as a decisive turning point in world history. He was familiar with the Glorious Revolution in England and valued its progressive impulses for the development of the English Constitution. He was also familiar with the fundamental facts of the American Revolution and considered its republican impetus legitimate in a country of such vast dimensions. But the Revolution that began in Paris was the real event: a terrifying revolution that brought with it a fundamental transformation—because, as he did not tire of repeating, it was not only a political but in its essence a "social" revolution. It wanted to topple the social order and the old law of Europe.

So far, discussions of what Metternich actually meant by the "social" have remained more or less superficial. An answer becomes clearer when we trace biographically how he came into contact with the Revolution; which events helped to form his judgment; which personal contacts were important; and in which sequence the immediate confrontations with the Revolution followed each other. For this, it is necessary to know where he was at each point in time.

A historian needs to distinguish between two perspectives. On the one hand, in hindsight we know today that the Revolution was not at all an immediate threat to the other European states and that it began as an internal affair of a politically weakened state. On the other hand, the sources show the changing contexts from which Metternich's perception of the Revolution emerged. The picture of an altogether novel phenomenon, which the adolescent Metternich then carried over into his adult life, built up only gradually out of his elementary experiences. Many of his remarks on "revolution," "radicalism," and the political actors practicing it, made during the pre-1848 period, the "pre-March" [*Vormärz*], appear in a new light when looked at against what we know about his early life. Which, then, were these contexts and contacts? We need to keep in mind that Metternich was present as a witness at all of the central places where the Revolution extended beyond the borders of France and affected neighboring countries: Strasbourg, the Rhineland (and here in particular Mainz and Koblenz), and then the Austrian Netherlands, where the war of the first coalition began. Each time, different aspects opened up to the young count, some seemingly attractive, some violent, some aiming to settle accounts, some instructive, and some promising.

The Family in Alsace and a Mother's Worries

During the time of his studies in Strasbourg and Mainz between the summer of 1788 and August 1792, Metternich regularly exchanged letters with his mother. She expected some news from her beloved son at least every eight days, no matter whether she was in Koblenz, Königswart, Prague, or Vienna. When Metternich later sorted his correspondence, he noted down on a bundle of her letters to him: "Letters from my mother which refer to the explosion of the French Revolution. They prove how little the significance and nature of the events were understood."[11]

Before the outbreak of the Revolution, his mother complained about the extent to which the war tax levied by the empire for the Turkish War had put stress on the family finances. These financial worries were to grow enormously. On July 28, 1789, she reacted to Clemens's "gloomy news" from the "theater of horror" for the first time. This reaction expresses a naive royalism: "What a revolution! It is torture to see how such a glorious monarchy is *troublé* by civil war." We may conclude from this that for his mother, the events in France were not just a case of insurrection, civil war, and unrest; they already constituted "the Revolution." Her worries turned to Alsace, where her parents lived and owned estates. She had heard rumors that towns had been burned down and destroyed there, and that all the castles in Alsace and in Franche-Comté had been ruined. She was concerned about her sister, who managed to bring all her furniture to safety and to flee to the Breisgau herself. She was also worried about the canonesses of Remiremont, who were losing their rights; the abbess was a sister of Prince Condé, who was cursed in France. That Beatrix's fears were not absurd becomes clear when looking at reports that appeared in newspapers in Strasbourg: "All of Alsace is in flames. Hordes of arsonist murderers move around the country."[12]

The mother recognized the fundamentals of what was happening: "Farewell to the prebends; they are off the table." Clemens must have felt personally affected when his mother asserted who the movement was directed against: "This is a cruel century, in all countries the nobility is on the ground, that is where people want to see it at all costs, and unfortunately in terms of numbers it is only a tiny minority."[13] She feared for the "droits seigneuriaux," the prerogatives or feudal rights. She referred to the situation of the imperial counts who still held property in Alsace. Their feudal rights had already been swept away by the famous sitting of the National Assembly on August 5, 1789—a fact that was discussed in Strasbourg only a week later and that Metternich would not have missed. His tutor, Simon, kept him informed on these matters.[14]

The Violent Revolution: The Storming of Strasbourg City Hall on July 21, 1789

The exchange on political matters between Clemens and his mother made him aware of his own threatened position as an imperial count, and at the same time must have distanced him from the Revolution. In Strasbourg, the sixteen-year-old experienced the outbreak of the Revolution in the form of the charge on the city hall, mimicking the storming of the Bastille in Paris. And this means he experienced its violent side, a fact whose significance should not be underestimated. Metternich later remembered that his "mind was then too young" to understand the deeper causes of the events, that he was "absorbed in the present." But with "all the force of youthful impressions" he captured the "first stirrings of Jacobinism." Metternich does not describe these experiences as traumatic, but the way in which the "revolution" and "the people" presented themselves to him at the time left indelible impressions in his memory. In his judgment, nothing could have been more damaging to the idea of the sovereignty of the people: "Surrounded by a number of dull spectators, who called themselves the people, I had been present at the plundering of the Stadthaus [city hall] at Strasburg, perpetrated by a drunken mob, which also considered itself the people."[15]

This description is not a royalist's propagandistic exaggeration. What exactly had Metternich witnessed? News about the revolutionary events in Paris, especially about the storming of the Bastille on July 14, 1789, had spread rapidly to Strasbourg. It took a courier on horseback three and a half days to travel the distance. As early as July 19, a Sunday, the king's speech to the National Assembly was put up on placards all over the city.[16] The king was celebrated because he had reconciled himself with the people; three days of celebrations were declared. Itinerant craftsmen and day laborers succeeded in having the city illuminated in the same way as the capital, Paris, and the fireworks and illuminations at the Paradeplatz (Place Broglie) attracted viewers from all social classes. An eyewitness observed that soldiers had also taken part in the celebrations and "in particular a group of about sixty young people from distinguished families."[17] Metternich was one of them.

The city's council assembled on July 20 and was confronted with the list of grievances submitted by the citizens and peasants, including their demand to lower the excise tax on bread and meat. When stones were thrown at the magistracy its members took flight, while the praetor of Strasbourg, Joseph Klinglin, tried to calm people down by assuring them that all their demands would be met. On July 21, the magistracy, with great hesitation, agreed to this, but then suddenly the erroneous rumor spread that it had retracted all concessions. The collective anger of the people erupted. Journeymen, pugnacious youth, and even women encouraged each other; day laborers and craftsmen armed themselves with their tools. As in many riots of the early modern period, they acted out of a sense of righteousness. E. P. Thompson speaks of the "moral economy" of the poor in this context. They decided to take the law into their own hands and to storm the city hall.[18]

The military from the Strasbourg garrison moved in. Metternich witnessed how his protective councillor, Prince Maximilian, now had to intervene in his role as the colonel of the "Regiment Royal." Judging from the circumstances, it was the lower classes who were responsible for the uncontrolled explosion of violence. Window panes were smashed, and the scaling ladders that had been left behind after the installation of the illuminations were used by the particularly courageous ones to help them storm the hated council chamber. The military took a wait-and-see approach in order to avoid further provocation, and Klinglin, the praetor, shouted: "Children, do whatever you like, but just don't burn things!" And the people obeyed him: nothing was burned, but furniture in the council chamber was smashed and thrown out of the windows, together with files, protocols, and documents from the archive. All this, in the end, filled the place in front of the city hall up to people's ankles.

The watchwords that were shouted revealed that the news from Paris had been a catalyst: "No taxes! Long live the Estates General!"[19] No city office was spared from the attacks; the municipal coffers were plundered and the carriages smashed. Some of the agitators stormed the council's cellar [Ratskeller] and "flooded" it with 17,000 liters of wine. The military was not sure what to do and intervened only sporadically, in order to avoid the worst. The neighboring alleys were filled with crowds of people who carried trophies from the city hall: curtains, files, letters, window frames, receptacles.

Hofmeister Simon Becomes a Revolutionary

The storming of the city hall looked like an elementary eruption of popular anger, fueled by economic needs, which certainly played a role. But in fact it was the result of a carefully calculated plan. In his published memoirs, Metternich obscures the true background—which he knew about at the time. His unpublished notes, however, reveal that his own tutor, Simon, was behind the events: "He was one of the leaders of the storming of the city hall of Strasbourg, the purpose of which was the destruction of the historical files, land registries, and all the documents that protected the ownership of land, which were kept there."[20] This adds a rationale and a revolutionary dimension to the events. The operation aimed at the remaining feudal rights of the nobility, what Metternich increasingly understood as the "old legal order"; and Simon showed how to agitate and utilize the masses.

On July 22, 1789, shocked by the unbridled anger of the mob, the citizens of Strasbourg began to arm themselves and to organize a bourgeois guard on the model of the one in Paris. It was composed of members of the magistracy, professors, merchants, and preachers. The principal of the university, Johann Lorenz Blessig, asked the students to assemble and form an armed group to guard the university's institutions. Simon volunteered to be a night guard, which appalled Clemens's mother. His duty, she said, was to look after the security of the disciples who had been entrusted to him, and not after the peace and quiet of the city. She was so displeased by the foolishness of Simon's misconceived courage that she threatened to dismiss him from his position.[21]

Metternich did not tell his mother about Simon's actual involvement in the revolt at Strasbourg, and it seems as if he did not want to let the posthumous world know about his closeness to this revolutionary educator either. In his unpublished notes, he says that Simon threw himself "with a fanatical enthusiasm into the ferment of the Revolution. At my reading desk, he wrote the most extreme newspaper which helped substantially in the revolutionizing of Alsace."[22] Simon translated the complete French Constitution into German. Metternich, for his part, was well acquainted with the original; he possessed a copy of this first French Constitution, which contains his notes in the margins; until the end of his life, he kept it in his library.[23]

Over the course of the following summer, Simon demanded that aristocratic titles be abolished, the carrying of coats of arms be banned, and the church's estates be confiscated.[24] As someone who was fully bilingual, he was pushed further and further to the center of events. In Strasbourg, beginning on December 6, 1789, he edited the *Patriotisches Wochenblatt* [The patriotic weekly], in which he provided his readers with a German version of the Declaration of Human Rights.[25] He encouraged his audience to embark on a European "holy war" in an appeal titled: "Allgemeiner Aufstand oder vertrauliches Sendschreiben an die benachbarten Völker, um sie zu einer heiligen und heilsamen Empörung aufzumuntern" [General rebellion, or confidential epistle addressed to the neighboring people in order to encourage them to show a holy and healthy indignation].[26] Simon's radicalization introduced him to the innermost circle around the leaders of the Revolution in Paris, Jean-Paul Marat and Maximilien Robespierre. Metternich knew: "In 1792, the deputies from Marseille in Paris elected him as the president of the Comité des dix, which presided over the events of August 10."[27] In other words: Simon was involved in the preparations for the storming of the Tuileries on August 10, 1792, in which rebels massacred the Swiss Guard and forced the king to take shelter in the National Assembly.

Simon enthusiastically welcomed France's declaration of war on the old powers, and in the same spirit returned to Mainz together with the French general Custine, who conquered the city on October 21, 1792. This led to the founding of the Republic of Mainz by the German Jacobins. Simon translated the general's appeals to the Palatine population. When the Prussians retook Mainz on July 22, 1793, Simon—who had for a while styled himself as the "The Grand Inquisitor of France at Mainz"—signed the capitulation and returned to Strasbourg. Before he left, he still tried to influence the elections to the "Rhenish-German National Convention" as a commissioner under the protection of the French bayonets.[28]

Once in Strasbourg, looking for help in the fight against the "traitors of the Revolution," Simon called on the all-powerful member of the Committee of Public Safety in Paris, the fanatical executor of the Revolution, Louis Antoine de Saint-Just. In October 1793, Simon was a member of a military tribunal that passed sixty-two death sentences.[29] Metternich's memory was correct when he wrote of Simon that "during the Reign of Terror he was a member of the revolutionary tribunal, . . . and he shared in the responsibility of those streams of blood shed by that abhorred tribunal in that unhappy province."[30]

Why should we dwell for such a long time on the role this one individual played in Metternich's biography? In his unpublished notes, Metternich provides the answer himself: "Under a more sophisticated schooling in a far-reaching radicalism I would probably not have been able to see its teachings, means, and methods. My straight mind allowed me to recognize the foundations of the goings-on as far as my educator's character was concerned. His personal madness and the vulgar nature of the activities became apparent to me. As I had received my education from the school of true radicalism, the later liberalism seemed a very *dull* creation to me."[31]

In Metternich's eyes, Simon was the prototype of a seemingly soft, committed do-gooder and revolutionary "fundamentalist," in today's parlance, with a propensity to violence. In Metternich's terms, he was the epitome of a "radical," but that means the same thing: in the one case, things are followed to their roots ("radix"), in the other to their foundation ("fundamentum"). Friedrich Simon was one of those characters who is easily inspired and gets carried away, who ruthlessly sacrifices victims in the name of the high ideals of humankind because the end seems to justify the means.

When Metternich later spoke about "radicalism" in the period leading up to 1848, then, for him Simon would always have been associated with this term—this is how deeply this man had preoccupied him—on the one hand, in endeavoring to steer clear of such emotions; on the other, due to his extremely one-sided experience of the Revolution. Lest we forget, the Revolution also had another face, one that remained alien to Metternich—namely, that of a movement propagating constitutional reform to whose initiatives Emperor Joseph II and Emperor Leopold II were not unsympathetic. A later judgment on his erstwhile tutor shows, however, how little Metternich was capable of, or willing to engage in, revenge or condemnation from a stronger position: "This Hofmeister was the best man in the world; he wept for joy, and filled the whole world with his love and his philanthropy. I was his pupil, and yet my soul sank into sorrow."[32]

Metternich saw himself as a "close observer" and subsequently an "adversary" of the Revolution, as having gone through a school of overly excited passion and of confusions to which wrongheaded spirits found themselves subjected. To have seen all this, he thought, protected him against error and strengthened his resistance against "the luring illusions of innovations and theories which my own understanding and conscience discarded as not fit to pass before the court of reason and of legitimate right [*des guten Rechts*]."[33] Here speaks the cosmopolitan enlightener; here we can sense shining through his reading of Kant, whose writings are also to be found in the Metternichs' library in Königswart (whereas we look in vain for those of Fichte, Hegel, or Schelling). Our introductory historical journey through the Holy Roman Empire and the rise of the Metternichs revealed to us what he understood by "legitimate right." The concrete meaning of "legitimate right" in 1789 had already become clear with the first attacks on the rights of the nobility.

Revolutionary Discussions and the Jacobins of Mainz

His tutor gave Metternich his first opportunity to observe how the ideas of the French Revolution changed people's political awareness and the horizon of values. And the Strasbourg professor for canon law Franz Anton Brendel— Metternich called him his "religious teacher"[34]—demonstrated to the young student the inclination of many academic teachers to reinterpret their traditional doctrines within the horizon of the Revolution. Here, the Catholic imperial count could see how the new teachings of the Revolution subordinated the Constitution of the church to the law of the state. While most members of the clergy refused to take an oath on the Civil Constitution, Brendel was prepared to do so in order to be elected the constitutional bishop of the Strasbourg diocese. And it was only logical that not the pope but the National Assembly in Paris removed his predecessor from his post.[35] In his first epistle to the faithful, Brendel acknowledged his changed values and recognized the hand of God in the way the Revolution dealt with the church and in the flight of aristocratic emigrants: "He, who rules all worlds . . . often choses great and sublime moments in the history of states in order to lead religion to new victories, and he renews it more or less in its outward appearance. . . . And thus the voice of the Highest God recently sounded out; he lowered the place of the powerful and drove away the proud."[36] This high spiritual flight did not last long. In 1797 Brendel renounced the honor of being a bishop. This was known to Metternich, who also described the dramatic staging of this step. After Brendel had forsworn "religion and the episcopate," he "publicly burned the insignia of his office in a revolutionary orgy."[37] In the end, he became the archivist of the Department of the Lower Rhine.

At the University of Mainz, Metternich, no longer accompanied by his tutor Simon, entered even deeper into the revolutionary debate. Mainz was the place where the emigrants met at the court of the prince elector as well as the focal point for the Jacobins. Metternich learned how the Revolution took total control over the hearts and the senses and evoked a collective enthusiasm: "The most beautiful sun beamed on a hundred thousand enthusiasts, almost all of whom believed in the dawn of the Golden Age."[38]

Metternich remembered one of these enthusiasts especially well, because in his teaching he practiced the method of historical contemporizing more efficiently than any other. Andreas Joseph Hofmann was professor of philosophy and natural law. In Metternich's words, he was one of those "who made it their business to lard their lectures with allusions to the emancipation of the human race, as Marat and Robespierre had done so well."[39] One might consider this libelous talk, unless one knows what the students, and among them Metternich, were exposed to in Hofmann's lectures, which were obligatory for all first-year students. Like Simon, he argued for teaching to take place in German, as Latin was an artificial language barrier and helped the rulers manipulate their subjects. He made derogatory remarks about prayers and *Pfaffen*,[40] while he called theologians *Hornvieh*[41]—as a university teacher in a religious state! He called the nobility "the smallest part of a population" and said they lived only "off the sweat of others."[42] Metternich rightly remembered him as "one of the heads of the club at Mainz"; the French general Custine had conquered Mainz on October 21, 1792, and two days later Hofmann helped found the Jacobin Club of Mainz—and later he helped found the first republic on German soil, which had an elected Parliament, whose president he became.

During the actual existence of the Republic of Mainz, lasting from the beginning of the French occupation (October 21, 1792) until its recapture by the allies (the French surrendered on July 22, 1793), Metternich was no longer there. He worked at his father's office in Brussels until the French occupation of the city on November 14, 1792, drove him into exile for the first time.

The Revolution as Perceived by the Nineteen-Year-Old Metternich

The Revolution of 1789 and Napoleon's military dominance were the two main factors in Metternich's life, and they therefore dominate his later memoirs. And yet the question remains, whether it is not possible to learn a little bit more about the decisive years of his youth when looking at immediate sources from that time. This may then allow us to measure the judgments and conclusions of the later politician against this knowledge, and possibly to determine with more precision which moments had a formative and lasting influence on the personality of the state chancellor. Up until now, when they were trying to understand how he experienced the words and deeds of the Revolution, historians have depended exclusively on the memories of the old politician looking back on his life. But how much of it did the adolescent Metternich consciously experience and take in at the time, and how much is owed to later recombination of events?

Metternich's library at Königswart holds a hitherto unknown collection of newspapers and pamphlets from the years 1792–1793.[43] As a passionate reader, Metternich had the lifelong habit of marking up the passages he found important, and it is no different here. And the selection of texts itself is equally interesting. All this shows what caught his attention and how intensely focused he was on keeping the phenomenon of the "revolution" in view and analyzing it thoroughly, even from the distance of his temporary exile in Wesel. Srbik's judgment that "in this phase of his life, Metternich showed neither particular originality nor particular depth in his reception of intellectual matters" is therefore completely misguided.[44]

Metternich's focus was clearly still limited to the electorate of Mainz, where the revolutionary troops under General Custine, who, ironically, was elevated to general [*Obergeneral*] by Metternich, operated. In his numerous pamphlets addressing the German population, General Custine had given France's military expansion the aura of a liberation of the people and salvation from the despots of the ancien régime. Metternich studied on a daily basis whatever newspapers from Mainz he could get.

There was, for instance, *Der Bürgerfreund* [Citizens' friend], edited by the professor of mathematics in Mainz, and namesake of Metternich, Mathias Metternich, with whom the imperial count was personally acquainted, having studied with him. Now, he held his revolutionary publications in his hands. In the first issue of October 26, 1792, Mathias Metternich, moved by the idea of freedom, promised the beginning of a divine "true bliss," and threatened: "We know your enemies who gave you misery instead of joy, who deprived you of all joys of life and kept them for themselves, while passing all the drudgery on to you, and despite all this still had the insolence of calling themselves your fathers." Kings, administrators, noble court officials, priests: these categories made up the enemy.

Our young aristocrat also followed *Die neue Mainzer Zeitung oder der Volksfreund* [The new paper of Mainz, or the friend of the people], edited by Georg Forster, whom he also knew very well from the time of his studies. In the first issue, January 1, 1793, Forster said there had been a turning point, and he declared the dawn of paradise: "At last, freedom of the press is established inside these city walls, where the printing press was invented. New contributions appear daily, aiming at the conversion of a good people, who, however, have ceased to be blindfolded only so recently that they still blink when looking at the sun of truth and must slowly become accustomed to its benevolent light. Soon our city will be transformed into one of those sources of light from which the bright and refreshing beams will radiate in every direction into the far distance." Here, we hear the enlightened prophets who saw themselves as revealing the one and only truth to the simpleminded masses. According to Metternich, they represented the "acolytes of the Revolution"; he had more than ample opportunity to get to know them in the lecture halls and in Jacobin circles. To one such circle, he had been introduced during a visit to the house of Georg Forster.

The *Mainzisches Intelligenzblatt* [Mainz paper for the intelligentsia] provided, to a certain extent, a counterbalance to this. From October 27, 1792, it had to pay tribute to the new spirit of the times, but until then it had still presented itself as an official organ published "under the gracious privilege granted by the prince elector." Then, suddenly, this changed to "under provisional authorization by the Franconian nation." The official organ published all announcements made by the new masters, in both French and German, and also told the citizens uncomfortable truths—such as the order, coming from Custine's headquarters, that provisions of wood and salt in the stores of Mainz would no longer go to the citizens but instead would go to the French army—for which, however, these supplies were "barely sufficient."

The fourth paper Metternich followed was the *Mainzer Zeitung*, which, on November 3, 1792, was renamed the *Mainzer National-Zeitung* by its editor, the theologian and scholar of canon law Georg Wilhelm Böhmer. Böhmer, the co-director of the Lutheran secondary school in Worms, had recently become the private secretary to Custine and the mouthpiece of the Gesellschaft der Freunde der Freiheit und Gleichheit [Society of the friends of freedom and equality]—the Jacobin Club of Mainz that he had co-founded on October 23. From this paper, Metternich learned the latest news from Paris, including the advance of the French troops in Belgium—whence he had to flee—and the latest proclamations made by Custine.

His collection of pamphlets shows what he learned about the Revolution beyond the newspaper reports. Among them, *Zuruf eines teutschen Bürgers an den Führer der Franzosen* [Call to the leader of the French by a German citizen] sticks out. It attacks the ideology of liberation and defends the existing Constitution: "We are free! We do not carry any dishonorable fetters put on by greedy tyrants! We love our magistracy not out of a slavish fear but because it takes care for the well-being of the citizens with fatherly love. So, why do you want to liberate us from fetters that we do not carry; why do you want to impose benefactions on us that we do not need? Why do you want to shake up a Constitution that is venerable not because of its age but because of its kindness?" At this point the author, who was from Frankfurt, alludes to the "old German freedom" that was guaranteed by the Constitution of the empire and applied to the orders of the imperial cities, and that was still a principle very much alive in Frankfurt. Metternich must have been close to the author and have supported and agreed with this open letter, for in addition to the printed version he possessed a handwritten copy.

It is important to know the detailed background to this letter of protest. After the occupation of Frankfurt on October 22, 1792, Custine had demanded a contribution of two million guilders from the city.[45] With the new revolutionary France in mind, the anonymous author points out: "A nation which acts in accordance with moral principles, which writes justice and philanthropy on its banner and adopts the motto 'War on the palaces, peace to the huts!,' for such a nation it is not fitting to pillage and threaten to burn." Custine's demand for contributions was backed up by his threat to burn down or pillage the city if they were not forthcoming. Apart from that, the author from Frankfurt continues, the contribution would not actually deprive the rich merchants of their bread; those who would suffer would be the hundreds of craftsmen and day laborers who lived off the merchants' businesses. The French nation "would have to act against the principles it so loudly preached; would have to reveal that it was looking for money, not friends, in Germany; would have to reveal that it considered sacred neither the property of the citizens nor the well-being of a quiet city." Custine responded with a printed pamphlet addressed to the "councillors of the people," which was also in Metternich's possession. In it, Custine announced that he would reduce the contributions by 500,000 guilders if he were provided with cannon and war provisions for the defense of this "highly important conquest made by the Franconian Republic."[46] The argument regarding an already existing liberal Constitution he ignored.

There are two leading members of the Jacobin Club of Mainz to which the young Metternich paid particular attention in his reading. On the printed *Anrede an die neu gebildete Gesellschaft der Freunde der Freiheit und Gleichheit in Mainz* [Address to the newly formed society of the friends of freedom and equality in Mainz], by Anton Joseph Dorsch, he wrote in his own hand: "Note: Dorsch had been professor at the University of Mainz."[47] He remembered the circumstances, which caused a stir at the time: in November 1791, the professor of theology, logic, and metaphysics was forced to leave the university because adherents to Catholic orthodoxy had severely attacked him, a representative of the Catholic Enlightenment who had promoted Kant in his lectures. Dorsch then went to Strasbourg, where he founded the Jacobin Club.[48] After the French had taken hold of Mainz, he returned at the beginning of November 1792 and gave an impassioned speech to the newly founded Jacobin Club. He praised the "hero Custine from whom the despots and repressors of the people take flight," who brings "the palm of peace and the protection of the Franconian Republic to the righteous citizens." He also described how the "societies of the people" fought against the traitors of the French king and the enemies of freedom.

He recommended the Jacobin clubs in France as "an example to be followed." Metternich has underlined this statement by Dorsch: "But the Jacobins were victorious, and France became and remained—a free state." What is of significance is the fact that Metternich learned that the German friends of the Revolution called themselves Jacobins, from which he drew a conclusion as to the extent to which they were, indeed, prepared to identify and sympathize with the radicalization of the Revolution in France. When, later—in his

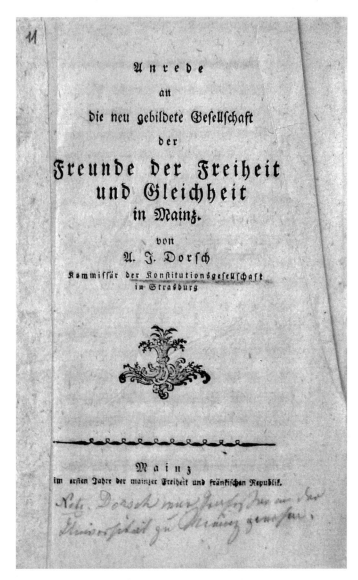

Pamphlet by the Professor of Theology and Jacobin, Anton Joseph
Dorsch (1792), with a handwritten note by Metternich.

memoirs, for instance—he spoke of the German "Jacobins" in the context of
the French Revolution, this was not a cheap catchword; he knew that this political avant-garde had direct exchanges with their French counterparts and had
declared themselves "Jacobins." Metternich's close personal relations with these
groups during his studies in Mainz and the intensity of his examination of their
writings have not previously been revealed.

The case of Dorsch also demonstrated to Metternich the collaboration of the Mainz Jacobins with the French general Custine, as the latter had called the former priest back to Mainz and, by a decree of November 18, 1792 (of which Metternich also possessed a copy), appointed him president of the new autonomous local administration with the power to dismiss all existing officials. Of the seven paragraphs, Metternich considered the sixth particularly important and underlined it:

> On the basis of the power given to us, we cannot yet declare the complete abolition of those troublesome rights under whose pressures the people have sighed for so many centuries; those rights which were created by despotism and which will be smashed by justice. But in the meantime, we eagerly seize the opportunity for lowering the burden of the people by appointing public administrators whose proven principles guarantee that wisdom and moderation will guide their actions and decisions.[49]

The fact that Metternich marked this passage shows that he was aware of the implications current events had for what was to come. Here, he came across a formulation which spelled out what later made him speak of the French Revolution as a "social" revolution: both the social structure and the legal Constitution were to be overthrown. And in 1792–1793 he clearly foresaw that this movement, which addressed itself to all "peoples," had to spread beyond the borders of France and across Europe and would radically topple all local administrations.

The second leading representative of the Mainz Jacobins whom Metternich considered particularly noteworthy was the aforementioned Mathias Metternich. On his pamphlet, the young imperial count noted down: "M. Metternich was professor of mathematics at Mainz University." He not only kept this address to the Jacobin Club, but reflected on it in detail. It was the "speech in which the concerns mentioned to the people of Mainz regarding giving themselves a new Constitution are answered." Mathias Metternich was several times president of the Jacobin Club; he was eloquent, passionate, and polemical (as in his *Bürgerfreund*), determined to revolutionize the peasants: in short, a "typical agitator."[50]

In the printed version of the speech, Clemens Metternich marked passages which told of how the new politics of the Revolution would bid farewell to the old politics: "This Franconian nation no longer wants any convoluted diplomacy, with which until now the courts pitifully thumbed their noses at each other.—And second, isn't every despot a natural enemy of France, following the declarations of the National Convention?" This must have provoked the

Metternich whose professional aim was to become a diplomat. What was there left to negotiate if all European monarchs were defined as despots and enemies?

And he must have been truly alarmed by the following doctrine, whose consequences he would witness throughout twenty-three years of war. The fact that he marked the passage is evidence enough of his surprising foresight even at this early age: "The great idea sworn to by the new Franconians, that their present war will end only when the eradication of tyrannies is complete; ha! to the shortsighted; to those who never conceived of true human greatness, could never conceive of it because their servility tied them too much to the ground; to those small-minded—that idea is a chimera."[51]

This was a call for a modern crusade; "eradication" was pursued, allegedly motivated by "true human greatness." Metternich would later experience déjà vu when he heard the same tone in the arguments of the assassin Sand. Reacting to the speech, Metternich emphasized that when the Jacobins discussed a new Constitution for Mainz, the professor of mathematics recommended waiting until the National Convention in Paris fully guaranteed "that they will receive us with open arms, protect us with all their power." The speaker suggested an expansion of the planned "free federation" to include the states between the Rhine and the Mosel. This, of course, touched upon the question of whether the Metternich estates would be integrated into the French state, and upon the question, much discussed in France at the time, of its "natural borders." The young nobleman also took note of Mathias Metternich's claim that the surrogate bishop of Mainz, Dalberg (i.e., the deputy archbishop), was his friend, but that to entrust him with the government of Mainz would only prolong the "sultan-like government." Instead, selected men should expose to the light of day all of the dealings between the prince elector and the cathedral chapter and search the archives thoroughly to that end. Should there be resistance to the opening of the cabinets, "citizen General Custine must be asked to break them asunder with his mighty sword."[52] One could not trust in "the upright ministers": "Princes and ministers—and the welfare of the people—for the one who can bring these things into harmony, I happily make room, because I cannot." In other words: the existing government did not have a chance of surviving.

Finally, the young Metternich studied with extreme care the initial French Constitution of September 3, 1791. The moment it had been published, he immediately purchased a copy,[53] in which he then entered later amendments; he must therefore have studied it sentence by sentence. With the same care, he examined the widely distributed pamphlet *Von der Staatsverfassung in Frankreich zum Unterrichte für die Bürger und Bewohner im Erzbistume Mainz und*

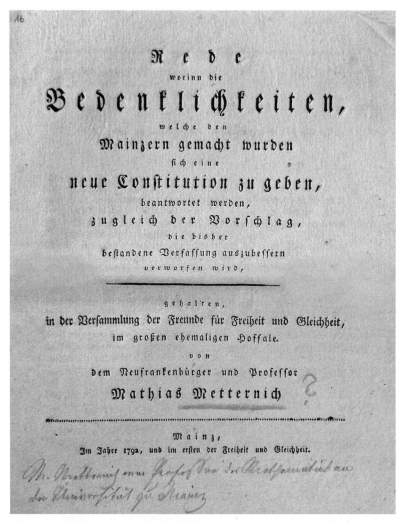

Pamphlet of the Professor of Mathematics and Jacobin, Mathias Metternich (1792), with a handwritten note by Clemens Metternich.

den Bistümern Worms und Speyer [On the Constitution of the state of France, for the education of the citizens and inhabitants of the archdiocese of Mainz and the dioceses of Worms and Speyer].[54] He underlined the following demand, put forward by the anonymous author: "After all, you need to know what is in it [i.e., in the Constitution]," and confirmed it with a "nota bene." Metternich stressed that the tendency to be critical of the nobility was justified by the equality of all before the law, and he noted its result—namely, that the son of a rural peasant might become a minister or archbishop, just like the "the son of a king"; it was not necessary "to have descended from old and high nobility, from the bloodline of a duke or prince."

In the passage on the removal of the royalty, Metternich noted the justification: "because he [the king] only carried out his duties to the detriment of the people, and the people abolished altogether such a superfluous, expensive office as that of a king or prince, which was a danger to freedom. Thus, France now calls itself a republic." Metternich highlighted the pamphlet's claim, too, that the new ideology was likely to spread across Europe. In the justification given for that expectation, he recognized arguments that had been given by the Romans when they built their vast empire: namely, that they had been called by oppressed peoples in order to bring them freedom. The text of this pamphlet saw the French republic besieged by enemies: "The emperor, the king of Prussia, the empire and such a vast number of enemies inside France, they all had united with the aim of ruining it [the present Constitution]."

The collection of newspapers and pamphlets the nineteen-year-old Metternich kept tells us a lot about the adolescent young man that up until now had not been known. He studied the early revolutionary publications in Germany, such as those produced in Mainz, which shows that he realized that the press was "the fourth estate" much earlier than Napoleon, who is usually credited with this insight and who began to manipulate the press in his own way. Metternich gained deep insight into the formation of the will of the Jacobins of Mainz and their political cohabitation with the French conquerors. And the functioning and further branching out of the Jacobin Club of Mainz, which had begun as a reading circle, stayed in his mind. For him, it became a "blueprint," so to speak, for all later secret societies as the core and germ of any "revolutionary party," as he would later say, whether it be the "Carbonaria" in Italy, the League of Outlaws [*Bund der Geächteten*] or the League of the Just [*Bund der Gerechten*] among the early German socialists in Paris, the politicized journeymen's unions [*Arbeitergesellenvereine*] in Switzerland, or the "Young Europe" of Giuseppe Mazzini in Upper Italy.

Metternich learned to see through the ideological character of proclaimed ideals, and gained an insight that would stay with him for the rest of his life: the passionate appeal to high values may well conceal material interests. When he later heard slogans talking of the happiness of the people, readiness to use violence, revolutionary impulses, or a centralist constitutional architecture, it brought back to him the days of the French Revolution, radicalism, and Jacobinism. For him, there was continuity between what had happened in 1789 and what followed. This explains why the Revolution of 1789, in principle, never came to an end for him and always, throughout his life, threatened to repeat itself. And part and parcel of his analysis was that intellectuals had to be considered the motor of the movement—the "proletarians of intellectual labor," as Wilhelm Heinrich Riehl would call them in the 1840s. The existentially unstable intellectuals (as opposed to those who were grounded by property, such as the publisher Friedrich Cotta), the writers, the advocates, the teachers at schools and universities, and the newspaper editors, all those who are filled with high-sounding ideas but do not take into account the "backward" population and think the people must be forced to do what is good for them—that was the "caste" that Metternich would never trust.

BRUSSELS AND THE AUSTRIAN NETHERLANDS

The times when Metternich stayed in Brussels, where, in the summer of 1791, his father had become the minister plenipotentiary to the States General of the Austrian Netherlands, form a distinct phase in his biography. Here, Clemens submersed himself in a historical landscape whose prehistory, from the sixteenth century onward, was closely connected with the House of Habsburg and the development of the empire. The serious religious conflicts between the Catholics in the south and the Protestants in the north of the Netherlands only ended with the Peace of Westphalia in 1648, when the Dutch "States General" left the empire. The southern Netherlands remained with the Habsburgs, first with the Spanish and then, from 1714, with the Austrian line. A governor and his wife represented the emperor in Brussels; the last couple were Albert Duke of Saxony-Teschen and Marie Christine, archduchess and a daughter of Maria Theresia.

In accordance with his enlightened absolutist policies, Emperor Joseph II had intervened in the internal politics of his provinces. From 1787 onward, he had questioned the traditional "Joyeuse Entrée"—the "Magna Carta" of the estates of Brabant, Limburg, and Antwerp that dates back to 1356.[55] At the same time, he wanted to put the education of priests at the strictly Catholic University of Leuven under the supervision of the state. This blatant break with historical precedent conflicted with the Belgian tradition of the autonomy of the estates and upset religious feelings. Henri Van der Noot, an advocate remembered by Metternich in his memoirs, collected all violations of the law committed by the emperor in a "Mémoire sur les droits du people brabançon" and demanded the reinstatement of the old law. He had to flee the Austrian government's persecution to the States General, but in the course of the Brabant Revolution the rule of the Austrians was ended. On October 24, 1789, opposition forces, fired up by the events in neighboring France, proclaimed the Revolution. On January 10, the Estates General declared the "United Belgian States," and for the first time those living in the Habsburg Netherlands called themselves

"Belgians." The inner tensions between the traditionalist party of Van der Noot and the democrats (who wanted to follow the French model), however, weakened the movement, and thus Austrian troops were able to retake Brussels on December 3, 1790.

The new emperor, Leopold II, distanced himself from the absolutism of his deceased brother. Even before 1789 he had gained a reputation across Europe as the first princc to rule on a constitutional basis (in his model state of Tuscany). Now, he wanted to bring peace to the reconquered country, and he promised to reinstate the old Constitution. In sending Franz Georg to Brussels, he intentionally chose a head of government whose own roots reached far back into the history of the Lower Rhine area. At the same time, he considered Franz Georg to be one of the empire's most experienced servants in dealing with the estates, the Imperial Diet, and religious conflicts, and he saw him as highly adept at mediating between warring factions. Upon his arrival, Franz Georg found a country riven by internal conflict and battles between royalists in the old estates and French-inspired democrats. Leopold afforded him comprehensive authority.

Here, however, we are not interested in the politics pursued by Habsburg and Franz Georg as such; rather, we want to know what Franz Georg's son, destined by him to become a diplomat, might have learned in Brussels and how his later policies might have been prefigured there. For that purpose, we need to establish, as precisely as possible, when he actually was there, something that has never been done before. To begin with, he stayed in Brussels during the university vacation in September and October 1791 while studying in Mainz. His parents had arrived at the capital only a little earlier, on July 8. During this time he witnessed in person how his father succeeded in "ending the execution of Liège" through an intense dialogue with the estates, through a well-calculated amnesty, and by mitigating legal proceedings. The Austrian state chancellor, Kaunitz, praised this successful pacification in the most glowing terms, saying it had "taken care of respect for the laws, of the preservation of the German imperial Constitution, and of the true well-being of the country in equal measure."[56]

At the beginning of September 1792, Metternich traveled to Brussels for the second time. From his memoirs one might get the impression that this was a short stay, but in fact he did not return to his studies in Mainz. Before the beginning of the new term at university, General Custine had been able to conquer the fortress and city of Mainz in a surprise attack on October 21, 1792, and Metternich remained in Brussels until his departure for London on March 25, 1794. His stay there was interrupted only by his exile in Wesel in the winter of 1792–1793. His stay in Brussels thus was an independent period in Metternich's biography and, accordingly, is more important than has so far been recognized.

What did Metternich learn in Brussels? His perspective was broadened beyond the horizon of Alsace and the Rhine, and for the first time he became familiar, in practice rather than from textbooks, with politics as an interplay between the European powers. In his unpublished notes, he provided an image of his acquisition of this new perspective:

> There are two ways of surveying an area: from a high mountain or from a point on the plane. On my journeys, I made it one of my rules to choose the highest tower in the middle of a city still unknown to me as the destination of my first excursion. Within a few minutes, I knew the city better than my fellow travelers who wanted to become familiar with it in a less arduous manner by walking through the streets. I was able to guide them from street to street without going astray, while they often did not get to the intended place even after a long time. My first glances at great affairs were from the point where they met. Of this perspective I have never since lost sight.[57]

From then on, whenever he had to find his way into a new subject matter, Metternich would adopt the intellectual method he discovered in Brussels—as we shall later see when, for instance, Metternich takes up his first position as an ambassador, in 1801. According to this method, whose ultimate practical test would be the Vienna Congress, Metternich first sought an observational point that afforded him some distance from the matters at hand and that allowed him to look at the fundamental facts. This furnished him with a "soberness" that he always demanded of himself "in the sciences and in political dealings." Indeed, this way of proceeding often allowed him to be ahead of his political colleagues and competitors, because he was able to evaluate the consequences of certain decisions before they could.

In his memoirs, Metternich introduces the "tower perspective," using the Netherlands at the time of his stay in Brussels as the example. With the Revolution having been driven back in the Netherlands, he describes his position as follows:

> The country had just passed through an internal crisis, the consequences of which were still felt in all directions, so that my position gave me the opportunity to observe and study at the same time two countries, one of which was given up to the horrors of the Revolution, whilst the other still showed fresh traces of what it had gone through. This position and the

instruction I gained from it have not been lost on me in the long course of my public life.[58]

In the Netherlands, Metternich became acquainted with three political dimensions. The first was crisis management within the domestic politics of an entity that—like the Holy Roman Empire—consisted of several states and was founded on an ancient traditional Constitution based on the estates. The second was international crisis management in foreign policy, where Metternich had the opportunity to study how war comes about and how it leads to the formation of alliances, and how difficult it is to achieve peace. And the third dimension was the way in which the domestic and foreign policies of Belgium became entangled as a consequence of the radicalization associated with the revolutionary war in neighboring France, a phenomenon that would from then on influence politics throughout the revolutionary age and into the following century.

The School of Diplomacy: Domestic Politics

The Austrian Netherlands were one of the composite states which were common in Europe in the early modern period. It consisted of semi-autonomous provinces, each with its own government seat.[59] In terms of legal rule, the state was connected in personal union with the House of Habsburg as the supreme rulers, represented, as mentioned above, by a governor couple. The present couple—Albert Duke of Saxony-Teschen and Marie Christine, archduchess and a daughter of Maria Theresia—had returned to Brussels after the city was taken back on June 15, 1791, and they traveled through all of the provinces for their inauguration, allowing the estates to make their oaths of obeisance and to present their complaints, thus confirming the federal structure of the country.

Franz Georg reorganized the internal administration and negotiated extensively and understandingly with the estates in order to regain their trust. His policies were mainly concerned with areas of domestic security that would later—after the Treaty of Schönbrunn in 1809—also be high on his son's agenda. Metternich learned from his father which institutional means were to be used in order to solve problems of this nature. Franz Georg established his own security office, the supreme police [*Hohe Polizei*], as he needed to know who was engaged in underground conspiracies, and where. Since the eighteenth century and especially since the revolutionary age, this kind of police, sometimes also referred to as state police [*Staatspolizei*], always entailed a secret political police in charge of espionage and postal and general surveillance. Franz Georg's security office was concerned with conspiracies led by royalist emigrants as well as with societies that were directed from France. These extreme groups also threatened the external security of Belgium because they could at any time provide a reason, or a pretext, for the French government to declare war on Belgium. Franz Georg waged a continuous internal battle against the emigrants, until he finally dissolved and expelled a corps of 5,000 officers.[60] A second instrument he used was a press office that was charged with inspecting letters and controlling newspapers; this office, too, was set up to combat the "inner enemy."

Apart from all this, Franz Georg had to permanently struggle with the estates, which were looking after their own interests, in order to raise the money needed to finance the war against France, a task of which he was persistently reminded by the government in Vienna. Following the French declaration of war on April 20, 1792, these reminders naturally became even more forceful. In contrast to the liberal policies of Leopold II, which were tolerant toward the estates, Leopold's son Franz, who succeeded him in 1792, strove to rein in the estates and insisted on the rights of the crown. Franz Georg considered this shift fateful, and he was altogether dismayed when, on February 27, 1793, Emperor Franz established a "Jointe"—a special office for Belgian matters—at the state Chancellery in Vienna. His horror increased further when he learned that it was to be headed by Ferdinand von Trauttmansdorff, who had been appointed court chancellor for the Netherlands. Von Trauttmansdorff became Franz Georg's personal enemy because he asked the emperor to bring statist measures to bear on Brussels and schemed to undermine Metternich's policies. The father, we may conclude, was able to present instructive examples in five areas (although he very likely would have preferred to have less to teach his son). These concerned the question of how to ward off a revolution; how to organize a political police; how to control the press; how to master conflicts between the estates; and how to deal with intrigues at court.[61]

The first reign of Franz Georg began with his entry into Brussels on July 8, 1791, and only lasted until November 8, 1792, when he had to organize the government's escape for the first time. Among other things, he had to secure the state treasury and the archive, and send the personnel and certified envoys from third countries at the Court in Brussels into exile in Roermond; when it was no longer safe to stay there either, he accompanied them to Wesel.[62] Clemens, who had by then broken off his studies in Mainz and was working in his father's office, thus experienced the first flight of a government from an enemy inspired by the Revolution. The scale of the operation was similar to the situation in 1809 when Napoleon approached Vienna and the court had to retreat to Komorn in Hungary; in that instance, too, the state archive had to be brought to safety.

During the crisis at the end of 1792, Emperor Franz suspended Governors Albert and Marie Christine and transferred the governorship to his brother, Archduke Carl. Carl argued for a program of reform that was altogether tailored to the ideas of Franz Georg and aimed at "putting an end once and for all to the disputes between the sovereign and the estates, but without at any point violating the Constitution."[63] The emperor reinforced this message and remarked: "You have an upright minister at your side." He must have been completely satisfied with Franz Georg's achievements up to that point because precisely at the moment of this crisis he honored him with the award of the Golden Fleece.[64]

During the French occupation, resistance in the Belgian provinces grew stronger. Pamphlets and placards circulated that described the fatherland as in danger and called on Belgians to drive out the barbarians who were destroying religion and the old corporations. There were calls to arm the people.[65] These protests had engulfed Belgium when, on January 31, 1793, the French National Convention demanded the integration of Belgium into the French state.

Meanwhile, the Austrians prepared to recapture the provinces, which they did with the victory at the Battle of Neerwinden, on March 18, 1793, under the leadership of the Prince of Coburg. In parallel, Clemens's father pursued a program to comprehensively restore the estates' historical rights that the French had abolished—that is, the "constitutional laws, customs and privileges of the country."[66] The state of affairs at the end of the reign of Maria Theresia provided the benchmark. The political program also included the declaration of a general amnesty, the prohibition of all illegal societies (including the Jacobin Club that had by then formed in Brussels), the surveillance and expulsion of French emigrants, and compensation for those who had suffered losses in the revolts of 1789 and 1790.[67] Metternich had to issue a proclamation to the Belgians, a message of peace, which was to be printed and distributed in large numbers during and after the entry of the imperial troops into the areas occupied by the enemy. And the son later proceeded in the same way when, in 1814, he issued a proclamation "To the French" upon the entry of the allies into France. The restoration of the constitutional rights of the estates after a period of military and revolutionary activity, which Clemens witnessed in Brussels and for which his father was responsible, has the look of a small-scale trial run, limited to domestic politics, for what he himself would have to master on a grand scale, in 1815, when "reconstructing" Europe. In terms of the principles, the battle remained the same.

The reputation Franz Georg had gained for himself in Belgium was evident upon his return to Brussels on March 29, 1793, a return witnessed by his son. The city council was waiting for him at the Leuven gate with a state coach,

Copper engraving from a brochure marking the celebration of St. Francis Day for the "Minister Plenipotentiary" Franz Georg and Emperor Franz on October 5, 1792, in Brussels.

received him with a welcoming speech, and then accompanied him in the coach, which was pulled by citizens, for a two-hour tour around the city. Along the route the citizenry was parading, and in the evening the whole city was illuminated in his honor.[68]

But it was not just because of their experiences with the French anticonstitutional centralism that the people of Brussels warmed to Metternich's father. Even before his temporary exile, they had shown signs of their reverence. On the occasion of his and the emperor's Saint's day, October 4 (St. Francis's Day), a celebration had been arranged for the following day in front of the Metternichs' house; included in the festivities was a performance of a musical couplet, printed in a booklet with a copper engraving.[69] Clemens witnessed how his father was celebrated, and it could not be overlooked that all the forms this took made use of stylistic elements taken from the French Revolution and adopted in a way that made them compatible with the estates and the aristocracy. This gave Franz Georg's government an aura that appeared more modern than it actually was.

This government skillfully engaged in propaganda, using the spirit of the age for its own legitimation. On the copper engraving of the pamphlet just mentioned, we find a cube, the iconographic symbol for stability, whose front shows the medallion of Franz Georg framed by the coats of arms of the Netherland provinces, the epitome of traditional federalism. The banner says: "Il est dans tous les Coeurs." [He is in everyone's heart.] The flag on the left proclaims: "l'expression général du Peuple Belge" [the voice of the Belgian people]. That sounded sensational because to speak of the one Belgian nation went beyond the traditional corporatism and adopted a stance that had first been expressed in the Brabant Revolution of 1789–1790. The allegorical figure in the center represents Minerva, but also suggests associations with the French figure "Liberté." The flag on the right declares: "vive l'Empereur / vivent Christine et Albert et vive Metternich le Chérie des Belges" [Long live the Emperor / long live Christine and Albert and long live Metternich, cherished by the Belgians].

Even more surprising is that the rhythm of the printed couplet follows that of the Marseillaise, which had been composed on April 26, 1792, during the campaign in Alsace, but had also been used as a melody announcing freedom at the end of the year in the Netherlands:

Allons, Amis, qu'on s'évertue
A concerter des chants joyeux!
Toute reconnoissance est due
A celui qui nous rend heureux.
　　Dans notre allégresse,
Aux accords des plus doux hautbois,
Qu'a répéter chacun de nous s'empresse,
vive François! vive François!

[Onward, friends, make sure
to let merry songs be heard!
All our gratitude belongs to him
who makes us happy.
　　In our jubilation
to the sounds of the most delicate oboes
each of us shall eagerly repeat:
Long live Franz! Long live Franz!]

The other stanzas praise Metternich's achievements: under his rule, the country has found peace; city and countryside have prospered; Metternich, it says, has ended the misery. And then the frightening image of the new spirit of the age is invoked, a spirit that must be defeated in a battle against the chimera that has been created, against a system that knows no respect and is brutal and subversive, that jeopardizes nature and all the world, and that threatens to turn the earth into one great cemetery. Banners are to be raised, the virtues of war mobilized in order to crush the murderous mob. Its defeat by the advancing troops of the Duke of Brunswick is near. The French are called upon to surrender and to celebrate the kings.

These proclamations expressed a Belgian patriotism that, backed by the Habsburg rulers, fought for an independent Belgian state. To dismiss this patriotism as a piece of "Habsburg restoration" would be to misjudge the will to independence and to create an image of the ensuing "modernizing" rule of the French (who did away with Belgium, as the three eastern powers did with Poland) that conforms more to the propagandistic fantasies at the time than to the reality as it was actually experienced.[70] The demonstrations of the estates and citizens of Brussels, incidentally, are a striking refutation of the judgment (always based on the defamations of von Trauttmansdorff) that Franz Georg "hardly had any success worth mentioning" in Brussels.[71] On the contrary: the aforementioned praise was proclaimed loudly in front of Metternich's house on October 5, 1792, at a time when the French troops were already marching toward Brussels. The threatening situation that would predictably arise afforded the young eyewitness Clemens a first opportunity to reflect on the new, modern way of war.

The School of War: International Politics

"Victoria! Victoria! We have defeated the French," Beatrix von Metternich wrote to Clemens, who was still in Mainz for his studies, from Brussels. This was April 30, 1792, ten days after the French declaration of war to the king of Hungary and Bohemia.[72] The French had attacked the Austrian Netherlands on April 20, 1792, immediately after declaring war, and thus was begun a war that might almost be called another Thirty Years War.

Following the storming of the Bastille in 1789, things had looked very different for a while. The European powers did not feel particularly challenged by the outbreak of the French Revolution, which took place in the middle of a European-wide crisis that affected each of the major powers in its own way. In the context of that crisis, other things seemed more important. The Russia of Catherine II was entangled in a war with the Ottoman Empire and saw the revolution in Poland as a welcome opportunity to divide that country yet again. Prussia was generally interested in extending its power in Europe, and also wanted to profit from the Polish crisis while, however, also supporting revolutionaries in Liège and Brabant in order to weaken the Austrian dominance in the Habsburg Netherlands and in the Holy Roman Empire. Austria under Joseph II and then, following his death, under Leopold II, wanted to make peace with Turkey and, just like Great Britain, considered the internal turmoil in

France as a rather welcome weakening of the country. Part of Leopold II's new political strategy was to withdraw from the permanent conflict with Prussia. With the Treaty of Reichenbach (July 27, 1790) he succeeded in bringing Prussia onto his side in order to secure the reorganization of Belgium, which had recently been recaptured by Austrian troops.

The fleeing of the French king from Paris to Varennes on June 20, 1791, changed all that. The king even eyed Brussels as a possible place of refuge. The legislature in Paris believed that he wanted to betray the Constitution. His difficult situation brought the two German powers even closer together. At a conference in Pillnitz (Saxony), they allowed themselves to be persuaded by Count Artois, the brother of Louis XVI and head of the emigrants, to make a declaration that intended "to enable the King of France, in perfect freedom, to establish the foundations for a form of government which corresponds to the rights of the sovereigns and the welfare of France" (Declaration of Pillnitz, August 27, 1791).[73] The declaration also contained a threat that military force would be used, provided all major powers agreed. Although this possibility could be ruled out on the grounds of Great Britain's stance alone, in the eyes of the French Parliament the declaration amounted to a declaration of war. The question of the emigrants provided propagandistic ammunition, and in the electorates of Mainz and Trier, as well as in Brussels, the emigrants actually attempted to gather troops for the purpose of a possible intervention in France.

The declaration of war on Hungary and Bohemia by the French National Assembly on April 20, 1792, to which Louis XVI had been forced to agree, fell during an interregnum in the Holy Roman Empire, and thus there was no emperor to serve as the addressee of the declaration. Initially the French side also assumed that this would be a regionally limited conflict. The French king believed that the gathering royalist troops would soon put an end to the nightmare in Paris, whereas the revolutionaries in the National Convention expected to be able to carry out some "land consolidation" in Habsburg territories and to reveal the king as a traitor. Not in anyone's wildest imagination was it expected that the country of the celebrated "Frédéric le Grand" would enter the war on the side of Austria: the two powers had been competitors rather than cooperators for almost half a century.[74]

Franz Georg, as one of the politicians in the Habsburg Netherlands who was most directly affected, was also one of the few who immediately foresaw the possible consequences: "On the basis of this state of affairs, we shall have to expect great events to take place shortly which will be decisive not only for the fate of the French but of all peoples."[75] Clemens's mother also saw the world-historical dimension of what was happening. Even before the French declaration of war, she sent a lucid analysis of the situation from Brussels to her son in Mainz: "There is general despair; in what a cruel situation the empire finds itself! Without a head at a moment of such crisis, I assure you, mon ami, that there will be plenty of speculation, and that subsequently everything might be carried away in the process. . . . The opinion is that we shall not stay in this country." She anticipated the end of the Austrian rule in the Netherlands.[76]

The French Emigrants

The attacks on the privileges of the nobility in Alsace; the people storming the city hall in Strasbourg; the discussions with his pro-revolution Hofmeister; the agitations of his academic teachers—all this made Metternich an eyewitness of contemporary events, which combined very different, and also opposed, words and deeds into a multifaceted kaleidoscope for which the term "revolution" served as an omnipresent metonym. At the same time, a parallel world was articulated in the letters that Metternich's mother sent him from Koblenz, Königswart, and Vienna. She did not take her eyes off that world, and she also neatly summed it up: "L'affaire de la contre révolution va tout doucement" [The matter of the counterrevolution progresses very slowly].[77]

The counterrevolution! One would suspect that the young observer would have fully and passionately sided with it. After all, at stake were the values of his social rank and the fundamental values of his conscience. But it was more complicated than that, because he had very different dealings with the French emigrants: in Koblenz, his hometown, to which many of them had fled; in Mainz, where he studied; and in Brussels, where they became a veritable problem, threatening a war, to the minister plenipotentiary. In Mainz and Brussels in particular, Clemens tried to engage with them. He delved into the French culture and mentality, something that would be of immeasurable value in his later politics: "In this way also I came to know the French; I learned to understand them, and to be understood by them."[78] (We shall later have the opportunity to consider the fact that among his French acquaintances there was also a young French lady.) He studied the royalist emigrants with the same attitude he took toward the Jacobins in Georg Forster's saloon: "From that school [of Jacobin "radicalism"] I fell into the one of the French emigration. It taught me the opposite side of the coin."[79] Interestingly, he felt that the politics of the emigrants was just as "extreme" and "radical"; inadvertently, they revealed to him "the mistakes made by the old régime."

Metternich provides only hints, behind which, however, there is always the concrete information provided by emigrants, the revolutionary press of Mainz, or Jacobin emissaries from Paris. Wherever he went, he came across emigrants: for example, in connection with the imperial coronation of 1792 in Frankfurt, where he observed their "lightheartedness,"[80] or in Koblenz, where the princes of the French royal family assembled, expecting to be able to return from exile within two months. Among those with whom he had conversations in Frankfurt were also prominent individuals in whom one could sense how their exile had changed their character. In this respect, Metternich mentioned in particular the famous priest and abbot Jean-Siffrein Maury. Previously Maury had been a principled member of the estates general in Paris and an opponent of the Civil Constitution of the Clergy. In 1791 he went into exile in Rome and was sent to the imperial coronation as the representative of the Holy See by the pope. In Frankfurt, Metternich already noted a fundamentally opportunistic streak in him; later Maury would become a faithful disciple of Napoleon.[81]

In Metternich's analysis, the emigrants bore a partial responsibility whose roots reached far back into the old political system. He concluded that "in France things had to turn out the way they did."[82] The emigrants imagined that the French would raise a white flag on every tower in the country, and the "*sans-culottes* would lay down their arms"[83] as soon as they caught sight of a few battalions of counterrevolutionary troops. According to Metternich, these were "lofty delusions" that contributed to the Prussians' believing in the emigrants, leading to the heavy defeat of their army at Valmy—a defeat not only in military terms (as they had to retreat) but also in terms of their reputation.[84]

The politics pursued by the emigrants also made it clear to Metternich that the Revolution would not remain restricted to France. In early September 1789, Beatrix already suspected that the "epidemic" would push beyond the French borders. Everyone was calling for "liberté," a phrase that sounds perfect but whose corresponding reality is difficult to ascertain. She still placed her hopes on the Comte d'Artois, who received a lot of support in Bonn. All this, she said, would have to come to an end soon.[85] But just half a week later she changed her mind: the declarations of the Comte d'Artois were terrible, and if he actually had committed all the crimes with which he was charged, he would deserve a grand inquisition and his *auto-da-fé* (i.e., being burned at the stake).[86] With avidity she followed the progress of the Revolution and overwhelmed her son with her worries and hopes. Later she considered the leader of the emigrants, Comte d'Artois, a political "obstacle" and the roughest person she had ever known ("le plus rude").[87]

The Path to War and the First Year of Fighting

How did the nineteen-year-old Metternich experience the path to war, and in which places did he have the opportunity to observe the development from an inside perspective? His published memoirs tell us much less about this than do his handwritten notes. In the company of his father, he personally witnessed the preparations for war. As the minister plenipotentiary for the Austrian Netherlands, his father was directly affected by the French campaign and had to be present to provide information at discussions of the further preparations for war. These took place following the imperial election in Frankfurt, when the monarchs gathered in Mainz for a Congress of Princes (July 19–21, 1792). Franz Georg held negotiations in particular with the Prussian king, Friedrich Wilhelm II. On this occasion, the emigrants who were present were already trying to push forward the preparations for the campaign and to draw up a manifesto declaring war.[88]

Clemens also witnessed further agitation by the French emigrants when he accompanied his father to Koblenz, where they visited the headquarters of the Prussian army near the village of Metternich. Scholarship so far has overlooked the fact that Clemens Metternich was present at each step, and experienced firsthand and through his father how the infamous manifesto of the Duke of Brunswick was initially formulated in Mainz and then was sent out from the Prussian headquarters in Koblenz on July 25, 1792.[89] Metternich leaves out this crucial fact in his memoirs and instead describes how, in Koblenz, he met for the first time the crown prince (who would later become King Friedrich Wilhelm III), with whom he would stay in permanent contact from 1797 until the latter's death in 1840. And he describes the impression King Friedrich Wilhelm II made on him: "Frederick William II was the picture of a king. In stature he was almost a giant, and stout in proportion."[90]

On the manifesto itself, by contrast, he remains silent, and anyone who is familiar with his later politics knows that he would never have accepted such a document, but instead would have condemned it as politically inane and unproductive. For what did this manifesto proclaim? It decreed the campaign as a common operation of Prussia and Austria as allies and handed the Duke of Brunswick the role of supreme commander. The reasons given for the campaign were the estates of German princes in Alsace and Lorraine and the invasion of the Austrian Netherlands. The intention was not, the manifesto declared, "to meddle in the internal government of France," but "merely . . . to deliver the king, the queen, and the royal family from their captivity." These were plausible aims and by no means dramatic. But traces of the emigrants' unbridled passion could also be sensed in the text when it threatened that "if the chateau of the Tuileries is entered by force or attacked again, if the least violence be offered to their Majesties the king, queen, and royal family, and if their safety and their liberty be not immediately assured, they will inflict an ever memorable vengeance by delivering the city of Paris over to military execution and complete destruction, and the rebels guilty of the said outrages over to the punishment that they merit."[91]

The text that Louis XVI announced to the National Assembly on August 3 referred to the previous threat against him on June 20. In order to protect himself against the *sans-culottes*, who were attacking the Tuileries, he had stepped out onto the balcony of the palace and put on the red cap of the Jacobins. The wording of the text had come from a French emigrant in Brussels, the former director of the treasury of the Duke of Orléans, Count Jérôme-Joseph Geoffroy de Limon. But for more than half a year, threats of this nature formed part of "the dinner-table conversations of Brussels and Koblenz" and were then publicized in royalist organs, much to the detriment of the royal family.[92] The manifesto provided a reason for the National Assembly to issue a passionate call to the peoples of Europe and to offer them the help of the French nation if they wanted to rebel against the tyrannies of their despots. In 1792, Louis Philippe, who later became the French king, commented that the manifesto mobilized more enthusiasm for the defense of the fatherland and for national independence in France than all the patriotic appeals coming from the National Assembly and the revolutionary societies taken together.[93] On August 10, 1792, the storming of the Tuileries, which Metternich's Hofmeister Simon helped to prepare, took place despite, or possibly because of, the manifesto. It ended with the king fleeing and seeking protection from the National Assembly. A day later, the Prussian and Austrian troops began their campaign by entering France from Luxembourg.

That was the situation to which Metternich refers in his memoirs: "In the latter part of the summer [of 1792] I went to Brussels. The war was at its height."[94] The time he subsequently spent in Brussels was crucial for his entire life, because there he "had therefore the opportunity of observing war very closely; and it is to be wished that all those who are called upon to take a leading part in the state could learn in the same school. In the course of my long public life I have often had reason to congratulate myself upon the experience thus gained."[95] This statement has been used to suggest that the young Metternich thought he could become a military expert purely by observing the war, that he wanted to gain "a practical education in the science of arms" but that his "amateur dabbling in siege operations was worthless."[96] This judgment is altogether wrongheaded. Metternich was actually concerned with the ways in which politics can transition into war, how traditional warfare functions, how strategy and tactics are developed and applied, and also what human suffering a politician must reckon with once he fails in his business.

After his arrival, Clemens worked in his father's office in Brussels. He was also involved in all military communications with the Austrian headquarters.

Franz Georg used him "for the most secret work for the cabinet, a fact which probably did not fail to have an essential influence on my subsequent career," as Metternich judged in retrospect.[97] His tasks in this context meant that he had to travel back and forth between the headquarters of the Austrian army and Brussels. He thus heard about the disaster suffered by the Prussian troops. Under the supreme command of the Duke of Brunswick, their intention of advancing to Paris had been thwarted on September 20, 1792, when they were brought to a halt at Valmy. For the French, the aborted battle developed into the myth that the revolutionary troops were capable of defeating the allied monarchs. The victorious wars of the monarchs had come to an end; those of the people had begun. In that sense, the famous dictum of Goethe, who had accompanied his Grand Duke Karl August of Saxony-Weimar-Eisenach to Valmy and thus was an eyewitness, was right: "From this place [i.e., Valmy] and from this day forth commences a new era in the world's history."[98] A day later the king was dethroned in Paris, and on September 22 France was declared a republic, inaugurating a new age with a new calendar, a change that became deeply engrained in the French mind.

As mentioned before, Metternich knew about Prussia's misconceived ideas, which had formed under the influence of the emigrants. He considered the campaign's plans flawed from the outset and, without mentioning a name, described it as led "by a man whose military reputation was founded simply on a flattering remark by Friedrich II."[99] The incompetence—as he saw it—of the duke had led to the "calamitous retreat." Information he gained at a later point in time brought Metternich to a judgment that corresponds to the knowledge we have today: If the Duke of Brunswick had not hesitated for days and had marched straight to Paris, then the French troops would not have been able to stop him.[100] But as matters stood, on October 10, 1792, the leading French general, Dumouriez, was able to appear in front of the National Convention and boast about the ideological character of the war and its expansive power. Freedom, he said, would triumph everywhere, would conquer every throne, would destroy despotism and illuminate the peoples. With its resolutions, the National Convention was laying the foundations for the welfare and brotherliness of the nations.[101] The retreat of the allies at Valmy opened up a space for Dumouriez that he could use in order to turn against Belgium and the Rhineland. This had fateful consequences: on October 21, 1792, General Custine conquered Mainz, and Dumouriez, following his spectacular victory at Jemappes on November 6, entered Brussels only a little later, on November 14, 1792.

In the published version of his memoirs, Metternich remains silent on the court's temporary flight from Brussels. In his handwritten "Hauptmomente meines Lebens," he reveals: "Emigration with the general government of the

Netherlands to Roermond and Wesel. Spent the winter 1792–1793 in Wesel."[102] The family had left Brussels during the night from November 8 to November 9.[103] Metternich experienced for himself for the first time the meaning of political emigration—that is, being expelled by revolutionaries—a catastrophic experience that he was to repeat in 1794 and 1848. For one and a half years he was engulfed by the turbulence in Belgium, during which time Austrian rule over the Netherlands was defended against and regained from the revolutionary troops. In the months of his exile in the Rhineland, as mentioned above, he studied very closely the newspapers and pamphlets from Mainz that kept him informed of the ruling power of the French and of the German Jacobins in the archdiocese. Similar Jacobin clubs were now also founded in Brussels.

During those months of reading and of observant restlessness, Metternich, despite his young age, came to understand the nature of the Revolution more deeply than most of those of his contemporaries who were inspired by the proclaimed values and aims. He also came to recognize the close connection between domestic and foreign policies, something he had already detected in the situation and agitation of the French emigrants in Mainz, Koblenz, and Brussels. The fact that in his memoirs he includes his deeper perception of the Revolution in the first chapter, on his apprenticeship years, also indicates that his time in Strasbourg, Koblenz, Mainz, and Brussels was decisive. In his judgment, the "Frenchmen of that day did not at all comprehend the Revolution,"[104] and in saying this, it was the emigrants he had primarily in mind. Their hope that the old rule could be reestablished with a campaign that would reach Paris, he also considered to be based on an error. Military means would not suffice; "moral remedies"[105] were needed, because in his eyes the mistakes lay far back in the past of the ancien régime. The real remedy he saw in the policies his father pursued after the revolution in Belgium, in the restoration of traditional rights and in approaching the estates. This allowed his father "to carry out the moral pacification of those provinces."[106]

Following the victory of the Austrian troops on March 18, 1793, at Neerwinden, Franz Georg, as previously described, returned with his family to Brussels. Clemens remarks on this: "Returned with the k.u.k. army to Brussels."[107] From then on, he kept his eye firmly on military developments: "attendant throughout the campaign." In this context, he experienced a spectacular situation. In Paris, Dumouriez's defeat had caused great consternation, leading to a conflict between the general and the National Convention, which was dominated by the Jacobins. Dumouriez, in consultation with the Austrians, therefore developed the plan to lead his troops to Paris and to topple the convention. That plan became known, and the Convention sent off the war minister, Beurnonville, and four of its members—Camus, Quinette, La Marque, and Bancal—with the task of arresting Dumouriez for high treason. It was clear to the defeated military leader that he might have to face the guillotine. When, on April 1, the members of the convention arrived at his headquarters, he explained to them: "I shall not go to Paris and allow myself to be treated unworthily by fanatics and find myself being condemned to death by a revolutionary tribunal." And when Camus, speaking for the members of the convention, responded by pointing out that in that case he failed to recognize the authority of the tribunal, Dumouriez retorted: "I recognize in it a tribunal of Blood and of Crimes, to which I will never submit as long as I hold an inch of iron in my hand. I moreover declare that, had I the power, I would abolish it, as being a dishonor to a free Nation."[108] The fate of General Custine after he had been driven out of Mainz later confirmed Dumouriez's fears and expectations: on August 28, 1793, Custine was taken to the scaffold in Paris.

The young Metternich saw for himself the drama of an adjutant of the commanding Austrian general informing his father that General Dumouriez had delivered the five emissaries of the National Convention to the Austrians. Clemens was even given the task of receiving them in Brussels and accompanying them to the prison. On this occasion, as before when meeting the Jacobins in Mainz, he tried to engage his opponents in direct conversation and to understand their thoughts. On his acquaintance with the messengers of Robespierre and his friends, he wrote in his memoirs: "I had many interviews with them in the prison to which they were assigned, and heard their complaints against the general, whom they had been ordered to remove and imprison."[109] Here in Brussels—in 1793, the year of the Terror—Metternich came as close to the Parisian Jacobins, the ambassadors of the Revolution, as his tutor Simon did at the same time in Paris. He met them on different terms, however. The Austrians finally had the five prisoners escorted to Moravia, where they remained in captivity until December 1795.[110]

The young Metternich learned even more about the peculiar dynamic of the Revolution when he witnessed how General Dumouriez, whose troops refused to follow him to Paris, defected to the camp of the Austrians on April 4, 1793, in order to escape the guillotine—the very general who had lent the war the spirit of a national battle for liberation, fought against the tyrants on the thrones, and been significantly involved in the declaration of war. His colossal about-turn caused Metternich to comment: "The French Reign of Terror destroyed its own commanders just as cartridges destroyed the soldiers."[111] This short succinct phrase is reminiscent of the words that the Girondist Victurnien Vergniaud is said to have spoken before his execution on October 31, 1793: "The Revolution is like Saturn; it devours its own children." Georg Büchner, the pre-

1848 revolutionary and poet, has his character Danton speak these words as he speculates about his possible end under the guillotine.[112]

Dumouriez was of a different ilk; he believed that he could enter the great political stage on the side of the Austrians. Once he had arrived at their camp on April 4, 1793, he revised, together with the Austrian general Mack, a proclamation of the Duke of Coburg which was due to be distributed on April 5. It was meant to announce that the intention of the Austrian emperor was not to conquer but to restore peace and order in France and that it was to this end that he cooperated with General Dumouriez.[113] In order to explain his motivation to him, Dumouriez also called on Franz Georg, as the "Ministre plénipotentiaire des Pays-Bas," at his home, where he felt that he was received "with the greatest friendship" and was given "a passport for Germany."[114] His war plans became politically highly explosive and led the young Metternich onto the great stage of international politics for the first time. Metternich had nominally arrived there already, as Emperor Franz had appointed him emissary of the States General of the Netherlands in The Hague.[115] But now he witnessed how a deserted general, in alliance with the Austrians, was attempting a coup in Paris. This whole episode from Metternich's life deserves to be given such special attention because it points to an event in his early biography that was unknown until now—namely, his participation at the Antwerp Conference that took place on April 8, 1793.

The Antwerp Conference and the First Coalition

Accompanying his father to Antwerp, the young Metternich for the first time saw what maintaining the power balance within European politics at the highest level meant—not in the textbooks of Koch and Vogt, but in reality. In this context, we need to remind ourselves of the following: the British government, led by Prime Minister William Pitt, had up to that point not seen the events in France as very serious, because they weakened the neighboring state. Ideological aspects did not initially weigh particularly heavily, as global maritime interests, such as the conquest of French colonies, seemed more important than what happened on the Continent.[116] This view of things changed after the National Convention decided, on November 19, 1792, to extend "support and brotherhood to all peoples who wanted to regain their freedom" and ordered the French generals "to bring help to these peoples and to protect those citizens who had been, or are going to be, mistreated because of their commitment to the cause of freedom."[117] For Edmund Burke, who would become important for Metternich a little later, this alone was reason enough to intervene militarily on the Continent.

The National Convention's commitment, in principle, to exporting the Revolution only confirmed hard political facts that had already been established when Dumouriez conquered Belgium. This was "the real break in British policy toward France after 1787,"[118] because it had been "since the middle ages a kind of law in foreign policy" that England took up arms whenever France conquered the Belgian coast.[119] The execution of Louis XVI on January 21, 1793, was a final signal for the British government to change its course. The eviction of the French ambassador from London on grounds of him conspiring with emigrants subsequently led to France's long-awaited declaration of war, which was made on February 1, 1793. Again, it was revolutionary France that declared war.

In Antwerp, the European powers now confronted this problem. According to Prussia's definition, the meeting was a "military congress," and it was the founding moment of the alliance that fought in the war of the first coalition. This meant that Clemens von Metternich would be the only leading European politician who experienced all six alliances and the resulting coalition wars against France, from the beginnings in 1792 to the end in 1815, mostly as an actively involved witness and then as a diplomat or politician. This experience put him in good stead in 1813–1814 when the survival of the sixth and last coalition, which would prove decisive, lay in his hands. Gathered in Antwerp on April 8, 1793, were representatives from Great Britain (the Duke of York, the ambassador Lord Auckland), Holland (the hereditary governor heir to the throne, the Prince of Orange—i.e., the father of the later king of the Netherlands, William I, who would give Metternich shelter in Brussels in 1848), Austria (the Prince of Coburg, the minister Count von Metternich, accompanied by Clemens, Count von Trauttmansdorff, and the ambassador to the Hague Starhemberg), and Prussia (Lieutenant General Baron von Knobelsdorff, and the emissary in the Hague, Baron von Keller). Information was exchanged on the exact number of troops available, their readiness, commanders, and the location of arsenals and equipment.[120]

The initiative for this congress had lain with the Austrian side—to be precise, with Prince Coburg, who had the intention of uniting the divergent interests of the allies. In particular, he wanted to discuss the plan that he had agreed to with Dumouriez and the draft of his appeal to the French. His intention to cooperate with a person like Dumouriez, who was seen as beyond the pale, caused pure horror all around, as is clear from the report of the Austrian emissary.[121] Dumouriez, it was believed, threw himself into the arms of the allies in order to save his own skin. He was a lofty and scheming character and wanted to call the shots within the alliance. The Duke of York felt personally betrayed by Coburg, and Auckland declared that he intended to leave the very same day, as the Austrian Court had misled the British. He threatened to end the coalition. Everyone else present was similarly forthright in their disapproval.

At this point the young Metternich witnessed how his father defused a situation that seemed entirely deadlocked, without the Duke of Coburg having to lose face. Earlier Starhemberg had repeatedly and insistently asked Franz Georg to take part in the conference, and he now called himself lucky to have a minister at his side whose "achievements, age, and political weight . . . , reasonableness and prudence" helped him calm the storm and, most importantly, reconcile York and Auckland. Starhemberg pointed out to the British how badly the name and reputation of a decorated military commander of the rank of Prince von Coburg would be damaged if, as they demanded, a formal public withdrawal of the plan was required of him. Metternich supported Starhemberg and made the decisive suggestion: the congress would formulate a common second declaration because, on the basis of the latest information, a new situation had arisen. The army on which Dumouriez had relied had deserted him, and the truce agreed on with him was invalid. Such a declaration would respect the reputation and self-esteem of the prince. The new declaration, drafted by Metternich's father, received general acclaim. The protocol of the congress did not mention Dumouriez by name at all. Metternich's experienced father had shown his son an example not only of how to deal with the Belgian estates but also of how to operate on the international stage. And at the same time, the son learned how important Great Britain was when it came to regulating international conflict.

In Antwerp the young Metternich developed a "firm foundation for his convictions" that remained a fixed point of reference for him in his subsequent diplomatic career. The decision against Coburg, however, may be interpreted in ways that differ from the judgment of those who were present, because there were two different "military schools" competing with each other in this matter. The rejection of the plan meant that there would not be a decisive common move toward Paris, but instead action would be limited to the occupation of the French border fortifications. This was a repetition of the mistake that Clemens von Metternich had already observed in the case of the defeat at Valmy ("If the Duke of Brunswick . . . had marched straight to Paris"). In the present context, he became familiar with a phenomenon that later critics called "the slavish adherence to an old military school." After all, it was known that there were men in Coburg's headquarters whose successes proved that they knew how to direct great masses of troops and were able to use them with boldness as well as with a sharp and clever eye for the situation.[122]

After his return to Brussels, Metternich observed the theaters of war himself and indeed had those experiences that he recommended to future politicians.

At the time, he did not yet know anything about the cruelty that characterized the more recent military conflicts or about how traditional campaigns that aimed to protect troops through positional warfare were to degenerate into wars of annihilation under the dominance of Napoleon in Europe. But because he observed them so keenly, certain theaters of war imprinted themselves particularly strongly in his memory during his time in Brussels. The places in question were three French fortresses that lay close to each other at the Belgian border in what today is the Departement Nord.

First, Metternich studied the siege of Condé-sur-l'Escaut, during which the new French commander and successor to Dumouriez, General Dampierre, was killed when he tried to break through the circle of the siege on May 8, 1793.[123] The strongest impression on the young observer was made by the siege of the neighboring Valenciennes, which lasted from May 24 to July 28, 1793, on which he remarked that he "was present at almost all the operations of the siege."[124] While the British, led by York, besieged Dunkirk between August 23 and September 8 in order to regain what was, for them, an important point of access to the Continent, Metternich moved with the Austrian troops toward Quesnoy. Their siege of the place began on August 19 and ended successfully on September 11. Thus, in 1793 Metternich experienced the last successes of the allies at the border with France. The time-consuming sieges, however, provided sufficient time for the French to recover from the earlier disasters of the spring, so that they were able to begin conquering large territories again. They profited from the principles of an old military school that limited activities to the circling of enemy positions instead of advancing over vast spaces. It was therefore only a matter of time before the French would reconquer Belgium and the left bank of the Rhine.

As Metternich was in constant contact with the soldiers, he learned about the execution of Marie Antoinette on October 19, 1793. There is hardly any other event at the time that shook him as strongly as this one, and it continued to have an effect on him into his old age. In Königswart, he kept the last book of prayers that the Queen, the daughter of Maria Theresia, had with her in prison. The young count, who, as a servant of the emperor's house in Brussels, felt personally attacked, vented his anger in a passionate outburst and in words of a kind he would never again commit to paper: he composed a "Call upon the Army"; it was not printed at the time:

> Soldiers! Your courage, your bravery needs not
> to be inflamed; redouble then your zeal and passionate
> desire to avenge the hideous crime, Maria Theresa's
> blood, upon the monsters who make war upon you.

Maria Antonia of Austria, Queen of France, they have murdered.
Innocence have they slaughtered on the scaffold, the
place of malefactors.
Ruin fall on the heads of these impious murderers,
murderers of their kings and of their Fatherland.
The blood of your immortal Theresa, the blood of
Austria herself, spilled upon a scaffold!!
Listen! that blood calls you to Vengeance. Heaven
and Earth cry out for Vengeance, even to—death!
Brave defenders of your lawful monarchs, rest not
Until that cry is accomplished![125]

After this, one never again finds revenge as a political motive in Metternich. When, in old age, he organized his personal papers, he wrote on the folder of this text: "The Sketch of an Appeal to the Imperial Army, composed in my youthful zeal in 1793."

Although in hindsight he claimed that at seventeen he had been "exactly" the man he remained thereafter, this eruption of emotion and his state of bafflement show how little his development was complete even at the age of twenty. He had not yet found his own position between the two forms of "radicalism" that he personally had experienced and rejected: Jacobinism and royalism. He summarizes his time in Brussels as follows: "From this school of thought ['radicalism' in the vein of Simon] I fell into the one propounded by the French emigrants. They taught me the reverse side of the coin. The feeling that there must be a middle ground between the extremes settled firmly in my young mind. To find this middle ground became an urge in me, and the extortions necessary to find it produced the conviction in me that I did not possess the skills for engaging in *world politics*."[126]

In light of the extremes and his urge for a politics of the middle ground, he thus felt that he was unsuitable for politics. However, he had yet to have one essential experience, which would also be provided for him by the great war against France. It was fundamentally to form his perspective and allow him to find the desired point after all: the political "middle ground" that made responsible political action possible. This position he would find during his upcoming travels to Great Britain.

This journey emerged from the war coalition's need for subsidies for further military action from the British allies. In March 1794, Franz Georg von Metternich instructed his treasurer—the "Trésorier général des Finances des Pays-Bas autrichiens"—Vicomte Pierre-Benoit Desandrouin, to negotiate a bond in London.[127] And his two sons, Clemens and Joseph, were to accompany him so that they would become acquainted with Great Britain and its leading politicians. It is a stroke of luck for us that Desandrouin invited his son-in-law, the Comte de Liedekerke Beaufort, to join them as company for the two Metternich sons, because the diary of the Comte tells us much more about the twenty-one-year-old Metternich's stay than do his own memoirs. In Liedekerke, Metternich was again close to an exemplary emigrant: he had served as a pageboy to the brother of Louis XVI before fleeing to Brussels in 1791.[128]

Franz Georg had announced the guests to the British prime minister, Pitt. It was Metternich's first journey to meet with the highest circles of British society and the British court. On March 25, 1794, the group departed from Brussels, not to return to the Continent until July of that year.

THE JOURNEY TO GREAT BRITAIN: THE FINAL PIECE TO THE YOUNG METTERNICH'S POLITICAL UNIVERSE

His journey brought Metternich to a country his teacher Vogt had introduced to him as the state in Europe that best preserved the "old German Constitution" and the "bourgeois freedom" enshrined in it. Following Vogt's instructions, Metternich also had to study the well-known promoter of this idea, Montesquieu. Both teachers of state theory had opened his eyes to the principle of the balance of powers as it is embodied in the English "Constitution." Would reality conform to this high ideal?

On March 25, 1794, Metternich began to write his first and only diary, which has remained unpublished to the present day. It ends on April 8, when the many new impressions overwhelmed him and left him no time to continue it. Nevertheless, it is one of the rare occasions where Metternich commented on his early years. It begins with the departure from Brussels. One of the first entries already—unconsciously—touches on the "Cato" of the British Parliament, Edmund Burke, who in 1793 had spoken out forcefully in favor of an "Aliens Act" in order to stem the free flow of French refugees entering the country. As a consequence, anyone arriving on the island had to be formally registered and reported to the local authorities. Metternich writes that the inspection of the passports during the crossing had led to "endless formalities since the beginning of the war." Their briefcase and the documents it contained had also triggered an extremely intrusive inspection from the authorities. It was a good idea to carry as little luggage as possible.[129]

Burke's speech, incidentally, inadvertently became part of parliamentary history because, in order to justify the Act, he warned that thousands of spies would come to the island and undermine the government. That claim was somehow not met with widespread belief. In order to make his point, Burke pulled out a dagger and cast it down onto the floor of the Parliament, exclaiming, "Such is the weapon which the French Jacobins would plunge into the heart of our beloved King!," upon which another member of Parliament, the writer Richard Brinsley Sheridan, "brought the house down with 'Where's the fork?'"[130] Burke, however, was not wrong in his admonition that French espionage had to be taken very seriously, even if he might have exaggerated the dimensions of the problem. An incredible coincidence meant that it was Metternich who ended up in a position to demonstrate the legitimacy of Burke's worries to the British, as we shall see.

Metternich's traveling companion Liedekerke also kept a diary, until the day of his return and in much greater detail than Metternich, so that by collating the two accounts we achieve a much better picture of Metternich's stay in England than has previously been possible. Which places did he visit on his journey? Following the crossing from Oostend to Dover, the itinerary brought him to Canterbury, Chatham, Rochester, Richmond, Hartford, Greenwich, Portsmouth, the Isle of Wight, Oxford, Stowe, and Blenheim. London was the base for his stay throughout. It might be tempting to follow his movements chronologically, but we must here ignore their sequence and instead concentrate on those outings and encounters that made lasting impressions on Metternich. Seven such experiences can be identified.

Connections in British Society (1)

The connections he was able to establish within British society are of chief importance for Metternich's future role as an internationally connected politician who was able to reap the benefits of his networks. A certain reputation preceded the affable young imperial count: he had already had something of an introduction not only by virtue of his appointment as an emissary to The Hague but also because his father had recommended him to Prime Minister Pitt. And Clemens already had supporters in London as well, such as Lord Thomas Elgin, whom he knew from his time at the embassy in Brussels, and most of all Ludwig Prince von Starhemberg, his predecessor at The Hague, whom he had met at the conference in Antwerp, and who now, as the Austrian ambassador to London, wanted, in the interests of the coalition, to improve the country's relationship with Great Britain. Starhemberg frequently invited Metternich to his home, and he opened up a way into British society for him. He showed him around London, organized tickets to the ministerial gallery at the House of Lords, and soon arranged an audience with King George III, on April 2. In St. James's Palace, the party walked along a hall with the royal guard, whose uniforms reminded Metternich of the Swiss Guard, and then entered the hall for the emissaries. The king walked through both halls and spoke to everyone, but Clemens he received with "unusual kindness and affability."[131] After meeting the king, they visited Prime Minister Pitt, all members of the diplomatic corps, and the ministers of the British Cabinet. The visit meant that Metternich came "into contact with the most remarkable men of this great epoch."[132]

The following day he would come even closer to the royal couple; he was invited to the "Cercle de la Reine," a reception hosted by the queen.[133] Here he experienced the ceremonial side of the court and the ladies-in-waiting in their grand robes. The queen was followed by one of the ladies, who carried her train; the princesses followed according to their rank. The king and queen went about the hall, and Metternich found it hard to imagine that anyone could outdo them in friendliness. They did not ignore a single person, spoke to everyone, and conversed altogether naturally in German. Afterward, they went to dinner at the home of Frau von Starhemberg, with Lord Grenville and his wife—the latter, Metternich wrote, "was the prettiest woman I have so far seen at the court."[134]

In Antwerp, Metternich had noticed from the outside the importance of Great Britain as an international player—here, in London, he learned from the inside why it was the Austrian raison d'état to close political ranks with Britain: the "public feeling manifested itself in both countries with the same energy against the horrors of the French Revolution," and "indeed their interests seemed to be identical."[135]

If we look at the men mentioned by Metternich individually, however, the harmonious perspective of the memoirs somewhat clashes with what we know of the reality at the time. He met politicians who were publicly engaged in the most vehement controversies over the direction British foreign policy should take with regard to the American colonies, East India, slavery, and especially the French Revolution. Metternich had personal exchanges with Prime Minister William Pitt, who for a long time underestimated the international danger emanating from the French Revolution. He also made the acquaintance of a Whig member of Parliament, Charles Fox, who was the most forceful critic of the British policies on East India but sympathized with the French Revolution, which led to his falling out with Edmund Burke. Burke was among the most radical critics of the French Revolution, and one of the first who recommended a decisive military intervention. Because of his influence on Metternich, we shall have to pay special attention to him. The Whig politician and poet Richard Brinsley Sheridan also entered into the fray with Burke.

Also of importance was Metternich's acquaintance with Charles Grey, later prime minister at the time of the July Revolution. Even more important, however, was his acquaintance with the Prince Regent, who, due to his father's illness, was to take office as early as 1811 and then take up the throne as George IV in 1820. This monarch, ostracized for his lifestyle but celebrated for his cultural policies, was particularly acknowledged by Metternich: "Our relations, begun at this time, lasted during the prince's whole life."[136] This was put to the test not least at the time of the "Carlsbad Decrees" and the persecution of demagogues, when the monarch and Metternich were both convinced of the European nature of the crisis to be confronted. For now, in London, Metternich caught the attention of the prince because of his unprejudiced attitude toward him amid the puritan environment in the capital ("He took a great fancy to me"). It was characteristic of Metternich that he did not judge on the basis of the "bad society" in which the Prince Regent moved, and which he condemned, but instead emphasized his positive traits: his "most charming manners" and his "sound intelligence," both of which "preserved him from being corrupted." Metternich did not shy away from pointing out to the Prince Regent, who was eleven years his senior, the dangers which surrounded him, and when he had become George IV and visited Hanover (as the ruling king of Hanover) in 1821 on the occasion of the royal succession, he still remembered Metternich's advice and said to him: "You were very right then."[137] This relationship with the Prince Regent shows that Metternich understood the battles between the factions at the time perfectly well, and within them he saw the prince having "taken up the side of the opposition." But this was of secondary importance compared to the lessons in politics he received from the British Parliament.

Encountering British Constitutionalism in Action (2)

The culture of political debate in the British Parliament was the fundamental impression left on Metternich by his journey to England. As often as possible, he attended meetings of Parliament, preferably those in the House of Lords. His fascination with the overall arrangement even led him to sketch the layout in his diary.[138]

In the sketch, he marked the positions of the individual dignitaries. At the front wall was the throne with a baldachin (1); next, at the front, sat the lord chancellor (2); in front of him, the "table of the house" for the five or six clerks in charge of protocol, who wore black wigs that reached down to their shoulders (3); next followed the row of ministers (5), and then the rows of lords who were not affiliated with any political party (6). On the left, the "temporal" side were the seats of the opposition (4), on the right, the "spiritual" side (not numbered in Metternich's sketch), sat the bishops and archbishops of the Church of England and the members of the governing party. There were barriers (7) separating the seats reserved for visitors from the House of Commons (9). The entrance (8) was to the left of the throne. The precision with which Metternich noted down the layout of the room shows how important it was to him to have an exact understanding of how the individual members of the upper house

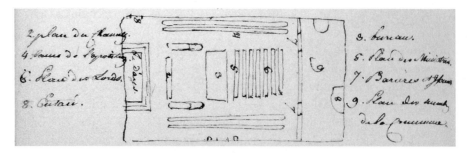

Sketch of the seating arrangement in the House of Lords in Metternich's diary of his journey to England (dated April 4, 1794).

were hierarchically placed according to rank, function, and title. The structure revealed the character of the complex balance in the constitutional architecture, from the throne down to the "commons." Metternich might well have been reminded of the Imperial Diet of the Holy Roman Empire, of which his lineage had become a member.

How accurately had the young imperial count represented reality? In 1834 the chamber of the upper house fell victim to the devastating fire at the Palace of Westminster, but a painting of it by a German-British bookseller, Rudolph Ackermann (who founded a printing press and drawing school in London one year after Metternich's visit), still exists. It shows the chamber's state in 1808, and it is amazing how precisely Metternich captured what he saw.

On April 8, Metternich observed in his journal that, even though the atmosphere was sometimes turbulent and strong words were used, "the sittings are highly impressive and conducted with great dignity." One of the conflicts left such a lasting impression on him that he remembered it well in to his old age and drew a lesson from it: "[I] followed with particular attention the famous trial of Mr. Hastings. I endeavored to acquaint myself thoroughly with the mechanism of the Parliament, and this was useful in my subsequent career."[139] Metternich became an eyewitness of some moments of the longest and most famous political trial in British history, lasting from 1788 to 1795, triggered by the "impeachment" of the Governor General Warren Hastings by Edmund Burke. Hastings had driven the native rulers out of Bengal in East India and erected a military dictatorship for the purpose of exploiting the country. In 1787 Burke wrote an indictment of this "tyrant," who had enriched himself; Burke fought as the "new Cato" (thus Burke's nickname) and the combative head of the prosecution for seven years, although in the end his opponent was acquitted. On April 10, 1794, Metternich attended the cross-examination of Lord Cornwallis, who had been called as a witness, and listened with fascination to the speeches made by the most famous British politicians of his time: Burke, Charles Fox, Charles Grey, and Stanhope. With amazement, he noticed how Hastings

The inside of the House of Lords, painting by Rudolph Ackermann (1808).

made casual notes and listened to Burke's incredibly heated diatribe against him, which lasted for more than half an hour and culminated in the declaration that the governor general of East India was a bloodthirsty oppressor of the people.[140]

During the weeks when Metternich was at the House of Lords, the debates in the upper and lower houses also dealt with crucial questions regarding the war against France, including the issue of the consequences of the occupation of Toulon in December 1793. In this context, Napoleon and Metternich were both involved for the first time in the network of international matters that had unfolded in the wake of the Revolution—Napoleon as an ambitious military leader and Metternich as an attentive observer and auxiliary diplomat in the service of Brussels. The British Parliament also discussed the raising of an army and the crucial problem of how the monarchy, the nobility, and the people should relate to each other. Edmund Burke was a prominent figure in all of these debates. As an aristocratic Whig politician with a long history in Parliament, he fought for the "freedom" of the estates against the absolutist and "despotic" ambitions of the crown. He had a reputation for defending the right of the Parliament against King George III. The impeachment of Hastings, the "oppressor of India," was thus of a piece with his politics. The expectation that he would, like his fellow Whig Fox, sympathize with the French Revolution as a movement for freedom, however, was dashed.[141] Burke turned out to be one of the most vehement critics of the Revolution, and in the debates that Metternich followed he categorically called for a military intervention.

The Convergence between Burke's and Metternich's Ideas

The first edition of Burke's best-seller *Reflections on the Revolution in France* had appeared in November 1790, thus some time before Metternich arrived on the island. It developed the "program of an aristocratic constitutionalism."[142] For the young Metternich, Burke's ideas had the quality of a political epiphany. Metternich was familiar with the individual ideas from the time of his studies, but here was a statesman who had formed these ideas about the state into a coherent conception and made them suitable for practical politics: all this in his battle against "the ideas of the French Revolution." At the same time, he discovered in Burke the "middle ground" between the radicalism of the royalists, whom he considered absolutists, and that of the Jacobins, whom he took to be demagogues. Originally written as a pamphlet, Burke's work became a key text on the Continent as well, especially after a later member of Metternich's staff, Friedrich Gentz, had translated it into German. Let us summarize, in the form of theses, those ideas of Burke's with which the young Metternich identified, for Burke's original mind had expressed what Metternich himself had not yet been able to put into words.[143]

- On Burke's interpretation, the Glorious Revolution was conservative: it was meant to preserve the existing Constitution, with its aristocratic orientation. The French Revolution was a repetition of Cromwell's Puritan revolution: both led to regicide, religiously intensified political fanaticism, and social anarchy.

- Burke, by contrast, appealed for cautious reform that respected historical traditions, slow and patient change that would not destroy the fundamental social structures. The value of functioning and legitimate institutions and social relations should not be underestimated. The law and Constitution must develop steadily and organically.

- This concept of reform was oriented by the historical manifestation of rights and freedoms—the "privileges" of each estate.

- Pre-revolutionary France—i.e., the ancien régime—had not been a despotic system characterized by arbitrary rule and economic stagnation. The nobility had not exploited and repressed their subjects.

- Burke put his finger on the economic interests that were at work behind the propaganda of the French Revolution. A bourgeois financial oligarchy—"bourgeois stock market speculators, bankers, wholesale buyers of land, and advocates"[144]—wanted to acquire the aristocratic estates and the land belonging to the church. And the men of letters, the intellectuals, offered them their help. These groups had hidden their "monied interests" from the lower classes and mobilized their hatred and envy of the crown, the clergy, and the nobility in the pursuit of their own interests.[145]

- The task of the nobility is to mediate between the "people" and the monarch. This would lead to a "balanced Constitution." Burke, too, had studied Montesquieu's critique of absolutism. He considered it a cardinal sin to strengthen the bureaucratic machinery of the state in the interests of the monarch and at the expense of the estates and historical privileges, because this undermines, and ultimately destroys, historically grown social relations and institutions.

- The French Revolution was a matter for all of Europe because it attacked the shared foundations of all of Europe.

- At the assembly of the States General in May 1789, the French would have had the chance to reinstate the old historical Constitution and to abolish the absolute monarchy of the seventeenth century—in other words, to pick up again the tradition prior to the age of absolutism, the "ancient principles and models of the old common law of Europe."[146]

Burke's overall conception was based on the idea of a structured, "composite" state, and it required the participation of the entitled estates. This order, for Burke, possessed the legal status of a "Constitution" and was therefore in competition with the French notion of constitutional popular sovereignty. In his arguments, Burke always presupposed a pan-European scope—in strict analogy to the Girondists, at the helm in Paris, and their Jacobin successors, who wanted to liberate all of Europe. Within the battle of ideas, Burke established a level playing field.

Metternich's View of Burke

For a long time it was not possible to say anything beyond "the level of the probable" when considering how important Burke was as a foundation for Metternich's convictions.[147] Burke's theses above, indeed, raise the question of whether Metternich actually consciously took note of them and perhaps even adapted them to his own understanding of matters. Since the publication of Liedekerke's diary in 1968, we know that Metternich studied the debates in Parliament, and thus necessarily also Burke's contributions, much more intensively than he makes it seem in his own notes—although he does say there that he "frequented the sittings of Parliament as much as possible."[148] In this context, his father's wisdom in asking the Hofmeister Abbé Bertrand to teach his pupil English paid off. It is inconceivable that Metternich would have had only an "incomplete command" of English.[149] He must have had more than a reasonable proficiency in the foreign language, to have attended and followed the parliamentary debates as regularly as he did.

There is further important evidence of Metternich's immediate impression of Burke. He had purchased a first edition of the *Reflections* of 1790,[150] and he had marked two passages in it that seemed important to him. These highlighted pages prove that he indeed read the text in the original, and they show the extent to which he saw Burke as sharing in his own political convictions.

The first marked passage refers to the question of how the French Revolution should be evaluated in relation to its chief concept of "liberty."[151] In Burke's view, freedom means the power of movement; it allows individuals to do what they please. Whether freedom will lead to happiness or misery will be clear only once it becomes obvious "how it had been combined with government." That Metternich concentrated in particular on what today's empirical sciences would call "operationalization"—the process which renders a theoretical construct measurable—reveals something of the young Metternich's intellectual acuity. In other words, "liberty," according to Burke, becomes a value only once it has been combined with "public force; the discipline and obedience of armies; the collection of an effective and well-distributed revenue; morality and religion; the solidity of property; with peace and order;[152] with civil and social manners": "Without them, liberty is not a benefit whilst it lasts, and is not likely to continue long." Burke put forward his cautious and skeptical approach as early as November 1790, and Metternich, who in the meantime had come to know the Terror, the degeneration of the revolutionary system, once again found reason to feel confirmed in his reservations. He would have remembered that his mother had written to him in Strasbourg as early as September 1, 1789, that everyone was calling for *liberté,* but that in reality this was only a fantasy, a phrase that sounded perfect, but the actual existence of liberty was difficult to ascertain.[153]

The second passage marked by Metternich stretches over three pages and is even more important.[154] In it, Burke describes the fate of Marie Antoinette. He had personally known her in her early, glittering years as the wife of the dauphin, the successor to the throne at the time, and compares this period to her "dishonoring" at the end of 1790. The feelings Metternich had expressed in his draft appeal of 1793 he must have found echoed in Burke's words: "I thought ten thousand swords must have leaped from their scabbards to avenge even a look that threatened her with insult." But the real heart of the passage is a reflection back on a time that was still harmonious. The reader's attention is at the same time drawn to the code of honor adhered to by Metternich's family throughout the ages but rarely mentioned explicitly by its most prominent member. Burke opens up a parallel for Metternich: France had once been a nation of men of honor, of gallant men and cavaliers. There is no doubt that he does not faithfully describe the system of feudal dependencies when he assumes that subservience to that system had been voluntary, an act of "proud submission," "dignified obedience," and "subordination of the heart" out of which had grown "the spirit of an exalted freedom." But now "the age of chivalry is gone," the "unbought grace of life, the cheap defence of nations, the nurse of manly sentiment and heroic enterprise"—all this is now gone. Burke's words read as if he had wanted to express the image that the Metternich family had of itself, and which was invoked in each of the official documents drawn up when another elevation in rank had taken place: he writes of a "mixed system of opinion and sentiment" that "had its origin in the ancient chivalry" and whose "principle, though varied in its appearance by the varying state of human affairs, subsisted and influenced through a long succession of generations, even to the time we live in." This system had "given its character to modern Europe." It had produced a peculiar and "noble equality": it "mitigated kings into companions, and raised private men to be fellows with kings." "Without force, or opposition, it subdued the fierceness of pride and power; it obliged sovereigns to submit to the soft collar of social esteem, compelled stern authority to submit to elegance, and gave a domination vanquisher of laws, to be subdued by manners." Metternich would later describe the position of the Habsburg emperor as a particular role in a "mixed system," because his rule only appeared as if it were absolute, but in reality he was bound by the customary laws as laid down in the statutes of the provinces. The same, Metternich argued, applied to the hierarchy between the estates, from the princes, to the nobility, to the bourgeoisie, and down to the peasants.

Beyond the passages Metternich picked out when reading the *Reflections,* there is a further piece of evidence that confirms the lasting impression Burke made on Metternich and shows that the young count found in this author and politician the answers to the great questions of the time that he found valid. In his private papers, Metternich kept an excerpt from a letter by Burke to W. Elliot (May 26, 1795).[155] The letter was a reaction to the collapse of the

First Coalition after Prussia had left it on April 5, 1795, by signing the Peace of Basel. Burke criticizes the European monarchies for betraying their principles in the face of the revolutionary propaganda. The passage Metternich excerpted is a manifesto on the condition of pre-revolutionary Europe. Again, Metternich communicates through Burke what he otherwise only hinted at when complaining that an exemplary order had been destroyed in 1789. Before, an unparalleled "prosperity" had characterized Europe. Now, a "false philosophy passed from academies into courts; and the great themselves were infected with the theories which conducted to their ruin." Science no longer was "in chosen hands" and as a result "diffused, weakened, and perverted." Interestingly, Burke again points toward economic interest as the real motor driving the social crisis, because "general wealth loosened morals": "Men of talent" began to criticize "the partition of the common stock of publick prosperity" and "found their portion not equal to their estimate (or perhaps the publick estimate) of their own worth." "Rapacity" turned against the existing Constitutions. For Burke, the inner principle of the French development was a general one: "A practicable breach was made in the whole order of things and in every country."

There it was, the "old order of things in the Holy Roman Empire" so frequently invoked by Metternich in his later years. The edifice, Burke writes, was eventually robbed of its "magazine to furnish arms for defence," first of religion, then of other norms that were decried as prejudices, finally of respect for property. The aura of the rulers' authority had been torn, the arcanum of power broken. From now on, governments had to convince the world and make themselves dependent on public agreement and "warm advocates and passionate defenders."

Burke saw a powerful "abuse of freedom." His reference to material interests was fundamentally an early form of ideology critique, and, as Fernand Braudel put it, he heightened the awareness of the forces of the "longue durée." His method may be seen as geared toward structures. The Frenchman Alexis de Tocqueville, someone at least as masterful as him, put it on an even broader basis. Tocqueville also detected vested interests behind high ideals. Both pre-revolutionary absolutism and the French Revolution, he said, aimed to establish a centralized institutional state, something that in Metternich's eyes did not amount to more "freedom." Metternich kept himself informed, and in conversation with an American correspondent he later referred not to Burke but to Tocqueville, with whose work he was well acquainted.[156]

Metternich's excerpt from Burke's letter goes on to say that "authority" needs to be at the same time aided and controlled—that, Burke says, is what "I call the true republican spirit." Patriots embodied this republican spirit by crowning any political Constitution. Steeped in their Constitution, they would not allow monarchs, senates, or popular assemblies

> to shake off those moral riders which reason has appointed to govern every sort of rude power. These, in appearance loading them by their weight, do by that pressure augment their essential force. The momentum is increased by the extraneous weight. It is true in moral as it is in mechanical science. It is true, not only in the draught, but in the race. These riders of the great, in effect, hold the reins which guide them in their course, and wear the spur that stimulates them to the goals of honor and of safety. The great must submit to the dominion of prudence and of virtue, or none will long submit to the dominion of the great.

In Burke's system, the "republican spirit" holds a position halfway between the monarch and the people. It protects monarchies from the ridiculous delusions of courtiers and the mad delusions of the people: "This republican spirit would not suffer men in high place to bring ruin on their country and on themselves. It would reform, not by destroying, but by saving, the great, the rich, and the powerful." Burke's ideal political system would replace the rule of intellectuals and economists with control by a responsible elite. The excerpt ends with a quotation from Horace: "Dis te minorem quod geris, imperas" [Because you (i.e., the Roman) subordinate yourself to the Gods, you rule].[157] Burke's letter draws the following conclusion from this quotation: "This is the feudal tenure which they cannot alter." In Metternich's mind, the only group that could fulfill the role of the elite in the middle between the "above" and the "below" could be a nobility defined by its achievements—like the British gentry, which one could join.

London as a Metropolis (3)

London triggered in Metternich very contradictory responses, ranging from impressions of understatement to those of grandeur. On his first trip around the most beautiful parts of the city—Piccadilly, St. James's Street, Haymarket, as recommended by the travel guide—he expected to see buildings similar to those in Vienna or Paris, but instead everywhere came across streets with small two-story buildings with a third floor, the basement, halfway below street level like a cellar. And these houses were built of bricks, not even painted, and without any architectural ornament.[158] A metal grid kept pedestrians from falling off the pavement into the basements. In Metternich's eyes, not one of the buildings deserved to be called a city palace [*Stadtpalais*]. He was also surprised to find that the name of the owner was displayed on a little sign above the door. St. James's Palace, the king's official residence in London, did not make much of an impression on him either: it resembled a prison or a mediocre municipal hall in a small town more than the "palace of the king of Great Britain." Seeing the inside of the building at the audience on April 2 did little to change his judgment. It was difficult, he said, to decide what parts of the palace were antiquated and what were simply derelict. Tapestries from Brussels were from bygone days and hung down in tatters, and the "rooms of Her Majesty" looked as if they had been covered in black coal.[159] Bourgeoisie, nobility, and the king presented themselves in a surprisingly unpretentious manner, in a kind of British understatement that was new and astonishing to someone who was used to the traditions of the Holy Roman Empire.

Metternich learned that greatness and understatement apparently can coexist perfectly well within a political system. As opposed to the unspectacular picture that London as a city had presented to him, the City of London—that metropolis of capital and economic power—impressed him greatly. Here, the resources that allowed the British to support the war against France on water and on land became clear to him.[160] At the stock market, he noted how the traders of all nations arranged their places underneath the arcades, and how the merchants and laborers put up their notices. The building of the Bank of England he found fantastic. Every financial transaction was dealt with in a separate office: "The activity and order in that place are astounding."[161] Metternich practiced his described method for exploring cities in London. He went up the sixty-one-meter-high Monument on Fish Street ("309 steps") in the center of the city, a memorial to the Great Fire of London in 1666, from where he could see the Tower, London, and the surroundings, but also the impact of London's industry: "The coal smoke hung like an impenetrable cloud above it all."

Walking through Savile Street (today Savile Row), he came across the ironmongers' market, which seemed to him "certainly the most beautiful in Europe." His eye for products of the iron industry he would develop in his later role as the owner of an ironworks in Plaß (Bohemia). The richness of the offerings overwhelmed him. It was difficult, he said, to find an article of which there did not exist twenty different versions. The shop owners were extremely friendly toward strangers, showed them all their goods without expecting at all that this would result in a purchase. This kind of integrity he found to be a common property of more or less all English traders. They seemed to be content if their products, usually perfect, were admired by a curious customer. Whether or not the sellers behaved differently toward their usual customers than they did toward strangers mattered little to Metternich; what he remembered was the inventive spirit and the richness of British trade.

Metternich sought out every opportunity to gain an even better understanding of the spirit of British manufacturing. The workshop of Europe's largest manufacturer and seller of coaches, Hatched, he found as attractive as the ironmongers' market.[162] In these early years, we can already see the combination of Metternich's curiosity and his nose for the most advanced trade, of the kind he found here in London. At the same time, he was specifically looking for the most modern scientific inventions—today we would say, for engineering competence. While Liedekerke, the courtier, was excited about Grey,[163] the most prestigious jeweler in London, Metternich visited the workshop of Jesse Ramsden, the mathematician, astronomer, and producer of scientific instruments. Ramsden—"le fameau Ramsden"—had already achieved great fame and the reputation of being the best optician in Europe. He wanted only to produce perfect pieces; all else, he said, angered him.

Metternich was baffled by the way such a commercial spirit could be combined with a historical awareness of one's rulers, heroes, and state that was unique in Europe. He came to realize this upon his first visit to Westminster Abbey, whose façade struck him as the exact opposite of the domestic and commercial architecture of London. The abbey was a monument, and evinced the highest mastery of the Gothic style. One entered the building, he writes, only with the greatest veneration, like a temple. Metternich felt an inescapable ancient aura that made him think he was surrounded by "Manes," the old Roman spirits of the dead. One walked around the monuments of the greatest heroes and the kings of England, whose storied lives were represented with the greatest artistic skill. Metternich did not attempt to describe all the masterpieces but concentrated on the one he considered to be the most splendid of all: the gravestone of Lord Chatham, created by the Flemish artist John Bacon. Chatham, Viscount Pitt, was the father of prime minister William Pitt the younger. No sooner had Metternich made his judgment than he found even higher praise for the design and quality of the gravestones made by the French sculptor Louis-François Roubillac, among which is the famous monument to Handel. All in all, to Metternich, Westminster Abbey, with its gravestones, monuments, and sculptures, was the centuries-old history of England immortalized in stone. Just the overwhelming number of royal graves, beginning with Edward the Confessor, who died in 1066, up to the father of the ruling king, George III, made England, in Metternich's eyes, stand out from all other European nations.

Metternich was shown that the most modern European state at the time succeeded in combining a deep sense of history with constitutionalism and the most advanced economy. His observations on Westminster Abbey are among the most detailed on any single item in his diary, and are therefore particularly telling regarding his sense of history. Liedekerke, otherwise often more eloquent, and always happy to talk about anything related to fashion, by contrast only remarked dryly that there were so many descriptions "of this old church (dreary and cold ever since Protestantism drove out the Catholic singing)," all that was left for him was to admire the magnificent gothic architecture inside the building.[164]

The Social Equality in Hyde Park (4)

Metternich experienced the atmosphere in Hyde Park on a Sunday, traditionally a day when, shops being closed, Londoners had the opportunity for outings. He watched, dumbfounded, the countless numbers of vehicles, riders, and curious pedestrians who flowed together on the broad promenades. There were three parallel avenues on which people moved, one of which had two lanes for coaches, one for those on horseback, and one for pedestrians.[165] There was no danger—no one got squashed. Liedekerke told his companion that it appeared to him as if the ancien régime was promenading. The coaches were of a select elegance, drawn by attractive, strong horses. The coachmen wore hats that were grooved on three sides and pointed, astonishing the visiting observers and making them laugh—to them, the coachmen looked like curates or students who had changed their social status but retained their hats. The servants were dressed very poorly, most of them without braids but with walking sticks in their hands of the kind that had been customary in the fifteenth or sixteenth century. They carried swords from the time of the Fronde conflict, when it had been necessary to defend their masters against enemies. Among the riders, they spotted the Prince of Wales, the successor to the throne, followed by a single adjutant on horseback and not drawing any more attention than an ordinary person.

This casual mingling of the different social ranks gave the visitors pause. They had just left a continent on which the different estates had begun to fight each other to the death. "In Hyde Park, freedom and equality existed on the old soil, and, contrary to the situation at home, there was no need for a revolution in order to bring them about."[166] Similar thoughts had come to Metternich when reading Burke. And our visitors were confirmed in their view even when—"in order to get to know all the ways in which one lived in London"—they dared to visit an ordinary pub frequented also by the middles classes.

Theaters and Concerts: London's Cultural Life (5)

Apart from the world of politics, the world of art was the main attraction of England for Metternich. His first experience was at the same time the most impressive: on March 28, he attended a performance of Handel's *Messiah* at the Theatre Royal in Drury Lane, which had opened only two weeks before.[167] Metternich was overwhelmed by the dimensions of the theater; he supposed (rightly) that the auditorium was the largest in Europe at the time. From their box the three visitors—the brothers Metternich and the Comte de Liedekerke— looked at an audience of more than 4,000. The 300-strong orchestra was arranged in the shape of an amphitheater on the stage. The stage decoration consisted of a Gothic church, with the choir being placed in the middle of the transept, the orchestra on galleries to both sides at the same height as the large organ in the background of the stage. Metternich even noted down the names of the most prominent of the performers.

In contrast to this serious work of art, Metternich attended a performance of the comical piece "Harlequin Faustus" at the theater in Covent Garden (today the Royal Opera House). This was a pantomime, a type of production invented by John Rich at the beginning of the seventeenth century and influenced by the Italian commedia dell'arte. For Metternich it was a "spectacle absoulment national." Pantomime, songs and dance, decorations, everything, he writes, was charming and of unlimited expressiveness.

Other highlights were the famous "Salomon Concerts" at the Hanover Square Rooms, named after the violinist and concert promoter Johann Peter Salomon. In 1794–1795, Haydn happened to be in London for his second stay there, during which he composed his "London Symphonies" and directed their premieres in person. Metternich attended one of these premieres on April 7, and it is astonishing how confident the twenty-year-old was in his judgment. Salomon, he says, was a "great violinist," and that it would be difficult to find so much talent concentrated in one place anywhere else. The young count attended many of the performances directed by Haydn and became friendly with him at dinners they both attended. At a soirée at the house of the Prussian envoy, Haydn performed a new string quartet, himself playing the viola. On that occasion, Metternich also came to hear the famous pianist Muzio Clementi.[168]

On June 2, at another of the Salomon Concerts, an audience member, reputed to be a Dutch merchant, caught his eye. He immediately recognized his old university teacher, Andreas Joseph Hofmann, whose course on "jus naturae et gentium" [natural law and law of nations] he had attended two years ago. Hofmann also recognized Metternich in a flash. He was in London under a false name as a French spy, tasked with gathering information on English troops and armaments on behalf of the French foreign minister, François Louis Deforgues. Metternich immediately informed the Prussian envoy of the true identity of the "merchant": that he was the former president of the Rhinish-German convention and former head of the administration in Mainz under the

Jacobins, a fugitive who had been put under the imperial ban and who was looked for by the police. From Metternich's gesticulations, Hofmann concluded that his identity had been revealed, and he quickly left the hall. When the police went to arrest him the next morning, they found his home deserted. Hofmann had gone underground in London, and he remained in hiding until he was able to leave the island safely in the autumn.[169] It is telling that Metternich does not mention this incident in his memoirs; it was not his style to present himself in a good light at the expense of others, but rather to remain silent about embarrassing moments. How easy it would have been for him to ridicule this chief Jacobin.

The event did not spoil Metternich's enjoyment of Haydn in London. He maintained contact with the composer in the years to come, and in 1802, during Metternich's time as an envoy in Dresden, he received a letter from the then seventy-year-old Haydn which reveals something of the cultural sophistication of the thirty-year-old politician who was its recipient. Haydn writes: "If a wise minister [i.e., envoy] who dedicates his time and talent to the welfare of his fatherland nevertheless finds moments in which he honors the arts and artists with his attention, then we may safely conclude that such a country will never be poor in works of art. And to this general encouragement from the side of the wiser part of the nation, the loveliest of the arts owes it that it stands at an advanced level in our fatherland at present."[170]

Visit to Oxford (6)

A visit to the old university town of Oxford was a crucial part of the itinerary, and it helped Metternich understand what England's admired capacities for achievement rested upon. Metternich and Liedekerke spent May 22–25 in and around Oxford.[171] Upon their arrival, they noticed the absence of fortifications. "Oxford is a place for studies," consisting mainly of colleges, as well as a significant printing press, many churches, and a beautiful theater. The remainder is formed by student accommodation, shops, coffee shops, pubs, and cabarets offering distraction. The visitors admired the age of the university, whose buildings sit on Roman foundations. At the same time, they were surprised by the robes the students wore, which reminded them of those of lawyers. As headgear they were wearing a kind of hood with a square roof. Apart from that, they enjoyed the same liberties as students on the Continent, although debauchery and libertinage were much more strictly controlled. The sons of the best English families studied here, and Oxford was the place where the members of the House of Lords, the House of Commons, and ministers were cultivated.

The first place they visited was the library near the center of town (the Radcliffe Camera). They went on to the main library, which held more than 150,000 books at the time and inside was decorated with ornaments, busts, paintings, and valuable statues. With some irony they noted what "new" meant at Oxford, where the "New College" dated back only to the fourteenth century. In this college, as in all the others, they admired the spaciousness and beauty of the buildings. The chapel, whose foundations were ancient, struck them as particularly magnificent. The town possessed a beauty that shone in both its historical and its modern buildings and inspired a deep respect for this place of human knowledge. Oxford was a "palace of science." Unfortunately, Liedekerke joked, they had neither the intention, nor the time, to metamorphose into "doctors." As we shall see, he was not exactly right.

A Maritime Power (7)

The war of the First Coalition caught up with Metternich in England, too. Metternich's experiences in England shone a new light on his view of the secular conflict between revolutionary France and its opponents. In direct contact with the military sea power of Great Britain, he recognized the conflict's global and imperial dimensions, which pointed beyond Europe. King George III personally saw to it that Metternich could be present at the departure of the fleet he so "eagerly desired to see."[172] Foreign Secretary William Grenville wrote a letter of recommendation to the commander of the British fleet in the English Channel and former first lord of the Admiralty, Richard Howe. Together with Liedekerke, Metternich departed for Portsmouth on April 20, but because April 21 was Easter Monday, he had to wait until April 22 for Howe to guide him to the pier. Such a visit from a stranger was exceptional for them: England was at war with France, and receiving any visitor from the Continent was almost like receiving a Frenchman. Metternich had to provide detailed proof of his identity and be registered in order to be allowed access to the gigantic harbor that was home to the Royal Navy: the place whence the force of the nation spread, and the heart of its power and wealth.[173]

An admiralty longboat brought Metternich, accompanied by Liedekerke, to the arsenal of the artillery and the well-stocked armory. Then they headed for the roads of Spithead, the Royal Navy anchorage. There the visitors had the opportunity to go aboard the frigate *Caesar* and to inspect its equipment: a hundred cannon over two decks. The ship was enormous, designed for 670 sailors. They were also able to take a look at four French warships with raised white flags that the allies had captured in mid-December 1793 in Toulon before Napoleon had opened fire on the allies' ships. The captured ships, now lying in the roads, were one more sign of how the revolutionary war had expanded. Admiral Howe personally received the guests aboard the *Queen Charlotte,* a flagship that bore 110 cannon over three decks.

The next day a ship took them to the Isle of Wight, where they enjoyed the panoramic view over the open sea from the famous Steep Hill. It was only here that they realized the dimensions of the enterprise. Twenty-six warships formed a convoy accompanying the merchant ships, one fleet sailing to the East Indies, the other to the West Indies. Hundreds of barques were bobbing in the sea; they belonged to curious onlookers who were watching how two different convoys of together more than 400 warships and merchant ships united into one, after the merchant ships had suddenly set their sails upon the signal given by the admiral. Looking back as an old man, Metternich would remember this as "the most beautiful sight I have ever seen, I might say, indeed, the most beautiful that human eyes have ever beheld!"[174] He was fascinated by the choreography of this spectacle, the amassed power operating in an orderly fashion, and the perfect harmony of it all made an aesthetic impression on him. In all this, he forgot the political context. Even before the inauguration of the Continental System ordered by Napoleon from Berlin in 1806, England and France were already engaged in a global trade war. The British warships had to protect the convoy of merchant vessels against attacks by the French.

The seriousness of the situation became apparent to Metternich a little later. In his memoirs, two separate events are conflated into one: he had made "earnest petitions" to Admiral Howe to be allowed to stay to witness the expected sea battle. But Howe rejected his pleas; in accordance with the king's wishes, Howe said, he had allowed Metternich to see everything, but he had to send him back alive and could not expose him to "the dangers of a sea fight."[175] This conversation must have taken place before Metternich's return from Portsmouth to London on April 24, and certainly not on the evening of May 30 (as he claims in his memoirs), because by that time Howe had long since set sail. On May 28, there had already been a battle near the French channel coast, and on May 30–31, Howe was immobilized by fog before the decisive battle, won by the British on June 1, 1794.[176] It went down in British military history as the "Glorious First of June."[177]

Metternich was in London when news arrived in the capital "of the great victory in the sea battle of June 1 at Quessant," which was greeted with joy among the population and inspired the arrangement of festive illuminations all around. What was the real background to the event? The British had used their battleships to intercept and destroy a French convoy of more than a hundred merchant ships—the very kind of attack against which they had sought to protect their own merchant vessels. The French ships had been transporting large amounts of grain from the United States destined for the starving population of France. This militarized trade war meant victims on both sides, and its grave consequences were to become clear to Metternich. He wanted to see the return of the victorious fleet, and he therefore traveled again to Portsmouth, by then without Liedekerke, who had left England on May 31. When the fleet entered the harbor on June 13, Metternich saw something he had not expected.[178] The admiral's ship, from which he had wanted to observe the battle, "had engaged the French admiral's ship, and presented the appearance of a ruin; the greater part of her crew had been killed or disabled."[179] And the victory was, moreover, only a half victory—the French had managed to sneak all their merchant ships safely home.

The Significance of Metternich's Stay in England

What was the significance of Metternich's stay in England for his personal development? Most of the details of this trip—let alone its importance—have been hitherto unknown. Only a few, mostly unpublished, studies have been dedicated to Metternich's attitude toward Great Britain.[180] In these, negative judgments dominate: Metternich and England are said "naturally" to contradict one another because it is erroneously assumed that the state chancellor dogmatically supported absolutism and lacked any appreciation of the values of having a constitution. He represented the institution of absolute monarchy, was preoccupied with the notion of legitimacy, and began in earnest to reflect on the insular state only relatively late, after 1814. Before 1821 he made no statements about the Parliament or the parties of Great Britain, and only after 1830 did such statements as he made become detailed. He eyed the British Constitution with suspicion, and by reform he understood nothing but the improvement of the existing condition. He knew nothing of English history, and all in all his reaction to the structure of the British state was one of incomprehension.[181]

All these claims may be considered refuted. His visit to England had a decisive influence, shaping and expanding Metternich's political universe. He detected and consolidated fundamental ideas that would go on to figure as permanent background influences over his political action, even if the realities of the Habsburg Empire meant that he did not always have the opportunity to put these ideas into practice. Among these ideas were an aristocratic constitutionalism (but we should note here how modern Metternich's concept of aristocracy was); the division of labor within the system of the estates, as interpreted by Edmund Burke; and a general appreciation for the English system, the British parliamentary system, and freedom of the press. Metternich did not support a "patriarchal absolutism based on estates"[182] (an absurd assertion, anyhow: the estates and absolutism are mutually exclusive). In short, Metternich's political stance throughout his life was, in a sense, that of a conservative British Whig, and he therefore found himself in a position for which there was no real counterpart within the context of the Habsburg Monarchy. The latter, in Metternich's view, was a fragile edifice that was beyond reform, and that could only be either kept together with great effort or rebuilt from the ground up.

It is worthwhile listening to what Metternich himself had to say about what England meant to him. In 1819, at the height of the so-called persecution of demagogues [*Demagogenverfolgung*], the forty-six-year-old reflected on his "fatherland" in a letter to Princess Lieven:

> In the end, I am not an Austrian if birth is sufficient for determining someone's fatherland. According to my principles, the fatherland is more than just the place of birth and the habits of youth. There can be an adopted fatherland [*une patrie adoptive*] which only depends on the heart, and anyhow: where birth and agreement with principles coincide, there is a perfect fatherland. Or Austria is my moral fatherland; that is so because the core of its existence is in perfect harmony with my principles and my feelings. In Austria I am like a fish in water. . . . *If I were not what I am, I would like to be an Englishman.* If I could neither be the one or the other, I would rather be nothing at all.[183]

Metternich's stay in England in 1794 shows us the source of this love of the country. His experiences of this first stay were consolidated and deepened by two later journeys there. The first was in 1814, after Napoleon had been wrestled to the ground for the first time and peace had been made in Paris in May; on this occasion, he received an honorary doctorate from the University of Oxford. The second took place in 1848, when he fled the revolution to England. Shortly after his arrival, on April 22, he noted down: "I have been here but two times twenty-four hours, and I already feel as if the thirty-four years that I have not set foot on English soil were no more than thirty-four days. This great country is the way it was, strong because of its unshakable belief in the value of the law, of order, and the kind of freedom which, if it truly wants to exist, must be based on these foundations. I also find my old friends again and the open hospitality which is not just a manner of speaking but a quality of this nation."[184] For a confirmation of the lasting effect of 1794, let us, finally, take a look at the end of Metternich's life, this time from the perspective of international politics. On October 23, 1858, eight months before his death, the eighty-five-year-old wrote to Benjamin Disraeli, whom he had met as the Tory leader of the opposition in 1848 (when Palmerston was prime minister), and who considered himself to be a "disciple" of Metternich:

> Eight years have gone by since we met in *England, the country which I love,* and with which I stood in closest contact over a long stretch of my public life. Many of the events which have conquered, and still continue to capture, the realm of politics could be of a kind that would confuse me in my train of thoughts if my convictions would rest on a less stable foundation. The great maritime empire, which is not a continental European empire, and the continental and central power which is not a maritime power, finally always meet each other where either truly general questions or questions pertaining to their direct interests are concerned.[185]

At the time of his departure from England, the political outlook of the young imperial count had crystallized, such that we are justified in calling his development "complete," a judgment he probably would have shared.

COLLAPSE AND FLIGHT IN 1794

With his return to the Continent, Metternich's life was altogether altered. He experienced a complete collapse—at the personal level in the form of his family's expulsion from their home in the Rhineland to exile in Austria (even if they still possessed their old feudal estate in Bohemia), and politically in the form of Austria's and the empire's retreat from the Belgian Netherlands and the left bank of the Rhine. His memoirs and even his handwritten notes seem to cover this period of his life under something of a conspiracy of silence, as if the author found it difficult to talk about it and to open one of the greatest crises in his life to public view. The loss of his parental home, the financial collapse of his family, and the uncertainty regarding his future—which would no longer necessarily follow the secure path of a career in the service of the emperor or rely on prebends from the church—all this must have led Metternich to despair. At one point he even considered emigrating to America.[186] But ultimately his family ethos prevented him from such an escape: he was by then the heir to the entailed estate, the future fee-tail lord of the family, and he already felt responsible for the whole family. His brother Joseph, who was conspicuous only by his absence, would never have been able to shoulder this responsibility had Clemens emigrated.

Caught in the Crossfire

The biographical uncertainties of this period already begin with Metternich's return journey, and they continue with the question of which places he visited between July and September 1794. His return immediately brought him into contact with battles of the First Coalition war, more precisely with the front with revolutionary France, which had begun to shift. French troops were about to occupy the Austrian Netherlands and then to turn toward the Dutch States General and the left bank of the Rhine, part of which were still heavily embattled. Everywhere, Austrian troops, Prussian troops, and troops from other parts of the empire were trying to hold their ground against the new revolutionary troops of the "levée en masse." Metternich was an eyewitness to the division of the allies' troops, and he saw how they retreated, in accordance with their old military doctrine, and thus missed one opportunity after another for toppling their opponent. This was another instance in which his military observations had afforded him important lessons.

The war was the reason he chose to set sail from the English harbor town of Harwich "at the beginning of autumn," as he would later write. He could no longer travel from Dover to Oostend in Belgium, which had already been captured by the French, so Harwich took him to the apparently secure Dutch city of Hellevoetsluis, near Rotterdam. It would be helpful to know more precisely when this was—it was certainly not as late as September or October, as is sometimes claimed.[187] A cannonade he experienced while at sea may help to date the crossing. Metternich's notes suggest the following circumstances: rather than reaching the Dutch port as intended, the ship was driven by a storm in a southeasterly direction toward Dunkirk. This brought it into an area in which British Admiral Sidney Smith was operating, having left for Dunkirk with two large floating batteries and fifty cannon ships "on a secret mission."[188] His fleet was controlling the passage through the Channel and warding off attacks on merchant ships. At the same time, it was supporting sieges near the coast. On the occasion of this "secret" mission, Smith was to support the troops fighting in West Flanders, around Nieuwpoort, near Dunkirk. On July 17, he bombarded the French besieger from his ships but had little success, being at too great a distance from the French.[189] The ferry that was to bring Metternich to the Netherlands came close enough to be endangered, and ended up spending more than two hours in the crossfire. Even though it was not so long ago that Metternich had implored Admiral Howe to allow him to experience a sea battle firsthand, it is unlikely he ever thought he would be directly involved in this kind of life-and-death spectacle. Newspapers reported that the French had arrested him, and his father was preparing to negotiate his release with the French government until he heard of his safe arrival in Holland.[190] We thus know that Metternich stepped on continental soil again sometime in the third week of July.

His return coincided with the final collapse of Austrian rule in the Netherlands, and the borders were shifting every week, even daily. Until June 13, Emperor Franz II was still present in Brussels and had even personally taken charge of the military command, doing everything to show his determination to defend Habsburg rule at all costs.[191] When leaving London, Metternich, however, had done well to avoid Belgium, "as the enemy had entered the [Habsburg] Netherlands." Even before and then during his journey, between June and August, the fortresses, towns, and cities toppled like houses of cards—among them Brussels on July 9—even if they were rarely handed over without a fight.[192] After Robespierre went to the guillotine, in July, the reign of terror in Paris collapsed, without, however, diminishing the intensity of the French attacks in the slightest.

At first, it seems, Metternich still believed that he might nevertheless be able to take up his post as an envoy in Holland: he wrote that he "remained in this country so long as was necessary to enable [him] to visit the Hague, Amsterdam, and part of North Holland."[193] But by September 10, at the latest, he no longer was an envoy, as French troops had moved into the States General from Meerle.

Franz Georg's End as Minister Plenipotentiary of the Netherlands

It had long since become impossible for Clemens to return to Brussels. His father had had a rough time, having been forced to flee from Brussels at the beginning of July. In the previous months he had had to master a welter of conflicting aims at the same time, a situation about which later historians have shown little understanding.[194] Franz Georg had remained faithful to his policy of approaching the local estates and respecting their wishes for relative autonomy. In this way, he had pacified the country, in the spirit of Emperor Leopold II and Austrian state chancellor Kaunitz, through a "conservative revolution" against Josephinian absolutism. And the new emperor, Franz II, had initially acknowledged Franz Georg's achievements. The latter had implored the provinces to contribute to the financial costs of the war and the common defense, but for a long time his pleas had fallen on deaf ears. Early on, in late 1793, he advocated arming the peasantry in the defense against the "levée en masse" at the Belgian border.[195] But this was a step too far for Emperor Franz II. He preferred a bureaucratic form of governance over negotiations with the estates. Count von Trauttmansdorff, of all people, the head of the court office in Vienna responsible for matters concerning the Netherlands, encouraged the emperor in his absolutist leanings. The count had carried out the violations of the law ordered by Joseph II and then, as one of Franz Georg's predecessors, had to flee the Belgian revolution from Brussels. He traduced Franz Georg's policy toward the estates as the "misfortune of Belgium," and early on called for the evacuation of the country, which Franz Georg opposed. Von Trauttmansdorff further defamed Franz Georg by claiming that he wanted to line his pockets with money from the Belgian coffers.

Thus dishonored, Franz Georg showed a side of his character that will be important to keep in mind when we see, later, how the family, facing financial ruin, was saved by Clemens. The father responded to the insinuations by saying that, in serving the emperor and the state, pecuniary interests had never been among his motives. He had himself assumed responsibility for a great deal of expenditure in connection with the elections of coadjutors in Cologne and Münster, the imperial coronation of 1792 in Frankfurt, and even recently as a Belgian minister. Then he added: "My wealth, which is that of my children, could tell a tale of this, but I never shall regret this. In accordance with my principles, I was already prepared to renounce my salary altogether for as long as this unfortunate crisis lasts, and to add this sacrifice to the voluntary present of 6,000 guilders which I have already contributed."[196]

Franz Georg had, in fact, done everything within his power to defend Austrian rule in Belgium. His flight from Brussels on July 4, with the French approaching, was the beginning of an odyssey that led him first to Mechelen (July 5), then to Averbode Abbey, near Diest to the northeast of Brussels (July 9), then to Roermond (July 14), and finally to Benrath, near Düsseldorf (July 18). On July 23, 1794, the emperor decreed: "As the Belgian provinces must unfortunately be said to be altogether lost by now, it is my intention that the government must be considered as altogether dissolved, from the minister down to the last civil servant, and that therefore their salaries are to be discontinued."[197] In early August, Franz Georg received secret notification of this decision; on August 14, he held the resolution in his hands; and on August 18, he communicated it to those members of the government who had traveled to Düsseldorf with him. His comments upon his departure for Vienna on August 27, though meant to sound cheerful, express resignation and disappointment: "As far as my own person is concerned, I shall now enjoy my freedom after a diplomatic career of twenty-seven years of which I dedicated twenty-two, without interruption, to the service of your noble House." Franz Georg felt hopeful that further uses of his person would be found in Vienna.[198]

The "General Arming of the People": Metternich's First Political Manifesto

Why do the exact dates of Franz Georg's movements matter? We had, of course, always the parallel movements of his son in mind. For Metternich, the turbulent weeks following his return from England ended with a bang. At the beginning of August, after his travels through Holland, he went to Benrath and experienced the dissolution of the government of the Austrian Netherlands firsthand at his father's place. He did not stay for long with the government in exile, but instead went to the headquarters of the Austrian supreme commander, the Prince of Coburg, in Fouron-le-Comte, between Liege and Maastricht. This can only have been before the prince was succeeded by General Clerfait on August 21.[199]

During that time, Metternich wrote and printed anonymously his second pamphlet: *Über die Notwendigkeit einer allgemeinen Bewaffnung des Volkes an den Grenzen Frankreichs von einem Freunde der allgemeinen Ruhe* [On the Necessity of a General Arming of the People on the Frontiers of France, by a Friend of Universal Peace].[200] Although the young Metternich was familiar with Franz Georg's practical efforts at arming the people, his text did not emerge from the "mind of his father" (and neither could it have been composed in August in London,[201] for Metternich had already left England). Rather, the text is part of an altogether different context that has so far not been appreciated: only a few days before Metternich's arrival at the headquarters, Prince Coburg had, on July 30, 1794, issued to the Germans on the other side of the Maas and along the Rhine and Mosel an appeal to arm the people.[202]

The revolt of the peasants of the French Vendée against being recruited to the army of the 500,000 in the context of the "levée en masse" in 1793 served as a model of the people arming themselves. With this example in mind, Metternich's father had sought to arm the peasants in Flanders at the border with France, and Prince Coburg made it clear as early as the end of December 1793 that the regular troops could not withstand the French attacks for very much longer without help from the "people."[203] In 1793–1794, with French troops advancing, the area of what is today Palatinate and large parts of Rheinhessen experienced the infamous "winter of pillaging," accompanied by robberies, arson, and hostage taking. At the beginning of 1794, the idea of creating peasant militias for the purpose of defending the borders gained wider public interest in Swabia and Franconia, and in the Upper Rhenish and Electoral Rhenish imperial circles. Prince Coburg sought to tap into this mood with his July pamphlet.

He asked the communities for money (in exchange for which he would hand out imperial promissory notes), food supplies, and volunteers to protect the borders. "Stand up in your thousands and fight with us to defend your altar, your hearth, your emperor, your freedom."[204] It would not be right for only the "remote people" to shed their blood for religion, property, emperor, and freedom. It is worth noting that Prince Coburg thus appealed to a nationalist sentiment. Addressing the people as "German brothers and friends!," he told them that the imperial armies were "a fortification of German freedom," and implored: "Surely, you Germans, we did not go wrong; we trust in the German spirit and German blood." Here, long before the patriotically colored appeals of Count Stadion of Austria in 1809, and before the emotionality associated with the wars of liberation of 1813, a monarch—"I myself a German prince"—was appealing to the sense of national loyalty of a German nation.

The appeal appeared in the form of a pamphlet and was at the same time printed in many newspapers.[205] Coburg's example motivated the young imperial count to take pen in hand himself, and a comparison of the two texts is revealing of Metternich's new political horizons. His pamphlet may be understood as his first systematic political confession and as pointing toward his future career. The distance from his emotional outburst in his "Appeal to the Army" of the previous year is striking. Now, there become visible the lineaments of a political program to which Metternich would remain faithful throughout his life. What were its fundamental traits?

The Repressed Mantra: Modern Total War

The autograph of the anonymously published pamphlet not only reveals to us that Metternich was its author but also includes a motto that was omitted in the printed version. It says: "Wherever they marched, their route was marked with blood. They ravaged or destroyed all around them. They made no distinction between what was sacred and what was profane. They respected no age, or sex, or rank. What escaped the fury of the first inundation perished in those which followed it."[206] This mantra describes modern warfare, which, as a murderous battle between masses, no longer distinguishes between the military and civilians and unleashes an unimaginable, unbridled violence.[207] This brings to mind the "orgy of killing" [Mordorgie], with more than 200,000 dead—men, women, and children alike—to which the peasants of the Vendée were subjected between January and May 1794, when the terror of the "colonnes infernal" reached its peak. The British Parliament and English newspapers had followed these horrors, and thus the events fed into the debates over the question of a military intervention.[208]

From this point on, it would be typical of Metternich to contextualize political insights historically and thus to extract from them the more general theoretical principles they contain. In the case of the motto above, he made use of one of his readings during his stay in England by quoting the Scottish historiographer royal, William Robertson, in English as well as in his own German translation. Robertson had referred to the violent raging of the Germanic tribes, who, he said, destroyed the great civilization of the Roman Empire, with all its art, science, and literature.[209] In Metternich's eyes, the revolutionary French were the vandals of his day; they did not bring civilization but haunted civilized Europe and laid it to waste. The old Imperium Romanum appeared to him analogous to the Holy Roman Empire of German Nations of his present. Metternich's chosen motto records a fundamental experience from which the ethos of his later politics follows: the commandment to foil war and create internal peace. He would later declare that law and domestic order were the real aims of his policies, and foreign policies were no more than a means to achieve them.

The war, he wrote in his pamphlet of 1794, had started as a conventional conflict, and things had been going well at the beginning of the year 1793. He had in mind the military successes of Prince Coburg, the recapturing of Belgium, the reentry into Brussels, which he had personally witnessed, and the second period of his father in government. The French army, "everywhere beaten, almost destroyed," had fled behind the line of their border fortresses. But with the introduction of the "levée en masse" in 1793, realized with the help of the enormous pressure of the Terror, the nature of the war changed fundamentally. It became a total war: "Old men and children, willing or unwilling, timid or brave, all fought in the same ranks. Peoples attacked armies, and small forces had to resist enormous masses. Thousands fell on one side, and thousands replaced them; hundreds fell on the other, and their places remained empty."[210] In the course of 1793, Metternich had personally experienced how the allied troops had been worn down by increasingly taxing "marches and countermarches" until eventually they were forced to retreat to the occupied fortresses for the winter. The campaigns had been a lesson in "what may be expected when armies have to contend against a whole armed people." Furthermore, because of their diverging interests, the armies of the Dutch, British, Austrians, Prussians, and Swedish had in fact weakened each other. In this context, it is again worth taking a look at a passage that is omitted in the printed version, for it neatly illustrates Metternich's analysis. In order to express the relationship between traditional armies and the new mass armies, he had originally used the phrase "a child's strength against a gigantic force," together with a footnote, also cut in the printed version: "This expression [the "gigantic force" of the French] may seem like a ridiculous exaggeration when we compare the force of a united Europe. I repeat it; it is adequate for a nation, even if that nation is internally disunited, if it is in conflict with the united armies of powers that are little united among themselves. The expression would be exaggerated if *one* people were to stand against *all peoples.*" In other words: at twenty-one, Metternich had already recognized the power of a nationalism that unites over the old cabinet politics. But he suspected already that the modern war would intensify and expand as a battle between "peoples."

In his pamphlet Metternich also alluded to his father's political practice, which he had experienced firsthand. A "general arming of the people" had been attempted in the threatened regions of the province of Flanders. The peasants and those "who possessed goods" had accepted the weapons with alacrity. This "newly made army," a rural militia of sorts, "was distributed among the troops" and successfully participated in the fighting. In the new situation, the "only means available" was that of "arming masses against masses." For Metternich what was important was not the enthusiasm of the French soldiers in battle—this he judged to be the "farce of Liberty" [*Freiheitspossen*],[211] which is the judgment that has been reached by modern research after protracted debate. It was not revolutionary energy, heroism, or political ideas that decided the outcome of the revolutionary wars: it was, first of all, simple superiority in numbers.[212] And the allies weakened themselves again and again, like the "incorrigible" Coburg, who commanded an army of more than 100,000 men but sent them simultaneously to Mons, Brussels, and Naumur, thus giving General Jourdan, who had fewer troops at his disposal, the opportunity to occupy Brussels on July 9, 1794.[213] Metternich had studied the war in his own way, which later allowed him to see through Napoleon's tactics, with the result that, at the Battle of Leipzig in 1813, Napoleon was not able to divide the enemies' lines and take them on one after the other, as he had done at Austerlitz in 1805.

Settling Scores with the "Old Diplomats" and the Social Character of the 1789 Revolution

If one recognizes the numerous subtle allusions in the pamphlet, it is clear that Metternich is settling scores with the "old diplomats," whom he holds responsible for the disaster of August 1794. Originally he wanted to write: "For a long time, the kings and their councillors were asleep; for a long time they thought the all-consuming fire [of the Revolution] was insignificant." But he crossed the sentence out, and replaced it with a more diplomatic formulation: "The conflagration was thought distant and unimportant." His insights into the changing forms of warfare led Metternich to seek to confront the "narrow minds." On the resistance to his father's call to arm the people, a call that was in his eyes justified, he commented as follows: "The aversion which narrow minds felt at the first steps toward acquiring this resource [i.e., arming the people], which promised everything, is inconceivable. An image of horror was held up before the eyes of the monarch, and this decisive measure of the government of the Netherlands was prohibited." This must be read as an admonition directed at von Trauttmansdorff for scheming against his father a few weeks earlier. He was the "narrow mind," the "old diplomat" of yesterday.

The pamphlet also explains for the first time why Metternich always understood the French Revolution as a "social" and not a political event, in contrast to the mere putsches that were the July Revolution of 1830 and the revolution of 1848, which he deemed only political revolutions. By contrast, the question of whether to arm the people revealed the altogether different character of 1789. Metternich was therefore, together with Burke, among the few who, from the very beginning, judged the significance of the events correctly: "Everywhere I hear old diplomats, men of that numerous class who consider the present war —like any other war, and like the Revolution in its commencement—mere child's play, ... exclaim—'What? Arm the people? Put arms in the hands of the mob? You are, then, resolved on your own destruction!'" In Strasbourg he had experienced in person how the masses could behave as a "mob," but this did not cloud his analytical acuity. Had not Burke already said that the deeper socioeconomic conditions must be taken into the calculation when making one's judgment, and that one should not be guided by superficial proclamations, such as the ones uttered by the "old diplomats"? Metternich located "mobs" in the large cities where they increased with "especial exceptionality" [*besonders außerordentlich*]." The mob consists, he said, predominantly of "the class of the unoccupied, so dangerous to the state, men who possess nothing, and are constantly ready for a revolt," as opposed to the class of the "real people," who have property to defend: the citizens and yeomen. The real people would take up arms in order to defend their money, possessions, and wives and children. They would usually vastly outnumber the uprooted lower classes.

For Metternich, "social revolution" meant the "mob" gaining the upper hand over the "real people," and thus "the dissolution of all social ties, the destruction of all principles, and the spoliation of all property." Putting it almost as a thesis, he writes: "The people finds its salvation in self-defense, in defense of its property, be it ever so small; the mob, who have nothing to lose but everything to gain in disorder, is found only in cities." Only in cities, because in the rural context those who were in dependent work were integrated into the life of the yeoman.[214] Metternich's social model assigned political rights exclusively to those with property. In this view Metternich, who had been educated by his tutors in the spirit of humanism, saw himself as agreeing with Cicero and with Burke, the conservative British Whig. The same attitude was later adopted in the period before 1848 by those liberals who saw legitimacy as resting on the sovereignty of the people and the representation of the people but who did not quite trust the "people" and therefore tied suffrage to specific selective criteria (census suffrage). Even a luminary of state law like Carl von Rotteck, who argued on the basis of human rights, opposed universal suffrage. Metternich might have preferred the nobility, but for him the nobility possessed their entitlements in virtue of their merits. Thus, Cicero, Burke, Metternich, and the liberals before 1848 all shared the ideal of a merit-based elite as the core of society. Metternich's judgments are remarkable: this sort of socially differentiating perspective distinguishes him from his peers and is not usually expected in him—or at least it is not noticed.

The Preservation of Europe

With keen insight, the twenty-one-year-old Metternich recognized how domestic and international politics had recently become connected with each other—that is, how France's material problems at home led to aggression against the outside: "Too narrow appear their boundaries to a people dying of hunger in a country formerly so blooming." The consequences were "destruction of all monuments and works of art, and subjugation of the nations." The French Revolution therefore threatened all European states with destruction. It was necessary, Metternich told his readers, to defend the fatherland, and he concluded the pamphlet by saying that it was to them that "Europe will owe her preservation, and whole generations their peace." Again, domestic peace was the ultimate goal. British politics had broadened and sharpened his perception of Europe; witnessing the reality of military campaigns waged by a "united Europe" had taught him not to appeal to a German national principle, as Coburg had. For how would that sound to a multinational allied force that included the Scottish, English, and Hanoverians?

What was the purpose of Metternich's pamphlet? Did he expect it to bring about an immediate change to the political and military situation in mid-1794? Having just returned from England, he recognized that continental politics had moved on. French rule in the regions belonging to the left bank of the Rhine and in southern German states, which was increasingly felt to be an occupation, had led to moves toward arming the people. The five "leading" imperial circles in the southwest—the Swabian, Franconian, Rhenish, Upper Rhenish, and Lower Rhenish-Westphalian circles—had decided in favor of arming the people at their Diets. Judging by signals from the population, they expected to mobilize at least 150,000 men.[215] On January 20, the emperor himself had passed a so-called commission decree, making the question "of whether, given the enemy's changed method of warfare, a general armament of all Germans living along borders is a necessity for securing the empire and its faithful subjects" a topic for debate at the Imperial Diet.[216] The initiative failed because of Prussia, which gradually withdrew from the war in the west in order to use its troops to make territorial gains in connection with the division of Poland. Prussia's answer to the question was: "If the empire wants to arm itself, then its defense by our troops ends, because provisions for them, even the conditions for obtaining them, would soon disappear."[217]

Metternich's appeal was a reaction to the fact that the military-political situation had reached a crisis point; the general arming of the people seemed to him the *ultima ratio*. At the same time, the pamphlet was his first major political manifesto and his first formulation of his guiding maxims. Whether intentionally or not, in publishing the manifesto he recommended himself as a man for higher tasks. Later, when the need was greatest and the methods of the "old diplomats" had conclusively failed, his name would be remembered— which, as we shall see, was the case in 1809. His principles were these: The old diplomacy is obsolete; modern, total war is a new type of war; the social dimension of the French Revolution makes it a pan-European matter; war signifies that politics has failed; and the ultimate purpose of politics is peace.

The pamphlet did not go unnoticed. In 1796 it was reviewed in an essay published in Vienna that addressed the "Fortune of Weapons" and examined the behavior of the population of the Rhineland at the moment when the enemy had arrived in masses. A general arming of the people, supported by a brave army, could have "averted all the evils of war and plunder and spared them, their wives, their children." A "warm and noble patriot" had called for this as early as 1794. He "overcame [*zerstäubte*] the dangers of a cautious politics and showed the paths along which the arming of the people could have happened. Alas, his plea remained unheard: not because the people lacked the courage to arm themselves, but because there was no one who would take the lead, no one who would have provided the necessary money and was prepared to give ten in order to save a hundred."[218]

Ultimately, Metternich established a dialectical relationship with the Revolution, a relationship that he also invoked in this text of 1794: the new situation "teaches you the necessity of applying stronger measures to avert the threatening danger close at hand. —Make use of the same means which have hitherto supported the common enemy."[219] What Metternich actually propagates— long before the Prussian military reforms during the wars of liberation—is universal conscription. His model of society, however, was not national but European, and it united the "well-intentioned of all classes"—not of "all nations," as falsely given in the published posthumous papers. What holds together the state is not the balance of power between warring parties, as Montesquieu postulates, but—fully in line with Cicero—the peacemaking consensus of the well intentioned: the *consensus omnium bonorum*.

Escape into Exile

In the summer and autumn of 1794, the advancing French troops conquered one place after another on the left bank of the Rhine: Trier (August 9), Cologne (October 6), Bonn (October 10), and finally Metternich's birthplace, Koblenz (October 23). Like other land-owning nobility, the Metternichs were left with no choice but to flee. The family divided among its members the burden of dealing with the chaotic situation. After Franz Georg's departure for Vienna at the end of August, Clemens's mother, Beatrix, stayed behind in Benrath, noting, skeptically, the movement of the allied troops, which suggested a retreat and the relinquishment of the left bank of the Rhine. Her salon took on the atmosphere of a military headquarters, becoming the meeting point for visitors such as General Bellegarde, Prince Moritz von Liechtenstein, and other officers.[220] She was given precise information on plans to move the Austrian headquarters to Aachen and on the intention to change the supreme commander. She sensed a growing restlessness, and therefore reserved horses for herself from the surrounding farmers, "just in case." Amid all the fear, she nevertheless managed to organize the removal of furniture and other belongings from Koblenz and Benrath; they were to be transported on a ship to Würzburg, and some of it on coaches to further destinations. They had lost everything, she wrote, they were ruined, and now, on top of this, she was to set off, at Franz Georg's insistence, on this expensive journey to Vienna.

The journey turned into an odyssey. On October 11, Beatrix had already reached Rüdesheim, where she received the terrible news from Koblenz regarding the Prussian withdrawal. She continued to Frankfurt in order to collect money for the journey from the financier Bethmann. On October 14, she reported that the Prussian army had completely retreated from the Hunsrück. During the journey, she was not yet entirely clear whether her final destination would be Königswart or, after all, Vienna. She worried constantly about the financial situation, and she was continually calculating which options would be more expensive and where money might be saved. Such was her financial distress that she had to sell her coach. She told Franz Georg: "Rest assured, I am economical, I do not waste anything, I promise."[221]

The political situation was constantly on Beatrix's mind, and now what she had prophesied upon the death of Leopold II seemed to be coming true. The empire had perished, she wrote; the left bank of the Rhine was in French hands, and if there were no peace, Germany would be altogether lost. "What a sad time, it breaks my heart, really, I can't bear it anymore. I have to move away from the sight of war, one dies of fear, so that one hardly feels anything anymore; I have never suffered that much before; the dismay could not get greater, and the prospects are terrible. Since this war began, the people have started to think angrily about the fact that the sovereigns, and the nobility along with them, are lost if they do not very quickly unite and use all available means."[222] All she longed for, she said, was peace [*Ruhe*]; she was getting old, and she was losing her powers. The house in Koblenz was deserted. The apocalyptic mood expressed in these letters was representative of the view of the whole family.

Metternich's First Review of the Family's Financial Situation

In September of that year the young Metternich was still in Mainz; later he would join his father in Vienna for the first time. The visit to Vienna was brief, as the father had instructed him to travel to Königswart in order to "arrange the estate."[223] This dry administrative formulation in Metternich's unpublished notes veils the real meaning of the words: Metternich was to draw up an account of the catastrophic financial situation the house was in, in order to establish what resources the family had left. It was a wise decision on Franz Georg's part to leave this business to his son, who was more adept at dealing with figures and finances. Clemens spent all of November in Königswart, issued orders to the administrator of the estate, and surveyed the state of affairs in his usual systematic fashion. He studied the situation in the imperiled regions of the left bank of the Rhine as well as the estate at Königswart.

From the Mosel and from Koblenz he received information from the cellarer Becker, who described his desperate attempts to sell the remaining stocks of wine: there were no buyers any more. In addition, the vine growers refused to pay their levies. Becker described the French confiscations taking place in the surrounding area, and the pillaging, especially of grain, cattle, and horses. In the face of extortion, the rural peasants feared famine. On the evening of October 23, Becker was present in Koblenz when General Marceau entered the city with his corps, following a short bombardment. The next day, the French troops followed. The population was treated as if it had been the headquarters of emigrants planning the military counterrevolution against France. The assets left behind by the fleeing emigrants were plundered.[224]

The house of the Metternich family was not spared. Those who had fled were threatened with the confiscation of their property and possessions if they did not return. The "representative of the people at the [French] army at Rhine and Mosel," Boubotte, carried out this threat on November 1, 1794, posting an official notice. His placard spoke "In the name of the French people" and bore the bellicose and fearsome headline: "Freedom, Equality, or Death." Becker sent Metternich a copy. Two articles in particular affected his family: "I. Art. All absent inhabitants of the land conquered by the French army are considered emigrants. . . . III. Art. All goods and securities of the previous regional sovereigns are declared the property of the French Republic."[225]

The regional administration implemented the measures by periodically announcing auctions in the local press "in accordance with the resolutions of the representatives of the people and the central administration of farmland from the Count Metternich estates."[226] The Metternichs' administrator in Königswart summarized what Becker reported from the Rhineland in a commentary that confirmed Beatrix's evaluation. Now, the young Metternich had written confirmation in front of him regarding his family's situation: "The unfortunate events on the other side of the Rhine . . . are part of the peculiar events of our age, and nothing is to be said about what happened beyond the expression of regret and general sorrow that so many have become unhappy in many ways." They were facing an enemy "who spares neither international law, religion, nor the laws of mankind, and thus is without fidelity and faith, as has been proven several times by the success of those who did not emigrate and nevertheless were not spared."

The Metternichs' private library, whose foundations had been laid by Prince Elector Lothar, met a particularly sorry fate. In the "war year" of 1794, it had been packed into boxes and deposited in the fortress of Ehrenbreitstein as a precaution. After the fortress had capitulated, the commissioners of the French Republic declared the library holdings, which were actually private property, "to be a good that belongs to an imperial estate and thus has been conquered by the Republic." That they were possessed by aristocrats thus apparently legitimized confiscation. They took from the boxes whatever they considered valuable enough for Paris, and transferred the remainder to the recently founded school in Koblenz. The books were transported from the fortress to Koblenz in heaps in open carriages, and many fell off. In 1818 some local citizens handed Metternich individual copies upon his return to Koblenz as "proof of ancient and inherited devotion to my family." After the acquisition of the Rhine province, King Friedrich Wilhelm III returned the library to the family, and it can today be admired at Königswart.[227] On November 13, 1794, Clemens had also ordered that the family archive was to be brought to safety in Bamberg. In this way, the cultural memory of the house was preserved.

In order to review the remaining possessions, Metternich requested topographic surveys of all the Bohemian estates and of the wine-growing estates in

Mainz, Rüdesheim, Oberehe, Koblenz, and Beilstein. He thus gained an over-view of all the vineyards, fields, meadows, forests, heaths, privileges, fiefdoms, farming estates, leaseholds, tenant farms, villages, and bailiwicks belonging to the Metternich family. He gained a deep understanding of traditional, inter-connected ownership and feudal structures. He had not written off the posses-sions on the left bank of the Rhine and, for now at least, still hoped they would be returned to the family.

The Metternichs' arrival in December 1794 was met with ambivalence from Vi-enna's high society. But their traditional ties with the emperor's house had continued into the recent reign of Maria Theresia, as well as those of the em-perors Joseph II and Leopold II. Franz Georg had accrued a substantial amount of moral capital during his twenty years of service to the House of Habsburg, even if an (undeserved) stigma attached to him because he was blamed for the loss of the rich Netherlands, a loss that was hard for the empire to bear. Bea-trix, for her part, had long been well connected with the court in Vienna. When-ever she had accompanied her husband on ambassadorial matters in Vienna, she had benefited from the benevolent support of the old state chancellor Kaunitz. He had died on June 27, 1794,[228] but Beatrix also entertained friendly relations with his daughter-in-law, Leopoldine, who was born into the von Öttingen-Spielberg family. In turn, Beatrix hoped to see Leopoldine's daughter, Eleonore, at her son Clemens's side as his bride. A marital connection with the Kaunitz family, she calculated, would open the doors to the insular Viennese aristocracy. Beatrix also made the acquaintance of Leopoldine's sister, Eleonore von Liechtenstein, and she would soon exploit that connection. After Leopol-dine's death on February 28, 1795, Eleonore von Liechtenstein became some-thing of a mother figure for the nineteen-year-old Eleonore. Social engagements and balls offered opportunities for them to interact—a carnival ball in the spring of 1795, for instance, allowed the young Clemens and Eleonore to get to know each other.[229]

A Marriage Blessed by the Emperor

There are many myths and half-truths surrounding Metternich's marriage. Ac-cording to some, the young and irresistible twenty-two-year-old conquered Eleonore's heart; others would say his mother made clever use of a long-standing relationship with the Imperial House of the Habsburgs in order to placate the upper echelons of Vienna's aristocracy. Or perhaps Eleonore used all her charm as a daughter in order to sweet-talk her skeptical father into agreeing to the marriage.[230] All these interpretations see the personal properties of individuals and their actions and decisions as crucial and are thus based on the bourgeois concept of marrying for love. They ignore the structural constraints to which an aristocratic wedding was still subject even at the end of the eighteenth century. A marriage united not individuals but family assets, and it created a new center of power that would also go on to pursue its own economic goals. The "noble house" represented "a unity that was founded equally on family relationships, relations of power, and economic goals."[231] A marriage, ideally, constituted such a new unity, and so, before embarking upon a marriage, it was necessary to examine whether the bride's dowry was sufficient and whether the groom was in a position to secure her existence in the long term. The first of these conditions was, in the case of the Kaunitz family, very quickly established; the second matter needed to be examined in a bit more detail. To be clear, the Kaunitz family wanted and was entitled to ascertain the financial situation of the Metternichs. And this was in 1795, the very year they had lost their possessions on the left bank of the Rhine. Their wealth was for the most part limited to the Königswart estate, and even that estate had been fairly neglected in the eighteenth century.

What has hitherto not been appreciated is the danger and risk the attempts at matchmaking actually entailed, and the fact that, at a particular point, these attempts looked like they might fail. Metternich himself saw no reason to speak about this in his memoirs. In any case, his mother's love and her matchmaking skills were, alone, not enough to secure success. In the final analysis it was Clemens who directed the negotiations. His stock-taking at Königswart paid off, for he came to be better informed about the family's financial situation than his father. The process of initiating the marriage stretched over five months, if we take as the starting point Franz Georg's first exploratory conversation with the head of Prince Kaunitz's Chancellery and as the conclusion the final financial audit by the prince's accountant, Peregrin Lobisch, on August 23, 1795.

Metternich kept the readers of his memoirs completely in the dark about this complicated business, so it is worth going through it step by step. The "project," as it is called in the files, developed at a metalevel—at the level of the oral and written dialogue between the two lovers.[232] At the same time, it also took place at a sublevel, the level of the tough negotiations that hammered out the marriage contract. Both dialogues were essential and had to be successful. If one of them had failed, then the whole "project" would have failed. Metternich had to use all his skill in leading both the amorous and the contractual conversations, yet—for the sake of Eleonore—keeping them as separate from each other as possible. Only once—and in dramatic fashion—did the two conversations overlap.

The Amorous Dialogue

The dialogue between the lovers seems to have been the easier part. Metternich's love letters gallantly and seductively courted Eleonore: "A thousand, thousand, thousand times, I kiss your hands." Locks of hair were exchanged. Metternich inquired compassionately about her condition after she had fallen down. The twenty-two-year-old clearly wanted to impress women by reading poetry and literature with them, meaning he expected his female partner to be intellectually engaging, something which came easily to Eleonore. He recommended a poetic novel by the French author Jean-François Marmontel (who had been a collaborator on Diderot's *Encyclopédie*), *Les Incas*, which dealt with the destruction of Peru. At the same time, he asked her to put in a good word for him with her father in order to hasten the arrival of their wedding day, which seemed to him "an eternity" away. The days he spent away on a trip to Königswart passed like centuries. In Eleonore, he expected "his life's happiness."[233]

The first decisive signal in the amorous dialogue was, however, provided by Eleonore. He was her suitor of choice—ahead of two others. She made her feelings known to him in a note in which she invited him to join her at the theater "if you really want it," confessing "that, between you and me, I love very much to do whatever you wish. . . . Do not simply forget me and remember, even if I am not as beautiful, as lovable, I love you more than anyone else you know, have known, or will ever know."[234]

In his memoirs, Metternich says that "the thought of marrying so young had never occurred" to him, but that it "was soon evident to me that my parents strongly desired this marriage."[235] Given these statements, and in light of the fact that Metternich had several long-standing affairs, the marriage is usually considered one of convenience. His declarations of love in the letters of 1795, however, are not at all just pretense. Eleonore had something about her that Metternich could not, and did not want to, ignore. Her aunt described her as follows: "She can wrap her father around her little finger, is spoiled, easygoing, open for all new impressions; I cannot easily think of another person with such a lighthearted and yet determinate character; it makes me tremble when I think of her future." In other words: she was not beautiful, but she was extremely charming, lively, seductive; and she was a rich heiress who could expect to receive an annual income of 47,000 guilders after the death of her father.[236] That sum was almost five times the annual salary of the best-paid civil servant at the court in Vienna in 1816.

Although the biographers do not want to admit it, Metternich honestly loved Eleonore and even confessed this to his lover Dorothea von Lieven:

> I did not like having to marry; my father wanted it and I went along with his wishes. Today, I am far away from regretting it. My wife is virtuous, has esprit, and all those properties on which domestic happiness is based are united in her. . . . My wife was never pretty, and she is charming only to close acquaintances. Those who really know her well cannot fail to love her; the majority of people find her stiff, unpleasant, and this is just what she wants. There is nothing in the world I would not do for her.[237]

On August 11, 1795, Metternich wrote to Eleonore that his father's court secretary, Kienmayer, was making arrangements for the house they were to move into in Vienna, that he himself would return to Königswart in mid-August, and that at the end of September their parents wanted to meet in Austerlitz, where the wedding was to take place. Metternich, however, was still urgently awaiting the arrival "de l'homme d'affaires du Prince," that is, of Prince Kaunitz's accountant, Lobisch. Later he reported that Kaunitz's representative finally arrived on August 14 and that matters would be dealt with within a few days. His father would write to Eleonore's father regarding certain questions that need not have concerned her. He loved her a thousand times more than himself.

Kienmayer had confidentially told Clemens that nasty rumors were being spread about him in Vienna. It is telling how important it was to Clemens to make clear to Eleonore that these were unfounded; he suddenly switches from French into German: "It goes in one ear and out another; I let them bark and continue my straight path." That, he said, was the easiest way to deal with the situation and the way that would do the most to confuse his enemies. This was a maxim that he later also applied in politics and that, indeed, continued to enrage his opponents.

The Business Dialogue

The subdialogue was the crucial one, and it resembled a hurdle race. Each time a hurdle was surmounted, another loomed. There were six such hurdles that had to be dealt with.

(1) Attempt to come to a preliminary agreement. The matchmaking process appears overall to have been more akin to the legal negotiation of a contract than a love story. It reveals a lot about the situation of the nobility, the court, and Viennese aristocratic society at the time. After the agreement of the loving couple had been established, it was—against what was generally deemed advisable—not

Beatrix, the mother, but the father, Franz Georg, who took the initiative. To begin with, he avoided a direct conversation with the man whom he hoped would be his son's future father-in-law. Instead, he secretly conferred with the head of the Chancellery, Councillor von Röper. On March 28, 1795, in a confidential evening conversation that lasted an hour and a half, Franz Georg got down to business: what had to be decided, if the two ancient noble houses were to come together, was what form the marriage contract would take. The conversation even touched upon the highly delicate question of the "Count's House's wealth."[238] Von Röper knew little about the rules of the empire and the Rhineland, and Franz Georg used the conversation to teach him some imperial law. Because of his imperial dominions, Winneburg and Beilstein, he told him, he had a seat and a vote at the Imperial Diet, and he was the proprietor of four cellars [*Kellnereien*]—estates with vineyards—which, apart from allowing him to engage in the lucrative trading of wine at home and abroad, also afforded him a wine tenth. In Bohemia, he owned the dominion of Königswart, which included the estates of Miltigau and Sandau. All this amounted to an annual income of 60,000 to 70,000 guilders in imperial currency.[239] Some of the estates were burdened with debts, but a sinking fund that had been especially arranged guaranteed that everything would be free of debt within seven years, he said, "if peace comes." His wealth would provide an "adequate establishment according to his rank" for his older son, and the younger son was provided for as a minor canon at Mainz, as a canon at Bruchsal, and through a prebend at Wimpfen. And his only daughter would "have to content herself with a moderate dowry and limited endowment [i.e., part of the real estate]." The marriage contract between Franz Georg and Beatrix should serve as the model, he said. It should stipulate an annual payment of 6,000 guilders in imperial currency; the furnishing of the town house, which came to 300 guilders per year; a coach and six for use in the city, plus provisions for the horses; and, in addition, annual pin money of 2,000 guilders as well as a morning gift of 2,000 guilders.[240] Because Beatrix's marriage contract was secured by estates in the empire, provision for the future bride was to be guaranteed by a mortgage on the Bohemian estates.

The marriage contract that was finally agreed was not as advantageous for Eleonore as these suggestions might lead one to expect. And the path toward it was tortuous. The negotiations reflected all the sensibilities and insecurities of a partly uprooted imperial nobility. Franz Georg had described his material circumstances in a rather rosy light, and tried to impress by mentioning his recent audience with the emperor, who had expressed his willingness to offer Clemens, currently a chamberlain at court, a position in one of the inner departments. For Franz Georg himself, Emperor Franz had promised "a higher post" if the Netherlands could not be recaptured. And regarding Beatrix, Franz Georg finally added that "the Countess, my wife, is of the most gentle character, and thus will not give her future daughter-in-law any cause for discontent." He asked to be introduced to Prince Kaunitz in the week before Easter, as he was due to travel to his estates in Königswart at the end of April.

(2) Disclosure of the financial situation. Franz Georg's confident assurances only served to make the smart privy councillor skeptical. From memory, the councillor produced for his prince a summary of the conversation in which he tactfully omitted the name and occasion of the conversation, replacing them with pointed lines. He recommended to Kaunitz requesting "an extract covering the dominion of Königswart from the Bohemian land registry in Prague." The land registry contained all possessions, including any encumbrances on them, and was certified by a notary.

It soon proved insufficient first to present the arrangements for the marriage merely in oral form to the councillor, and then reach a final agreement in a conversation with the father of the bride. Instead, what was needed was certified documentation that clearly laid out the financial situation of the Metternich family. In this highly sensitive matter, Clemens took the initiative. He succeeded in winning the favor of Prince Kaunitz's court secretary, Kienmayer, who became a reliable ally of Eleonore's in the efforts to make the marriage a reality. In other conversations, Clemens explained the financial situation of his family to Kienmayer. He went so far as to summarize the result of all these conversations in a document on the "possessions and wealth of the House of the Imperial Counts of Metternich Winneburg,"[241] which included a tabular list of the family's income and capital (Table 3.1).[242] Kienmayer told him that it made no sense to keep to himself "a secret so valuable to the family" instead of handing it to the prince. Clemens gave his consent, but requested that Kienmayer would "counteract adverse rumors regarding his [Clemens's] material situation," as he was now in a position to prove them wrong. Such rumors were indeed floating around, in a Viennese society that looked at the Metternichs, rather suspiciously, as refugees. On May 9, Kienmayer handed the documentation to his employer, Prince Kaunitz. Alas, this was only the beginning of the scrutiny the Metternichs were to come under, and this examination would be truly painful and embarrassing.

Now the optimistic version of the figures was on the table, accompanied by explanations and information regarding existing debts ("liabilities"). The "capital value" was also based on an optimistic calculation that assumed that the income represented 4 percent of the capital value.

(3) Initial objections. Head of the Chancellery von Röper carefully examined the submitted documents and then formulated "objections regarding the state-

Table 3.1. Draft of a survey of capital and interest of the Count Metternich-Winneburg entail and allodial assets based on disclosure of incomes expressed in the imperial currency (guilders)

Assets of the entail	Net income	Capital value	Allodial assets	Net income	Capital value
In the Empire			In Bohemia		
1. Earldom Winneburg and Beilstein	8,000 on the opposite side of the Rhine	200,000	1. Dominion Amonsgrün and Markesgrün	4,800	120,000
2. Winery Mainz	6,000 on this side	150,000	2. Dominion Miltigau	6,000	150,000
3. Winery Koblenz	6,000 on both sides	150,000	3. Private assets: capital and Austrian funds	5,200	130,000
4. Winery Trier	2,000 opposite side	50,000	Sum	16,000	400,000
5. Winery Oberehe	4,000 opposite side	100,000			
6. Reinhardstein and Pousseur near Liege	1,500 opposite side	37,500			
7. Dominion Königswart and Sandau in Bohemia	24,000	600,000	Furniture		30,000
Fixtures		60,000	Fixtures		20,000
Tableware		20,000	Tableware		10,000
Total sum of entail	51,500	1,367,500	Total sum		460,000
			plus entail		1,367,500
			Total assets		1,827,500

ment of Count Metternich's assets."[243] A particularly sensitive issue was the property on the left bank of the Rhine, which Franz Georg wanted to see included. The objection to this was that they were "in the hands of the enemy, and thus at present practically not existing, upon return much diminished, and in the long run not profitable." Of the Bohemian estates, Amonsgrün and Markesgrün were mortgaged for more than half of their value, and Miltigau for almost its entire value. They were, therefore, it was concluded, entirely unsuitable as securities in the context of the marriage contract. These arguments reveal that the conscientious von Röper had already gathered information from the land registry in Prague. There were 74,000 guilders in debts that had been kept secret. And if the estates on the left bank of the Rhine were lost, the councillor asked, would the creditors not want their repayment to come from the remaining estates east of the Rhine, thus depreciating the value of these assets?

These were serious accusations, and they could not but dent the apparent trustworthiness of the Metternichs. The final judgment was altogether damning: it so happens, it said, "that the family promises to give more to its son than it will be able to fulfill, especially now during times of war." In plain terms, if these "objections" could not be rebutted, the marriage could not go ahead. On May 27, the secretary, Kienmayer, passed to Clemens the papers setting all this out. Eleonore was also informed about it, and apparently her reaction was one of panic and desperation—she urged Metternich to explain himself to her. His response was to try to tie the two levels—the amorous and the financial— together: he declared that his love was the highest guarantee for the trustworthiness of the information provided about his wealth. He sent her the following letter:

> Judged by the proof of personal trust and convinced that the latter is the fundamental pillar of happiness in marriage, I affirm that the assets as submitted by my father are a fully correct assessment of how things are, and that on the basis of the most detailed knowledge which, over several years, I have gained of them, and the concepts of honor which are inborn in me and the guarantee of my future happiness.
> Clemens Metternich, 30 May 1795.[244]

But his declaration was to no avail. On the very same day, May 30, that Metternich desperately tried to calm Eleonore down, Prince von Kaunitz sent his court councillor, Röper, to Franz Georg in order to establish, on the basis of the original bills and documents, whether the "objections" were to be upheld. Franz Georg composed a formal reply; after all, it was an all-or-nothing situation.[245] Before discussing the objections in detail, he gave an account of the principles that he thought should guide proceedings. Alluding to his situation as an expellee, he pointed out that he could not possibly have all the necessary documentation at hand, and he made clear how deeply he felt his honor had been challenged, warning that he would have to "rely on that faithfulness and trust which, under certain circumstances in human life, must serve as the substitute for legal evidence, and without which the most solid tie that holds society together must cease to exist."

In terms of detail, he added that he had not even included the substantial income from new woodcutting areas in his list of assets. The real stumbling block was undeniably the debt relating to the dominion Miltigau, situated between Königswart and Eger. Miltigau, Franz Georg wrote, had been bought as a secure investment from Emperor Joseph's religious funds [*Religionsfonds*],[246] and the family profited from the income it generated, gradually paying off the

Metternich's handwritten declaration of honor of May 30, 1795, to
Eleonore von Kaunitz, in the face of the faltering marriage
negotiations.

loans through an amortization fund. This showed, he added, that systematic
efforts were being made at increasing their existing wealth. This line of argument, however, did not alter the fact that the estate was not suitable as a security. As regards the possession on the left bank of the Rhine, there was no reason
to be skeptical, Franz Georg said, because "on the basis of the current state of
political affairs one may be almost absolutely certain that the owner would soon

be taking charge of his property again." This hope was not unfounded, as Brussels had been recaptured twice, the Rhineland once. The request to specify his private wealth Franz Georg felt downright "indecent." At any rate, the income from the wineries, which were still part of the empire, and from the Bohemian estates, was sufficient to provide for his son.

(4) Proving the income from the Bohemian estates. In the meantime, Röper had had close consultations with Clemens and had reported to the prince that Metternich was thoroughly knowledgeable regarding the economic affairs of his house. Kaunitz responded positively, saying the news gave "the most assuring prospect for his future conduct of his affairs." Kaunitz insisted that he did not harbor any suspicions about the oral or written assurances from "a House like Count Metternich's." He therefore would not require that the imperial estates outside of Bohemia, fixtures, silverware, or private assets serve as securities for the marriage contract. The latter should be secured exclusively on the basis of the Bohemian estates. But for these, the documents required "according to our law" were still missing. On June 4, Franz Georg acceded to the demands to provide the necessary documentation.[247]

(5) The emperor as deus ex machina. All the calculations proved to be pointless: the financial basis would remain insufficient as long as the substantial loans on the dominion Miltigau were not repaid. This was where Emperor Franz II came in. Following Franz Georg's arrival from the Netherlands, he had paid him a *Gratifikation,* a bonus of 40,000 guilders. Franz Georg now wanted to use this sum to reduce his debts to the emperor's private treasury, from which he had originally bought Miltigau. The emperor explicitly authorized this, and thus helped to cut through the Gordian knot.[248] Without him, the marriage might well have failed.

(6) Successful cash audit. There was only one task remaining: an audit of all the accounts. In Königswart, Prince Kaunitz's accountant, Peregrin Lobisch, proceeded in a conscientious, purposeful, and thorough manner, as one might expect of a financial auditor. The wedding couple, meanwhile, felt that time was running out for them. From Königswart, Clemens wrote almost daily to Eleonore about the progress of their authorized representative. Lobisch had arrived on August 14, and on August 23 he finally issued the "certificate" they had so longed for. He had closely examined the dominions of Königswart and Miltigau; he had been shown all the original bills; and all incoming and outgoing payments between 1789 and 1794 had been documented. Clemens wrote

to Vienna: "*Je vous aime,* almost too much," and added that the accountant had left on August 24.

They still had to wait for the official marriage contract to arrive from Prague. Originally, Eleonore's father had had grave misgivings regarding the groom. But Eleonore had been Clemens's passionate advocate throughout, and now the father said: "For all I care, you will have to live with him, I warn you, if you want to, I am happy to agree, I give you my blessing, it happens at your peril."[249] As a consequence of the negotiations Clemens had orchestrated with such tact and authority, at least the gravest of his reservations had dissipated, and nothing now stood in the way of matrimonial harmony. The result was captured in form of a magnificent document.[250]

What was the outcome of these difficult negotiations? The contract stipulated the following: after the wedding, performed by a priest, the father of the bride would hand 6,000 guilders as a dowry to the groom, which was to be secured against a deposit of 12,000 guilders. The bride was to receive a morning gift of 400 ducats. The father of the groom would provide his son with an annual maintenance grant of 17,000 guilders, and in addition 2,400 guilders of pin money. These sums were to be secured against the dominions of Königswart and Amonsgrün. Clemens must leave to his wife the free possession, administration, and use of her inherited dominions of Kojetain, Witzomierzitz (in the county of Olmütz),[251] and of a part of Dieditz. Were she widowed, she would receive 6,000 guilders per annum in maintenance and, in addition, six horses, 700 guilders for fodder, and "adequate" lodgings in one of the count's houses. Strict separation was agreed for all independently hereditable goods, including any gains.

Prince Kaunitz had made sure that his daughter would remain financially independent in her marriage. Franz Georg had the emperor to thank for the fact that the marriage could take place at all. The experiences of the six months leading up to the wedding, on September 27, had made painfully clear to the Metternichs, however, the consequences for the family of the Revolution and the war. It seems understandable that, in his personal notes and writings, addressed to a posthumous audience, Metternich remained silent about all this— only the wedding itself he considered worthy of mention.

The Wedding in Austerlitz

After all the details had finally been sorted out, under great time pressure, Ernst von Kaunitz set out how the wedding would go. He wanted "a quiet wedding in the country, and as soon as possible,"[252] inviting only the closest family. On

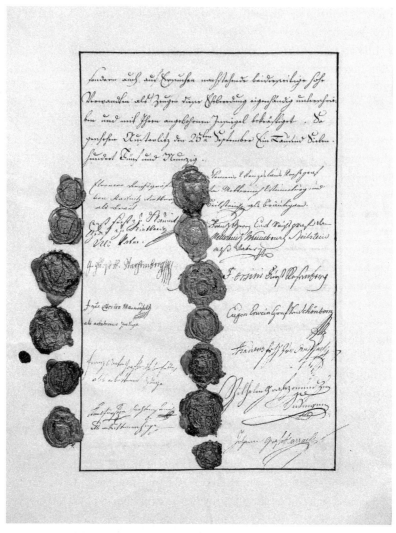

Last page of the marriage contract between Metternich and Eleonore von Kaunitz
of September 25, 1795, bearing the signatures and seals.

August 19, while the audit of the accounts was still ongoing at Königswart, he
suggested September 26 as the day, after first dates in October had been considered. Eventually, it took place on Sunday, September 27.[253] He also insisted
that it should take place at his palace in Austerlitz, where the chapel in which
the wedding took place can still be visited inside the beautifully restored Kaunitz
Castle. We know some details about the event from Princess Eleonore von
Liechtenstein, who was in charge of her niece's bridal wear.[254]

A few days before the wedding the bride and groom and their parents arrived. The day before the wedding, they were joined by Clemens's sister, Pauline; Eleonore's aunt, the Princess of Liechtenstein, accompanied by her son Moritz and his wife; and Count Sickingen. After attending mass, the bridal couple and the witnesses signed the marriage contract. The next day, the Sunday, the church wedding took place in the chapel of the palace. The ceremony was performed by the palace's chaplain, Pater Canal, whose sermon had a personal touch. He dutifully praised the quality of rank "of the high nobility of your lineage, which over so many centuries has led from the purest sources to the blood that runs entirely undiluted in your veins." He then, however, described the sort of bourgeois ideal of love that led to this marriage, "because where the unity of marriage is altogether left to the free choice and decision of two hearts, and is only formed by them, as is the case with the two of you, love comes by itself."[255] These words did not necessarily contradict the sorts of pressures of social rank that had been brought to bear in the production of the marriage contract.

The courtly choreography also followed the social etiquette: civil servants and peasants were allowed to watch the wedding feast, after which the chaplain wedded six bridal couples from the peasant estate for which the "lordship" [Herrschaft] provided a banquet at the inn and a separate peasants' ball. After their dinner, the noble wedding party watched a Singspiel, with dance, pantomime, tambourines, and flowers, performed by three young girls and two younger children. They declared: "Today's celebration is about conjugal love and good housekeeping," and the performance was followed by a humorous song whose stanzas described Eleonore as an ancient goddess who had lost her freedom. One of the ballads, sung in costumes of antique mythology, celebrated the bridal couple as "Minerve et L'amour." A ball followed in the evening, and the next day the wedding celebrations were concluded with pheasant shooting. That was certainly not Metternich's idea. His usual response upon seeing the caught animals displayed in the courtyard at Königswart was: "The poor animals!" Hunting in general he thought "an abomination."[256]

After the wedding, the young couple could move into the Viennese villa in Rennweg that Ernst von Kaunitz had acquired ten years previously from the Vienna Hof- und Kammerjuwelier[257] Franz Mack for 15,000 guilders.[258] The house was from now on to be the Viennese Palais of Clemens Metternich's family, whenever they were not in the upper floors of the Palais Kaunitz at the Heldenplatz. (Today, the Rennweg villa is home to the Italian embassy, and the Heldenplatz palais houses the Austrian Federal Chancellery.) On December 8, 1795, the young couple invited the members of Vienna's courtly high society for a large wedding dinner at the Rennweg villa. The Kaunitz name may have helped to dissolve any doubts guests might have had regarding the Metternichs, who were, after all, refugees in Austria.[259]

TIME OF TRANSITION: THE DIPLOMAT IN WAITING, 1796–1801

Metternich the Private Individual—and Keen Scientist

Until his flight to Austria, Metternich had come to know the political world primarily from the perspective of foreign policy: through France's war against a powerful alliance of European states; then in the service of the First Coalition, as a personal witness to the negotiations in Antwerp; as an outside observer of the Continent during his stay in England; and finally as an emissary appointed to The Hague. This last point would have confirmed his entrance into the international political stage, if the Revolution and the conquest of Holland had not thwarted it. His move to Vienna withdrew him from this scene and taught him to look at the Habsburg and German situation from the inside for the first time. During the years 1795 to 1801, he could be called a diplomat-in-waiting.

This seems to contradict a claim he repeatedly makes in his memoirs— namely, that at that time "public service presented few attractions" for him, and he would rather have dedicated his life to science.[260] And, indeed, in Vienna he gave in to his inclinations toward the sciences and medicine. He attended lectures in geology, chemistry, physics, botany, and medicine in order to study "man and his life."[261] We should interpret this, not as dilettantism, but instead as a basic motivation to get to the bottom of things on the basis of every method available to the age. Research has established that Metternich's interests reached deep into the empirical sciences.[262] The knowledge he acquired also helped him to engage with modern technology, as he already had done in London. He later continued to indulge these interests in the form of the herbariums and collections of minerals and insects at Königswart, which turned part of the palace into a natural history museum. In Vienna, he attended the lectures of several professors of medicine: Johann Peter Frank, the founder of hygiene as an academic discipline and a promoter of a public health service; Joseph von Quarin, a specialist in anatomy and pharmacology; and the anatomist and pioneer in neurology Franz Joseph Gall. Metternich's medical studies so engrossed him that he later considered himself to be "half a physician." Once, anxiously reporting to Wilhelmine von Sagan about the state of his son Victor, who had fallen ill with tuberculosis, he wrote: "Since my earliest youth I had a very decided inclination toward the sciences, and during my years at university, apart from my other studies, I also learned most of what a physician needs to know."[263]

Metternich also attended lectures by Nikolaus Joseph von Jaquin, a professor of chemistry, mineralogy, and botany, who introduced the Linnaean system in the Habsburg Monarchy. While Metternich was in Brussels in 1793, a French edition of Linnaeus's *Systema naturae* was published, and Metternich bought it for his library. Jaquin was also in charge of the Botanical Gardens of Vienna University, where Metternich found inspiration for the design of the gardens at Königswart and on the Johannisberg.

But why would Metternich later, when joining the diplomatic service, deny these interests? According to his memoirs, the failure of his first diplomatic mission to The Hague filled him with "a feeling of bitterness."[264] The position thus must have meant something to him. The key lies in his evaluation of Austrian policies after 1792, which, according to him, should have been guided by altogether different principles. He complained about the inadequacy of the key personnel and disapproved of the path they had chosen. He criticized the "weakness and vacillation of the Austrian cabinet."[265] The war of the First Coalition, he thought, had been badly conducted: "The Imperial court had raised a barrier, sometimes stronger, sometimes weaker, to the destructive principles of all the governments of France," and the success of one measure had been undone the next day. After the death of State Chancellor Kaunitz, the core problem had been "the utter want of consistency of plan." In retrospect, he writes that he wanted to pursue such a consistent plan when the opportunity arose. We shall have to examine this claim against his policies regarding Napoleon, as he was accused by his contemporaries—including Napoleon himself—and by historians of the caliber of Heinrich von Treitschke of possessing an opportunistic, chameleon-like, and scheming character, devoid of principle. Metternich criticized just these properties in what Srbik called the "system of Thugut" (Srbik). And Karl Otmar von Aretin labeled Thugut the "war baron" who had followed "the great statesman"—that is, Kaunitz—in 1794. Thugut's ministry "displays nothing but an unbroken series of mistakes and miscalculations . . . , all of which contributed to support and advance the preponderance of France."[266] Thugut, according to Metternich, had employed the wrong tactics, but Metternich "agreed with him in his principles."[267]

If we consider all these judgments together, the result is such a devastating picture that it is easy to see why, at that time, "public service presented few attractions" for him. His participation would have meant being "constrained to move within limits conflicting with [his] spirit of independence and cramping [his] conscience."[268] In other words, if the emperor wanted Metternich to enter into his service, then this would be on the condition that Metternich could decide the guidelines himself, or—as would later be the case during his time as an envoy—at least could be certain that the general policies being pursued agreed with his principles. Under Thugut's leadership, that was unimaginable.

Upon closer scrutiny of the internal affairs of the governmental machinery, it seemed to Metternich that there were war-supporting and peace-supporting factions in competition for the favor of the insecure and inexperienced emperor. It was the period in Austrian imperial politics between 1792 and 1801 when the emperor sought to achieve three partially incompatible goals at the same time: to defend the "integrity" of the empire; to use Austria's power to expand territorially; and to lead a successful war against revolutionary France.[269] With this in mind, on July 13, 1794, following the death of von Kaunitz, he passed the state Chancellery and the responsibility for foreign policy to Johann Amadeus Franz de Paula Thugut—from 1772 Baron von Thugut—the first bourgeois Austrian minister and for that reason an object of hostility from the court nobility. Metternich was one of the few who occasionally met with Thugut, who was something of a lone wolf. Thugut pursued a close alliance with Russia, continued the war against France, and veered a confrontational course with Prussia, which was a rival when it came to territorial expansion.

Another aggravating factor was that the emperor's domestic policies also lacked a plan. It was "a play with experiments in the administration which must be called an enlightened abundance of governing without enlightened substance."[270] He appointed as cabinet minister his former tutor Karl Baron von Colloredo, who was completely without political experience, which led to numerous political failures. Metternich wrote of Colloredo that he "was no great statesman."[271]

The Congress of Rastatt 1797–1799: An Education in Imperial and Peace Policies

On one occasion Metternich interrupted his existence as a private individual in order to participate in a major international peace congress for the first time. Despite the fact that Prussia had left the coalition after making peace with France in Basel in 1795, one year later the Austrian troops under Archduke Carl defeated the French so decisively at Amberg and Würzburg that the French had to again evacuate the southern German regions east of the Rhine. The glory of these victories—traces of which can be found even in Goethe's *Hermann and Dorothea*—waned, however, after the young French general Bonaparte, having conquered Mantua, advanced into Styria and threatened Vienna. Austria then agreed—in the words of the preamble—"for the future and for all times . . . a solid and inviolable peace," the so-called Peace of Campo Formio (October 17, 1797), near Udine. Austria renounced Belgium, which became French territory, as well as northern Italy to the river Etsch and Lombardy, with these two now forming the Cisalpine Republic. In return, the empire received regions belonging to the Republic of Venice, which had not been involved in the war at all.

The peace treaty stipulated three principles that threatened the very roots of the empire. First, Austria accepted the formation of a new state on what had been its territory and recognized it under international law. It thus endorsed Napoleon's practice, which began to take shape during these months, of populating the European map with new satellite states as he saw fit. From the German perspective, this climaxed in the formation of the Confederation of the Rhine, which led ultimately to the disintegration of the empire. Second, in a secret article of the treaty, the emperor recognized the surrender of the regions of the left bank of the Rhine, reaching to the river Nette, near Andernach, and of the fortress of Mainz. Because the article agreed only to the empire's support for these points at the upcoming peace congress in Rastatt, this did not yet amount to a violation of imperial law. But it opened up the path toward such a violation. Third, Austria also agreed that compensation of those who were dispossessed on the left bank of the Rhine was to come from secularized estates belonging to the empire.

Franz Georg's Role

The Metternichs were involved in the planned peace congress between France and the empire because Emperor Franz appointed Franz Georg as imperial plenipotentiary to the congress. In older works of history, the congress is usually dismissed as merely an opportunity for magnificent balls, amusement, and amorous affairs. And it is treated, in light of its result, as ultimately insignificant, especially because one of the main actors, Napoleon, did not take part in the negotiations.[272] We must evaluate the congress differently. As more recent research into the history of the empire has emphasized, to contemporaries, the congress revealed the true situation of the empire. The participating imperial estates paid close attention to the composition of the delegations. Many of those not represented in these delegations sent their own individual representatives to Rastatt.[273]

The received judgment that Franz Georg was playing a predominantly representative function at the congress and that he did not gain any insight into the affairs of state is wrong.[274] He had to open and close the congress. He acted as the mediator between the imperial estates and the French delegation. Every official document that was exchanged had to go through his hands in order to become legally binding. This is an important fact because it means that his son, as "secretary," was also privy to all the documents. When Franz Georg, as the representative of the emperor, refused to receive a document, this led to impassioned debate. This happened more than once: for instance, when the question of the surrender of the left bank of the Rhine came up. In the discussions over whether the fortress Ehrenbreitstein should be razed to the ground, Franz Georg refused to give his (imperial) approval. He argued that it did not matter "what the French say; what matters is: what does the law say, what is appropriate to the imperial Constitution and has continually, without being contradicted from within the empire or in negotiations with foreign powers, even with the French, been adhered to?"[275] That was the seasoned and experienced expert and defender of imperial law and "German freedom" speaking. Upon formally opening the congress, on January 19, 1798, he emphasized the importance of imperial law, communicating to the delegates that the guideline for the negotiations was the official decree of the emperor. The decree told them "to promote and hasten an equitable and decent peace on the basis of the integrity of the empire and its Constitution."[276] In concrete terms this meant that the empire's borders, be they in Alsace, in Lorraine, the left bank of the Rhine, or in Italy, were to be diminished only as a very last resort.[277]

Franz Georg had to perform a balancing act. The fourteen additional, secret articles of the Peace of Campo Formio put the integrity of the empire's borders and the estates into question in more than one sense. When it became known what was at stake—the handing over of the left bank of the Rhine and the fortress of Mainz, as well as secularization as a tool for compensating the dispossessed secular estates on the left bank of the Rhine—the drawn-out negotiations took a rather unexpected and dramatic turn, at least by the standards of the usually circumspect estates. In mid-March, Franz Georg found himself in an extremely uncomfortable predicament: he had to use his influence in order to persuade the hesitant imperial delegates that the emperor would agree to the surrender of the left bank of the Rhine. It was only then that the imperial deputation began to realize that the basis for this had already been established by the Peace of Basel, and that the Peace of Campo Formio had not changed anything about it.[278] Some of the delegates were truly outraged; they spoke of scandal, treason, and a violation of the law. Trust in the emperor's imperial policies was radically shaken. This was the work of Thugut.[279]

Clemens's Role at the Congress; Bernadotte and the Vienna Flag Riots

The substance of the peace congress went right to the heart of the imperial Constitution. None of the Metternich biographies, however, consider at all whether the young and traditional imperial count seriously reflected on this, or if so, what he made of it. Instead, the cliché is perpetuated that he had abundant free time "to give in to his inclination toward amusement of all sorts."[280]

But how important can the alleged "debaucheries" have been to him when he interrupted his stay at Rastatt on January 23, 1798, to spend two months with his wife and be present at the birth of their child, or when he invited his wife and child in mid-1798 to come to Rastatt?[281] Shortly after his arrival in Vienna at the end of January 1798, Clemens spoke with all the politicians who held positions of responsibility, especially with Thugut and Ludwig Count von Cobenzl, before having a very long and detailed discussion with the emperor. In carefully chosen words, he presented his father with a critical picture of the center where decisions were taken at Rastatt. In light of this, it is certainly not possible to claim that he "hardly gained . . . a full insight into the depth of the state affairs at Rastatt."[282]

Before presenting his political analysis of the court, Metternich explicitly emphasized that his father knew him well enough to know that he did not form his opinions precipitately and that he made a definitive judgment only after careful reflection. Metternich claimed it was imperative always to act in agreement with Cobenzl and Lehrbach, because otherwise all his father's best intentions would be thwarted. He then launched into this devastating description of the state Chancellery: "The Chancellery of the Empire, the only one on which you depend and from which you receive your advice and orders, is of such complete ignorance and apathy that nothing similar has ever existed before. It looks at everything from a perspective that stands in full contradiction to all other ministries. Its orders can represent the thinking of the government only either seemingly or through opposition, and they cannot lead you, especially not on the difficult paths you will have to take."[283] Clemens emphasized that there was satisfaction at the Chancellery with the way his father was conducting affairs and that he should not reveal what he had told him.

If we are to do justice to Metternich, we should ask the political question: What did this first international (imperial) peace congress really mean to him? His own answer is clear enough. We should, however, first clarify whether he was only a spectator or whether he actively intervened in the negotiations. Austria had no fewer than three representatives at the congress: Franz Georg, the imperial plenipotentiary; Count Cobenzl, the representative of the king of Bohemia and Hungary; and Count Lehrbach, the representative of the imperial circle of Austria.[284] Lehrbach had declared that the participation of the young Metternich was "highly worrying," and Thugut, when pressed by Lehrbach, agreed with him. But the emperor himself had decided that Franz Georg's son "may gain practice in political affairs" and should participate. To begin with, this only implied the role of an observer, but on December 18, 1797, Clemens was also assigned an official position as the representative "of the Catholic part of the Bench of Westphalian Counts," turning the purely observational role into one that potentially entailed participation as a representative of the estates. And he proved himself so well in this role that Lehrbach, who had been so skeptical about him at first, on one occasion, when Clemens was traveling to Vienna, even entrusted him with his diplomatic correspondence. Lehrbach added that he had "high praise for his talents, his knowledge, and his good manners."[285] We may therefore exclude the possibility that Metternich was simply idle. In a letter to Eleonore, he mentions an instance in which he intervened in the negotiations. He emphasized the "inestimable advantage" of having the position of the deputy of the Bench of Counts, which gave him "the opportunity to act by and for myself." His "project of an indemnity on the right bank [of the Rhine]," he wrote, "has been accepted by the French, especially given that they had conceived the same idea themselves some time ago."[286]

The available documentation reveals that Clemens was, in fact, much more involved in the work of the congress than has so far been assumed. He wrote to Eleonore that he worked all day and was inundated with "demands and requests" from his "constituents": "Everyone thinks only of indemnifying himself."[287] Franz Georg had, indeed, been swamped with queries and requests for "protection," as it was called. All estates of the empire were among the supplicants, from the imperial princes to the Imperial City of Frankfurt, and the municipalities that sought material compensation for the dispossessions and the quartering of French soldiers. Dinkelsbühl presented a precisely calculated demand of 1,792,584 guilders and 38 cruisers.[288] All this passed through Clemens's hands as well, and it demonstrated to him the complexity of the imperial estates system. From today's perspective, one may also see it as a small-scale rehearsal for the Vienna Congress, which was even more beleaguered by lobbyists seeking protection.

During the time when the congress was taking place, there was a scandal that agitated the city of Vienna, despite the scandal, as such, being politically insignificant. But it developed a public explosiveness and provides a nice example of how deeply Clemens was familiar with the affairs in Rastatt and how he was able to intervene in them. On April 13, 1798, the French ambassador in Vienna, Bernadotte, hoisted the tricolor on the balcony of his house. The Viennese population felt so provoked that a great mass—reportedly some 50,000—gathered in front of the embassy shouting "Long live the emperor!" After an hour of noise and protest, the windows were broken, and then the building was stormed. It was like the storming of Strasbourg's city hall in 1789, only in reverse. Coming in the middle of the peace negotiations at Rastatt, these events had the effect of a belligerent act. Bernadotte could not be appeased by any means and departed on April 15—for Rastatt, where Clemens von Metternich was already expecting him! The international stir caused by the scandal was massive. In

Berlin there was talk of a plot instigated by the French in order to embarrass and bring down Thugut.[289]

Metternich was soon involved. He was keen to get further information on the affair from Eleonore, and he took action on April 29 by composing, in carefully chosen words, a letter of solidarity to Thugut. Franz Georg expressed his indignation over the incident and called it a well-planned plot. The reactions of the French papers, he said, would only confirm this. He spoke of perfidiousness, conspiracy, and excess, and offered his resignation in order to preempt Thugut's dismissal. Franz Georg, Clemens wrote, could not imagine a more honorable way of retreating from political life.[290] He was playing with fire: had Franz Georg actually resigned, this may have been used as a reason for abandoning the congress. This case once more demonstrates Clemens von Metternich's role in the congress.

The Congress as a Stage for a Clash between Empire and Revolution

The negotiations motivated the young imperial count, who had been personally affected through the recent dispossessions of his family's estates, to learn more about the legal situation in the empire: "Certainly the lot of the proprietors is very sad, and if ever the condition of being a composite Empire was valuable, it is so at this moment. I have gathered together information on the internal state of this unhappy country."[291] Metternich also received practical instruction on the peculiarity of the empire's Constitution. The empire's representatives at the congress confirmed what he had learned from his teachers in state law at the universities of Strasbourg and Mainz; they argued against the surrender of the provinces of the left bank of the Rhine on the basis of the "different languages, customs, and ways of thinking" of these provinces. The Holy Roman Empire, they said, stood at the center of Europe and possessed a particular Constitution that France explicitly recognized in the Peace of Westphalia. Enlightened policies would recognize in this Constitution "one of the most important means for maintaining the balance in this part of the world."[292]

Given the experiences he had had with enthusiasts of the Revolution in Strasbourg and Mainz, Metternich had an experience of déjà vu when he saw the French delegates in Rastatt. It seemed like a clash of cultures: "I thought I saw a group of the men of September and it turned my stomach."[293] He was constantly reminded of those earlier days. From Rastatt, Metternich traveled to Strasbourg, and he was struck by how the places he had known before and during the Revolution had completely changed. On his Sunday excursions from Rastatt along the Rhine, Metternich spoke with peasants who crossed in small barques to the opposite bank of the river where they had the opportunity to attend mass. Metternich approached them and asked how they were. They all assured him that they now paid twice as much in levies compared to the worst times of the ancien régime, and if that were not to end soon, they said, they would pack up their belongings and leave the country. Metternich offered, ironically, "Fine regeneration and fine liberty!" And he reported: "Everyone jeered or wept when the word 'liberty' was pronounced, or 'equality,' which they mocked the most."[294] This snapshot from the lives of the common people confirmed his experiences of contributions, pillaging, and confiscations described above: in accordance with the motto "The war will feed itself" the advancing French troops plundered the country and revealed their promises to be lies.[295]

The dress and manners of the French delegates with whom Metternich dined seemed to him to indicate the same attitude of arrogation and possessiveness. But more important, at least in terms of his future biography, is the political substance he extracted from the circumstances and negotiations at the congress. At the beginning of 1797 he prophesied a dark fate for the empire and spontaneously fell into German when writing to Eleonore: "It [the end] . . . cannot be otherwise than terrible for the empire. Über dieses muss man das Kreuz machen [All one can do is bid farewell to it],"[296] adding, however, that he did not wish to be quoted on this. And on December 9, still before the official opening of the negotiations, he categorically declared: "But certainly the Empire has gone to hell."[297] He felt surrounded by ignorant people who were incapable of understanding his perspective. He thought the events so exceptional, the never-ending military operations of the French against the empire so unspeakable, that he was already imagining all of Vienna going up in flames. And, he wrote, there was no other place where so little was known about the empire than in Vienna; the government there had a completely false picture of the threats facing the empire.

Earlier than others, Metternich had recognized an inner necessity within French politics. The French were progressing "on all sides; they have blockaded Mainz and taken possession of the bishopric of Basle." And they had revolutionized Italy: "Heaven knows where it will stop; but there is certainly no reason why the rest of Europe should not be shaken to its foundations by forty million men aiming at the same mark."[298] As someone immediately affected by these developments, he felt the political force of the Revolution; but having absorbed Edmund Burke's insights, he was also quicker than others to evaluate surface events as manifestations of deeper, epochal trends. By Christmas 1797 he was certain that "Mainz has gone to hell" and that one had "to bid farewell" to the whole of the left bank of the Rhine, not just the stretch up to Andernach. He wrote that many people "do not believe it yet" but "come what may, I shall be astonished at nothing."[299] The French occupation of Basel revealed to him the underlying spirit of the Revolution: "Of what horrible augury is this unheard-of infringement of people's rights for all the countries near the whirlpool! The Revolution will have carried away in its torrent nearly fifty million men in less than seven years, and where will it stop? I pity these poor Swiss; but they are lost, and we shall have the Revolution in all the frontiers of Tyrol. The French yesterday entered Mainz."[300] In other words, he expected that the revolutionary war that began in 1792 would take on the dimensions of a new Seven Years War of the kind that had struck Europe, and in particular the center of Germany, forty years earlier.

Even before the opening of negotiations at Rastatt, Metternich's prognosis that the left bank of the Rhine was utterly lost implies only one conclusion: he must already have known the content of the secret articles of the Peace of Campo Formio. As early as January 6, he wrote that in Vienna many people believed "que ce congrès de Rastatt ne serait qu'un jeu [that the Congress of Rastatt is nothing but a farce]: everything is already arranged."[301] And we may go further: he must also have learned about an incident that threw a spotlight on Napoleon's unpredictably violent character. Cobenzl, the leading member of the Austrian delegation at Rastatt, had personally negotiated the contract agreed to at Campo Formio. When it finally came to actually signing it, Cobenzl sought a few more advantages, which prompted Napoleon to issue the following warning: "The French Republic will never give up any of its legal borders; given the means at its disposal, it may conquer all of Europe within two years."[302] And when Cobenzl still hesitated, Napoleon lost his temper and threatened him. "So the truce is broken and war declared; but remember that I shall have shattered your monarchy before the end of the autumn, the same way I now shatter this porcelain,"[303] he said, lifting a porcelain figure from the table and smashing it on the floor. The figure was a present from Empress Catherine II to thank Cobenzl for his diplomatic work in Saint Petersburg, and it meant a lot to him—and Napoleon knew as much. Cobenzl signed the peace treaty the same day, October 17, 1797. The Austrian diplomats were speechless. The Peace of Campo Formio had been agreed to under duress. The emperor might have wanted to retain the "integrity of the empire," but the decision had been taken out of his hands then and there. This background makes Metternich's visions of looming catastrophe a good deal more plausible. In 1809 he would find himself in a comparable situation when the Treaty of Schönbrunn was negotiated and the Napoleonic sword of Damocles hung over the Habsburg Monarchy once again.

The blackmail surrounding the peace agreement necessarily had an effect on the process and result of the congress. Metternich therefore avoided the temptation to dismiss it as "treason," "scandal," or a "violation of the law," as

historians sometimes do. He simply stated: "My stay in Rastatt only strengthened me in my opposition to a career which in no ways satisfied my mind and
disposition."[304] On March 12, 1799, France declared war on Austria. The victories of Archduke Carl led to the dismissal of Franz Georg von Metternich by
Vice-Chancellor Cobenzl on April 1, 1799. On April 7, Metternich communicated this decision to the deputation, and a day later he informed the French of
his dismissal, saying that the truce had been broken and the War of the Second
Coalition had, indeed, been declared. With the removal of Franz Georg, the
delegation lost the authority to communicate officially with the French, as this
could only be done through the representative of the emperor.[305]

Again, Clemens's summary account found arguments for the muddled policies of the monarchy. He criticized not the congress as such but Thugut's overall
political strategy. At the same time, he managed to gain such a degree of respect
and acknowledgment from Cobenzl and Lehrbach for his work at the congress
that the emperor came to consider him suitable for higher diplomatic offices. In
May 1798 Cobenzl had already taken over the Foreign Ministry, although only
temporarily. Thugut remained active as an influential *éminence grise,* and took
charge of foreign affairs again when Cobenzl was appointed to Saint Petersburg
for the second time. Thus, Thugut continued to hold the reins when it came to
foreign policy—until his definitive dismissal in 1801.

4

BETWEEN PEACE AND WAR

Life as an Ambassador, 1801–1806

The Circumstances of Metternich's Appointment

For the Holy Roman Empire, the Peace of Lunéville of February 9, 1801, meant the end of the War of the Second Coalition with its neighbor, the Republic of France, headed by its First Consul—the position to which Napoleon had had himself elected in 1799. A little later, in 1802, France and Great Britain signed the Peace of Amiens. The path toward general peace in Europe seemed at long last to have been prepared. Without a doubt there were losers and victims: Poland was not restored as an independent state; Venice fell to the Habsburg Monarchy; the Piedmont fell to France; the Prince of Orange became a ruler without a country; and the German ecclesiastical princes and numerous smaller dominions within the empire became pawns to be moved about on the chessboard of the powerful. At that point, though, the old German empire was still alive as a political organism; it even passed another fundamental law, stipulating for all imperial estates how the secular property owners on the left bank of the Rhine would be compensated, to be added to its already complicated constitutional structure. This law was the famous Principal Decree of the Imperial Deputation of 1803, the last constitutional law passed in the old empire.

Paul Schroeder's judgment on the peace treaties of Lunéville and Amiens is plausible: as contracts, they were technically insufficient, but from an eighteenth-century perspective, they were not useless as a foundation for lasting peace. It was not the way the peace was constructed as such that carried the seed of the wars that were to follow and continue until 1815; it was the personality of Napoleon, his ambitiousness, that led to the next war and the many others that would follow.[1] And this is exactly how, in 1813, Metternich retrospectively interpreted the logic of Napoleon's policies in suggesting to him that his peace treaties were never anything but a prelude to the next war: "Your peace is never more than a truce."[2]

In his memoirs, Metternich interprets the Peace of Lunéville of 1801 as a historico-political rupture and, connectedly, as a turning point in his biography. The peace between the Holy Roman Empire and France marked the failure of Thugut's wartime policies. The unhappy successor to the great Kaunitz resigned from all his offices in 1801, and thus paved the way for Ludwig Count von Cobenzl, who then, until 1805, dominated Austrian politics as the state and conference minister and as court and state chancellor.[3] The end of the "Thugut system" dissolved Metternich's reservations about pursuing a diplomatic career. The newly established peace also offered more room for diplomatic maneuvering and meant that important posts at embassies—in London, Berlin, and Saint Petersburg, for instance—were filled again. Emperor Franz tried to convince the young imperial count, at this point only twenty-seven years old, to join his diplomatic corps. But Metternich's real patron was Cobenzl, who had had plenty of opportunities to observe him at the Rastatt negotiations. After Metternich's appointment as minister to Dresden, Cobenzl gave him the stamp of diplomatic maturity, so to speak, by treating him as his disciple, telling him personally: "You know that I wished for a long time to see you embark on a diplomatic career, and I am highly pleased about the good appointment we have made. The feelings I harbored for you all along mean that should never doubt your utility in everything that might depend on me."[4] Before his appointment, Metternich was still plagued by self-doubt. Emperor Franz personally helped him overcome his misgivings by appealing to Metternich's "patriotism" and offering him a choice between the diplomatic mission in Copenhagen or Dresden, or the role of representative of the Bohemian electorship at the Imperial Diet in Regensburg. Denmark, it seemed to Metternich, was too far away, and he ruled out Regensburg, he later wrote, because it was "repugnant" to him to go there "only to witness the obsequies of the noble German Empire."[5] For a budding diplomat, Dresden was, indeed, the most attractive place—possibly next to Munich—among the embassies in the central states; it had the value of being an "observation post." Saxony was the venerable electorate in which the Reformation had begun and therefore represented the leading voice of Protestantism in the empire, even if its rulers had somewhat weakened this reputation by converting to Catholicism in the context of taking on the elective monarchy in Poland. Due to its traditional ties with Poland, Saxony's perspective went beyond that of the central states and looked further east. Within imperial politics, it was considered, as a neutral central power, to have a guiding role among the imperial estates, and it was therefore eagerly wooed, but also critically observed, by Prussia, France, and Austria.

In his memoirs Metternich connects the beginning of his service for the state with his criticism of the policies pursued by Austria after 1792, criticisms we have already discussed. In his eyes, the main fault had been "the utter want of consistency of plan."[6] This was by no means a "harsh, unjust verdict" motivated by "sad memories of his youth"[7] but instead an objective and unflinching judgment. More recent research has not only confirmed it but also gone further than Metternich, describing Thugut's leadership as involving "serious mistakes," "chaotic government," "willfulness," "rigid wartime policies," "clueless dilettantism," and general "failure."[8] Metternich's verdict also suggests that he wanted his own politics to follow a "plan." It is for this reason that, at this point in his memoirs, he inserts his "confession," in which he candidly states "the principles on which the actions of [his] political life have been based" (touched upon above).

Metternich's "Self-Instructions" of November 2, 1801: Program for a New Diplomacy

This does not yet answer the question of whether Metternich himself had a "consistent plan" in 1801. Did he already have those guiding "principles," and did he already have—as he would later claim—the political vision and farsightedness that he would demonstrate at the height of his career—namely, at the Congress of Vienna and during the era following it? This question has never seriously been asked. Fortunately, in 1801 Metternich took his own principle fully to heart: "I could never do anything by halves; once a diplomat, I decided to be one thoroughly, and in the sense which I connected with diplomacy."[9] In order to demonstrate to himself, the court, and in particular the emperor the true qualities of a diplomat, he did something probably unique within the history of diplomacy and international relations. In a document officially dated November 2, 1801, he composed for himself a set of binding instructions for his post in Dresden: a major political manifesto of no less than 105 pages.[10] This is an invaluable document because it allows us to judge how diplomatically competent Metternich was at the beginning of his career and whether his early methods and principles endured into his later career. At the same time, it allows us to discover whether he still took the Holy Roman Empire seriously or whether he was one of those who considered it a moribund political entity.

In January 1801, following the redeployment of the minister in Saxony, Count Emmerich zu Eltz, to the Spanish court, Metternich was appointed his successor in Dresden. As he did not have to take up the post until November, he had ample time to prepare for his new role, and he did so in characteristic manner. For months he buried his head in files on diplomatic communications at the archive of the state Chancellery; he wanted to "have a thorough knowledge of the circumstances," and in particular of whatever had "led to the present state of European politics." In this document, Metternich developed a method he would apply in his later years as foreign minister and state chancellor whenever he had to explain a political question of fundamental significance to the emperor or justify a political decision that followed on from his analysis of such a question. He always developed a problem against its historical background and inferred the measures to be taken accordingly. Before taking a final decision he presented the emperor with the available options and the risks associated with them, rejecting each until only one plausible option remained. This is how he explained to the emperor the path that was supposed to lead the monarchy out of its nadir in 1809; this is how he justified the strategy to be adopted in confronting Napoleon between 1810 and 1813; this is how he explained the project of getting Marie Louise, the daughter of the emperor, to wed Napoleon (in 1810); and it is how he identified the right point in time for ending the alliance with Napoleon and joining the war coalition against France (in 1813).

In the official terms of the administration, the form in which this took place was called a "presentation" [*Vortrag*]. Such presentations to the emperor were also given by the heads of other court offices, and they might concern anything from matters of everyday business to questions on which the existence of the monarchy depended. In his presentations, Metternich revealed his thoughts to the emperor without reservation. This is worth bearing in mind if we are to gain an appropriate understanding of the document Metternich presented upon taking up his post. At first glance, it seems to be nothing but a set of instructions, but it is in fact the text that ends the time of Metternich's political apprenticeship, and with it he put himself forward for higher office—even the office of a minister. That he was given the freedom to do so indicates not only the level of trust people had in him but also the weakness of the government in providing leadership and orientation.

Metternich divided his inaugural manifesto into four sections. The first section gave a survey of the historical and political events between 1790 and 1801, "an epoch which saw the most striking changes take place in the system of European states." The second section described the role of the Court of Saxony during that period. The third presented "the present state of European politics," and the fourth, finally, listed concrete instructions for how the envoy should act.

European History between 1790 and 1801

It will suffice for our purposes to take a look at the first year from Metternich's historical analysis, for that was the one most ridden with conflict. The analysis reveals him to be very much a pupil of his teachers in state theory, Koch and Vogt, concerned with the transformations of the European empires. But he also made use of his own political experiences. We have seen how intimately connected Metternich was to the consequences of changing social forces between 1789 and 1799. For this reason, he went beyond the intellectual framework of his teachers and identified the core of the events, the epicenter of the social earthquake, in the "innermost organization of society." This was, among other things, a reference to the Revolution unleashed by the Jacobin terror. His interpretations no longer rested on the old concepts of estates, privileges, or corporations—which belong to the "old world"—but were based exclusively on the new guiding concept: the modern collective singular, "society."

Metternich painted a complex picture of the crises in 1790 in which internal and external circumstances—effects of the Revolution, power politics, military matters, social processes—are interlocked. He looked at all major European states, and interpreted the climactic crisis points as the result of interconnected processes across all of Europe—whatever happened at one end of the Continent had an effect at the other end. In 1790, Russia, Austria, and the Ottoman Empire were at war with each other; so were Russia and Sweden; between England and Spain war was looming; the Netherlands had declared their independence from the Habsburg Monarchy; Hungary was on the way to doing the same; and Liege had descended into anarchy. The French Revolution, Metternich wrote, spread "its branches" on all sides. Prussia, "true to its congenital hatred of the dynasty [*Erzhaus*] of Habsburg, thought only of expanding its territory and power, and did not shy away from supporting the revolution in Liege, against the interests of the Holy Roman Empire, fomenting an uprising in Hungary, and intervening in the Polish crisis to achieve some "territorial gain." Prussia's conduct toward the Holy Roman Empire was also hostile: it supported the German League of Princes, which aimed to prevent the election of a Habsburg emperor following the death of Joseph II. Russia, on the other hand, after having made peace with Sweden, became more aligned with Habsburg policies toward Prussia. Metternich saw the "German empire" in 1790 as divided by the "unconstitutional League of Princes," but the loyalty to the House of Habsburg shown by the estates faithful to the empire nevertheless made possible the election and coronation of Leopold II as emperor.

The History of Saxony between 1790 and 1801 in the Context of Imperial Politics

Metternich treated the past eleven years of the Court of Saxony under Prince Elector Friedrich August I with the same thoroughness. He again proceeded chronologically, and the report shows how thoroughly he had acquainted himself with the history of Poland and, in particular, with the complications associated with the Polish imperial Constitution, which was passed on May 3, 1791. One of these was the—ultimately unsuccessful—election of the Saxon prince elector, Friedrich August, as the hereditary king. At the time, there was no better place than Dresden for Metternich to become familiar with the complicated balance between the three major powers in Eastern Europe, where Prussia and Russia pursued the sole objective of making territorial gains at the expense of Poland.

The intensity with which Metternich reflected on the dilemma in which the Electorate of Saxony was caught—between its commitments to the empire and the coercion coming from Prussia—makes it clear to the reader how personal this question was for him. Even in its final years, the old Holy Roman Empire still meant something to him. In his memoirs, he later gave the impression that he had held "the firm conviction that the grand creation of Charlemagne was tending inevitably to its end."[11] His instructions paint a very different picture. On the basis of original quotations from the reports of emissaries, he attempted to prove that one side had behaved blamelessly, in line with the imperial Constitution (Saxony), and that another side had systematically tried to destroy the Constitution in order, among other things, to reduce Austria's influence in Germany (Prussia). In the eyes of the Saxon Cabinet, Prussia was a threat, hence the Saxon efforts to build a military cordon against it and the recall of Saxon imperial troops to strengthen the military at home. Metternich illustrated the seriousness with which the court in Vienna viewed the intended withdrawal of troops, quoting verbatim from an instruction that had been sent to the Austrian emissary in Dresden that said that "if His Imperial Majesty were deserted by all larger estates of the empire and each individual imperial estate sought only to look after its own immediate interests, then His Imperial Majesty would also have to give up the defense of the empire's borders and would be justified in the eyes of God and the world to limit himself to the defense of the borders of his own states, which would, however, necessarily have the saddest consequences for all of the empire."

According to Metternich's analysis, one should not equate the Austrian and the Prussian policies and claim—as, for instance, Karl Otmar von Aretin does—that "Austria was ultimately only interested in an expansion of its territory. . . . In the politics pursued by the two major German powers, the fate of the empire was not worth being taken into consideration."[12] Metternich, by contrast, was of the opinion that the empire was at that point in time still capable of consolidation and reform if the imperial estates could reach unanimous agreement. In his summary, he defined the goal to be sought as "the preservation so far as possible of the Constitution of the Empire and the protection of each member of it."[13] At the same time, almost prophetically, he recognized that another option was that Austria might inadvertently move out of the imperial federation altogether.

Metternich's Insights and Conclusions

In an extensive summary of the third section, Metternich developed his conclusions, which display his particular talent for seeing through complex constellations, putting them into historical context, and abstracting from them principles to guide practical politics. His insights were the following:

- The transformations of the previous eleven years caused by the French Revolution had changed the political situation in Europe more than the three "great wars" of the eighteenth century, which Metternich understands as forming a unity (the War of the Spanish Succession, the Northern war, and "the Prussian war with us in 1740, the consequence of which was the Seven Years' war").[14] The alliance with France, which Kaunitz had forged as state chancellor in 1756, no longer existed.

- The contemporary situation between the European states was a "chaos of elements" from which no "settled European state system for the immediate future" could be drawn. The "still pending struggle of political principles" meant "the hope of a general peace" would have to wait until "a very distant period."[15]

- The original English stance of neutrality toward the Continent had given way, and England had become "the most active member of the Coalition" in the context of the revolutionary war.[16] Because England had become a maritime power and a global player, European politics had to be seen within a context that transcended Europe. England wanted to maintain its "world monopoly in trade."

- The traditional friendship with Russia during the reign of Catherine II, based on Prussia and the Ottoman Empire being common enemies, also no longer existed. Although Alexander I had ascended the throne only four months before the "Instructions" were composed, Metternich already had a pretty accurate picture of his mentality: his "fickle character, easily distracted by small matters and not to be won over by even the greatest effort" made a stable, peaceful relationship with his empire impossible. In 1801, Metternich already recognized in Russia the second European power, next to France, that would continually threaten the continental center of Europe from the wings with its hegemonic ambitions.

- Prussia had "since the reign of Friedrich II shown the ambition of becoming a power of the first rank,"[17] albeit with a population of a secondary power, and through only minor financial reforms. The "desire for aggrandizement" had led to the violation of "all acknowledged international and moral principles. The alliance of the year 1791 hardly deserves mention," having been abolished very quickly. Metternich's long-term prognosis for Prussia in 1801 was that it intended to subject all imperial matters to its own idiosyncratic guidance and finally to sacrifice the fate and existence of large parts of Germany in the interests of its own expansion—and all this "under the pretense of German patriotism."

- As Metternich had already realized during his stay there in 1794, England continued to be a firm partner in any alliance: "The often-renewed alliances with England had a natural ground in the political and geographical relations of the two countries; between a merely commercial and an exclusively continental power there was no natural ground for rivalry."[18] However, what guaranteed this commonality of interests—the Austrian Netherlands as a transmission place for English trade and a bastion against France—had been lost.

- The fate of the States General of Holland would be, at a "more or less distant point in the future," to lose their independence and be relegated to the status of French provinces (as happened in 1810).

- The overall rule of Habsburg in Italy would dissolve. Instead, there would be a range of smaller Italian states as French republics (as Napoleon later, indeed, managed to achieve). Metternich, in fact, declared the end of all the traditional alliances of the Habsburg Monarchy.

- The partition of Poland was "contrary to all principles of sound policy" and derived from the "blind desire for aggrandisement" of the Prussian and Russian Cabinets. For Metternich, as a count who believed in imperial law, it was simply a violation of European international law and of political morality. At the same time, the young envoy displayed a deeper, pragmatic streak: "The existence of Poland was equally important for us, for the interests of the adjacent states, and for the general peace of Europe. Situated between three major powers, Poland prevented the frequent collisions which always occur if there is immediate contact, and for that reason alone it had a decided value for each of the three Powers."[19]

Metternich's analysis is penetrating, and it demonstrates his ability to predict future developments. His evaluation of Prussia's and Russia's expansionist tendencies is correct, as is his judgment of England as a permanent counterforce. But which conclusions should be drawn from the disintegration of the traditional alliances and relationships? General peace, Metternich said, could be established only through a European balance of powers, but this was a long way off. The reason for the imbalance in the system was "extraordinary acquisitions of France, to which belong all surrounding, altogether subordinate republics." Metternich early on saw this imbalance as a technique of rule that Napoleon practiced, using the satellite states he had set up: France's hegemony was to be secured through a circle of dependent states that were lowered to the status of medium-sized powers. The urgent goal of Austrian politics in Europe, according to Metternich, was to mitigate this "excessive situation"—that is, to bring it to a level compatible with a balance of power. This was Metternich's enduring aim in all his dealings with Napoleon, right up until the Congress of Vienna reduced France to the status of one power among others.

At the Court of Saxony: Observations and Experiences

Metternich had thus prepared himself intellectually for his first diplomatic mission. But he also knew that at the court of the prince elector great emphasis was placed on adhering to ceremonial etiquette, and he therefore ensured he was prepared for that as well. To this end, he asked the chancellery of the imperial court to provide him with information "on the guidelines": court attire, the days on which gala dresses had to be worn, and the manners to be followed in general. It was as though the world had stood still in Dresden, as if time had stopped in the mid-eighteenth century. While the French Revolution had abolished the monarchy and Napoleon had introduced the dictatorship of the consulate, in Dresden women still wore rococo dresses. In the face of the tense unrest in Europe, Dresden appeared like an "oasis in the desert" to Metternich.

As there were no important contracts to be negotiated, Metternich used his contacts with the Cabinet and the prince elector to encourage their loyalty to the empire and to warn them against getting to close to Prussia. He also sought contacts and information wherever he could find them. This brought him to the salons of the city, where he made acquaintances that would prove useful in his later career.[20] He visited the salon of Princess Izabela Czartoryska, the wife of the rich Polish magnate Adam Kazimierz Czartoryski, whose estates had been confiscated after the failed rebellion in 1794, although his involvement in the rebellion was never proven. Czartoryski traveled across all of Europe in order to gain friends for Poland. One of his sons, Adam Jerzy, was a friend of the young tsar, Alexander, and later became his foreign minister. The fifty-six-year-old Princess Izabela, who knew Rousseau, Voltaire, and Benjamin Franklin, took to the young envoy from Vienna at once and tried to support him whenever she could. In her salon, Metternich also met the Russian general Prince Peter Bagration. His nineteen-year-old wife Katharina and Metternich would later produce an illegitimate child in Dresden, an episode to which we shall return.

Another attraction was the salon of the widowed Duchess Dorothea von Kurland, who had inherited the rich duchy of Sagan in Silesia from her deceased husband. Now the Duchess of Sagan, she lived in Dresden with her three daughters, Pauline, Wilhelmine, and Dorothea. Wilhelmine von Sagan later became Metternich's great love. We shall look at Metternich's relationships with women in more detail in a separate chapter. For now, suffice it to say that his wife, Eleonore, accepted her fate with a measured irony. To Napoleon's great general, Marshal Auguste de Marmont, she remarked that she did not understand how a woman could resist her husband.[21] Metternich did not neglect his marriage while in Dresden. On January 3, 1803, the longed-for male heir, Victor, was born here (the two earlier sons, Georg and Edmund, born in Vienna, had both died in 1799). Eleonore also fell pregnant with their daughter Clementine during Metternich's time at the embassy in Dresden. Clementine was born in Berlin on August 30, 1804.

The most entertaining salon for Metternich, however, was that of the English ambassador Hugh Elliot, who was at Dresden between 1792 and 1803. Metternich spoke of him in superlatives: "A pleasanter man in society I have never known."[22] Indeed, in his memoirs Metternich describes Prince Elector Friedrich August in one sentence but spends two pages on the English diplomat. He was impressed by Elliot's quick-wittedness, his vivacity, and his self-confident brashness—he did not pay any attention to etiquette, not even when it came to the delicate social scene of the Dresden court. Metternich's memoirs describe a scene at the court of the Prussian king Friedrich II that clearly amused him. Preferring the French, the king had ordered his chamberlain to introduce each French diplomat to him individually at receptions, whereas the English were introduced only as a group. When on one such occasion the chamberlain turned to the king and said: "I have the honor to present to Your Majesty twelve Englishmen," Elliot interrupted him, "exclaiming in a loud voice, as he turned to leave the room, 'You are mistaken, Herr marschal [sic]; there are only eleven.'"[23] The Prussian king remembered this éclat when, some years later, Elliot was appointed as ambassador extraordinary to the court in Berlin; the king sought to express his "ill-humor" to the court in London by sending someone of mediocre rank to London and having him introduced with the ironic remark that his "Majesty flatters himself that your Court will be satisfied with this choice." The Prussian chamberlain informed Elliot about this, whereupon the latter "answered without hesitation: 'The King, your master, evidently could not have chosen anyone who would have better represented him.'" Metternich dryly commented: "With such manners as these, Mr. Elliot was not likely to make himself a favorite in Prussia."[24]

Metternich frequently visited Elliot's home, and he would later recall fondly his relationship with this idiosyncratic character. Again we see his admiration for the Anglo-Saxon way of life and its mentality and intellectuality, which he would seek out whenever he could. The two ambassadors even exchanged ideas on how best to fulfill the duty of regularly sending reports to the court at home when there was nothing to report. Elliot, who was Metternich's senior by almost twenty years, let him in on a secret: "If anything comes to my knowledge which may interest my government, I tell it; if I do not know of anything, I invent my news, and contradict it by the next courier."[25]

Elliot, ignored by Srbik, is worth mentioning not only because he reawakened Metternich's love of England but also because it was in his salon that the imperial count met the then Prussian civil servant and "war councillor" Friedrich Gentz, who was the famous translator of and commentator on Edmund Burke's *Reflections on the Revolution in France*. Each immediately recognized in the other a kindred spirit. Gentz's *Fragments upon the Balance of Power in Europe*, written in 1805, shows which political questions exercised Gentz at the time. We can also see from the text what it was about Gentz that must have caught Metternich's attention. The title already suggests something that fits the coordinates of Metternich's political system, and the principles developed in the book reveal an astonishing intellectual affinity with Metternich's thought. Gentz wanted to illuminate the path that had led to the War of the Third Coalition (1803–1805) after the Treaty of Lunéville. Gentz set out from the "former federal system of Europe" and from the colossal superiority of France, which was repressing Europe and destroying its old Constitutions, and needed to be limited. This, Gentz wrote, was "a just and necessary war." He saw the danger that Germany would be brought under the French yoke like Holland, Switzerland, Italy, and Spain before it. He spoke, he said, with "genuine patriotic and true cosmopolitan feeling," and wrote for "our native country, the commonwealth of Europe, the liberty and dignity of nations, the reign of law and order."[26] On the horizon, he saw the utopia of a "world government" [Weltregierung], including a "league of nations" [Völkerbund]. His interest was a commonwealth grounded in international law that would be capable of protecting the rights of the less powerful. Gentz juxtaposed the French universal centralist monarchy—toward which Napoleon was moving—with the English "mixed Constitution."[27] Like Metternich, Gentz used historical retrospection, in this case the history of the French revolutionary wars, as a catalyst for his reflections. Metternich would also not have failed to notice, with approval, that Gentz complained about the fact that France and Russia had taken it upon themselves to transform the imperial Constitution in order to be able autocratically to administer the compensation for the areas on the left bank of the Rhine, rather than leaving this business to the emperor and the Imperial Diet. Gentz's political acuity also shone where he discussed the partition of Poland and the transformations of Switzerland and Italy under the direction of the French. In short, given so much common ground, it is not surprising that during his days in Dresden Gentz mainly spent time at Metternich's house and became a friend. Together, they moved in the diplomatic circles of Dresden and visited its salons, such as those of Countess Hohenthal and Duchess Czartoryska.[28]

The Principal Decree of the Imperial Deputation and the Rescue of the House of Metternich

Although Metternich experienced the court in Dresden as an oasis, he remained alert to the unrest elsewhere in Europe, to the fragility of the peace created by the treaties of Lunéville and Amiens, and to the existential crisis of the Holy Roman Empire. There was evidence of that crisis in Regensburg, where, from 1802, a special commission of the Imperial Diet prepared the so-called Principal Decree of the Imperial Deputation. Metternich conspicuously avoided this term and instead spoke of a "French-Russian mediation," because he saw, quite rightly, where the responsibility for the inner revolution that "destroyed the last foundations of the old German Empire, and thus greatly accelerated the moment of its utter dissolution" lay.[29] Metternich's judgment on the future of the empire differed in an unusually radical way from his father's. After the law was passed, the son saw the empire as shaken to its very foundations and as effectively nonexistent: it had been dispersed into its elements, and these could not be put together again.

Between the summer of 1801, when he composed his "Instructions," and the summer of 1803, when he was appointed to the embassy in Berlin, his judgment changed fundamentally. This can be explained only if we take into account that during that period father and son exchanged many letters on the topic of the Principal Decree of the Imperial Deputation. At the end of his instructions, Metternich had only addressed the question of how an imperial deputation should be composed if it were to regulate the issue of compensation for those of the nobility with possessions on the left bank of the Rhine. This problem continued to exercise him while in Dresden. He observed, from afar, how his father in Regensburg intensely—and ultimately successfully— lobbied throughout the negotiations "to watch over the interests of his family"; Franz Georg fought for "compensation for the loss of his hereditary estates on the left bank of the Rhine."[30] From the way Metternich expresses himself, it sounds as though he wanted to distance himself from the business of compensation altogether, although as a member of the family and the future master of the entailed estate he profited from it. Thus developed this strange, but probably very convenient, division of roles between father and son that lasted up to the negotiations at the Congress of Vienna: the father took the part of the head of the imperial counts and acted in their interest, and the son the role of a disinterested, neutral—almost aloof—mediator.

A historian cannot simply accept this division of roles. Franz Georg, after all, acted in the interests of the whole family. We therefore have to take a brief look at the special position he had at the Imperial Diet, if we want to explain why the Metternich family did not end up on the losing end following the dispossessions on the left bank of the Rhine. Franz Georg might not have been very astute financially, but he was masterly at navigating the jungle of imperial law and its institutions: in this, he had decades of experience. The Catholic faction of the College of Imperial Counts had been in a state of complete inactivity before Franz Georg von Metternich was elected as head of the Catholic counts[31] and revived its institutions (the committee, the chancellery, and delegation). He reestablished the counts' Diet, made sure that the coffers of the collegiate were filled again, and now, in 1802, took charge of lobbying activity in relation to the question of compensation.

In order to establish the total value of the estates he had lost on the left bank of the Rhine, Franz Georg asked his councillor and chief magistrate for the "dominions in the empire," Knoodt, to draw up a comprehensive tabular list, on which we find two imperial dominions (Winneburg and Beilstein), four dominions (Oberehe, Rheinhardstein, Pousseur, and shares in the fiefdom Monclar), three offices, three towns, thirty villages, eighteen "Burgfriede" [a jurisdiction associated with a castle] and verges [*Hofbezirke*], nine local jurisdictions [*Gerichtsbarkeiten*], fifty-eight farms, fifty-four mills, and four wineries (in Mainz, Trier, Beilstein, and Koblenz). Various privileges were associated with these, the most important being the sovereign right to coinage, many dependent fiefdoms, fifteen patronages, and many foundations. The dominions and estates produced an annual yield in rent of 62,611 guilders. For all possessions, including the buildings and capital claims, the sum was 3,127,066 guilders. Reparations for war damages sustained during the years from 1792 to 1802 were listed separately and came to 438,850 guilders.[32] Reparations were not under discussion at Regensburg. But in the case of the remaining three million or so guilders, we may assume that the calculation was generous. In terms of territory, the Metternich family had lost two and a half square miles, with a population of 6,400, left of the Rhine.[33] Franz Georg encouraged others to make similar calculations so that he could present a survey of the total demands to the deputation at Regensburg.[34]

On March 2, 1801, Franz Georg gathered together the Catholic imperial counts to discuss a shared strategy. He wrote notes, protocols, and memoranda to the emperor; to his plenipotentiary at the deputation, Baron von Hügel; to influential members of the deputation; to the Russian ambassador in Regensburg, Baron von Bühler; to the French ambassador, Laforest; and to the Prussian state and cabinet minister, von Haugwitz.[35] He also sent a personal note to the French foreign minister, "Citoyen Talleyrand," who replied, in very polite terms, that he had presented Metternich's letter to the First Consul—that is, Napoleon—who had gladly received the gratitude that Franz Georg, as the head of the Westphalian Catholic Bench of Counts, had shown toward him. Napoleon was also grateful for the mediation offered, and said he would help every single member of the German empire.[36]

Franz Georg made use of the full arsenal of tools he had acquired over a long life in politics, a life that had given him the self-confidence to write to the highest political representatives as though he were their equal. Without his lively initiative, the interests of the imperial counts, and of his own house, would simply have been ignored. He was at the center of all activity, and this gave him a self-confidence on which his son commented as follows: "My father hoped that his love of the fatherland would find an opportunity in the immediate future of contributing to the strengthening of the Empire."[37]

Following the Principal Decree of the Imperial Deputation, Franz Georg received the former imperial abbey Ochsenhausen, near Ulm, as compensation. Its status and size meant it afforded the Metternichs imperial immediacy, and they thus regained an imperial estate that gave them a seat in the Imperial Diet—a legal substitute for the dominions of Winneburg and Beilstein on the left bank of the Rhine. Franz Georg might well have considered it promising that the emperor, as described above, at the same time raised him to the rank of an imperial prince. This awakened in him the false hope that the empire might continue to exist in a consolidated form, as all the rituals of the Constitution, such as his elevation, were carried on as before. In the summer of 1803, Clemens visited his father when he officially took charge of Ochsenhausen as its new sovereign lord.

From his "observation post" in Dresden, Clemens learned to take on a more realistic and therefore more critical perspective. He used his position to learn more about diplomacy, and he made the most of the special advantages attached to the post of ambassador at Dresden: the Cabinet in Berlin, which, when it came to imperial politics, preferred to keep its intentions hidden, had to reveal them to the Court of Saxony in order to persuade it to take its side against Austria. The relationship between the Russian court and the Cabinet in Vienna was tense. Dresden offered various possibilities for contact with the Russian ambassador to Saxony, and so for gaining some insight into the tsar's deeper motivations. Metternich was soon able to use these experiences in practice: not long after his visit to Ochsenhausen, he was appointed to the embassy in Berlin.

BERLIN, 1803–1806: THE AMBASSADOR ON THE GRAND DIPLOMATIC STAGE

The Initial Situation: The Path into the Third Coalition

His appointment to Berlin turned Metternich from an observer into an active negotiator. He joined the highest level of diplomacy: the level at which the major powers negotiated war and peace in Europe and, in particular, at which they formulated their strategy for dealing with the French First Consul, then pushing for hegemony over the Continent. As a young man, Metternich had partially observed the War of the First Coalition (1792–1797) from his father's office in Brussels. The War of the Second Coalition, during which Napoleon had taken charge of French forces, he had predicted while at the congress in Rastatt and then observed as a private imperial count in Vienna. After a short peace, he observed renewed hostilities between France and England, which broke out in May 1803, while Metternich was in Dresden. The War of the Third Coalition (1803–1805) was looming. This war took on broader dimensions: Napoleon began to challenge England's maritime superiority in the Mediterranean, in the Ionian islands, at the Bosporus, in Alexandria, and in North and

Central America.[38] This conflict turned into an imperial and commercial competition on a global scale. In order to be able to sustain it, Napoleon expanded the French fleet significantly and strove to establish his dominance over the European Continent. There was only one way of resisting this, and that was to find allies and form coalitions. Vienna, Saint Petersburg, London, Berlin, and Paris were the five centers of European politics at the time, and Metternich was in the most important of them, for it was in Berlin that it would be decided just what form the coalition would take.

Three aspects that would become important for Metternich's career must be highlighted at this point. First, his new post meant that he was now at the political center of Austria's "arch-enemy," which he had described—and witnessed, while in Dresden—as the destroyer of the old empire. He now had to use his political skill to keep his views hidden while looking at the disastrous chasms between different factions in the Cabinet in Berlin. There was a split between a peace grouping and a war grouping, in the middle of which an anxious monarch, Friedrich Wilhelm III, and his similarly anxious foreign minister, Haugwitz, pursued their policies with even less of a plan than Thugut—of whose politics Metternich had so disapproved. The ambassador nevertheless worried about Prussia's persistent attempts at territorial expansion at the expense of its neighbors; and he was right to be concerned, because "in no other period of its history" had the Prussian state grown as much "as in the two decades between the death of Friedrich and the catastrophe of Jena" in 1806.[39] Second, in Berlin Metternich came into close contact with Russian politics, meeting the young Russian tsar, Alexander I, for the first time, and gaining his trust. And third, he was able to study how the War of the Third Coalition failed because of Haugwitz's misguided diplomacy, Alexander's misdirected ambitiousness, and the dilettantism with which the war was conducted. This led to catastrophic results for Austria, both on the battlefield and in the field of diplomacy.

The (Self-)Instructions of November 5, 1803

Upon taking up his second post as ambassador, Metternich again received a document with instructions. It reveals both the political goals that his patron, the foreign minister, Cobenzl, had set out for him and, at the same time, his own expectations and intentions: the writing style and manner of argumentation are such that we cannot but conclude that Metternich had been personally involved in its drafting.[40] The instructions emphasize that Metternich had—just as he had done before taking up his post in Dresden—studied in the archive of the state Chancellery, reading up on the most important negotiations with the Prussian court and deepening his already "thorough familiarity with European matters in general."

The instructions set out a new political rationale for the Habsburg Monarchy, one that had developed out of the Peace of Lunéville. The surrender of the Austrian Netherlands and Lombardy was seen as positive because these areas were far away from the core countries and therefore difficult to defend; furthermore, as they were an arena for the clash of Austrian and French interests, they were always exposed to foreign assault. The policies of Austria and the allies of the coalition after 1789 had predominantly aimed at "the repression of the principles of the French Revolution at their source," and had undoubtedly failed in achieving this aim. Yet it could not be denied that this very same goal had largely been achieved by the First Consul, Napoleon, for he had succeeded in restoring domestic order to France and in reestablishing a "form of government similar to a monarchy." It was important for peace in Europe, the document said, that Napoleon continued to be successful in this.

The instructions were uncertain regarding Napoleon's broader plans and did not exclude the possibility that he had "dangerous intentions" that aimed at the "establishment of a lasting despotic rule over the other European empires." Resistance mounted by one country alone, however, would only exacerbate this situation by granting Napoleon further victories. The only means of setting limits to his ambitions was an alliance among the major European powers. This expresses the goal and the principle informing Metternich's politics with regard to France up to 1815, whether in his actions as an ambassador or as a minister.

The Policy of Appeasement toward Napoleon and the Rapprochement with Russia

The instructions spelled out two concrete aims. On the one hand, the idea was, whenever the opportunity arose, to convince Napoleon of Austria's peaceful intentions. On the other, the old unanimity between Russia and Austria was to be reestablished, as it was only the disagreement between them that made Napoleon's superiority possible. When the document says that the rapprochement between Russia and Austria had to be seen as "the first and most indispensable step toward securing a European balance," it sounds as though this came from Metternich's mouth verbatim. The first aim provided the framework for a policy of appeasement. In order to appease Napoleon, Austria had of its own accord guaranteed its complete neutrality in the case of a war between England and France, and it even documented this in form of a "patent of neutrality" [Neutralitätspatent] for all Austrian harbors and ships. If French troops were to occupy Hanover, the instructions said, Austria would refrain from commenting on this in diplomatic or public contexts or at the Imperial Diet. Because the prince electors—including the prince elector of Hanover, who was also the English king—were authorized to go to war with foreign powers, the emperor was not obliged to interfere. Because the French government, and its ambassador in Berlin, Laforest, were already watching with suspicion the first signs of a rapprochement between Russia and Austria, the Austrians would have to achieve an almost impossible feat: to behave with reserve toward Laforest, without giving the impression of being aloof, but also to avoid giving the impression of any rapprochement with France in order not to be compromised in the eyes of Russia. Under no circumstances, however, should the French ambassador be permitted to notice that Austria was about to prepare "the way for future . . . friendly tripartite relations" between Austria, Russia, and Prussia.

This was the art of high diplomacy. In the terminology of the day, instructions of that nature were called "the official version" [Sprachführung]. When Metternich was later accused of being two-faced, scheming, or even mendacious, especially by Napoleon, this was actually no more than a description of this diplomatic practice: one did not reveal one's intentions publicly, for fear of undermining one's plans from the outset. We shall have ample opportunity to demonstrate how Metternich strategically pursued long-term goals under the veil of diplomacy, and along the way proceeded pragmatically and made the best possible use of emerging situations in order to achieve shorter-term goals.

The instructions describe the second goal—that of establishing a consensual relation with Russia—as a particularly sensitive task. The relation had, however, recently improved, because the Russian side had made attempts to draw Austria into an alliance against France. The very optimistic expectation in Vienna was that Napoleon would soon become more moderate if the old trust between the tsar and the Austrian emperor were rekindled.

England's interests were judged, soberly, as a potential threat. The British Cabinet wanted free rein in the conquest of further colonies in order to expand their maritime power and thus the country's monopoly in trade. This, however, would be possible only if Napoleon gave up his planned invasion of Britain and instead directed his troops toward the Continent (i.e., Austria). The instructions acknowledged very clearly that the struggle for superiority in Europe was ultimately a preparation for the battle to become a "global player." Of these there could be only two—one continental and one maritime—and Napoleon wanted France to be one of the two. With keen foresight, the instructions noted that Napoleon would never accept the tsarist empire or the

Habsburg Empire as powers equal to France, and thus he would wage wars to reduce both to the status of middle-ranking powers. The instructions recommended a preventively defensive posture in order "to avoid everything that might give him the opportunity to transform the difficult and unpromising naval war into land warfare."

Napoleon, the Enigma

The degree of ambivalence one discerns in the pictures of Napoleon formed by political observers between the time of the Peace of Lunéville (1801) and the Battle of Austerlitz (1805) is remarkable. Metternich also was not yet clear in his judgment of the man. For this reason, it makes sense that he later seized the opportunity to get a closer look, first as ambassador in Paris and then as the ministerial escort to Princess Marie Louise. In 1803 he was undecided on the matter of "whether Bonaparte really carries the insatiable imperiousness and desire to conquer in his heart of which he is being accused from England [e.g., by Burke] and the English followers [in Germany], or whether this man, who is so savvy in matters pertaining to the state, . . . might not be persuaded in future to welcome a moderate system of states." Here we have him: the Janus-faced Napoleon by whom so many opponents were still puzzled during the campaign in France in 1814. As far as prudence permitted, the instructions said, one should examine whether the second interpretation was the correct one, which was the secret hope. The position taken in the document was that Austria was exposed, and it was essential to buy time. The mission required exercising the highest art of diplomacy because all communications had to take place in secret in order not to provoke Napoleon.

Agreement with Prussia

The most difficult task with which Metternich was charged was to reach "a genuine understanding with Prussia," which seemed unlikely for many reasons. The memories of Prussia's expansive power politics had been kept alive in the Habsburg Empire ever since the wars in Silesia in the 1740s, most recently by Prussia's conduct during the revolutionary wars, which was seen as selfish. This dim view of Prussia can also be felt in the instructions: "Fish in troubled waters, and then wait for a gain that may be had with no effort or danger: that is the secret of Prussian politics." However, the text continued, the mutual interests of the two states required the attempt to establish a peaceful relationship. Tensions between the two major German powers were damaging to the public good, benefited troublemakers, and would ultimately be disadvantageous to both states. Nevertheless, one should not harbor any illusions or false hopes. In the face of all the "nonsense" going on in Prussia, it seemed a "moral impossibility" that Ambassador Metternich should display the customary diplomatic friendliness. Malign intentions, especially when it came to legal matters pertaining to the empire, he should pass over in silence, feigning indifference.

Finding His Feet

In December 1803, equipped with the instructions of November 5, Metternich arrived in Berlin. Having familiarized himself with the political situation on the ground, he applied his usual method of getting to know a new city. He provided his superior in Vienna, Colloredo, with a bird's-eye view of Berlin politics that demonstrated his keen insight into the political landscape, even after only a short period of time. On the basis of the geopolitical situation, he concluded that there were only two major European powers whose competition, via their dependent states, could change the shape of Europe: namely, France and Russia.

As early as the spring of 1804, the figure of Napoleon, who had not yet been crowned as First Consul, exerted such a powerful and intimidating influence that any reports that Metternich sent about him were in code. Let us look at a particularly informative example of this.[41] On March 16, 1804, Metternich sent to Vienna an anonymous publication that had been a great "sensation" in Berlin because it alluded to a failed conspiracy in August 1803 in which three royal generals had plotted to attack Napoleon at his residence, the Château de Malmaison.

Bearing in mind that two years later Napoleon had the publisher Palm executed because he refused to reveal the name of an author who had attacked Napoleon in print, it was not at all absurd to write the letter in code. The fear of Napoleon, at this point still in its early days, would soon take hold of almost every politician on the Continent.

The conclusion of Metternich's analysis was that Austria and Prussia, being situated between France and Russia, would be capable of asserting themselves against the powers at either end of the Continent only if they cooperated. By overcoming their characteristic rivalry, which had persisted for more than half a century, the two dominant German powers could found "a new system" on the basis of common interests.[42]

Despite all the crises that ensued, the fundamental consensus with Prussia would be the linchpin of Austrian policies from then on. This was the only way in which Austria under the House of Habsburg was able to remain part of German politics for more than half a century. It lasted as a part of what was

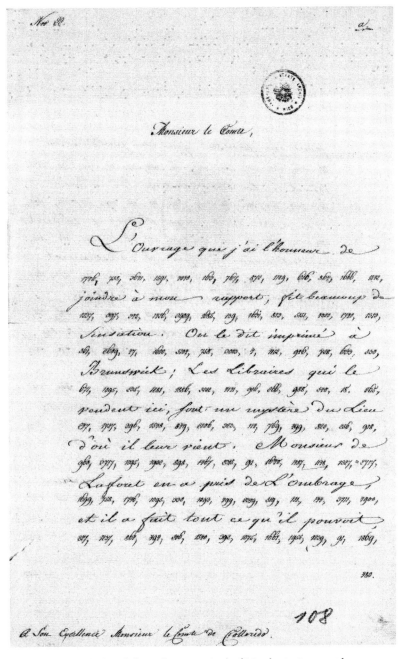

Coded letter (with decoded interlinear version) of March 16, 1804, sent by Metternich as ambassador from Berlin.

understood at the time to be Germany. This also formed the basis of the German Confederation after 1815. On the Austrian side, Metternich, a strategist looking to the long term, was the first to provide a programmatic and diplomatic foundation for this.

The Prussian "Cabinet System": The Paralysis of Politics

Over time, however, Metternich learned that Prussian politics followed its own rules and these followed from the temperament of Friedrich Wilhelm III. With a surprising psychological sensitivity, the ambassador observed that there was one sentiment that ruled over the emperor: fear. He was no longer afraid of Austria. Whichever power succeeded in inducing terror in him would in all likelihood be the one that succeeded in directing the Prussian Cabinet. France and Russia were capable of exerting such influence. Accordingly, after the Peace of Basel in 1795, Prussia pursued a policy of neutrality in order to avoid any provocation. Mere mention of the word "coalition" was therefore enough to make the king defensive and indignant. All this led to what was Metternich's most difficult task in Berlin: bringing Austrian and Prussian politicians close enough together that a written agreement would become possible.

In this endeavor, Metternich for the first time displayed his diplomatic skills at the highest level. He first identified potential opponents to his policies, and he found them in the "cabinet system" that operated at the court. Within this system, the king surrounded himself not only with his ministers but also with personal advisors in whom he placed almost unlimited trust. An advisor could therefore thwart any action from a minister. Among these *éminences grises* were the king's personal secretary and cabinet councillor, Johann Wilhelm Lombard, and the cabinet councillor Karl Friedrich von Beyme. There was also the impracticality of two politicians being responsible for foreign policy: the official foreign minister, Christian Count von Haugwitz, and Karl August Baron von Hardenberg, who would later become state chancellor. Metternich viewed Haugwitz as completely devoid of principle, as perfidious and incapable; Napoleon confirmed this judgment: "Napoleon knew Haugwitz and all the weaknesses in his character, and called him a rogue."[43] When Tsar Alexander I asked Metternich whether he considered Lombard or Beyme to be "the worst," he "could only tell him that one being a French Jacobin, and the other a German Jacobin, the only thing to do was to distrust them both."[44] Both subordinated themselves unconditionally to French politics and believed that if Prussia behaved in a strictly neutral way, it would be spared in Napoleon's drive to expand. The successful enlargement of Prussia over many years seemed to confirm this. Haugwitz, as the third party of the trio, agreed with their evaluation. From Metternich's perspective, it was necessary to circumvent the three of them and approach the king directly, or, failing that, at least to get through to Hardenberg.

Hardenberg was open to the idea of a European balance of power. And he could also be persuaded that an alliance against Napoleon was needed. In his eyes, it would be best for Prussia to join the Third Coalition, which England and Russia had formed on April 11, 1805, and which Austria had subsequently joined on August 9. Hardenberg warned, however, that were Berlin openly to consider joining this alliance, which Napoleon would see as a provocation, the French ambassador could not fail to find out about it, and therefore this way of proceeding was impossible, given the king's reservations. Hardenberg unwittingly confirmed the pernicious effects of the shadow cabinet system when he implored Metternich to avoid those circles close to Friedrich Wilhelm III and meet with the king alone.

The Treaty of Potsdam, November 3, 1805: A Vain Victory for Metternich

It has not been fully acknowledged before that in Berlin Metternich proved for the first time how well he understood how to guide negotiations in such a way that potential opponents come to see themselves as partners in a contract of mutual assistance. Indeed, he succeeded in achieving the impossible: drawing Prussia away from its position of neutrality and bringing it onto the side of the coalition against Napoleon. Emperor Franz expressed his satisfaction with his ambassador by awarding him the St. Stephen medal upon the signing of the Treaty of Potsdam on November 3, 1805. The treaty turned out to be a vain victory for Metternich, for it failed to achieve its aim of uniting the military forces of the countries. But that was not Metternich's fault; rather, the problem was Prussia's disloyalty to the alliance. As we shall see, Prussia did not keep its promises.

We are relatively well informed about the way the alliance came about. Given how diplomats at the time normally negotiated contracts, we can say that the circumstances leading up to the Treaty of Potsdam were nothing short of adventurous. The background to this was the perilous situation of the allies. Approaching simultaneously from the southwest and northwest, Napoleon's forces had very quickly moved toward the center of the old empire—the heart of the Continent. Following the unimaginable disaster of the Austrian army under General Mack at Ulm, his troops had to capitulate on October 17, 1805. Mack had allowed himself to be militarily outwitted by Napoleon. Metternich knew Mack from the War of the First Coalition; in 1793 Mack had had the bold idea of entering into a conspiracy with General Dumouriez of France and

marching toward Paris, a plan that had been roundly condemned at the Antwerp conference. In 1799, after Mack had failed miserably in Naples during the
War of the Second Coalition, Napoleon made this withering assessment of
him: "Mack is one of the most mediocre individuals I have met in my life. Full
of a sense of superiority and full of vanity, he believes himself to be capable of
everything. It would be desirable to see him put on a mission against one of
our good generals one day; he would get to see nice things."[45] In 1805, near
Ulm, Napoleon was that "good general."

Austria's vulnerable position after this defeat implied the urgent need for
an alliance with Prussia. Tsar Alexander's troops had advanced to the border
with Eastern Prussia and threatened to invade if King Friedrich Wilhelm IIII
did not join the alliance. Metternich correctly judged that this would only drive
Prussia into the arms of France. In the end, the tsar made a personal appearance in Berlin, and Metternich spoke with him for the first time. At that point,
his judgment of him was not yet as critical as would later be. Metternich spoke
respectfully but frankly, encouraged by the tsar, who told Metternich that he
was well aware of him from the reports of his envoys. The young ambassador
warned the tsar of the plotting by royal Prussian Cabinet councillors and described the picture as he saw it: it was necessary to sign a common declaration as soon as possible. Napoleon would head straight toward Vienna, and
Austrian and Russian troops needed to confront him together as quickly as
possible. In this, Prussia must lend its support, Metternich said, as the well-
being of all of Europe was at stake. The disaster of Ulm had to be undone as
soon as possible. In his report to Colloredo, Metternich was generous in his
praise for the tsar; Alexander's view of things, his principles and ideas about
how one should act, would have been fully in agreement with those of the
ambassador.[46]

For three days and three nights (November 1–3) the Russian and Prussian
foreign ministers, Prince Czartoryski and Baron Haugwitz; the Austrian ambassador, Metternich; and—highly unusually, given diplomatic custom at the
time—the tsar and occasionally the Prussian king discussed the possibility of
Prussia joining the alliance. The tsar wanted Prussia simply to join the alliance.
Friedrich Wilhelm III, by contrast, wanted, at the most, to offer Prussia's cooperation, an "armed mediation" for which the foreign minister, Haugwitz,
would then be responsible. During negotiations Metternich found his earlier
judgment of Prussia's conduct confirmed: "Prussia is only accustomed to work
when it is clearly for her own benefit; that is all she looks to, and Europe would
disappear before her eyes if it depended on her efforts to save it."[47] Prussia, he
continued, "would have been immovable" were it not for Tsar Alexander's
insistence that it was a matter of personal dignity for him, that he could not

return empty-handed after having agreed to play the role of a "simple negotiator" and having put up with "delays and annoyances of every kind."

The level of courage and perseverance Metternich showed in the course of
these difficult negotiations is clear when we consider the moment when he
risked their failure by insisting on an amendment relating to the possibility that
Napoleon might march on the Austrian capital. In that case, he said, should it
come to an "armed mediation," it would be necessary to insist on a definitive
answer from Napoleon within forty-eight hours. Further, this demand had to
be accompanied by a Prussian declaration that took the form of an ultimatum.
During the slow-moving negotiations, Haugwitz kept coming up with new
ways of corrupting the text; either he ignored from one day to the next the corrections and amendments that had been agreed to, or he found a way of
turning their meaning into the opposite. His overall strategy was obstruc-
tionism. He refused to present to the king the demand for a fixed time for the
ultimatum, which, he said, was "injurious . . . to his dignity" because "the thing
is taken for granted." Metternich countered that "an injury to the king could
never be taken for granted." Haugwitz's evasiveness bordered on the ridiculous: "'We could not fight the enemy,' said he to me [i.e., to Metternich], 'before we had reached him.'"[48]

Metternich himself noted the exceptional course the negotiations took. The
tsar finally began to doubt whether they should be continued in the presence
of the Prussian king. Only once Metternich began to dictate the rhythm of the
negotiations and meet for consultations with the tsar at hourly intervals was it
possible to push through Metternich's amendment. When Haugwitz refused
to present it to the king for final approval, Metternich made a—threatening—
declaration, alluding to Prussia's damaging behavior within the empire, and in
doing so put himself forward as the European politician of the future:

> The Emperor, my master, has always been ready to make sacrifices; we
> have defended your cause as much as our own, and if the approach of the
> enemy to our capital—in case of a reversal in fortune always possible in
> the chances of war—does not alarm us when it is a consequence of de-
> fending the independence of Europe, it seems to me that we have a right
> to demand that it is not left to the good pleasure of the negotiator to hasten
> the matter. We want to finalize all negotiations—within the space of four
> weeks.[49]

Metternich's evaluation is by no means tendentious. He refers to the historically proven fact that during the years following the Peace of Basel, Austria had
"done much more for the defense of the empire and for fighting the growing

French superiority" than had Prussia, which—"shying away from taking action and indecisive"—had retreated from the bloody wars.[50] In the end, on November 3, 1805, the Prussian king signed the treaty on the alliance between the three courts.

The Third Coalition: An Object Lesson in Failing Alliances

Subsequently Metternich watched from Berlin as the policies of the alliance, which were in principle the right ones, gradually failed because of the allies' failure fully to appreciate the threat coming from France. Napoleon had made the formation of a more effective alliance necessary by bringing about the French-Bavarian military pact, which was then joined by Württemberg and Baden. All three southern German states now provided soldiers for Napoleon's army and allowed Napoleon to march through imperial territory toward Ulm and into Bohemia.

Metternich was now deeply involved in military planning, just as he would later be before the Battle of Leipzig. Together with the Russian ambassador, for instance, he took part in a "military conference" arranged by von Hardenberg. Also present at this conference were the British special envoy, the Earl of Harrowby, representing the prime minister, Pitt; the English ambassador, Jackson; General Crenneville of Austria; General von Kalckreuth of Prussia; and the Prussian officers Scharnhorst, Kleist, and Pfuel. At this point Metternich still believed there was a need to speed up the implementation of the measures taken by Prussia and to advance them to the best possible point.[51] He had precise information about the number of Prussian troops and reported the figure to Vienna: 270,000.[52] The Third Coalition still seemed sufficiently united to withstand Napoleon. Metternich was also privy to the deployment plans according to which the Prussian and Russian troops were to unite.[53]

The Third Coalition, however, gradually fell apart, because the obstructive delaying tactics of Foreign Minister Haugwitz, who followed Napoleon from Berlin, via Paris and Brünn, to Vienna in order to arrange the "armed mediation," thwarted the intervention of the Prussian troops. Tsar Alexander, grotesquely overestimating his abilities as a military commander, was not prepared to wait for Archduke Carl's army, which was approaching as rapidly as possible from Italy, despite Emperor Franz's attempts to prevent him from entering into battle. In his memoirs, Metternich made it sound as though the opportunity to surround and defeat Napoleon through the coordinated movement of troops in 1805 outside Vienna had been missed; the chance would arise again only with the "Battle of the Nations" at Leipzig: "If the allied armies, instead of offering battle at Austerlitz, had halted at a suitable distance, the French army would have been forced to fall back upon Vienna, and the Allies would then have been able again to take the offensive with vigour. . . . Thus the chances of war were all in favour of the Allies, and never was a position more grave than that of Napoleon."[54] In fact, Metternich anticipated the judgment arrived at, after thorough research, by Paul Schroeder—namely, that Napoleon's army was highly vulnerable outside Vienna: it was deep into enemy territory, shortly before the beginning of winter, with its flanks and lines of communication unprotected.[55] Metternich had also already recognized Napoleon's simple recipe for success: compensate for numerical inferiority by dividing the enemy's armies and defeating them one after another.

Metternich urged the unification of military forces not only in hindsight but also at the time. Even after the defeat at Austerlitz (December 2, 1805) he implored Hardenberg not to come to an individual agreement with Napoleon but instead, in line with the Treaty of Potsdam, to unite the Prussian troops with those of Austria and Russia as soon as possible. It was necessary, he said, to mount a stubborn and energetic resistance to the common enemy, lest Europe lose all hope of being saved: "the moment for conquering or perishing has arrived."[56] The situation was Metternich's first opportunity to stand up for his understanding of Europe. He argued that Europe should be treated as more than a mere object for tactical maneuvering that focused only on whether Russia, England, or France ended up as the dominant power on the Continent. Rather, he considered Europe to be a space that belonged to the five major powers and had to be regulated by international law, a space in which the five powers should stand in balanced relations with each other and be accorded equal rights. The well-being of Europe, at this point, appeared as Metternich's lodestar, and it already appeared in his firmament in his second memorandum of 1794.

THE PEACE OF PRESSBURG AND THE BEGINNING OF THE END
FOR THE HOLY ROMAN EMPIRE

An Enforced Peace and the Lessons Metternich Drew from It

Metternich experienced the disastrous end to the War of the Third Coalition at the Battle of Austerlitz in Moravia on December 2, 1805, from a distance, in Berlin, as he did Napoleon's entry into Vienna on November 13 and the Peace of Pressburg, which was virtually a coup, on December 26. With these developments Austria lost any power in southern Germany, Tyrol, and Italy (Venice), and was forced to recognize that the prince electors of Bavaria and Württemberg now had the status of kings. It had to recognize, too, the Kingdom of

Italy, newly created by Napoleon. In addition, there were reparations that had to be paid—although the peace treaty did not give an exact figure, they would run into the millions. The end of the Holy Roman Empire had not yet been confirmed, but the path toward it had been prepared. All this made the positions of Foreign Minister Johann Ludwig Baron von Cobenzl and of Cabinet and Conference Minister Karl Baron von Colloredo untenable, and they had to go. Even in these hours of dire need, the emperor and the empire could still draw on the almost inexhaustible functional elite of cosmopolitan imperial counts, barons, and imperial knights. Colloredo and Cobenzl were followed by the forty-two-year-old imperial count Johann Philipp von Stadion, who came from Warthausen in Upper Swabia. As Metternich's predecessor in Berlin, he also had had the opportunity to come to grips with the situation in Prussia. Like Metternich, he was a conceptual thinker with keen foresight, and Metternich therefore now sent him reports from Berlin that went beyond the usual dispatches, developing ambitious programmatic plans for the future of an Austrian politics that would be in the interests of Germany and Europe.

As soon as Metternich had received the exact wording of the peace treaty, his thoughts turned to the empire and especially to Europe, because the contract with the French Empire, as a separate peace treaty, did not end the War of the Third Coalition. The consequences of this seemed to Metternich of incalculable significance: Which side would Russia take? What would be the result of the Prussian negotiations with France? The peace and existence of the Austrian monarchy depended on these questions.[57] At that moment, all Metternich saw was elements "in combustion": "Nothing is in its place" and "one man alone in Europe is at the helm with an all-powerful hand."[58] His country, he wrote, was in a state of "the most complete dependence."[59] Metternich felt that they had been betrayed by Prussia because Prussia had used the enforced peace negotiation as a pretext to deny Austria any military support.

As there was no master plan for peace in Europe, and Napoleon was not even interested in developing one, Metternich set out a political plan in an article that dealt with the form Europe had to take after Austerlitz and Pressburg if a halfway stable balance between the powers was to prevail. In this article, Metternich again showed that he wanted more—and was capable of fulfilling more—than just the role of an ambassador. At the time, an ambassador would normally act as a medium through which the will of his court and the responses of his host country would be communicated, and if possible he also reported back on the mood of the country or relayed accounts of the various characters in his surroundings. Metternich, by contrast, attempted to actively participate in politics, providing his government with papers—a "plan," a "memorandum," or "pro memoria"—with data, tables, and sketches. In this way, he recommended himself, should another catastrophe occur, as a natural successor for the office of foreign minister. In 1809 he was appointed to that very post.

The fundamental points of his plan of January 1806 provided answers to the open questions regarding the Peace of Pressburg. It was Metternich's intention to provide a solid foundation for Austrian politics. What he in fact achieved is difficult to assess. He was also not acting entirely on his own, as Friedrich Gentz, at the state Chancellery in Vienna and thus at the very center of things, participated in the development of plans. With 4,000 guilders Gentz was a well-paid but not permanent employee. The two mostly agreed in their aims and norms, and this did not change when Gentz began working for Metternich at the state Chancellery, although the Prussian Gentz was more doctrinaire, emphatic, and suggestive in the way he argued, while Metternich was more rational, pragmatic, and disinterested.

From Berlin, Metternich analyzed how it might still be possible for the old partners in the alliance, Austria, Russia, and Prussia, to reaffirm their pact. They should enter into a purely defensive alliance. Metternich suggested creating three lines of fortresses between the mouth of the Weser in the north and the delta of the Tagliamento in Friaul, northern Italy. Western Europe beyond these lines should be entirely abandoned to be ruled by France, whose power was impossible to counter at present. Further, the integrity of the Ottoman Empire should be guaranteed, as it was increasingly coming under threat from Napoleon's expansion in the Mediterranean. The allies would offer to mediate between France and England with the aim of establishing peace. Russia would make peace with France and recognize the title of emperor and king for Napoleon and also for any subsequent French kings. The military system of the three powers, Austria, Prussia, and Russia, would be divided into three zones: the right wing was to be formed by the Prussian and Saxon armies; the center and the left wing by the Austrian army; and the Russian army would form a reserve standing army of 100,000 in the Polish possessions. The remaining Russian army could be placed in lines farther east, permanently at the ready.

This concept was based on the idea that there were western and eastern confederations facing each other. The latter, Metternich thought, should proclaim its aims and foundations in a manifesto. This is how Metternich conceived of a system with a structured balance in which France, as the dominant power, would be contained. Of course, Napoleon would never have entered into a contractual relation of this nature voluntarily, and in his unbridled and potentially global ambition to expand, he could not be tamed. Although this sketch never made it beyond the planning stage, it nevertheless shows us how Metternich would think in the future. His thinking always cast Europe as a whole and sought to balance the interests of the major powers. These he wanted to tie together in a lasting, contractually agreed-upon system of peace, backed by military arrangements and zones of influence that were also to be contractually agreed upon.

The German Question and the Continued Existence of the Holy Roman Empire

Metternich's plan for Europe pointed toward Franz I renouncing the office of emperor of the Holy Roman Empire, but it had nothing to say about how to solve the German question. The Treaty of Pressburg, which included Bavaria, Württemberg, and Baden "as allies" of Napoleon, was the extreme unction of a dying empire. But it was not dead yet, for the princes of Bavaria and Württemberg, who had become kings, and the margrave of Baden, who had been promoted to grand duke, were now, as the contract stipulated, formally sovereign "but without ceasing to be members of the German federation." In the French original: "sans néanmoins cesser d'appartenir à la Confédération Germanique." The term "Holy Roman Empire" was no longer used. The text of the contract spoke instead of the Habsburg ruler as "His Majesty, the Emperor of Germany and Austria."[60]

From his post in Berlin, Metternich had to find out the Prussian stance on the German question after Pressburg. For this, Hardenberg was the only person to turn to, as he had distanced himself from Haugwitz and his politics in confidential conversations with Metternich. During those weeks, Hardenberg had put forward his own plans, which showed that he considered it necessary to find a new Constitution for the German empire, one that would combine within a federal system the interests of the Prussian state, French predominance in southern Germany, and the tradition of the old empire, thus transforming the old imperial federation into a federal association.[61]

Hardenberg had allegedly been ill in bed during the lively negotiation of the Potsdam alliance. The most serious provocation for him was the offensive and defensive alliance that Haugwitz had single-handedly agreed to with Napoleon in Schönbrunn on December 15, 1805, thereby terminating the alliance of the War of the Third Coalition. For the second time, Hardenberg offered his resignation to the king, and for the second time the king did not accept it. Friedrich Wilhelm III refused to sign this contract agreed to by Haugwitz because he still believed that he could maintain a position of "armed neutrality." In Paris and Berlin, the strictest silence was kept regarding the deal. Metternich recognized that this agreement between Prussia and France fundamentally put into question Prussia's role within the alliance—Prussia "could no longer be counted among those who only desired repose and stability in Europe."[62] The Prussian occupation of Hanover necessarily led to a military and trade war with England. It was of more than just symbolic significance that early in 1806 the French foreign minister, Talleyrand, received the star of the Prussian Order of the Black Eagle; the medal was for the first time made of diamonds, worth 60,000 crowns.[63]

Metternich was already preparing to leave Berlin for Saint Petersburg, where he was to take up the post of ambassador, when he learned, with alarm, of the secret alliance between Prussia and France. He needed to find out more before leaving, and he delayed his departure in order to confront Hardenberg in person on March 7, 1806. He pointed out to him that Prussia had completely isolated itself and had given up its independence by becoming "directly included in the devastating progress of Bonaparte's policy."[64] The Constitution of the German empire would soon be fully destroyed as a result. Because Metternich was certain that Hardenberg would give evasive answers, he deployed a strikingly modern technique, one that journalists today sometimes resort to for particularly difficult interviews: he sent Hardenberg a list of questions in advance. In this way, he aimed to force Hardenberg to make binding statements. Hardenberg's answers served as the basis for his memorandum to Stadion, the drafting of which kept Metternich in Berlin until mid-April.[65]

The core of Metternich's questioning concerned the future of the empire. Metternich wanted to know whether the new situation would still allow for a close association with Austria that would enable the two powers to defend themselves against "foreign pressure"—that is, pressure from France. Did the new contract with France still allow "a mutual guarantee of possessions" between Prussia and France? And would Prussia "agree to a convention by which the influence of the two powers in the German empire can alone be equally maintained?" Hardenberg gave identical answers to each of these questions, referring Metternich to opinions of his of which Metternich was already well aware, but then also evasively to "the feeling of the future ministry." This answer, repeated through the use of "idem," was unhelpful. As Metternich assumed, quite rightly, that the empire still existed, he pursued the matter more concretely by asking whether Prussia would "instruct her Comitial ambassadors in their future deliberations of the empire, to agree with the Imperial voice" (i.e., to not to support French interests, as Haugwitz had done). Hardenberg declared "that the King is personally much inclined to such an alliance."

As a political realist who was yet committed to principles, Metternich always kept an eye on the military situation. Thus, he also asked Hardenberg about "the possibility of a system of Imperial defense," alluding to the suggestion of a line of fortresses he had put forward in his European plan. "It cannot be concealed," he wrote, "that a line from the North Sea to the Croatian frontier, and formed of the united forces of Austria, Prussia, and Saxony, must be a great advantage for that part of the kingdom, and prevent it from being so easily threatened by France." In this context, too, Hardenberg revealed the paralyzing division in Prussia's foreign policy. He quite agreed with Metternich, and he assured him that his own efforts were directed in a similar way but that he feared "that Count Haugwitz was so in love with his work that he was under the illusion that he had gained all guarantees that Prussia needed."[66] Metternich's final question, whether Prussia would "in no case allow the French army to march through her states to the obstruction of trade," reveals his determination. Hardenberg was left with no other choice but to openly admit Prussia's political and military failure, saying that this question "can only be answered according to the measure of the weakness shown so far."[67] The answers Metternich received made it clear to him that the monarchy of the Hohenzollern could not be seen as a political partner at that moment in time.

His time as ambassador in Berlin marked an important step forward in Metternich's career. He had the opportunity to negotiate vital questions about the fate of Austria at the highest level; to prove his competence as a diplomat and politician by making programmatic suggestions and showing superior skill in negotiation; and to establish close ties with future leading figures in Europe, such as Tsar Alexander and Hardenberg. But the greatest test of his abilities still lay ahead, and it could come in no other form than a confrontation with Napoleon. It took place sooner than expected because the French emperor himself had set in train developments that would see Metternich go, not—as planned—from Berlin to Saint Petersburg, where the post of ambassador had become vacant after Stadion's departure, but instead to Paris.

5

WORLD WAR

Outset and Intensification, 1806–1812

The Napoleonic "World War"

The year 1806 began a new chapter both in the history of Europe and in Metternich's biography. We give it the title "world war." This may sound like an artificial attempt at making the past more relevant to the present and therefore more important, but such a suspicion would be unfounded. Recent research has become less reluctant to identify "world wars" that occurred before those of the twentieth century. "On the lookout for traces of early 'globalization,'" such research has discovered "transnational, transcontinental, or transcultural elements."[1] This perspective moves away from a narrow focus on national traditions and identifies global dimensions in events as early as, for instance, the Seven Years War in the mid-eighteenth century.[2] Strangely, this sort of approach is rarely adopted in works on the Napoleonic Wars, even though the subject matter lends itself to it. In 1876 the historian Wilhelm Oncken, a representative of national liberalism from Giessen, wrote: "The world war of 1813 was about the very existence of the Prussian state."[3] But his perspective was limited to this one year, and furthermore was captivated by a romanticized vision of the "Prussian uprising" that lost sight of the fate of Europe and the wider world. From a British perspective rather than a Prussian, that of Tim Blanning, the limited deployment of Austrian and Prussian divisions in 1792 was a spark that ignited a conflagration that could easily have "escalated" into a "world war."[4] This thought, however, was not pursued further at the time. Only more recently has the more fundamental question of whether the Napoleonic Wars, taken together, constitute a "world war" been asked.[5]

It is indeed the case that the effect of these wars reached beyond Europe to the Americas and Asia. And they possess two characteristics—beyond their sheer geographical dimensions—that suggest that they were something more significant than the Seven Years War and that it is even more plausible to think of them as constituting a world war. First, Napoleon's wars aimed at global dominance, something of which he wanted to deprive the British empire and the tsarist empire. And second, according to Christopher Bayly, the Napoleonic system of states and military system created an "explosive combination of military ambition and financial need which had driven on the world crisis from its origins."[6] His "global history" of "the birth of the modern world" is informed by the perception of a "world crisis" between 1780 and 1820 that culminated in a "world war." The first impulses were provided by the American and French revolutions and "penetrated deep inland in every continent. Cairo, Moscow, Delhi, Jogjakarta, and Paris, all great and famed political and commercial centers, had fallen to conquering armies."[7] To this list should be added Vienna, Berlin, Madrid, Lisbon, and Rome.

In the context of this "world war," the period between 1806 and 1815, dominated by the figures of Napoleon and Metternich, forms a unity. Its substance can be defined in terms of the establishment and consolidation of the Napoleonic Continental System and its subsequent destruction. In more concrete terms, the period includes the final collapse of the Holy Roman Empire, the creation of the Rhenish Confederation as a system of alliances, the degradation of Prussia and Austria as major powers in the Wars of the Fourth and Fifth Coalitions between 1806 and 1809, the attempted degradation of the tsarist empire during the campaign of 1812, and finally the defeat of Napoleon in the War of the Sixth Coalition between 1813 and 1815. Any peace agreement into which Napoleon entered during this time was only a truce before the next campaign. This is the story to be told in this and the following two chapters.

The Lasting Importance for Metternich of His Recollections of the World War

Metternich felt that taking up his post as ambassador in Paris was a fundamental turning point in his biography: "This was, in fact, the beginning of my public life."[8] This might have been an exaggeration, but it correctly reflects what the consequences of this step were, because in Paris "destiny had placed [him] face to face with the man who at this epoch ruled the affairs of the world."[9] In all his written recollections and, years later, in his memoirs, Metternich returns again and again to the battle over the fate of Europe during the years 1806 to 1815, a battle that, in his own view, was a personal duel between him and Napoleon. For Metternich, the climax of this was the unparalleled and famous trial of strength that was his meeting with Napoleon at the Palais Marcolini on June 26, 1813, in Dresden, which lasted more than eight hours. At that time, Austria had to decide whether to become actively involved in the war. For Metternich, this period of his life and this period of world history formed a unity. If we employ the image of a "duel," then Metternich probably would have thought that he had emerged victorious, and he would, accordingly, remember this time more fondly than any other. The editorial presentation of his memoirs may be inadequate, but it reflects fairly accurately the uneven weights Metternich assigned to the different phases of his life. The thirty-three years from his birth to the end of his time as ambassador in Berlin, in the spring of 1806, take up one-fifth of the text, whereas two-thirds of the text is devoted to the time of the world war, the period 1806–1815. Under the title "The Dawn of Peace," the following thirty-eight years, between 1815 and the date of the last entry in his memoirs in 1853,[10] make up less than a tenth of the text, while the chapter on 1813 and 1814—"History of the Alliances"—makes up just about a third.

It is not that Metternich did not have time to devote himself to his memoirs. He lived a long life, and he had a good decade in which he was no longer holding any position: ample opportunity for writing. He used this time to compose from memory various vignettes of political personalities and events, only some of which have been published. But he was not prepared to combine these pieces into a coherent account of the time after 1815. The reason for this was not that he considered this period of his life less important than the period before; rather, he considered it self-evident that the documents in the state archives would shed sufficient light on these events for future historians. The same did not apply to the war years, especially 1813–1814. For these years, he felt justified in drawing on his insider knowledge to provide much more forthcoming autobiographical reflections.

AMBASSADOR IN PARIS, 1806–1809: IN THE "LION'S DEN"

There is probably no other period in Metternich's life about which we know as much as his time as Austrian ambassador in Paris.[11] From there, he observed and commented upon fundamental upheavals, even those as distant as the Prussian catastrophe at the Battle of Jena-Auerstedt, the formation of the Rhenish Confederation in the context of the decline of the Holy Roman Empire, the degradation of his own house of imperial counts through mediatization, the Treaty of Tilsit, the war in Spain, and the Congress of Erfurt. These events will be discussed in separate sections of this chapter, but only to the extent that they help to explain the development of Metternich's thinking and action. Most importantly, this chapter aims to make clear the extent to which his close engagement with Napoleon during this time awakened and consolidated the "strategist and visionary" in him.

His time in Paris was dominated by the central figure of Napoleon, and thus a biographical account of that period must take heed of this fact. Our guiding question will be: To what extent do Metternich's principles, judgment of Napoleon, and political aims truly correspond to the picture he painted of these as an aging statesman? Did he really have the insight, at the time, that Napoleon was striving for "world domination"? And did Metternich from the very beginning systematically pursue the aim of subverting the emerging French hegemony in Europe?

Paris, the Political and Cultural Capital of Europe

The office of ambassador brought Metternich to Paris for the first time, in a career progression that catapulted him into the highest diplomatic post of the foreign ministry.[12] Paris must have stirred ambivalent expectations and feelings in him. In political and social terms, the metropolis appeared to him a revolutionary hot spot, the very source of the attempt to destroy the European social order. The threat of Napoleon's dominance and the failure of the Third Coalition, especially of Austria, which was made clear by the Treaty of Pressburg, had filled Metternich with forebodings. For Metternich, on December 2, the day of the Battle of Austerlitz, Europe had taken on a new shape. He considered the date to be as crucial as July 14, 1789: the latter date, he wrote, had begun what had now been completed. In his analysis of the contemporary moment—January 1806—he fell, as he always did when he reflected on history and on the future, into the role of the visionary who looks far beyond his own generation, sometimes to the end of the nineteenth century, and on one occasion even into the twentieth century: "The world is lost: Europe will now burn down, and a new order will emerge only out of its ashes, or rather, old order will make new empires happy. We shall not experience it any longer, the epoch in which laws assert their eternal rights against blind imperiousness; a change in the form of all European states is unavoidable; it will, it must come about; and we shall witness this complete overthrow."[13]

For a member of the German aristocracy who was influenced by the Enlightenment, however, Paris also had another side. Culturally, it still had the aura of intellectual superiority that made it a model for others. Germany's princes, aristocracy, and intellectual elite felt committed to this model from the age of Louis XIV onward. We have seen that Metternich, as an educated aristocrat, was thoroughly steeped in French culture through his parents, his studies in Strasbourg, and—as his library impressively demonstrates—his books. This influence can be seen in his family's correspondence: in letters between the parents and between parents and children, French was taken for granted. And in diplomatic circles, French was of course the lingua franca. To the Parisians, Metternich's French sounded "impeccable."[14]

Metternich's Appointment

Metternich's appointment to Paris was enough to associate him with Napoleon, even if the connection was not as close as would often later—following Metternich's own account in his memoirs—be assumed. It is not exactly that Napoleon had wanted to see him appointed. The actual prehistory is slightly more complicated. Through Talleyrand, Napoleon had communicated that he did not want to see Cobenzl, who was originally meant to take up the post, in Paris. From the negotiations in Campo Formio and Lunéville he knew him as a promoter of anti-French coalition policies under Russian leadership. His name, Napoleon said, was "odious" to Paris. He considered unacceptable all individuals who were associated with "Cobenzl's plotting" and who had favored an alliance with Russia, and he instead wanted "someone from the House of Kaunitz, the genuinely Austrian House, which was associated with the French system for a long time."[15] That Napoleon was thus able to dictate to a foreign government its choice of ambassador and expect close cooperation from the future envoy demonstrates his power.

The suggestion of Clemens von Metternich as ambassador was, however, made by the French ambassador in Vienna, Comte Alexandre de La Rochefoucauld, who had previously been a diplomat in Dresden and had become close friends with Metternich.[16] In April 1806, Metternich's appointment was a fait accompli, but the Frenchman had first to tell Stadion that he had to fill the post in Paris, and the formal appointment of Metternich by the emperor did not take place until May 18, 1806.[17] In Berlin, Metternich had acquired a reputation as a nondoctrinaire, reliable, and able partner in negotiation, and, despite being involved in the formation of the Third Coalition, he had carefully avoided any hostility toward the somewhat marginalized French ambassador, Laforest. Metternich would later write in his memoirs of his diplomatic code of honor, saying that it had "always been [his] habit not to mingle business affairs with personal matters," and that he therefore "endeavored to maintain relations with [his] French colleague on a footing of frank courtesy."[18]

This paid off in the long term: Laforest was a confidant of the foreign minister Talleyrand, who then supported Metternich's appointment.

With ten sections in total, the instructions of July 8, 1806, were more comprehensive than the previous ones.[19] They described the political relations between Austria and France as being in limbo, a fact that would change dramatically in the following two weeks. There were three areas marked as problematic: the resolution of certain questions left open regarding the Treaty of Pressburg; the question of the German Constitution; and the question of Austria's position within the international system of powers, because a peace treaty between the states that took part in the War of the Third Coalition, France, Russia, and Austria, was to be agreed to in Paris. In order to prepare for his new task, Metternich had again studied the diplomatic correspondence between the major courts at the archive of the state Chancellery. In the instructions, Stadion pointed out to him the critical situation faced by the Habsburg Monarchy. Given the continued presence of enemy troops in the countries of the Habsburg Empire it was necessary to assure the French emperor that the intention was to have a friendly and trusting relationship with him. The instructions, however, warned against a formal contractual alliance, because Napoleon's understanding of an "alliance" was that his partner submitted entirely to his will, as the Treaty of Schönbrunn of December 15, 1805, between France and Prussia demonstrated. Yet it was also dangerous to reject such advances outright. A trusting relation was possible only once Napoleon no longer wanted to undermine the imperial authority of the empire.

The Imperial Constitution, said the instructions, would "still exist according to the letter of the contract [i.e., the Treaty of Pressburg], the Empire still enjoys a certain independence, and the head of the Empire still exercises his privileges, though only to a reduced degree, and is able to fulfill his legal obligations."[20] Meanwhile, through its "creatures and agents," France had granted further rights to individual estates of the empire, and the "Constitution of the Empire" came "closer to dissolution day by day, individual members of the Empire are deprived of their political existence, and the head of the Empire every day finds himself more impaired in the enjoyment of his privileges." The instructions spoke of the willfulness of the French court. The appointment of General Murat of France as Duke of Berg and Cleves was nothing other than a use of French military power to assign to "two imperial fiefdoms" to a prince, ignoring that fact that only the emperor had the right to authorize the elevation to a higher rank. A similar provocation, according to the instructions, was the appointment of Cardinal Fesch—one of Napoleon's uncles—as coadjutor to the archchancellor of the Holy Roman Empire, placing him—an outsider— next to the highest office in the realm and thus making him a possible successor to the present holder. The Treaty of Pressburg did not stipulate anything regarding the mediatization of the immediate imperial knighthood; the mediatizations carried out by Bavaria, Württemberg, and Baden were in contravention of the law. Through these violations of the law, France knowingly dealt a "deadly blow" to the empire. The fact that archchancellor of the empire, Dahlberg, personally applied for these mediatizations did not change anything about their status, because Dahlberg had breached his duties and acted against the Constitution.

Given the power relations between the defeated emperor and the victorious *empereur,* it might seem bizarre that Emperor Franz still insisted on the rights enshrined in the Imperial Constitution. In Clemens von Metternich, he had in Paris an imperial count to whom the legal order and the aura of the empire meant a good deal, given the role his family had played in it, and who was himself one of the members of the empire who had been deprived of his political existence. French power did not respect imperial law; it trumped it. This could be seen in practical terms in the question of military recruitment. The German middle states now claimed the old imperial right to recruitment for themselves and provided their new master with troops. When the instructions explained the French behavior as being the result of "the new international law that has been created on the basis of his [Napoleon's] willfulness and superior strength," Metternich recognized in them his own understanding of the law.

The instructions already suggested the possibility that Napoleon might intend "to give the empire an altogether different Constitution." The emperor also hinted that, if worse came to worst, he might abdicate. Thus, the fact that Metternich was tasked with instilling "serious reflection and at least some awareness of injustice in Emperor Napoleon" suggests a certain naivety. At the end of the instructions, in the form of a separate "Resolution," the emperor emphatically ordered Metternich to "do all he can to find out the exact detail of Napoleon's plans regarding Germany, but in such a way that My Monarchy does not get entangled in fresh quarrels."

The Formation of the Rhenish Confederation and Metternich's Delayed Departure for Paris

Metternich departed from Vienna on July 11, 1806. He traveled via Frankfurt am Main to take care of some personal business at a bank before being prevented from continuing his journey by a border authority on French soil, in Strasbourg, on July 23. On this occasion, he experienced for himself for the first time how ruthlessly Napoleon violated diplomatic custom in the pursuit of particular political aims. In his memoirs, Metternich attributed the delay to the

French emperor's wanting to exploit the inexperience of the young Russian ambassador Oubril at the peace negotiations with Russia, something that would have been much harder for him in the presence of Metternich, who was by this point diplomatically savvy. Even if this suspicion was right, the even deeper reason lay in the exceptional energy with which the German princes at Napoleon's court were attempting to get involved in the new foundation of the empire. The actual representative of the old empire, Metternich, would only have been in the way.

Let us remind ourselves of all that happened in the days between Metternich's departure on July 11 and his arrival in Paris on August 2.[21] On July 12, the envoys of sixteen German states signed the draft for a federal Constitution, which had been prepared by Talleyrand. On July 16, all ministers of the allied courts came together in Paris to sign the original document, which had by then been ratified by the French emperor. Napoleon, however, could not be fully certain that the contract was formally valid until the members of the new "Confédération du Rhin" had also ratified the federal contract. That ratification was to take place on July 25 in Munich, and that was reason enough to let Metternich wait in Strasbourg.[22] The whole affair had the character of a ploy to take the emperor of the Holy Roman Empire—the one who was mainly affected— by surprise and to complete the business without him. This by itself was already an unprecedented affront, but Napoleon found a way to top it: on July 22, he threatened Emperor Franz II with a return to war if Franz did not abdicate. He explained this to Austria's special envoy in Paris, at the same time setting a deadline of August 10 for the abdication.[23] On August 1, one day before Metternich's arrival in Paris, the declaration of the sixteen allied states that they would secede from the empire was read out at the Imperial Diet in Regensburg. Franz relented on August 6 and declared that he no longer held the title of Emperor of the Holy Roman Empire. He released the imperial estates from all obligations. "With this, the ancient imperial union was shattered." Napoleon had achieved his goal of "disintegrating Germany."[24]

The Imperial Counts as Victims of the Rhenish Confederation and the Metternich Family

During this time the high politics and the fate of the empire Clemens von Metternich served were once again bound up, dramatically, with the fate of the House of Metternich, for which Clemens's father, Franz Georg, fought. The events in Paris also decided the fate of the ruling immediate imperial princes and counts, and, as in 1802–1803, Franz Georg drew on all of his connections, writing to Talleyrand, to the French ambassador in Vienna, and to the foreign minister Stadion. Stadion replied to him on April 3, 1806, praising his patriotic mind-set and his commitment to the Imperial Constitution and the independence of the counts, and promising "any conceivable protection from the Head of the Empire and all support possible."[25]

The imperial counts had their own plenipotentiary at Paris who fought for the preservation of their elevated social status: Count Friedrich Carl Rudolph von Waltbott Bassenheim.[26] On July 3, even before the draft document on the Rhenish Confederation was made public, Bassenheim reported to Vienna that he had been able to speak with Napoleon in person and explain to him how important it was to preserve the imperial counts as a political estate. But Bassenheim concluded his report saying: "Everything points toward the fact that we are close to the unhappy moment of our political demise."[27]

This evaluation was accurate. The document on the Rhenish Confederation even explicitly mentioned the Metternich family, because it said that "His Majesty the King of Württemberg" now held the sovereign rights over the possessions of the Prince of Ochsenhausen.[28] But the Metternichs were not alone in meeting this fate, and when a French courier, on July 24, brought news of the forthcoming secession of the states of the Rhenish Confederation, a world collapsed at the Imperial Diet. The legation clerk Jacob Chrétien, for instance, wrote in desperation to Franz Georg in the hope that he, as head of the imperial counts, might be able to help him: "It has finally arrived, the unhappy hour at which the German Imperial Constitution is almost entirely unraveled, and the Imperial Diet which existed for so long in this place is even completely destroyed, thus throwing an enormous number of innocent people into utter ruin." As a father, he had to look after three children, and in these expensive times, he had debts of 400 guilders.[29]

Notwithstanding his helplessness, Franz Georg reacted in a seemingly professional manner: he wrote a memorandum. But the form of the memorandum reveals his desperation in a way that moves the present reader, for the only addressee he could think of was, apparently, the posthumous world. He reminded his reader that since the sixteenth century his ancestors, "as free dynasts," had had a vote in the German Imperial Diet and had produced two prince electors, at Mainz and Trier—in fact, there had been three—and he himself had been a faithful servant to the emperor for thirty-six years. His self-perception, that he is nobility of his own right, he justifies by criticizing the "submission to estates which are nothing but . . . subsidiary estates," among which he counts the king of Württemberg. The argument of the memorandum suggests a last, desperate cry for help directed at Prince-Archbishop and Archchancellor Karl Theodor von Dalberg, whom Franz Georg knew well. Dalberg's position as a leading figure in both the old and the new federal order gave Franz

Georg hope that he might be able to act as a "preserver of the Imperial Consti-tution." Massively overestimating what Dalberg might be able to do, he sug-gested to him a change in the Constitution of the Rhenish Confederation in order "to include the congregation of counts cumulatively as an independent constitutive subsidiary estate of the new federation."

Given that Napoleon himself had thought about the question of whether the imperial counts should retain their old independence and be given a voice in the federal assembly of the Rhenish Confederation, Franz Georg's suggestion was utopian. Napoleon's expectation was that if they remained independent, they would vote against France, because they were either Austrians or, at the very least, too closely associated with Austria. The small princes could not be brought into harmony with the sovereigns of Bavaria, Württemberg, and Baden. What France really hoped was that the German empire ("l'Empire Ger-manique") would reorganize itself under a strong and powerful leadership.[30] The two kingdoms and the grand duchy could not have their usurpations le-gitimized in legal terms by the imperial authority of the emperor; they owed their possessions to Napoleon alone and therefore were obligated to him.

In the case of the minor imperial counts, Napoleon was not, however, inter-ested in the principle involved. Dominions such as Hohenzollern-Hechingen, Hohenzollern-Sigmaringen, Salm-Salm, Salm-Kyrburg, Isenburg-Birstein, Ahremberg, and von der Leyen survived as sovereign states. Why, then, not the Metternichs' dominion? In April 1806, Napoleon reminded Talleyrand of the Third Coalition in 1805 and those who took part in it, Austria, Russia, and— almost—Prussia; but most importantly England. For these countries, he said, there was no sacrifice too great to achieve the humiliation of France. He capped his remarks by saying: "It is altogether impossible that the Prince von Metter-nich, who is wholly Austrian, and von Fürstenberg, who is wholly Austrian, remain in Swabia"—we need to add: as independent princes.[31] This makes it clear why, before taking up his post as ambassador, Clemens von Metternich was right to be worried about the continued existence of the Habsburg Mon-archy; Napoleon was obviously already proceeding unscrupulously and will-fully in this matter.

For a long time it has not been clear what the son's attitude to his father's activities as a political lobbyist for the imperial princes and counts was—or even whether he knew about his plans at all.[32] In the context of the Congress of Vienna, Franz Georg would later still appear as a prominent representative for the mediatized. Some have even suggested that Clemens had dedicated him-self so much to high politics and the interests of the Austrian state that he had no particular interest in the fate of the mediatized.[33] As we shall see, we now know that Metternich was in close contact with his father on this matter.

In Paris, Metternich was at the very source of the proceedings that would dictate the fate of, among others, his family, and at the center of it all was Talleyrand, who was at that very moment working on the wording of the document on which the Rhenish Confederation would be based. On August 3, the day after Metternich's arrival in Paris, the new ambassador went to see Talleyrand and, on that occasion, raised the sensitive point that he had been appointed by the emperor of the Holy Roman Empire—not the Austrian emperor. At the earliest opportunity, two days after his arrival, he wrote to his father.[34] He had learned of the official declarations his father could expect to hear in Regensburg: "Our lot has been decided. Although the act which destroys our political existence is an unheard of monstrosity through and through, it is nevertheless no less awful to be the victim. It is a fact that our personal fate could not be sadder; among the new sovereigns, Württemberg is the worst. [In order to justify this judgment,] it certainly suffices to convince oneself that it is especially this court which has brought matters to the point where they are now." Later, Metternich's judgment on the "chicanery" of the king of Württemberg became even more extreme: "We are at the moment worse off than the last peasant in Württemberg."[35] This anticipated a lament that the "red" nobleman of Württemberg, Constantin von Waldburg-Zeil, later expressed even more starkly: "Better a swineherd in Turkey than a nobleman in Württemberg."[36]

Even at this early stage, Clemens von Metternich urged his father to take a step that could ultimately be realized only in 1825—namely, to sell off Ochsenhausen, the dominion in Württemberg, and instead to look for a dominion that enjoyed continued sovereignty within the Habsburg Empire. Clemens pointed out another difficulty the family faced: according to article 27 of the Treaty of the Rhenish Confederation, if they wanted to sell the estates to interested parties from outside the confederation, they had to first offer them to the king of Württemberg.

Even more humiliating was the disciplinary supervision, the resident's duty [*Residenzpflicht*], which stipulated that no prince whose principalities lay within the Rhenish Confederation was allowed to be at the service of any "power foreign to the Confederation" (art. 7). And this was precisely the situation of Franz Georg and—next to him in the hereditary line—his son Clemens. The king of Württemberg informed the newly mediatized Franz Georg of this in a wounding personal letter that asked him to relinquish the title of Royal and Imperial Privy Councillor and Conference Minister in Vienna on the grounds that he was not entitled to serve at other courts if he held estates in a state of the Rhenish Confederation.[37] Clemens assured his father that he would do whatever he could to resolve the matter. "May God grant," he wrote, "that I shall not fail in this nigh on impossible task!" He would follow the principles laid down in the memoranda that the diplomatic secretary Rieff, Franz Georg's legal advisor, had compiled. Clemens had thus actively assimilated the material on the mediatization process that his father had put together.[38]

Both Metternichs, however, would surely have been aware that they were issuing their complaint from what was still a highly privileged position. One of the memoranda, known to Franz Georg, explained that even in the words of the Treaty of the Rhenish Confederation, the once self-governing nobility continued to be a "privileged estate." In concrete terms this meant that all existing domestic and family contracts, entails, orders of succession, and inheritance contracts remained in effect. The innermost core of the nobility had been preserved, and even after 1806 it still retained its status as an estate with the authority to rule. The Treaty of the Rhenish Confederation continued to guarantee the new class of "mediatized princes" significant sovereign rights, such as inferior jurisdiction in civil and criminal matters, local and forestry policing, hunting and fishing rights, the operation of mines and smelting works, tithes and feudal privileges, patrimonial rights over the church, and separate criminal courts for the nobility. Heinz Gollwitzer rightly talks of this bundle of "seignorial and feudal rights" (art. 27 of the Treaty of the Rhenish Confederation) as implying a kind of "subterritorial sovereignty" [Unterlandesherrschaft].[39]

First Meeting with the Empereur: A Lasting Impression

When Metternich introduced himself to Talleyrand on August 3, 1806, he also handed him his letter of credence. Metternich had learned from the "Grand-Maître des Cérémonies," Count Louis-Philippe de Ségur, just how seriously the new French empire took matters of ceremony and etiquette. Ségur had served the Bourbons as ambassador to Saint Petersburg and Berlin, and he now prepared Metternich for the grand ceremony that had recently been reintroduced and that he was about to experience upon his initial audience with Napoleon.[40]

Historians have recently come to see symbolic forms of rule in early modern times not as mere secondary accessories to the "real" Constitution—as they were often seen by older constitutional historians. Rather, the institution of the Roman-German emperor, as an element within a richly articulated system, worked "proactively to bring events under its control, in order successively to present itself as the judge and mediator, as the head and highest authority."[41] Napoleon granted Metternich his initial audience at the very moment that the competition between the "empereur" and the "emperor of the Holy Roman Empire of the German Nation" had been decided. On the day of the audience, August 10, Metternich already knew that Franz II had abdicated. But Franz II's instructions still insisted on Metternich introducing himself to Napoleon as the "Ambassadeur de Sa Majesté l'Empereur des Romains et d'Autriche." Ségur, however, made it clear that Napoleon viewed him as the ambassador of the emperor of Austria only.

On August 10, Metternich faced Napoleon for the first time, in the audience chamber of the Palace Saint Cloud—the palace Louis XVI had acquired for his wife, Marie Antoinette, and the location in which the first consul had been declared French emperor on May 18, 1804. Metternich's later account of his audience with Napoleon painted a picture of the emperor's character through a description of how he presented himself. Metternich had experienced the imperial coronations of 1790 and 1792 and was therefore well aware of the political significance of the symbolism of a genuine tradition; now, however, he watched as Napoleon used such historically authenticated forms of symbolism as a cloak for his imperial, transnational claims to power.

An 1820 essay by Metternich described the audience: Napoleon stood in the middle of the room, surrounded by "the minister for foreign affairs and six other members of the court."[42] Given the significance of the ceremony, we may assume that these were holders of important offices, the archchancellor (Jean-Jacques Régis de Cambacérès), the archtreasurer (Charles-François Lebrun), the grand marshal of the palace (Géraud Christophe Duroc), the master of the horse (Armand de Caulaincourt), the marshal of the empire (Louis-Alexandre Berthier), and the grand master of ceremony (Ségur). Napoleon was dressed in the uniform of the infantry of the imperial guard and wore a hat. Metternich, who was sensitive to issues of ceremony, felt that the latter was "improper" given that the audience was not a public one. For a moment, he was unsure whether he, too, should cover his head. Against the background of this parody of the old imperial offices of state, the hat seemed to him a "misplaced pretension, showing the *parvenu*," a term that Metternich usually avoided using: the emperor was not of "equal social standing," did not possess "standesgemäße Ebenbürtigkeit," as aristocrats called it.

The ambassador thus recognized a psychological weakness that Napoleon, try as he might, could not conceal from a nobleman of an ancient lineage. Napoleon did not remain loyal to his humble background, and he adorned himself with the trappings of the aristocracy. His conduct revealed self-consciousness, even embarrassment. Whereas some today attempt to claim that Napoleon was of average height, Metternich described him as "short and square" ("sa figure courte et carrée").[43] At a later point in his essay, Metternich said that he was "satisfied" that Napoleon "would have made great sacrifices to add to his height and give dignity to his appearance. . . . He walked by preference on tiptoe." His bearing seemed to Metternich to be an attempt to copy the Bourbons.[44] Here, Napoleon gave away one of the fundamental traits of his character: his inclination to put on a show and take on a role. This trait was revealed in many ways. There is the famous portrait by Ingres, which shows him in full regalia on the emperor's throne; there was his inclination to disguise himself in costumes at masked balls. On these occasions, as Metternich remarked, his costumes made use of the contrast between extremes: they showed either extreme simplicity (e.g., the uniform of a soldier) or magnificence (e.g., regalia). As Metternich reported, in order to increase the expressive power of his gestures, he made the famous actor François-Joseph Talma "come to teach him particular postures."[45] Even his use of language in public, especially his army bulletins on victorious battles, involved careful fabrication and fakery. When Metternich pointed out to him "the palpable falsehoods which formed the chief part of his bulletins," Napoleon replied "with a smile, 'They are not written for you; the Parisians believe everything.'" Indeed, he "privately regarded the Parisians as children, and often compared Paris to the opera."[46] His propaganda was part of a grand work of art that aimed to ideologically justify his rule. From the very beginning, Metternich saw through his opponent, saw him as a master of "roles and masks," and this knowledge gave him a secret superiority in his dealings with him.[47]

Metternich spoke of the way Napoleon was dressed at this audience as "ignoble" and yet as intended "to make an imposing effect."[48] Ambassador Metternich observed in his own person what modern developmental psychologists call the "primacy effect," the phenomenon that first impressions often have a lasting influence on one's judgment.[49] He later said that his first impression from meeting Napoleon "had never been entirely effaced from my mind,"[50] and he recalled it even during the most heated meetings with the French emperor. For Metternich, the picture, always present in his mind, of a "parvenu" striving for equality of greatness and social standing in front of an imperial count freed him from any illusions about the "man before whom the world trembled."[51]

And yet there was a mutual fascination between the two. For Napoleon it stemmed from the experience—rare, for him—of being confronted with an independent mind who was intellectually his equal, someone who dared to contradict him, and of whose physiognomy, aura, urbanity, and heritage he was jealous. For Metternich it stemmed from the charisma of a man of deeds and unbridled willpower—something felt by many in Napoleon's presence. Metternich's eyes were always on the future; he already foresaw that, however threatening and powerful Napoleon was, his "rare intellectual gifts"[52] (which were undeniable) would not protect him from his own downfall.[53]

Metternich's recollections of Napoleon do not suggest a "hostile stance" toward him,[54] but nor do they glamorize him. In his letters Metternich often commented on the murderous consequences of Napoleon's politics of war, a topic he even raised openly in conversation with Napoleon in 1813 in Dresden. In Metternich's essay of 1820, one year before Napoleon's death, he examined his erstwhile opponent without prejudice, without emotion, in a distanced and discerning manner. He repeatedly referred to him as a "genius": Napoleon had a sharp mind, was quick to comprehend, and had an extraordinary talent for judging causes and predicting consequences; in addition, he had a particular way of recognizing individuals who might be useful to him. Conversations with Napoleon had a "charm" for Metternich that he found "difficult to define."[55] Napoleon, he said, was able to strip conversations about complex issues "of useless accessories" and reduce them to their essential points. He always found "the fitting word for the thing," and "where the usage of the language had not created it," he invented it: "By the wealth of his ideas and the facility of his elocution, he was able to lead the conversation, and one of his habitual expressions was, 'I see what you want; you wish to come to such or such a point; well, let us go straight to it.'"[56] At the same time, he listened to the remarks and objections directed at him. He took them on board, discussed them, and, if necessary, rejected them. Metternich, for his part, "never felt the least difficulty in saying to him what [he] believed to be the truth, even when it was not likely to please him."[57]

In his essay Metternich also took up the often-asked question of whether Napoleon was fundamentally evil. In answering this question, he again judged like a psychologist. He did not adopt a moral perspective but attempted an analytic explanation. He therefore considered the question inappropriate; instead, he described Napoleon as a divided personality with two faces: as a private person, "without being amiable he was good-natured, and even carried indulgence to the point of weakness,"[58] a good son and father, with the traits one would expect in someone from a bourgeois Italian family. He tolerated excessive behavior within his family circle and was incapable of denying anything to his sisters. His wife, Marie Louise, even erroneously concluded from his conduct that he was so much under her spell that she could direct his behavior. As a statesman, by contrast, Napoleon "admitted no sentiment," Metternich said. He did not make his decisions on the basis of passion or hate: "He crushed or removed his enemies, without thinking of anything but the necessity or advisability of getting rid of them." Once that had been achieved, he forgot them and did not pursue them any further.[59] Obsessed by the mission of representing the interests of a large part of Europe, he did not shrink from the immeasurable individual suffering the execution of his plans entailed; he was like a chariot that, once set in motion, crushes everything that gets in its way.[60] He showed no consideration for those who did not place themselves under his protection—those who did not submit—even accusing them of stupidity. As he was indifferent to the views of all those who were to the left or right of his intellectual and political path, what happened to them was, to him, neither here nor there. This divided personality meant his empathy extended only to cases of petty bourgeois mishaps that occurred in his family and circle of close friends.

There is an incident that confirms the dissonance between the private and the public Napoleon Metternich described. Witnessing Marie Louise in the excruciating pain of childbirth, he turned deadly pale and fled into the adjacent room. Later he said: "If that is the cost, I do not demand any more children."[61] In the face of the unhappiness and human suffering brought about by politics, by contrast, he showed an indifference that bordered on contempt for humankind.[62] His favors and kindnesses he dispensed "in proportion to the value he put on the utility of those who received them."[63] Napoleon himself also confirmed the split in his personality that Metternich observed in him. In a conversation with his minister of justice, Louis-Mathieu Molé, who had been appointed in 1813, he confessed, ahead of the great battles of that year: "Yet don't think that my heart is less sensitive than those of other men. I'm a very kind man [un assez bon homme]. But since my earliest youth I have devoted myself to silencing that chord within me which never yields a sound now."[64]

Metternich recognized in particular the calculating nature in Napoleon's policies regarding the aristocracy. These policies did not follow exclusively from Napoleon's feeling of social inferiority [Gefühl mangelnder Ebenbürtigkeit]. Metternich looked at the foundation of a new aristocracy, and the self-enrichment and redistribution of wealth associated with it, with particular clarity, for he was one of the dispossessed who had to provide the means for making the new riches possible (something he did not say in public). In 1808 he already possessed astonishingly detailed information on how Napoleon's new aristocracy functioned and how the new elite in Europe were able to get rich. Although Napoleon's system is often contrasted with the ancien régime in terms of the lasting "modernization" it introduced, Metternich saw its dark side:

> Europe has been hunted, raped, and it is still being hunted down at the present moment [1808]; ambition, vanity, cupidity, all the passions are put in movement in the accomplices of the great work of destruction. Many will be satisfied by it, but not all; some bait will be necessary in the future: this bait will be sought in every direction, and history offers too many examples of the success of the system of dividing the best of the spoils among the collaborateurs to have escaped the attention of Napoleon.[65]

Marshal Ney had personally told Metternich that he had received 500,000 livres in lease and rent from the estates given to him—in Italy, Poland, Westphalia, and Hanover. The arch-offices alone were worth princely sums: Archchancellor Cambacérès received 150,000 francs annually "ad perpetuum" from Parma, together with the title of duke, the same amount as Archtreasurer Lebrun as the Duke of Piacenza. Master of Ceremonies Ségur, Champagny, who became foreign minister in 1807, and First Secretary Maret—the "Duke of Bassano"—received an income of 50,000 to 100,000 francs each from estates in Westphalia and Hanover. One would have assumed, as Metternich did in 1808, that the intention was also to award the title of duke to Grand Marshal of the Palace Duroc, Master of the Horse Caulaincourt, and the head of the secret police, Savary. The list of regions from which those of Napoleon's marshals elevated to the rank of duke received their income reveals the extent to which Europe was being exploited: Augerau became duke of Castiglione and Masséna; Ney of Elchingen; Davout of Auerstedt; Duroc of Friaul; Caulaincourt of Vicenza; Colonel Arrighi, a cousin of Napoleon, of Padua; and Juno of d'Abrantès.

Fully in line with the methods of the old empire, Napoleon created hereditary titles for his followers, gave them fiefdoms and primogenitures for their families. In addition, there were the rewards for the imperial guard. All officers received a perpetual pension, which could be passed on in direct line to the descendants: 2,000 francs for a captain; 1,000 for a lieutenant; 500 for a second lieutenant. Napoleon's imperial rule, Metternich reported, not only reached as far as the Weichsel river but also diminished the power and resources of the subservient sovereigns who ruled under his protection in the vast empire's provinces. Napoleon, he said, increased his power by placing the extracted wealth in the hands of French citizens, who thus became the richest proprietors in the states of the Rhenish Confederation. Metternich saw the "génie de Napoleon" in the way he seized the new opportunities for enrichment in order to bind others to his person, his heirs, and the spatial expanse of his conquests. Looking back at the War of the Third Coalition, Metternich stated that Napoleon had arranged all his measures such that he now had a huge number of dominions at his disposal. Once again, we see what Metternich meant when he spoke of the overthrow of the old social order, and why he called the French Revolution more social than political.

The French Empire and Napoleon's Emperorship

There can be no doubt that the roles which the old empire and the end of the eighteenth century played in Metternich's biography have so far not been taken sufficiently into consideration in the literature. On the one hand, Metternich owed his self-confidence and his socialization to the European Enlightenment (that is what made him a cosmopolitan), but on the other hand, he also owed them to the legacy of the complex and convoluted legal system of the old Imperial Constitution. This should have become clear through the description of his development so far. It would be too simplistic to look only for mono-causal "influences" that affect a life in a linear fashion. For Metternich, who was historically knowledgeable as well as an attentive observer of contemporary events, the old empire became, in his time at the court of the "nouveau" Emperor Napoleon in formerly revolutionary Paris, a kind of kaleidoscope. Looking through the medium of the old empire at the new one, he saw at least six elements, which stood in sometimes parallel, sometimes coordinated, and sometimes oppositional relation with each other. They were: (1) the great historical tradition of the empire, which he had studied at the universities of Strasbourg and Mainz; (2) the living imperial tradition, which he experienced at the imperial coronations in Frankfurt; (3) the still politically existent Habsburg Empire, which, since 1792, had fought a war against the French revolutionary troops as part of a coalition of the old Europe; (4) the empire as protector of his family, the Count Metternichs and their dominions; (5) the empire that his own father served as one of its highest-ranking servants; and finally (6) the empire that had been transformed into the "Confédération du Rhin," protected by the emperor of France. The latter styled himself as the successor to Charlemagne, and he created a sense of continuity by appointing Dalberg—the last archchancellor of the Holy Roman Empire and prince elector of the most important electorate in the old empire—the prince primate [*Fürstprimas*] of the new Rhenish Confederation.

What, then, did the old empire mean to Metternich? Because he was aware of all these aspects and also had become familiar with the destructive power of the princes of the empire's states, Metternich, unlike his father, considered it impossible that it could still be saved or resurrected at a later point in time. For him, the old empire was no more than a canvas onto which he could project his idea of a future "Germany." In the years between 1806 and 1815, he must have been particularly irritated by the way Napoleon used the elements of that old transnational empire to conjure up his own plans.

Napoleon liked to engage Metternich in conversation about historical topics. Such discussions revealed Napoleon's limited knowledge but also his exceptional talent for identifying causes and predicting consequences. What he did not know, he was able to guess, lending individuals and events his personal coloring in the process. All the while, he returned again and again to the same quotations, which he had taken from a small number of works—in particular, short history books—and within these he would draw specifically from passages dealing with heroic moments in ancient and French history. Metternich reported: "His heroes were Alexander, Caesar, and, above all, Charlemagne. He was singularly occupied with his claim to be the successor of Charlemagne by right and title. He would lose himself in interminable discussions with me in endeavouring to sustain this paradox by the feeblest reasoning. Apparently it was my quality of Austrian Ambassador which I had to thank for his obstinacy on this point."[66] Napoleon saw in Metternich the embodiment of the old empire, and therefore he felt all the more keenly the need to convince him. Metternich was right to speak of a paradox, and it was one of which, of course, Napoleon was also aware: If one is always only one defeat in battle away from losing one's throne, how can one talk of being part of a tradition? The emperor himself acknowledged: "Your sovereigns, born to the throne, may be beaten twenty times, and still go back to their palaces; that I cannot do—the child of fortune; my reign will not outlast the day when I have ceased to be strong, and therefore to be feared."[67] Metternich reached the conclusion that "few men have been so profoundly conscious as he was that authority deprived of this foundation is precarious and fragile, and open to attack."[68]

When in Metternich's presence, Napoleon did not miss any opportunity to protest against the opinion that he had usurped the French throne. The throne, he argued, had been vacant because Louis XVI did not know how to hold on to it. After the king was overthrown, the republic had seized the French territory and abolished the throne: "The old throne of France is buried under its rubbish; I had to found a new one. . . . I am new, like the Empire; there is, therefore, perfect unity between the Empire and myself."[69] With movable pieces of the historical scenery, Napoleon built the backdrop for the stage on which he presented himself as emperor. Following Eric Hobsbawm, modern historians call this the "invention of tradition."

Napoleon revealed to Metternich just how little he thought of continuing or resurrecting the old German empire, despite all his talk about Charlemagne, when on one occasion he mocked the former archchancellor of the empire and now prince primate of the Rhenish Confederation, Dalberg. Having just released Dalberg from an audience, he turned to Metternich:

"Well, what would you have?" said Napoleon smiling: "this man is full of empty dreams. He torments me continually to arrange the constitution of what he calls the German Fatherland. He wants his Regensburg, his Imperial court of supreme judicature with all the traditions of the old German Empire. He tried to speak again of these absurdities, but I cut him short."[70]

In this scene, Napoleon gave away the "secret" of his rule:

> "Monsieur l'Abbé," I said to him, "I will tell you my secret. In Germany the small people want to be protected against the great people; the great wish to govern according to their own fancy; now, as I only want men and money from the federation, and as it is the great people and not the small who can provide me with both, I leave the former alone in peace, and the second have only to settle themselves as best they may!"

Napoleon confessed this to Metternich shortly after he had taken up his post as ambassador in Paris. The former imperial count knew what his own estate should expect from Napoleon in the future: nothing. But from their new masters, like the king of Württemberg, they could expect everything. And knowing how the king of Württemberg treated his nobility, this did not bode well.

Even more astonishing was Napoleon's idea that he derived his supreme authority from a divine origin. In this context, he also referred to the title of the Habsburg emperor: "by the grace of God elected Holy Roman Emperor," on which, according to Metternich, he commented: "It is a fine custom, and plausible. Power comes from God, and it is that place alone where it is outside the reach of men. From there I shall adopt the title in due course."[71] And this was indeed what happened in November 1807 when Napoleon introduced the Constitution of the Kingdom of Westphalia with the formula: "Napoleon, by the Grace of God, and by the Constitution, the Emperor of the French, King of Italy, and Protector of the Rhenish Confederacy"; and this was despite the fact that, as Metternich pointed out, Napoleon was not particularly religious. Catholicism as a religious cult appeared to him as a useful means of preserving law and order in the moral world. Thus, Napoleon's treatment of religion, like his treatment of political power, human beings in general, and the printing press, expressed his opinion that these should all be considered not as values in themselves but only insofar as they can serve an instrumental purpose. Metternich's claim is therefore plausible that Napoleon looked for orientation, not from the authors of the Enlightenment, certainly not from Voltaire, whom he disliked, but from the prophet of early modern power politics, Niccolò Machiavelli, who had also fascinated Friedrich II.[72]

Metternich's instructions for Paris had already described the Janus-faced character of Napoleonic submission, saying he had subdued the Revolution and the European Continent alike. To Metternich, Napoleon seemed to be "the incarnation of the revolution";[73] at the same time, he was "a born conqueror, legislator, and administrator."[74] In one of their intimate conversations, the emperor was revealing: "'When I was young,' he said to me, 'I was revolutionary

from ignorance and ambition. At the age of reason, I have followed its counsels and my own instinct, and I crushed [*j'ai écrasé*] the Revolution.'"[75]

In summary, we should take note of the following points. Between 1806 and
1809, Metternich, as Austrian ambassador, was in a uniquely privileged position in terms of his proximity to the French emperor. It was an "immediate
contact over years—such contact as never existed between Napoleon and any
other person not a Frenchman."[76] This enabled Metternich to pursue the task
he had set himself of impartially weighing the conditions on which Napoleon's
career rested, convinced "that the analysis of this personified product of the
Revolution must necessarily explain to me how this man, from so mean a
starting point, could have raised himself to such a height."[77] The way Metternich approached the object of his investigation in his essay of 1820 revealed him
to be a follower of the historical-critical method of his teachers Koch and Vogt.
He created an impartial distance from his subject by reflecting on "the conditions on which his existence rested."[78]

At the same time, this addressed the question of Napoleon's greatness. It
did not suffice, Metternich said, to emphasize the important characteristics of
strength, power, and superiority that allowed Napoleon to rise from obscurity
in such a short amount of time. Metternich was critical of the fact that "many
useless attempts have been made, and much learning vainly expended in order
to compare Napoleon" to his great forerunners, in the hope of gaining a better
understanding of him, whether the comparison was with "the heroes of antiquity, the barbarian conquerors of the Middle Ages, . . . or a usurper of the stamp
of Cromwell." The "mania for [historical] parallels" distorted real history by
separating the individual "from the setting in which he was placed, and the circumstances under which he acted." The specificities of times and situations
"admit of no analogy."[79]

In order to judge Napoleon's "genius," Metternich wrote, it was necessary
to have the measure of the age in which he lived.[80] With complete detachment,
he described how the judgment would depend on the position taken by the
judge. For those who think the era of the Revolution was "the most brilliant,
the most glorious epoch of modern history, Napoleon . . . was, certainly, one
of the greatest men who have ever appeared." For those, on the contrary, who
thought that he "only had to move like a meteor above the mists of a general
dissolution," that he "found nothing around him but the debris of a social condition ruined by the excess of false civilization [*fausse civilisation*]," and that
he "only had to combat a resistance weakened by universal lassitude, feeble rivalries, ignoble passions, in fact, adversaries everywhere disunited," for those
there was "no danger of exaggerating the idea of Napoleon's grandeur." Antici-
pating the concept of the "invention of tradition," and in allusion to Napoleon's

desire to present himself as aristocratic and imperial, Metternich stated: "The vast edifice which he had constructed was exclusively the work of his hands, and he was himself the keystone of the arch. But this gigantic construction was essentially wanting in its foundation; the materials of which it was composed were nothing but the ruins of other buildings; some were rotten from decay, others had never possessed any consistency from their very beginning. The keystone of the arch has been withdrawn, and the whole edifice has fallen in."[81] Metternich was therefore right in concluding: "I do not think it was a good inspiration of Napoleon's, which called me to functions which gave me the opportunity of appreciating his excellences, but also the possibility of discovering the faults which at last led him to ruin and freed Europe from the oppression under which it languished."[82] Looking back late in life, it seemed to the state chancellor that, by appointing him to Paris, Napoleon had sown the seeds of his own downfall. The story of Metternich's political life that follows seeks, ultimately, to answer the question of whether Metternich's unique insider knowledge from his personal dealings with the *empereur* between 1806 and 1813 allowed him to develop a long-term strategy that, in turn, led to the downfall of Napoleon's "universal monarchy."

Jena and Auerstedt (October 14, 1806): Prussia's Failure to Learn the Lessons from the Battle of Austerlitz

Metternich's main tasks in Paris were to keep track of how Napoleon influenced German affairs and to provide his own judgment of these matters. A further task was to observe closely how Napoleon dealt with other European powers and, wherever possible, to infer from this what next steps the emperor might have in mind, especially with regard to the Habsburg Monarchy, which was just one more ball in this great game of billiards. During his three years as ambassador, Metternich looked at all the old and new areas of conflict on the Continent: the traditional Spanish Empire of the Bourbons, the Prussia of the great Friedrich and his less-great successors, the Ottoman Empire, which was shaken by numerous wars, the vast Russian Empire under young, ambitious Tsar Alexander, the global British maritime empire, and Italy, the peninsula on which the interests of all major powers, except for Prussia, met. All these empires and regions became part of Napoleon's imperial politics, the rationale of which Metternich had to discover. This was going to be the great overarching theme of his time as ambassador in Paris, the aim to which all else had to be subordinated.

We have to keep in mind that the shock of Austerlitz represented a watershed in Metternich's political consciousness. Before Austerlitz, his understanding of how a "universal monarchy" could be prevented by establishing a European balance of power on the basis of political agreement was of a rather theoretical nature. The experience of Austerlitz taught him the principles informing the political worldview that grounded his foreign policy from then on. According to this view, a power like the France of Napoleon could be defeated and dismantled only by a strong and strictly coherent coalition of the other powers. Until 1815 this remained his unchanging mantra. The repeated failures of powers that went to war with Napoleon by themselves confirmed to him how right he was in this conviction. In January 1806, while still in Berlin and with Austerlitz still fresh on his mind, he wrote to Friedrich Gentz:

> With some thirty years I have grown old [Metternich was actually thirty-three at this point]; in terms of conclusions to be drawn my last three years count as much as three decades from any other century. I have seen things from too close up; I know Prussia and Russia as well as I know Austria; I enjoyed extracts of English politics. And what else should save us, if no help springs from the closest union between these powers! . . . Such a union would be necessary in order to topple the colossus of the whole united south and west of Europe. I say *topple,* because *resistance* never helps under such circumstances . . . ; the intention was to *set limits* to the man, to *build a fence* around him; one should have wanted to conquer him, destroy and dismember his Empire.—Who does not want to conquer, he will be conquered.—*The only man in Europe who wills actively* has provided us with terrible proof of this eternal truth.[83]

This passage can be taken as setting out a program that Metternich followed strictly until 1815, even if he sometimes had to make various concessions to Napoleon, concessions that outside observers have erroneously interpreted as opportunism. He pursued a *realpolitik* guided by principles, so to speak, that in the long term did not allow for any compromises with the usurper. The reason for Metternich's strategy, as his explanation reveals, lay in the person of Napoleon, in his untamable and insatiable urge to expand his power.

On September 16, six weeks after his arrival in Paris and barely four weeks before the Battle of Jena-Auerstedt, Metternich declared that war between Prussia and France was unavoidable, but, knowing the Hohenzollern Monarchy from the inside from his time in Berlin, he did not consider it sufficiently prepared for the conflict. At that very moment, he recalled the lesson of Austerlitz, and, with Prussia in mind, leveled an accusation: "If they are prepared to show such character in 1806, why did they not help to save Europe in 1805?"[84] The upcoming war, and every war that was to follow, Metternich viewed not as an individual conflict but as a crisis of the overall system: "We are at a point where Europe is in a horrible crisis."[85] One might almost be tempted to think that he anticipated a criticism of Austria's military adventure of 1809 when he complained about the lack of coordination in the way the Prussian king threw himself into a war that was "not premeditated, but rather the effect of an agitation."[86]

Sheer logic dictated that the war effort had to fail. There was a coalition between Russia, Prussia, and England—the fourth of its kind—against Napoleon, but Napoleon succeeded in breaking it up. For Prussia, the catastrophic but by no means unavoidable defeat at Jena and Auerstedt became the paradigm for military indecisiveness, uncoordinated warfare among the allies, and bad communication between the different troops. England remained at war, but Prussia and Russia, against whom Napoleon had pursued his usual tactic, fighting against them individually and in succession, each signed a separate bilateral peace treaty with Napoleon in July 1807 in Tilsit—treaties, moreover, that stipulated entirely different conditions.

The Treaties of Tilsit (July 7 and 9, 1807): Universal Monarchy instead of the European Concert of Great Powers

For Metternich, the agreement negotiated between Napoleon and the tsar in the Peace of Tilsit on July 9, 1807, meant the final collapse of the European pentarchy, because the two powers distributed continental spheres of influence among themselves, which thus suspended the balance of power among the five major powers, not least because it meant that Russia joined the Continental System. Since 1794, Metternich had learned to think in a global context. Now, he observed Napoleon's splendid and symbolically charged staging of the new dispensation. For the negotiations in Tilsit he met with Alexander on a raft in the middle of the Memel (the Neman), where the edges of the spheres of influence of the two global players met: "They remodelled the whole of Europe. Two empires, one in the west and the other in the east, would draw round them the small confederate States to serve as reciprocal intermediaries."[87]

While the peace treaty between France and Russia was based on the fact of their equality, the treaty Napoleon agreed to with Prussia on July 7, also in Tilsit, was one of submission: it reduced Prussia to a third of its former territory and fixed the tribute Prussia had to pay at an enormous 120 million francs. In his report to Stadion, Metternich rightly judged that the Hohenzollern Monarchy had been relegated from the first league of powers to the third tier of states. This would also worsen Austria's situation. The Rhenish Confederation surrounded it on both sides, and any military conflict with France was necessarily a war on two fronts between the Weichsel and Inn rivers. From this point onward, Metternich would always warn against a bilateral war with France. As these warnings suggest, he was no warmonger, an accusation still leveled against him because of the events of 1809.

It cannot be stressed enough just how peculiar Metternich's reports as an ambassador were. Instead of just exchanging facts and sending materials as an intermediary—which he also did—he used his reports to develop perspectives on the political options open to Austria. He prophesied that the situation in Europe already bore within it the seeds of destruction. The government in Vienna only needed to wait for the right moment because the whole system rested on the life of a single man who had no plan for what was to come after him.

In Metternich's eyes, it was not the Spanish uprising of 1808 that first brought about the turn of events. Napoleon's great "political mistake," the event that began his decline, was for Metternich—not only in hindsight but at the time—the Peace of Tilsit. In his memoirs, he reiterates this judgment, saying that Napoleon's decline "was chiefly the consequence of the false idea he had formed of the thorough exhaustion of the Prussian power."[88] Napoleon's "enormous edifice" did not gain "strength and solidity" because the conditions of the Peace of Tilsit "were so hard and overstrained."[89] Metternich was not alone in offering this evaluation. The French foreign minister, Talleyrand, who had pleaded for the treaty conditions to be more lenient, was also of the opinion that at Tilsit Napoleon had begun to go too far. He had "triumphed, and was therefore inflexible. The promises he had caused to be broken, and those he had obtained, had intoxicated him."[90]

Metternich's judgment was indirect praise for the Prussian reforms and for Prussia's ability to unite all of its social forces in a resistance against Napoleon. He combined this insight with his fundamental principle that only a coalition of the other powers in full agreement could topple Napoleon: "The mistake which the Prussians made in 1805 in not uniting their strength with that of Austria and Russia was renewed in the rising of 1806; and yet it was to this repeated mistake that we owe the liberation of Europe from the yoke which Napoleon's love of conquest had imposed upon it."[91]

The Treaty of Fontainebleau (October 10, 1807): Witnessing Napoleon's Negotiation Tactics for the First Time

One of Metternich's tasks in Paris was to clarify questions that had been left open by the Peace of Pressburg. This was the first time that he took personal responsibility for Austrian negotiations. Essentially, they needed to reach a contractual agreement about the border between the new Kingdom of Italy, which Napoleon had "invented," and Austrian territory. Here, Metternich had his first experience of the ruthless manner in which Napoleon pushed weaker partners around, violating the fundamental rule of international law, the principle of equality [*Ebenbürtigkeit*], or "reciprocity," as Metternich called it.[92] He had "never found more bad faith, more impudence, in any of the tortuous negotiations with which [he had] been charged." Again and again, he was confronted with "new demands and pretensions altogether unjust."[93] Napoleon flatly refused direct talks and negotiated through his foreign minister, Champagny. Champagny presented a map on which Napoleon had personally marked a border running along the Isonzo, adding that there was nothing further to discuss.

Metternich tried to influence Napoleon through the Italian ambassador, Count Ferdinando Marescalchi, to whom he complained: "You demand everything and give nothing."[94] The ambassador, however, warned Metternich that there were many Italian people around Napoleon who might try to get him interested in Trieste as well. Trieste, Austria's only access to the Adriatic, drove a wedge between the new Kingdom of Italy and Napoleon's new conquests in Dalmatia. It was easy for Napoleon to issue threats, as his troops were still in Austria. Marescalchi's advice was to agree to the suggested borderline as soon as possible—before further demands were put on the table. Metternich judged that Napoleon did "not know any limits" and, further, that he had "now completely let the mask slip."[95]

Despite all this, the ambassador also saw advantages for Austria resulting from the negotiations, because Napoleon thought this was the beginning of a new era in their relationship, which would now be characterized by a spirit of understanding. And, indeed, Austria for the first time found itself in a situation in which all questions of borders and possessions had been completely resolved and Napoleon could not make further demands. He even wished for a future alliance,[96] something that worried Metternich; he immediately suspected that the intention behind these overtures was to ask Austria to fulfill its duties and provide military support to help achieve France's aims.

The Continental System (November 21, 1806): Napoleon on the Way toward a Universal Monarchy

In order to conquer the Continent, Napoleon needed an enormous war machine. French military power at times reached 2 million men in arms, recruited from the revolutionary masses, the troops of satellite states—the so-called allies—and mercenaries who hoped to profit from Napoleon, or, like many

Poles and Italians, hoped to achieve national unity and freedom. Napoleon's troops, however, would hardly bring such freedom, for in order to finance the war efforts they had to ask the "cowed or conquered territories" for compensation, contributions, or payments in kind, and rich cities they literally pillaged—as Metternich had seen in the case of Frankfurt in October 1792. In order to compensate for the overseas colonies that had been lost to England, France in addition needed "control of the European economies."[97] The Continental System, proclaimed on November 21, 1806, in Berlin and expanded at the end of 1807 in Milan, was meant to achieve this control by prohibiting the import of any English goods to continental Europe. After the Royal Navy under Nelson, in the War of the Third Coalition, had inflicted a devastating defeat on the French-Spanish fleet in the Battle of Trafalgar (October 21, 1805), making British naval supremacy unassailable, Napoleon needed this tool more than ever.

Napoleon's aim remained to wrest global dominance from the British. He wanted to force them to capitulate through an economic war. This was his reason for trying to hermetically seal the Continent from the influx of British goods. This strategy was popular inside France: it got rid of inconvenient British competition, creating new economic opportunities and giving a massive boost to the French economy.[98] As early as 1808, it caused a severe economic crisis and social unrest in England. The price for the strategy, however, also had to be paid by those countries who did not abide by the Continental System: Napoleon waged war on them—first on Portugal, later on Russia.

With the Treaty of Tilsit in 1807, Napoleon was initially able to include the tsar in the Continental System. For Portugal, however, the system would soon mean war. On August 2, 1807, Metternich witnessed Napoleon threaten the Portuguese ambassador, Don Lorenzo de Lima, at the great diplomatic audience: "That cannot continue; we must have peace or war."[99] Peace, here, meant Portugal joining the Continental System. Napoleon demanded that Portugal at once close its harbors to the import of English goods, confiscate all English property, and arrest all English nationals, regardless of age or sex, as prisoners of war. The Portuguese prince regent was prepared to close the harbors to English imports, but he refused to arrest innocent people on the grounds that to do so would violate their human rights.

At this point Metternich was for the first time personally confronted with Napoleon's untamable will to conquer. Initially Champagny had informed him of Napoleon's ambition to institute a "universal monarchy." The emperor thought that, as Britain was the sovereign at sea, the time had come for a "ruler of the Continent."[100] Anyone who opposed or offered the least resistance would be destroyed, and because he was acting in agreement with Russia, no one would dare to do so. At a large audience on October 15, 1807, Napoleon again addressed the Portuguese ambassador directly: "If Portugal does not do what I wish, the House of Braganza will not be reigning in Europe in two months."[101]

This introduced a new, menacing note into Napoleon's policies, which now not only degraded other states but began threatening to remove their ruling houses, no matter how old these might be. Bolstering even further his demand for adherence to the Continental System, the emperor said he would not tolerate any English ambassadors in Europe and that he would declare war on any power that still received an English ambassador, adding that he had 300,000 allied Russian soldiers at his disposal. Metternich's sober judgment was that Napoleon's impetuousness and his thirst for universal dominance had no limits.

After declaring war on Portugal, Napoleon dispatched troops under the command of General Junot, which traveled to Lisbon via Spain, arriving on November 30, 1807, and declared the House of Braganza dismissed. Prince Regent Johann fled to Brazil, taking his whole court with him. Napoleon would again find himself at war in Portugal when, a year later, the British under Wellington landed there, resisting the French until the end of Napoleonic rule and, finally, in 1813, managing to drive Napoleon's troops out of the Iberian Peninsula altogether.

Napoleon's War against Spain: A Shock for All the Crowns of Europe

Metternich followed with great concern how Napoleon's will to expand his empire led Napoleon to set his sights on the Iberian Peninsula. Spain joined the Treaty of Basel in 1795, entered into an alliance with France one year later, and in the following years stood by its side, even in 1805 in the devastating defeat by the British at the Battle of Trafalgar. On October 27, 1807, a contract was signed at Fontainebleau that contained the details on how Portugal, once defeated, should be divided up between the two countries. Thus, with the full consent of the Spanish government, Junot's troops marched through Spain in order to conquer Portugal.

Intrigue at the Spanish court, however, offered a welcome opportunity for Napoleon to intervene in his own interest in Spain and to turn the political situation in the country upside down. The starting point was an attempt by Infante Ferdinand to dismiss the ruling premier, Manuel de Godoy, who was a favorite of the politically inactive Karl IV—and the queen's lover. Napoleon invited all the members of the royal family to the Castle of Marracq in Bayonne, in the French part of the Basque country on the Atlantic coast, for mediation. When, on May 2, 1808, French soldiers went to collect Ferdinand's younger brother Francesco in Madrid and bring him to the meeting, rebels tried to prevent them from doing so. The following day, Marshal Murat took revenge for the French soldiers who had been killed by the rebels, overseeing a blood-bath in which hundreds of civilians were shot. This was the catalyst for the Spanish resistance against Napoleon, which lasted until 1813.

The Spanish theater of war tied up a large part of Napoleon's military forces and from then on played an important role in Metternich's political calcula-tions as he tried to figure out how strong the French forces at the center of the Continent might still be. But for the most part Metternich was angry about the way Napoleon, in Bayonne, had used threats of violence to force Karl IV to hand him the crown. The French emperor had achieved his goal through a "coup," with "guile and brutal force." On June 6, 1808, Napoleon then con-ferred the Spanish crown on his brother Joseph.[102] Even Talleyrand, in his memoirs, distanced himself from this way of proceeding: "If ever the success of an enterprise should have appeared infallible, it was assuredly an enterprise in which treason had combined everything in such a manner as to leave nothing to be done by force of arms."[103] On August 9, 1807, Napoleon had already ac-cepted his foreign secretary's resignation, but he had kept him on as a political advisor, including at the Congress of Erfurt. When Talleyrand tried to prevent Napoleon from carrying out his "assassination" and warned him, frankly, that the public would take him for a thief and cheater, Napoleon ordered him to bring the Spanish royal family to Talleyrand's renaissance castle in Valençay, to the east of Tours, and to house them there at the castle owner's expense. This event was the beginning of Talleyrand's increasing alienation from Napoleon.

The removal of the Bourbons from the Spanish throne alarmed Metternich. In establishing his "Continental System," the French emperor was not only un-scrupulously sweeping aside dynasties with rich traditions but also replacing them with his own dynastic rule. He thus created a new system of legitimacy in which, wherever possible, members of his family should rule—such as his brother Louis, who became king of the Netherlands in May 1806; Joseph, who was king of Naples from March 1806 and then of Spain from June 1808; and his brother-in-law Murat, who became king of Naples in July 1808. Napoleon's brother Jérôme received the newly formed Kingdom of Westphalia in August 1807, deposing the German prince elector of Hanover and Hesse-Kassel and the duke of Brunswick-Wolfenbüttel. In 1806 Napoleon's step-uncle, Cardinal Joseph Fesch, became the coadjutant of Dalberg, the prince primate of the Rhenish Confederation. And his adopted son, Eugène de Beauharnais, the French emperor appointed vice-king of Italy in 1805.

Napoleon also gave his dynastic policies an ideological dimension that made the systemic change look even more dangerous. This is clear from the famous letter of November 15, 1807, from Napoleon to Jérôme. This manifesto of

Napoleonic imperialism expressed a revolutionary and missionary force that posed an additional threat to the old European dynasties:

> Your subjects must enjoy a degree of liberty, equality, and prosperity hitherto unknown to the German people! . . . In Germany, as in France, Italy, and Spain, people long for equality and enlightened ideas. I have been managing the affairs of Europe long enough now to know that the grumblings of the privileged classes does not represent public opinion. Rule constitutionally. Even if the reason, and the enlightenment of the age, were not sufficient cause, it would be good policy for one in your position; and you will find that the backing of public opinion gives you a great natural advantage over the absolute kings who are your neighbors.[104]

Of course, these fine words were contradicted in all the states mentioned—by the presence of a political police, by censorship, and by the enrichment of the new elite. Metternich, who was familiar with the old Europe, saw through all this very quickly. If we are to understand how Metternich must have felt in August 1808, we must truly appreciate how many old princes were replaced by new arch-monarchs in the short time between 1805 and 1808. Who, in this situation, would have doubted that Napoleon had even grander plans? Which of the remaining powers would be next? These were the questions continuously going around in the ambassador's mind. Napoleon lent further credence to Metternich's fears regarding further expansionist plans when he sought a discussion with him, allegedly in confidence, about how the Ottoman Empire was to be divided. After such a division, and once the Spanish uprising had been quelled, Metternich assumed, it would be the Habsburg Monarchy's turn, and Napoleon would look "upon Austria as a prize in prospect for one of his new German allies."[105]

In a special audience on August 25, 1808, Napoleon approached Metternich with a gesture of seeming confidentiality and discussed the question of war with him, for Napoleon had been informed that Austria had, since April, begun to reorganize its army and territorial army [*Landwehr*]. Napoleon rightly remarked that without Russia as an ally, Austria could not risk a war, and its relationship with the tsar's empire was not good. Without beating about the bush, he said: "Grant that it was the affairs in Spain which alarmed you; you already imagined your throne overturned, as I had overturned that one."[106] Though Napoleon immediately moved to reassure Metternich that he had no such plan, Metternich must have perceived it as a threat that the Habsburg throne existed entirely at Napoleon's discretion. He claimed that he had occupied the throne of the Bourbons because they were his personal enemies: "They and I cannot occupy thrones at the same time in Europe. The other dynasties have not that peculiarity. I make a great distinction between the House of [Habsburg-]Lorraine and that of the Bourbons."[107]

The matter of the Bourbons posed a difficult dilemma for Metternich because Napoleon demanded that Austria recognize Joseph in Spain and Murat in Naples as legitimate rulers. Metternich told Stadion that this was inconceivable on the basis of existing legal standards, and not even justified on the basis of right to conquer, as neither throne had been vacant. (This was Napoleon's argument in his own case, as Louis XVI had been executed.) But if Austria were to argue against recognition, then it would have to criticize those European powers who had recognized Napoleon as the successor to the throne of Louis XVI. "That was the first, the grand usurpation; all the others are but corollaries."[108] In the interests of pragmatism, and in order to avoid creating any vulnerabilities, Metternich therefore suggested recognizing the new kings who had gained their crowns "by the grace of Napoleon." The tsar, incidentally, had already beaten Austria to it. Metternich, however, wanted to offer Austrian recognition of the kings in exchange for an end to all discussions regarding Austrian armament and a renewal of amiable relations between France and Austria. But Emperor Franz and Stadion did not go along with his proposal, which appeared to them to be breaking a taboo.

The Congress of Erfurt (September 27 to October 14, 1808): Austria Threatened on All Sides

Metternich was on high alert when Napoleon, following his return from the victorious campaign in Spain, started preparing a further meeting with the tsar, similar to the one in Tilsit the previous year. This time it was to take place in Erfurt in the autumn. He did all he could to persuade Napoleon also to invite Emperor Franz, or at least to admit Metternich himself to the meeting. The manner in which Metternich was rejected was, by diplomatic standards, humiliating, and must have deepened his concerns.[109] Talleyrand was the only one to provide Metternich with more detail on those attending, and he strongly encouraged him to try to get an invitation for Franz through the foreign minister Champagny or Napoleon himself. He even suggested that Emperor Franz should simply turn up in Erfurt unannounced. It was indeed the case that scores of German princes went to Erfurt without being invited because they believed they might get the opportunity to present their interests. But for the Austrian emperor such behavior would have been undignified, and was thus impossible.

Metternich explained to Champagny how embarrassing it would be for him if Austrian interests were discussed at Erfurt in his absence. His participation would at the same time demonstrate to Europe how warm relations between

Austria and France actually were; Napoleon himself, he said, had emphasized this at the last audience. Finally, he even offered to attend not as Austrian ambassador—after all, he did not have instructions—but simply as a private individual. Champagny twisted and turned in embarrassment, answering monosyllabically and stressing that it was not the emperor's habit to travel to such meetings with the entire diplomatic corps. And, apart from all that, it was just a conversation between friends that would not touch on any Austrian interests. Also, the Spanish or the Persian ambassador might then just as well express the same desire, an argument to which Metternich responded, with an ironic smile, "I cannot, either from a moral or political point of view, agree to your comparing an ambassador of Austria with the envoy of a khan of Persia; we form a veritable diplomatic antithesis."[110] Champagny noticed that he was treading on dangerous ground and simply told Metternich that he would communicate his ideas to the emperor.

Given the little information he had, it is astounding how sharp Metternich's analysis was of the deeper motivations behind the meeting, even in the run-up to it. He studied the official organ and mouthpiece of Napoleon—the *Moniteur*—the speeches given at the senate in Paris, and the public announcements of the government. The style and the phrases he came across reminded him of the situation in 1793 at the Jacobin Convention. Now, as then, a two-faced game was played: the ministers paid some respect to Austria in their speeches, but the orators at the Senate addressed the "French nation" and "reviled" Austria. At bottom, what drove Napoleon was the aim of compensating for mistakes he had made, both at the domestic and at the international level (Spain), improving the public mood through propaganda, and most of all securing himself against an attack from Russia or Austria while he was still engaged in Spain and Portugal. The aims at Erfurt were to distance Russia from Austria, to discuss the division of the Ottoman Empire, and "to force England to peace." The last point meant the imposition of an even more effective and comprehensive Continental System. Champagny explained to Metternich that, from a geographical point of view, it was Russia, not Austria, that was needed in order to achieve this. No matter how often Metternich repeated that a general peace in Europe also required Austria, his protestations were in vain.

Metternich had hit the nail on the head. At Erfurt, Napoleon openly admitted to Armand de Caulaincourt—his ambassador in Saint Petersburg and later his closest adjutant—that he had intentionally not invited the Austrian emperor. If Alexander was his friend, then Russia had to make common cause with France, and should not worry about "Germany" ("l'Allemagne"), even less about Spain.[111] Before his departure for Erfurt, Napoleon explained the aim of the meeting as follows: "I wish, in returning, to be free to do what I wish in Spain. I wish to be assured that Austria will be afraid and hold back, and I do not desire to be engaged in too precise a manner with Russia concerning the affairs in the East."[112] Later, in Erfurt, he referred to Austria as a "true enemy."[113] Throughout all his consultations with Caulaincourt, one can sense Napoleon's concern that Austria might build up its military and go to war against him. Yet even though Emperor Franz was not invited, his presence was felt at all the conversations in Erfurt. He had been able, after all, to send General Karl von Vincent as an observer. Having been to Paris on special diplomatic missions, Vincent was familiar with the situation there and also personally known to Napoleon.

To an external observer, the congress and the associated propaganda effort fulfilled their purpose. In contravention of international law, Napoleon, following the Treaty of Tilsit, had, on August 4, 1807, passed a decree declaring Erfurt an imperial domain, making it a French enclave on German soil, and so Napoleon was inviting attendees to a congress on home turf, so to speak. Beforehand he had personally arranged all the events in minute detail and consulted with Talleyrand, to whom he said: "I wish to astonish Germany by my splendor." He spent a lot of time on the theater program and ordered the famous Comédie Française to come to Erfurt. He wanted only tragedies—not comedies—to be performed, because they were suitable for the Germans with their "melancholy ideas": "Their moral concepts must be enlarged," as they always "stick to the same ideas."[114]

The program for the congress followed the pattern of courtly celebrations under the ancien régime, including battues, visits to the theater in the evening, and carefully choreographed official dinners. The princes of the Rhenish Confederation were seated at an elliptical table (which had been specially built) as the dynast's "expanded family" with Napoleon presiding as "pater familias."[115] The ambivalence of this event has rightly been highlighted: it was a courtly ceremony imitating baroque forms, and the approved press reported on it as a sensational media event.

A chronicler from Leipzig, however, reported that not a single word had been heard about what had actually been negotiated.[116] In actual fact, the event did not turn out the way Napoleon had wanted. Tsar Alexander was not prepared to make himself dependent on France alone through a contract. Napoleon's courting of Alexander's sister, Katharina, also failed, but at least the "secret contract of Erfurt" referred to England as "the common enemy of themselves [France and Russia] and of the Continent" with whom "no treaties of peace" were to be made "but by common consent."[117]

Talleyrand had already tried to influence the Treaty of Pressburg in Austria's favor. Now, in Erfurt, he contradicted Napoleon's claim that Austria was a true enemy: "Your enemy, Sire, at present, perhaps, but at heart her policy is not in opposition to that of France; she is not aggressive, but conservative." Napoleon responded: "My dear Talleyrand, I know that this is your opinion; we will speak of that when the Spanish business is over."[118] Napoleon realized that Talleyrand took the side of Austria, and on one occasion he even ironically told him: "You are still an Austrian!"[119] The other member of the old nobility who was very close to Napoleon, Caulaincourt, also confronted Napoleon at Erfurt, and with Talleyrand's knowledge. Referring to the relations with Germany and Prussia, and the occupation of the territory that had been conquered since the Treaty of Tilsit, he warned him that everyone felt threatened by him. Caulaincourt went even further, recommending to Napoleon that he moderate his system by withdrawing his troops from Germany. It was necessary to calm Europe down, not to scare it further, and anything that would contribute to such pacification would ultimately consolidate Napoleon's gains. The emperor replied that Caulaincourt's suggestions amounted to weakness; he would forfeit what had already been gained at great cost in his attempts to defeat England. Napoleon thus continued to follow his Continental System, which, indeed, required complete domination of the whole Continent.[120]

After the Congress of Erfurt, Metternich asked Talleyrand, Count Peter Tolstoy (the Russian ambassador at the court in Paris, whom he knew well), and the Austrian special envoy General von Vincent to tell him what had taken place. He found his predictions confirmed, especially when it came to the dangerous diplomatic isolation of the Habsburg Monarchy and Napoleon's increasing readiness to attack Austria. The project of attacking England in her Indian possessions, he thought, "existed only as an eventuality, dependent on the concurrence of circumstances as yet remote." Napoleon "occupied himself instead with perfecting his Continental System and with the expulsion of the Bourbons from the throne of Spain."[121] For Metternich, the rapprochement between the two empires, the French and the Russian, had "no real basis";[122] it was an "illusive alliance"[123] whose aim was to neutralize Russia so that France could carry out further assaults.

Talleyrand, an Advocate for Austria "in the Lion's Den"

As Austrian ambassador in Paris, Metternich had to master a difficult situation for his country, and in Talleyrand he found a person he could trust. As a descendant of ancient nobility, Talleyrand thought differently from Napoleon, the parvenu. Both Metternich and Talleyrand were perfectly familiar with the details of international power relations and the principles of the balance between European powers. Both considered the "European Concert" the only possible foundation for a stable order. In their eyes, the "universal monarchy" Napoleon had in mind could not be maintained or defended in the long run. Talleyrand was twenty years older than Metternich, and he despised the sacrifice and cruelty of modern war just as much as Metternich did, if in a different way. This was well expressed by a declaration of his after a walk across the battlefield of Austerlitz with the French marshal Lannes: "Marshal Lannes . . . was about to faint when his eyes gazed on the dead and maimed soldiers of all nations; he was so moved that, when showing me the different points where the principal attacks had been made, he said to me: 'I cannot stay longer.'"[124]

Even before the Congress of Erfurt, Metternich presented an analysis to Stadion in which he identified two "factions" at the court in Paris. Those following the emperor owed their influence to military violence and to "a degree of nepotism."[125] There was one estate [état] in France that opened the way to everything—to "fortune, titles, and constant protection of the sovereign"—and this was "the military profession; one might say that France is peopled entirely by soldiers, and by citizens created to work for them by the sweat of their brows."[126] The other "faction" was composed of "the great mass of the nation"; this was the bourgeois, more precisely the civil faction, headed by "the most eminent persons of the state, and principally M. de Talleyrand [and] the Minister of Police"—that is, Fouché.[127] This faction had existed since 1805: that is, since Austerlitz, the end of the empire, and the foundation of Rhenish Confederation. The campaigns in 1806 and 1807 against Prussia and Russia had further strengthened this faction, and the enterprise in Spain in 1808, with its devastating battles and the immoral removal of the Bourbons, moreover, had taken its toll on France domestically, not least because the financial resources necessary for the maintenance of the troops could not be acquired from Spain itself and therefore petered out.

Talleyrand had also distanced himself from the system by not pleading for the recognition of the new kings "at the grace of Napoleon." With his typical astuteness, Metternich recommended that Stadion "separate the moral man from the political man."[128] Talleyrand's playing fast and loose with women and his venality could not be denied, but on the other hand he was an eminently political man who was guided by principles [homme à système]. This could be useful or dangerous—and if dangerous, much more so than in the case of an incompetent minister like Champagny: "Men like M. de Talleyrand are like sharp-edged instruments, with which it is dangerous to play; but for great wounds great remedies are necessary, and he who has to treat them ought not to be afraid to use the instrument that cuts the best."[129]

In this report Metternich was already hinting at the fact that Talleyrand might become an ideal ally in removing Napoleon and his system (the "wound"). In the course of long conversations, the two men cautiously drew nearer to each other, until Talleyrand trusted Metternich enough to risk everything by passing on secret information, regarding, for instance, the condition, location, and numbers of French and allied troops or Napoleon's whereabouts. Both masterfully employed the art of diplomacy in order to veil their connection from Napoleon, who did not learn about this duplicity until his political demise in 1815.

Napoleon's behavior, however, also fostered their arrangement. At the end of 1808, he was in the Spanish theater of war when he got wind of Talleyrand and Fouché's plans for succession in the event that Napoleon was killed. Murat was discussed as the preferred successor.[130] After a forced ride from Valladolid to Paris within six days, the emperor arrived in the capital on January 23, 1809, and called Talleyrand, Fouché, Cambacérès, Lebrun, and Admiral Decrès to his study. There, he performed one of his well-known calculated outbursts:

"You are a thief," he cried, "a coward who has no respect for anything; you've never in your life performed any duty faithfully. You don't believe in God; you've betrayed and deceived everybody; nothing is sacred to you; you would give away your own father; I have loaded you with gifts, and you would do anything to harm me. . . . You deserve to be broken like a glass tumbler. I could do it if I liked it, but I despise you too much to do it!"

Several sources confirm this scene.[131] According to one of them, Napoleon even uttered this famous insult: "You are nothing but shit in silk stockings." Whether or not he really said this, Talleyrand was deeply hurt by his public humiliation in front of the court; he left the room in perfect accordance with etiquette but muttered to himself: "What a pity—such a great man and so ill-mannered." But he could not resist adding: "There are things one never forgives."[132]

Now Talleyrand had personal grievance as well as political principle as grounds for seeking to secretly undermine Napoleon and for taking the side of Austria. And to Talleyrand Metternich, who had become the trusted representative of Austria. In Metternich's ambassadorial correspondence—ideally encoded—Talleyrand, in turn, was mentioned as a "reliable source," and would often not be described in more detail; sometimes he was simply the mysterious "Monsieur X."[133] Metternich heard the news about Napoleon's performance, and he also knew that Napoleon was angry with Talleyrand for spreading, behind the emperor's back, his opinion that the Treaty of Pressburg was "infamous and the work of corruption." Metternich reported to Vienna that Talleyrand had fallen from favor and had lost his title of grand chamberlain and the annual payment of 40,000 francs that came with it. Unbeknownst to Napoleon, Talleyrand was now practically an Austrian spy. He offered Metternich the mobilization plans for the army, and offered to collaborate closely with Austria; there was nothing left for him, he said, but either to be victorious on its side, or to perish. At the same time, he asked for several hundred thousand francs in order to compensate for his lost income and the costs incurred by having to take care of the Spanish Bourbons at his castle in Valençay. In a letter of February 23, 1809—thus, even before the outbreak of war—Metternich asked Emperor Franz to transfer 300,000 or 400,000 francs in bills of exchange into the accounts of fictitious payees in Holland: "Considerable as this sum may appear, it stands in no comparison to the sacrifices one usually makes. And what will be gained may have enormous effects."[134]

Metternich, the "Main Instigator of the Glorious, Unhappy War of 1809"?

When would Napoleon direct his bellicose intentions toward Austria? Metternich's main task during his time as ambassador in Paris was to answer this question. Whenever he met with Napoleon in person, this uncertainty was in the air or the emperor explicitly brought it up. Napoleon eyed with suspicion Austrian attempts to reorganize its army. He interpreted these efforts as rearmament, preparation for yet another war—the fourth—against him. Metternich did all he could to allay his suspicion. Here, as ever, Metternich demonstrated his willingness to inform himself in great detail about military matters, which he understood to be an essential part of international politics. In September 1807 he arranged for "a tabular survey of reforms and changes which have taken place in the army since the Treaty of Pressburg" to be sent to him by secret courier via Mainz.[135]

   For Metternich, who was always on his guard, Napoleon's foreign policy offered many causes for concern. Austria was systematically isolated—as the Congress of Erfurt had shown—and surrounded by the states of the Rhenish Confederation, who were allies of Napoleon and were in any case compelled to provide him with troops, but also, since the Treaties of Tilsit, by Prussia and the tsar's empire. Napoleon's alliance with his alleged "friend," Tsar Alexander, was a way of neutralizing Russia while Napoleon's armies marched against Spain, Portugal, the Ottoman Empire, the arch-enemy England, and ultimately also the Habsburg Monarchy.

   Metternich's attention was mainly directed at the strength and movement of French troops and troops of the Rhenish Confederation, as well as the situation on the Iberian Peninsula, where a strong royalist movement, consisting of the nobility, the clergy, and the peasant population, offered unexpectedly stubborn resistance. Napoleon's enemies used a novel way of fighting, guerrilla warfare—lying in wait and ambushing. The occupying force, by contrast, tried to intimidate the population with punitive acts of retaliation. As a result, Napoleon could not achieve a quick victory and peace treaty, and therefore he was not able, as he usually was, to extract contributions from the country. He had to finance the war himself, and this weakened his position in France. Furthermore, the English succeeded in making Portugal their bridgehead on the peninsula, and from there the talented military tactician Arthur Wellesley, later Duke of Wellington, began to push back the front from the west.

Metternich closely followed the developments in Spain and sent to Vienna appeals, proclamations, and also the text of a Napoleonic Constitution for Spain, drafted in Bayonne.[136] He reported on the popular outrage and included the text of an appeal to the Spanish people that commented on the removal and deportation of the king. The tone of this statement, a tone one also encounters in texts from later underground German publications, must have been an extreme provocation to the Napoleonic censors: "The monster from France has decided in its deceitful heart to tyrannize our independence with the most abominable means, which are without parallel in the annals of the world. Its infamy lies open for all to see, its betrayal is obvious, and the removal of our king confirms all this."[137]

Regarding the information Metternich provided to Stadion, Talleyrand was the best source he could have wished for. In July 1808, for instance, the ambassador sent "a detailed and very trustworthy [*surtout très sure*] list of the French army corps which are at the front line in order to attack us from Prussia,"[138] along with the quantitative distribution of troops in Silesia, Brandenburg, Berlin, Pomerania, and Denmark. Metternich was also able to provide excerpts from secret French military bulletins from Spain that contained evaluations of the situation and accounts of troop movements in the country.[139] At the beginning of 1809 he sent information, culled from the English press, on the strength of troops and the equipment of the units that the English had shipped to Spain.[140] The most important news, which could have cost Talleyrand his head, Metternich sent in encoded form in February 1809, complemented by very detailed lists referring to the condition of the Spanish and Rhine armies and to the French troops in Italy.[141] Among all the documents Metternich sent, the crown jewel was a nineteen-page tabular survey that gave the exact locations of all regiments in the French empire as of March 10, 1809. Together with other encoded letters, it was dispatched from Paris on March 23.[142]

At the time there was probably no other ambassador at any of the European courts who held such a key position as Metternich. His astuteness, his wide-ranging network of contacts—which he had already begun to establish while at the courts of Dresden and Berlin—and his knowledgeability made him indispensable for the Viennese court. He said that Napoleon had once warned him that one false word, or one misstep, from the ambassador could mean war.[143] This was a dramatic exaggeration from Napoleon, meant to intimidate Metternich.

It is this vulnerable position Metternich was in that has sparked debate about his responsibility for war, a debate that still continues today. The historian Adam Wolf started it in 1875 when he, rather offhandedly and without evidence, claimed: "He was the creator of the war in 1809. In Vienna, his wife spoke and rabble-roused in favor of it."[144] Without examining the actual sources in the archive, Srbik uncritically adopted this judgment and expanded it into the thesis that Metternich was the "main instigator of the glorious, unhappy war of 1809." Metternich, it is said, was under the spell of "fateful misconceptions" that led him to "repeatedly ask for war in the most fervent memoranda and dispatches of the highest rhetorical zest and of surprising force."[145] This is a particularly striking example of the obvious mistakes caused by Srbik's method of avoiding the sources in the state archives. Meticulous examination of the documents in Vienna and Prague shows that "there is no evidence that Metternich at any point before his stay in Vienna in November and December 1808 thought Austria should begin the war against France of its own accord."[146]

Having followed Metternich's career up to this point, we have seen the kind of logic he discerned in the dynamics of large international conflict and war. He was convinced that only a close alliance of all other major powers could tame and crush a primordial force such as Napoleon's system of rule. Three failed wars of coalition had demonstrated this at places such as Valmy, Marengo, Hohenlinden, Austerlitz, and most recently Jena and Auerstedt. In Paris, Metternich tried to convince the Russian ambassador, Count Tolstoy, that they had to unite against Napoleon in order to survive. But he did not succeed, despite the fact that Tolstoy, in contrast to Tsar Alexander, shared Metternich's political convictions unreservedly. At that point Alexander had not yet reached the correct assessment of Napoleon; he thought that he was by far Napoleon's superior, and initially thought they could share the European Continent between the two of them.

In some of the perspicacious analyses that were so characteristic of him, Metternich explained to his foreign minister that only an alliance of the major powers could achieve anything against Napoleon. He warned Stadion in no uncertain terms: "It would be madness on our part to provoke a war with France."[147] His evaluation of the political situation in mid-1808 reads like a prophecy of the failure of the war in 1809. Only one week later, he explicitly repeated his warning: "To provoke a war with France would be madness; it must therefore be avoided, but it cannot be avoided with middle-sized forces . . .

but our army, however strong, good, and well ordered it may be, is it in number sufficient to prevent the final ruin of a monarchy . . . ? It is, therefore, not in ourselves alone that we must seek our safety."[148]

Are these words that call for war? More specifically, are they words that call for the sort of bilateral war waged by an individual state without allies that Austria then, indeed, decided to begin?[149] On the contrary: in the months before and after the Congress of Erfurt, Metternich sensed that plans for hasty attacks were being made in Vienna, and he advised against them. And he told his father that for eight weeks he had stood at the center of politics and had saved the peace.[150] This remark no doubt alluded to the audiences in the summer of 1808—still before the Congress of Erfurt—at which he tried to rebut Napoleon's accusations regarding Austria's efforts at arming itself. Now, however, he no longer felt sufficiently well informed. He therefore requested permission to travel to Vienna in order to be brought up to speed; otherwise, he could not possibly fulfill his responsibilities in Paris properly.

On November 12, 1808, he arrived in the capital of the Habsburg Monarchy.[151] He went immediately to see Stadion, who told him that war had practically been declared. This is confirmed by Metternich's later judgment, in his memoirs, that "war was nearer than [he] had supposed" in October 1808.[152] In a conversation with the emperor that lasted several hours, he realized that the emperor himself was not yet fully aware of how far the preparations for war had advanced. But Metternich, the ambassador, was expected to provide a precise evaluation of the situation: he was closest to Napoleon in Paris and thus had the most up-to-date information. Within three weeks he prepared three extensive memoranda; he presented them on December 4.

The first memorandum was the most important in Metternich's eyes ("mon Mémoire principal"), because it concentrated on the political and moral perspective and confined the military aspect to the background.[153] In the form of a panorama of the contemporary political landscape, Metternich characterized the time after 1806 as a time of radical change in the European system and explained what the individual turning points—Tilsit, Bayonne, the war in Spain, and the Congress of Erfurt—meant for Napoleon's position. He drew his reader's attention to the way in which external and internal power relations condition each other, and described in detail the domestic opposition to Napoleon, in particular the resistance from Talleyrand and Fouché, and also the distance kept by critical observers such as the Russian ambassador, Tolstoy. Whoever was interested in finding arguments against a hasty entrance to war would have found them here, in particular in Metternich's warning "that Europe can be saved only by the most intimate alliance of Austria and Russia."[154] This insight categorically ruled out any action by an individual state.

The second memorandum concentrated on the role of Russia and its relations with Austria.[155] This document also expressed reservations about a precipitate entrance into war. Metternich reported that the Russian foreign minister, Nikolai Romanzov, had argued in favor of maintaining the peace, as he thought that, if Austria attacked France, Russia would have to intervene in support of Napoleon in order to honor its obligations under the Treaty of Tilsit. On the eve of his departure from Paris, Metternich wrote, Romanzov was still cautioning him: "Do not do anything; you would bring Russia into a most embarrassing situation."[156] The minister wished for a rapprochement between Russia and Austria; the tsar was not prepared to let himself be influenced by Napoleon. Talleyrand had conveyed the same impression from Erfurt. But, Metternich said, Alexander's political fickleness and the extreme instability of his character meant that it was not possible to depend on him. In the present situation it was altogether inadvisable to count on a change in the Russian attitude or on the domestic weakness of France: "We must look solely within ourselves for the means that save us." Because Metternich considered individually waged wars against Napoleon unwise, this statement can only be interpreted as Metternich distancing himself from the prospect of war.

The third memorandum reflected on the extent to which Napoleon's problems with Spain might be advantageous to Austria. Metternich asked whether Napoleon would be able to fight simultaneous wars against Spain and Austria, and he registered very clearly how religious loyalties, commercial interests, but most of all national sentiment and passion fueled the resistance to Napoleon. But he admonished his reader to keep in mind the differences between a war on the Iberian Peninsula and one at the Rhine and the Alps: Germany consisted of twenty different peoples that had never constituted a unity, would not be unified in the future, and were accustomed to tearing each other apart.[157]

The overall situation Metternich depicted for the emperor and the cabinet in December 1808 in Vienna invited an evaluation of the military balance of power between the two camps. Because of the comprehensive information he had received from Talleyrand, Metternich alone was in a position to provide such an evaluation. His honest conclusion was: "Thus the forces of Austria, so inferior to those of France before the insurrection in Spain, will be at least equal to them in the initial phase."[158] But even here he refrained from giving unequivocal advice, because "calculations on military operations are so little in [his] line" that he made them "only with great reserve."[159]

On the basis of these documents—which were meant to be decision-making aids—it appears altogether mistaken to count Metternich as a member of the "war faction." Stadion had found himself in a tight spot because he believed that Austria's financial situation required that an attack on Napoleon would have to come before the spring of 1809; Stadion had become a "prisoner of his own war politics."[160] Metternich would never have risked a war without the backing of a reliable alliance. But Stadion had the Spanish example in mind and counted on support from an ally who was not a power in the traditional sense: he expected a national war. For a long time, deep into the days of the later truce, he maintained contacts with Prussia and hoped that rebellions in the north of Germany would further paralyze Napoleon's troops. In hindsight, Metternich commented: "The preparations for the war had now been decided upon, and an element was added to them by the rising of patriotic feeling in north Germany after the defeat of Prussia in 1806. Events have proved how illusive this assistance was." It had also been erroneous to assume that the "energetic support from German patriotic feeling [*Volkssinn*] that had been evoked in north Germany" was a real help, rather than illusory, because—as Metternich predicted—if there was an "unfortunate beginning of the war," southern Germany would turn "not against Napoleon, but against Austria."[161] More recent research has, indeed, confirmed how little the south of Germany got caught up in these national German sentiments; it was more prone to be suspicious of an Austrian intervention. The uprising in Tyrol during the war of 1809 was more anti-Bavarian than anti-Napoleonic.[162]

In this phase of Metternich's political life, he had the opportunity to observe, as one of the actors involved, how not only facts and decisions but also character and temperament can set a country on the path toward war. At least, this is how we may interpret his choice of words in this depiction of the foreign minister's character: "Count Stadion was one of those men of lively imagination and quick understanding who are easily overcome by the impressions of the moment. Men of this sort always incline to extremes: for them there are no transitions, and since these nevertheless lie in the nature of things, they anticipate events instead of knowing how to wait for them, and thus too often act on the basis of guesswork."[163] Historical research has concurred with this judgment of what Manfred Botzenhart called Stadion's "politics of a fiery heart and passionate will," a politics that led to failure.[164] In 1813, in the midst of war, Metternich was in a position to demonstrate the different, strategically superior characteristics that were needed in order to be successful against Napoleon for the first time.

AMBASSADOR ON BORROWED TIME AND NAPOLEON'S CAPTIVE UNDER HOUSE ARREST

Metternich was very uneasy about returning to Paris: "The passive part I had to play was a contrast to the excessive activity of the military preparations, of which I was condemned to be a mere spectator."[165] The court in Vienna was aware that the situation of the ambassador would be extremely precarious, and there had been discussion about how he should conduct himself. In his *Memoirs,* Metternich erroneously claimed that he "received no instructions from Vienna."[166] But in fact, Stadion had provided him three pages with nine detailed points to be followed. The general rules set out in these instructions were: "Say nothing; be prepared to hear anything; do not believe anything unless you have proof." He was not to change his behavior toward Napoleon. The official line he was to provide was that Austria wished for nothing but peace, that it saw itself as isolated and therefore as reliant on its own powers, and that it wanted nothing from anyone but was prepared to defend its sovereignty against the whole world. According to the instructions, it was likely that Napoleon would raise the issues of the division of the Ottoman Empire and the recognition of the kings of Spain and Naples. The ambassador was to treat questions on these matters as entirely new and hence "ad referendum"—that is, as questions simply to be passed on without comment. Metternich should be evasive in all matters. He was also charged with finding out how serious Talleyrand's offers were.[167]

Metternich traveled day and night in his coach in order to arrive in time for the great diplomatic audience. As Napoleon was still in Spain, Empress Josephine stood in for him. Metternich was greeted joyfully: his return seemed to dispel worries about an imminent war. There were, indeed, rumors circulating in public that Austria would begin a war in the spring at the latest. Metternich faithfully followed the strategy outlined in his instructions: he assured Champagny that Austria wanted nothing but peace and was awaiting the withdrawal of French troops from Germany.

Over the coming weeks, whenever Metternich met Napoleon at audiences or meetings of specific court members, he tried to detect in his behavior toward him any deviations from the familiar script. Everyone present was aware that the emperor's conduct had a significant effect on those present. Napoleon used to pass down the line of assembled diplomats twice, and it was noticed if an ambassador was not addressed on the second pass; or, at a soirée, people took note if he addressed only Madame de Metternich and ignored her husband.[168] Napoleon also studded his addresses with indirect threats, as during an audience of February 21, 1809, when he asked Metternich about his wife's health—always a sign that he had nothing to say to him—but then asked the Bavarian ambassador whether the Bavarian fortresses were prepared for the defense of the state, especially the fortress in Passau, close to the Austrian border.[169]

Metternich confronted the Russian foreign minister, Romanzov, with the question of how Russia and France, as allies, could secure peace in Europe if they systematically shut out Austria as the third major power. Romanzov replied that the Austrian court should not be led into erroneously believing that it was encouraged to go to war from the Russian side. But on another occasion Romanzov candidly reported Napoleon's intentions:

> the Emperor of the French does desire it [the war], because he needs more or less virgin soil to explore, because he has need to occupy his armies, and to entertain them at the expense of others. M. de Romanzow did not dispute my argument. He came to visit me two days after this conversation, and repeated, nearly word for word, the arguments which I had made use of on my visit to him, as if he had been inspired with them that morning in a long conversation he had had with the Emperor. He wants money, he said—he does not hide it; he wishes for war against Austria to procure it; but when he has finished that, will he not come and seek it from us?[170]

This frank assessment shows that Napoleon's system cannot be explained as simply the result of his psychology, his unbridled will to rule. It was also characterized by a logic that depended on resources; what the system needed to achieve was what in economics is called the "takeoff" of an economy, a self-sustaining growth that occurs once the startup investment is sufficiently large. Romanzov's prediction that, in the long term, Napoleon's self-sufficient military system also posed a danger to the tsarist empire was correct.

Bleak Visions of the Future

Metternich understood this logic, and in his last reports from Paris after the outbreak of war he described it with great clarity. He presented one of his typical visions, in this case of what would happen if Austria were to lose the war: Austria is struck off the list of major powers, and "her vast states are dismembered. Europe undergoes a complete reform." A monstrous central government "weighs down feeble tributaries," who lead a miserable existence and rivet their own chains. Napoleon's long-term plan has succeeded: "He is the Sovereign of Europe: his death will be the signal for a new and frightful revolution . . . ; a real civil war will establish itself for half a century in the vast Empire of the Continent the very day when the iron arm which holds the reins shall fall into dust."[171]

Metternich saw Napoleon's master plan with equal clarity. It would ultimately amount to the creation of a global empire, which presupposed the "division of Europe into Powers, of which the strongest would not have more than three or four millions of subjects." Napoleon would "become chief and protector of twenty or thirty small states." This would require "frightful convulsions which Europe would necessarily experience before the realization of this plan," and, not being "held back by any moral principle," Napoleon would not shrink from this. The empire would extend to "the borders of the Niemen, Borysthene, and to the confines of Hungary and Turkey," and finally "fall with all the power of ancient Europe upon Russia, and drive her back into the steppes of Tartary and behind the Volga—such is the plan of universal dominion which Napoleon dreams of, and in which his confederates frankly support him." Napoleon would destroy the old Europe and put his princes on newly created thrones to create a great federation [*la ligue napoleonienne*]: "The jealousy among political allies [*confrères*], the military, and police, spread by France on all the surfaces of the great federation, will discover schemes and annul them before they can be tried." Even if he became mentally feeble and without strength of character, the emperor of the French would "maintain order solely by his position, by the need that the entire federation will have of him and of his authority."[172]

In Metternich's view, the Treaty of Tilsit had been the turning point. After that, Napoleon had had the choice of toppling either Spain or Austria. His attack on the Spanish dynasty was proof for Metternich of Napoleon's revolutionary European imperialism. But Napoleon even looked beyond Europe, toward the colonial world, where he hoped for handsome compensation for the lost French colonies on the American continent.[173] From this perspective, ultimately, there could be only two "global players." Once Russia had been pushed aside, France, as the only remaining power of continental Europe, would have to enter into competition with the British Empire. The Continental System was designed to pave the way for that conflict, and it was only logical that England, since 1793—with the one exception of the short-lived Peace of Amiens in 1802—had been permanently at war with France and also fought it globally at sea. England therefore had to be the most reliable ally for Metternich's future policies for the regeneration and reconstruction of Europe.

Austria at War in 1809 and Metternich's Peculiar Role in It

In the space of half a year during the war of 1809, Metternich must surely have united in one person more disparate roles than any of his contemporaries: ambassador on borrowed time, political prisoner of Napoleon under house arrest, neutralized peace negotiator, interim minister, and, finally, accountable minister of the imperial household and of foreign affairs.[174]

After the final decision to go to war had been taken on December 23, 1808, Austria's intention was initially to begin the campaign on March 15, moving from Bohemia toward Franconia. But subsequently the direction of attack was changed toward Old Bavaria, which delayed the beginning of the campaign until April 10. On that day the Austrian troops crossed the Inn. Napoleon learned about this, via semaphore telegraph, at ten o'clock in the evening on April 12. Five hours later, he was on his way to Strasbourg. After a five-day battle (April 19 to 23), Archduke Carl was finally forced to give in to Napoleon's robust advance and withdraw to Bohemia. The archduke's appeal "To the German Nation" (April 8) ahead of the battle turned out to be ineffectual in spite of its stirring patriotic rhetoric: "Germans! Honor your situation! Accept the help we offer you! Participate in your salvation!"[175] None of the Bavarians or Swabians, who were the first to be addressed, lifted a hand.

This opened the way for Napoleon to advance on Vienna, and he entered the city on May 13. On May 21–22, however, the archduke was able to inflict a surprising initial defeat on Napoleon near Aspern, the very same day that plans for a rebellion in northern Germany, spearheaded by Colonel Wilhelm von Dörnberg and the major of the hussars in Berlin, Ferdinand von Schill, failed. Metternich knew about the planned rebellion,[176] and his prediction that there would be no significant German national movement turned out to be correct. As opposed to Spain, there were no further attempts at revolt.

Metternich's Arrest in Paris

Metternich was not at all certain how he would be treated in Paris once the war had begun. If this treatment should have to be painful to him personally, he would happily accept that as part of his duty. He realized that Napoleon might make use of the symbolic significance of his dealings with him as a representative of a state with which Napoleon was at war.[177] Metternich did countenance the possibility of things turning ugly; he ordered the destruction of the documents held at the embassy, and bade farewell to Stadion on April 10 with words that were probably intended to be ironic: "Good-bye, my dear Count. I write to you at four o'clock in the morning, and shall go to bed now, expecting that I shall be woken up in order to be shot. If you learn that the whole embassy has been reduced to rubble, please arrange a spiritual and diplomatic requiem mass for so many victims!"[178] Such worries were soon dispelled.

In Paris, before Champagny's planned departure on April 15, Champagny invited him to his house, allegedly because he wanted to hear whatever news he might have for him. Metternich replied dryly that, as his correspondence had been interfered with and read, Champagny already knew everything. Champagny did not deny this. He informed Metternich that the emperor did not consider it appropriate for the members of the embassy to remain after ties had been cut off, and he offered to give him a passport.[179] Napoleon had also asked Champagny explicitly to tell Metternich that he had been satisfied in every respect with Metternich's conduct and behavior throughout his time as ambassador. Napoleon also offered Metternich's wife and his family his personal protection; they were allowed to stay for as long as they wished.[180] Metternich happily accepted this offer: he did not want to have his wife and children travel amid the large troop movements, and they might face hostile public reactions. Besides, he "knew the ground too well to be uneasy as to the welfare of those I left behind me in Paris."[181] Metternich left his family behind at the embassy's hotel and planned his own departure for April 21.

But things did not go quite as smoothly as planned. On the day he was due to depart, the postmaster general denied Metternich the horses for the carriages. From Champagny, who was by then in Munich, Metternich learned the reason for this. There had been an embarrassing episode: after the departure of the French ambassador, Count Andréossy, the Austrian government had arrested his representative, the first secretary of the embassy, Claude Dodun, and the personnel at the embassy, and had brought them to Hungary. This was meant to be in the interest of Metternich's safety, but he considered it an "unusual, and also quite unnecessary" measure that was "a fresh example of the false estimate the Austrian cabinet made of Napoleon's character and attitude."[182] Champagny wrote that Metternich had to stay in Paris until Dodun had been released.

Napoleon's Hostage in Vienna

The matter, however, took an unexpected turn when Napoleon joined the military action, and it struck him that Metternich might be useful as a bargaining chip in political and military negotiations. This changed Metternich's status into that of a political prisoner who was soon to be deported. On May 16, Fouché told him of Napoleon's orders and announced that Metternich would from now on be under the guard of an officer of the gendarmerie.

On May 26, 1809, Metternich had to depart together with the personnel at the embassy. The manner in which this happened shocked Parisian society. The respected French writer Laure d'Abrantès, a lady at Napoleon's court and the wife of General Junot, expressed her indignation thus: "No ambassador had ever left the capital under such circumstances as Herr von Metternich . . . his most valuable rights compromised; forced to leave Paris like a criminal! . . . in a carriage—invisible to anyone behind drawn curtains—an innocent person, a noble face which blushed only to us."[183]

Soon, on June 5, Metternich arrived under guard with his entourage in Vienna and was sent to the Palais Esterházy. At this point he already had a clearer understanding of how Napoleon was seeking to use him for his own purposes. He was confronted with another hostage-taking by the French emperor, one

Passport issued by Fouché for Metternich's wife, who stayed behind in Paris; the passport allowed her to leave the country, even during the war of 1809.

that must have personally shocked and intimidated him: His own father, Franz Georg, Minister of Police Count Pergen, Major General Duke Hardegg, and the archbishop of Vienna were all placed under house arrest by the directorate of the French army. This scandalous blackmail was reason enough for Metternich to get in touch with Champagny as quickly as possible. In his memoirs,

Metternich incorrectly recounted Napoleon's reasons for taking the four civilians hostage, saying that Napoleon had ordered the deportation of the hostages to France and instructed that they be kept there until the city of Vienna had paid the contributions imposed on it.

But sources from the time suggest a different interpretation. The next morning, the matter became clear to Metternich when he visited Champagny. It was just two months since Metternich's visit to Champagny in Paris, the occasion on which he had been expelled from France. Now Napoleon's minister received him in the rooms of the Habsburg empress in the Hofburg with "honeyed phrases, in which, nevertheless, a great feeling of anxiety was perceptible."[184] Following the unsuccessful battle of Aspern on April 21–22, the French intervention forces felt insecure. In Vienna they met with a spirit of opposition, and Napoleon was eager to learn more details about Austria's war aims, as these could not be deduced from any of the official proclamations.

At the time, Metternich prepared a summary of his conversation with Champagny, which reveals Napoleon's true motivations in bringing him as a political prisoner to Vienna and into the enemy's camp.[185] The real reason was not to secure the contributions from the city of Vienna—this may perhaps have been the reason given to the political prisoners themselves—but to secure the release of two French officers, Brigadier General Jean Auguste Durousnel and Major General of the Cavalry Albert-Louis de Fouler, who had been taken captive by the Austrians. Napoleon hoped to use the four mentioned Austrian hostages in the bargain. To this end, he wanted to use Metternich in the negotiations with the Austrian authorities.

As the summary reveals, Napoleon's foreign minister received Metternich "in a very amicable manner" and, on Napoleon's orders, presented him with three letters. The first demanded the exchange of the diplomatic representatives—that is, of Metternich and his entourage for Dodun and his. The second suggested how this exchange might take place. The third concerned the "affaire du Général Chasteler" and was thus the most delicate point.

In the third week of April, Lieutenant Field Marshall Johann Gabriel von Chasteler had conquered Innsbruck and the Trentino with an army corps under the general command of Archduke Johann, arresting the two generals mentioned above as he did so. On May 13, however, he had suffered a defeat in the Battle of Wörgl. Napoleon had Chasteler sentenced to death in absentia by a French military court as the instigator of the unrest in Tyrol. Metternich told the foreign minister that this contravened all laws and rules of war and of international law. And, he continued, as it was not feasible to put four civilians on one side, and two military officers on the other, in front of a firing squad and execute them, Napoleon's hostage-taking was pointless. From this conversation we can already see how Napoleon was seeking to draw Metternich into these events.

Champagny even invited Metternich to dinner, and he had Metternich sit next to him. From Metternich's point of view, this was a bizarre situation: "I found myself in the enemy's camp, in the capacity of an unconcerned spectator."[186] This made sense if the plan was to use him as a compliant middleman, and everything seemed to give the impression that this was the case: Champagny hinted at the fact that the French side was interested in exchanging the diplomats quickly. He even raised the prospect that he might again be welcoming Metternich as ambassador in Paris in the winter. Metternich rejected this idea vehemently; after an existential war had been declared on the Austrian dynasty, it was impossible. If Napoleon was going to carry out the extensive plans he had announced to the world, then Metternich would never set foot on Parisian soil again. Apart from all that, he was sure he must have been unbearable (odieuse) to Napoleon by now. But Champagny was unmoved, and, seeking a political deal, he continued to attempt to win Metternich over, saying: "Think, meanwhile, on the possible issue of the impending drama: you will find the Emperor in good humour about it."[187] And in the aforementioned summary Metternich reported Champagny as directing this compliment at him: "You are the only one who is able to maintain good relations with us. The Emperor has given you his full trust before the war; he will also give you back peace." But Metternich categorically insisted on his status as a prisoner, which, he said, meant he was not permitted to become involved in such matters.

Under House Arrest in Grünberg

Because Metternich wanted to be freed from French captivity as soon as possible, he arranged the very same day for the letters he had received from Champagny to be passed on to the headquarters of Archduke Carl. On June 9, the archduke replied that he accepted the conditions for the prisoner exchange, which, he demanded, had to take place man for man and according to rank. He selected two responsible officers and suggested Eger as the place for the transfer. Emperor Franz himself also wanted to see the exchange take place as swiftly as possible, so that Metternich could be released; he did not mind where the exchange took place.[188]

But Metternich's suspicion that the French intended to delay his exchange was confirmed. Napoleon had appointed Andréossy, well known to Metternich as the former ambassador in Vienna, as the city's new governor. Andréossy sent his adjutant to see Metternich to tell him he could no longer stay in Vienna and should choose alternative quarters near the city. Metternich suggested a country residence owned by his mother. The house was located in Grünberg, today a part of Hietzing, immediately adjacent to the park of the Palace of Schönbrunn, where Napoleon had been staying since May 13. Metternich went there on June 8, still accompanied by the officer of the gendarmerie from Paris. He assumed that he would remain in the hands of Napoleon and prepared himself accordingly. And Napoleon, indeed, attempted a second time to influence him—this time through his chief of police, General Savary, who was now in charge of police matters at Napoleon's headquarters.

Savary asked Metternich's father, Franz Georg, about his son's whereabouts, and he then went to visit Clemens on the—clearly false—pretext that he simply happened to be passing by the country house. He quickly turned the conversation toward politics. He lamented the condition of perpetual war and emphasized that it was high time that Austria and France came to a lasting peace. And finally he dared to suggest: "Why do you not use the opportunity of being in the [French] emperor's neighborhood to obtain a meeting with him? You have two or three steps from one another, the gardens are adjacent to each other: instead of taking the air on your own, go over into the Schönbrunn gardens; the emperor will be delighted to see you."[189]

In his summary of their two-hour conversation, Metternich said he had made sure throughout "not to be taken in."[190] Nevertheless, he took away from Savary's remarks information that was instructive for the Austrian side. First of all, Napoleon was pondering about the Austrians' motivation for war, assuming—astonishingly, to Metternich—that Austria wanted to claim ancient rights of the Habsburg Monarchy over Spain, rights that had been obsolete "for centuries" since Spain had become the inheritance of the Bourbons. And now that Napoleon had taken over "all of the inheritance of the Bourbons, the thrones of Madrid and Naples [were] his by right." Second, the French were having great problems with the rebellion in Tyrol, which is why Savary suggested putting it down. Metternich replied that it was not possible for him to say anything on this matter as the country had been in the hands of a foreign power (Bavaria) for the past three years.

One of Savary's comments, however, hit at the heart of Metternich's convictions: "Admit that it was unwise of your Court to lead a war without Russia's backing. And Prussia, which is actually a proud power, was not even able to prevent the desertion of Schill or to comment on it; this, it will come to regret." Thus, Savary pointed out to Metternich that the Austrian cabinet was not capable of forming the alliance that was needed. And he showed himself to be excellently informed on the domestic situation in Germany. Metternich categorically rejected the suggestion that he should negotiate, from his position, as a representative of Austria: "This is a matter to be agreed between the sovereigns."

Metternich was fully aware of his precarious situation, and also of how the public would see it if he entered into a negotiation with Napoleon in the park of the Palace of Schönbrunn. Let us remind ourselves of the symbolic significance of the overall situation. The Habsburg emperor had been forced to flee from his residence in Vienna and seek refuge in a fortress in Komorn, Hungary, and the French foreign minister, Champagny—an ordinary minister—now resided in the empress's rooms in the Hofburg. Napoleon himself had taken Schönbrunn as his residence, where he enjoyed his court proceedings and staged pompous weekly parades in front of the Vienna public. It was altogether without precedent that a potentate should have left his own court for almost half a year (from May 13 to October 15) and set up camp in a foreign country. Metternich knew how suspicious it might appear if he were seen to be present among the French in Vienna, and he therefore categorically refused all the tempting overtures from Napoleon—which he knew were self-serving. Instead, he insisted that it remain clear to the outside world that he was a prisoner. He rejected an offer of a conversation with Napoleon, saying: "If I am a prisoner, I behave myself as a prisoner; if I am free, I shall make use of my freedom; but if I had my freedom at this moment, I should certainly not use it in order to go and walk with Napoleon in the garden belonging to the emperor my master."[191] Saying this took some courage.

The Prisoner Exchange: Part Comedy, Part Jeopardy

In his memoirs, Metternich devoted more than seven full pages to his time as a prisoner. If we compare this to other events that are barely touched upon, we may conclude that this was an overwhelming experience for him. On June 17, Napoleon relented and informed Metternich that his captivity was over. The following morning, there began the rather risky exercise of the exchange of the imprisoned diplomats—between the frontlines, in the midst of battle. Colonel Avy, a general staff officer, had been charged with organizing the exchange. Five carriages, carrying Metternich and his Paris diplomatic corps, escorted by fifty mounted cavalry, set off, proceeding first to the castle of Count Harrach in Bruck an der Leitha, where they stayed for the night. On June 28, after several delays and detours, they reached Raab (Györ), and thence continued to neighboring Ács, where the French outpost was located. Ahead lay the Austrian front, marked by a line of artillery near the village of Gönyö, at the mouth of a branch of the Danube. When he saw the striking equipage and large escort, the Austrian commanding officer mistook it for the entourage of Viceroy Beauharnais, who was expected from Italy, and he fired the cannon. One cannon-ball passed between the wheels of Metternich's carriage; another missed its roof by a few centimeters. In the course of their crisscrossing itinerary, Metternich observed that large parts of the French army were moving toward Vienna. He concluded that Napoleon was preparing "a strike."

After further delays, the exchange at long last took place on July 2 at Zichy Castle. Here there was a bizarre scene. The castle, which previously had been in the hands of Brigadier General Duke Louis-Pierre Montbrun of France, was now under the rule of Count Palatine and Archduke Joseph, the imperial representative in Hungary after it had been taken by Hungarian rebels and thus become Austrian again. Suddenly, Colonel Avy was a potential prisoner of war. When he realized this, he leapt out of his carriage to find a horse and flee. Metternich's conduct in this episode is striking; he held back the colonel, saying: "You forget . . . that our parts are exchanged. I have been under your protection; now you are under mine, international law protects you; you will not be made a prisoner."[192] The colonel stayed, left his escort behind and personally accompanied Metternich. They met Dodun, the captive French diplomat, and Avy went with him to join the French corps while Metternich moved across to the Austrian.

THE INTERIM MINISTER: SIDELINED BY NAPOLEON

Foreign Minister ad Interim

After his release, Metternich went straight to Austrian headquarters in Wolkersdorf, where Emperor Franz was staying. On July 3, Franz was visibly relieved to receive Metternich there, and he made it clear that he wanted Metternich to be at his side from now on. In Wolkersdorf, Metternich experienced the decisive battle at Wagram on July 4 and 5 from very close by. As he had expected, it ended with defeat for the Austrians. This afforded him the opportunity to study their military weaknesses directly: the striking lack of internal coordination among the troops; the premature attacks; the delayed arrival of the army under the command of Archduke Johann; the withdrawal of Archduke Carl's army without the prior agreement of the emperor; and the truce that Carl agreed to with Napoleon on July 12, unauthorized by and against the will of the emperor. Because the truce stipulated that all Austrian troops would leave Tyrol, it meant that Emperor Franz was forced to break his promise to the Tyrolians not to agree to a peace without them.

Stadion was still hoping for Prussian support and for rebellions in northern Germany, but he was disappointed in all his expectations and was forced to admit to Metternich that he had failed. His position had become untenable, and on July 8, after it had become clear that that they had been defeated at Wagram, he offered his resignation to the emperor. Metternich's moment had arrived. As a politician is judged in part by the manner in which he entered into office, it is necessary at this point to disprove the insinuation that a sly Metternich plotted against Stadion and toppled him, that he was finally satisfying his overweening ambition by taking up the office of foreign minister. This insinuation is repeated again and again, or only halfheartedly rejected.[193] This is the context in which Srbik inserts his scathing picture of Metternich's character, according to which he lacked "imagination," was un-German, had no sense for the moral character of "a peoples," and did not possess the exalted ethos that "forms characters"—that is, of those around him. According to Srbik, Metternich lacked all the things possessed by those he praises: Stein, Fichte, and Wilhelm von Humboldt.[194]

The way in which the transition was ultimately arranged suggests another story. Metternich initially rejected the offer of becoming foreign minister, and when the emperor insisted, he accepted on one condition: he did not want to take over the foreign ministry as such but merely to become the functional equivalent to the French foreign minister, in order to sound out the possibilities of a peace treaty. He himself suggested that he should be appointed only provisionally and that Stadion should remain in his post as minister. Were Stadion to resign immediately following the defeat at Wagram, Metternich argued, this would weaken the Austrian negotiating position—a "great mistake."[195] The emperor accepted Metternich's suggestion and Stadion was kept in his post as foreign minister, in case the war should end victoriously after all.

This is not the style of argument of someone who is eaten up with ambition. Metternich knew about his contemporaries' insinuations about his motives, and he rebutted them in his memoirs.[196] Austria thus temporarily had two foreign ministers, one who held the official title but did not act as one, and one who acted as one but did not hold the title. In terms of rank, Metternich was meant to be on a par with his French counterpart, and on July 31 the emperor therefore formally appointed him "state and conference minister" for the negotiations.[197]

Emperor Franz and Metternich: The Foundation of Their Working Relationship

Metternich's reports and memoranda from Paris had given Emperor Franz an ever clearer picture of his ambassador's intellectual qualities and analytical nature. After the failures of Cobenzl, Colloredo, Thugut, and Stadion, the political situation had reached a nadir, and the monarch needed to try a minister who thought and acted differently. Metternich's appointment represented a total change in direction. And Metternich himself saw it that way, too. The scruples he expressed by saying "that [he did] not consider [himself] fit for the post" have always been completely misinterpreted as a case of— allegedly typical—vanity, and this interpretation is allegedly further strengthened by reading Metternich's declaration "I do not think myself capable of steering the vessel of the state in so great an Empire" as a case of fishing for compliments.[198]

These statements can be properly understood only against the background of his conditions for taking up the post. We need only remind ourselves of the reasons he avoided taking up an office during the Thugut era (which lasted up to 1801), even though he had been told that it would have been the start of a great career. He did not want to be in a position of responsibility and yet also have to follow others. His scruples were not caused by transitory political problems, no matter how grave the crisis of July 1809 might have been. He did not doubt his political competence. The actual hurdle he faced is expressed in the following statement: "I would do nothing the way that I have seen it done by others with more insight than me."[199] Here, he spoke with appropriate respect for the emperor. To put it less diplomatically, he would have had to have said: the policies of all politicians before me who held this position after Kaunitz, were wrong; they acted without principles, without competence, and without consistency; if I were now to assert the policies I consider to be the right ones, I would have all these individuals as my opponents. Metternich would have faced opposition in the face of which he could only have failed. This is the meaning of the diplomatically worded sentence that follows: "I should run the risk of advising badly [*auf falsche Wege zu geraten*], and my conscience does not allow me to bring this danger upon Your Majesty and the state."[200] But his suggestion of adopting new policies was met with open ears by the emperor, who felt that Metternich's reservations—and here Metternich quotes him verbatim—had "the value of determining reasons, and confirm my choice of your person."[201]

Metternich wanted a clear and reliable basis for his dealings with the emperor. An unusual occurrence meant he soon had the opportunity to find out whether such a basis existed. He accompanied the emperor, by himself, in his carriage on the way from the headquarters in Znaim to the Hungarian fortress Komorn. At this point a truce had not yet been agreed to, and due to the distribution of enemy troops, the carriage had to take a detour via the Jablunka Pass in the most eastern part of Moravia. Metternich, the new minister, recorded that he therefore had plenty of time "to lay before his Majesty my view of the present state of affairs."[202] It is no coincidence that Metternich, at this point in his memoirs, inserted an extensive characterization of the emperor, because during this journey the crucial question of whether he would have the emperor's backing at all times would be answered. We should therefore look more soberly at his somewhat rapturous evaluation, and we should look to the evidence that gave Metternich the hope that he would have the emperor's support, despite the criticism to which his policies were subjected in public.

Metternich was convinced that what guaranteed his support were the emperor's "great qualities": his "calm," even in the midst of the most serious crises; his inner strength; his "calm and clear line of thought"; the charisma of "his strong and pure soul."[203] Today we would speak of the integrity of his character. Metternich became "convinced that in all important questions my views would always be in harmony with his, and that his great qualities would always insure me the support without which a minister, be his views ever so good, can make no certain plan and carry out no project with prospect of success." This is how Metternich remembered the impression he gained from the conversation during the journey in the emperor's carriage, and he had nothing to change about it in hindsight. No doubt there were particular matters on which the emperor and his minister did not agree entirely. Nevertheless, they agreed in all matters that concerned threats to the existence of the state. In July 1813 there occurred another extraordinary situation, similar to the one in July 1809, in which Metternich asked the emperor for unconditional loyalty in the face of Tsar Alexander's forceful demands for Metternich's resignation.

The cooperation between the emperor and his minister was to last until the final hours of the emperor's life, when he entrusted Metternich with organizing his testament. What was the secret of their cooperation? It would be wrong to suspect that Franz was a naive, servile monarch who succumbed to the art of a superior persuader.[204] He acted of his own will, independently, and was downright stubborn if someone tried to manipulate him or to force him into doing something. But he was not intellectually flexible enough to discern a clear line of action in a complex situation that required a decision. He knew what he wanted and what he did not want, but complexity made him insecure and hesitant. That was the point where Metternich, his congenial partner, stood by his side. In his testament, Franz even called him his "friend." Metternich's theoretical talents, intellectuality, ready comprehension, and breathtakingly retentive memory allowed him to enumerate the available options clearly. And on this basis the emperor could then develop his arguments and opinions and come to an independent decision. Metternich drew up hundreds of preparatory papers to aid decision making, so-called presentations [*Vorträge*], which, in the case of extremely important decisions, took the form of exemplary memoranda or manifestos. He did not manipulate the emperor; he waited for his "imperial decision," which the emperor usually appended to the "presentation" in the form of an imperial resolution [*Signat*].

Metternich's conduct was endearingly loyal, but he acted without fear and was faithful to his principles. The character traits he found in his emperor guaranteed that he could discuss matters freely and did not have to hold anything back. This, too, he was able to discover during the journey in the emperor's carriage: "We examined the situation of the empire with thorough impartiality; we reviewed the prospects which the war still presented, as well as those promised by a peace concluded under the most unhappy auspices."[205]

Metternich's Comprehensive Political Analysis upon Taking Up His Post: Instructions "under the Most Unhappy Auspices"

On July 20, 1809, in a comprehensive political analysis of the situation of the Habsburg Monarchy, Metternich summarized everything he had been discussing and evaluating in his private meetings with the emperor during the two weeks following his release.[206] The truce of Znaim on July 12, together with the appointment of the peace negotiators, was the point of departure. His presentation proved straightaway why the provisional foreign minister was so valuable to the emperor. The newly appointed minister needed guidelines— "instructions"—that could be authorized only by the emperor, but the emperor required assistance in this, and Metternich provided him with clear principles and suggestions about what could be negotiated and what was under no circumstance to be put up for discussion.

Metternich began by comparing the current balance of forces with that after the Battle of Austerlitz at the end of 1805. After Austerlitz, Austrian forces had been almost wiped out; now, there was still an army of some 250,000 men, and Austria had almost succeeded in "utterly destroying the enemy."[207] Whereas in 1805 there were still the allies, Russia and Prussia, in the background, and Napoleon had not yet achieved complete control of Germany, now "Prussia is destroyed, Russia is an ally of France, France the master of Germany."[208] Because of this complete isolation, Austria's position in 1809 was much worse than in 1805. Back then, the peace negotiations discussed the question of territorial concessions; now such concessions could possibly "bring ruin to the empire," destroy "the very life of the state."[209] The truce was of crucial importance, Metternich thought, because if there were another failed military campaign, "the present association of states that make up Austria would be in danger of being entirely disunited."[210]

Beyond this general risk, Metternich discussed the consequences of conceding particular territories. In military terms, Salzburg was more important
than West Galicia. The concession of the Dalmatian coast, the Littorale, would
hit the state at its core: "Financially considered, the Littorale has the first position, the most eminent one in my view." With the loss of this region, the state
would lose access to the Adriatic and would become an exclusively continental
power. Metternich even feared the breakup of the empire.[211] It is often forgotten
that the Habsburg Monarchy had a fleet and was a maritime power; it did not
sail the seas out of colonial aspirations but instead understood the Mediterranean as its economic and trade area, on which the commercial power of the
monarchy was completely dependent. In the years following 1809, this dependence increased even further. The Habsburg Monarchy shared its longest external border with the Ottoman Empire, with which it was economically closely
connected.[212] Their influence in the Mediterranean was significant; the
Habsburg emperors traditionally considered the Italian peninsula as their
exclusive zone of influence. The demand for a reduction in the size of the army,
on the other hand, Metternich saw as less important because the catastrophic
financial situation of the monarchy required it anyway. And, at any rate, the
reduction would in a sense be in name only, if the bulk of regiments were retained and support from reserves and the system of territorial troops was taken
into account.

The Russian foreign minister, Romanzov, had already foreseen how urgently
Napoleon would need money for the opulent furnishing of the new military
nobility and his own family, as well as for financing further campaigns, and
now this had come to pass. Metternich pointed out that Napoleon's demands
for contribution payments, if sufficiently "extravagant," would hamper Austria's economic prosperity, and that—should Austria default—they would also
provide Napoleon with a pretext to renew hostilities if he so chose, as he had
done in the case of Prussia.[213]

Metternich knew about the importance of political symbolism for imperial
supremacy. Thus, he insisted that they retain the title of Emperor. Without the
addition of "Holy Roman," the title "until recently had been an empty word,"
but after Napoleon's appropriation of the title, this had changed. The title now
defined the position of a ruler in Europe: "It is noticeable that Napoleon connects the concept of supremacy and independence with the title of Emperor.
By losing it, Austria would lower itself . . . to the class of tributary powers."[214]
With this observation, Metternich was keeping in mind Napoleon's strategy
of dividing up European states; for Austria, resisting this strategy meant
defending its status as an imperial power.

Even as a beginner in his office, Metternich already thought beyond its confines, as is demonstrated by his criticism of the domestic administration of the empire, which, he said, needed to be centralized in order to "remove the unhappy influences of divided powers."[215] He was thinking of the paralyzing effect of competition from court offices that should have no say over decisions of war or peace. But most of all he was of the opinion that the army command should under no circumstances involve itself in the negotiations of the conditions of peace. He suspected that it would be Napoleon's intention to sideline the new foreign minister, and he would soon be confirmed in his suspicion.

Metternich's New Strategy: The "Keuner Method"

Metternich's new strategy consisted, first, of a precise strategic plan for his own way of proceeding toward his political goal (the actual strategy), which was to rescue the state in its entirety through the rapid development of resources for its reconstruction. Second, at the tactical level he acted with cool calculation, subordinating his behavior to his purpose. Taking these aspects together, one might call this strategy the "Keuner method," after Bertolt Brecht's *Stories of Mr. Keuner,* in particular the one titled "Measures against Power." This is actually a story within a story, for in it Mr. Keuner relates the story of a Mr. Eggers, who had to let a very powerful agent stay in his house during a time of despotism. The agent asks him: "Will you be my servant?"[216] Mr. Eggers remains silent but serves the agent for seven years until he becomes fat and dies. Mr. Eggers carries him out of the house, and only then does he answer: "No." This parable illustrates vividly how a form of behavior that may be mistaken for weakness or opportunism finds its true explanation only once it is seen in light of Mr. Keuner's maxim: "I don't have a backbone to be broken. I'm the one who has to live longer than Power."[217]

This is how we should understand Metternich's policies toward Napoleon in the years between 1809 and 1815, or at least up to 1813. Whoever has not understood his method is easily misled into identifying his strategy and tactics with his character, as has been done by Srbik, for whom Metternich was "the supple man"—as opposed to the "strong-willed," often difficult, high-minded Stadion, who for Srbik, given the "master race" he favors, is the "nobler" of the two.[218] The more appropriate categories for a historian, one should assume, are political acumen and professionalism. Metternich was no Haugwitz, who turned into putty in Napoleon's hands and consequently betrayed the interests of his king and state. He was also no Cobenzl, who allowed himself to be intimidated by the choleric fit in which Napoleon smashed a valuable porcelain figure at his feet. Rather, on many occasions, Metternich faced the French emperor and stood his ground so fearlessly that he earned Napoleon's respect. The famous meeting of the two in Dresden, in June 1813, is a classic example of this.

Even before the beginning of the peace negotiations in Altenburg, Metternich inculcated the "Keuner method" in the emperor, who was then residing in Komorn. Metternich suspected that the method would make him many enemies in Vienna, but he was not prepared to let the monarchy's "backbone be broken." A future peace, he thought, had to take into account the following "evidence": "Initially, and leaving aside unpredictable events, we shall find our safety only by accommodating ourselves to the triumphant system of France."[219] To Metternich it was obvious that this system, "being entirely contrary to all sound principles of policy—being opposed to every great union of states," was most unsuitable for the Austrian situation: "My convictions are expressed in the body of papers I produced as ambassador. My principles are unchangeable, but to necessity we must yield. . . . From the day when peace is signed we must confine our system to tacking, and turning, and flattering. Thus alone may we possibly preserve our existence, till the day of general deliverance. . . . Therefore . . . for us there remains but one expedient, to preserve our strength for better days, to work out our preservation by gentler means, without looking back upon our former course."[220] This tactical program amounts to a confession of faith, and without it Metternich's subsequent decisions are unintelligible.

According to Metternich, in the long term it was necessary to lead the Habsburg Monarchy out of its international isolation. As even Napoleon's own police minister had said, in order to act against Napoleon, Russia's support was needed. Metternich had an underhand way to achieve this: he would aim to loosen the ties between the fickle Russian court and France and bring Russia closer to Austria by appearing to be in fierce competition with the tsar for the role of Napoleon's ally. As early as 1809, Metternich thought of the marriage project as a "soft" means to that end. The daughter of the Habsburg emperor, Marie Louise, won out over the favored daughter of the tsar, Katharina, and became Napoleon's future wife. In December 1809 the plan began to take a more definite shape.

Metternich also considered joining the general Continental System unavoidable, however harmful this might be. A further taboo he thought had to be broken was the recognition of the "usurpation of Spain"—the replacement of the Bourbons in Naples and Madrid with Napoleon's kings, Marat and Joseph; both Stadion and the emperor had vehemently opposed this. Metternich also foresaw that Napoleon's dissolution of the Papal States would force Austria to make a statement, which was, however, only to engage with political and not with ecclesiastical questions. Contributions, finally, were unavoidable.

Metternich Sidelined at the Peace Negotiations in Altenburg, Hungary

The truce of Znaim created a state of limbo for as long as it remained unclear whether a peace treaty would follow and make the continuation of the war impossible. The negotiations for the treaty began on August 17, 1809. The emperor had withdrawn to the Hungarian Palace of the Ésterházy in Totis (in Hungarian Tata), which was now serving as the headquarters. The supreme command of the military had been transferred from Archduke Carl to Prince Johann Liechtenstein, and Metternich had been given the role of "chief plenipotentiary for peace negotiations." It had been agreed that the negotiations would take place in Altenburg, Hungary. Altenburg lay within the French sphere of influence and thus was declared neutral.

In his memoirs, Metternich revealed details that until then had been unknown about the negotiations which show how his expectations of Champagny and Napoleon had been painfully confirmed. After all, he knew how they would set about cornering an inferior opponent. In the cases of the Spanish Bourbons in Bayonne and King Friedrich Wilhelm III of Prussia in Tilsit, Napoleon had demonstrated his tendency to design agreements in his own favor. This time the negotiations were about what land and people Austria would concede as the price for peace and what level of contributions Austria would have to pay—with regard to the latter, Napoleon, notoriously, tended to demand exorbitant sums.

The treatment Metternich received in Altenburg was dramatically worse than even his experiences in Fontainebleau. When he demanded formal protocols of the meetings, Champagny refused, saying he had not been instructed to produce such protocols. Some fourteen days later, he presented Metternich with edited protocols for Metternich to accept and sign. Among them were a number of protocols of meetings that had never taken place. Metternich saw what Napoleon was doing: foisting false protocols on him that he could later use to justify the continuation of the war if the negotiations failed. When Metternich, indignant, told Champagny that simple common sense could have told him that this way of proceeding was futile and compromised him, Champagny sought to defend himself but at the same committed the indiscretion of admitting that Napoleon had indeed dictated the protocols. The French emperor realized that, faced with Metternich, this strategy would not work, and he broke off negotiations at Altenburg and recalled Champagny to Vienna. This whole undignified affair confirmed for Metternich that this was a "pretend negotiation" and that Napoleon was simply playing for time in order to allow him to reorganize and reequip his troops.

Right at the beginning of his time as interim minister, Metternich had an experience he would have liked to forget. The Austrian emperor had acted without consulting his minister and opened up a parallel series of events.[221] Franz noticed that, as long as the negotiations continued, Napoleon was able to consolidate his army, and Franz feared that this increasing military strength would mean that Napoleon could impose an even less favorable peace on Austria. Without discussing it with Metternich, he sent General Bubna as a negotiator to Napoleon's camp in order, finally, to settle the conditions of the peace treaty. In the absence of Metternich's input, no one took into account Napoleon's sly, calculating nature. Napoleon suggested to Bubna: "The diplomats . . . do not know how to get through an affair like the present; we soldiers understand one another better. Let the Emperor send Prince Liechtenstein to me, and we will end the matter in four-and-twenty hours."[222]

The emperor consulted with the new supreme commander, Prince Liechtenstein, Field Marshal Count Heinrich von Bellegarde, and Stadion, without involving Metternich, who was still in Altenburg. Their advice was that he should give Napoleon's offer a chance.[223] The minister whose responsibility it would have been to take this decision learned of it only when Liechtenstein stayed with Metternich in Altenburg on his way to Vienna.

The emperor had explicitly ordered Metternich to hand over to Liechtenstein the documents containing Austrian demands and henceforth to abstain from negotiations with Champagny. It was even taken into consideration that the undertaking might fail, in which case the war would have been resumed and Stadion would have taken charge of his ministry again.

Having learned of the operation, Metternich immediately recognized the risks contained in Napoleon's suggestion. Liechtenstein was not an ordinary negotiator: he was the supreme commander of the Austrian army, and it was in this capacity that he entered the territory controlled by the enemy. This put the French emperor in a favorable position, because if Liechtenstein refused to accept his conditions, he could force a peace on him. Metternich prophesied that Liechtenstein would be held captive, and the army would become leaderless, and thus hardly able to fight the war. Liechtenstein was so shocked that he wanted to return to Totis, but Metternich talked him out of it. Up to this point, Prince Liechtenstein had believed that when meeting Napoleon he would confront an upright soldier. Metternich, for his part, found himself limited to taking "an observant and passive attitude"[224] because the emperor had resorted to his old ways, moving responsibilities to and fro and, in this case, putting the matter in Liechtenstein's hands.

A Peace Treaty in Contravention of International Law

After the negotiations in Altenburg had been broken off on September 25, Metternich still tried "to save what could be saved." He knew that the gullible Prince Liechtenstein was hopelessly out of his depth and suggested to the emperor that he say the conference had been moved from Altenburg to Vienna and authorize Metternich to accompany Liechtenstein to the meeting with Napoleon.[225] He went even further, indirectly criticizing the emperor's actions by saying that "here [in Altenburg] my word was the only one that counted, while in Vienna I can only appear as second to Prince Liechtenstein." The whole operation therefore had to be modified, and the emperor ordered the general "to follow [Metternich's] lead in the course of the negotiations."[226] However much Metternich had felt in agreement and harmony with the emperor, this marked an early instance of a structural problem with which he had to battle until the monarch's death in early 1835—namely, the antagonisms between him and the other officials the monarch consulted. The emperor liked to consult different authorities and to play them off against each other, often without their knowledge.

The newly appointed minister experienced a textbook case of governmental paralysis, which resulted, to its own disadvantage, in the spoliation of the peace negotiations. This shocked and embittered him. In a subsequent review, he wrote that because Napoleon had faced, on the Austrian side, a military man, a dilettante in questions regarding statecraft who had not mastered "all the detours and retreats known to the science of diplomacy," a man who—in his simple gullibility—knew nothing about the means of falseness, duplicitousness, and deviousness, the French emperor was able to steer the negotiations to his advantage.[227] Champagny, who played a leading role in the negotiations, repeatedly gave Prince Liechtenstein new hopes and promised new concessions that, it was clear, would be retreated from in the next round of talks. On this occasion Metternich described the dark side of the business of diplomacy, the side of which Napoleon was a master; one had to be able to deal with such business. Metternich knew how to deal with it, and this is something people often resented in him if they mistook the techniques of diplomacy for traits of his character. Prince Liechtenstein came to agreements in the course of one night on issues that Metternich had been unable to settle over the course of six weeks in Altenburg. Champagny later claimed that he had handed Napoleon peace overnight as a "present."[228]

Why did Metternich speak so openly and publicly about the "so-called" peace treaty, as he referred to it, even when he had been in such an unfavorable position, sidelined and helpless? He wanted to send out a signal about the political morality that was, for him, embodied in European international law. Napoleon had committed unprecedented violations of this law. In 1809 the predictions the sidelined Metternich had conveyed to Prince Liechtenstein were confirmed. When Liechtenstein sought to leave Vienna and the negotiations in protest at the continuous trickery of the opposite side, he was told that, as the supreme commander of the Austrian army, this would be considered a breach of the truce, which would make the prince a prisoner of war and deprive his army of its leader. Such was the effect of this blackmail on the prince that, during the night of October 13, he accepted everything that Champagny had demanded, and finally sealed it all with his signature.

The next morning, Liechtenstein, upon departing from Vienna to Totis in order to receive instructions, heard the thunder of Napoleon's cannon—fired to mark the signing of the peace treaty, even though the Austrian emperor had yet to agree to its terms. When Metternich learned of this, he was so deeply shocked that it altered his picture of Napoleon: "A Treaty of Peace full of unworthy artifices, having no foundation in international rights. . . . What had just taken place disclosed a side of Napoleon to me which placed him far lower in my eyes; and before my conscience the cause I had to uphold rose in like measure."[229]

Metternich was not exaggerating his indignation in hindsight. At the time, Napoleon's methods caused disbelief; it seemed impossible that he should have presented the contract as already agreed to with his unannounced departure. At a conference in Totis—two days after the cannon were fired—the minister of foreign affairs (Metternich), of war (Count Karl von Zichy), and the president of the court chamber (Count Joseph O'Donel) discussed possible ways the contributions might be reduced. They condemned the fact that negotiations had been delayed and had become almost impossible "on the assumption of an ill will on the part of the French government in light of the emperor's departure."[230] All in all they concluded that, "in its present form," the peace treaty had suffered "essential deteriorations." But in fact there was nothing left to negotiate.

Why did Emperor Franz ultimately agree to the harsh peace that had been signed at the Palace of Schönbrunn on October 14, 1809? In his later summary, Metternich enumerates six reasons: first, the evils of all kinds visited upon the provinces that were occupied by the enemy; second, in addition to contributions, the enormous cost to the population of French troops being maintained in the country; third, the poor condition of the army, which had shrunk by a third through injury and was not fit for another campaign; fourth, a revolt in Galicia at the same time that opened up a second front; fifth, the willingness of the Russians to enter Hungary; and, sixth, the uncertainty that resulted from the fact that the existence of the monarchy as such might otherwise depend on the outcome of a single battle—that the last independent barrier to French aggression in Europe might fall.

Conclusions from a Lost War

It is possible to understand the change in Metternich's strategy—henceforth to flatter France—only if one takes into account his view of the lost war of 1809. An account written shortly after the end of the war reveals what Metternich had learned from the disaster—if he had not known it before.[231] It is not that Metternich was a warmonger who suddenly adopted a defensive stance; these texts do not show—as Srbik claims—that there was a "quick transition from political hatred to dispassionate calculation, from whipping up sentiment in the agitation for war to a rejection of everything excessively provocative, extreme, or violent."[232] It was not a matter of Metternich changing but of him wanting to correct the course steered so far by Austrian cabinets, a course he judged to have been disastrous.

According to Metternich, there had been two reasons for Austria's declaration of war. Napoleon's gradual subjugation of the European Continent made the Austrian cabinet fear for the existence of the empire. The first reason was thus that the weakening of the French by the war in Spain presented their last chance for self-preservation, a "hint that the moment had arrived in which Austria had to believe that it was called upon to play its last card, hopeful of success."[233] The second reason was that, given the "elevation of a national feeling of the people" in northern Germany after 1806, they could count on them as allies, and this justified launching an attack even without a formal alliance. The outcome of the war, Metternich wrote, proved this to have been an illusion.

At this point Metternich touched upon his doubts regarding the power of the national political movement in Germany. His skepticism in this regard has been misunderstood, and he has therefore been accused of being an enemy of national movements for reasons of principle. Metternich understood nationality to be an essential part of human nature. But he condemned national movements when they ended up influencing important political decision—in particular because of the possibility of war. He was convinced that Napoleon could be overcome only by consolidated military power and the largest possible numbers of troops. He recognized that when national identity became political, different ethnic groups were separated from each other and turned into enemies. All the major powers' armies at the time were based on troops of mixed nationalities. One had only to look at Napoleon's allies: the states of the Rhenish Confederation, the Italian and Polish legions. And when Napoleon sought to use national sentiment for political purposes, he addressed the French to strengthen support for him, or he addressed the nationalities of the states against which he fought in order to destabilize them. This is what he tried to do with the Hungarians in 1809, for instance, by promising them national independence if they broke away from the Habsburg Empire.

From Metternich's perspective, passionate politicians such as Baron vom Stein overlooked the fact that war could be won only through the unity of the allies: if the princes of England, Russia, Prussia, Austria, Sweden, and—who knows—possibly even the renegade states of the Rhenish Confederation united their troops against Napoleon. For Metternich, the "world war" against Napoleon was too large to be won by national impulses. It was Napoleon himself, of all people, who confirmed Metternich's doubt that national uprisings could be effective against France. In June 1813 Napoleon told him: "Do you count on Germany? See what it did in the year 1809! To hold the people there in check, my soldiers are sufficient; and for the faith of the princes, my security is the fear they have of you."[234]

At the heart of Metternich's criticism of the war of 1809 are the convictions that it was the wrong moment in time; that there was a lack of coordination regarding the plan for war; that the withdrawal came too early; and that there were no allies.[235] Metternich's account came close to the conclusions reached by modern military analysis. On this view, from an outside perspective, the chances of an Austrian victory were not too bad: with 400,000 soldiers, they had more troops than the French. Napoleon, however, had an advantage over his enemy, because he was able to move and coordinate large military units over vast geographical distances. Austria's military leaders were still applying an eighteenth-century strategy, only moving their armies over limited distances. They were not able to unite their forces in battle at crucial points, and they did not chase retreating enemy troops.[236]

The Burden of the Treaty of Schönbrunn

The Treaty of Schönbrunn is usually evaluated in terms of the territory and people the monarchy lost. That evaluation betrays the thinking of the age; states did not yet have the tool of reliable statistics fully at their disposal, and so the "power of states" was measured in terms of their area and population, not in terms of nationalities.[237] For Metternich this method of calculation seemed important enough that he asked for a precise list of the territories and populations Austria had lost, which he filed in the family archive (today housed in Prague).[238]

But more important than the territory and population question is the political significance of the peace treaty. In this respect, one aspect of the treaty is usually overlooked, an aspect that was of great importance for the Metternichs' family history. The Treaty of Schönbrunn was a historical watershed after which the restoration of the Holy Roman Empire had become impossible. Stadion was the last politician in the service of the Habsburgs who attempted such a restoration—at least, this is how it appears from his conduct in the war. He wanted to restore the Germany of the period immediately after the Principal Conclusion of the Extraordinary Imperial Delegation of 1803. The mediatization (although not the secularization) that had taken place since then was to be reversed, and there is evidence that there were also plans to revive the sort of imperial rule there had been under the Holy Roman Empire, which would have brought Germany under the hegemony of the Habsburgs rather than of France. This scenario would also explain the appeals to the "German nation," as Stadion, who was himself a mediatized imperial count, could not have had a unified nation-state in mind.[239]

Metternich was conscious of this historical turning point. He no longer evaluated the peace treaty from the perspective of the Holy Roman Empire; all that counted for him now was "the empire," and this meant the Habsburg Empire. He thought that it was "most destructive for the empire" that it was now encircled by "countries which were under the scepter of Napoleon, or subject to his direct influence."[240] The members of this cartel were rewarded by Napoleon at the expense of Austria. Salzburg, Berchtesgaden, and the Inn province were given to Bavaria, a faithful ally of the Rhenish Confederation. Western Galicia, Cracow, and the county of Zamosk became extensions of the Dukedom of Warsaw. A part of Eastern Galicia became Russian. And the French military administration took charge of the newly formed "Illyrian provinces," which meant that the port city of Trieste and all access to the Adriatic had been wrested from Austria.

Metternich had already analyzed what this meant for the country's economy. The peace left Austria weakened in both military and economic terms, hobbled by the 85 million franc contributions, the impact on trade of joining the Continental System, and the reduction of the Austrian army to a maximum of 150,000 men. All these factors meant that the new Austrian politics would have to adopt the "Keuner method," described above, which meant: to stay calm, to be cautious, and "to keep open for Austria the chances which the greatest of all powers, the power of circumstances, might offer sooner or later (under the strong government of its monarch) for the much-threatened prosperity of the Empire."[241] The power of circumstance, sooner or later, would lead to the collapse of the French system of universal domination.

THE MINISTER IN CHARGE OF THE NEW DIRECTION: A DEFENSIVE
STRATEGY IN DOMESTIC POLICY AND MATCHMAKING ABROAD,
1809–1810

Crisis Management: The Situation following the Treaty of Schönbrunn

On November 27, 1809, Emperor Franz and Metternich arrived in Vienna only
hours apart. The people of Vienna lined the streets and greeted the monarch
with a genuine enthusiasm; to them, he seemed to guarantee that the French
occupation was over for good. Metternich went straight to the chancellor's
palace, the Palais Kaunitz, to take up office as the now-permanent foreign minister and the most important servant of the emperor. He arranged his rooms
on the first floor and was already designing plans for the level above, where his
family was to live. At such watersheds in his life, he always reflected on the path
he had taken and his place within the maelstrom of contemporary events. It
was one year since he had gone to Paris, before the war, and seven months since
his departure from Paris:

> Think of all that has happened in this time! The world has never been
> closer to salvation, never closer to the abyss. What events and challenges!
> Fortunately, heaven has given me health and an unwavering mind, nothing
> will ever set me off my course; it is as straight as my heart. . . . And I, truly,
> will be the happiest being, once—with my existence secured, but inde-
> pendent—I can follow my inclinations, which are altogether contrary to
> the horrible movements by which I find myself permanently surrounded.
> I pay no regard to the burden Austria may have to bear, or to how much
> I can take of what I have to carry at present.[242]

He was now playing "the main role." Clearly aware of the significance of the
moment, Metternich summarized: "It is no minor task to be the foreign minister of Austria in 1809."

Many biographers interpret such statements as self-centeredness, smugness,
or arrogance, without acknowledging the essence of what is being said. The foreign minister entered into office at a time of transition; the state was experiencing its worst crisis. Metternich had in mind a program that he expected
would meet with great resistance. He was in all matters completely dependent
on the emperor's support, but otherwise, unlike his time as ambassador, he now
was able to act independently and suggest political guidelines—or so he thought.

It has never been truly appreciated just how the emperor and Metternich
perceived the situation in which the state found itself after the catastrophic

Treaty of Schönbrunn, nor how they digested this political trauma and advanced a program they—and in particular Metternich—thought necessitated by this situation. Following the peace treaty, this program emerged within a few months, while the Chancellery still resided in Totis. The fact that the new policies were consistent, were implemented systematically, and were oriented toward a clearly defined goal, absolutely contradicts Srbik's picture of a "maneuvering" minister for whom the time between 1809 and 1813 was only one of "transition."

Metternich used his authority to begin attacking the root cause of the evil, reorganizing the Chancellery in November, while it was still in Totis, and thus getting rid of the chaotic procedures and distribution of authority under Stadion. His mind preoccupied with the French Revolution and Napoleon's rule, he also at this point established the basis of his future political course in a thus far little-noticed analysis: "I considered the Revolution, as it burst forth in France in 1789, as the starting point of all the misfortunes of Europe."[243] During the previous twenty years, the "wars occasioned by the Revolution had preserved Germany and Austria from the infection of social theories." For Metternich, the real challenge was the attack on the social order, not the political program for a new Constitution (though he criticized that as well). The German states had remained to a large extent unaffected, "for nations are averse to adopt as benefits those doctrines which are presented to them by the force of arms."

In France, by contrast, the "social revolution" had led to a civil war and the guillotine. When the young Napoleon aimed cannon at demonstrating and rebelling citizens in 1795, he was reacting to a situation that offered him an opportunity to seize power by military means. Metternich called the rise of his great opponent an "inevitable result" of the social revolution, because this revolution had led to "military despotism, which found its highest expression in Napoleon." Napoleon himself had been "a barrier against the encroachments of anarchical theories in France and in those countries upon which lay the weight of his iron arm." Napoleon himself had explained it to Metternich: "I crushed the Revolution" ["J'ai écrasé la Révolution"].[244]

This analysis was still valid in 1809, and it justified the new minister in placing "social questions . . . in the background," as he explicitly said.[245] This does not mean, however, that he did not have a sense for social problems. In France, he said, Napoleon tamed such problems with dictatorial measures; thus, for the time being Germany did not seem to be threatened with social unrest coming from France. Metternich therefore placed "in the very first rank . . . the preservation of what remained of the Austrian Empire, even after its unsuccessful campaigns."[246] What did he mean by that? What in his list of priorities held more importance than the social question? While the population "did not look beyond the present moment"—they were rejoicing over the emperor's return to Vienna, believing they were liberated—Metternich looked toward a more distant future: "Napoleon, in the eyes of Europe, passed for an irresistible power, under the yoke of which all must bow."[247] From now on, this fact informed Metternich's policies. It was necessary carefully to avoid anything that might give the *empereur* the slightest reason to intervene again in Austria, which seemed to be at his mercy for the foreseeable future. The emperor and his minister became convinced that they had to secure the country by using repressive measures on the domestic front and precautionary measures against Napoleon on the foreign policy front.

During the French Revolution, Metternich had followed the maxim of studying the enemy and learning from him. He now followed this maxim again, imitating the structure and efficiency of the Napoleonic system of repression in Austria. Political change after 1809 was not informed by principles of feudal absolutism but by Napoleon's new, "more modern" educational dictatorship, which pretended to be enlightened but rested on intimidation. It may sound like a paradox, but if one does not identify "modern" with "progressive," and instead sees this "modern" dictatorship as simply a new, technical, instrumental way of organizing politics and ruling over people, then Napoleon and Metternich can both be seen as pursuing modernizing agendas in relation to the public sphere, propaganda, the control of communication, infrastructure, and homeland security. Between 1809 and 1813 Austrian politics was influenced by the Napoleonic system in two respects: in foreign policy, it found itself under a sword of Damocles—Austria as a major power could be wiped off the map at any moment; domestically, it sought to preserve what was left of the monarchy's independence by keeping the population under control with a system of domination that copied essential elements of the Napoleonic system. These new policies began to spread a defensive network of control across the country, not for any anti-Enlightenment reasons but instead to fend off Napoleon. Let us take a look at the most important aspects of this strategy.

Controlling Opinion as a Protective Measure against Napoleon

There was a tradition of censoring the press and printed material in the Habsburg Monarchy. Autocratic rule, no matter how much it might have been inspired by idea of the Enlightenment, could not be made compatible with a free public sphere. The emperors Joseph II and Leopold II learned this very quickly during their temporary experiments with press liberalization. Their successor, Emperor Franz, was considerably more skeptical, and reinstated a full-blown, traditional form of censorship. This was deemed especially necessary after suspicions arose that secret political or even revolutionary associations, such as the Rosicrucians, Illuminati, Freemasons, and "Jacobins," were seeking to abolish the existing social order.

Censorship of the press by itself, however, no longer seemed sufficient to Franz. How, for instance, was he to deal with the many foreign pamphlets and newspapers that were published every day? After the peace with Napoleon, could he let them circulate freely inside Austria if they expressed "obvious harmful tendencies"? Franz had in mind newspapers from France, Italy, and the Rhenish Confederation. Thus, he wondered "whether it would not be useful and of no disadvantage to foreign relations if such writings were disproved and invalidated straight after their publication." He wanted to take the initiative and influence public opinion through creating a press that was loyal to the government. Metternich was asked to draw up a report on the matter.[248] This contradicts the traditional view of "how little the government was inclined to express or to explain itself to any public."[249] Quite the contrary, at the beginning of November 1809, Emperor Franz launched an active press policy initiative. He needed people to mastermind the project, and he found them in Metternich and his father.

During his time as an ambassador in Paris, Metternich had already drawn up plans to influence the foreign press, especially the German-speaking parts of it. As early as mid-1808, Metternich warned that it was a colossal mistake—and one made by Austria in particular—for the government to consider addressing the public [*parler avec le public*] in a manner that was superfluous or beneath its dignity. It was necessary to tell the public the truth, and to stop talking to it as if doing so were a danger in itself. Since the beginning of the French Revolution, the French government had made things easier for themselves by filling positions in journalists' offices. They had picked up the weapons the authorities of the ancien régime had previously disregarded, and now they turned their fire on the governments of other states.

As a modern thinker, Metternich understood the press as a progressive mass medium. He was one of only a few politicians of this age to realize that his time—he spoke of the "century of words"—had seen a transformation in the media that would fundamentally change "society": the press was becoming a social power. Prophetically, he declared: "Public opinion is the most powerful of all means; like religion, it penetrates the most hidden recesses, where administrative measures have no influence. To despise public opinion is as dangerous as to despise moral principles; . . . it requires peculiar attention, consistency, and untiring perseverance. Posterity will hardly believe that we have regarded silence as an efficacious weapon to oppose to the clamours of our opponents, and that in a century of words!"[250] From his perspective, what mattered was to manipulate the press, to deprive it of its semblance of authority, and nothing could be easier than that. The example of Napoleon, to whom he referred by name, taught him that newspapers were as powerful as an army of 300,000 men. The emperor's November 1809 initiative reminded Metternich of the *Österreichische Zeitung*, which had been under the editorship of Friedrich von Schlegel since June 24, 1809, and had been launched by Archduke Carl.[251] But much more was needed. It was "a task of any government that had existed for more than a day" to do all it could against a party that had been attempting for years "to kill the public spirit or at least to poison it." The Austrian government used only one newspaper for its official announcements, the *Wiener Zeitung*. Metternich argued that this was not enough to satisfy the masses' hunger for news, especially in times when "every day brings a fresh catastrophe." As the organ of the government, the *Wiener Zeitung* could not be impartial, and so was lacking a counter-voice. What was needed, therefore, was "a periodical that was seemingly not influenced by the authorities."[252] From then on, Metternich focused on setting up a "literary bureau" that would be a center for press manipulation. He tried to influence well-known intellectuals and get them to write favorably of Austria's politics: in Leipzig there was Adam Müller; in Prague, in 1813, Friedrich Gentz; and in Vienna, Friedrich von Schlegel.

Metternich looked at the problem within the wider historical context. In 1808 he had already warned that, since the French Revolution, papers from France had influenced public opinion in Germany and that, in the interests of gaining control over the situation, they should seek an agreement with France in order "to remove the daily diatribes." It was again the French who decided the goal pursued by the Austrians: "The weapon, no matter how primitive, is nevertheless too strong in the hands of Napoleon for him ever to be prepared to give it up." Metternich advised against an overly strict censorship, though, because that would only cause unrest. He therefore recommended that the censors be "reasonable men with strong principles who acted impartially and without subsidiary motives." He wanted to permit a "larger press" to form so that its "large power" could be even more effective against the enemy.[253]

At the same time, Metternich brought it about that an imperial resolution was sent to all regional rulers reminding them that Austria was now at peace with France and its allies. The resolution asked "that the tone and language of the newspapers appearing in the monarchy shall be adapted accordingly, and be kept free of anything that may give rise to reminiscences [i.e., bitter memories that may be seen as complaints]."[254] This was another way of avoiding any "expression of displeasure" from Napoleon.

These were the real motivations behind Metternich's press policies. The policies were initially inspired by external factors, and these factors have thus far been overlooked because the press policies were interpreted through the lens of the pre-revolutionary period of the pre-March—that is, they were read as an effort to compete with liberal outlets and to increase patriotic attachment to the "fatherland." This interpretation is right for the later period, but the initial adoption of these policies was born of the fear of the all-powerful external enemy at the time, Napoleon.

It was not just Metternich but also the emperor, in particular, who kept the issues of the press and censorship continuously in mind, and it was the emperor who demanded, promoted, and drove forward a more systematic arrangement of supervision and control. He was afraid of "not sufficiently prudent" contributions in the *Wiener Zeitung* (which was, after all, perceived as the government's official organ), afraid of articles that might make "an impression and cause a stir in my provinces as well as abroad." When Metternich was away in Paris for several months, in connection with the marriage between Napoleon and Marie Louise, the Habsburg ruler temporarily appointed Metternich's father, Franz Georg, as his proxy in Vienna. He instructed the long-serving imperial duke to document the current censorship rules and make suggestions about how the supervision of the press might be organized even better.[255]

During Metternich's absence, Franz Georg became the real architect of the administration's first official press policy. Beginning in February 1810, he designed plans for this organized form of opinion control. On October 31, 1810, when he transferred responsibility for his official business back to his son, the plan was fully developed. Franz Georg referred explicitly to his forty-five years of experience, during which time he had headed the government in Brussels and, inspired by England's media policies and revolutionary France, begun to develop ideas for counterpropaganda and censorship. Clemens was thus able to build on this preliminary work when he began to restructure and centralize censorship and propaganda as the minister in Vienna.

Franz Georg explicitly pointed out that states like England and France "made every effort to influence the general opinion through newspapers, journals, and pamphlets."[256] It was also Metternich's father who had suggested creating a "literary bureau"—as he called it—to collect data and information. Under the supervision of the state Chancellery, the bureau would cooperate with the Austrian and Bohemian court Chancellery and the court's police constabulary. Furthermore, there were plans to create three organs: "first, a general Austrian imperial gazette which would report domestic news and influence opinion abroad regarding Austria's intentions; second, a government publication for public announcements that would be sent to all regional authorities; and, third, a general official journal covering social and economic topics (industry, agriculture, currency issues, the arts)."

In April 1810 the bureau began its work. It had its own library, had subscriptions for periodicals—"journals and learned papers," political papers, and domestic and foreign weeklies—and had its own budget and personnel.[257] In the form of so-called business journals [Geschäftsjournalen] it provided a daily press review of the domestic and international press, accompanied by warnings and analysis. The view on which Franz Georg based the whole project is worth noting, as it reveals a completely new orientation in political thinking: "The imperative necessities of our times determine and justify the utmost efforts by governments to bring the developments in international politics into a continual connection with the domestic situation."[258] Foreign and domestic politics were intertwined in the medium of the press and public opinion. The problem of Napoleon meant it was no longer possible to distinguish between foreign and domestic questions.

A "Political Police" Fighting the Foreign Enemy at Home

Napoleon influenced Austria's domestic situation in still other ways. Metternich referred to these as "French machinations inside our countries." In Vienna and all larger cities that experienced periods of occupation by French troops, he wrote, there was "a formally organized secret police." These had to be removed or at least rendered harmless. To do this without provoking Napoleon was possible only "by proceeding very purposefully and with perfect steadiness and silence, by organizing a counter-police which moved in step with the other police." This was the way to find and silence the spies and secret agents. In Prussia, Justus Gruner, the head of the Berlin police, founded a similar secret counterespionage service in the same year—1809—and under similar circumstances (i.e., because of French soldiers and agents operating inside Prussia).[259]

Metternich clearly copied the French model, especially Fouché's system, but for the Habsburg Monarchy he was introducing something entirely novel, for which he also introduced a new term: "This body, which I consider to be independent of the normal police insofar as the latter is only concerned with the internal administration of the state, I would almost like to call the political police—all the more so as this is how it is actually treated in France."[260] Metternich went on to say that he did not want to offend anyone, but he was certain that he was the only person in the whole monarchy who knew "the most secret springs that drive the French domestic and foreign governmental system."

Because no one apart from Metternich understood the French police system, there was also no one else who knew how France influenced foreign countries. Metternich's structural innovation consisted in the fact that the police office at the court was from now on to be in permanent contact with the foreign ministry. The emperor agreed to this without any reservations, and Metternich was given the authority to give orders to the police minister, Hager.

One should not, however, lose sight of the fact that the emperor ultimately wanted to maintain control of all investigations and initiatives. There are many instances that serve as evidence of this fact, and it follows that one cannot simply speak of an omnipresent "Metternich system." Even in important "foreign" cases, such as the machinations of the "League of Virtue" in Prussia, or on the "sect" of a certain Professor Fichte in Berlin, the police minister first informed the emperor. Hager knew about these goings-on from correspondence that had been opened—"intercepts"—that Franz passed on (or not) to Metternich as he saw fit. Metternich was sometimes forced to undertake further research even though the emperor had already acted without Metternich's knowledge.[261]

Peace and Order [Ruhe] *Everywhere, except for the Resistance to Napoleon in Tyrol*

After the Treaty of Schönbrunn, peace and order were meant to reign, and there were to be no public utterances insulting to the French emperor. The new organization of the police and the press was designed to guarantee this. In one instance, however, Emperor Franz faced a moral dilemma that weighed heavily on his conscience. After the outbreak of war in April 1809, the Tyrolians were such stubborn opponents of Napoleon and the Bavarians (who were members of the Rhenish Confederation) that, when visiting Metternich in Grünberg, Savary had urged him to intervene as an arbiter. After the peace of October 14, the Tyrolians continued to fight, because they simply could not believe that Emperor Franz would have given away his beloved Tyrol. And even once they did believe it, they continued to sing the "Andreas Hofer Song": "Long live my good Emperor Franz, and with him Tyrol." And there was good reason for this: in an appeal to "My dear and faithful Tyrolians" of April 18, 1809, Franz had asked them to fight with him for the reunification of old Habsburg rule with Austria.[262] On May 15, he had even ennobled their leader, Andreas Hofer, in recognition of his decisive actions and personal courage.[263] And after the victory at Aspern on May 29, the emperor had gone so far as to swear to his "faithful Dukedom of Tyrol" that "it shall never again be separated from the body of the Austrian imperial state, and that I shall not sign any peace but one that ties this country inseparably to My Monarchy."[264]

As we know, under the Treaty of Schönbrunn, Tyrol remained with Bavaria; but the treaty granted "those inhabitants of Tyrol and Vorarlberg who have taken part in the insurrection a full and unlimited pardon"—that is, full amnesty without any trials or confiscations. In an appeal "To the peoples of Tyrol" on October 25, Eugène Beauharnais, the viceroy of Italy, informed the leaders of the insurrection of the peace treaty and the amnesty, asking them to lay down their arms.[265]

For Austria, the question of Tyrol was an issue both domestic and international. Since 1805 Tyrol had belonged to Bavaria and stood under the supreme rule of Napoleon as the protector of the Rhenish Confederation. Historically, however, it was associated with the Habsburg Monarchy. As the new foreign minister, Metternich could not be indifferent to this conflict. In order to defuse the crisis, he formulated an appeal in the name of the emperor: "I hear that you want to continue your resistance until you hear from me that we now really have peace. I give you this assurance." At the same time, he referred to the total amnesty. Alluding to the emperor's previous promise, he said he was forced into his actions by a desperate situation in which he was "surrounded by enemies, attacked at several main points."[266]

Metternich wanted to entrust this appeal to the imperial court inspector, Count von Wrbna, who was to send it via the French army high command to the commanders of the Tyrolians. On this occasion, Metternich again expressed, through the words he formulated for Emperor Franz, that he was acting under pressure from Napoleon: "The French Court must recognize in this step irrefutable proof of the honesty of my intentions as well as of my wish no longer to see a good people exposed to the horrors of war and its devastations." Metternich rarely explicitly expressed his disgust at war in official documents; in his private letters, he frequently confessed to it. But the emperor turned out not to be the puppet he is often taken to be. He did not follow Metternich's advice at all, but instead remarked drily: "As we do not know anything about the situation of Tyrol with certainty, this matter has to be rested, at least for the time being."

But Metternich did not let the matter rest, because the Tyrolian resistance continued; finally, on January 1, 1810, the emperor agreed to a modified version of the appeal:

Tyrolians

You have made innumerable sacrifices and given innumerable proofs of your dedication to me; I ask you for one more thing. Give peace to yourselves and to yours. A peace has been signed on October 14, 1809. I cared for you as much as the sad circumstances allowed. Now think of your

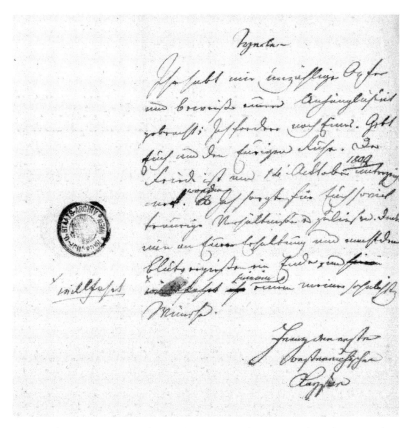

Appeal of January 1, 1810, to the Tyrolians, written by Metternich in the name of the emperor.

own preservation and end the bloodshed, and in this consent to one of my fondest wishes.

Franz the First

Austrian

Emperor

Metternich considered every word of this appeal carefully. The text was designed to make the Tyrolians look toward the future, to encourage them to cease hostilities while avoiding hurting their feelings. The wording was also meant to avoid giving any impression that Austria wanted to take hold of Tyrol after all, which would not have gone down well in France or Bavaria. It is against this background that we should read the explanation Metternich sent to the emperor: "I attach great importance to the word *preservation,* which says everything without being in any way compromising."[267]

In the case of Andreas Hofer, Metternich witnessed the merciless workings of Napoleon's system of military justice. Emperor Franz had learned that French soldiers had arrested the "famous Tyrolian publican of the Sandhof, Andreas Hofer," and he knew that the death penalty awaited him: the rebels had rejected Beauharnais's offer of an amnesty and instead continued the fight. The emperor ordered Metternich: "You will set in train everything suitable for his liberation and rescue from death, making everything you do appear as though it is an expression of our friendly relations with France."[268] With this, he alluded to the imminent marriage of Napoleon to his daughter Marie Louise. On March 22, 1810, he learned of Hofer's execution; Hofer's petition to Archduke Johann had arrived too late. The emperor pointed out that "the established friendly relations with France" had made impossible what Hofer had really been asking for: the return of Tyrol to Austria. The emperor would ensure that Hofer's family would be taken care of. He concluded his resolution with a declaration that again makes clear how we ought to interpret his policies: "As much as I feel inclined toward supporting the just cause, this must nevertheless be done with such prudence and caution that any adverse impression is avoided."[269] Anyone familiar with the way Napoleon operated would surely be skeptical about his later expression of regret, to Metternich, over Hofer's death: "This is an ugly story and happened against my wishes and interests. Hofer was a courageous man, and I counted on him to pacify Tyrol. Tell your Majesty, I offer my apologies."[270]

Napoleon's Search for a Bride

The court in Vienna was always preoccupied with the same questions: What were Napoleon's plans, and would his dominance in Europe last? The archetypal climber, who presented himself as a man of progress, ended up mimicking the rule of the very ancien régime that he despised and against which he fought, for he was looking to found a dynasty, and this meant, in concrete terms, that he required a son and heir. And Empress Josephine, born in 1763, could not be the mother. The mother should come from one of the most respected and ancient royal houses of Europe, to be grafted, so to speak, on to the Napoleonic family tree so as to ennoble it. Several members of the family had already married into sovereign houses from the middle-sized German states, or at least into the traditional ancient nobility. For instance, the king of Westphalia, Jerôme, had chosen the daughter of the king of Württemberg, Katharina (1807); Napoleon's adopted son, Eugène Beauharnais, had chosen the daughter of the later king of Bavaria, Auguste (1806); and his sister Pauline had chosen an officer from the old noble family of the Borghese. Marriages to women not of the appropriate rank, as in the case of Napoleon's brother Lucien, could lead to rifts. For Napoleon, only the best would do: a bride from the House of the Romanovs (Russia), the House of Habsburg (Austria), or the Albertine House (Saxony / Poland). He was perfectly aware of the anachronism; after all, in 1807 he was still talking of the "superiority" of constitutional kings—such as his brother Jérôme—over "all absolutist princes." Now he claimed that it was "necessary to make concessions to the customs of the times one lives in, to the usages of other States, and above all to the propriety which policy makes it a duty to observe."[271]

In the autumn of 1809 at the latest, there was speculation at Napoleon's court and among the people of Paris over whether the emperor would divorce his wife and look for a new bride—and speculation, too, about who such a new bride might be. During the peace negotiations in Vienna, the secretary at the Paris embassy, and close confidant of Metternich, Engelbert Joseph Ritter von Floret, was already suggesting that the French were considering Marie Louise as an option.[272] But until the first week of February 1810, the tsar's sister Anna was also still in the running after another sister, Katharina, had rejected the offer. Marquis Alexandre de Laborde, a confidant of Napoleon, was the first to make Metternich aware of the possibility of a marriage involving the House of Habsburg. He was an *auditeur*—master of requests—on the Council of State, the administrative court of the French emperor, and he had very good relations with the Austrian court and spoke excellent German. But initially Metternich did not take the idea seriously; he considered it a "fantastic dream."[273]

This changed after Metternich's successor as ambassador, Prince Karl Philipp zu Schwarzenberg, arrived in Paris at the end of November 1809 and heard of all the rumors and speculation. The attempted assassination of Napoleon by the seventeen-year-old merchant Friedrich Staps on October 12 in Vienna had shocked the Bonaparte family, and this intensified the search for his successor. The favorite was Napoleon's adopted son-in-law, Eugène Beauharnais, the son of Empress Josephine. But a "party of Beauharnais opponents" within the family began to push for a divorce and a new marriage that might provide a natural heir to the throne.

At his first audience, on November 26, Schwarzenberg witnessed Napoleon in a bad mood—Josephine had sent her apologies because she was indisposed—and he learned that there was a question about who might be Napoleon's new wife. To begin with, only a very few people knew that the House of Habsburg was being considered, and the Austrian ambassador was made aware of this on the condition of the strictest secrecy. Schwarzenberg's report of December 4 relayed to Metternich the suggestion that a family tie between the two dynasties might be a real possibility.[274] The new ambassador requested new instructions on how he was to conduct himself in regard to this sensitive matter.

A little later, on December 15, 1809, the matter of Napoleon's new marriage was made public when Napoleon invited the family council to meet in the great cabinet, next to the throne room in the Tuileries; in the presence of Josephine, the kings and queens of Holland, Naples, Spain, and Westphalia, the viceroy of Italy, and Princess Pauline, Napoleon declared definitively that he would annul his marriage and enter into a new one. The next day, this was publicized in the *Moniteur,* and the senate was called to sit and formally announced the divorce, sending the ex-spouses to separate palaces: Napoleon to Trianon, Josephine and the royal household to Malmaison.[275]

A Habsburg Marriage according to the "Keuner Method"

Metternich knew of all these events, but only now did he begin to wonder whether this might be a unique opportunity to be seized without hesitation. A lot was still unclear. One could not be sure of Napoleon's motives, for he also had his mind on Saint Petersburg; nor could one be certain that Emperor Franz and Marie Louise would agree, not least because the courted archduchess saw in Napoleon the "Antichrist" and found strong support for her view in Empress Ludovika, her stepmother.[276] There was also a broad resistance at the court to be contended with: first of all from the archdukes, but also from a strong "Russian faction" represented in particular by the ambassador from Saint Petersburg and the princesses Bagration and Sagan.

The arrangement thus had to be backed up by irrefutable arguments. These Metternich set out in his instructions of December 25 to Schwarzenberg—a key document for understanding the reorientation of Austria's policies.[277] They are marked *reservé* ("For official use only") and contain an evaluation of the European situation: following the subjugation of Spain, it was to be expected that Napoleon would move toward the European east again. Napoleon's future actions were obvious. Given Napoleon's incessant need to be active, it was natural that the states he founded and that were entirely subjugated to his system would as little escape destruction as those outside the system. Holland was the first example of this. The smaller confederated states would likewise succumb unless Napoleon granted them some sort of existence. The so-called independence of these peoples was limited by their ruler—Napoleon—whose title was calculated to evoke in the people the traditional idea of the emperor. Metternich's bitter conclusion was:

> Too weak from now on to resist the destructive will of the French Empe-
> reur by ourselves, we no longer have a fixed perspective on the role we
> would have to play if the unified power of the French Empire were to

appear at the Eastern border. The day Russia will awaken is too far off for any calculations. . . . While our role in future . . . is subject to a large number of incalculable possibilities, our role at present is dictated by the nature of things themselves. We have to avoid all complications and adopt an attitude that ensures we do not fail at the precise moment that new problems appear in front of us.

Metternich's bleak analysis implied the following political maxim: In trying to extricate oneself from isolation, be cautious and careful, and in waiting for the moment when the alliance against Napoleon becomes possible, be patient. A marital connection with Napoleon was a way of making Austria less isolated and therefore more secure. In the same letter, Schwarzenberg received instructions to that effect. From his time as ambassador in Paris, Metternich knew that there was a party at the French court that had "for a long time tried to limit the violent changes in Europe."[278] He was thinking of Talleyrand, who would later play an important part in the marriage plans. Metternich told Schwarzenberg that His Majesty the emperor, who always had the "well-being and tranquillity of the state" in mind, ordered him "to refuse no overtures which may be made on the subject" from the French side, although he was to receive any such overtures "in a non-official manner."[279]

Circuitous Matchmaking

As was Napoleon's style, the time between the first cautious moves toward proposal and the final decision on the marriage was extraordinarily short. There were many anecdotes abroad at the time about Napoleon; it was said, for instance, that at a costume ball in Paris a disguised Napoleon asked Eleonore "whether she thought that Archduchess Marie Louise would accept his hand, and whether the emperor, her father, would agree to this alliance."[280] But Napoleon would not have required her assurances. He received hints from various sources, not least from the well-connected Marquis de Laborde, and he was able to find things out for himself.

The daily news from the court, the *Bulletin de Paris,* was almost exclusively concerned with the complications of the separation and speculation about Josephine's successor.[281] After a visit to Napoleon, the empress said he could not make up his mind between a Russian and an Austrian princess (December 25). Metternich's wife, Eleonore, who had stayed in Paris at the outbreak of the war, felt the change in the mood at the court most keenly; her family had been ostracized, but suddenly she was welcomed again—even at court and by Napoleon's closest family.

Eleonore had received an invitation to appear at a ladies' audience at court on December 31. When she entered the room, she found Napoleon engrossed in reading, but, seeing that she had arrived, the bad temper he had displayed apparently dissolved, and he approached her with a smile. He spoke warmly to her, even alluding to a possible bright future for her family: "Well, Madame, you have stayed here all of this time; you have seized all the opportunities you could. Your husband holds a nice position; he can do himself proud, knows this country well, and can do good things for it—how are your children?" The *Bulletin* from which this quotation is taken confirms Eleonore's memory of the encounter almost word for word. In her letter to her husband, she tells him that Napoleon said that Metternich could be "useful" for the country. She had been astonished by this, and because of what she experienced in the days that followed, she came to interpret it as a significant hint. She explained to her husband that she could not say anything concrete regarding the marital matter, but that within a short period of time she was so overwhelmed with offers that she could not possibly list them all. She was invited into the most intimate "circle" of the emperor, who complimented her and began to interrogate her in detail about her family and relatives. This attention from Napoleon was so striking that, afterward, all the dignitaries, marshals, and ministers had sought her out and surrounded her. With her typical dry irony, she said this had given her "opportunities for philosophical reflection on the vicissitudes of human affairs."[282]

Eleonore conveyed to her husband just how serious the matter had become after this was confirmed to her by the highest authority, and someone personally affected by it. A courtier of Empress Josephine had told her the empress urgently wanted to see her. On January 2, when Eleonore arrived at Malmaison, she found that the queen of Holland, Napoleon's stepdaughter Hortense Beauharnais, was also there. The queen took Eleonore to one side and told her: "You know we are all Austrian at heart, but you will never guess that my brother has had the courage to advise the emperor to ask the hand of your Archduchess."[283] While Eleonore was still reeling from this news, Empress Josephine entered the room. She spoke openly about how much she had suffered: "I have a plan which occupies me entirely, the success of which alone could make me hope that the sacrifice I am about to make will not be a pure loss; it is that the emperor should marry your archduchess. I spoke to him of it yesterday, and he said his choice was not yet fixed; but," added she, "he believes that this would be his choice, if he were certain of being accepted by you."[284]

Eleonore replied that she personally would "regard this marriage as a great happiness," but "could not help adding that it would be painful for an Archduchess of Austria to establish herself in France."[285] This allusion to the fate of Marie Antoinette could not have gone unnoticed. The empress responded: "We must try to arrange all that."[286] And she expressed her regret that Eleonore's husband, Clemens, was not in Paris to help. Then she added a remark whose significance cannot be overestimated: "It must be represented to your Emperor that his ruin and that of his country is certain if he does not consent."[287] She would breakfast with Napoleon today and would let her know of any positive developments.

There is no doubt surrounding the question of "whether Napoleon or Metternich was the originator of the plan" to make Marie Louise the bride.[288] Eleonore's letter to her husband proves beyond any doubt that it was Napoleon who had taken the initiative, and that Metternich, as a minister, played the role of a mediator who was strongly in favor of the plan for raisons d'état; further, he knew that it was not wise to oppose Napoleon. Given Marie Louise's views, Metternich felt that success was far from certain and that he would have to use all his diplomatic skill in order to get this sensitive "business" under way. Because it was not possible to negotiate such a delicate matter directly with Champagny, not to mention with Napoleon himself, he had to find ways to express Austria's willingness without appearing importunate.

As Napoleon had chosen the indirect route and had used Eleonore as a mediator, Metternich responded, on January 27, with two letters, one addressed to the ambassador, Schwarzenberg, the other privately to Eleonore but with a copy sent to Schwarzenberg. Metternich wrote that Schwarzenberg was to hand Laborde the letter to Eleonore in confidence; that way, he could be certain that it would end up in Napoleon's hands too. In this private letter, Metternich provided a euphemistic description of what was, in fact, a precarious situation in the family of the Austrian emperor, and he expressed optimism that the family would agree to the marriage. Metternich gave grounds for his optimism by pointing out that Austrian princesses were hardly accustomed to choosing their husbands with their hearts; and the respect that a child as well brought up as the archduchess had for her father's will meant that it was unlikely that she would present any obstacle. And as far as her father was concerned, he was "on this occasion, as on all others, without prejudice, fair, loyal, strong in principles and will"—the "sovereign of a vast empire."[289] Metternich suggested that the monarch would heed the raisons d'état, and he emphasized the point with an admission that was clearly intended for Napoleon's eyes: "I regard this affair as the greatest which could at this moment occupy Europe. I believe the choice which the emperor has made will prove as conducive to the general interests of the numerous peoples who, after so many and such frightful revolutions, long for peace, as to the private interests of that prince."[290]

It was only on February 14, after the decision in Paris had long since been taken, that Metternich found out for certain that Marie Louise would accept.

Now he could tell Eleonore "that we have the acceptance of the archduchess; if I ever had to lead difficult negotiations, then these were probably among the most difficult—but thankfully they ended with a full success, and I think I may claim that only I would have succeeded and that I needed the full strength of my attitude for it."[291] In his memoirs, Metternich does not write a single word about the vehement resistance to the marriage. At that point, February 14, he already knew about the strange way the decision had come about in Paris.

A Fast Move to Secure the Bride: Napoleon Dictates the Marriage

Although Napoleon's preference for Marie Louise was becoming increasingly clear, he still remained undecided. On January 28, he convened the great family council and presented his options: a princess of Russia, Austria, Saxony, or another German sovereign house, or a French woman. A majority of those present advised in favor of Austria, but the emperor did not want to commit himself yet. That changed once the long-awaited courier from Saint Petersburg arrived on February 6. Napoleon learned from the letter from his ambassador, Caulaincourt, that the tsar had again not reached a decision after another period of reflection on the matter had elapsed on January 16, which meant that the plan to marry the tsar's sister was off. Napoleon's attention now turned to Marie Louise.

Napoleon now wanted a quick decision, and he called another meeting of the great family council for February 7. Talleyrand was also present, and from him we know that the question was treated as if it were a matter before a state conference: the pros and cons for every argument were weighed, and then decisions were taken by a vote.[292] The archchancellor of the empire Cambacérès, Murat, and Fouché voted for the Russian grand duchess, Anna. Charles François Lebrun voted for the royal family of Saxony. Talleyrand made the greatest impression, as the occasion gave him an opportunity to talk about his "favorite topic," as Napoleon had referred to it, disapprovingly, at Erfurt—namely, an alliance between France and Austria. In his memoirs, Talleyrand admitted: "My secret motive was that the security of Austria depended on the resolution the emperor was going to take, but that was not the place to say it."[293] Talleyrand's final argument was the decisive one: that if an Austrian princess appeared in their midst, this might "absolve France in the eyes of Europe and in her own eyes, of a crime that was not her own, and which belonged entirely to a faction. The term 'European reconciliation' that I employed several times, pleased several members of the council, who had had enough of war." He could see, he wrote, that despite some objections from Napoleon, his advice "suited him."[294]

The emperor ended the meeting without further comment, and he dispatched a courier to Vienna the very same evening. Even before that, he had sent for Schwarzenberg, and at the foreign ministry Schwarzenberg was forced to sign the formal marriage agreement in the name of his monarch; Champagny signed it on behalf of Napoleon. Schwarzenberg was shocked, and he protested that he did not have the authority to perform such an act. What Champagny's response to this must have been may be inferred from the entreating language with which Schwarzenberg later tried to convince Metternich: He had had no other choice; a refusal would have invoked the ire of Napoleon and the French people as a whole; as great as the archduchess's sacrifice might be, it would appear to suffering humankind as the radiance of the angel of peace who with one hand stems the flow of the rivers of blood, and with the other heals all fresh wounds; all prejudices had to discarded when the well-being of the fatherland was at stake; it was "necessary to obey without hesitation."[295] Schwarzenberg sent the documents to Vienna with Floret, the secretary of the Paris embassy and a close confidant of Metternich. But three days before he arrived, the French ambassador, Count Otto, had learned of the developments and, at eight o'clock in the morning on February 15, rushed to the Chancellery to see Metternich and inform him that he had received dispatches containing information of the greatest importance.

For the emperor and Metternich, these developments were scandalous, hurtful, and humiliating. This was especially true of the emperor, for the minister was familiar with this kind of domineering behavior from the negotiations at Fontainebleau and Altenburg; this new incident confirmed his opinion that, if one were not able to build a special relationship with Napoleon, he would be highly dangerous. Their hopes of gaining a political advantage in exchange had clearly been dashed by this *coup de main*. Franz felt hurt because a parvenu had imposed a marriage on the oldest house of rulers in Europe without having proposed, without—as was the custom among aristocratic houses—agreeing to a formal marriage contract, and without following the tactful ceremonial etiquette that was appropriate between courts. Despite all this, he was prepared to ratify the agreement soon afterward on February 21.

The wedding took place in the sort of style that is familiar to us today only from the weddings of the British royal family. And even that comparison is not quite right, for the ceremony was performed not just once, but twice: on March 11, in the Augustinerkirche in Vienna, and on April 2, in the Tuileries in Paris. At Napoleon's explicit request, at the ceremony in Vienna, Archduke Carl—who had been victorious at Aspern—stood in for the groom, as his procurator, so to speak. Metternich is sometimes accused of tactlessness or insensitivity for retrieving the files on Marie Antoinette's marriage of 1770 from the imperial archives and using them as the template for the ceremony. This interpretation is wrong. He was charged with organizing the donations and presents for the French dignitaries and others involved in the wedding because he had the most knowledge of individuals at the French court. Money was always a sensitive issue for the emperor, who was notoriously anxious when it came to financial matters and therefore economical with his means. To ask for funds thus required a certain effort. In order to get an idea of how much the Austrian embassy in Paris had received in additional payments in 1770, Metternich consulted the figures for that year, although he considered them insufficient because of inflation; and, in addition, this time the groom was the French emperor and not a crown prince.[296]

The Old Symbolism of Empire and Emperor: The Golden Fleece and the Metternichs

From the perspective of political and historical symbolism, Metternich, in a strange parallel, experienced the symbolic world of the Holy Roman Empire, which was still authentic for the former imperial count, at the same time that Napoleon staged his wedding as an artificial costumed spectacle. For Metternich, the symbolic world of the Holy Roman Empire was the world that was actually important and the model to be followed. One day before the marriage ceremony, in a particularly solemn ceremony, the Austrian emperor awarded his minister the Order of the Golden Fleece. The ceremony tells us a lot about the Metternichs and the imperial house. The minister was to be decorated for his services to the empire in reaching a peace with France. This referred less to the actual wording of the Treaty of Schönbrunn, which Metternich considered the result of bad negotiation, than to the new peace between the empires, which rested on the new family connection and secured the existence of the monarchy.

The highly respected Order of the Golden Fleece can be traced back to fifteenth-century Burgundy. Within the Habsburg Monarchy, it could be awarded only by the emperor, who became the head of this chivalric order after the line of dukes of Burgundy had died out. Metternich proudly told his wife in Paris about the event and hinted at the fact that the French delegates were astonished by what they experienced—for they had known only Napoleon's new form of nobility.[297] Metternich was fully aware of the contrast, and also competition, between the two ceremonies. "It is a fact, that once we take something seriously, our splendor compares to the French like vermeil to plated"—that is, like gold-plated sterling silver to gold plating on some cheap base material.

Document of March 15, 1810, awarding Clemens von Metternich the Order of the Golden Fleece.

The unique coincidence of the two ceremonies has never before been described. The Vienna ceremony demonstrated to court society the importance that now attached to the Metternich family. In 1794 they had arrived as refugees from the Rhineland, stranded in the Habsburg metropolis; now they stood at the epicenter of imperial splendor. Together, Franz Georg and his son Clemens embodied all the symbolism, ceremony, and tradition of the empire. Clemens stood out on this occasion in particular because the emperor did not choose any other candidates; Metternich alone was accepted into the order. This meant he was the center of the order's magnificent court spectacle, overseen by the emperor in the new ballroom of the Hofburg.[298] As he was older than Franz Georg, Prince Karl von Ligne—who would later give the Congress of Vienna its dictum: "The Congress dances"—acted as the dean of the order, but he had the official acts carried out by the vice-dean, Franz Georg. Traditionally the son would wait for his father to lead him into the knight's hall and up to the emperor's throne—the monarch and four knights, who were present in their full regalia, surrounded Metternich. Franz Georg presented the collar of the Order of the Golden Fleece to the emperor on a cushion. After receiving the accolade from the emperor, the father put the collar around his

Portrait of Metternich by Thomas Lawrence, 1819. Metternich is wearing the collar of the Order of the Golden Fleece.

son's neck. In the most famous portrait of the later chancellor, by Thomas Lawrence, the collar can be seen.

A contemporary observer of the scene experienced a "strange" déjà vu. He was reminded of a time, seventeen years before, when the Belgian court, headed by Franz Georg, had fled for the first time from the French to Wesel.[299] Back then, on December 12, 1792, the nineteen-year-old son, and knight of the Order of St. John, had performed a similar ceremony, handing his father the honorary sword, putting the chain around his neck, and giving him the brotherly kiss.[300] Now, witnessing Clemens himself receive the honor from his father, and seeing the regalia, the members of the order, and the emperor on his throne, the scene appeared to him "like the Court of Karl V," the great political rival of the French kings. As his father carried out the responsibilities of the dean of the order, Metternich believed he saw a third of those in the hall in tears; Napoleon's marshal, Louis-Alexandre Berthier, the prince of Neufchâtel, was "so moved that he wept incessantly." Soon, at Napoleon's wedding banquet in the Tuileries on April 2, 1810, Metternich would experience Napoleon's competing symbolic order.

THE FOREIGN MINISTER ON TOUR: 181 DAYS WITH NAPOLEON

Plans for a "Short Time" in Paris

Napoleon and Marie Louise's wedding was special because it took place twice, once "by proxy" in Vienna, and once—the "real" wedding—amid great splendor and exuberant celebration in Paris. For this, it was necessary to "bring home" the imperial bride. This required an extremely complicated courtly ceremonial that stipulated the ways in which French dignitaries of the highest rank would meet their Austrian counterparts. To begin with, the bride had to be ceremoniously handed over at the state border in Braunau. Then, still in Braunau, the bride's accoutrements, garments, and her court had to be transformed from those of an Austrian archduchess into those of a future French empress. Metternich was responsible for classifying the foreign dignitaries, whom he knew very well, by rank, and providing them with the customary gifts.[301]

Thus, Metternich stood at the center of conjugal diplomacy. In the run-up to the event, the French foreign minister suggested a significant idea to his Austrian counterpart. On February 18, after the decision to go ahead with the marriage had been taken, Champagny, who was in Vienna at the time, invited Metternich to dinner. He disclosed to Metternich that Napoleon had decided to withdraw his armies from Germany and reduce troop numbers in the Rhenish Confederation to peacetime levels. Work on extending the fortress in Passau was to be halted, and the troop numbers in the Illyrian provinces were to be reduced to a quarter of their present level.[302] The good news led Metternich to wonder whether the new family ties might not also persuade Napoleon to consider revising the dictates of the Treaty of Schönbrunn. If so, why not accompany Marie Louise to Paris on the pretext of seeking to help her settle into her new surroundings, and at the same time pursue political negotiations with Napoleon? Given the exceptional circumstances, it was an opportune time to get close to Napoleon and take advantage of the situation politically.

At this point, a situation emerged that is probably unique in the history of diplomacy. From the day of his arrival in Paris on March 28, 1810, until his farewell audience with Napoleon on September 24, Metternich—the Austrian foreign minister, whose proper place was at the Chancellery in Vienna—stayed continuously at the court of a foreign potentate. This half year—181 days, to be precise—in Paris even exceeded the 153 days Napoleon had held court at Schönbrunn. Metternich told the emperor that he would be "absent for a short period of a few weeks."[303] His actions make clear how little he believed his own words: he suggested to the emperor that during his absence his father should take over his duties and become deputy minister.[304] If it were to be just a few weeks, the head of the Chancellery, Hudelist, might just as well have coordinated the business to be done in Vienna, as he did on many subsequent occasions when Metternich was traveling. In this case, Metternich had bigger plans.

The minister understood his project as a highly political "mission." The seriousness with which he took his mission is clear from the fact that although he was now the authorized minister and no longer needed instructions, he formulated a government program in the form of instructions for himself. As in all important cases, he wanted to get the emperor's written approval of his plans. He knew that, in the absence of his minister, Emperor Franz was liable to be influenced by his surroundings. Metternich explained to the emperor that accepting the marriage plans had achieved three goals: first, the alliance between the families guaranteed the monarchy's "peace and order for the time being"; second, this peace and order would hopefully also spread to the rest of Europe; and, third, the empire now had the necessary peace and time to consolidate itself domestically and to arm itself and so defend itself against future external attacks, which were to be expected.

Metternich wanted these three aims to inform his political negotiations in Paris. In concrete terms, he wanted the French to drop the conditions stipulated in the secret articles of the peace treaty, namely the 85 million francs in contributions, which were sapping "our inner strength," as Metternich put it, and the limitation of the army's size to 150,000 men. He also wanted to negotiate a strip of land that would guarantee Austria's access to the Adriatic, financial regulations for loans, and a trade agreement in case the contributions were not canceled. Finally, Metternich dreamed that Austria might become "party to securing maritime peace" and thus confirmed as a major power mediating between the global players, France and England, in the interests of international peace. Regarding the financial matters, he had already asked for assurances from the court's treasury.[305] The emperor supported him on each point and expressed his full confidence in him. What Metternich did not mention to the emperor was that, with the new, supposedly more compliant Napoleon, the emperor's new son-in-law, he thought he might also be able to negotiate the return of his own estates (which the king of Württemberg had confiscated during the war in 1809).

On March 28, Metternich arrived in Paris. With a red pen he marked the note in the Parisian *Journal de l'Empire* of March 31 that reported his invitation by Napoleon. The note mentioned that his father would be taking care of business in Vienna during his absence, and said that both "famous personalities" had rendered exceptional services to the House of Austria. The French newspaper did not fail to mention Franz Georg's activities in Brussels, in Frankfurt at the imperial election of Leopold II, and as plenipotentiary in Rastatt. It is worth noting how the son's activities were described: "His son, the present minister, has the good fortune to be involved in the imperial alliance which is going to be formed between France and Austria."[306] There was not a word about the imminent wedding.

The Wedding Ceremony in Paris: New Wine in Old Bottles?

Metternich had left Vienna on the night of March 15, 1810. While on his way to Paris, he had learned how the imperial bride's journey had been received. The reactions were rapturous and had the effect of straightforward propaganda for the House of Habsburg. The journey "was like a triumphal procession," Metternich wrote, noting that it also had the effect of achieving social unity, of "benefiting all classes"; he listed, in particular, the citizen, the peasant, the merchant, and the proprietor as all joining in the jubilations.[307]

In Munich, the Bavarian king hosted a splendid celebration for Marie Louise. From there she went on to visit the former prince elector of Trier, Clemens Wenceslaus (Metternich's godfather), in Augsburg. On March 23, having traveled via Stuttgart, she arrived in Strasbourg, where Metternich paid her a courtesy visit. Thereafter, their ways parted. Marie Louise continued along the road from Soissons to Compiègne, at the side of which three magnificent tents had been erected on a common between poplar and willow trees. There Napoleon and Marie Louise celebrated their first meeting. On March 28, Metternich also arrived at Compiègne, where his wife, Eleonore, accompanied by Ambassador Schwarzenberg, joined him. These three, considered by Napoleon's family to have been instrumental in bringing about the marriage, were guests of honor, and were invited to join the family at their table for dinner during the following days.

Metternich observed carefully how Marie Louise settled into her new surroundings. He assured her worried father how comfortable she felt, and that she had every reason to feel so because Napoleon paid almost exclusive attention to her and fulfilled her tiniest wish. About the eighteen-year-old he said: "Her conduct is in every respect excellent; pleasantly, affably, and with great dignity she wins all hearts." As a guest of honor Metternich was present at the civil wedding on Sunday, April 1, in Saint Cloud, and at the religious ceremony the following day in Paris. He noted that all the festivities were "celebrated with an almost unparalleled splendor. . . . The arrangements of every kind are of such vast proportions that it is difficult to give an impression of them to someone who has not seen them."[308]

Napoleon did not choose a house of God for the religious ceremony, as he had done for the imperial coronation on December 2, 1804, which took place in Notre Dame. The emperor wanted to present himself as the creator of a new age, as an aficionado of art and culture. He selected as his stage the Diana Gallery in the Louvre, intended as a new European temple of culture. The rear of the building had been redesigned as a chapel, which was reached, in solemn procession, through the large exhibition hall, lined with paintings. For a Frenchman like the Baron de Barante, the prefect of the Vendée, who assisted as master of ceremonies, nothing could have given a more splendid impression than this long imperial court procession, the march of the kings and queens who accompanied the empress, the high dignitaries, the marshals decked out in gold and adorned with their medals, between two rows of spectators, resplendent in their dress and uniforms.[309]

At the ceremony, Metternich observed the disharmony between church and state. Napoleon had great difficulty suppressing his anger when, upon entering the building, he noted that more than half of the twenty-nine cardinals present in Paris had refused to attend the ceremony, and the surplus—magnificent—chairs set out for them had to be hurriedly removed shortly before the ceremony began. Napoleon later exiled the non-attendees to the provinces and, in the case of the leading cardinal, Consalvi, who was, in Metternich's eyes, a model of civil courage, he even threatened to have him shot for lèse-majesté and conspiracy.[310] Metternich would later come across the very same Ercole Consalvi as the chief diplomat of the pope at the Congress of Vienna; after 1814, Consalvi became Metternich's most important contact when the relationship between state and Catholic Church had to be put on a new footing.

In contrast to the church wedding, this time Napoleon did not choose a cultural temple for the banquet. He chose the Tuileries, the palace of the French kings, presenting himself as an emperor who creates his own tradition and founds his own personal nobility. The painter Alexandre Benoît Jean Dufay captured the scene. The true significance of Napoleon's self-staging becomes apparent only when one determines who had the honor of sitting at his table. This is possible with the help of the "Plan de Banquet Imperial du 2 Avril 1810"; Metternich had a copy of this on the occasion, and he later took it with him as a souvenir.[311]

In front of the spectators, who were standing up, sat the members of the Bonaparte family, with Napoleon at the center—as befitted the successor to Charlemagne (since the imperial coronation of 1804) and the Holy Roman Empire (since the coronation in Milan with the Iron Crown of the Lombards in 1805). Within five years Napoleon had dethroned numerous rulers from old European houses—the House of Welf in Hanover, the Bourbons in Naples-Sicily and Spain, the Habsburgs in Tuscany, the popes in the Papal States. Their places had been filled with members of his family as new kings and queens. If anyone remained in any doubt, they could now see Napoleon's system of imperial rule in Europe in the choreography of the wedding banquet. The extent to which his understanding of what it meant to rule served the purposes of family politics was also betrayed by the selection of guests: not even the prince primate of the Rhenish Confederation, Karl Theodor von Dalberg, had a place at this table, whereas the representative of the Habsburg family, Ferdinand, did, and not in his role as an ally of the Rhenish Confederation but as Marie Louise's uncle and as brother of the father-in-law.

Because the diplomatic corps, the standing spectators, were not being provided with food, Metternich offered the Austrian embassy for that purpose. At the embassy, when the Russian ambassador entered the room, all the seats had been taken, which provided the occasion for many knowing jokes about "Russia arriving too late." After the dinner, Metternich stepped out onto the balcony, underneath which a curious crowd had gathered, and, with a glass of champagne in his hand, he offered an ambiguous toast to the heir to the throne that Napoleon desired so much, the child that would be half-Habsburg by birth: "To the King of Rome!" Like the French observers at the time, later German historians saw this as an inappropriate ingratiation [*courtoisie*], an homage to the "destructor of the Empire," Napoleon, and a betrayal of the "memory of the venerable traditions of the deceased Holy Roman Empire."[312] But they were ignorant of Metternich's true role as a "Mr. Keuner," of the inner distance that the minister kept from proceedings, and they also knew little of his talent for irony. Part of this story, incidentally, was that Napoleon paradoxically declared the soon-to-be-born grandson of Emperor Franz, who had resigned as the emperor of the Holy Roman Empire in 1806, the "King of Rome."

The wedding banquet at the Tuileries on April 2, 1810. Painting by Alexandre Benoît Jean Dufay, called Casanova.

A sharp observer, such as Metternich, must surely have asked himself which further goals this ruler, who seemed to be at the height of his powers, was pursuing. Ultimately Marie Louise appeared like a foreign body within this circle, because she descended from the genuine imperial tradition of the Habsburgs. In his memoirs, Metternich did not spend many words on the character of the wedding he witnessed. He was in a precarious position: he could hardly criticize publicly what was, after all, the result of his own matchmaking work—still less something that concerned the daughter of his revered emperor. But given that it was only two years earlier that he had described with such perspicacity what he thought of the nouveau riche nobility of Napoleon, who, on pain of the bayonet, exploited Europe for his personal enrichment, we can easily imagine the kind of thoughts that must have gone through Metternich's mind. He shared the view of Talleyrand, who, as someone who could remember the magnificence of "the ancient court of France," felt that the "luxury of these courts founded by Napoleon" was "absurd," and spoke of Napoleon's weak spot as revealing a lack of propriety, something perverse and meaningless: "The luxury of Bonaparte was neither German nor French; it was a mixture, a species of learned luxury; it was copied from everywhere. It had some of the gravity of that of Austria, with something European and Asiatic belonging to St. Petersburg. It paraded some of the mantles taken from the Caesars at Rome. . . . That which this kind of luxury set off, above all, was the absolute lack of propriety; and, in France, when propriety is too much lacking, mockery is near at hand."[313]

To Metternich, the theater of the banquet revealed Napoleon's psychological weakness. The "dynastie de Napoléon" embodied "les parvenus sur les trônes"—and this was a view that Metternich, the spectator, would never give up, despite all the conciliatory gestures he made.[314] Three years later, in Dresden, the French emperor revealed to Metternich the significance that his marriage held for him: "When I married an Archduchess, I tried to weld the new with the old, Gothic prejudices with the institutions of my century."[315] That was Napoleon's perspective. He was really fighting for "equality of rank" [Ebenbürtigkeit], as the aristocratic norm would have it.

Travels to the Netherlands: Metternich's Memories of His Years in Brussels

After the wedding celebrations, Napoleon took the new empress on a journey to the occupied Netherlands, including Brussels, so that the population, the estates, and the local magistrates had the opportunity to greet and honor him.

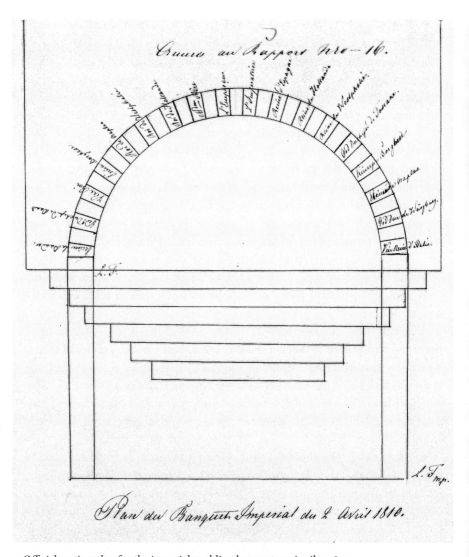

Official seating plan for the imperial wedding banquet on April 2, 1810.

Members of the party at the table (from left to right, year of enthronement in parentheses):

- Prince of Baden: Karl Ludwig Friedrich, married to Napoleon's adopted daughter, Stéphanie de Beauharnais
- Grand Duke of Baden: Karl Friedrich
- Viceroy of Italy: Eugène Beauharnais, Napoleon's adopted son (1805)
- Prince Borghese: Camillo, husband of Napoleon's sister Pauline
- King of Naples: Joachim Murat, Napoleon's marshal (1808)
- King of Westphalia: Jérôme, Napoleon's brother (1807)
- King of Holland: Louis, the disgraced brother of Napoleon (1806)
- Madame Mère: Laetitia Bonaparte, Napoleon's mother
- The Emperor: Napoleon (1804)

Scholars have paid scant attention to this journey, which Metternich joined in parts. Metternich's company was important to the emperor, and Metternich emphasized in his memoirs that Napoleon had explicitly asked him to join the traveling party and also to take part at an audience: "'I wish to show you,' said he, 'how I am wont to speak to these people.'"[316] Metternich continued: "I saw that the emperor was anxious that I should perceive how many-sided was his administrative knowledge."[317] This may be partly correct of Napoleon, especially given his craving for recognition; he always thought he needed to prove himself to Metternich.

Metternich avoided openly discussing the significance of these travels, as he really saw it. The destinations were old Habsburg countries, and by taking Metternich with him the victorious Napoleon could show him how much better off they now were. The journey made the ambivalence and distance that Metternich had felt throughout his stay in Paris particularly acute. In one of his "presentations," he told Emperor Franz, alone, how he had spent the days with Napoleon "almost from morning to evening with his closest family" and had learned, on these occasions, how Napoleon would receive various deputations and question them in great detail until late into the night.[318] To his emperor, Metternich revealed how far he was from admiring Napoleon, even at this time when he was courted by everyone as the matchmaker; and he made clear how the imperial tradition of the Holy Roman Empire lived on in the background of his thought:

In the month of May, the French emperor traveled through the former Austrian Netherlands, accompanied by the empress. The latter was received with an incredible enthusiasm, whereas the emperor was met with remarkable coldness. Every step convinced the monarch that the former subjects of Your Majesty, who once were so happy, now were sighing under an unbearable

---

- The Empress: Marie-Louise (1810)
- The Queen of Spain: Julie Clary, the daughter of a merchant and wife of Napoleon's brother Joseph (1808)
- The Queen of Holland: Hortense de Beauharnais, Napoleons stepdaughter (1806)
- The Queen of Westphalia: Katharina von Württemberg, daughter of the King Friedrich of Württemberg (1807)
- "Grand Duchess" of Tuscany (honorary title): Governess General Elisa Baciocchi, Napoleon's sister (1809)
- Princess Borghese: Pauline, Napoleon's sister
- Queen of Naples: Caroline, Napoleon's sister (1808)
- Grand-Duke of Würzburg: Ferdinand, Marie Louise's uncle and brother of Emperor Franz
- Vicereine of Italy: Auguste of Bavaria, daughter of the later King Maximilian I. Joseph of Bavaria (1805)

yoke due to the lack of commerce, the introduction of conscription, and the many laws and institutions that are alien to the Dutch spirit. The presence of a princess from the ancient dynasty brought these feelings out into the open with the greatest clarity.[319]

These friendly reactions to the Habsburg princess were so obviously unwelcome to Napoleon that, in Cambrai, after three days of traveling, Metternich decided to leave the imperial couple to themselves and return to Paris. He had been brought to his decision also by the fact that during the public parades, members of families who had served Austria had stood in the first line, giving loud expression to their discontent. Metternich wanted to avoid any provocation. Nevertheless, Napoleon's experiences in the Netherlands had consequences. Metternich noted how, upon his return, the emperor tightened his policies toward the Netherlands, removing an experienced and much-liked servant who was responsible for domestic security there and putting General Savary in charge of the police. At the same time, he now wanted to intensify the "assimilation between the population of the Netherlands and the French." In numerous conversations with Napoleon, Metternich argued the discrimination of Austrian and French nationals who served the House of Habsburg, and even secured the release of General Rousseau, formerly an officer under Bellegarde, from French captivity. Metternich also put to Napoleon the case for the right of "officers with property in the former Austrian Netherlands to evade the threat of the confiscation of their estates."[320] Thus, during his travels with the imperial couple he lived in two separate worlds: in that of the memory of the old Habsburg Belgium, and in the contemporary world, in which a subdued population, suffering under the Continental System, feared for its nationality and autonomy.

False Hopes

Despite the fact that he certainly kept his distance from Napoleon's political system and his ambitions, Metternich nevertheless observed very carefully how the relationship between Marie Louise and Napoleon developed. To Emperor Franz, he described Napoleon as being passionately in love, as someone who catered to his bride's every wish, no matter what the cost. Napoleon claimed that his life had only now truly begun. Metternich remarked that he "dreamed only of a successor."[321] It was important to see that, at least from the outside, the imperial family was well disposed toward Marie Louise, even if Napoleon's three sisters found it hard to stomach the fact that they had to carry the young archduchess's train on the way to the altar. Napoleon's mother, Laetitia, was even moved to tears by Marie Louise, and the young empress excelled at courtly etiquette. Napoleon praised her sweet temper and tact [*mésure*]. She, in turn, believed that she already knew her husband well enough to be able to tell Metternich: "I am not at all afraid of Napoleon, but I begin to think that he is afraid of me."[322] As Metternich was later to find out, he was wrong in assuming that he might be able to manipulate Napoleon through Marie Louise. But for the time being he still wrote about him: "He may have more weak sides than many others, and if the empress continues to make use of them the way she now begins to see that she might, she can do herself and Europe the greatest favors."[323]

During his stay in Paris, Metternich had the opportunity to experience Napoleon with his closest family, and occasionally he saw him for days at a time. It sometimes happened that Napoleon engaged him in conversations that lasted until four o'clock in the morning, conversations in which he related to him every little detail of his whole life history. Metternich considered the information he received on these occasions important enough, "in certain historical respects," to make notes of them to present to Emperor Franz orally later. These conversations were also the source for his later psychological analysis of Napoleon.

Emperor Franz's response to the presentations Metternich sent from Paris was ambivalent, as can be seen from his extensive marginal remarks on the documents. The emperor rarely wrote much when adding his resolution to the documents presented to him, so when he did, it signaled that he thought the matter important or that he was burdened with something. Franz told his minister that the enthusiastic reports about the heartfelt welcome Marie Louise had received at the court in Paris were a "true consolation" to him—and yet that they also caused him misery, given the shortcomings of the agreed-upon peace. He thought of the Tyrolians and the other imperial subjects whom he was not able to retain; he hoped for the suspension of the confiscations, death sentences, and penal measures imposed on those who had served him. Finally, he hoped for the release of the Austrian officers and soldiers who were still in France or in the states of the Rhenish Confederation. All this serves as a reminder of why the Austrian ruler had agreed to a family tie between his dynasty and the seemingly almighty Napoleon.

During his negotiations in Paris, Metternich had his own house in mind at all times. He hoped that in his confidential conversations with Napoleon he might take advantage of the emperor's honeymoon mood to secure the return of possessions confiscated by states of the Rhenish Confederation from individuals who had served Austria. Metternich had already asked his wife to find an opportune moment in her conversations with Napoleon's stepdaughter,

Hortense, or even with Napoleon himself, to bring up the topic of Ochsen-hausen. In editing his posthumous papers, Metternich's son mostly omitted any passages relating to this. For the minister himself, however, the return of confiscated possessions was so important that he filed a draft of the negotia-tions in his house archive, together with all the documents relating to the family's dire financial situation.[324] Indeed, he successfully negotiated a conven-tion with Champagny that was ratified on August 30, 1810, as a protocol to the Treaty of Schönbrunn.[325] At that time, the Metternich family was a highly vis-ible presence at the court in Vienna: the son Clemens had been able to nego-tiate the return of the estates in Württemberg through Napoleon, and his father, deputizing for the minister, presented Emperor Franz with the contract in order for him to ratify it, which he did.[326]

The Deeper Purpose of Metternich's Stay in Paris

All negotiations with Champagny and with Napoleon himself oscillated be-tween a conciliatory approach on the personal level and an iron obstinacy on the level of the subject matter itself, with the result that Metternich was disap-pointed about how little reward the family ties between the French emperor and the Habsburgs had actually reaped in the short term. In his memoirs he said that "to discover the emperor's motivations" was the "next and most important task" of his time in Paris.[327] This sort of declaration might lead one to suspect that Metternich was retrospectively attempting to ascribe some higher usefulness to an enterprise that, from the point of view of the problems at the time, failed pretty miserably. This makes it all the more important to look at Metternich's statements about himself from the time in question.

At the time, Metternich was convinced that his stay in Paris would provide him "with important and significant clarifications about the future." It struck him that he was in Paris at a time when the larger European states were en-tering into new relationships with each other. Shortly before his departure, he judged that he found himself in "such an important, but therefore also com-promised position," referring, no doubt, to the many critics waiting for him in Vienna, some of whom—those among the emperor's closest family—would have liked very much to bring him down. He therefore described his pri-mary intention to Emperor Franz, who, during Metternich's absence, had been exposed to continuous criticism of his minister—especially from his wife, Ludovika. Metternich insisted on the real benefits of his stay in Paris, saying that his "perspective is mainly toward *investigating, toward determining the nearer and farther intentions of Napoleon*," and that he would "certainly achieve this purpose *without compromising in any way any position that it might be necessary to take in following the highest intentions in the future.*"[328]

Shortly after his arrival in Paris, Metternich had admitted to Napoleon that, in accompanying Marie Louise on her "introduction" to France, he had been carrying out the wishes of Emperor Franz, but he added that his own wishes went further—that he wanted to "find a guiding principle for [his] political action in a more remote future."[329] Napoleon replied that this agreed wholly with his own wishes and that in "a few weeks" Metternich would leave Paris with satisfaction. Metternich, for his part, took great care that the crucial condition for practicing his international politics was not affected—his "freedom of action which would have been hampered by a closer intimacy with the conqueror."[330]

"A veil was spread over the future of Europe, which I longed to raise," Metternich wrote.[331] But what was the clarifying insight he was waiting for in the week after week that he postponed his return to Vienna? The key to this can be found in a conversation Metternich had with Napoleon on September 20, 1810, in Saint Cloud. The importance of this conversation for Metternich's actions as a minister before 1815 has so far not been recognized. Its significance can be compared to that of the dispute of 1813 in Dresden. By September 1810, Metternich had sufficiently understood the principles of Napoleon's politics to know how bold Austria could be in its dealings with France without jeopardizing itself, until finally, in the summer of 1813, Austria was able to change sides and enter into a victorious alliance against Napoleon. Metternich's memoirs show how important the conversation in question was to him. Unusually for him, he did not describe the conversation from memory but inserted the exact wording of a note he wrote while he still had the dialogue fresh in his mind.[332] This makes the text relatively more authentic because it reflects Metternich's judgment at the time. The great significance of the conversation is clear from the fact that Napoleon demanded, categorically, that all his deliberations and calculations about the future be treated as "altogether confidential," that no one except Emperor Franz was to learn of them; even Champagny, he said, was not familiar with the details. Napoleon's intention was, he said, to "not let slip the rare opportunity when a monarch can converse with the Foreign Minister of another Power, and offer a new point of view to another Government, without expecting an answer."[333]

The key point was that Napoleon's thought was centered on an upcoming war with Russia, despite the fact that, since the Treaty of Tilsit in 1807 and the magnificent meeting in Erfurt in 1808, he was in principle in an alliance with the country, whose tsar he had declared "his brother." Although the failed marital arrangement with Saint Petersburg was only slightly responsible for the increasing tensions Napoleon perceived between France and the tsarist empire, and which he mentioned to Metternich, the new marital connection with the Habsburgs had, indeed, shifted Napoleon's geopolitical perspective. In addition, there was the fact that, in Bernadotte, one of Napoleon's marshals now sat on the Swedish throne, which meant that France was interfering in Russia's zone of influence. Napoleon's tendency to favor a strong Polish kingdom at the border with Russia amounted to the same thing. Metternich recognized that the crucial point was that "the continental prohibitions against trade steadily increased"[334]—in other words, that the Continental System was increasingly harming Russian trade. Three matters dominated the conversation: war aims, the question of alliances, and the question of whether the war was necessary at all.

Napoleon emphasized that in the case of a campaign, he "should have a great and powerful ally in a king of Poland," to which Metternich correctly responded that to speak of a kingdom of Poland was simply to give a new name to the existing Duchy of Warsaw, albeit at the expense of Austria because the new kingdom would involve enlarging the duchy by adding parts of Galicia. King Friedrich August of Saxony took a central position in this matter, as he had been, in personal union, the head of the duchy since 1807. By way of compensation, the French emperor offered to return the commercially important Illyrian provinces to Austria. If, on the other hand, Austria wanted to insist on Galicia, it would have to side with Russia.

Concerning the prospect of war, Napoleon asked Metternich a straight question: "What part will you play then?"[335] Finding himself so directly addressed, Metternich skillfully managed to wriggle out of the situation, pointing out that, as a minister, he was not authorized to make a judgment on the matter, and that everything he might say "should be considered as coming from the lips of a cosmopolitan, and not from the Austrian minister";[336] in other words, he wanted whatever he said to be seen as independent of any interests dictated by raison d'état. Only in hindsight did he fully realize what Napoleon had actually offered to guarantee to the Austrians, because it was only when going through his handwritten notes shortly after the conversation that he added Napoleon's assurance:

I do not desire from you any active co-operation, because I have made up my mind not again to join any coalition. I have had enough of the trial I made of it in 1809 [i.e., the coalition with Russia that should have actively fought on the side of France]. I should have made quite another war for you, if I had been alone. I have never reckoned much on the Russians, but they have at any rate taken the place of fifty or sixty thousand Frenchmen, who would have treated you to quite another sort of war from the Russians.[337]

Even though Napoleon later ended up demanding a contingent of 30,000 troops from Austria after all, Metternich learned on this occasion that, in Napoleon's mind, they were not intended to play a decisive part in the war. It was important to know this in advance because it allowed Metternich to calculate the extent to which he needed to agree with Napoleon's war plans.

The most important effect of the conversation was, however, that it turned what was a hypothetical war into a fact, something Metternich could take into account in his calculations: "I shall have war with Russia on grounds which lie beyond possible human influence, because they are rooted in the peculiarities of the matter itself. The time will soon approach . . . when hostilities will be inevitable."[338] Metternich heard from Napoleon himself what his advisor Laborde had already predicted in February 1810 while the marriage was being arranged: France would "in less than five or six months entertain cooler relations with Russia, and in less than eighteen months be on a war footing with it."[339] The first of these predictions had come true: in September 1810 Napoleon saw war with Russia as inevitable.

Directly after the memorable conversation in Saint Cloud, Metternich finally felt certain "that [he] had at last obtained sufficient light. The object of [his] stay in Paris was attained."[340] Four days later, on September 24, he had his final audience before taking his leave of Napoleon. On that occasion, Napoleon paid his new father-in-law a dubious compliment that assumed an equality of rank between his family and the Habsburgs and presented him as the ruler of the thrones of Europe: "Even if I could put one of my brothers on the throne tomorrow, I would like that less than to see the present ruler on it."[341] Looking back, Napoleon saw Metternich's stay as of the greatest political importance and as something he needed to use for propaganda purposes. He wanted it to be publicly known just how good the relations between the two powers already were. He therefore told Champagny to arrange a report in the *Moniteur* on the presents he had given to Metternich on his departure—a Gobelin, a marble bust of the emperor (himself), and a set of Sèvres porcelain.[342]

For Metternich, the most important conclusion from all this was that Austria was again playing a role in international power politics: in Napoleon's plan for war against Russia it mattered whether the Habsburg Monarchy was on his side. On the last day of September, Metternich embarked on his return journey, arriving in Vienna on October 10.[343]

DOMESTIC AND INTERNATIONAL CONSOLIDATION, 1810–1812

An Evaluation of the Situation in 1811

Following his return to Vienna, Metternich first had to reacquaint himself with the domestic situation before he could, with help from the insights he had gained in Paris, describe "the true position of the monarchy in the present political system of Europe."[344] This he did in an extensive report of January 17, 1811, which may be considered his first major programmatic government declaration since he took office in 1809. He himself called it "one complete piece of writing," one "work," and indeed the text reads like a treatise presenting an argument that is to serve as the basis for "a political plan."

The Habsburg Monarchy, Metternich wrote, was the only European power still left with a choice. To make this choice in a reasoned way required an insight into the nature of the Napoleonic system of rule, a system in which the French emperor was the "centre of all power," acting according to a grand plan that was hidden from the other rulers and the ruled: "Each of his steps is from the beginning part of a whole." From the early days of Metternich's diplomatic career—that is, since 1801—Napoleon's political calculation and intentions had remained the same: "the monstrous idea of ruling alone over the whole continent," followed with "admirable coolness in the conception of expedients." At the time of the Treaty of Tilsit, Austria's dissolution into "a number of realms to be dissected," as had happened in the case of Prussia, had been decided. The ultimate result of that plan, as Metternich saw it, was "that Napoleon intended to advance over the ruins of Austria and Prussia in order to drive Russia back into the deserts of Asia."

Surprisingly, Metternich first set out the commercial nature of the system in order to characterize it as an exploitative despotism. France, he wrote, lived "under an iron rule, an unparalleled fiscal system, a tremendous load of regulations, and entire destruction of commerce." The "state coffers are empty," and yet "France is undeniably the richest state on the continent, and can bid defiance to any other from a financial point of view." The paradox was explained by Napoleon's financial policies. The coffers "of the sovereign are full": "The latter, by the establishment of a *domaine extraordinaire,* which receives all foreign contributions, has made it possible for him to grant extensive assistance in any state emergency, apparently from the private resources of the crown." Metternich here had in mind institutions such as the Monte Napoleone in Milan, a kind of mortgage bank that collected the confiscated properties of the Kingdom of Italy and the debts on them.[345] By meeting the state's needs with seemingly private means—that is, with the wealth of the crown—Napoleon was thus able to present himself to the French as a bene-factor. This also enabled him to overcome internal resistance, for the French citizen saw "one state after another fall around him" and could expect that this would increase French wealth.

Looking around him at the other states, Napoleon had no reason to fear that the German rulers would unite against him, for they had secured too many per-sonal benefits through being his allies. And, after the experience of the past twenty years, no one could count on "the voice of the German peoples." The only point Metternich found difficult to gauge was the question of how conse-quential continued Spanish and British resistance would ultimately be, in par-ticular as the defeats Napoleon suffered on the Iberian Peninsula "could at any time be the signal for fresh disturbances in other directions." Russia, without money and devoid of inner coherence, was powerless, and Prussia was "no longer to be reckoned among the powers."

In Metternich's eyes, this overall situation was caused by "an uninterrupted succession of moral, political, military, financial mistakes made by all the Eu-ropean Powers" over the past twenty years. The coalitions all failed due to their own inner weaknesses and lack of unity. The system of Tilsit had been the "highest triumph of French policy," because now the two great powers, Aus-tria and Russia, "who *united* were invincible," were separated, and Austria was driven into a "system of isolation." Only the marriage of Napoleon and Marie Louise had prevented the certain dissolution of the Habsburg Monarchy. Met-ternich saw the significance of this marriage as deeply anchored in Napoleon's way of thinking, and he was probably the only European statesman who was able to analyze the psychology of the French emperor with such precision. He recognized Napoleon's particular need to secure his rule and dynasty and, to that end, to rely on "guarantees." The marriage therefore achieved the same goal as would have been achieved by the initial plan to "overthrow . . . the Aus-trian throne": the Habsburg Empire no longer appeared to be a potential threat. As a result, Austria's position within Europe, especially toward France and Russia, had fundamentally changed. The alliance between France and Russia began to crumble, and Austria had escaped its isolation. It was now able to choose the alliance it wanted to join.

The three options Metternich had suggested to Emperor Franz in January 1811 offered themselves again, in almost unchanged forms, in the crucial year of 1813. A proper understanding and appreciation of these three options and the per-spectives they offered absolves Metternich of the charge that he practiced a poli-tics that pursued only the state's self-interest—as the rulers of the Rhenish Confederation in fact did. For his political vision took its bearings from what he called "Europe's peace."

According to Metternich's philosophy of power, the *first option*—a new alliance with Russia, the sixth—should really have been the "means of deliverance." But he predicted that it would, in fact, be a death sentence for Austria, because Napoleon, at the beginning of his campaign, would be diverted south while moving toward Russia. And while Russia would be able to concentrate its forces, an unprepared Austria would be exposed to the first attacks, with "not the most remote prospect of success." Austrian forces were still practically paralyzed. There would be an uprising in Galicia before the 70,000 men there were ready to take their positions, and Napoleon would quickly enter Vienna for a third time. A popular uprising seemed a chimera, given the experiences of the past. Thus, Austria would have to depend entirely on the determination of Russia and possibly Prussia, and the history of the previous wars and the unstable character of the Prussian king and Russian tsar had shown how little Austria could rely on such determination.

The *second option*—an alliance with France on the model of the Rhenish Confederation, including an integration of Austrian troops into the French army under the direct command of Napoleon—was rejected by Metternich for a noteworthy reason: the armies under Napoleon intended to lead "a war against holy immutable principles, and against Austria's direct interests." Austria, Metternich wrote, held a unique position in Europe by embodying a "moral height from which the most adverse circumstances were not able to displace her. Your Majesty is the central point, the only representative left of an old order of things founded on eternal unchangeable law." In this passage, Metternich thematized the radical change in Europe and described the front lines, as he perceived them, between an old and a new Europe. He subjected the categories of "old" and "new," not to some utopian idea of progress, but to his understanding of the law, as it is developed in detail in this biography. Metternich's sympathy for English, historically grounded constitutionalism (which we already touched upon) was central here. At this point in time, he was already distinguishing between his "morality," which he adhered to in the long term and on which he did not compromise, and the short-term tactics he adopted, tactics to which his opponents and critics seek to reduce him. By opting against an alliance with France, he distanced himself from the allies in the Rhenish Confederation—the "confederate mob" [*konföderierte Haufen*], as he called them—who integrated their troops with the French and participated in the "war of destruction."

Thus, the remaining *third option* was the only possible one: "neutrality, in the strictest sense." The space for this had been opened up by Napoleon when he disclosed to Metternich his operational plan against Russia in the conversation of September 20, 1810. In that context, he also mentioned the key role to be played by a resurrected kingdom of Poland, which the emperor wanted to see on his side in a campaign against Russia, leaving Austria the option of remaining neutral. That meant that, following a successful campaign, Austria would lose Galicia to an enlarged Poland. In that case, Metternich banked on getting the Illyrian provinces (Corinthia, Krain, Görz, Croatia, the Hungarian Littoral, Dalmatia) back as compensation.

Metternich and Napoleon had discussed several times in Paris the illusion that popular movements might play a significant role. Napoleon was thinking of Spain, and also of Germany, where Austria's hopes had been dashed twice before, in 1794 and in 1808–1809. Napoleon taught Metternich that anyone who relied on a popular uprising in his fight against the French would fall into a trap. On September 20, the minister responded to Napoleon, saying: "Many, among them sober observers, whose insight into the peculiar condition of affairs in Europe, however, is rather limited, believe that the beginning of a war against Russia must, given the popular feeling at the present time, be the signal of a general rebellion—and hence the forerunner of Russian victory."[346] Napoleon revealed his strategy to Metternich. At the most, 80,000 to 100,000 of the troops taking part in the campaign against Russia would be French; the remaining troops would come from countries between the Rhine and Oder— that is, from the Rhenish Confederation and Poland. But he would move 300,000 French troops to Germany and Italy, and these, Metternich said, would "more than suffice to hold Germany and Italy in check, and stifle every popular movement in its birth."[347] The good-hearted liberators of the people in 1813 did not foresee this, but Metternich did; he had been provided with military information by Napoleon and thus knew that the armed popular movements were without a chance of success. This is why he relied entirely on coordinated military operations and the numerical superiority of the traditional armies united in a war coalition.

Russian Attempts at Forging an Alliance

After his return from Paris, Metternich was deeply concerned about negotiations, conducted by his father while deputizing for him in his absence, regarding an alliance with Russia. These had reached the stage at which contracts could be drawn up and signed. Metternich, the son, considered this an "extremely important matter which exerts the most direct influence on our future political development."[348] Metternich responded to Russia's offer of a return to friendly relations with Austria by pointing out how Russia had damaged Austria with the Treaty of Tilsit and, furthermore, had contributed to the devastating result of the last war. Napoleon's marriage and his journey to Paris, he added, had changed the situation fundamentally. In the end, the tsar's adjutant general, Count Paul Shuvalov, and the foreign minister, Romanzov, only wanted to find out how Austria, and in particular Metternich himself, would react if there were a rift between France and Russia. But this was precisely what Metternich wanted to keep secret for as long as possible. Most of all, he did not want "to betray the secret of our weakness." He told Shuvalov, who had come on a diplomatic mission, that there was only a family tie between Austria and France, not a defensive or offensive alliance. The family connection rendered a political alliance superfluous. Metternich considered all expansionist intentions—such as Russia's aim of conquering Moldavia and Walachia, both formally still under the supreme rule of the Ottoman Empire—as particularly critical. Emperor Franz followed the explanations and suggestions of his ministers on every point.[349]

Metternich detected in Russia the same expansionist tendencies that he saw in Napoleonic France. Since the time of Peter the Great, the tsarist empire had continuously expanded at the expense of Austria's allies and friends; it had enabled the rise of Prussia and, with the destruction of Poland, had disobeyed "all idea of true European policy," establishing "in its stead a system of destruction and robbery."[350] Without Austria's resistance, the Ottoman Empire would long since have been destroyed by the Russian attacks. Russia participated actively in the dissolution of the Holy Roman Empire in 1803.

Domestic Consolidation: Metternich's Take on Economic Questions

In Paris, Metternich had negotiated a convention that was ready to be signed and that was meant to make transit trade possible in the Illyrian provinces and at the economic center of Fiume. Now, he had for the first time the painful experience of the resistance he would come to expect from other parts of the court. The president of the court chamber, von Wallis, produced a devastating report on the convention. He predicted that the French would abuse the right to found, for commercial reasons, new consulates—which formed part of the agreement—for spreading an espionage network across all of the territory of the Habsburg Monarchy. Metternich was humiliated, and he was accused of having acted without seeking the advice of the court chamber. The convention, the report concluded, must under no circumstances be signed; otherwise, Austria would suffer enormously.[351]

This judgment and the fact that the convention was not signed are at the root of the claim that Metternich did not understand anything about economic affairs. The domestic situation of Austria, according to Srbik, was still alien to him at that time, and he therefore was not able to "say anything of importance regarding the organization of the state's economic situation."[352] What this evaluation leaves out is that, before setting off to Paris, Metternich had consulted with the president of the court chamber and had asked for material relating to the issue so that he could take it with him. Metternich defended himself by pointing out that, despite the fact that the convention was now coming under heavy criticism from the court chamber, it was mainly based on these materials. The court chamber "apparently . . . had changed its mind."[353]

Apart from that, Metternich very much did have important things to say about the "organization of the economic situation," in fact about the most important economic question of them all—namely, the restoration of a stable currency, even if that would entail a state bankruptcy, which actually occurred in 1811. The task was to put an end to recent increases in paper money and to the volatility of the currency by reducing the amount of such money in circulation. The president of the court chamber presented a report that suggested reducing the value of the currently circulating paper notes to a fifth of their current value by December 31, 1810, at the latest, and accepting them as legal tender only until December 31, 1811. Under conditions of the utmost secrecy, the emperor sent his minister, Metternich, a sealed package containing said report. The strict secrecy was intended to make Metternich "realize the great confidence I place in you." The emperor then addressed his most important man with words of a kind he had never before put to paper: "By contrast, I have to tell you that in case anything regarding this secret proposal should become known through you, I would remove you without hesitation from my services: you therefore must not mention this to anyone and must maintain the strictest silence on it."[354] Is it still possible, then, to claim that Metternich had no part in the reorganization of the economic situation?

The conflict between Metternich and the court chamber is evidence, not of Metternich's lack of economic understanding, but of a structural problem. The president of the court chamber, von Wallis, relentlessly insisted on parsimony when it came to the state's finances, whereas Metternich, as the foreign minister, could not avoid having to advocate for expensive conflicts such as wars and interventions. In some years of crisis, such as in 1813 or in 1830, during the July Revolution, financial demands necessarily increased. In 1810, Austria was already looking back over an almost uninterrupted sequence of years of war, reaching back to 1792, and in addition there were the oppressively high levels of contributions to be paid to Napoleon. During those years in which Austria aimed to consolidate its financial and military forces, Metternich therefore demonstrated to the emperor in a very fundamental way that domestic parsimony and military expenditure were compatible. For this was another of the lessons he drew from the various personal conversations he had in Paris: that the independence of a state could rest only on its military power.

A memorandum by Metternich on the state of the army in October 1810 expressed the stark economic dilemma well: "Every state rests on two bases: a) on industrial power of wealth and goods from national capital; b) on the independent preservation and safeguarding of these goods, on the power to wage war. Both condition each other, both are one. No wealth is grounded that cannot preserve and, it follows, defend itself; and no power to wage war is lasting that undermines the wealth. Finding the right proportion between the two, balancing them out so that they mutually strengthen each other, that is the genuine economics of the state."[355] This could be called Metternich's financial doctrine of military policy. The experience of Napoleon ruthlessly basing his rule on military power led the peace-loving Metternich, who abhorred war, to the development of an economics based on the principles of *realpolitik:* "It cannot only want peace; it must also want war, because the one does not exist without the other." The citizen had to be persuaded of this, and all forces had to be combined. Metternich invoked the "spirit of the nation," which was a way of bolstering the capacity to wage war without diminishing wealth. At the same time, he pleaded for an extension of conscription "to several estates"—he had in mind the "educated estates"—and for an expansion of the military reserve. What concerned him was that inflation and rising prices were making it more difficult to provide for the army.

Changing Course: "Active instead of Strict Neutrality" toward France

From the very beginning of 1812, there were expectations of a major Franco-Russian war. This forced Metternich to revise his beliefs about "taking sides" because he thought, rightly, that Austria's existence depended on it. On November 28, 1811, he presented Emperor Franz with a new summary, looking both backward and forward, and added his earlier report from January to aid the ruler's memory.[356] Metternich reckoned that 1812 would see unprecedented change in Europe: "The time has come which Napoleon has long calculated on, in which the final struggle of the old order of things against his revolutionary plans is unavoidable." It was a question of victory or defeat, of to be or not to be; no matter how the war ended, "the whole position of affairs in Europe" would be altered. Napoleon was busy secretly organizing his plans for attack, and would, without a thought for Austria, move toward the "ultimate destruction of the old order of things."[357] There would be a "continental war."

On the basis of new information provided by the ambassador in Paris, Schwarzenberg, Metternich had begun to have doubts about the Austrian concept of "strict neutrality." His mind was continually preoccupied with thoughts of the coming war. The possibility that Prussia would be drawn into the war as an unconditional ally of France, like the Rhenish Confederation, caused him great anxiety. That anxiety turned out to be well grounded: on February 24, 1812, the state of Friedrich Wilhelm III did, indeed, enter into a pact with France that committed it to full military allegiance in case of war and promised generous compensation in case of victory—compensation that would come, in part, at the expense of Austria.

Metternich was particularly concerned that a situation might come about that forced Napoleon—strengthened by the military potential of Prussia—to take up arms against Austria. Such a situation was conceivable given Schwarzenberg's information from Paris, especially the warning he had received from Napoleon: "If Austria is neutral, I shall not revolutionize Galicia; but if that were done by my allies the Poles, I could not hinder it, and then we should certainly quarrel over it."[358] This led Metternich to offer Napoleon an "auxiliary corps" for his campaign against Russia in return for Austria setting up an "observational corps" in Galicia.[359] He knew from previous conversations that as long as Austria remained neutral, Napoleon would never grant it such a corps; Austria could not even carry out policing measures in Galicia while maintaining neutrality. It was therefore necessary to take part in Napoleon's campaign, but as little as possible, and to enter into a strictly limited alliance. Within the framework of such an alliance, it would then be possible to set up an Austrian corps in Galicia. The auxiliary corps was to be made up of 30,000 men and stationed with the outmost right wing of the French army. It would have to be under the command of an Austrian general.

With characteristic clarity, Metternich defined Austrian participation in Napoleon's campaign neither as a "war of defense," because Austria was not under attack, nor as a "war of conquest" of the kind Napoleon had in mind, but as a *war of self-preservation* in order to "prepare [for Austria] a better future by actively interfering in the future course of European affairs."[360] Metternich's strategy deserves to be called dialectical, because by participating in the war, he was attempting to avoid a war against Austria that might have been triggered by Poland. His objective was to do all he could to prevent Poland's being revolutionized, and this was the purpose of the Austrian military bridgehead in Galicia. It is important to take this into account when assessing Austria's policies, for Austria is often charged with having recklessly followed Napoleon's lead. In fact, Austria's participation served the purpose of keeping Napoleon at arm's length.

Just how seriously the emperor and Metternich took this objective was clear even before they reached a conclusive agreement with Napoleon. On December 18, 1811, Emperor Franz sent a resolution, based on a draft by Metternich, to the vice president of the court's police constabulary, Hager, saying that the daily increases in troop numbers in the states adjacent to Austria's northern border required a heightened level of vigilance. These troops were not directed at Austria, but "for political and policing reasons," in order to preserve "peace and order," they necessitated measures in those border areas closest to them. The emperor ordered that Hungarian—not German—troops be sent there; there were more Hungarian troops available, and, unlike the option of recalling soldiers on leave, this would not require any additional expenditure by the state.[361] In this case, too, Metternich was seeking to strike a compromise between military expenditure and the need to consolidate the state's budget.

The Franco-Austrian Alliance of March 14, 1812

Between the autumn of 1811 and the spring 1812, Metternich's political calculations were in an unstable limbo. He did not know whether Napoleon would actually show an interest in his virtuoso balancing act, the strictly limited alliance that was designed to make Austria unassailable and, in the case of victory, ensure that she would be treated as a joint partner rather than a passive element to be maneuvered around. But at the same time, the Habsburg Monarchy was not to be reduced to a satellite state; its potential sphere of action was to be preserved. Metternich harbored the justified concern that the existence of the entire monarchy depended exclusively on him and his advice. This was by no means an exaggeration, because, given the way Napoleon dealt with weaker powers, nothing could be ruled out. In this situation, Metternich, in the somber context of a ministerial presentation, revealed to the emperor a rare glimpse of his inner condition:

> What is to be done? I try to answer this question, which is comprehensive, affects all of the future, and determines the weal and woe of the state, with the feeling of an incalculable burden resting on me. In front of Your Majesty stands a man for whom only God, His Majesty, and his duty count, and who therefore does not take anything into his calculations that would be alien to these. But the truth of this defines in just a few words the burden of my situation! What is at stake is the existence of the state; every false step must and will threaten it; any deviation from the course, once set, is a false step.[362]

Metternich added to this dramatic address an imploring and urgent appeal to the emperor: "Whatever we decide, we must follow through on it." The minister expressed himself with such directness only in cases in which momentous decisions needed to be taken—as when later, in April 1813, he sought to align the emperor firmly with the course toward war with Napoleon. But on this occasion the result was a package of programs that ended in a formal alliance with France. In the phase leading up to it, Metternich compared the proposed alliance—article by article—to the one that Kaunitz, who was admired by both Metternich and Napoleon, had agreed to with France in 1756, thereby implying that the Austria of 1812 was also acting as an independent, sovereign state.[363] What made the whole process peculiar was the fact that Metternich suggested a military initiative and the emperor approved it, but its execution was put in the hands of a commission that was charged with voting on it and informing the emperor of its decision. Chaired by the war minister, Karl Count Zichy, the commission consisted of the foreign minister, the president of the court chamber, and the president of the court's war council.[364] Thus, Metternich was by no means the only one outside of the office of the emperor to wield power. This explains why he always found it necessary to employ such passionate appeals in order to secure Emperor Franz's support for the political course he pursued.

On March 14, 1812, France and Austria sealed the pact in a formal contract that corresponded precisely to Metternich's line of "active neutrality." It also was proof of the extent to which Austria's international position had solidified, because Austria wrung the following concessions from the most powerful man in Europe:

- An assurance of the mutual inviolability of the territories of the two states

- A promise that the integrity of the Ottoman Empire would be respected

- An agreement on an Austrian contingent of (only) 30,000 men (24,000 infantry; 6,000 cavalry)

In secret additional articles it was also stipulated that:

- The contingent would serve under an Austrian commander chosen by Emperor Franz and could not be divided.

- Austria was not obligated to join a war against England or the states on the Iberian Peninsula, only against Russia.

• If that the kingdom of Poland were restored, Galicia would remain a part of Austria.

• Austria could exchange Galicia for the Illyrian provinces if it wished to do so.

Metternich's claim that the negotiations had achieved more than could have been wished for "during the past twenty years"—that is, since the beginning of war in 1792—makes it clear how much they meant.[365] The example of Prussia had shown what a completely dependent alliance with Napoleon might look like. Prussia's pact of February 24, 1812, had locked it into the kind of unconditional offensive and defensive alliance that every state of the Rhenish Confederation had entered into.[366] Metternich had been able to prevent Austria from becoming such an unconditional brother in arms.

The Dresden Conference, May 16 to 29, 1812

In Dresden in the spring of 1812, Napoleon was setting in motion preparations for the great campaign. He had arrived there on May 16 and stayed until May 29. Every day he gave instructions to his chief of staff, Berthier.[367] He used his stay to hold another meeting of monarchs, at which the spectators witnessed a strange castling of the political forces. Whereas in 1808 Russia had been invited as an ally and the French empire had been planning the war against Austria, now Russia was the isolated power and Austria the ally. The whole meeting had the atmosphere of a high-level family gathering; Napoleon had communicated through his ambassador in Vienna that he would "consider himself very fortunate" to meet his father-in-law when arriving in Dresden with Marie Louise. The party who had been explicitly excluded in 1808 was now the guest. Metternich considered this a significant improvement in Austria's position.

Prior to the arrival of Napoleon and Marie Louise in Dresden on May 16,[368] Metternich had taken care of the guest list and found suitable accommodation for the high nobility and their court entourages.[369] On his list of guests were:

• Emperor Napoleon and Empress Marie Louise of France

• Emperor Franz and Empress Ludovika of Austria

• Archduke Johann of Austria

• the King of Naples, Marshal Joachim Murat

• the Prince of Neuchatel, Louis-Alexandre Berthier, Napoleon's Chief of Staff

• the Queen of Westphalia, Katharina von Württemberg (King Jérôme was already on his way to the battlefield)

• the Prince of Benevent, Charles-Maurice de Talleyrand

• the Duc de Bassano, Hugues-Bernard Maret, Napoleon's new foreign minister

• the Grand Duke of Würzburg, Ferdinand III, formerly of Tuscany, brother of Emperor Franz

• Clemens and Eleonore Metternich

• the King of Prussia, Friedrich Wilhelm III

Although this meeting is not much discussed in the literature on the Russian campaign, it was nevertheless important if we are considering Metternich's role. It gave him another opportunity for detailed meetings with Napoleon and for sounding him out regarding his further plans. He found confirmation of his view that Napoleon still did not attach any great importance to military support from Austria, whose army he wanted kept artificially small. The imposition of an "auxiliary army" of 30,000 men he considered "a moral guarantee for the restraint of the other part of the Austrian army within the boundaries of their own kingdom."[370] And Napoleon, indeed, allowed his ally to deploy an "observational corps" in Galicia and Bohemia, as previously agreed.[371]

Metternich himself felt that this pretense of active participation while at the same time maintaining neutrality and enjoying the guaranteed inviolability of Austrian territory was an absurdity, an "eccentric political situation" that was unique in the history of diplomacy and "a remarkable illustration of a period fantastic in every respect, and afflicted with every kind of abnormal condition."[372] From their confidential discussions in Dresden, Metternich extracted Napoleon's vision of a "Carolingian Empire under a Bonapartist dynasty."[373] He judged this undertaking to be "fantastic—the *va banque* of a gambler who had become foolhardy because of former gains."[374] For this envisaged empire, Napoleon was also prepared to risk a march toward Moscow in order to force Alexander into a decisive battle, for he assumed, Metternich wrote, that the tsar would under all circumstances protect his most magnificent city against an

Meeting of the monarchs in Dresden, May 1812. *Left to right:* Emperor Franz with
Ludovika, Emperor Napoleon with Marie-Louise, King Friedrich August I of
Saxony with his wife, Maria Augusta, Metternich with Eleonore.

invading enemy. In any case, Napoleon told Metternich that he was certainly
prepared for a split campaign, divided by the winter and to be continued in
the spring of 1813, which was how things did eventually turn out.

In Dresden, Napoleon for the first time met his father-in-law, who was visibly impressed by his Corsican son-in-law ("That is a proper man!") and
through his behavior confirmed the *empereur* in his view that Austria would
never join an alliance against him. In 1813, again in Dresden, Napoleon would
reveal to Metternich that this belief had been the greatest error he had made.
Ludovika, "the Empress whose disposition toward Napoleon, as is well known,
is utterly hostile,"[375] did not alter her disposition one iota, a forceful reminder
for Metternich that a hostile front awaited him in Vienna, a front that included
Archduke Johann, who left Dresden in protest after forty-eight hours.[376]

Awaiting the Catastrophe, a Signal to Change Course

News of the outbreak of war reached Metternich in Prague on June 28, when
he learned of the French proclamation to the army of June 22. In Dresden, Napoleon had already mentioned to Metternich that people would be talking
about him on June 23.[377] During the campaign—even while in Königswart in

July—Metternich also engaged with the difficulties of financing the army, in particular the auxiliary corps, whose task was to support the campaign under the supreme command of Schwarzenberg. During a presentation to the emperor, Metternich's anger toward the president of the court chamber, von Wallis, erupted: "The court chamber always assumes that Austria no longer needs an army. An attempt at refuting this proposition would be like tussling with a chimera. It seems undeniable to me that our military constitution at present is the worst possible because the state pays many individuals and in the hour of danger no one is available."[378]

Metternich followed military developments closely. To him, the progress and outcome of the Russian campaign was a barometer that would show him if and when Napoleon had been weakened enough that a coalition against him was feasible. But so far, no one has examined in detail what information the minister had at his disposal and when he received it. The following chronological information should therefore be seen as the pieces of a puzzle that gradually revealed a picture of crisis; this picture finally made it clear that Napoleon's power had been diminished enough that Metternich could take his policies in a different direction. We must remind ourselves of the sources of information the minister could draw upon in Vienna. The French ambassador provided him with the always overly optimistic military bulletins. He also intercepted the mail of the French embassy and thus learned, for instance, what the Russian military bulletins contained. But he also received information from the Austrian privy councillor von Baum, who had been sent to Napoleon's headquarters as the Austrian contact.

As early as August 14, Metternich was haunted by gloomy premonitions: he identified Smolensk as the place of an important event even before Napoleon's forces encountered the Russian army in their first battle there on August 17–18, and he already judged that one should not be preoccupied with the organization of Napoleon's headquarters and the so-called *Conseils militaires* "in order to understand all the disasters that have happened and to foresee endless disaster to come. One 'Pfuhl'[379] is enough to destroy a whole army forever."[380] This was an allusion to Karl Ludwig von Pfuel, the hapless Prussian chief of staff who was serving in the Russian army at the Battle of Auerstedt in 1806. On September 8, Metternich learned from French military bulletins and reports from von Baum that the Russians were "now trying to enter into battle" but were everywhere being defeated by Napoleon's maneuvers. The consequences of the likely march toward Moscow, he learned, were unpredictable.[381] On September 16, he saw to it that Schwarzenberg's troops were equipped with winter coats, and he knew that the French emperor was "incessantly" progressing toward Moscow. On September 20, he was made aware of the bloody conquest of Smolensk by Napoleon's troops. On September 24, the secretary of the Austrian embassy in Saint Petersburg, von Berks, arrived in Vienna and brought fresh news. He had traveled via Moscow and Kiev, and his report led Metternich to comment: "Error everywhere. It would be difficult to give an idea of the state of affairs, if it could not be calculated on the basis of the individuals in charge."[382]

The enemy troops entered Moscow on September 14; between September 14 and 18 the city was in flames. On September 30, the French ambassador in Vienna handed Metternich the nineteenth *Military Bulletin,* of September 16, which had been issued in Moscow. It contained information on the army entering the city and, with the French reader in mind, compared the metropolis with the splendor of their own capital. But it also reported on Russian tactics: "Thus, complete anarchy devastated this great and beautiful city and the flames consume it."[383] To this, Metternich's desperate response was: "This exhausts everything, and the only hope for peace is left to us."[384]

No more than a week later, on October 4, Metternich held in his hands the twentieth bulletin, of September 17. Despite the fact that it had been censored by Napoleon, it contained enough to make Metternich "shudder," even if some of the numbers it contained were too high. Within three days, a sea of flames had destroyed five-sixths of the city, whose houses were all built of wood, including 1,600 churches, 1,000 palaces, and enormous food stores that had held enough provisions for eight months. Some 30,000 injured and ill Russians had burned to death, and the richest trading houses had been ruined. The army had therefore found very little to pillage—the bulletins spoke euphemistically of "resources."[385] In Metternich's judgment, the withdrawal of Russian troops into the country's heartland had been the only possible military option. The campaign now appeared to him "like a war between the Siberian empire and Europe" in which the Russians had been pushed onto the Siberian side and out of Europe, so to speak. At that point Metternich still found it difficult to say who should be considered the winner, who the loser: "It is altogether impossible to give a proper idea of what has happened. What is certain is that Russia has been beaten back for the next hundred years."[386]

Napoleon left Moscow on October 19, but even before that, on October 2, Schwarzenberg had taken the precautionary measure of retreating beyond the Bug River in order to protect his troops. For Metternich a precarious situation emerged: he had to send troops from Galicia in order to restore troop numbers to 30,000 after they had been decimated. But there was no longer any victory to be had. In the course of October, there were wild rumors coming to Vienna from all sides, among them that Napoleon had been blown up inside the Kremlin. Schwarzenberg's reports contradicted this. On December 15, Metternich found out that Napoleon, having left his army, had arrived "all by him-self" in Vilnius on December 5. On December 17, Metternich handed Emperor Franz a personal letter from Napoleon, "set in a moderate tone," that he had received through the French ambassador. At that point, Metternich knew that Napoleon was already back in Paris.[387]

Among the Chancellery files from December 1812, there is an undated hand-written note from Metternich to the emperor relating to the news that was coming from the Russian theater of war. This note is the earliest clear sign that the minister thought the moment had come to take action and to build up arms against Napoleon. In great haste, he had written: "Your Majesty! Among all measures the one that must not be delayed is the fastest possible organization of the army, which needs to be formed in Bohemia. I therefore suggest most obediently to decree what is appended in copy."[388] He had formulated the necessary order for the emperor. The signal of the major change of political course had been given. Armament could begin.

6

WORLD WAR

Climax and Crisis, 1813

METTERNICH DISCREETLY ASSEMBLES THE FORCES

Metternich's Overlooked Role in the Events of 1813

There are periods in history, and in the lives of individuals, when the sequence of events is so concentrated that what would normally take decades happens in a single year. For those affected by this experience, this as an incredible acceleration of time, something that causes them enormous psychological stress. This is how Metternich experienced the year 1813, the turning point that determined the course of the history of the whole epoch of 1789–1815. Historians find it difficult to disentangle the web of political and military actions in this year, with their parallel, opposed, and combined natures, and to find out which were the decisive fields of action, the fields that truly guided developments. Thus it is all the more strange that the true significance of the Austrian foreign minister within this web is practically unrecognized. His role is either completely ignored or considered only in relation to particular points; overall, it is underestimated and misinterpreted.

The thesis to be developed here is the following: Metternich not only steered negotiations over the course of a few months but also, in a way that has hitherto not been recognized, steered the whole period of the wars of liberation. Without his power of political insight, and without the attention he paid to the overall military situation, the new coalition would have failed, just as all the others had. This apparently daring interpretation can be defended only through a fresh and more comprehensive reading of the unpublished sources and by screening them systematically for evidence of Metternich's participation. Did he really possess the potential of a strong-willed, target-oriented strategist? Was Tsar Alexander the "savior of Europe?"[1] The dominant opinion suggests: "At the beginning of 1813, Metternich had no general plan, although he later wanted to make people believe otherwise." He was "devious" and practiced "betrayal, political bigamy."[2] Only over the course of the year did he change his mind; he joined the coalition against Napoleon when the situation seemed propitious. This view of Metternich focuses on his diplomatic activities. It entirely ignores his participation in military affairs, especially his involvement before and during the Battle of Leipzig, and also in mediating conflicts between the generals and the monarchs who tried to direct the course of the war.[3]

Distancing Himself from Napoleon: The Truce with Russia, January 24

As early as the end of January 1813, Austria altered the orientation of its military policy. Metternich and the emperor saw this as justified after they received crucial information on the outcome of the Russian campaign. They now knew that Napoleon's marshal Berthier (the prince of Neufchâtel) was retreating; that, from January 14, 1813, the headquarters of the allied troops of the Grande Armée was in Posen; that Murat (the king of Naples) had returned home. The emperor and his minister were worried about Schwarzenberg's auxiliary corps, having received no news from him. They feared an engagement with Russian troops and wanted to avoid this at all costs. On January 24, the emperor therefore ordered "the arrangement of a temporary truce of the shortest possible period and without written agreement." This actually constituted a breach of the contract with Napoleon. Field Marshal Ludwig Count Yorck von Wartenburg set the example of this kind of transgression when, on December 30 in Tauroggen, he single-handedly agreed to a truce between his Prussian auxiliary corps and the Russians. But now the person who took this step was the emperor, which was significantly more important. He adopted Metternich's strategy of cautiously but systematically withdrawing from the alliance, and he gave the decisive signal to the Russian side that he would no longer be the enemy. Having in mind the further aim of armament, Emperor Franz also ordered that, under all circumstances, the auxiliary corps should be kept together and moved toward Galicia.[4]

An anonymous pamphlet on Metternich's desk indirectly revealed how far his operational planning had already advanced. It urged the government to free Austria from Napoleon's grip, take on the role of a mediator, and, to that end, establish contact with Russia, England, and France. On February 3, the minister said of the text that it only advised "what had already begun and been partly executed." Indeed, he had already put out his political feelers in order to weave a diplomatic network that would be strong enough to support a war coalition against Napoleon.[5] It was a paradoxical situation: the other powers—Great Britain, Russia, and later also Prussia—were all at war with France and were moving toward an alliance, but Metternich was the only one who, from a position of "active neutrality," maintained relations with all the belligerents. His endeavor was highly risky, and, in the worst case, might have provoked an immediate war with Napoleon. Metternich therefore conducted himself in a way he thought diplomatically unassailable, offering himself as a mediator between the warring parties in the interests of a general European peace treaty. From the very beginning, he used the offer of peace as a tactical tool to increase his room for maneuver. His real aim was to forge a resilient coalition against Napoleon.

Metternich's way of proceeding has been misunderstood as an attempt to avoid a military conflict for as long as possible. The fact that he finally joined the war coalition in August, the argument goes, must be interpreted as the failure of his dovish policies.[6] This is wrong because Metternich was enough of a realist to know that, without the use of force, France under Napoleon would never have allowed itself to be reduced to its "normal" dimensions—as a major European power on the left bank of the Rhine within its 1792 borders. The declared aim of establishing peace had only instrumental value. If Napoleon had accepted it, Austria would have regained its freedom to act, because a conference participant who has the generally acknowledged authority to lead peace negotiations is also in a position to negotiate political settlements, such as territorial concessions, or military agreements, such as truces and their length. And Metternich's suggestion of acting as a mediator had a further effect: it forced the allies to get clear about their war aims and what they wanted to achieve in negotiations, and so it forced them to unite properly against Napoleon. Metternich's intention was that this would lead to the formulation of a shared program. If the negotiations failed, this would provide grounds for a declaration of war. And that is what Metternich expected to be the ultimate outcome. That was his master plan.

Preventing an Alpine Revolution, February 1813

When Metternich was just about to introduce a raft of measures to put this master plan into action, his delicately woven strategy came under threat from an adventurous project, already well in progress, to promote a patriotically driven revolution in the Alpine region. There were three dangers. The first was that an uprising against Napoleon in central Tyrol would once again draw French troops into the heartland of Habsburg, something Metternich wanted to avoid in order to keep the theater of war in central Germany, in Saxony, if at all possible. The second was that the connections of the rebels to the most important European courts, once revealed, would seriously interfere with the diplomatic work to be achieved. But, third, by far the most compromising fact was that the emperor's brother, Archduke Johann, figured as the *spiritus rector* of the rebellion.

The archduke had committed the most secret plans to his diary. As early as mid-December 1812, he wrote: "My plan is beautiful, if only I could execute it. I am willing to use any means, be it amicably or with the sword against Napoleon, I only have one purpose in mind, namely the old "German freedom," revenge for Austria—and happiness for my beloved Tyrol."[7] He no longer believed in Napoleon's invincibility. Tyrol was to liberate itself by its own power. Russia and England strongly supported a rebellion in Tyrol in order to cut France off from resources coming from Italy.[8] In Metternich's view the plan for this rebellion was the result of a patriotically enflamed but politically naive mind that did not appreciate how dangerous Napoleon was, and did not even remember how effortlessly he had defeated the Tyrolians when they fought on their own in 1809–1810. In 1811 Metternich was already fearing that rebellions were likely in Tyrol and Switzerland. He was highly critical of such plans, saying that the result would be "a lot of innocent sacrificial victims." He thought about things in broader contexts and further in advance, and from this perspective what needed to be taken into account was "how much we may need the support from these provinces in possible future situations."[9] Archduke Johann was not perturbed by such considerations. He wanted to pursue his fine intentions, and between January 29 and February 3, 1813, he developed a surprisingly concrete plan for rebellion.

Metternich must have been shocked by this: here was someone practicing politics by bypassing the Austrian government. And Johann placed his bets on the so-called *Zundfünkentheorie*: that a spark would start a conflagration. But the plan was not even properly thought through. The archduke expected that he would be thought a "fool" or regarded as "lost," and he naively promised: "If I am happy, the cause will progress, then everyone will open their eyes in amazement, admiration, and say: Who would have thought this?"[10] But what would happen if the plan failed? That question he left unanswered.

The exact sequence of events in the revolutionary conspiracy need not detain us here. The core actors, apart from the archduke, were the director of the

Haus-, Hof- und Staatsarchiv in Vienna [the imperial archive], privy councillor Josef Baron von Hormayr; Anton Schneider, privy councillor at the court of appeal; and the district commissioner Anton von Roschmann, who, familiar with all the details, betrayed the enterprise to Metternich. The beginning of the attack was planned for Easter Monday, April 19, 1813, but Hager, the deputy head of the court police office, preempted the leaders' action by having Hormayr, Schneider, and—as cover—Roschmann arrested on the night of March 8. The reliability of the information provided by the informant was confirmed to Metternich after the conspirators' courier was captured on his way from Vienna to Saint Petersburg on the night of February 25. The explosive documents found on the courier provided conclusive evidence of the connections the conspirators had already established. The documents were deposited at the Chancellery in the strictly secret section of the "Acta Secreta," where they still are today.[11]

The intercepted documents brought to light the fact that individuals from the highest level of politics were involved in the conspiracy. An English agent in Vienna (John Harcourt King) was the leading diplomatic coordinator; the British ambassador at the court in Vienna (Viscount Cathcart) was involved, as was a British national at the Russian headquarters (Horatio Lord Walpole) and a confidant of Johann's in northern Germany who was commander of the Russian-German legion (Field Marshal Lieutenant Ludwig von Wallmoden). Finally—and this was the most sensational disclosure—the British foreign minister, Viscount Castlereagh, was involved. The British were prepared to contribute £30,000 to the enterprise. The fact that Russia and Britain were acting behind the back of the Austrian government certainly made the future negotiations with Metternich about an alliance more difficult. The minister must also have been worried by the fact that the Bavarian envoy, Count Rechberg, had known about a forthcoming Tyrolian uprising as early as February 1813. As Bavaria was part of the Rhenish Confederation, one could be certain that Napoleon would soon get wind of the plans.[12]

With the agreement of the emperor, Metternich reprimanded the archduke, who, on the morning of March 9, appeared before the minister and, contrite and subdued, delivered "a kind of general confession." He declared that he "had erred greatly."[13] The whole Tyrolian resistance movement [*Alpenbund*] affair taught Metternich that in the future he would have to be even more vigilant when it came to national tendencies. Later, in Dresden at the end of June, Napoleon, who was closely observing the stirrings in Germany, discussed with Metternich how little one could rely on national movements in the context of great wars.

"We Have Reached the Day of Decision": The Fundamental Shift in Austrian Policy

"Alea iacta est"—the die is cast. Thus spoke Caesar after he had crossed the Rubicon in northern Italy on his way to Rome. For Metternich, the die was cast on March 3, 1813. On this day, a day of great personal significance for him, the emperor made him Grand-Chancellor of the Order of Maria Theresia, the most important Austrian military order, founded by Maria Theresia in 1757 to recognize acts of courage. The head of this order was the emperor himself, who was its Grand-Master, with the Chancellor of the Order having the second most important role. That the emperor acknowledged Metternich as an advisor also in military matters in this way makes it clear just how much he trusted him. This is also how Metternich himself understood it, weaving the following reminiscences into his thank-you speech: "Your Majesty has known me for a number of the most troublesome years of recent history. I have stood by Your Majesty with faithful loyalty in the days of danger. I have gathered courage and strength from Your Majesty's high-minded, firmly law-abiding character; we have reached the day of decision."[14]

From that moment on, Metternich was guided unswervingly and consistently by a single thought: namely, that this time he would be politically and militarily victorious in a coalition against Napoleon, and that he would not—no matter how frequently this was insinuated in the course of that year—allow himself to be lured out of the intended alliance by Napoleon. The fact that in February 1814, in his role as Grand-Chancellor of the Order, Metternich awarded the Grand-Cross of the Order of Maria Theresia to the later victor of the Battle of Waterloo, Wellington, in recognition of his victory over Napoleon at Vitoria in Spain, was perhaps an augury.[15]

There has never before been a systematic analysis of the measures Metternich introduced at this point. Within only a few weeks, in several stages and in accordance with a clear plan, he very determinedly introduced policies that faced great resistance in Vienna. In the course of this, he also coordinated the rearmament at home with Austria's international policies.

Police and the Intensification of Domestic Control (March 4). On March 4, just one day after he had been made Grand-Chancellor of the Order, Metternich pleaded with the emperor to raise Hager from the rank of interim head of the court's police office to its official president—making him the head of "an at present particularly important office."[16] This was an allusion to Archduke Johann's Revolution in the Alps [*Alpenrevolution*], which had just been uncovered and foiled. Metternich furthermore secured more powers for himself in order better to control the political goings-on in Vienna and Austria and make sure that they did not work against his own political and military plans.

Military Preparations: The Path toward "Armed Mediation" (March 14, 1813). Metternich was not at all the hesitant tactician he is often portrayed to be. In March 1813 he urged haste because "every moment lost is irreplaceable." If one takes into account the fact that Metternich requested the right to always be part of discussions about political and military decisions, and that he either insisted upon or gave his blessing to the measures that were taken, then this throws an entirely new light on his role in the war in the year of 1813. The beginning of his involvement was a resolution of March 14, addressed to the president of the court's war council, Bellegarde, which he drafted in the name of the emperor. The resolution suggested proposing to all belligerents an "armed mediation." The emperor could thus redefine "the political state of [Metternich's] relations with other states."[17]

Because the result of the mediation could not be anticipated with certainty, this proposal required that Austria be prepared for a military confrontation. Franz gave the order ("The appended handwritten letter is decreed") to have the corps at the border with Silesia and the not-insignificant corps in Galicia at the ready. Having these troops on standby would strengthen Austria's negotiating position: they served as a constant reminder to the opposed parties that Austria's decision to side with the one or the other could be crucial. The emperor also made detailed plans for a possible war with France, which would involve mustering troops to fight in southern Germany and northern Italy. The troops that were still in Transylvania and Bukovina were to be moved to Galicia, and Schwarzenberg's auxiliary corps was to be sent to Bohemia. Bellegarde was charged with "making immediate preparations" and presenting drafts of the troops' positions.

As a result of this order, Bellegarde was hurrying to secure the border between Bohemia and Saxony. To that end, Field Marshal Lieutenant Duka, who was charged with carrying this out, requested an imperial order, and this order, again, went through Metternich. Metternich declared himself "entirely in agreement" with the draft because he considered it "appropriate given the present circumstances."[18] All this took place during March—that is, before the allies' spring campaign against Napoleon began in April.

The Emperor's Financial Diktat (March 17, 1813). Metternich's strong influence could also be felt in the finances. The "inner conference" [Enge Konferenz], which was normally in charge of financial matters, had not been able to agree "on the possible creation of extraordinary resources for the state," and this angered the emperor, who agreed with Metternich that this was completely unacceptable "at the present, highly important moment." In this instance, too, Metternich formulated an imperial resolution, addressed to Stadion, who in the meantime had become finance minister. Metternich was unusually blunt, given that this was an official communication: "I see it as my duty to give you the order to. . . ." On March 17, in the name of the emperor, Metternich ordered the creation of a new commission, to be chaired by Stadion, to look at these matters again. Metternich would determine who would be on the commission. He explicitly stressed that he "expected of the commission a ruthless consideration of the most practicable and fastest means that might allow the state to secure at this extraordinary present moment free disposition over 30 million guilders in Vienna currency in order to cover extraordinary expenses."[19]

Where was a state that was highly indebted and that had just—in 1811—gone through bankruptcy to find that sort of money? Within the sensationally short time—compared to the leisurely pace at which such institutions usually proceed—of three weeks, the commission suggested a solution to the problem that could yield not just 30 million but 45 million guilders for the state. On April 10, Metternich presented the plan to the emperor. It proposed the immediate creation of a fund based on the state's future income—a so-called anticipatory fund [*Antizipationsfonds*]. This fund was to be credited with 3,750,000 guilders annually for a period of twelve years. The annual sum was to be drawn as an advance on the property tax in the German, Bohemian, and Galician provinces, to be repaid later. The most dependable element of the state's income thus served as a security. This meant, however, that for the next twelve years the budget had to be presided over by a master of thrift. Metternich again invoked the present situation to plead with the emperor: "Extraordinary times and conditions require extraordinary measures. And how much more is that true of the most extraordinary of all times and all situations!"[20] He vehemently contradicted Stadion's suggestions for alterations to the plan that would have postponed creating the required credit. Metternich prevailed, and by April 25, 1813, the establishment of the fund was already being reported in the press.[21] Surprisingly, Napoleon knew as early as May 16 about the 45 million "billets," although in his opinion it was not enough to fight a war against him.[22]

Metternich's Vision for Systemic Change in Austria's Foreign Policy. Because Metternich always viewed domestic and foreign policy as connected, his measures relating to the police, military, and finances also tell us something about his plans for Austria's foreign policy. We are perfectly justified in calling this plan a vision for a peaceful European order. Metternich had in mind a new system, and, in this momentous March, the time finally appeared to be ripe for it. In his usual manner, he formulated the plan as a systematic design complemented by a historical contextualization. The best opportunity for doing so was the reappointment of an ambassador to the embassy in Paris, a post that had remained vacant until then. Prince Schwarzenberg left his role as a general to return to that of an ambassador, and because the situation had shifted so fundamentally, Metternich considered it necessary to give him fresh instructions, which the envoy received on March 28 before departing to Paris.[23] To return to the image we introduced earlier, one might say that Metternich thought that now—after Napoleon's fiasco in Russia—the moment had come for Mr. Keuner to say "No," even if in a somewhat more gradual way than in the parable. It is also important to note that, with these instructions, Metternich converted to his vision the man who would go on to be the field marshal of all allied armies in the war coalition against Napoleon, and thus gained, at an early point, a politically like-minded collaborator.

In the case of a Metternich, such a plan had to refer back to history. French dominance, he wrote, had done away with all the old ideas about European balance.[24] After the wars in 1806–1807, the two allied powers of France and Russia had, between them, held the Continent in their grip. But more recent events—Metternich meant the Russian campaign—had rendered all previous calculations obsolete and brought about a significant shift in the situation. France was in the greatest of crises, in an "enormous catastrophe" of a kind hitherto unseen in modern history. But the evil also contained the remedy: "the idea of a condition of peace, the return to an order of things of the kind which all peoples of Europe, except for one, desired." Now was the moment for an initiative that none of the warring powers could have carried out alone. The new alliance between Prussia and Russia, which was formed in February, had created an altogether new political situation.

Metternich developed the "design" for a possible future European order, a force field, so to speak, made up of four continental powers. On the wings there were two empires, France and Russia, which were constantly in competition for dominance over the Continent and were a permanent threat to the two realms between them, Austria and Prussia. These two "intermediary" powers owed the valuable good of their independence to their unity of sentiment. Every violation of one of the powers in the middle of the Continent also immediately threatened the existence of the other. Peace in central Europe, in turn, guaranteed peace for the other two empires. The Austrian emperor, therefore, could never gain an advantage from the ruin of Austria's sister state [état ami], Prussia; to pursue that would be to pursue his own decline.

Metternich was far from wanting to return to the old power politics. He strove for a condition of peace "based on a just balance [*juste équilibre*] between the major powers and on the independence and well-being of second- and third-rate powers." The protection of the less-powerful states had not been a goal of the old balance-focused policies. Properly understood, the European interest also spoke in favor of preserving the Ottoman Empire. Metternich identified as the most urgent goal the establishment of a continental peace that would spread to England and Russia. The further aim was a maritime and general peace that would allow for a bilateral solution, between France and England, to the problem of Spain. In concrete terms, Metternich hoped that Napoleon, like Russia, would seize the opportunity to accept Austria's dovish intervention. Metternich thus implicitly hinted at Austria's independence—and thus also at its withdrawal from the alliance with France—as a more distant goal.

Establishing Contacts with the Other Major European Powers. Since 1812 Metternich had been thinking about how he could improve Austria's connections with the other major powers involved in the war. He never broke off relations with England, especially not after the unavoidable alliance with France on March 14, 1812. Ever since his first stay in London, in 1794, he had had a special, trusting relationship with the prince regent. He would make use of this fact whenever he needed to preempt the possibility of Austria being seen as England's potential enemy. He therefore sent the prince regent a note saying that the alliance with France would change nothing about Austria's relationship with England and that it would not affect Austria's relationship with the Iberian Peninsula, part of England's sphere of influence, because both were explicitly excluded from the contractual agreement with France. He did wish, however, that England would discontinue "its plans for insurrections in northern Italy and the Illyrian provinces," as they threatened unnecessary political ferment and put Austria "in a most compromising situation."[25]

Now, in 1813, Metternich sought to cultivate his contacts in England. To the Swedish ambassador's expression of interest in Sweden joining the war alliance, Metternich responded, on April 24, 1813, by reaffirming their common interest in a peaceful order in Europe, in its "balance," and in reconstituting the freedom of Germany. On April 26, he signaled to Russia the lifting of the narrow restrictions on trade with the tsarist empire, imposed because of the war, so that Austria could adopt its role as an "armed mediator of peace" amid the changing circumstances. At the beginning of May, he also tried to reach an understanding between the Austrian and Russian troops stationed at the Weichsel. And in April 1813 he had revived relations with the Prussian chancellor, Hardenberg, having already assured him in October of the previous year that the independence and well-being of both states was in their mutual interest.[26]

The issue of how Napoleon would react to the attempt at "armed mediation" must have been particularly important to Metternich. Initially, on April 21, he still thought the French emperor would accept the idea.[27] But this was going to change completely with Russia and Prussia's campaign, as new allies, in the spring of 1813. Between April 17 and 24, Napoleon had held a military review with his allies in Mainz. He was forced to acknowledge the fact that one of his most faithful allies, the king of Saxony, had agreed to a convention with Austria and, having been wooed by Metternich, had left the Rhenish Confederation in order to join the "armed mediation." This was a first sign of Metternich's long-term strategy: he was not only depending on a coalition against Napoleon but also destabilizing the Rhenish Confederation by enticing member states to leave it and join Austria's side. His greatest coup in this effort came on October 8, 1813, when the most important member of the Rhenish Confederation, Bavaria, left just before the Battle of Leipzig. The king of Saxony, though, witnessed Napoleon recapture his country—including Dresden, where Napoleon set up his headquarters—through victories at Großgörschen and Lützen (May 2) and Bautzen (May 20).

After fighting had broken out between Napoleon, Prussia, and Russia, Schwarzenberg's former deputy in Paris, Count Ferdinand Bubna, visited the French emperor in Dresden on May 16, 1813. As far as Napoleon's judgment and manner of conducting himself are concerned, this rather neglected conversation can be understood as something of a dry run for the dispute between Napoleon and Metternich that was to take place just six weeks later. The conversation was the acid test for Metternich's idea of "armed mediation." Unlike later historians, Napoleon immediately recognized the strategy behind the suggestion; he suspected Austria was trying to distance itself from him and move closer to the war coalition against him. He considered the truce that Schwarzenberg and his auxiliary corps had agreed to with Russia in January as a breach of the contractual alliance of March 1812. According to a report from Bubna, he therefore no longer saw Austria as an ally, and, as it was pursuing its own interests, he did not think it a credible neutral mediator. The ruling house was Italian (with this he alluded to Emperor Franz's having been born in Florence), as was the family of Archduchess Beatrix (i.e., the wife of the emperor, Ludovika Beatrix, who came from the Duchy of Modena). Moreover, Austria was the only power that had suffered great losses in Italy: "How could I accept as a mediator a power with interests in that region, a power that has experienced losses there and thus has claims to make?"[28] That was an understandable argument, and Napoleon complemented it with a list of Austria's sins—offenses that, in his eyes, made Metternich's peace initiative ring hollow, which he told Bubna to communicate to Vienna: he was appalled at Metternich's attempt to persuade Saxony to leave the Rhenish Confederation, and Austrian efforts at armament in Bohemia alarmed not only him but also the courts of Bavaria and Württemberg. It all culminated in the sentence: "I do not want your armed mediation."

Napoleon must have been beside himself with rage. He talked to Bubna "with a blistering intensity" that was "difficult to describe because no expression is able to capture it." Metternich was clearly on thin ice. Napoleon's emotional outburst was staged; as we know from Metternich, Napoleon intentionally used such incidents in order to influence and test his opponents. The next day, he received Bubna again, but this time, "with kindness and a very friendly face," he asked him to forget his fervor of the previous day, adding that he did not speak so openly to just anyone. He even explained to Bubna the Russian positions in the forthcoming battle at Bautzen; he asked Bubna, who was a general, about the strength of the Prussians and Russians and revealed the maneuvers he had planned against them. The central message of the seven hours of this dispute was, however, that he was prepared to accept a truce, even if the details remained to be agreed upon. At the same time, Bubna was able to tell Metternich, on the basis of a letter Napoleon had sent to Stadion, that the French emperor would, through gritted teeth, accept an armed mediation. As a military expert, Bubna added that, given the present situation and the condition of Austrian forces, any time they could gain would be beneficial.

THE TACTICAL PATH TO AN "ARMED MEDIATION"

Metternich's Role in Assembling the Alliance against Napoleon: First Draft of the War Aims, Early May 1813

The catastrophe Napoleon experienced in Russia and his return to Paris in December 1812 figure in historical consciousness as a turning point. Yet he had simply ended a campaign; the war between France and the Rhenish Confederation and Russia continued. Russia and Prussia agreed to a truce on December 30, 1812, in the Convention of Tauroggen, before confirming the peace and their alliance with the Treaty of Kalisz, signed in Wrocław on February 27 and Kalisz on February 28. The way to Berlin was thus open to the Russians, who entered the city on March 4 as liberators after the French had given it up without resistance. The Prussian king, who had retreated to Wrocław, declared war on France on March 17 after the tsar arrived in the city.[29]

Prince Kutusow, the famous Russian field marshal and victor over Napoleon, could now turn to the Germans as supreme commander of "the allied armies" and, in his famous proclamation of Kalisz, offer "the princes and peoples of Germany a return to freedom and independence." On March 17, the Prussian king seconded this in an appeal addressed "To my people." Even though neither was of anything like a democratic persuasion, both had learned from Napoleon and his opponents, the Spanish, how much of an advantage could be gained by igniting patriotism within the population. It seemed perfectly possible, however, that the inexperienced volunteers thus attracted would prove counterproductive in battle with the efficient traditional armies directed by Napoleon. Metternich, for good reason, was among those who doubted their helpfulness.

The people of Hamburg had already learned the hard way the price one could end up paying for liberating the people. In March the "Hanseatic League," supported by Russian troops, tried to end the Napoleonic occupation. At the end of May, French troops recaptured the city and brutally slaughtered the poorly trained civil militias and inexperienced officers. Napoleon ordered his commanding marshal, Davout, to raze the houses outside the city gates, thereby enabling a clear shot at anyone who approached, and to require all inhabitants to dig trenches, thus turning the former Hanseatic city into a fortress. Forty-eight million francs in contributions and the cost of maintaining tens of thousands of French soldiers brought the city to its knees.[30] Hamburg became the German Aranjuez. Learning of Hamburg's fate, Metternich recognized the risk of drawing the population into a "people's war," as was advocated in particular by Prussia. Moreover, the French military continued to control northern and central Germany by holding the fortresses of Gdansk, Szczecin, Küstrin, Glogau, Magdeburg, Wesel, and Mainz. Overall, though, the French troops that remained in northern Germany were on the defensive. This did not change until Napoleon rejoined the theater of war in Saxony again at the end of April.

This military limbo was the background for the introduction of Metternich's "armed mediation." Metternich saw, correctly, that Austria was now a sought-after ally, even if, from his perspective, Austrian troops were nowhere near ready for engagement, given their relative weakness and the state of their equipment. At the beginning of May, he therefore sent Stadion to Russian headquarters in Reichenbach as his special envoy, with a personal letter from Emperor Franz to the tsar. The mission was crucial: Metternich was attempting to get the allies to commit to a common set of war aims, which for the first time included a vision of a peaceful reconstructed Europe. Even if his fellow politicians—as well as Tsar Alexander and Friedrich Wilhelm III—did not yet completely understand all the implications of the offer, Metternich, in his instructions for Stadion (dated May 7, 1813), presented a framework that anticipated the fundamental principles and architecture of the order later agreed to at the Congress of Vienna in 1815.[31] This draft of the future was structured into a general part and a specific part. The following four general principles were to be applied:

1. The common goal was peace in the form of a general agreement in which the geographical and political relations between the powers were to be put on a just, and therefore lasting, foundation.
2. A new order was to be founded that took account of everyone's interests; there was to be no return to the status quo ante.
3. True peace and order could not exist without a general peace that included maritime peace. This peace, which had to include England, had top priority.
4. General peace could be achieved through an agreement concerning continental Europe that confined France within appropriate borders.

The specific points for securing a solid continental peace were the following:

• The reconstitution of the countries that once made up the old Kingdom of Poland, in the form it had before the Treaty of Schönbrunn. This was a roundabout way of saying that the Duchy of Warsaw would cease to exist and that the regions that had made up the three divisions of Poland should be returned to Russia, Prussia, and Austria.

• The reconstitution of Prussia by restoring to it its old northern German territories.

• France had to relinquish the German territories on the left bank of the Rhine.

• Holland would become independent of France.

• The reconstitution of the former territories in Italy that were currently French provinces.

• The reconstitution of the papacy by returning its Italian properties to it.

• The border that existed between Austria and Italy before the Treaty of Lunéville was to be restored; Tyrol and the Innviertel, the Dalmatian provinces, and all regions beyond the latter that had been lost since the Treaty of Schönbrunn had to be returned to Austria.

- Napoleon's supreme rule over Germany had to end; the Rhenish Confederation was to be dissolved and a system introduced that united the interests of the German states with those of Europe.

- Napoleon had to give up the Kingdom of Italy.

The whole design was implicitly informed by the idea of a European power balance, an idea Metternich already had explained to Schwarzenberg in March.

The design had now been put out into the world, but at first it did not elicit the desired response. In any case, Metternich had made it clear that Austria would enter into a coalition only if there were a certain degree of unity regarding the war aims. In May, while this proposal was on the table, Napoleon's military fortunes and the fragility of the new coalition between Russia and Prussia led to a fundamental change in Metternich's role and importance.

Lützen, Bautzen, and the Coalition in Crisis, May 1813

Over the course of May, the fate of the allies' spring campaign was decided. On April 24, Napoleon had left Mainz and put off his original plan to march to Berlin; he rushed to the rescue of his threatened marshals Ney and Marmont, who were struggling to defend themselves against the united Russian and Prussian troops under the supreme command of Wittgenstein.[32] After arriving on May 1, he managed to win the Battle of Lützen, on May 2, although not decisively, for he did not have sufficient cavalry to pursue the enemy. On May 8 he took back Dresden and set up his headquarters there.

During these weeks, the Austrian conference diplomacy previously described began to make itself felt at the headquarters in Reichenbach and Dresden, with visits from Stadion and Bubna. At this point, however, these efforts were not successful because Metternich ignored the pleas to join the alliance without the political conditions having been fixed first. Two further battles on May 20–21 at Bautzen changed the situation fundamentally. According to Munro Price, Napoleon had hoped for a repeat of the success at Austerlitz but achieved another Borodino—a bloodbath—with the loss of 20,000 men, twice as many as his opponents. The defeat nevertheless had a morally and militarily devastating effect on the allies. In military terms this was evident from the rifts within the allies' camp. In the Russian camp, Wittgenstein's orders competed with those of the older imperial generals (Miloradowitsch and Tormasow), who took their lead directly from the tsar and encouraged him to take control more or less completely during battle. How little Alexander understood about directing an army he had already demonstrated on December 3, 1805, at Austerlitz, when his numerically superior troops were deceived on the famous Pratzen Heights and had to flee from

Napoleon. Now, at Bautzen, Alexander again contributed decisively to his army's failure, even if they managed an orderly retreat.

What happened next added a political dimension to the military failure. Some Russian generals, among them Barclay de Tolly, who continued to play an important part, argued in favor of retreating to Poland. But this would have left Berlin defenseless against the French troops. Blücher and Yorck therefore threatened to move their units north in order to protect the capital. The Russo-Prussian alliance was at the point of complete disintegration. The truce offered by Napoleon—agreed on June 4, 1813 in Pläswitz, Silesia—must have been manna to the defeated allies. The truce was initially to expire on July 20. Then, on Metternich's initiative, it was extended to August 10, giving enough time and opportunity to refresh the forces and regroup.

Metternich's "Diplomatic Revolution": The Emperor and Chancellery Depart for the Allies' Headquarters

As someone directly involved, Metternich recognized early on that, in the final battle against Napoleon, the conventions of international politics and diplomacy would undergo revolutionary change, and that such change was absolutely necessary in facing an opponent like Napoleon. On June 1, 1813, the Austrian emperor and his minister thus left their residence—unbeknownst to the Viennese public—in order to be close to the action in the Bohemian part of the empire. World history was now being made through uniquely intense communication at the very heart of the continent: between the Palais Marcolini in Dresden (Napoleon's headquarters); Reichenbach (Dzierżoniów) in the Silesian Owl Mountains (the Russian and Prussian headquarters); Gitschin Castle (Jičín), eighty-five kilometers north-east of Prague (the Austrian headquarters); Opotschno Castle (Opočno) in eastern Bohemia, belonging to the Counts Colloredo (temporarily used for negotiations by the tsar); and Ratiborschitz (Ratibořice), the summer palace of Duchess Wilhelmine von Sagan in Northern Bohemia. On June 3, Metternich and the emperor arrived in Gitschin.

Why exactly had they decided to go there? It was not news of defeat at Bautzen that had led Metternich to change his strategy, even if this is how he later portrayed it in his memoirs,[33] but news of an imminent truce. On May 27, a report from Stadion had arrived from Dresden that mentioned that only the Russian side was asking for a truce. The very same day, the minister advised his emperor: "Your Majesty may now want to be silently prepared to go to Bohemia yourself and to be closer to the negotiations should the truce be accepted."[34] There were three reasons Metternich wanted to be there in person very soon: first, the Russo-Prussian coalition was threatening to fall apart and had to be saved; second, there was a danger that the tsar and Napoleon would

Table 6.1. List of Metternich's carriages during the campaign of 1813–1814

Suite		
1.	Large calash for His Excellency + 1 cavalryman	6 *Hofpferde*[a]
2.	Small calash: Leyder, Giroux + 1 hunter	4 carriage horses
3.	Four-seater calash: cook, waiter, valet of Baron Binder	4 ditto
4.	Large *Fourgon* (carriage for provisions), domestic servant	6 ditto
5.	Kitchen carriage, scullion	4 ditto
6.	Small *Wurst*[b]	2 ditto
Chancellery		
7.	Baron Binder + 1 hunter of Baron Binder	4 ditto
8.	Councillor von Wacken, Baron Kruft + servant of Kruft	4 ditto
9.	Schweiger, Gigel	4 ditto
10.	Officials of the Chancellery, Huissiers [bailiffs]	4 ditto
Total number of horses		42

a Horses belonging to the court.

b An open carriage, shaped like a sausage, on which one sat astride.

Source: NA Prague A. C. 8, Krt. 7, 41.

agree a bilateral alliance, with all the disadvantages to Austria that that would entail—a second Tilsit, so to speak—and that had to be averted; and, third, the truce meant there was a window of opportunity for intense negotiations aimed at forming an alliance of the four major powers—which, eventually, with Sweden, would become five—against Napoleon.

Metternich broke new ground with his policies. He formed a mobile Chancellery around him, complete with an office, employees, servants, a cook, and his own equipment, so that he could follow the Austrian and the Russo-Prussian headquarters around and be close to them at all times. When all the Chancellery servants and employees who made up Metternich's staff traveled together, they required ten carriages and forty-two horses (Table 6.1).

Unlike the five previous coalitions, for the sixth Metternich ensured that there would be, by the standards of the time, enormously efficient communication between the various parties. It was "without precedent in the annals of history" for the emperor of Austria, the Russian tsar, the king of Prussia, and the British secretary of foreign affairs to be present on site and meeting in person. "The most difficult affairs, and the arrangements most complicated in their nature, were, so to speak, negotiated from one room to another,"[35] without the need for couriers, the exchange of documents, or envoys to serve as intermediaries. The monarchs and the leaders of their cabinets at first discussed the essential matters confidentially. As soon as an agreement about a particular matter began to take shape, the ministers met for regular conferences at which memoranda and protocols were produced that determined the form and scope of the agreement. Following negotiations with the Russian foreign minister, Nesselrode, and the Prussian state chancellor, Hardenberg, Metternich claimed: "I think that in some negotiations I have achieved more than in three weeks of correspondence."[36]

Metternich's innovation offered three advantages. First, the political chancelleries and the military headquarters were able to exchange their news, views, and decisions as quickly as possible. This helped to unite and strengthen the coalition. Emerging disagreements could be dealt with immediately. Second, the agreements that were reached provided points of reference and outlines for the future order. It has perhaps not always been sufficiently acknowledged that the essential outcomes of the Congress of Vienna were determined in advance in this way, and that its real substance—including all its points of contention—had already been negotiated in 1813–1814, so that they could then be ratified at the congress in a relatively short period of time. In what follows, it is worth taking note of the extent to which the decisions taken during the war prefigured the Vienna System of 1815. This also demonstrates the extent to which room for maneuver began to shrink in 1813–1814: it was not at all possible to "construct" the European order from scratch in November 1814; to a large extent, its principles were already determined.

Third, Metternich was able to coordinate proceedings and facilitate communication between all the parties, and this allowed him to mediate conflicts between rival generals when they flared up. Looking back at the path that was successful in bringing about the decisive Battle of Leipzig in October 1813, which pushed Napoleon and his troops back across the Rhine, Metternich was fully justified in saying that he deserved all the credit for it, for he "had been the helmsman of the coalition over the past months and had prevented it from striking many a shoal."[37] After having witnessed Metternich's skills and determination in the most difficult parts of the negotiations—especially in meetings with Tsar Alexander and the advisors to the Prussian king—the British foreign minister, Castlereagh, went as far as to say: "You are the prime minister of the world, and I beg your pardon that I did not always trust you accordingly."[38] Castlereagh had at first, indeed, deeply distrusted Austria because of its alliance with Napoleon, and this by no means changed immediately when he personally met Metternich, the mastermind of this policy. This makes his judgment of the role of the minister, with whom he later developed close, friendly relations, all the more credible.

In what follows, my focus will be on the crises and turning points on the way from the scenes in Saxony and Bohemia to the first Treaty of Paris on May 30, 1814, and on Metternich's role during this period. Following his arrival in Gitschin on June 3, 1813, the minister, in a fashion altogether unique for a politician, practiced his peripatetic conference diplomacy for a whole year.

On the Way to an Alliance: The Opotschno Summit between
Tsar Alexander and Metternich, June 17–20, 1813

Dorothy McGuigan has given us a vivid day-by-day description of Metternich's shuttle diplomacy between the castles of Bohemia in June 1813, weaving into her account his enthusiastic courtship of Wilhelmine von Sagan.[39] We shall consider this episode at a later point. Metternich benefited from the fact that, during his time as ambassador in Berlin, he had come to respect Hardenberg and, during the heated negotiations over Prussia joining the third coalition in 1805, the tsar had also come to trust Metternich. Metternich's faith in the reliability of Russian politics, however, had suffered—particularly as a result of the events at Austerlitz, Tilsit, and Erfurt. Now he had to fight hard in order to be accepted in his role as mediator at all.

The Prussian and Russian sides were convinced that, as soon as their troops were reinforced by those of Austria, they would be able to defeat Napoleon, and so they thought they could do without a frustrating truce. But given how much attacking power, military cunning, energy, and capacity for regeneration Napoleon would draw upon in the next year, and given that he would still go on to achieve worrying victories against his enemies, it is clear that the hopes of Prussian and Russian decision-makers were fanciful. Metternich was right to be more cautious, and he knew better than anyone else the threat posed by Napoleon. Tsar Alexander, Wilhelm von Humboldt, Hardenberg, and the Prussian military did not see any point in negotiations; they wanted to resume the battle as soon as possible. Metternich, by contrast, was looking for a way to buy time, mindful of the deficient combat strength and equipment of the Austrian army. Offering to open negotiations with Napoleon could do just that. At the same time, Metternich outlined the essential conditions that had to be met for Austria to join the war alliance. All parties involved wanted a contractual agreement, Metternich because, as mediator, he needed binding conditions to present to Napoleon, Prussia and Russia because they wanted to get Austria to commit to joining the war, in case Napoleon rejected the offers made.

Metternich had to negotiate with both extremes—Napoleon and the Russian tsar. He arranged an audience with Alexander in Opotschno Castle, eastern Bohemia. Emperor Franz hastily had the castle's salon redecorated, and between June 17 and 20 it became the scene for conversations between Metternich and Alexander that, in terms of their world-historical significance, can be compared to those the minister would later hold in Dresden. Metternich had, while still in Vienna, judged the situation perfectly in recognizing that he could only master the complicated procedure of simultaneously distancing himself from Napoleon and joining the alliance against him if he was present on site: no amount of diplomatic correspondence could do what face-to-face meetings did.

At this point it is important to say something about the roles that Metternich and Alexander played in securing the stability of the coalition. An influential interpretation of the sixth coalition claims that it only was successful because of the leadership of the British foreign minister, Castlereagh, on account of his wisdom, determination, ideas, and negotiating skills; Castlereagh, this story goes, was the man who ultimately held the coalition together.[40] But the British foreign minister only entered the scene in January 1814, and the coalition was founded in June 1813. Castlereagh knew very little about the internal matters concerning the Continent and only became a pivotal support of the coalition through his "entente cordiale" with Metternich. Metternich remained the man who was indispensable in times of crisis. It is important to emphasize this in the present context if we are to understand the two alpha-male figures Metternich and Alexander, who were, in 1813, laying the groundwork for their trusting relationship, a relationship that would be tested repeatedly. The success of the coalition depended on these two being able to resolve their conflicts. Right up until the allies entered Paris in April 1814, these two engaged with one another's differences in a way that often threatened to open up an irreconcilable rift: over the question of who should have supreme military command, over military operational plans, over the reorganization of Germany, and over the matter of the successor to the French throne. And it was always Metternich who was able to build bridges with the egocentric, impulsive, wavering, and unpredictable character of the Russian ruler, and thus to maintain peace within the coalition.

Metternich's role could only be so thoroughly misjudged because his politics seem so completely two-faced. The tsar was driven by bitterness, even by the desire for revenge; he wanted to avenge the destruction of Moscow by having Russian troops conquer their enemy's metropolis. He was supported in his military inclinations by Hardenberg, Humboldt, and the circle around his advisor, Baron vom Stein. They were deeply suspicious of the Austrian minister given that he had promoted the marital connection between the House of Habsburg and Napoleon and had formed an alliance with Napoleon before the start of the Russian campaign. Metternich's habit of always stubbornly insisting on establishing contacts with Napoleon and seeking to open negotiations with him led them to suspect that he was ultimately out to get the best result for Austria and would be prepared to leave the coalition at any time. He knew that he was being traduced, in particular, by the circle around the former Russian foreign minister and Chancellor Count Nikolai Romanzov.

Before their meeting, Metternich was prepared for Alexander's "personal bias, always so powerful with the Emperor."[41] Metternich's whole project depended on his ability to gain people's trust and make a plausible argument for the necessity of negotiations with Napoleon. He therefore assured Alexander that he wanted to talk to him "with the greatest frankness"; only with "unbounded confidence" in Austria could the allies be successful.[42] Metternich had to explain to the tsar that the Austrian emperor was facing a political quandary when it came to the decision to go to war: "Emperor Francis believed in the sincerity of Napoleon's mood; but I was convinced of the contrary."[43] Metternich followed his fundamental conviction "that the idea of peace was far from Napoleon."[44] He tried to get the tsar to agree to the fact "that nothing could distract us from the path we had taken for the salvation of Europe and which had put us in the position of becoming its savior."[45] These words may sound lofty, even pompous, but the rhetoric of Metternich as the "savior of Europe," which frequently occurs in his private letters, must be understood in relation to his long-term plan to abolish the Napoleonic system and take down its originator. Metternich knew Napoleon too well to believe that he might ever have resigned himself to ruling within France's old borders. It is therefore wrong to claim that in 1813–1814 Metternich was still desperately trying to reach an accommodation with Napoleon; rather, he was at this point the architect of a coalition for which he had longed for more than a decade.

At the meetings with the tsar in Opotschno, Metternich put his cards on the table: "I was ready to lay the whole plan before him."[46] He intended to fight Napoleon to the end. Asked what he would do if Napoleon accepted the offer of negotiations, Metternich replied that "the negotiations will most certainly show Napoleon to be neither wise nor just, and then the result will be the same."[47] Metternich thus left the tsar without any doubt that, for him, the negotiations served only a tactical purpose. But they were needed, he claimed, because of Emperor Franz, and also because of the French public and Napoleon's situation. Napoleon's grand dignitaries, ministers, and generals were speaking out in favor of peace. By this point, the atmosphere in France was similar to that "during the Terror," that is, 1793–1794.[48] But Metternich also warned against insisting on conditions that were too specific or strict, because Napoleon would simply set his propaganda machinery in motion and have the press and his diplomats shout about the dishonor that France was being asked to endure.[49] Metternich wanted to drive a wedge between Napoleon and the French nation and avoid at all costs the danger that would arise from the nation's solidarity and identification with Napoleon. Later developments proved him right. When Napoleon fled from Elba, his old generals and their soldiers defected to him in droves—and this at a time that was much more hopeless than the present one. For the tsar, it was particularly heartening that Metternich offered to send an able officer to Schwarzenberg's headquarters so that the tsar could be kept abreast of all operational developments. On May 8, upon Metternich's suggestion, the emperor had made Schwarzenberg the generalissimo of the main Austrian battalion that was to be formed in Bohemia.

Apart from Metternich's memoirs, we also have another account of the dialogue that corroborates Metternich's recollections. A day after Metternich's departure, Friedrich Gentz had a three-and-a-half hour conversation with the tsar in which he presented striking arguments for the minister's particular considerations and real intentions.

From 1813 until the early 1820s, Gentz was intimately involved in Metternich's policies, just as he was at Opotschno. I shall therefore present a short characterization of his role here. As a rule it is exaggerated. He loved elegant rhetoric, being close to power, money and women. "Without an aristocratic title, without an academic degree, without a pronounced sense for the . . . virtues of disciplined labor," he did not conform to the "prototype of the modern professional civil servant."[50] He therefore was not happy in his position as a war councillor and councillor for estates in Berlin, and in 1802 he accepted an offer from Cobenzl to enter into Austrian politics. He received a regular salary but, to his chagrin, no state position. He was in demand as a journalist and propagandist, and as an intellectually talented advisor in financial matters and on international, especially British, politics. Metternich, himself having been a minister since 1809, drew him into a long-term association with the Chancellery—as a collaborator, advisor, writer, secretary, and minute taker at congresses. He was Metternich's tool, not vice versa. The minister valued him, trusted him even in sensitive and delicate matters to do with Wilhelmine von Sagan, and yet he never acknowledged him as of equal rank [ebenbürtig]. Gentz, an ambitious journalist, helped to draft dispatches, memoranda, proclamations, and newspaper articles, and the minister therefore liked to have him nearby and to use him as a go-between.

To the tsar, in Opotschno, Gentz's words lent credibility to those of his master: "'If M. de Metternich were your Majesty's minister, and consequently situated as a minister of your Majesty's now is, your Majesty would perhaps find in him one of the warmest advocates of the war.' As Austrian Minister he must look on things differently and act differently."[51] With Napoleon, it would remain impossible to restore a balance of power in Europe.

Finally, Metternich impressed upon Alexander how crucial it was for the Austrian army that there be a further delay in order for the army to become fully operational. All in all, the minister managed to convince the tsar completely. When, in November 1813, the allies decided to march into France, there were—as we shall see—voices that urged continuous negotiation with the opponent even while the campaigns and battles carried on.

The Treaty of Reichenbach: The Foundation of the Alliance, June 27, 1813

Before departing from Gitschin for Dresden, Metternich gave Emperor Franz some advice about how to argue with the Russian foreign minister, Nesselrode, but he implored him to keep in mind that mutual trust was more important than any quarrel over this or that issue. To remove any doubt, Metternich said, the emperor should assure the tsar that he was prepared to "support [the common cause] with arms in hand, and that, once war had broken out, Your Majesty will not be distracted by any subsidiary considerations from achieving the highest goal."[52] And he also asked him to refer to the previous conversation Metternich had had with the tsar, the conservation in which Metternich had not only revealed his master plan to him but also convinced him that negotiations with Napoleon were necessary in order to gain time for Austria's armament and to be able to portray Napoleon as the aggressor.

The agreements Metternich approved before his departure for Dresden on June 25 were laid down as the so-called Reichenbach Convention on June 27. They stipulated 1. the dissolution of the Duchy of Warsaw and the distribution of its regions among Russia, Prussia, and Austria; 2. the expansion of Prussia by adding Gdansk, the withdrawal of French troops from all fortresses in Prussia and the Duchy of Warsaw and the return to Prussia of other areas in northern Germany (this, in fact, by itself implied the dissolution of the Rhenish Confederation); 3. the return of the Illyrian provinces to Austria; and 4. the reinstatement of the Hanseatic cities of Hamburg and Lübeck. Historians always mention the second set of stipulations. The first point is in most cases ignored, but it is the one that bears Metternich's stamp most clearly, as it relates to Austria's new role as a leading power between the major powers and to the picture of a future peace in Europe based on a balance of power. It was absolutely essential that the agreement remain secret because, by dictating conditions to Napoleon, it obviously violated Austria's alliance with him.

The Summit with Napoleon at the Palais Marcolini in Dresden, June 26–30, 1813: Metternich's Ulterior Motives in the Dispute over War and Peace

Metternich's contemporaries were already puzzling over his intentions at this world-famous meeting. Historians today are rather fascinated by the almost cinematographic quality of the situation, a scene no director could have constructed more effectively. World history seems to have been condensed into two individuals, and one day seems to have been the pivotal moment for the future distribution of political power on the European continent. The reason for this view of that day is certainly not the allegedly embellished narrative provided by Metternich's 1829 retrospection. As a former diplomat he possessed an exquisite ability to memorize oral negotiations, which was important when opponents might take a single sentence as grounds for war. There is hardly anything to doubt about Metternich's account of the conversation. A meticulous recent comparison of all existing records, those of Metternich, Napoleon, and those around Napoleon, revealed "a surprisingly high degree of commonality" between them.[53] The numerous insinuations from historians that Metternich, motivated by vanity, sought to present himself in a good light can be considered unjustified.

Nevertheless, his true intentions at Dresden have not yet been identified. They only become apparent once we take into account the whole compass of his political views as they had developed up to this point. What is clear is: as soon as he arrived at the imperial headquarters in Gitschin (Bohemia) at the beginning of June, he made contact with Napoleon and with Tsar Alexander to organize meetings with them. After the French emperor had learned of Metternich's meeting with the tsar, he immediately invited Metternich to come to see him in Dresden. Metternich arrived at the Palais Marcolini in Dresden on

Prince Metternich meets Napoleon I in Dresden on June 26, 1813. Painting by Woldemar Friedrich, 1900.

Saturday, June 26, 1813 in order to see Napoleon, carrying with him the baggage of all of the voluntary commitments Austria had made in the Reichenbach Convention. The Chinese room in which the conversation took place can still be seen today.

It is true that Metternich's retrospective notes cannot be read as a verbatim record. As he himself says, he did not seek to reproduce all that Napoleon, who was at times verbose, had said in the course of their almost nine hour discussion: "I have no intention of reproducing here all that Napoleon said during this long interview. I have only dwelt upon the most striking points in it which bear directly on the object of my mission."[54] For a biographer it is, of course, to be welcomed that the minister's remarks here reveal what seemed most important to him politically. There were two main problems that concerned him: Napoleon's current military capacity and how willing he was to negotiate. Because of the world-historical significance of this dispute, we must analyze it in the minutest detail, even if there is supposedly nothing more left to be said about it.

Metternich's primary goal was to glean information from Napoleon himself regarding the first issue—his *present military capacity*. We know that Metternich had, since his "self-instructions" for his time at the embassy in Dresden in 1801, and most certainly since his time as ambassador in Paris, recognized Napoleon's aspiration of a "universal monarchy" as a threat to world peace. With great determination, Metternich pursued the plan to construct anew a peaceful European order on the model of a balance of power. In such an order, there was no place for Napoleon unless he changed his character. The most recent conversation Count Bubna had had with Napoleon in Dresden revealed that he would consider himself dishonored had he to renounce territory or give up his supreme rule over Germany. He confirmed this again in Dresden by requesting that Metternich give him 300,000 soldiers on the grounds that this was the number it had cost him to conquer Illyria and Dalmatia. In his conversation with the tsar, Metternich had already mentioned that he did not expect Napoleon to consent to the peace conditions. What is clear is that Metternich wanted a mandate for an "armed mediation" not only from the tsar but also from Napoleon, even though six weeks earlier the latter had still categorically denied him such a mandate in the conversation with Bubna.

But the underlying meaning of this conversation was far more significant. This meaning emerges from the situation Metternich had left behind when he left the headquarters in Gitschin. The Austrians were already fully engaged in bringing together their various army corps and in intense preparations for war. All resources that might possibly have fallen into the hands of the enemy were removed. Towns were fortified; Prague, which was to serve as an arsenal, was sealed off; bridgeheads were established at the Elbe and the Vitava river, as were magazines for the provision of the Austrian and allied troops that were to be assembled in Bohemia. At the same time, food depots were created. "The east and north part of Bohemia now had the appearance of a great camp."[55] Metternich had left the headquarters just as an assessment of the army's preparedness for war had begun. This is where the real impulse for the conversation came from: "I wished to ascertain a certain point which would greatly affect the issue of the war."[56] Metternich meant the military strength of the opponent, and he thus again demonstrated his strategic thinking and his ability to think simultaneously along political, diplomatic, and military lines.

If we keep this in mind, some passages in the conversation between Napoleon and Metternich suddenly take on a momentous significance. Because Metternich knew his counterpart's psychological make-up, he knew his weak spots—and so precisely how to provoke him. And he made powerful use of the opposition between their temperaments: he himself composed, distanced, controlled, authoritative, imperturbable—Napoleon excitable, choleric, spontaneous, irascible, uncontrolled, and, in addition, irritated by the composure demonstrated by his diplomatically experienced opponent. Metternich thrust his first banderilla by quoting the figure of 250,000 as the strength of the Austrian troops (a figure Napoleon had calculated at no more than 75,000), adding that he thought that it should have been easy for the *empereur* to get hold of precise statistics,[57] given that he, Metternich, was able to give him an exact list of the French battalions. Napoleon—who thought himself the master of military calculation—allowed himself to be provoked, and he revealed the source of his information, the French ambassador in Vienna, Comte de Narbonne, who, Napoleon said, had deployed a network of spies to the field. The resulting lists were complete down to the last Austrian drummer boy, and Napoleon's headquarters had carried out the same calculations. His calculations, Napoleon said, rested on "mathematical grounds." He even went so far as to lead Metternich into his study and show him the lists of Austrian "forces as they were daily sent to him."[58] Napoleon spoke in great depth ("a long digression") about "the possible strength of our army" and allowed himself to be tempted into revealing to his potential enemy military information that should have remained secret.[59] When Berthier, the French foreign minister, asked Metternich as he was leaving whether he was satisfied with his meeting with the emperor, he received the reply: "Yes, he has explained everything to me; it is all over with the man."[60] The most valuable insight Metternich had gained he expressed thus: "my conversation with Napoleon himself had raised the doubt in my mind whether it would not be desirable to gain some weeks' delay, in order to bring our *ordre de bataille* to its greatest possible completeness."[61]

Metternich sent a courier to Schwarzenberg's headquarters that very same night—June 26—to ask whether Austrian troops could still be reinforced if the truce were extended, and how much time would be needed. Only two days later, in the afternoon of June 28, Metternich held Schwarzenberg's response in his hands. It said: "My army would in twenty days add to its strength seventy-five thousand men: I should consider reaching that point in time a happy circumstance, the twenty-first day would be a burden to me."[62]

This information created a completely new situation for Metternich, and it led him to stay in Dresden for three days longer than he had originally planned. Keeping Schwarzenberg's message at the back of his mind, he continued to have discussions with Napoleon, his foreign minister Maret, and the various French marshals and generals who happened to be present. His aim was to gain time for further armament by extending the truce. When, on the evening of June 29, he had still not achieved a concrete result, he announced to Maret that he would be departing the very next day. Only then did Napoleon relent, asking him to come at eight o'clock in the morning first to the garden at the Palais Marcolini and then to his private office. This second conversation in Dresden— on June 30—is not usually taken into consideration. It did not develop the same furious dynamic as the one four days earlier, but its outcome may have decided the result of the war that followed and been the reason that Napoleon later, on Saint Helena, complained that the truce had been the greatest mistake of his life.

On this occasion, Metternich revealed himself to be a brilliant military strategist, working in the interests of the emerging coalition. The facts were complicated. Napoleon encouraged Metternich to commit his demands to paper. The most simple of these concerned four concessions to be obtained from Napoleon: recognition of Austria's armed mediation; a meeting of the belligerent countries and Austria, as a mediator, at a peace conference in Prague on July 10; a deadline for negotiations of August 10; and, finally, a stop to all acts of war until that date.

This contract, signed by Napoleon, was actually purely bilateral—and therefore not a truce (as Austria was not at war with France). Napoleon rightly pointed out that his truce with Russia and Prussia ended on July 20, and Metternich had to acknowledge that he was not authorized to agree an extension. That was more than a sheer formality because Prussian and Russian forces were stationed, in high concentration, in the Prussian Upper Silesia, and this was an extremely unfavorable location as far as food was concerned, for Emperor Franz had prohibited all food exports to Bohemia and Moravia after the beginning of the spring campaign of 1813. This was intended to prove his neutrality in the conflict, but it created conditions for Metternich's future allies that he could not reasonably prolong for another three weeks by extending the truce. He therefore wrung from Napoleon the concession that enemy troops would be allowed to be provided with food from Austrian territory. Napoleon agreed not to interpret this as a breach of Austria's neutrality, which, strictly speaking, it certainly was. But here Metternich again demonstrated his assertiveness and far-sightedness. Given Napoleon's assurances, he considered himself authorized "to guarantee the prolongation of the truce" not only in the name of the Austrian emperor but also in the names of Friedrich Wilhelm III and the tsar.[63]

Commentators have hitherto considered the main theme of the Dresden conversations to be what is identified above as the second main problem Metternich had in mind, namely the question of *Napoleon's willingness to negotiate*. As Metternich seems to have indicated as much by committing himself to the Reichenbach Convention, it may be that this question was originally the central one for him. But Napoleon's subsequent openness in providing him with information must have shifted his priorities, and military considerations and planning moved into the foreground. Because scholars have so far looked at the conversation predominantly as a negotiation, Metternich has been seen as not playing a particularly assertive role in the dispute: he did not confront Napoleon with tough political demands, such as the dissolution of the Rhenish Confederation. Metternich knew that this would have been completely pointless. He was familiar with Napoleon's position from the conversation Bubna had had with him: if Austria wanted provinces, blood would have to be spilled.[64] Feeling elated by the two victorious battles at Lützen and Bautzen, Napoleon confirmed that he would "not yield one handbreadth of soil."[65]

Metternich rather avoided touching upon territorial questions and instead invoked Europe: "The world requires peace. In order to secure this peace, you must reduce your power within bounds compatible with the general tranquillity."[66] He envisioned "a concert of nations,"[67] or, more precisely, the picture of a future Europe in which "a spirit of moderation and respect for the legal rights and possessions of states, which they themselves exercise, rules," as the secretary, Fain, summarized what he took from Napoleon's oral report after Metternich's departure.[68] "Austria wants to found an order which creates peace through a division of power under the protection of an association of independent states. According to Fain, it was Napoleon who became concrete when he sarcastically rejected the demand of "moderation." In the scene in his study mentioned above, he made it clear to his opponent that this was not just about Illyria, but also about Central Italy, the reinstatement of the Papal States following the return of Pope Pius VII from his exile in the French castle Fountainebleu, the dissolution of Poland, the renunciation of Spain, Holland, the

Rhenish Confederation, and Switzerland. Austria wanted Italy. Russia desired Poland. Sweden demanded Norway. Prussia asked for Saxony, and England wanted Holland and Belgium restored. Peace was only a pretext. "You demand no less than the dissolution of the Empire Français." With the stroke of a pen, the fortresses of Küstrin, Glogau, Magdeburg, Wesel, Mainz, Antwerp, Alexandria, and Mantua were to be abolished, and French troops pushed back across the Rhine, the Alps, and the Pyrenees.[69]

His rage over Metternich's role in the conversation, later led Napoleon to reveal himself to Caulaincourt, so we have a further account of the exchange.[70] According to this version, which was only discovered much later, it is true that Metternich put forward the conditions themselves for discussion. From Metternich's perspective, however, these were ultimately of no significance, because Napoleon was of the opinion that to demand moderation of him was itself to ask for capitulation. Recently, Munro Price, in his interpretation of the conversation, has rightly recognized Metternich's normative vision of the future in contrast to Napoleon's politics of naked self-interest. For Napoleon, the only possible foundations for diplomacy were power and violence. For Metternich and Emperor Franz, by contrast, what was at stake was the lost balance of power ("equilibrium")—and so the fate of Europe. Price argues that they envisaged a new contractual system that would guarantee the rights of all European states. Price's suggestion that this picture of the future was at least partly realized in the context of the Congress of Vienna is highly plausible.[71]

Metternich has been criticized for being prepared to negotiate with Napoleon. But this misses the point: he always took the possibility of the failure of negotiations into his calculations. He was Mr. Eggers of Brecht's parable: he concealed his long-term strategy for getting rid of Napoleon behind the screen of his outward behavior. By April 1814, in Paris, Metternich no longer needed to hold back. Asked by M. de Vitrolles whether Napoleon should continue to reign with limited powers, he confessed openly—as Talleyrand testifies—"that they [the allies] recognized that Napoleon was a man with whom it was impossible to continue to negotiate; that the day when he had reverses he appeared to yield everything; but that as soon as he obtained a slight success, he again assumed pretensions as exaggerated as inadmissible."[72]

The reason for this was the *empereur*'s incorrigible willfulness. Once, in Dresden, he provided an impressive demonstration of this willfulness by confirming to Metternich, with brutal honesty, that he was striving for universal power in Europe; at the same time, this demonstration confirmed to Metternich that he had been right in his psychological analysis of the *empereur*'s personality, one part of which had killed off any propensity for empathy he might have had. The scene occurred when Metternich touched upon what was for

Napoleon another sore point: namely, the moral discrepancy between his image of himself as someone promoting progress and human happiness and the unimaginable human suffering of the countless victims of his continual warfare. Metternich pointed to the risk of yet another war if the truce were to expire without the negotiations having yielded any result, and he made reference to the French nation's longing for peace.[73] Metternich was acutely aware of how the nature of warfare had changed; war had become total war: "In ordinary times armies are formed of only a small part of the population, to-day it is the whole people that you have called to arms," he told Napoleon.[74] And the new soldiers were actually a "future generation," children in fact.[75] Metternich was right: in the autumn of 2001, a mass grave with more than 3,000 soldiers was discovered near Vilnius, and upon closer inspection it turned out they were members of the "Grande Armée" of 1812 who had just about managed to drag themselves back to this point on their retreat. The examination of the skeletons showed that there were, indeed, very young soldiers among them—with broken toes, diagnosed by orthopedic consultants as stress fractures suffered during brutal forced marches.

Metternich's remarks touched upon the very core of Napoleon's being: his identity as a general. He responded with fury. "You are no soldier," he said, "and you do not know what goes on in the soul of a soldier," adding, allegedly: "I was brought up in military camps, and a man such as I am does not concern himself much about the lives of a million of men."[76] This is also the version in the printed edition of Metternich's memoirs. In the manuscript,

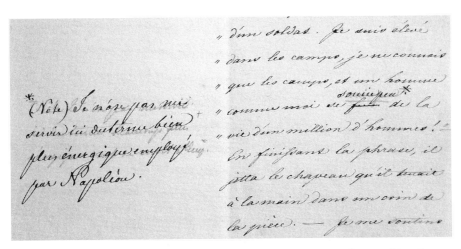

Note from Metternich's hand in the margin: "Je n'ose pas me servir ici du terme bien plus énergique employé par Napoléon." ["I do not dare to make use here of the much worse expression employed by Napoleon."]

Metternich's note: "un homme comme moi se f[out] de la vie d'un million d'hommes!"

however, Metternich added in the margin: "I do not dare to make use here of the much worse expression [*du terme bien plus énergique*] employed by Napoleon."[77]

But in the written copy that is kept in Prague—in which Metternich recorded the conversation in French—he uses an abbreviation that is omitted in later fair copies. This abbreviation makes it possible to reconstruct the actual words Napoleon used.[78] Napoleon said the following, part of which Metternich omitted in his account (which thus cannot be found in the published version): "Je suis élevé dans les camps, je ne connais que les camps, et un homme comme moi se f[outre] de la vie d'un million d'hommes!" ["I was brought up in military camps, and know nothing but military camps, and a man such as I am does not give a fuck about the lives of a million of men."]

There is no reason why historians should remain silent about Napoleon's way of thinking, especially as he did, indeed, accept more than a million killed by the wars he provoked as the price to be paid for the achievement of his goals. He saw himself as the man of the "century," the one who, by marrying an archduchess, wanted "to weld the new with the old, Gothic prejudices with the institutions of [his] century."[79] His statement in Dresden was also not just a rhetorical slip; he had also emphasized his nature as a soldier in the conversation with Bubna, and here he topped it off with a threat to take everything with him into the abyss:

I do not concede anything, not a single village which I have constitutionally united with France. A man who was a simple private person and has ascended to the throne [*parvenu*], who has spent twenty years hailed with bullets, is not afraid of projectiles, he does not fear any threats at all. I do not value my life above all else, nor that of others very much. I do not waver to and fro in order to save my life; I do not rate it higher than that of a hundred thousand people. I sacrifice a million if necessary. You will not get anything by violent means; we shall battle each other in many campaigns. You will only force me through many victories. I may decline and my dynasty with me. That is all the same to me. You want to take Italy and Germany from me. You want to degrade me.[80]

Metternich knew what to expect from Napoleon in Dresden because he was prepared for it by this report from Bubna. For Napoleon, as for Metternich, negotiating meant accepting conditions. That alone, the emperor thought degrading. Caulaincourt's report shows the full extent of Napoleon's wrath after he took Metternich's peace initiative—correctly—as mere pretext. The minister, Napoleon asked, no longer wanted to be his ally; would he now become his enemy? While Metternich tried to gauge the extent of Napoleon's willingness to negotiate, Napoleon was furious that he could no longer feel assured of Austria's support. He recognized Metternich's intention to limit the power of France. Metternich, he said, wanted to humiliate France, weaken him, paralyze his troops, and hold him at gunpoint. The word "peace" veiled the intention to regain Italy, Germany, and everything else the Habsburg Monarchy

had lost; the word obscured the wish to fundamentally overturn everything—
it was a cover for betrayal. While Metternich's real aim was a lasting European
peace, Napoleon always insinuated that he was only driven by the urge to make
petty territorial gains; and Napoleon himself never tired of dangling the lost
Illyria before Austria's nose as bait.

All in all, the conversation must have confirmed Metternich in his conviction that it would never be possible to discipline and control Napoleon through
treaties. History has confirmed how right Metternich was about the French emperor's inability to take a politically moderate course. Napoleon could have
survived as a ruler on Elba within certain political limits. Instead, he seized
the first opportunity to begin the power game anew. Metternich had foreseen
this in April 1814 in Paris, and had therefore been enraged about the decision to
send him to Elba. But by the time Metternich arrived in Paris from Dijon,
Alexander had made it a fait accompli—against Metternich's explicit will. We
may infer that, notwithstanding the proposals for a peace congress in Prague,
Metternich's intention in the Palais Marcolini was to hold on to his plans for
war against Napoleon.

AUSTRIA JOINS THE WAR: THE QUADRUPLE ALLIANCE

*A Farcical Peace Congress in Prague: Metternich Prepares for War,
July–August 1813*

From Dresden, Metternich went to the "Areopagus of Ratiborschitz," as Wilhelmine von Sagan now called her summer residence. This place was developing "into a center of European diplomacy at a moment in which this poor
Europe became a focal point for the unrest in the world," as Metternich put it
to her in a letter.[81] On July 4, 1813, Chancellor Hardenberg, Wilhelm von Humboldt, Foreign Minister Nesselrode, and Stadion met there to hear what Metternich had achieved in his encounter with Napoleon. When they were told of
the extension to the truce, they reacted with unconcealed rage.[82] They accused
Metternich of having broken his word, and were utterly determined to end the
truce on July 20. In his memoirs, Metternich skips over this scene as if there
had been no problems at all. In fact, he had to fight hard to get his agreement
with Napoleon accepted, and it is instructive to consider the extent to which,
while under attack, he argued on the basis of military interests. He pointed to
a military memorandum by Schwarzenberg that said that, if there were an early
end to the truce, Vienna would be vulnerable to attack by French troops that
were already on their way from Italy; Emperor Franz, it said, feared that the
whole burden of the war would immediately fall on Austria. He would therefore

not give up Austrian neutrality prematurely. If the allies wanted to begin their campaign before August 10, they would need to do so without Austria, and this would also mean, because of Austria's neutrality, that they would not be able to cross Bohemia.

Metternich had to muster all his powers of persuasion to win Prussia over. A day later, Metternich's representative, Ritter von Lebzeltern, had to make a similar effort to get the agreement of the tsar. Lebzeltern also argued that it was not in the allies' interests for Austria to be so vulnerable when the first attack took place. Just how right Metternich was about this is confirmed by a contemporary report on the military situation by Field Marshal Count Radetzky: only the former auxiliary corps and a third of the army in Bohemia was made up of experienced soldiers, and two-thirds were inexperienced recruits that had first to be trained to use their weapons; in addition, the number of available firearms was, at the time, insufficient. It was imperative to acquire more firearms and to train the troops.[83]

Metternich had to fight a war on two fronts. He had to hold back the allies, who were pushing for action, and he had to bring a hesitant Emperor Franz over to the hawks' camp. On July 12, 1813, before the actual start of the negotiations in Prague, Metternich strained to get the monarch to commit to his course of action, employing all of his rhetorical skill. In one of his distinctive "presentations," he called on the emperor's resolve: "Can I count on Your Majesty's steadfastness in case Napoleon does not accept Austria's conditions for peace; is Your Majesty unwaveringly determined, in that case, to entrust the cause of justice to the arms of Austria and of all the other united European states?" And as if that were not enough, he again insisted: "Your Majesty, however, will only be able to save yourself and the monarchy if Your Highness is utterly at one with yourself and if I can have full confidence that the course I see ahead of me, once chosen, will be followed with the greatest steadfastness and tenacity. Without such steadfastness, from tomorrow onward all the steps I take will be wrong, incoherent, and thus extremely dangerous."[84]

Metternich later reviewed the path his policies took after 1809, when "all means of the monarchy had been destroyed." Within four years, Austria had regained "the prime position in Europe." But he also warned against recklessly ignoring or underestimating the weakness of the monarchy. Austria's strength rested on a unique situation that Metternich had brought about with his masterful sense for the right moment and for power relations. As he formulated it: "In the abstract sense—if we take the monarchy by itself—we are far from being as powerful as we once were—but as a weight added to the scales, the side chosen by Austria is the predominant one."

The emperor's response was exceptionally lengthy, and he prefaced his resolution with the following praise: "I mostly owe the present glorious political condition of my monarchy to you." But this was followed by moderating qualifications that indicated that the Emperor wanted the offer of a peace to be a serious one. What he wanted most was a lasting peace. Franz demanded that they "avoid as much as possible anything that might harm Napoleon's honour." He ordered Metternich to insist only on a minimum in the negotiations; if the other parties demanded more, he should support them, avoiding any potential rifts. If necessary, the emperor was also prepared to renounce Illyria. He essentially sought to avoid war, whereas Metternich, by contrast, with his tactical argument for peace, engaged in what Wilhelm Oncken called a "diplomatic double-campaign." Talk of peace was a necessary salve for the emperor's conscience, for he wanted to negotiate for as long as possible, and saw war as only ever a last resort. But this pretense of a peaceful purpose was also necessary in order to avoid Napoleon prematurely taking up arms.

In mid-July, the authorized representatives began to arrive in Prague for the conference: Caulaincourt and the French ambassador in Vienna, Count Narbonne (for France); Wilhelm von Humboldt (for Prussia); Baron Johann von Anstett (for Russia); and Metternich (as mediator). By not even sending Hardenberg and Nesselrode, Prussia and Russia made it clear, from the outset, how little hope they held out for the negotiations. Napoleon matched them by not issuing the required authorization documents for his representatives, and continually delaying this despite the fact that they desperately needed them. Metternich refused even to open the congress before the legitimacy of all participants had been formally established. Even on August 5—with the end of the truce threatening—he reported to the emperor: "Our negotiations are marked by perfect silence." Even Caulaincourt spoke unambiguously of Napoleon's "blindness."

Despite all the caution of the diplomatic negotiations, Metternich was pursuing only one goal, namely, as he told the emperor, "to present ourselves before God and world as having right on our side, and to place responsibility where it really lies." The emperor concurred energetically: "We must do everything so that we are not held responsible if the result is not peace."[85] The emperor and his minister considered it crucial to negotiate with Napoleon, even if only to win the favor of the public. As long as Napoleon was seen as the real warmonger, there would be no solidarity with him among the French. Napoleon also paid attention to public opinion and, because of the enormous sacrifices he asked of the French, he had to prove that he was willing to accept peace. More recently, we have learned that reports from the regional prefects prior to the negotiations made it clear to him that the longing for peace was spreading and that the upcoming congress in Prague was being eagerly awaited.[86]

Napoleon made full use of every tactical means at his disposal, including using the offer of territory to attempt to lure Austria out of the alliance. On the evening of August 6, Caulaincourt turned to Metternich "in the strictest secrecy" and told him that Napoleon wanted to know what France needed to give Austria "in order [for Austria] either to unite with it or remain neutral."[87] Metternich immediately relayed this to the Russian and Prussian representatives: what better opportunity could there have been to affirm, beyond any doubt, the "loyalty which we declare toward our allies." When Caulaincourt, who shuttled back and forth between Prague and Dresden, arrived with Napoleon's instructions, he was told that they were already at war.

When assessing Metternich's decision making, which from the outside seems opaque, one aspect is often overlooked: he had to take into consideration the family ties between the Austrian and the French monarchs, which made the relationship between the two powers a special one. The feeling of loyalty was probably even more keenly felt by Napoleon, whose mindset was anchored in the tradition of the Corsican family clans, than by the Habsburg emperor, with his sense of dynastic values. Ultimately, Napoleon could not really imagine that his father-in-law would lead a war against him. In Dresden he said to Metternich: "Send three hundred thousand men to Bohemia; the word of the Emperor that he will not make war against me before the negotiation is ended is sufficient." And a little later: "would Emperor Francis then dethrone his daughter?"[88] A few weeks earlier, in his conversation with Bubna, Napoleon had been even more emphatic: "What will become of the child in whose veins runs Austrian blood?" He had, further, tried to intimidate the Austrians, threatening that France would descend into anarchy if he lost, that his wife and their two-year-old son, the daughter and grandson of Emperor Franz, would perish. Emperor Franz would be destroying himself.

So sure was Napoleon of the security guaranteed by his family connections with the Habsburgs that, just one day before the truce ended, August 9, 1813, he was still warning that he should not be pressured. He did not just write down what he had to say, but Bubna had to communicate it in person. He wanted to give Metternich, he said, a good route out of a tricky situation.[89] Because of their close family ties, he still hoped to be able to get Austria to defect and to renew its alliance with France. He was thus all the more shocked when he heard that war had been declared. As Metternich wrote to the head of his Chancellery in Vienna: "After all the news the most terrible consternation over our declaration of war has taken hold of the French. Eight days ago Napoleon still proclaimed à l'ordre du jour that there would be peace, or that Austria would declare itself on his side."[90]

When the clock approached midnight on August 10–11, Metternich's thoughts turned to Eleonore, and he wrote to her. He could look back with satisfaction at the military advantage he had secured through his discussions with Napoleon in Dresden. His main concern at this point was the strength of the army. He wrote that he awaited the cannon fire that had been agreed as the signal for the start of the war, at midnight, and the following day 150,000 Austrian soldiers would join the Russian and Prussian troops. Together, they would amount to 340,000 men, amassed in Bohemia under the command of Schwarzenberg.[91]

Metternich as "Reluctant Chief of Staff"

Even during the truce, the allies had begun to develop a common plan for the expected campaign. Between July 10 and 13, Tsar Alexander, King Friedrich Wilhelm III of Prussia, Crown Prince Bernadotte of Sweden, and Count Stadion met at Trachtenberg Castle—today Żmigród—north of Wroclaw. The purpose of the meeting was not to develop the operational plan but rather to familiarize the Swedish crown prince with the basic ideas on which it rested—Sweden, like England, having joined the coalition in June 1813. Military historians have traced back the various stages in the development of the plan to March of that year and have suggested that the Prussian general, Gneisenau, and the Austrian general, Radetzky, also had a hand in it. When it came to military theory, the sharpest mind was Radetzky, as Alan Sked's recent biography has shown. But, as far as the operational plan was concerned, all of the allies shared the same fundamental idea. At least three large army divisions were to be established in order to surround Napoleon's troops; they would operate according to the principle: "Attack on Napoleon by those not attacked, in order to help those attacked by Napoleon."[92] The basic—and correct—idea was that the French troops were weakest where they were under the command of his marshals and that a direct confrontation with Napoleon should be avoided.

This plan was not at all under the spell of the military ideas of the eighteenth century, as if the major lessons of the Napoleonic campaigns had not yet been understood.[93] The old doctrine according to which it was imperative to occupy strategic positions, such as high points that overlooked the landscape or fortresses that could not be captured, had been abandoned. The goal was no longer to maintain invincible defensive positions behind a fortress or a fortified camp. In the famous Trachtenberg war plan, the most important principle was rather: "Should Emperor Napoleon, in order to anticipate the attack from the allied army in Bohemia, march toward it in the hope of defeating it, then the army of the Crown Prince of Sweden will proceed in forced marches and attack from the back. Should, by contrast, Emperor Napoleon turn toward the Crown Prince of Sweden, the allies' (main) army will launch a vigorous offensive and move toward enemy units in order to engage him in battle. All allied troops will go on the offensive and the enemy's camp will be their rendezvous."[94]

Radetzky is given credit for the operational plan that was ultimately used.[95] Its fundamental guiding idea, however, corresponded to Metternich's earlier observations regarding previous failed campaigns. Since the era of Thugut, Metternich could justifiably claim to be the real expert in the principles of Napoleon's operations. The allies' new rule was that any army attacked by Napoleon was not to respond but to withdraw. This required the allied armies to be constantly mobile, and that meant, in turn, uninterrupted coordination and communication among them. This is precisely what Metternich had seen as lacking in the previous campaigns. The modern aspect of this mode of operation was the principle that every commanding general had to judge the situation independently at every point in time, and then had to decide how and where to support those troops that were under attack. Napoleon's generals were not used to operating independently; they awaited their master's directives. When these did not come, they made grave mistakes. If one looks at all the campaigns between April 1813 and March 1814, it is clear that, whenever the allies' plan was actually followed, it always led to victory. As soon as they deviated from it and faced Napoleon in battle, he got the upper hand.

What role did Metternich play in military planning? To begin with, in the Austrian war manifesto [*Österreichisches Kriegmanifest*] he provided the public justification for the war.[96] Although Gentz actually wrote it, Metternich went through it in detail and edited the final version. The rhetorically gifted journalist congenially described what the minister had, from 1809 onward, systematically and persistently inculcated in his emperor through his presentations: Napoleon had destroyed the whole social system of Europe with his lawlessness and willfulness; had erected a pernicious system that was choking the whole continent; had ruined Europe's economic and financial system; had turned half of Germany into a French province; and had imposed a "system of helpless inactivity" on Austria. From December 1812 onward, however, Austria had taken important steps toward resisting this system, and since March 1813 had systematically developed them further. The armed mediation under Austria's lead had offered Napoleon the opportunity for a general peace. The manifesto described, in painstaking detail, how Napoleon was responsible for the failure of the peace congress in Prague. The only conclusion could be: "The justification for this war is written in the heart of every Austrian, every European, no matter under whose rule he lives, in such large and easily read letters that no art is required to show its validity. The nation and the army will do what they have to do. An alliance with all powers who have armed themselves for independence, founded on common need and common interest, will give our efforts their full force."

And so Metternich had reached the goal he had been working toward for years. He could publicly present himself as part of a European alliance ranged against Napoleon's universal monarchy. The formal contracts for the alliance with Prussia and Russia were only signed on September 9, in Teplitz, and the contract with Great Britain on October 3. But Gentz's words ensured that the public "saw [the manifesto] as a clear pane of glass behind which that political system which I should certainly never have invented" could be seen. Friedrich Schlegel commented: "Now I understand and feel that everything had to be conducted precisely in this way, that nothing, absolutely nothing, could have been different."[97]

The manifesto was part of Metternich's core competency as foreign minister. But what of his involvement in genuine military matters? Until recently, historians' accounts of the campaigns of 1813 have had them taking place in his absence. Some biographers simply deny that he had any military talent or accuse him of being a dilettante, a wiseacre. Only in the specialist military literature has a rethinking begun: here he is, for instance, referred to as a "reluctant chief of staff" who shared with Radetzky the capacity to combine strategic considerations with political aims.[98] But in particular Munro Price's account of the last two years of Napoleon at war in 1813–1814 and Alan Sked's biography of Radetzky have resulted in significantly more emphasis being placed on Metternich. Supreme Commander Schwarzenberg, whose importance has previously been somewhat diminished, is now acknowledged, along with Radetzky and Metternich, as playing an indispensable role in the solidification of the coalition, insofar as the coalition depended on military success.

Metternich experienced the first test of his abilities in this area when, after Austria had joined the coalition, Tsar Alexander demanded that he be allowed to lead the allied troops as their supreme commander. Metternich still had vivid memories of how the tsar's willful, amateurish operations had led to the disaster of Austerlitz, when Napoleon slyly and mercilessly outmaneuvered the tsar, finally leaving him weeping at the edge of the battlefield. Metternich threatened that, if Alexander became the supreme commander, Austria would not participate in the alliance. Metternich made sure that Field Marshal Prince Karl Philipp zu Schwarzenberg, an Austrian two years Metternich's senior and thus of the same generation, would take over the supreme command. Schwarzenberg knew Napoleon from his time at the embassy in Paris, and he had succeeded in bringing back his auxiliary corps more or less unscathed from the campaign in Russia, something for which he had been commended by Emperor Franz. Schwarzenberg had no stomach for risky operations that staked everything on one victory, but rather proceeded cautiously, avoiding unnecessary losses wherever possible. He was the perfect fit for Metternich's strategy, which combined warfare and politics at a higher level, and was the only adequate response to Napoleon's ruses. Schwarzenberg, better than anyone else, was able to defuse the tensions resulting from the allies' diverging interests, mutual rivalries, and petty jealousies, and—as Metternich would have wanted—he showed patience where others followed their blind patriotism and ran into a trap.

Later, on November 11, 1813, three weeks after the Battle of Leipzig, Gentz emphasized that Metternich had defended and supported Schwarzenberg against all the "malcontents and detractors." Without Metternich, Schwarzenberg would neither have accepted nor kept the supreme command. Metternich, Gentz said, had been the soul of the political process and the guarantor of all military operations. He had personally kept track of all the army's movements and had been at Schwarzenberg's side throughout all combat operations.[99] In the context of the major crisis of 1814 in Troyes, when there had been yet another a deviation from the operational plan, Metternich acknowledged his special relationship with the supreme commander in a statement: "I and Prince Schwarzenberg have so far kept it [the coalition] together, because in our characters there is a lot of calm and coolness." In the same breath he referred sarcastically to the actual troublemakers: "Both our relationships with the Russian emperor are on a good footing. I, in particular, am standing by him, where none of his ministers are standing."[100] Metternich—not without Emperor Franz's help—had seen to it that the Prussian generals Gebhard Leberecht von Blücher and Friedrich Wilhelm von Bülow obeyed Schwarzenberg's orders, though Blücher tended to ignore them from time to time, as he was wont to do.

Helping to make Field Marshal Radetzky Schwarzenberg's chief of staff can be considered a stroke of genius on Metternich's part. On May 9, 1813, the emperor then promoted him further to become the quartermaster general in Schwarzenberg's army. In this role, Radetzky would be responsible for bringing together all allied units—from Swedish Pomerania to Italy, from the Pyrenees to Russia—and, while taking into account their national peculiarities, direct them toward a common goal. Closer to home, it had only been, in Hubert Zeinar's phrase, the "art of the Minister Metternich" that had made it possible to create, within the space of three and a half months, an army out of Austrian troops who had been mostly decommissioned during the period after 1809—in such a way that even drew admiration from Napoleon.[101] By August 1813, Radetzky had created an allied army of 479,000 men.

How deeply Metternich interfered in these processes has gradually become more well known, and to describe this in detail would lead us too far afield. He noticed the difficulties in creating an efficient command structure for the motley group of representatives of different nationalities and from different military traditions. He took the lead when agreement on war aims had to be established—and in formulating them in the first place. He knew the effects these aims would have on actual operations, and he was the only one who was able to head off the potential conflicts arising from the permanent interferences from particular leaders, most notably from Tsar Alexander. In the crucial phase following the declaration of war on August 10, he was always close to the army and the headquarters and followed troop movements closely. On one occasion, when the tsar wanted Austrian troops, as the ones being closest by, being sent as reinforcements to Dippoldiswalde to fight against General Vandamme's men, Metternich even took on military responsibility himself. When the Austrian troops' commanding general, Count Coloredo, refused to follow the tsar's orders, Metternich—who happened to be present at the scene—ordered Coloredo to grant the tsar's request. Metternich thus actually contributed to an impressive victory over Napoleon's general.[102]

Metternich reported the incident to the head of his Chancellery in Vienna, Hudelist, whose task it was to relay military information to the president of the court's war council, Count Bellegarde. Together with Bellegarde, Metternich had helped to secretly rebuild and reorganize the military between 1810 and 1812. In his memoirs, he writes of him: "With a thorough knowledge of military matters, familiar with my turn of mind, and quite agreeing with my political views, he was anxious not only to maintain the Imperial forces, but to strengthen them to the utmost, for every imaginable contingency, while avoiding everything that would attract attention. He alone was thoroughly acquainted with my views, and he knew how to raise himself, with me, above the illusions which assume the appearance of public opinion. He understood as well as I did the value of letting men talk."[103] In this passage, Metternich again characterized his long-term plan for war, his ever-present "bellicose ulterior motive" as August Fournier put it, his readiness to strike at the right moment.

Metternich's Leadership after Defeat at Dresden on August 26–27, 1813

With the defeat at Dresden, on August 26–27, 1813, the coalition had to endure the first true test of its resilience. The defeat revealed a deep crisis in the military command: Alexander had insisted on the attacks against the orders of

Supreme Commander Schwarzenberg. Up to that point, the strategy of the Trachtenberg plan had been followed to the letter, confrontations with Napoleon had been avoided, and his generals had been beaten: Nicolas Oudinot at Großbeeren (August 23), Field Marshal Jacques McDonald at the Katzbach (August 26), General Jean-Baptiste Girard at Hagelberg (August 27). A brilliant victory was again achieved at Kulm over General Dominique Joseph Vandamme (August 30), who was arrested, along with 10,000 soldiers, and deported to Siberia by the tsar. That measure was an expression of Alexander's anger at having just caused the spectacular defeat at Dresden.

The episode helps to illustrate both the fundamental problem of the coalition and the way Metternich acted within it. The troops concerned were those of the main army under Schwarzenberg, and he did not want to use them in a direct confrontation with Napoleon. At headquarters, however, Alexander prevailed upon him—with devastating consequences.[104] Schwarzenberg was so angry that he turned to Emperor Franz. He described conditions at the headquarters—not only in general but also during battle. Tsar Alexander did not obey the supreme command and allowed his generals to do whatever they wished. Alexander's general Barclay de Tolly was disobedient, lacked knowledge in military matters, and in addition was driven by personal jealousy. The generals Wittgenstein and Kleist, who were subordinate to Barclay de Tolly, received their orders either too late or not at all. The tsar himself continually interrupted Schwarzenberg with comments and advice, confusing him with his many contradictory opinions. Schwarzenberg demanded that Alexander leave the army, Barclay be removed, and Wittgenstein and Miloradowitsch put under his command. If these requests were not granted, the emperor "would have to find another supreme commander—someone who combined the talents of a general with the superhuman physical and moral strength that was required for working on important operations under such altogether adverse circumstances."[105]

Metternich had to mediate, as he often did when Schwarzenberg, Alexander, and various other commanders found it impossible to reach agreement.[106] Metternich, who according to Srbik was allegedly so accommodating and unable to assert himself, was the only politician who dared to openly defy Alexander; as a consequence, the tsar several times asked Emperor Franz to dismiss his minister. Alexander provoked one such encounter immediately after Schwarzenberg had offered to resign from the supreme command if necessary. On September 1, three days after the defeat at Dresden, the tsar called Metternich to a meeting and informed him he would be assuming the title of supreme commander (Generalissimo). The actual military command he would leave to General Moreau, a former French general who had been persecuted by Napoleon and had joined the Russians in the spring of 1813. Metternich warned him that this would mean the immediate withdrawal of Emperor Franz from the alliance. The tsar relented. Two days later, Moreau was struck and killed by a bullet while standing next to him.[107]

The ultimate lesson of the affair was that everyone involved had to adhere strictly to the Trachtenberg plan. Immediately after the Battle of Dresden, Metternich had reported to Vienna what this plan would achieve. He was the supreme crisis manager, operating at a meta-level whenever strategic, emotional, or irrational conflicts among the monarchs and generals at lower levels threatened to sunder the coalition.

Teplitz and the Sixth Coalition against Napoleon

"If a large state is condemned to act in a way that puts it in danger, it must at least secure the right to take the position of the supreme leader in the undertaking. How much this requirement dominated our feelings is demonstrated by the protocols of Teplitz from the year 1813."[108] This diplomatic axiom was Metternich's later commentary on the alliance that England and France formed on December 2, 1854, which Austria joined in the Crimean War. But it also described the role that, as he saw it, he had played in relation to the political balance of power after Austria had joined the war in 1813. Since March, he had pursued a strategy for which he coined yet another axiom: "The power of Austria within the hopeless entanglements of the day rests on the freedom of its movement and not in being bound."[109] This freedom he had created for himself.

The formal accession to the coalition provided the foundation for this freedom in international law. On September 9, 1813, Russia, Prussia, and Austria signed identical bilateral treaties of alliance "in the name of the most holy and indivisible Trinity." On October 3, Great Britain joined them. The preamble was inspired by Metternich's vision for peace: the intention, it said, was to end Europe's misery and to restore its peace by creating the right balance of power. The powers assured each other of military support if one of them came under attack. None of them was allowed to enter into a one-sided peace treaty without including the others in it. It is striking that there were six bilateral contracts but not one overall contract. On September 3, the British representative, the earl of Aberdeen, also arrived in Teplitz. These contracts have been judged vague and unclear because they excluded important territorial questions. Castlereagh, in London, saw reasons to be concerned: this was not the way to secure a lasting peace in Europe.[110]

While this may have been the view of contemporaries, it did not correspond to the facts. Usually, analyses of the contractual arrangements of Teplitz overlook the separate secret articles. But these were substantial because, even before the war ended, they had marked effects that may be seen in the European architecture designed at the Congress of Vienna.[111] In particular, they stipulated:

1. The restoration of the Austrian and Prussian monarchies on a scale that matches the extent of their territories in 1805.
2. The dissolution of the Rhenish Confederation and the complete and unlimited independence ("l'indépendence entière et absolue") of the states, which were to be restored (reconstruites) on its territory between the borders of the Austrian and Prussian monarchies, and between the Rhine and the Alps, on the 1805 borders.
3. The return of Hanover and its other possessions to the House of Brunswick-Lüneburg—that is, the restoration of the personal union between the former prince electorate of Hanover and the British crown.
4. A mutual agreement between the courts of Russia, Austria, and Prussia on the future of the Duchy of Warsaw.
5. The restoration of those countries that formed part of French territory and were designated as "32 division militaire"—that is, the Hanseatic cities and the Grand Duchy of Oldenburg.
6. The restoration of the countries in the possession of French princes.

The words *l'indépendence entière et absolue* were like a "magic spell" that opened the door for Napoleon's allies to leave the Rhenish Confederation, knowing that their possessions had been guaranteed.[112] The formulation prefigured the federal structure of the later German Confederation, as defined in the German Federal Act of June 8, 1815, which was passed as part of the Congress of Vienna: a league of "sovereign princes and free cities of Germany." In his posthumous papers, Metternich revealed that at Teplitz he was already demanding that, "as a political body," Germany must not be constituted "in any other form but that of a confederation." For him, this had "the value of a fundamental condition for the entry of Austria into the Quadruple Alliance." This means that the concept of a "federal tie" uniting the future Germany was laid down before the First Treaty of Paris of May 30, 1814, and it is clear that the idea and the will to implement it originated with Metternich.[113]

All these agreements contradict Paul Schroeder's thesis that it was only with "Castlereagh's leadership" and his "Grand Design" of August and September that there emerged "a greater degree of union and consistency" among the allies when it came to their most important war aims.[114] It is true, though, that the British government was informed by its envoi, Viscount Cathcart, about the negotiations between Metternich and the tsar in June 1813 in Opotschno and about the considerations regarding a general peace. Castlereagh told Metternich in July 1813 that the prince regent was extremely interested in participating in the upcoming peace negotiations in Prague. He was, at that point, already adumbrating a program for the reconstruction of central Europe that paralleled that of the contracts of Teplitz: the restoration of the Austrian and Prussian monarchies and "complete and absolute Restoration" of the kingships of Hanover and the rest of Germany.[115] He also demanded the restoration of Holland, Switzerland, and Italy, matters not touched upon in Teplitz. In Spain, Portugal, and Sicily, the legitimate rulers were to be reinstated. In Metternich's eyes, it was obvious that these points should later be incorporated. The debate over whether Castlereagh or Metternich was the instigator is therefore likely to be fruitless. In the summer of 1813 there were already striking parallels between British and Austrian interests and plans. It is therefore not surprising that after Castlereagh intervened personally in the negotiations on the war aims in January 1814, he and Metternich became steadfast allies in the attempt to make a success of the coalition.

The agreements of Teplitz were thus central to the long and bloody path toward the reconstruction of Europe. Metternich found himself where he had aimed to be for many years: "My attempts to gain accurate knowledge of my opponent and of our forces before embarking on the great work to be done had not been in vain."[116]

The Battle of Leipzig

The reports Metternich sent to Vienna confirm how carefully he monitored military developments and how he tried to influence them, as on September 1, after the disaster of Dresden: "The further operations are now being designed, and I hope that my influence on them will not be a bad one. We shall try to avoid all major battles and wear down Napoleon, who is sitting in a tight spot"[117] Two days later, Metternich repeated his prediction, which turned out to be correct: "How long he will continue to play this game in a country where he is already living off horse meat, is difficult to say. So much is certainly clear, that he runs the risk of being completely worn down, and our war, which is entirely based on the avoidance of major field battles, is very well suited to that end."[118] At the end of September, the "reluctant chief of staff" managed to persuade Tsar Alexander of the common—and ultimately successful—strategy. Metternich explained:

> God has given me enough cold-bloodedness to bring the project to this point politically, and now I shall also realize it in military terms. The situ-

ation of the army is the best possible. Among the highest authorities there is the greatest unanimity. E.(mperor) Alexander, who initially wanted to rush ahead a little bit too much, and believed that Napoleon must be devoured within eight days, now fully agrees with me and Schwarzenberg. As soon as the right hour for battle comes, I shall be the first to advise in its favor; but I first want to see Napoleon lose half his army without any danger to us.[119]

This unanimity in the run-up to the Battle of Leipzig was to endure.

Two sketches drawn by Metternich—one of them previously unpublished, the other already known—illustrate how closely he followed the movements on the battlefield. The previously unpublished drawing was sent to Eleonore on October 10; it showed the current position of the troops, making it plain how Napoleon was surrounded by the troops of Blücher, Bennigsen, Schwarzenberg's main army (who had Bohemia at their back), and the Swedish crown prince, all of which operated independently but struck together.[120]

Four days later, on October 14, Napoleon withdrew from Dresden and united his army at Leipzig. On that day, Metternich sketched the "position of the army on the 14th" in a presentation for the emperor.[121] At the center was Leipzig. The division of the general of the cavalry, Count Johann von Klenau, was stationed to the south at Borna. A Russian reserve was waiting at Altenburg. The infantry regiment of the quartermaster general, Colloredo-Mansfeld, was waiting at Chemnitz. The main army under Schwarzenberg was positioned near

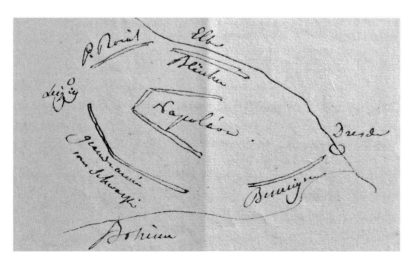

Metternich's sketch of October 10, 1813, for Eleonore, showing the position of the troops between Leipzig and Dresden.

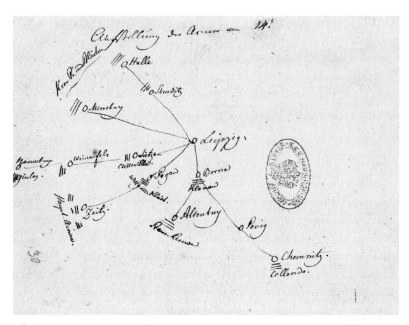

Metternich's sketch of October 14, 1813, for Emperor Franz, showing the position
of the troops before the Battle of Leipzig.

Zeitz. The northern army under Crown Prince Bernadotte of Sweden and the
general of the cavalry, Blücher, had taken up position before Merseburg and
Halle. The infantry regiment of Count Albert von Gyulai of Hungary had set
up camp at Naumburg. The troops of the general of the cavalry, Ludwig zu
Sayn-Wittgenstein, and the corps of Lieutenant General Friedrich von Kleist
of Prussia, under the command of the Russian general of the cavalry, Barclay
de Tolly, had taken up position outside Pegau. Field Marshal Lieutenant Crenneville's division was stationed at Lützen.

The sketch clearly shows how the allied army was able to encircle Leipzig
and advance on it. The complicated positioning made the situation difficult
to survey, with the result that on several occasions Napoleon followed false
information on the location of units and gave the wrong orders. In these
cases, too, the allies' approach of mutual aid worked well. In his conversation
with Metternich in Dresden, Napoleon had displayed an arrogance that betrayed how little he had appreciated the fact that his military situation had
changed fundamentally. He declared that he would defeat his opponents one
after the other:

> I have annihilated the Prussian army at Lützen; I have defeated the Rus-
> sians at Bautzen; now you wish your turn to come. Be it so; the rendez-

vous shall be in Vienna.... You think to conquer me by a coalition, then ... how many are there of you—four, five, six, twenty? The more you are, so much the better for me.[122]

Napoleon had miscalculated. The coalition he scorned taught him a lesson. At eleven o'clock on the crucial day, October 18, Metternich was with the three allied monarchs at the location Schwarzenberg had chosen for them to observe the battle with him. Metternich wrote: "I did not leave this point of observation till the end of that bloody day, about six o'clock in the evening, when I returned with them."[123] The very same day, he judged the battle a "bataille du monde," but he was not jubilant or joyful. He recorded the military detail, the more than a hundred cannon captured from the enemy. For him, it was a "bloody day." At eleven o'clock in the evening before the last day of the battle, he found time to write a short letter to Wilhelmine von Sagan, in which he lamented over the battlefield covered with the dead.[124]

The following day, October 19, Metternich informed the head of his Chancellery in Vienna, Hudelist, and through him the president of the court's war council, Count von Bellegarde. Metternich's letter conveyed his feelings of release and satisfaction, but one can also sense in it evidence of the internal disputes among the allies over how to fight against the greatest military commander of the times—who was still not yet completely defeated: "Now all those who have protested will after all finally realize that our operations were very justified and *well* calculated. If you think about the difficulty of bringing together on one battlefield four armies coming from all corners of the world, and how much needed to be done to arrange everything so that none of these armies could be defeated individually [*en détail*] and a commander like Napoleon became caught between them all, then the merits of FM [Field Marshal] Prince von Schwarzenberg are surely beyond doubt."[125]

The scene the day after the battle is instructive, for it revealed Metternich's determination to pursue Napoleon and to use peace negotiations with the French emperor only as pretext. On the first day of the Battle of Leipzig (October 16), Count Merveldt had been captured. Napoleon released him on the evening of his defeat (October 18). He had had a conversation with him over several hours before releasing him "on parole," using him as a messenger to communicate an offer of peace. Metternich recognized Napoleon's desperation: "He was in the position of a field commander who had been beaten, and was prepared to concede a lot of things—if not anything." The minister rejected the offer: "We shall give our response at the Rhine, and Wrede's army will hurry there ahead of us." Metternich thus wanted to continue to pursue Napoleon and to wait and see what the result of that would be.[126] Had he been the politician of appeasement he is always taken to be, he would surely have seized this moment, when Napoleon was at his most desperate, to accept the offer of a peace.

The End of the Rhenish Confederation and the Constitution of a New Germany

Military acumen alone, however, was not enough to beat Napoleon. What is sometimes overlooked is the extent to which Metternich's behind-the-scenes diplomatic activities also helped to degrade Napoleon's military capabilities. The war was also decided by the fact that Napoleon could no longer draw freely on troops from the Rhenish Confederation, particularly those from its most important member, Bavaria. Metternich's skillful negotiations on October 8, before the Battle of Leipzig, led to the Treaty of Ried, under which Bavaria left the Confederation. It was not Montgelas but General Count Wrede of Bavaria who pushed for this move, and it reinforced the allies' troops with some 36,000 men.

The treaty was pointed to by experts on German history as evidence that Metternich promoted the particular interests of individual states and under-mined impulses toward a larger, united Germany. The treaty listed the dissolu-tion of the Rhenish Confederation as the most important war aim, but at the same time guaranteed—in its first secret article—"the complete and uncondi-tional independence of Bavaria in the sense that it shall, freed of any foreign influence, enjoy its full sovereignty."[127] This has been judged by historians as "a questionable anticipation of the later solution to the problem of a German Constitution, a serious obstacle . . . to the creation of a German Reich."[128] Granted, the article defined the room for maneuver that would later, at the Congress of Vienna, be left for solving the "German question." The example of Bavaria, the most important member of the Rhenish Confederation, showed how lenient the potentially victorious allies could be toward those they defeated—those who, but a moment ago, were still fighting them. Those who complain about the allegedly forfeited German unity, however, overlook the fact that coalition troops were confronting an extremely dangerous opponent. The coalition could gain advantages from the members of the Rhenish Confederation changing sides only if they showed goodwill toward them by respecting their territorial integrity. As Metternich's ally, Count Schwarzen-berg, said of the treatment of former members of the Confederation, "it is true that preserving the [political] form made it infinitely easier for us to activate the military means [*moyens*], and the creation of German troops must at pre-sent remain our main aim." That was Metternich's thought, too.[129]

Metternich noted that Bavaria joining the alliance caused "an exceptional sensation" in the army.[130] Even before the Battle of Leipzig, he hoped for a domino effect, with further members of the Rhenish Confederation defecting, and so he suggested that news of Bavaria's defection on October 14 be marked with an artillery salute along the allies' front lines, to inform friend and foe alike. And he then, indeed, witnessed a Saxon battalion and two battalions from Württemberg change sides during the battle. The whole state of Württemberg followed, formally, on November 2, through the Treaty of Fulda. On November 7, two days after Metternich had arrived in the old imperial city of Frankfurt am Main, the Rhenish Confederation collapsed entirely.

In Frankfurt, on November 6, he had witnessed an incredible clash between the ages—the past of the perished Holy Roman Empire and the present of the moribund Napoleonic empire. On that day, Emperor Franz, the former Holy Roman Emperor, entered Frankfurt, amid much ceremony. The old imperial city, the scene of coronations, had been chosen as a staging point where further campaign planning was to take place. Metternich had been charged with preparing the ceremonial entry into the city, and he had the idea of giving the procession the look of the old Adventus, the ceremonial entry of the emperor-elect that preceded the coronation of the Holy Roman Emperor, and so he chose the very same parade route as would have been taken during the Adventus. In the same place where he had, in his youth, participated in two imperial coronations, he now watched as the former emperor of the Holy Roman Empire proceeded along an old route now "soiled by rogues": "Never before has the triumph of good over evil, of beauty over the bad, of the sublime over the ridiculous—never before have such contrasts become so visible more quickly." Back then, in the old empire, before the incomprehensible catastrophes that followed, the "Emperor of Germany" had not been a holy being, a savior, a messenger from heaven. But now the people were shouting: "Old luck, old memories, age of happiness and wealth—come back!"[131]

Then, from seven o'clock in the morning until two o'clock in the afternoon on November 7, Metternich was present for a highly unusual spectacle. It resembled the gathering of German princes at the court in Paris in July 1806 upon the formation of the Rhenish Confederation—the occasion when Napoleon had ensured that Metternich was kept at the border in Strasbourg. Metternich now sneeringly reported how all the ministers and little princes of beautiful Germany had come and knelt before him in order to enjoy the pleasure of an audience. He had already made agreements with Baden, Nassau, and Hesse: "Due to a lack of confederates there is no longer a confederation . . . How I enjoyed letting it [the Rhenish Confederation] die its orderly death—this monstrous association."[132] Within three days he had to draw up fourteen treaties with states that wanted to join the coalition.

But the new arrivals were not allowed to jump ship without paying a price. They had to enter into a contractual obligation to provide soldiers and to pay for a part of the war effort. Although their sovereignty had been guaranteed, in financial and military terms they were made to feel part of the united Germany. For the new members of the confederation [*Bund*], as the association was already called, in anticipation of the Congress of Vienna, the following was stipulated: "In order to guarantee the future independence of Germany, and to give greater unity and power to its military means, it has been agreed to establish a uniform system for all states of Germany."[133] In the coming weeks, the Chancellery in Vienna monitored whether the required payments had been received and sent reminders to those who had not paid.

The Relationship between Austria and Bavaria as a Paradigm for Metternich's Peace Policy

From an outsider's perspective, Paul Schroeder has explained perceptively that the way in which relations between Austria, Prussia, and the former states of the Rhenish Confederation were reconfigured was not a matter that concerned only Germany. Rather, it was a model for the solution to the "German question" in the context of the new European order developed at the Congress of Vienna. Whereas in German one speaks only of a "political equilibrium," Schroeder distinguishes between a "political equilibrium" and a "balance of power." The latter, suggesting the image of scales on which the powers are weighed, could be paraphrased as a "respected equality of rank" [*respektierte Ebenbürtigkeit*]. The politics of power balance was practiced within the pentarchic system of major powers of equal rank that competed with each other and pursued conflicting interests. A single major power could not impose its will on the others because if it attempted to do so, they would, almost mechanically, throw their weight on the scales to redress the balance. This model characterized European politics after the Treaty of Westphalia in 1648. It did not rule out wars of conquest, but the aggressor in such wars was ultimately always brought back into the system by the weight of the superior number of opponents, as Prussian King Friedrich II learned in the Seven Years War. A "political equilibrium," by contrast, could exist under conditions of single-state hegemony. It did not work in a purely mechanical fashion, but had—as Metternich would have put it—a "moral core." It involved the acknowledgment of each other's interests, respect for agreements among powers and the (international) law, and the need for independence and security.

Understood in these terms, the European balance corresponded perfectly to Metternich's political philosophy, the fruit of his intellectual development, as it has been unfolded here. According to Schroeder, the Vienna System of 1815 relates to this idea of a political equilibrium. After the idea had been accepted in the Treaty of Ried, it proved able to serve as the foundation for a system that worked on the basis of "respected equality of rank" and not according to a mechanical balance of power. Unfortunately, Schroeder only ever refers to Austria in general, but it was in fact Metternich who fundamentally shifted European politics by providing a new definition of Europe's security interests and a new means of realizing them. If enough major powers were to strive for it, he thought, a qualitatively new system of European politics could emerge. He would later refer to international law as its basis.

For the new relationship between Austria and Bavaria, this meant the following: Bavaria no longer had to fear that its large neighbor would intervene in it, conquer it, or exchange it for other territories. The Treaty of Ried had indeed "ended a century-old rivalry." Austria reined in its territorial ambitions and respected Bavaria's independence and its concerns; it also left the territories gained during the Napoleonic era untouched. This came about without any use of force from the Bavarian side or from any other European state. Metternich followed a principle Paul Schroeder expresses as follows: "The decision by this big fish [Austria] not to swallow the middle-sized ones left the latter free to digest the lesser fry they had gobbled up earlier." This created "a less dangerous and conflictual international system."[134]

Provisional Answer to the "German Question": Stein versus Metternich

A central administrative council in Frankfurt, headed by Baron Karl vom Stein, determined how the relations involving the former states of the Rhenish Confederation were to be reorganized. A short historical recapitulation will be useful at this point. At the beginning of September in Teplitz, when the Sixth Coalition was being forged, the allies were already considering what to do with the states of the Rhenish Confederation when they captured them. Hardenberg and Humboldt had the idea for a "German administrative council," to be led by Karl vom Stein, which would rule over the conquered countries. This council would act as a Prusso-Russian occupying body and be authorized to carry out far-reaching regulatory intervention. It would collect tax revenue, recruit soldiers, and organize the armed forces. Tsar Alexander insisted on taking the lead on this, and on October 20, one day after the allies had entered Leipzig, he sought to involve Metternich: Austria was to join the administrative council and accept Stein as the director of its central administrative department.

Metternich vehemently protested against the proposals—and for good reasons, as far as he was concerned. He was in possession of a memorandum Stein had produced at the end of August 1813 for the tsar and Humboldt. This memorandum was one of the "most controversial documents of his [Stein's] constitutional work," in the words of Ernst Rudolf Huber, and goes a long way toward explaining what it was about Stein that Metternich feared. It promoted the kind of ethnically based and power-oriented German nationalism that saw Prussia as the better German state, the state with the right to lead. The suggestion of elevating Franz, a member of the House of Habsburg, back to the status of German emperor altered nothing about that, because "due to its geographical position, the mentality of its inhabitants, its government, the degree of education that has been reached, Prussia remains an important state for Europe, and in particular for Germany." By comparison, to Stein the Habsburg Monarchy appeared a lot less suitable to the purpose: "In Prussia, the German spirit is maintained much freer and purer than in Austria, whose population is mixed with Slavs and Hungarians, whose territory is delimited by Turks and Slavonic nations, and whose development would therefore be made difficult in any case, even if progress had not been impeded by intellectual repression and intolerance in the 17th and 18th centuries." From this, Metternich could tell already that Austria would become a country foreign to Germany, as he put it in 1833 upon the founding of the German Customs Union [*Deutscher Zollverein*].

The following suggestion of Stein's must have appeared downright scandalous to Metternich: "In order to round off and strengthen Prussia, it would have to incorporate Mecklenburg, Holstein, the Electorate of Saxony—on the latter two, the right of conquest decides."[135] In Teplitz, Metternich demanded the "removal of the idea of conquest from the purposes of the Alliance"—a demand that must have been made in the knowledge of Stein's aforementioned suggestion.[136] Stein threatened German states with occupation, mediatization, and dispossession, and all this at a point when the great battle against Napoleon was still far from over. The states of the Rhenish Confederation were still on the French side. Stein's aggressive rhetoric about the "fifteen little despots" and the fifteen million Germans who were at their mercy raised the gravest fears. A wild desire for change, a mad sense of self-importance, profligacy, and beastly lust, he said, had destroyed the happiness of those living in their territories. Stein's lament over the division of Germany, which he saw as detrimental to the nationalist sentiment, suggested that he longed for a major territorial reconstruction. In addition, he wanted to reinstate Germany according to the borders prior to the Imperial Recess of 1803, reviving the small estates and states that were faithful to the emperor in order to bolster his power.

These coarse, threatening suggestions would have destroyed Metternich's finely spun diplomatic net, into which he wanted to bring, in particular, the states of the Rhenish Confederation. He was not able to prevent Stein becoming the head of the central administrative department because the tsar had already promised his minion the post: conceding would have meant seeing himself—yet again—publicly humiliated. Metternich prevailed, in his own way, by severely limiting the efficiency of the central administration and tying it to the allied powers' Leipzig convention of October 21, 1813.[137]

In sum, one can say that, long before the Congress of Vienna, the answer to the "German question" was a federation—because of the Treaties of Teplitz and the Treaty of Ried, the convention on the central administration, and finally Baden joining the alliance. All this happened in the spirit of Metternich's idea of an equilibrium that secured domestic peace in Germany and Europe. What the middle-sized fish "had gobbled up earlier" they were allowed to retain; the clock was not turned back to a point before 1803, nor did the Austrian ruler want to become a German emperor. This was no "restoration." Metternich's ideas and political measures pointed the way toward a federalist reconstruction.

In principle, Metternich and Stein underwent the same political socialization and shared essential political convictions. Both came from the tradition of the old Holy Roman Empire and, at the same time—strangely enough—admired the British Constitution as a model for a liberal political order based on participation. And yet the imperial count from the Rhineland put "Stein and the Prussian Particularists or abstract Germanists [Deutschtümler]" in the same category: "the revolutionary spirit which in 1807 had disguised itself under the cloak of Prussian patriotism, and afterward in Teutonic colours." Metternich supposed that "aristocratic tendencies blended with the democratic in the mind of Freiherr von Stein."[138] Friedrich Gentz seconded Metternich's view of Stein in a piece about the Congress of Vienna, calling Stein "a true disturber of the public peace in Germany and Europe."[139] Metternich's judgment was so harsh because he considered Stein's ruthless and, in part, vengeful treatment of the states of the Rhenish Confederation extremely dangerous. Ultimately, what we have here is the opposition between what Max Weber refers to as an ethics of conviction versus an ethics of responsibility. Stein aggressively promoted his fundamental political principles, regardless of whether they could be realized. According to Heinz Duchhardt, "In many cases, what was doable was of only secondary importance to him." Metternich knew how to deal with this attitude, but he considered it completely unsuited to achieving political success.[140]

7

WORLD WAR

Catastrophe and Resolution, 1814

THE FINAL BATTLE AGAINST NAPOLEON AND THE PREFIGURATION
OF THE VIENNA ORDER

Metternich divided the Sixth Coalition's war against Napoleon into three "campaigns." The first began with Austria entering the war on August 10, 1813, and lasted until the allies moved into Frankfurt. The second campaign stretched from the allies' decision to continue the war and intervene in France, which was taken in November 1813, to the occupation of the strategically important heights in the French Langres region in mid-January 1814. The third and final campaign consisted of the battles on French soil before the allies entered Paris in April 1814. These three campaigns are probably unique in the history of international relations, in that the military engagements were accompanied by uninterrupted diplomatic exchange between the belligerents. According to Tsar Alexander and the Prussian military leadership around Gneisenau and Blücher, the right thing to do would have been to defeat Napoleon in one great campaign and to dictate the terms of peace to France. From his study of the emperor and the previous five coalition wars, all of which had failed, Metternich was all too aware of the extent to which this expressed a naivety and an ignorance regarding Napoleon's power and military skill. Up until March 1814, it was Metternich alone who, in the name of the allies, ensured that the campaigns were always accompanied by proposals for a peace agreement.

After reaching Frankfurt, the allies were divided over whether to continue the campaign and carry it into France. The Prussian king was decidedly against crossing the Rhine. And the Russian generals, who had resented even having to cross the Weichsel, also tried to prevent Alexander from continuing on. Metternich took a different stance and, together with Schwarzenberg, expressed his support for continuing the war. After all we have learned about him, this is only to have been expected.[1] On November 9, 1813, in Metternich's quarters in Frankfurt, the decisive conversation between the Prussian and Austrian generals took place, and a common operational plan was agreed to. Schwarzenberg's main army was to march into France from the south, via Switzerland, and to make contact along the way with the Austrian troops in Italy and Wellington's British army coming from Spain. Blücher was to cross the Rhine from the east at Mainz, and Crown Prince Bernadotte was to arrive from the occupied Netherlands in the north. The intention was thus to encircle Napoleon while advancing and retreating in a coordinated fashion, and to engage him in a full battle only once this strategy had sufficiently weakened him. Following the meeting, Schwarzenberg summarized it in a document for the tsar.[2]

Metternich's Pretend Peace Initiative

The meeting had settled it: war would continue. But Metternich insisted that this should not mean cutting off communications with Napoleon. A response to the offer of peace negotiations that Napoleon had made at Leipzig was still outstanding. After defeat at the Battle of Leipzig, Napoleon had used the captured Austrian general Merveldt as a messenger. The allies now proceeded to do the same with the arrested French emissary to the courts of Gotha and Weimar, Baron Saint-Aignan. Metternich considered this arrest a "contravention of international law" of the kind he himself had suffered at the hands of Napoleon in Paris.[3] But he thought it was possible to compensate for the injustice by sending the captive to Paris with an offer of negotiations.

The very same day, November 9, 1813, Metternich gathered together Prince Schwarzenberg, Lord Aberdeen, representing Great Britain, and Count Nesselrode, representing Russia and, as proxy for Hardenberg, Prussia. Metternich pursued a shrewd strategy: he did not present anything in writing to the assembled representatives but, in the presence of Saint-Aignan, simply outlined a peace plan then and there. The baron took notes—on, among other things, the offer that France remain a nation-state within its "natural borders"—that is, the Alps, the Pyrenees, and the Rhine. The offer demanded independence for Germany, Spain (under its old rulers), Italy, and Holland. There would be the prospect of a peace congress, but no firm offer of a peace agreement. The offer ruled out an armistice or a peace agreement limited to the European Continent.[4]

Castlereagh, along with some parts of the British public, was appalled at Saint-Aignan's mission. But they had misinterpreted it. The view that Metternich acted in a "slippery" way—first by ignoring British and Prussian interests and then, once his mission had failed, denying, as usual, that he was maneuvering—has become a received wisdom among historians.[5] But this judgment becomes untenable once we consider Metternich's long-term strategy; he clearly anticipated that his offers of negotiations would be rejected—something he pointed out to the tsar in June 1813 in Opotschno, when he presented him with his "great plan." In the case of Saint-Aignan, Metternich handed him a message for Caulaincourt that read: "Mr. Saint-Aignan will tell you about our conversation. I do not expect that anything will come of it, but once again I shall have done my duty—*Napoleon ne fera pas la paix, voilà ma profession de foi* [Napoleon will not make peace; this is my profession of faith]."[6]

Just as Metternich had enticed the states of the Rhenish Confederation to leave the Napoleonic system, he now proceeded with Napoleon's last remaining allies: Switzerland, Denmark, and Naples. But once he had succeeded in severing their ties with Napoleon, there was no mention of peace negotiations. Saint-Aignan's secret mission had the same purpose as the conversation in Dresden: namely, to buy time for troop mobilization. That is what Metternich told his chief secretary at the chancellery under the pledge of absolute secrecy: "I do not believe that Napoleon will genuinely pursue this matter. But, in every respect, we had to make a move in order to see clearly and at the same time to acquire weapons from the nation."[7]

The new allies who had joined from the Rhenish Confederation had had to commit themselves to raising troops for the continuation of the battle against Napoleon. Here, Metternich's federal policies regarding the German states paid great dividends; and here, too, he had been the catalyst: "All of the provisional organization of Germany we have planned and implemented with the military aspect in mind. In less than two months, Germany will provide 120,000 line infantry, 120,000 active militiamen [*Landwehr*] and a home guard [*Landsturm*] in the cities of the Black Forest, the Odenwald, the Westerwald, and the Spessart and Harz Mountains, reaching from the Swiss border to the North Sea."[8] During the months of November and December, Stein, as the head of the central administrative department, was invaluable when it came to the business of getting the states previously belonging to the Rhenish Confederation to fulfill their duties. However, this did not make him "a key figure in the coalition war."[9] The war lasted nine months, during which time Stein was not always a key decision maker. Like Gentz, his effective role was that of a writer, a provider of ideas, and a behind-the-scenes promoter of the cause. But others called the shots.

The Declaration of Frankfurt, December 1, 1813: A Manifesto Addressed to the French

Metternich had not been wrong about Napoleon. On November 25, he received his response in a letter from the foreign minister, Maret. The letter completely ignored all the suggested peace conditions and consisted of generalities about the independence of all nations and the emperor's desire for peace. This was just the basis Metternich needed for his next tactical move. He suggested to the allies that they address the French people in a manifesto. The real meaning of this proclamation—that is, the political and historical connections Metternich associated with it—becomes apparent only when we take into account Metternich's public career from 1792 onward, something that has never been done before.

We need to remind ourselves that in 1792 Metternich had been in Mainz, where he witnessed the birth of the notorious manifesto of the Duke of Brunswick. Only a few months later, he had observed how the manifesto's threat to destroy Paris had enraged the city and had been used by the National Assembly as justification for war against the "king of Bohemia and Hungary."

Metternich considered himself someone "thoroughly acquainted with the public feeling in France," and he therefore thought that it was important that the manifesto should be "flattering [to] the national vanity instead of embittering the feelings of the nation."[10] He was worried that another intervention by allied troops could lead to a similar revolutionary radicalization inside France, as in 1792–1793. This catastrophic scenario made an indelible impression on his political thought, which he still felt twenty years later, and this explains why he declared that his manifesto of 1813 was the most difficult piece of work in his life and that he had written it "from the bottom of my heart."[11]

When a few weeks later Metternich was confronted with the impatient Blücher, who set off to Verdun in order to march straight to Paris, this immediately struck Metternich as an operation "like the one which ended so unfortunately in 1792," by which he meant the withdrawal following the cannonade at Valmy.[12] At the time of the formation of the alliance in Teplitz, Metternich was already thinking that France might view the treaties as the forging of an aggressive alliance similar to the one in 1792. He made a point of consulting the exact wording of the pact of 1792 in the archive of the chancellery in order to improve the design of the new contracts "in every respect": "I have made sure that we appear moderate to the highest degree, so much so that I even put the only articles which attack France directly into a separate convention which is only known to the three Courts."[13] In an unpublished section of his memoirs, Metternich reveals the true motives behind his tactical peace policies of 1813–1814: "In my eyes Napoleon was the bearer of the Revolution, and the

Revolution still lived through him. If the [allied] powers had given their undertakings, which were directed against the cravings for conquest shown by the
bearer of the Revolution, the character of intentions to conquer, they would
have strengthened the force of the enemy when what was needed was to weaken
them."[14]

No repeat of 1792—this was also the criterion Metternich applied to the
manifesto. In it, he flattered the "national vanity" of the French by assuring
them that the allies would guarantee France "an extension of its territories as
France never knew it under their kings, because a chivalrous nation does
not sink because it has suffered accidents."[15] Metternich paraphrased the suggestion that the Rhine, the Alps, and the Pyrenees were the "natural borders" of
the country. He asserted that the allied powers were at war not with France
but with Napoleon, who had upset the balance of the Continent to the detriment of both Europe and France. Napoleon, he said, had also rejected all offers of a peace. In his memoirs, Metternich later wrote that his intention was
"to separate Napoleon still more from the nation, and at the same time to act
on the mind of the army," because he knew that the majority of the generals
were tired of war.[16] He also made mention of a fact that would have been uncomfortable for the audience: namely, that a further 300,000 French soldiers
were to be recruited.

The manifesto ended with Metternich's vision of peace for Europe: not only
France but "also the [allied] powers want freedom, happiness, and peace. They
want a condition of peace which will use a wise distribution of power and a
just balance to protect the peoples against the endless suffering that has burdened Europe for the past twenty years. They will not lay down their arms before a new order for the states of Europe has been agreed upon, unchanging
principles have gained victory over arbitrary attacks, and the sacredness of contracts finally secures true peace for Europe." With this passage, the minister
anticipated the idealistic goal he pursued at the Congress of Vienna, and gave
voice to a vision he had already adopted as a young man.

The manifesto worked. Metternich soon learned how well it had been received. He had had 20,000 leaflets distributed in France. Caulaincourt later told
him that he had hit a nerve with Napoleon. The police minister, Savary, had
immediately passed one of the first copies on to Napoleon, and the French emperor commented: "No one but Metternich can have concocted this document; talking of the Rhine, the Alps, and the Pyrenees is a thorough piece of
cunning. It could only enter into the head of a man who knows France as well
as he does."[17]

The Alleged Violation of Swiss Neutrality

At the beginning of December 1813, the alliance between Switzerland and Napoleonic France still existed. Under Radetzky's military planning, however, a march across Swiss territory toward Langres was unavoidable. Tsar Alexander objected forcefully and, as was his habit, declared the matter to be a matter of honor. He had publicly committed himself to defending Swiss neutrality and feared that he might lose face. The conflict became another instance in which Metternich's political calculations and actions ended up steering the military operations.

The neutrality argument was absurd. Since 1798 the Helvetic Republic had been in a defensive and offensive alliance with Napoleon—much as the Rhenish Confederation would later be—and had to contribute a contingent of 16,000 troops. The assembly of representatives from the cantons—the "Tagsatzung," "Diète fédérale," "Dieta federale"—which insisted on the alleged neutrality, had just recruited another 300 soldiers and sent them to the Swiss regiments serving under Napoleon. An Austrian officer who had fled France for Switzerland had been extradited.[18] Metternich conducted himself as he had in the case of the Rhenish Confederation, and justified the imminent intervention to Emperor Franz by arguing that it was in truth no intervention:

> It is not us who want to intervene in Swiss matters—but we must exterminate the French influence which has suffused all internal affairs of Switzerland. We must topple the French edifice not in order to erect an Austrian one in its stead: we want to provide a new foundation for Swiss freedom. The Swiss themselves, however, must give us the means to do this.[19]

In secret negotiations Metternich had persuaded the canton of Berne to seek the help of the allies. Metternich's initiative sought to support the "independents" in Switzerland against the "French faction." The minister also assumed that the cantons of Graubünden and Zurich would follow the example of Berne. After Schwarzenberg and Radetzky came out in support of Metternich's position, the emperor agreed to the plan for military intervention. On December 21, 1813, the Austrians crossed the Rhine over bridges at Basle, Laufenburg, and Schaffhausen without encountering resistance. The rift with the tsar that resulted would take time to heal, although he had to admit that in military terms the operation was necessary and justified. The allies could not tolerate a state allied to Napoleon that lay like a hostile bridgehead between the Austrian troops in Italy and Wellington's army, which was approaching from Spain.

Between the Battlefield and Diplomacy: Metternich on His Way to Paris

The past is more complicated than any historian can appreciate. This is especially true of the events on the battlefields of France between January and
April 1814. Diplomatic and military actions were inextricably bound up with
each other. Numerous actions were initiated by army headquarters, which kept
moving. Schwarzenberg's headquarters were located for longer spells in Lör-
rach, Langres, Troyes, Chaumont, and Bar-sur-Aube, and for briefer periods
at places such as Vandœvres, Colombey, and Bar-sur-Seine. The quarters of
the monarchs and ministers were sometimes in the same place as the headquarters, sometimes in different locations. Allied delegates held parallel meetings
with Caulaincourt (who in the meantime had succeeded Mauret as the French
foreign minister) during February 3–9, and again between February 17 and
March 19, to negotiate conditions for a peace. At special conferences of the
monarchs and ministers, negotiations were particularly intense, especially at
the beginning of March when the pact for a lasting Quadruple Alliance was renewed and solidified.

In addition, the locations of the armies were changing, and the regiments
were shifted continually in order to attack Napoleon from the flanks or the
back. Also, apart from Schwarzenberg's headquarters, there were those of the
generals Blücher, Wittgenstein, Wrede, and Bernadotte. If we wanted to assess
what happened at this time in military terms, we would need to descend to the
level of day-to-day detail. The reader who is interested in this should delve into
one of the older military authors, such as Carl von Plotho, who chronicles the
events day by day.[20] More-distant activities had to be coordinated if individual
units were to avoid being worn down by Napoleon—particularly given that it
was the middle of winter and troops were struggling with miserable nutrition.
The French were grappling with similar issues, something about which we are
now much better informed thanks to the work of Munro Price.

Historians have hitherto failed to describe in a holistic manner the developments that led to Napoleon's abdication. But such a description is needed if
we are to calculate precisely the contributions made by individual actors. It is
therefore not surprising that partial perspectives have tended to dominate and
Metternich has hardly been noticed. In this context, a biographer is in a privileged position: he knows where Metternich was at what time and to what extent he was involved in moderating particular conflicts (Table 7.1). For these
conflicts continued: What were the right military tactics? How should France
and Europe be organized? Who was to rule over Napoleon's empire once it had
been defeated? Which territories were to remain French? Only a few people had
both the sangfroid and the intellectual acuity to master this situation. The tsar,

Table 7.1. Metternich's itinerary in the spring of 1814

Freiburg	December 14, 1813–January 12, 1814
Basel	January 12–24, 1814
Langres	**January 25–February 2, 1814**
Chaumont	February 3–4, 1814
Vendœvres	February 5, 1814
Bar-sur-Aube	February 6, 1814
Bar-sur-Seine	February 7, 1814
Troyes	February 8–24, 1814
Bar-sur-Aube	**February 25, 1814**
Chaumont	**February 26–March 14, 1814**
Troyes	March 15–19, 1814
Bar-sur-Seine	March 19, 1814
Bar-sur-Aube	March 21–24, 1814
Dijon	March 25–April 7, 1814
Paris	April 10–June 3, 1814
London	June 5–30, 1814
Paris	July 2–7, 1814
Arrival in Vienna	July 18, 1814

Note: Bold type indicates three crucial events: the Langres conference, the war council in Bar-sur-Aube, and the consolidation of the quadruple alliance in Chaumont.

Gneisenau, Blücher, and Stein were certainly not among them. In military matters, Schwarzenberg and, in particular, Radetzky were,[21] and in operational matters Metternich was too. But when the conflicts came to a head, they chiefly played out between the tsar and Metternich, although from January 19 onward the minister also had a strong ally in the British foreign minister, Castlereagh.

Three crucial sequences of events well illustrate Metternich's ability to manage crises: the crisis conferences in Langres between January 27 and February 1, the great war council in Bar-sur-Aube on February 25, and the consolidation of the Quadruple Alliance at the beginning of March in Chaumont. We shall also take a few brief looks at the conferences in Châtillon, which took place at the same time.

The Main Crisis: Tactical Peace Offer or March on Paris? *(Langres, End of January 1814)*

According to Metternich's schema, the heights at Langres, in the Departement Haute-Marne, mark the end point of the second campaign. Having arrived there, a decision had to be made about whether the troops should march on or, as it was wintertime, be given time for recreation and to await the arrival of fresh supplies. Tsar Alexander, Gneisenau, Blücher, and Stein advocated the former; Schwarzenberg recommended the latter in a memorandum that Metternich supported.

The military question was connected with a political one: Should they still engage in peace negotiations, and, if so, was Napoleon actually an acceptable partner in such negotiations? Tsar Alexander made the surprising—and provocative—suggestion that they should proclaim Napoleon's former general, Bernadotte, the French ruler or even let "the French people" decide Napoleon's successor. Alexander wanted to convene community meetings that would elect representatives to a parliament in Paris that would draw up a Constitution and decide on a head of state. Metternich protested vehemently against this: "That would be a repetition of the [National] Convention, a renewed unleashing of the Revolution which Napoleon has once crushed!"[22] There was a clash of worlds here, underlain by the different experiences of the two. While a—precocious—youngster, Metternich had experienced the outbreak of revolutionary violence, its efficacy in moving the masses, and its radicalization and escalation, to the point of attempting to physically destroy its opponent. By contrast, Alexander, who was four years younger, had lived in faraway Saint Petersburg at the time; he was educated by Frédéric-César de Laharpe, an admirer of Rousseau and a liberal-minded freemason. He could see no danger in the situation in 1814, and suggested that the allied armies would intimidate the voters. Napoleon's power, Alexander said, was broken and no one wanted to have anything to do with him any longer. The tsar even wanted to leave the practicalities to his old teacher, Laharpe. Laharpe would present the delegates with a choice: republic or Bernadotte, and no doubt the decision would be for Bernadotte.

Metternich and Castlereagh resisted this plan with all their might. They feared it would encourage Jacobin or other dictatorial coups. That this fear was not at all far-fetched is confirmed by Talleyrand's prediction that Bernadotte, were he to ascend to the throne, would only be "a new phase of the Revolution."[23] For Metternich and Castlereagh, the only viable candidates were the Bourbons. After Metternich threatened that Austria would leave the coalition, the tsar was temporarily dissuaded from pushing for his idea. But the really crucial question was whether they should still negotiate with Napoleon. Up to that point the tsar had agreed to Metternich's strategy of tactical negotiations, but now, in January 1814, he no longer wanted to hear of the strategy. He was animated by a wild urge to defeat Napoleon in a battle and ride into Paris as the victor.

We have already mentioned Metternich's proposed tactic of winning over the French public and public officials in Paris and making them turn against Napoleon by bringing it about that Napoleon was seen to be repeatedly rejecting offers of a peace. In his crucial presentation in Langres (January 27, 1814), Metternich again developed the argument for Emperor Franz: "The powerful weapon which the coalition has used against Napoleon was to rip from his face the mask of peace [*arracher la masque pacifique*], under which he had piled conquest upon conquest." Metternich went on to explain the emperor's policies, which were actually his own, as the result of a long-term strategy: "Your Majesty has given your policies this orientation from a long-term perspective. And the allies have followed it entirely, and only a partisan spirit could deny the evidence provided by the enormous successes which the allies have had as a result of those steps taken, which bore the character of moderation, legality, and peace."[24] And now, Metternich said, they must not let this powerful weapon slip out their hands. If used the wrong way, it could also be turned against the allies. At this point Metternich revealed, more clearly than usual, that the peacefulness he promoted was nothing but a propaganda tool that concealed the actual goal of his policies.

In deviation from his usual practice, Metternich composed this presentation not in German but in French. This made it clear from the very beginning that he wanted to present it to the participants at a forthcoming conference. It was part of Metternich's propaganda strategy that the allies define themselves as the representatives of Europe and address their peace offers directly to the French public, circumventing Napoleon. It was a case of Europe negotiating with France, not with Napoleon. This Europe saw itself as a system that was to be rebuilt on the firm basis of the principle of the balance of power.

It is characteristic of Metternich's diplomacy that he tried to establish a consensus. Initially he distributed his presentation to Castlereagh, Nesselrode, Hardenberg, Stadion, and Count Andrey Rasumovsky, who had been the Russian ambassador in Vienna until 1807 and now accompanied the tsar as his advisor. They were due to discuss the presentation in a conference on January 29. The presentation also suggested holding a separate congress in Châtillon with the purpose of discussing with Caulaincourt possible conditions for a peace. The delegates from all four allies finally agreed at the conference in Langres and left it to Metternich to prepare the instructions for the representatives at the conference in Châtillon.[25]

Because modern historians are still unanimously of the opinion that Metternich tried until the very last to reach a peace agreement with Napoleon in order to keep him on the throne, it is important to look in detail at Metternich's instructions for the delegates at Châtillon. He formulated a program of war aims for them, the most provocative of which was "the return of France to its borders before the Revolution." There was no more talk of "natural borders." The program amounted to a complete dismantling of the Napoleonic empire.

France was asked to renounce any claims to influence outside of its borders—
that is, to renounce the protectorates of Italy, Germany, and Switzerland. All
legal titles of rulers relating to these were to be revoked. The Ducs de Bassano,
de Tarente, de Reggio, d'Elchingen, de Castiglione, d'Abrantès; the princes de
Neufchâtel, de Parme, d'Eckmühl, de Vicenze—they all would lose the prebends that came with their colorful, artificial titles. The old Austrian influence
in Italy had to be restored. The Bourbons, led by Ferdinand VII, were to rule
Spain again, and Holland was to be reconstituted under the Prince of Orange.
Metternich's instructions set out a forward-looking definition of Germany
that anticipated the scope of the negotiations at the Congress of Vienna: "Germany consists of sovereign princes, connected by a federal tie which assures
and guarantees the independence of Germany."[26] This is the first time this
formulation appears in Metternich's writings—not, as is usually claimed, a
month later, in the contract of Chaumont and under the allegedly critical influence of Castlereagh. In any case, the formulation had already appeared at
Teplitz as Metternich's fundamental condition for Austria's joining of the alliance. When looking at the instructions in their entirety, they can only be understood as "an order to Napoleon that he should abdicate which is dressed in
unfulfillable demands."[27]

And this was exactly how Napoleon interpreted the message coming from
Châtillon. He had before him the oath he swore as emperor on May 18, 1804,
in which he had vowed to protect "the integrity of the territory of the Republic."
From his secretary, Fain, we know of Napoleon's indignant reaction when he
received the instructions for the congress in Châtillon. The *empereur* at once
understood what was demanded of him. He was expected to renounce not only
the territories he himself had captured but also those that had been captured
before his reign. He had to leave behind a smaller France than he had found,
and thus would have to break his oath. He felt this to be an unbearable affront,
and he described it as cowardice, betrayal, humiliation, scorn.[28] Metternich
could not have hoped for a better reaction. His evaluation of Napoleon's political character was exactly right.

However, Metternich wanted to avoid any impression among the Parisian
elite or the French population that the interventionist powers were trying to
impose a ruler on the nation. This is why, in his presentation for the conference in Langres, he included only the hedged question which other dynasty
should be installed if Napoleon were to be removed from the throne. Did the
allied powers have the right to directly intervene in this matter? Were they allowed to raise the question now or only if the French did not come up with
their own solution? Were they entitled to initiate a change of the ruler or only
to support it?

The presentation also serves to refute the widespread opinion that Metternich wanted to keep Napoleon on the throne until the very last moment, and that he abandoned this attitude only after Schwarzenberg fought the decisive battle of March 21, 1814, and the victorious allies marched toward Paris.[29] For Metternich it was clear that Napoleon was not to be kept on his throne. He expressed himself most openly about this to Wilhelmine von Sagan in his reports about the conferences in Langres: "For years I have told myself: 'I shall kill Napoleon' and I shall establish peace in the world . . . and if Napoleon lives, if he rules—he will be smaller, as if he had never ruled!"[30]

The Coalition Faces the Abyss: Metternich's Crisis Diplomacy, February 14, 1814

On February 3, the delegates to the Congress of Châtillon had arrived, among them Stadion as the spokesperson for the coalition. Castlereagh participated as the head of the British delegation, which consisted of himself, Aberdeen, Cathcart, and Stewart. Humboldt attended for Prussia, Rasumovsky for Russia. On February 9, when signs emerged that Caulaincourt might be prepared to agree even to the harsh conditions set out in Metternich's instructions, Alexander withdrew his representative so as to interrupt the congress. He referred to a clause in the instructions that permitted changes to the conditions if there were major developments in the war. Some allied successes had inspired him to no longer be held back by Schwarzenberg and to march directly on Paris. He wanted to destroy Napoleon's army—and the man himself—and arrange for the free election of the future head of state in Paris. He pointed to the numerical superiority of the allies' troops and ignored the 50,000 or so wounded soldiers among them. Likewise, he ignored the miserable situation they were confronting when it came to supplies and provisions, something Schwarzenberg took into account.

This once again demonstrates the central role Metternich played in keeping the alliance together and in steering its course. The tsar threatened that the alliance would break apart if it did not pursue his policies, policies that were in his case ultimately emotionally driven. Ministers met for hastily convened crisis conferences in Troyes between February 10 and 15. Castlereagh made a personal effort to change the tsar's mind—but in vain. Further communications from conference participants went unanswered by the tsar. Everything came to rest with Metternich, and he declared his willingness to negotiate with Alexander directly. When they met on February 14, Metternich gambled; he threatened to withdraw the Austrian troops and to agree to a separate peace with Napoleon. The tsar relented—in part because, in the meantime, Blücher had suffered a few more defeats at the hands of Napoleon. On February 17, the negotiations in Châtillon resumed.

The following day Metternich adopted a slightly ironic tone in describing the burden the allies had thus managed to shed: "A bunch of fools have taken hold of *your beautiful friend* [Alexander] for some time now, and if they continue along the same vein they will ruin the world." He had taken it upon himself, he wrote, to confront Alexander face-to-face, and he had scored a major victory.

> My friend Castlereagh told me: You are the prime minister of the world [*le premier ministre du monde*], and I beg your pardon that I did not always trust you accordingly. The chancellor [Hardenberg] embraced me, my Emperor [Franz] took me by the collar, the king of Prussia smiled at me, and your *beau* [Alexander] told me he loved me because there was no other man who knew what he wanted and never strayed from his path.[31]

The War Council in Bar-sur-Aube, February 25, 1814

In Schwarzenberg's eyes, the mistakes the allies had made during the previous year, which had culminated in the defeat at Dresden at the end of August, were repeated during the campaign in France. The supreme commander repeatedly lamented Blücher's shortcomings: "He yet again begins to storm ahead pointlessly without considering that the enemy in front of him might be weak but has the army waiting at his flank; it would be a miracle if this piecemeal approach should not again end in a calamity for him."[32] In mid-February, Napoleon was able to prove his exceptional military talent once more, capitalizing on a lack of coordination among the allies and winning several battles, despite being outnumbered. The allies found themselves in a desperate situation in a foreign country; Schwarzenberg summed the situation up by saying: "If I divide up my army, I may be beaten *en détail*; if I collect it in one spot, I starve to death."[33]

The crisis led to a meeting of the allies for a major war council, hosted by King Friedrich Wilhelm III in Bar-sur-Aube on February 25. In attendance were Emperor Franz, Tsar Alexander, Schwarzenberg, Metternich, Castlereagh, Nesselrode, and Hardenberg, as well as the generals Count Radetzky (quartermaster general of the Austrian army), Prince Wolkonski (the tsar's chief of staff), von Diebitsch (quartermaster general of the Russian army), and von Knesebeck (adjutant general of the Prussian king). Alexander took notes. The list of those attending gives us an idea of how dramatic the crisis was. To his wife, Schwarzenberg described the tsar's conduct as follows: "Emperor Alexander is experiencing another fit of sublime tomfoolery from which he suffers so frequently."[34] He envied Napoleon and Wellington, who were sole commanders: "We are made up of all nations, suffer from the sad predicament of carrying three sovereigns on our shoulders . . . to be tormented by proud, vain, and ignorant sovereigns who play soldier is a terrible form of torture."[35]

In the end, it was agreed that they would return to the old strategy, which had been so successful in the run-up to the Battle of Leipzig—namely "to avoid risking the fate of the campaign on the chance of one general battle, but gradually to exhaust Napoleon's strength."[36] The return to the successful strategy, which had been repeatedly questioned, illustrates Metternich's key role in managing conflict. He backed the Austrian military leaders, Schwarzenberg and Radetzky, against the Russian and Prussian resistance. At the same time, the decision was taken to march on Paris. The complex difficulties of the situation at the human, political, and military levels led Metternich and Castlereagh to consolidate the foundation of the pact again.

The "Entente Cordiale" between Metternich and Castlereagh

Metternich eagerly awaited the arrival of the British foreign minister, who reached Basel on January 19. From there, they together continued the journey to Langres, where they arrived on January 25. After a few hours of intense conversation, the two had discovered a large area of mutual agreement. They shared the political vision of a European peace based on a balance between the major powers and bolstered by principles and alliances. Metternich felt that his British partner understood him as the Burkean conservative Whig that he really would have liked to be. Both wanted to disempower Napoleon and reinstate the Bourbons, and both feared that another Jacobin Revolution could occur in Paris and spread across France. In his dealings with politicians, Metternich rarely spoke of friendship. Castlereagh, and soon after Wellington, were the great exceptions. Langres was the first time Metternich and Castlereagh fought together in the diplomatic arena for the same political project. It was here that they founded their "entente cordiale." These two must be credited as those most responsible for the success of the Sixth Coalition from Langres onward; they were the ones who energetically and resolutely fought for it. At the beginning of March in Troyes, Stadion described Metternich's position in the negotiations to a messenger from the French royalists and Dalberg by saying: "Besides, you cannot achieve anything here except through him. Herr von Metternich is the tie that binds the sovereigns together. At the present moment, he is a minister of the Emperor of Russia as much as a minister of Austria."[37]

Because of the positions he had held in Brussels, Rastatt, Dresden, Berlin, Paris, and Vienna, Metternich's political understanding far outstripped that of Castlereagh, who had no experience of continental politics. But the British minister was a political heavyweight in his own right. It was unusual for a foreign secretary to leave the island at all, and even more unusual to engage in months of political negotiations on the Continent.

We may learn quite a bit about Metternich by describing in more detail the exceptional relationship between the two men. Metternich was already familiar with the peculiarities of English dress compared to the French fashion at the time. Castlereagh turned up at Basel in red knickerbockers and a blue coat with laces that resembled the livery of a prelate from 1780. Metternich, however, did not smirk at this attire—as, for instance, Wilhelm von Humboldt did when he first met Lord Aberdeen. Rather, he considered it a charming British eccentricity that was to be tolerated. Castlereagh sensed this immediately and, having worked with Metternich for a couple of hours, told Aberdeen that he had worked with many men of great reputation but had never met someone who possessed such "gallantry" in his manners as Metternich. Aberdeen, in turn, relayed this to Metternich, who was quite surprised; by his standards, he had treated Castlereagh rather undiplomatically and informally:

> Milord, we do not have the time for cautiously getting to know each other. I do not have the right to know what you think before you know what I think. I shall tell you in four words—that is all, no more and no less. If you think the same as I do, when you want what I want, the world is saved—if you do not think the same, it will be lost. You will spend a few weeks with us. You have the choice either to bring about what is good at once, or to prepare what is bad for the long term.

Without raising his eyebrows, Castlereagh answered: "If that is what you want, are we principally agreed?" "Yes," Metternich responded, and, according to a letter to Wilhelmine von Sagan, he added: "Since then we work like two employees in the same office."[38]

Immediately after Castlereagh's arrival in Basel on January 19, Metternich tried to keep him close. They talked for hours; they talked until Metternich's voice was hoarse. He spent a full day "dissecting Europe like a piece of cheese" to him. He noted that Castlereagh was satisfied, and wrote enthusiastically: "My relationship to him is as if we had spent our whole lives together. He is calm, prudent, has the heart in the right place, he stands his ground and keeps a cool head." Castlereagh placed so much trust in Metternich that he called him "mon honorable ami" and showed him a letter from Wellington. With amazement,

Metternich noticed that it fully reflected his position and even contained formulations of his.[39] This is all the more surprising given that, while he was conducting Britain's continental politics from London in 1813, Castlereagh had harbored the greatest mistrust toward the Austrian politician. At that time he knew nothing about Metternich's long-term strategy, which Metternich had to hide from Napoleon. The conjugal relation between the Habsburgs and Napoleon, the alliance of spring 1812, the open and seemingly friendly contacts at the meeting in Dresden in the summer of 1812 before Napoleon's Russian campaign—all these, in Castlereagh's mind, were so many good reasons not to trust Metternich as a reliable ally.

Their mutual appreciation, which developed very quickly, was nevertheless not the result of a momentary mood. It reactivated Metternich's inner political compass, which had had a British orientation ever since 1794. The two ministers possessed the same cool and distanced view on things, a view tinged with a sense of irony; they were committed to political empiricism and pragmatism and recognized each other as members of the cosmopolitan generation of the 1770s. Even though, on the way to Paris, Castlereagh still had to learn quite a few things from Metternich regarding the empirical facts of continental politics, their principles would be at the heart of the order created at the Congress of Vienna.

The British prince regent later confirmed that the two were, indeed, bound by a proper friendship. In a conversation with Metternich during a visit to Hanover in 1821, he said of Castlereagh: "He understands you; he is your friend: that says everything."[40] In private letters from the end of 1822, following Castlereagh's terrible death, Metternich confessed how much he had meant to him:

> It is a great misfortune. The man is not to be replaced, especially not for me. Someone of high intellect may replace everything, except [Castlereagh's] experience. Londonderry [Castlereagh] was the only man in his country who had gained any experience abroad; he had learned to understand me. . . . The catastrophe is one of the most shocking that I have ever known. He was devoted to me in heart and spirit, not only from personal inclination, but also from conviction. . . . I awaited him here [at the Congress of Verona] as my second self. My work would have been reduced by half, because I should have had him to share it with me.

Metternich considered the Duke of Wellington "the only man who can in a measure replace him."[41] And, indeed, the duke became the second British friend he could count on to remain loyal to him at all times, including during Metternich's exile in London in 1848–1849.[42]

The Treaty of Chaumont, the Moment the Concert of Europe Was Born
(Early March 1814)

The major war council at Bar-sur-Aube was not the only effect of the sequence of victories Napoleon managed to achieve in February 1814. As the politicians of the allied states began to suspect that the war might still continue for a substantial amount of time, in the first week of March in Chaumont—where Metternich, Nesselrode, Castlereagh, and Hardenberg, as the ministers of the four major powers, were meeting—the idea was floated of setting up a new contractual basis for the alliance. It is difficult to establish whether the initiative came from Castlereagh or Metternich. The two politicians' thoughts regarding this topic ran in parallel. In a memorandum of 1805, Castlereagh had already advocated the idea of a peaceful order in Europe; in 1813 he gave the text to the British ambassador in Saint Petersburg, Cathcart, for use in negotiations.[43] Ever since his studies with Koch and Vogt, Metternich had entertained visions of a peaceful European order anchored in international law. In Chaumont, Metternich and Castlereagh were part of a fragile war coalition and confronted an emergency in which they were looking for more stability than a defensive or offensive alliance alone could offer. In their negotiations during the first week of March 1814, Metternich and Castlereagh lent a new quality to Metternich's negotiating tactics, which had been criticized up until that point.

The allies agreed that they would not cease cooperating before Napoleon was defeated. The contract adopted, verbatim, parts of their Teplitz agreement of September 1813. At the same time, they produced something entirely new by agreeing a "parfait concert"—a system that aimed to provide a foundation for general peace in Europe and under whose protection the rights and freedoms of all nations were meant to be guaranteed. The contract consolidated the Quadruple Alliance. It set out the troop numbers and subsidies that were to be provided. The main goal, according to the contract, was safety from France. That included mutual assistance in case one of the members was attacked by France. The contract gave as its objective the formation of a defensive alliance "with the purpose of maintaining the balance [*l'équilibre*] in Europe, of guaranteeing the peace and independence of the states, and preventing attacks, which have for so many years brought disaster to the world." The four powers therefore committed themselves for the next twenty years to meeting whenever the circumstances required it.

A secret article repeated in identical wording the war aims and the conditions for a peace agreement that Metternich had formulated in the instructions for the Châtillon congress, which again indicates the major part he was playing. The main focus was, again, on the fate of Switzerland, Italy, Spain, and Holland.

It also mentioned the constitutional formula for a Germany of sovereign princes and a federal tie that guaranteed its independence.[44]

Paul Schroeder rightly calls the Treaty of Chaumont a "vision." It imagined a Europe of independent and sovereign states that had the same rights, status, and level of protection, even if they were uneven in terms of power, responsibility, and influence.[45] Metternich had already implemented this model in October 1813 when he lured Bavaria out of the Rhenish Confederation. Whoever celebrates the treaty as a solely "British triumph"[46] misjudges Metternich's achievements in the course of its preparation, the actual formulations he contributed, and his part in the treaty's realization. As we have seen, Metternich's word meant a great deal to the tsar—more than that of Castlereagh. In his memoirs Metternich did not boast that he sealed the alliance; to Wilhelmine von Sagan, he revealed how unnerving Alexander's fickleness had been, how tedious and tiring their continual disputes. It would also be wrong, however, to assume that everyone simply did what he wanted. Instead, at Chaumont Metternich again used his talent for creating a consensus out of conflicting opinions through continuous argument and counterargument.

Metternich now saw himself on the road to a general peace: that is, not only to peace on the Continent but to a peace that included Great Britain and the colonies. That was the aim he had already announced in May 1813 through Stadion's mission to Reichenbach. All in all, Metternich understood that this was an exceptional historical moment; the negotiations in Chaumont seemed unique in the annals of world history. The Quadruple Alliance had two faces. It worked toward a future in accordance with Metternich's, and Castlereagh's, political philosophy, and at the same time it was, as Metternich saw it, a medium for propaganda. Because of its moderate principles, the minister thought, it could "make the best impression on the European public."[47]

Metternich Isolated: The First Treaty of Paris, May 30, 1814

On March 19, the allies broke off negotiations with Napoleon, represented by Caulaincourt, in Châtillon. They considered their demands unfulfilled. Now the final battle of the great "world war" began. These decisive days marked a turning point; Metternich, for the first time since June 1813, was not the center of events at a time when decisions regarding strategy and war aims—even regarding the definitive result of the "world war"—had to be finalized. The closeness between Schwarzenberg's headquarters and the imperial Chancellery, which Metternich had up to that point thought desirable, now turned into a handicap, because after March 19 it exposed the imperial court to the extreme danger of falling into the hands of the enemy. It was forced to relocate continually.

On March 19, it moved from Troyes to Bar-sur-Seine; on March 21, it moved on to Bar-sur-Aube; and on March 24, it finally moved to Dijon. On the evening of that day, Napoleon spent the night in Bar-sur-Aube in the very house his father-in-law had left that morning, as Hardenberg noted in his diary.[48]

From Bar-sur-Aube, Emperor Franz and the ministers and diplomats witnessed Schwarzenberg's decisive victory in nearby Arcis-sur-Aube (March 20–21). This gave Metternich his last opportunity to influence events once more before his arrival in Paris on April 10. On March 23, late in the evening, the members of the alliance who had gathered at Bar-sur-Aube composed a "Declaration of the Allied Powers after the Aborted Negotiations of Châtillon."[49] This manifesto explicitly emphasized that the allies' intention was not conquest but the restoration of Europe on the basis of a just balance between the powers in terms of their size.

Schwarzenberg's military breakthrough allowed the allies to march straight on to Paris; Napoleon could no longer offer any resistance. Nevertheless, he could still pose a threat to the headquarters of the Austrian court. Schwarzenberg therefore recommended to Emperor Franz to move with his entourage to Dijon, which was within the reach of the southern army, and to wait there until it was safe. In his memoirs, Talleyrand reports that the Austrian emperor was going to Dijon, and not with the tsar and the Prussian king immediately to Paris. We may suspect that it suited the Austrian emperor not to be personally present when his son-in-law was toppled and his daughter, the French empress, was forced into exile.[50] Schwarzenberg, for his part, united his main army with that of Silesia and, together with Friedrich Wilhelm III and Alexander, marched toward Paris.

From March 25 onward, the following personages were assembled at Dijon: Emperor Franz, Metternich, Castlereagh, Aberdeen, Hardenberg, Humboldt, and Stein. Metternich found himself transported from a theater of war into a peaceful and idyllic rural landscape. The foreign visitors, he wrote, received a wonderful welcome in royalist Burgundy—not as enemies but as liberators. Having experienced the cruelty of war, he was moved by the sights of ordinary life: an ox cart drawn by four animals, a cock with twelve hens, and a peasant woman spinning on her doorstep. Within twenty-four hours the city changed its appearance: the tricolor cockades were replaced with white ones, the color of the Bourbons.[51]

In this remote place, far away from the world, Wilhelm von Humboldt tempted Metternich into reflections on the different ways in which people experience happiness and love. While writing his letters, the minister fell into a romantic longing for Wilhelmine von Sagan, to whom he described the peaceful idyll of Dijon. To his wife, Eleonore, he depicted similar images of life in a rural place, and declared how much he loved and cared for his family. And with a fatherly devotion he corresponded with his seventeen-year-old daughter, to whom he also described Dijon.[52] He also sent her the declaration of the allies of March 23 and told her about the developments in the war. His love for his lover, for his wife, and for his daughter contrasts with the love life that the pioneer of classical education, Wilhelm von Humboldt, recommended to Metternich. Every evening at seven, Humboldt told him, he received a young woman from the city who stayed until six in the morning. While he was busy with writing tasks in his study, she was sitting in the next room. "And she is writing as well?" Metternich innocently asked. "No, she is watching the fire in the fireplace. Afterward we sleep with each other, and she is really charming." Humboldt was of the opinion that Dijon was more beautiful than any other city in the world because its ladies were so forthcoming. Metternich drily remarked: "If the world goes under—assuming it makes him an offer while doing so—Humboldt would be content. I am surrounded by a number of people who are no less happy about some other things—everyone according to his own taste, his enjoyment, and what makes him happy, but many of them are more reasonable than Humboldt."[53]

During the two weeks of their enforced isolation, Metternich, Castlereagh, and Hardenberg met regularly for meals and conversations in which they began to discuss the problems that the Congress of Vienna would have to solve. They concerned in particular the future of Italy and of the Duchy of Warsaw. They eagerly awaited news from individual battles, and with particular excitement news from Paris. They knew that Alexander, along with Friedrich Wilhelm III and Schwarzenberg, had been in the capital since March 31. They also knew that Swedish Crown Prince Bernadotte had sent a messenger to the tsar in order to "advise" him on the peace—"his [Bernadotte's] intrigues in Paris," is how Hardenberg referred to this in his diary.[54] Metternich had every reason to suspect that Alexander might renege on the allies' agreement regarding the question of the successor to the throne.

After Napoleon's marshal Marmont had handed over Paris on March 30, Alexander entered the city and went straight to Talleyrand's palace, where he also took up residence. The allies were altogether uncertain about what to expect in Paris after their troops had taken the city. At how many conferences had they rehearsed what might happen? Would there be a Jacobin revolution? Would the population show solidarity with Napoleon if he succeeded in presenting himself as the savior of a nation surrounded by enemies? And what would become of the throne? Could one take the risk of making Louis XVIII the successor to Napoleon, given that he was the younger brother of the Bourbon Louis XVI, who had been beheaded in France? Would civil war break out between Napoleon's followers and the ultraroyalist Bourbons? And was it true that the French were tired of war?

In fact, the allies could rely on a practically omniscient advisor. Talleyrand's hour had come. From this point onward he held the reins—fortunately, Metternich would have said, because he was the most experienced and probably the only man in the French political elite who knew how to handle the transition from the Napoleonic empire to a monarchy in a peaceful way. He had connections everywhere: with Napoleon's men; with the Bourbons; with the state authorities, especially the crucial Parisian Senate; and with the allies. He was regarded by all as an authority, and he knew the steps that had to be taken. The tsar, in his naivety, believed he could use Talleyrand, whereas in fact it was he who became a pawn in Talleyrand's politically subtle game. Talleyrand encouraged Alexander to write a public manifesto. Although the tsar had not asked Emperor Franz for his agreement, he boldly claimed that he was speaking in the name of the allies, and he had 1,000 copies of a declaration pinned to the walls of houses across the city. It proclaimed that the allies would "no longer negotiate with Napoleon Bonaparte, nor with any member of his family, but that they will recognize the Constitution which the French people were going to give themselves."[55]

Talleyrand made sure that the Senate would see this declaration, and he used it in order to introduce a motion to dismiss the emperor and reinstate the Bourbons, if with some constitutional guarantees. Following a nominal vote on the motion, the Senate decreed this on April 1. Among those in favor, there were senators who had also voted for the execution of Louis XVI.[56] The Legislating Body (as the assembly of delegates from the regional *departements* was called) confirmed the vote, and the high imperial offices, first of all the Audit Court and the Court of Cassation, changed sides. The accession of Louis XVIII to the throne could now be presented as a result of the free decision of the French people. On April 4, Napoleon's most faithful generals—Ney, Macdonald, Lefebvre, and Oudinot—presented the emperor with the draft of his resignation, and he signed it.

The tsar again suggested Bernadotte as a possible successor to the throne, but Talleyrand was able to persuade him—in line with Metternich's thinking on the matter—that if France wanted a military man at its head, it might as well keep the one they had at the moment, as there was none better. The Bourbons were therefore the only candidates. In his memoirs, Talleyrand tells us the real reason he favored the Bourbons: as a former marshal in Napoleon's army, Bernadotte would have had far less influence in the expected peace negotiations compared to the Bourbons, who had a legitimate right to the throne. Talleyrand wanted to retain as much as possible of France's international importance.[57] The French Senate recognized this and charged Talleyrand with forming a provisional government, allowing him to complete the change of the political system by implementing the decrees it had passed. On April 11, Napoleon, Austria, Prussia, and Russia ratified the Treaty of Fontainebleau, in which the *empereur* resigned in his name and in the name of his family. The immediate relatives of the emperor were allowed to keep their titles and received rich appanages. Napoleon received Elba, which was elevated to the status of a sovereign principality, and Empress Marie Louise was given the Duchies of Parma and Guastalla. The document of April 11 was also signed by Metternich and Hardenberg.[58]

The two politicians, however, had only arrived from Dijon on April 10. Alexander's actions had taken them by surprise. Metternich was convinced that it would be impossible to keep a character like Napoleon confined to Elba, given how close it was to the French mainland. He therefore requested a consultation with Schwarzenberg and Castlereagh prior to the signing of the contract. But because the tsar had already committed himself in public, he again treated the matter as one of personal honor. At the same time, he threatened that war would break out again immediately if the contract were not accepted. In his memoirs, Metternich formulated in very diplomatic terms his judgment on the conference preceding the signing of the contract, saying that he would always count it "among the most remarkable scenes of my public life."[59] In his correspondence, he was more direct: had he arrived in Paris three days earlier, he would have prevented Elba. But as things were, he found that Alexander had "done many silly things and behaved like a pupil who has escaped his teacher. The teacher is back, and now it will get better again."[60] In another letter, he was even more outspoken about Alexander: "This is the biggest child on earth! He has begun to turn what is good into something bad. Now, we shall have to repair a lot, but we shall still have to suffer from the maladies caused by the first moment when he had escaped us!"[61]

In the weeks that followed, Metternich sat in meetings from morning until the evening working out the peace treaty. And when it came to defining conditions for Europe, these continued into the night. Metternich saw only two alternatives for the shape a peace could take. It could be motivated either by vengeance or by the "perspective of the greatest possible political balance among the powers." The latter meant moderation, because it was the only way to secure a lasting peace in Europe. This was also the reason Metternich discarded the "system of conquest." It is illuminating that, when looking at the future order, he spoke not of a system of restoration but of "the establishment of the system of restitution and equivalents [equivalent compensation] in the reestablishment of kingdoms and states."[62]

The first Treaty of Paris of May 30, 1814, ended the Napoleonic system of contracts: all rights to sovereignty, of supreme rule, and possessions outside of the
borders of French territory were declared legally invalid.[63] The authors of the
contract wanted "to eradicate all traces of the unfortunate events which had burdened their people." In this, we may recognize Metternich's influence. In two
complementary articles, he explicitly added that the Treaty of Vienna (1805) and
the Treaty of Schönbrunn (1809) were now also legally invalid. The Treaty of Paris
also announced that it created the basis for a "future congress" in Vienna.

The Bourbon dynasty was reinstated, but it found itself at the head of a state
that had changed completely. The major redistribution of ownership that had
taken place since 1789 remained untouched. Files, maps, and documents of all
kinds that had been removed from archives all over Europe under Napoleon
had to be returned to the relevant states at once. The stolen artworks, by contrast, remained in the Louvre. France did not have to pay any reparations to the
allies. The borders of the French state were those of January 1, 1792. National
estates from the left bank of the Rhine that had been sold—among them those
of the Metternichs—remained the property of the buyer.[64]

Only six weeks after the Bourbons had been returned to the throne, foreign
troops had withdrawn from French soil. The text of the treaty, however, also
contained regulations that went beyond France. As far as the German states
were concerned, the formula that Metternich had first suggested in Langres in
January 1814 was retained, although the famous and much-cited article 6 no
longer spoke of sovereign princes but only of independent states that were to
be united by federal ties. The treaty declared the independence of Holland
under the rule of the House of Orange and the independence of Switzerland.
Italy partly became Austrian again, and the remainder became sovereign states.
Malta was placed under English sovereignty. The colonies were divided up according to the distribution of January 1, 1792. The stipulations regarding the
distribution of the colonies took up more space than those pertaining to Europe: France was clearly meant to continue being a "global player" alongside
England and Russia.

METTERNICH'S SECOND VOYAGE TO ENGLAND AND PREPARATIONS FOR THE CONGRESS OF VIENNA

Public Perception of Metternich in London

On March 26, 1794, a young prospective diplomat and student of political science and imperial history had stood at the port of Oostende waiting for the
regular crossing to England—a simple traveler on a Belgian government mis-

sion. Twenty years later, on June 5, 1814, the same man—now one of the most important politicians in Europe—sailed from Boulogne on a royal frigate that the British prince regent had sent especially for him and that was to bring him to Dover. His name—Metternich—was widely heard in political circles. The frigate belonged to a fleet of seventeen warships under the command of Rear Admiral Duke of Clarence, the younger son of King George III, and later King William IV. The fleet carried the sovereigns of the Treaty of Paris, Tsar Alexander and King Friedrich Wilhelm III, and their ministers, across the channel for a state visit.[65] Metternich was there as a representative of Emperor Franz.

Metternich was humble about this turn of events, although he did refer to his elevated status by describing the honors he received. In high spirits, he described to his wife how, upon landing at Dover, he received the same treatment as the sovereigns. There were daily articles about him in the newspapers. When he left the palace of the prince regent at midnight of June 10, people in the streets followed him, pressed up against his coach, and shouted: "Hurray Prince Metternich forever!" The people wanted more than just to see him; they wanted to touch him, wanted a handshake, and all of a sudden there were three hundred hands all over his coach. The coachman was thrown from his seat, and Metternich fled to his accommodation to save himself from being crushed "by love."[66]

Metternich used the celebrations, rallies, appearances, and parades in London through which the ruling European aristocracy celebrated itself as welcome material for the press at home. He personally wrote articles for the *Wiener Zeitung* in which he cited as one of the reasons for the journey to England that Austria wanted to thank the country for its enduring support and participation in the liberation of Europe. Between June 22 and July 17, the *Wiener Zeitung* reported on the state visit almost daily, under the heading "Great Britain." This would have given Metternich the opportunity to present his own role in the work of liberation in a flattering light. Instead the paper almost exclusively reported on the sovereigns, and when it came to Metternich, mentioned only his arrival and departure and his trip to Oxford. It reported that the British prince regent had been awarded the Order of the Golden Fleece for his achievements; Metternich had personally conferred it. Emperor Franz, in return, received the Order of the Garter, the most exclusive and respected honor of the United Kingdom. *The Times* of June 10, 1814, carried an article on the award of the Order of the Garter to the emperor in recognition of the "powerful contribution of his arms to the common cause," confirming the excellent state of relations between the two countries, as the now preferred choice of words had it—after a long time during which Austria's closeness to Napoleon had been regarded very critically by British politicians.[67]

A special gesture of appreciation was the award of an honorary doctorate to Metternich by the University of Oxford. He arrived in Oxford on June 15 and the following day was awarded a doctoral degree in *jus civile*. Metternich described Oxford to Eleonore with the same admiration he had felt twenty years earlier, as an extraordinary place that he also counted among the most beautiful. With all the old monuments still intact, he wrote, it was as though one were back in the twelfth century.[68] The thirty colleges lent the place a peculiar character. Some of the walls had been built under King Alfred, others under the Norman kings, and in the way they were inhabited and maintained, they appeared as though they had just been built. To complete the illusion, the professors and students, he said, were dressed in unusual attire of a kind one did not see on the Continent. He himself had been given an enormous coat made of scarlet silk and a beret of black velvet.

In this outfit he received the doctoral degree from the university, in the presence of Tsar Alexander, the king of Prussia, Wellington, and Blücher. The whole ceremony struck him as magnificent. It took place in an enormous Gothic hall with galleries for the spectators. The prince regent was sitting on his throne with the sovereigns seated on either side of him. All the doctors were lined up on cushioned benches and the chancellor of the university was standing on a podium. When it was Metternich's turn, the master of the ceremony ad-

The Dean and Chapter of Christ Church, with the gracious permission of His Royal Highness the Prince Regent, request the company of *Prince Metternich* at dinner to-day, in Christ Church Hall, at *five* o'clock.

June 15th, 1814.

Invitation from the Dean and Chapter of Christ Church for dinner on June 15, 1814, the day before the award of an honorary doctorate to Metternich in Oxford.

dressed him in Latin and conferred the degree upon him. The whole auditorium erupted in cheers.

England Still the Role Model; Metternich Works on the "Great Plan"

Metternich was overwhelmed by the effect the British metropolis had on him, just as he had been twenty years earlier. It appeared the most unusual city in the world to him, as little comparable to other European places as Beijing. Beyond London, Metternich again made excursions to other parts of England. He was amazed by the richness of both the culture and the vegetation. The meadows stretched like carpets; the fields seemed to him like flowering gardens enriched by huge trees of very different shapes and small houses that could be seen everywhere across the plains. And nowhere did he see any beggars or poor people. Farmers went on horseback.

But Metternich also used his time in London as an opportunity to further pursue his great plan for an order that would guarantee lasting European peace. For here the ministers of the four major powers who had won the war were all present: Metternich himself, Hardenberg, Castlereagh, and Nesselrode. At his audience with the prince regent on June 9, Metternich was promised what he had wished for from his journey—namely "influential consequences for the next steps in the development of political matters." As far as their other commitments allowed it, the four ministers met for conferences. Metternich made the case for presenting a united front at the forthcoming peace conference, and worked on the central issues of the future of the Duchy of Warsaw, the fate of Saxony, as well as the "balancing of German matters." The four powers should at least not part before the main principles had been clearly articulated. The Polish question caused Metternich headaches because of the "unparalleled inclination to be lenient" that the Prussian king was showing toward the tsar. Metternich's impression was that the various English opposition parties were strongly preoccupied with the Polish question. Most of them, he wrote, were in favor of restoring a kingdom, but none was in favor of its unification with Russia.[69] In London, too, it was the tsar who made it impossible to reach more detailed agreements and commitments on the fundamental problems.

In London, Metternich and Hardenberg also met for bilateral discussions in order to find a common position on the future of Germany, even before the actual negotiations were to begin in Vienna. They paid special attention to the goal of "ameliorating the situation of the subjects in the smaller despotic states of middle and southern Germany."[70] The two agreed that by August, Austria and Prussia would have formulated a "definitive plan for a German

Constitution" and would then include Hanover, Bavaria, and Württemberg in the discussions.[71]

Among the questions discussed in London there was one that particularly worried the allies: Was the new regime in Paris strong enough to resist any attempts at a coup? Before his departure for London, Metternich had urgently advised the emperor "that we should retain a respectable military attitude at least for some more weeks. . . . Only if we remain armed will we be able to avoid complications."[72] Ultimately, everyone doubted the stability of the French regime, and it was therefore agreed that they would remain "on a war footing"; every power was to hold 75,000 men in reserve. Napoleon's "hundred day" return the following year proved them right, and proved the wisdom of the four powers' keeping their armies at the ready. Metternich also considered it desirable to have "the largest possible" military presence as a trump card at the forthcoming negotiations in Vienna. In the future, he expected to be busy primarily with the "battle against the mad ideas of the Russian emperor."[73]

At their conferences, Metternich, Hardenberg, Castlereagh, and Nesselrode agreed on a start date of October 1 for the Congress of Vienna. This would allow the tsar time to travel to Saint Petersburg before the congress. On the English side, it was important that Parliament was not sitting, so that Castlereagh would be able to attend. Metternich had already developed very concrete ideas about how the congress was to be organized; as far as possible, he wanted to leave nothing to chance. In London, the four ministers thus agreed the following: The four great courts had to arrive in Vienna ahead of the congress on September 10 in order to settle the distribution of territories. They would be asked to present their plans to the monarchs by September 27. Metternich recommended to the emperor that he should also be in Vienna from September 10 onward; as the only monarch present at the preliminary talks, that would give him a very welcome home advantage.[74]

At the opening of the congress, Metternich told the emperor, he would suggest forming a committee of seven members selected from the body of plenipotentiaries. They should represent the powers that agreed the peace with France on May 30, 1814: Austria, England, Russia, Prussia, Sweden, Spain, and Portugal. The committee was then to develop a "general organizational plan" for the agendas at the congress. Here, Metternich described his wishes rather than reality: he thought that the four main powers could reach an advance agreement so that they would be able to control and thus accelerate proceedings (given their majority within the committee of seven). Metternich's greatest worry was again that the tsar might "go astray" and irritate people—if that did not happen, he wrote, the whole congress would be over and done within the space of six weeks.

Metternich's Strategy of Creating Sympathy for Austria

In contrast to the tsar, Emperor Franz had not traveled to London, in part because he was afraid that he might encounter public animosity on account of his apparently friendly previous relationship with Napoleon. In London, however, the tsar and his sister Katharina, who accompanied him, were surprisingly aloof, and they took every opportunity to commit faux pas. As a result the mood at the English court and among the public became more favorable to Austria. The tsar caused further anger by visiting the estranged wife of the prince regent, who now moved in the circles of the Whig opposition. He also played down the role of the British in the victory over Napoleon and publicly criticized the government, despite the fact that it was very popular. In the face of this tactless and arrogant behavior the prince regent fell out with the tsar completely. From Metternich's perspective, this discord could be used to Austria's advantage.

As early as June 8, Metternich had been received by the prince regent, who treated him "with the most exceptional kindness." It now paid off that in 1794, at the age of twenty-one, he had established an exceptionally close and trusting relationship with the then crown prince, who had been a controversial figure among the public. By now he ruled as the prince regent because in 1811 his father, George III, had been declared unfit to govern on health grounds. After George III's death in 1820, his son ascended the throne as George IV. In 1814 he was therefore merely the de facto ruler. It was all the more important that Metternich was able to use his trusting personal relationship with him in order to again raise the issue of the role that Austria played in British foreign policy.

The extent to which Metternich succeeded in this was confirmed by the prince regent himself, who on the day of the tsar's departure revealed his anger to Metternich: "If your emperor would have come here, England would have seen a prince, while at present it is being shown the spectacle of a barbarian from the north who is unfortunate enough to act the part of a Jacobin of the political middle ground. I see that Tsar Alexander wants to do me harm; I should pay it back to him ten times over."[75] Metternich thought that he had noticed a swing in public opinion: all the political parties appeared to favor Austria, England, and Prussia uniting in order to keep Russia and France reined in. For him, that was the ideal situation, and in Vienna he wanted to make sure that it would last throughout the next epoch. This hope was later significantly dampened, however, by Prussia's desire to occupy Saxony.

Diplomatic Work Prior to the Vienna Congress

On June 30, Metternich traveled with Hardenberg from London to Paris; he finally arrived back in Vienna on July 18. He used the whole journey from London to Vienna to gain strategic allies ahead of the congress. Originally he had planned to return directly to Vienna, but the impressions he got from the conferences of the ministers in London had persuaded him to include a few days in Paris in order to meet Talleyrand. Talleyrand shared his basic idea of the major powers exercising self-restraint within a European Concert, a fact that had made him an uncomfortable critic of Napoleon. Metternich wanted to confer with King Louis XVIII regarding the arrival of the French plenipotentiary—that is, Talleyrand—at the congress. While in London, the four ministers agreed that they did not want him to arrive in Vienna before September 20, so that they could have negotiations among themselves before-hand. This calculation of Metternich's did not work out in practice. But his audience with the king on July 6 at least had the effect of bringing the king closer to the Austrian position and distancing himself from the Russian court. Met-ternich saw Russia as politically isolated: "I was entirely content with the king in every respect."[76]

During his return trip from London, Metternich also urged Emperor Franz to push forward the Italian situation in a way that served Austrian interests. He had seen to it that there was "provisional occupation" of those Italian states whose fate had already been determined in the Paris treaty or earlier treaties between the allied powers. The emperor was now to give orders to the effect that the temporarily occupied states were to remain under Austrian influence. Nothing spoke against taking definitive possession of the provinces between Po and Ticino, Metternich wrote.[77]

Metternich considered the two southern German kingdoms of Württemberg and Bavaria as important strategic partners in the federal reorganization of Ger-many. From Paris he therefore traveled via Stuttgart and Munich, where he met with the kings of Württemberg and Bavaria, trying to win over the two courts in the run-up to the congress.[78] He called the relationship with Bavaria the "only fixed point of reference in our relationship to Germany." That was an astonishing judgment, given the previously hostile relation between Aus-tria and Bavaria. The Habsburg Monarchy, despite being a multiethnic state, wanted to remain integrated into "Germany," but it did not look toward Prussia as support for this policy. On June 3, 1814, in Paris, Bavarian field marshal Count Wrede and Metternich had signed a convention that again guaranteed the vested rights of the Bavarian state. Metternich considered the time between the Treaty of Paris and the opening of the Congress of Vienna to be a "very

Metternich's proposal for a cross of honor to be awarded to Austrian
soldiers (1814).

dangerous second period." He feared that in the course of those long months
the "definitive arrangement for Europe may become unstable again." Russia
and Prussia would use that in order to return to their old ideas and might possibly try to influence Bavaria as well.[79]

Symbolic Domestic Politics

Overall, Metternich's activities following the first Treaty of Paris suggest a well-
calculated strategy that sought to remove any conflicts between the major
powers in the run-up to the congress and thus get closer to achieving his overall
goal. He also practiced symbolic politics at home in order to create the right
"public mood." He aimed to consolidate the population's loyalty to the monarchy. Metternich proposed new military and civil medals of honor, to be cast
from the iron of captured enemy cannon, in the shape of a cross surrounded
by a laurel wreath, bearing the inscription: "PRO PATRIA SALVATA 1813 [or
1814]." Metternich wanted to confer 100,000 crosses on soldiers. The civil medal
was to be awarded only rarely: a hundred in silver and two in gold (Metternich

had originally suggested 200 golden crosses to the emperor). Military and civil authorities were to nominate candidates for these honors. Metternich also arranged the public announcement of the honors in an official article in the *Wiener Zeitung*.[80]

Further, Metternich wrote a speech for the emperor, addressed to the delegates of the provincial assemblies of the estates. The speech recalled the twenty long years of sacrifice and suffering. The delegates, it said, had been from time immemorial pillars of love and steadfast loyalty of his people. The speech invoked the firm connection between the monarch and his people and expressed thanks in particular for the enduring loyalty of those provinces that had temporarily been torn away from the empire and were now reunited: "Love the state whose members you are. Love your fatherland. Trust your monarch and never forget that common welfare is the only purpose of my life." With these words, the monarch reminded the addressees that he was the connecting center of his complex, multiethnic state. The wars of liberation had produced enough examples of speeches in which monarchs had addressed themselves to their "people." Metternich was cautious when it came to such propagandistic gestures out of fear that he might thereby arouse the impudence of those addressed. Thus, he explained to the emperor: "I have kept this speech short because feelings never find long-winded expression, and because it is always risky to go too deeply into questions when faced with delegates of the people, something one should not lose sight of, in particular in our times."[81]

All these activities were steps on the way toward the goal Metternich wanted to achieve at the forthcoming Congress of Vienna. What exactly this goal was, he revealed in the description he gave Eleonore of the character his welcome ceremony in Vienna should take: "Nothing military, because we no longer decorate ourselves with soldiers, but altogether peaceful. My festivities shall cast a light ahead on twenty years of peace."[82]

METTERNICH, THE WAR, AND VIOLENCE IN POLITICS

We shall now interrupt the chronological tour of Metternich's life for the first time and take the opportunity to look at a specific theme from an elevated position that allows us to take a wider view. Altogether, there will be four such interruptions, dealing with the topics of war, women, economics, and political rule. Because all four play a part throughout his life, their meaning for Metternich becomes clear only when one adopts a synoptic view, a view that looks back as well as ahead, and thus allows one to see what is essential. The end of the great "world war" is an opportune point to pause and ask what war actually meant for Metternich. In the existing biographies one looks in vain for a chapter on this question. How did he react to the human suffering caused by this method of disciplined physical destruction? In the case of Srbik, the absence of such a chapter is not surprising, because to Srbik bellicosity is the sign of a strong will and the power of affirmation in an exceptional political character—a "leadership figure" [*Führergestalt*]. Had this misinterpretation not exerted such influence, we might have been content to take note of it and leave it at that. Where Metternich appears in the context of a larger historical narrative, authors tend to continue to rely on Srbik's judgment, adding to it the view of Metternich as a superficial courtier. Thus, in an important recently published account of Napoleon's fall we read: "Metternich was also surprisingly unaffected by the horrors of war," a statement accompanied by judgments regarding the chronic hypertrophy of his ego, his self-centeredness, and his vanity; in addition, the author claims that Metternich was "not highly intelligent."[83]

Was Metternich capable of empathy at all, then? Did he take the other person seriously in conversation; did he show honest, impartial interest and curiosity? In person, he frequently surprised his visitors with his integrity and unpretentious conduct—that is, the total absence of any vanity. In those times, Americans traveling on the Continent were the most likely to remark upon aristocratic and arrogant behavior and social conceit. The American George Ticknor wrote of his meeting with Metternich that he "listened with great readiness" to all he had to say, "for he is eminently elegant and winning in his ways." He answered eloquently and behaved in such an informal manner that he even invited his guest to stay for dinner. This is how he treated a card-carrying Republican whose judgment of Metternich was almost ecstatic: "The Prince was consistently courteous to the last, followed me to the door with kind compliments, and then, turning back, ceased, I dare say, in five minutes, to think or remember anything more about me, as Sancho says, than 'about the shapes of the last year's clouds.' I take him to be the most consummate statesman of his sort that our time has produced."[84] In addition to Ticknor, we could mention many witnesses who confirm his view, including, in particular, opponents and critics of Metternich who were surprised by his integrity and friendliness—such as Carl von Rotteck, Ludwig Kossuth, Honoré de Balzac, and Louis Blanc.

It cannot be denied that Metternich described and thought of himself on certain occasions as the "savior of the world." A historian, however, should not make use of these statements independently of their concrete contexts, as if the one who uttered them were making a universal claim. And unless you are a follower of Napoleon, he was, in a certain sense, even right to make the claim. But—and this is an important point—he expressed himself in these terms only in private, in fact secret, correspondence with his (female) confidantes, who knew that Metternich kept an inner distance from everything: other human beings, political matters, even himself. His addressees therefore heard an ironic undertone in his pompous self-descriptions. These were never intended for the public, which as a rule fails to notice such irony because it sees only the literal text and does not know its author well enough.

In the case of Metternich's attitude toward war, we are faced with a similar problem regarding sources because he expressed his views hardly ever in diplomatic contexts but almost exclusively in his private letters to his wives, daughters, and lovers—letter that are kept in the family archive. Those who are sensitive to the issue of gender within the writing of history will take note of the fact that Metternich usually revealed his feelings to women. What would have happened had he revealed such empathy in the presence of the kind of men praised by Srbik, Metternich knew from Napoleon's reaction when he had the courage to point out to him how many hundred thousands of lives his wars had cost.

But a chance discovery has caused historians writing about Metternich to think again. A hitherto little noticed letter of June 28, 1813, sent by Metternich to his wife Eleonore from Dresden, led Munro Price to conclude that Metternich possessed more admirable qualities than had previously been thought: "These were a basic humanity, and a view of war and its effects very different to Napoleon's."[85] When Metternich wrote the letter, he was still reeling from his conversation with the French emperor, the battle of words in which Napoleon had been "swearing like a devil."[86] To Eleonore, Metternich declared that it was impossible to form a picture of the misery and horror that Dresden had witnessed since the last battles. There were more than 80,000 dead and wounded Frenchmen alone. All suitable houses had been turned into hospitals. Then there were a further 25,000 wounded and sick in Dresden and the surrounding areas. The bridge across the Elbe was covered with palisades and cannon; the mall between the "Weißes" and "Schwarzes Tor" was filled with artillery units.

In Metternich's mind, the picture of horror was made utterly grotesque by its juxtaposition with a parallel illusory world of harmony: "Meanwhile the Japanese garden" of the Palais Marcolini, where Napoleon was staying, "is filled with the most beautiful roses." This illusion of harmony was further heightened by the park's orangery, where the emperor had put up his theater company, made up of the same actors and using the same stage settings as in Saint Cloud, his home. The emperor had Racine's *Phèdre* performed in Dresden, as he had had Voltaire's *Oedipe* performed in Erfurt before, and continued to pursue his inclinations toward moving in the fantasy world of costumes and antique empires. In his efforts to undo his previous calculated bursts of rage, Napoleon declared in the ninth hour of his dispute with Metternich: "that I [Metternich], of all human beings on earth, was the one that he loved most, and that if we declared war on each other tomorrow, he would not love me any less." From his time as ambassador in Paris, Metternich was familiar with Napoleon's oscillations between brutal threats and generous compliments, between the horrors of war and the intimate trust within the court and family clan. We can rest assured that Metternich's contradictory experiences of the Napoleonic lifeworld in Dresden confirmed his idea of Napoleon's split personality. Writing to Eleonore about the rose garden, he revealed to her what he inwardly felt but outwardly knew how to hide: "I went in there for a moment and could easily have wept over these continual upheavals that are called the histories of empires."

Against the backdrop of these critical remarks on the sources, Metternich's dismay and horror at the human suffering of soldiers and the civil population during wartime appear genuine. This becomes even clearer when we look at his attitude not as the result of a momentary mood, expressed in a single letter, but as a part of his moral core, a part that also influenced his politics. The details of this unknown side of Metternich deserve to be known more widely, and we therefore shall for the first time present a synopsis of the most important statements he made about his experience of war.

During the last weeks of August 1813, Metternich spent the better part of each day on the battlefields at Dresden and Kulm. He revealed his feelings and thoughts to Wilhelmine von Sagan:

> It causes horror, but I love it to expose myself to great terror as much as to true beauty. Ten thousand dead soldiers on the battlefield do not have the same effect on me as one wounded soldier on his bed. The effect of the former is that I regret not to be among them, and produces an abysmal hatred in me against the being who, in the service of a delusion and out of the most undignified feelings, has the throat of hundreds of thousands of people cut. I believe, my friend, that my deep feeling that I am called upon to end this great tragedy will be fulfilled. For years now, this idea has not left me. It has been the driving force in all of my political actions. I have sacrificed everything for it—everything a human being can set his heart on.[87]

With these sentences, Metternich characterized himself as a strategist and visionary who spent many years pursuing the ultimate goal of breaking the politics of Napoleon's inhuman system and installing an enduring peaceful order. Ten years ago, he wrote, he had begun to lay the foundations for this great order, while his predecessors had still been busy destroying the state. For many years he had worked in secret. Peace had not been established yet, but the "hydra" had been struck—not only in her ten heads, but in her heart.[88]

In hindsight, the peace of 1815 appears to many historians as a mechanically engineered, logical conclusion to an epoch without any particular ideational substance of its own. For Metternich in 1813, however, engaged in a battle against a system that for two decades had seemed practically impossible to defeat, the desire for peace grew into a vision: a hope for a future that was anything but certain. This peace, to him, meant not only the absence of war but also the absence of despotism.

On October 20, 1813, after the Battle of Leipzig, Metternich was still conducting some minor negotiations in the city with the tsar and Crown Prince Bernadotte. Although he had a horse at his disposal, he could not make his way back to Köthen. Everywhere around Leipzig, he wrote to Wilhelmine Sagan, one had to step over the dead and, even worse, the dying. He hated the war and detested battle. He noticed, he said, how war numbed the soul and made the existential experiences of misery and deprivation impossible. His remark that this was the only positive thing about war sounds despairing.[89]

At the end of October, Metternich followed Schwarzenberg's headquarters, which moved to Fulda along the same route Napoleon had taken with the sad remnants of his army: "His army disintegrates; the roads he takes are marked by the dead, by hunger and misery." A stretch of ten miles, he wrote, was strewn with the dead bodies of humans and horses, and mixed in with them the living, who got down on their knees in "worship (because this is the only fitting expression for it) in front of the old head of the Holy Empire which the barbarians want to destroy. Ask the people of Fulda who is the successor to Charlemagne."[90]

But during the continuing campaign toward the Rhine, things got even worse:

> Even a character that was less easily and quickly affected could only be repelled with horror and dismay when looking at the main road from Leipzig to Frankfurt. You cannot take ten steps without coming across someone dead or dying, or someone captivated whose face looks worse than those of the dead. Dear God, this man has no right to reproach you, who sacrificed the blood of so many millions out of a vain feeling of misguided fame. How is it possible that, having witnessed a scene like this just once, he does not have to move away from himself in horror! And—Napoleon has equally covered the road from Moscow to Frankfurt with wreckage.[91]

Because historical accounts place such enormous importance on the Battle of Leipzig, it is forgotten that Napoleon continued for another six months to leave a trail of destruction in his wake. Metternich witnessed this in December on his way from Frankfurt to Offenburg: "Along this way you find everything that has been invented by hell to cause misery to human beings and travelers, a class of people who are unhappy at the best of times. Across this exceedingly narrow country road there are strewn heaps of pontoons, cannon, and boxes."[92] On his way across the Rhine into France, the atrocities of war continued to follow Metternich. The difficult traveling conditions in a carriage during a bitterly cold winter, the demanding negotiations between monarchs, ministers, and the headquarters, the lack of sleep, all exhausted his psychological and mental energy. While in Chaumont, he described his state thus: "I hate the war and all that it brings with it: the killing, the pain, the muck [la cochonnerie], the pillaging, the corpses, the amputations, the dead horses—and also the rape."[93] His worries deprived him of sleep. A lot came together: serious discord with the tsar; the series of victories won by Napoleon in mid-February 1814, which almost led to an offer of a truce because Alexander and Blücher had deviated from the agreed strategy.[94] This brought Metternich to the edge of despair, and he was seized by a deep depression: "My thinking is concentrated on one point. I let the moments that are no longer pass by and drift into the future. My friend, in the end tears came to my eyes."[95]

On his way to the next conference in Bar-sur-Aube, the atrocities did not stop: "I got here fairly quickly. The road is covered with dead horses and dreadful things to such a degree that I would have preferred to travel even faster. The incessant spectacle of destruction is horrific and hurts my heart. Heaven did not build me for war, or maybe it has after all: if I were a general I would support it strongly so that I would end it quickly and not begin another one for a long time."[96] Metternich witnessed the worst destruction outside Troyes; it reminded him of the parts of the southern German landscape that had repeatedly been visited by French troops since 1794:[97]

> There is no stretch of land, no house that would still be intact; no upright tree, no horse, and I would almost say no human being that is not dead. There were four battles on one single country road; everything was geared toward killing, and no one takes care of burying. It is a nasty thing that war! It sullies everything, even the imagination, and I fight hard that this may not happen to me. This is why I work for peace, ignoring all the yelling of the stupid and the fools—I want peace fast and a good one.[98]

It is noteworthy that Metternich perceived the nature of war as a gender-specific phenomenon and explained it as the result of an anthropologically based peculiarity of men. He also observed how the war changed the psychology of the soldiers in a peculiar way. This is evident in these words, directed to his daughter Marie: "If all the world were like us, my dear Marie, there would be no war. It is a pretty evil thing to experience, but unfortunately it follows from human nature: among thousands of dead or wounded, you can see the troops dance and laugh, and complain if three days pass without battle."[99] Metternich's lover Dorothea von Lieven indirectly confirms this gender-specific perspective by declaring that a military upbringing would be incompatible with Metternich's character: "What an ugly [*vilaine*] necessity soldiers are! How inhumane these mechanical movements look, to lift the right foot when, really, one wants to move away to the left! What a wonderful aim in life to spend it like that! I bet you never had the idea to become a soldier, not even when you were a little child; even then you had too much intelligence [*Geist*] for that."[100]

So close was Metternich to war and the havoc it wreaked, and so dramatic his writing about it, that we may compare the horror and empathy evoked by his words to that we find in the contemporaneous *Horrors of War* series of prints by Francisco de Goya. Without taking sides, the painter took the motifs for his horrific images from the Spanish theater of war between 1810 and 1814, and represented war as a human catastrophe independent of the question of whether the victims or perpetrators were Spanish or French. In the context of war, Metternich showed himself to follow an "ethics of conviction," in Max Weber's sense, and to be a person driven only by humanitarian impulses. But as a statesman he was not allowed to simply follow his basic feelings; instead, he had to react to the war that had been imposed by Napoleon in accordance with an "ethics of responsibility." How did he do that, either during the wars of liberation or, to look ahead, in the policies he pursued in international relations after 1815? The classical author on the theory of war, General Carl von Clausewitz, coined the well-known phrase: "War is merely the continuation of policy by other means."[101] This had been uniquely and ruthlessly demonstrated by Napoleon in the way he constructed his continental empire. In their Dresden conversation, Metternich was therefore right to tell him that, for the French emperor, any peace agreement was nothing but a truce on the way to the next campaign. Metternich would never have signed up to Clausewitz's dictum because he considered war to be the result of radically misguided politics. In 1824 he illustrated this with regard to an area he thought to be the most crisis-prone in nineteenth-century Europe: the Ottoman Empire and the part of the Mediterranean over which it ruled, especially the straits at the Bosporus, the Balkans, and the so-called Levant—the historical Syria and Palestine. In this area, between the 1820s and 1840s, the interests of the major powers Russia, France, and Great Britain conflicted. The first focal point was the Greek question, and, at various conferences between 1824 and 1832, the powers tried to find a strategy for preventing war over the matter.[102] Metternich commented as follows on the explosive situation, which threatened to descend into war:

> War can only be the result of enormous mistakes, and Mr. Canning [the British foreign minister], who does not want one either, may lead us there. War would mean the loss of the social body [*la perte du corps sociale*] of Russia, of Austria, of the whole world. The war—the only one conceivably happening—would not be one in which the people simply see Russian and Turkish rivalries, and expect that it will mutually produce wounded soldiers and foster or fight against prejudices ... No, my friend, this war would be one of those great natural catastrophes [*des grandes catastrophes de la nature*] that turn everything upside down. All elements would clash and upon meeting crush everything between them, that is, Europe as a whole. But it will not come about, unless Mr. Canning would play the deus ex machina which sets this great work of destruction and death in motion. He is capable of it.[103]

In this passage, Metternich anticipated the "great seminal catastrophe" of European civilization, triggered by clueless politicians who believed that they could contain a war within the limits of a local crisis but slid inadvertently into a conflict that they did not want.[104] The later British prime minister Lloyd George thought the Great War started because the powers "slid into" it. Metternich, in 1824, did not simply invoke an imaginary catastrophe but based it on hard political realities. In 1853 this was borne out by the way the Crimean War erupted and pulled in the major powers. In historical accounts, this war is described as a "world war that was not fully executed and fought."[105]

Because during Metternich's times the Habsburg Monarchy did not pursue any expansionist policies, it considered the threat of war purely as a means for avoiding war, not for making territorial gains. In the context of the aforementioned Greek crisis, Metternich professed, "*Si vis pacem para bellum* [If you want peace, prepare for war] everyone understands. ... This saying, and nothing else, have I applied throughout the whole history of the Greek affair, but only in the way of negotiation. This men do not understand. I have filled my diplomatic arsenal, completed and trained my troops, not in order to come to war, but to prevent it."[106]

In Metternich's view, conflicting international interests are not the only cause of war. His experiences with the French Revolution taught him how to detect powerful bellicose motives in ideologies of liberation. Violence in the service of a just cause meant that the reasons for war were partly to be found in the thinking of the actors. For them, the ends justified the means, and this prepared the path toward revolutions and attacks on politicians and monarchs. Terrorism—intentional intimidation through unpredictable violent attacks—was also part of the modern arsenal; Metternich already used the concept. In his mind, this kind of action related to the category of the "Jacobin." The Jacobin still believed he was acting as a cosmopolitan. In the post-Napoleonic era, this type mutated into a holy warrior inspired by nationalism, as exemplified by, for instance, Carl Ludwig Sand. Metternich was aware that the legal system would be destroyed if every individual were free to take up arms on the basis of his or her subjective conscience. With respect to the assassin Sand, he made the following judgment: "I find it repugnant when murder is committed in the name of philanthropy; I have no liking for madmen and mad deeds of any kind, and even less for those who threaten the life of good people who sit peaceful in their chambers." In the same letter, he clearly expressed his pessimistic analysis of the times: "The world is sick, my friend; there is nothing worse than an ill-advised thirst for freedom. It kills everything and in the end itself."[107]

Before the outbreak of the revolution in France in February 1848 and the ensuing revolution in Germany in March, Metternich wrote about revolutionary violence: "Revolutions march fast! This saying invariably reminds me of that young, very popular poet [Gottfried August] Bürger in Germany: *The dead ride fast* [*Die Toten reiten schnell*] in his ballad 'Leonore.'"[108]

In Metternich's case, coming to terms with the war meant considering the suffering he had witnessed endless times on the battlefields and along the roads—unnecessary, pointless, even a crime, caused by human delusions of grandeur that, he thought, could pull down the walls protecting civilization and the law (as he understood it) at any time and in any place. It was the duty of politics to erect enduring barriers against this possibility. Only if one understands Metternich's fundamental experience of a European war that lasted more than twenty years as the force that shaped his life will one understand him or his political goals after 1815. He opposed this catastrophe on humanitarian grounds, and his lasting commitment was: "never again." That fundamental experience determined everything for him: his attitude toward revolutionary acts, attacks on monarchs, calls for violent action in the press, and secret organizations and associations that conspired to subvert the law. It is easy to accuse Metternich of repression, but it is difficult to ignore his experience of how a civilization can collapse.

8

THE END OF AN ERA AND A NEW BEGINNING FOR EUROPE

The Congress of Vienna, 1814–1815

THE INITIAL SITUATION: THE EXPERIENCE OF WAR AND A LEGAL VACUUM

War, and nothing but war, battles, and battlefields, mountains of corpses such as the world had never seen before: that was what politicians had to bear, and depending on how they had digested it emotionally or intellectually, it was a burden or trauma, or it acted as a warning that a better future could not be taken for granted. A war worse than the Thirty Years War lodged itself in the memory of a whole generation, members of which set off to the Congress of Vienna in order to dismantle and rebuild what was left of Europe. Today, we are quite shortsighted when we look back at the nine months of negotiations and celebrations in Vienna—with the slogan "the Congress dances" in our heads. This phrase, to the present day, evokes memories of the popular German UFA film for which it provided the title. As a musical comedy from the early days of the talkies (1931), of which an English and a French version were also produced, it gives the impression that the Congress of Vienna consisted of nothing but grand ballroom scenes and glorious melodies, love affairs and intrigues.[1] We overlook how deeply the experience of war and destruction determined the actions of those affected, both of those who wanted to save parts of the past and of those who wanted to build something new. The American historian Paul Schroeder reminds us that, proportionally, the Napoleonic wars had cost Great Britain more casualties and more resources than the Great War.[2] This means a lot, given that the Great War left deeper traces in the British cultural memory than the Second World War.

Over September and October 1814, the delegations arrived in Vienna for a congress the likes of which the world had never seen. At the major peace congresses in the early modern period, diplomats and envoys had met for protracted negotiations that were often carried out in written form. But now the monarchs and their ministers appeared in person at the meeting and were therefore able to reach definitive conclusions in a much shorter time, even in the case of complicated questions. The Congress of Vienna, however, was not actually a peace congress, because peace had already been agreed upon in the Treaty of Paris of May 30, 1814. What, then, was its purpose?

The usual picture of the devastated landscape left behind by Napoleon shows only half of the truth, because he had not only led wars and destroyed countries but also built a new legal and constitutional order in Europe. In France, the Constitution of the Consulate, with Napoleon as first consul, formally was valid between 1799 and 1804, followed by the Constitution of the Senate of 1804, when Napoleon became emperor. Napoleon had annexed territories of other states as departments of the empire (Catalonia, Illyria, Tuscany, the North Sea coast, including the Hanseatic cities, Belgium, Holland). He had created model states according to his political principles, such as the Kingdom of Westphalia. The Metternichs had personally been driven into exile by the French and witnessed how they annexed Belgium from the Habsburg Empire and then turned the Dutch States General first into the central state of the Batavian Republic, and then into the Kingdom of the Netherlands. Napoleon replaced old European dynasties such as the Bourbons (Spain, Naples), the Houses of Orange (Holland) and Habsburg (Tuscany) with rulers from his own family or his general staff. With the Rhenish Confederation—whose supreme protector he was, and for which he created its own Constitution—he made the "third Germany" (apart from Prussia and Austria) a part of his empire. The Duchy of Warsaw and Switzerland were connected to him in similar fashion. Almost all European powers had officially recognized him as emperor, and many of the ruling dynasties had established family ties by marrying into his family—including the rulers of Bavaria, Württemberg, Baden, and finally the Habsburg dynasty through the emperor's daughter. All of Napoleon's wars ended with bilateral peace agreements that became part of the corpus of contemporary public law. His empire, built around him as a person, represented a system of states founded in international law, and it also permeated the societies of the states in the form of the Code Napoléon and the model Constitutions of the satellite states—at least this was the intention. The wars Napoleon fought together with his allies not only asked the allies to make severe human and financial sacrifices. They also provided rich territorial gains for them. As a result, the territories of Bavaria, Württemberg, Baden, Saxony, and Warsaw were repeatedly extended. Napoleon was aware that his empire rested entirely on his person, such that, when he died, it would become subject to the equivalent of the Wars of the Diadochi.

In 1813–1814, this whole system collapsed within half a year. An autocratically based state order disappeared, much as the German Democratic Republic and the surrounding Warsaw Pact countries disappeared in 1989–1990. It is necessary to have the concrete problems created by this situation in mind when we attempt to understand the task the Congress of Vienna had set itself. Only then will it be possible to see why more-recent historical accounts have dropped the idea that "restoration" was the goal of the Vienna System.[3] This political battle cry from the Bern state law jurist Karl Ludwig von Haller could at best pull wool over the eyes of the losers and dreamers and assure them they would get back what they had lost: the Catholic Church, its theocratic regime within a reconstituted Holy Roman Empire; the imperial counts and knights, their dominions; the imperial cities, their independence; and so on. "Reconstruction" or "restitution" were the concepts used at the time, and they come much closer to the reality of the matter. "Reconstruction" entailed the element of a potentially continual constructing and building. "Reconstruction" [*Umbau*] seems to be the most fitting concept, because it denotes building on existing foundations and at the same time the integration of new elements.

The collapse we have described above created a state of limbo. Did the territories that were formerly ruled by Napoleon exist in a legal vacuum? The rulers and ministers of the states of the Rhenish Confederation, in particular, were exercised by this question. Was what they had appropriated under Napoleon still legitimately theirs? And were the inhabitants on the west bank of the Rhine allowed to keep the possessions that they had acquired from the French "national property"—that is, from the dispossessed estates of the aristocracy and church? Metternich, himself dispossessed, was acutely aware of this limbo, and he repeatedly summed it up as "the difficulty of erecting a society on new foundations, when the old are destroyed."[4]

THE "COSMOPOLITANS": INSTIGATING A NEW LAW BASED
ON IMPERIAL LEGAL ORDERS

The "Metternich Generation" and European International Law

"A world picture loses its world"—this is Wolfgang Burgdorf's pithy characterization of the process that took hold of Europe between 1789 and 1815. The world that was disappearing was the old Europe, which we may roughly indicate with the keywords "ancien régime" and "Enlightenment" as its intellectual coordinates. Burgdorf's formula also suggests that the experience of a vacuum was typical of the historical experience at the time. At this threshold point, the exciting question was: Who would put what, and with which means, in place of the old world? If we want to understand the Congress of Vienna, we need to be familiar with the thinking and the fundamental assumptions of the important politicians who took part. Many of them were not even aware of their "categories," as Kant would have put it. A historian, by contrast, must establish the axioms followed by those who steered the Congress of Vienna.

Even in very recent publications on the occasion of the congress's two-hundredth anniversary, the architects of the Vienna order of 1815 are criticized for not having based their work on the foundation of nation-states. They are charged with not having respected the will of the people and of having proceeded solely by haggling over territories: "The Congress of Vienna of 1815 created an altogether deficient Europe in which the Italian, the German, and the Polish questions, and the question of the Balkans, were in the end all solved by war. The post-revolutionary, post-Napoleonic order and restoration was the real seminal catastrophe, not the Great War. The Great War was waiting to happen because it broke up something that had been ill-conceived: the system of the Congress of Vienna."[5] Such admonishing of the politicians at the time, however, is an unhistorical retrospective projection of later perspectives onto earlier events.

The intellectual imagination of 1814–1815 was tied to the historical epoch into which these politicians had been born. The generation of the two antipodes—the "Generation Metternich" and the "Generation Bonaparte"[6]—dominated the Congress of Vienna. The members of this generation were born around 1770. They shared the experience of the Enlightenment, the ancien régime, the French Revolution, and more than two decades of world war. From the perspective of global history, the politicians at the Congress of Vienna acted under the impression of a recent worldwide political as well as social and economic crisis that had grown out of a world war, which had just ended. Following Napoleon's attempt at universal domination, what was to be brought back into balance, and what could be brought back into balance, was the system of empires to which the other European states had to adapt. That was the pre-given structure. There was no other basis on which to act. Which of the politicians present would have conceived of an alternative order? Only on the premise of an imperial order could there be a guarantee that a peaceful European order and a European international law could emerge. The politicians who dominated the congress had in mind a "European law of a pre-national character," a uniting idea of a "public law of Europe." Palmerston, Cavour, and Bismarck

only later pushed through the new doctrine of "international law" as a law between competing nation-states. This law was no longer negotiated in a collective and collegial way at the imperial level of congresses. It was fought over *inter
nationes* in the context of mostly militant competition between nation-states.[7]

The Vienna order was possible only because the reconstruction of states was
not subjected to the national principle—in contrast to Woodrow Wilson's
"fourteen points" of 1918. The decision makers at the Congress of Vienna all
belonged to a cosmopolitan generation. Wilhelm von Humboldt was born in
1767; Emperor Franz, in 1768; Castlereagh, Wellington, and Napoleon (as it
were, a virtual participant), in 1769; Friedrich Wilhelm III and George Canning, in 1770; Schwarzenberg, in 1771; Metternich and Dalberg, in 1773; Tsar
Alexander, in 1777. Born earlier were Hardenberg (1750), Talleyrand (1754),
Stein (1757), and Friedrich Gentz (1764). But they all practiced politics against
the backdrop of the old European empires.

Empire as the Basis for Negotiations

At the same time that historians started to study eighteenth- and early
nineteenth-century processes of globalization, they also started to become more
aware of the pre-national foundations of the transformations during the saddle
period [*Sattelzeit*][8] between 1770 and 1830.[9] These foundations were the empires. If we consider the period between the French Revolution and the Congress of Vienna as a whole, then all major powers competing during that time
were empires: Great Britain, Russia, the Habsburg Empire, the Holy Roman
Empire of German Nations, the Ottoman Empire, and also France if we include the French colonies; the exception was the monarchy of the Hohenzollern. Four of these empires, Austria, Russia, Prussia, and England, called
the shots at the Congress of Vienna.

If we keep in mind the imperial character of the political orders at the time,
it becomes easier to understand why the congress reconfigured the world according to the size of populations and territorial expanses and not according
to "nations." We may summarize the difference between empires and modern
centralized territorial states in five points:[10]

1. Blurred territorial boundaries: As a rule, empires lacked precise borders;
at the edges, they faded into open space. We can easily visualize this in the case
of the tsarist empire, the Ottoman Empire, and Great Britain, who extended
themselves into the vast spaces of Siberia, the expanses of the Sahara, and the
almost infinite space of the seven seas, respectively.

2. The absence of concentrated rule: From the center to the periphery, there
was diminishing integration. In other words, empires were not hierarchically

organized around a center. Toward the periphery, the legal integration became weaker and so did the ability to respond to the center's policies and to have a say in their formation.

3. Multinationality: The tendency toward integrating the population did not take the form of granting all members of the empire identical rights, independent of their location in the core area of the state or in border regions. They enjoyed different rights that established their specific status. This enabled the empires to be multiethnic or multinational.

4. Composite states: An empire did not unite political units with equal rights; rather, it was characterized by gradations of power and influence. Imperial structures were sometimes superimposed on the political orders of several states, and sometimes they tied states as client or satellite states to the center.

5. Accidental emergence: Empires existed in the "longue durée," within the temporal horizons of whole epochs. They owed their existence to "a mixture of coincidence and individual decisions," not to a single imperial impetus or a great strategic plan. The maxim of the Habsburg Monarchy, to expand the empire through convenient marriages, expresses this vividly.[11] But there was also the belligerent route—such as the never-ending sequence of Russo-Turkish wars in the eighteenth and nineteenth centuries. In that case, two geopolitical neighbors continued to attack each other without a need for any master plan to bring this about.

These were the premises that the politicians attending the Congress of Vienna had in mind—not ideas about a "spring of nations," or a much-needed *risorgimento,* or a hoped-for national unity in freedom. In 1815 these concepts were untimely, because they would have put into question the whole existing world of states, something that was inconceivable because no one knew how to construct a "nation-state." The vague designs for a nation suggested by people like Stein, Arndt, Jahn, or Görres were ideological confessions rather than practicable political programs, because they entirely bracketed the question of national borders, which would have been the central topic in 1815. Thus, they ignored issue of the intractable conflicts that would thus have been created. In 1848–1849, when the attempt was made to found German, Polish, and Italian nation-states, the question of nationally defined state borders quickly led to bloody conflicts over Schleswig, Posen, Bohemia, and northern Italy. The interests represented at the Congress of Vienna were those of the victorious major powers, who were not looking for new conflicts but wanted and needed to consolidate their states and Europe. But who actually had the power to create law? Who had the last word on which topic was discussed and decided in a particular committee?

Imperial Dominance at the Congress

Who actually called the shots at the congress became clear very quickly when a decision had to be taken about how the congress was to work. This was uncharted territory because there was no precedent for a diplomatic conference of such dimensions, where ministers and, in the background, their monarchs operated, and which was confronted with such a complicated network of problems left behind by the Napoleonic empire. Territories, countries and people, the law and future wealth: everything was at stake.

From the very beginning it was clear that the four victorious powers were demanding the right to set the direction and pace. The first meeting of the great four took place under Metternich's auspices in Vienna on September 16, a week later than had originally been planned in London. Hardenberg only arrived the following day. In several strictly secret meetings at the Chancellery at the Ballhausplatz, the first decisions on how to proceed were taken. Present at these meetings were Nesselrode (Russia), Hardenberg and Humboldt (Prussia), Castlereagh (Britain), and Metternich (Austria), men who knew each other from many months of close contact and who had grown into what Reinhard Stauber called their "role of main decision makers." They embodied the normative core of the congress.

After his arrival in Vienna on September 23, Talleyrand was the one who explicitly raised the question of how the congress would go about achieving a consensus. On September 30, he attended another secret meeting of the four powers in Metternich's Rennweg villa. Metternich had invited him in order to inform him about how the preparations were progressing. Talleyrand's appearance was a perfect display of his fine diplomatic skills. He called Metternich a new Mazarin or Richelieu who, together with his allies, sought to rule the universe. That was a clever polemical point, with a truth at its heart, because the allies, indeed, wanted to control everything at the congress and steer it from above.

Talleyrand called into question their whole approach by making himself out to be the advocate of the allegedly less powerful states. In this, he pursued the obvious tactic of also elevating the role of France as an outsider. He rightly claimed that, following the Treaty of Paris, it was wrong to continue excluding him from the inner circle. In modern terms, he initiated a discussion about whether the congress should be organized in a "bottom-up" or "top-down" fashion, himself pleading for the former. At the Rennweg meeting, he was indignant at talk of the "allies," on the grounds that a peace had been agreed to. He demanded that a plenary of the congress participants be called, and that this general assembly would decide upon the formation of committees and questions of principle. The eight powers who had signed the Treaty of Paris, he argued, were not the whole body of the congress but only a part of it. Talleyrand also wanted to see the principles of public law adopted as guidelines for the negotiations.[12] He spoke for the hopes of many rulers from small- and middle-sized states, former imperial counts, and church dignitaries at the congress. Metternich decidedly rejected the idea of subjecting the major powers to the majority vote of an *assemblée délibérante* [deliberating assembly]. Talleyrand made concessions only when Metternich threatened to call off the congress, signaling therein what he considered his role to be. Talleyrand completely accepted that role by subsequently suggesting Metternich as the head of the negotiations *(présidence de cette assemblée)*.

Ultimately, four levels of interaction emerged:[13]

1. The conferences of eight, chaired by Metternich: They dealt with matters pertaining to the whole of Europe. The eight members (Austria, Prussia, England, France, Russia, Sweden, Spain, Portugal), as the signatory powers, turned the Final Act of the Congress into valid international law.
2. The conferences of the five—namely, the former allies and France: They were the actual power center of the congress and dealt with the most difficult questions—territorial questions. Gentz called them "the only and real congress," "the center and seat of all matters."
3. The German committee, chaired by Metternich: This was the only body that consisted exclusively of German members (Austria, Prussia, Hannover, Bavaria, Württemberg), and it was charged with drawing up a federal Constitution. On October 16, Metternich presented the Austrian-German draft Constitution. In May 1815, after an interval of several months, the committee was extended to include the other German states. At the beginning of June, Metternich urged a speedy conclusion, and on June 8 he chaired the final reading of the German Federal Act.
4. Twelve special committees, which were points of contact for the various lobbyists who had come to Vienna.

The congress had various streams, and mastered what Reinhard Stauber called a "multi-centric working mode" with surprising efficiency. The complex procedures in commissions and at conferences, which partly took place in parallel, were successfully translated into resolutions. The congress's crowning achievement was the collection of all individual results in one final document, a Treaty on General Peace *(Traité de la paix générale)*. The act kept Metternich at the Chancellery until the evening of June 9, 1815, when he oversaw the initialing of the document while the other congress participants were already heading to the battle against Napoleon, who had returned from Elba, or back to their headquarters. The Final Act of the Congress of Vienna retained its binding force for the European states at least until 1866—that is, until the end of the German Confederation and the exit of the Habsburg Monarchy from the arrangement of German states agreed upon in Vienna.

A Peace Congress in Metternich's Sense?

There is wide-ranging agreement among historians that the Congress of Vienna was not a peace congress, because a peace had already been agreed to in Paris on May 30, 1814.[14] It is seen as, at best, a "peace-instantiating congress" [*Friedensvollzugskongress*].[15] According to this perspective, no peace was agreed to in the conventional sense—as in, say, the Peace of Westphalia—because the congress did not end a war.[16] This, however, contradicts the understanding of the participants themselves. They distinguished between the Treaty of Paris, whose original title was *Traité de paix et d'amitié*, and the Treaty on General Peace *(Traité de paix générale)* or general document on peace *(instrument général de la paix)*.[17] Because the Treaty of Paris stipulated that an ensuing congress in Vienna should "complete the dispositions of the present tractate" (art. 32), the document of May 30, 1814—one might say—only represented half a peace, one that was basically incomplete. Only the Final Act of the Congress of Vienna turned it into a complete peace.

All this also fit with Metternich's political view of the world. From his perspective, only a peace treaty that took the place of the Napoleonic empire and did not stop at the Rhine could be considered conclusive. Given the vastness of the Napoleonic empire, the peace could not be a bilateral one between France and the allies, like the Treaty of Paris; it could also not be limited to the European Continent. It had to be general. The global perspective on peace was the only appropriate one for Metternich and his contemporaries, and it is the only appropriate one for historians today. Metternich had adopted this perspective as early as May 1813, when he included general peace as a long-term goal in his instructions to his ambassador Stadion. Two years later, he had reached that goal.

The negotiations at the Congress of Vienna were characterized by continuous discord. Friedrich Gentz, who took the official minutes of the congress, spoke bluntly of the "great battlefield" on which the principal powers met.[18] The negotiations that had been begun in Paris in May 1814 were seen, after all, as still to be completed, and as having various potential consequences. The major powers no longer looked to end the war by military means. They looked to do it by political means, although their disputes with each other took them to the brink of war, and even encouraged them to speculate on a new coalition—which would have been the seventh coalition—because the Napoleonic empire was not fully liquidated until a new order had been established on its territory.

A MASTER PLAN? METTERNICH BETWEEN REALPOLITIK, STRATEGY, AND VISION

Metternich's Approach

There have been doubts about whether Metternich had a master plan at the Congress of Vienna.[19] In order to form a judgment on this question, it is necessary to consider Metternich's character as a strategist and as a visionary. Following the collapse of the Napoleonic empire, Metternich had to master the political problem of finding a new foundation for the states of Europe and their relationships with each other. For Metternich, "politics is the science of the vital interests of states. Since, however, an isolated state no longer exists . . . we must always view the society of nations as the essential condition of the present world."[20] If we apply this to the Congress of Vienna, it meant that Metternich's task was to identify the interests of the states who took part or were represented, and then to moderate them, and constructively to combine them.

The term *vision,* in this context, denotes the long-term design for the future that, for him, amounted to a political "confession"—we have already discussed the origin and form of this political declaration of faith. A vision in this sense has a normative quality. In Metternich's case, this normativity was contained in the moral core of the principle of balance. The nature of the latter was not the oft-invoked "law and order."[21] For Metternich, who remembered the rule of the Jacobins and the Terror, those two requirements were obvious givens, meaning the absence of war and civil war. Metternich was convinced that without "law and order" there could be no freedom or wealth. By balance, on the contrary, Metternich understood the principle of solidarity and a balance between states on a shared legal basis. The desired balance entailed the possibility of forcing a state that sought dominance over the others back into the common legal framework.

The form in which the Vienna order was finally established fulfilled Metternich's vision. It was a European order based on shared laws and guaranteed by the eight signatory states. The Final Act of the Congress of Vienna represents a bundle of contracts that redefined the world of the European states—it has even been called the "invention of Europe."[22] The foundational Quadruple Alliance of the Sixth Coalition had created an instrument for intervening when the system was threatened. As late as 1853, Metternich retrospectively said that the Vienna order had fulfilled its purpose of preventing another great European war of the kind that had been possible before 1815.

Metternich's strategy was to work systematically over many years, and under changing circumstances, toward achieving his design for the future. So far, we have tried to demonstrate the systematic nature of his politics by looking at his own statements and actions. From the time Austria joined the alliance in June 1813 until the beginning of the Congress of Vienna in November 1814, Metternich took important steps toward developing and defining the "design" of the Vienna order. Even if he did not achieve all he wanted, he nevertheless decisively influenced how participants' room for maneuver was limited and hedged. This applied to France and the states of the Rhenish Confederation as much as to the allies themselves. It was Metternich who insisted that the allies reach an agreement on the war aims while at the same time never breaking off negotiations with Napoleon altogether. It is in large part thanks to Metternich that, after June 1813, the monarchs and ministers within the alliance were always in close physical proximity to each other, and, in an ongoing series of conferences, congresses, summits, and ad hoc personal meetings, worked on the fundamental questions that would later be addressed at the Congress of Vienna. The sixteen months leading up to the gathering in Vienna were one long stretch of conflict management and problem solving.

We therefore need to ask about the extent to which the solutions reached at the Congress of Vienna were predetermined at these earlier negotiations. Without going into the detail again of what had already been decided, let us briefly recall the places where negotiations had taken place: Reichenbach, Teplitz, Ried and Fulda (including the alliance treaties with Bavaria and Württemberg), Leipzig (where the central administrative council had been established), and Frankfurt (where most of the states of the Rhenish Confederation had joined the alliance, Saint-Aignan's mission had been planned, and the manifesto to the French composed). Finally, there had been conferences at Langres, Châtillon, Bar-sur-Aube, Chaumont, the first Treaty of Paris of May 30, 1814, and the discussions in London in June. On all these occasions, pieces of the Vienna puzzle had already been put into place. It was agreed to at Langres that the Rhenish Confederation would not continue to exist as a national umbrella organization; instead, a new "federal" tie would unite the individual German states. Apart from that, Napoleon's former allies were allowed to keep their possessions and sovereignty. The Netherlands was to continue to exist, extended by the incorporation of Belgium, which formerly belonged to the

Habsburgs. Switzerland had already been guaranteed the neutrality it craved so much. And the Bourbons were to return to France, Spain, and the throne of Naples.

Metternich's Role at the Congress

If Metternich—allegedly such a vain show-off—had wanted his achievements to be lauded by posterity, the Congress of Vienna would have been the ideal opportunity for him to ensure that this would be the case. In his memoirs, he could have presented himself in the glamorous role of someone of historical importance. Instead, once we get to the actual congress there is a striking gap in his memoirs. The run-up to the event, the "history of the alliances," takes up the greatest amount of space of all his reminiscences. They are followed by a few more pages on the "The Dawn of Peace." But, except for a couple of sentences, Metternich leaves out the congress—the most important event of his long political life, the place where he really had made world history. He was aware of that, but all he wrote about the event is one terse sentence: "The history of the Congress is written in its Acts and in its results, and has no place in these pages."[23] The editor of the memoirs, Metternich's son Richard, filled this gap only by including a report on the congress written by Friedrich Gentz in the second volume of the memoirs on which Metternich had commented: "Overall, the account is true to the facts," with the caveat, however, that Gentz was easily influenced by "changing impressions" and by his temperament, and so did not write with the requisite impartiality.[24]

It would be possible to fill a whole library with the books that have been written on the Congress of Vienna, and in the year of its 200th anniversary, in 2014–2015, a good few were added to it. We therefore need only sketch the framework conditions, the main moments, and the principles according to which the congress worked, with Metternich's role and importance at the center. For various reasons he was the guarantor of the congress's success, even if he could not ascribe it to himself alone—he had powerful and indispensable collaborators, among them his *ami* Castlereagh, whom he once described as his "second self." Careful consideration of the facts reveals that Metternich's character, intellect, and long international experience enabled the successful outcome of the congress.

In terms of his *character*, he provided the distance, composure, and polite openness toward everyone that we have already discussed. He was able to ignore personal emotions, and this allowed him to recognize the motivations behind another's actions. Even if his political relations with another person were confrontational or hostile, he always remained polite at the personal level.

He also proved this several times in the case of his encounters with French ambassadors, as with La Tour in Berlin, or later Saint-Aulaire in Vienna. The most striking examples are probably his dealings with Napoleon and the tsar. In contrast to the choleric Alexander, for instance, he never ended up in tight argumentative corners, felt that his honor had been violated by the impertinence of others, or went off into the proverbial corner to sulk. Derogatory judgments about Metternich are often the result of envy, and often of male rivalry or pure ill will, as in the case of the embittered Hormayr, who is still being used—or, more correctly, misused—as a contemporary witness in drawing conclusion about Metternich's role at the Congress of Vienna.[25] More reliable is the judgment of Metternich's colleague Nesselrode, who found in the thirty-three-year-old, apart from his polite manners, "more esprit [*Geist*] than in three-quarters of the Viennese excellencies."[26]

In *intellectual terms,* Metternich possessed the talent of being able to consider complex problems from the perspective of how they had developed—taking a historical approach—and then to disentangle them and infer from them the possible actions available. We have already come across his major "presentations" on questions that were vital to the Habsburg Monarchy as key examples of this capacity for conflict management. In this way, he was able to make the participants at conferences aware that they had a variety of choices, allowing them to weigh these and then make their decisions. This way of working through problems created the foundation on which compromises could be made, as Metternich proved numerous times after Austria had joined the Sixth Coalition.

Experience, finally, was the medium in which he mastered politics. Not only did he gather information on the history and contemporary condition of international relations from the files at the Chancellery whenever he took up a new post—as he did, for instance, before he went to Dresden and Berlin. He also made contacts wherever he could, while away or on travels, in order to learn more about a country, its customs, and its Constitution. The stations of his career so far suffice to document his rich experience—Koblenz, Strasbourg, Mainz, Brussels, Antwerp, London, Rastatt, Dresden, Berlin, Paris. In addition, there were, of course, stays at residences and central places in Germany, such as Frankfurt, Karlsruhe, Hanover, Stuttgart, and Munich. There was no other participant at the congress who had, over the course of twenty-five years, been so consistently present at the places where history was being made. Metternich had been in contact with members from all parties and knew their arguments from personal exchanges with them: the Jacobin commissaries of Robespierre; the glowing admirers of the French Revolution, such as his erstwhile tutor; ultraroyalist French emigrants, including their leader, the Prince of Condé;

ministers, diplomats, generals, and monarchs, including Napoleon, Tsar Alexander, and the British prince regent.

For the duration of the congress, right up until the completion of the Final Act in his office in the Chancellery on June 9, 1815, Metternich, in contrast to all other participants, had to be, according to Reinhard Stauber, "omnipresent." With regard to the areas in which he had to intervene most forcefully, either as disputant or as mediator, two sorts may be distinguished: There were *crises*, which resulted from antagonisms among the four allies and sometimes could affect the substance of the alliance. These topics always raised the question of dominance in Europe and required a form of crisis management, which then became part of the Vienna System. Then there were *conflicts*, which were discussed at a broader and lower level. The allies intervened in these only in part, and it was much easier to reach a consensus about them. The "German question" played a special role for Metternich because of his biography; it appealed most strongly to his own commitments to the traditions of the old Holy Roman Empire.

THE CONGRESS ON THE BRINK: CRISES TEST THE PRINCIPLE OF BALANCE

The Polish Question

Where serious conflicts emerged during the congress, the major powers had to practice the system of balance while they were still in the process of establishing it. That was the case, for instance, with regard to the Polish question. At Teplitz it had been agreed that it would be settled peacefully between Russia, Austria, and Prussia by restoring the status quo before the formation of the Duchy of Warsaw. After the successful campaign in France, however, Tsar Alexander no longer felt bound by this agreement and indicated that he wanted to turn all of Poland, including the Austrian and Prussian parts, into one state, which would then be incorporated into the Russian empire under his rule. In Metternich's and Castlereagh's eyes, this would have created a power shift significant enough to create a Russian hegemony over the Continent and thus threaten the Continent's independence.

It is important to remember that, in the European context, and especially within Austria, Metternich represented a minority position regarding the Polish question. He had condemned the divisions of Poland from the very beginning, and had already expressed this unambiguously during the first days of his political career in 1801. For him, they violated international law and political common sense, which suggested that a larger buffer state between the tsarist empire and the central European powers Prussia and Austria was desirable. As early as July 1814, upon his return from London, he mentioned to Archduke Johann: "What keeps Austria from setting free its Poles and guaranteeing a free king?"[27] At the end of October 1814, during the preparatory negotiations in Vienna, he recommended the full restoration of Poland to its state before the first division in 1772 and its being ruled by an independent sovereign. So did Castlereagh and Hardenberg. If the tsar believed that he would have to forfeit too much territory under this option, then an independent Kingdom of Poland was to be formed along its 1791 borders. Back then, Poland had given itself its own Constitution under Stanislaus Poniatowski.[28]

For Metternich, the fate of Poland was a topic that went to the root of the territorial problems in Europe. One option was that the provinces that belonged to the various powers who had divided Poland would be united as one independent state situated between the three major powers (réunies en un corps politique indépendant). Another option was to divide up the Duchy of Warsaw between the three powers.[29]

Given that people continue to claim that Metternich was a politician of restoration, it cannot be emphasized enough that he was not interested in keeping Poland divided. It was the tsar, with his ambition of expanding the Russian Empire, who thwarted Metternich's ingenious suggestion. But there was also Prussian resistance to it, because the renunciation of the Prussian parts might have triggered an interest in gaining other territories as a substitute. Jean Gabriel Eynard, an intelligent Swiss banker and observer at the congress, noted, after attending various meetings and gatherings during the weeks of December, that a war between the allies was being considered more and more likely. On December 26, his evaluation of the situation was especially bleak: "We are at a crucial junction which is of the greatest importance for the future peace [Ruhe] in Europe. The general affairs are in the worst possible state, and resentment begins to grow among the rulers. A war cannot be excluded, and on both sides [i.e., Russia and Prussia on the one hand, and Austria, Britain, and France on the other] the reasons for leading it multiply."[30]

The conflict between the tsar and Metternich regarding the Polish question had come to a head on October 24, 1814, in a dispute between them that lasted two hours. Metternich declared that he no longer wanted to negotiate with the tsar tête-à-tête. In Vienna it was rumored that Metternich, at one point, was not sure "whether he should leave by the door or the window."[31] The tsar, for his part, told Emperor Franz of his "decision to challenge [Metternich] to a duel."[32] Metternich had taken the precaution of immediately informing Franz about how little Alexander had been prepared to make concessions regarding the Polish question: "He was full of great words and assurances that his will would not change. It would be nigh impossible to describe all the nonsense he presented at this conference, and in form as well as expression it reminded me of the many earlier meetings I have had with Emperor Napoleon."[33]

This confrontation between the tsar and Metternich, which was by no means a one-off, suggests we should shift the emphasis when it comes to the question of who played the major role at the congress. So far, Paul Schroeder, who is more familiar with British than with Habsburg sources, has set the tone. According to him, it was mainly Castlereagh who determined the course of the negotiations. At a superficial level, Friedrich Gentz's statement regarding Lord Castlereagh seems to confirm Schroeder's view. In mid-February 1815, Gentz said: "He has been the most active and the most influential minister of all." But then Gentz qualified his judgment. Castlereagh, he said, lacked the energy to maintain his positions, and he had been "a little too cold toward Austria, and a little too warm toward Prussia and France." Metternich, in our view, would not have shared Gentz's judgment on the way Castlereagh distributed his sympathies. But for Gentz, the conclusion was that England, "although having held the first place at the Congress, has nevertheless played a part mediocre enough [*un role assez médicocre*] as to its results."[34]

Metternich, by contrast, was the only one who dared to confront the tsar head-on and who could persuade him to withdraw his unreasonable demands. As usual, Metternich made sure that he had the necessary allies. The tsar's wish to dominate was so extreme that he inadvertently brought into operation the system of balance that was still to be established. The crisis emerged when the Polish question became bound up with the Prussian intention to annex all of Saxony. At this point, on January 3, 1815, Austria, England, and France held a strictly secret meeting at which they agreed to a defensive alliance in order to confront the imbalance threatened by Prussia and Russia. Talleyrand was ecstatic, because from this point on he was admitted to the conference of the five major powers, something Metternich and Castlereagh pushed through "with a forceful advance" in the face of resistance from Alexander and Hardenberg.[35] Metternich applied his principle of threatening war in order to avoid war, and in the end the tsar gave in. It was agreed that an enlarged Duchy of Poland (but excluding the Prussian and Austrian parts) was to become the Kingdom of Poland, ruled in personal union with Russia, making Alexander at the same time the king of Poland, just as previously he had been the king of Saxony. But this "Congress Poland," as it would later be called, was to get its own administration and Constitution. It is noteworthy that it was Metternich who recommended the "constitutional form, which limits the Russian influence as much as possible."[36] The importance of the Polish question is clear from the Final Act of the congress, which opens with an article concerning Poland.

The Question of Saxony

The discussions on the Polish question, which continued over several months, concerned the redistribution of power in the eastern parts of central Europe, but this was part of the overall European situation. If Russia expanded into Poland, then Prussia, in a sort of "package deal," would extend toward Saxony and the Rhine.[37] The monarchy of the Hohenzollern wanted to regain its rights to its old territorial status of 1805. In Hardenberg's eyes, and even more so in Stein's, this provided sufficient justification for the annexation of Saxony. The fact that the king of Saxony, Friedrich August, had remained loyal to Napoleon for so long was only a pretext. After all, Metternich had enticed the Saxon king to leave the Rhenish Confederation with the convention of April 20, 1813, and had guaranteed his possessions, including military protection when necessary.[38] Without help from the coalition, which was only emerging at that point, the middle-sized state of Saxony would suffer a renewed occupation by Napoleon. But the king could hardly be blamed for that.

Metternich identified in Prussian politics a structural tendency toward "expansion" [*Verdickung*] and a tendency to develop into a "expanding system" [*Verdickungssystem*].[39] He had already seen this in the time of the old Holy Roman Empire, and he was right in his analysis: Prussia continually tried to grow at the expense of neighboring territories. In Vienna, this created a serious dilemma for him. He saw Prussia as an ideal geopolitical ally for counterbalancing the power of France and Russia, who were striving for dominance. At the same time, however, his own plans for the pacification of Germany required him to prevent Prussia from expanding at the expense of individual German states and so undermining the trustworthiness of the future federal association—the German Confederation. Only after tough battles between the five powers—including Talleyrand—and with a deeply disgruntled Prussia, was it possible to persuade the latter to be content with half of Saxony and thus to save the throne of the House of Wettin, one of the oldest German dynasties. In this case, too, the principle of balance proved itself to be capable of protecting the "less powerful," if only in part.

THE END OF THE HOLY ROMAN EMPIRE: THE HABSBURG EMPIRE AND THE GERMAN QUESTION

Restoring the Old German Empire under the House of Habsburg?

The enforced peace treaties of Pressburg (1805) and Schönbrunn (1809) meant that the Napoleonic empire had also made the Habsburg Monarchy smaller, although its losses were not as great as those of Prussia. The loss of Trieste and

Dalmatia, and with it of access to the Mediterranean, and the loss of the old Habsburg heartland of Tyrol, had hurt Emperor Franz the most. In 1815 the Habsburg Empire also had to be reconstructed, and alongside this issue was the question of whether the Holy Roman Empire should be resurrected under a Habsburg emperor. Earlier, in the spring of 1813, even the tsar had made plans for the restoration of the old empire under Habsburg rule, and his closest advisor, the imperial Baron vom Stein, for some time dreamed of reviving the Imperial Constitution of the tenth to thirteenth centuries. These prominent spokesmen were joined by the chorus of the "dispossessed" and "less powerful"—the old mediatized imperial estates.[40]

Emperor Franz and Metternich were well aware of the problem. Metternich's published "posthumous papers," unfortunately, leave out several pages of the original manuscript in which he explained why reinstating the old empire was not an option. His reflections on this are connected to Austria's joining the coalition in September 1813 in Teplitz. This fact is highly significant because it means that the question of the coalition at the same time decided the future shape of Germany, something that has not been known with such certainty until now. Metternich's unpublished recollections revolved around two arguments about the future of Germany, both of which excluded a new Roman-German empire.[41]

The *first* had to do with the question of what to do with the states of the Rhenish Confederation and other territories that had been annexed by France, once the war had been won. From the perspective of the allies, the resurrection of the Holy Roman Empire would have required either that the princes of the Rhenish Confederation be expelled from their recently acquired estates or that they be mediatized. In the case of expulsion, the countries would have had to be distributed among the allies; in the case of mediatization, the German territories of the princes would have been allocated to the newly founded central sovereign power. With this, the allies, Metternich wrote, would have put themselves "morally and materially" on the same plane as Napoleon by applying the principle of conquest. They would themselves have been practicing what they were actually fighting against. The conclusion could only be that the states making up the Rhenish Confederation had to be retained.

Every political body, Metternich wrote in a lecturing mode, is based on the principle of unity. But it is also necessary to respect the differences between a political body's individual elements. That, he wrote, was the foundation and guiding principle of "our plan" in 1813. This norm was one of Metternich's fundamental convictions and rested on the idea of composite statehood. It also found expression in his understanding of sovereignty. In the Holy Roman Empire, sovereignty had been divided between the emperor and the empire.

The princes, the imperial estates—to which Metternich, as a member of the old imperial estate of counts, saw himself as belonging—and the free cities possessed regional sovereignty. Through the dissolution of the empire, the princes of the Rhenish Confederation, however, had been given full sovereignty. Would the future members of a newly inaugurated empire, in particular Prussia, be prepared to give up the sovereignty they had acquired—"the most important of all acquired rights"—in order to approve of the "revival of the *privilegia Austriae*"? Moreover, Emperor Franz and Metternich could not forget the obstructionist politics practiced by Prussia and other imperial estates during the empire's war against revolutionary France, politics that had led a still-young Franz, in a letter to his envoy in Dresden, to threaten his withdrawal from the empire if the situation did not improve.

Metternich summarized the situation by saying that, with the end of the Holy Roman Empire in 1806, "the name of a German political body had disappeared from the map."[42] What had formerly been called Germany, for him, appeared to have disintegrated into four parts: the Austrian and the Prussian Monarchies, the states of the Rhenish Confederation, and the regions that had been incorporated into the French empire as *departements*. From the perspective of the emperor and Metternich, "the violence of facts" provided an answer to the question of "whether a German central political body should be called into life."[43] The experiences Austria had had in the wars of 1805 and 1809 left it feeling "deserted" and doubtful of the existence of any "*German feeling*" in Prussia, which, back then, had kept its distance. In Austria, the propaganda of the Prussian nationalists, who in 1813–1815 were so vociferous in their German patriotism, had, Metternich wrote, "no more meaning than a myth,"[44] and thus was not good evidence of a general sense of Germanness that would have included Austria.

The *second* arose in the context of the events of August 1813, when the coalition was thinking about its war aims. Metternich had already dismissed a restoration of the old empire at this early point: "The German Empire of a thousand years was dissolved in 1805 and 1806, and indeed, strictly speaking, as much from the want of inward vitality as from external influences. If earlier defects had crippled the strength of the Empire, its continuance had become a sheer impossibility by the results of the Regensburg mediation in the year 1803. Not only had the German Empire been extinguished in the year 1805, but the German name had disappeared from the map."[45] At that point in time, "the name [of Germany] itself had only a geographical value."[46] In concrete terms, the restoration of the Holy Roman Empire would have required the emperor to demand that the sovereign rights that had passed to the princes of the individual states be passed back to him. This would have been possible only by exercising compulsion, and "the moral consequences of this constraint would have been but an addition to the fundamental evils of the former state of the empire," namely "the unavoidable collisions between the sovereign head and the supremacy of the separate states."[47] All in all, such a reconstruction of the empire would have effected precisely what Metternich wanted to avoid with his idea of a new order: a discord inherent in the structure from the very beginning.

While in exile in London, Metternich was again confronted with the question of a German empire, which was at that point being planned at the National Assembly in Frankfurt. In a memorandum of August 1848, he emphatically warned the newly elected imperial regent [*Reichsverweser*] against it, reminding him of the historical situation between 1813 and 1815.[48] The "German question" never left him. In January 1849 he addressed the topic again, with particular intensity. In three different, highly edited drafts, he recalled the options that had been available between 1813 and 1815, and provided an explanation that—as far as I can see—has so far not been considered in discussions of the arguments against a German empire. In hindsight, Metternich saw four options for a future Germany: (1) complete independence of the German states after the dissolution of the Rhenish Confederation, (2) the creation of a new German empire under a common leader, (3) the unification of the members of the former empire in a federation of states, and (4) a "hostile assimilation of princely territories" into Austria and Prussia, directed against the former states of the Rhenish Confederation.

The last of these options had appeared altogether unacceptable to Metternich and the emperor. The first one had been prevented by the Treaty of Ried between Austria and Bavaria. The argument against the restoration of the empire was that "too many of the pieces from the collapsed edifice had been lost," and that it would have been impossible to reconstruct a similar edifice from the remaining ones. A "new empire" would have had to be erected and the joining of the coalition would have had to aim at conquests. Such an empire would not have been accepted by the other powers in the alliance—England, Russia, and Prussia. Because Metternich's strategy in Teplitz aimed at "the protection of a peace that promises to last," the Austrian system had to distance itself from the "system of the French emperor." The means for doing that "lay in the steadfast unity among the four allied powers. The German question, put as a question concerning empire and emperor, would not have been compatible with the concept of a unity between the powers, and would have made the fulfillment of the great task impossible *ab ovo*."[49] For Metternich, this analysis was as valid in 1848–1849 as it had been at the Congress of Vienna. At the congress, Russia, England, Prussia, and France would have opposed the

Habsburgs as a broader European power with its center in central Europe, and Metternich therefore ruled out this option from the very beginning.

The Continued Existence of the Holy Roman Empire in the Habsburg Empire

The emperor and his minister resisted the temptation to revive the Holy Roman Empire. Nevertheless, the Austrian Empire that came into existence in 1804 remained constrained by the history of and, most of all, its structural continuities with the Holy Roman Empire. This fundamental fact was to influence all Austrian decisions and aims at the Congress of Vienna. In this context, it is important to remind oneself of the shape of the Habsburg Empire, which is what Metternich did during the run-up to the congress.

An empire declares itself with its name. The "Empire of Austria" [*Kaisertum Österreich*] had been baptized on August 11, 1804. This seemed to be a step further into modernity for Austria; it had previously been an aggregate of many individual territories, each with its own laws, without a name for the overall structure. Metternich considered it altogether unusual for Europe at the time that a state should call itself after the ruling family, that is, the House of Habsburg. That would have suggested a hotchpotch of states held together only by the figure of the emperor. The "name of the 'Empire of Austria'" was chosen out of necessity and "removed the appearance that the parts were united to the whole and to each other only in a personal union."[50] Emperor Franz would have preferred to uphold the fiction that he did not possess supreme power but stood in bilateral relations with all of his sub-states. With the new name "Empire of Austria," by contrast, the empire claimed a rank equal to that of the Empire of Napoleon, which had been founded by the Constitution passed on June 4, 1804. The French centralist monarchy, decreed from above and hence only pseudo-constitutional, however, seemed to be the exact opposite of the historically grown unity of a monarchical state on a quasi-federal basis. The monarch was the capstone that connected all parts of the imperial edifice. Metternich described the new—and yet old—"Empire of Austria" so perfectly that his words are superior to any paraphrase:

> The Empire, without being a federal state, had yet the advantages and the disadvantages of a federal shape. If the *head* of the *House of Austria* was in the modern sense of the word *absolute,* this notion was restricted in its sovereign power, according to the different Constitutions of the several countries whose crowns he united on his own head. The greatest limitations applied to the large regions which belonged to the Kingdom

of Hungary and its other parts. . . . That this situation was a most peculiar one cannot be doubted; and it is no less certain that it would have
been untenable, if it had not been founded on the most important of
powers—namely, the interest of the different parts of the Empire in
being united. These facts, which were clearly seen by the Emperor and
myself, exercised a pervasive influence on the reconstruction of the Empire
in the years 1813 to 1815.[51]

Research into the early modern period has by now learned again to appreciate this kind of state order and has given it the somewhat complex but fitting
description of a "composite and complementary statehood" with "multiple
identities."[52] This old structure, which lasted until 1848, was also expressed in
the title of the ruler, which we shall give here in its old form—there being no
better way to invoke the complexity of the structure, which was quite distinct
from what was once referred to as the Habsburgs' "absolutism." The "Great
Title" of the emperor in 1806 was:

Wir Franz der Erste, von Gottes Gnaden Kaiser von Oesterreich, König
von Jerusalem, Hungarn, Böheim, Dalmazien, Croatien, Slavonien, Gali-
zien und Lodomerien, Erzherzog zu Oesterreich, Herzog zu Lothringen,
zu Salzburg, zu Würzburg und in Franken, zu Steyer, Kärnthen und Krain,
Großherzog zu Krakau, Großfürst zu Siebenbürgen, Markgraf zu Mähren,
Herzog zu Sandomir, Massovien, Lublin, Ober- und Niederschlesien, zu
Auschwitz und Zator, zu Teschen und zu Friaul, Fürst zu Berchtoldsgaden
und Mergentheim, gefürsteter Graf zu Habsburg, Kyburg, Görz und
Gradiska; Markgraf zu Ober- und Niederlausnitz und in Istrien; Herr der
Lande Vollhynien, Podlachien und Brzesz, zu Triest, zu Freudenthal und
Eulenberg und auf der windischen Mark.[53]

This "highest majestic k. k. title"[54] was used on those occasions when power
and dominion were to be represented and celebrated.

"My Italian States"

For the Habsburg Empire, the Italian states were comparable to the German
Confederation. Both were part of the legacy of the Holy Roman Empire. Even
before the Congress of Vienna, Emperor Franz made it clear that Italy was exceptionally important to him, also as far as the politics of the monarchy were
concerned. It was for him not only his birthplace—he was born in Florence in
1768—but also the place where he spent the first sixteen years of his life, until his
uncle, Emperor Joseph II, called him to Vienna. After Lombardy and Venetia

had been recaptured at the beginning of July 1814, he spoke to Field Marshal Lieutenant Bellegarde, who was operating in the area, of "his Italian states."[55] At this point, however, it was already clear for him that all of Italy belonged to the Habsburgs' "hegemonic sphere."[56] He had already stationed troops in the resurrected states: in the Kingdom of Sardinia, the Grand Duchy of Tuscany, in the Duchies of Parma and Modena, and in the Papal States, which were now again under the control of the pope. And he ordered that the states under the Habsburgs' protection had to provide for the soldiers.[57]

Given this initial situation, Metternich's tactic at the congress was to avoid making the fate of all of Italy a part of the negotiations.[58] He opposed the suggestion of forming a special commission, comparable to the one on the reorganization of Germany. As he saw it, only the emperor was entitled to make decisions on Italy, and the congress only needed to guarantee the restitution of the individual states. This is why we shall discuss what Reinhard Stauber called Metternich's "master plan for Italy" only when we come to look at the period after the congress. The emperor's guiding idea, which did not necessarily correspond to Metternich's, can be seen in the way in which the Italian states—as so-called secundogenitures, dependent territories—were provided with rulers from the dynastic sidelines. The emperor behaved toward the Italian states as a patrimonial power, using them to provide for his family members, not unlike Napoleon. Metternich had succeeded in getting assurances from England and France regarding the way Italy was to be restored. These were recorded in a memorandum of February 18, 1815,[59] which showed how the House of Habsburg was connected with the Apennine Peninsula through a dynastic network, which turned it—with the exception of the Papal States—into a patrimony of the Habsburgs. The following resolutions found their way into the Final Act of the Congress of Vienna:

- Following the expulsion of Murat, both Sicilian kingdoms were to be handed back to the Bourbons—namely, to Ferdinand I, whose wife was a daughter of Maria Theresia.

- Parma, Piacenza, and Guastalla provided for the former Empress Marie Louise, as had already been agreed upon with Napoleon in the Treaty of Fontainebleau (April 11, 1814).

- The pope was to be allowed to return to the reconstituted Papal States.

- Tuscany, enlarged by Lucca, Piombino, and Elba, was returned to the brother of Emperor Franz, Ferdinand III, about whom we have already heard in connection with Napoleon's wedding celebrations.

• Modena was to be ruled by Archduke Franz IV of Este, a grandson of Maria Theresia and cousin of Emperor Franz.

• The reconstituted Kingdom of Piedmont-Sardinia did not have a Habsburg ruler allocated to it, but had been connected with Austria since June 1, 1815, by a military treaty, in part for the purposes of fighting together against Napoleon.

After 1815, Italy became one of the main stages of Austrian politics. How Metternich came to terms with this strange composite statehood is a question we shall consider in Chapter 10.

"GERMANY—UNITED BY FEDERAL TIES": METTERNICH'S PART IN THE FOUNDATION OF THE GERMAN CONFEDERATION

"German Freedom" in the Context of Composite Statehood

The articulated nature of the Habsburg Empire mirrored that of the other great empire, the Holy Roman Empire. Both contained the person of the emperor and the imperial institutions, such as the Imperial Diet, the Imperial Chamber Court, and Aulic Council. And yet they represented two different powers and orders. Their rich historical legacies presented the peace negotiators of 1814–1815 with innumerable problems when it came to avoiding the collapse of the central European order. In all situations, Metternich's inner compass told him to defend what he first had called the "federal ties of the German nation." As an aristocrat and cosmopolitan with deep roots in the Holy Roman Empire, he retained a sense of patriotism and national identity.

In 1813, Goethe provided a felicitous description of the politically educative and freedom-enhancing quality of the old order: "The Constitution of the German empire resembled that of the Greek in the many small states it comprised. The least, inconspicuous, even invisible city, because it had interests of its own, had to nurture and preserve these within itself, and had to defend them against its neighbors. Thus, its youth were alerted and asked to think about political matters from early on."[60] Goethe had no problem in seeing himself as a German within a richly articulated empire, and he embodied a German patriotic attachment to the empire that existed long before 1789. It was not the case that people began to define themselves as German only from the time of the wars of liberation onward. Contemporaries spoke of the "old German freedom" in the "German Imperial Constitution." The cosmopolitan Goethe lived with the same national self-understanding as Metternich. Metternich displayed it on June 26, 1813, in Dresden, when Napoleon, in the context of his disastrous Russian campaign, had boasted: "The French cannot complain of me; to spare them, I have sacrificed the Germans and the Poles. I have lost in the campaign of Moscow three hundred thousand men, and there were not more than thirty thousand Frenchmen among them." Metternich's retort was: "You forget, sire, that you are speaking to a German."[61]

There are certain spiteful judgments of the Holy Roman Empire, such as the one of the frustrated, resentful Bavarian servant at the Chancellery, Karl Heinrich (Knight of) Lang, who characterized the old world as a carnivalesque historical masquerade.[62] The bourgeois son of a priest, who owed his knighthood to the Bavarian Order of Merit of 1808, had been present at the imperial coronation in Frankfurt in 1792, which Metternich attended as a young imperial count. If Lang would not have been so narrow-minded, he could have learned from his contemporaries that in the late eighteenth century, foreign observers—such as the founding fathers of the American Constitution—still thought the Imperial Constitution exemplary. Thomas Jefferson, who was in Paris as an ambassador, sent his friend, and architect of the U.S. Constitution, James Madison whole boxes of books on the German Imperial Constitution. And Madison saw in its federal system of "checks and balances," with an elected emperor—or: president—at the top a model for the American Constitution. In the *Federalist Papers,* he explicitly recommended the Constitution of the Holy Roman Empire as a model to be followed.[63] While working on the Constitution, Washington and Madison also used Montesquieu's treatise *The Spirit of Laws,* in which they found the core chapter on the separation of powers to be particularly important. In it, Montesquieu, too, described the German Imperial Constitution as an example to be followed, and called the old empire "la république fédérale de l'Allemagne" [the Federal Republic of Germany].[64] Montesquieu saw realized in it his fundamental idea, which he expressed in his dictum "Every man invested with power is apt to abuse it, and to carry his authority as far as it will go. . . . To prevent this abuse, it is necessary, from the very nature of things, power should be a check to power."[65] Montesquieu knew what he was talking about: he had traveled to Germany in the years 1728 and 1729.[66]

Through the interaction between the elected emperor, prince electors, the Imperial Diet, the Aulic Council, and the Imperial Chamber Court, the complicated political order of the empire seemed to regulate itself in an almost miraculous fashion that its critics saw as cumbersome. This order guaranteed the rights of the less powerful estates, who were entitled to defend their rights at the courts. Seen from today's perspective, this empire combined progressive elements with old-fashioned ones. One of the old-fashioned elements was the idea of theocracy: spiritual dignitaries—archbishops, princely bishops, imperial abbots, or grand masters of knightly orders—exercising secular power. Except for the case of the Papal States, the Congress of Vienna irrevocably put an end to this ancient ecclesiastical system, which went back to the times of Otto the Great.

Metternich, Founding Father of the German Confederation

Metternich was familiar with this disappearing heritage, and as a pragmatic politician he had to transform it into something fit for the future. He intentionally made sure that he would head the committee on German matters at the congress. The history of previous attempts at giving a new shape to "Germany" has actually only been rediscovered, and only in part, since Europe's epochal shift in 1989–1990. The solution to the German question in the form of reunification also rehabilitated the German Confederation and put it in the right historical perspective as a precursor of, in Dieter Langewiesche's phrase, a "federalist nation."[67]

Until now, however, Wilhelm von Humboldt's plans received the most attention from historians. He is said to have given birth to the idea of a Constitution for Germany that would have given Prussia and Austria hegemonic positions.[68] There is no doubt that, from December 1813 onward, Humboldt put a lot of energy and imagination into plans for a future Germany, but his thought followed on from that of others, rather than itself setting the tone. I would like to argue the case that the real impulse for the solution to the German question in the form of a confederation came from Metternich. But the minister's ideas would not have been successful had it not been for Hardenberg, the cosmopolitan chancellor twenty-three years his senior, who shared his outlook.

The many steps Metternich took on the path toward the creation of the German Confederation reveal just how determined he was in pursuing the federal idea. Metternich reestablished contact with Hardenberg, whom he knew well from his time at the embassy in Berlin, on October 5, 1812, when Prussia had hit a low point. He presented to him the idea of Prussian-Austrian hegemony in central Europe. News of the devastating fire in Moscow had led him to this step. Metternich openly acknowledged that the interests of the two states were identical—namely, to gain independence and, as geographically "intermediary powers" between France and Russia, to become as strong as possible in order to be able to pursue common policies.[69] At the end of March 1813, Metternich deepened his vision for central Europe (*l'Europe intermédiare*): only Austria and Prussia—the "other two large empires" apart from France and Russia—would be able to guarantee peace [*Ruhe*] in the area.[70] In May 1813, he sent his special envoy, Stadion, to Reichenbach, the headquarters of allies Russia and Prussia, where Stadion presented Metternich's plan for Prussian-Austrian "intermediary" hegemony to Hardenberg, this time connecting it with the establishment of a special system for Germany.[71]

Metternich ultimately ensured that the concept of a federation of states prevailed by making Austria's entry into the Sixth Coalition, on September 9, 1813, in Teplitz, conditional not only on the states of the Rhenish Confederation becoming independent (which was stipulated in a secret article) but also on Germany becoming a federation of states. Metternich thereby also gave the allies a guarantee that the House of Habsburg had no ambition to create a new German empire. This was initially only an oral agreement, but it was nevertheless binding. Metternich then provided the conclusive formulation of the plan for a German confederation at the end of January 1814 in Langres. Hardenberg and King Friedrich Wilhelm III signed the agreement. The formula was taken over into the Treaties of Chaumont and the first Treaty of Paris, and thence became a task to be completed at the Congress of Vienna. On the basis of this prehistory, Metternich can be considered the founding father of the German Confederation.

Beyond this prehistory, Metternich also, in the end, was the one who made sure that the federalist solution prevailed. It would lead us too far afield if we were to trace in detail the well-documented roads and side roads that led to this goal. It would also be misleading, however, to present Metternich as a victor over active opponents. The negotiations of the German committee were often passionate and intractable, but Metternich always continued to operate skillfully, keeping the facts in mind, with a view to achieving a consensus. In the eyes of the participants, that made him credible. Neither did he use his position to pursue the urgent demands from his mediatized colleagues—among them his father—or act in the interests of the old imperial aristocracy. On the contrary: "Metternich presided over all meetings and gained general recognition for his liberal style in chairing the negotiations."[72]

Originally he shared the aim with Hardenberg and Humboldt of building more centralist elements into what Eckhardt Treichel called the "hegemonic protective confederation" of Germany: a directorship of the five member states of the German committee; a mediatization of the middle-sized and smaller states by a regional constitution; a federal court; and so on. But after the Polish-Saxon crisis, he moved away from the idea of such a close cooperation with Prussia. Prussia's unscrupulous desire for "expansion" [*Verdickung*], following the annexation of Saxony, made Hardenberg and Humboldt's position a marginal one within the German discussions. The middle-sized and smaller states, keeping in mind the example of Poland, felt threatened by divisions that might destroy them. Metternich used these fears to create a "third Germany" as a counterweight to the expansionist Prussia.[73] In May 1815, he even opened up the German committee to include representatives from all the states that were candidate members of the confederation. One might call the way in which he forced seemingly incompatible stances together a kind of dialectical politics: he combined a cautious distancing from Prussia with the necessary cooperation with that other dominant power in Germany, the power without which the federalist system would fail. The idea of a double hegemony, which Metternich had already mooted in his instructions of 1801, thus continued to be pursued. The German Confederation became frail and finally disintegrated once this partnership between Prussia and Austria could no longer be maintained. That process began with the Prussian succession in 1840 and the revolution of 1848–1849, and was completed in 1866 when Bismarck asked the question of who the leading power was.

The Broader Picture: How Metternich's Principles and the Vienna Congress Secured International Peace

The progressive element in the constitutional order of the Holy Roman Empire was the ultimately successful system of "checks and balances" within a composite state. The German Confederation of 1815 was characterized by the same principle. It still treated the German question in a typically old-European fashion. The way the confederation was embedded within Europe was a continuation of the Holy Roman Empire, so to speak, and ran counter to any design for a rational institutional state.[74] At the political level, the order agreed upon in Vienna combined two state territories: that of the German Confederation and that of the Habsburg Monarchy, only part of which belonged to the German Confederation. The Federal Act of June 8, 1815, declared the territory it covered to be "Germany." It explicitly referred back to the old Imperial Constitution by defining the parts of Austria and Prussia that belonged to the confederation as "their possessions formerly belonging to the German empire" (art. 1).[75] The territory of the confederation, however, was not a national state because three foreign heads of state were members with full rights: the king of England (because he was also king of Hanover); the king of Denmark for Holstein and Lauenburg; and the king of the Netherlands for Luxembourg. The confederation was a legal subject under international law, but had no head of state. It integrated individual states of which some had republican Constitutions, some were based on estates, and some had representative Constitutions or an absolutist form of organization. On its territory lived Germans, Poles, Slavonic Wends, Czechs, Slovenians, and Italians. From the perspective of the concept of a nation-state, a legal order in which legal spheres, territories, and nationalities overlap in such a seemingly bizarre fashion can only appear anachronistic.

It would be wrong, however, to assume that the politicians at the time were ignorant of or indifferent to the principle of national identity. The most striking illustration of the fact that this was not the case is the way in which the Polish question—the most difficult one, from a national perspective—was resolved. The Final Act of the Congress of Vienna of June 9, 1815, stipulated: "The Poles who are respective subjects of Russia, Austria, and Prussia shall obtain a representation, and national institutions."[76] In principle, the article guaranteed the Poles living in the three empires national representation in each of them—in the Russian Congress Poland, in Prussian Posen, and in Austrian Galicia—and thus formed a composite state.

In short, this means that the Vienna order guaranteed national identities *within* the state; the Swiss Confederation, which was guaranteed at the same time, remains, even today, the paradigm for this, and it was also invoked by Metternich. The European Union follows the same model, guaranteeing national identity, under the umbrella of composite statehood, within the state, that is, *within* the European Union—there is no European national identity. The nation-state, as the countermodel, proclaims a national identity *of* the state. The state becomes the bearer of the nation and acquires as its essential trait that it is a *nation* state. It is a necessary consequence of this that the state must present itself as a homogeneous nation because the state is conceived as belonging to only one nation.

Metternich continued to reflect on the federalist solution to the German question, especially in 1848–1849 when the German Confederation, the order of central Europe, threatened to collapse, just as the Napoleonic system had before it. And he always ended up with the same conclusion: If Austria was to continue to exist as an empire and at the same time to remain a part of Germany's "body politic" [*politischer Staatskörper*], there was no alternative to the German Confederation. Around 1849 Metternich wrote down an aphorism that captured his dilemma regarding the national question, not without some irony: "As a monarchy, Austria is a giant whose forces cannot be sucked up by democratic children and revolutionary dreamers; it even overcomes the administration introduced by fossils like Metternich, weaklings like Pillersdorf, and stubborn Schwarzenbergs—but the Achilles heel of this giant is Germany!"[77] Franz von Pillersdorf and Felix Count Schwarzenberg were his ministerial successors.

Everyone involved in 1815 wanted a Germany that included Austria. Even Stein, who favored Prussia, wanted a Habsburg Empire. This was an expression of the influence of the Holy Roman Empire. The German Confederation seemed to make the impossible possible: retaining Austria as a part of the rest of Germany. But any further centralization meant an existential threat to stability, as the revolution of 1848 later showed. As late as December 1848 the Austrian prime minister, Count Felix zu Schwarzenberg, dogmatically insisted that he was at one and the same time German, a Habsburg, and Austrian, postulating: "Austria is a German federal power still today. This position, which has emerged from natural developments over a thousand years, it does not consider giving up."[78] He confirmed what had already been visible in 1815—namely, that the only alternative to a confederation of states was disintegration into a bundle of middle-sized and smaller sovereign states at the heart of Europe. Since the wars of liberation, it had been Metternich's maxim that this needed to be prevented.

Metternich recognized, more clearly than his contemporaries, the fundamental problem that arises when national strivings and imperial orders clashed. "Unity and freedom" was the catchphrase. That sounded innocuous enough. But it was the question of national territories that was explosive, because an answer to it required the drawing of borders. Metternich, and the other midwives of Europe at the Congress of Vienna, still resisted the primordial sin of the coming nineteenth century. To put it concisely: They refused to accept the unity of nation, language, and territory—the unity that led only to war.

The Holy Alliance, a "Loud-Sounding Nothing"

Those who have understood Metternich's view of the world will hardly deny his seriousness of intention when it came to avoiding war defensively and securing peace actively. They will also agree with his harsh judgment on another form of supranational peacekeeping, the so-called Holy Alliance. This treaty, a manifesto proposed by Tsar Alexander, aimed to put forward Christian commandments as maxims for a peaceful European order. It was signed in Paris on September 26, 1815, by Alexander, Franz, and Friedrich Wilhelm III as a pact of peace inspired by Christian values. Emperor Franz, and even more so Metternich, would have preferred to thwart this initiative. Metternich's judgments are well known: he called the Holy Alliance a "loud-sounding nothing," a politically worthless "moral demonstration," and the "overflow of the pietistic feeling of Emperor Alexander." According to Metternich, the term did not occur in the official correspondence between the governments. He consistently refused to characterize the international alliances after Chaumont as "holy." And what is even more, he realized what a devastating public perception this alliance caused, as it seemed to be the product of a dynastic conspiracy, "an institution to keep down the rights of the people, to promote absolutism or any other tyranny."[79] Politics, as Metternich understood it, had to follow rational criteria and to respect the principle of balance in the relationships between states and within societies. For him, the concept of the tsar could not be separated from its religious context, and he would certainly have rejected, either indignantly or with irony, an interpretation of the religious fraternization between Catholicism, Protestantism, and the Greek Orthodox Church as a "league of nations."[80] Metternich himself had formulated a vision of a league of nations as a distant goal, but his vision was not permeated by ideology. In August 1840, at the climax of the Rhine crisis, he initiated with numerous diplomats who were staying with him at Königswart intense discussions concerning a possible European league of nations. This "League of Nations" was envisaged, not as another "Holy Alliance," but as an institutionalized system of communication based on international law that would have the aim of permanently preventing war in Europe.[81] Ultimately, the initiative failed because of opposition from Palmerston, but it is an episode worth mentioning because it shows how closely Metternich's political thinking was bound up with practical politics, and how strongly he remained committed to the cosmopolitan attitude of his student days. Metternich was right to make a connection between the tsar and the tenor of the Holy Alliance, on the one hand, and the Pietist writer Juliane von Krüdener, on the other. Krüdener had accompanied the allied armies to France on their campaigns against the "anti-Christ," as she called Napoleon, and, following the victory at Waterloo, she took an apartment in Paris close to the tsar's residence. They sang psalms and prayed together every day, and they discussed the great project of creating a union of all Christian peoples.[82] But no matter how subtly one traces Alexander's religious leanings and deep desire for peace, and analyzes his avowed commitment to constitutionalism,[83] the fact remains that—like his predecessors, among them the famous Katharina—this tsar also pursued expansionist policies. He wanted Russia to swallow up Poland and extend his empire toward the Balkans and the Mediterranean, as well as into East Asia. His avowed desire for peace went hand in hand with his hawkishness. Metternich disliked this.

The Detailed Picture of the Congress of Vienna: The Aristocracy and the Metternichs Retain an Elevated Social Status

In the context of a biography, our view must also descend from the large-scale issues decided at the Congress of Vienna to the smaller-scale issues that immediately affected the House of Metternich. The meetings of the German committee also discussed what status the nobility should have within the German Confederation. In 1806 the imperial nobility had survived its first existential crisis relatively well, because under the Act of the Rhenish Confederation it continued to have a privileged social position as a ruling class. After the dissolution of the Rhenish Confederation, however, there was no legal basis for the nobility's continued existence. At the beginning, the states formerly belonging to the Rhenish Confederation could not risk invoking the Napoleonic Act as a model. But, surprisingly, the German Federal Act of 1815 ended up preserving pretty much the same position for the nobility that had been secured in 1806.

Metternich's father, as well as Metternich himself, was involved in the political processes relating to this. In 1805–1806, they had coordinated their activities. But now the situation was very different: the son strode the corridors of power. In short, father and son worked in parallel. The son played the role of a neutral administrator, something the conflicting parties happily conceded to him. The imperial nobility's preferred solution—the reversal of all the changes that had taken place since 1803—was not going to happen, but there were three core points that were intended to allow it to retain its special status as an estate: the continuing existence of its legal privileges; representation in the "upper house" of the new German Parliaments that represented the estates [Ständeparlament]; and a vote in the planned central body of the confederation in Frankfurt. At times it looked as if the voice of the old imperial nobility would simply be drowned out in the debates about the federal Constitution. The representatives of the estates had been alarmed for some time and had founded an association for the mediatized as early as December 1813. When the meetings of the German committee—from which the imperial nobility had initially been excluded—entered their decisive phase in May and June 1815, the mediatized founded a common committee and made Metternich's father, Franz, its head.[84]

The amount of energy, time, and concentration invested by all those involved in the German committee and related activities is documented by the corpus of memoranda, drafts, motions, rectifications, and mutual correspondence between Hardenberg, Metternich, the ministers of Bavaria and Württemberg, and the so-called less powerful, which has now been published in its entirety.[85] The mediatized, among them Franz Georg, were particularly prolific in producing such documentation, as the Metternichs' posthumous papers at the Prague archive show. In contrast to the way in which the major powers approached critical topics, the German committee's method of dealing with controversial points was a process of opinion formation that seems democratic and almost modern. It was an open discussion in which the former states of the Rhenish Confederation, in particular, made known their resistance to an overly centralist organization of Germany and to the prospect of the former imperial nobility gaining too much influence.

As far as the position of the imperial nobility (mainly, that is, the members of the old Imperial Diet) was concerned, the result of the meetings was not as catastrophic as it was portrayed to be by some of those affected—above all Franz Georg. If we compare how the Act of the Rhenish Confederation and the German Federal Act each treated the status of the imperial nobility, we get the following picture:

Act of the Rhenish Confederation July 12, 1806; articles 27 and 28 (Princes and Counts)	German Federal Act June 8, 1815; article 14 (Houses of Princes and Counts)
Membership of the "most privileged class"	"Most privileged class" in the state, still "high nobility"
Right of equality of rank	Right of equality of rank
Free choice of place of residence within all states of the Rhenish Confederation	Free choice of place of residence in all states of the German Confederation
	Family covenants and inheritance law (entails) guaranteed
Lower civil and penal jurisdiction	Lower civil and penal jurisdiction at Courts of First Instance
Medium civil and penal jurisdiction	Civil and penal jurisdiction at the Courts of Second Instance, provided the dominion is of a sufficient size
Jurisdiction over forestry matters [Forstgerichtsbarkeit]	Jurisdiction over forestry matters [Forstgerichtsbarkeit]
Patrimonial policing rights	Local policing rights
Jurisdiction over hunting matters [Jagdgerechtigkeit]	Hunting rights
Jurisdiction over fishing matters, right of disposal over mining and smelting works, tenth part, income from said domains and rights	Assurance of all rights and privileges deriving from possessions
Right of patronage	Church patronage, authority over clerical and educational matters
Privileged place of jurisdiction	Privileged place of jurisdiction, dispensation from military service, privileged taxation
No confiscation of estates	Right to defend one's rights in person at the Parliament of the federal state [Landtag]

Metternich intervened several times in the negotiations regarding the fate of the mediatized. At the meeting on May 31, 1815, for instance, he suggested at least giving them a collective vote [*Kuriatstimme*] at the Federal Assembly. That granted them the political status they had enjoyed at the Imperial Diet. Metternich also submitted a proposal to include the equality of rank [*Ebenbürtigkeit*] of imperial nobility in the Federal Act. This put the high imperial nobility formally on a par with the ruling nobility. The move was a clear signal that the imperial nobility should still be awarded the dignity of rank of sovereigns. This made it easier to legitimize the continued existence of sovereign rights.

The discussions of the issue of the mediatized at the German committee, however, became rather delicate toward the end when, on June 3, 1815, Metternich's father, Franz Georg, lodged a "declaration of legal protest." It concerned a reference in the draft of the Federal Act to a Bavarian regulation of 1807. Franz Georg's vehement formal protest against the clause containing this reference was not successful; it sounded like it was based on a far-fetched legal nicety. But from the perspective of the old imperial nobility, the clause was a scandal: in it the Federal Act defined the status of the former imperial nobility with reference to "the Act of the Rhenish Confederation as the foundation."[86] In an indirect way, articles 27 and 28 of the Act of the Rhenisch Confederation thereby remained valid law under article 14 of the German Federal Act. The old imperial nobility considered it offensive that the Act of the Rhenish Confederation was honored in this way even after Napoleon's rule had ended.

This legal continuity, however, could also be evaluated in a positive light (Franz Georg's son Clemens certainly saw it that way), because it meant that, despite being diminished in 1806 under Napoleon, the imperial nobility was able to secure its still considerably privileged position under the conditions of the emerging new age. This is what the reference amounted to. And it was far from obvious that the old imperial nobility would continue to enjoy authority over territory and people through what Heinz Gollwitzer calls sovereignty at a sub-state level [*Unterlandesherrschaft*]. For the peasants in the southwest of Germany, this special status of the "most privileged class in the state" was still scandalous enough to justify setting fire to castles and storming revenue offices in 1848. They wanted to destroy the files containing their feudal encumbrances and thus remove the double taxation by state and feudal lords that they felt was unjust.

Franz Georg, the former head of the Rhenish-Westphalian Bench at the old Imperial Diet, relished his role as an elected representative. He intentionally avoided the term "feudal lords" [*Standesherren*] and the even worse term "the mediatized" [*Mediatisierte*]. Instead, he defined his peers and himself as the "former regional sovereigns of the imperial estates who are now subordinated to the various German sovereigns." For as long as possible he ignored the new reality—that they were no longer sovereign ruling nobility; on the contrary, he kept repeating the demand that the members of the imperial nobility "most of all be given back a representation at the German Federal Assembly that corresponds to the age, importance, and reputation of their houses, and that they be given proper justice."[87]

The open disagreement between father and son regarding this matter is instructive for us, because it helps us to characterize them both. Franz Georg was a principled nobleman of the Holy Roman Empire who followed an ethics of conviction, whereas Clemens was a traditionalist yet pragmatic statesman. The son framed things against a broader horizon: he had to achieve political results in a situation in which, until only a short while ago, and for over a hundred years, Germans had led war against Germans; imperial estates had formed an alliance of princes against the empire; Bavaria had fought with France against the empire; Austria had tried to annex Bavaria; Prussia had conquered Silesia, a part of Austria; the prince elector of Hesse had sold off the native children of his state to North America as soldiers; and so on.

Clemens von Metternich, himself one of the mediatized, secured what he could for his group. With his vote for *Ebenbürtigkeit,* their equality of rank with the ruling monarchs, he sent a clear signal. But the southern German kingdoms would have liked to diminish even further their inconvenient new members, who had now become "subjects." One of them, from Württemberg, was so strongly provoked by this that he coined the desperate catchphrase we already quoted before: "Better a swineherd in Turkey than a nobleman in Württemberg."

On June 8, at one o'clock in the morning, Metternich was looking back at the long final day of negotiations over the creation of the confederation, and he contemplated his differences with his father. Although he had to set off early to travel to the headquarters in Heidelberg—to see firsthand what fate Napoleon would meet (the Battle of Waterloo took place on June 18)—he still took the time to write a few comforting lines to his father. They touched upon his father's main focus: "There have been no changes to the article which concerns the mediatized (art. 14)—and the movement of the question regarding the collective votes (which is referred to Frankfurt) from its place in article 11 to the end of article 6, where it follows the list of votes at the plenary [the Federal Assembly], is a great improvement."[88] There was thus still a chance that the controversial question of whether the mediatized should be represented at the Federal Assembly in Frankfurt would be answered in the positive.

Franz Georg congratulated his son on "the victory of peace" and expressed his wishes that the agreement would give "at least the hope for a condition of

peace [*Ruhestand*] that lasts for several years." He considered the Vienna order
"the great work": "As a father and as a cosmopolitan I follow this most important event with too much interest, not to add to my congratulations my devotion, care, and joy."[89] Nevertheless, on November 9, 1815, he addressed a "*Note
Verbale* to the Minister of Foreign Affairs," that is, to his own son, in which he
informed him that even after the congress he would have to continue his work
on behalf of the interests of the princes and counts of southern Germany, and
that he wanted it recorded for posterity that the estates had suffered an injustice against which he would continue to fight.

At first Franz Georg had been prepared to wait and see what effect the resolutions of the Congress of Vienna would have "on the anarchic situation regarding German matters." But now he noted a remarkable contrast: in the north
of Germany, the princes and counts enjoyed all the rights and entitlements that
the Congress of Vienna had guaranteed, while in the south, "willfulness and
arbitrary power ruled as much as in the darkest times of the reign of the
Rhenish Confederation, if not more so." This caused Franz Georg to take up
the "role of an active spokesperson" for his peers again. The Court of Württemberg refused to give them the rights that had been granted, citing as justification that the state did not agree to the Vienna resolutions. Franz Georg
saw in Württemberg a "pernicious violent system of willfulness" and demanded that the Viennese court intervene.[90] He thus rekindled his lingering
conflict with the king of Württemberg, who had temporarily confiscated
Ochsenhausen from the Metternichs during the time of the Rhenish Confederation. Their conflict now continued on a new level. It was finally ended when
Metternich, who by this point was the head of the entailed estate, following the
death of his father, sold the dominion near Ulm and exchanged it for a Bohemian dominion in Plaß. We shall come back to this in Chapter 12.

"THE CONGRESS DANCES"—ESPECIALLY IN METTERNICH'S HOUSE

Politics and Celebrations

When Metternich returned to Vienna on July 18, 1814, he had an audience with
the emperor in Baden and then returned to the Chancellery on July 20 to receive the members of the diplomatic corps. In the evening he was surprised by
music being played on the square in front of the Chancellery by the orchestra
of the court theater together with the choir of the Theater an der Wien. The
director of the court theater, Count Pálffy, opened with the overture to
Beethoven's *The Creatures of Prometheus,* followed by a violin concerto composed and conducted by the musical director of the orchestra at the Theater

an der Wien, Louis Spohr. The performance ended with a cantata that had been especially composed for the occasion by Johann Nepomuk Hummel, with libretto by Johann Emanuel Veith. During this concluding cantata, a moved Metternich appeared on the balcony and endured some "crude homages," as a critical observer remarked. Metternich, for instance, listened to the following antiphony between soloist and choir:

> FIRST VOICE: Who stood unmoved
>   Amid the stormy seas of the times?
> CHOIR: Prince Metternich!
> SECOND VOICE: Who carried it out, the heroic deed?
>   Who led the federal troops?
> CHOIR: Prince Schwarzenberg!
> FIVE VOICES: Whose names are mentioned with deep gratitude
>   In the oh so happy fatherland?
> CHOIR: Metternich and Schwarzenberg![91]

This concert may be seen as evidence of the "dancing congress," the picture that would soon come to dominate perceptions of the Habsburg metropolis.

From the newspapers Metternich was familiar with the "witty bon mot" [*Witzwort*] of Prince Ligne: "Le Congrès ne marche pas, il danse" [The congress does not work, it dances]. But he rejected the view. He later wrote: "During the Congress a number of crowned heads with numerous retinues and a crowd of tourists assembled within the walls of Vienna. To provide social recreation for them was one of the duties of the Imperial Court; that these festivities had no connection with the labors of the Congress, and did not interfere with them, is proved by the short duration of the Congress, which accomplished its work in five months."[92] By ignoring the preparatory talks, Metternich thus saw the congress as beginning with the meeting on November 3. But if we take this as the starting point, and the initialing of the Final Act of the Congress of Vienna by the representatives of the eight powers on June 9, 1815, as the end point, the congress took seven (rather than five) months.[93]

In the light of the efforts of the Viennese court to make its noble guests feel as comfortable as possible and to impress on them the regained importance of the Habsburg Monarchy within the "European Concert"—for which Metternich seemed to play the role of conductor—the expression "to provide social recreation" is, to put it mildly, an understatement. In charge of the festivities was not Metternich, however, but the head of the office of the Lord Chamberlain, Prince Ferdinand zu Trauttmansdorff-Weinsberg. On May 28, 1814, Emperor Franz had already given instructions for how his own reception was to be conducted upon his return to Vienna on June 16, and he asked von Trauttmansdorff to translate them into a concrete program. In August the emperor then passed on Trauttmansdorff's "presentations" and plans of the Hofburg (indicating the allocation of rooms to the noble guests) to Metternich in Baden so that he could make sure that the sensitive etiquette concerning the accommodation of important guests had been respected.[94]

In preparation for the great Adventus [arrival] of the emperor, who was returning from battle victorious, von Trauttmansdorff solicited ideas for what the celebrations should involve. These included the erection of an arch of triumph, the decoration of buildings, and a general illumination of the city and the suburbs. A plan to "celebrate the memory of the great battle for liberation with an entry into Vienna on horseback" emerged. The lord chamberlain set up a commission with representatives from the court offices.[95] Everything was planned with military precision: the role in the celebration of the estates, the district governors, the military, the clergy, schools, and communities, as well as the parade route, which would finally end at Saint Stephen's Cathedral, where a *Te Deum* would be sung in gratitude.

The celebrations showed grandeur of overwhelming proportions, akin in their repertoire and choreography to those of the ancien régime. Von Trauttmansdorff revealed the deeper meaning of this and the upcoming festivities in a statement that also made it clear that the state's bankruptcy in 1811 and the burden of the "anticipatory fund" [*Antizipationsfonds*][96] were no object for the emperor (despite his usual tightness) when it came to demonstrating the epochal mission of his monarchy—even if the cost amounted to a tenth of the annual budget:

> The indescribable splendor of the Court, the magnificence and wealth of the uniforms worn by the accompanying nobility, especially the national costume of the Hungarian cavaliers, the innumerable members of the population and of foreigners from all empires; the emperor's expression of how moved he was by all proclamations of joy; and finally the thought of all the events that have come to pass in the short period of a year, which are not matched by centuries, and the calm prospect of a happy future that will create welfare, elevated this day, favored by the most splendid weather, to an immortal moment in the history of the empire whose brilliance will always shine on the future generations of the Austrian dynasty.[97]

This was the official message of the state propaganda, a message infused with patriarchal care. The culture of festivities, though, took hold of Viennese society as a whole, including the noble salons, the coffeehouses, the Prater, the Auwiesen, the palais in which the politicians lived, and the apartments of the "Grandes Dames," such as Bragation, Sagan, and Arnstein,[98] and even the public houses and brothels. The individuals who populated these places can be understood as elements in a comprehensive communicative network, as a recent study has shown.[99] The life that took place away from, and in parallel to, the political negotiations had always kindled curiosity in, and passion for, the congress. As exciting as all this may be, a biography does not have the space for it.[100] Metternich is often viewed as flitting about almost everywhere within this colorful environment. But this impression is misleading, as he resisted most temptations. He devoted very little of his precious time to such distractions and worked much harder than anyone else to make sure that the many parallel congress activities were always brought back together again.

The Festivities at Rennweg (October 18, 1814)

It is true, though, that Metternich himself contributed to the impression that he gave more attention to the festivities and entertainment on offer than to the tough diplomatic work. Only four days after the signing of the Treaty of Paris, on June 3, 1814, he asked the emperor for an advance of 10,000 guilders to prepare festivities for the monarchs.[101] This was the beginning of the planning for the greatest and most magnificent event staged during the congress. That was the judgment of all the observers, and even the tsar freely admitted it.[102] The celebration was also going to cost more than all previous events of its kind. We do not have the space for a comprehensive discussion of the festivities surrounding the congress, but this event demonstrates in exemplary fashion the function such court-directed festivities had. They meant more than just a bit of "social recreation." The background planning for the event—which has never previously been discussed—reveals its actual purpose.

While in Paris for the peace negotiations, Metternich got in touch with an old acquaintance from the time of the Napoleonic festivities while he was ambassador: the inspector general of l'Académie Royale de Musique of Paris, Jean-Étienne Despréaux. Metternich returned to London, and Despréaux immediately began to develop ideas for a party. The stage artist was steeped in the theatrical culture of the ancien régime. Under Louis XV and Louis XVI he had been a celebrated dancer and then master of dance at the Académie Royale de Musique. He survived the Revolution. Napoleon's wife, Josephine, introduced him to the circles around Napoleon as a dance teacher, and made him her protégé. He became professor of dance at the academy and finally its inspector general.[103] He organized great balls and banquets for Napoleon and taught his adopted children, Hortense and Eugène. He was also the teacher of Napoleon's sister, Caroline, with whom Metternich notoriously had an affair. Metternich asked Despréaux to make suggestions for a magnificent "festivity of peace." This set the general tone of the event: nothing military. By June 19, Despréaux had already worked out a complete program and sent it to Metternich in London.[104]

Because pantomime formed an important part of the program, Despréaux warned that it would take an intelligent and excellently trained mime, and recommended the best of them all, Jean-Pierre Aumer, who had been employed by Jérôme Bonaparte for some time as the master of ballet at the court's theater in Kassel. Metternich appointed him to Vienna. He probably knew him from London, where Aumer, in 1794, had performed with a dance ensemble and then joined the king's theater; Metternich had developed a fondness for pantomime at the time. In the end, the whole courtly classicist repertoire was performed. Part of the program involved a procession of the royalty present through the garden grounds, past temples of Mars, Apollo, and Minerva. Peace, the arts, and industry were personified. The pantomime showed the movement from the allegory of Discordia to the temple of peace. The guests watched from a large banquet table while dinner was served.

The location for the event was Metternich's villa in Rennweg. In preparation for the event, Metternich not only directed the performances but also decided on the layout. With its large park, his villa provided numerous possibilities. But in order to accommodate the 1,700 invited guests, the internal space did not suffice. As was often the case at such courtly celebrations, pavilions, tents, and other architectural structures were erected especially for the occasion. For that, Metternich asked the most competent festive decorator of the time, the Paris-born architect and painter Charles de Moreau, for advice. Moreau had been trained at the studio of the famous Jacques-Louis David, a former Jacobin and the court painter of Napoleon who had subsequently changed his ways. Like Despréaux, Moreau fitted with Metternich's classicist leanings, an inclination that had become even more pronounced during Metternich's time in Napoleonic Paris. Metternich expressed his wishes down to the level of fine detail, such as how the monarchs should enter and where they should be seated. He arranged the lighting (including Bengal lights and a wheel of fire that was lifted into the air by balloons), decided where the orchestra should be seated, and determined where the ballet was to perform. The most important, most expensive, and most indispensable project was a large two-story wooden construction that housed the ballroom. The illustration shows Moreau's design for it, seen from the front. The ballroom was on the ground floor, a café was on the first floor, and the orchestra was located above it on a gallery. Royalty were provided with a special tent in the ballroom bearing the coats of arms of the four major powers Austria, Prussia, Russia, and Britain. When Metternich said that he wanted to spend no more than 30,000 guilders, Moreau responded that the enormous ballroom alone would cost 60,000 guilders.[105] In the end, the total costs for the event came to 318,000 guilders![106]

Beyond its sheer ostentatiousness, the party, which took place on October 18, 1814, had three important aspects:

First, it symbolically expressed the importance of the Metternichs and showed everyone that the family had fully arrived in Vienna. By covering the costs of the event and supporting it with his authority, the emperor turned the event into an integral part of symbolic politics. Having been driven out of the perishing empire before coming to Vienna almost exactly twenty years before, the Metternichs were now at the center of the courtly aristocracy and of Habsburg politics, and they were now receiving—due to Clemens's congress—public recognition at the European level. The Metternichs had had earlier opportunities to put themselves forward in the eyes of the Habsburg court and the aristocratic society of Vienna—for instance, on April 10, 1810, when the emperor awarded his thirty-six-year-old minister the Order of the Golden Fleece in a ceremony with all the trappings of courtly dignity and honor.[107] But what Metternich created on October 18 in Rennweg outshone all this. No one could ignore the youngest representative of this dynasty any longer. A week after the Battle of Leipzig, the emperor had also formally expressed Metternich's increasing importance by making him a prince. And unlike his father, he was exempt from the substantial taxes associated with such an elevation.

Second, the enormous effort and expense meant that the event was a symbolic representation of "the entire European courtly society and monarchic order." Metternich experienced himself there as a part of a European cosmopolitan aristocracy.[108] The Swiss banker Eynard wrote in his diary: "Almost all of the highest dynasties of Europe were present at this festivity; fifty crowned heads and ruling princes and the entire high nobility of Germany."[109] But the event appeared to be a paradox: the task of the Congress of Vienna had been to constrain the common enemy, France, and to undo Napoleon's restructuring of Europe, and yet it celebrated itself in French language, culture, and visual arts, down to the classicist style of the theater performances and choreography. Napoleon's empire was laid to rest—at least at Metternich's villa—in the style of the empire.

Third, the event fit with Metternich's vision of peace and intentionally provided a counterpoint to the official commemoration of the anniversary of the Battle of Leipzig, which the court had arranged to take place in the morning of the very same day, October 18, 1814, in the Prater. At the commemoration, the

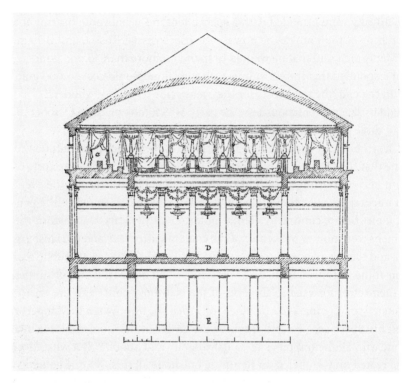

Charles de Moreau's design for the two-story wooden construction, built especially for the event.

military had the opportunity to present itself publicly in all its pomp—a solemn church parade, artillery and cannon fire upon the arrival of the monarchs, infantry men lined up and firing one after another, and a military parade in which all parts of the army were involved. Pontoon bridges were laid across the Danube, with banisters made of collected French rifles and decorated with captured French cannon. The monarchs and their entourages dined in a pleasure house [*Lusthaus*] decorated "richly and tastefully" with French trophies.

As Talleyrand noted, Metternich provided the contrast to this. Tsar Alexander liberally praised the splendor of the event, but objected to having two celebrations in one day. He did not understand Metternich's intention, but Talleyrand did, as we know from his report to King Louis XVIII: "All of yesterday was devoted to two celebrations, one of them a military commemoration of the Battle of Leipzig at which the delegation of Your Majesty could not be present; I attended the other which Prince Metternich had staged in honour of peace."[110] The Frenchman had understood that Metternich had found his own way of rejecting the purely military commemoration of glorious victors and

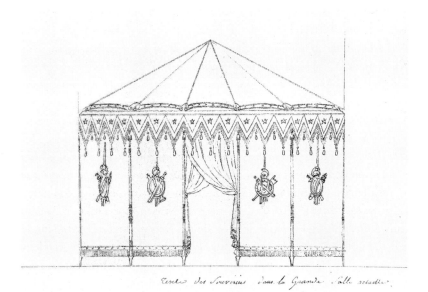

Charles de Moreau's design for the princes' tent in the ballroom on the ground floor.

deserving losers. As the moderator of the congress, he showed the participants a vision of the future.

Reward for the Peacemaker: Johannisberg at the Rhine

In personal terms, the crowning glory for Metternich was the emperor's exceptional gift, following the congress, of the Domaine Johannisberg in Rheingau. In an *Allerhöchstes Handschreiben* [personal, handwritten letter by His Highest Majesty] of July 1, 1816, the emperor gave the following reasons for the endowment: "In order to give you a lasting sign of my content and gratitude for the services that you have provided me and the state during the last phase of the final resolution of the European matters, I award you the dominion of Johannisberg am Rhein, formerly belonging to Fulda."[111]

This was a strange coincidence. The roots of Metternich's family were at the Lower Rhine, at the Mosel, and in the area around Koblenz, Mainz, and Rüdesheim. Metternich, a former imperial count, had taken a leading role at the great European congress where the loss of his family's estates, among many others, had been legally confirmed. The dispossessions could no longer be reversed, especially as Metternich had been compensated with the dominion of Ochsenhausen. But article 51 of the Final Act of the Congress of Vienna contained a key that opened a way back to the area at the Rhine again. This article dealt with "territories and possessions, as well on the left bank of the Rhine, in the old departments of the Sarre [Saar] and Mont-Tonnere [Donnersberg], as in the former departments of Fulda and Frankfort," and stipulated that they "shall pass in full sovereignty and property, under the Government of His Majesty the Emperor of Austria."[112]

Johannisberg had been a monastery until 1563, and until its secularization in 1803 had remained the property of Prince-Bishop Fulda, serving as a baroque summer residence and generating a substantial income through the associated winery. In 1803 it became part of the Duchy of Nassau. The Duke of Nassau was an ally of Prussia, and when in 1806 he defied Napoleon, the French simply occupied the country and turned it into a "pay reservé"—French territory under state law. The expensive wine of Johannisberg was sold on behalf of the French treasury. Napoleon particularly liked to get his hands on such luxury estates in the conquered territories in order to provide for his followers. On August 20, 1807, he gave the former monastery of Johannisberg to Marshal Franz Christoph Kellermann, who, together with Dumouriez, had been in charge of the cannonade of Valmy, for which Napoleon had made him Duc de Valmy in 1804. After the Battle of Leipzig, this jewel of Rheingau became the responsibility of the central administration for the territories to be recaptured— that is, it became Stein's responsibility. Subsequently, the First Treaty of Paris formally annulled Napoleon's endowments to his generals. This led to conflict over the question of who should receive the property. The Final Act of the Congress of Vienna made the Austrian emperor its owner, although he did not want to administer it from Vienna.

In the discussions about potential recipients, many prominent names turned up: Blücher, Gneisenau, and especially Stein.[113] On October 7, 1815, Hardenberg wrote personally to Metternich and advocated Stein. Because of its distant location at the Rhine, he said, the estate was most likely "the least convenient for the emperor of Austria." The tsar, he continued, wished for the dominion to be given to Baron vom Stein as a "present of honor" from the allied powers. Stein's special public reputation spoke in favor of his being the recipient; after all, he had been appointed head of the central administration for the countries conquered by the allies. His descent from Nassau was also an advantage.[114] But the Prussian chancellor had picked the wrong person to ask, because Metternich was eying the dominion himself. In 1815 he was in a financially precarious situation, a crisis that—in 1816—threatened to widen into a catastrophe for his house. On May 22, 1814, he had already explained to the

Schloss Johannisberg, following its renovation by Metternich in classical style; watercolor by Carl Hemerlein (1841).

emperor that he was struggling with the "sad state of the wealth of my House, without this being in any way my fault."[115] (We shall discuss this economic crisis in more detail in Chapter 12.) In short, his father had accrued a mountain of debt, some 900,000 guilders, and Metternich had tried to persuade the creditors to accept an extension to repayment. The debts were secured by Ochsenhausen, but there was a possibility that the Württemberg estate would have to be sold because the Metternichs could not comply with the duty of residency required by the king of Württemberg. Metternich therefore needed an asset that could be mortgaged. In that situation, Johannisberg was a tempting proposition.

Johannisberg, however, was not a mere gift. Metternich offered his ruler a deal. A report by the finance minister, Stadion, had explained to the emperor that it would be impossible for the emperor to run the estate in a commercially successful way in the style of a private person, and especially not from such a distance. That would be uneconomical and would not befit his position. But if he were to sell the estate, that would diminish his reputation in Germany. This was where Metternich came in. Using Stadion's arguments, he suggested that, as the owner, he would pass on a tenth of the annual yield to the emperor.[116] This way, the emperor would have the court cellars filled with more quality wine than he could possibly need. Metternich also explicitly addressed the competition between him and Stein. He countered the argument of the latter's native origin by saying: "These possessions, incidentally, are situated halfway between those which my House inherited five centuries ago and which the recent stormy times ripped out of its hands." And then—in 1816—he played the national card: "As the Russian emperor decided to give this estate to Baron Stein, its award to a state servant of Your Majesty would, in the eyes of Germany, certainly be the clearest proof of Your Highness's satisfaction with that servant. The question is in itself altogether a *German* one, and Germany would never forgive it if the first of the wines from the Rhine would remain at the disposal of the Russian Tsar."[117] Apart from all that, he added, he would be much better able to fulfill his duties to the emperor if he were to be in an economically comfortable position. Metternich's arguments seemed plausible to the emperor, and he asked him to compose the donation document. After that, everything happened very quickly. As early as August 1, 1816, Metternich could take possession of the dominion and enter on his account the income it generated.

On his first visit to Johannisberg (September 12), Metternich was overwhelmed by the place. He had arrived in the late afternoon and later tried to describe the scenery to his wife in Vienna: "I arrived early enough to be able to see twenty miles along the shores of the Rhine from my balcony, with eight or ten towns, close to a hundred villages and vineyards, which will this year yield wine for twenty million, interspersed with meadows and fields, like gardens, imposing forests of oak trees, and a wide plane covered with fruit trees bending down under the weight of their excellent fruits."[118] The southern character of the landscape provided a hint of Italy at home, Italy being a country he had learned to love on a recent trip in the spring of 1816.

Throughout his life Metternich was captivated by the Rhine valley, its history, which he knew so well, the well-kept cultural landscape, the mild climate, the rich vegetation, and the sublimity of the vistas. As late as 1857, on his last visit to the river, he got carried away and composed a declaration of love: "This river, all things considered, is one of its kind because it unites everything that nature and civilization have to offer in terms of attractions." For him, this insight was condensed in Nikolaus Becker's popular song on the Rhine, "They shall not have it, the free German Rhine," the first five lines of which, he wrote, provided "proof of this truth [in the experience of the Rhine] and of the national feeling it evokes." At this point Metternich added the oft-quoted phrase: "The Rhine is flowing in my veins, I feel it, and therefore the sight of it delights me."[119]

The panoramic view of Schloss Johannisberg also attracted many visitors, and Metternich kept an open house. Visitors could enter their names and comments in a visitors' book, and by 1857 their entries filled two large folio volumes.[120] Trivial remarks are followed—very occasionally—by examples of aphoristic wit. Metternich commented with subtle irony on the range of literary outpourings: "My beloved Germans, especially those from the North, find it entertaining to show their wit everywhere. There is a whole litany of bad verse next to unknown names. The only signature in my book that gives me joy is by one of our most talented poets, Jean-Paul; he is famous in Germany." Metternich is referring to the line: "Remembrance is the only paradise from which we cannot be expelled."[121] The phrase dates from 1811, and Jean-Paul used it for entries in visitors' books. In 1851, after his return from exile, Metternich mocked the fact that numerous delegates from left-wing factions and the center left of the National Assembly in the Paulskirche had memorialized themselves in his visitors' book. We also owe the artful depictions of Johannisberg to Metternich's hospitality; he liked to welcome artists to his place. The painter of landscapes and historical motifs Carl Hemerlein, born in Mainz and educated at the Vienna Academy of Fine Arts, went on to continue his training in the studios of Paris before he returned to Germany in 1837 and got to know Metternich. As a thank-you for a longer stay at Johannisberg, he compiled a valuable portfolio of watercolors of the place. This collection also allows us a glimpse

The view from Schloss Johannisberg toward the south, watercolor by Carl Hemerlein (after 1837).

into the castle, which was partly destroyed in the Second World War, but has since been restored.[122]

The greatest praise for Johannisberg, albeit couched in gentle irony, came from that sharp-tongued and feared citizen of the world, Heinrich Heine: "I know that Metternich thinks of me often and likes me; I like him, too, and do not allow myself to be deceived by his political aspirations. I am convinced the man who owns the mountain on which the fiery, liberal Johannisberg wine grows, cannot possibly still love servilism and obscurantism in his heart. Could it possibly be the wine that inspired the idea in him that he wants to be the only free and clever mind in Austria?"[123] And: "I have always considered the wine which grows there as the very best, and regarded the Lord of the Schloss as a crafty old bird, but my respect has greatly increased since I know how highly he esteems my poems, and that he once told Your Highness that while reading them he had at times shed tears."[124]

This is the irony, we should remember, of a poet of the Young Germany whose writings were prohibited by the Federal Assembly in 1835. By then, Heine had already gone into exile in France. His political poems were famous—such as his *Night Thoughts* ("When, Germany, I think of thee / At night, all slumber flies from me"),[125] or the bitter social criticism of his weaver-song, *The Silesian Weavers*. But for Heine, as for his famous Austrian contemporary Franz Grillparzer, it would have been too simplistic to assume that Metternich had been the sole originator of their experiences of censorship and repression.

Soon after Johannisberg was ceded to him, Metternich was appointed state chancellor. The castle was more than a personal summer residence: it also served as a Habsburg bridgehead in Germany. The assembly of the German Confederation in Frankfurt was close by, as was the fortress of Mainz, where Prussia and Austria each provided half of the troops, and where Metternich's intelligence office, the Central Commission on Revolutionary Activity, was established in 1833. Metternich visited Johannisberg regularly, whenever possible every year, often in connection with important political negotiations, but also when he was on his way to other places, such as Paris or the Congress of Aix-la-Chapelle. Monarchs and ministers, current and former alike, came to see Metternich at Johannisberg and receive advice from him or present their concerns and requests. The leading statesmen of the German Confederation regularly met here.

The Celebrated Peacemaker: The Watercolor by Johann Heinrich Ramberg

In 1822 Johann Heinrich Ramberg, the court painter of Hanover and famous illustrator of works by Goethe, Schiller, and Wieland, provided Metternich with a very special honor. The year before, at the end of October, Metternich had stayed in Hanover during a visit by the former British prince regent, who by now, following the death of his father, had become king. On that previous occasion, Metternich had visited Ramberg's studio. Now, in the spring of 1822, Ramberg came to Metternich with a petition on behalf of his son, strengthening his case by including, as an homage, a watercolor dedicated to the minister.[126]

The allegory depicted by the watercolor follows a model that had existed since the Baroque period and was still common around 1800, as can be seen in the fresco by Tiepolo in the Imperial Hall at Würzburg. The fresco shows Barbarossa in front of his throne, towering above two sculptures (Hercules and Minerva) standing to his left and right.[127] The reference to the Congress of Vienna is impossible to miss. Metternich is styled as a peacemaker, draped in classical garb. On his right stands Pax with her traditional olive branch. On his left, Hercules symbolizes strength, while the god of war keeps watch in the background, holding a shield with the Austrian double-headed eagle on it. Mars is looking up at an aureole with the imperial crown shining at its center. It is no longer the crown of the Holy Roman Empire but that of the Habsburg emperor, whose uniting force rules over everything.

There are further remarkable allegorical figures that point beyond the role of the peacemaker toward the commercial world that was now able to flourish.

Metternich as the Prince of Peace; watercolor by Johann Heinrich Ramberg (1822).

Metternich is shown as its patron, helping Industry (industriousness) to raise herself up from the ground, while Mercury, who should actually be responsible for trade and industry, is busy counting money. There are subtle references to shipping and commerce. Agriculture is represented by a cherub holding a sheaf of wheat and a sickle. Finally, the sciences are also included (geography with a globe, and astronomy with a quadrant), as are the arts: a cherub holding up a brush stands for painting; a second cherub with a hammer can be associated with sculpture; and a woman in a red dress touches a capital, thus alluding to architecture. In addition to this trio of painting, architecture, and sculpture, there are representations of acting and music. Metternich's own role is indicated very subtly; it is clear only to the expert: he holds the helm in his left hand—a representation normally fit only for rulers. In his toga he is presented as an ancient "governor." This association must have reminded Metternich of a catchphrase that was coined around that time. His wife had told him from Paris of a conversation between the prime minister, Jean-Baptiste de Villèle, and the general and foreign minister, Mathieu de Montmorency, in which the latter had called Metternich the "coachman of Europe."[128] Thus, Metternich did not himself invent this description, as has repeatedly been claimed.[129] The more important aspect of Ramberg's watercolor is, however, that with this picture of Metternich an observant contemporary celebrated the idea of peace in Europe and at the same time connected it to the promotion of "industry" and commerce.

9

CONNOISSEUR OF WOMEN AND

HEAD OF THE ENTAIL

Love in a Different Time: A Challenge to Our Understanding

If we were to represent the level of public attention that Metternich received throughout the course of his life in a graph, then this graph would rise steeply in the years of the Congress of Vienna (1814–1815) toward an apex. During that time, he was at the center of European public life as a politician, a star of courtly society, and a divinely gifted master of ceremonies. And at no other time were so many people interested in the alleged "coachman of Europe" as a lover of women. Regarding this topic, it is again Heinrich von Srbik who set the trend that was subsequently followed by others. On Metternich during the time of the congress, he wrote that "his inclination toward superficial pleasure and perfunctory behavior again showed very strongly, and his 'affairs with women' [*Weibergeschichten*] yet again made disproportionate demands on his time and mind."[1] Srbik mentioned the numerous "cliques" in the Viennese aristocracy that were hostile toward Metternich and eagerly received and passed on gossip and rumor about him. Even Metternich's closest collaborator, Friedrich Gentz, fanned the flames when, at the beginning of April, he complained: "At seven I went to Metternich for dinner. As usual, he hardly listened to me. The whole crowd of whores from Courland was there, hence Metternich had no time for anyone else. For eight days, M. has filled these women in on all political secrets: the amount they know is incredible."[2] And a voluminous documentation with an accompanying commentary by a disciple of Srbik, titled *Metternich und die*

Frauen [Metternich and women], serves up every possible cliché, making any historian aware of how sensitive and awkward this topic is.[3] It is therefore appropriate to treat it thoroughly in a chapter of its own.

Because everyone thinks they know what love is and how it finds expression in relationships, everyone is very confident in their judgment or condemnation of Metternich. Female historians have only recently begun to raise critical voices against this kind of confidence.[4] Before that, male historians dominated the discussions. They treated the historical sources in a strikingly unhistorical—naive—fashion, because they read the letters in which Metternich spoke as a lover as if his words belonged to and were addressed to their own age. They then freely vented their feelings about the letters' oddness, called his language "florid," sentimental, frivolous, mendacious, vain, or boisterous, and quickly reduced him to a "womanizer" or "Lothario," a "salon philanderer" and "cavalier."[5] Both male and female historians must, however, leave aside the moral ideas of their own times and try to adopt the mentality and sensibility of the period in question. Like ethnologists, they must consider that love between human beings, beyond its anthropological foundation, has a historical component, and that forms and expressions of love that at first appear strange must therefore first be deciphered. No art historian would ever look at a painting as if it were a photographic reproduction of reality, but historians, by contrast, sometimes like to treat their sources as such simple representations. The art historian asks questions about the iconography of their object, the studio of the artist, and the stylistic traditions in which the artist worked. Metternich's "love," as expressed in his courtly socializing and his letters, also followed a pattern he did not freely choose, whether he liked it or not, because the women expected him to adhere to a historically specific arrangement.

Metternich's Cult of Love: "Abelard and Heloise" and "Amor and Psyche"

A fortunate discovery pertaining to Metternich's early life allows us for the first time to capture the beginnings of the pattern he followed. At a hidden place in the library at Königswart Castle, a framed drawing hangs on one of the walls. Its broken glass points to the journey it made from Strasbourg, where it was produced, to the castle, a journey not free of danger at the time. It takes the form of a tondo, known from the Florentine art of the fifteenth and sixteenth centuries, and bears the caption: "The Meeting of Eloisa and Abelard in the Elysian Fields." On the left and right hand at the bottom one can make out the words: "Dessiné par le Comte Clément de Metternich / A Strasbourg ce 4 May 1790." The young imperial count had drawn it during the time of his studies in Strasbourg, just two weeks before his seventeenth birthday.

"The Meeting of Eloisa and Abélard in the Elysian Fields," signed drawing by Metternich, May 4, 1790.

The drawing shows the reunion of Abelard and Heloise in paradise. Dressed in classical garments, they greet each other against the backdrop of an idyllic landscape. In the left foreground they are accompanied by two cherubs, one of which seems, by the way Abelard's clothes fall, to acquire wings, making him look like a cupid. On the right hand side in the background, separated by a brook, is a group of figures listening to a female harpist. Two upright figures accompany the harpist with a song, reading the words off a sheet. The main motif of the drawing is the passionate love between Abelard, the theologian and philosopher of the twelfth century, and his pupil. In the historical reception, the fate of the two was taken as a symbol for intellectual equality between the sexes, for being prepared to ignore social convention and hold on to love under all circumstances—even after having been violently separated.

In the drawing, the young Metternich tried his hand at rococo artistic forms. In poetry and literature, these could be found in the so-called Anacreontics, named after the Greek poet Anacreon. Literature and the visual arts alike valued the classical model and a sensitive, "tender" style whose purpose was no longer to teach for practical purposes. Far away from everyday life, the playful handling of classical motifs was meant to develop the senses and aesthetic taste. Love, wine, and friendship were typical topics, and the setting was usually a soft landscape with brooks, bushes, grottos, and wells, often populated by fawns, nymphs, and female and male shepherds who lived in "a serene and decisively secular" way.[6] Metternich, the precocious student, devoted his time to the ideal of a swooning, gallant, sentimental [empfindsam], and as yet unfulfilled love. The longing was more important than the fulfillment. As Metternich depicted it, two attributes of the love between Abelard and Heloise seem important: the erotic attraction between the bodies and the equality [Ebenbürtigkeit] between them—she puts her hand around his shoulder and pulls him close in a commanding way.

Metternich's sketch is a remarkable artistic achievement, albeit one based on a template. It can be found in a painting by Giovanni Battista Cipriani and as an engraving (1784) by Francesco Bartolozzi, who was born in Florence but lived in London and was a friend of Cipriani.[7] With his drawing, Metternich thus participated in the Italian classicism that was taught at the academy in Florence. The academy was characterized by its "enthusiasm for the beauty of the human form and especially for female grace."[8] It took the inspiration for its goddesses and bacchanals, its nymphs and cupids, from Greek and Roman mythology. The exceptional knowledge of human anatomy and the sensitivity for female beauty found expression in the quality of their work, in the brilliance of the light, the graceful lines and beauty of expression. Metternich developed his lasting preference for such classicism early on. Later, he had "Singspiele" containing motifs from Greek and Roman mythology at his wedding to Eleonore in 1795; he adapted his castles in Königswart and Johannisberg to the classicist style; and he decorated his gardens and the reception rooms in the Rennweg villa with classical sculptures.

The original copper engraving was based on two stanzas from Alexander Pope's poem "Eloisa and Abelard" (1717), which created an enthusiasm for the lovers all over Europe; it inspired Rousseau's *New Heloise,* a copy of which Metternich kept in his library. It is likely that his English teacher in Strasbourg introduced him to Pope as the literary messenger of the age of sensibility, and also to the copper engraving.

Metternich's taste and his preference for this artistic motif endured. Thirty-two years later his drawing was complemented with a striking thematic counterpoint. In February 1822, a copy of a marble sculpture of Amor and Psyche was delivered to his Rennweg villa. The original had been made by the famous Italian classicist sculptor Antonio Canova for Napoleon's castle Malmaison. Metternich's copy, which he had set up in the villa's pavilion, had also been made by Canova. "It is one of the most tender and at the same time one of the most voluptuous creations of the artist. He has modeled the marble into love and grace." With his typical irony, Metternich described the worries that the life-sized sculpture caused him: the "very pure and innocent" among his visitors might see the first kiss that Amor gave his Psyche, requiring him to "hang a dressing-gown round Amor and throw a sheet over Psyche." But "except on such occasions," he wrote, "I will leave them in their simple god-like forms."[9] Today the work of art is in the large hall at Königswart castle. In a discreet way, with this sculpture and his early Strasbourg drawing, Metternich revealed his ideal of the relationship between the sexes: it united erotic attraction, gallantry, tenderness, and equality [*Ebenbürtigkeit*].

The Rhetoric of Love in the Age of Sensibility

Even more instructive than these aesthetic influences are the linguistic patterns on which Metternich drew. These have so far mostly been overlooked by historians examining the letters he wrote to women, who often believed they found the most intimate and personal confessions in them. Let us look at just a few examples of formulas that misled later readers. To Wilhelmine von Sagan, for instance, Metternich confessed: "Do not forget me: keep me in your memory just a little bit, and tell yourself that I love you from the bottom of my heart and, oh!, much more than that." "Adieu mon amie, whom I love a hundred times more than my own life." "I shall not tell you what went on inside me; my heart is the victim of so many confused sentiments, unfathomable—I feel so insecure over what might be the right way, that I no longer care to investigate my sentiments."[10]

The letter Metternich wrote to Wilhelmine von Sagan on August 16, 1813, not long before they planned to meet, is a telling example of the love rhetoric he used in courting a woman. Because it can be deciphered only as a whole, I quote a longer passage:

Antonio Canova, *Amor and Psyche,* around 1820; displayed at
Metternich's Rennweg villa from 1822.

You do not love me. If you would love me, you would be happy! . . . I love
you with painful passion; I nourish the pain; I glorify it. I am the unhap-
piest creature on earth, and away from you I do not want to be happy. I
shall not yet do anything to ease my pain. . . . My love, I no longer imagine
what life without you might be like. Time—maybe—will teach me! If I
die, let me die far away from you—I shall spare you painful moments. Be
happy! I would give my life for you a hundred times over—I can easily let
it go, if I die for you. . . . Adieu. There is no longer any happiness for me
in this world—all that is left, it may be yours! My love, think of me as little

as possible—so that the image of me may not become attached to an idea that is painful to you; let me suffer, let me carry my pain alone.[11]

Metternich used the same language when he later turned to Dorothea von Lieven, the successor "in his heart" to the Duchess of Sagan, writing to her: "I love you the way that I breathe, and I find you in my heart as if you had been born there!" The next sentence calls to mind one of Heinrich Heine's ironic twists: "One day I shall explain this to you with a nice thesis from my philosophy, which is not generally followed, but would deserve to be universal."[12]

This distancing irony—which is in fact rather typical of his style—suggests that it would be altogether inappropriate to infer from his emotional form of expression conclusions about his psychological state by interpreting the former as a spontaneous, uncontrolled, "passionate outpouring."[13] The eighteenth century had developed a culture of letter writing in which a letter could serve various purposes: the purpose of setting oneself apart, aware of one's worth; of presenting oneself in a good light; of suggesting closeness; of expressing cultivation; of hinting at physical intimacy. All this gave letters "the character of a little work of art which could not just be read as an individual communication . . . but asked to be read as an artful expression of a longing."[14] Letters were part of a culture of friendship, and certain rhetorical elements in them laid claim to intimacy. The "theatrical," the "performative," was as important as the content. "The basic interest of the sentimental letter [empfindsamer Brief] is not the content, in the sense of information or news, but the communicative effect it achieves."[15]

If we decipher Metternich's letters, we find what Tanja Reinlein called a "code for communicating love." This code includes the fiction of the letter as representing the soul of its writer, rejections, justifications, the yearning for the physical presence of the partner, and invocations of a longing for death. The world-famous prototype of this kind of writing was Goethe's Sorrows of Young Werther, and if we take all of Metternich's letters from the correspondence with Wilhelmine von Sagan or Dorothea von Lieven, they form a similar "epistolary novel." Metternich's narrative was similar to the one in Werther: the unfulfilled love of a married—in his case aristocratic—woman. On one occasion, in order to prove his "faithfulness"—ultimately, lack of fulfillment—he explicitly asserted, "I have never interfered in a marriage."[16]

In essence, the tone of Metternich's language derived from a new experience that his contemporaries summed up in the concepts of "sensibility" and "tenderness." "Sensibility" was a European phenomenon whose origin lay in the emerging bourgeois class of academics and civil servants, but which took on an aura that transcended these classes and was attractive to enlightened aristocrats as well.[17] A theoretician of "empirical psychology" [*Erfahrungsseelenkunde*] wrote in 1788: "More *subtle* sensibility is predominantly found in tender and educated people who are endowed with a lively imagination, which is actually the mother of sensibility. It mostly finds expression in an exaggerated and enthusiastic feeling for friendship and love, in a highly excitable feeling of empathy with the other's pain." Especially sensitive women [*empfindsame "Frauenzimmer"*] directed their wishes at "anxiously attentive, and deliberately sympathetic men." These women, the author critically remarked, have an ideal of perfection in their mind and had expectations regarding the conduct of men, which the men were only prepared to meet "during the courtship."[18] All in all, the author distanced himself from the "unfortunate epoch of Werther," which had made "all mores softer, more tender and delicate."

Metternich's relationship to the age of sensibility was mediated not only by literature—that is, by a certain moment in cultural history—but also by the close connection between his parental home and the author Sophie von La Roche in Koblenz. La Roche's husband was a conference minister in Mainz at the same time as Franz Georg. We know that Metternich's father frequented the salon of the author, who propounded the style of sensibility both in her works and in her life.[19] The pedagogical reformer Basedow, who was the role model for Metternich's tutor Johann Friedrich Simon, could also be found in La Roche's salon. And one of Goethe's real-life models for Werther's Lotte was her daughter Maximiliane.

There were thus more than enough elements in the young Metternich's education and upbringing to bring him into contact with the intellectual movement of sensibility. One particularly interesting detail is that the people who moved in these circles tended toward the same categorical criticism of war that we have already found in Metternich. "War shows itself to be a monster, a barbarism in the age of the century's enlightenment," was the judgment of one adherent of sensibility; he pointed toward the Napoleonic wars and the "ruins Dresden and Saxony." He denounced "the devastation of the German Rhineland, Switzerland, and Italy," the gruesome scenes, inhumanity, the horrible descriptions of the conquest of Holland, the "example of the cold-blooded murder of unarmed prisoners, which appalls human sensibility," especially in wars that were led "in the name of human rights."[20] At the same time, the author described sensibility and the warmth of philanthropic enthusiasm as moral counterbalances to "lazy repose and cold indifference," to tyranny and "deliberately created human misery."

The attitude of the age of sensibility toward war goes some way to explaining Metternich's dialectic between sentimental affection [*empfindsame Hinwendung*] toward his lovers and revulsion at the age of war and its "soiling of thinking." It was not unusual for him to express both attitudes in one and the same letter. It seems that he found psychological relief from the brutality of political affairs and the empirical world by living in an alternative literary world of feeling and the imagination. Otherwise it would be difficult to understand why he would have added private psychological stress to the stresses of his public life. He reflected on the precarious relationship between the two, which made Gentz suspect that the minister might be neglecting his important political duties. Metternich described to Dorothea von Lieven what he had observed about himself in this respect:

> The thought of my [female] friend does not leave me even amidst the most arduous tasks; it does not distract me from my duties, quite the opposite, it deepens my feeling of responsibility. It does not weaken my energy for action, but strengthens it. Love, for me, is a conscience; and conscience has always been the most important element of strength and willpower. What I say is in no way applicable to all men, but those to whom it does not apply are feeble, and a feeble soul is not capable of powerful surges of emotion. It succumbs before it has reached its goal.[21]

The clarity of this self-analysis is stunning. On the one hand, Metternich recognized that the way in which he expressed his love for the other sex was the result of a special disposition; on the other, he used this disposition as a means to come to terms with life.

Metternich's Understanding of "Faithfulness" and His Chosen Ones

Mozart's Don Giovanni has a servant, Leporello, who is able to list, in the "catalogue aria," all his master's love affairs. Such an attempt would necessarily fail in the case of Metternich. To begin with, he was no driven Don Juan, even if he is often portrayed as such a character. Apart from the woman to whom he was married, he always only entertained one other love at a time, and these changed over time. This explains his at first baffling claim: "I was never unfaithful; the woman I love is the only one in the world for me."[22] He lived in a double monogamy, a sentimental love and his marriage. In his own way, he remained faithful to his wives as long as they lived; he survived all three of them. He truly loved them as well as his lovers. The contradiction can only be resolved if we keep in mind his idea of an emotionally highly charged "true love." This love is the great "heavenly power" that takes hold of the whole person; it belongs to the realm of sensibility and emotion that is separate from all domestic bliss and exists more in an imagined than a real space.

A "catalogue" à la Leporello would also be impossible to compile because Metternich knew very well how to remain discreet. Among his posthumous papers in Prague are numerous letters from women that clearly contain signs of love, admiration, or personal intimacy, but they never show the sender's name. When Metternich began to sort through his papers, he often added names on the cover of the files, as a form of commentary or explanation. In the case of women he avoided this. He himself explained to Dorothea von Lieven why any accountant of love affairs would fail in his case: "Many women have been mentioned in connection with me who were not even in my thoughts. By contrast, I have entertained relationships with many women that were anything but romantic, without the public ever learning anything about it."[23]

His biographers, most of all Srbik, look at his relationships with women from the perspective of the petit bourgeois world of the nineteenth century, in which the nuclear family emerged as the ideal of love and marriage. They neglect the social conventions that influenced Metternich and informed his behavior. As we have already seen in the case of his wedding in 1795, within European aristocracy marriage was a business deal that was sealed with a formal contract. When Dorothea von Lieven showed her dissatisfaction with her marriage, Metternich consoled her with the words: "Fulfilling love within a marriage is the privilege of very few individuals. It can never be found, in my opinion, in the case of early marriages."[24] Within aristocratic society the solution was the mistress, a figure that in Metternich's case already took the "refined" bourgeois form of a "lover."

Metternich did not choose his female partners at random. They were all economically independent; they could freely choose how and where they wanted to spend their lives, unless, as in the case of Dorothea von Lieven, who was married to an ambassador, they had to follow their husbands around on business. Like Metternich, most of them belonged to the aristocracy, were themselves married, but took the liberty to emulate their spouses and keep a *maître*. If only on an extremely limited scale, they experienced a kind of female emancipation that other women experienced only in the twentieth century.

With the age of Enlightenment, women cultivated a form of hospitality that developed into the culture of the salon, where, across the estates, the elite met: ministers, monarchs and their advisors. Here, networks were formed and news was exchanged. For Metternich, women in salons had a special role: "At the center of a circle of men has to be an intelligent woman. Then, everything takes on a different look; the ideas are fresher; and nothing is comparable to the special tact and peculiar wisdom which a superior and graceful woman can produce at private gatherings. I have spent the best years of my life in this form of life."[25] At the salons he experienced elegance, a cosmopolitan spirit, the art of conversation, the "creation of a common emotional and cultural space," the equal participation of women, and their emancipation in the sense of liberation from the roles of late feudal society.[26]

In the remainder of this and the following chapters, we shall introduce the most important women in Metternich's life. In each case, a striking trait or perspective will be highlighted that helps us to better understand Metternich the politician and the man. Our guiding thread shall be a confession of Metternich's. In mid-November 1818, he had said farewell to Countess Lieven in Aachen. He had made her acquaintance during the Congress of Aix-la-Chapelle, and from then on a correspondence developed between the two. At the beginning, Metternich thought he should make himself better known to Dorothea through his letters: "You know my heart as it is now, but you do not know the least about the history of my life."[27] To that end, he composed his "general confession,"[28] at the same time courting the attention of his female partner. His desire was "that my friend knows me, . . . to hand over to her all the weapons she may use against me. It seems to me, there are even sharp weapons among them, I should not love you!"[29] Metternich knew about the reputation he had earned since his time in Paris. He therefore thought he should proactively explain his past love life, including the role of his wife within it, in order to remove any doubts that may have prevented Dorothea from getting closer to him.

"There have been two love relationships in my life," Metternich wrote on December 1, 1818, referring to the emotional love of sensibility. Part of this form of love for him was necessarily a continual exchange of letters. Another category was "being in love." In those cases, he adhered to the rules of courtly gallantry. Nesselrode, the Russian diplomat and later minister, noticed this in his young colleague in Dresden early on: "He is very charming if he wants it to be, of handsome appearance, almost always in love, but even more often absent-minded, something that is as dangerous in diplomatic as in love affairs."[30] As far as the absent-mindedness is concerned, Nesselrode was wrong, but he correctly realized that Metternich used his innate and acquired attractiveness to the female sex in order to pursue political objectives. In order to distinguish between the two kinds of amorous relationship, Metternich also used the concepts of "l'amour" and the less intense "liaison." In the case of the latter, he held, it was possible to sleep with each other without "amour," even without "amitié," and while having different tastes, inclinations, and desires.[31]

The third form of love was marital love, which in Metternich's case found expression in an impressive number children—twelve. His correspondence with his wives, which he always maintained whenever he was apart from them, shows how seriously he took this kind of affection. The fourth kind of love Metternich knew, finally, was fatherly love; this he showed toward his sons Victor and Richard, but in the case of his daughters Marie and Leontine—in particular, Marie—it rested on a kind of spiritual kinship.

Through the Eyes of the Rococo: Constanze von Lamoignon

At his birthplace (Koblenz), during his university studies (Mainz), and when staying with his father out of term time in Brussels: everywhere, the young Metternich met French emigrants. Emigrants also came to his father's house, and in the autumn of 1791, on one of his visits to Brussels, he made the acquaintance of "a young woman of my age, with a flexible mind, intelligent and tasteful, a French woman of very good stock. I love her the way a young man loves. She loved me with all the innocence of her heart. We both longed for what we never requested of each other."[32] These are the words the forty-five-year-old Metternich uses to describe the love of his youth. They made plans for a long future together—longing, swooning, talking, in their rooms during the day, in their thoughts during the night—and "postponed the fulfillment of this tender love to better times." Metternich experienced his first love exactly as he imagined it in his rococo drawing of Abelard and Heloise in Strasbourg. This relationship went on for three years, and during the times that they were separated the young lover wrote letters. They became a medium for his courtship and admiration of women, and his letters to Dorothea von Lieven reveal him to be a master of the form.

We would not know who the mysterious French woman was were it not for the reminiscences of one of Metternich's fellow students in Mainz, the Marquis de Bouillé, who developed the same passion for the Countess Marie Constance de Lamoignon as did Metternich. In 1791 she was only seventeen years old and married to the Comte François Pierre Bertrand de Caumont, with whom she had fled to Mainz. The marquis and the imperial count both adored her, with Bouillé describing her in the same classical manner that Metternich adopted in his drawing of his imagined lover in Strasbourg: lively, young, winsome, with an almost childlike, virginal aura, a slim figure, elegant and nimble. Bouillé thought that for a painter she would have been the ideal model for a Hebe or Psyche.[33] He and Metternich did not consider each other as competitors; rather, they almost formed a friendship over their shared passion. They spent time at the house of Madame de Caumont at the Mainzer Rheinallee almost every day.

The Apex of Emphatic Sensibility: Countess Julie Zichy, née Festetics

Metternich kept his second great love—of the emphatic-sensibility kind—as much a secret as his first, and he did not reveal her name. He described her in almost divine terms, speaking of

> a phase in my life . . . in which the full reality of the heart seemed to me contained forever. I loved a woman who descended onto the earth only in order to hover away immediately like spring. She loved me with the all-encapsulating love of a soul that is close to heaven. The world has hardly noticed any of it. Only we knew about the secret. . . . She died. . . . My life ended at the time; I neither had the will nor did I want to live any longer. My soul was broken, I no longer had a heart.[34]

The object of his worship was the Hungarian Countess Julie Festetics (1778–1816). She was the second wife of the Hungarian president of the court chamber, count Karl II Zichy von Vásonykeő, the son of the famous state and conference minister count Karl I Zichy von Vásonykeő. It was an unhappy marriage.[35] During the Congress of Vienna she hosted a popular salon where the most important people met: Tsar Alexander, the king of Prussia, Napoleon's stepson Eugène Beauharnais, Gentz, Friedrich Schlegel, Wilhelmine von Sagan, Vienna's high nobility, and, of course, Metternich. To the Prussian author and diplomat Karl August Varnhagen von Ense, who was by no means uncritical, we owe an appreciation of the countess. Although he was not biased, as Metternich might have been, he used similar words to describe her: "In her, the greatest beauty, an expression of innocence and virtue amidst rich worldly wisdom, shone from the purest noble femininity."[36]

Varnhagen's judgment makes clear how discreet Metternich's behavior in Countess Zichy's salon was: he was "of a tremendous friendliness and natural composure . . . , as if the state had nothing to worry about in the world." No one suspected a relationship between Metternich and the countess. Before her death, she wrote a testament and an accompanying letter in which she explained to her husband why she had not been able to love him. The testament contains a passage that refers to Metternich, and only he was able to understand it. She left Metternich a small sealed box. Upon opening it, he found that it contained the ashes of his letters to her and a ring from Metternich, which she had broken. This shows, again, that correspondence was central to this kind of relationship. Metternich related all this to Countess Lieven two years after Julie's death, so as to be able to claim credibly that Dorothea was the third in the exclusive sequence of his great loves. He thus began a correspondence with her that lasted for over eight years. At times, they exchanged letters daily.[37]

LOVE AND POLITICS: AT THE COURTS OF DRESDEN, BERLIN, AND PARIS

Dresden: Princess Katharina von Bagration

The attractive and influential women Metternich had relationships with at the courts come under the category of "liaison"; they were, however, not mentioned by name in his "general confession." Because an envoy at a foreign residence was a conduit for news, any information he might glean about the center of power through intimate channels was welcome. One might say, if one wished to sneer, that this was a way of combining the pleasurable with the useful—a double-edged, sometimes dangerous method, if pursued, for instance, at Napoleon's court. But his first experiences of this kind Metternich had at the harmless salons of Dresden. While there, he often visited Princess Izabela Czartoryska, who was well-disposed toward him. She was the mother of the Polish patriot Adam Jerzy Czartoryski, and in her house Metternich was directly confronted with the fate of Poland, whose partitioning he condemned. After the failed Polish uprising in 1794, her husband, Prince Adam Kazimierz Czartoryski, had come to the Russian court as a hostage and befriended Tsar Alexander. Between 1804 and 1806, he became Alexander's minister, and he accompanied him to the Congress of Vienna as his advisor, encouraging Alexander to give Poland a constitution. At Izabela's salon, Metternich also met the grandniece of Tsarina Katharina I and the Russian field marshal Potemkin, Princess Katharina Pawlowna Bagration (1783–1857). Her husband was eighteen years her senior and descended from the Georgian dynasty of the Bagratid kings. He had fought against Poland several times before battling Napoleon.

Everything that had to do with Russian politics interested Metternich. His instructions for Dresden and his own analyses suggested that it would be wise to revive the friendly relationship with Russia that had once existed under Catherine II, and to be circumspect about the expansionist tendencies of this vast empire. Any contacts with leading members of the Russian nobility could only be useful, and it seemed likely that such contacts could be established through the just nineteen-year-old Princess Bagration, especially because she caused a stir at the court in virtue of being well educated (she spoke fluent French, German, English, and Italian), and even more so because she wore very delicate, gossamer clothes that earned her the title "the naked angel," which even became the name of a novel.[38] Lady Castlereagh allegedly coined the oft-quoted phrase "her neckline reached her stomach." Admittedly, Metternich rather overdid his advances. When he met Princess Bagration again in Vienna at the turn from 1809 to 1810, their short but intense affair resulted, on September 29, 1810, in the birth of a daughter, whom the princess tellingly christened Marie-Clementine, in a nod to the father.[39] Metternich acknowledged his fatherhood when he met the princess again in 1825 in Paris. In 1828, Marie-Clementine married, and one year later she died of a miscarriage.[40] The paths of Metternich and Princess Bagration crossed numerous times, right up until Metternich's old age, but there is a conspicuous absence of any signs of a continual correspondence. This relationship appears to have been more fleeting than that with the next competitor for his interests, Wilhelmine von Sagan. During the Congress of Vienna, the two women lived in opposite wings of the same palace. Even after the congress had ended, Metternich kept in touch, and there was a sporadic exchange of letters. As late as July 1852, Melanie von Metternich, the chancellor's third wife, recorded an ironic remark in her diary: "We were also visited by Countess Bagration, who spent six weeks in Vienna and came almost daily to our house. Her cosmetics and equipage are of unparalleled originality."[41] Only a few days before her death on May 21, 1857, the eighty-four-year-old Metternich had had dinner with her. When he learned of her death, he commented: "I cannot be surprised that she passed away. What was miraculous was the fact that she was still able to live, given the way she was. Her appearance exceeded all imagination. It cannot be compared to anything else but a walking, eating, and talking mummy."[42]

Paris: Caroline Bonaparte (Later to Become Queen Murat)

As far as we know there were no comparable female adventures in the field of diplomacy during Metternich's time at the Berlin embassy. This changed dramatically once he moved to Paris. The young court of Napoleon at Saint Cloud attracted him because it was dominated mostly by men and women of his own generation. New and old nobility mixed, and there were no arrogant attempts to distance the court from society through etiquette or an exaggerated sense of class difference—nothing like the reservation, or even rejection, that the Metternichs had experienced from the court nobility in Vienna when he arrived there in 1794. Metternich moved within these circles "without aristocratic conceit and without consciousness of class, without prejudices and resentment."[43] Although he rejected Napoleon's political system, he was strongly influenced by the Parisian idea of the empire as a modern variation of classicism. On the basis of many meetings, the famous actress Mademoiselle Georges, who was Napoleon's mistress for some time, confirmed how well Metternich was received by this environment, and reported that he could frequently be seen near the court: "This famous diplomat was very cheerful [*fort gai*], very informal, very natural [*très simple*], and a very witty mocker. He liked to laugh, the great diplomat."[44] During the great dispute between Metternich and Napoleon in Dresden, Mademoiselle Georges happened to perform on one of the city's stages.

Metternich considered it his main task to find out about Napoleon's true intentions. He therefore sought to get close to the court whenever an opportunity arose. The women in particular thought that he was "a reincarnation of Casanova in an Austrian version."[45] Caroline Bonaparte's biographer describes the look of the youthful envoy as the exact opposite of Murat: tall and slender, elegant gestures, even facial features, blond hair (mildly powdered to appear older), blue eyes with attractively drooping eyelids. He had pale skin, she writes, so pale, in fact, that Caroline spoke of a "cream face" after their first meeting—in any case, he was an attractive man.[46]

The French painter François Gérard, who worked at the studio of Jacques-Louis David, painted a portrait of Metternich around this time, in 1810. In it Metternich, then thirty-seven, appears even more youthful, sensitive, with a lingering, scrutinizing expression that is somehow forthcoming and restrained at the same time. Gérard was born in 1770—almost the same age as Metternich—and knew about the effect that Metternich had on women. He painted him, as it were, from their perspective. The painter's model liked the result so much that, during his long stay in Paris in 1810, he had a copy made that he took with him to Königswart, where it can still be admired today. This is how we must imagine Metternich as looking when he confidently pitted himself against Napoleon—the "world soul on horseback" (Hegel)—in Paris, and worked on his long-term plan to replace him and his empire with a balance between the main powers of Europe.

One look at Gérard's portrait makes it clear how the resolute and rather rough Napoleon could have come to underestimate this envoy. He even said to his sister Caroline: "Entertain this simpleton [*ce niais*] well, we need him at the moment."[47] According to Bertier de Sauvigny, Caroline—"selfish, not very cultivated, cold, calculating"—the woman with the big nose and the hard eyes, posed a problem for official portrait painters at the time. Metternich did not share this opinion at all. Because of her political proximity to Napoleon, she appeared promising enough to the envoy to make his advances. He later remembered: "Caroline combined a pleasant exterior with somewhat common powers of mind. She had carefully studied the character of her brother, and did not deceive herself as to his defects, or the danger to himself of the excess of his ambition and love of power. . . . Caroline exercised great power over the mind of her brother, and it was she who cemented the family bonds."[48] Metternich very quickly found some success. It was through Caroline that, at the end of November 1806, he learned that her husband, Murat, hoped to become the king of a newly founded Poland; in February 1807 he had news about Napoleon's mistress in Warsaw—Countess Marie Walewska—and he learned earlier than others about Napoleon's plans for a divorce.[49] One should not, however, overestimate the importance of, in Manfred Botzenhart's phrase, "women as a source of information." Napoleon, who was always cool and calculating in his personal conduct, rarely revealed genuine secrets; if he did, it was likely to be in conversation with Metternich, who knew how to use his rhetorical skill to provoke and manipulate him, as he did so well at their encounter in June 1813 in Dresden. When one looks ahead to the time when the queen of Naples and her husband were expelled, and, following the execution of her husband, the demoted Caroline had to choose a new name, one does not quite want to follow Sauvigny in his harsh judgment of her. She called herself Countess of Lipona—an anagram of "Napoli." Metternich remained in touch with her by letter and saw to it that her exile in upper Italy, then part of Austria, was as comfortable as possible.

Laure Junot, the Duchess d'Abrantès

Among the many salons of Paris, one stands out in virtue of the twenty-two-year-old host's attractiveness, grace, and intelligence, and because she was at the same time the wife of a courageous general who was as devoted to Napoleon as "a hunting dog" to his master.[50] Napoleon had ennobled his former adjutant Andoche Junot, as he tended to do in the case of his most faithful military leaders, and he became the Duc d'Abrantès. In 1806 he was still the governor of Paris; one year later, Napoleon appointed him commander of the campaign in Portugal. This left Junot's wife with the time and opportunity to surrender to Metternich's advances; in this case, Metternich once again knew how to combine the pleasurable and the useful. In Laure, he found a glowing admirer who memorialized him in her twenty-five volume memoirs.

Metternich's relationship with this court lady and author is particularly exciting for the historian. Despite being discretion incarnate, Metternich became entangled in a scandal that is ideal for depicting the slippery ground Metternich was on as soon as envy, passionate love, anger, public attention, gossip, and politics all became entwined.[51] Metternich made the mistake of secretly exchanging letters with Laure Junot, using a chambermaid and Viscount Pierre-Benoît Desandrouin as messengers. Metternich knew the latter very well from his youth; by now quite old, he had been the imperial treasurer of his father's government in Brussels. Back then the viscount had taken Metternich as a companion on his official trip to London. Now, he told Metternich in strict confidence what had happened: Caroline, Napoleon's sister, who had in the meantime become Queen Murat of Naples, nevertheless was in jealous rivalry with Junot's wife. Through a bribe, she had made sure that the letters ended up in the hands of Junot's husband, the general. Although the general was himself romantically interested in Caroline, he nevertheless vented his anger at his wife—and also to Metternich's wife, whom he summoned especially. Eleonore thus also learned of Metternich's affair, and so did the public at court because Napoleon's sisters, Talleyrand, and of course the emperor himself got wind of it.

Nothing could have been more inconvenient for Napoleon than a high-profile scandal, because just at that time—the end of January to early February 1810—he was putting out feelers to Metternich regarding the potential marriage into the Habsburg dynasty. Metternich was no longer only a simple envoy but a minister with full responsibility, and his wife, Eleonore, had just reached out to Napoleon in Paris in order to facilitate this difficult business. Without further ado, Napoleon sent Junot, along with his wife, to the Iberian Peninsula with the task of taking back Portugal.

Eleonore shrugged off Junot's fit as that of a petit bourgeois parvenu, and told her husband in Vienna about the incident. In his reply of February 14, Metternich praises Eleonore for having kept a very clear and sober head.[52] His relationship with Laure Junot did not suffer either. She remained steadfastly attached to him, became more and more estranged from the Napoleonic milieu, and after 1815 acted as one of the most prominent French defenders of Metternich's policies. The so-called "1793" argument—an allusion to the general's Jacobin past—also moved her. She was aware that there were prisoners in the fortresses of Hungary and Bohemia as well: "But I ask the people who try to excuse '93 how it is that the prisons of the world were overflowing without a wrong having been committed."[53]

In June 1817, the Duchess d'Abrantès left Paris for Italy, where she met with Metternich in Florence and again, one last time, in Rome. He provided her with the references she needed in Rome, and in the twenty-third volume of her *Memoires,* published in 1837, she confessed that she never forgot him. He knew this, she wrote, "but I want the testimony of a thankful friendship to reach him through this book."[54] This is followed by a confession in a style typical of the cult of friendship of the age. This cult was not limited to the German phenomena of "sensibility" and "Sturm und Drang," but had also gained a foothold in France. The duchess declared herself to Metternich as a kindred soul, pointing out that friendship is not something produced at will but a matter of the heart. She herself, she said, was proof of how much it means to have a true friend. "Monsieur Metternich is a friend for whom his word is sacred, whose handshake means certainty; he is a man on whose moral support one can always rely, and this is what I seek when I suffer."[55]

The background to this public declaration has so far not been uncovered. We know of a significant yet mysterious remark Metternich addressed to the duchess on December 1, 1836, thus before the publication of her book: "You have therefore not at all been wrong when you relied on me."[56] As a result of her son's gambling debts, the duchess was in a desperate financial situation— so desperate that it threatened her reputation. On September 10, 1836, in the midst of her crisis, she confidentially *(confidentielle expressée)* turned to Baron James Rothschild, asking him to issue her a fixed-term bill of exchange for 3,500 francs. State Chancellor Metternich would guarantee it, and she turned to him, she wrote, because the Rothschild banking house had connections to Austria as well as to Metternich. The passionate letter ends with a postscript: "For thirty-six years now, Metternich has been my best friend" [*mon meilleur ami*]. Rothschild was understanding and, in principle, was prepared to grant the request, but—as one might expect of a banker—required confirmation from Metternich. On October 8, the duchess handed over a very personal and desperate letter for Metternich ("Mon ami, mon cher Clément . . .") to the Austrian ambassador, Apponyi. The ambassador passed all letters to the state chancellor. When Apponyi read these lines, he considered the matter sensitive and delicate enough to take it into his own hands. He assured Rothschild of Metternich's authorization, without having spoken to the latter, and encouraged the banker to sign an appropriate declaration and authorize the credit. To Metternich, Apponyi explained discreetly that he intentionally left aside the kind of relationship between him and the duchess, but he thought that if she were refused help it might lead to a scandal—a desperate woman, and, to make matters worse, a female author, had powerful means at her disposal to bring about such a scandal.[57] We know how Metternich replied to his former lover: he supported her call for help. This is a particularly striking example of how Metternich's relationships ended in agreement, not in discord—that there always remained the possibility of further contact, and also of reunion. Even after the relationships had ended, he continued to exchange letters with Princess Bagration, Countess and later Princess Lieven, and Duchess Sagan.

WILHELMINE VON SAGAN AND THE CONFUSION OF FEELINGS

His relationship with Wilhelmine von Sagan was the most complicated he ever had with a woman, and it made clear, even to him, his limits in amorous matters. In the transitional period of world history between 1813 and 1815, politics and passion, the public and private, became mixed up as never before or after, and rarely do historical sources allow such a deep insight into this mixed sphere as in the case of the correspondence between the two. Wilhelmine came to "international fame already during her lifetime" and would need a biography of her own.[58] She was born on February 8, 1781, into an old aristocratic family of the Courland. Her father was Peter Biron, Duke of Courland, Livonia, and Semigallia. In 1786 Friedrich Wilhelm II gave him the Prussian fiefdom of Sagan in Silesia with the explicit right of female succession. With the third division of Poland in 1795, the Duchy of Courland became Russian and the duke abdicated, but he received an annual rent of 25,000 ducats and, in addition, 2 million rubles from the sale of his estates in Courland. The inherited annual rent explains why Wilhelmine felt like the tsar's subject and felt obliged to him. The tsar was also in personal contact with her, a fact that later made her even more appealing to Metternich.

Following her father's death in 1800, Wilhelmine received the fiefdom of Sagan from Friedrich Wilhelm III. She took over the dominion in 1805, once she had reached maturity at the age of twenty-four. The Bohemian town of Náchrod with its castle, Ratiborschitz—the summer residence which served as a center of wartime politics in 1813—also belonged to Sagan. As was usual in her milieu, Wilhelmine grew up multilingual. She spoke German and Russian, and also learned French and English. Her teacher, Antonina Forster, shows striking similarities to Metternich's Jacobin tutor. She was the daughter of the natural historian and ethnologist Georg Forster, in whose house Metternich had encountered German Jacobin thinkers. The Enlightenment was therefore also part of Antonina's cultural heritage. All the men who later got to know her praised the seemingly ideal unity formed by her intelligence, attractiveness, and elegance.[59] Wilhelmine, who was portrayed as a princess at the early age of three by the German painter Angelika Kauffmann in Rome, represented the very idea of female self-determination, including the condition of female succession and complete economic independence, something that in that aristocratic age could exist only under exceptional circumstances.

Metternich made her acquaintance in the salons of Dresden while ambassador. At that time he was still captivated by the Russian princess Katharina Bagration. He shared Wilhemine's criticism of Napoleon, whom she detested and called an "arch-monster" [Erzungeheuer].[60] This was hardly surprising, giving that French troops had captured her dominion, Sagan, several times in 1806–1807 and 1813. Over long periods of time Metternich's relationship with Wilhelmine developed in the realm of the imagination, spurred on by letters that had to substitute for the lack of meetings. The emotional rhetoric of love and "sensibility," however, was disturbed by very earthly anguishes. Violent fits of jealousy triggered by his competitor Alfred von Windischgrätz confused his feelings. He wrote to her about his fever and cold, which seemed to cure him of his real malady of the soul. A letter from Wilhelmine appeared to still his emotional turmoil. On August 19, 1813, after she had started to open up to him, Metternich for the first time addressed her using the intimate and informal *tu* rather than the formal *vous*, and he hoped that she would now dedicate "the full powers of her mind, her reason, the strong and essential elements of her character" to him: "Always write to me the way you wrote on the 17th, properly of you, always you and nothing but of you."[61]

Wilhelmine reciprocated Metternich's florid affirmations of love, but without ever losing sight of the political situation. In the same letter, she asked about the war—Metternich was, of course, close to the sources. And in letter after letter Metternich followed her wish to be informed. His courting was successful, and she revealed just how successful when she suddenly fell into German when talking about her feelings: "Je sens eine wahre Sehnsucht [a true longing]—de Vous revoir."[62] Although she did not use the informal address *(tu)*, she was prepared to confess her love: "You understand so well how to be a lover, and I truly love with all my heart—well, dear Clemens, in truth I love you much more than you think. In this respect, I think you are very unjust—I think very, very often of you, just as you would like it to be. . . . Tell yourself that you could not have a better lover than me. . . . Your love is a necessity for my happiness."

These letters brought the two closer together and built up trust to the point at which, for Wilhelmine, the courtship and gallantry suddenly turned into something more serious. She shed her reticence, left her role within the context of courtly rhetoric, and for the first time said that, for a genuine loving relationship, she required exclusivity and commitment, something for which she did not really dare to hope and that, according to the conventions of the age, could be guaranteed only by marriage. Her letter of August 31, 1813, from her summer residence, Ratiborschitz, betrayed her mounting hope that Metternich might want a more serious relationship with her, by involuntarily, and movingly, dropping the language of courtly culture—French—in which she began the letter:

> There was never anything noble that I would not have expected to find in your soul, your heart, but if you are going to surprise me I shall be all the more touched. [At this point, the letter changes to German.] So few [men] keep what they promise, or what we [women] expect of them, and you, dear Clemens—you who I call with delight and pride, and the fullest satisfaction, my friend, you did not fulfill my expectations but the dreams of my imagination. With a feeling that rises far above this earthly life and lifts its pleasures and pains, I hold the friend which God in his grace has

let me find to a heart which has no other claim on such happiness as to feel your value. My dear and good Clemens, I love you with all my heart; should this love be all you could possibly ask for; in some respect it is more, the love itself assures me of this.

Wilhelmine then made plans for them to change their travel itineraries so that they would meet as soon as possible. More than once, she used the end of the letter to affirm her love, saying, among other things, in German: "Now you know that you only have to ask—you can count on me. Fare thee well—Adieu mon Ami, mon cher Clément, Adieu—j'ignore, pourqoui je Vous ai écrit en allemand, je ne m'en étais pas apperçue."[63]

Metternich, for his part, immediately arranged accommodation in Laun [Louny], northern Bohemia, and gave orders to his chef de cuisine. The letters following their meeting were increasingly made up of mutual declarations of love. Wilhelmine signaled that she wanted a firm relationship, writing: "I am no longer alone in the world with my wish for a being that will *always* love me. Judge accordingly, dear Clemens, whether I am really sincerely attached to you."[64] Such frankness must have also characterized the moment when she handed Metternich a token of her love—a lock of her reddish-brown hair, which Metternich kept like a sacred object in his desk.[65] A little later, Wilhelmine declared her love even less unequivocally, by addressing the topic of their relationship directly: "Remind yourself what I told you about my situation: there are pretty strong ties, but none of the inseparable kind that are forged in front of an altar—that is the perspective from which to look at our situation."

Metternich, however, obviously wanted to underplay the seriousness of the situation. He replied that there were stronger ties even than those formed in front of an altar—namely, those that were derived from divine wisdom as laws. These, he wrote, were the ties of the heart. Human laws exist only to hold together what otherwise could not maintain itself. The heart does not need laws, because it stands above laws and above reason.[66]

From October 31 onward, Wilhelmine at long last uses the informal *Du,* "this sweet, familiar attribute behind whose heartfelt use in the language of all countries expresses genuine intimacy."[67] But Wilhelmine did not stop revealing her secret desires to Metternich: protection against all the vicissitudes of life, security, happiness, and hope—that was all she wanted, she wrote.[68]

Metternich involuntarily fueled these hopes further by describing the warmth and hospitality of the Bachofens, a married couple who ran the inn at Basel where he had stayed in January 1814 while following the advancing front line. The sixty-year-old couple seemed to him as harmonious as Philemon and

Baucis in Ovid's *Metamorphosis*. Everything in their home had an air of the Biedermeier about it: it was very clean, well kept; it had beautiful furniture and paintings and lacquered walls. They had four children and eighteen grandchildren, and lived their lives with a stoic serenity; Metternich had the idea that he might want nothing else than to be a Monsieur Bachofen to Wilhelmine's Madame Bachofen.[69] With this suggestion, Metternich touched upon Wilhelmine's sore spot. She responded by saying that she would wish every good Christian woman such a happy home, but that she was deprived of it, and that the idea would only trigger useless wishes in her. Along her path, she always encountered "illusions of happiness but never happiness itself." And then she wrote something that Metternich was incapable of understanding because, despite his considerable empathy, he was not willing or able to acknowledge the wish for unconditionality: "Beloved, you may love me less; that's natural; it is also the case that you may stop loving me, but ... the thought of becoming a stranger to you causes me terror. You would destroy my whole existence if you decided no longer to be interested in me. My love, I must be loved not only with all the imperfections that you are aware of, but also with those you do not know. I can no longer renounce your heart."[70] With Mr. and Mrs. Bachofen in mind, she confessed that she loves the big world only out of despair. She could find real happiness if she could withdraw, surrounded by a few friends, and live for the one with whom she found happiness.[71] Her character, she wrote, was such that she permanently desired the presence of her beloved. The mistake was not that she had married but that she had chosen the wrong person.[72]

Metternich avoided providing further nourishment for these desires. He would have had to give up his marriage, the domesticity that was indispensable to him—in other words, precisely the stability that Wilhelmine was seeking, which, after all the emotions and ideas he had stirred in her, she sought with him and only with him. Besides, an ongoing relationship with another partner whom she had known even before she knew Metternich was a permanent provocation to him. That partner was Alfred von Windischgrätz, who took part in the campaign of 1813–1814 as a lieutenant colonel under Schwarzenberg. Wilhelmine constantly asked Metternich, of all people, about the officer's fate in battle. Wilhelmine's insistence that she would only renounce her freedom if Metternich committed to her unequivocally was not plausible to Metternich. His jealous rivalry with Alfred von Windischgrätz did not fit into Metternich's conception of love.

Friedrich Gentz further fomented Metternich's restlessness by continually providing him with rumors from Vienna about who else Wilhelmine might have her eyes on, adding such wise advice as the following: "My main and basic premise remains unchanged: W. is too intelligent and has too noble a mind not to put everything in second place compared to the happiness of a solid connection with you. But she should not be left to herself for too long."[73] Neither Metternich nor Gentz understood what Wilhelmine really wanted. The secret correspondence between the two men reveals how anxious the situation made Metternich. The editor of Metternich's letters, Friedrich Wittichen, had no access at all to this correspondence, and the "posthumous papers" do not mention them. With regard to the publication of Metternich's works, the family archivist noted on each single letter: "Excluded in its entirety." In the letters, Gentz regularly reported on the situation in the Sagan home and on Wilhelmine's mood and worries. There is every reason to doubt that Gentz was the right person for this job, given his inclination toward gossip, drama, and exaggeration. It is likely that he caused further damage, confusion, and misunderstanding of the kind that third parties almost invariably produce when interfering in precarious amorous relations. Metternich later said that he struggled with an "educational project" for Wilhelmine. If so, then statements such as the following from Gentz probably provided rich material for it: "W. is not yet *disciplined* enough herself for leading a regular, calm, pure, and solemn life. She spent her early life under the influence of fierce passions which only ever gave her short and spasmodic pleasure and then a long sequence of pains. If she is still susceptible to happiness at all, then she will blossom only in the sunshine of confidential contacts with you."[74] And when he observed her despondent, Gentz knew the right therapy: "Let her spend eight days with you—and all will be in perfect harmony."[75]

Politics was an essential and permanent part of their relationship. Metternich was fascinated by Wilhelmine's independence of mind, and he fascinated her because he was close to the corridors of power. At her salon during the Congress of Vienna, Wilhelmine continued to fulfill her mediating role in the communication between the powerful individuals of Europe. Varnhagen, as a neutral outside observer, described how discreetly she operated: "As always, the Duchess of Sagan was at the center of a lively circle that, on this occasion, was heightened even further by noblesse and importance. The engaging nature of this beautiful lady, as mild and benevolent as she was strong and energetic, had the effect of a conquering power, and it seemed to depend only on her whether she wanted to influence important decisions." The diplomat added that she did not have any ambitions in this direction, although she would have been very well capable of fulfilling such a role.[76]

The love that Metternich was looking to receive from Wilhelmine and the love she wanted from Metternich could not be made to agree, and as a result the elevated tone of the beginning of their courtship deteriorated into deep bitterness; the conventional, distanced *Vous* replaced the more intimate *tu*. A psychologist would probably speak of phenomena such as transference, projection, and misdirected role expectations, and of the function of personal constructions. Metternich, who would probably have been sympathetic to such ideas, explained his turning away from Wilhelmine von Sagan as being the result of major disappointment:

> Everything has changed so fundamentally between us that it is not at all astonishing that our thoughts and feelings do not meet at all any more, and that we find ourselves in a situation in which the one is more than alien to the other. I begin to believe that we never knew each other. We each followed a phantom. You think that you see a model of perfection in me and I see in you every kind of beauty and intellectual greatness that exists, a matter far above ordinary values. As a natural consequence of these illusions, you found it right to lower my worth in your imagination as much as, earlier, you had found it right to elevate it.[77]

After the end of July 1814, Metternich and Wilhelmine von Sagan once again became closer to each other, seemed to have reconciled themselves with each other.[78] But in October, problems began to reemerge that could no longer be solved. Alfred von Windischgrätz successfully rekindled his relationship with his former lover, and Metternich suffered the pains of a truly torturous jealousy. The tsar even managed to top this. He offered to help Wilhelmine get her illegitimate thirteen-year-old daughter away from the influence of her father, a Russian governor in Finland. Only the tsar, it seems, was able to do anything about this custody battle.[79] Metternich was deeply hurt by the fact that Wilhelmine turned to the tsar at the very moment when Metternich was having the most bitter political dispute with him over Poland and Saxony. He felt betrayed by both of them. Alexander, for his part, was driven by a "strange, almost pathological interest" in Metternich's love affairs and gleefully used them to gossip about him and to expose him publicly. In October 1814 Metternich and Wilhelmine's relationship was broken off completely.[80] He continued to speak to her and correspond with her, even helped her formulate a request to the Russian finance minister regarding her appanage, but their relationship now remained cool and distant.

By March 1815 Metternich's aloof attitude to Wilhelmine had given way to a deep bitterness. The woman he had once thought he could never live without he now accused of always having been distant from him. This distance, he claimed, never bothered her very much because he had never been more than an object of superficial interest for her. His whole life, all his moral qualities, all the strength he ever felt he possessed, he had given to her. He had given all to her, and she had only wanted a little bit of it.[81]

There is only a small step from here to the claim he made in his "general confession" to Wilhelmine's successor when asked how he could possibly have been in love with this woman: "I never was: I was in love with my impossible intention. . . . I fell out with myself because of her. I do not hate her, because I never loved her; I hate the time I wasted with the pursuit of erroneous ideas."[82] In his confession, he revealed that his long-term strategy had been to persuade Wilhelmine to give up on her "stupidities" [*Dummheiten*], meaning her relationships with other men. He then went on to make a remark that can be found, shorn of context, in practically every book on Wilhelmine von Sagan, and that is often used as if it would suffice on its own as a characterization of her: "She sins seven times a day, behaves like a lunatic, and engages as easily in love adventures as other have lunch." But then, surprisingly, he immediately corrects himself and reaches a positive judgment that seems to undermine this disparaging remark: "Lady Sagan is a highly intellectual person, full of strong self-confidence, of an infinitely healthy power of judgment and an almost inexhaustible physical calm."

DOROTHEA VON LIEVEN: "THE NEARNESS OF THE BELOVED"?

Encounter on a Business Trip

Among all of Metternich's love affairs, the last important one, with Dorothea von Lieven, is the most peculiar. Although he had the longest and therefore most voluminous correspondence with her, stretching from November 1818 to July 1826, the two lovers met in person only during three brief periods. The Congress of Aix-la-Chappelle was the context for the beginning of their relationship in October / November 1818. They then met again in October 1821 on the occasion of the English king visiting Hanover, and finally one more time in October / November 1822 during the Congress of Verona. What the two told each other about their love over hundreds of pages demonstrates that this relationship was no superficial affair, as Metternich's relationships with educated and politically knowledgeable aristocratic women are usually classified (and thus trivialized). There has to be a different explanation for a sustained and intense exchange of letters over eight years, despite there having been just three brief periods, amounting to no more than a few weeks in total, during which they met in person.

Dorothea was born on December 28, 1785, in Riga, Latvia, and came from an aristocratic German Baltic family, the von Benckendorffs.[83] Her brother was the tsar's adjutant general and one of the leading generals in the campaign against Napoleon. In 1800 she had married Christoph von Lieven, who was eleven years her senior. He was a Baltic German and general of the Russian army. During his long time as Russian envoy to London (1812–1834), Dorothea developed such a presence at the court that she became a social and political figure of the first order, a "grande dame par excellence." In 1816 she wrote to her brother: "No event is considered fashionable if I am not present, and I have even arrived at amusing the English and myself at the same time."[84] Diplomats who were well disposed toward her called her "the mother of the diplomatic corps."[85] Everyone was careful not to fall out with her, because she was friendly with Castlereagh and Wellington, and later with Canning, and a close confidante of the prince regent. Ambitious, intelligent, funny, in possession of a sharp mind, quick-witted, and quickly bored—these were the traits ascribed to the "cosmopolitan aristocrat." Nesselrode even experienced her as a charismatic personality.[86] Metternich would have had the opportunity to meet her on his visit to England in 1814, but back then he ignored her, whereas the countess at the time considered the minister intimidating and aloof.

Then, at the meeting of the monarchs at the Congress of Aix-la-Chappelle, which was also attended by Christoph von Lieven and his wife, Metternich and Dorothea were placed next to each other by their dinner host, Nesselrode (October 22, 1818).[87] They were immediately struck by one another. Within a few moments, Dorothea von Lieven was captivated by Metternich's openness, and she immediately noticed how often his witty remarks made her laugh. She, in turn, immediately hit upon the topic that was best suited to getting Metternich talking with the greatest intensity, namely Napoleon. They discovered that they liked the same authors, paintings, furniture, books, and music. Dorothea revealed that she was in the habit of playing pieces by Metternich's favorite composer, Rossini, on the piano, just like Metternich's daughter Marie. Later Metternich sent her the autobiography of Benvenuto Cellini. Both loved children, agreed in their political judgments, and were convinced that their countries should be allies. The thirty-three-year-old and the forty-five-year-old were moved so deeply by their encounter that they felt their souls were destined for each other. Wherever there was an opportunity, they each sought the harmonious presence of the other, even if just during a ride in a carriage from the Belgian Spa back to Aachen at the end of a conference outing. But there were also other opportunities to get closer to each other. After being apart for only a few days, Metternich described to his new lover how he had been struck by a natural force:

> The stories of *our* lives are condensed in a few moments. I have found you just to lose you! The past, the present, and perhaps the future, are contained in these few words. In less than eight days, I have concluded a

period of my life. That would appear like a dream to me if I would not know myself. Others are either all or nothing to me. My soul is neither sensitive to anything half-felt, nor half-thought. I spent the past weeks in your presence. I have spoken little with you, and you are today a part of my existence. . . . The day I saw that my thinking and yours met, the day that no doubt was left in me that you understand me, that your mind and your heart altogether follow the direction that I consider my direction, I felt that I could become your friend. . . . I had to affirm that for my friend: for you—my friend for eight days and for life.[88]

The Peculiar Correspondence

As in the days of his youth, Metternich gave expression to his new love with the evocative emotionality and the linguistic forms of sensibility. That was the right tone to meet the expectations of his female counterpart and to win her lasting attention. It was the beginning of an apparent romance that lasted eight years.

In fact, however, Metternich was unable to switch off the soberly calculating politician in him, and he saw in Dorothea not only the worshipped *amie* but also the influential—almost omniscient—lady at the very court in Europe that he considered, in the long term, the most important one for the interests of the Habsburg Monarchy in a European balance of power. Dorothea more than fulfilled Metternich's expectations. Her letters reported almost everything she knew about developments in Britain's politics, about conversations between the prince regent, Castlereagh, and Wellington that she either witnessed or had heard about from one of those present.[89] Metternich received background information from her that even the liberal English press did not provide, such as the circumstances of Castlereagh's suicide or the details of the plan that formed the basis of the Cato Street Conspiracy.[90] Metternich, in turn, always returned to three themes:

First, he expressed and explained to Dorothea the fundamental political convictions on which he based his behavior in times of political crisis, such as after the assassination of Kotzebue or in the case of press censorship. He discussed his ideas of personal freedom and legality and why he considered political murder, assassination, and revolution to be wrong. But in this context he also mentioned background information on concrete political events that was not contained in official documents and so is valuable to us.

Second, he described how he understood his own role within politics, how he tried to master it, how much of a burden it was to him, and how little he made himself dependent on the judgment of others. He would design an image of himself through thought experiments and hold it up against the image that others had of him—his public image—in order to attempt to expose the latter as a cliché, prejudice, or the product of revolutionary propaganda. Such attempts are rare in his official correspondence. Provided these private letters are read with a critical eye, they therefore help the historian to better evaluate and understand Metternich himself, as opposed to the image his contemporaries had of him. This sort of letter also explains why women who were closer to Metternich tended to evaluate him more positively than did his professional colleagues.

The third topic was women in general and the women in his life in particular, which is, of course, the focus of the present chapter. This theme ran through all of his confidential correspondence with women, but in the case of Dorothea von Lieven it was clearly dominant, perhaps because he could now treat it without any kind of jealousy, unlike in the case of Wilhelmine von Sagan.

On November 17, 1818, at the Congress of Aix-la-Chappelle, Metternich saw Dorothea for the last time. This meeting represents another development in their relationship: from this point on they used the informal *tu* instead of the usual *vous*—a development that occurred much more quickly than with Wilhelmine von Sagan. Within courtly society it normally took a long time to move toward informal address. There was a strong emphasis on keeping one's distance; it was often unusual to adopt such informal modes of address even with members of one's own family. It is therefore significant that, in the case of the German-Russian countess, and later princess, from London and the leading minister of the major power of Austria, this transition happened within days.

Gender Stereotypes and the Intellectual Equality of Women

What did Metternich find in Dorothea that so transformed him, and what did his chosen one discover in him to make her trust him so quickly? What made them even talk of lifelong love after such a short time? These are not trivial questions. Rather, they lead us right to the fundamental problems of relations between the genders, to ideas of emancipation and assigned roles. Metternich was permanently reflecting on these and tried to explain to Dorothea why he was so certain of her after only a few days. Hinting at the power of erotic attraction at the beginning of a relationship, he said: "What attracts most men, has no effect on me; I do not know whether I need more than the others, but I am aware that I desire something else."[91] What this was, he illustrated by reporting a conversation about "the fair sex" that he had had in a public house in Aix-la-Chapelle with the Russian envoy from Torino. They both praised what they liked in a woman. For the Russian it was plumpness, round cheeks, chubby arms; he was little interested in the mind, he had said; he opted for "volup-tuousness," for the well-fed who liked their food. Metternich replied that he only cared about the mind, heart, and soul (*l'esprit, le coeur et l'âme*), no matter how slim or round the cheeks were. This was certainly true in the case of his wife Eleonore, about whom there was universally agreement that she was no beauty.

Metternich believed that there was a difference between the sexes regarding the degree to which they were captivated by love. Even if the intensity of feeling was the same in both, it was nevertheless the case that "love fills the whole life of women, but only part of the life of men."[92] The more men left their youthful age behind, the more they became attracted by young women, a trait that, how-ever, Metternich claimed not to have himself. Dorothea was twelve years younger than him, but when they met she was already thirty-three. He assured her "that her age was one of her attractions for him." His experience with women told him that there was "a delay of ten years" between the two sexes, with women being ten years ahead in terms of intellectual development. Or, to put it differently, if both were of the same age, then the woman was intellectu-ally superior to the man: "The foundation for any happy relationship must be a roughly equal capacity for thought; and just that is rarely given in the case of two people of the same age but opposite sex."[93]

Metternich illustrated this delay of ten years in the development of men in the form of a scale. In parallel with the seasons and the times of the day, he distinguished between the stages of life: (1) childhood and youth (spring, morning); (2) sexual prowess (summer, midday); (3) sexual decline (autumn, evening); (4) infirmity (winter, night). According to Metternich, men reach their sexual zenith at an age of thirty-one or thirty-two years, women at twenty-four or twenty-five. The age of sexual death for men is sixty-three; for women it is forty-nine. He sent this scale to Dorothea on May 15, 1823—his fiftieth birthday.

At first sight this diagram is surprising: Metternich paid attention only to sexual vitality. But given that he talked about intellectual capacities only in the context of his overall views on gender issues, he must implicitly have consid-ered intellectual and physical conditions as two independent forms in which one and the same individual became manifest. In any case, he mostly stressed the intellectual equality [*geistige Ebenbürtigkeit*] of women and men. Women even appear to have the upper hand in that they develop more quickly and therefore are more advanced at a given age.

With these views Metternich was a complete outlier. The overwhelming ma-jority of his male contemporaries would have scorned such a position. The much-praised, supposedly progressive Code Napoleon, for instance, is backward

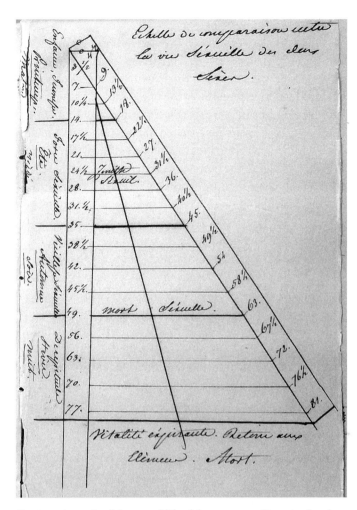

Comparative scale of the sexual life of the two sexes. Conceived and
drawn by Metternich (May 6, 1823).

by comparison. In the discussions over the codification of the law, Napoleon
himself had removed the legal capacity of women before the law. On his explicit request, article 213 read: "The husband owes protection to his wife, the
wife obedience to her husband." A wife was not allowed to enter a plea without
authorization by the husband. In Prussia, women could get a divorce in accordance with the rules of state law, and women like Wilhelmine von Sagan or
the popular novelist Fanny Lewald actually did. In France, the Code Napoleon
prohibited this.

Choice of Partners and Women in Politics

Metternich's view on choosing a partner also diverged from the customs of aristocratic society. These customs were intended to secure or expand possessions through family contracts. Metternich's ideal was the free choice of one's partner. But on this question in particular he saw women confronted with an almost insuperable problem. Whereas men approached their goal—the courted woman—directly, youthful women were looking for something "that mature experience and a deep knowledge of the human heart hardly succeed in recognizing." Women tried to anticipate the future, to know whether their partner would be reliable, loving, just, and honest:

> A woman's heart wants to know in advance how the heart of the man whom they wish for is made. A man, in most cases, has reached his goal at the point where, for the woman, a beginning has undeniably been made. The man desists, where the woman starts. Love appears too protracted an affair to him, and to her life appears too short. . . . It [love] consists mostly of contradictions and oppositions; it is strengthened by difficulties, *it is only crowned through complete parity.*[94] It must move through many phases and overcome many difficulties. Most people lose their breath halfway when dealing with difficult matters—happy he who perseveres![95]

These reflections on love, the constraints of gender roles, and how to choose one's partner complicate the common picture of Metternich as an adulterer, courtier, and superficial womanizer. They speak to his life experience and demonstrate his aim of equality [*Gleichberechtigung*] between the sexes, even if the men and women had to take on different roles because of social compulsion. He was ahead of his time in transposing the question of equality [*Gleichberechtigung*] onto the political arena, thereby undermining the conventional norms for equality within the feudal hierarchy. This was in opposition to the nineteenth-century bourgeois trend increasingly to limit the space in which women could act by extending the rights of men. Men won the right to take up arms, to organize, to take on political office, even the right to vote and to stand for election in regional parliaments and, finally, the national Parliament [*Reichstag*]. All this was withheld from women. Metternich wanted to treat women as equals [*gleichwertig*]. He still saw them, at least in the exceptional cases of women who were economically independent, as respected personalities who were consulted by men for political advice. For Metternich, the minister with responsibility for the Habsburg Monarchy, it was conceivable for a woman to take a leading role in politics. There could be no better example than Maria Theresia. He criticized the division between the sexes in politics, assuring Dorothea: "If you had been born a man, you would have risen to the heights where fateful decisions are taken. With an understanding like yours, courage like yours, one is in a position to do anything."[96]

Metternich had encouraged Wilhelmine von Sagan to give him political advice. At the end of November 1813, just before the invasion of France, he was occupied with the important matter of the declaration to the French nation. He drafted the memorandum we discussed above, in which he developed his view on matters. He sent it to her, adding: "I count on your approval; it serves me as a safeguard." He went even further, expressing his wish that she were the envoy and he the minister, or vice versa.[97] And he thought Dorothea von Lieven should sit on the throne: "My liberalism and at the same time my despotism convince me that the best monarchic system would be a female sovereign with great esprit [Geist] and tact, which women possess to a much larger extent than men; in addition, a grand vizier, a personality that possesses intelligence, a heart, and honor."[98]

This was not just rhetorical flourish or an attempt to ingratiate himself with Dorothea. Instead it fits with his fundamental convictions regarding the political ability of women, which—as we have seen—Metternich expressed several times in identical form. Archduke Johann's indignant reaction on one of these occasions is a proof, so to speak, that these ideas of Metternich's were taken seriously and not considered ironic or playful. The archduke decidedly disapproved of the idea that women should take up leading political positions, and he suggested that Metternich spent too much time in salons, which were dominated by women: "In these circles of our so-called 'refined ones' [Feinen], he once lectured for two hours about the question of whether a woman may be minister for foreign affairs."[99]

The fatal distance between the two lovers forced both to reflect on their relationship. Dorothea developed her own "theory on their liaison." She suspected Metternich of worshipping the ideal of "Platonism." He rejected this vehemently and emphasized how much he suffered because of her absence and the physical distance between them. But, he added, for principled reasons he did not want to strive for something that could only lead to deep regret. Without a doubt, he was cut off from his happiness by a distance of hundreds of miles. But he knew a secret: "Hundreds of miles are a truly enormous obstacle; one would be robbed of one's happiness by a far lesser distance. My soul knows of no distances at all; my heart shortens them. I can be wholly with my female friend and at the same time in another part of the world; only in her proximity do I know myself happy."[100]

This imagined proximity had earlier found expression in Goethe's poem "Nearness of the Beloved" of 1795. The last four lines of the four-stanza poem run: "I'm near thee, though far away mayst be— / Thou, too, art near! / The sun then sets, the stars soon lighten me. / Would thou wert here!"[101] This lyrically evoked longing seems to express the general mood that, from Metternich's side, runs through the whole correspondence.

Metternich's Urge to Write

Given that there were few opportunities for personal meetings and the whole relationship was apparently Platonic, it is understandable that Metternich's engaging literary style and his repeated affirmations of love raised Dorothea's suspicions. Dorothea might well have asked herself whether she was the real interest or whether there were other, more important purposes Metternich was pursuing. Why did the busy state chancellor sacrifice so much time for her? Metternich answered this by explaining how letter writing was integrated into his daily routine. He wrote very fast, he said. In only a few minutes he had determined "what is going on in me." The half-filled sheet of paper was always within easy reach, and he used every spare minute between trivial matters or serious meetings to write down another passage: "I take refuge with you; I get my strength from you; with you I am happy." This was the way he left work, trouble, and all sorts of nuisances behind. The imagined conversation gave him a feeling of understanding that provided him with psychological support. Looked at from a sober perspective, this probably had little to do with love. He was engaged in a kind of self-referential dynamic that involved guiding himself through pictures of the imagination that he had himself chosen. The other person was the screen onto which his own present condition was projected, and so stabilized.

Metternich delved into this parallel world of thought at various times throughout the day. The habitus of the writer of letters enabled him to constantly reflect—self-critically—on his political principles and the role he played in public life. Women were the ideal addressees for this because they were not competitors for the distribution of political power, and they were therefore less biased in their feedback. This interpretation of his habits seems plausible because Metternich did not limit this form of self-reflection to one lover at a time. He also practiced it with family members, and in particular his wives, his favorite daughters (Marie, Leontine), and his favorite son (Richard): whenever he was apart from them, he was in continuous correspondence.

Literary scholars have put forward an "epistolary theory" that might explain quite well the motive behind Metternich's letter writing. German authors of the Enlightenment, most notably Christian Fürchtegott Gellert, developed practical theories of letter writing that illuminate what the authors gain through their correspondence. Letters, it is said, imitate conversations and create a "stretched-out communicative situation," which forces the writer to search for the simplest and most apposite expression. Most importantly: "Writing organizes one's thoughts anew."[102] Historians have been irritated by passages in his love letters in which Metternich evaluated his political and historical role, reading them as expressions of his alleged vanity. Examples are: "Every error I make has an effect on 30 million people" or "My name has become associated with so many enormous events that it will go down in history together with them."[103] However, if we keep in mind his need to reaffirm his stances before his conscience, such sentences should appear in a different light.

In his private correspondence, Metternich heeded the advice of an intelligent contemporary: "If you want to know something and can't find it through meditation, then I advise you, my dear quick-witted friend, to talk it over with the next acquaintance you happen to meet."[104] Metternich practiced the method Heinrich von Kleist suggests in his "On the Gradual Formulation of Thoughts While Speaking."[105] The medium of letter writing allowed him to engage in an ongoing inner monologue. Even the imagination of the bodily presence of another person only served this purpose. Metternich was aware of this connection between love, thinking, writing, and his political duty and energy. In a passage already quoted above, he is lucid on this point: "The thought of my [female] friend does not leave me even amidst the most arduous tasks; it does not distract me from my duties, quite the opposite, it deepens my feeling of responsibility. It does not weaken my energy for action, but strengthens it."[106]

His love for Dorothea von Lieven was put to the test by a crisis that ensued when, following the death of Castlereagh, Dorothea's political convictions became more closely aligned with those of his successor, Canning. Metternich condemned these views. Regarding the Greek question, the tsarist empire had canceled its agreement with Austria and formed an alliance with England instead. Metternich feared that the system that guaranteed Europe's security would disintegrate as a consequence. He must have been greatly irritated by the role played by Countess Lieven in all of this. Dorothea herself spoke of a "bad mood" [*Verstimmung*] between them. She was well informed about events in Vienna and knew that, following the death of his wife, the fifty-three-year-old Metternich had turned his eyes on the twenty-year-old Antonia von Leykam, although she was not sure whether she should think of the young lady as his future wife or present mistress: "What a strange man you are! Taking notice of a little girl! I would expect to be seen as ridiculous, if I were to bother myself with a little boy!"[107] Metternich's last letter is dated October 30, 1826. Dorothea replied one last time, on November 22, suggesting: "Let us start again from the beginning. We should be hard put to it, you and I, to find anywhere in the whole world people of our own caliber. Our hearts are well matched, our minds too; and our letters are very pleasant. . . . I repeat: you will find no one better than me. If you meet your like, show him to me."[108] There is no known reply from Metternich.

WIVES AND CHILDREN: FAMILY TIES AND TRIBULATIONS

Eleonore von Kaunitz

We have already discussed Metternich's first wife, of course, in connection with their marriage. And we heard from Eleonore's aunt, Princess Eleonore von Liechtenstein, who characterized her as not beautiful, but graceful, lively, seductive, intelligent, and a rich heiress. Metternich himself gave the most fitting description of her—to, of all people, his beloved Dorothea von Lieven. There was no sign that he wanted to diminish his wife in the eyes of his lover in order to make the latter feel more important, like the real chosen one. Quite the opposite: he praised his wife to Dorothea, calling her an "excellent woman."[109]

In precarious situations, Eleonore always showed presence of mind and even courage—even toward Napoleon, who occasionally made efforts to present himself to her as a great conversationalist [causeur] but could often display an unsurpassable tactlessness. Metternich's granddaughter Pauline once heard her grandfather tell of such an episode. The French emperor—thinking it a joke—told Eleonore several times: "Princesse Laure, nous vieillissons, nous maigrissons, nous enlaidissons!" [Ah, Princess Laure, we are getting older, we're getting scraggy, we're getting ugly!] To Napoleon's delight, Eleonore laughed, and he continued: "Décidément vous avez plus d'esprit que toutes ces grues qui vous entourent!" [There's no doubt about it; you've got more brains than all those clodhopping women around you!][110]

In this, Napoleon was right. In delicate situations, Eleonore acted vigorously in support of her husband: most notably in the arrangement of Napoleon's marriage with Marie Louise, and, with great strength and confidence in the case of the public scandal brought about by General Junot. Metternich wrote to his wife whenever they were apart, just as he wrote to his lovers, and he took great interest in his children and in their upbringing; he shared in the worries and necessities of keeping a house. In addition to political discussion, his letters to his wife also contained numerous comments on other people, events, and his present intentions regarding, for instance, problems at conferences and how they were progressing. He kept her informed about preparations for the Karlsbad decrees. He looked at his wives as co-regents, so to speak, whose opinions he actively sought out. The third wife, Melanie Zichy-Ferraris, was a presence at the Chancellery and read the most secret dispatches to him; Metternich also read out the first drafts of his memoirs to her.

It is sometimes claimed that Eleonore did not have enough of a social network to host a first-rate salon, but this judgment overlooks the great hospitality she extended in her own suite of rooms on the first floor of the Chancellery and in their stately home, the Rennweg villa, where every Monday members of the diplomatic corps were invited for dinner, not to mention the many social gatherings that took place in the house. This was also the place where Metternich surrounded himself with greenhouses and monkey and parrot cages, and where he grew plants from Italy and Brazil. He thus created a kind of private domesticity into which he could disappear from his daily work. Here, he entered into the world of classicism, a world he had learned to love even more on his journeys to Italy. The first thing a visitor would have seen upon entering the villa was Canova's "Amor and Psyche" at the opposite end of the room.

In his mind, Metternich lived in two different worlds. The one was filled with memoranda and protocols, and belonged to his country, his office, his duties as a statesman.[111] This side of his life he spoke of as ghastly: attending at court,

"Musaeum" at the Rennweg villa. Engraver: Eduard Gurk. Lithography: F. Dewerth. Printing: Johann Höfelich (1836).

Gallery at the Rennweg villa. Engraver: Eduard Gurk. Lithography: F. Dewerth.
Printing: Johann Höfelich (1836).

the arrival of Tsar Alexander, having fifty people for dinner or three hundred
visiting in one evening, the endless receptions, the scores of tiresome garru-
lous characters, fake glamour, fake honors, empty speeches, and false fame.[112]
He hated everything to do with courtly life: the stiffness, the evening receptions, the long, cold corridors, the overheated salons, the stilted behavior, the
lack of feeling, the conversations that served no other purpose but showing off
or doing business. All this he summed up as "the swamp of business."[113]

The other world was the private one, a counter-world that he called "my real
capital, the one that sustains my life, provides the foundation for my happiness." Part of this world was having breakfast with his wife and children; part
of it was writing to his lovers. He considered it unbearable to be wholly dependent on others in life, and with this he was referring to his professional life.
Personal happiness, he held, could not be found in the hustle and bustle of the
world.[114] Ballroom events he considered a duty to be fulfilled. If his presence
was not indispensable, he left them after one or two hours, between eleven and
one o'clock.[115]

Metternich's private world consisted of a few friends, a lover, his wife, and
his children. He summed it up neatly: "A few very reliable friends, very devoted
ones who count on me no less than on themselves, a female friend [*une amie*],
these make up my state of happiness; an agreeable and calm domesticity, an

excellent wife, the mother of good children which she brings up well, that makes up my life overall."[116]

Metternich's Attachment to His Children and the Death of Clementine

The strong attachment Metternich had to his children is demonstrated by the events of the summer of 1820, when two of his daughters died of tuberculosis within the space of just two months. This put him in a desperate situation. In the months between November 24, 1819, and May 24, 1820, delegates from all the German states met in Vienna in order to add the Basic Law that had been promised at the Congress of Vienna to the Federal Act of 1815. Metternich had invited the politicians to the cabinet room of his Chancellery for the negotiations. While he was chairing the concluding negotiations in that room, his daughter Clementine, not quite sixteen years old, lay dying in the private rooms on the floor above. In addition to tuberculosis and pneumonia, she had developed pleurisy, and despite her having lost so much strength already, the doctors did everything they could to weaken her even further, bleeding her on three consecutive days. Metternich saw that, after three months of illness, the excessive loss of blood was draining her completely, and he doubted that the doctors could still save her: "There are cases where the remedy seems worse than the disease itself."[117]

Amid the emotional stress of the situation, Metternich's inner life expressed itself as it never had before: "Nothing breaks me down like a sick child. . . . It is not enough for me to know that those I love are content. I want them also to be happy. . . . Elegies do not belong to my character. I cannot lament. Heaven has doomed me to suffer in silence."[118] He found himself torn between political business, which tied him to the conference table, and the feeling that called him to his daughter's side. He was able to cope with the distress this caused only by returning to his typical way of reflecting on his situation and thus understanding it. Recording these reflections and communicating them, in this case to Dorothea von Lieven, helped him to keep his countenance to the outside. He knew how he was judged by others, and the situation brought this to mind: "In painful moments like the present it is more than ever necessary to turn my second nature outside—that nature which makes many people believe that I have no heart."[119]

The situation was almost impossible to endure. On one occasion, during a meeting with the plenipotentiaries in his office, doctors asked him to come to his daughter's room. One of the delegates, not aware of the situation, insisted: "Pardon me, allow me to draw your attention to some of the Rhine tariffs!"

Metternich "assured him that [he] would leave him now even if the Rhine should flow back to its source!"[120]

On May 1, 1820, the famous portrait of Clementine by Thomas Lawrence arrived from Florence. Metternich had made up his mind not to open the box for several months, but Clementine—in a state of semi-consciousness—had noticed the painting's arrival and asked for it to be unpacked and shown to her. She smiled and said: "'Lawrence seems to have painted me for the heavens, for he has surrounded me with clouds!' She wished to have the portrait placed beside her bed." She was granted her wish, even though, as Metternich writes, "this was unbearable for us; you cannot place life and death so close together."[121]

Clementine von Metternich, detail from portrait by Thomas Lawrence (1820).

Worst of all were the presentiments Clementine expressed regarding her impending death. Her room had a second bed so that she could change between them. One day she asked for her bed to be turned. "[When asked why, she explained:] 'I do not want always to see the same things,' adding immediately: 'Look at that bed . . . is it not extraordinary that they give me a stone bed?' I replied that she was mistaken: that the second bed was hung with muslin. 'Stone or muslin,' said she, 'both are alike to me; both are white, and that pleases me.'" Her look made Metternich shudder: "Her face is quite disfigured, and Lawrence himself would not know her. Her features are only to be recognised if she smiles; but this smile comes from a heavenly rather than an earthly being."[122] Eleonore was crushed by her death. She did not leave the room where Clementine had died, and she collected all of her daughter's belongings and kept them close to herself. Metternich also found it difficult to keep his composure: "I cannot enter the room without tears, and I soon return to my business, which makes a barrier between me and myself [*entre moi et moi même*]."[123]

At this point Metternich said something that is worth quoting in its entirety, for it demonstrates how sensitive and at the same time sharp-sighted his observations on women were:

> I was right to say that I always feel a certain anxiety about young girls who are too beautiful. The cause of their beauty is in most cases the cause of their death. Too great a delicacy in the features, a quite transparent skin, a certain flow in the figure, are all proofs of an extremely tender organism. A climate like ours acts on such a one like the north wind on the flowers of spring. I have, happily, the gift of keeping my senses, even when my heart is half broken. Of this I have given certain proof during the last months. The thirty men with whom I sit daily at the conference table have certainly never guessed what I was going through while I talked for three or four hours, and dictated hundreds of pages.[124]

The Death of Marie

Only a short while later, Metternich was again torn between political exigency and personal suffering. Following his annual stay at Königswart in June 1820, he traveled via Karlsbad to Vienna, setting off on July 11 and arriving on July 13. The next day, he went to see his family in Baden. On July 15 he received news of the revolution that had broken out in Naples earlier on July 2. Emperor Franz was at his summer residence in Weinzierl (lower Austria). The emperor immediately summoned Metternich to join him there, and Metternich arrived in Weinzierl on July 16.

In Baden he had seen his favorite daughter, Marie, who had recently married and was pregnant. She now also had all the symptoms of tuberculosis: "I found her terribly altered, so broken, so weak, that I have no more hope for her."[125] Five days after his departure, on July 20, she died. Metternich wrote: "How much I have loved this daughter, she on her side loved me more than as a father. For many years she has been my best friend. I had no need to confide my thoughts to her: she divined them. She knew me better than I knew myself. She had never a thought which did not become mine, never spoke a word which in her place I would not have said. I was constantly impelled to thank her, that she was what she was. I have sustained an irreparable loss."[126] During the preparations for his journey to Italy at the beginning of 1819, a journey he had rather been avoiding, it had been a consolation to him that Marie would accompany him. Once again he described the similarity of their natures: "I always find understanding with her, nothing is more soothing than this fact for my soul, which is lonely amid the hustle and bustle of the world." He recognized a special talent in her, the art of expressing something with aphoristic exactitude: "Recently, on her birthday she wrote to her mother: 'I write to you on my knees in order to thank you for twenty-two happy years!' That was all, but I prefer this one line to a whole sentimental novel."[127]

If we ask to what extent Metternich's Catholic faith consoled him, we find a peculiarly abstract attitude that corresponds to a sort of Enlightenment Kantianism. But he did not altogether want to renounce hopes for a life beyond this one, something Kant, after all, did not exclude a priori either: "Heaven sends me hard trials; I submit to its decrees, and I hope they will be imputed to me in a better world."[128] There was no revolt of a Job against a cruel God: "The burden which Providence lays upon me is very heavy, and would crush many men." Work was his therapy: "I throw myself into my task like a desperate man on the enemies' batteries. I no longer live to feel, but to act."[129]

The Metternich Family Stays in Paris

Up to that point Metternich had only played with the idea, but now, with his wife's agreement, he took action: he considered it necessary to remove his family from the atmosphere of Vienna. "During the last twenty years eight persons have died in my house, seven of them from lung disease."[130] But which place would be more suitable than the metropolis on the Danube? Metternich's reflections show that he was very able to provide a distanced analysis of the political situation of the world—he had just identified members of the secret order of the Carbonari, who were spread all over Italy, as being behind the revolution in Naples: "The main character of the Carbonari, the party which has led all the others, is the anxiety."[131] But such intellectual distance did not prevent him from developing this intentionally caused "anxiety" himself. When Eleonore suggested that they might spend some years in Italy, and that their son Victor could finish his studies in Padua or Siena, Metternich countered by saying that Italy was not an option under the present circumstances. And with the assassination of Kotzebue in mind, he wrote to Dorothea von Lieven: "Neither could I send my son to Germany; he might be murdered. I am far too exposed to the attacks from Radicals of every country to consider such plans."[132] Thus, Metternich drew the paradoxical conclusion that he had to send his family to Paris, meaning that he trusted that his family would be safe in the very country that was the source of revolutions in Europe.

Metternich's wife and children departed in the last week of September 1820. We would not have needed this experience to tell us how much he depended on his family, even if there was no other politician in Europe—with the possible exception of Nesselrode—who had spent more time on stagecoaches crisscrossing all over the Continent. But if he was at home, he regularly spent the time between nine and ten in the morning with his wife and children. That hour now needed to be filled. He had sealed off a whole section of the apartment above the Chancellery. He could not enter the room in which Clementine had died "without shivering," and he could not bring himself to set foot in Marie's house at all after her death.

Eleonore, his daughters Leontine and Hermine, and his son Victor returned three years later, on May 17, 1823. The idea had been that the geographical distance would enable Eleonore to enter the house with which so many terrible memories were associated. Metternich had in the meantime changed the house a great deal, removing everything that might have brought back memories of the sad times. On this occasion, too, Metternich was not inclined toward prayer and Christian ritual; instead he thanked "providence" that it "has given to the lapse of time great power over human feeling."[133] Metternich returned to his old life, with its "domestic happiness" of shared breakfasts and lunches. He referred to this in one of his trademark aphorisms, which he introduced with an allusion to the Old Testament: "Man is clearly not intended to be alone, and those who assert the contrary have a sick mind or heart."[134]

Eleonore's Death in Paris

The domestic bliss did not last long. Eleonore's poor health led Metternich to persuade his family to go back to Paris again. But his hopes that Eleonore's condition would stabilize there were not fulfilled. Metternich's personal court calendar shows that he spent the summer months of June and July 1824 at

Johannisberg, while Eleonore was in Bad Ems suffering pulmonary problems. On July 21, Metternich went to see the emperor in Bad Ischl. Eleonore and the children did not return to Vienna, but—with an interruption in Johannisberg— traveled to Paris, arriving in September shortly after Louis XVIII had passed away on September 16. They thus arrived at a time of political transition. Europe watched as Karl X ascended the throne.

At the beginning of 1825, worrying news reached Metternich. He suspected— rightly—that the doctors and his family were seeking to avoid making him anxious,[135] and he resolved to travel to the French capital at once if Eleonore's condition deteriorated. Although he could not be certain, Metternich feared that the lungs were affected—as we know today, she indeed suffered from tuberculosis. That, he knew, would have meant certain death. The uncertainty paralyzed him.

As in the summer of 1820, personal life and political crisis overlapped. Back then the crisis had been the consolidation of the federal Constitution and then the revolution in Naples; now, at the beginning of 1825, it was the Greek question, a conflict that threatened to divide the major powers. Metternich was afraid that Canning's ministry in London would interpret his journey to Paris as a pretext for discussing with the French government how to sabotage the London-backed common front of major powers against the Ottoman Empire, and for utilizing the new situation in France following the succession to promote Austrian interests generally. This particular instance proved very clearly how important his correspondence with Dorothea von Lieven must have been to the English court; he described his personal crisis to her in great detail and thus made it clear that he had no political reasons for going to Paris. In this situation, however, the judgment of "the world" did not matter to him. He knew the commentaries that would appear in the French press.

Even before his departure, he feared it would end in catastrophe. The way in which he digested the upcoming events shows, again, how much his wife meant to him. He knew that "after thirty years of undisturbed married life" he would now be "reduced to a frightful isolation. What shall I do with my daughters? To give them over to a governess is a very insufficient remedy, although I will never separate myself from my children." He contrasted the blows of fate that his family suffered with the public image of himself as a "fortunate man," and asked, half in desperation and half ironically: "What must it be like to be one of the so-called unfortunate ones!"[136]

On February 8, he made his final decision to travel to Paris. He had received a letter Eleonore had sent to Vienna on January 28. She knew about his travel plans. The letter was written in the knowledge that the end was near. She expressed her hope that God might still give her "a bit" of time with her loved ones, and then, addressing Metternich directly, confessed: "It would have cost me a lot to leave this life. Apart from the terrible misfortunes which put me down, I was always happy. I owe this to you, to you alone, my dear, my noble friend. You never caused me even a moment of grief. You only ever cared about my happiness, and you were successful, because I was always very happy, and I would with great pleasure begin my life for the next forty years again."[137] One cannot be skeptical about this sort of death-bed statement: it was meant sincerely.

Metternich now had to change all his travels plans. He had planned a meeting with Emperor Franz in Milan, which had now to be shifted to the first week of May. On March 5, he left Vienna and traveled directly to Paris, where he arrived in the early morning of March 14. He immediately went to his wife's side, and saw that she only had hours, or at best a few days, to live. On March 19, she passed away. Metternich, one last time, expressed all of his admiration for her in a letter to Dorothea von Lieven: "I have sustained an irreparable loss; Providence has so ordained. It is not for the survivors to give way to expressions of just lamentation when the best of mothers has parted from her children without a word of complaint."[138]

Antonia von Leykam: Why Did Metternich Marry a Twenty-One-Year-Old Woman?

Metternich's second marriage, in 1827, broke several taboos of the closed world of Vienna's high aristocracy simultaneously. Antonia von Leykam's mother was an Italian singer, née Caputo de Marchesi della Petrella, who performed in the theaters of Naples. Her father, Ambros Baron Leykam, was a chamberlain in Baden and a former member of the imperial knighthood of the canton of Ortenau in Baden.[139] The previous year, Dorothea von Lieven was already carefully listening to the rumors that the extremely beautiful young woman had been seen with Metternich. Being the daughter of an artist was disreputable enough to put one's moral credentials into question. It was also resented that it was Metternich, of all people, who showed such a relaxed attitude toward the principles of equality of rank [Ebenbürtigkeit] and legitimacy.[140] The emperor, by contrast, publicly announced that he supported his state chancellor: by decree of October 8, 1827, he made Mademoiselle de Leykam a Countess Beilstein. As bitter as it was for the ladies-in-waiting, by decree of December 21 the empress furthermore granted Antonia access to the court chambers [Großer Kammerzutritt]—that is, she gave her the status of a lady-in-waiting.[141]

According to Metternich, his children were happy about the marriage. To his son Victor, he later explained what had motivated him to take this step—namely, "the necessity not to be alone."[142] But this explanation is not enough for some. Historians, in particular, have been quick to trot out the usual cliché: an old man going for a young thing. The voices of Dorothea von Lieven, Friedrich Gentz, and the Viennese aristocracy began singing this tune, and it was later developed into a full-blown chorus of mockery by Srbik and Corti. Among the British public, Dorothea von Lieven began what could be called a smear campaign against the minister, and she did not hesitate to ridicule him. The Austrian ambassador in London reported that she had brought the catchphrase into circulation: "Le chevalier de la Sainte Alliance finit par une mesalliance." [The knight of the holy alliance ended up in a misalliance.] Metternich must have been particularly embittered by this—Dorothea knew that he rejected the Holy Alliance, this "loud-sounding nothing." At the same time, she denounced Castlereagh by spreading the following gossip: "Whatever has happened to Metternich's talents and intelligence? For he was intelligent, and exceptionally so. I remember that Lord Castlereagh occasionally called him 'a political harlequin,' that was not a bad remark." And she now joined the ranks of his critics, who, whenever they disagreed with Metternich politically, associated him with "intrigues . . . , malice, a foolish character and dishonesty."[143]

Metternich tried to let the rumors and reproaches bounce off him as so much "mud-slinging"—the business of the other, public half of his world. But when the reproaches began to come from his closest friends and his family, they touched upon his private life: the half of the world that was really important to him. We have heard him tell Dorothea von Lieven that his wife, children, and reliable friends were his true support. Now he felt compelled to explain himself. A remarkable letter to Countess Molly Zichy-Ferraris suggests the answer to the question of what led him to marry again, what counted more than erotic attraction—even if that exerted a strong influence, too.

The countess belonged to his small circle of "reliable" friends. Two weeks before the wedding, he sent her an excerpt from the only letter he had written so far in which he had defended his decision to marry, without saying to whom this defense had originally been addressed.[144] That person had to be of exceptional importance to him, and we today know that it was his cousin, Countess Flora Wrbna, née Countess Kageneck. For a long time she had been the *éminence grise* at "Villa Metternich"; she pulled all the strings, and she organized festivities and receptions and looked after visitors. Apart from "Flore," as she was called in the family, Metternich had such a close relationship only with his wife and children. Her rejection hurt him deeply.

He wrote to Flora that he had decided in favor of this marriage "with the reason and the calmness which are in my heart": "In great decisions I ask

Table 9.1. Metternich's children from his three marriages, with birth and death dates

Date of birth	Child	Date of death
January 17, 1797	Marie	July 20, 1820
February 22, 1798	Georg	November 22, 1799
April 6, 1799	Edmund	July 15, 1799
January 3, 1803	Victor	November 30, 1829
August 30, 1804	Clementine	May 6, 1820
June 18, 1811	Leontine	November 6, 1861
July 1, 1815	Hermine	December 1890
January 7, 1829	Richard	March 1, 1895
February 27, 1832	Melanie	November 16, 1919
April 21, 1833	Clemens	June 3, 1833
October 14, 1834	Paul	February 6, 1906
September 12, 1835	Lothar	October 2, 1904

counsel from no one." He was no longer twenty-five, and he knew exactly what he ought to do. And then follows a strange sentence: "The conduct of men may be influenced by the circumstances which form the setting in which they are placed."[145] Instead of declarations of love, Metternich referred to the circumstances on which one's wise calculations must be based. Which circumstances he had in mind we may deduce from his situation in 1827 and his strong commitment to family.

To understand his position we must consider the slings and arrows of fate he endured—not in public life but in his far more important private life. To Molly he complained: "I have lost all which constitutes the happiness of man."[146] A list of all his children from the three marriages documents how many painful events he had already suffered in his life before his second marriage (Table 9.1).

By 1827, the year of his second marriage, he had lost his wife and four of his seven children, among them two sons. When looking at the long history of the Metternich family, we saw how indispensable it was to have at least one son and heir, and since the founding father, Sibido, each generation of Metternichs had produced one. As the head of the entail, Clemens, the fourteenth generation in this ancestry, felt equally duty-bound to his dynasty. Now, in 1827, he saw the signs of an impending catastrophe.

Metternich's letter to his twenty-four-year-old son and heir, Victor, in which he announces his marriage must be read against this background.[147] The passages containing the information on the wedding sound like two dry entries in a dossier. Instead of adding some flourish on the forthcoming happy event, Metternich talked about the worrying health of his son. His advice reads like a déjà-vu: "Your constitution requires care, and I entreat you not to spare it. Ask

Gall what he recommends, and follow exactly what he prescribes." Metternich warns that winter is about to begin, and should Gall recommend "some months in a warmer climate than that of Paris, do not hesitate to go—let nothing stop you." Metternich suggests "Hyères [at the Côte d'Azur], Nice, or some place near Genoa, perhaps Genoa itself" as possible destinations. Although he spoke of precautionary measures, it would be more fitting to say that he had had premonitions of another misfortune, that of losing his last son on account of his "delicate chest."[148] What that would have meant to him he had already described eight years earlier: "I have only this one son. . . . The thought of losing him, or to see him becoming infirm, could cost me my own life."[149] The medical knowledge that Metternich had acquired at the university in Vienna in the late 1790s led him to believe, almost with certainty, that he would sooner or later see this son die, too. The only possible course of action was to enter into a marriage, not with someone like Wilhelmine von Sagan or Dorothea von Lieven, but with someone as young as possible, who was free of the deadly disease, someone who could bear a male heir and thus would help his family maintain the "strength" we mentioned in the beginning. The year 1827 also offered itself as an opportune moment because a year earlier Metternich had sold the dominion of Ochsenhausen to the king of Württemberg and had used the money from the sale to buy an old domain belonging to a Cistercian abbey in Plaß (Plasý), in Bohemia. The time was therefore right to begin a new life centered in Bohemia.

The wedding took place on November 5, 1827, at the royal castle Hetzendorf, the residence of Metternich's brother-in-law, Duke Ferdinand Friedrich August von Württemberg, and Metternich's sister Pauline. The celebrations did not take place under auspicious signs: a cold November wind blew throughout the ceremony, and during the wedding feast an imperial adjutant delivered the news that the united fleets of Russia, France, and England had destroyed the Turkish fleet in the harbor of Navarino. Metternich saw this as a result of the policies of Canning, who thus contributed to the destabilization of the Ottoman Empire.

Antonia fulfilled her husband's expectations and, on January 7, 1829, gave birth to a strong and healthy son, Richard, who, following the death of Victor in the same year, would soon become the only hope for an heir. His full name was Richard Clemens Joseph Lothar Hermann.[150] Metternich's brother Joseph was the godfather. The name Lothar demonstrates that the chancellor still upheld the heritage of the archbishop who had laid the foundations for the dynasty. But death now struck unexpectedly elsewhere: On January 12, 1829, only five days after Richard's birth, Antonia died of puerperal fever.

Victor's Death

Metternich was left with Victor as the only other adult member of the family. To him he could confide his unspeakable grief. All he could do was commend himself helplessly into the hands of God: "What the Lord gave the Lord can take away, and man must bow the head without question. My confidence is in Him, and I bow to His immutable decrees. My life is over, and nothing remains to me but my children. This idea sustains me and gives me courage to live."[151]

In the promising Victor, Metternich discovered all of his own talents: an ease of thought, an ever-present sense of humor, a measure of savoir vivre, and a carefree attitude toward love—like his father, Victor was a favorite with women. But neither was Victor spared. He suffered from an illness so protracted as to become an ordeal. At the end of it, he would not permit his father leave his side. On November 30, 1829, Metternich listened to his last words, spoken in German: "You, too, will now soon be relieved!"[152] A bad omen seemed to hang over the house, threatening the Metternichs with the same fate suffered by thousands of aristocratic families before them: their demise.

Melanie von Zichy-Ferraris

The chancellor's third wife was the niece of Count Karl Zichy-Vásonykeő, the Austrian state, conference, foreign, and—from 1813 to 1814—interior minister. Throughout the wars of liberation he had always been known to Metternich in some official capacity or other. His son, Count Franz Zichy-Ferraris, fought as a colonel in the Austrian army. Franz and his wife, Marie (called "Molly") Zichy-Ferraris, had a salon in Vienna that the Metternichs visited regularly. After Antonia's death, Metternich became even more anxious about Victor, who was working at the embassy in Paris. When Victor's health deteriorated, Metternich shared his worries with Molly, who was his only confidante. He appeared at her house more and more often.

Molly and her young daughter Melanie, born in 1805, had already set their eyes on the widower in 1825. Melanie wrote a moving letter of condolence to Metternich upon Eleonore's death, and he remembered her. She judiciously kept all his letters, which she received in increasing numbers from 1827 onward. They usually corresponded in French, but Metternich's letter of October 2, 1830, ends with the German: "And after all this, love me a lot, quite a lot, because I am not at all afraid it might be too much."[153] On October 22, he again ended with a confession in German: "I love you with all my heart." And on October 31, he almost formulated a marriage proposal, including a declaration of his faithfulness: "The path through life ne me semble moins conforme à mes gouts [could not conform less to my tastes]. *With you* yes; with others no!"[154] The wedding took place, with all the formalities, on January 30, 1831. The twenty-five-year-old's admiration for the fifty-seven-year-old was without limit, and she drew him so close to her that from then on he lacked the time, strength, or opportunity to have another lover. Metternich's personal doctor, Jäger, incurred her displeasure by suggesting she should go easy on her husband, referring to the pregnancies that had followed in quick succession. But they gave him the certainty that the male line was secured.

People had contradictory reactions to Melanie: enthusiastic, idiosyncratic, dominating, lively. The negative judgments came mostly from Gentz, who considered interventions by a woman in the core business of politics to undermine the honor of his own role—and simply as dangerous: "She wants to understand all business, reads all dispatches that are sent out, many of those arriving she even opens."[155]

He was right about the last point. On February 17, 1831, she openly confessed to her diary (which she kept from 1819, without interruptions, until her death in 1854): "To-day I breakfasted alone with Clement for the first time since my marriage. He spoke much on business, and initiated me into all his views and plans. I was astounded at my excessive ignorance. I should like to get to understand him at the first word, to be of use to him in every way, to follow his discussions, and be able to enter into them myself; in a word, I should like to be more than merely a loving wife, which is certainly a far too easy task."[156] Metternich remained faithful to himself in his choice of a partner. Melanie was an independently thinking woman who did not just want to be "her master's voice."

Two events illustrate well how Metternich and his young wife behaved toward each other. Metternich condemned homeopathy out of a deep conviction, and it would sometimes happen that he would lecture at length on this topic over dinner. Count Prokesch zu Osten noted on this regarding Melanie: "Heavy quarrel of the Countess with him over homeopathy, which has become a kind of religion to her for which she burns with the fanaticism of a heretic."[157] She even picked a fight with the whole medical profession over this. Whenever she publicly quarreled with him over the merits of this practice, which he considered to be nonsense, he calmly let it go, suffering it gracefully.

The second event was described by Melanie in her diary. At a dinner on New Year's Day 1834, she wore a striking diamond diadem in her hair. The French envoy, Count Saint-Aulaire, who was sitting next to her, attempted a compliment: "Why, Princess, your head is adorned with a crown!" She replied: "Why not? It belongs to me; if it were not my own property I should not wear it."[158] This was an allusion to the crown of Louis Philippe, and expressed

Princess Melanie von Metternich. Miniature portrait on ivory by
Moritz Michael Daffinger (around 1836).

her well-known aversion to the July Revolution of 1830 in France. She indirectly
declared the ascension of the "citizen king" as unlawful. Her words quickly
made the rounds, and finally ended up in the French press and with the foreign minister, Victor de Broglie; the French then protested the scandalous remark to the court in Vienna. The envoy sought to take Melanie to task for her
slight. She demanded that her husband be present. In the end, Saint-Aulaire
formulated a formal protocol that was to provide a proper account of the conversation. Metternich fiercely resisted the insinuation that Melanie held hostile
opinions about the French government, and he came to his wife's defense. His
argument deserves to be highlighted. He said: "Une femme peut, tout comme

un homme, avoir des opinions." [A woman, just like a man, may have opinions.][159]

Melanie's vivacity turned Metternich's house in Rennweg into a focal point of social life again. There were great balls with up to 800 guests. Almost daily they had guests to dinner, frequently groups of some twenty people. The Hungarian woman, who had a sense for the arts as well, left behind a visitors' book that documents well the range of prominent people who frequented the house over the years. It contains small portraits of influential, or at least respected, personalities—all of them male—little masterworks created by artists such as Moritz Michael Daffinger or Josef Kriehuber.[160]

On June 3, 1833, Metternich suffered another shock when Melanie's firstborn son died after six weeks. On April 21, the parents had christened him Clemens Franz Ferdinand Lothar Gregor Bonifaz, names that tied him to the family dynasty. Was the series of dying sons to be continued? The uncertainty over this question led Metternich to take an unusual step. He ordered an autopsy in order to rule out the old family disease as the culprit. The forensic examination established that the six-week-old had "died of a nervous-periodic cramp of the lungs (suffocation periodica) resulting from a congenital pathological condition of both lungs."[161] Following the later births, however, the worrying clinical picture did not show again.

The vault of the Metternich family crypt in St. Wenzel, Plaß.

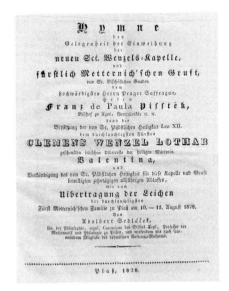

"Hymne bey Gelegenheit der Einweihung der neuen Sct. Wenzels-Kapelle, und fürstlich Metternich'schen Gruft" [Hymn on the occasion of the inauguration of the new St. Wenzel Chapel and crypt of the Princes Metternich] by Adalbert Sedláček, in German and Czech (August 10–11, 1828).

The Family Crypt in Plaß: A Memorial to the Metternich Dynasty

Whenever Metternich was confronted with death in his own family, he turned to his remaining children to find the courage to carry on. After Antonia had passed away, he confessed to Victor: "What value [what remains] has still for me arises from my love for my children; the feeling of the great importance of my life for their dear sakes the feeling, in fact, that I am not a useless piece of furniture in the world!"[162] With life and death so close to each other, and with the thoughts of the future of the Metternich lineage in mind, the head of the entail began to think about the idea of building a family crypt. From his point of view, this was only appropriate for a ruling aristocratic family. Up until then, the ancestral counts were buried in various places, some from the seventeenth and eighteenth centuries in St. Margaretha in Königswart and in St. Ursula in Königsberg an der Eger (Kynšperk nad Ohří), Bohemia.[163]

Metternich wanted a new beginning, a central memorial site for the family. He had pondered this idea for a long time, and the year 1820, with the deaths of Clementine and Marie, gave new impetus to it. He thought of the ruin of Miltigau Castle in his dominion of Königswart, which had burned down, along with the whole village, in April 1820. The intended building was to serve not only as a crypt but as a visible sign of his dynasty: "A mausoleum shall be erected to which there shall be no second in Bohemia, and perhaps not in Europe. . . . I will therefore make an Egyptian monument, not, indeed, a pyramid, but a chapel with a vault in the Egyptian style."[164]

Remarkably, in this case Metternich moved away from his beloved classicism, which he deemed too historically specific. The Egyptian style, by contrast, he deemed the only one that defied time and withstood the power of the elements. Metternich's recourse to an archaic, pre-European, in a certain sense natural, architectural style anticipated an idea the architect Bruno Schmitz later, in 1913, sought to use for a monument commemorating the Battle of Leipzig.

The purchase of Plaß opened up entirely new possibilities. The former Cistercian abbey had a cemetery with its own chapel, St. Wenzel. In the chapel's subterranean vault Metternich had the burial ground for the family installed and denominated the whole arrangement as the family crypt. He transformed the chapel's main façade in a "non-Egyptian" style—namely, in the style of the classical empire, in line with Königswart and Johannisberg.

The inauguration was given a sacral dignity: Pope Leo XII had personally presented Metternich with a relic of the Holy Valentina as a sign of his appre-

The family crypt in Plaß, with Clemens von Metternich's coffin in the central chamber.

ciation for Metternich's support on numerous occasions.[165] On July 4, 1828, the population gathered together, curious to see the arrival of the relic and watching while it was embedded in the altar together with its sarcophagus. The official opening was celebrated with a religious ceremony during which Metternich's father, Franz Georg, his wife Eleonore, and his daughters Marie and Clementine, united in death, were laid to rest in Plaß. The inauguration of the vaulted chapel took place on August 10 and 11.[166] Adalbert Sedláček composed a hymn especially for the occasion. The cultural potency of the region was embodied in his person: he was a doctor of philosophy, professor of mathematics, and philologist in Pilsen, as well as the canon of the Abbey Tepl and a member of the National Museum of Bohemia.

Metternich used the celebration to express his ideal of the equal value of different nationalities. He respected their differences by handing out a German and a Czech version of the hymn's text. In the form of an eulogy, it invoked a picture of the prince that kept the old alliance of altar and throne alive.

> By your Prince's pious mind and holy church alliance
> I see a thousand pilgrims come to you each year,
> From all sides the praise and accolade, and songs I hear,
> Blessing this house of God, and exclaiming Hail to the pious one,
> Who brought so much happiness to this quiet valley by what he's done;
> Who cared for Plaß with paternal love and wishes that one day shall rest
> his mortal veil here among his children, as pious custom does request;
> Who with this ancestral crypt completed a work of highest resplendence,
> And laid to final rest four of his, peacefully passed away, father, wife,
>   descendants.

The hymn honors the ruler as the patriarch of his subjects, one in a long chain of ancestors, and as an authority who still took seriously the feudal right derived from church patronage (*jus patronatus*). But Metternich was neither a stranger to the world nor a nostalgic character. The place of the ceremony also embodied the spirit of modernity, with its factory workers from a state-of-the-art ironworks. Even if the family crypt, completed in 1828, was not recognizably "Egyptian"—its external appearance was rather classicist—it served its purpose: it can still be visited today, a fact that surely would have pleased Metternich, who wrote to Dorothea von Lieven: "I like everything that defies time."[167]

10

THE CONSTRUCTION OF A NEW BEGINNING

Reform and Reconstruction, 1815–1818

METTERNICH'S IDEAS AND POLICIES ON THE NATIONALITY QUESTION: THE CASE OF ITALY

Defensive and Constructive Security Policies after 1815

The Final Act of the Congress of Vienna on June 9, 1815, marked an epochal threshold within European history, and because three of the major powers— England, Russia, and France—continued to strive for an expansion of their spheres of influence beyond Europe, this threshold was also significant in the context of global history. If we try to imagine the immediate future through the eyes of the politicians at the time, it very quickly becomes obvious how misleading it is to describe the ensuing epoch as one of "restoration." It would be much more appropriate to describe their aims, and the constraints under which they acted, as giving rise to "security policies." These consisted of two components. One component comprised *defensive* security policies aimed at defending the system of international law established in 1815. As, following the French Revolution, there was no longer any distinction between foreign and domestic politics, the attention of the major powers was also directed toward threats to the Vienna System from attempted revolutions and rebellions, or assassinations and seizures of power, within individual states. The Greek revolution, which aimed to form a sovereign state out of a part of the Ottoman Empire, is one example.

The second component was a *constructive* security policy. Here, the aim was to build on the rubble of the past age of war and complete what had been left undecided at the Congress of Vienna. The post-Napoleonic world was a constitutional world. On June 4, 1814, France was given its *Charte Constitutionnelle*.[1] It "not only confirmed essential achievements of the Revolution; it was also far more liberal than the Constitutions of the French Empire. It marked the transition from a state that in many respects had been despotic . . . to a modern state with a liberal Constitution," as Volker Sellin puts it. The Constitution's motto was not to "roll back" the Revolution but to incorporate its results.

Being constructive and pushing developments forward was the plan of the Prussian reformers. The heirs to the Rhenish Confederation began looking for their place within the national mosaic as the "Third Germany," and reorganized the territories that had been gained through Napoleon into modern, middle-sized states. The outstanding minister Montgelas set a glowing example in Bavaria, followed by others such as Sigismund von Reitzenstein in Baden and Eugen von Maucler in Württemberg. Metternich also followed this trend. Between 1815 and 1819, he developed promising plans for policies to be implemented by the Habsburg Monarchy in Italy, for the reorganization of the monarchy generally, and for the relationship between Austria and "Germany."

During the time of the wars of liberation, Italy had already had an important place in Emperor Franz's vision for the monarchy after Napoleon. Italy was the only case in which Metternich developed ideas that were important for domestic matters—something that, strictly speaking, lay outside of his competence as a foreign minister. In the case of Italy, however, his services were required, because despite the fact that the larger part of the Apennine Peninsula was foreign territory, the Kingdom of Lombardy-Venetia had been an immediate part of the Habsburg Empire since 1815. What Metternich said about the question of different nationalities in the case of Italy can also be straightforwardly applied to his treatment of other nationalities within the monarchy more generally. The Italian example can therefore be used to illustrate the fundamental ideas that informed Metternich's practical attitude toward the question of nation and nationality. As we saw in the Introduction, Srbik, for ideological reasons, put forward the absurd claim that "nation and state were alien concepts" to Metternich and that he had a "non-national" attitude. Had Srbik's authority not been so overwhelming, and had people not been so ready to bow to it, then a different picture of Metternich on this issue would surely have emerged some time ago. As early as 1963, a study fundamentally refuted Srbik's judgment regarding the question of nationalities. This work, which has only been studied by experts, had been undertaken because Hans Rothfels, the founding father of contemporary history in Tübingen, had doubted the evaluations of the biographer. Rothfels had chosen nationalism as his topic and encouraged a doctoral student to check Srbik's conclusions, which were based on printed documents, against the originals in Vienna. For reasons of historical justice, the name of this excellent but underrated American PhD student deserves to be highlighted here: it was Arthur G. Haas.[2]

The Kingdom of Lombardy-Venetia as a Model State

Having arrived in Milan on December 29, 1815, Metternich began to develop his principles for new Italian policies. From talking to people in Milan, he knew of the fear in Lombardy-Venetia that the Habsburgs might treat the regained provinces as entirely subordinate political entities. And he observed that the civil servants who had been sent by Vienna were appreciated. Metternich made concrete proposals to strengthen the autonomy and self-government of the country. The third-instance court was to remain in Milan. The greatest fear, he wrote, was that Milan might deteriorate to the status of a mere provincial town. The people there did not want their city to become like Brünn or Graz, or to see it fall behind Turin or Florence. They therefore wanted the court to sit in Milan. The administration, he added, had made significant progress in recent years—that is, during Napoleonic times. The civil servants were well educated and the administration worked efficiently. But the fear was that the local administration would be "jettisoned" for a "hereditary" [erbländische] one—imported from Austria—and that the posts for local civil servants would disappear. The desire was for an independent intermediate instance representing Milan. Metternich's recommendation to the emperor was "simply to establish an Italian chancellery" in Vienna. When doing so, however, it would be important to avoid certain mistakes:

> The countries here must be governed from here, and their local governments must be represented in Vienna. If the running of the local business is done from Vienna, Your Majesty will soon not see a single penny coming from these countries and everything will come to a halt. If, by contrast, Lombardy and Venice are governed under the strict responsibility of the governor according to principles that must be formulated and controlled in Vienna, Your Majesty will have spread calm [Ruhe], happiness, and peace among the countries this side [i.e., south] of the Alps. . . . The question actually can be reduced to the following: does one want five-hundred or fifty questions arriving monthly in Vienna?[3]

This statement already contained a political program. Metternich was also highly critical of the policies the Austrian administration had pursued so far, which, he wrote, had gone against its own instructions by not respecting existing legislation. An organizational committee had been set up whose mem-

bers had no knowledge whatsoever of local affairs; the administration was paralyzed and the "public most severely disgruntled." Metternich was concerned to
rectify the mistakes that had been made in the past, "in order to enlighten the
people about the true intentions of Your Majesty." Metternich was sensitive to
the "momentary wishes of the nation," as he called them. He urgently recommended that the emperor instruct the governor not to abolish any of the existing institutions. Were such plans to be suggested in the future, the emperor
would need to examine them before their implementation.[4]

In October 1819 Metternich presented the emperor with a provisional summary of the developments in Lombardy-Venetia since the dissolution of the
Kingdom of Italy and the "reunification of the Italian provinces with the Austrian monarchy," as he put it.[5] He had tried, he said, to satisfy "the wishes of
the inhabitants of this beautiful country," but had been only partially successful
because among the educated of Lombardy "the principles of the Revolution
that had only just ended" still had an influence. The "class of the independents,"
with their connections across the whole country, pursued "the phantasm of a
unification of all of Italy under one scepter." In this connection Metternich
made an insightful observation: those who were politically active engaged in
agitation among the Italian people "and showed them in the case of every
popular movement in other countries, in every political constellation in Europe, the moment when the realization of this chimera becomes possible."

Metternich was describing the revival of nationalist movements and nationalist demands in the various regions of Europe. He recognized that the national idea—the unity of nationality, language, and territory—was being proclaimed across Europe, that it was perceived across borders and thus continually
reinforced itself. What Metternich in October 1819 identified as a phenomenon
of political communication, the revolutionaries of 1820–1821 put into practice.
Beginning in Spain in 1820, the rebellions spread to Portugal, Italy, and Greece.
Common guiding principles—most importantly the Spanish Constitution of
Cádiz of 1812—connected the otherwise geographically dispersed events. This
was not a figment of Metternich's imagination; it was not a case of absurd conspiracy theories. It was a reality that has been affirmed by subsequent historical
research. All the revolutions of 1820–1821 "connected the three Mediterranean
peninsulas like a system of communicating tubes."[6]

Metternich, however, was wrong to believe that he could manipulate the nationalist stirrings in Northern Italy. His idea was "imperceptibly to drain politics of these superfluous activities and to provide them with an object that is
not harmful and possibly even useful." He referred to the renowned poet Vin-
cenzo Monti, who was celebrated among the Italians as "Dante redivivo," Dante
reborn. It did not irritate Metternich at all that Monti had previously been

Napoleon's poet laureate of the Kingdom of Italy; from 1814 onward, he had sung songs in praise of Emperor Franz. Monti was engaged with the Academia della Crusca in a "literary feud" regarding the purification of the Italian language. Metternich wanted to transform this personal battle into a general and national one between the competing centers of Florence and Milan. His expectation was that the "literary jealousy will morally solidify the political division between the regions. The more heated the literary feud becomes, the weaker the effects which the contemporary political events will have on the minds of the educated parts of the population."

A Plurality of States within Cultural Unity

Metternich's intention to keep Italy politically divided while considering it a cultural unity might easily be misunderstood as cynical. For him, it was a case of pragmatism, of realpolitik, because he believed that the only feasible Italy was an Italy of regions. He considered the country to consist of competing political entities of the sorts he also saw in Germany: "Therefore, in Italy provinces are against provinces, towns against towns, families against families, and men against men. If a movement broke out in Florence, the Pratoian or Pistoian would take the contrary side, because he hates Florence; thus Naples hates Rome, Rome Bologna, Leghorn Ancona, Milan Venice."[7]

It is remarkable that, given all this, Metternich spoke of a nation and its wishes. His strategy assumed that the cultural promotion of nationalities led to their depoliticization. He overlooked the fact that the concrete conflict did not weaken the fundamental idea of a national commonality, but even strengthened it. He suggested to the emperor that he should promote the Accademia di Belle Arti di Brera, the Academy of Fine Arts in Milan, which had been founded by Maria Theresia, but more importantly that he should reorganize the already existing, but deteriorated, "Literary Institute" by filling the vacant posts of "this national institution." With this, Metternich also pursued a particular cultural policy that was designed to disarm the opponents of the Austrian government by undermining their argument that the Austrians harbored "hatred against any kind of enlightenment and science." As the public honoring of Italian artists in Rome had been greeted as a pleasant surprise, a similar measure in the case of scholars and artists in Milan was likely to elicit a similarly positive response. Metternich already had concrete plans for reforming the Academy of the Arts and for the reorganization of the Imperial and Royal Institute of the Sciences, Literature, and the Arts. The Austrian Viceroy of Lombardy-Venetia, Archduke Rainer, was to preside over both institutions.

Metternich also suggested relaxing regulations in order to make it easier for Austrian students to study at the universities in Florence and Parma, especially given that Tuscany, being a secundogeniture of the imperial house, could hardly be considered a foreign state to which the prohibition of studies abroad categorically applied. Metternich was thinking in particular of the humanities and the Italian language as subjects of study. Metternich made the case for Austrian subjects to have the opportunity "to dedicate themselves to the study of the Italian language, which has acquired its most developed form in Tuscany." He considered it a necessity that civil servants coming from Austria to Lombardy-Venetia had a command of the Italian language.[8]

The Central Observation Agency

From Count Bubna, Metternich regularly received secret reports on the mood in the Kingdom of Lombardy-Venetia, which he sent directly to the emperor. From the perspective of the Austrian administration and military, the mood was significantly calmer by the end of 1818. It should not be overlooked that these reports on the general mood served the purposes not only of the modern "political police" but also of the old traditional "administrative police"—that is, it allowed them to detect administrative shortcomings. Police measures aimed at stopping violent fights and thefts from "getting out of hand," for instance, appeared insufficient. The judicial processes were too slow, they said. The viceroy and archduke were too cut off from the population. Metternich expected the archduke to use his public appearances to promote the good standing of the Austrian government. But the main purpose of the strictly secret Central Observational Agency, which Metternich established in Milan, was to keep an eye on the political situation in the other states on the Italian Peninsula.[9]

Metternich engaged the services of Tito Manzi, who was born in Tuscany, as a source of information about all of Italy. During the reign of Grand Duke Ferdinand III, he had been a professor of criminal law at the University of Pisa for nine years. He then worked for Napoleon's brother-in-law Murat, the King of Naples, and was a judge at the Court of Cassation in Naples. He was also appointed a state councillor. This career did not keep Metternich from calling Manzi a man who was praised in all of Italy for his talents and knowledge. He was always loyal toward the present regent and had the reputation of being an "entirely selfless, moderate man." Metternich recommended to the emperor that he should appoint this civil servant as a court councillor at the highest court in Verona.[10]

At the Central Observation Agency, Manzi's memoranda were also seen by counts Guicciardi and Bubna, who were in charge of the institution. Metternich told the emperor that, in his opinion, Naples was developing well and there were no signs of a revolution there. The weaknesses of the Papal States

Metternich considered obvious, but he thought Manzi exaggerated them. Tuscany had distanced itself from the Papal States and followed Austrian policies. There were no changes in Lucca, Modena, and Parma; all was quiet there. In Piedmont there was still an expansionist appetite that seemed ludicrously strong, given the size of the state. In Genova, Sardinia, and the Dukedom of Nice there was great dissatisfaction about the desperate financial situation. In this context Metternich made a judgment that illuminates the fundamental framework of his European politics: "If general peace is consolidated in Europe, the expansionist intentions of the court in Turin are hardly a cause for serious concern." In Metternich's eyes, Piedmont's hostile policies toward its neighbors required continual surveillance. Bubna, he wrote, was exceptionally well suited for this task because he knew the country and had many secret contacts there. For Metternich, there were two signs that seemed to guarantee calm [*Ruhe*] in Italy: the decreasing activities of secret societies and the disappearance of Russian agents. He saw these tendencies as the result of his determined intervention against Russian agitation in Italy at the Congress of Aix-la-Chapelle in 1818.[11]

In April 1819 Metternich learned that the situation in Northern Italy was set to change. This, he wrote, was not the fault of the government but instead was due to events in France and Germany—more precisely, efforts in those countries aimed "at the phantom of independence omnipresent in a nation."[12] The people had been duped by talk of "alleged rights." Like any other country, he said, Italy was dreaming of a "so-called liberal Constitution." Bubna was of the opinion that it would be easier to calm people down if the emperor visited and a much-needed contribution were made to the preservation of the Scala and an educational institution for boys. The government should give Lombardy and Milan "something useful and pleasant." The arrests in Venice had been premature and had made a bad impression. The sources make it clear that the person who was actually fully informed and, in turn informed the monarch, was the president of the police, Sedlnitzky, whereas Metternich was not even familiar with the background details. It seems that there was also unrest because of the continuous conscription of soldiers. The question of how far back in the line of generations the recruitment should reach, Metternich explained, was also outside his remit.

Metternich granted the secret service a unique special status. Its center had to be in Milan because this was where postal traffic from all of Italy crossed over, and the control of letters—the so-called *Perlustrierung*[13]—was to be carried out only by special civil servants who were directly under the command of the imperial secret cabinet. This meant that even Metternich had to go via the emperor to receive information from this source.

Italy under the Habsburgs

Emperor Franz and Metternich looked beyond the borders of Lombardy-Venetia to all of Italy. Metternich developed various ideas, all of which contradict the view that he defined the country only in terms of a "geographical concept." Although he occasionally used this expression,[14] what he actually had in mind was an integration of the individual Italian states into a "Lega Italica," similar to the German Confederation. On June 12, 1815, in a letter to Bellegarde—from whom he kept no political secrets—Metternich wrote that he was "occupied for a long time with the project of creating a federal system of defense [*un système fédératif de defense*] in Italy that would be able to secure a solid and also lasting peace and domestic calm [*Ruhe*] in this important part of Europe. I am only waiting for the first opportunity to carry out this plan."[15]

In the style of an empirical social scientist, Metternich set about getting a survey of the conditions and problems across the whole peninsula. On March 28, 1817, Manzi presented a voluminous dossier to him.[16] It was also Manzi who first provided him with information on the secret association of the Carbonari. But the information about the social and economic shortcomings in the country was more important. Metternich produced a lengthy memorandum for the emperor from Manzi's material.[17] It is noteworthy that Metternich was concerned about the country's level of socioeconomic development and pointed out its backwardness. There was "little taste for manufactures: most of the articles in daily use Italy imports from foreign countries." France and England, by contrast, had made the "greatest advances" in "industry" and supplied "all the markets of Italy." In Austria, the manufacturing spirit was also "in a torpid condition," and manufacturers "care but little to make themselves known in foreign countries."[18] This was the task of the Board of Trade at the court.

The most striking aspect of the memorandum is Metternich's presentation of the achievements of Austrian policies in Lombardy-Venetia. The administration of this kingdom, he wrote, must serve as a model for all other Italian states. Metternich considered the following points important:

- All classes of the population were subject to the same laws.

- Nobility and rich individuals could not exploit their positions.

- The clergy had to obey the state.

- The changes in possessions that took place during revolutionary times, and were later sanctioned by the law, were respected.

- There was no restoration or reactionary politics because "a veil of oblivion had been drawn over the past—that is to say, that no one was exposed either to public or private persecution."[19]

But Metternich also found points to criticize:

- the "progress of business" was too slow, and

- the emperor was seen as "wishing to give an entirely German character to the Italian provinces, . . . where the Italians daily see with sorrow German magistrates appointed to offices."[20]

Metternich here expressed a maxim regarding the treatment of non-German nationalities that he heeded consistently throughout his time in office. He decidedly disapproved of all attempts at a "Germanification"—of pressure being used to bring about linguistic assimilation—in any part of the Habsburg Monarchy. Metternich advised his emperor "to flatter the national spirit and self-love of the [Italian] nation by giving to these provinces an administrative shape which might prove to the Italians that we have no desire to deal with them exactly as with the German provinces of the monarchy, or, so to speak, to weld them with those provinces."[21]

Metternich put this conviction into practice in all his dealings with the nationalities of the monarchy. Together with Emperor Franz he supported, for instance, the foundation of a Chair for Slavonic Languages in Laibach and similar chairs for the cultivation of the national language, in this case Czech, in Bohemia (University of Prague) and Moravia. He demanded a Chair for Polish at the University of Lemberg and promoted professorships of Italian at German universities and professorships of German at Italian universities.[22]

JOURNEYS TO ITALY, A HAPPY, UNGOVERNABLE COUNTRY

Metternich's Three Italian Journeys, 1816–1819

"Beautiful Italy"—this was how Metternich described it in a presentation for Emperor Franz. Italy was the country to which they both, from 1815 onward, devoted the greatest attention, sometimes even more attention than they paid to the situation in Germany. Before the outbreak of the revolution in Naples, which then spread across the peninsula up to Sardinia-Piedmont, Metternich traveled around the country for several months on three occasions.

The first occasion was Emperor Franz's tour of the region to mark his re-gained—or newly gained—rule over the various countries, and give the local communities and their dignitaries the opportunity to pay homage to him. In this context, Metternich was developing his plans to redesign Austrian rule on the Apennine Peninsula. Between December 29, 1815, and mid-May 1816, he joined the emperor in visiting Venice, Milan, and other parts of the country in preparation for the organization of the Kingdom of Lombardy-Venetia.

The second journey was undertaken as a political mission in the service of the monarchy. History seemed to repeat itself: Metternich was again acting in the capacity of the "k. u. k. Übergabekommissär" [imperial and royal handover commissioner], accompanying the daughter of the emperor, Leopoldine, on her way to her groom, Dom Pedro de Alkantara, the second son of King Johann VI of Portugal and Brazil. Metternich's task was to accompany the princess and her court on their way from Vienna to the harbor of Livorno, where he had to hand her over to the royal Portuguese commissioners. From Livorno, the princess then sailed to Rio de Janeiro. The party left Vienna on June 3, 1817, and Metternich carried out the handover ceremony in Livorno on August 12. He also visited the city's synagogue—the most splendid in It-aly—and reported that 12,000 Jews lived in the city, where they enjoyed great privileges. He went thence to Lucca, where he stayed until the end of the month. His problems with his eyes cleared up, and he had the opportunity for a meeting with Marie Louise.

The third journey was the most curious. It had the character of one of the "grand tours" taken by nobles in early modern times. The emperor had initi-ated it, and it gave Metternich a welcome opportunity to make up for what he had not been able to afford as a young aristocrat. The emperor set off from Vienna with a large traveling party of about ninety-eight people in fifty-four carriages.[23] Political meetings could not be avoided altogether—for instance, in Rome, Florence, and Naples—but the main focus was on visits to art collec-tions, natural history museums, and libraries. There were also family meetings, including in Florence, which were attended by Grand Duke Ferdinand III, Archduke Franz IV of Modena, Marie Louise of Parma, or Archduke Joseph, Palatine of Hungary, who also made the trip.

For an astute observer such as Metternich, all three journeys provided valu-able insights into the country and its people, and they provided the basis for his plans for policy reform. In addition, they allowed him to form a personal image of Italy, which is less well known, but which we may deduce from his private letters to his wife Eleonore, Beatrix, his mother, his daughter Marie, and—during the third journey—Dorothea von Lieven.

The Myth of Italy

Italy had its own myths. For half a century Rome had been the mecca for modern artists and art historians such as Winckelmann, David, or Canova. By the time of the appearance of the second volume of Goethe's *Wilhelm Meister's Apprenticeship* in 1795, at the latest, the members of the educated class knew what was meant by the longing for Italy, swooning over the lines of Mignon's song: "Do you know the land where the lemon-trees grow." Scores of German painters and sculptors went to Rome to be inspired by the masters, and Caroline von Humboldt, the patroness, for a long time provided them with accommodation, contracts, and upkeep.[24] Shortly before Metternich sojourned in Italy, the so-called Nazarenes, disciples of the Vienna Academy of the Arts, had founded an artists' colony in Rome.

Metternich took in the country with all of his senses. The three feet of snow on the Simplon Pass still in mind, the landscape appeared even more beautiful, the sun even friendlier, when he descended into the Po plain. To his mother he wrote that she would certainly prefer the Isola Bella to her house in Grünberg.[25] Venice, which he had seen for the first time in December 1815, now, in June 1817, appeared an altogether different city.[26] The heat was moderated by the nearby sea. Every evening a mild breeze set in. The Piazza San Marco was filled with large tents. People were out in the streets until the early morning hours, and the cafés stayed open until five in the morning. He walked about Venice "as if it were a city of the 'Thousand and One Nights.'" It was warm. The women no longer had "red hands; blue noses have disappeared."[27]

Metternich visited all the attractions along the way: the library in Bologna, Palazzo Pitti and the Academy of the Fine Arts in Florence, the Uffizi—everything he saw exceeded his expectations. Florence had everything beautiful and grand one could wish for. He was amazed by what he saw: "Great God! What men they were in past times."[28] Cultivation, he wrote, "has made Tuscany one of the most productive countries in the world." The climate he considered "divine; there is great heat from eleven till five, but the morning, the evening, and the night are like what a day in Paradise will probably be."[29] It was understandable, he added, that this country produced so many painters and poets. Everywhere he admired the vegetation, the olive groves, the fig trees, the catalpa, the peasants' orchards with their orange trees, the jasmine hedges, the pomegranate trees, the grape vines, the flowering plants, which lined the paths and roads and filled everything with their scent. He was less enthusiastic about the millions of midges in the night.

In Pisa he visited the cathedral, the leaning tower, and the Baptistery of St. John. He felt that the "sovereign of all Italy could not be received as" he was, and that the "Jacobins hide themselves." To Eleonore he wrote: "If I have ever been inspired in any step I have taken, it was in deciding to come here; and you are witness that I made up my mind in a quarter of an hour."[30] He also visited Rome and the Etruscan Fiesole, with its remains of an amphitheater in an olive grove nearby. Everywhere he was overwhelmed by the landscape and the echoes of antiquity—as in the valley leading from Pistoria to Volterra, where Catiline had been defeated.

While on his Italian journey in the summer of 1819, he reported in more detail about his experience of Rome. He understood why it had been the center of the world. Everything there, he wrote, was gigantic and superior; everything made one's thoughts turn toward the past. He was enthusiastic about the extensive remains of the emperor's palace, the arches and remaining walls on the Palatine Hill, the Colosseum, which had a capacity of 80,000, the Caracalla thermal baths—a closed room built of marble that was large enough for 3,000 visitors and had a basin the size of a swimming pool. Metternich dryly commented: "How small does our present life appear. I am afraid the freedom of the press will not restore the former condition of human society."[31]

Metternich felt that the civilized behavior of the people of Tuscany was remarkable. Every peasant, he said, spoke an Italian as sophisticated and elegant as any member of the Accademia della Crusca in Florence. It was curious to speak to these upstanding people: their language was that of the salon, wholly without jargon, and without the exclamatory and temperamental intonation that one found in the rest of Italy. A vine dresser, who appeared to him to be half African, was his guide. He explained everything to him, he wrote, as an archaeologist would. What we learn from Metternich's report is that he spoke and understood Italian, and did not shy away from contact with ordinary people. He was not the haughty courtier—uninterested in the opinions of the common people—to whom "the innermost reasons for the social movements were a closed book," and who was incapable of feeling the "need of the people."[32]

The Ambivalences of Christianity

Particular experiences Metternich had in Italy help us to understand further the happy picture he formed of the place. One of his observations deserves to be highlighted because of what it says of him as a person. It concerned his idea of what Christianity should be like. He remembered a small painting, which he thought he had seen in Padua, whose fundamental idea surprised him. It showed Christ as he,

> with an air simple though triumphant, holds up the cross in the middle of a vast grotto. It is the entrance of Limbo. On the right of the picture are the patriarchs weeping with joy and love. St. John the Baptist calls to

him a number of beings, who are coming from all parts of the interior of the cave, and shows them the cross. There is an inspiration in this picture which is quite magical. It is no longer Christ suffering on the cross, but Christ having triumphed over death, and sharing His triumph with the just, who are entering into His kingdom. Expectation and happiness are equally depicted on the faces; Christ alone is calm, and St. John more inspired than ever. We hear him cry from the abyss, "The hour is come!"[33]

On his Italian journey two years later, when visiting the Basilica of Saint John Outside the Walls (Basilica papale San Paolo fuori le mura), Metternich engaged with Christianity even more intensely. The architecture, he wrote, was crude, the mosaics "in extremely degenerate taste." He judged this to be a sign of decline and explained it—a thought that had come to him while looking at the monument—in terms of the "complete descent of the arts in the Middle Ages." He saw the reason for this decline in the Christianity implemented by Constantine:

The Christian elements were unable to unite with heathen ones; Christianity had to destroy in order to purify and order its realm before taking possession of it. . . . The first Christians . . . had to take it upon themselves to eradicate, root and branch, those arts which produced temples and depictions of heathen deities. . . . The image of the mother of God was not allowed to be reminiscent of the lure of a Venus or the majesty of Juno; it could not be veiled by the graceful robes of Roman matrons. . . . The Christians took advantage of the decay of the empire by destroying the monuments of the cult they hated. Nothing is more common than to see victims turn into hangmen; the Christians took revenge on the residues of heathen life.[34]

These insights express something of Metternich's anthropology, and they reveal him to be a free spirit with the same fundamental pessimism regarding human nature that is expressed in Kant's image of the "crooked timber"[35] of humanity.[36] Metternich thought along similar lines when speaking of the trail of destruction Christianity had left behind: "This shows that nothing good ever prevails without surrounding its victory with the traces of destruction. Human nature, my friend, is a highly endangered thing, it is made up of opposites, feeds on extremes and acts through them, and reason will always be only a late final solution."

A Conclusion: "Internal Improvement"

At the end of August 1817, Metternich came to a very positive conclusion about Italy:

> I am leaving a little country which is in every way very interesting, and from which I carry away a remembrance very dear to my heart. My departure from here—I have been told—is like a public catastrophe. I have had the happiness of repairing many faults and follies, and I have prevented new ones being committed in a time more or less remote, which is very important for a country about to pass under another Government. I am more and more convinced that one only does well what one does oneself, and that one ought to be everywhere to do well.[37]

Metternich's aim was thus not to keep Italy calm through efficient surveillance. He aimed to use agreements to establish a trans-regional infrastructure, such as agreements on taxes, on trade relations, on the expansion of the postal network and roads; none of this suggests a striving for political domination. He afforded the Kingdom of Lombardy-Venetia a special role within the Habsburg Monarchy: it should be allowed to correspond directly with all Austrian embassies in Italy. It is worth noting that Metternich distinguished between political and diplomatic matters of a general kind that could be directed only from the center—that is, from his Chancellery—and other diplomatic business pertaining to Italy that could be dealt with in Milan, where, he said, there were numerous individuals who spoke Italian and were privy to diplomatic matters.[38]

At the time, Metternich—rightly—did not think that Italy could be a united nation-state. In a strange way, he might have seen his opinion confirmed today. In 2011 the city of Rome organized an exhibition on the occasion of the 150th anniversary of the founding of the Italian state; the slogan for the exhibition—"1861–2011: Regioni e Testimonianzi d'Italia" [Regions and testimonies of Italy]—expressed the very opposite of the idea of unity.[39] But the conviction that it was impossible to unite the country contradicted the nationalist sentiment of the "Risorgimento" movement of the time before 1848. In a sort of dialectical move, Metternich devised a method through which, in the long term, the peninsula could nevertheless come together politically in its own best interests. This method has been observed in the context of the formation of multiethnic states within composite states, as in the United States. In the nineteenth century, the United States and Italy both had weak central governments. Impulses toward unity came from the debts incurred by individual states because of wars, debts that had to be met with the help of the political center. Like Metternich in Italy, Jefferson used infrastructure measures in order to integrate the country—building postal roads, removing trade barriers, and pursuing other projects that were in the national interest. He thus created what Wolfgang Knöbl called a "society-wide communication sphere," on which the internal formation of the nation was mainly based. In the individual states of the German Confederation, the constitutionalism of the countries' Parliaments served this function. Modern sociology places all this in the category "internal improvements."[40] Metternich also opted for gradual evolution and not abrupt revolution. The wave of revolutions in southern Europe between 1820 and 1822, and further such waves in Europe following the July Revolution of 1830, ignored this option. They forced Metternich to move from a constructive to a defensive security policy.

METTERNICH'S PLAN FOR A REORGANIZATION OF THE MONARCHY

A Federal Empire

On October 27, 1817, Metternich presented the emperor with a draft plan for the reorganization of the monarchy. The plan was based on the system of modern ministries, which was to replace the archaic system of parallel court offices. Metternich suggested adding to the existing Foreign Ministry and Finance Ministry a Ministry of the Interior and a Ministry of Justice. The latter should direct four departments led by "four chancellors, one for each nationality." These would complement the already existing Hungarian and Transylvanian Chancelleries at the court.[41]

Metternich was aware that these were unusually wide plans. He assuaged the emperor's doubts by reminding him that the emperor knew "from a long history that any desire for unnecessary changes in the administration or risky innovations" was alien to Metternich. "There is nothing crass, nothing revolutionary, not a single risky principle in my suggestion," he assured him. "I demand some reordering, because an overly complicated administration must lead to disorder." He invoked the "glorious government of Maria Theresia" and diplomatically distanced himself from the "theoretical initiatives of her successor," and with this actually implied a condemnation of Joseph II's experiments with centralist reforms, which had ultimately failed. Since then, "a true communal spirit has enlivened the nation," and Emperor Franz could present himself "as the most felicitous legislator in the interest of the good of the people."

Metternich referred to information he had gathered in the meantime, and which gave him an overview of the existing "ills." He had thought for a long time about these issues, and had communicated them one-by-one to the emperor "in many confidential conversations." Now he presented his results in their totality. He did not wish to "express in a light-handed, unconsidered, or unexamined way something that had to have very weighty consequences." His aim was to introduce an order into "the already existing organized parts of the central authorities of the state." In this context, Hungary played a special and separate role for him. Metternich appealed to "enlightened principles" and "the experience of past centuries."

In Metternich's opinion, the present system worked only because "a monarch capable of governing" was at its top. But it was also necessary to think ahead and plan for a possible catastrophe: "Your Majesty must imagine today's way of dealing with matters without His Majesty's presence, without Your Majesty's influence, on which it is almost exclusively based!" With this, Metternich alluded to the possibility that the mentally unstable Crown Prince Ferdinand might—in accordance with the law—become the emperor's successor.

Metternich again took up his old idea of Austria as a federal state, a "composite state," ruled by a single monarch. In line with his usual method, he developed two options, ideal types that could guide the emperor's actions. The *first option* was a "complete unification of all elements of the monarchy in one single form of government." This is what Emperor Joseph II had attempted to do—and what he had had to undo within a few years of governing. The reason, Metternich argued, was that a "complete unification of mutually alien elements could only be the result of a violent revolution."[42] In addition, Metternich thought that too radical a centralization would "necessarily [evoke] the idea of a central representation of the nation," and such a representation he considered altogether impossible, given the many different languages and "peoples" [*Volksstämme*] in the empire.

As part of his *second option*, he set out political areas of responsibility for the different ministries, an approach that was now being adopted, he wrote, by practically every larger state. The departments were as follows: (1) Foreign Affairs; (2) Domestic Administration; (3) Finance; (4) War Office; (5) Justice; (6) Police; (7) General Accountancy. The head of the domestic administration would bear the titles of "Colonel Chancellor" [*Obrister Kanzler*] and "Minister of the Interior." He would have four chancellors beneath him, corresponding to the different nationalities. Each of these chancelleries would be defined by "the nationality of the province and the interests that result from their local conditions."

This does not sound like the suggestion of an absolutist of the kind Metternich is often made out to be. Rather, these were the ideas of a statesman who

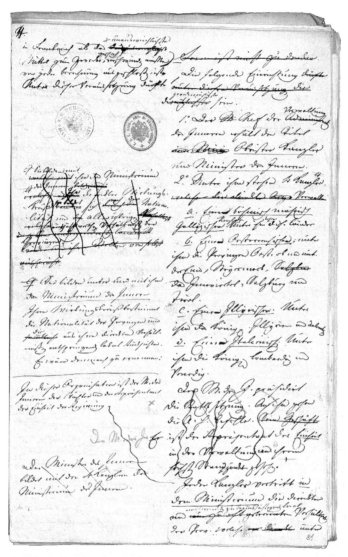

Page from the manuscript setting out a draft organizational statute for the Habsburg Monarchy, dated October 27, 1817. It shows the division into four court chancelleries, and corrections by Metternich.

thought that the principle of political participation was the foundation for political action. He did not have in mind, however, elected bodies, but the modus operandi of the administration. Traditionally, the latter operated only "top-down." But by taking into account the different nationalities, Metternich also suggested the very modern idea of "bottom-up" processes.

Metternich distinguished four regions of the monarchy that were defined by a particular nationality:

1. A Bohemian-Moravian-Galician chancellery, which covered the northern Slavs
2. An Austrian chancellery, which covered the German provinces: Austria above and below the Enns, Styria, the Inn region, Salzburg, Tyrol
3. An Illyrian chancellery, which covered the Kingdom of Illyria and Dalmatia, and the southern Slavs of that region
4. An Italian chancellery, which covered the Kingdom of Lombardo-Venetia

Each chancellor was to fulfill a double role within his ministry: toward the ministry, he would represent the immediate interests stemming from the specific conditions in the province that had to be taken into consideration; and toward the province, he would have to defend the principles followed by the government, which would aim at political unity. In this second role, he would still have to keep in mind, in an "enlightened sense," the conditions in the province. There would be equality between the chancelleries.[43] Each would have to be provided with the necessary number of consultants and subordinate personnel. This "reform," as Metternich called it, would have the effect of increasing equality because it would see the Hungarian and Transylvanian chancelleries "descend from the elevated position where they are today to the level of the common administration." This would also pave the way, Metternich said, for "a reformation of these two countries that must be gradually prepared."

Metternich showed a surprising degree of political sensibility and perspective in dealing with the problem of the different nationalities. His idea of a decentralization from the top down would establish a kind of "equilibrium." It would maintain a balance between equally weighted parts. Metternich thus avoided the grave mistake of the later Austro-Hungarian Compromise of 1867, which led to the Austro-Hungarian double monarchy in which the other great nationalities—the Czechs, the Poles, Croatians, and Ruthenians (Ukrainians)—felt disadvantaged and second-rate.

Metternich's reform program pursued the idea of "unity within plurality," a formula that was neatly illustrated by the example of German federalism. It showed him to be a farsighted, reform-minded politician who sought to solve the central problem of the nineteenth century: integrating different nationalities within a single state. As he saw it, only a decentralization of the state could forestall conflicts between the nationalities.

Metternich's suggestion of forming a Kingdom of Illyria showed how hard he strove to take into account the different nationalities of the populations in the Habsburg Monarchy. His justification for the existence of such a kingdom was incredibly modern. He had gathered information from "everyone reasonable" in the region, and the result was: "The majority of this nation here is of Slavic origin and naturally harbors a predilection for [Slavic] stock. A *Southern Slavic realm* can only bring advantage, especially where this nationality coincides with the Roman-Catholic religion." Metternich thought that the provinces of Illyria and Dalmatia, on which the kingdom was to be based, could be retained and the Dukedom of Krain added. He also had the surprising suggestion of investigating "which coat of arms there might be that would point toward some old and perhaps more significant memory of the Kingdom of Illyria."[44] In this way, he attempted to uncover some historical legitimacy for an Illyrian national identity. He thus revealed that he understood all of his political actions as involving an "invention of tradition," to use the formula of the famous British scholar of nationalism Eric Hobsbawm. As Hobsbawm recognized, the emergence of nationalism in the nineteenth century had to be understood as the result of such construction.[45]

The Habsburg Empire as a Patrimony, and the Case of Marie Louise

The fate of Metternich's draft proposal provides further insight into his role as a statesman of the Habsburg Monarchy. The reorganization of the administration was published on December 24, 1817, in the *Wiener Zeitung* and became law.[46] But what had become of Metternich's daring plans? They had been diminished, even deprived of their essence. The terms "nation" and "nationality," which, as guiding values, were meant to give life to the reorganization, had been taken out altogether, leaving behind talk of different needs, special situations, and particular conditions. The whole setup was reduced to exchanges between the Ministry of the Interior (which was created, at least) and the subordinate authorities. The parity between the central state and the provinces that Metternich had demanded gave way to the hierarchical, top-down functioning of the bureaucracy. The suggested Kingdom of Illyria was also only partially realized. The separate interests of the southern Slavs were played down to such an extent that they did not get their own Austrian-Illyrian chancellery in Vienna.

All this reflected a peculiarity of the Habsburg state that can be seen as its main structural feature. Emperor Franz considered the Austrian-Illyrian regions as old family property and was only prepared to let go of parts of them.[47]

In Roman law, property that is inherited, distributed, and passed on by the fathers is called patrimony. Emperor Franz, the patriarch of the ruling dynasty, viewed the monarchy, in line with his premodern way of thinking, in terms of the idea of the family clan. He treated it as his family's property, and he provided his numerous sons, and also his daughter Marie Louise, with dominions from his empire. The fecundity of Maria Theresia, Emperor Leopold II, and Emperor Franz created a vast number of princes and archdukes. The secondary lines of the dynasty, the so-called secundogenitures, were usually given prebends on the Italian Peninsula, although we should keep in mind that, in terms of nationality, Emperor Franz was also an "Italian," having been born in Florence. We have already discussed the detail how the parts of the country were distributed among the members of the family in the context of the Congress of Vienna.

The case of Marie Louise reveals in particularly dramatic fashion how deeply the patrimonial claim to ownership was anchored in the thinking of the emperor and his family. With Napoleon's abdication, she became an empress without an empire. During the peace negotiations in Paris, Metternich demanded, on Emperor Franz's orders, that the allies agree to let her keep the status of a ruler, albeit over a reduced territory. The contract of Fountainebleau (April 11, 1814) assigned her Parma, Piacenza, and Guastalla as heritable dominions.

On November 6, 1816, the emperor candidly admitted that the costs for "the maintenance" of his daughter—which he had paid until March 7, 1816 (the date she formally took up her rule) from his "Kameralärarium," his private account—were pretty expensive. He officially told his finance minister to draw up a report, in consultation with the foreign minister, on the question of "whether and to what extent the expenses incurred before my daughter entered into the full enjoyment of income from her dukedom [i.e., March 7, 1816] qualify for reimbursement."[48] This order set in motion a great bureaucratic machinery and produced a voluminous file: all Marie Louise's expenses between April 11, 1814, and March 7, 1816, had to be calculated. In the end, a sum of 799,982 guilders and 40 $^1/_{28}$ cruisers was given for the slightly shorter period between May 1, 1814, and the end of January 1816. The precision of the sum is astonishing, given the imperfect basis for its calculation.

The case of Marie Louise was but one of many. We must consider the emperor's interests in as much detail as possible if we are to decide whether Metternich really was the almighty state chancellor that he was claimed to be by, for instance, Viktor Bibl, who hated him.[49] Metternich's attempts at a modernizing reorganization of the monarchy as a whole, in fact, were futile.

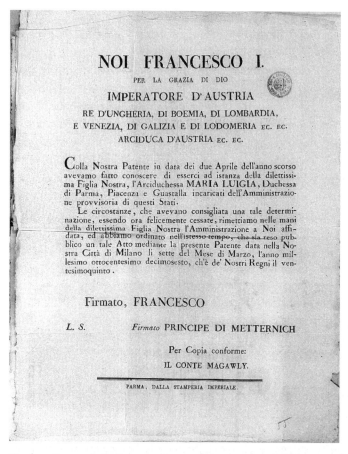

Proclamation made by Emperor Franz on March 7, 1816, in Milan regarding the Duchy of Parma passing to his daughter Marie Louise.

The weight of the territorial hereditary courts overruled the criteria of nationality, and rationality, which would have guided Metternich's decentralization. His comprehensive proposals, supported by the detailed information provided by Manzi, asked too much of the emperor, who recognized very well that the reforms would set him on a collision course with the interests of his house more broadly. Metternich waited in vain for the imperial resolution and comments that Franz would give at the end of his presentations. Even if there was no decision to be taken, he usually added: "Dient der Wissenschaft" [Improves knowledge]—"noted," in other words. In this case, he did not even write that.

Competing Options for National Integration: The German Confederation Is Put to the Test

Between 1815 and 1819, Metternich recognized that things were still in flux. Many developments could still be shaped further, and Metternich was constructively planning for the future. Even the issue of the organization of the German Confederation presented multiple questions that still needed to be answered. The participants at the Congress of Vienna had felt that the foundation of the German Confederation had inaugurated an indisputable new "Germany," but in 1817 a situation emerged that would have been a sensation had it been public knowledge. Prussia questioned the fundamental principles of the federal organization in a way that seemed, to the Habsburgs, to throw everything into doubt. Metternich was shocked, and a debate ensued that represents such a radical attack on the foundations that it must be discussed in a biography of Metternich. As far as I can see, there has never before been such a discussion.

On November 5, 1816, the Federal Assembly had its first session and, after a promising address to the "German nation" by the Austrian presidential envoy, formally began its work. The Vienna and Berlin cabinets nevertheless discussed all options regarding the "German question" once again at the turn of 1817–1818, as if the organization of the German Confederation might still be changed. In particular, they discussed what relation Prussia and Austria should have with the German Confederation. It all began with a special mission of the Prussian royal councillor Johann Ludwig von Jordan, section head in the Prussian Foreign Ministry and a close collaborator of Hardenberg at the Congress of Vienna. He was the man to be trusted with unusual tasks. Upon the personal suggestion of the Prussian king, Jordan went to Vienna for several meetings in the first week of January 1818. On January 5, he even had an audience with Emperor Franz.[50] He confronted Metternich with a proposal from King Friedrich Wilhelm III that left the minister speechless. During his time at the embassy in Berlin and the campaign against Napoleon, Metternich had already found the Prussian king to be indecisive and easily influenced. Now, as he had before, the king was being guided by "the impulses of the revolutionary military party" in Berlin, as Metternich told his emperor. Metternich was mostly thinking of Gneisenau, but probably also of Stein. The Prussian king, he wrote, had allowed himself to be misled into making "a proposal bordering on the insane": Either

Prussia as a whole—that is, including the provinces of Eastern Prussia, Western Prussia, and Posen, which were not part of the confederation—should join the confederation, or, if this option were rejected, Prussia should join the confederation with the exclusion of Silesia and Lausitz. Hardenberg had at first, with great effort, managed to dissuade the king from going along with this idea, which treated the difficult compromise between the German states found in 1815 as if it did not exist as a legally binding part of the Vienna System. But now the Prussian state chancellor was seeking support from Vienna. Jordan attempted to persuade Metternich to oppose the king with "the full weight of the Austrian cabinet" in the hope of thwarting the plan.[51]

Metternich obliged with a memorandum that probed with great precision each option's capacity to define the relationships of Austria and Prussia to the German Confederation. In this text, he was already considering all the arguments that later became the controversial issues discussed by the members of the National Assembly in Frankfurt in 1848–1849 and ultimately led them to split into factions. Metternich knew exactly what the German Confederation meant and had achieved for Habsburg and Central Europe, and he knew what the collateral damage would be for any option that dissolved the order agreed to in Vienna. Without having thought about it in any great depth, the spokesmen for a unified German nation-state believed that it could include Austria. It would only be with the debates during the revolution of 1848, not least those at the National Assembly in Frankfurt, that the impossibility of such a solution would be revealed. Long before they began to recognize the options available, Metternich had seen them clearly. In his memorandum, he described the three politically conceivable alternatives to the German Confederation.[52] For each of them, he also mentioned the disadvantages that the abandonment of the previous order would have.

He began by briefly setting out the common interests of Austria and Prussia. Due to their geographical positions, both major powers were in a unique situation in Europe that forced them to develop and organize themselves in a similar way to one another. Both states were under the same "pressure" [Andrang] from the east (Russia) as well as from the west (France). Russia was pushing up against the Ottoman Empire and the lower Danube, which had a direct impact on Austrian interests; Hungary had "a peculiar Constitution"; Italy was in a process of permanent revolutionary or political ferment directed against Austria. Prussia, he wrote, did not face the same challenges; it was in an "alert alliance" with the Netherlands against France. Europe needed Prussia and Austria to fulfill a double function: as major European powers and as predominant powers in the German Confederation. This alone could guarantee stability in the heart of Europe. Then Metternich went on to present the various possibilities:

First option: *Prussia and Austria join the German Confederation with all their provinces.* This proposal represented almost the same idea that the later Austrian prime minister Prince Felix zu Schwarzenberg would moot in 1848–1849 when he offered an "empire of 70 million." There were three arguments that spoke against this solution:

First, Austria and Prussia had to retain their independence and were not to "dissolve their whole political existence into their relationship with the German Confederation." If both states were absorbed into the German Confederation, they stopped being independent European powers and left the stage of European politics to the remaining three major powers. Their voices would no longer be able to influence the European equilibrium, which would thus be weakened; this would threaten to undermine peace.

Second, this solution would mean that both states, along with their Polish provinces (Eastern Prussia and Western Prussia, Posen, Galicia), would join the German Confederation. The tsarist empire would then have the right to demand the same for the Kingdom of Poland, with which it was associated. Metternich observed that the different Constitutions of Poland under Russian rule and the tsarist empire made it difficult for Emperor Alexander to consolidate his political power. The accession of the Kingdom of Poland to the German Confederation would allow the tsar to avoid the differences in organization and administration between Russia and Poland, and to resolve the daily difficulties that emerged between the old and new Polish provinces. Metternich correctly saw that the Polish question would immediately reemerge as a subject for negotiation if there was a deviation from the statutory arrangements of the German Confederation. He needed only to invoke the Congress of Vienna in order to draw attention to the potential conflicts that could again arise here. Furthermore, as there was personal union between Russia and Poland; the German princes could call on new member Russia as a protective power against Prussia and Austria.

Third, under this option Austria and Prussia would also lose the military advantage they had gained from their relationship with a separately existing German Confederation. And apart from all that, Austria could never join the confederation and take its provinces Hungary, Transylvania, and Lombardy-Venetia with it. This constituted a difference from the Prussian situation. As things stood, the German Confederation was a "palladium of their common security." If Prussia were to be dissolved in the confederation, the latter would lose its protective function, and Austria would inexorably be pushed out of it.

Second option: *Prussia alone, with all its provinces, joins the German Confederation.* This is what the National Assembly in Frankfurt later tried to achieve in its Imperial Constitution of March 1849, which stipulated the unity of Germany—without Austria but with the annexed Prussian provinces of Eastern Prussia and Western Prussia and a divided Posen. That was the so-called Lesser Germany answer to the German question. Metternich opposed it by pointing out that the stipulations of the Final Act of the Congress of Vienna protected all relationships between European states. This applied in particular to the first article of the German Federal Act, which stipulated that the German major powers had "entered into a permanent alliance in the name of all of their possessions that formerly belonged to the German empire." Neither the German princes nor all of the powers who signed the Congress Act would agree to an accession of the kind Prussia desired. It would provoke other states that were prepared to join the confederation, such as Denmark or the Netherlands, who could demand the same right for themselves. And if everything became fluid again, some German princes might also leave the confederation.

In addition, the German princes were not very likely to welcome the admission of the Prussian monarchy, with all its territories, into the confederation. At present, the mutual advantage and commitment on which the confederation was based was "in a well-known and calculated balance." If a predominant Prussia frightened the German princes, this well-balanced equilibrium would be lost.

Third option: *Prussia and Austria together, on the basis of their territories outside of the German Confederation, enter into an alliance with the confederation.* This option anticipated, at least in part, the makeshift solution to German unification that was adopted in 1849, in which a narrower confederation, including Prussia's and Austria's German provinces, was supposed to enable the formation of a *Greater Germany*, including Austria's non-German provinces, in a wider confederation.

In 1818 Metternich was again compelled to explain the main advantage of the confederation for Europe. He spoke of a "powerful association of states," a "great political body" that, because of its defensive orientation, maintained peace at the center of Europe. It did not need any alliances because it did not look to form aggressive alliances. But it was able to raise its voice "for those threatened and against the aggressor." This is how Metternich expressed what he saw as the special political value of a German Confederation that excluded Prussia's three eastern provinces. Austria and Prussia thus had an ally—in concrete terms: they could draw on additional military resources—if their non-German territories were attacked. As there already existed a federal Constitution that guaranteed support in the case of an attack on one of its members, there was no need for additional military alliances. The character of this "federal defensive system" meant that in times of peace there was no federal army and no supreme command. In other words: the federation as such was of a defensive character, but if there were a threat, it could form an army out of its members and appoint a common supreme commander. Metternich here hinted at a potential attack by Russia and described the military cooperation that might result from it: "In that case, the two monarchies, backed by the confederation behind them, would be able to position all their troops in the provinces of Eastern and Western Prussia, Posen, Galicia, and the Bukovina."

The possibility of drawing on military support from the German Confederation gave Austria and Prussia an advantage that no other major power in Europe enjoyed. Both would lose this exclusive advantage if they turned the German Confederation into an ally of the kind that any other European state might be, for other European states could then also enter into alliances with the German Confederation. On this point, Metternich was specific: France, England, Russia, Sweden, Spain, Naples, Sardinia, even Portugal and the Ottoman Empire might wish to form a defensive alliance with the German Confederation. If the confederation were to open itself up to such new members, it would have to prefer some powers and reject others—it would lose its "eminently peaceful character," would be drawn into the competition for alliances, and would have to take sides. With these reflections, Metternich explained very clearly why he considered appeals to turn the German Confederation into a nation-state to be so dangerous. Metternich asked Hardenberg to keep this memorandum strictly secret; only the king was to see it.

Which Parts of the Habsburg Monarchy Actually Belonged to the German Confederation?

This was a question Emperor Franz asked himself in February 1818, immediately after he and Metternich had formulated the memorandum. Was it really the case that, at the beginning of 1818, the emperor still had to clarify what his minister had settled with the Federal Act of June 8, 1815? That act answered the question of the federal territory. Prussia and Austria were part of it, "with all their possessions formerly belonging to the German empire" (art. 1). Now Emperor Franz wanted certainty about what this meant, and he ordered Metternich to convene a conference with the finance minister (Stadion), the president of the court's military council (Schwarzenberg), and the minister of the interior (Count von Saurau). They were to establish "how Bohemia once had become part of Germany; whether military contingents or payments had ever been provided for the German empire; then consider Fiume, including the ter-

ritoriis belonging to it under the name of a county, namely Flaum [Rijeka], and which parts of it belong to Germany; finally whether, and what kind of adverse or disadvantageous impression it would make on the Galicians if Auschwitz and Zator were declared parts of the German Confederation."[53]

Because of his deep knowledge of the Holy Roman Empire, Metternich was the best man to chair the conference. The aforementioned participants met on March 5, 1818, at his Chancellery, accompanied by the court councillors Kübeck and Spiegel. Metternich opened proceedings with a legal-historical presentation that, in the case of Bohemia, went back to the times of Charlemagne.[54] He emphasized Bohemia's electorship as the most important sign that it belonged to the empire; the Hussite Wars and later religious unrest had loosened the originally close ties. Since the accession of Hanover to the electoral college in 1708, however, Bohemia's electorship had also been revitalized. Bohemia (the territory included Moravia and the Austrian part of Silesia) had to be considered an "integrating part of Germany." Metternich reminded his listeners that on March 6, 1795, the Imperial Diet had asked the Bohemian estates to provide the outstanding troops. He knew this very well because, as a member of the Bohemian imperial estate, he had had to provide soldiers himself. He was in Königswart at the time, looking into the financial situation of his dominion, and in this context he also looked at the imperial register of 1795, the list of estates that were required to contribute to the imperial army. As a member of the Holy Roman Empire, Bohemia had also taken part not only in wars within the German empire but also in European wars. Metternich also confirmed to the conference participants that Bohemia had paid taxes to the empire.

On the emperor's other questions, he remarked: Fiume is not to be counted as part of the empire, while the dukedoms of Auschwitz and Zator are Bohemian-Silesian possessions and thus should be included in the German Confederation. This step was, indeed, taken in 1818. Through this measure, the German Confederation had a common boundary with the tsarist empire. From Metternich's perspective, there were therefore arguments that spoke in favor of assigning the dukedoms to the confederation not only of a "geographical-public" kind—that is, arguments to do with public law—but also of a "military-strategic" kind. The archivist of the Chancellery provided additional information in support of Metternich's presentation in the form of a statistical table that gave a "general survey of the elements, size, and population of the Austrian imperial state." Tellingly, he did the same, and with the same thoroughness, for Prussia. This documented unequivocally what the term "non-German territories" meant for both major German powers.

In a biography of Metternich, these detailed expositions may appear a digression—but they are not. Here we see Metternich engaged in concrete work on the national question. Throughout, talk is of the German empire and German territories, a fact that is often overlooked. But this was a nationality that was not primarily defined in terms of language, or even ethnicity. It was nationality on a constitutional basis: membership of decision-making bodies (the electoral college), the provision of soldiers, and the payment of taxes—those were the factors that decided who was part of Germany and who was not. This repeated the principles that we saw operative at the Congress of Vienna: German and other nationalities formed part of the state, but they were not essential to it—they were accidents, not essences. The conference clarified the territories that belonged to the Habsburg Monarchy and, at the same time, to the German Confederation.

11

DEFENSIVE SECURITY POLICIES

Averting Threats under the Vienna System, 1815–1829

NAPOLEON'S "HUNDRED DAYS": ACTIVATING THE EUROPEAN
SECURITY SYSTEM

Napoleon's Final Legacy: The Allies' Crisis Scenario

What is the significance of the intermezzo of the Hundred Days, triggered by
the abdicated French emperor returning to mainland Europe, forcing the participants at the Congress of Vienna back to their military headquarters?
Accounts of the Congress of Vienna usually treat his return as an irritating
episode at the end of the great Vienna gathering. Descriptions of the "Concert
of Europe" locate the beginning of the system's working in 1818—namely, at
the Congress of Aix-la-Chapelle.[1] But the significance of Napoleon's return is
instead that it marked the moment when the European security system began
to operate as a fixed element of international political practice.

This resulted from the simple course of events. Metternich described the beginning of the episode vividly in his memoirs.[2] At three o'clock in the morning
on March 7, 1815, one of the conferences of the five powers' plenipotentiaries
had just ended at his house. He ordered his servant not to wake him should
couriers bring dispatches later in the night. Metternich thought that they could
not possibly contain anything of importance, because the representatives of the
major powers were all in Vienna. He had been asleep for just two hours when,
at six o'clock, the servant, despite his orders, brought him a dispatch from an
express courier from Genoa, marked "urgent." At first he put the dispatch on
his nightstand, but when he could not get back to sleep, curiosity finally got
the better of him. At seven thirty he opened the envelope and learned that

Napoleon had disappeared from Elba—just as Metternich had foreseen in April of the previous year in Paris.[3] The memoirs give the exact chronology of the events that followed: at eight o'clock he was with Emperor Franz; at 8:15 with the tsar; at 8:30 with Friedrich Wilhelm III; and at nine o'clock he was back at the Chancellery, where he informed Field Marshall Prince Schwarzenberg, who was already waiting for him. The military units that were in the process of returning back home were ordered to halt. Metternich concluded: "Thus war was decided on in less than an hour."[4]

This succinct sentence expresses the fact that the Quadruple Alliance of Chaumont had unanimously prepared to act immediately. The serious disagreement regarding the Polish and Saxon territories, which had only recently been resolved, did not impact on the agreement at all. Metternich immediately coordinated the action to be taken by the political agents, calling a conference of the ministers for ten o'clock. On March 25, the allies formally renewed the Treaty of Chaumont, which had established the conference system. They defined their goal as follows: "calmness [Ruhe] for Europe and general peace, and protected by it the rights, the freedom, and the independence of nations."[5] The armies of the four major powers were more or less at the ready; the Seventh Coalition had been agreed to. But the outcome of the war was decided on June 18, 1815, near the small Belgian town of Waterloo to the south of Brussels, which gave its name to the world-famous battle in which the British army, led by the Duke of Wellington, and the Prussian army, led by Field Marshall Blücher, encountered Napoleon's troops and inflicted a decisive defeat on him.

The immediate agreement of March 7, 1815, and the renewal of the alliance on March 25 must be seen as the beginning of the European security policies that were applied by the major powers for the next ten years. Historically, the campaign against Napoleon after his return from Elba must be seen as the first common intervention for the protection of the European system; it was the first time that the Concert of Europe defended the Vienna order, the order based on international law, against rebellion from within, despite the fact that that order was not formally agreed upon until the Final Act of the Vienna Congress on June 9, 1815. There was never the intention of entering into new negotiations with Napoleon. He was viewed simply as someone who was disturbing the peace of Europe, and the allies took him as the model for the various subversions, assassinations, and revolutionary uprisings that were to follow. Their way of proceeding did not take the sovereignty of states into account. Their actions were the "anticipation of the doctrine of intervention" that was later explicitly formulated at the Congress of Troppau in 1820.[6]

The negotiations following Waterloo were conducted on the basis of the new European security policy. This is confirmed by the rhetoric and measures of the second Treaty of Paris, agreed to on November 20, 1815.[7] The preamble proclaimed that the allied powers had, "by their united efforts, and by the success of their arms, preserved France and Europe from the convulsions with which they were menaced by the late enterprise of Napoleon Bonaparte, and by the revolutionary system reproduced in France, to promote its success." They had protected France and Europe against rebellion. Napoleon's deeds are here seen as an "assassination"! The measures of the alliance had been directed against a "revolutionary system" that had supported this assassination. That was precisely the perspective taken under the system of the Concert of Europe. There was no "Metternich system" that would have been responsible for the political decisions taken. Rather, these decisions were determined by the common will of Great Britain, Russia, Prussia, and Austria as allies. This will had already been invoked earlier at Chaumont. The Habsburg Monarchy, represented by Metternich, was only one of the four actors that made up the alliance. Metternich assumed that the alliance would be stable, because he thought that, even if the Battle of Waterloo had been won by Napoleon, "the cause of Napoleon would nevertheless have been irretrievably lost." The Austrian and Russian armies "would have spread over France."[8]

A comparison with the first Treaty of Paris shows that the military operations against Napoleon until the Battle of Waterloo and the peace of November 20, 1815, marked the beginning of a new epoch. Contrary to the stipulations of the first treaty of the previous year, France was now also subject to the principles of the security policies. According to the wording of the treaty, France was secured by an allied "occupational army" that France had to maintain. The number of troops was not to exceed 150,000, and the measure was limited to five years, although it could be shortened if, after three years, the allied sovereigns and the king of France agreed that enough progress had been made toward the "reestablishment of order and tranquillity." France also had to pay reparations of 700 million francs and hand over some militarily important fortresses. The allies practiced exactly what they later practiced under the principles of the European Concert: they intervened where a ruling government could not guarantee domestic peace—and thus not peace in Europe.

On November 20, 1815, the day of the signing of the second Treaty of Paris, the four powers also renewed their Quadruple Alliance. They referred to the original Treaty of Chaumont (March 1, 1814) and the follow-up Treaty of Vienna (March 25, 1815). In the preamble, they again invoked Europe's tranquillity [*die Ruhe Europas*].[9] The German has only one word, "Ruhe," where the French has two: "repos" (rest, calm) and "tranquillité" (tranquility). The French text distinguished two aspects: "repos de l'Europe" expresses the moment of recovery following an exhausting effort and refers to the consequences of warfare; "tranquillité générale" expresses undisturbed peacefulness, and one can detect in it the idea of an order for world peace, which is "the object of the wishes of humankind and the constant end of their efforts" (preamble). The partners in the alliance were "desirous moreover to draw closer the ties which unite Them for the common interests of Their People" (preamble). They wanted to establish principles for the future "which They propose to follow, in order to guarantee Europe from the dangers by which She may still be menaced" (preamble).[10]

Why is it of such importance to see Napoleon's last appearance as part of a new epoch in European security policy? His reappearance created the image of a possible crisis. He provided the experiences and patterns of expectation on the basis of which the allies from then on concluded which signals might indicate that the peace in Europe is threatened. The same revolutionary principles, under a different guise, might disturb its peace again. The allies were on the lookout for similar situations that might lead to similarly unhappy events.

A military cordon was therefore to be extended around France in order to forestall any potential attacks. It was promised that these troops would be reinforced if they proved to be insufficient. Napoleon's return had made it clear to Europe that a usurper might gain revolutionary support within a very short span of time and topple the existing order. Napoleon thus provided the allies with the model of a possible catastrophe that became a fixed part of their mental map from then on.

The allies' view of the situation was also shared by the British—they did not follow a special path. Whether they were older or were members of the Metternich generation,[11] all signatories to the conventions, and the monarchs on whose orders they acted, had experienced the Janus-faced nature of the Revolution: its lofty ideals and its inhuman degenerations; the dominance of a violent ruler who could almost not be defeated; the ever-increasing risk of a "world war" after 1789; and the threat of the diminution of their territories. These four shared formative experiences gave the Concert of Europe its unifying moral impetus.

FAULT LINES IN THE SOCIETIES OF EUROPE AFTER 1815

When historians look at the post-Napoleonic era from a European perspective, they usually argue at the level of international relations. They look at individual actors, the major powers as acting subjects, and sometimes at institutions such as the ideal type of what Matthias Schulz called a "security council." The politics that matters takes place on the stage of large international congresses, unless it ceases at times of war. But the influence of social and economic factors and crises should not be forgotten. Taking them into account is also the only way to answer the often-asked question of whether the possibility of crisis was real or was invoked only as an ideological pretext to justify certain measures. To put the question in a different way: To what extent was European security policy after 1815 a reaction to a real threat? The final judgments on the so-called Metternich system and on the Carlsbad Decrees, with which he is also associated, depend on the answer to this question. It is therefore appropriate to preface a discussion of these two core themes with some remarks on the conditions that the collapse of the Napoleonic system had created in Europe.

The Legacy of the Napoleonic Wars: Enduring State Debt

Accounts of economic and social history typically fail to explain the extent of the disruption and destruction that the Napoleonic age wrought. They give the impression that, with the deportation of the French emperor to Saint Helena, his politics disappeared, without any lasting consequences. The opposite was the case. "On the Complaints of Our Times" is the title of an analysis of the economic situation in the agricultural sector at the beginning of the 1820s, and what the author observed in the case of Württemberg also applied, as he claimed, to "all of Germany." Farmers experienced "ever increasing need and paucity" and ever-growing debt. The same applied to urban tradespeople and "capitalist" bankers. The author was also able to explain the reasons for this:

> We further see the reasons for this ill in a disproportion between national income and public income of the state. We also looked for them in the excessively high demands the governments place on their subjects, which—when we look back over the rising public debt of states as well as individual municipalities during the more than twenty years of war that destroyed so much capital—they mostly have to demand.[12]

In the absence of other measurable consequences of the destruction of war and of Napoleon's "robber economy," as Hans-Peter Ullmann called it, the lasting deficits in public finances provide some evidence. In the case of the Habsburg Monarchy, we have already come across the method of financing the war of 1813 by drawing on future tax income from the next fifteen years. That represented only a small proportion of the accrued state debt, as the Habsburg Empire also had to pay twice—for the quartering of French troops and for the reparations agreed to in the treaties of Pressburg and Schönbrunn.

In 1807, Prussia's debt ran to 48 million reichstaler, compared to an annual income of 25 million. After the Treaty of Tilsit in the same year, the income decreased to 12 million for the following year. But Napoleon took 200 million reichstaler out of Prussia in the two-year period between 1806 and 1808, in addition to war contributions Prussia had to pay of some 30 million. In 1811, Prussia's debt had risen to 112 million, and in 1820 it was running at 217 million. It was still at 216 million in 1833. In the mid-nineteenth century about two-thirds of the Prussian population lived at subsistence level.[13] For the epoch after Napoleon this meant, in Ilja Mieck's phrase, "modesty imposed by budgetary constraints." Until the revolution of 1848, the state's administrative spending remained continually below the level of 1821.

The results of more than twenty years of war were an enormous loss of human life and of material goods in the form of devastated landscapes, confiscated property, contributions to be paid, and, most importantly, the financing of armies on an unprecedented scale. Between 1796 and 1809, Aichach, a village of 220 houses in the Bavarian part of Swabia, had to cater for 18,699 officers, 194,086 ordinary soldiers, and 95,784 horses.[14] And everywhere was like Aichach. The cost, in the years after 1815, was an impoverished and decimated population. One part of the male youth had been lost, and another part—the politically active part—was, as we shall see, often prone to the use of violence and susceptible to the new nationalist doctrines that promised salvation amid pauperism and civil service job cuts. For decades the Napoleonic legacy of large government deficits aggravated economic stagnation because it led states to adopt austerity policies. Many states were not able to consolidate their financial positions, more or less, until the mid-1840s. The southern German states valued their sovereignty, and their motivation that led them to join the German Customs Union, which was dominated by Prussia, was not nationalism but a simple lack of money: they wanted to profit from the payments that, from 1834 onward, they would receive from the Customs Union to redress imbalances. According to Ullmann, the parsimonious state remained the default model until the mid-nineteenth century.[15]

From Budgetary Poverty to the "Proletarians of Intellectual Labor"

The empty coffers had a fatal consequence: there were job cuts, and as a consequence those leaving the universities were less likely to get one of the hotly desired positions in the civil service. In Bavaria, state pension payments between 1819 and 1825 still amounted to 1,436,000 guilders in total, whereas between 1849 and 1851 this figure had come down to 571,000 guilders. These figures indicate a reduction in civil service staff.[16] Because of state debt, public investments that would have been necessary for the transition from the feudal manorial economy to capitalist agriculture could not be made. How effective state investment would have been is demonstrated by an exception to this rule. The inventor and industrial entrepreneur Friedrich Koenig revolutionized the print media with his printing machines and gained an international reputation for his product. But he had had to go to London to find the necessary capital for his development. The first newspaper ever printed with his rotary press, based on a principle still in use today, was the *Times* of November 29, 1814. Only after his return to Germany did the Bavarian king provide him with a credit that allowed him to set up his own, soon-flourishing factory in a former monastery in Oberzell, near Würzburg.[17] But as a rule there was economic underdevelopment and a lack of money. This self-imposed need was complemented by a terrible natural companion, the eruption of the Indonesian volcano Mount Tambora in 1815, which had worldwide consequences: the "year without a summer" in 1816. As a result, corn prices exploded between 1815 and 1817, and the whole of Europe was struck by famine and inflation.[18] In addition, after Napoleon's continental system was abolished, British goods flooded the Continent and domestic markets collapsed.

Of these crises, it was the crisis in the state finances that was structurally long-lasting. It led to the lasting picture of the German states as backward. The younger generation, however, especially the critical intelligentsia, did not blame the legacy of the war and their originator—that was before their time—but considered the policies of the princely states after 1815 responsible for the stagnation and backwardness.

The opposition forces Metternich was mainly concerned with were the journalists, authors, and poets, who were under pressure to publish and be successful. They lived with the contradiction of an "arrogant elitist self-understanding" alongside meager material living conditions. Journalists became the "tribunes or apostles of collective reason."[19] The "typical journalist of the *Vormärz* period" (i.e., during the period leading up to 1848) was often a doctor or professor, and thus had both a national mission and a low social status. Academics who were not fortunate enough to get positions as civil servants survived as freelance writers and occasionally projected onto Jews their "discontent over their own status as literati without any prestige,"[20] leading to an association between the spirit of modern liberal opposition and a strong anti-Semitism, especially where these writers were in direct competition with Jewish authors seeking to emancipate themselves.

Private lecturers, trainee lawyers without income, authors who could barely survive as free producers without a patron—these groups formed the class of what Wilhelm Heinrich Riehl called the "proletarians of intellectual labor," and they blamed the "Metternich system" for their situation. They were supported by apprentice craftsmen who had no hope of becoming masters because of the famine and inflation of the pre-1848 period. In 1848 they could be seen manning the barricades. They all felt that they were suffering an injustice. Due to their economic, social, and psychological situation, they were predestined to become the apostles of the new religion of nationalism.

Nationalism in Backward Regions: Assassination as a "Propaganda of the Deed"

Modern research into nationalism has found that aggressive and xenophobic nationalism is particularly easy to trigger in backward areas. That was precisely the situation during the time after 1815. Whether in individual German cities, especially those with universities, or in southern European regions, Poland, or France (where the wars had also left their marks)—everywhere we find cells, unions, and associations attacking their governments with revolutionary and nationalistic zeal. In the 1820s they called themselves fraternities [*Burschenschaften*], Deutscher Bund,[21] Jünglingsbund [association of young men],[22] *Griechenvereine* [Greek associations], and after the July Revolution they were called Young Europe, Young Germany, Young Poland, Young Italy, and so on, or the League of the Just, the League of Outlaws, or the Communist League.

The Napoleonic empire was European, and the socioeconomic basis in the transitional period that followed it was also European. The movements to which this gave rise took place in three widening waves of rebellion—in 1820, 1830, and 1848—in the context of European-wide communication that was dominated by a common vision of the future: a free Constitution, a united nation-state, a European "springtime of the peoples," and—as a rule—a constitutional monarch as the head of state. The classical themes of nationalism—the role of the "chosen people," the "holy fatherland," and the "historical mission," and, importantly, the concept of an enemy—were invoked in the face of economic backwardness. In order to appear effective, nationalism needs the myth of the regeneration of a people, exaggerated through images of "resurrection," "risorgimento," or a "springtime of the peoples" that promise salvation.[23]

There was an immediate connection between economic backwardness and the spread of nationalism as a social movement. This is supported by the "fact that all original nationalisms were established before industrialization."[24] To adopt a functional understanding of these doctrines of salvation, we can say that they emerged as crutches on which all those who felt weak, disadvantaged, or defeated—in short, the latecomers to the process of modernization—could lean.[25] Nationalism was in part an answer to the weakening of the public finances caused by Napoleon and his system. Inferiority and weakness in the face of Napoleon provided the initial impulses. After 1815 the supporters of nationalism believed that a collective German identity could provide them with strength. Nationalism brought about a "mobilization in the name of solidarity among individuals not personally known to each other."[26] Mobilization, participation—everything seemed to point toward what Dieter Langewiesche called a longed-for "community of resources," and thus power.

This was the context in which Metternich started to worry about the attack on "society" in Europe. Conspicuously, he did not talk about the social entities that had been the basis of the estates: corporations, guilds, orders, and so on. He used the modern collective singular "society." This was why he called 1789 a "social revolution." In his eyes, this revolution continued after 1815. But by then, he believed, the radicals knew that they could no longer reach the "masses." It was not easy, and in some parts of Germany it was impossible, to bring about an "uprising of the masses." Despite this, "the situation is different when it comes to violent attacks on persons, events that spread terror, which people hope will produce confusion and discouragement."[27] Metternich thought the real danger to the stability of the system was not the outbreak of a revolution, but terror attacks by underground groups. At the European level, attacks on the prince regent[28] and on Wellington, and the assassination of the playwright August von Kotzebue, who was in Russian service, were meant to send a signal. We shall have reason to look at these events in more detail later. All this resulted in a new form of political activism, which had established itself in Europe after the French Revolution: the assassination attempt as the nationalistically motivated "propaganda of the deed."[29]

Our consideration of the wider context has established a link between the burdens of the postwar period, the economic and financial crises engulfing the states, and the fear of social demotion among social elites. As a result of this fear, the elites became critical of the "system" and developed an inclination to reject evolutionary progress and opt for targeted political violence (assassinations, revolution) instead. Only against the background of this European context is it possible to understand Metternich's way of dealing with "the revolution" after 1815. Once we realize that the reactions in France, England, and the tsarist empire were similar, and sometimes even harsher, than in Austria, Prussia, and the smaller and middle-sized German states, Metternich no longer appears in an ahistorical and personalizing guise as the isolated "reactionary." The hitherto unwritten history of this European-wide terrorism, which developed between 1817 and 1825, is part of this story. It was only because of this terrorism that nationalism was able to become an unassailable social power.

Metternich and Modern Nationalism's Bellicosity

Metternich was very aware of the pan-European crisis, the collapse of the old European order, and the transition to an altogether new age. He saw that the Habsburg order was brittle. It could not be saved by piecemeal repair: the whole edifice had to be built up again from scratch. As a politician and observer of the contemporary scene, he felt that he was living through a time of transition whose end he would not live to see. Whether the topic was monarchy versus republic, absolutist versus constitutional state, the freedom of the press, the rights of the estates versus sovereignty of the people: in his view, all these problems came together in the phenomenon of nationality. Nationality was the element that continued to spur on the bourgeois educated elites after the Congress of Vienna. Historical research has typically contented itself with presenting Metternich as an enemy of national movements and as the leader of the "persecution of demagogues." But what exactly was it that prejudiced him against these new tendencies? It is important to have an answer to this question in order to be able to evaluate whether the judgments of him as a "reactionary" and of the epoch as one of "restoration" are appropriate.

His posthumous papers contain two pieces from his time in exile in which he provides explanations of his attitude toward the problem of nationality and the nation-state. With regard to the revolution of 1848–1849, he wrote: "Among the most remarkable contemporary phenomena is the emergence of nationalities."[30] He asks whether this phenomenon meant the revival of a lost good or whether the word was just an "empty sound." He found the basis of the concept of nationality "in the tribe [*Volksstamm*], in the geographical delimitation of a country"; both elements, he held, find their expression in language. He also mentioned the history of a people, their peculiar customs and laws as the product of history, and climatic influences. Following Johann Gottfried Herder, he defined his understanding of nationality in cultural and ethnological terms.

From this he distinguished the modern "urge for nationality" as a weapon in political struggle. He locates this transformation at the end of the rule of Emperor Joseph II, when the Hungarians began to invoke their nationality at the Diets of 1790–1791. But more decisive was the following fact: "The battles which the French Revolution brought to all of Europe increased to fever pitch the same feeling in the subjugated German states." After the "general peace" of 1815, this feeling moved into the world of theory and found a place under the roof of liberalism. "Radicalism," by contrast, which had lost faith in the words "liberté" and "fraternité," used nationality as a political weapon in the sense of the French slogan: "Everything by and for France" ("Tout par et pour la France").

Metternich recognized in this the abuse of the concept of nationality. 'It no longer served the purpose of protection from external enemies but the subordination of internal minorities by the state in the name of the "national interest." The reference to nationality was used to stir up feelings against those forces within states that protected minorities, and these forces became paralyzed.

While in exile in the English seaside resort of Brighton, Metternich looked back over the changes that had taken place in the period between 1815 and the revolution in 1848. He reached the following conclusion: "Two elements have appeared in society which are suitable to shatter its calm [*Ruhe*] to the core. I call these elements the extension of the *fundamental concept of nationality* to the realm of *politically and legally defined territories* and to their signification through *language*."[31] Thus, for Metternich, the perennial source for political and military battles lay in the idea of a linguistically defined nationality that was used by states to make territorial demands in the name of a unitary nation-state.

In speaking of the "rule of a progressive spirit of the times," meaning the modern urge toward the nation-state, Metternich anticipated, with breathtaking precision, the potential for violence that later expressed itself in the wars surrounding the formation of nation-states. For him these processes amounted to "schemes of conquest under the pretence of aiming at so-called natural frontiers, an aim which any self-contained State can oppose with equally rightful claims, so that peaceful agreements are to make way for the rights of might alone."[32] In other words, he recognized as erroneous the assumption that national (ethnic, linguistic) homogeneity is a suitable principle for building a state. In Central Europe, any state that sought to define itself on the basis of linguistic homogeneity thereby created a problematic minority within its territory. And if these minorities, in turn, demanded their own nation-state, there would be war.

In 1848 Metternich witnessed the arrival of what he had prophesied since 1815. The nationalities, which now presented themselves not just as bearers of culture but as engines for the creation of their own statehood—for their own "self-contained" state—could only end up coming into conflict with each other.[33] In 1849 Franz Grillparzer, one of the most important poets of the Habsburg Monarchy, neatly summed up the same insight in the following lines: "The path of recent education / leads from humanity / through nationality / to bestiality."[34]

At the domestic level, the new nationalism that Metternich feared increased the separation of the majority from the minorities; it even created the problem of minorities in the first place. This separation was the necessary "mirror image of the creation of the nation."[35] The conformist nation created two enemies for itself. The first—external—enemy had been proclaimed by Ernst Moritz Arndt as early as 1813, during the wars of liberation, in his famous song, which Metternich knew: "That is the German's fatherland, / . . . / —Where every Frank is held a foe, / And Germans all as brothers glow." As a companion piece, Arndt had published a brochure, *Über den Volkshass* [On hatred among peoples]. The dream of the homogeneous nation also created internal enemies. The erstwhile cosmopolitans who shied away from nationalism were among them, as were the European aristocracy, the Jews in general, and Catholics at times, as during the years of the Civil Constitution under Napoleon or of the *Kulturkampf* [culture struggle][36] of the Bismarck era. Nationalism thus created frontiers that the multicultural empires had been able to do without and, in Metternich's view, should do without.

Metternich's analysis of the concept of nationality was untimely: it contradicted the tendency of the nineteenth century toward sovereign nation-states. In that sense, he was a visionary. Against the spirit of his times, he anticipated an insight that historical accounts of the modern state would reach only some two hundred years later. Wolfgang Reinhard sums it up as follows: "The self-contained nation-state as the standard model in modern times since the French Revolution is no more than a fiction. . . . Theoretically, there are only nation-states, but practically there are almost exclusively multinational states. . . . It is obviously high time to bid farewell to this unrealistic model of the nation-state."[37] The risks that resulted from the trinity of language, nationality, and territory in the nineteenth century have been sufficiently analyzed in modern comparative research into nationalism, which speaks of, for instance, "nationalism as the duty to be intolerant," "nation-states as the children of war," "springtime of the peoples" and the "nightmare of nations," "territory as the source of conflict," and "exclusion of what is alien."[38]

It is necessary to take this circuitous route to Metternich's understanding of nation and nationalism in order to appreciate the background against which he acted in the months during which he was confronted with ever-greater numbers of nationalistically motivated deeds of conviction [*Gesinnungstaten*]—in short, with political assassinations taking place in Europe. This was also the atmosphere in which the proclamations of the Wartburg Festival and the infamous "Carlsbad Decrees" belong. By thus reconstructing Metternich's reflections on "nationality," we are not reading later insights into his earlier stance—early on he pointed out with great clarity the explosive potential of this unity of language, nationality, and territory.

He also thought about Arndt's song "The German Fatherland." Upon its publication, he wrote, he had wondered whether it should be opposed. Arndt's intention was the return of those parts of Germany that had become parts of

France. He did not, Metternich believed, think beyond that aim, but it was not the song that opened the door to the later abuse. "The Polish insurrection and the Hellenism, which was already widespread at the Congress of Vienna, are the true ills which intensified into nonsense during turbulent times."

The Greek revolt in 1821 was the most significant, because it led to the foundation of a new state and thus shook the Vienna System. It was part of a series of revolutionary uprisings that affected the Mediterranean countries between 1820 and 1823, beginning in Spain and Portugal, and moving to the Peloponnese. This wave of revolutions and uprisings brought into operation the coordinated defensive security policies of the system agreed upon at the Congress of Vienna. We shall take a look at these policies shortly. Metternich considered Greece a more important zone of conflict than any of the other countries mentioned, because it threatened the existence of the Ottoman Empire as a whole, and it was supported by some of the allies.

The Warsaw uprising of November 1830 during the July Revolution was just as grave a threat, because a revision of the partition of Poland meant a reordering of the Polish territories of Prussia, the tsarist empire, and the Habsburg Monarchy, and thus it meant intervening in the sovereignty of three major powers. In accordance with his values, Metternich assigned priority to the integrity and stability of the European state order and the general peace associated with it over the interests of individual nationalities. A nationality, as we have seen, could also flourish within the traditional multinational orders. The Swiss Confederation, for instance, proved that a good state was possible without linguistic homogeneity.

METTERNICH AND BRITISH SECURITY POLICIES, 1817–1820: PRETEXT OR DEFENSE AGAINST A REVOLUTION?

Contradictory Interpretations of Metternich

With the European security policies that were implemented after Napoleon's defeat at Waterloo, our biography of Metternich reaches a point that serves as a sort of watershed between conflicting judgments of him. Was not this the beginning of the police state and the interventionist "Metternich system," the inauguration, under his leadership, of the "restoration" that lasted until he was defeated by the constitutional and liberal resistance of the Western powers—namely, England and France?

This is the almost canonical received wisdom, and it has recently been repeated yet again. Matthias Schulz personalizes the internationally coordinated policies that were implemented after 1815 in opposition to a revival of the Revolution. He constructs a "Prince Metternich congress system," which Metternich allegedly used between 1815 and 1823 to subjugate everything to his "antirevolutionary dogma."[39] And Schultz is not alone: from the perspective of more recent historical accounts of Prussia, there is still today, as there was in the times of Treitschke, a conflation of "Metternich and . . . the reactionary system of the Holy Alliance." This view presents Prussia as having been seduced into becoming a "compliant, overzealous executioner of Metternich's reactionary policies," as if the Prussian politicians did not have wills of their own.[40]

This interpretation constructs a dichotomy between the "reactionary Eastern powers" of Austria, Russia, and Prussia—personified by Metternich—and the "progressive" Western powers of England and France, which took the constitutional and liberal path, initially represented by Castlereagh, later by George Canning and Lord Palmerston. This schematic perspective on international policies casts Metternich in the role of the almighty orchestrator of the reactionary position; it looks at the men responsible for the Concert of Europe without paying attention to the social and economic conditions—not to mention the fundamental psychological orientation—they shared owing to the experiences their generation had in common.

This tunnel vision shown by German historians, sometimes still Prussian in their outlook, when it comes to Metternich is a step backward compared to the view established by older, undogmatic English research as early as the 1920s. In 1925 the British doyen of diplomatic history, Harold Temperley, opened the first chapter of his book on Canning with these words: "At the beginning of 1820 Europe was still governed by Alexander, by Metternich, and by Castlereagh. They were a trio not unworthy of fame, for they had overthrown Napoleon. . . . Their union and friendship still remained to ensure the peace in the world in 1820."[41]

He describes Metternich as a politician who tried to mediate and maintain a balance between Castlereagh (who had to take Parliament and the public into consideration) and the vague cosmopolitan mysticism of Alexander. Temperley nowhere uses the term "reaction." In his view, the three politicians sought to prevent a restoration of the Napoleonic dynasty; if a revolution or unrest broke out in France, they would have to come together at conferences to decide what to do.

The aforementioned judgments that Metternich had put his "reactionary" stamp on the epoch, by contrast, rest on a different assumption—namely, that his warnings about revolutions or violent "Jacobins" were nothing but a veil for his restorationist intentions. The uprisings and assassinations mentioned by Metternich are seen by some as merely regional events without broader significance. On this interpretation, revolution is a praiseworthy expression of civil courage in the fight for freedom, a Constitution, and national unity, and "1789" is taken as a symbol of the struggle for a better future. This naive cliché disregards the experiences of human beings who were looking back at twenty-five years of war and revolution. The question contemporary witnesses asked themselves was whether the more than three million dead on the battlefields of Europe had died for any meaningful goal. In many peasant families, there were no male youths left: in Bavaria, for instance, 30,000 young recruits in the service of Napoleon did not return from Russia; they were later honored with the official inscription on the obelisk on Karolinenplatz in Munich—"They, too, died for the liberation of the fatherland."

No Special Liberal Path: British Fears about a Revolution

Looking at how the British dealt with revolutionary violence serves to refute the old stereotype of the reactionary and antirevolutionary East, especially Metternich, versus a progressive and liberal West that tolerated the constitutional demands of revolutionary movements. We find this cliché in, for instance, the following claim: "As a precaution, Great Britain had opposed the development of automatic antirevolutionary interventions on the basis that such an automatism would violate the independence of states and thus the fundamental pillar of international law."[42] This claim contains two assumptions: that Metternich pursued antirevolutionary policies and that the British adopted an anti-interventionism. Let us look first at the thesis of Britain's anti-interventionism.

All the differences of opinion here turn on the picture of Castlereagh. How did Metternich's contemporary view the French Revolution, and how did it influence his decisions? When the allies began to march into France in January 1814, Metternich and Castlereagh were both seriously concerned that a wave of solidarity with Napoleon might lead to a renewal of the Jacobin terror, and that revolutionaries might seize power again following Napoleon's defeat. Then, in May 1814, Castlereagh saw the victory in France as associated with "a great moral change coming on in Europe"—the "principles of freedom," he said, "are in full operation."[43] "Freedom" was used by Castlereagh, as by Burke, in opposition to the myth of revolution.

With his signature to the first Treaty of Paris, Castlereagh had, like Wellington, committed himself to the antirevolutionary principles of the Quadruple Alliance. All the leading ministers of the alliance between 1815 and 1822 assumed, in light of the experiences of their generation, that there was a continuing revolutionary threat across Europe. They saw their assumptions confirmed when, from the 1820s onward, uprisings spread in the south of Europe—

uprisings that cloaked themselves as revolutions but were often no more than coups rather than popular movements. The ruling elites feared that a new Jacobinism could break out and suspected—correctly—that followers of Napoleon were behind it.

After the outbreak of the revolution in Spain, Wellington reported from Madrid that Jacobinism was rapidly spreading around the clubs. The behavior of one such club, he said, was as repellent as that of the Illuminati in Germany.[44] The general could still remember the guillotine and the bloodbaths in the Vendée, all in the name of revolutionary reason. Regarding the revolution in Naples, Castlereagh received a report that found the events incomprehensible because the country was well off, the government restrained, and the taxes moderate. The kingdom was crumbling "before a handful of insurgents that half a battalion of good soldiers would have crushed in an instant." The author of the report feared that the revolution might spread to the rest of Italy and suspected that it would lead to "bloodshed and confusion everywhere." The "watchword" was "the Constitution," but what was actually happening was nothing less than the triumph of Jacobinism, the "war of poverty against property"; "the lower classes have been taught to know their own power."[45]

The Attempted Assassination of the British Prince Regent, 1817: Canning and the British "Carlsbad Decrees"

Castlereagh's successor, Canning, is particularly celebrated among historians as an adherent of noninterventionism and a representative of the allegedly democratic bloc of major Western powers, for he was of the opinion that he should not prevent other states from pursuing a liberal and constitutional path. Regarding domestic policy, by contrast, he was far more repressive than Metternich ever was at Carlsbad. Among Metternich's posthumous papers is a hitherto unknown document that sheds new light on European politics after Napoleon and on the role the protagonists played. Metternich had asked for excerpts from Canning's speech to the House of Commons on February 24, 1817; the document contains these excerpts with Metternich's annotations.[46]

In the years 1816–1817, the economic crises and social unrest mentioned above had also reached England and had led to "mass meetings"—that is, mass demonstrations—which were very popular in England. On November 15 and December 2, 1816, there had been incidents of significant unrest in London: the "Spa Field Riots" in the park of the same name in Islington. A leading radical, Thomas Spence, had planned an attack on the Tower of London and on the Bank of England. He and Arthur Thistlewood, who would later become notorious in connection with the Cato Street Conspiracy, were arrested and convicted of high treason. The situation escalated on January 28, 1817, when the prince regent's carriage was attacked while he was on his way to Parliament. Secret committees of both houses gathered evidence of widespread discontent in London and the country's industrial cities. They saw a treacherous conspiracy at work that aimed to topple the government, engage in general looting, and establish a new distribution of property. Canning's speech was based on the special report of an inquiry carried out by a committee of the House of Commons (the "secret committee"), and it was a passionate plea, in accordance with the committee's advice, for an exceptional law to limit freedom of assembly.[47]

The excerpts from Canning's speech that Metternich received proved a number of things. The attempted attacks were being perceived not as isolated incidents but as part of a Europe-wide phenomenon. Metternich saw this as confirmation of his assumption that there was a common European interest in security. He read the text in English, made his notes in the margins, and underlined passages. He was struck by the parallels between Canning's and his own views regarding the provocative acts of revolutionaries and the appropriate responses for the state. It is striking that Canning, whom Metternich had accused of being a Jacobin, and Metternich himself, Canning's harshest critic, invoked the possibility of the same catastrophic scenario for Europe and used it to justify identical restrictions in the name of security. Table 11.1 juxtaposes the most important passages in Canning's speech with Metternich's comments in the text's margins.

Like Metternich, Canning saw that there was a threat not only to the state— "the Constitution"—but to all of society. The problem was a small, manageable circle of fanatical doctrinaires. Canning angrily rejected the suspicion that all this was just a pretext, a clever and devilish invention by the government, a conspiracy, in order to be able to change the law so as to crack down on the people. He complained that the real, existing danger was being denied, or at least downplayed. In actual fact, these opponents wanted to undermine the state. They abused the desperation and need of the suffering classes in order to prepare for a rebellion. The existing laws, he argued, were not strict enough to deal with the plans that were hatched in Spa Fields. Bad men were plotting "secret cabals" in "midnight counsels." Canning recognized them as the activists of the French Revolution. "They have lain by these twenty years now, without being found to produce mischief." But while "when dormant" the doctrines of 1789 might be harmless, revived they strove for their violent implementation.

Everything turned on property. The much-feared "Spenceans" might not "really wish to partition the whole property of the kingdom" or "carry into effect their scheme for an agrarian division of land," but they would "labor hard

Table 11.1. Excerpts from George Canning's speech of February 24, 1817, with Metternich's marginal notes

Canning's speech (passages which Metternich underlined in italics)	Metternich's marginal notes
"What is the nature of this danger? Why, Sir, the danger to be apprehended is not to be defined in one word. It is rebellion; but not rebellion only: it is treason; but not treason merely: it is confiscation; but not confiscation within such bounds as have been usually applied to it in the changes of dynasties, or the revolutions of states;—*it is an aggregate of all these evils* *; it is all the dreadful variety of sorrow and of suffering which must follow the extinction of loyalty, morality, and religion; which must follow upon the accomplishments of designs, tending not only to subvert the Constitution of England, but to overthrow the whole frame of society."	*"This evil, so well described, is the same that England allows and protects in the case of more than one power on the Continent."
"The Executive Government do not ask for these additional powers as a boon . . . [but] only for the conservation of the public safety. * . . . It has been asserted, however, that Ministers call for these powers, the better to enable them to make war against the people. We repel the accusation with disdain. *We ask them for the people—for the protection of that sound and sober majority of the nation, for that bulk and body of community, which are truly and legitimately the people.* ** . . . But when this incredible resurrection [of the doctrines of 1789] actually takes place, *when the votaries of these doctrines actually go forth armed, to exert physical strength in furtherance of them, then it is that I think it time to be on my guard, not against the accomplishment of their plans (that is, I am willing to believe, impracticable), but against mischiefs which must attend the attempt to accomplish them by force.*" ***	*"This is the same language which demands power as necessary for itself in order to keep others from using it and doing with it what one has described so well for oneself." **"That is indeed absolutely central to the interest of the population, that the government preempts the outbreak of the volcano which captures all huts just as much as the palaces. It is the duty of government to protect the mass of the reasonable against this group of a hundred doctrinaires who lead some into misery, others to the scaffold or into exile, but all into the most lamentable anarchy." ***"An argument that tells a great truth, because the evils associated with these matters are most lamentable, even without any damage to their object."

Source: "Extraits d'un discours de Mr. Canning en demandant des pouvoirs extraordinaires pour empêcher ou reprimer des casseurs elements séditieux en Fevrier 1817" [Extracts from a speech by Mr. Canning asking for extraordinary powers for preventing or repressing seditious elements], NA Prague A. C. 8, Krt. 8, 44. English translation: Canning, *The Speeches*, pp. 445–46.

to accomplish the spoliation of its present possessors." Canning hoped to be able to "recall the wavering" and "restrain the half-resolved."[48] Metternich approved of this, noting down: "This follows the same principle according to which preventive measures are demanded in order to avoid having to use repressive ones."

Canning warned against being deceived by the fact that the "would-be reformers and revolutionists are but few in number."[49] Without "vigorous measures for its suppression," the attempt would lead to the same results as the French Revolution: "Can it be forgotten how frequently, in the course of the French Revolution, the world has seen sanguinary minorities riding in blood over the necks of their prostrate countrymen?" He suggested to his listeners that it would be wrong to believe that "the monstrousness of any doctrine is a sufficient security against the attempt to reduce it into practice."

Atheism "was professed in France as a faith," and, though it seemed ludicrous, "proselytes *were* made, and a great nation, robbed of its religion and its morality, was thus stripped of the armour and of the shield which might have protected her from anarchy and desolation."[50] The "'sovereignty of the people' was preached up not as a doctrine of abstract theory only, but as a principle and ground of practical political experiment." Canning reminded his listeners that in the name of the "'sovereign people' . . . France saw the whole of the upper orders of society swept from the face of the earth": "crimes followed by crimes, in a long train of horrors, which ended at last in an overwhelming but comparatively salutary despotism." In Canning's view, "bad men reciprocally corrupt each other," and thus "Robespierre grew from crime to crime, and became gradually familiarized with blood" until he ended up the incarnation of terror.[51]

Canning also drew attention to the large number of antireligious pamphlets, which were circulated "wherever there is distress to be aggravated, or discontent to be inflamed." "In the nightly councils of the disaffected . . . the overthrow of the state [is] being settled."[52] One passage Metternich found particularly worth underlining—Canning's rhetorical question: "If then, the Government demands extraordinary powers, I ask, on the other hand, are these or are they not, extraordinary times? Have we, has England, ever seen the like before?"[53] And Metternich added the remark: "a question that is very precisely put and very appropriate today." Canning concluded his speech by saying that the aim was to defend the Constitution and "that system of law and liberty, under which England has so long flourished in happiness and glory."[54] The House of Commons passed the bill 190–14.

In his speech Canning referred to the spokesman of the Spa Fields assemblies, the radical Henry Hunt, who had tried in vain to hand a petition from the demonstrators to the prince regent. Hunt had openly declared himself part of the revolutionary tradition by attending the assemblies carrying the symbols of the French Revolution: the pike of the *sans-culottes,* the Phrygian cap (the Jacobin symbol of freedom), and the tricolor.[55] For the secret committee of the House of Commons, and for Canning, these were all unmistakable signs of the formation of an organized revolutionary movement that had to be opposed with extraordinary measures. Canning implemented his preventive security policies in England, but the frame of reference was the enduring tendency toward revolution in Europe. Canning considered the spokesmen to be intellectual arsonists who wanted to overthrow the English Constitution, society, and the system of 1815.

The Attempted Assassination of Wellington as a Representative of the Security Policies, 1818

What concerned Metternich after 1815 was the fact that the members of Napoleon's family and his most faithful acolytes were distributed all over Europe. Many of them had found shelter in the Habsburg Monarchy—in Bohemia, and preferably in Italy. Metternich's caution was by no means exaggerated, as was later proved by Napoleon's nephew, Louis Napoleon, who twice (in 1836 and 1840) tried in vain to stage a coup in France, before—following his uncle's example—becoming Napoleon III, emperor of France, following a successful coup d'état in 1851.

The first attempt to bring about a Napoleonic restoration through a violent attack was carried out by Louis Joseph Stanislas Marinet, a follower of Napoleon and a Jacobin exile in Belgium.[56] Originally a lawyer, first in Lyon, then in Dijon, he had been employed as an auditor in the State Council during Napoleon's Hundred Days; as a champion of Napoleon's return, he was forced into exile and given a death sentence in absentia. Later legal investigations uncovered his Bonapartist network in Brussels.[57] Marinet had recruited a thirty-five-year-old corporal and jeweler's apprentice, Maria Andreas Cantillon, to carry out the assassination of Wellington, the supreme commander of the allies' occupational forces in France. After Napoleon's return from Elba, Cantillon had been an infantry colonel in the Napoleonic guard. He carried out the attack on the night of February 10–11, 1818. When Wellington returned to his hotel in Paris at one o'clock in the morning, the hired assassin shot at his carriage.[58]

On February 22, Metternich learned of the attack from the Paris newspapers that arrived in Vienna and immediately informed the emperor, who—in his inimitable terse style—expressed his horror and gave Metternich a task: "It is with pleasure that I hear of the failure of this planned gruesome deed, and wish to convey my liveliest sympathy to the Duke of Wellington."[59] The next day Metternich wrote to the duke and told him that he would make sure that the most important Austrian newspaper would carry a report on the event. Metternich was interested in keeping the public informed in as much detail as possible about the circumstances and perpetrator of this deed. The *Öster-reichischer Beobacher* published a series of articles on the incident and an extensive report on the indictment in May 1819. It was important to Metternich to publicize such assassination attempts and the internationally growing tendency to carry them out. It seems absurd to insinuate that, for Metternich, the fear of revolution was but an instrument that he "played with virtuosity in front of the European monarchs,"[60] as the attack on Wellington was an attack on all representatives of the Vienna order. In that respect, Wellington was in the same position as Metternich: both energetically pursued the coordination of allied security policies, pushed back against the followers of Napoleon, and—as Metternich saw it—sought to dampen the still-glowing fire of the Revolution.

There were reactions to the attempted assassination across Europe, and even from beyond. The political public was aware that Wellington had been targeted as the most important representative of the allies in Paris and as the person who was acting as their responsible head in control of the military occupation, which had been limited to five years. A Parisian legal scholar called him "the general of all European armies, one of the arbiters of the world."[61] It was also well known that he was the one who would determine how and when the allies' planned withdrawal would proceed.[62]

The danger posed by a Bonapartism that was ready to strike at any moment was, bizarrely and yet unmistakably, confirmed by Napoleon himself. In his will of 1821, he bequeathed 10,000 francs to the subaltern Cantillon, citing as his reason that he

> has as much right to assassinate that oligarchist as the latter had to send me to perish upon the rock of St. Helena. Wellington, who proposed this outrage [*cet attentat*], attempted to justify it by pleading the interest of Great Britain. Cantillon, if he had really assassinated that lord, would have pleaded the same excuse, and been justified by the same motive—the interest of France—to get rid of this General, who, moreover, by violating the capitulation of Paris, had rendered himself responsible for the blood of the martyrs Ney, Labédoyère, etc.: and for the crime of having pillaged the museums, contrary to the text of the treaties.[63]

Metternich probably knew of the content of the will through bureaucratic channels. And if not, the French version was published in Brussels in 1824 and, only a year later, also appeared in German. Metternich read everything related to Napoleon that he could (including the memoirs of Las Casas and of Napoleon's secretary, Fain), so he would certainly have learned, as soon as copies of the will were available, of the strange act of revenge that the former emperor managed to commit from his deathbed.

THE RADICALIZATION OF THE GERMAN NATIONAL MOVEMENT: THE WARTBURG FESTIVAL AND SAND'S ASSASSINATION OF KOTZEBUE

The Wartburg Festival: From Verbal to Political Violence

In Metternich's view, it was not only Greek and Polish patriotism that threatened the European order. The national movement in Germany would also become dangerous if it began to question the carefully balanced construct of the German Confederation. As Metternich emphasized repeatedly, in 1815 the overwhelming majority of Germans still thought of themselves as primarily Prussians, Austrians, Westphalians, Mecklenburgians, Silesians, Württembergians, from Baden or Hesse. Prussians and Bavarians would at times refer to their compatriots as forming a "nation." After the secularizations and mediatizations of 1803 and 1806, many who had lived in the Holy Roman Empire "under the crosier" [*unter dem Krummstab*], as the rule of the clergy was called, still did not feel properly at home in their national identities. During the wars of liberation, the nation was more of an "imagined community," in Benedict Anderson's sense—a design for the state of the future. Before 1815, even the leading minds had hardly any concrete ideas as to how this German nation was to be imagined as a state in concrete terms. The group closest to having such an idea was the German Jacobins, but they were not in a position to command a majority.

The most active disciples of this "imagined community" were German students. In the beginning they were the only social group with a national network, because they could move at will between universities and between the countries of the confederation. They carried the enthusiasm for the national idea into the postwar period. Following the foundation of the first student fraternity [*Urburschenschaft*] on June 12, 1815, in Jena, they became ever more organized. The welcome occasion for such further consolidation was the commemoration of the Battle of Leipzig.

October 18, the day of the Wartburg Festival, took place around the time of the anniversaries of two crucial events, and this attracted particular public attention. Three hundred years before, on October 31, 1517, Martin Luther allegedly nailed his theses to the door of the All Saints' Church in Wittenberg,[64] marking the beginning of the Reformation. And October 18 was the fourth anniversary of the second day of the Battle of Leipzig. Because of Luther, about five hundred students had chosen the Wartburg Castle as the location for a spectacular celebration. Despite the fact that schoolbooks often praise this event as an important milestone of Germany's national history, it was the expression of a nationalism that even contemporaries were already highly ambivalent about—even viewing it as dangerous. Celebrating Luther as the incarnation of German unity obviously meant forgetting German Catholics. Luther's translation of the Bible constituted a common German heritage, but his rejection of Rome created a religiously divided nation. The texts of the speeches given at the Wartburg, and the especially the songs that were sung, were quickly circulated among the population.[65] The ceremonial address by the philosophy student Ludwig Rödiger, delivered next to one of the nightly bonfires, offered the typical admixture of compensatory nationalism: on the one hand, the basic experience of inferiority, frustration, and weakness, and on the other—by contrast—the enthusiasm, the continual emotional appeals, the expressions of preparedness to give one's life for God and fatherland, to fight to the last drop of blood.[66] There were only two options: one could be with those who were good and for the good, the heroes of the fatherland, the prophets, light, truth, and justice; or one could be with those who were evil and for what was evil, darkness, servitude, shame, the poisonous odor of imperious aliens, the shamelessly sycophantic princes, cheats, humiliation.

In coded allusions, the present was described as a vale of tears and a call for action issued: "But first the time of strength must return! Because the misery of the souls also enslaves the bodies and pushes them to the ground. Thus, gradually, whole generations of defiant ancestors pass into slumber and endure all violence and deceit with a dull mind, until an alien sword slays them."[67] This was followed with a threat of conflict: "We have not come together in order to adorn ourselves with the harvest wreaths of quietude [*Ruhe*] but with the oak leaves of dying, and merrily to anoint body and mind—for a fierce battle is still to come with the bad and vain."

We have to imagine that among those listening by the bonfire was the later assassin Carl Sand, who must have felt called upon to act when he heard the following: "In the supreme calling of these times in which the earth purifies itself again and the peoples bow to the waving hand of unchanging universal justice; proud that our hopeful fatherland also looks trustingly toward us; and everyone prepared to become a martyr for the holy cause, we here, surrounded by your spirit, forge a pure and strong bond [*Bund*]."[68] According to Hans-Ulrich Wehler, the national patriotism of the Wartburg Festival united vague ideas, a "horizon formed of eschatological expectations," militancy, and the willingness to conduct a national "foundational war." Its legitimacy was that of a political religion, and it drew on all the elements of such a myth: rituals, symbols, and an origin myth that reached back to the old Germanic people.

But what attracted public opprobrium was the book burning. Heinrich Heine alluded to the burning in his tragedy *Almansor* of 1821, in which a copy of the Qur'an is burned and the main character says: "This was only the prologue. Where books are burned / humans will in the end be burned as well."[69] These words should not be subjected to an ahistorical or overcharged interpretation that relates them to the experience of genocide in the twentieth century. Rather, the book burning was at its heart a terrorist deed because it was presented as the act of an individual conscience, a conscience that considered itself justified in everything by its religious and nationalist motives. Heine's prophesy proved correct in the case of at least one of those present at the Wartburg. It was here that Carl Sand came across Kotzebue for the first time: he cast Kotzebue's book *Deutsche Geschichte* [German history] into the flames. Later he would take Kotzebue's life not by fire but by dagger.

Saul Ascher, a German Jew whose treatise *Germanomanie* [Germanomania] was also burned at the Wartburg, was among those who recognized most clearly the partisan nature of the event. His treatise had criticized the fraternities by pointing out, among other things, that Christianity was not an exclusively German religion. Ascher saw the Wartburg Festival as a Protestant event that was imbued with the spirit of "anti-Judaism." He asked what it said of supposed scholars that they burned books they disagreed with, rather than refuting them.[70] He was perturbed by the fact "that these nefarious activities . . . have not already been opposed long ago and that it is tolerated when teachers at universities, on their lecterns, take the liberty of animating young men of limited knowledge with eccentric opinions and ideas to such a degree that the latter's eagerness can turn into deeds and actions taken against their opponents."[71] Ascher here anticipated Metternich's idea of placing commissaries of the sovereign at the universities. Instead of "teutonism," as he called it, he recommended "tolerance, cosmopolitanism, and universal education."[72]

The *Österreichischer Beobachter,* which appeared under Metternich's auspices, scorned the "intolerance of the new primitive vandals": Professor Oken, who was present at the Wartburg, "and his fellow believers [have] also clearly shown what they mean by the freedom of the press for which they always call at the top of their voice, and that they only want it applied to natural philosophical and demagogic nonsense, but not for reason and order." Their book burning replaced censorship with "terrorist martial law."[73]

Nevertheless, the *Österreichischer Beobachter* judged the students rather mildly, referring—somewhat as mitigating factors—to surges of youthful liveliness and feelings of strength, rapture, exaggeration, to the statements of fiery youths caught up in the moment, speeches full of immature thought, half-baked ideas, extraordinary demands, and misunderstood desires and strivings. The students lacked experience and knowledge of the world. The article acknowledged their love of the fatherland and patriotic mentality [*Gesinnung*], and said they only needed to be steered in the right direction. The students' teachers were not granted any such clemency. It was the duty of those who were present to intervene. The professors should have taught them better.[74] This was the line Metternich would later pursue in the "Carlsbad Decrees."

At the Margins at the Conference of Aix-la-Chapelle (1818):
A Call for National Struggle

The original aim of the first major conference of monarchs and ministers after Vienna, which began in September 1818, was to put a conclusive end to the war era. The allies wanted to end the occupation of France, as the contributions they had demanded had been made. The Quadruple Alliance turned into a system of the five major powers again, including France. This development, however, did not mean the end of European defensive security policy. Because a revolution in one state could affect the European system overall, domestic and foreign affairs could no longer be kept separate, and attention was—increasingly—drawn to the domestic situation in the individual countries. The attacks in London and Paris suggested an unstable situation that might be further fueled by what was happening in Germany. At least this is what the Russian state councillor Alexandru Sturdza feared might happen. He presented to the conference a memorandum on the unrest at German universities, which described the domestic situation in Germany, against the background of a broad historical context, as a cause for concern. The tsarist empire, which had signed on not only to the Final Act of the Congress of Vienna but also to the German Federal Act, claimed the right to have a say on internal affairs if necessary. Stourdza suggested controlling the universities and limiting the freedom of the press through decrees passed at the Federal Assembly.

This initiative served Metternich's ends. Metternich and the Prussian police minister, Wittgenstein, had received worrying information on the universities, especially on the fraternities. The pamphlet, *Teutsche Jugend an die teutsche Menge* [German youth to the German masses],[75] which fell into Wittgenstein's hands, caused particular anxiety because it seemed to signal a continuation of the agitation of the Wartburg Festival and refer to the special effectiveness of the fraternities. As head chamberlain and a close confidant of the Prussian king, Prince Wilhelm Ludwig zu Wittgenstein was an *éminence grise* of Prussian politics. He bypassed the ministry and corresponded in strict secrecy directly with Metternich, who in this way maintained a direct connection to Friedrich Wilhelm III, whom he knew well anyway from his time as an envoy in Berlin and from the time of the wars of liberation. Wittgenstein was the head of the Prussian police from 1812 until he resigned this office in 1819, at which point he apparently retreated into the background as a minister of the royal household. He provided Metternich with all the documents relating to the fraternities—their protocols, announcements, appeals, and constitutional documents. This allowed Metternich to form a detailed picture of this movement as it emerged within the German Confederation. In the view of both men, its cardinal sin was that it formed a "state within the state."[76] The author of the pamphlet presumed—not unlike the crushed Prussian "League of Virtue"—that he had a right to an independent judgment on political matters and the right to influence politics, just based on the existence of his own organization.

The poem served as a *pars pro toto* of the crude nationalism that was spreading around Germany. Without any concrete political goals, this nationalism produced in its disciples an irrational compulsion to act. It constructed a simplistic friend / enemy schema and encouraged fanatical action. Its topic was the people's battle for a free state—a term that might evoke the idea of a republic without princes—and the opponents were called "tyrants" [*Zwingherrn*], princes, and the masters of Babel. Talk of a divine mission gave this battle a religious air. Faced with the prince as the incarnation of evil, only one means counted: the sword. Some 6,000 copies of the pamphlet had been distributed. Experts call it the "first case after the Congress of Vienna of a pamphlet calling for a violent coup that explicitly aimed at all of Germany."[77]

Leaving aside the poor quality of the political lyric, it nevertheless contained the stuff of which assassins are made. The text can be ascribed to Karl Follen from Jena, and we know from the questioning following the assassination of Kotzebue that Carl Sand also distributed copies of it. Wittgenstein's description of the lyrical style at the same time characterized the habitus of this nationalism that radicalized the students: "The sequence of ideas and the style of this text appear to me beyond all criticism. Half metaphysical, half trivial, but always confused ideas, endless repetitions of what has already been said, feeble efforts at appearing strong, everything inspired by presumption and dyed in a ridiculous pretense at nobleness, all this would have no effect in another age and in another generation."[78]

In this case Metternich, unusually, attached the pamphlet on the left side of the title page of a presentation for the emperor. He immediately recognized the revolutionary tendency it represented. This did not fail to have an effect on the

Teutsche Jugend an die teutsche Menge,

zum 18. October 1818.

————

Dreißig oder drei und dreißig — gleichviel!

(Weise:)

C 85313582 | 3018765 | 6628 |

87302 | 287662 | 3−r : ‖ 5456 7823 |

428765 | 8822 | 3885 | 624282 | 3−r : ‖

624287 | 8−r ‖. Zum 2. Mal:

Menschenmenge, große Menschenwüste,
Die umsonst der Geistesfrühling grüßte,
     Reiße, krache endlich, altes Eis!
Stürz' in starken, stolzen Meeresstrudeln
Dich auf Knecht' und Zwingherrn, die dich hudeln,
     Sey ein Volk, ein Freistaat! werde heiß!

Bleibt im Freiheitskampf das Herz dir frostig,
In der Scheide wird dein Schwert dann rostig,
     Männerwille, aller Schwerter Schwert;
Wird es gar im Fürstenkampf geschwungen,
Bald ist es zerschroten, bald zersprungen:
     Nur im Volkskampf blitzt es unversehrt.

Thurmhoch auf des Bürgers und des Bauern
Nacken mögt ihr eure Zwingburg mauern,
     Fürstenmaurer, drei und dreimal zehn!
Babels Herrenthurm und faule Weichheit
Bricht mit Blitz und Donner Freiheit, Gleichheit,
     Gottheit aus der Menschheit Mutterwehn.

————————— • —————————

emperor. Franz reacted with a particularly extensive and emphatic resolution: "The societies in question are so harmful that they must not be tolerated, and therefore an end must be put to them as soon as possible, something that is likely to become more and more difficult, the longer they exist." He asked Metternich to provide him as soon as possible with up-to-date information, especially on the extent to which Austrian students at German universities might come under the sway of these groups. There certainly were such students, because Protestant students from Hungary did not have any universities in Austria where they could have studied theology and therefore were allowed to study abroad. The emperor also at once involved Police Minister Sedlnitzky in the investigations. Metternich had originally planned, together with Wittgenstein, to prevent the meeting of the fraternities on October 18, 1818, but they realized that there was not enough time left to put this plan into operation, and therefore they recommended strict surveillance of the event instead. By October 1818, then, the ground was prepared for an assassination as well as for

---

Pamphlet of 1818, commemorating the Battle of Leipzig.
German Youth to the German Masses,
On October 18, 1818

Thirty or thirty and three—it does not matter!

A mass of people, a great desert scene
Greeted by the spirit of spring in vain
Crack and open up, old ice, at last!
Strong and proud your waters tumble
Onto servant and tyrant who keep you humble,
Be a People, a free state! Hot and fast!

If the battle for freedom leaves your heart cold
Your sword in its sheath will soon grow old,
The will of men, the sword of all swords
If it is wielded in battle for the prince's matter
Soon it will rot, soon it will shatter
It only shines wholly in the people's battle against their lords.

As high as towers on the citizens' and farmers' back
You may build your strongholds on their neck,
Princes' masons, three and three times ten!
Babel's tower of masters and languid passivity
Are broken by the flash and thunder of freedom and equality,
And the deity is born from mankind's labor then.

control of the universities. Then, in 1819, in light of the positive public and press reactions to Sand's assassination of Kotzebue, there was also a new impetus to limit the freedom of the press.

The Assassination of Kotzebue: Sand's Journey from Jena to Mannheim

On March 9, 1819, an inconspicuous and introverted twenty-three-year-old student of theology embarked on a journey from Jena, where he was studying, to Mannheim.[79] Carl Sand was on his way to commit a deed that would make him a household name in the more educated circles of Germany and at the European courts. More precisely, "Sand" became the byword for a new phenomenon in Germany: a political assassination in the name of the German nation, of which his act became the archetype.

Everyone who met him during his two-week journey described him as a polite, calm, at times somewhat distracted young man. No one knew the plans he had harbored for more than a year and had confessed only to his diary. In hindsight, many of his casual hints suddenly made sense. He went by foot, in accordance with his social status, viewed various places along the way, and was in no rush; one might have gotten the impression that he was a tourist.

Via Erfurt and Eisenach, his itinerary brought him, as it had in 1817, to the Wartburg again, where, on March 12, he was shown the sights of the castle and had lunch. He wrote some suggestive remarks in the students' book whose meaning immediately becomes clear in light of the subsequent assassination: "What are *the old sleepyheads* likely to achieve? Trust in yourself and build an altar for God and fatherland in your own heart." This was followed by his favorite line from Theodor Körner's poem "Aufruf 1813" [Call 1813]: "Push the spear into your pious heart / A breach for freedom." One can understand how Sand felt at this moment only if one adds the other lines, which the student must also have had in mind. It continues: "Wash the earth, / Your German land, clean it with your blood! / It is not a war the crowned would know / It is a crusade; it is a holy war! . . . / Thus, pray that the old strength may awaken, / That we stand again as the old victorious people! / The martyrs of the holy German cause." His entry in the students' book reveals the essence of his conviction: he acted where politics was idle; he pursued a holy mission—driven by his personal conscience; Germany had a holy character; in his understanding, his deed was an act of war.[80]

On March 23, he confronted the poet Kotzebue at his home. He stabbed him with a long dagger, shouting, "Take this, you traitor of the fatherland!" Afterward, he stabbed himself with a shorter dagger. This has been interpreted as a suicide attempt. This is wrong. It was a knee-jerk reaction triggered by the poet's four-year-old son, who witnessed the scene and began to scream. Sand himself said during his questioning: "His screaming caused me—in the midst of such mixed feelings—as a substitute for the boy, so to speak, to give myself a stab with the small sword."[81] This fits with the fact that he tried to flee and to nail a text justifying the deed—titled "A mortal blow to August von Kotzebue"—to the door with the same smaller dagger. Because of his wound, he could only hand the text to Kotzebue's servant.[82]

Sand's Personality: How He Became a Political Icon

If one views Carl Sand as merely a narcissistic martyr and dreamer, his attack appears to be no more than an "event of tertiary importance."[83] This judgment misunderstands the nature of the new kind of European terrorism, whose attacks were isolated but followed a consistent ideological pattern. According to his own testimony, Sand sacrificed himself not only for Germany but also for the struggle of the Greeks. Viewing his actions as of marginal importance also neglects the fact that Sand acted with a cool head and after careful planning. He styled himself in such a way that his actions became a media event and he came to embody the idea of a new type of terrorist.

Comprehensive questioning of Sand's academic friends and acquaintances, and numerous conversations between the chair of the investigative commission and Sand, produced an irritating picture of his character that showed nothing of a brutal treacherous murderer. He is described as a calm, well-behaved, and prudent person whom one could not help but like. He was not considered an enthusiastic character, but instead someone who spoke with calm reflection. A great inner calm emanated from him.[84] It is, however, telling that he calls the war of liberation in 1813–1814, referring to his taking part in it, as a "holy war."[85]

The copper engraving shows Sand after four months in prison. It is based on a painting that was done on August 1, 1819, in his prison cell and is allegedly very faithful to how he actually looked. The chair of the investigative commission was well placed to judge this, because he saw him almost daily. He found him mostly friendly, not particularly witty, but with an open face; he was well behaved. The long curly hair, his youthfulness, the old German style of his dress, the melancholic, serious, rather hesitant facial expression, with the only determinate gesture being the hand reaching for the hidden dagger—all this made him an appropriate icon for the young bourgeois men who were eagerly striving for national enthusiasm and identification.

In addition to this picture, there were press reports that described Sand as someone of keen understanding and broad knowledge. He was not a dreamer, the reports said, even less a madman. The deed was presented as the consequence

Carl Ludwig Sand, copper engraving, after a painting done on August 1, 1819, in his cell.

of a thought-through system. Sand gave the impression that he had sacrificed himself for a good cause. The only category of murder a German judge at the time was familiar with was murder by bandits with base motivations. When questioned, Sand emphasized that he committed his deed out of love for his fatherland and insisted that he did not intend to bring about a violent political revolution.

Sand was born on October 5, 1795, the son of a civil servant at court in the Bavarian town of Wunsiedel. He hated Napoleon. In 1812, he witnessed the retreat of the French on the great army route that led through Hof; he joined the war of liberation as a volunteer, and then, in the winter of 1815, he took up the study of theology in Erlangen, where, a year later, he founded a fraternity. His participation at the Wartburg Festival gave his life a new direction. He subsequently transferred to the University of Jena, where he joined a fraternity. In the autumn of 1818, he traveled to northern Germany, including Berlin, where he apparently distributed the pamphlet by Follen discussed above, copies of which turned up in Berlin in October 1818. From Berlin he returned to Jena. In lectures by the private lecturer [*Privatdozent*] Karl Follen, he became acquainted with Follen's doctrine of the "unconditional act of conscience" [*unbedingte Gewissenstat*], which removed any scruples he may have had. Sand now called Kotzebue a seducer of the youth, desecrator of the history of the German people, and a Russian spy. Because of his puritanism, Sand despised the erotic allusions in the scenes of gallantry in the poet's works.

At the beginning of March 1819, before the attack on March 23, Sand had explained the reasons behind his action in a confession titled "An Alle die Meinigen" [To all those close to me].[86] It was time, he wrote, to stop dreaming: "The need of the fatherland urges action." Thousands had given their lives for "God's cause" in 1813. The renewal of German life had begun, "especially during the holy time of 1813 with the confident courage given by God." He called Germany "the fatherly house" and "a true temple of God." Kotzebue, he claimed, was a traitor to the fatherland. Sand said that he was not really made for murder, but all his waiting and prayers that someone else might do what needed to be done were in vain. He knew that his deed would not cause a revolution. What he hoped for was straight out of the terrorist's playbook. He wanted to spread terror [*Schrecken*], which he said had a twofold function: The "strong youth" could use it to direct "the revenge of the people" [*Volksrache*] against their governments, who brought only "dishonesty and violence." And it could also affect the governments directly and motivate them to adopt policies in favor of the fatherland. Sand gave as his motivation the following: "In order to save our common fatherland, Germany, this still-torn and ignoble confederation of states, from the great danger that is near, I want to bring terror to those who are evil and craven, and courage to those who are good.—Shouting and talking have no effect—only acting can unite—I want at least to hurl a fire into the present slackness and help to maintain, to strengthen, the flame of the feeling of the people, of the beautiful striving for God's cause among humankind, which has been kindled among us since 1813."

Thus, Sand was dedicated to his own—German—people. But his horizons were broader. He saw himself as a fighter for the rights of Europe's repressed people, and the Greeks seemed to him a prime example. "So many Greeks have fallen already in order to free their people from the punishing rod of the Turks, and have died almost without having had any success or prospect of it, and hundreds of them, sanctifying themselves through education also among us, do nevertheless not lose courage and are prepared to give their lives straightaway for the salvation of their country—; and I should not want to die?" With these words, Sand unwittingly confirmed Metternich's analysis: It was the Greeks who challenged the Vienna order by raising the national question.

Political Murder as an Act of Conscience and Divine Mission

It is also striking how much effort Sand expended on making sure that his motives came to be widely known. He systematically avoided, however, making statements about others. The core of his political ideology was contained in the statement: "I have to follow my free will, and what my convictions determine me to do, I have to do, even if I shall be defeated and complete derision will be my lot." The investigating judge commented on this: "In the case of a collision with secular laws, no one must be deterred by them when something should be done for the fatherland."[87] For Sand, the ends justified the means, the investigating judge added, and it was beyond doubt that Sand had put his personal convictions above positive law: under the given Constitution of Germany, Sand thought, the people could not flourish; the existing laws were therefore invalid. According to the investigating judge, Sand considered the existing federalism as a "condition of separation between the German people." Violence against those who opposed the conviction of the individual was legitimate. Sand, the investigating judge wrote, assumed that the acts of men and the acts of God had to coincide: "If everyone were a self-determining being, then all, as it says in the scripture, would be one in God.—No government and no leadership but that of the good, of God in the breast of each individual . . . could be of help."[88]

In his justification on the day of the assassination, the "mortal blow" text, Sand went even further. He addressed the people like a prophet: "My German people, gain self-confidence and the high courage which some of your heroes have already shown! This is life's true spirit of celebration, that you do what the holy scriptures of Christianity and ancient times teach; that you do what your poets sing about. . . . 'A Christ you may become!'"

He who fought for the fatherland could bring freedom as a martyr and thus gain a likeness to Christ and God. The last sentence is a quotation from the revolutionary "Großes Lied" [Great song] by Karl Follen.[89] Sand's confession makes him out to be the prototype of a "holy warrior" for whom the interpretation of the holy scriptures and political action were one. He was the typical revolutionary fundamentalist: he believed, unwaveringly, to have recognized the truth from one source, and he wanted to impose it on others. Sand understood himself as being at the vanguard of the revolution; his "mortal blow" text ends with the following promise: "Up! I see the great day of freedom! Up my people, bethink yourself, take courage, liberate yourself!"

As a justification of his deed, Sand again pointed to the general political apathy that he had already deplored in his entry in the student book at the Wartburg. He wanted to shake people up, wanted to send a signal: "*There is nothing I hate more than the cowardice and laziness of today's spirit [Gesinnung].* I have to send a signal to you, have to declare my opposition to this slackness—I know of nothing nobler to do but to strike you down, you who are the *corrupter* and *traitor* of my people, August von Kotzebue, and the *arch-servant* and *palladium* of these corruptible times."[90] No one in Germany had spoken like that since the religious wars had ended. But those wars had been concerned only with God; now the concern was also the German nation. That was something absolutely new and something that, together with the strangely contradictory mixture of character, politics, and religion in Sand's views, gained a great deal of attention. As Metternich immediately became aware from his reading of the official documents, the perpetrator and his deeds were of far greater than merely tertiary importance.

METTERNICH'S HESITANT REACTIONS: THE PRESS, THE PROFESSORS,
AND THE STUDENTS

The murder of August von Kotzebue by Carl Sand led to the infamous Carlsbad Decrees. Many hold that 1819 was an epochal turning point at which the originally liberal development of Germany was cut off. In this view, what Wehler called the "perfidious" policies of Metternich, the "Metternich system," subjugated the German states and enforced an "almost cemetery-like silence [*Ruhe*]" on them. Whole books have been written on the topic.[91] And yet not all has been said. To gain a more nuanced understanding of Metternich, it is worth considering him from five possible angles: (1) his moral evaluation of the assassination, (2) his political evaluation of it, (3) his strategy for establishing a consensus on a more defensive course for federal policies, (4) the limitations on freedom of the press, and finally (5) the measures taken against the universities.

*Metternich's Moral Judgment: The Freedom of Those Who Think
Differently Is Denied by Violence*

Metternich's moral judgment of Sand reveals Metternich to be a principled follower of the "golden rule,"[92] which for him had its foundation in the Bible, and according to which everyone may do as they wish as long as it does not violate the rights of others—a principle which, of course, rests on mutuality. The spokespeople in the struggle for freedom of the press, to which Sand also committed himself in his emotional texts, violated this principle. Measuring the high-minded goals of the revolutionaries against the reality of their deeds, Metternich ironically stated: "The liberals behaved pretty badly on this occasion, and the principle of a free press is hardly defended very well by men who answer their literary opponents by stabbing them with a dagger. At least, it gives the impression that they did not want to accept any freedom but the one that suits them." The principle invoked by Sand according to which the ends justify the means also violates the "golden rule." Immediately after hearing of the assassination, Metternich wrote: "I don't like it when murder is committed in the name of philanthropy; I don't like madmen or mad deeds of any kind, and even less those who murder good people who are sitting quietly in their rooms."[93]

Metternich only had to think back to his tutor Simon to remind himself of his disgust at those who kill others in pursuing their good intentions: "The world is genuinely sick, my friend; nothing is worse than the spirit of freedom led astray. It kills everything and ends in killing itself." Metternich could only think in the categories of the revolutionary age. That also applied in the case of his earlier remark to his wife regarding the time before the Revolution: "I assure you that the world was in perfect health in 1789 in comparison with what it is now."[94] He repeated this argument while in exile during the revolution of 1848: "Murder is a very bad weapon; bloodshed calls for bloodshed, and it is in its nature to soil what it touches, and not to purify it. God help poor humankind!" He had just learned of the lynching of the Austrian war minister Theodor Count Latour by the Viennese. They had hung his body from a streetlamp.[95]

The Political Evaluation: Individual Act or Conspiracy?

Now it had been proven that a terrorist attack was possible in Germany, Metternich could not hide from the fact that he was in as much danger as Kotzebue had been. When he presented the information on the assassination, provided by Gentz, to the emperor, the monarch prophesied that the students would now deal with Metternich in the same way they had dealt with Kotzebue. Metternich replied that for a long time he had thought of himself in the role of a fearless general facing a battery of cannon fire. Emperor Franz replied: "Well, then we shall both be murdered." The remark in the original French uses the term "assassiner," which—in line with Metternich's image—can also mean "bombarded."[96]

Metternich found himself in a difficult situation, and thought about the fastest and most effective strategy for responding to this extraordinary challenge. He received the news of the assassination on April 9 while in Rome, far away from the central German places of importance: Vienna, the capital; Mannheim, where the atrocity had taken place; and Frankfurt, the meeting place of the Federal Assembly. He even suspected that his absence might have encouraged the assassin to strike at the particular time that he had. Friedrich Gentz had already learned of the incident on March 31 from an article in the *Allgemeine Zeitung*, a newspaper published in Augsburg, and the next day he sent a lengthy dispatch to Rome, including some official documents, which Metternich received on April 10.

The most urgent question was whether the assassination had been the act of an individual perpetrator or whether there was a conspiracy. Gentz and Metternich disagreed over this. Gentz thought that there was little point in continuing to interrogate Sand: "A conspiracy in the true sense of the word will certainly not be found."[97] Metternich held on to the idea that there might be a conspiracy. He had a more accurate picture than Gentz because from the very beginning he assumed a connection between the Sand and the University of Jena. He reminded Gentz of the secret files on the fraternities that Gentz had given to him many months ago. On April 10, Metternich already had at his disposal first results from the interrogations in Mannheim. Early on, he had the measure of the assassin: "Sand was a young man at the University of Erlangen who was calm and well-behaved. In 1817 he moved to the University of Jena, and he stood out at the Wartburg. In 1818 he returned to Erlangen and preached for the fraternities. He was in raptures over the life of the free ones [the so-called *Unbedingten* around Karl Follen], preached loudly, and returned to Jena again."[98] In support of his theory, Metternich used the following oft-quoted words: "I, for one, do not doubt that the murderer acted, not on his own impulses, but within the context of a secret society. In this case, true evil will also produce some good because poor Kotzebue serves as an *argumentum ad hominem* which not even the liberal Duke of Weimar is able to defend.—My concern is to give the matter the best possible direction in which to develop, to gain the maximum advantage from it, and I shall not waver in my efforts to pursue this concern."[99] Argumentum ad hominem is originally a concept of Roman law and means that the personal fate of a person is used as evidence. Kotzebue's death could not be denied, and it weakened the position of Duke Karl August, at whose university in Jena the threads of the investigations were converging. Metternich also had the European context in mind: "The assassination of Kotzebue is more than an isolated fact. This will be seen by and by, and I shall not be the last to take advantage of it [*tirer un bon parti*], . . . I do not allow myself to be distracted; I go my own way, and if all the ministers did the same, things would not be as they are."[100]

Defensive National Integration as a Strategy: The Wait-and-See Approach

These statements from Metternich draw our attention to his strategy of establishing defensive measures at the federal level. The usual interpretation is that he simply waited for a situation to arise that could serve as a pretext for implementing the measures, that he never really saw the situation as particularly threatening. It is assumed that he used scaremongering to corner the German governments. This interpretation is wrong, although it does fit Gentz's conduct. In contrast to Metternich, Gentz was often in the doctrinal vanguard. In his first letter on the matter, on April 1, he urged that the situation be viewed as "useful and even beneficent" for pushing forward measures that one otherwise might never have been able to introduce. He developed a three-point program: first, Tsar Alexander should be used to exert pressure on Prussia, Bavaria, and Germany as a whole; second, measures should be taken against the press, and the "eternally unforgivable article" on freedom of the press should be removed from the Federal Act; third, at the Federal Assembly one had to move against the universities before the effect of the assassination had dissipated—while the "blood of Kotzebue" still demanded revenge.

Metternich, for his part, first wanted more detailed information, and he urged the government of Baden to be as thorough as possible in its investigations. The government was in an embarrassing position because it was notoriously liberal, and the assassination had happened on its territory. The grand duke had therefore quickly set up a commission to investigate the background of the perpetrator, possible accomplices and confidants, and, most importantly, Carl Sand's motive. The investigation was headed by the state councillor Karl Georg Levin von Hohnhorst. His work was so thorough, free of prejudice, and detailed that following the publication of the results—the first part in September, the second part after Sand's execution on May 20, 1820—it was immediately prohibited.[101]

In contrast to Gentz's intentions, Metternich did not want to play the role of "coachman of Europe"; instead, he waited for the reactions from the German governments. And he was right. On April 23, he was able to tell Gentz, with satisfaction and a good dose of irony: "Among the rare things that have occurred in my life, incidentally, is the fact that I am called upon in Rome to work for hours on end on the German universities, and that I receive cabinet letters from all quarters of Germany with the urgent request to do my best to finish the nonsense that every German prince has provoked and fueled in his country, and now does not know how to appease."[102]

Metternich even planned to have the statutes of fraternities printed secretly, that is anonymously, and then distributed in Germany. They were meant to be evidence he could use in his negotiations with the princes. Again unlike Gentz, he did not consider it worthwhile to involve the Federal Assembly from the outset; instead he suggested first meeting for preliminary talks in Carlsbad with representatives from selected governments—that is, representatives of those governments that had urged him to take the matter into his own hands. Meanwhile, Gentz provided him almost daily with newspaper articles from the extensive press coverage of the assassination. Gentz strongly recommended keeping them all on file as it was likely that they would need to make use of them. Metternich, indeed, followed his advice, and today they form a separate section in the posthumous papers in Prague, titled "Gentziana."[103]

Preparations for the Press Measures: A Compromise Proposal

The task of reining in the press appeared more important to Metternich and Gentz than any other political task. Both were masterful in their handling of policies for the press within German-speaking territories. Metternich had learned these skills from Napoleon in Paris, where he became familiar with the press as the "fourth estate." The multilingual Gentz had made a name for himself in Berlin, London, Paris, and Vienna as a sharp-witted analyst of the contemporary scene; he was renowned for his rhetorical brilliance. Popular writers or journalists like Joseph Görres or Ernst Moritz Arndt, who reached only the German market, could not compare in terms of their success.

After the assassination of Kotzebue, the press landscape abruptly changed. Far too little attention has been paid to the fact that, in particular, the more or less explicit glorifications of the act in the press had led to many calls for censorship. There was both a formal and a material aspect to the matter. In terms of substance, the question was whether it was permissible to print anything one liked, and whether that constituted true freedom of the press. If, however, limits were to be set to what could be printed, the formal problem arose of how narrowly or widely these limits were to be drawn and what procedures should be in place for administering the regulations.

The laws on censorship in the various states differed widely. In Württemberg, censorship had even been abolished in 1817. Laws for the whole of Germany were therefore uncharted territory. Article 18 of the Federal Act only charged the Assembly with a task: "The Federal Assembly shall at its first meeting concern itself . . . with the formulation of uniform orders regarding the freedom of the press."[104] This had so far not happened, and as far as dealings with the press were concerned a legal vacuum existed at the federal level. It was an open question what would happen if writings were banned in one federal state but circulated freely in another. It was therefore by no means a case of reactionary politics when the Austrian emperor and other rulers approached the question of the limits to the freedom of the press.

It would actually be more accurate to speak of "freedom of communication." The old term "freedom of the press" referred to all printed products: images and illustrations as well as texts. A common misunderstanding is that any limitation on the freedom of communication counts as censorship. As paradoxical as it may sound, censorship within an authoritarian state and the fundamental right of freedom of expression in a constitutional state have to solve the same problem: they have to find a formula and a procedure for drawing a line between what is prohibited and what is permitted. In both cases, the same process of "regulation" is concerned.[105] In the constitutional state the line is drawn in criminal law. In the case of present-day Germany this is laid down in about thirty articles that deal with a range of offenses, from high treason and incitement of the people to violations of professional and fiscal secrecy.[106]

In modern criminal law there are no doubt some new elements, but fundamentally the same six offenses have been identified from the time of the invention of the printing press. These were also the decisive categories for Metternich and his contemporaries. They marked out the following categories as worthy of protection: monarchs and authorities; state and Constitution; the honor of foreign regents and governments; religion, customs, and morality (under which came prohibitions on gambling and pornography); and the honor and reputation of private individuals. In the age of enlightenment, protection against stultification, superstition, and delusive religious doctrines [Schwärmerei] were added to these.

This material content of the traditional regulations was incorporated into criminal law through legal codification, with independent courts deciding on individual cases. The British used court-based procedures after the abolition of censorship in 1695. In the case of authoritarian continental states, the regulation was administered by the state—that is, a censor examined works before they were printed, instead of—if appropriate—banning them afterward as a judge would. If there is a justified accusation to be leveled against Metternich and his contemporaries, it is that they did not have sufficient courage to transfer the decision-making responsibility in this area to the law and the independent judiciary, following the successful example of the British and the attempts that were made in France after the Revolution.

But the notion of "censorship in the Vormärz"—that is, during the time leading up to the revolutions of 1848—should not distract us from the fact that there were certain publications that had to be prohibited in the interests of domestic peace. The political bards of the wars of liberation, pamphleteers and poets belonging to the radical political opposition, and the extreme wings of the fraternities all produced bloodthirsty texts that called for murder. Those who, to the present day, want to instrumentalize history in order to forge a tradition of national unity like to overlook these texts, or to play down their significance by seeing them as the products of youthful enthusiasm. Carl Sand's pamphlet *Teutsche Jugend an die teutsche Menge,* which we discussed above, belonged alongside these texts, even if it is a milder example of the genre.

Knowing what we know today about the regulation of the freedom of communication, we can say that Metternich's approach to the problem of regulation, which was pragmatic, reflective, and based on international comparisons, is astonishingly modern.[107] He conceded to modern states such as France and Britain that they could easily "allow freedom of the press and even postulate the principle that this freedom is an indispensable condition for a pure representational system." As centrally organized states, he argued, they could regulate post hoc, through the courts, in order to avoid abuses of press freedoms.

The conditions in Germany required a different solution. Metternich's suggestion distinguished his legal and political form of argumentation from the authoritarian, even absolutist, rigorism of Gentz, who simply wanted to see article 18—on freedom of the press—removed. Metternich explained that Germany, unlike Britain and France, consisted of sovereign states that guaranteed each other protection and help. To the external world they appeared as one power because of their confederation, but internally they were administratively divided. If one of them sought to interfere in another because of some undesirable publication, this would necessarily disturb the inner peace of the confederation. Metternich, incidentally, did not have to remind Gentz that German states waged wars against each other, something that had still been the rule in the seventeenth and eighteenth centuries. After 1815 it was no longer a possibility.

Metternich then presented a surprising argument: There was, of course, "a nationality that stretches across all of Germany." He essentially called for a degree of national integration within the German Confederation through common legislation that subjected dealings with the press to shared—national—principles. He considered the type of regulation practiced in France or England as impossible for Germany because that would require "the unification of Germany into a single body that is not internally divided." This would be conceivable only under the umbrella of a single German monarchy or of a "German free state." Metternich thus also countenanced a unified German republic. What led him to discard that option was the counterargument. Metternich's opponents always accuse him of "obscurantism" and reactionary intentions, but this argument had nothing reactionary about it and had nothing to do with the wish to persecute agitators. The counterargument sets out from the idea of German federalism, which would have to be sacrificed if the British or French model were adopted. One had to assume "that there will be no German government that will allow that it is chased out of its home and possessions for the sake of Germanness."

Metternich did not hide the fact that he would have liked it best for all writings, without exception, to be censored. Here, too, his thinking followed the logic, not of restoration, but of the existing law—he respected the different systems of regulation in the German states. He accepted that the freedom of the press might sometimes be controlled by courts as well as through a method of pre-censorship: "Every German state is free to decide whether it wants to retain or introduce an institution for censorship or a censorship law [operated through courts] dealing with all intellectual material produced within its borders."

The public political agitation following the assassination had left its marks on Metternich. For the identification of material that was to be subjected to censorship he suggested a criterion that was not material—that is, did not concern content—but formal. He distinguished between "works" that appeared once—books that contained "scientific content" and had a volume of at least 25 print sheets (equaling 400 printed pages)—and periodicals, such as "newspapers, pamphlets, etc." It was later agreed that the required length for the former would be 20 print sheets, equaling 320 printed pages. The latter, Metternich argued, were characterized by their political or moral content and had to be generally presented to a censor before being printed. This rule has been seen as a social clause which exempted the educated from pre-censorship.

Metternich's suggestion became part of the general press law of the federation of September 20, 1819, as had already been agreed to in Carlsbad. It was a compromise that put the two preeminent German powers, Prussia and Austria, under considerable strain, as they had reserved the right to carry out pre-censorship in all of their states. Metternich's liberal solution, intended to accommodate differences between states, created unforeseen gaps, and so we cannot speak of a closed system of repression or the policing of the press.[108] The best proof of this is the never-ending series of initiatives to strengthen the censorship rules through the Federal Assembly. That was necessary only because the existing system did not work efficiently, and, again and again, loopholes had to be closed. And after 1825, with the invention and introduction of the high-speed printing press, daily publications in Germany increased to such an extent that the conventional censorship bureaus were hardly able to keep up. In 1842, Prussia even experimented with so-called censorship courts.

The Reaction to the Assassination of Kotzebue: National Mobilization

Why did Carl Sand's assassination of Kotzebue provoke new legislation on the regulation of the press in Germany at all? Gentz provided the answer in an almost prophetic vision of the kind of mood Sand's act would trigger in the German public. He predicted that the trial against Sand would be taken very seriously and that he would be punished with all the force of the criminal law. Gentz expected that in the press, "thousands and thousands will become exalted to the point of rapture, will present him as a hero, a martyr for the good cause, the sacrificial lamb of the obscurantists, and will become ten times as raging and as guilty as they already are."[109]

Indeed, Gentz's collection of newspaper articles provides convincing evidence that sympathy for Sand was building in the press. The articles begin by routinely distancing themselves from the "terrible act" and assuring the reader that murder is not an acceptable means in politics. But then Sand's noble character is emphasized, followed by—most importantly—praise for his selfless patriotism. This is combined with advice and warnings to the princes to revise their misguided policies. The papers trotted out variations on this narrative, depending on what kind of new information had emerged. Upon closer scrutiny, it becomes apparent that the papers were eager to soak up any information they could: eyewitness reports, whose distribution multiplied exponentially as the papers copied them off each other, and details from the files of the investigation, among them Sand's proclamations and letters. The *Rheinische Blätter*, published in Wiesbaden, can be taken as a good example of this trend. Gentz underlined the following passage from the edition of April 5, 1819, highlighting for Metternich what was particularly objectionable:

> But in the case of Kotzebue's catastrophe everyone seems to have a silent feeling that the real deed only begins where in similar cases it ends, namely *after* the perpetrated murder. This was not a matter of individual fighting against individual; the spirit of the new age entered the ring against the spirit of the age that has just ended. . . . This deed proves that the spirit which in 1813 rose up for Germany's independence of *alien* rule, control and discipline is still alive in 1819. The impression the deed makes in all areas of Germany shows that the matter is not perceived as concerning an individual but as a national matter.[110]

As this commentary reveals, one of the effects of the assassination was to encourage criticisms of the political system directed at the rulers. Further, Sand became a symbol, an icon, a myth, and the object of cultlike devotion. This is expressed well by Karl Hase, a fraternity member. In 1820, after he had visited Sand's parents, he wrote an obituary in his diary that, though it was only one voice, was representative of the collective sympathy that Metternich and Gentz feared:

> Sand appears to me to be one of the greatest men of his century. He freely chose a hero's death for the salvation of the fatherland, the greatest deed known to humankind, and hence his grave be given a citizen's crown. This is why his name will be celebrated by posterity; therefore, whatever evil the deed may have presently brought about, it will not be lost in the workings of providence, as no great deed ever is. . . . But he has become a treacherous murderer, and therefore I would decide for the death penalty if I was sitting among his judges. Justice be done, and if it means humankind as a whole must climb the scaffold; for what worth does human life possess without justice? You tender women may weep for him, he deserves them. . . . Sand wanted to sacrifice himself for the fatherland, how will you execute him for that?[111]

Even Archduke Johann had some sympathy for Sand, although he did undoubtedly condemn the act. In his diary the archduke wrote about Sand and Kotzebue: "A pity about him it is not at all.—The murderer, a young man called Sand—a dreamer [*Schwärmer*]—pity about him, that he makes himself guilty of such an act—murder remains murder."[112] All of Sand's own statements, however, contradict this idea of the fundamentalist holy warrior as a mere "Schwärmer." What Sand was interested in was attention, impact, publicity—in a word: sending "a signal." In this, he had succeeded. For instance, in those days illustrations in daily newspapers were very rare, and when they appeared it meant that an event had received the highest level of attention; an article in the *Aarauer Zeitung,* "The Execution of Carl Ludwig Sand on May 20, 1820," was illustrated with a lithograph. It showed his execution, alongside a depiction of the death sentence being handed down to Sand while tied to his bed, still suffering from his wound.

The newspaper article expressed not the slightest trace of disgust at the political assassination. But it revealed that Sand envisaged his execution as a staged demonstration. He had been offered the option of executing himself with a dagger, but he insisted on a public execution. "To die on the scaffold, clearly, was a kind of triumph for him." The paper called him a "young man whose fate is deeply to be bemoaned," and stressed that he showed the "greatest calmness in his soul." Before the execution, he was allowed to receive "people who wished to see and speak to him." He wanted to go to the place of execution on

Illustration in the article "Karl Ludwig Sand's Hinrichtung am 20. May 1820" [Execution of Carl Ludwig Sand on May 20, 1820], *Aarauer Zeitung.*

his own, without a priest accompanying him, and dressed in a "German black coat." Before his execution, he said: "My hope in God is unshaken"; then he raised his right hand toward the sky, as if taking an oath, and spoke in prayer: "I die with the force of my God!" and then as his last words: "God, you have taken me into your grace."

Sand presented himself as a holy warrior and martyr, and the newspaper went along with this glorification, describing his last public appearance in an almost Christ-like fashion: "He only wanted the good with all his will, and was prepared to sacrifice his life for it. That is why it was possible to respect and love him. That he nevertheless committed a crime was the fault of the unfortunate error which captivated him. . . . His crime is now atoned. Sand, the criminal, no longer is, but Sand, the noble and unhappy young man, will continue to live for a long time in the memory of many."

As soon as the scaffold was opened to the public, many of those present rushed to it to dip their handkerchiefs in his blood, tear off parts the scaffold itself, or try to take a lock of his hair. Someone who had traveled to Mannheim especially for the occasion took the execution seat, and the calash that had brought Sand to the execution was sold at a profit. But the fraternity from Heidelberg beat all the other relic hunters: a democrat from the Palatinate used the beams and boards from the scaffold to build a garden house at a vineyard in Heidelberg, and secret meetings were held there "in Sand's scaffold as guests of his hangman."[113] To Metternich, who was thinking instead of the family of the dead Kotzebue, this was indicative of the suffocating nationalism that was dividing the nation. He knew well that the assassin was worshipped like a holy figure; he kept the article and illustration from the *Aarauer Zeitung* with his personal papers.[114]

Measures Taken against the Universities

As in the case of the measures taken against the press, when it came to the universities Metternich arrived at his concrete ideas about what to do with the encouragement of Gentz and of the Leipzig consul and political observer Adam Müller. These ideas were connected with Metternich's judgment of the students' political actions and of where the real dangers lay. In his opinion, there was no federal state with a university that was not at risk. Even in Vienna, which was allegedly well shielded from these phenomena, Karl Follen and his "Giessener Unbedingte" had their followers. And in a large-scale raid in which 140 students were arrested, the diary of a Sand devotee turned up. It revealed just how easily the idea of terrorist attacks as noble acts of conscience in the service of holy, patriotic purposes had caught on: "Travel plans, battles, booze-ups, revolution, the murder of tyrants, all this constantly drives me around. Only someone who is able to give up for a holy purpose even what the world calls honor makes a truly great sacrifice. This is why only Sand stands as high as he does, because he did not shy away from appearing to the common crowd like a common murderer."[115] There was a community of sentiment [*Gesinnungsgenossenschaft*] emerging that reached all the way from ordinary students to the sympathetic tributes of the archduke.

But where should one try to intervene? For Metternich, the real sources of danger were not the students, not even those who were members of fraternities: "The member of a fraternity, taken by himself, is a child, and fraternities are impractical puppet shows."[116] The danger emanated from the professors, who, as academic teachers, also influenced the students on a personal and moral level, as the example of Karl Follen showed. They created the ideological networks. No one provided better confirmation of this than the Berlin professor of theology Wilhelm de Wette, who had known Sand personally. He did not suspect that his words of consolation for Sand's mother would fall into the hands of the police. He defended her son's honor against the "opinion of the common masses" that he was a murderer. Of course, he wrote, in secular terms his act was unlawful and punishable by a judge. Her son had erred and been carried away by passion—but then he added what many people thought, and what deeply troubled Metternich:

An error is excused and compensated, so to speak, by firmness and sincerity of conviction, and passion is sanctified by the goodness of the source from which it flows: I am firmly convinced that both cases apply to your pious and virtuous son. He was sure about his concern, and he thought it was right to do what he did, and thus he has done right. Everyone should act in accordance with their conviction, and then everyone will do the best. . . . A young man gives his life in order to eradicate a human being whom many revere as an idol. And this should really have no effect at all?[117]

In the eyes of the theologian the assassin was a pure young man who was pious and confident that he had done something good that his conscience had told him to do. His deed was therefore "a beautiful sign of the times." The professor lost his position over the letter. He was one of the first. After him, other more or less prominent professors were dismissed for corrupting the youth, among them the prophet of nationalism, Ernst Moritz Arndt, who had only recently been appointed a professor of history in Bonn.

In Metternich's view, when these professors strayed beyond their fields, in these cases theology and history, and became politically active, they became intellectual arsonists. But he also thought that they were altogether incapable of staging a coup. He knew "no conspirators who are as miserable and superficial as professors, individually as well as taken as a group." They were men of theory and put forward propositions, but revolution was not a theoretical pursuit. Scholars and professors did not know how to overthrow existing institutions because they had no sense of the value of property. Advocates, as practitioners, had such a sense, and Metternich saw them as the conspirators who were genuinely capable of achieving their aims. He might have been right—the most-wanted Italian revolutionary, Giuseppe Mazzini, for instance, had studied law and initially practiced as a lawyer for the poor, and had thus learned firsthand about the importance of the distribution of property.

Metternich drew the following conclusion: "I therefore never feared that the revolution might be *created* at the universities; but that a whole generation of revolutionaries must form there if no barriers are set up against the ills, seems certain to me."[118] On the question of what had to be done, however, he contradicted the eager proposals of Adam Müller, who advised a "purification of the academic chairs, in sober fashion and without noise." Müller wanted to "quietly remove" the small number of "ringleaders . . . and substitute them with calm, well-behaved scholars"; the latter, he held, had more talent anyway, and they could, in this way, at the same time contribute to a reform of the universities.[119] This proposal would have implied an evaluation of the quality of the professors' work. Adam Müller traced the whole "university nonsense" to the Reformation, and thought that only an undoing of the Reformation could provide a genuine remedy. When he said this he certainly had in mind Protestant theologians such as de Witte and the theology student Sand. In essence, Metternich agreed with Müller's idea; for him, Luther had been a revolutionary because he, too, had placed the justification of his deeds solely in his conscience, independent of what the laws of state and church demanded. But Metternich was a politician and not an impractical theoretician of the kind Müller had become. With a subtle sense for the irony of being asked to pass judgment on Protestantism from Rome, Metternich replied to him: "Being at the Quirinale, I cannot engage with Dr. Martin Luther, and I hope that nevertheless something good may happen without pursuing Protestantism back to its original source." Metternich therefore stipulated that "questions of discipline" had to be separated from "questions concerning study." The latter concerned the content of studies, and the confederation had to leave this alone. The confederation was only to establish formal rules for the supervision of universities, and Adam Müller had suggested how this could be done. A "curator" should be appointed to every university. In the decrees that were eventually passed, this curator became a "representative of the sovereign"—that is, the arm of the state within academic life. This institution can still be found at many universities in the role of "chancellor."

FROM TEPLITZ TO CARLSBAD: THE CONFERENCES ON DOMESTIC SECURITY, 1819–1820

Preparations for the Carlsbad Conferences: Security Pact with Wittgenstein

Metternich learned of the assassination of Kotzebue on April 9, 1819, while in Rome. From then on, he was in intense consultations regarding how to proceed with the "German matters"—as the files call it—with Friedrich Gentz, who was in Vienna. Metternich observed that the public mood in Lombardy-Venetia had deteriorated, but he thought that mistaken measures introduced by the government were only partially to blame, and that the unrest was being stirred by recent events in Germany and France. His awareness was now heightened, and he registered every attack and every sign of unrest ever more acutely, integrating them all into his picture of the progressive revolutionizing of Europe.

Although Kotzebue's assassination struck him as a dramatic event, he did not let it distract him from his travel plans. His stay in Rome ended in the last week of April, and he went on to Naples, where he spent all of May—even climbing Mount Vesuvius. At the beginning of June he returned to Rome, in mid-June he traveled on to Verona, and in the last week of June he went to Florence, where he stayed until mid-July. Finally, after two days in Verona again, he set off for Carlsbad.

On July 18, he stopped over in Munich and used the opportunity to present the situation to King Maximilian I. After Prussia, Bavaria was the second most important partner when it came to establishing a consensus on a future legal framework for domestic security in the German Confederation. Metternich made contact with the ministers and the king, and he noticed that the mood in Bavaria had shifted. Half a year ago the state had still "lived in a dream of political greatness." Now he found the government "without ideas, without hope, lying prostrate on the floor." The hope that they would be able to help themselves had gone. Bavaria was just one of the states whose representatives flocked to Metternich asking for his advice. After the assassinations, the princes and their ministers were now fearing for their lives. Metternich informed Field Marshall von Wrede about his plans for Carlsbad.

At the same time, more worrying news reached Metternich. He knew about investigations in Berlin, Karlsruhe, Darmstadt, and Nassau. From Berlin he learned of a "Black league" [*Schwarzer Bund*] that had been identified and arrested—this was actually a radical fraternity, the "Blacks of Giessen" [*Gießener Schwarze*]. After an apothecary named Karl Löning attempted to assassinate the president of one of Nassau's seven regional governments, Carl von Ibell, Metternich asked the minister in Nassau, Baron von Marschall, to keep him abreast of the results of the interrogation. Only two and a half weeks later, Metternich knew that the assassin had connections to the "Giessener Schwarze" and that he was dealing with more than sixty suspected sympathizers. Metternich arranged for copies of the files to be sent to the emperor and simultaneously made contact with the minister of police, Sedlnitzky.

In his preparations for Carlsbad, Metternich relied mainly on the Prussian minister of police, Wittgenstein, who had contacted him at the end of June with a cry for help. Wittgenstein felt pretty much left alone with his investigations in Berlin, and wrote that he "therefore need[ed] a strong ally. I therefore very much hope that Your Liebden will come to my aid, and in Your own noble person [*hohe Person*]."[120] The assassination carried out by Sand led to a close and strictly secret alliance against terror between Metternich and Wittgenstein. With this alliance, Metternich now had a direct line to King Friedrich Wilhelm III. Wittgenstein organized a personal meeting between the king and Metternich in Teplitz. The police minister urged Metternich to attend; the king, he said, would "certainly enjoy it very much" to see him there and to arrange "a rendezvous" with Hardenberg. This would give Wittgenstein the opportunity to have Metternich "as a faithful ally supporting him."[121] Metternich also passed on to the emperor this offer of an alliance. It is crucial to note just how much this Prussian initiative bolstered Metternich's plans. It shows, also, that a battle over strategy and over who could influence the king was taking place at the Prussian court.

Within only a few months, worrying news of successful and failed attacks, as well as of the conspiratorial activities of the fraternities, reached Metternich. At the same time, he was shocked by the wave of sympathy that was triggered among allegedly patriotic bourgeois individuals by acts like Sand's. He did not doubt for a moment that these sorts of events exerted an amplifying effect across Europe. The declarations of solidarity with the Greeks, issued by Sand, among others, revealed just one dimension of this dynamic. The other dimension became visible in August, when the Carlsbad conference took place and when (on August 16, 1819) English cavalry charged into a crowd protesting against the Corn Laws, causing the so-called Peterloo massacre near Manchester.[122] The "Six Acts" for the protection of domestic security passed in London were the exact equivalent of the decrees for which Metternich and Wittgenstein fought in Carlsbad. Given the way Metternich summarized his concerns, it is really not plausible to speak of a mere "pretext" here: "Today, more than ever, I am convinced that the evil [*Übel*] will be beyond any human remedy if the German governments do not come close together and take very appropriate and especially uniform measures between now and a few months' time."[123] The path toward such measures led via Teplitz.

Teplitz: A Common Platform for Austria and Prussia, July 27–August 2, 1819

Metternich arrived in Carlsbad on July 21, 1819. The most important preparations had been made. He had formed a circle of insiders through diplomatic channels. In terms of the program to be pursued, he was very well prepared; he knew exactly what he wanted to achieve. But before the conference, he still went to Teplitz. "I obey the invitation of the Prussian king," he wrote to Emperor Franz, thus revealing whose idea the meeting was. Nevertheless, a consultation between Prussia and Austria fit with the ideal according to which he had constructed the German Confederation, which implied steadfast agreement between the two.

The joint political program agreed upon at Teplitz rested on two pillars. One of them found expression in the Carlsbad Decrees and concerned "the reining in of parties in Germany"—measures against the press, the universities, and the fraternities, and for the investigation of the assassination carried out by Sand. The other concerned the process of constitutional legislation in Prussia. On May 22, 1815, the king had passed a "decree on the representation of the people to be formed," in which he called the state an "empire" in which the "Prussian nation is given a pledge of our trust" in the form of a "constitutional document."[124] To form a "representation of the people" meant nothing other than the establishment of a central Parliament. For Metternich, this was an alarming sign that the idea of "people's representation" had taken hold in Prussia. Although the decree talked about "provincial estates" [*Provinzial-stände*], the new Parliament was to embody "the people."

In November 1818, during the Congress of Aix-la-Chapelle, Metternich had already explained to Wittgenstein, in a confidential letter, why a "central representation" was not suitable for Prussia. If one reads Metternich in the right way, it is clear that he did not fight against the political participation of social forces—he was not an absolutist—but that his concern was always that the political system serve the purposes of internal peace. If it was not able to do that, then it was no good in his eyes. He considered the Prussian Monarchy to be, like the Habsburg Monarchy, a "composite state" as an empire: "The Prussian state, although united under one sceptre, consists of several parts, separated by geographical position, climate, tribes [*Volksstämme*], or language. It has in this respect an essential similarity to the Austrian [state]."[125]

Metternich argued that the centralization of the monarchy in a purely representational system would have led to its disintegration into its already existing constituent parts. As proof, he pointed toward the Netherlands, which was, he said, politically paralyzed by such a system. A central Parliament inaugurated "a composition of individual, mutually alien and hostile deputies—which are far from being united for the *One* purpose of being a state." A state council or central committee of the estates could serve as an alternative central institution, which was doubtlessly needed. What the maintenance of a kingdom required was, apart from the person of the monarch, a strong standing army, as the example of the Netherlands showed. At this point in his letter to Wittgenstein, Metternich called the "arming of the people" a "senseless system" and predicted that "the Prussian state would approach its internal dissolution if ever the king of Prussia should appear, not at the head of an army, but as the leader of seven or eight separate masses of men."[126] Because of the experiences they had had, because of "the dreadful abuse of power of which the German princes, in their sovereign arrogance, have been guilty since the year 1806," the Germans desired guarantees against despotic rule.[127]

Metternich considered "the restoration of *estate-based Constitutions*" to be the best means for preserving domestic peace, whereas the centralist former states of the Rhenish Confederation tended toward absolutism. One does not have to sympathize with Metternich's political ideals in order to admit that he was hostile toward absolutism, and that he sought ways of guaranteeing legal forms for political participation that were grounded in regional and provincial traditions. Toward Prussia, he essentially argued for a constitutional conservativism in line with Edmund Burke's philosophy. That was precisely the spirit in which he tried to persuade the Prussian king and Hardenberg in Teplitz "not to introduce a representation of the people, but to limit themselves to representation of the provincial estates in a purely monarchical sense."[128]

Many critics of Metternich will be astonished that his defensive security policies, which came to dominate after Carlsbad, were based on the idea of the unity of Germany. In his presentation for the emperor, he pushed the problem to its dramatic conclusion: "The first of all questions is—will Prussia be drawn into the stream of revolution, or has the king enough strength to save himself, and thus Germany?" How should we understand this claim? Metternich had now realized that there were ideologically motivated people prepared to murder heads of state, and that their actions could not be predicted; they could show up at any time. The uncertainty alone was enough to produce insecurity. What was at stake, in Metternich's view, was therefore "the preservation of the monarchy." The experience of the French Revolution, which had demonstrated how societal violence could transform into an all-powerful military dictatorship, could not be forgotten. It was the matrix behind his political predictions.

Metternich did not seek to draw trivial analogies between the present and the times of the French Revolution. He was looking in particular for the differences. It was the same monarchy now "which [was] threatened in very different but surely no less dangerous ways compared to the ways it was threatened between 1792 and 1814." For him, Austria had a decisive and very specific role to play in connection to the issue of whether another revolution would take place. If a revolution were to take hold of all of Germany, it would soon also reach Italy, and then Austria. That would also mean the end of the German Confederation. Austria, however, was a major European power as much as a German one. If Germany was lost, Austria would remain a major European power. For Metternich, all this brought a sense of déjà vu. When the emperor had lost the backing of the other member states in the imperial war—the Peace of Basel in 1795 was a turning point in this process—he threatened to withdraw from Germany. Metternich recognized this sort of situation as a recurring challenge. The year 1819 was therefore a crucial one. The problem would persist. The German Customs Union in 1833 and the revolution in 1848 were markers of the gradual distancing of Prussia and Austria from each other. It seems like a dialectical paradox of history—a compatibility of the incompatible—that in Metternich's view the maligned, allegedly antinational Carlsbad Decrees were intended to preserve the federal German unity he had helped create in 1815. To the emperor, he implored: "Our *first* duty is to try to save Germany, which is still possible, because in this alone still lies a certain and true good for us."[129]

On July 27, 1819, Metternich arrived in Teplitz and found himself in the same room, even at the same table, where, six years earlier, he had signed the Quadruple Alliance. It was also almost the same time of the year. On this occasion, he thought the sorry world had committed even graver errors and mistakes than it had made six years ago.[130]

The next day Metternich had a long conversation with King Friedrich Wilhelm III. The king, too, looked back: "Six years ago we had to fight the enemy in the open field: now he sneaks and hides."[131] Metternich disregarded diplomatic custom and spoke frankly about what he saw as the problems at the Prussian court. Hardenberg, he said, was "now old and feeble both in mind and body. He desires what is right, and only too frequently supports what is bad."[132] Metternich further criticized the state chancellor for surrounding himself with second-raters who would have to be dismissed. Metternich's posthumous papers suppress the urgent questions he added: "Given that only one *Jahn* has yet been arrested, whose activities have been known for years;[133] that a new university was built in Bonn, which was then filled with everything known to be bad in Germany; that only after my reporting a *Varnhagen* was removed from his post at the embassy, after he had revolutionized a whole country; how then should well-meaning people support this administration?"

The king agreed with everything Metternich said and asked him for help. Metternich made his help conditional on a categorical demand being met: "not to introduce a representation of the people in your state, which is less suited to it than any other." The priorities, he said, were measures against the press and the fraternities. Friedrich Wilhelm III ordered that Metternich be allowed to access to all his administration's documents, "even the most secret."

Having looked through all of the information he received, Metternich was convinced "that there is a very widespread conspiracy which aims at the overthrow of all German governments *without exception*." Independent of Metternich's conclusion, the police and the Justice Ministry were charged with a systematic investigation that was to establish whether there was a more-organized enterprise behind the violence. What was incontrovertible was that copycat attacks had obviously been planned and executed by individuals who sympathized with one another's attitudes (Sand, Löning, Cantillon and Marinet, later Thistlewood and Louvel). It was also obvious that the attacks had a European character and that there was communication across the Continent; everywhere the attacks were justified with reference to the same values: the national liberation of the Greeks, Germans, Poles, Italians, and so on, and the demand for Constitutions. Metternich took calls for the murder of princes very seriously.

A proclamation, for instance, had been uncovered that said that if there were twenty-one German princes, then twenty-one heads had to roll. Metternich ironically asked why the prince of Liechtenstein had been refused the honor of appearing on the list—that "odd compilation"—together with the Austrian emperor.[134]

In Metternich's view, the conspiracy was far-reaching. Most higher civil servants in Prussia, he thought, were playing crucial roles in it, as were the universities of Jena, Heidelberg, Giessen, and Freiburg. The whole "gymnastics club" [*Turnanstalt*] served the same purpose, especially Dr. Jahn. The "Unbedingten" (the radical and revolutionary core of the fraternities), Metternich thought, were "the real assassins"—all of them young men between twenty and twenty-four. Metternich referred to the fanaticism revealed by the many confiscated diaries, "which overflow with the happiness of wading in blood, handling a dagger and being a regicide, with being called upon to do God's work, etc. Many of the young people wrote down prayers in which they ask God for forgiveness because they have not acted yet—have called upon him soon to offer them an opportunity to die like Sand."[135] The professors encouraged the young men to hold on to their good intentions and to prove themselves worthy of their fatherland. There were also alleged connections to French Jacobins. The information Metternich had provided to the Prussian king made Hardenberg highly anxious. He urgently asked Metternich to stay in Teplitz until August 2. Metternich corrected his earlier judgment: the state chancellor was "not in mind but in feeling close on childhood."[136]

Metternich considered the current moment, August 1819, to be "the most important for Germany as a whole."[137] He had succeeded in changing Prussia's political course, steering it away from the introduction of popular representation, establishing a trusting relationship with the king through Wittgenstein, and inviting the important ministers of the German states to Carlsbad. Metternich had, let us recall, been very uncertain as he traveled to Teplitz. Given Prussia's weak king, frail state chancellor, and the unruly, reform-minded faction at court, he did not know if Prussia was ready to exercise joint supreme rule over the German Confederation. The reformist faction were centralists, and they had no interest in supporting the ancient inner plurality of the monarchy or the representation of provincial estates in the capital.

To Emperor Franz, Metternich repeated the only option they had: "To save Germany by the help of Austria, or to leave Austria the possibility, difficult as it may be, to save herself."[138] The emperor agreed unreservedly with Metternich, and Metternich was able to dispel his usual worries. It was an overwhelming success. Metternich could be certain of Prussia's unqualified support at the upcoming Carlsbad Conference.

Metternich could now pursue both defensive and constructive security policies. He recognized the need to correct mistakes and uncertainties in the federal Constitution, and to develop it further—to "point out the appropriate ways and means to improve the defects in the Bund."[139] He drew up a timetable for the emperor showing what he had contractually agreed to with Prussia in order to achieve that end. In a first period in Carlsbad, questions regarding the press, universities (including fraternities), and the investigative commission for the Sand case were to be dealt with. These were defensive measures that roughly corresponded to the "Six Acts" passed in London. In a second period, in Vienna, the federal Constitution was to be amended in light of those questions that were still controversial.

The Carlsbad Conference, August 6–31, 1819

Metternich had invited to Carlsbad only the ministers of a select group of states, and this he had done as secretly as possible. He was afraid of the as-yet unregulated press, and passionate discussion in the papers could bring the federal states into conflict and might have derailed the undertaking before it had even begun. On August 31, at the very end of the negotiations, Metternich was still claiming: "No one in Germany yet knows what the essence of our negotiations here will be."[140] All of Metternich's preparations and his experienced handling of the negotiations paid off. In addition to Austria and Prussia, the others of Metternich's chosen eleven were Bavaria, Saxony, Hannover, Württemberg, Baden, Mecklenburg, Nassau, Kurhessen, and Saxony-Weimar. These states Metternich considered sufficiently important or reliable to be invited.

The eleven ministers, assembled like conspirators, agreed upon four pieces of draft legislation that were to be presented to the Federal Assembly for ratification. There could be no talk of taking the waters, as Metternich had originally planned.[141] He had underestimated the difficulties. For more than three weeks he had to chair meetings, work on plans, and study documents for twelve to fifteen hours every day. He felt "like a hunted deer." In the end he felt infinitely relieved; he had not been as sure of success as his outward appearance might have suggested. To the emperor he confessed that something had, in the end, been achieved that "a short while ago might have seemed impossible." Looking back at this achievement, Metternich explained how he had fought for the right formulation of every point. The text was "strictly scrutinized and calculated to fit not only the situation in Germany, but in Europe."[142]

1. The law on the universities prohibited student associations, especially fraternities, and regulated the universities themselves. Each of them had to have a "commissioner of the sovereign" [*Landesherrlicher Beauftragter*] who would,

in particular, control the teaching. Metternich had previously warned against revolution and "parties," but the decree did not yet actually target political associations, the real bodies behind social movements. Those were prohibited only after the July Revolution of 1830.

2. The federation now finally possessed a legal framework for regulating the freedom of the press. Smaller texts, especially periodicals, were subject to pre-censorship in all states of the federation. For printed matter of more than 320 pages, states could individually choose whether to practice pre-censorship. Metternich had pushed through the compromise he had designed in Italy.

3. The law on investigations created a federal institution, the Central Investigation Commission, located in Mainz, which was to find out whether there really was a conspiracy behind Carl Sand's assassination of Kotzebue.

4. An executive order gave the German Confederation the authority to force individual states to comply with the jointly agreed decrees—through military force if necessary. The confederation could thus threaten the use of force, a means it sometimes employed to bring states into line. Württemberg had to give up its own press law of 1817, which had abolished censorship altogether. Later attempts at abolishing censorship, such as in Baden in 1831, also failed; in this case, the law had already been passed by the state Parliament, but had to be revoked in order to avoid the risk of federal retaliation.

There is a widespread view that Metternich imposed the Carlsbad Decrees on the German states through his infamous "system." But as we have seen, in the days after Sand's attack Metternich was besieged on all sides by people urging him to take the initiative. At the end of the negotiations, the ministers' statements made it clear that nothing had changed in this respect. In a farewell letter, they offered him a "unanimous expression of [their] unbounded respect and gratitude." They praised Metternich's "prudent guidance, [his] ceaseless efforts, and the confidence [he had] so kindly shown in [them]." He had helped them to fulfill "their most sacred and indispensable duty toward the common fatherland."[143] The minister, thus, was clearly believed to have acted not only in the interest of their princes but in that of their common fatherland. Metternich took this letter not merely as a product of official business but as an expression of personal appreciation—he marked it: "to be filed ad acta familiae."

At the crucial sitting of the Federal Assembly on September 20, 1819, the Austrian presidential envoy, Count von Buol, asked the members "to direct their whole attention to the restless agitation and fermentation of feeling prevailing in the greater part of Germany," which "was unmistakably revealed in sermonising writings, in widespread criminal confederations, even in single deeds of horror." The decrees they were asked to pass would secure much-needed "order

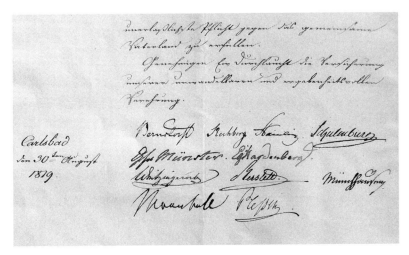

Signatures to the "Letter of Thanks from the Ministers assembled at Carlsbad to Prince Metternich, Carlsbad, August 30, 1819": Bernstorff, Rechberg, Stainlein, Schulenburg, Count Münster, Hardenberg, Wintzingerode, Berstett, Münchhausen, Marschall, Plessen.

and peace, respect for laws and confidence in Governments, general contentment, and the undisturbed enjoyment of all the benefits which, under the protection of a durable, secure peace, would fall to the share of the German nation from the hand of their princes."[144]

Like the British laws, the four decrees that the Federal Assembly finally passed on September 20, 1819, were time-limited. When Metternich heard the news, he wrote to Dorothea von Lieven that "the child which I have carried nine months has at last seen the light and is well."[145] If this is right, then he must have had his initial ideas for this legislation in December 1818, immediately after the Conference of Aix-la-Chapelle and before the assassination of Kotzebue. This is certainly plausible: the theme of domestic and European unrest was touched upon at the conference. Metternich knew that this legislation was controversial: "Each party will wish to baptize the child by a different name. Some will call it a monster, some a good work, some a piece of stupidity. The truth lies in between. The first legislative words spoken for thirty years that are uttered from a sense of reason, justice, and experience, . . . these words are a great act, one of the most important of my life."[146] Given that it wholly contradicts the widely shared judgment on the Carlsbad Decrees, this self-evaluation will no doubt come as some surprise. It can be properly understood only if we bear in mind what the experience of war, and the regaining of domestic peace, meant to him, how much he valued the unity of Germany and the fact that the

Habsburg Monarchy was a part of it. "The first legislative words spoken for thirty years," Metternich wrote—in other words, since 1789. He never managed to shake off the past when designing the future.

METTERNICH'S SUGGESTIONS FOR THE DEVELOPMENT AND EXTENSION OF THE GERMAN FEDERAL CONSTITUTION: THE FINAL ACT OF THE GERMAN CONFEDERATION, MAY 15, 1820

From Carlsbad to Vienna: Consolidation and Developments

Only a few weeks had passed since the negotiations in Carlsbad. With the decrees, which aimed to rein in the press and control the universities, Metternich wanted—like the British—to counter potential revolutionary activity in the country. The purely defensive measures strengthened the power of the confederation. It would be possible to speak of a negative national integration. But Metternich did not forget that the Federal Act was only provisional, and he therefore embarked on the second part of his constitutional policies, which he had announced previously. He energetically pushed ahead with the extension of the federal Constitution. Even constitutional historians who view Carlsbad as nothing but a "conservative-restorative regression of the federal Constitution" find the tendencies of the subsequent Vienna conference "peculiar and remarkable."[147]

On November 18, the emperor granted an audience to the group of ministers who had been invited to Vienna. Metternich provided him with the appropriate wording for the occasion. The conferences in Vienna had been initiated "in order finally to make a direct attempt at putting the confederation on the right track."[148] The only opposition to be expected might come from Bavaria or Württemberg. Such opposition rested either on misunderstanding, which could be easily dispelled, or on diverging principles, which could be combatted with the help of the rest of the confederation. "A common good" had "to be preserved." One or two participants, Metternich wrote, wanted to vote against everything on the basis of their private ideas. "In this case, the opponents will have to bow if the rest of the assembly agrees and has right on their side." When thus addressing those gathered, he was to direct his gaze at those for whom these remarks were intended, without showing any further emotion.

The meetings in Vienna differed from those in Carlsbad in every way. Metternich took the initiative and did not wait for the other governments to call upon him. He did not exclude any of the states, officially inviting all seventeen of the "inner council" [Engerer Rat] of the Federal Assembly to Vienna for negotiations on the federal Constitution. The council was the body in which all federal states were represented, whether in the form of an individual vote [*Virilstimme*] or a collective vote [*Kuriatstimme*]. It would be misleading to suggest that Metternich bypassed the Federal Assembly as the actually authoritative body in constitutional matters, because the latter was a permanent assembly of envoys who first had to ask for instructions regarding any decisions to be made. A matter as complicated as the amendment of the Constitution could not be negotiated through envoys; it was necessary to have the responsible decision makers—the ministers—present at the table.

Metternich held all cards. For the negotiations, he invited the delegates to his Chancellery. He proposed the agenda and handed the participants a thorough paper that set out his approach. On November 25, 1819, there were two opening speeches written by Metternich, one given by the emperor and expressing the emperor's general support for the confederation, and another given by Metternich as the host minister, in which he outlined the aims of the conferences ahead of them. His own speech lasted two hours, and Metternich regretted that he did not have a stenographer on hand, because, as he told Dorothea von Lieven—as usual with some irony—"I spoke like a God."[149]

At the beginning of the negotiations, Metternich felt that he was achieving great things: "I am in a very decisive phase of my public life—I shall either perish along with society or I shall have a substantial hand in its salvation."[150] He quoted Talleyrand as saying: "Austria is the upper house *(chambre de pairs)* of Europe. As long as it is not dissolved, it will rein in the lower house *(les communes)*"—that is, the smaller states. Metternich repeatedly emphasized that the Carlsbad Decrees and the decrees to be passed now were important not only for Germany but also for Europe as a whole. He was thinking of the strong defensive central region that the German Confederation was destined to form.

As Metternich had also written the speech he gave on behalf of the emperor, we can interpret both speeches together. Metternich reminded his listeners of the motivations that had led to the foundation of the confederation. It is striking that he described it "as the only possible meeting point for the whole *German nation*."[151] He referred to the "federal Constitution" [*Föderativ-Verfassung*] of Germany.

At the same time, he warned about a "party hooked on revolution that is spread across all of Europe," including in the lands of the German Confederation, that had made worrying progress over the past two years. To begin with, there had been only a few dissatisfied individuals, political dreamers, but then whole generations had been caught "under the treacherous cloak of holy words and philanthropic intentions, so that the passion of the crowds were roused with feeling."

The confederation, he went on, guaranteed external and internal peace [*Ruhe*] for Germany; it guaranteed the independence of the individual allied members and protected them against threats from one another, as well as from abroad. In his opening speech, Metternich made the case for the German Confederation, explaining to the participants the implications of its foundation in international law. All existing public law in Germany depended on it: it guaranteed not only the rights of the confederation but also the sovereign rights of the individual states. The existence of the confederation no longer depended on arbitrary decisions, but it was necessary to make sure that it did not continue to carry on in an incomplete, unsatisfactory, and uncertain form. One must not allow it, he concluded, to sink into powerlessness and irrelevance.

A Program for Confederate Policies

Metternich, the allegedly restorationist minister, formulated a brief for reform: "It is therefore an obvious necessity and common duty to give the confederation the perfection which, according to its foundation and the basic idea on which it rests, it was destined to acquire." That more progress had not been made so far was down to the specificity of the confederation itself, the influence of local opinions—that is, of the federal components. Metternich wished the confederation "the perfection, the solidity, and thus the reputation that the association of thirty million Germans, equal in rank and influence to the foremost European powers, deserves."

At the same time, he identified ten tasks to be addressed by the conference. For each of these, a working commission was formed.[152] The catalogue of tasks expressed Metternich's determination to strengthen the confederation's character as a united federal state by giving it central authority in legal, executive, constitutional, military, and even economic matters. This can certainly be interpreted as a progressive step forward for the federal union—as a form of national integration. Metternich himself revealed his political priorities by adding his name to three of the commissions: article 13 [*13. Artikel*], political-military situation [*Politisch-militärische Verhältnisse*], and federal fortresses [*Bundesfestungen*]. Minister Zentner, from sovereignty-obsessed Bavaria, wanted to join no less than seven commissions, closely followed by the equally suspicious representative of Württemberg, Mandesloh, on five commissions. Prussia opted for the permanent court [*Permanante Instanz*]—that is, the high court (Hardenberg)—competencies [*Kompetenz*], article 13, federal fortresses, and trade [*Handel*] (all Bernstorff). From the wide range of topics, we shall select two in which Metternich intervened strongly through written submissions, and which show well what his political convictions and his particular interests as a member of the nobility were. They concern the question of the Constitution and the role of the mediatized within the framework of the federal Constitution.

Metternich, Constitutionalism, and Article 13

At the fringes of Carlsbad and then at the Vienna conferences themselves, the participants conducted heated debates regarding the correct interpretation of article 13 of the Federal Act: "All Confederate states will be given an estate-based Constitution." At one end of the spectrum of interpretations was an interpretation based on the "old estates" [altständisch], and at the other, one based on "representatives." Friedrich Gentz had deployed all of his rhetorical skill in arguing for the interpretation based on the "old estates," but he failed, mainly because of resistance from Württemberg and Bavaria. It was agreed that the question would be resolved at the Vienna meetings.

In light of these previous debates, the conference participants were curious to see what position Metternich would adopt on the commission. It was well known that he saw the term "sovereignty of the people" as a demagogic catchphrase. Would he turn the Vienna conferences into a battlefield of restoration? Metternich knew that his question was on the minds of quite a few participants, and he therefore declared to Bavarian Minister of Foreign Affairs Rechberg:

> The whole of Germany—her right-thinking men as well as the others—is deceived as to the object of our meeting at Vienna.
>
> Everybody thought we were going to overthrow all that is connected with the forms which unhappily have been transplanted to the German soil (that soil so historical, so classical, and so great) in the course of the two or three last years. Some have thought we were right to do so, others have raised a great outcry. Now, we are not doing what they expected, and I declare frankly that in my soul and conscience I do not allow myself to regret it, because I cannot regret what is impossible.[153]

Metternich did not consider the recently passed Constitution of Württemberg to be workable, unlike the Constitution of Bavaria, and he added, ironically, that he believed that "the result of our Conferences will be most disastrous for the King of Württemberg and for his people, seeing that they will be condemned to preserve their Constitution."[154]

At the Vienna conferences Metternich himself presented a memorandum on the question of the Constitution.[155] The content must have surprised everyone, because he did not touch at all on the controversial issue of the "old estates" versus "representatives." He considered the Constitutions of the individual states only to the extent that they affected the confederation, and formulated some general rules on that basis. Because the confederation was an association of princes, only a monarchical principle—not a democratic one—could achieve its goals. A Constitution was not to infringe the independence of the confederation in its dealings with external actors, or the inviolability and independence of the individual federal states and their domestic security. To break either of these rules would undermine the confederation's purpose of safeguarding external and internal security. The participation of the estates in taxation was not to negatively impact on the military expenditure of the confederation. The estates were also not to try to influence questions of war or peace, which were a matter for the confederation. Ironically, it was the Bavarian representative who spoke for the commission on the constitutional question. He thanked Metternich emphatically for his clarifications and drew the inescapable conclusion: "On the basis of the principle that the Constitutions of individual federal states, as *inner* matters of these states, are outside the competence of the confederation and their order is left to the governments of the individual states, neither are the already existing Constitutions to be subjected to revisions, nor are future Constitutions to be subjected to different rules." In other words, the existing law remained in place, regardless of how it had become law.

Metternich made sure that this principle was secured further. In the previous months the Bavarian king sought his advice about whether he could repeal his country's Constitution—and if so, how. Metternich had categorically denied this possibility. In Vienna it was now agreed that an existing Constitution could "be altered again only in accordance with the rules of the Constitution"—that is, under the participation of the estates, not by a diktat of the monarch alone. The Final Act of Vienna represented great progress, because it allowed the states to adopt their own Constitutions and at the same time stipulated that the confederation guaranteed these Constitutions. Apart from that, it remained the duty of all members of the confederation to introduce a Constitution. A "violation of the law from above," as Ernst Rudolf Huber put it, or a "restorationist coup" were from that point on impossible. It was now the duty of the ruler to maintain the Constitution.

The supplementary constitutional law strengthened state Parliaments. The so-called monarchical principle, which was now anchored in the Constitution, did not change that at all, although it is often presented as a sign of restoration. It did, indeed, insist on the fact that "all of the state's power remains united in the head of the state," with the estates presented as participating only in the decision process. This was not a genuine separation of powers. But with this principle, the delegates forestalled any constitutional crises that might have resulted if the votes of the parliamentary chambers clashed with the will of the monarch. Between 1861 and 1866 in Bismarck's Prussia, the political process was paralyzed because the House of Delegates refused to agree to the necessary taxes for the reform of the army. But beyond that, monarchies were the rule in the nineteenth century.[156] Even states that had just formed in the wake of revolutions retained a king—Leopold of Coburg became King of Belgium, and Otto of Bavaria became King of Greece. The Swiss Confederation and the United States were the exceptions, and the latter only to a certain extent, given the unique position of the president, with his absolute right to veto legislation and his role as commander in chief.

The discussions in Vienna, especially with delegates from middle-sized German states that already had a Constitution, motivated Metternich to explain in more detail what he understood by the law and a Constitution. He wanted to make clear that he was not the absolutist he was often taken to be, and to that end he consciously chose to speak with the envoy from Baden, a state with a particularly active Parliament. Metternich once again unambiguously stated that by preservation he meant "not only the old order of things as they have been preserved in some countries since times immemorial, but also all the new legally established institutions."[157] Metternich's overriding aim was to avoid unrest; a return to something that no longer existed was just as dangerous as the transition from the old to something new. He surprised Berstett with his view that the Constitutions established so far (by May 1820) had to be recognized, saying by way of justification: "Every order of things legally introduced bears in itself the principle of a better system."[158] This sentence expresses Metternich's categorical commitment to reform and to evolutionary progress in accordance with the law.

A genuine Constitution "is made only by time." Metternich was thinking of the case of Britain. He assumed that the British legal order is historically founded, hence has a historical origin and is anchored in reality. In a private letter, he wrote: "The English Constitution is the work of centuries, and, moreover, streams of blood and anarchy of every kind supplied the means. Social order ever progresses in this way; it cannot be otherwise, since it is the law of nature."[159] In 1847 he warned against a general Prussian Constitution, saying: "I have nothing against Constitutions; I admire the good ones and pity the state which is subjected to a bad one, that is, to one that does not suit it. Constitutionalism I condemn to hell; it only lives on deception and fraud."[160] He hated words that ended in "-ism," he explained, because this suffix turned them into ideological concepts and rendered them useless for factual description—his examples were: *communitas* and communism; *societas* and socialism; *pietas* and pietism, and, accordingly, Constitution and constitutionalism.

The Cortes Constitution of 1812 was for Metternich no Constitution at all, but "the work of caprice or of a wild delusion."[161] Anyone familiar with Metternich's way of thinking will see that he was not being purely polemical. This Constitution, in particular, served as an example during the revolutions in southern Europe between 1820 and 1823, and those countries imitating it failed because it did not fit with their specific conditions.[162] This applied even to Spain, because the Constitution only had space for one Parliament, one nation, but not for the countries out of which this great state was composed.

The Mediatized and the Metternichs

We have become familiar with the Metternich family and its venerable tradition of barons, counts, and finally even princes of the old Holy Roman Empire. Metternich's father, Franz Georg, had continued this tradition and always acted as an energetic representative for the interests of the estate to which he belonged—the former aristocracy that enjoyed imperial immediacy. As far as the interest of the estates was concerned, his son acted cautiously in the background as a minister who stood above these political matters but still was effective, as in the case of the special allowances made for the mediatized nobility in the Federal Act, which preserved most of their rights and made them, in effect, as Heinz Gollwitzer put it, "sub-rulers" [Unterlandesherren].

Franz Georg had died on August 11, 1818, and all rights as the head of the family and the entailed estate had thus passed to Clemens von Metternich. It is therefore not surprising that in the context of the constitutional work to be done in Vienna, he took on the task of compiling the report on the situation and rights of the mediatized.[163] This report is a rare piece of evidence for how he understood himself in his role as a mediatized prince. According to his interpretation, the former imperial nobility had lost everything associated with rule; all other rights, however, had to be retained. The Congress of Vienna and the Federal Act (especially article 14) had confirmed that "in a no less advantageous sense" than had the Imperial Recess (1803) and the Treaty of the Rhenish Confederation (1806). As Metternich saw, however, the stipulations of this article had not yet been fulfilled. This was now being remedied with article 63 of the Viennese Final Act. The expectations of the mediatized were met. The confederation now had the authority to make sure that the legal rights of the imperial nobility were secured. And if their rights were not being upheld, they now had the right, enshrined in law, to lodge a complaint with the Federal Assembly. In this way, the nobility had been able to maintain an old right even within the new confederation, a right that under conditions of the old "German freedom" all members of the empire had had in the form of the right to appeal to the Imperial Chamber Court [*Reichskammergericht*]. Forfeiting this democratic right had been a step backward that had damaged the reputation of the German Confederation in the eyes of the people. For those mediatized there nevertheless remained points to be clarified and further demands. There were six points:

1. The promised "equality of rank" [*Ebenbürtigkeit*] with the ruling aristocracy had to be made clear so that it would not be forgotten. Princes therefore had to be legally awarded the title "serene highness," counts the title "noble." The federal Chancellery had to establish and continually keep a record of births, marriages, and deaths occurring in the families concerned. Later, in 1848, a majority at the National Assembly in Frankfurt found this demand so objectionable that they discussed whether to abolish the aristocracy as an estate and to deprive it of its titles.
2. The mediatized had to have the right to enter into the services of any of the federal states without being limited in the disposition of their property. Regarding this question, the Metternichs had bitter memories from dealings with Napoleon and the king of Württemberg, especially as the Act of the Rhenish Confederation insisted on the need to be resident.
3. Protection against "sequestration"—the confiscation of property—had to be guaranteed. According to the Act of the Rhenish Confederation, in criminal cases it was not permitted to confiscate the estates of the mediatized—only the income they generated. That was "not unreasonable" and had to be assured.
4. If the estates of a family were distributed over several federal states, it had to be possible, in the case of minors, to arrange a common custodial administration.
5. The family contracts and regulations of family inheritance law were to remain valid.
6. Where formerly imperial estates were sold to individuals who were not of equal social rank [*Nicht-Ebenbürtige*], the titles associated with the rank had to remain with their former owner, because all equality of rank [*Ebenbürtigkeit*] was tied to families and not their possessions.

Metternich added that the Austrian emperor approved of all these demands, and that he wished that all delegates would lobby their governments to provide them with instructions to the same effect.

Difficulty and Resistance: Bavaria and Württemberg

Metternich was prepared to encounter resistance in Vienna, and as in Carlsbad he expected it to come from Bavaria and Württemberg. The Bavarian government had to be convinced of the federation's right to decide on matters of war and peace. The rule that had been agreed upon "deprived smaller courts of the possibilities for pursuing political intrigues with foreign countries," Metternich wrote.[164] But the greatest resistance in the negotiations came from Württemberg, which, after four months of discussions, raised the prospect of the whole conference ending in failure. Württemberg did not want the negotiations in Vienna to end with a final, fixed document—"a definitive resolution," as it was put. It wanted for the results of the consultations to be considered only preliminary work that would then be completed at the Federal Assembly after extensive discussions. As an experienced diplomat, Metternich knew that the most difficult questions could be solved in Vienna, while he was moderating the negotiations. In Frankfurt, this would be very different; he expected disruption. Metternich assumed that the king of Württemberg's proposal was an attempt to present himself as liberal and everyone else as authoritarian. He simply wanted to appear populist, Metternich thought. After his negative experiences of Württemberg at Carlsbad, he now noted that whereas all the other courts had sent their best men to Vienna, Württemberg had chosen someone, Count Mandelslohe, who, although he could not be faulted personally, did not enjoy the trust of others or any ability to influence them. And behind Mandelslohe's back operated a clever, dishonorable adventurer who had been personally involved in criminal proceedings. Count Mandelslohe was subordinate to this character in all of his actions. But the German Confederation could only "prosper under the rule of a firm and united will."

Württemberg's most substantial objection was that the conference could not supplement the Federal Act without the involvement of the powers that had backed the Final Act of the Congress of Vienna, because the Federal Act was a part of the latter. Metternich had more than enough reason to treat the Württemberg government with great caution, especially King Wilhelm, who had a powerful ally backing him. His second marriage was to Grand Princess Katharina Pavlovna, who had died on January 9, 1819. But close family ties were retained between the courts in Saint Petersburg and Stuttgart.[165] Alexander's father, Tsar Paul, had been married to Duchess Sophie Dorothea of Württemberg (who called herself Maria Fjodorovna after her conversion to the Orthodox faith). Alexander thus had a mother from Württemberg, and he made sure to visit his family in Stuttgart each time he passed through. He was one of the signatories of the Final Act of the Congress of Vienna, and he had a lively interest in interfering in the way German political affairs were handled. Only recently, the behavior of his state councillor, Stourdza, at the Congress of Aix-la-Chapelle had proved as much.

Metternich knew that foreign countries were paying close attention to the negotiations in Vienna. The interpretation of article 13 was followed with particular interest. Metternich received an article from the French press that registered with astonishment that every German sovereign was allowed "to interpret this famous article according to his whim—whether in the sense of the princes who are absolutist rulers, or in the sense of constitutional princes who take the interest of their people as the main point of reference."[166]

Metternich countered the warnings against interventions from abroad, not without some satisfaction, by pointing out that the government of Württemberg had earlier completely ruled out any toleration of foreign interference in the questions discussed in Vienna, calling it incompatible with the independence and dignity of the German Confederation; like any other sovereign power, Württemberg had argued, the German Confederation had the indisputable authority to arrange its domestic affairs according to its own opinions and interests. Württemberg's demand that the signatories of the Vienna order should now participate in the deliberations was in clear contradiction to this.

The representative for Württemberg was steadfast in his refusal to sign the declaration that said that the resolutions agreed to in Vienna did not need any "further consultations at the Federal Assembly." He explained in great detail why his court would not agree to the declaration. On March 31, 1820, Emperor Franz personally approached the king of Württemberg, who finally capitulated: on April 14, 1820, Count von Wintzingerode, the minister of foreign affairs, declared to Metternich that he agreed to the procedures and that he recognized the resolutions passed at Vienna as definitive and not in need of further deliberation at the Federal Assembly. On May 14, Württemberg's approval of the Final Act arrived in Vienna. Thirty meetings had taken place between November 25, 1819, and the official date of the document, which was the following day, May 15, 1820.

Metternich was pleased, but also relieved. The document achieved "the maximum that can be achieved today." At the Federal Assembly, all states agreed to adopt, as a whole and without further deliberation, the sixty-five articles agreed to in Vienna as supplements to the Basic Federal Law. Austria's reputation had been so bolstered by the negotiations and their results that Metternich got carried away: "A word spoken by Austria will be inalienable law in Germany. Only now will the Carlsbad measures truly come to life, and all measures needed to maintain calm [*Ruhe*] in Germany will naturally follow."[167]

All in all, the sixty-five paragraphs of the Final Act of Vienna represented great progress when measured against Metternich's ideal of the powers and role of the German Confederation. The federal Constitution was only now complete.

The act strengthened the character of the confederation as a state and equipped it with an army of 300,000 soldiers. These could only be employed defensively: this was guaranteed by the federal structure of the confederation, which meant that a supreme commander would have to be elected each time a conflict arose. Germany, which Metternich had referred to as the "fatherland" several times in conference texts, was now in a safer position among the major powers. As one of these powers, its role, in virtue of its geographical location between France and Russia, was to strengthen peace in Europe without itself taking an active role in the Concert of Europe. This had been Metternich's plan for many years. Germany was now also on the way toward constitutionalism and had opened the door toward common trade and a common economy, even if these initiatives would later fail.

The question of who was responsible for thwarting the promising possibilities for progress is a matter of controversy among historians. Was it the allegedly well-meaning assassins and rebels (until 1848 one can hardly speak of genuine "revolutionaries"), the Simons and Sands? Thomas Nipperdey warns against trivializing them as pathological cases or failing to recognize their revolutionary aspirations, including the "potential for direct terrorist actions."[168] Or is Hans-Ulrich Wehler right when he identifies the "existing despotism," "the governments' errors of judgment," and most of all Metternich himself as really responsible? Metternich, Wehler says, "used the entire repertoire of his Machiavellian art in all directions and at different levels," and used the fear of revolution for "clever manipulation." In that case, it would after all have been the short-sighted and obstinate princes and their followers, who did not understand the historical situation, that were to blame. Our discussion of the post-1815 era, however, has shown how difficult it was to find the right interpretation of the present against the background of past historical experience. That present was characterized by dire public finances following decades of senseless war, by famines and inflation, and by feelings of hopelessness amid economic backwardness.

TERRORISM AND SECURITY POLICIES AS A EUROPEAN PROBLEM: ENGLAND, FRANCE, AND METTERNICH

Britain's View of German Security Policies

German historians such as Nipperdey and Wehler look at the attacks and other forms of social violence from a national perspective. But this is not how politicians at the time saw them. The British and the Russians carefully followed the German Confederation's reaction to the attacks. An example of this is the exchange between Castlereagh and the Russian ambassador in London, Christoph von Lieven. They considered the "pre-conferences" in Carlsbad to be characterized by a spirit of exceptional unity and agreement. Now they were eager to see whether this would also be the case in Vienna, because the cabinets in Saint Petersburg and London sincerely, and with equal enthusiasm ("avec sincérité et une ardeur égale"), welcomed the German powers' efforts to arrest the revolutionary tendencies. They also welcomed the fact that at Vienna the connections within the German Confederation were extended in order to secure general peace [*Ruhe*] in Germany, which they saw as inseparable from that in Europe. In this way, the great political expectations that accompanied the signing of the Federal Act in Vienna would be fulfilled. The same principles of security policy had also guided the Court of St. James, which had also followed German politics with the question of European security in mind. The courts in Vienna and Berlin also reported regularly to London on the measures taken.[169]

After the Carlsbad conferences, Metternich had even sent the British prince regent a personal summary, explaining the future plans to him. "A new era is beginning," he wrote, "and it will be an era of salvation if the German courts do not go beyond the limits assigned to them." Metternich invoked their common principles, "which would have achieved great work if they had not so often been lost sight of in many negotiations of the years 1813 up to the disastrous epoch of 1815." He thanked the prince regent for sending Count Ernst Friedrich zu Münster—the head of the German Chancellery in London and representative of the prince regent in the Kingdom of Hannover—to Carlsbad and requested that he be sent to Vienna, as he would "consider the direct support of Count Münster in the course of the negotiations of Vienna a real benefit."[170]

These exchanges and Castlereagh's comments document clearly that the oft-invoked "East–West contrast" in European security policy did not exist in the early years. On the contrary, in a long programmatic dispatch to the English ambassador in Vienna, dated January 14, 1820, Castlereagh reached the conclusion that the four allied cabinets were fundamentally in agreement, even if there were slight differences when it came to the question of the means for achieving the shared aims. The setup of the British government made it necessary to proceed with more caution when it came to its dealings with other powers, and—hinting at its dependence on the Parliament and the public—he added that it also had to be aware of other considerations.[171]

During May 1820, Castlereagh continued to follow the consultations on the federal Constitution in Vienna and supported them, saying that enormous progress had been made in the fight against radicalism, but that "the monster still lives, and shows himself in new shapes." But they would not despair over the task of "crushing him by time and perseverance. The laws have been reinforced, the juries do their duty."[172] Castlereagh approved unreservedly of the substance, intention, and stringency of the measures. After the Final Act of Vienna had been signed, Castlereagh congratulated Metternich on his moderation and persistence. Metternich, he said, had achieved a result that was "honourable" to him and "beneficial to Europe at the present critical conjuncture." Those who "most actively presided" over the negotiations had "added important additional securities to the European System."[173]

On May 28, 1820, a week after Sand's execution, the British ambassador in Frankfurt, Frederick Lamb, reported on the press reaction to the judgment. He was surprised by the passionate sympathy for the murderer, who was seen as a victim, and by the lively outrage against the princes. He approved of the measures to protect domestic security taken by the Federal Assembly, which appeared to have established tranquility. He concluded that the "really dangerous part of the community consisted in some thirty periodical writers, and in the large proportion of the professors in the schools and universities." But since the introduction of censorship, "the former [i.e., the writers of periodicals] have become comparatively harmless." He mentioned an account of Sand's death as "one of the worst articles I have seen," and blamed the government for allowing it to go to print. The universities of the Grand Duchy of Baden, and especially that of Heidelberg, he considered to be "in a worse state than most others." The students there "still wear the absurd dress which is the rallying sign of their party." The students of Göttingen had in the last three days "filled the town of Cassel in the same costume, and their appearance in it in numbers is always attended by a feeling of their strength, and by their proportionate insolence and obnoxiousness." But in general the "measures of compression" had succeeded. Lamb welcomed the aims and the effects of the federal resolution of September 20, 1819.[174]

The Assassination of the Duc de Berry (February 13, 1820)

Even if there is occasional mention in the literature of the international character of the attacks,[175] it is never asked whether Metternich learned about them, or, if he did, how he interpreted and reacted to them. The closer we look at this, the more obvious it becomes that the one-dimensional approach that equates Metternich's attitude with the Carlsbad Decrees is insufficient. This approach does not allow us to see the context within which the actors made their decisions at the time, because it ignores their perception of potential crises, and because it entirely ignores what it meant for politicians to feel that their lives were permanently under threat. The greatest international uproar was caused by the assassination of the Bourbon Charles-Ferdinand d'Artois, Duc de Berry, the potential successor to the throne. His father, who ruled from 1824, was Charles X—the brother of the Bourbon king Louis XVI, who had been executed, and of Louis XVIII, who was at that time on the throne. On the evening of February 13, 1820, Louis Pierre Louvel, a saddler, attacked the Duc de Berry with a knife while the prince was walking from the opera to his carriage. He was not killed immediately, but bled to death, fully conscious, in front of the assembled court in the early morning of the following day. This event left a deep impression on those present as well as on later aristocrats who learned about it. It created a traumatic image of regicide as unpredictable, as potentially occurring anywhere and at any time. "War on the palaces! Peace to the shacks!" went the slogan, from the time of the French Revolution, of the writer Nicolas Chamfort; it spread from Paris and frightened the high nobility of Europe. How else should we make sense of the fact that Melanie Zichy, a descendant of a Hungarian noble family and later Metternich's wife, noted the event in her diary in faraway Vienna? She described how, on February 21, her mother had entered her room in a panic. Her notes show that the assassination dominated the family's conversations for days.[176]

The inconspicuous appearance of the assassin contributed to the fear. Chateaubriand, the leading French diplomat of the 1820s, was an eyewitness, having rushed to the scene. In his memoirs, he described the assassin as "a little man with a dirty and sorry face, such as one sees by a thousand on the Paris streets." He thought it probable that he was not a member of any society, but instead an individual fanatic, a member of a sect rather than of a conspiracy: "He belonged to one of those conspiracies of ideas, the members of which may sometimes come together but most frequently act one by one, according to their individual impulse. His brain fed on a single thought, even as a heart slakes its thirst on a single passion. His act was consequent upon his principles: he would have liked to kill the whole Dynasty with one blow."[177] The type of perpetrator witnessed and described by Chateaubriand was like a terrorist who, as a "sleeper," may strike at any time. Because he justified his politically motivated act [Gesinnungstat] on the basis of an ideational community, it was not possible to get close to such individuals by infiltrating organized revolutionary networks. In this way, he appeared strikingly similar to the German prototype, Carl Sand.

Chateaubriand had been appointed ambassador in Berlin in November 1820. He loved to walk through the parks of Berlin, and on one of his walks he came across the young assassin's name. He found hearts carved into the beechwood benches and "pierced by daggers: under these stabbed hearts one read the name of 'Sand.'"[178] Chateaubriand thought that "under the sky of Germany" the "love of liberty becomes a sort of sombre and mysterious fanaticism, which is propagated by means of secret societies." This new terrorism, he summed up in the phrase: "Sand came to strike terror into Europe."[179]

When questioned in court, Louvel revealed himself to be a convinced antimonarchist. He said that he had pursued his plans for years, admired Napoleon, and hoped to be able to take revenge for the foreign invasion of France. He did not feel any personal antipathy toward his victim, but he wanted to eradicate the Bourbons. He had, indeed, killed the only direct heir to the throne.[180] His deed proved that the "murder of tyrants" propagated by bloodthirsty revolutionary lyrics and by radical fraternities, including the followers of Friedrich Hecker, was an actual option. Anyone who carved the hearts described by Chateaubriand belonged to a community that celebrated political assassination as the individual acts of a national conscience.

On February 20, 1820, Metternich received an initial, still sketchy, report about "a not very promising event" in a letter from the banker Rothschild in Paris, dated February 14. At that point Metternich was in the middle of the negotiations over the Final Act of Vienna. At first he recommended complete silence regarding the matter.[181] On February 23, the emperor approved Metternich's suggestion that Count von Wallmoden should personally deliver a letter of condolence to the royal family. To Dorothea von Lieven, Metternich wrote very frankly: "Liberalism is doing fine. It is raining Sands ["des Sands"]. This is the fourth one in less than nine months. I still have about sixty like them on my lists, and that is for Germany alone."[182] Metternich was thus immediately struck by the parallel between Paris and Mannheim—both assassins shared the same political motive. And he lived under the constant fear that he would become the target of an attack himself. While the impression of Sand's assassination of Kotzebue was still fresh in his mind, Metternich admitted: "My daily battle is against ultras of any kind, until the dagger of some fool will find its way to me as well. But unless the rogue approaches me from behind, he will get a slap in the face that he will remember for a long time—even if he catches me—Until then, fare thee well."[183] The feeling of being permanently threatened stuck with him; fresh attacks intensified it. In 1831, he warned Gentz at one of his dinner evenings: "I shall be killed in three months; I know it; but I would be killed later as well; better that way."[184]

By February 26 Metternich had received the report from Vincent, the envoy in Paris, along with a newspaper article. It said that it was too early to form a final judgment, but the French government was now in a position to change an article of the Constitution—the Charte Constitutionnelle—that "had been attacked in equal measure by both extreme parties." The French equivalent of the Habeas Corpus Act—the rule that citizens who have been arrested must be brought before a judge and can be imprisoned only if that is what the judge rules—was also to be suspended. Finally, the introduction of censorship for a period of five years was suggested. Metternich commented: "These two last laws are fundamentally nothing but an imitation of our Carlsbad Decrees."[185] But he had his doubts about whether the suggested legal initiative would pass through the Chamber of Deputies without further resistance. He reacted with skepticism to the formation of Richelieu's government. Although he welcomed the fact that, politically, it occupied the center ground, he did not consider it assertive enough: "The Jacobins think he is an ultra-socialist weakling, the royalists think he is a weakling without a clear position [*ohne Sinn*]."[186]

The Cato Street Conspiracy of Arthur Thistlewood, February 1820

While Metternich was still thinking about the Paris attack and its consequences, news reached him of a much larger attack that had been planned in London. Had the plot not been thwarted, the entire Cabinet would have been killed. Metternich was now facing the fact that the most prominent advocates for the revolution in Britain were about to become perpetrators. He knew them all from having studied Canning's speech and policies three years earlier. He was well informed. Around thirty of the best-known popular speakers from the "time of the radicals' machinations" (at the end of 1816 and the beginning of 1817) had planned to strike on February 13, when a Cabinet dinner was scheduled to be hosted by the president of the Council, Lord Harrowby. The conspirators—all of them heavily armed—had met in a nearby hayloft that could be reached only by a ladder. Suddenly several constables appeared and asked the assembled to lay down their arms. The "ring leader," Arthur Thistlewood, one of the closest friends of the aforementioned Hunt, had previously appeared as a popular speaker at Spa Fields. The conspirators resisted arrest, and most were able to flee; only nine could be detained by the police.

Metternich again evaluated the events by way of a comparison: "This event, and possibly many more, are the best commentaries on the Carlsbad Decrees. In England, incidentally, all is quiet [*herrscht vollkommene Ruhe*]."[187] In his comments on the presentation, the emperor asked that they also monitor the "situation in Spain."

Metternich had not even mentioned the cruel detail of the planned attack, about which he had learned from Dorothea von Lieven. Wellington had given her information about the way in which the attack was meant to be executed that he not dared give the press. The assassins had intended to cut off their victims' heads, and they had quarreled over who was allowed to cut off which head. Thistlewood had chosen Wellington; there had been longer disputes over Castlereagh. Two people were meant to cut off the heads, a third to hold a bag. From the place of the attack, the conspirators would have headed to the Bank of England and occupied it. Then they had planned to seize six cannon from the artillery firing range and issue prepared proclamations that they had the ministers in their power and that the people should join them. The conspirators would "announce the overthrow of tyranny and establish themselves as the popular government." There were lists with signatures in support of the plan that included the names of wealthy families, citizens from all classes, and even foreigners. Confiscated papers had provided the details of the plot. The plans were foiled only because a spy had infiltrated the group. At the end of her report, Countess Lieven, hinting at Brutus's murder of Caesar, commented with irony: "It appears to me that a foible for antiquity must have influenced these Brutus characters."[188]

THE DOUBLE-EDGED SWORD OF INTERVENTION AND THE CONCERT OF EUROPE

Reluctant Intervention

The question that still lingered—not only for Metternich, but for all politicians—was whether "the Revolution" had really ended with the Vienna order. Unrest in all of Europe and attempted uprisings pointed toward a continuation of the Revolution. When confronting social unrest and successful and attempted assassinations, the British government showed that it was prepared to act as energetically as the Habsburg Monarchy, and even temporarily to curb the civil rights of freedom of movement, of assembly, and of the press. Metternich's comparison with Carlsbad was not arbitrarily chosen.

But what about the principle of intervention in cases in which peace in Europe seemed under threat—an intrinsic part of the Quadruple Alliance's agreements after Chaumont in 1814? Received opinion draws a strict line of demarcation between Metternich and Castlereagh with regard to this question. But is it a correct description of Britain's role, and thus also of Castlereagh's, to say that following the conference of Aix-la-Chapelle it opposed an "automatic antirevolutionary interventionism," that its aim was to defend "the independence of the state and thus the central pillar of international law"?[189] It all depends on how Castlereagh's position is seen. In the context of the Carlsbad and Vienna conferences, he indeed said (including to Russia): "The two courts share the same care not to allow themselves any interventions in German affairs— interventions that could be seen as a violation of the right and the independence of the German Confederation."[190]

The Australian historian Hafner has argued for a significant revision of Castlereagh's image.[191] It is correct that the British minister opposed intervention, but it is only half of the truth. He did not oppose intervention categorically. By intervention he meant primarily a joint military intervention of all the major allied powers. That, for Castlereagh, could only be a highly exceptional case. Individual interventions, in contrast, he considered appropriate. As long as states were able to solve their domestic problems themselves—as, for instance, the German Confederation managed to do with the help of its laws for the protection of the state—the powers should stand back. But if states were too weak, Castlereagh considered intervention appropriate. He shared Metternich's opinion that not just any European conflict demanded the kind of force used in the case of Napoleon. In Metternich's eyes this would have given the tsar much too much of a voice in Europe. "Metternich had no desire to see Cossacks restoring order in Germany, but he might want to see Austrians restoring it in Italy."[192] According to Castlereagh, the question of whether to intervene had to be decided on a case-by-case basis; in one case, such as Naples, it could be left to Austria; and in another, such as Spain, to France. While Castlereagh distinguished very carefully between cases in which the use of the double-edged sword of intervention was called for and cases in which it was not, he did not change his opinion regarding internal federal politics. In this, he remained in full agreement with Metternich, his friend.

Castlereagh, though, was mindful "that we have to live with a Parliament." The Parliament needed to be taken into consideration and forced the government to tone down statements against its better judgment. He considered the meeting of the monarchs and ministers beneficial, calling it "a new discovery in the European Government, at once extinguishing the cobwebs with which diplomacy obscures the horizon, bringing the whole bearing of the system into its true light, and giving to the counsels of the great powers the efficiency and almost the simplicity of a single state."[193]

Interventions as a Question of Ideology: Canning and Palmerston

Under Castlereagh's successors Canning and Palmerston, the question of intervention became confused. Canning followed Castlereagh as foreign minister in 1822. He proclaimed a policy of nonintervention and used it as a propaganda tool. He distanced himself from his predecessor and eschewed the politics of the higher European interest, of peace on the continent. Canning increasingly formed British policies with the interests of world trade in mind, and he looked at the European Continent as a place where he could gain allies in the competition with major powers. He declared that the Parliament had to help ensure that Britain's international policies could enable the principles of freedom and constitutional government to spread. In the long term, the spirit of democracy would destroy the monarchies, he said—excluding, of course, his own.[194] He saw a fight between two camps, and his biographer, Harold Temperley, took that at face value, writing of a war between the "three Eastern despots" and the "two Western or parliamentary states."[195] Canning, born in 1770, should have been part of the Metternich generation, but his social roots lay not in the nobility but in the merchant class of London. He knew how important it was to be popular, and many of his statements in the lower house were addressed to the press.[196]

From the moment that Palmerston began to influence the fate of international politics in 1830, a divergence between Britain and the Continent became increasingly apparent.[197] Metternich went as far as to call him a mouthpiece for revolutionary propaganda, speaking up for the Greek revolt and the struggle for independence in the Spanish colonies.[198] Metternich perceptively criticized a contradiction between domestic and foreign policy. In domestic affairs, Tories and Whigs were equally conservative and did not practice the principles they preached to the continental powers: "The government, in full agreement with the Parliament, has just taken strong measures for maintaining order in Ireland. Government and Parliament are right. But they were wrong when back then [i.e., at the time of the Carlsbad Decrees] they resented the governments on the Continent for agreeing to the same resolutions for the protection of public welfare. What is right and proper cannot be limited by geographical borders, and the sentence 'Everything for me and nothing for you' is categorically wrong."[199] Metternich observed how British politics fundamentally changed after Castlereagh's death. Under Palmerston, it was conservative ("for home consumption") and revolutionary ("for export"), a system which, Metternich thought, was more suited to British industry than to British politics, and which undermined European law.[200] He blamed Palmerston, but also cited deeper reasons for the situation: "British politics has become purely functional. Lord Palmerston was the outstanding representative of these doubtful policies."[201]

Metternich, trained in Burke's social analysis of the French Revolution, always looked at which economic or power-political interests were associated with attractive-sounding political principles. He knew from experience that it was possible to call for "freedom and equality" as a human being and citizen, while at the same time having one's own advantage as a trader or landowner in mind, eyeing the estates of the aristocracy and clergy. For him, this also applied to the policies of Canning, whose fundamentally conservative, antirevolutionary convictions when it came to domestic politics he had extracted from the speech Canning gave in the lower house in February 1817.

Historians should once and for all bid farewell to the view that the so-called progressive powers fought against the "Holy Alliance," especially given that this term seems to be justified only in the minds of its critics and of Tsar Alexander. The juxtaposition of "constitutional and Western" with "anti-constitutional and autocratic" assumes that the Western side had a superior political ethic, and is just as obsolete as talk of a "phantom terror." In fact, Western politics was just a different kind of interest politics. Anselm Doering-Manteuffel rightly evaluates Canning's representation of himself as being "constitutionally minded" as liberal propaganda: "Liberal arguments cloaked the politics of a 'Canningite chauvinism.'"[202] In truth, what took place was a fundamental change in politics. Castlereagh and Metternich both still saw themselves bound by a European "general interest," a "public law of Europe." Metternich always spoke of the need to respect international law. Canning and his successors replaced this with the "national interest." They turned "national egotism into the most important point of reference for British foreign policy."[203]

The most telling example is France. It is counted as a member of the constitutional and anti-interventionist power bloc, but the invasion of Spain by French troops—authorized by the Congress of Verona (1822)—is ignored.[204] The French state of the July monarchy and Napoleon III used the ideology of freedom in order to advance to the Rhine, to justify conquests in North Africa, Nizza, and Savoy. The tsarist empire invoked the freedom of the Christian Orthodox faith in its battle against the "heathen" Ottoman Empire, and expanded into southeast Europe on that basis, conquering piece by piece important parts of the Balkans and seeking access to the straits of the Bosporus.

Talk of blocs also ignores the alliance of the "Western powers," England and France, with the "Eastern power" of Russia, an alliance that intervened on behalf of Greece in the Ottoman Empire. The British Empire propagated the idea that its colonial expansion and the expansion of its overseas trade were the triumph of freedom. The three major powers competed for influence in the Mediterranean. The Habsburg Monarchy did not pursue any such expansionist policies. It was too fragile for that, and it would have cost it too dearly. Its rulers nevertheless insisted on their right to the Apennine Peninsula as their sphere of influence. Prussia took the path toward a domestic colonialism by trying to push through territorial and "moral conquests" (Wilhelm I) within Germany. It either tried to occupy other territories, as, for instance, in the case of Hanover and Saxony, or to economically infiltrate them, as in the case of the German Customs Union.

One phenomenon persisted in Europe throughout all of the changes after 1789. As foreign and domestic policies were interwoven, a revolutionary uprising in the interest sphere of one major power could have repercussions for

all of Europe. In order to avoid a great war in Europe, the Metternich generation, having lived through an age of war, had established a system of international communication that involved regular conferences for the purposes of
crisis management. The Metternich–Castlereagh duo must be credited with
having invented this system. Their noble idea was repeatedly subverted
by powers who got carried away with their expansionist tendencies—as, for
example, in 1839–1840, when France's expansion into Egypt was halted by the
concerted efforts of the other four major powers, which subsequently led to
the Rhine crisis.[205] The system was undermined whenever a situation was no
longer susceptible to negotiation and arbitration, as in the case of the Russo-
Turkish war of 1828–1829, the first one after 1815 that threatened to expand
into a pan-European war, when England and France allied themselves with the
tsarist empire against Turkey.

After the collapse of the Napoleonic system, the social and economic basis
of Europe was so destabilized, and parts of the bourgeois elites, as well as soldiers who had been released from service, were so susceptible to the provoca-
tions of agitators that protest movements, rebellions, and attempted coups triggered the chain reaction of 1820, 1830, and 1848. Optimistic thinkers such as
Georg Gottfried Gervinus, trained in Hegel's philosophy of history, interpreted this as part of the trend of the age toward greater freedom. More-
pessimistic contemporaries, including Metternich, interpreted these chain
reactions as a warning sign: "It is going to start all over again," by which they
meant another revolution. The French Revolution had become a myth; but
the reappearance of its symbols, rituals, and media, including the Jacobins' red
caps and the guillotine, was enough to rekindle fears of new revolutions.

For Metternich it was not an empty phrase when he spoke of "Jacobins." The
first wave of interconnected rebellions at the beginning of 1820 in Spain originated among dismissed soldiers. After the collapse of the Spanish colonial empire they had returned home and began an uprising under the leadership of
their field marshal, Rafael del Riego. Their rallying cry was the famous Constitution of the Spanish Cortes of Cadiz of 1812. The conceptual tools of modern
history would describe this Constitution as a medium of cultural transfer. In
Sicily, Naples, and Turin, the rebels took this document as a model for their
own constitutional state. What particularly irritated the governments was the
fact that a bourgeois elite, helped by liberal aristocrats, was able to communicate very quickly across state borders and agree to common goals.

Encouraged by the example set by the Spanish, the secret society of the Car-
bonari in Nola, Avellino, and Salerno started their rebellion on July 2, 1820.
From there it spread to Naples, and then they took the island of Sicily.[206] By
August and September 1820, the movement had also reached Portugal, and

finally in March 1821 Piedmont in northern Italy. The Carbonari formed the backbone of the rebellion. They had gained a foothold in the army, and thus the uprising began with a "Pronunciamiento," a military coup. Napoleon's empire was still playing the role of a midwife in this case: the Europe-wide agrarian crisis after 1816 came together with a trade crisis caused by governments abandoning the old protectionism and opening the corn markets to competition from abroad, which, in turn, damaged the landowners at home. Those landowners who had gained their possessions during the Napoleonic era protested against overproduction, the influx of foreign goods, and declining prices. The rebels were what Werner Daum called "agrarian bourgeois provincial elites"—that is, landowners, civil servants, members of the higher military ranks, literati, and scholars. Under Murat's rule they had gained property, offices, aristocratic titles, and prestige.

There was a striking contradiction between the local character of the southern European "revolutions," with their regionally based protests against a new administrative centralism, and the effect they had on the outside, where the perception was that of ever-growing revolutionary potential. This effect came about because all the groups appealed to the example of the Spanish Cortes Constitution. It was based on a unicameral system, the limitation of the rights of the monarch (who had only a suspensive veto), and the principle of popular sovereignty. For a short time, Europe was split into two "constitutional spaces," with the French "Charte Constitutionnelle" of 1814 as the alternative model.[207] This was a bicameral system based on the monarchical principle. For Metternich, the real culprits were therefore the adoption of the Spanish Constitution of 1812 and the prohibited secret society. Because he based his views on the collateral effects of the sequence of revolutions in southern Europe rather than on the specific regional situations from which they arose, he considered European peace to be under threat. This required the conference system of the "big five."

THE CONCERT OF EUROPE AND THE DEFENSIVE SECURITY POLICIES OF THE 1820S

The Conferences of Troppau (1820), Laibach (1821), and Verona (1822)

When regional revolutions threatened to develop into a pan-European conflagration, international peace was threatened—more than enough reason to convene the agreed congresses of the monarchs. The first congress of the pentarchy after the one in Aix-la-Chapelle (1818) took place in the winter of 1820 in the small town of Troppau (Czech Opava), located in the most easterly part of what was then Austrian Silesia. The uprising in Naples had forced the monarchs to meet to discuss their defensive measures. If we look at the finer detail of how the meeting came about, the old cliché of the East–West opposition is quickly revealed to be unfounded. Castlereagh and Metternich thought that under the Vienna order Italy belonged to Austria's sphere of influence. Austria could therefore intervene on its own, and a large congress was not necessary. It was Tsar Alexander, urged on by his foreign minister, Capodistrias, and a faction at the court that supported Capodistrias, who was seeking to gain dominance within the alliance through a European congress.[208] In the end, Metternich gave in. Between October 19 and December 25 three of the monarchs met at Troppau: Emperor Franz, Tsar Alexander accompanied by Grand Prince Nikolaus, and King Friedrich Wilhelm III with the Prussian crown prince.[209] Among the diplomats present were Metternich, Gentz, Nesselrode, Capodistrias, and Hardenberg. The British representative was Stewart—Castlereagh's brother, who was the British envoy to Vienna at the time; he only wanted to have the status of an observer. That has been misunderstood as a rejection of any kind of intervention. But the British did not oppose a military invasion; they only rejected the idea that it was necessary to call the entire pentarchy for a meeting. The same is true of the French representative, Comte de La Ferronays.

At Troppau, two differences between Austria and Russia emerged (further evidence that there was no "Eastern bloc"). The tsar demanded that Emperor Franz immediately launch a military attack. In drawn-out conversations with the tsar and Nesselrode, Metternich vehemently opposed the suggestion, arguing: "We employ the principle that there is no basis in international law for the intervention of a monarch in the moral territory of another, and that *advice* must not be confused with *action*. We may wish for the best of the Kingdom of Naples, but we cannot decide its internal administrative laws. We can tell the nation that we wish for the best and shall never oppose the best. But we cannot determine what is best for others."[210] The initiative had to come from the king of Naples, who knew his country better than outsiders.

The second difference emerged when the exact wording of the public announcement of the congress results was discussed. Metternich had formulated three principles, which sounded moderate enough. The first was that the three allies' "aim and object . . . is not limited to giving liberty of thought and action to legitimate power, but is also to enable that power to consolidate and strengthen itself in such a way as to guarantee peace and stability to the kingdom and to Europe." The second and third principles stipulated that the power should, "in its reconstruction, consult the true interests and needs of the country" and that "what the King in his wisdom considers satisfactory for the interests of the kingdom, and consequently satisfactory to the sound part of the nation, will be taken as the legal basis of the order to be established."[211]

These principles were formulated specifically with Naples in mind. That was not the case with another text, which was edited by Capodistrias. We are in the fortunate position of being able to reconstruct how the infamous "Troppau protocol" of November 19, 1820, came about. The sentence that sparked the most outrage expressed the alliance's categorical right to intervene. The alliance would "initially take friendly steps in order to return the states which are in sedition back into the fold of the great alliance, and in a second stage will use coercive measures should this be unavoidable."[212] The passage was later compared to the so-called Brezhnev doctrine of 1968, which was used to justify the invasion of Czechoslovakia by troops of the Warsaw Pact in order to suppress the "Prague Spring." Such a general statement actually contradicted Metternich's cautious and shrewd political thinking. For instance, it made it possible for the tsar to intervene with his troops at any time and in any place in Europe. The example of Naples demonstrates that this was exactly what Metternich, and also Castlereagh, wanted to rule out. They also did not want to take the tsar up on his offer to involve one of his diplomats as a mediator either between the government of Naples and the major powers, or in the negotiations among the major powers; they believed that Austria on its own should solve the problem of Italy.

One day after the text was passed, Metternich reported in a half despairing, half ironic tone how it had come about: "If I must sit opposite to Capo d'Istria at the Conference table for hours on end and read his elaborations, which is worse than to hear him speak, I am so confused, and my thoughts wander so much that I am always uneasy lest I perpetrate some stupidity. In all the documents sent forth the thoughts are mine; but the drawing up is by Capo d'Istria, in consequence of which I very often do not recognise my own thoughts."[213] A few days later he added that he did not like the results of this enforced working as a group. As if he had anticipated the effect of the "Troppau protocol," he wrote: "I shall gain 85 percent of the victories, and with the rest he will deprive the world of its peace, reason of its good reputation, and common sense of its dignity. Capo d'Istria is not a bad man, but, honestly speaking, he is a complete and thorough fool; . . . He lives in a world to which our minds are sometimes transported by a bad nightmare."[214]

Such a nightmare was apparently also caused by an official circular to the European courts sent from Troppau that was intended to justify the resolutions passed at the conference.[215] Castlereagh criticized the document, and it irked the lower house. Here, too, he has been misunderstood as condemning intervention as such. That was precisely not the case, because Britain sent to

Naples a frigate that brought King Ferdinand I to Trieste, from where he traveled to the next conference venue, Laibach (Ljubljana) in Slovenia. The British government would hardly have been prepared to do this if it had condemned intervention. In the course of long and intense conversations, Metternich had convinced the tsar that it was necessary to invite Ferdinand and seek his personal approval. After one of these conversations, Metternich told the emperor: "He was very firm and *very much in agreement with me,* and this is how I left him."[216] Between January 4 and May 21, the consultations continued in Laibach, where the Bourbon Ferdinand I provided legitimacy for the crushing of the uprising in Naples and for abolishing the Constitution, which he had previously amended: he did not swear the oath on it voluntarily, he said. On May 15, 1821, two weeks after the occupation of Naples by Austrian troops, Ferdinand returned to his kingdom. Metternich had equipped him with serious plans for reforming his country. It was Ferdinand who thwarted these promising, forward-looking initiatives.

During the meeting in Laibach, another revolution broke out, this time in neighboring Sardinia-Piedmont. Here it was not necessary to take the same circuitous route as in the case of Naples, because the government had immediately turned to the Austrians for help. The uprising collapsed when Austrian troops, supported by loyal troops from Piedmont, appeared at the gates of Turin.

The major powers also dedicated a conference to Spain, the trouble spot where the wave of revolutions had originated. Metternich was against an intervention, but this time constitutional France took the initiative and abolished its neighboring country's Constitution. The tsar had again offered to bring in his troops to support the operation. This case shows with particular clarity how the self-serving interests of the state could be dressed up in the rhetoric of freedom. The restorationist Bourbons saw Spain as belonging to their natural sphere of influence and were clearly following their own national interests.

For four and a half months Metternich had been occupied with international crisis management in Laibach. The uprising in Naples had been successfully put down, and King Ferdinand had returned to his throne. On May 26, 1821, Metternich was back in Vienna, where, to his great surprise, he found a letter addressed to him from the emperor himself. It was, as Metternich saw at once, composed in a warm and cordial tone that the reticent ruler rarely adopted. The letter evoked memories of July 1809, when Stadion had resigned from office after a lost war and the emperor had appointed Metternich as "state and conference minister," first provisionally on July 8 and then formally and definitively on July 31, so that he had the requisite status to negotiate the peace with Napoleon. With this low point in the history of the monarchy clearly in mind, the emperor wrote:

Dear Prince Metternich! The achievements, on behalf of both myself and the state, that you have earned during your twelve years as minister and in the course of your efforts at restoring general peace and consolidating the friendly ties between myself and the European powers, have multiplied further through the diligence with which, especially during the past two years, you have preserved, with prudence and courage, general tranquillity [*Ruhe*] and ensured the victory of right over the passionate machinations of the disturbers of the domestic and external peace of states.

At a moment which was so decisive for the future preservation of tranquillity [*Ruhe*], I consider it a duty to give you a public proof of My satisfaction and My trust in you.

I therefore appoint you to the position of My Court Chancellor and Chancellor of State, whose tasks you have already directed with such happy success and faithful loyalty.

Vienna, May 25, 1821,   Franz m[anu]. p[roprio].[217]

Anyone familiar with the reserved and sober diction of the emperor would have been able to tell that this document expressed exuberant praise and overwhelming commitment to his minister. The rank of state chancellor allowed Metternich in effect to take on the role of a prime minister. But because the emperor continued to insist, anachronistically, on his personal rule, he also still reserved the right to play off his ministers and heads of court offices against each other as he wished. Nevertheless, the appointment increased Metternich's standing; he had always liked to see himself as a second Kaunitz, and now he had effectively been publicly acknowledged as such by the emperor. In private Metternich claimed that he was not interested in such distinctions: his only ambition was to do good, and if he could achieve that without titles and while dwelling in a mole hole, he would be just as happy and content. He further showed his modesty by saying: "But in my new position neither a wig nor an ermine mantle is necessary. That would indeed have been the worst of all miseries."[218] He did admit, however, that his new position brought an immeasurable extension of his sphere of action ("La sphere d'activité en est infiniment plus étendu").[219] After Emperor Franz's death, however, it became clear how little his impressive title meant in the absence of a strong monarch.

The Greek Question as the Catalyst for the Problem of the Century

The image of an Eastern bloc and a Western bloc is further discredited if we look at the way the three Eastern powers, which were allegedly operating as a monolithic, autocratic unity, became divided over the "Greek question." The crisis threatened to destroy the Vienna System because in its context the other major powers wanted to sideline Austria and exclude it from their conferences. Apart from the Polish question, Metternich considered the "Hellenic question" the problem of the century because of the way it was inseparably bound up with the existence of the Ottoman Empire. At the Congress of Vienna, he had already failed to find an audience for his analysis of the dangers associated with the situation, because the major powers assembled there, except for Britain, refused to include the Ottoman Empire as a sixth imperial power in the Vienna order. Metternich and Castlereagh had unsuccessfully suggested its inclusion.

The Czech historian Miroslav Šedivý has sifted through the entire diplomatic correspondence between the major powers between 1820 and 1840 to see whether it contains anything that may shed light on the importance of the Ottoman Empire within the Concert of Europe. The results of this meticulous work were pathbreaking new insights into an under-researched period and its tensions that have transformed our understanding of the geography of European conflict at the time.[220] With the exception of Paul Schroeder,[221] the scholarship traditionally looked mostly toward Europe's south and southwest (Naples-Sicily, Sardinia-Piedmont, Portugal and Spain) and considered the congresses of Troppau, Laibach, and Verona. It overlooked, or at least underplayed, the dramatic tension in Europe's southeast—namely, the explosiveness of the "Hellenic question." This question found expression, not in the form of conferences, but in the unusually dense diplomatic correspondence that Šedivý systematically examined. This correspondence reveals where the real focal point and catalyst for a major war in Europe was to be found, a war that had the potential to draw in all the major powers. As we know, Metternich worried about a new type of war that would, like a natural catastrophe, turn everything upside down. His prophetic declaration quoted above was made in 1824, the very year when the Vienna System's peacekeeping function began to falter.

It is important to appreciate just what a tinderbox this was—between 1568 and the Crimean War in 1853, there were ten wars between Russia and Turkey, with four of them occurring within Metternich's lifetime. The first European war after 1815 was between the Ottoman Empire and the allies Russia, France, and England, in 1828–1829. In 1840, it was again the eastern Mediterranean, beginning in Egypt, where conflict broke out, and with the Crimean War in 1853 the system threatened to become derailed for a third time. In the 1820s all of Metternich's initiatives to counter Russia's and France's expansionist tendencies in the Mediterranean failed. The manner in which the tsar systematically destabilized peace in the Near East, as well as the functioning of the alliance, with what Miroslav Šedivý called his initially "discrete imperialism," should serve to dispel whatever was left of the image of the benevolent Russian ruler.[222]

All the complications that make the conflicts in the southern Balkans so intractable, and make simple judgments about them impossible, were already present in 1822 and 1823. Not only did the Russian, Turkish, and Austrian spheres of interest overlap in Greece, Serbia, and the Habsburg duchies of Moldavia and Walachia; in the same regions there were also religious differences, between Christians and Muslims, and national differences. These differences developed an unpredictable dynamic of their own as the ensuing atrocities of war were registered across all of Europe, leading to misunderstandings, aversions, and irritations among the major powers. There were divisions even within particular courts, as is clear from the existence of the war faction at the court in Saint Petersburg, which was striving to break up the Ottoman Empire, although the tsar's inclination toward restoration initially made him susceptible to Metternich's influence and led him to support putting down the uprising in Greece in order to stabilize the sultanate. To put it bluntly: Russian imperialism lurked always in the background, and was active only sometimes. The political immobility of the "Sublime Porte" (as the Ottoman Empire was sometimes called), Russia's readiness to go to war, France's pro-Russian inclinations, British indifference, and Prussian passivity all paved the way for war.[223] Metternich immediately saw through the duplicitous rhetoric of Russian politicians, who claimed not to have any expansionist or bellicose intentions but insisted on receiving compensation for Russia's military expenditure, and, as the sultan was not able to pay, would take hold of land instead—that is, temporarily occupy the duchies along the Danube. For the same reason, it was argued, Russia would have to extend its influence into Serbia.

This was a textbook case of two factions marching toward a war in a way that made it increasingly difficult for either to turn back, even though, after the war had broken out, each would insist that this was not their preferred outcome. Two of Metternich's traits can be highlighted as crucial in the context of this complicated conflict: his insistence on adherence to international law and his pragmatic willingness to deflate the conflict—even by recognizing an independent Greek state if necessary.

It is often claimed that Metternich was possessed by a "dogmatic" attitude in favor of "legitimacy" that meant that he took the rights of legitimate rulers to trump those of rebelling peoples. This was not Metternich's political logic or way of thinking at all. He explained what the principles of international law meant to him in the Greek crisis as follows: If the European powers did not want to act in accordance with international law, then they could intervene not only to support the Greek rebels, but also to support the Irish and Finnish rebels. On what grounds could the British king or the Russian tsar oppose such support? The revolutionary power of the rebels would, in principle, be put on a par with the legitimacy of the state. Metternich asked whether the British government would be prepared to consider the next best rebellious Irish group as a power with rights equal to the British king, if that self-declared group proclaimed itself the government of Ireland.[224]

It was in line with Metternich's pragmatism that, as a result of the revolutionary uprising, he supported an independent Greek kingdom on the former territory of the Ottoman Empire. This actually contradicted the fundamental principles of the Vienna System of 1815. The restoration of a functional pentarchy—as opposed to the latest triple alliance excluding Austria (and with Prussia remaining inactive)—was more important to him than the repression of a revolutionary movement. In contrast to the image of a reactionary focused on legitimacy, Šedivý makes it clear that it was Metternich who pleaded for the independence of Greece ("sovereignty"), instead of its autonomy ("suzerainty"), and that he wanted to see it established as quickly as possible. The complete independence of a Greek state would more effectively block Russia's desire to expand than would autonomy under Ottoman suzerainty, because the latter would always provide grounds for Russian intervention. How little Metternich thought in rigidly doctrinal terms is also demonstrated by the fact that he argued in favor of taking the United States as a model for the creation of a new Greek state: that is, it could be created through collective international recognition rather than authorization by conference.

The Greek rebellion was preceded by the successful uprising of the Serbs, who had gained partial autonomy under Ottoman suzerainty in a struggle that lasted from 1804 until 1817. The Greek rebellion began in 1821, and their fight lasted almost a decade. It had a strong social revolutionary character; the poor mountain peasants felt disadvantaged by the Greek merchants and sailors. During that time the Turks were launching repeated military campaigns in the Peloponnese. The Greek question revealed, like no other, the power of an overarching European public, and it became a medium for utilizing political conflict for ideological purposes. In this instance, too, modern nationalism presented itself as a form of religious salvation and exploited a context of social and economic backwardness. The political and social unrest after 1815, it was claimed, was a continuation of what started in 1789—namely, supposedly "national revolutions," which became a universally usable myth. Paradoxically, its sympathizers and propagandists became victims of the same warped perspective as their antirevolutionary ruling opponents. In the case of Greece, the regional fight of the mountain peasants for independence mutated into a religiously motivated struggle for independence from Ottoman suzerainty, with its different religion, which was about to restrict the rights of the Greek Orthodox patriarchs of Constantinople. All of a sudden the premodern protest over "moral economy," as E. P. Thompson put it, took on the dimensions of a national struggle for "freedom, equality, and fraternity."

The modern agrarian Greeks, who had nothing in common with the Hellenes of antiquity, suddenly appeared to be the repressed descendants of the fathers of democracy and the inheritors of classical Greece, for which the Bavarian king Ludwig I, together with the Philhellenes, showed great enthusiasm. The English poet Lord Byron lamented the lot of the Greek people in lyrical poems; the Germans discovered their sympathy for the Greeks—as they later did for the Poles—because it allowed them to support another people's movement for national freedom and secretly dream of their own German movement at home. The "springtime of the peoples" was a universal utopia.

The common European policies of the alliance, which had worked between 1815 and 1823, were now obsolete. The real goal of these policies had been to put France in its place, were it to become a revolutionary country again. The Treaty of Adrianople of 1829 stipulated that the entire estuary region of the Danube, parts of Armenia, and the duchies at the Danube Moldavia and Walachia—the later Romania—was to come under Russian influence. With this, Russia became a power in the Balkans in competition with the Habsburg Monarchy. And this peace of Adrianople already guaranteed the autonomy of Greece. It was not clear at that point what concrete form this would take, but the conference in London in 1830 recognized the full sovereignty of the new nation-state. Metternich fought in its corner.

12

THE ECONOMIST

Metternich as a Capitalist with a Social Conscience

The Transformation of the Economic System: From Personal Ownership to a Capitalist Economy

Previous biographies of Metternich do not have a chapter on Metternich as an economist. Such an idea does not fit well with the cliché, spread by Srbik, of Metternich the hedonistic courtier, Metternich the idler who could barely organize his own life. Gentz, who, along with some others, spread such slander—and managed to lead Sbik astray—took himself far too seriously, was preoccupied with socializing with important individuals who admired his rhetorical skill, and hardly paid any attention to Metternich's everyday business outside of politics. But Metternich himself also contributed to the fact that this part of his activity remained hidden. When he compiled his personal posthumous papers in the form of the voluminous "Acta Clementina," he did not include any of the documents concerning his family's economic situation, leaving them instead as part of the general family archive.

The aforementioned misconceptions are connected to a further misunderstanding: that Metternich did not understand economics and had no insight into the lower social strata. The two claims are connected because in Metternich's times the social and the economic were still united under the concept of *gute Policey,* the good general order of the polity and domestic welfare. It is necessary to distinguish between the old estate-based social order and that of the newly emerging market capitalism. The aristocracy experienced this shift as a fundamental threat to be countered with a fight to "stay at the top."[1] In this respect, Metternich was only one of many. One of his contemporaries, the Prussian landowner August Ludwig von der Marwitz (1777–1837), expressed the economic challenge of the emerging agrarian capitalism particularly well in a speech he gave to his peasants in 1818. He pointed out the disadvantages that resulted "when the ownership of land, like the merchants' commodities, is passed on perpetually from one hand to the next . . . and everyone is only interested in financial profit. The fortunate ones will prevail, the unfortunate ones will be on their own."[2] Marwitz had in mind the lot of "the poor and weak" when he lamented the social consequences of the market radicalism behind the so-called liberation of the peasants in Prussia and in other states. This liberation created favorable conditions for the "Bauernlegen"—the acquisition of smaller farms; it deprived these farmers of social protection and pushed them into the proletariat. Metternich's contemporaries thus witnessed the "pauperism" that proliferated in the run-up to 1848. Did all this really pass Metternich by?

The Metternich family's dominions, especially Winneburg and Beilstein, and the Bohemian entail Königswart, gave them the authority of lords. From 1803, the dominions on the left bank of the Rhine were replaced with Ochsenhausen, near Ulm, which was at that point turned into a principality. When the position of fee tail lord moved from father to son—as happened, for instance, in 1764 when Franz Georg became the head of the entail—the manager of the estate assembled the "subjects" to take the oath of obeisance [Huldigungseid]. When Clemens became fee tail lord in 1826, he no longer required that oaths be taken, but the way he was greeted by the population, in particular by the Jewish population, still resembled a tribute [Huldigung].

The transition from the estates-based social order, with its emphasis on sovereignty, to the capitalist agrarian economy was a slow process. In Prussia, for instance, this process was subject to more than forty regulatory edicts in the time before 1848. It is important to realize that capitalism and industrialization are not the same thing: this new capitalism took hold of the land itself, land that, under the estates-based order, had mostly been tied to personal ownership by sovereign rights and inheritance laws. The new idea was to render the land fully subject to the law of things, in the Roman law sense—that is, to turn it from property tied to social status into a commodity that could be divided, sold off, and turned into capital. In the case of the Habsburg Monarchy, this happened at a stroke when the Imperial Parliament in Vienna abolished the old property law with the famous Kudlichgesetz.[3] But there were also manorial lords who, even under the estate-based order, had granted their "subjects" the right to "shed" their obligations and levies, as Metternich had done in the case of the vintners at Johannisberg.

In other words, an aristocratic landowner necessarily dealt with the so-called ordinary people and with social problems. In preindustrial times, the latter mainly had to do with agriculture. The peasants and their levies, services, rent, debts and legal disputes were part of an aristocratic landowner's daily life. And Metternich showed himself to be liberal in his dealings with his people, unlike some of his peers—the Bavarian Prince Karl von Öttingen-Wallerstein, for instance, invoked allegedly historical feudal rights in order to get even more levies out of his subjects.

It is also important to distinguish between the different economic roles Metternich had to play. He was always simultaneously active in four areas: as a vintner and wine producer who acted as a merchant; as a forester; as a lessor of large manorial estates—so-called *Meierhöfe;* and finally as a manufacturer, or more precisely, as an entrepreneur running an ironworks. He usually had capable administrators and advocates in all of the places concerned, but he always steered the business himself and regularly received reports on the economic situations of the estates and enterprises. Continuously dealing with these sorts of activities—at the same time as the power politics in Vienna—required diligence, energy, and strong organizational acumen. A more detailed look at these individual areas of activity reveals just how much this man had to manage simultaneously—and that he did so with seeming ease.

The Difficult Point of Departure

During the second half of the eighteenth century, the pall of permanent debt hovered over the House of Metternich. This debt had resulted from a combination of financial incompetence, the pressures of keeping up social appearances, and the dispossessions suffered through the revolutionary wars.

Metternich had to take over responsibility from his father early on, and he was faced with great financial difficulties from the very beginning. Debts were piling up, and they embroiled the fee tail lord in legal disputes with creditors who were desperately trying to collect their money. The permanent lack of money was not only the result of Franz Georg's luxurious lifestyle; Franz Georg had lost his father at the age of four, and the family fortune that was bound up in the entail was run down while he was under guardianship, before he took charge of the estates at the age of twenty-two, having been declared legally of age early by the emperor in 1764. His work for the emperor forced him to travel frequently, and this meant leading a particular kind of lifestyle as an imperial representative. In order to meet the high expectations, he often made contributions from his personal funds, whether to pay for accommodation, for oiling the axles of his coaches, or for the special attire that had to be worn by someone of his social rank.[4]

The expulsion from the dominions on the left bank of the Rhine aggravated the situation even further. As in the case of the difficult negotiations concerning Clemens's marriage contract in 1795, the family constantly had to calculate the value of what had been lost. The situation appeared to become a little more relaxed when the family received the former Cistercian abbey Ochsenhausen, near Ulm, as compensation under the German mediatization in 1803. But this was an illusion: the debts kept rising until Franz Georg's disputes with his creditors ended at the Imperial Chamber Court, to which one of them had turned in desperation. The creditor was looking to collect two debts ("promissory notes"). On June 3, 1806, the court decided in favor of the plaintiff. Franz Georg was ordered to pay 7,000 guilders, along with default interest and fees.[5] It was a bizarre situation because the judgment was made just before Emperor Franz ceased to be Holy Roman Emperor on August 6, 1806. It must have been one of the court's last judgments.

With this judgment, the financial situation of the Metternich family officially became public knowledge. But this was only the tip of the iceberg. While Clemens worked as an envoy in Dresden and then in Paris, exchanging anxious letters with his father, Franz Georg's continued spending was steering the family further toward the abyss. The situation became serious when the king of Württemberg confiscated Ochsenhausen in the course of the war of 1809. Responsibility lay more and more in Clemens's hands, and in 1810 he reluctantly presented his father with a balance sheet, suggesting that Franz Georg should make his son the fee tail lord early. It is clear that Metternich was torn between his love and admiration for his father and the need to assume responsibility for the family finances—which made public his father's failure.

The Spiral of Rising Debt

On December 23, 1810, Clemens von Metternich took the remarkable step of making a declaration addressed to the present and future members of the family.[6] As the next fee tail lord and head of the family, he felt responsible "for the future well-being, even the existence, of my house." He therefore wanted to express as frankly and unreservedly as possible how he saw the family's financial situation. Such declarations, including the later one of 1814, are key moments in the crisis-ridden history of the Metternichs. The historian faced with meter-long rows of files, filled with the evidence of the continual disputes over outstanding bills, thick bundles of documents telling the story of the repeated attempts to get out of the jungle of "liabilities," is grateful for these summaries. They were always the initiative of Clemens Metternich, who was looking for ways to gain an overview of the situation and to stop the decline.

In this particular document, Metternich mentioned that previous fee tail lords had, over several generations, managed the entail rather poorly. His own father, as an orphan, lacked the support of his father during the long time he was under guardianship; he thus confronted the worst possible starting point. He owed his career, which saw him elevated to the highest ranks, solely to his own efforts, and in return he deserved to be held in the fondest memory by his descendants for this. He blazed the trail for future generations. Metternich himself, for his part, had the impression that he had not done enough to save the family, not even to save "its present head," who was no longer in control of the situation, because he had wanted to avoid hurting his father.

In 1801, he wrote, he began dealing with the debts during a short stay in Königswart. In 1799 he had already taken some cautious steps in this direction. Since then, however, the debt had again risen sharply. He had accepted everything—as the successor and hypothecary creditor: he accepted that the appanage he was due to receive according to the marriage contract would be used as a security for the creditors' mortgages. He let it come to pass that a third of the entail was encumbered in this way. In 1803 the family met in Dresden, while Metternich was an envoy there, and gave its approval for encumbering the second third with a mortgage. Metternich went along with this only because he hoped that the debts in Bohemia could be paid off in better times.

Metternich was present when his father took possession of Ochsenhausen in 1803. At that time Clemens began to calculate the total debt of the family across the whole empire. In 1804, as Clemens came across more and more unclarity in the accounts, Franz Georg instructed the privy councillor of Württemberg, Weckbecker, to come to Ochsenhausen as an authorized commissary and establish the total debt. Weckbecker calculated a sum of 1,055,796 guilders. Weckbecker sold off two estates and Rhenish plots of land for 430,000, reducing the debt to 625,796 guilders.

But the situation did not improve. The commissary involved the Mühlens brothers in the transactions, and the bankers' inept financial strategies with the Metternichs' funds led the creditors to appeal to the imperial courts. Not knowing what to do, Franz Georg asked for an imperial commission to be established. Just when the family was on the way toward consolidating its finances, the whole process was threatened. In 1806 the commission called in all the creditors. The debt had risen by 284,501 guilders to 910,297 guilders.

In the war of 1809 the family once again lost their possessions in Germany. In 1810, after four years, the debts in the Rhenish areas had multiplied and the

Bohemian part of the entail had not been disburdened at all. For a second time, the Metternichs faced ruin. An extraordinary political situation—that is, Napoleon's personal intervention—allowed Metternich to reverse the confiscations ("sequestrations") in Württemberg. Given the situation, action was needed to pay off the debts and thus remove the burdens from the estates.

The debt now stood at, in Metternich's own words, "the enormous sum" of 1,210,500 guilders. Compared to 1807, the debt had risen by 300,203 guilders. The sale of the Rhenish wetlands and of the silverware yielded 47,000 guilders. In less than seven years, debt had risen by 613,704 guilders. The only remaining solution was for Metternich's father to hand over responsibility to his son. Clemens set up another commission in which he, as its commissary, would be able to overcome the deficiencies of his father's administration once and for all. The only solution, he said, was to hand him complete responsibility for the administration. They could no longer count on good will and flexible creditors. The past seven years had shown that dealing with the debt was possible only if one adopted a unified approach, which meant all operations being in one person's hands. Metternich was afraid that he would later be criticized, by his children and grandchildren, for not being assertive enough with his father. He added: "For my justification I demand that the present declaration will be part of the family archive for eternal times. In it, I shall always find consoling reasons for myself and reasons for my pardoning by the members of my family."[7]

Metternich's Determination to Deal with the Debt

Metternich had been compelled to act. He composed the "Consolidation of the Fortunes or rather the Creation of Fortunes," which set out the common goal to be achieved by the family. All assets had to be brought together, including his wife's possessions in Moravia. The family finances, including the repayment of debts, had to be centrally administered. He promised the following five points:

1. He would take on all the debts of the Metternich family, but might decide on his own how they were to be reduced—through negotiations, settlements, or other means.
2. He would guarantee the head of the family an adequate upkeep for life.
3. He would fulfill all existing obligations toward his mother and siblings, and would also pay the appanages for the latter.
4. He would make his personal assets part of the overall administration of the debts.
5. The newly formed assets were to become part of an entail and thus to be secured for the descendants.

This declaration of August 4, 1814, had no explicit addressee but could only have been written with his father in mind. Metternich expected him to agree to these proposals. The offer was a discreet way of urging the father to act.[8] Honor and public reputation were important to Franz Georg, and for that reason his son could only persuade him to resign in stages. In a family contract of December 23, 1808, Franz Georg handed over the entail of Königswart and other estates, including all the debts and mortgages associated with them, to his son.[9] In a further contract of January 3, 1815, Clemens became the owner, prematurely, of all the family's assets.[10]

After the handover contract had been signed, it was clear from the words he chose to justify himself that Metternich's father had been shaken by the whole process, but also that he trusted his eldest son completely. He recognized that Clemens had sacrificed himself in order to save the honor of the family—and, of course, to improve its creditworthiness. He declared that "in order to avoid all disadvantages in my private family matters and not to ruin my private assets even further, I fully agree to be legally declared incompetent to enter into further debts or any other obligations, and placed under the guardianship of my son."[11]

In the *Wiener Zeitung* of October 8, 1816, Metternich had made his father's financial ruin public. He was determined to restore order to the family assets and to Franz Georg's private finances. In order to bring these debts in order, he was prepared to use his private assets to establish a fund that would make payments to creditors and, where appropriate, agree to settlements.

In order to lend credibility to the procedure, the emperor, upon Metternich's request, had arranged a special commission at the court's Supreme Judicial Authority. The commission invited the creditors to register their demands and to agree to a timetable for repayment. The public declaration [*Kundmachung*] is dated September 27, 1816.[12] The commission presented the results of the negotiation of settlements on May 29, 1818, and at the same time provided an overview of all of the creditors who had lent to Franz Georg and still hoped to see their money paid back. Altogether, there were 106 of them. The debts fell into two categories. The first were the so-called *Chirographar* creditors—individuals who had lent Franz Georg minted coins against promissory notes signed by him. There were 36 of them, and the sums involved ranged from 61 to 15,333 guilders. The remaining 70 creditors presented bills that they expected to be settled with paper money. Here the sums ranged from 57,307 guilders to 18 guilders and 36 cruisers—owed to a locksmith, Jakob Prener. The impression one gets from the wide variety of demands is that there were creditors and unsettled bills from every sort of craft and trade in the Habsburg Empire. The demands of 106 creditors taken together came to 211,056 guilders; the final debt after the settlement negotiations came to a total of 166,980 guilders.[13] The commission noted with satisfaction that rarely had a settlement out of court been so successful.

Metternich had also inherited from his father an ongoing trial over the estates of Reichardstein, Poußneur, Weismes, and Wanne. The dispute with the Wachtendonck family over the inheritance of these estates reached back to the time of Johann I—the beginning of the fifteenth century. The trial was so complicated that the president of the Supreme Judicial Authority, Baron von Gärtner, wrote a "History of the Trial" for Metternich. It concluded that the Wachtendoncks, as the complainants, had little chance of success. The dispute only ended with a judgment passed by the Imperial Court at Leipzig on May 27, 1884, twenty-five years after Metternich's death. The fiefdoms were awarded to the Metternichs.[14]

From Ochsenhausen to Plaß: A Risk-Taker

Clemens von Metternich succeeded in turning his family's financial situation around. His success depended mainly on the decision to sell Ochsenhausen and invest the money in something that promised better returns. It was a stroke of luck that he moved the family's commercial center to Bohemia, where he bought a new dominion with the money from the Ochsenhausen sale.

That sale was carried out by the authorized representative of the king of Württemberg, the privy councillor and minister of finance von Weckherlin, and Baron Salomon von Rothschild, as Metternich's representative. The price was 1,200,000 imperial guilders. The library, furniture, and artworks were excluded from the sale; they were moved to Königswart. On January 27, 1825, the representatives signed the contract in Stuttgart, but it had already become effective on January 1. This was relevant when it came to the levies to be paid after that date, or the logging done. King Wilhelm sealed the contract on March 8 with his personal signature.[15] The move also had the advantage of allowing Metternich to escape from the exasperating policies of the king of Württemberg, which did not favor the estates and had been a burden to Metternich for a number of years.

In 1826 Metternich bought the alodial dominion of Plaß, which in 1146 had been given to the Cistercian abbey located there by the Bohemian king Wladislaus II. During the Baroque era it developed so well that it came to be known as the "Bohemian Escorial," reminiscent, in its splendor, of the glorious Spanish royal site and monastery El Escorial. In 1785 Emperor Joseph II's religious policies had led to the closure of the abbey, and the estates and possessions were put into a "religious fund" created for the purpose of improving the general welfare. Metternich bought the dominion in 1826 after it had been publicly advertised for sale.

On February 5, 1826, the commission for the sale of state-owned property at the Imperial Court gave permission for the sale of the dominion of Plaß, including all estates belonging to it. The contract took effect retroactively on November 1, 1825—that is, from that moment Metternich had the right of use of the dominion. The purchase price was 1,100,050 guilders in conventional coins [*Konventionalmünze*].[16]

Because of the debt repayments that his father, by this time deceased, had agreed to with his creditors, Metternich could not use all of the money from the sale of Ochsenhausen for the purchase of Plaß. A year after the purchase had been made, there was still a considerable financial gap in the financing of it that needed to be closed. To that end, the director of the administration of his estates arranged a credit of over 500,000 guilders (in conventional coins) with Mayer Amschel Rothschild in Frankfurt.[17] That money went to the Bohemian religious fund and the credit was repaid by Metternich in annual installments, at an interest rate of 4 percent, until it was finally repaid in full on December 31, 1858. The state chancellor certainly did not receive any preferable treatment in this matter as far as the financial terms were concerned. It was only thanks to the renown and importance of his political office, however, that he was able to get a credit of this magnitude at all. Around the same time, Friedrich Koenig, the entrepreneur and technological pioneer who invented the high-speed, steam-powered printing press, could not find anyone in Germany to lend him money to build a factory—he had to go to London and convince financiers there by presenting them with a prototype of his machine.[18] Metternich, in contrast, received credit of over half a million guilders from the Rothschild banking house in Frankfurt for an ironworks project that carried at least as much risk.

METTERNICH AS AGRARIAN ECONOMIST: FARMER, VINTNER, FORESTER

Metternich as Landowner and Landlord

As opposed to Königswart, the dominion of Plaß was a so-called alodial dominion: it was freely possessed by its owner, who could use it as he saw fit, and there were no levies or other obligations associated with it, as was the case with fiefdoms. In other words: Metternich leased his lands to others, yet they remained his dominion.

The dominion of Plaß comprised a large amount of landed property. About two-thirds of the property was field, meadow, and pasture. Thanks to the quality of the soil (clay soil with some sand), the *Meierhöfe*, or large farms, produced good yields, and grew all kinds of grains, feed crops, and tubers. Fruit and hops also flourished. In addition, there was livestock: according to the figures from 1844, there were 4,620 cattle, 13,850 sheep, and 957 horses. Altogether, Metternich leased out sixteen *Meierhöfe*.[19]

1. Meierhof Biela	9. Meierhof Rohy
2. Meierhof Bikow	10. Meierhof Schlössel
3. Meierhof Hubenow	11. Meierhof Sechutitz
4. Meierhof Katzerow	12. Meierhof Tlutzna
5. Meierhof Lednitz	13. Meierhof Třemoschnitz
6. Meierhof Lohmann	14. Meierhof Wollschan
7. Meierhof Mlatz	15. Meierhof Wrtwa
8. Meierhof Plaß	16. Scattered communes

As a minister in Vienna, Metternich employed a chief commissioner to administer Plaß, but he became personally involved whenever there was a change of tenant farmers. He would even get involved in matters of detail—for instance, whether a large meadow should be part of the lease, which levies and obligations the tenant farmer had to enter into, and whether a farmer's skill and reputation were such that he could be trusted with the property.

Leases were initially for a six-year period. Before the signing of the contract, an evaluation was carried out together with the future lessee. He had the opportunity to inspect the living quarters and farm buildings, and an inventory was drawn up. As a regular rental contract, the lease contained stipulations regarding the use and maintenance of the property. When an estate became available, Metternich advertised it in the classified section of the *Prager Zeitung*. In such cases, the Metternich's central administration [*Oberamt*] had to examine, for instance, whether two *Meierhöfe* were each productive enough or whether they should be leased out together.[20] The details of leases were fixed in so-called lease protocols, which were sent to Metternich in Vienna in order to be examined and confirmed by him.

Throughout the dominion of Plaß, Czech (in the terminology used in the sources: "Bohemian") was the language of everyday life. Many of the workers in the mines and ironworks also spoke German. We may observe, in this local context, how Metternich dealt with people of different nationalities. He treated them with respect and as equals, in a way that no longer seemed appropriate to those partisans of the emerging modern nationalism Metternich labeled *Teutomanie* [*Germanomania*].

Metternich's respect for the Czechs was particularly evident when it came to legal disputes, which he, as the local authority, ordered a legally trained bailiff in Plaß to deal with. If one of the parties in the dispute wanted to present

Advertisement in the *Prager Zeitung* for the leasehold of Meierhöfe,
belonging to the dominion of Plaß, April 1835.

their case in the Czech language, this was permitted, and the protocol reflected
this. Metternich's openness in dealing with different languages was clear from
early on in his lordship at Plaß, when he "brought home" the family's dead to
be buried in the crypt underneath the St. Wenzel church, which he had designated as the family burial ground. On this occasion, "his subjects" also paid
homage to him in German and Czech.

Jewish Communities

The "Jewish community of Neustadl"—*Judenschaft*, as they called themselves—had thought of a special way to greet Metternich upon his taking up
the lordship at Plaß. The parish of Neustadl (sometimes also called "Neustadtel"
or "Unter-Biela"), with its sixty-four houses and a population of 511, belonged
to the dominion of Plaß, and was located close to Metternich's Meierhof Biela.[21]
Metternich held the legal patronage not only over the parish and its school but

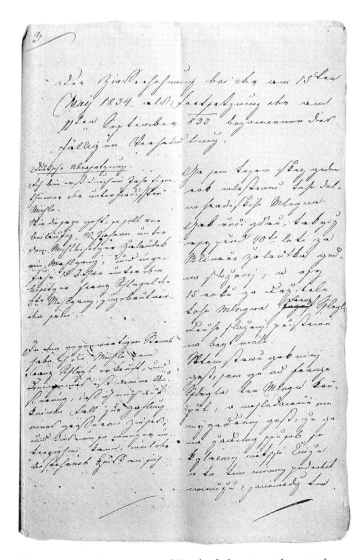

Bilingual protocol in German and Czech of a hearing at the central administration of Plaß; continuation, on May 15, 1834, of the trial begun on September 11, 1833.

also over the Jewish community. In 1838, fourteen Jewish families, 82 people altogether, lived there. One of them, who is not named in the sources, addressed the new ruler as if he were facing Moses. He opened his speech with a verse from the prophet Joshua and ended it with "Amen." The Joshua quote from the Tanakh was: "Just as we fully obeyed Moses, so we will obey you. Only may the LORD your God be with you as he was with Moses."[22] He praised

Metternich's work for the good of Europe. But, he said, the minister not only looked after the millions: for him, "it will not be too trifling a matter to give his attention to a much smaller number that is directly subservient to him," and he, who "like [Moses], knew how to meld the interests of so many nations into one," would also "tie the well-being of his Israelite subjects to that of his other subjects."

There were other Jewish communities in Metternich's Bohemian dominions. In Königswart there were 74 families, in the village of Amonsgrün 16 families, and in the parish of Miltigau 6 families.[23] Metternich's reputation as a patron of the members of the Jewish faith, which was noted at the Congress of Vienna,[24] had also reached these provincial regions, where he was warmly welcomed with a poem praising him and thanking him for his support for the Jews.

Metternich also revealed himself to be a patriarch with a social conscience in general. He had bread baked for his rural subjects and sold it at reduced prices; he arranged support for widows and orphans. Where a family, through no fault of its own, such as the death of the family father, was unable to pay the levies, he did not insist on them; instead, he thought of ways to alleviate their hardship. His administrator kept him informed about such cases and, from Vienna, Metternich attended to each and every one of them. He also set up a fund for the establishment of a poorhouse. Before it was completed, Metternich and his wife supported the poor with donations that, annually, came to more than 1,100 guilders.[25] It is therefore utterly false that Metternich had no sense of or feeling for the lives of ordinary people.

The Vintner, Wine Merchant, and Publican at Johannisberg

As already mentioned, Emperor Franz gave the lucrative vineyards and Baroque castle in Johannisberg, situated in the Rheingau near Koblenz, to his invaluable aide as a thank you—although with certain conditions attached. As he later did in Königswart, Metternich here carried out restoration work on the buildings. What Schinkel was for Prussia and Klenze for Bavaria, the court architect and master builder Georg Moller was for the Grand Duchy of Hesse, and it was Moller who redesigned the Baroque castle in the classical style. That work was also made possible by a credit from Mayer Amschel Rothschild in Frankfurt: on November 19, 1819, he provided Metternich with 18,000 guilders for the purpose. Metternich wanted to repay the credit within four years from the yields of the vineyards.[26] The restructuring work not only corresponded to Metternich's taste; it also was commercially useful, because the modernized castle with its public house became a popular destination for visitors at a time when the Rhine was turning into a tourist attraction. Metternich, the passionate gardener, created a park with Mediterranean plants, in which visitors to the present day can enjoy walks under the pergolas.

The founder of the Bädecker publishing house, Karl Bädecker, was among those who advertised the castle, praising it for the splendid views from the oriel, which the hospitable prince even opened to members of the public.[27] Visitors could take a break on the large terrace, enjoy the Johannisberg, but were also able to see the rooms. The travel guide listed the place as a rewarding destination.[28]

From "Feudal Lord" to Economist

Metternich retained the Benedictine friar Karl Arnd as his administrator. Together with Arnd, and from 1826 with his successor, Metternich introduced a modern way of selling the wine. Instead of putting the annual production up for auction by the barrel, which was how it was typically done at the time, he had it bottled and sold it only to selected buyers, mainly monarchs. This increased turnover considerably. Metternich rearranged the accounting, even determined and controlled the payment of the wages for the peasants working in the vineyards, the chimney sweepers, and sextons, as well as arranging the improvements to the country road leading up to the castle.[29] In these dealings Metternich employed a modern marketing sense: he advised against labeling the different types of vine simply with numbers—1, 2, 3, and so on—because the buyer would think only number 1 made really good wine. Instead, the wine was to be marked by differently colored seals on the top of the bottles, making the wine recognizable only according to the type of grape, but not according to quality. In 1830 he even ordered that the administrator and cellar master had to sign the label of each bottle, to guarantee to the buyer the high quality the wine.

It is particularly surprising to observe the business acumen Metternich brought to winegrowing, and to the overall administration. In 1836 he introduced a so-called cultivation plan [*Cultur-Plan*] and a tree-felling plan [*Holzfällungsplan*].[30] The administrator had to present an annual report listing the strengths and weaknesses of the yields and forms of cultivation in two separate columns, thus providing an evaluation of the previous business year. As a rule, Metternich used the wine merchant Leyden in Cologne to organize the distribution. Leyden was his "agent" in questions of trade, and he was in constant correspondence with him, including during the revolutionary years 1848–1849, when Leyden sent to him in London all the pamphlets he could lay his hands on from revolutionary Cologne.

Due to a legal particularity, Johannisberg was to become the reason for an enduring dispute between Metternich and the government of Nassau. Although

Original label of 1819, sent by Metternich from Vienna to the office of the administrator at Johannisberg (March 2, 1819).

the Holy Roman Empire was gone, Metternich had received his "domain" under the old legal form, which stipulated that he was—as in the case of König-swart—the ruling sovereign. But the emperor defined the estate using the cat-egory "lordship" [*Obereigentum*], which was a category of feudal law. The right of the feudal lord was opposed to the "tributary possession" [*Untereigentum*], which gave the right of use to whoever took the fiefdom. This was more than just hair-splitting: it meant that Metternich was not allowed to sell the estate, and if there were no heirs it would become the property of the emperor again. As it counted as the "sovereign property" of the emperor, the emperor retained a territorial enclave in Germany even after the demise of the Holy Roman Empire. As Metternich interpreted it, with the bestowal of the estate the sover-eign right had also passed to him. He possessed the *iura regalia,* the sovereign rights to exercise civil and criminal jurisdiction. To begin with, he was still an aristocratic landlord and not a capitalist owner of an estate.

The parish council of Johannisberg used the opportunity of Metternich's presence in September 1841 in order to propose the abolition of the tithe on fruit. The same day, September 20, he replied that this would be possible only if the tithe on wine were also abolished—in that case, he would, in the name of the Austrian emperor as the "supreme feudal lord" of Johannisberg, be pre-pared to accept the proposal. He had the relevant contracts drawn up,[31] but it took some time—until July 1843—for Metternich's administrator to complete and send out the documents for the Rheingau parishes of Johannisberg,

Rüdesheim, and Eibingen. The redemption payment was financed by the Duke of Nassau's bank. With this move, Metternich proved himself to be ahead of his time. He paved the way for his "subjects" to become free owners, and thus renounced his position as "feudal lord"—before others were compelled to do so under the threat of violence in 1848. Metternich nevertheless continued to see himself as the authority; he performed the rights of patronage—that is, he took care of the priests and the parish churches, which he also equipped financially with foundations.

Metternich's Battle for Johannisberg during the Revolutionary Year 1848

An intractable dispute between Metternich and the government in Wiesbaden developed over the legal status and the taxation of Johannisberg. The government considered the estate to belong to a subject of the Duchy of Nassau—namely, Metternich—and, as such, demanded he pay his taxes. In this conflict, two legal worlds collided. For understandable reasons, Metternich adhered to the older of the two and refused to pay. His exemption from taxation rested on an ancient contract between the Archdiocese of Mainz and the Prince-Bishopric of Fulda. It had been bought for the price of 2,000 guilders. The population did not know that, but they did know about the outstanding taxes to be paid. During the revolution in March 1848, popular anger grew, and followers of Jahn from Mainz and Frankfurt prepared to storm Johannisberg Castle. On March 31, at eleven o'clock at night, a civil guard of nineteen men from Johannisberg and the surrounding villages, supported by the bailiff of Nassau in Rüdesheim, took preemptive action. The bailiff ordered that the castle's cellars be sealed and arranged for the entrance to the castle and the wine cellars to be blocked.[32] Two flags were raised, one at each of the castle's wings: one was the colors of Nassau, the other the colors of Germany. Metternich's coat of arms was painted over with the colors of the House of Nassau, as it was too heavy to be removed quickly. Up to that point, the corners of the castle had been painted in black and yellow as a sign of Austria's supreme rule. Johannisberg was temporarily confiscated—"subject to sequestration" was the term used.

The legal claim regarding the unpaid tax was taken up again, and the matter was discussed at the assembly of the estates in Wiesbaden. The assembly set up a "commission for the investigation of the legal situation of Johannisberg Castle regarding state law." The resulting report is dated March 15 and was presented to the assembly on May 28, 1849. It was still imbued with the emotion of those days of the previous March, and invoked the "new transition in all things," and the long-suppressed anger of the people, especially those of the

Rheingau, that had been vented at all the "old injustices." The report calculated a sum of 55,353 guilders in unpaid state tax, and of 17,738 guilders in unpaid communal tax. The communities even demanded payment for war contributions reaching back to 1792.[33] It would have been altogether impossible for Metternich—at that point in exile in London—to pay the overall sum: about 73,000 guilders.

After the revolutionary period, the dispute could finally be settled at the highest level. The words of the Austrian prime minister, Prince Felix zu Schwarzenberg, backed by the young emperor Franz Joseph, were enough to persuade the small state of Nassau to accept a settlement. On December 20, 1850, a contract was signed between the Austrian emperor and the Duke of Nassau that clarified the legal position of the domain Johannisberg. In January of the same year, Metternich signaled his acceptance from Brussels. The contract included the payment of outstanding taxes from 1818 onward, which were put at 7,000 guilders. That was no trifling matter either, given that the overall annual profit of the Johannisberg estate was 15,000 to 18,000 guilders. From his exile, Metternich could not, of course, raise this amount of money himself—especially as his Bohemian estates had been confiscated in 1848. Metternich was able to pay the sum only because he received more credit from the M. A. von Rothschild and Sons banking house in Frankfurt.

On February 3, 1851, the emperor and the duke ratified the contract.[34] The emperor forfeited the sovereign rights over the domain of Johannisberg, which had been guaranteed in article 51 of the Final Act of the Congress of Vienna. But he retained the "lordship" [*Obereigentum*] under feudal law, which entitled him to pass on the property, over which the Metternich family had the right of use (*dominium utile*), if the family line became extinct. The "canon," the annual proportion of wine to be delivered to the emperor in Vienna, remained in place. Under the terms of the settlement, the emperor and Metternich forfeited the right to be exempted from taxation, and Metternich, additionally, agreed to forgive the repayment of the 2,000 guilders originally paid for this right. From now on, the domain of Johannisberg was fully subject to the laws of taxation "like any other possession under the sovereignty of His Highness the Duke of Nassau." Modern times had finally reached the winegrowing estate, and Metternich had saved this treasure for himself and his descendants.

The Forester

Metternich's Bohemian estates not only provided him with a handsome income from the local commercial enterprises, but also included large forests that his forestry officials cultivated according to the newest methods and principles.

Johann Nußbaumer, the prince's forester in Plaß, made a name for himself by increasing the yield of wood using new methods of planting and cultivating. Metternich's competent management involved giving his administrators and civil servants a degree of discretion in their actions and decisions. This encouraged the director of mining and metallurgy, for instance, to invent a technical instrument for pulling the trunks of felled trees out of the soil. The invention was officially recognized with an imperial patent.

In his forward-thinking policies for the development of his lands, Metternich made use of new methods in economics, technology, and engineering. This becomes apparent not only to the historian; open-minded and unprejudiced contemporaries of Metternich also remarked on the effects of these policies when they traveled through Bohemia. It is astonishing that a report like that of the American Peter Evan Turnbull, who recognized Metternich as a "great and influential landowner," could have been so easily forgotten: "On his Bohemian estates, which have of late years been augmented by very extensive purchases, he has established experimental farms. He has introduced from other lands a better system of agriculture and of rural economy. He has erected villages; established schools; and, exerting the powers of his wealth, his influence, and his intellect, for the improvement primarily of his own land and of

Stockrodemaschine [machine for clearing tree trunks], k. k. exclusive privilege of the director of mining and metallurgy of the Metternich estate, Josef Em. Blümel (patent dated October 9, 1858).

the cultivators on it, he is contributing secondarily, but most importantly, to the benefit of the kingdom at large." Turnbull observed with astonishment "the facility with which his mind can discriminate the smallest details, while grasping the mightiest objects," and he noted, correctly, that "from the cabinet of state at Vienna he can give directions for the management of his farmyard in Bohemia."[35]

FACTORY OWNER AND INDUSTRIAL ENTREPRENEUR

The Ironworks at Plaß

The Bohemian dominion of Plaß also attracted Metternich's attention because he hoped to find mineral resources there that would allow him to erect a new ironworks near the abbey. He used elaborate methods to search for natural resources, and the search succeeded. It is telling how, in this case, he dealt with the central administration in Plaß, which was subordinate to him. He had intelligent civil servants there who were capable of thinking for themselves. They suspected there were iron ore deposits in the dominion, and they secured mining rights. They had sent samples of ore findings to Metternich and asked whether they should undertake test drillings at the dominion's expense. Metternich weighed the potential commercial advantages against the costs involved in taking the necessary systematic approach, necessary "because in mining everything depends on conviction, and one cannot rely on what nature accidentally happens to present in terms of hints, and I also understand the necessity to try all that is possible to give the forests a greater value."[36]

Metternich left the decision to the central administration but told them to treat the initiative as a "preliminary investigation" that aimed to establish the location, quality, and extent of the existing iron ore. In the end, the expectations of Metternich in Vienna and his subordinate civil servants in Plaß were exceeded: the dominion had not only layers of ironstone, but also black coal deposits, making it even more profitable. That was a stroke of luck: in the early industrial period in Bohemia, there was not yet a railway network, and the close proximity of the ore and coal, along with a supply of wood, made Plaß an ideal place for industrial exploitation in the form of an ironworks. As it could be used locally, the wood was more valuable and did not have to be transported, at vast expense, to other locations. We know how open-minded Metternich was toward new commercial and technological innovations, and what a great pupil of English engineering he had been, ever since his first trip to London in 1794. In this way he was able to take up the role of an early German industrial pioneer and entrepreneur.

The St. Clemens ironworks at Plaß in 1844.

The ironworks gradually developed into a substantial enterprise. We have precise figures relating to its equipment for the year 1844. At that point in time, it consisted of a blast furnace and a so-called cupola furnace coupled with a steam engine. This type of furnace, invented by the Englishman John Wilkinson in 1794, allowed it to melt the iron at a lower temperature than a blast furnace, and thus it was more economical. It turned raw iron into cast iron. The name relates to the dome-shaped top from which the long furnace shaft emerges. The steam engine drove various hammers that transformed rough bar iron into so-called *Zaineisen,* semi-finished iron products that were then turned into nails or spoons in smithies. All this was produced by the prince's ironworks itself. To that end, it also had a foundry and a mechanical workshop with three machines for turning and drilling and six machines for planing, screw cutting, and pressing. The coal for the ironworks came from two coal mines, the ore from sixteen iron-ore mines. The enterprise had a commercially structured workforce: there were more than 124 miners, 26 laborers at the ironworks, 75 casters and grinders, 45 blacksmiths, 46 locksmiths, turners, and carpenters (pattern-makers), and 32 charcoal makers. The total workforce came to 348 employees, and they annually processed 80,000 centner of iron ore into 18,000 centner of raw iron, 8,000 centner of cast iron products, and 7,800 centner of bar and higher-grade *Zeugeisen.*[37] The annual turnover for 1842 was 280,000 guilders.[38]

The Range of Products

A price list from 1856 details the broad range of available products, which corresponded to the modern needs of an economy about to enter the age of industrialization in earnest.

The cast iron section produced rails, axles, and wheels for railways; plough-shares and ploughshare wheels for farmers; and barrel hoops for coopers. The cast iron products, in contrast, aimed at the domestic economy and included ovens, pots, weights, kettles, pestles and mortars, hot plates, fire grids, pavement slabs, water pipes, lattice fences, nails, and garden chairs with side arms and canopies. For an extra fee, the ironworks would make products to order, if corresponding drawings and models were provided. Often these special commissions were machine parts. Even highly unusual products could be made, such as the funeral monument Metternich ordered for the deceased clergymen of the former abbey. It still stands today.

The impressive cast iron fountain in the inner courtyard at Königswart Castle, which catches the eye of every visitor, was also made by the ironworks of Plaß. Its products were distributed across the Bohemian region. The main storage site for all products was the warehouse of the Saaz-based merchant Adolf Mendl, who delivered goods to all of Bohemia. Metternich did not lease the ironworks to someone else but operated it himself, through the leadership of his director. The income thus went straight into his own account.

The Industrial Patriarch with a Social Conscience

When Metternich returned from exile in 1851, he continued to maintain his estates with the same prudence and diligence as before, even up until the last weeks of his life. He paid special attention to the ironworks, and on the occasion of its expansion the workers collectively thanked him in a letter presented to him at the celebration.

In 1854 the flourishing ironworks acquired a steamroller. Upon its inauguration, the choir of the workforce sang a "Bohemian hymn" in honor of Metternich. The chaplain of Plaß, Father Wenzl Pokorny, had composed and translated it into German for him. The cover page of the sheet music that was handed out bore the title—translated from the Czech—"Song performed by the schoolchildren during the inauguration of the steamroller at Plaß in honor of His Serene Highness, the noble Clemens Wenzel Lothar Prince Metternich of Winneburg."[39]

Like later early industrialists—such as the Krupps—Metternich felt obliged to his workers, and, following his paternalistic instincts, he took care of them.

Price list for the goods offered by Metternich's ironworks at Plaß in 1856.

In Metternich's case the century-old family tradition also played a role: he conceived of himself as a ruling prince who, on the basis of a feudal relationship, was responsible for his "subjects," for his "people." In the context of the new age of capitalism, this attitude prevented him from becoming exclusively focused on profits in the style of Manchester capitalism. For the entrepreneurs of the latter kind, Zwanziger, Metternich's contemporary, became infamous in 1844 because of his treatment of the weavers of the Silesian cottage industry. (In Gerhart Hauptmann's play "The Weavers," he is called "Dreißiger"). As a patriarch with a social conscience, Metternich anticipated the principles that

Memorial for the deceased monks of the monastery, St. Wenzel
cemetery in Plaß. The figure of the angel was produced at the iron
works ("IN MEMORIAM COENOBII PLASSENSIS DEFUNC-
TORUM CISTERCIENSIUM").

would later undergird the modern welfare state; in Plaß, for instance, he built
single-story homes near the ironworks for his workers. One row of these houses
is still inhabited today; a part of the ironworks is a museum. Individual examples of the products of the lucrative ironworks—from lattice fencing to ovens
and sculptures—are also on display at the museum.

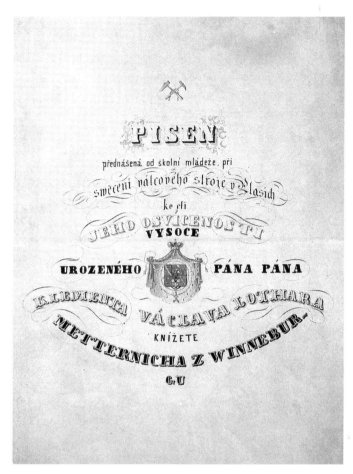

Thank-you document for Metternich on the occasion of the celebration to mark the expansion of the St. Clemens ironworks in Plaß in 1854.

An Industrial Pioneer with One Eye on the Monarchy

It did not fall under Metternich's competency as minister to intervene in the commercial development of the Habsburg Monarchy. He nevertheless drew on his experiences as an entrepreneur in order to do so, and he helped to foster an early industrial spirit even beyond his own dominions. Metternich knew what the new iron industry was capable of doing if energy sources and iron ore could be combined in profitable ways. He was aware of the coal deposits in Istria and suggested the creation of a joint-stock company with the aim of establishing a coal-mining enterprise. He also helped this enterprise overcome some early setbacks. Our wise observer Turnbull called this the path toward "increasing opulence."[40]

A memorandum Metternich wrote in 1844 that sketches Hungary's path toward prosperity and industrialization shows how seriously Metternich took the economic development of the empire.[41] To his mind, there was too little "urban sense" in the backward agrarian country: "Cities develop only in the context of a progressive civilization," and this for him meant development through "the stimulation of national industry." The memorandum described a five-point program for such a stimulus that would have made any finance minister of the pre-1848 era proud: (1) the liberalization of landed property (in strict contrast to von der Marwitz's position); (2) the establishment of a mortgage bank to provide financial support and thus investment in the estates—he supported, he wrote, moves toward making property independent of feudal ownership; (3) the increased use of the labor force and a higher intensity of work; (4) the improvement of "means of communication" and "inner lines of communication," meaning more roads, railways, and river navigation, creating infrastructure to allow for sustainable growth; and finally (5) a program of "industrialization"—the capital should be used for building factories.[42] He described these points, rightly, as the path out of economic backwardness, and they were exactly what he had practiced on his estates. The memorandum was discussed at the state conference and then—a popular strategy in the Habsburg Monarchy—handed to a commission, where it was quietly ignored. The commission rejected the suggestion of a mortgage bank for the general population. Metternich once more experienced what it means to say that a prophet is not without honor save in his own country. His program became known to the public only in 1850 through a series of articles, and Metternich registered from his exile, not without some amusement, how people could not believe it came from him.[43]

In 1844, just as he was making his proposals for Hungary, Metternich also pushed ahead with plans for his ironworks that aimed to bring about what the policies of large-scale agrarians pursuing their shortsighted interests and—until 1835—an overly anxious monarch could not. Metternich was not the only one among the Bohemian aristocrats who had adapted to modern economic changes and left behind agrarian feudalism for the sphere of industrial production, but he was the only one of them who was also a state minister. In this context, his interest in modern machinery and industrial forms of production, which was evident as early as his first visit to England, bore rich fruit at home and also had an impact at the highest political levels. Metternich vigorously promoted the expansion of the railway system, and he also promoted the industrial development of Austria more generally. In his 1844 memorandum on

Hungary, he declared that the country—like all other backward regions—had to be transformed from an agrarian society into an industrial one. "Industrial development," he wrote, "is the natural result of civilization, whose edifice must be built from the ground up."[44] Metternich described the steps along the path toward this "civilization" in his five conditions for infrastructural improvements, discussed above.

While in exile in Brussels, Metternich wrote more about his little-known ideas on economic policy. He was looking back at the pre-1848 period and commenting, with approval, on a submission made by Friedrich List, who had made the same suggestions regarding Hungary—namely, that before any industrialization, it was necessary to build the appropriate infrastructure: roads, river navigation, canals, and railways. According to List, what mattered was "the stimulation of means and paths of communication."[45] If Metternich was prepared to count even Friedrich List as a kindred spirit in economic matters, then quite some revision will be necessary to the picture of Metternich as a man of the "restoration." From his roots in the estate-based society of the Holy Roman Empire, he went through a change of mind and mentality that only a few who lived through the transition from ancien régime to the beginning of modernity managed to achieve.

13

THE SPRING OF NATIONS AMID POVERTY, 1830–1847

THE JULY REVOLUTION IN 1830 AND METTERNICH'S INTERNATIONAL CRISIS MANAGEMENT

The July Revolution in Paris: The Initial Situation

As far as Metternich was concerned, the summer of 1830 was no different from any other. On May 28, a bit earlier than usual, he set off from Vienna to Johannisberg, where the first worrying news from Paris reached him. He was particularly concerned by the news because the French political conflict yet again linked foreign with domestic matters. On April 20, 1830, King Charles X had declared war on the Dey of Algiers—the governor of the Sultan—for trivial reasons. Publicly, he claimed that the military was going to end pirate raids in the Mediterranean—and the pirates were operating from Algerian soil. In fact, the move was just the first step toward an imperialist policy in North Africa, where France occupied Algeria as a colony from 1830 onward.

The king's decision was motivated by the desire to sideline his domestic political opponents, who were opposing his plans in the Chamber of Deputies. The war would allow him to limit voting rights and curtail freedom of the press using "ordinances"—emergency decrees. As in the case of the later "Rhine crisis" in 1840, victories on the international level were intended to increase the ruler's prestige at home—"with the idea of saving the Royal government," as Metternich put it.[1] The plan to change voting rights was bound to fail and lead to the most dangerous complications, Metternich wrote to his envoy in Paris on June 5. He added, almost prophetically, that the king would be toppled: "Everything in France is at stake—everything is in a state of acute crisis. I have long had a presentiment of the existence of danger, and seen it gradually increasing; for a long time, too, I have thought it my duty to call the serious attention of the principal Courts to this subject."[2] In other words, he was thinking of an international conference within the framework of the Concert of Europe.

On July 7, Metternich was back in Vienna briefly before heading to Königswart on July 22 for his usual August vacation. He traveled via Prague to Teplitz, where he paid the Prussian king a courtesy call. On July 29, three days after the outbreak of the July Revolution, he arrived at his summer residence. The very next day he read an edition of the *Moniteur* that ran articles about the ordinances passed on July 25 and the rebellion of July 26. Further news allayed his fears temporarily: the Count of Orleans had "put himself at the head of the revolt." We shall see shortly why this would have reassured Metternich. In any case, King Charles was "still with the army."[3] The situation was severe enough for Metternich to consider ways and means *"by which a basis of union between the Great Powers, and especially the old Quadruple Alliance, might be found."*[4] This required a restoration of the old conference system, which by this time lay in ruins. Metternich nevertheless did not consider the situation in Paris to be as serious as in 1815 or 1789, because he recognized in it the "stamp of the English Revolution of 1688."[5] And the "Glorious Revolution" had happened without bloodshed, with only the ruler being substituted.

Analyzing the Danger for Europe

Metternich saw the sea battle of Navarino in 1827, in which a united Russian, British, and French fleet was fighting against Turkish and Egyptian forces, as a turning point. The allies forced the Ottoman Empire to recognize Greece as an independent state. From Metternich's perspective, this situation, from which Austria was excluded, marked a nadir for the system that the major powers had held in place together from 1813 to 1815. What kind of state was to be created on Greek soil? What did the July Revolution in Paris mean for Europe? These questions could be dealt with only on the basis of the ailing European Concert, which had to be resuscitated immediately. In this highly impenetrable global situation, Emperor Franz once again asked Metternich to analyze the crisis and calculate the extent to which the European state order was indeed threatened by events in Paris. Metternich responded with one of his trademark presentations, setting out the fundamentals of the situation for the emperor.[6]

Metternich thought that Italy and Galicia would be danger zones in the case of an interventionist war. After the Treaty of Paris of 1814, the system of communication between the monarchs had guaranteed a stable order for many years. Looking back, the years 1824–1825 seemed to have been a "transitional period," characterized by the self-serving policies of Canning; in addition, there had been the increasing weakness of the French government and the death of Alexander. The earlier "great alliance offering general protection" was shaken to the core, and with it any remaining confidence Austria had in it. Austria's political security could no longer be guaranteed exclusively by the alliance. Russia had been seriously weakened by the losses suffered in 1828–1829 and needed several years of peace in order to recover. France was so divided domestically that the monarchy might even be threatened. The relationship between the Prussian and Austrian cabinets was the "most intimate." Austria thus only needed to take defensive measures. Metternich assumed that the peace would last for several more years. The triple alliance, without Austria, he saw as no more than a sad interregnum. England and Austria now enjoyed an understanding that was as "intimate" as the relationship during Canning's time had been estranged. The courts of England and France treated each other considerately. There was no longer a dangerous connection between France and Russia "for the promotion of isolated ends." Russia and Austria had shared interests in the preservation of the monarchical principle in France and the continued existence of the Ottoman Empire. Prussia would always genuinely support these interests.

Since the Congress of Vienna, Austria had had one coherent political body, in contrast to the times of the old German empire. Sardinia and the German Confederation protected them toward the west. Toward the east, the monarchy was vulnerable. The Ottoman Empire had become weak, making the duchies along the Danube—Moldavia, Walachia, and Serbia—part of the Russian zone of influence. Austria's military situation had significantly improved because of the unity established at the Congress of Vienna. Metternich saw Tyrol and the Alps, as well as Bohemia and Transylvania, as a bulwark; the Danube valley, Galicia, and Lombardy were weak points. His overall analysis of the geostrategic situation was not likely to reawaken the old fears of a revolution. There was no reason to follow the emphatic advice given to Metternich by Field Marshall Wrede and march straight into France as they had in 1792 or 1814.[7]

Should the Concert of Europe Intervene? Metternich the Appeaser

In this unpredictable European crisis, everything spoke in favor of reviving the conference system. The most difficult problem was to find a way for Austria to resume friendlier relations with Russia, which had suspended cooperation with Austria over the Greek question. A happy coincidence came to Metternich's rescue: when Metternich ended his stay in Königswart early, on August 5, in order to travel to Vienna via Carlsbad, Foreign Minister Nesselrode, by coincidence, was in Carlsbad to take the waters.

At a memorable meeting on August 6, Metternich succeeded in reestablishing relations with the Russian court. This was the basis for revitalizing the Concert. They discussed the revolution in Paris, and Metternich's Russian colleague was surprised "about the extreme moderation of [Metternich's view]."[8] The conference system, moreover, would have had to discuss the conditions and aims of an intervention because there was already a conflict requiring action—namely, the revolution in France. Metternich was fully aware of the contradiction between his wish to reactivate the Concert and his intention to prevent an intervention. There was a similar contradiction, though, in the conduct of Louis Philippe, who owed his throne to a revolution, yet insisted that he wanted to respect the conservative—preserving—principles on which the alliance had been based.[9]

How could Metternich be sure that, this time, there was no danger to Europe emanating from France? The answer—which has not been revealed before—is that he had a bargaining chip to use against Louis Philippe that gave him unconditional control over him. Only he and the French king knew about it, which is why this document was filed under "Acta Secreta" in the state Chancellery, rather than with the diplomatic correspondence.[10] It is a letter of August 3, 1805, written by the Duke of Orleans and sent from his exile in London to the Austrian general Mack. In this letter he sought permission to join "the strongest army in Europe" and reminded Mack that he had offered his services to the emperor before, in 1801. (Nothing had come of it back then, because of the Treaty of Lunéville.) The prince had thus been prepared to join the Third Coalition, which had been agreed to in Berlin while Metternich was the Austrian envoy there.

Metternich had personally handed a copy of the letter, rolled up and kept in a container separate from other documents, to Count Anton Apponyi, the Austrian ambassador in Paris, adding a coded letter with instructions that began: "You will find enclosed an extremely interesting piece of writing; simply reading it will prove to you that it contains an enormous means for compromising Louis Philippe [*un moyen de compromission immense*]." He ordered the envoy to ask Louis Philippe for an audience if the French showed any intention of planning to attack "us" materially—that is, militarily. The envoy was to show the king the letter and warn him that, should he take military action against Austria, it would be published and that, in addition, Austria had several other equally sensitive items at their disposal. In the case of King Ludwig I of Bavaria, Metternich, incidentally, possessed a similarly embarrassing document—a

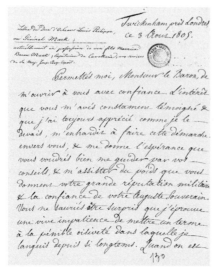 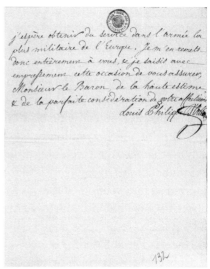

Lettre autographe du Louis Philippe d'Orléans au Général Mack, en date de Twickenham près Londres ce 3 Aout 1805 [Handwritten letter from Louis Philippe d'Orleans to General Mack, dated August 3, 1805, Twickenham near London], note by Metternich (shown are the first and last page of the letter).

whole dossier—on Lola Montez. But he would not be forced to make use of the dossier—or of the Duke of Orleans's letter.[11]

Amid all these details, we should not forget the wider context. It was only because of Metternich that the institution of the conferences between the five major powers became functional again. As soon as he had built bridges with Russia, he made contact with Great Britain. And he kept in communication with the Prussian king as well, following their meeting in Teplitz. The first piece of evidence of the results of Metternich's initiative is a small piece of paper on which he had noted down details of the agreement reached with Nesselrode: "To adopt for the general basis of our conduct not in any way to interfere in the internal disputes of France, but, on the other hand, to permit no violation on the part of the French Government either of the material interests of Europe, as established and guaranteed by general transactions, or of the internal peace of the various States composing it."[12] This unassuming but important note was diplomatically christened the "chiffon de Carlsbad."

Thus, the plan to recognize the July monarchy did not come from Britain, and nor did Austria quickly follow suit because of its parlous financial situation, as some have thought.[13] In fact, Metternich's actual role was that he sent the decisive signal to Russia, where events in Paris were being closely monitored and the mood was by no means averse to a possible intervention.

Metternich used the alliance between the five major powers to prevent an intervention, despite the fact that there was a case for one under the contractual rules. He decided against it in the interests of securing peace in Europe. This contradicts the traditional view of Metternich as one of the most prominent representatives of the "Holy Alliance for the defense of the rights of legitimate rulers against their rebellious peoples."[14] Metternich had despised the legitimate Bourbon king, Charles X, since in his youth, when he witnessed how the ultraroyalist—then the Count of Artois—initiated the fateful declaration of Pillnitz, which was instrumental in further fueling the war of the First Coalition. Back then Metternich had already distanced himself from this kind of ultraroyalism; and in 1830 he did not hold back in his criticisms of the king, whose foolish government measures, he said, had sealed his own fate. It served Metternich well in this instance that, ever since the battle at the Belgian Jemappes, he had followed the career of the Duke of Orleans, who was his age, and formed a picture of his character.[15]

Metternich's central role in the international response to the July Revolution is clear from the fact that, at the end of August, Louis Philippe sent General Augustin Daniel Belliard (1769–1832) to Vienna. The general had already fought under Dumouriez, but now supported the new king. In three intense conversations with Metternich and at an audience with the emperor, Belliard tried to convince them that the ruler who had ascended the throne through a revolution would entirely abide by the Vienna contracts and ensure that the revolutionary movement would not spread beyond France. He also had a letter from the king in which the king praised himself as a pillar of order compared to Charles X. The emperor promised in return that he would not under any circumstances intervene in the internal problems of France. In addition, Metternich sent a dispatch to all Austrian embassies telling them that the emperor recognized the new French government and would entertain diplomatic relations with it.[16]

A REVOLUTION IN COMMUNICATION, THE SPRING OF NATIONS, STATE SECURITY

Europe as a Public Space

There were fundamental differences between the situation in 1830 and the fight against the first French Revolution and Napoleon. In the intervening fifteen years, the gradual dissolution of the old order of estates had progressed further. After the famine and inflation of 1816, there occurred in 1830 another dual crisis which created a common ground for social protest across Europe. In

Germany, too, even in the absence of coordinated actions, social unrest spread rapidly, like a conflagration, and chaotically. In Aachen, craftsmen and workers stormed the grounds of a factory owner. In Leipzig, apprentices and journeymen attacked the universally unpopular police and cheered the July Revolution.[17] In Dresden, demonstrators stormed city hall and burned records. Finally, the peasants also expressed their indignation, as did the weavers of the cottage industry in the Oberlausitz. In Brunswick, even the castle was burned down; in Kassel the poor stormed the bakeries after the price of bread was raised. In Hanover, the students rebelled. These were all signs of the emerging poverty caused by preindustrial crises in food provision and inflation, which sparked protests because they violated the "moral economy."

The new revolution in communication provided welcome services: events happening in different places could be perceived almost simultaneously and linked up in the discourses associated with them. The number of daily publications shot up; there was an explosion of critique and satire. As early as 1853 the Heidelberg historian Georg Gottfried Gervinus recognized the deeper causes behind the symptoms of modernization: "The changes in property, the equal right of inheritance, educational institutions open to all, facility of intercourse, everything tends to the approximation of classes; the most opposite qualities and inclinations combine to assist in the elevation of the lower classes."[18] And then he added the sentence that would see him tried for high treason: "The emancipation of all the oppressed and suffering is the vocation of the century, and the force of this idea has been victorious over mighty interests and deeply rooted institutions, which may be perceived in the abolition of serfdom and villeinage in Europe, and in the liberation of the slaves in the West Indies."[19] In contrast to his successors Heinrich von Sybel and Heinrich von Treitschke, Gervinus still thought in European and even global terms and, as he put it, "as a citizen of the world."[20] This enabled him to recognize how the space for action and communication within Europe had broadened after 1789—for a first time in 1820, then in 1830, and for a final time in 1848. With the revolution of 1848, the cycle of bottom-up, European-wide social movements ended. Contrary to the opening statement of the *Communist Manifesto,* no "specter" haunted Europe after that date, and the "world revolution" took place only in the texts of socialist and communist theoreticians: Europe as a whole was consumed by the wars that built nations—just as Metternich had predicted. Despite sharing a common European perspective, Metternich did not share Gervinus's optimism that Europe would progress inevitably toward the realm of freedom. To Nesselrode, Metternich intimated what the July Revolution had triggered in him: "But, after all, the thought I secretly cherish is that ancient Europe is at the beginning of the end. My determination being to perish with it, I shall know how to do my duty; nor is this my motto only—it is that of the Emperor too. New Europe, on the other hand, has not as yet even begun its existence, and between the end and the beginning there will be a chaos."[21] He expected this chaos to arise in two spheres: within society and between states. Here, too, he thought in European terms.

The signal from Paris released patriotic energies in the rest of Europe of the kind that had last been seen between 1813 and 1815 in Poland, Spain, Germany, and Italy. Back then Napoleon had offered himself as the symbol to be fought against or admired. Since the July Revolution, a front opened up within public discourse: on one side stood the spokesmen who in their publications styled themselves as freedom fighters; on the other side stood, as Gervinus put it, "fortresses of the principle of conservation," "despotism," and the "monarchical politics of conservation." Good and evil were neatly and clearly divided.

The "Spring of Nations" as "Time Bomb"

From 1830 onward, the principle of nationality served as both fuel and social cement. With sincere conviction, Giuseppe Mazzini, the advocate for the poor, preached about the "spring of nations" that would lead to the peoples living in peace and harmony. He invoked the "Young Europe," "Young Italy," "Young Germany," and so forth. At the same time, he beat the drum for revolutionary war against the "Metternich system." Once again it was confirmed that the principle of nationality succeeded wherever the desolation of the present required something that instilled hope in people. That hope was now placed on the romantic utopia of an "awakening of the people" and on "national rebirth." It is impossible to overestimate the naïveté of those enthusiasts who believed that their nationality, which they experienced in cultural and political terms, would be considered peaceful by their neighbors once it was organized as a state. The spiritual, religious, social, and economic crises and uncertainty led to a flourishing of nationalism everywhere. To that extent, the term *Vormärz* is a fitting name for the time leading up to March 1848, during which European societies became dynamic and involuntarily moved toward an even greater European revolution.

Helmut Rumpler rightly talks of a "Pandora's box" in his exceptionally dense and revealing survey of the colorful plurality of vociferous nationalisms that proliferated in the Habsburg Monarchy during that period. In the end, the painful realization was that "national self-determination implied national separation." This was the "time bomb." The optimistic national narratives were blind to the overall picture—namely, that within the political reality in which they operated, war could be avoided only if individual nationalities and their movements "made concessions in their demands."[22] And why make concessions when there was something to conquer and gain? They looked first to their own interests. That provided the energy and desired confidence, and in that respect all nationalities were the same. According to Rumpler, the spring of nations developed centrifugal force in the form of an "oppositional or secessional nationalism." Rumpler's discussion reads like an account of Metternich's worst nightmare. "Poland is not yet lost"—the line, which today appears in the Polish national anthem, called for a Polish national state, and it was like an axe coming down on the Vienna System as a whole. The Poles found themselves faced with the cultural awakening in Galicia. The Magyars, who only wanted to allow the Hungarian language to be spoken in the Imperial Assembly at Pressburg, experienced problems with the Transylvanian Saxons, Szekler, Croats, and Serbs, while Czech nationalism moved away from the bilingual foundation in a common "Bohemian nation," which could live with regional patriotism but not with ethnic nationalism, and it also found new opponents in the Slovaks, who also wanted to "find" themselves. The Croats were still looking for their proper place within the great monarchy, while their Slavonic brothers in the south began to develop a pan-Serbian program, which was, in turn, resisted by an emerging "Illyrianism." And the "awakened" Illyrians themselves had to deal with their Italian neighbors, who were celebrating their own "rebirth" (Risorgimento).

Only now is historical research slowly beginning to look deeper into the Habsburg Monarchy's agrarian, legal, and institutional plurality. The empire's regions were as diverse as its different nationalities. During the first half of the nineteenth century, the agrarian conditions in the German and Bohemian crown lands were relatively good, and hence there was little cause for social protest.[23] In these regions, Joseph II's reforms were already having positive effects, whereas Prussian reforms were only just beginning to be implemented. The emperor and Metternich had in mind these regions of relative social peace [Ruhe] when they reacted with incomprehension to the social unrest in the German Confederation. But the Habsburg Monarchy also had backward regions, such as the Ruthenian and Slovenian East, which can still be detected in an east–west gap in the imperial statistics of 1910.[24] The monarchy was socially and economically divided, and for Metternich this meant the need for targeted support for particular regions. For Illyria, and northern Italy generally, he had developed ideas for how this could be achieved, and later he developed plans for Hungary, even though this was not within his purview. The precise details of when and where particular nationalisms were mobilized are even more difficult to determine for the pre-1848 period than for the post-1848 era.

The Germans were ignorant of all of this, because, like everyone else, they looked only at themselves—their philhellenism and their friendship with

Poland were mainly mirrors in which they could see their own nationalism reflected. These Germans celebrated their dreams of unity as a state—in 1817 on the Wartburg; in 1832 at the festival at Hambach Castle; in songs on Schleswig-Holstein; in gymnastics clubs; in fraternities; and in German Catholic communities. For them, the German Austrians naturally belonged to their state, and they did not understand that they themselves were only one voice in the chorus of nationalities whose volume was increasing across the European Continent.

It is important to imagine the growth of this plurality of nationalities as vividly as possible if we are to understand aright Metternich's political calculations, presentiments, and concerns. He never thought in terms of individual nationalities, but always in terms of complex connections. He had two ways of dealing with national movements: they needed to be culturally supported and politically tamed—that is, domestic policies had to put up barriers and dams, and then one might hope that, with increasing prosperity, tranquillity [*Ruhe*] would return.

Tightening of the Federal Domestic Laws

Metternich knew where to apply political pressure in order to get things done. In this case, as in the case of the Carlsbad Decrees, we must remember that he had the backing of the overwhelming majority of German princes. The work they had begun in Carlsbad they now perfected in the context of the July Revolution, with further decrees at the Federal Assembly. These dealt with the issue of too much public reporting on the discussions in the regional parliaments (1830) and with public political activities—associations, parties, meetings, and national festivals (1832). Metternich interpreted the attempted attack on the Federal Assembly in Frankfurt (April 3, 1833) according to his idea of interrelated terrorist activities, with which we are already familiar. This attack actually had more supporters than is suggested by Wehler's remark—that it was an "attack by a few idealists and radical hotheads."[25] It afforded the governments the opportunity to establish a second national investigative institution: the Central Investigative Office in Frankfurt, the successor to the Central Investigative Commission in Mainz. At the ministerial conferences in Vienna (1834), Metternich made another attempt, by way of further federal resolutions, at improving the domestic security policies that had been agreed on at Carlsbad.

Independently of the federal policies, Metternich established his own secret service, the Mainz Central Police [*Mainzer Zentralpolizei*], as it was called in the files of the state Chancellery. In other official documentation, it was also sometimes called the Mainz Intelligence Agency [*Mainzer Informationsbüro (MIB)*], a term that appears more modern and sheds the association with today's police.[26] A week before the attack in Frankfurt, Metternich had explained the concept for this institution to the Bavarian field marshal Wrede. After its inauguration, the agency became a hub for political espionage and policing and for collaboration between the courts of Berlin, Wiesbaden, Darmstadt, and Vienna. It was the first institutionally independent, centralized secret service, organized as a state authority, on German soil. The operations covered all German federal states as well as focal points in neighboring countries, such as Paris and Zurich. In the period between its foundation in May 1833 and its dissolution in February 1848, it collected vast amounts of information on individuals, associations, events, the movements of suspects, and so on. The office thus functioned as an efficient observation post that made Metternich the best-informed politician on the Continent as far as political developments, the politically committed literary world (the Young Germany of writers like Heine, Börne, and Gutzkow), and the politically interested public were concerned.

In Vienna, the state Chancellery combined the information from the Mainz bureau with information from the court's ministries of police and finance. The diagram of political emigration shows how the information was used to infer the existence of communicative networks from press information. This rendered talk about a "revolutionary party" superfluous; now they could track what was actually going on with much more precision. In this sort of research, domestic policy and foreign policy overlapped. Metternich could not direct all activities himself, but he was the central mediator. As part of the surveillance work, printed materials were sent to Vienna, where they were screened and marked with a red pen either by civil servants or by Metternich himself. As an ardent reader, he could thus form for himself a picture of the existing threats. He had more reason to be fearful than anyone else: he learned more about the blood-curdling threats to hang the princes or to chase them out of the country. He had learned in the early 1820s that these were no idle threats.

The pamphlet *The German Tribune* [*Der deutsche Tribun*] was written in Zurich and printed by the well-known printing house in Herisau; some 2,000 copies were smuggled into Baden. As the head of the intelligence agency reported, the pamphlet was the precursor to a proclamation that would call for a rebellion. The pamphlet advocated a republic and anticipated that the princes and their civil servants ("repressors and bloodsuckers") would be driven out of the country. In the final passage, it openly called for murder.

Another pamphlet that was found in March 1847, "A German Model Calculation," talks of the "princely idlers" and calls princes and their servants "incurable misanthropists," before adding the correction: "Incurable? *One* remedy there is, and this remedy—*is made of iron!*"[27]

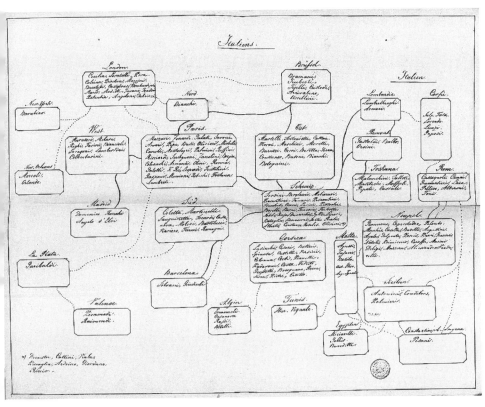

"Tabular survey of political emigration," here: Italy, Mainz, June 6, 1845.

Metternich and the "Police State"

In the case of the federal investigative authorities in Mainz and Frankfurt, the purpose was not only to identify the ringleaders of possible conspiracies. The potentially more important purpose was their function as intelligence services. They did what every modern state does: they collected information in order to defend the state and its Constitution. Why should Metternich take attacks on the German Confederation any less seriously than the representatives of modern states take similar attacks on their own states? Here we reach the real basis for the picture of Metternich as a "reactionary." The Carlsbad Decrees and the "police state" both form parts of that picture. A historian must point out an awkward methodological problem in this context, a problem that, if denied, means we will never be able to reach a historically faithful judgment on the past. It is a simple problem: The same name does not necessarily signify the same thing. For someone living in the twentieth or early twenty-first century,

Pamphlet *The German Tribune* with three passages marked; accompanying letter "from Lake Constance, November 23rd, 1846."

the expression "police state" is loaded with associations: the "Gestapo," the "Stasi," the "Gulag," the "concentration camp," secret arrests and executions. But these associations do not fit either with the heterogeneous Habsburg Monarchy, which was not really centralized before 1848, or with the German Confederation. The emperors Franz and Ferdinand enjoyed broad popularity among the wider population, something that was regularly confirmed—particularly in the case of Franz—at weekly audiences with "the people." Their rule can be called a benevolent patriarchal dictatorship; they spoke of *Policey* and *Policeystaat*[28]—the different spelling alone suggests that this must have been quite a different phenomenon from later police states. In the older language of state administration, *policey* referred to the totality of the domestic administration, and accordingly there was a *Medicinal-Policey* that was responsible for medical policies, and a *Wohlfahrts-Policey* dealing with welfare policies. If we wanted to find modern equivalents to the activities performed by the police during the pre-1848 period, we would need to think of the work of "secret intelligence services" and of the Office for the Protection of the Constitution [*Verfassungschutz*]. The interception of mail and the screening of state and private correspondence was part of this work. This was called *Perlustrieren* (literally: to shine a light into something) and *Interzepieren* ("confiscation," "withdrawal"). The latter referred to the secret interception and disposal of a letter before delivery. An *Interzept* was a copy of a letter that had been secretly opened. All of this required a lot of expertise, and Metternich had a special office at his state Chancellery for that purpose called the *Ziffernkabinett*. It was responsible for the interception, opening, and copying of letters and their discreet return into the postal system. It also had to decipher encoded letters from foreign diplomats, and from time to time it translated arriving correspondence that was written in unusual languages.

If we understand the Habsburg "police state" in this way, parallels with modern security measures become obvious, and the question of how far a state may go in order to defend itself arises. As in the case of the control of communication, the problem is not surveillance as such, but surveillance without independent judicial oversight. This shortcoming relates to our description of the Habsburg Monarchy as a benevolent patriarchal dictatorship: states of this kind tend to reject independent judicial control. The Habsburg Monarchy, however, was similar in this regard to all the other German states during the pre-1848 era—and most certainly to Prussia. With regard to Metternich, another little-known factor must be taken into account: within the Austrian administration, censorship and police were part of the Ministry of the Interior's brief, and this ministry was, from 1826 onward, headed by the Bohemian count Kolowrat, who was also the finance minister. Emperor Franz thwarted any attempt at establishing a council of ministers, headed by a prime minister, as an independent governmental body, and reserved the right for himself to treat every minister individually as the holder of a so-called *Hofstelle,* a court office. The holder had direct—"immediater"—access to the emperor and wrote his own presentations for him, while the emperor was always able to play his ministers off against each other, an ability he frequently made use of.

As someone who thought and planned for the long term, Metternich must have been close to desperation when the emperor rejected his suggestions, as he did in 1816–1817 when Metternich proposed federal reorganization and rationalization of the monarchy. The concrete example of the "police" showed us that Metternich was by no means the all-powerful figure within the political system of the Habsburg Monarchy. We shall have occasion to revisit this point in more detail later.

TOLERATED REVOLUTIONS AFTER 1830

King Leopold of Belgium: A Second Revolutionary Prince Legitimized

The rebellion in Brussels on September 28, 1830, came in the wake of the July Revolution. It fit with Metternich's predictions of ensuing chaos. How should one deal with the emergence of a new state? A part of the Kingdom of the United Netherlands, which had been established and legitimized at the Congress of Vienna, tried its hand at rebellion. This was a repetition of the same pattern, typical for the nineteenth century, which Metternich considered a core evil: claims of nationality aiming at establishing a separate territory. The situation was paradoxical: the national principle was invoked to legitimize a future nation-state, while undermining the existing state from within.

The governments of Russia, England, and Austria seriously considered a military intervention.[29] Metternich, however, took the overall geopolitical distribution of military power into account: If Austrian troops were engaged in Brussels, they would no longer be available in Italy, where he also expected uprisings to occur—and, as it turned out, he was right—and the Habsburg Monarchy would also lose its capacity to respond to the situation in Germany. Metternich also expected unrest in the Polish regions. He calculated like a chess player (an image he himself used): If one moved pieces to one side, this created a vacuum of power on the other side. Because of all the interconnections between the potential conflict areas, the states paused, despite their readiness to intervene. This ultimately made possible the formation of a sovereign Kingdom of Belgium, which was then legitimized by a conference of the five major powers in London on November 15, 1831. The Concert of Europe diplomacy still worked, even if the kind of conference politics familiar from the 1820s was no longer practiced. Leopold von Saxony-Coburg-Gotha—a compromise candidate to avoid a Bourbon king—seized the opportunity (a rare one for the prince of a small German state) to become the ruler of a kingdom. He would later be one of the most reliable supporters of Metternich during his time in exile after 1848.

The Drive toward Constitutionalism in Germany

In the German states the July Revolution drove forward constitutionalism, which had begun to gain ground in 1814. By 1848 there were only four states that still had no written Constitution: Austria, Prussia, Mecklenburg, and Hesse-Homburg. But in the pre-1848 period, Prussia and Austria were, because of their provincial estates, no longer absolutist states—contrary to what one usually understands from school textbooks. Prussia's domestic policies suffered from an enduring problem. Still with the Napoleonic wars in mind, the Prussian king, Friedrich Wilhelm III, had issued a written promise in 1815 that the country would receive a (modern) written Constitution. Metternich saw this as potentially explosive; he considered Prussia, like the Habsburg Monarchy, to be a heterogeneous, composite state that would be blown apart by central parliamentary representation. After the succession of Wilhelm IV in 1840, he repeatedly told the new king that he should under no circumstances grant the country a Constitution with central representation. All the same, in 1847 what Metternich had consistently warned against came to pass. The king called a meeting of the "united parliaments" for the purpose of discussing the financing of the railroad to Eastern Prussia. This parliament, based on the model of the French estates general of 1789 and thus old-fashioned in its form, could then no longer be diverted from its aim of becoming the "national" Parliament of Prussia.

In Austria, too, the regional parliaments were trailblazers in the fight for more political participation. And here, again, there had been no central representative body before 1848; the one established by the revolution was only short-lived, and the monarchy took the path toward a central parliament only after Metternich's death—namely, after 1861 and, in particular, after the Austro-Hungarian Compromise of 1867. Metternich rightly expected that in the multinational Habsburg state, central representation would unleash destructive centrifugal forces, but the German states, and in particular the Napoleonic kingdoms of Bavaria and Württemberg, expected the result to be a new and integrating confidence in the state. A new constitutional patriotism was to unite the diverse new regions and diverse parts of the population. Some nevertheless used the generic adjective "German"—as did the Bavarian king, Ludwig I, when he built the grand national monument of the "Walhalla" at the Danube. But this national consciousness was supposed to be cultural and historical, not political, because apart from the much-invoked "German fatherland," there were also Prussian, Bavarian, Württembergian, and Hessian "nations" in the contemporary consciousness. It is not often remembered today that the original purpose of the much-discussed "national festival of the Germans" in Hambach in May 1832 had been to celebrate the anniversary of the Bavarian Constitution, something that, in the end, it did not do.

Metternich also interpreted the disturbances in the German states within the overall European context. The attack on the main police station [*Hauptwache*] in Frankfurt on April 3, 1833, was directed at the Federal Assembly. Although the attack failed miserably, it had to be seen as an attempt at a revolution, because the plan had been to take the members of the Assembly hostage. And there were many hints that suggested connections with Polish and Italian activists, even though the Frankfurt bourgeoisie very efficiently covered up the most important of these.

A Revolution in Poland?

All the European uprisings that followed were interconnected. The whole Continent felt the movement. A parallel was drawn between the bombardment of Antwerp during the uprising in the Belgian Netherlands and the uprising in Warsaw. The commentators in the press saw the Poles, like the Greeks in the 1820s, as an *Aufstandsnation*—a nation that was rising up. All rebellious activities targeted state power, and in the extreme case the monarch himself. The Russian crown prince, Konstantin, who was in Warsaw as the representative of the tsar, fled the danger to the safety of the Russian troops that were stationed there—about 15,000 of them. Metternich reacted logically and ordered 10,000 troops to be moved to the border with Galicia in order to be prepared for any attack. The Prussians did the same. After the rebellion had been put down, Metternich tolerated Polish fighters who had fled to the Austrian part of Galicia. They were disarmed and their equipment handed over to the Russians. There was a kind of informal agreement between the major powers of the pentarchy not to take any action, as it was in all of their interests not to change the status quo—to ensure that, unlike what happened in Belgium, an independent Polish state was prevented. At the same time, Metternich reflected on the situation in the Habsburg countries. The population, especially the peasants in Galicia, showed no signs of planning a rebellion, and so he concluded that there were no sympathies for a revolution or unrest in the Slavonic countries. He interpreted this as being due to the success of his policies. The uprisings that emanated from Warsaw certainly posed a problem for the Vienna System of 1815; the Poles tried to cast off the yoke of Russian supremacy and restore their own kingdom. This would have implied changing the three Polish divisions and would have challenged the territorial claims of three of the major powers—Austria, Prussia, and Russia.

FROM THE ORIENT TO THE RHINE: THE CONCERT OF THE MAJOR POWERS AS A CHALLENGE

Because of the general tumult in Europe after the July Revolution, Metternich wanted to see the old system of regular conferences restored—even if that meant long and tiring coach journeys across Europe for all the participants. Such journeys involved a good deal of physical stress: traveling for weeks on the road in coaches that did not have much in the way of suspension. Metternich complained about this in his letters, but he continued to advocate for the conferences. At the beginning, he only managed to bring the Eastern powers together. In September 1833 they met in Münchengrätz (Czech Mnichovo Hradiště) to the northeast of Prague; Tsar Nikolaus rushed to the meeting from Warsaw. Prussia (represented by the crown prince), Austria, and Russia agreed to a joint convention that apparently intended to restore the original system of 1815, which had been created to deal with France. With this alliance, Russia adopted a policy of preserving the Ottoman Empire as long as Russia would be able to extend its sphere of influence into the Balkans and the straits at the Black Sea. That was the reason Russia joined the convention. The powers mutually guaranteed their respective Polish possessions, and they agreed to come to each other's aid in the case of another Polish independence movement. Mutual assurances of aid in the common battle against rebellious "liberalism" were also given, for the powers feared that "the revolution" would continue. Police reports on "terrorism" were to be exchanged, and, were the revolution to extend into the German Confederation, the Habsburg Monarchy, or Prussia, the allies agreed to intervene if called upon for help. This happened in 1849 when Russian troops came to the aid of Austria; without their help, the revolutions could not have been quelled. This antirevolutionary league was also designed to secure the monarchical system generally; in Münchengrätz in 1833, Tsar Nikolaus guaranteed, for instance, that the crown prince and future emperor, Ferdinand, would succeed to the throne—despite his physical and mental disabilities and legal incapacity. Overall, these policies stabilized the Vienna System of 1815; they did not serve any particular interests. The three powers supported these coordinated policies up until 1841.

Superficially, however, it did look like a resuscitation of the conservative league of Russia, Austria, and Prussia. But this view is incorrect. Münchengrätz was another attempt to secure the European system of 1815, whose continued existence depended on the preservation of the Ottoman Empire. This was unambiguously Metternich's achievement. Shortly before Münchengrätz, a contract between Russia and the Ottoman Empire (Hunkiar Iskelessi) had made the old enemies into partners in a defensive alliance. In this contract, the tsar guaranteed the existence of the Ottoman Empire, and in a "secret supplementary article" he agreed to a blockade of the Bosporus strait for warships of third countries.

Metternich knew about this secret article. It constituted an affront to France and especially to Great Britain, which saw in it a threat to its interests as a naval power. The bilateral contract between Russia and the Ottoman Empire was, in fact, an expression of a Russian imperialism that was independent of the Vienna System and was gradually moving further and further west. Metternich did not see a problem with this because the Bosporus strait did not immediately concern the Habsburg Monarchy, while the support for the Ottoman Empire and the secret article convinced him that the mutual understanding between France and tsarist Russia that he had feared was no longer possible. Metternich's long-term aim was still a peaceful understanding between the powers of the pentarchy on the basis of the consensus achieved in Vienna. If this solidarity was temporarily unachievable, the major powers were at least to adhere to rational policies to secure peace in Europe.

During the period 1839–1841, Metternich's policies were successful. A thorough examination of all embassy archives has recently shown how instrumental Metternich was in controlling the European crisis by deflating the conflicts that arose from problems within the Ottoman Empire.[30] Because of the one-sided policies pursued by the French foreign ministry, this conflict threatened to grow into a great European war. The possibility of a dangerous expansion of the conflict, which began as a regional conflict in Syria and Algeria, became clear when the major powers—apart from France—guaranteed the continued existence of the Ottoman Empire in the Convention of London of 1840, thus demonstrating to the Egyptian viceroy the limits of his power. In a mixture of prestige-seeking and nostalgia for the great Napoleon (whose mortal remains had just been transferred from Saint Helena to Paris), the public opinion in France's daily press scorned this agreement of the Quadruple Alliance. The convention was seen as a national humiliation because it seemed as though the old allies were conspiring against France again, as they had done during the period 1813 to 1815. That stirred thoughts of revenge, and an overheated press called for the recapture of the left bank of the Rhine and northern Italy. There was a wave of national passion in the German press, and German songs were sung ("They shall not have it / the free German Rhine"); on both sides there was talk of a war for the fatherland.

In 1840, plans for troop mobilization became more concrete in both France and the German Confederation. In something of a master stroke, Metternich succeeded in ending France's diplomatic isolation and bringing about an agreement between the powers of the pentarchy and the sultan in the second London Convention of 1841, which prohibited warships from entering the Dardanelles and the Bosporus during peacetime. Early on, Metternich understood that excluding France from the agreements of the major European states risked war—even if, in truth, France had excluded itself.

This international conflict showed that Metternich considered the German Confederation an important military element in the Rhine crisis. He did not view the public nationalist fervor during the crisis as "revolutionary"; he explicitly welcomed it as something that strengthened the German Confederation. Austria's renewed dominance within the Austro-Prussian relationship also became clear. Metternich, however, was becoming aware of the limits of the system he had helped to create in 1815. The status quo could no longer be maintained: the independence of Greece and Belgium, the division of Luxembourg, and the revolution in Paris could not be prevented. Stability, the status quo, could not be maintained.

METTERNICH AND CUSTOMS POLICIES

The peculiar order of the German Confederation—which was in part Metternich's work—meant that the Habsburg Monarchy could enter into a quasinational relationship with the other German states and form something like a state, an entity that was called "Germany," without having to sacrifice its own independence. We have seen how this created spheres of influence and areas of competency that sometimes overlapped. In principle, the Austrian emperor stood in the same relation to the German Confederation as the kings of England, Prussia, Denmark, or the Netherlands did. Each German ruler only had one foot in the German Confederation. But the market cannot stand such barriers for long. Trade requires the free exchange of goods and the removal of obstacles to it—such as customs borders. Prussia had removed such obstacles with the trade, customs, and excise law of May 26, 1818, which created a uniform internal market in the Prussian provinces. The Habsburg Monarchy was far from having such a market: the inequalities between Bregenz at Lake Constance and Chernivtsi in the Bukovina were so vast that trade and agriculture still required protection and called for customs barriers—not to mention the customs border that separated Hungary from the rest of the empire. From 1816 onward, there had been a *Kommerz-Hofkommission,* an imperial commission for commerce at the court in Vienna, but it had not yet succeeded in creating a standardized economic area for the monarchy as a whole.[31]

As a consequence of the rules agreed upon at the Congress of Vienna, Prussia "had grown far into Germany," but it was territorially split between its eastern and western parts, and therefore it sought regulations that could be applied across all of its states.[32] The idea of a free trade area created through a customs union seemed to be a way of achieving this. Other German states were attracted by the potential income that could be generated by the external borders of a customs union. Metternich observed this trend with great concern. We shall not go into the subtleties of the financial policies involved, but instead shall concentrate on two questions: What was Metternich's attitude toward the emerging free trade area? And to what extent did he see the development fostered by Prussia as a problem for the "Germany" he had designed—that is, for the "federal nation" with multiple identities?

In conversation with the American Ticknor, Metternich expressed his interest in the systematic promotion of trade and industry.[33] He talked very fondly of the Polytechnic Institute—"its *élèves* were already at the head of the principal manufactories in the empire." The factories were improving, and there was "an increasing demand for improved factories, so that the manufacturers are now constantly urging the reduction of the tariff, on the ground that they can better enter into competition with foreign nations than with smugglers." The Austrian government maintained a tariff, "not at all as a fiscal measure, but merely to protect and encourage manufactures." The system, Metternich said, had been introduced in the time of Joseph II, but "if he had been minister at the time he should have advised against it," even though it could "not to be denied that it has effected its purpose and made Austria a manufacturing country." He added that the government had "already abolished that part of the laws which excludes entirely any article whatever."[34]

As the idea of the German Customs Union began to pick up steam, Metternich alerted Emperor Franz to this development in one of his presentations, dated June 24, 1833.[35] Demonstrating a remarkable grasp of economic policy, he set out, without prejudice, the reasons Prussia was pursuing these policies. Metternich sat up and took notice when "two Southern German states, Bavaria and Württemberg, who usually guard their independence with such jealousy," signaled that they were prepared to enter into an association with Prussia "as satellite states" and accept losing the sovereign right to set their own tariffs. Metternich recognized the financial attraction of the Customs Union for states that were in financially difficult situations. For the German Confederation generally, and for Austria, however, he considered the "minor German" Customs

Union to be highly disadvantageous—even potentially disastrous. If imperial Austria were excluded from the trade arrangements, he expected them to hinder Austrian industry. Even more worrying to him than the commercial consequences were the political ones: The increasing power of one state, he said, undermined the federation. The federation's stability depended on its internal equilibrium, which he thought was threatened by Prussia's increasing economic influence. A new relation between patron and client, between protector and protected, was emerging. Because ten of its seventeen members were part of the Customs Union, the power relations within the Central Council [*Engerer Rat*] of the Federal Assembly had already begun to shift. Prussia, Metternich said, was seeking to weaken Austria's influence in Germany, adding, prophetically, that Prussia wanted the German states to "direct their view in fear as in hope only toward Berlin, and to see Austria at long last for what it actually in commercial terms already is to all these states, and as what the fashionable Prussian writers are again and again eager to present it, namely as a foreign country." Metternich's view went even further: the relationships between the German federal states and Austria would, in the long term, fray more and more, until finally a rift with Prussia would open up.

Metternich saw himself and Austria as fighting for "Germany." But there were clearly two types of Germany. Plausible arguments have been put forward in historical research—especially against Heinrich von Treitschke—for the view that there was no straightforward or irreversible development from the Prussian finance minister Friedrich von Motz to the "founder of the Reich," Otto von Bismarck. There are countless examples, so the argument goes, that show that an economic unity does not necessarily lead to political unity. But listening to Metternich and Motz casts doubt on this argument. Why do both speak of "Germany" when they talk about tariffs, trade, and the economy? Metternich was thinking about ways of "dealing the Prussian customs system a most devastating blow." Motz, in contrast, hoped that through the Customs Union "a genuinely united, internally and externally truly free, Germany, under the protection and umbrella of Prussia, would develop and be happy."[36]

The fundamental question was how to organize the state: as a composite empire or as a centralized institutional state [*Anstaltsstaat*]. Paradoxically, Prussia at the time conformed to the latter form more in idea than in reality; the monarch was still fearful of the aristocratic owners of the feudal estates, and in Ostelbien the police, the judiciary, and village schools were still under the authority of the manorial lord or the aristocratic commissioner of the regional council.

Metternich's presentation for the emperor was a revealing political confession regarding the way he envisaged the ideal functioning of the German Confederation. He was aware of how unpopular the German Confederation was among the people—as, indeed, was the Federal Assembly, which had "too often received the thankless task of having to take repressive and disciplinary measures due to the restless mood of the times." Metternich was appealing to the confederation's true nature: to serve the welfare of the nation. He responded to Prussia's trajectory, which led it away from the confederation, by arguing that the German Confederation should become the center of trade, and he reminded the emperor of the task set out in article 19 of the Federal Act: "to enter into negotiations . . . regarding trade and commerce between the different federal states."[37] This task still remained unfulfilled.

In an alternative to the Customs Union, Metternich put forward the goal of free trade and commerce between the federal states, and equal treatment for natural and artificial products that originated from German federal states rather than from "outside the confederation." These were the sort of "benevolent measures" that were required to promote "public well-being in Germany."

With regard to Austria, Metternich recommended changing the existing customs system and bringing it into line with the other states of the German Confederation. Austria might even have to be prepared to make sacrifices, he said, in order "to prevent a larger evil which might eventually affect the well-being and influence of the monarchy at the roots." We saw how inventive Metternich was in promoting the economy, wealth, and infrastructure of his own estates, and how he used the latest technological and agricultural methods in farming, forestry, and winegrowing, and at his ironworks. It is plausible to assume that he also had the capacity to create a similar vision for the state as a whole. Unfortunately, though, he was only the foreign minister, and he found himself in a situation in which all possible actions would turn out to be wrong, no matter what one chose to do. If Metternich had chosen to push through Austrian membership of the custom union, which he actually considered to be the right move, he would have fallen out with the political elite at home and failed in the face of their resistance. If he had decided in favor of a customs union internal to the Habsburg Monarchy, as his great opponent Kolowrat wanted, Austria would have lost its ties with "Germany" (in Metternich's sense) and become a foreign country.

Metternich, the reformer, had suggested more than enough measures for economic improvement. He distanced himself from his adviser, Adam Müller, who was generally hostile to industry and advocated a conservative agrarian economic order. Müller railed against the "dreadful large factories" and declared his support for the family-based crafts. Metternich had also entered into negotiations with the liberal Friedrich List in Vienna to try to accommodate the economic interests of the middle-sized and smaller federal states. And finally he tried to secure the free trade of foodstuffs.

Metternich failed because of opposition from the emperor, who said that his "monarchy, notwithstanding the fact that it joined the German Confederation, must always remain an independent body."[38] Metternich also came up against the isolationist and conservative tendencies within the monarchy. The emperor himself represented these tendencies, and he was the only one who could have brought about a fundamentally different approach. And, keeping in mind the fate of Joseph II, even that seems questionable. Metternich also underestimated the power and influence of his aristocratic peers. The crucial point, it turned out, was the tariff on sugar. It would have been necessary to lower this tariff for imports to Bohemia, but the Bohemian owners of the large sugar-producing estates stubbornly resisted this in order to protect themselves from unwelcome competition. In Kolowrat, they had a voice who had the ear of the emperor. The fate of Metternich's memorandum can easily be deduced by simply looking at the original: it lacks the usual "decision of His Majesty"" [*Allerhöchste Entschließung*], which the conscientious Emperor Franz never withheld without good reason. When he did withhold it, and the initiative had come from Metternich, it was the emperor's habit simply to pass over the presentation without making any comments. That was enough for Metternich to understand. One can only agree with Heinrich Lutz: "Metternich wanted a different outcome."[39]

14

THE ORGANIZATION OF RULE

Power Centers, Networks, Interests, Intrigues

THE MASTER OF THE STATE CHANCELLERY

The Networks of Power and Political Rule

At first glance we might think that what we have witnessed so far has been merely the continual advance of a political career, an advance that has seen our subject, in 1821, appointed to the position of state chancellor of the Habsburg Empire. We now come to the threshold of the revolution of 1848. At the end of October 1847, a young diplomat from Saxony visiting Vienna found the then seventy-four-year-old Metternich to still be an impressive figure, with a sturdy posture (like the "iron" Wellington), fresh, exuding a youthful friendliness— in short, an exceptional personality of the sort the present times, in the diplomat's view, rarely produced.[1] But Metternich was also seen as the embodiment of his eponymous "system." The contemporary author Ferdinand Kürnberger wrote that at the heart of those "times of intellectual slavery" were the "tyrants Sedlnitzky and Metternich."[2] Despite these opposed views, both sides saw him as the all-powerful ruler over the European states. Keeping in mind the battles he fought and the policies he pursued up to this point, it is therefore necessary to take a closer look at the networks and centers of power within the Habsburg Monarchy that formed the background conditions within which Metternich acted. In his career as a civil servant, Metternich experienced both extremes on the spectrum of monarchical rule: from the personal rule of Emperor Franz, who, in his manic need to control everything, wanted to make every single decision himself, to the rule of his successor, Ferdinand, who had no talent for rule at all. As a result, Metternich had the experience of working under completely different sets of conditions. Emperor Franz—whose will immortalized Metternich as his "friend"—built a wall around his minister that protected and supported him, especially from the rest of the imperial family, the majority of whom were not well disposed toward Metternich. This wall protected him against Empress Ludovika, for instance, who could not comprehend Metternich's plans for a tactical appeasement of Napoleon, and against Archduke Johann, who thought he could single-handedly start a revolutionary war against Napoleon. The wall also protected him from dismissal when this was demanded by someone inside the imperial family or by the powerful tsar. Metternich was therefore not dependent on allies, and as long as he was in agreement with his ruler, he was largely able to operate autonomously.

Ferdinand's reign created precisely the opposite situation. Metternich was no longer shielded by a protective wall, and he needed allies. He found himself faced with powerful opposition from the imperial family and from his main opponent in domestic politics, Franz Anton Count Kolowrat-Liebsteinsky, a Bohemian aristocrat and former Prague burgrave, who possessed large estates in Bohemia. Emperor Franz had appointed him as a state and conference minister in Vienna on September 26, 1826. As an expert in financial matters, he knew how to make himself indispensable to the emperor, who was always worried about the state's finances.[3]

We therefore need to shed light on the roles Metternich played under both a strong emperor and a weak one, the complex system of conferences, ministries, and court offices, and the influence of the estates, especially of their economic interests. As a rule, these factors are ignored in biographies of Metternich and other literature on the "statesman of Europe," especially in publications from outside of Austria, but understanding these aspects will enable us to answer central questions regarding Metternich's scope of action.

Initial Impressions of the Administrative Jungle

By the time of his appointment as ambassador to Dresden in 1801, Metternich had already gained sufficient insight into the machinery at the top of the state, under Thugut, to be repelled by the intrigues, rivalries, and self-importance on display; he even questioned whether he should actually embark on a career in the civil service. It was only when the supportive Colloredo took up his post that Metternich changed his mind. After the emperor appointed him state minister in 1809, he also had regular personal contact with the emperor, gaining an even deeper insight into the political process.

Governmental authorities of the Habsburg monarchy until the beginning of the nineteenth century.

		Central Authorities						Provinces		Sub-authorities	
		Supreme Governmental and Advisory Authorities	External Administration	Judiciary and Judicial Administration	Internal Affairs	Finances	War	Administration and Finances	Judicial Matters	Regional Authorities	Municipal Authorities
Maria Theresia	Initial Situation						Court War Councillor (since 1556)	Governments			Mayors
	1740				Court Chancellery (2 Divisions)	Court Chamber					Municipal Councils
	1742										
	1. Period of Reforms (Haugwitz) 1748		Haus-, Hof- und Staats-kanzlei	Supreme Office of Justice	Directorium in publicis et cameralibus			Representation of Chambers	(Regional) Offices of Justice		
	1749	State Council	Chancellery of Court and State		United Bohemian Court Chancellery	Court Chamber		Gubernien (governments) with Judicial Senates		Local Authorities	
	2. Period of Reforms (Kaunitz) 1760										
	1765				Verein. Hofstelle (United Court Office) Court Chancellery	Court Chamber of Accountancy	General Treasury				
Joseph II	1780	Imperial Cabinet				Court Chamber		Government Districts	Courts of Appeal		Mayors
	1782							Gubernien (sometimes divided into regional authorities)			Magistrates
Leopold II	1790										
Franz II/I	1792										
	1806										
	1814	State Conference									

Provincial Law

Careful observation here reveals a complicated state structure that still bore marks of the times of Maria Theresia and Joseph II—not only the plurality of internal Constitutions in the provinces but also the top-down style in which the court in Vienna ruled. The monarch stood at the center, and around him were various authorities and bodies. The State Council held a central position, evaluating presentations from the court and provincial offices on behalf of the emperor. As a rule, the authorities communicated in written form and provided their information directly to the emperor. Politicians in the Foreign Ministry or the War Ministry did not know what the heads of the Finance Ministry, the Ministry of the Interior, or of the Ministry of Trade were doing, and vice versa. Ministers, the presidents of court offices, and leading civil servants were in competition for the emperor's favor, because there was no council of ministers with a president where joint consultations could take place. Such a council would have weakened the monarch's power. He always had the final say; his civil servants advised him in a collegial way, but they did not take individual responsibility as ministers with specific portfolios. Even after 1815 the emperor did not deviate from this strict separation of competencies. Within such a system, the allegedly all-powerful minister Metternich could quite easily find himself being reprimanded.

For instance, in July 1817 the Federal Assembly in Frankfurt discussed a law on *Nachsteuer- und Abzugsfreiheit*—the guarantee that assets that were moved from one federal country to another were exempted from tax in cases such as inheritance, gifts, sales, or dowries. Metternich was the superior of the Austrian representative at the assembly and therefore in a position to instruct the representative. But although the matter concerned taxation, and was thus relevant to domestic politics, the representative in Frankfurt had voted without asking for specific instructions from the Austrian ministries. And the instruction Metternich had provided single-handedly, the emperor considered null and void. The emperor reprimanded Metternich, saying he had to be mindful of problems that might arise because of his ignorance of certain matters. He must know, Franz added, "that the state Chancellery is not informed, and cannot be informed, on matters to do with the inner administration of My monarchy, and therefore is under instruction always to seek agreement with My court offices on such matters, which also makes any further discussion of your presentations superfluous and always allows all matters to be thoroughly presented to me."[4] If a ministerial council had existed, the foreign minister and minister of the interior would have been informed about each other's work—but in Emperor Franz's empire this was not the case. In the absence of such a council, there was also no filter mechanism to separate important and unimportant matters at the outset.

The influence of the provincial aristocratic estates cannot be overestimated—especially when it came to issues of taxation. The provincial states successfully resisted a strengthening of the central state. Metternich came to recognize this ever more clearly in the course of his career, until finally, in the 1840s, he resigned himself to the resulting paralysis; or, to put it differently: he was sidetracked and no longer had any say in domestic matters.

When he entered his ministry in 1809, he still believed in the possibility of reforming the "disorganized state administration."[5] Metternich saw himself as a modernizer, and from the very beginning he had to fight against the disorganization of the administration, as we know from the unpublished part of his memoirs.[6] He noticed that the government was not organized into the separate ministries that had become increasingly common since the French Revolution. The business of government was conducted between colleagues, and each area was headed by a president, who sometimes carried the title of chancellor of whichever court chancellery he was in charge of. There were chancelleries for Hungary, Bohemia, Transylvania, Italy, and the Netherlands. As the governing minister in Brussels, Metternich's father had had to settle quite a few disputes with the chancellery for the Netherlands. The most prominent chancellery was the Chancellery of Court and State [*Haus-, Hof- und Staatskanzlei*]. Throughout his whole time in office, Metternich was trying to work his way up to the superior position of prime minister, and thus beyond the competition between the various court chancelleries. Emperor Franz prevented that.

The Reorganization of the State Chancellery

Metternich got his first taste of the sorts of problems that lay in store for him when he was appointed state chancellor, and found that the Chancellery had been left in a pretty chaotic condition by Stadion.[7] At the beginning of 1809, Stadion had followed the army headquarters to Upper Austria without appointing anyone to head the Chancellery, reserving the right to direct it even in his absence. The work ended up being carried out by three court councillors who stayed behind and divided up between themselves the responsibility for correspondence with other courts and embassies. Each of them submitted his reports independently and directly to the minister and received his instructions from him; but none of them knew what the others were doing, and there was no central directorate in charge of personnel at the Chancellery. Nothing was known about the registry or the files that were archived there, except that the registrar and expeditor held the keys. Years before they had been told to organize the files, but they had not done it because they were always busy dealing with the daily business. And to make matters worse, in 1805, during the war, all the files had been sent to safety in Pressburg, which meant they became even more disorganized. There was no inventory. Because of this, no one knew where any particular file could be found.

As Napoleon marched toward Vienna in 1809, court councillor Hudelist made a vital intervention. Stadion had not countenanced the possibility of military defeat, and so he had not considered the possibility that the archive would have to be brought to safety. He thought it was an "altogether excessive worry," something one should not mention because it might undermine the will to victory. When the danger nevertheless became imminent, he passed all responsibility to Hudelist, who ordered that the files be packed into sixty-one boxes (weighing at least six centner each), which, along with twenty-six boxes of documents from the chancelleries of the Netherlands and Italy and the treasury of the state Chancellery, were, in a matter of days, loaded onto a rented ship that, with two civil servants, sailed from Vienna to Pressburg, setting off on May 4 and arriving in Temesvar on May 10.

Returning with the exiled court from the Hungarian Totis, Metternich learned that the parsimonious emperor would quibble over the hiring of the lowliest office messenger. The emperor's comments on such occasions were often so detailed that they were as long as the request they were a response to. Metternich wanted to hire more personnel, but post after post was declined because, as Metternich read: "the financial situation makes it indispensable to implement every further saving that can be done without the services having to be discontinued."[8]

Metternich nevertheless still hoped that he might have the state Chancellery at the Ballhausplatz renovated before returning to Vienna. Two basement vaults, the ground floor, and three further floors formed Metternich's universe, the location from which his policies reached all of Europe. The wine from Johannisberg was stored in the cellar. The ground floor was taken up with the kitchen (including a confectioner's), the stables and coach house, and accommodations for the house officer, household servant, cook, and coachman. The civil servants worked on the first floor, which also housed the registry, the *Ziffernkabinett* (the office where letters were read and encoded or decoded), the Chancellery's library, and a meeting room. The second floor housed the state rooms (which also were the venue for the Congress of Vienna), a reception room, an audience room, a dining hall, a private library, and bedrooms for Metternich and his wife. The third floor, finally, was the home of the children, the chamberlain, the master of the stables and the servants; in addition, Metternich's private chancellery for his estates and the domicile of his brother Joseph, an eccentric character known to all of Vienna, was also situated on the third floor.[9]

Metternich continued to employ the fifty-year-old court councillor Josef von Hudelist, who had worked at the embassies in Florence, Rome, Naples, Berlin, and Saint Petersburg, and had been court councillor at the state Chancellery since 1803. In 1813 Metternich promoted him to state and conference councillor. In this position, immediately below Metternich, he stood in as head of the Chancellery when Metternich was away. Every document Metternich received was also seen by Hudelist. When Hudelist was criticized for the condition of the Chancellery's archive, he justified himself by saying that "in sacrificing my health and every pleasure in life I have only caused the envy of my colleagues."

Metternich rationalized the state Chancellery and ordered a new inventory for the archive to be drawn up. A court councillor was given sole responsibility for this task. Metternich also made sure that clear structures and areas of responsibility for the five sections were introduced. The Chancellery's sections were divided up as follows: (1) correspondence with the major powers; (2) correspondence with the Rhenish Confederation; (3) correspondence with the Ottoman Empire; (4) correspondence with domestic authorities; (5) mail department and registry.[10]

After 1815 Metternich had to adapt this basic structure to new needs; the empire had become bigger again, having reacquired old embassies that had been lost under Napoleon, and more diplomatic personnel were required. Every pay raise and every new post had to be justified and argued for in minute detail, before the emperor would be prepared to make an exception to his general rule of parsimony.

Metternich presented the emperor with his sketch for the reorganization of the state Chancellery, including the elevations in rank and substantial increases in salary associated with it, during the Italian journey in the first half of 1816 when the emperor was inspecting his kingdom of Lombardy-Venetia. Metternich argued that "during the years of French predominance" Austria had maintained correspondence in only four areas: France (including the princes of the Rhenish Confederation), Russia, Prussia, and the "Sublime Porte" (the Ottoman Empire). Now the state Chancellery was in correspondence with thirty courts. There had usually been about thirty staff, reduced to twenty-three before 1815. The vacant posts needed to be refilled. As the minister in charge, Metternich defended his Chancellery and praised his employees as loyal and diligent workers who "showed the most dutiful devotion to their monarch"; they deserved a "well-earned encouragement."

In response to requests during the Napoleonic era, the emperor said the salaries should be such that "the civil servants do not have to starve." Now he wrote that he "approved all the posts and salaries suggested here," although adding, of course, the condition "that you will seek to reduce this numerous

Table 14.1. Personnel and salaries at the Privy Chancellery of Court and State (1816)

Name	Rank	Old Salary (florins)	New Salary (florins)
Section for Foreign Affairs			
Graf Mercy	Court Councillor	4,000	4,000
Hr. v. Wacken	Court Councillor	4,000	4,000
Freiherr v. Spiegel	Court Councillor		4,000
Baron Kruft	Councillor	2,000	2,500
Hr. v. Hoppé	Director of the Chancellery	2,500	3,000
Baron de Pont	Court Secretary		2,000
Hr. v. Schweiger	Court Secretary	1,500	2,000
Hr. v. Mekarski	Scrivener	1,000	1,200
Hr. v. Stradiot	Scrivener	800	1,000
Hr. v. Dilg	Official	400	800
Hr. Raimond	Official		800
Section for Domestic Affairs			
Hr. v. Hudelist	State and Conference Councillor	10,000	10,000
Hr. v. Perin	Court Councillor	2,500	4,000
Hr. v. Brenner	Court Councillor	2,500	4,000
Hr. v. Lebzeltern	Councillor	1,800	2,500
Baron Bretfeld	Councillor	1,600	2,500
Baron Ottenfels	Court Secretary	1,500	2,000
Hr. v. Kesaer	Court Secretary	1,200	1,600
Hr. Spengler	Scrivener	1,000	1,200
Hr. Casaqui	Scrivener	1,000	1,200
Hr. v. Swietczki	Court Councillor and Director of Chancellery	2,500	4,000
Hr. Obermayer	Expeditor	1,800	2,000
Hr. Augé	Adjunct Expeditor	800	1,000
Hr. de Hoze	Official	800	800
Hr. v. Sieber	Official		800
Hr. v. Kesaer, Joseph	Official		800
Registry			
Hr. Anton v. Kesaer	Councillor and Registrar	2,500	2,500
Hr. Böhm	Registry Adjunct	1,000	1,200
Old Registry			
Hr. v. Lefevre	Court Secretary	3,000	2,000
Hr. Springer	Scrivener	1,000	1,000
Haus-, Hof- und Staatsarchiv [archive of the court as well as the emperor's family]			
Hr. v. Rademacher	Archive Director	5,000	5,000
Hr. Knechtl	Councillor and Privy Archivist	2,000	2,500
Baron Reinhard	Privy Archivist	1,000	1,500
Hr. Delitsch	Official	800	800
Hr. Rosner	Official	700	700

Source: Metternich, Presentation, dated May 19, 1816, HHStA Wien StK Krt. 202, Fol. 96–119.

personnel as soon as the circumstances allow for it."[11] Metternich produced a unique survey in support of his request (Table 14.1). It reveals, like an X-ray, the internal structure of the state's most important authority, how much it had grown in 1816 at the beginning of the era of the new empire, and what the overall costs were. The structure and division of the sections and areas of competence reflected Metternich's rational and efficient approach to leading the Chancellery.

At subsequent annual budget consultations, Metternich would always end up clashing with the Court Chamber and the finance minister, especially beginning in 1826 when Kolowrat, the former Prague burgrave, was appointed to the court and made responsible for the state finances. Kolowrat became Metternich's opponent, and he knew how to form an internal front against the seemingly all-powerful state chancellor. As a result, the monarchy was thrown into a systemic crisis that, in the end, made it the victim of revolution. Metternich's ongoing conflict with Kolowrat is a chapter in Metternich's biography that is often not examined enough.

CONSTRAINED BY EMPEROR FRANZ'S "PERSONAL REGIME"

First Attempts at Reforming the Empire

In 1811 Metternich made a first attempt at reforming the upper echelons of the empire. This was an overly daring plan that took him well beyond his purview; it contradicted the principles of the emperor's "personal regime," and therefore did not make it past the draft stage. Metternich suggested an imperial council and a committee made up of all the state councillors, who at that time were working separately from one another. He wanted "to give the central power more central sense of purpose [*Zentralsinn*]" and to unite the heads of the court offices in one body at the top.[12] He repeatedly pointed to the example of France. What Metternich wanted amounted to a governing ministerial council, with separate areas of responsibility for ministers, headed by a prime minister. But he avoided calling this arrangement by its name. One sentence, nevertheless, must have provoked the emperor: "The monarch deposits a part of his executive power in the hands of a minister, chief of a department, and that minister must therefore be free, very free indeed. . . . Lastly, there lies in the existence of a well-organized council, filled with able men, ready to advise the monarch on every occasion with enlightened and impartial counsel, so high a degree of security for the whole body politic that this feeling will soon become general, and secure to the government strength and repose in equal measure."[13] It was altogether inconceivable to Franz that he might relinquish any power.

Metternich was not yet disheartened. In the autumn of 1817 he presented the emperor with an even more detailed and substantial design. He proposed a federal structure, taking into account the individual nationalities, for the monarchy as a whole, complemented by a further centralization of the administration at the top. This plan, too, was left to gather dust among the emperor's papers; it did not receive "Supreme Approval." Yet again, Metternich was condemned to remain the visionary whom reality—the emperor—refused to follow, not least because Metternich's ideas ran counter to the familial interests of the emperor's dynasty.

The Emperor's Personality

We lack a competent modern biography of Emperor Franz, this important if rather uninventive monarch.[14] It must be acknowledged as a substantial achievement that he was able to hold his large and complex empire together and safely guide it, over a reign of more than forty-two years (1792–1835), from the ancien régime through the Napoleonic wars and into the nineteenth century. As Metternich found out at the start of his career, under Thugut, the emperor was an idiosyncratic, yet easily influenced, character.

It was only with Metternich that the emperor's foreign policies became more purposeful and acquired an internal logic. Metternich defined his special relationship with his ruler in a oft-quoted aphorism: "The emperor always does what I want him to do; but I never want him to do anything else but what he has to do."[15] If the emperor was not, as is sometimes claimed, a mere marionette operated by Metternich's hands, then he must also have known what "he had to do."

It is complicated to explain this, because the emperor was not so much someone following specific ideas and plans. He rather knew what he did not want. But it is possible to draw conclusions from all the things he did not want, as they become apparent in the thousands of "supreme resolutions"—the *Signate*—he appended to the ministerial presentations. We may construct a picture of what he wanted as the mirror image of all these unwanted things. He was filled with an almost pathological fear of any change or risk. We have seen how in August 1813 Metternich could persuade him to take the epoch-making decision of declaring war against Napoleon only by apparently leaving the door open to negotiations at all times. The emperor's character was steadfast, loyal, predictable, and principled, but even with those very few people he was warm toward he still maintained a distance. His caring side showed in his genuinely felt sympathy for Metternich upon the deaths of his children and wives. Metternich, who sometimes had conversations with the emperor almost daily, interpreted his few gestures and dry comments correctly. Metternich was reliable, always kept an appropriate distance, and was open with the emperor, and in this way he gained his master's trust.

Given the emperor's character, Metternich was the best thing that could have happened to him. As we have seen, Metternich was always able to explain complex situations to his scrupulous, insecure, and therefore suspicious ruler by presenting him with the available options and their consequences. This enabled the monarch to make decisions and then carry them out with resolve.

We should not take Emperor's Franz's reserve, and his often monosyllabic responses, to suggest an uninterested, semi-educated, or small-minded dilettante. This is how German nationalist historians tend to present him. There are sides to him that are little known.[16] He was an acute observer of the times, studied nature closely, and was a connoisseur of Italian art. He was possessed of a photographic memory, and he was interested in business and in social and medical institutions. He personally drew sketches of important matters. He was able to digest documents thoroughly and remember them well for future use. Metternich knew all of this. His admiration for his "chief," as he sometimes called him, was genuine, not just a superficial adulation.

EMPEROR FRANZ'S LEGACY: A SYSTEM "HEADED BY A HALF-WIT WHO REPRESENTS THE CROWN"

With the death of Emperor Franz on March 2, 1835, in Vienna, the Habsburg Monarchy faced the worst-case scenario. The monarch had strictly adhered to the normal line of succession, making his firstborn son—Archduke Ferdinand, who was unfit for rule—his successor. In a confidential letter to all embassies of the Habsburg Empire, Metternich officially announced the death of the emperor. The people who revered him honored him as a "father," a title he truly deserved. In order to allay any suspicions, Metternich described the night of February 27–28 in detail. The monarch partly dictated his last will (and subsequently edited it), partly wrote it himself. In a separate letter to his son, the emperor formulated some brief instructions for legislation under the new government. The central passage said: "Disturb nothing in the foundations of the edifice of the State. Govern, and change nothing. . . . Honor the properly acquired rights . . . Maintain harmony in the family, and look upon it as one of the highest blessings."[17] Emperor Franz set out three unambiguous principles for Ferdinand to follow; they defined the future structure of rule:

1. Regarding Archduke Ludwig: "Place complete trust in my brother, Archduke Ludwig, who always assisted me in so many important matters of government with his advice. Take from now on his counsel in important domestic affairs."

2. Regarding Archduke Franz Karl: "Keep the friendliest relations with your brother, and also keep him informed of all business."

3. Regarding Metternich: "Repose in Prince Metternich, my truest servant and friend, that confidence which I have bestowed upon him through the course of so many years. Decide no question relating to public affairs or to persons, without first hearing what he has to say. And I call upon him, in his turn, to act towards you with the same rectitude and devotion which he has always exhibited to myself."[18]

According to the emperor's will, a governmental body was to be created—a state conference—in which a triumvirate took on the role of a regent for the formally appointed Emperor Ferdinand. As Metternich's opinion had to be heard on all questions—whether pertaining to domestic or foreign affairs, or to persons—he took on the role of a prime minister with the authority to set policy guidelines. On the basis of his seniority, Ludwig represented the dynasty as a blood relation from the father's side *(Agnat),* but as the superior over Franz Karl, who was informally involved.

This well-considered construction was designed to help overcome the weakness of the successor to the throne. There was no question that Ferdinand had to be considered a problematic case. He suffered from several physical ailments: epilepsy, rickets, and hydrocephalus. He was, however, not at all the feebleminded ruler the older literature portrays him to be. He spoke five languages, among them Hungarian, played the piano, and dedicated himself to botany.[19] His father had prepared for him to be his successor by, for instance, having him crowned king of Hungary in 1830 at the Diet in Pressburg. The family archive holds moving letters that Ferdinand sent to his sister Marie Louise; they are warmhearted and truly brotherly.[20] During the revolution of 1848, he kept a diary in which he tried to reflect on the events. He also liked to keep diaries during his travels—for instance, in Pressburg, Innsbruck, and Olmütz.[21] Metternich knew him well because he had given him lectures, such as "On Diplomacy" (in 1825), with the crown prince taking notes.[22] We have even more detailed knowledge of Emperor Ferdinand through his principal chamberlain, Count August Ségur-Cabanac, who described him as selfless, dutiful, friendly, and kindhearted, even toward his inferiors. All this, however, did not make him any more fit to govern.[23]

Ferdinand had to formally comment on all governmental acts that required the emperor's supreme resolution. One of his ministers, Metternich or Kolowrat, formulated these for him, and he signed them. He was nevertheless capable of developing a will of his own, as on the question of which among a group of Italian prisoners who had been sentenced for political crimes should be granted amnesty.[24] But he was incapable of governing independently in the

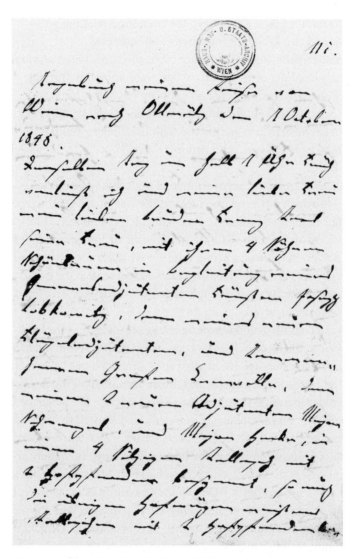

First page of diary, Emperor Ferdinand I, "Tagebuch meiner Reise von
Wien nach Ollmütz den 1 October 1848" [Diary of my journey from
Vienna to Ollmütz on October 1, 1848].

way his father had done. Metternich always treated Ferdinand with the respect
due to someone in his position, but the quality, substance, and volume of his
presentations for the emperor steadily declined. Whereas in the case of Franz
he had covered the whole spectrum of politics, the presentations for Ferdinand
increasingly limited themselves to formulaic summaries of the reports received
from the embassies.[25]

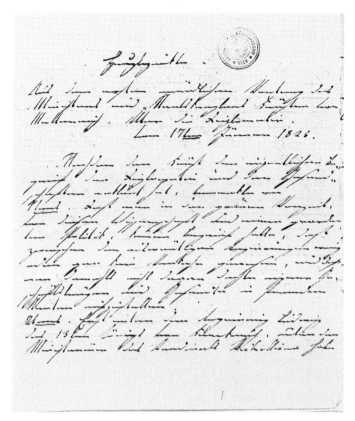

First page of Ferdinand's notes on a lecture by Metternich, titled:
"Hauptpunkte Aus dem ersten mündlichen Vortrag des Ministers und
Staatskanzlers Fürsten von Metternich. Über die Diplomatie. Vom
17ten Jänner 1825" [Main points of the first oral presentation of the
minister and state chancellor Prince Metternich. On Diplomacy.
January 17, 1825].

Ferdinand's adjutant general was Karl Johann Count Clam-Martinitz. He
called himself Metternich's "friend," something only few people could dare to
do. As we shall see, in his thinking and acting this shrewd general was on the
same wavelength as Metternich, and this expressed itself both intellectually and
in their personal dealings with each other. Metternich therefore had a first-class
source of information not only on the emperor but also more generally on the
court, which, following Emperor Franz's death, increasingly distanced itself
from Metternich, and even became hostile toward him.

After Emperor Franz fell seriously ill in 1827, years before the worst-case scenario was to come to pass, Metternich had recommended finding a solution

to the problem of his successor. He felt it was necessary to act preemptively to "create a government machinery with the help of which Your successor to the throne will be called upon to rule."[26] This did not necessarily rule out Ferdinand as the successor; it instead meant creating an institutional framework that would compensate for his potential inability to govern. It is important to emphasize this point, because Metternich is sometimes accused of wanting simply to impose a will on the dying emperor. Franz himself had previously been unable to bring himself to create one. He also had refused to consider his younger son, Archduke Franz Karl (1802–1878), as his successor.

The will did not mention Kolowrat at all. He was deeply hurt, for he thought he had had a particularly intimate relationship with the monarch—many personal notes to him from the emperor seemed to suggest so.[27] He was therefore the first of many to insinuate that the self-seeking, devious Metternich had persuaded an almost completely passive emperor, on his deathbed, to write his will and make him a kind of substitute emperor.

This view overestimates Metternich's influence on the emperor and underestimates the emperor's strong-mindedness. He had the full capacity to act. Although there is a draft of the testament written in Metternich's hand, it deviates so markedly from the final version that it actually confirms that the emperor must, at that point, still have been fully capable of making up his own mind.[28] Metternich only formulated general principles; he did not mention any names (e.g., "He [i.e., the successor, whoever it would be] should trust only tried and tested righteous men"). And unlike Franz's version, his considers the possibility that changes would be suggested ("always examine whether what is suggested to him as an improvement does not threaten this fundamental pillar of the state"). Metternich provided a formula that intentionally left out the name of the person in whom confidence was to be placed: "As the man I recommend to My son as a faithful advisor worthy of his full trust, I name. . . ." He would have had himself in mind, but Archduke Ludwig would have been another candidate for filling this space. Someone needed to perform this role, but Metternich did not necessarily think it should be him. And, as it turned out, the result was very different and far more detailed, involving a state conference of three individuals who advised Ferdinand.

In order to understand the emphasis the will placed on Metternich, it is necessary to keep in mind the emperor's personality and the experiences he had had with Metternich over more than four decades. Ever since their first meeting in Belgium during the war in 1794, the emperor had gradually become familiar with Metternich's political principles, and had judged them to be the right ones. He had learned that Metternich always managed to find a solution, even in times of great crisis, even amid defeat, and that he always had the unity of the monarchy as a whole in mind. He had observed how he was able to hold his own when facing a Napoleon or a Tsar Alexander. He could be sure that Metternich would not seek to change the "foundations of the edifice of the state." He was wrong, however, when he thought that Metternich would not promote the development of the empire through evolutionary change. About that issue, Metternich had too many ideas, and he knew too much about the many social and economic problems facing the empire.

By invoking the idea of loyalty to the dynasty, the emperor revealed that he expected problems in this area. The arrangements for the succession to the throne were indeed highly controversial within the family. As a result, Metternich faced such powerful opposition that the system was from then on administered on an ad hoc basis rather than governed with a plan in mind. Archduchess Sophie, in particular, harbored an abiding grudge against Metternich, and held him responsible for the emperor's will. The effects of this could be felt as late as 1851. On September 24 of that year, Metternich and his wife returned from exile to Vienna. Sophie invited Melanie for a meeting at the Hofburg on October 6. In the course of a long conversation, they also spoke about Metternich's involvement in the succession to the throne. Clearly unaware of what actually happened, Sophie said: "What I accuse your husband of is that he wanted something impossible, namely to lead a monarchy without an emperor and with a half-wit embodying the throne."[29] When asked who should have replaced Ferdinand, Sophie responded that it should have been someone who was born with the qualities that were required for ruling. No doubt she had in mind the emperor's younger son, Archduke Franz Karl, her husband and the father of the later emperor, Franz Joseph I. However, the *Posthumous Papers* document this meeting in line with their overall tendency of protecting the imperial house from criticism, and thus the archduchess's reproach is redacted. Instead, they invent a passage that does not exist in the original diary and that ends by saying that they parted "in the friendliest mood."[30]

The disabilities of the legal successor to the throne were clearly visible. His simple mind could not be hidden in public. Then there were his epileptic fits, which were often misinterpreted by the outside world. He was unable to present himself well in public or to perform representational duties. The best he could do was simply to appear in his full imperial regalia and let the people hail him, because he had a knack for looking gracefully at people that earned him the epithet "Ferdinand the benevolent." But conversations with him were filled with embarrassing moments. The wife of Tsar Nikolaus I, Tsarina Charlotte of Prussia (Alexandra Feodorovna)—the sister of the Prussian king, Friedrich Wilhelm IV—met Ferdinand in 1835 in Teplitz, and afterward noted in her diary: "Good Lord, I had heard a lot about him, about his short, ugly,

Section of a redacted passage from the diary of Princess Melanie relating to
October 6, 1851: ". . . with a half-wit representing the throne."

stunted figure and his large head without any expression but that of dim-
wittedness, but the reality exceeded all descriptions."[31]

CRISIS INSTEAD OF REFORM: METTERNICH VERSUS KOLOWRAT

*Metternich's Reforms of the State Conference (October 31, 1836): A
"Prime Minister"?*

There can be no doubt that, after the emperor's death, Metternich sought—
on the basis of the emperor's will—to use his position at the state conference
in order to reform the monarchy and take control of the internal administration. In the autumn of 1836, he developed a plan for his reforms. Srbik's account of these plans for redesigning the government draws on the sources in
Vienna, and even those in Plaß, in unusual depth, and he reaches a very positive image of Metternich that contrasts starkly with the one he previously had
painted on the basis of a rich array of various published memoirs, attesting to
the "important statesmanlike substance," clarity, and rationality of the reforms.[32] Metternich does not appear here as the superficial, unimaginative,
doctrinaire character that Srbik describes elsewhere.

Metternich wanted to reconstruct the system under which the heads of court
offices communicated with top government officials through uncoordinated
written submissions. In the case of competing projects, this system always led
to "intrigues," as Metternich put it. These he wanted to eradicate. There were

special circumstances that confirmed him in his intentions.[33] Kolowrat increasingly complained about health problems that were hindering him in his work, and in September 1836 he decided to retreat to his Bohemian estates for six months. On this occasion, as on many others, Metternich noticed how governmental processes stagnated. For several months, the most important man when it came to finance, censorship, police, and internal affairs could do only limited work, or sometimes could not work at all, and it was impossible to predict when normal conditions would resume. Metternich was looking for a solution that would take pressure off Kolowrat and at the same time introduce more rational and efficient processes at the top. He was not seeking to sideline or outmaneuver his colleague. Kolowrat, for his part, explicitly declared that he did not want to be involved in reform and that "given the circumstances" of how the work was distributed at the state conference, was happy to leave everything to the state chancellor and Archduke Ludwig.

On September 30, 1836, Metternich presented a memorandum in which he explained his plans for reform.[34] He then called two conferences to discuss it. On October 6 and October 28, the conference ministers, section heads, and Metternich gathered for meetings, chaired by Archduke Ludwig. Metternich opened proceedings with a survey that took in the history of how the administration had been organized at the top since Kaunitz. Metternich's model, with some minor modifications, was welcomed by all and passed into law with a "personal resolution" from Emperor Ferdinand on October 31, 1836.

The reform aimed at creating a strict separation of administration and government, and it introduced a central body for each. The governmental body was to be the *State Conference*. It would have to make decisions in response to requests from ministers and the presidents of court chancelleries, and whenever a dispute arose between different court offices. The major innovation was that Metternich would be installed as the "chief of the State Conference" and that its members would all be ministers or civil service administrators (section heads). Careful examination of the plans reveals that no members of the royal family are mentioned. The governmental body would therefore be a pure civil service institution, independent of dynastic influence and interests. The members of the imperial household were to be relegated to the second tier, so to speak; they were, however, happy with that. The construction would have given Metternich influence in *all* political questions, whether domestic or international; he would have had to have been consulted on all of them. At the State Conference, he would have had the final say, much as Emperor Franz had signed off on all proposals.

Metternich had a very good justification for having all matters come together in one person in this way. Before Franz's death, that person had been the monarch himself. Metternich was not driven by personal ambition; rather, he saw this construction as necessary because of the peculiarity of the Habsburg Monarchy, which set it apart from other European states, especially from the French "centralization system," as he called it. This peculiarity was the Habsburg Monarchy's "composite nature, made up of elements that differ with regard to language, customs, Constitutions, and historical origins." Unity in such an empire could emerge only through "the confluence of these parts in the person of the regent."[35]

Because Emperor Franz's will did not mention Kolowrat, Metternich was in the superior position. After Kolowrat protested, however, the triumvirate of Metternich, Ludwig, and Franz Karl had originally agreed to accept him as a fourth member of the executive body. Metternich's reform proposals went back on this decision. This was not a plot against Kolowrat; instead, Metternich thought he was accommodating Kolowrat's wishes—Kolowrat had, after all, declared himself to be only partially able to work.

The State Conference was complemented by a separate *State Council* in charge of administration. This council was to be made up of the state and conference ministers and their section heads, among them Kolowrat, who thus did not have to attend the regular meetings of the State Conference. Metternich was also the president of the council, and so, had Kolowrat been a part of the council, he would have been his subordinate in two different capacities—in his role at conference and at council. In contrast to the executive State Conference, which had the authority to set guidelines, the State Council was meant to have only advisory powers. In sum, these reforms would have seen Metternich outmaneuver his opponents in the domestic context and deprive of power a troublesome opponent, an opponent who had consistently resisted his demands for such things as more money for the army or economic sacrifices in the interests of liberal economic development.

After Emperor Ferdinand had formally approved the proposals, Metternich even took the step of making the planned reorganization, and his new position in government, public knowledge in order to further consolidate the resolution. The news was officially published across the German Confederation: "The Austrian Monarchy exists under conditions that make it difficult to distinguish between domestic and foreign politics. It is necessary for a master to direct the whole machinery in accordance with the council of the monarch, and Prince Metternich has proved at all times that he, and no one else, possesses the true skills of such a master."[36]

The opposition between the two "alpha males" seemed to come to a head in the form of a conflict over finances: Kolowrat wanted to make savings in order to eliminate the deficit in the state budget. For this to happen, spending on the army would have to be reduced. The year of the July Revolution, 1830, was the first year in which he had achieved a balanced budget, albeit on the basis of some imaginative accounting.[37] The emperor was ecstatic, and Kolowrat rose in his estimation accordingly. But military interventions and troop movements were expensive, and reducing military expenditure at a time of international crisis would have significantly weakened Metternich's influence in Europe. Although Metternich was not inclined toward war, he needed Austria to have military strength if it was to be a major player in the Concert of the main powers.

Kolowrat's Minor Coup (December 12, 1836): Metternich's Disempowerment

When Kolowrat saw the plans for the new political order, he immediately recognized that for him they meant a demotion. His change of mind is nevertheless difficult to understand. He quickly returned to Vienna. What happened next may be regarded as a minor coup. The interior and finance minister used all the means at his disposal to destroy the core of the administrative reforms, which had been agreed upon in the legally correct form. He did not shy away from indulging in defamation, and an unprecedented battle of wills ensued. Crucial for a proper understanding of the shifts in the distribution of political power is the fact that Kolowrat succeeded in turning Archduke Johann and, through him, a large part of the imperial family against Metternich.

Archduke Johann initiated the series of events. Their background has been meticulously laid out by Srbik. Because of his use of quotations from Johann's diaries, some of which—especially the parts covering the years around 1836—were destroyed during the Second World War, his account has status of a genuine source. Without Srbik's work, we would be unable to reconstruct the background dynamic of the conflict between Metternich and Kolowrat. For various reasons, it is important to understand the front that was coalescing against Metternich: it explains the subsequent paralysis of the system and shows Metternich's role in a new light. Kolowrat's threat of resignation once again did its work—he knew that it would have been considered a scandal by the public and would have made the crisis public.

Kolowrat provided Johann with one-sided information.[38] A situation emerged that was to be repeated many times under the "Ferdinand system" and explains why the monarchy became paralyzed. Kolowrat succeeded in gaining the trust of the emperor's brother, Archduke Johann, who had returned to Styria from the exile into which Metternich had sent him. Kolowrat played a duplicitous game, abusing the archduke's trust in order to traduce Metternich. Johann was all too eager to believe the opinions Kolowrat fed him and pass them on. Johann, of course, knew Metternich as the man who had undermined his unquestionably noble intentions in 1813 by sidelining him. Johann accused Metternich of being supported by the "Rothschild Jewish factions."[39] In everything he did, Kolowrat systematically presented Metternich as reactionary and himself as liberal.

Metternich's plan to lift the prohibition on the Jesuit order, for instance, was motivated by his wish to establish an agreement with the Catholic Church. It was the result, not of a piousness suddenly brought on by old age, but instead of a recognition that unity between throne and altar conduced to domestic peace. He wanted to keep the monarchy free from the kinds of cultural-political battles Friedrich Wilhelm III would soon (in 1837) be provoking in Prussia by taking a side in the "dispute over mixed marriages"—that is, interfaith marriages—in opposition to the bishops. Kolowrat denounced Metternich—who had a generally liberal worldview and was rather indifferent when it came to matters of faith—as a supporter of the clergy with ultramontane convictions. Whenever Metternich suggested reforms, as in the 1840s in connection with Hungary, regarding questions of free trade or infrastructural developments, Kolowrat blocked them using his authority over domestic policies, and then accused Metternich of being inflexible in his policies. He stoked resentment against Metternich in Johann and among the somewhat intellectually limited and mostly indecisive archdukes.

In this way he built a majority against Metternich. Johann became the vociferous spokesperson for the imperial family. He fought against the "ministerial government"—against Metternich's supreme governance of the state—and against the male members of the imperial family being pushed aside.[40] In his diary he wrote: "We do not want a major domus"—*major domus* being the term used for the chief civil servant in the Merovingian Empire. In his eyes, the idea that Metternich, rather than a member of the imperial family, was the head of the State Conference was an insult to the honor of the dynasty. Srbik traces the networks within which Johann moved. He consulted with the archdukes Ludwig and Franz Karl, with the latter's wife, Sophie, with the emperor's mother, with Clam-Martinitz, and finally—as the climax, as it were—with the state chancellor.

Johann reprimanded him for the "colossal blunder of wanting to become president, so to speak." Metternich, he said, "wanted to bring back the time of the Merovingians and be like Pipin." He put Metternich under so much pressure that he gave in and, despite being indignant at the accusations, declared his willingness to rewrite the reform plans in accordance with Kolowrat's wishes. Kolowrat thus succeeded in foiling the plan for a major internal reorganization of the top-level administration—a plan that was actually legally binding, having been signed off on by Archduke Ludwig, as the head of the

State Conference, and by Emperor Ferdinand. Feeling the pressure from Kolowrat and the court, Ludwig blinked and withdrew his signature.

In place of Metternich's reform there was the revision of December 12, 1836. On that day, Ferdinand passed an "imperial resolution" that Kolowrat had dictated to him. It ordered Archduke Ludwig to redesign the State Conference in line with Emperor Ferdinand's words, which had the force of law ("As it is my will . . ."). This constituted a new statute.[41] The conference was henceforth to be chaired by the emperor himself. The archdukes Ludwig and Karl Franz were made members of the State Conference again, alongside Metternich and Kolowrat. State and conference ministers, section heads, state councillors, and the presidents of court offices could be invited to join it on a case-by-case basis.

This statute was accompanied by another "imperial resolution," of the same day, that was concerned especially with Kolowrat. This note was the real scandal—the minor coup.[42] On Metternich's plan, Metternich would have been the chair of both bodies and he would have been consulted on all matters—domestic as well as foreign. Now it was stipulated that all matters pertaining to finance, domestic policies, and the secret state police [*Hohe Polizei*] would be shown only to Kolowrat, who would then decide whether they needed to be discussed at the State Conference, in which case they would be handed directly to the chair, Archduke Ludwig—without being seen by Metternich. Kolowrat now had the opportunity to give his opinion and decide on all matters; Metternich's influence was limited to foreign affairs. Kolowrat had betrayed the emperor's last will.

It makes little sense to speak of a "Metternich system" before December 1836, but to speak of one after would simply amount to a caricature of reality. Metternich's intended reforms had involved plans to move away from written communication and to introduce weekly meetings. He wanted immediate communication within a single body, so as to speed up decision making and to make unilateral actions, rivalry, and secretive operations impossible. Now there was to be no talk of regular conferences or oral consultations; what mattered was whatever the erratic Kolowrat judged mattered. No one knew when he would leave for Bohemia again and stop his work. Under the new design, Kolowrat could delay any item, or even paralyze the State Conference at will. That was the key factor in the indisputable paralysis of Habsburg government from then on. The deeper reason for this stagnation we still have to identify.

Metternich soon felt the consequences of all this. He was no longer given any documents on domestic questions, and he complained about this to Kolowrat. Kolowrat brushed off his complaints, dryly responding that he was no longer the president of the State Conference and had himself agreed to entrust Archduke Ludwig with that function. He would therefore now send all papers to the latter, and the president then had to decide which of them the conference would discuss.

Because it had already been publicly announced that Metternich would preside over the State Conference, Kolowrat's coup was a snub and humiliation for Metternich, and this was noted at the courts of Europe. In France, for instance, it was reported that Kolowrat's return to the cabinet in Vienna was bought at the price of his increased influence and elevation in status in comparison to Metternich.[43] The conflict between the two ministers is usually treated as an internal power struggle, but this is far too narrow a view. Within Europe, the shift in the distribution of power that Kolowrat had achieved with his coup was interpreted as an epochal shift in Austrian politics. The *Journal du Commerce* of Paris wrote: "In these days, all the world can see that the energy and activity of Mr. Metternich is paralyzed [*étaient paralysées*]. Rumors are spreading that he might even hand over his position to Prince [*sic*] Kolowrat."[44] At the end of December, these rumors stopped; nevertheless, the impression remained that Metternich's position had been fundamentally weakened.[45] The paper also reported, though, that Metternich was extremely irritated about the fact that secrets from the innermost circles of the cabinet had been made public, and spoke of a Slavonic "parti Kollowrat." The events were also interpreted in the context of Austria moving closer to (Kolowrat) or further away from (Metternich) Russia, which gave the dispute an international dimension.

The most intelligent mind of the Habsburg ruling elite on matters of commerce and trade, Karl Friedrich von Kübeck, quickly understood what the coup had achieved for Kolowrat. Kübeck, who later became the president of the court chamber, wrote of Kolowrat: "The effect is that he is the supreme head of the State Council, master over the power of money and all appointments and the fate of all civil servants (through the police), master of the camarilla and due to this position the decisive voice at the State Conference."[46] Clam-Martinitz even spoke of an "absolutist ministerial cabinet."[47] Kübeck's concise summary of Kolowrat's power in domestic affairs was no exaggeration.

The claims about Metternich's all-powerfulness overlook the fact that, after his appointment in 1826, Kolowrat was responsible for police, censorship, the economy, and finances (including the state budget), and that he also had a say whenever posts had to be filled—his voice was heard on all matters that involved money. An additional office boy to carry files between the various buildings for Metternich had to be justified just as much as did an additional accommodation allowance for Gentz so that he could afford to reside in expensive Vienna.

Those who complain about censorship in the Habsburg Monarchy—at least after 1826—are wrong to pick on Metternich: Kolowrat and Sedlnitzky were chiefly responsible. Franz Grillparzer, who was personally affected by censorship, noticed the difference. In 1848 he wrote: "Prince Metternich, pleasant and witty by character, but in the first phase of his life careless, and all his life determined by his desires (in the better sense of the word), was the most decided critic of those suffocating measures of his masters during the reign of Emperor Franz. He joked with those he trusted about the small-mindedness of the Austrian state, and his enthusiasm for Lord Byron and similar spirits clearly showed how much all humiliations of human nature were alien to his original nature."[48]

Kübeck's statement gives us more insight into what Kolowrat's unassailable position rested on: the influence of the Bohemian nobility as a lobby that infiltrated the whole monarchy, and the power of the imperial dynasty.

LOBBYISM, THE POWER POLITICS OF THE IMPERIAL FAMILY, THE ESTATES

Bohemian Lobbyism Blocks the System

It is altogether misguided to reduce the domestic crisis of 1836 to a merely personal conflict between two men. The role of lobbying in the economic and social history of the pre-1848 era in the Habsburg Empire has not been researched enough. There were obviously very significant material interests being promoted, as is already clear from our look at the time of Emperor Franz's rule. At the time when Prussia was pursuing the idea of a free trade area through the German Customs Union—before 1833—Metternich was observing, with great concern, that the long-term alignment of tariffs would, indeed, produce a free trade zone. We already touched upon the inhibitive role played in this context by the Bohemian large-scale landowners.[49]

Kolowrat openly and unscrupulously used his ministry to support Bohemian interests.[50] As the minister responsible for new appointments, he granted his fellow Bohemians preferential treatment when new posts had to be filled in the monarchy (unless they were in Hungary and Italy). That was so well known that people joked about it. An applicant, it was said, did not need to argue for his position; it was enough for him to say: "I am Bohemian and my name is Wenzel."[51] Kolowrat had also developed a system for smuggling Bohemian aristocrats into the civil service. They were first appointed without salary (as so-called supernumeraries)—they could always support themselves independently in these first years. During that time, they were gradually promoted until, after three or four years, they had reached the rank of a district commissioner, at which point they received regular salaries. By contrast, a non-aristocratic intern usually still remained an intern after twelve or sixteen years. Within only a few years, Kolowrat had also succeeded in increasing the influence of the aristocracy on the legislature. In 1843 his successor in Prague, High Burgrave Count Carl Chotek, was forced out of his position in disgrace because he was too interested in enforcing in Bohemia the legal regulations coming from Vienna.

Kolowrat's Bohemian peers must have been shocked when they learned that he intended to leave the civil service. Metternich's close confidant, Count Clam-Martinitz, predicted "that the party which needs his firm [the Ministry] for their plans and his power for their interests will want him back. This party has expressed its dismay in the first days."[52] This group encouraged their man in Vienna to become "an unrestricted directorial minister for domestic affairs and finances." "The party" had already announced Kolowrat's return, and with this return, Clam-Martinitz prophesied, the "patronage regarding posts, salaries, and emoluments"—in other words, nepotism—would also return. Metternich expressed the same suspicion personally to Archduke Ludwig. He asked him how it was possible that Kolowrat could have recently declared the civil service "insufferable," yet now apparently wanted to return to it. This contradiction, Metternich said, was easily explained: "First, it was Kolowrat who spoke, now others are speaking through him who think their power can only be maintained cloaked in fog; and they are right about that."[53]

Clam-Martinitz urged Metternich to prevent his opponent from returning or else to organize government business so as to reduce his influence.[54] He also had to watch out for Kolowrat's allies in the central administration in Vienna—"Eichhof's liberal faction." With this he referred to the *éminence grise* who was the president of the Court Chamber, Joseph Eichhof; the use of the term "liberal" was an ironic comment on the fact that Eichhof had used his position for risky speculations on the stock market, investing in shares in the Milan–Venice railway, even implicating Archduke Franz Karl in his dealings.[55]

Kolowrat's lobbying on behalf of Bohemia must be seen within an even broader context. Metternich and Clam-Martinitz thought that the constant complaints about the financial distress of the state, which supposedly made spending cuts compulsory, were in part ideological, a pretext for making certain things impossible from the outset. Emperor Franz had a long-term aim of carrying out economic and financial reforms: more precisely, to create new foundations on which the land tax—the main source of income for the state—could be calculated more accurately. To that end, he had begun a program in 1817 under the title "Franzian Land Registry" [*Franziszeisches Kataster*]. Helmut

Rumpler was the first to draw attention to this important initiative and to its consequences.[56] The emperor sent civil servants to all parts of the monarchy in order to collect statistical, economic, geographical, and demographic information. This information was to be used for the creation of a land registry. It is not hard to see why this idea was highly unpopular with the owners of large estates. The large-scale aristocratic landowners expected—correctly—that the results would show that they were paying far too little in tax. They tried to sabotage the information-gathering process using every trick in the book—they were even prepared to deploy, if necessary, armed hunters to chase the civil servants away.

His alliance with these interests meant that Kolowrat used his position as the head of the internal administration to make sure that all of Metternich's ideas, after Franz's death, for progressive changes to the monarchy would fail. It was no accident that the *Hanauer Zeitung* hoped that Metternich's original reform plans would have stimulated Austria's commerce and trade with the other federal states.

Eichhof's Downfall: A New Start with Kübeck as President of the Court Chamber

Metternich did not yet admit defeat. He was encouraged by Emperor Ferdinand's adjutant general, Clam-Martinitz. Clam-Martinitz suggested to Metternich a strategy for beating Kolowrat: namely, by hounding the narrow-minded president of the court chamber, Eichhof, out of office. Eichhof was a heavyweight in the financial administration because he was responsible for the annual budgets. This conversation between Metternich and Clam-Martinitz was strictly confidential and top secret. Thanks to a lucky coincidence, however, we know what it was about. Clam-Martinitz had prepared a written account of the situation for Metternich, which he read out at their meeting. Afterward he had wanted to destroy the text because "it probably belongs to the category of confessions whose main points remain lively enough in the imagination to make the not altogether risk-free preservation of their written traces obsolete."[57] Metternich considered what he heard to be important enough to ask Clam-Martinitz for a fair copy. Clam-Martinitz trusted him unreservedly—he spoke of "our important matters."

In the posthumous papers, Metternich's son Richard was only prepared to publish an abridged version of the text, which did not mention the author; the critical remarks on Archduke Ludwig were omitted.[58] That version does not convey that the overall aim was to topple Eichhof. Their secret conspiracy was absolutely necessary; both thought that their task was the "most difficult and

complicated." Metternich appreciated outspoken friends who told him everything, and Clam-Martinitz was one of only a few of them. Clam-Martinitz told
him that "daily the divergence and heterogeneity between the views and tendencies of the two most senior ministers [was becoming] more and more an
open secret." The consequences, in Clam's view, were a lack of direction; delays, because the government's intentions were not clear; a lack of determination; uncertainty in the higher state offices; and information being held back
or incomplete. At the highest level of the state's administration, core questions
regarding finances and appointments were left unresolved. The result was an
absolutism that "rested not on a decisive preponderance of intelligence and
will-power but on cleverness and the spirit of intrigue." The small-minded vani-
ties and selfish plans of schemers and egoists won the day. It would not have
come to this, Clam-Martinitz thought, if Archduke Ludwig—the head of the
State Conference—had not been deceived about Kolowrat and did not have
exaggerated ideas about the latter's intellectual abilities: Ludwig did not recognize Kolowrat's "moral worthlessness as a statesman." Clam-Martinitz also
included his judgment of Metternich: he wanted "to reform the ills" of the
empire; he did not lack perseverance or willpower, but he was not prepared to
use the means employed by Kolowrat—duplicity, lies, or shameless defamation. Kolowrat called Metternich's views on church, state, and legislation timid,
retrograde, and Jesuitical. According to him, Metternich sacrificed his own
country for other countries, and he sacrificed finances for the state Chancellery. He who was prepared to use whatever means he had at his disposal, Clam-
Martinitz wrote, would win out. It would be impossible to achieve anything as
long as the power of Metternich's opponent, who shied away from all formal
organization and procedures ensuring accountability, had not been undermined. It was necessary to demonstrate to Archduke Ludwig Eichhof's lack of
moral worth, for it was Eichhof who served as "a head and base for the whole
Kolowrat faction." It was also necessary to "prove the bad use or abuse of
power." Without Eichhof, Kolowrat would lack support; he would be helpless.
In order to undermine Eichhof, they had to look into how he conducted his
business, even at the risk of toppling Kolowrat.

The conversation between Metternich and Clam-Martinitz took place in
January 1838. Over the following year, Melanie watched her husband become
increasingly desperate and dispirited, and in her diary she noted: "Lethargy,
apathy, and carelessness are getting worse every day. The conferences are abhorred because everyone knows that after them the proposals of my husband
must be accepted, which Count Kolowrat dislikes. Thus, our beautiful monarchy disintegrates into rubble, that is, it begins to molder, because there are
only destructive elements in it, and none of preservation."[59] With Clam's death
on January 29, 1840, Metternich lost his strongest ally at the court. At that time

he was in such poor health that Melanie began to expect the worst: "He feels too old to fight; he does not think he has enough strength left to continue the battle, and does not know how to lead the petty war that would be needed."[60]

Ultimately Metternich succeeded in pushing Eichhof out and installing Kübeck. Metternich then again attempted to bring the Habsburg Monarchy closer to the Customs Union. It was Metternich—the same Metternich Kolowrat accused of not understanding economics—who, toward the end of 1841, developed an impressive economic program that highlighted Austria's commercial strengths and weaknesses. A program for domestic development, he said, might make Austria more attractive to the Customs Union, "if, that is, we are able to organize a system of internal connections which offers shorter and more convenient lines of communication with Italy to the states of the Customs Union."[61] The Rhine crisis of 1839–1840 stirred up patriotic emotions in all of Germany. Metternich wanted to exploit this moment; it seemed to him the last opportunity to foster "the development of German trade and thus provide a decisive impulse for the future trade of Germany as well as Austria." This opportunity, he thought, was not to be wasted. He also thought it essential to link up the railway systems. And he repeated something he had said in 1833: he wanted to prevent anything that might make "Austria look excluded and treated as a foreign country." On November 17, 1841, a secret ministerial conference took place. Metternich encountered unwavering resistance, and his initiative came to nothing—or, more precisely, it resulted in the establishment of a commission to produce a survey of Austria's commercial situation. That meant, in effect, indefinite postponement.[62]

Metternich's failure teaches us several things: When looking at Germany, he adopted a national perspective; he was prepared to reform the confederation, something that was also desired by other German states in the 1840s; he thought intensely about economic questions and had an expert knowledge in questions concerning the economy, trade, and customs; and again, foreign and domestic policies were inextricably linked. Because the two spheres were divided at the state conference, he depended on Kolowrat's approval of his domestic policy. And Kolowrat again showed how the system could grind to a halt, in this instance because he and his Bohemian peers had no interest in adopting free trade policies. Metternich told Kübeck how seriously he took these matters, and he urged him to be assertive: "These Bohemian stories are symptoms and must be quashed. The means for that is to make people *walk away*. Eichhof was a bad wound; today he is no more than scab. He will fall off! Stamp your foot down and we shall achieve the best possible result."[63]

In January 1850, while in exile in Brussels, Metternich told a confidant of many years, Count Franz von Hartig, that he had recommended fundamental reforms of the empire to the emperor as early as 1816. These early plans for reform would have served the purpose of, among other things, dealing with the "unrest [*Unfrieden*] in the social field." The emperor had simply filed the proposal away, and ten years later, when faced with his life-threatening illness, he confessed to Metternich that his inaction had been "a sin." In 1835 the emperor reproached his earlier self: "Today, deliberate lying and ignorance burden me with those things I was not even able to set in motion."[64]

The good, however, did not happen; the emperor did not prepare the way for reforms. The diplomat Alexander von Hübner, who was present during Metternich's final hours, reported conversations in which Metternich retrospectively evaluated his position within the political system after the death of Emperor Franz in 1835. "His initiatives failed due to the resistance coming from a powerful clique which held the strings of the administration in its hands. Their head was seen as a champion of liberal ideas, while he was actually nothing but the head, guided by others, of an ossified bureaucracy. Prince Metternich, still apparently powerful, felt, and actually was, paralyzed."[65] Indeed, Metternich went even further, judging that the rebellion of 1848 could have been avoided had it not been for this political paralysis—or, to put it differently, the paralysis abetted the revolution by frustrating Metternich's reform plans. His failure on the matter of the Customs Union is a particularly convincing piece of evidence for this view.

Imperial Power Politics: The Empire as the Patrimony of the Habsburg Family

Kolowrat would never have had as much power as he did if the majority of the imperial family had not backed him. In the background, interwoven dynastic interests were exerting their influence, and in the absence of the strong Emperor Franz, that influence had grown. Metternich now had to resist more influential opponents—including most of the archdukes—without the backing of the emperor. In 1835, five of the emperor's brothers were still alive: Carl, Joseph, Rainer, Ludwig, and Johann. Next to them stood the emperor's sons: the successor to the throne, Ferdinand, ruled until 1848, and then abdicated when the emperor's nephew, Franz Joseph, came of age, and Archduke Franz Karl, who could have laid claim to the throne in 1848 but renounced his claim in favor of his son, Franz Joseph. Franz Joseph was therefore the great hope for the future, and he came of age in 1848. His mother, Archduchess Sophie, remained in contact with Metternich over all those years—years during which almost all of the archdukes were opposed to him. She also entrusted him with the education of the young prince, who as an adolescent received daily lessons in politics from Metternich.

When political power has been wielded by the same hands over decades, it is not surprising for there to be feelings of hurt, sensitivity, and even enmities so hostile as to make understanding or civil relations impossible. *Archduke Carl*, who won the battle of Aspern and was the president of the court's war council, was also the first one to have inflicted a defeat on Napoleon. He was an exceptional military talent and an internationally acknowledged figure. But Metternich refused to accommodate his wish to be supreme commander, generalissimo over the military of the Habsburg Monarchy as a whole. That would have been an extraordinary move that would have affected the overall distribution of power within the monarchy. Metternich thwarted Carl's plans and in the process made himself an enemy (until Carl's death in 1847), because he hoped to be able to use the weakness of the system after the emperor's death to his own advantage. Metternich created another grievance when he prevented the marriage of one of Carl's daughters to the French crown prince, the son of Louis Philippe.

We have already mentioned Archduke Johann's deep-seated reservations about Metternich. Emperor Franz's brother *Archduke Ludwig*, who received special mention in Franz's will and presided over the state conference, was indecisive, had no particular talent for politics, and was therefore easily influenced—a fact on which the overall weakness of the system was based. He also lacked the formal sovereignty that was invested in Ferdinand, who was susceptible to all sorts of subtle cajolery. *Archduke Joseph*, the emperor's representative in Hungary (the so-called Palatin), always maintained good relations with Metternich. This had something to do with Metternich's wife, Melanie, whom Metternich had married in 1831. She was born Countess Zichy, and Metternich thus married into one of Hungary's most important families from the high nobility. *Archduke Rainer* was delegate to the Kingdom of Lombardy-Venetia as viceroy, but played only a very minor role in Milanese politics. Franz Karl, finally, was important because he was the father of the future emperor, but he had no political profile and was easily influenced despite being a member of the state conference. The emperor's widow, *Karoline Auguste*, was also part of the anti-Metternich opposition.

At this point one might have the impression that historical analysis has completely given way to the reporting of merely personal jealousies and court intrigue. But the dynastic clan was at the center of the system, and it contributed to its dysfunctionality. Politics rarely pursued the interests of the overall state anymore, revealing the weakness of a system whose roots reached back to the times of Emperor Franz. Recall how the case of Marie Louise revealed that Franz also considered the empire the patrimony of the dynastic family. But amid the power vacuum that followed his death, the preponderance of the power of the dynasty over the well-being of the state was revealed dramatically. To put it bluntly, the fate of the Habsburg Monarchy in the nineteenth century was determined by the fertility of two emperors: Emperor Leopold II, who produced sixteen children, including twelve sons, of whom nine were archdukes. Once they were old enough, they all took up positions within the monarchy: Ferdinand III (Grand Duke of Tuscany, died 1824), Carl (president of the court's war council, died 1847), Joseph ("Palatin" of Hungary, died 1847), Anton (*Hoch- und Deutschmeister*, Grandmaster of the German Order in Austria, died 1835), Johann (imperial regent 1848–1849, died 1859), Rainer (viceroy of Lombardy-Venetia, died 1853), Ludwig (head of the state conference until 1848, died 1864), and Rudolf (cardinal and princely archbishop of Olmütz, died 1831). The son of Leopold II, Emperor Franz II (from 1806: Franz I), had thirteen children, among them four sons. Only the successor to the throne, Ferdinand and Archduke Franz Karl, however, survived. Franz Karl was a member of the state conference until 1848 and died in 1878.

This system treated the empire as a large ancestral estate and used the state to provide for the members of the dynasty. The empire served the purpose of a gigantic family entail. Given this fact, any attempt at rational integration or the introduction of federal principles would clearly run up against the self-interest of the numerous members of the imperial dynasty. Metternich had already failed to overcome this obstacle in 1817. Any ideas of a representational system or more rights for the individual nationalities would have been considered a disturbance to this status quo. This is why there was no impetus for reform from the top of the monarchy, despite the fact that Metternich had already urged Emperor Franz to make changes. And unlike Prussia or Bavaria, the bureaucracy did not develop into a motor of modernization after the dynastic leadership had failed in its task. This was prevented by the "Ferdinand system."[66]

Political Participation, Constitutions, the Estates in the Run-Up to Revolution

The prospect of revolution was already casting its shadow, and in some German states in 1830 there were again calls for parliamentary representatives elected by the "people" to supplement the Federal Assembly. Metternich took note of all this. He had always insisted that he was not an absolutist; he took seriously the existence of the provincial estates of the Habsburg Monarchy. They also formed part of the question of how to organize power. As former parts of the Holy Roman Empire, estates were elements of the political cosmos in which Metternich too had his own fixed place: the College of Imperial Counts. In his archive he kept the imperial register that had been established and maintained by the Imperial Chamber Court. It listed all imperial estates falling under the empire's legitimate sphere of interest, for the purpose of collecting the *Zieler*, the imperial tax in support of the Imperial Chamber Court.[67] Even after the demise of the Holy Roman Empire, Metternich retained the political right to rule over his estates and remained a regular member of the Bohemian estates. He felt committed to them and regularly received the protocols from the sittings of the provincial diet.

In October 1847, he pleaded for the establishment of a commission to deal with matters arising from the provincial diets. He once more convinced himself that the Habsburg Monarchy needed the representation of the estates, and he was decidedly against any form of absolutism, including the form of "neo-absolutism" pursued by the minister of the interior, Alexander Bach, from 1852 onward. (Bach was ennobled in 1854 and became von Bach.) But for Metternich the kind of representation that was needed depended on the individual country. In Austria's case, the decisive point for him was its character as "an aggregate of parts with representation of the estates."[68]

In England, France, Bavaria, and Baden, the body of the estates covered the whole state. In Austria, Prussia, Sweden (including Norway), Denmark (including Jutland and Holstein), and the Netherlands (including Luxembourg), "the bodies of the estate only represent parts of the whole, while the governments comprise the whole." For Austria, the unity of the empire rested on contracts that made the monarch the center of the overall edifice. But Metternich saw this as peculiar to the Habsburg Monarchy, and something that did not exclude the possibility of different solutions for other states.

Particularly interesting in this connection are the revealing statements Metternich made about matters of political principle during conversations with intelligent foreigners. On those occasions, he proved that the horizons of his political thought were far broader than the day-to-day business of imperial politics. In June 1836, for instance, in a conversation with the American George Ticknor, from Boston, he made some fundamental statements about political systems and denied being "a great absolutist."[69] He said that he did not like democracy because it was always "a dissolving, decomposing principle; it tends to separate men, it loosens society. This does not suit my character. I am by character and habit constructive [Je suis par caractère et par habitude constructeur]."[70] These remarks hinted at the fact that democracy leads to competition and the formation of antagonistic factions.

This is why monarchy, he said, "is the only government fitted to my mind. . . . . Monarchy alone tends to bring men together, to unite them into compact and effective masses; to render them capable, by their combined efforts, of the highest degrees of culture and civilization."[71] This makes monarchical rule the functional countermodel to the nation-state. We may conclude that, in his view, while a monarchy also developed a potential for integration, a nation-state developed a significantly more powerful potential because it tended toward homogeneity.

The American countered by saying that in a republic, individuals are bound to act much more on the basis of their own intelligence and responsibility, whereas in monarchies everything is done for them. Metternich's response makes clear his context-specific approach to these sorts of judgments. He was aware that the United States had been able to make such significant progress in so short a time only because of their democratic system. Democracy, he said, "separates men, creates rivalries of all kinds, and carries them forward very fast by competition among themselves." Americans, compared to the French "or our old Austria,—*notre vieille Autriche,* as he constantly called it," had "more marked and characteristic individualities." They were "more curious, too, more distinct, more interesting—even, perhaps, more efficient—as individuals; but they will not constitute so efficient a mass, nor one so likely to make permanent progress." For Ticknor, Metternich continued, democracy was "a reality—*une vérité*—in America. In Europe it is a falsehood, and I hate all falsehood,—*En Europe c'est un mensonge.*" Metternich had always been "of the opinion expressed by Tocqueville, that democracy, so far from being the oldest and simplest form of government, as has been so often said, is the latest invented form of all, and the most complicated." It seemed to Metternich that in America democracy was a permanent tour de force [*un tour de force perpétuel*], and he told Ticknor: "You are, therefore, often in dangerous positions." Ticknor suggested to him that a young Constitution might easily brush off ills that would destroy an older one, to which Metternich responded: "True, true, . . . you will go on much further in democracy; you will become much more democratic. I do not know where it will end, nor how it will end; but it cannot end in a quiet, ripe old age."[72] If he were an American, he would be "of that old party of which Washington was originally the head. It was a sort of conservative party, and I should be conservative almost everywhere, certainly in England and America."[73]

France appeared to Metternich "like a man who has just passed thoroughly through a severe disease. He is not so likely to take it [i.e., a return of the illness] as if he had never had it." He called Louis Philippe the "ablest statesman they have had for a great while," but France was in "such a want of stability." During his time in the civil service, Metternich had "had dealings with twenty-eight Ministers of Foreign Affairs in France. I counted them up the day I had been here twenty-five years, and there had been just twenty-five; but in the last two years there have been three."[74] To Ticknor he confessed: "I do not like my business—*Je n'aime pas mon métier*. If I liked it, I should not be able to preserve the quietness of spirit—*le calme*—necessary to it."[75] At the age of just twenty-five, he "foresaw nothing but change and trouble" for Europe, and was considering going "to America, or somewhere else."[76] He labored "chiefly, almost entirely, to prevent troubles, to prevent evil."[77]

And on the theme of the past and the future, his words were clearly not those of a partisan of "restoration": "I care nothing about the past, except as a warning for the future. The present day has no value for me, except as the eve of to-morrow,—*Le jour qui court n'a aucune valeur pour moi, excepté comme la veille du lendemain*. I labor for to-morrow. I do not venture even to think much of the day following, but to-morrow, it is with to-morrow that my spirit wrestles,—*mon esprit lutte*."[78]

15

REVOLUTION, ESCAPE, EXILE, 1848–1851

Europe in Crisis: From Unrest to the Revolution in Vienna

We have accompanied Metternich on this journey through his times and have arrived in the first weeks of 1848. Let us try to imagine what the aged state chancellor would have found on his desk in those days. As the best-informed politician in Europe, he received the usual dispatches from his envoys in all four corners of the Continent, police reports from Sedlnitzky on the turbulent regions within the monarchy, and secret dossiers and news from his Central Commission on revolutionary activity in Mainz. Finally, there were the newspapers from France, Great Britain, and the states of the German Confederation, which Metternich read regularly, adding to the files the articles he deemed important. The signals he was now receiving crystallized into the perception of a threat of an altogether different kind. One of the organizers of the large exhibition at the Schirn Kunsthalle in Frankfurt to mark the 150th anniversary of the revolution chose the apposite image of the "Sheet Lightning of the Revolution" as the title for her contribution to the exhibition's catalogue.[1] We only have time for a brief look at the general historical context,[2] before narrowing our view and considering what this fourth European revolution—following those in 1789, 1820, and 1830—did to Metternich, and, in turn, how he dealt with it.

Throughout the 1840s the symptoms of a deeper, structural social and economic crisis in Europe were becoming more and more obvious: there were the unfulfilled bourgeois demands for political participation; the aspirations for national self-determination and independence; the distress in the preindustrial crafts; the effects of overpopulation and proletarianization in the major cities and in many rural areas. Friedrich Engels even thought he could interpret the proletarianization of the "working classes" of London, Manchester, and Birmingham as signs of a general European crisis that would also take hold of Germany. Karl Marx had expressed this idea pointedly in his now-famous declaration: "A specter is haunting Europe."

Social inequality was increasingly widening because of an unprecedented agrarian crisis that hit not only the poor in Ireland but also many German states. It was expressed most obviously in the potato blight, which decimated what was for much of the population the main source of nutrition and led to bread shortages and riots at markets. Speculators caused public outcry. Bourgeois journalists again decried the suffocating censorship and reported the scandal of the treatment of the Silesian weavers as a sign of Germany's woes. The provincial parliaments of the states of the German Confederation became more and more courageous: in 1847 they even called for a German parliament, or at least for the supplementation of the Federal Assembly with a national representative body.

In 1847, the unrest had already spread to the Habsburg Monarchy, where, at the assemblies of the estates in Lower Austria (Vienna) and Hungary (Pressburg), politically active members of the bourgeoisie started to express their demands publicly, often in petitions and pamphlets. The Vienna regional assembly had not quite reached this point, but on March 13 its members were called for a meeting at the House of Estates [*Ständehaus*]. It was then and there that Metternich's fate was to be sealed.

Metternich knew that there had been successful revolutionary uprisings in Palermo and Naples before the signal of revolution had spread across all of Europe through the Parisian rebellions in February 1848. In the Habsburg Monarchy, Italian and Hungarian subjects raised their voices, but the so-called March demands [*Märzforderungen*] were also heard in Galicia, in Bohemia, in Ilyria at the Adriatic coast, and from the Serbs, Croats, and Slovenians, who were under Hungarian rule. Everywhere there were calls for freedom of the press, freedom of association, independent regional representation, and, often, the liberation of the peasants.[3]

The reports from the Austrian envoys in Italy had reached Metternich early, and they contained surprisingly up-to-date information on the growing unrest. In December 1847, on the basis of the hard facts, Metternich was expecting the revolution. When Prince Schwarzenberg, still an envoy in Naples at the time, asked for military intervention, Metternich appeased him, but urged him to use troops only defensively. Even though the state chancellor correctly predicted the revolution, he did not know the exact day it would come or what would trigger it. Both took him by surprise.

An early proponent of a more nuanced picture of Metternich, Hanns Schlitter, director of the archive in Vienna, and later Srbik, both unearthed so many details and so much background information on the outbreak of the revolution that it is possible to trace, day by day, sometimes hour by hour, the developments that would finally force Metternich out of office. Princess Melanie's diaries are also revelatory, and her judgments on various members of the imperial family were slightly too passionate to make their way into publication. The editor of the diaries, Metternich's son Richard, "upon highest order had to delete important passages—or had to falsify them—because they exonerated Metternich and compromised a few other individuals."[4] It was a bitter experience for the state chancellor: he watched as the imperial family used him, often with some satisfaction, as a pawn.

Kolowrat's Later Ambitions and Metternich's Political End

A newly found document allows us to piece together a lot of the evidence about Metternich's resignation into a picture that, again, suggests that the state and conference minister Count Kolowrat played an inglorious role in the events. Everything points to his having sought to use the growing discontent and protest in Vienna to push Metternich out of office and usurp his position; he even had plans to then make that position still more powerful. The question of whether he would be able to take up a position at the top of the state in the midst of a revolution, especially given his continual health problems, does not seem to have occurred to him. Metternich, for one, disputed Kolowrat's leadership qualities: "Although he is an excellent businessman, he lacks that quality which alone makes the statesman. He is incapable of seeing a question as a whole, to capture it, determine how it will develop, and not be distracted by coincidences."[5]

Kolowrat was discovered, much to everyone's astonishment, to be present at a meeting of the bourgeois opposition in the juridical-political reading circle [*Juridisch-politischer Leseverein*] and the Lower Austrian Trade Association [*Niederösterreichischer Gewerbeverein*] in Vienna, where the critically minded members of the estates met. At its monthly meeting on March 6, the trade association made a risky move, passing a motion addressed to the emperor and handing it to the association's patron, Archduke Franz Karl, who was in attendance. Kolowrat condemned a newspaper article that had been inspired by Metternich. "Two members of the state conference served as a foil for this demonstration against the governmental system."[6]

In the days leading up to March 13, derogatory remarks about Metternich were often heard in court circles, and people talked openly about wanting to get rid of him. Archduke Johann, Kolowrat, and also Archduchess Sophie knew that there would be stormy protests against Metternich on March 13 when the estates assembled. Metternich must have known what would happen. In a passage in her diary dated March 12—a passage that was later censored—Melanie wrote about an event at the salon of the state Chancellery at which the rather naive Countess Felicie Esterházy confronted her with the question: "Is it true that you are leaving tomorrow?" "Why?" the princess responded. "Well, Louis Széchény just told us that we should buy candles for an illumination tomorrow, because you will be sent away!" In her diary, Melanie commented on the episode by saying that Széchény had spent all his life at court and that one could not ignore the things he said.[7] He was, after all, the head of the court household [Obersthofmeister] of Archduchess Sophie.

On Monday, March 13, the protests escalated, as expected, in front of the building where the assembly of the Lower Austrian Diet took place. The Diet convened on that day in order to present the emperor with demands for a Constitution. Over the course of the day, the masses gathered. Soldiers fired at random into the crowds, killing several, and finally violence also broke out in the suburbs, where impoverished workers ripped gas pipes out of the ground at the defensive wall (the so-called Glacis) around Vienna, starting a fire that could be seen from across the city, a sign of the social uprising. Kolowrat's hour had come. In a clever operation, he succeeded in using the influence of the archdukes to put enough pressure on Metternich for him to offer his resignation. He was sacrificed in order to restore calm [Ruhe]. At the Hofburg, the idea of removing Metternich, the embodiment of his "system," was welcomed. The state chancellor found it difficult to accept either the way in which his resignation had come about or all the plotting against him. In his posthumous papers there are numerous unpublished manifestos and justifications in which he declares that reforms were all he could ever have accepted, and that he would not have objected to his resignation if his remaining in office would have meant a revolution.

Metternich's Escape from Vienna to London via Germany

In the heated atmosphere, Metternich feared for his life. He decided to flee. Melanie's diary describes in great detail their adventurous journey through Germany to Brussels and The Hague to England.[8] On March 17, the family found its initial refuge in Feldsberg (Czech Valtice), southern Moravia, where they stayed at the castle of Prince Liechtenstein, who had always been close to the family. The local community council, however, requested that Metternich leave the place within twenty-four hours. Metternich was not sure where to turn. It was his daughter Leontine who gave him the idea of fleeing to England. The Metternichs tried to move incognito—with a passport in the name of a merchant, Friedrich Mayern. The destination was London. The supposed wholesale trader from Graz was traveling with his wife and son "Joseph" to spend six months in London on "private business." This travel document rescued Metternich, and it meant so much to him that he kept the original in his personal papers.[9]

The family traveled, in part by train, on to Olmütz, where the commanding officer and archbishop refused to take Metternich in. They traveled by train to Prague, and, by an extraordinary coincidence, sitting in the next carriage was the Polish politician Burian, the very same man who had given the speech in front of the state Chancellery on March 13. In Teplitz, despite traveling under three different aliases, Metternich was recognized by people in a tavern. One of them shouted: "Away with the cockades, there is Prince Metternich," and let him pass without hindrance. He could thus still command a certain degree of deference. Metternich was recognized in Dresden, too, but people merely looked at him with curiosity (March 24). In Leipzig, soldiers could be heard singing patriotic songs, and the family spent two hours in fear of their lives because of a large gathering of workers (March 26). The journey continued to Magdeburg, where the police commissioner explained to Metternich that he could not guarantee his safety if he tried to quench his agonizing thirst; in the end, Count Rechberg, who accompanied Metternich, managed to organize some water without Metternich having to show himself in public (March 27). The escape route continued into Hanover, where the king had been arrested and a price put on the head of the prince of Prussia (March 27–28), and thence to the peaceful Minden (March 28), and to Fürstenau, where the innkeepers recognized the princely crown on Metternich's clothing. They commented: "That is probably another king who had to abscond." On March 30, the family finally reached the Dutch border. Metternich would have been entirely without means at this point if Baron Rothschild had not extended him some credit along the way. The family had other frightening moments: at an inn in Arnhem, for instance, a waiter declared that he would kill Prince Metternich were he ever to meet him. On April 4, they took the steamboat from Arnhem to The Hague, where they met the king of the Netherlands, before continuing their journey on April 19 with the ferry from Rotterdam to Blackwall in England. On April 20, they arrived safely in London.

Passport for Metternich's escape, issued in the name of the wholesaler Friedrich Mayern from Graz.

A Nasty Plot Metternich Never Knew About

Metternich had to flee from Vienna without any means, and in London he learned that his Bohemian estates had been confiscated ("sequestered") and he would not receive any pension. He was left to wonder why he, an old state chancellor and with thirty-nine years of service—the longest serving among the ministers—was treated differently from the other leading politicians who had resigned, such as Sedlnitzky, and soon Kolowrat and Ficquelmont, especially as, in the days after his resignation, Ferdinand had signed a resolution that was supposed to have guaranteed his pension.[10]

Metternich's resignation triggered an unprecedented campaign of vilification against him. He was presented as the villain responsible for everything regrettable about the past. The free press indulged in slander and character assassination.[11] The chronology of events is important:

- On June 23, 1848, the journalist Ludwig August Frankl, writing in the *Wiener Abendzeitung,* accused Metternich of having received, since 1815, between 50,000 and 75,000 ducats annually from the Russian tsar as a bribe so that he would act in Russia's interests. The article also claimed that Metternich had continually embezzled and squandered public money. This was all flatly false.

- Then the former director of the archive at the state Chancellery, Josef von Hormayr, listed a number of accusations in a diatribe entitled "Emperor Franz and Metternich." Metternich, he said, had enriched himself with public money. He received Plaß in 1826 for free, he claimed.[12]

- These accusation were reproduced and repeated in the press, and thus they snowballed. On August 14, the German-Bohemian delegate in the newly elected Imperial Diet in Vienna, Ludwig the Noble of Löhner, thought he might follow democratic custom by using the parliamentary tool of interpellation to ask the finance minister of the new government, Philipp Baron von Krauß, whether the financial dealings of the state chancellor—that is, his use of public funds—had been formally investigated. Löhner's astonishingly detailed knowledge should have been available only to employees at the office of the Court Chamber. How did he know that the foreign minister had not been discharged following the audit of the monies he had received, and that there was "no indemnity" in his case? Löhner also repeated the claim that Metternich never paid for Plaß.[13]

The purpose of an interpellation was to instruct the relevant minister to clarify certain issues. At the same meeting the finance minister declared: "I also kept an eye on this matter, and there are pending proceedings in place." This was a hint that the government was about to open a so-called fiscal investigation [*Fiskalitätsverfahren*]—what today we would call a financial audit. Because of the unresolved situation, the government now refused to pay Metternich's pension and confiscated—as a security, it was said—his Bohemian estates.

Metternich's expenses since he took up his ministerial office in 1809 were to be audited. The absurdity of this is clear from the fact that the audit would also look into expenses from the years 1813 to 1815, when the court and the state Chancellery traveled with the military in theaters of war, sometimes—as in France—risking their lives as they did so. A request some thirty years later, in 1848, for pedantic bookkeeping under such circumstances can only be interpreted as motivated by malice. Those who dealt with the matter should have realized as soon as they looked at the files the real reason no official discharge had taken place: the Court Chamber, under Kolowrat as its president, had delayed it for years because of the usual way in which it conducted its business. Thus, what remained was the accusation of embezzlement.

In December 1849, after much delay, the finance minister established a commission to examine whether all bills had been properly accounted for. Without any sense of urgency, the president of the Directorate of the Audit Office [*Generalrechnungsdirektorium*], three privy councillors, two ministerial councillors, and a procurator of the Court Chamber set about their work with a fastidious thoroughness. Meanwhile, Metternich had no money. His Rennweg home in Vienna was about to be sold in order to cover 200,000 guilders of debt. Without the 100,000 rubles from the tsar, which Metternich received as an interest-bearing loan, he would not have been able to subsist.

Negotiations at the ministerial council could not sway the finance minister—not even the argument that Metternich had, at the time under consideration, been "entrusted with the greatest interests of the state, during an epoch when the existence of the state was at stake every day, and when he followed the headquarters to the borders of the battlefields and into enemy territory, and when he was frequently separated from his office and it was physically impossible for him to control the details of the business performed."[14]

After two years of patience, Metternich used the last means available to him. He instructed his lawyer in Vienna, who appealed to the law "that every notice must be made legally valid within fourteen days by bringing formal charges."[15] Now, finally, the matter was being dealt with; it was discussed at two meetings of the ministerial council. The outcome was a successful one for Metternich.

On November 14, 1850, he was granted the legal annual pension of 8,000 guilders and the mortgage was canceled.

Kolowrat's Plan for an Attack on Metternich

The still-unresolved question is who originated this whole train of events. Who was the source for the insider information about supposed embezzlement of traveling expenses more than thirty years ago? A note throws light on these questions and suggests the culprit. The files of the minister of the interior and finances for the years 1826 to 1848 (the so-called Minister-Kolowrat-Akten) fill 228 large boxes. Only someone familiar with them could have fished out, with the help of an index that ran to twenty volumes, a "presentation" made by Ritter von Eichhof, then vice president of the Court Chamber, on November 28, 1834.[16] That document was concerned with Metternich's invoices submitted in 1813–1814 and 1818, which document his expenses for "business travel." It includes a note, written in Kolowrat's hand, which he added on April 25, 1848, to the original document. In other words, Kolowrat arranged for the document to be retrieved from the archive of the Court Chamber on that day, and then, as the note tells us, passed it on to the finance minister, Baron von Krauß, adding: "On this, as well as on the presentations 100 and 4107 [from the year] 1835, the finance minister will probably be asked to comment." Kolowrat had clearly planned ahead and taken the initiative: no one had asked him to provide evidence. Also: Why did Kolowrat subsequently take the file to his home, Ebreichsdorf Castle, near Vienna, as he himself noted on the back of it? That was not at all normal practice at the office. On April 30, Kolowrat was back in Vienna and penned a "supreme resolution" for Emperor Ferdinand saying the file had to be passed on to finance minister Krauß.

We also have to keep in mind that on March 17, 1848, Emperor Ferdinand had established a ministerial council and had made Kolowrat its (provisional) prime minister. Kolowrat appointed Baron von Krauß as finance minister in his government. Kolowrat's old health problems soon came back, and after the second sitting of the council on April 3 he was already signaling that he had to suspend the meetings. He stayed in Vienna until the emperor dismissed him on April 18.[17] Kolowrat was therefore no longer officially in his post when he retrieved the document from the archive of the Court Chamber on April 25. The point is worth stressing: Already dismissed, Kolowrat still penned an order for the emperor. Because of Ferdinand's intellectual disabilities, he never initiated actions—he simply agreed to them. We must conclude, then, that the former minister manipulated him for his own purposes. He was targeting Metternich. He had insider knowledge, and it was he who drew the finance

Kolowrat's note on a document concerned with Metternich's travel expenses between 1813 and 1818 that Kolowrat retrieved from the archive on April 25, 1848.

minister's attention to it. Löhner, the delegate at the Imperial Diet, was obviously too well informed about the fact that Metternich had not been discharged of (had not received *Indemnität* for) the expenses he had incurred. There can be no doubt that Kolowrat was the originator of the plan to push Metternich into financial and existential distress, a situation from which Metternich could escape only with the help of others. At court, no one lifted a finger.

METTERNICH'S ENGLISH SELF: IN EXILE, 1848–1849

The German Question from an English Perspective

Even in exile in England, Metternich continued to think about politics. The seventy-five-year-old restlessly sought out whatever news he could about Germany and Europe from the papers. He became a popular center of British society, and he was soon welcoming an almost uninterrupted stream of visitors: his old companion the Duke of Wellington, victor of Waterloo, who visited him daily; the leading English politicians Aberdeen, Disraeli, and Londonderry; and even his political opponent Palmerston—they all turned up. So, too, did another prominent exile, Prince Wilhelm of Prussia.

Metternich remained in permanent contact with the Continent, and he wrote one memorandum after another.[18] Srbik dismisses these memoranda as the worthless products of a rigid and intransigent doctrinal thinker. On July 10, 1848, Metternich wrote a memorandum, titled "Über die Lage des Tages" [On the situation of the day], to Archduke Johann upon his appointment as Emperor Ferdinand's deputy. In August the archduke, who had entered his office as the German imperial regent on July 12, 1848, received a memorandum on "Die deutsche Frage: Genesis, Verlauf und gegenwärtiger Stand derselben" [The German question: Genesis, development, and the present situation]. In his usual fashion, Metternich developed the problem against its historical background, and concluded that there was only one possible way to secure peace between Austria, Germany, and the other nationalities: by restoring the German Confederation. Carefully, skeptically, he observed the work of the National Assembly in Frankfurt, which was still deliberating about the possibility of a federal state. Metternich tried to give advice to the new Austrian prime minister, Prince Felix zu Schwarzenberg, when he announced his plans for a "Greater Austria" that would see the monarchy become part of the German Confederation and thus create an "empire of seventy million." The exiled Metternich also followed the strange attempt of the Prussian king, Friedrich Wilhelm IV, to put himself at the head of a constitutional union of lesser German states, which confirmed Metternich's long-standing suspicion that the dominant northern power aimed to "swallow up" Germany. The Prussian king's slogan, "Prussia from now on dissolves into Germany," despite literally expressing Prussia's dissolution into Germany, seemed to point toward Prussian hegemony over the other German states.

Metternich remained faithful to his view that, given the political situation, the only solution would be the restoration of the German Confederation. This view was based on three premises: (1) the national tie had to be preserved, (2) a political order without Austria had to be ruled out, and (3) the state was not to be defined by a national principle. From the last of these conditions it followed that, in the newly organized state, no nationality could be superordinate to any other, and this requirement, Metternich thought, could be met only by a loose federal association that respected different historical traditions and was held together by a monarch at the top. Indeed, this was a solution that the Czechs, under František Palacký, would also have tolerated. They were vociferously protesting against the nation-state being planned in Frankfurt. They did not want to be part of a German empire in which they would have been a national minority, rather than part of a Habsburg Monarchy consisting of nothing but national minorities.

Further developments confirmed Metternich's analysis. The formation of a German nation-state in 1866–1871 was only possible without Austria, and Austria disintegrated under the influence of the politicization of the principle of nationality. The German Reich that was founded in 1870–1871, in turn, turned the battle against national minorities into an internal one with the so-called *innere Reichsgründung*:[19] against the Danes, the Poles, the French Alsatians, and against the Jews, who—despite having equal legal rights—were increasingly deprived of their German nationality in public discourse.

Metternich's third stay in England was also his longest. This time he did not just come as a visitor, as in 1794 and 1814; England became his temporary home. He knew that he would have to settle for a longer period of time. The Metternich who lived in England was a different character. After March 13, 1848, he was no longer a statesman with political responsibility operating within a network of dependencies and limitations. His time in England—and, indeed, everything that Metternich the private person thought and did during his restless retirement—can be seen as part of an extraterritorial space of intellectual freedom.

How did exile change Metternich? He had his own method of coping with the psychological pressure—not by repressing it but by dealing with it actively. "I find my state of mind relieved when I can communicate things that painfully impact on me to another mind that I know proceeds in parallel with mine."[20] He was a prolific letter writer, and after 1848 certain individuals were in more or less permanent correspondence with him, even into the last year of his—or his correspondent's—life. We should mention his daughter Leontine, his son and heir Richard, and also his grandson Roger von Aldenburg, who was the illegitimate son of Metternich's son Victor and for whom Metternich was a guardian. He had special relationships, too, with his other regular correspondents: Alexander von Humboldt; the Englishmen Disraeli, Wellington, Travers Twiss, and Edward Cheney; the field marshals Alfred von Windisch-grätz and August von Jochmus; Dorothea von Sagan, the younger sister of Wilhelmine; and his kindred spirits, Alexander von Hübner and Karl von Kübeck.

A Declaration of Love to England and to Freedom

Later, in a retrospection of December 31, 1849, after having left Britain, Metternich expressed what England had meant to him.[21] It is important to remember, when reading it, just what he had left behind in Austria. He was still hurt that the court and the inner circle of the aristocracy had seen him as merely a nuisance, and that the government had seen him as a compromising factor. In England he found an alternative world that—to speak in old-fashioned terms—soothed his embittered heart.

We can see Metternich's English self expressed in the following judgment: "Everything in England is organized differently from the way it is done in the continental states which are today wasting away. In England, regulated strength still rules; it still counterbalances the dreams which do find the air to breathe across the country but turn into a mist under the pressure of the truth." In this "great country" about which Metternich rhapsodized, he lived in particular in three places: London, Brighton, and Richmond. It bears repeating, if only to finally break down the stubborn prejudices that still surround Metternich: It is impossible for someone of such an anglophile conviction to be an admirer of absolutism or a hater of Constitutions. And, for Metternich, it was the British Constitution, rather than the abstract and artificial Constitutions that, in his view, had been mass-produced in the wake of the French Revolution, that was the ideal.

On April 12, 1849, he wrote in a private letter from England: "I live here amid a commonwealth which not only is ordered in the way required for the protection of life and property, but also values freedom so highly that it knows how to fend off with great determination any licentious attacks on public order; and I therefore daily come into contact with men who cannot comprehend the anarchy ruling on the Continent, by which I am not surprised."[22] In one of his

Adelaide Terrace (today Adelaide Crescent), King's Road, Brighton (around 1849).
Metternich lived at 42 Brunswick Terrace, to the right of the first house on the left.

letters he ironically suggested that the students of Vienna should come to England in order to see what a properly constructed state actually looks like.

Metternich repeatedly praises English freedom and culture: "Because in England—the freest country in the world, because the most orderly—all customs follow a certain rule, an hour before dinner a bell is rung."[23] "The concepts of freedom and order are so inseparable in the English mind that even the lowest stable-boy would laugh into the faces of the alleged reformers when they wanted to preach them freedom! The English spirit is mainly characterized by a sense of the simple and practical. That sense shows up everywhere one looks. It is always the matter at hand in which the English are interested; they don't care about the form."[24]

A Somewhat Different Nobility

Considering the "English" Metternich allows us to dissolve another prejudice. He is seen as a representative of the old aristocratic—ossified—society of the ancien régime. But the allegedly "doctrinal" Metternich despised empty phrases. Instead, he looked to the social foundations of ideas. His evaluation of the English aristocracy shows that he was, ultimately, not really a traditionalist or legitimist. He distinguished between nobility by birth and the peerage: "The term 'English aristocracy' is often associated with the concept of nobility. That is not quite right. The foundation of the English aristocracy does not lie in this concept, but in the concept of property," and therefore "a bourgeois of today may be elevated to the rank of high nobility tomorrow."[25] "The titles are the equivalent of offices, and everyone can make his way toward them through his achievements. This constitutes an equality which is useful through its successes, one that elevates rather than degrades as the equality of misery does."[26] Metternich—who was himself a social climber within the aristocracy, moving from the rank of baron to that of prince—praised this modern conception of nobility, one that was derived from the bourgeois principles of performance and merit and did not seek to defend birth rights. This focus on the English conception of nobility once again demonstrates that Metternich's convictions were those of a conservative constitutionalist; they were a far cry from those of a backward-looking traditionalist or legitimist who was hostile to change.

Political Parties

Reflecting on the British political party system, Metternich applied the same method of looking for the social interests that underlay each of the parties. His way of speaking about continental parties—where, for instance, he referred *grosso modo* to the liberal party or the party of those supporting revolution—was rather blunt, for he considered them mere products of the intellect, a phenomenon to which his prohibitive policies at the Federal Assembly contributed. Here we confront a riddle: Metternich did not think that the Germans could develop a civilized way of dealing with political parties, but in the case of Britain, he accepted political parties as unproblematic, as freely operating social groups.

It is interesting to observe the objective and nuanced way in which Metternich described the party political system and how intelligently he analyzed the contradictions in British politics. First of all, he did not simply side with the allegedly "good ones," the Tories. In an instruction to the envoy in London, he explained to him:

I have noticed with great clarity that the terms Tories and Whigs have ceased to signify clearly defined ideas. When I reflect on the question of what these parties represent in practical politics, I find that who says "Tory" says "conservative," while the same does not apply to the term "Whig" as the Whigs are split into conservatives and radical reformers. In this respect, the Tories would have a moral advantage over their opponents, but this advantage has very much shrunk due to the splitting of the Tories into moderates and ultras. To try and find the difference in opinions between a moderate Tory and a conservative Whig is, as I see it, a useless exercise.

According to Metternich, the parties differed "[not] in what they want but [in] how they want to achieve it."[27] This is not the language of an ideologue.

The Press and Public Opinion

In England, Metternich learned that there could be freely expressed public opinion, and he was a voracious reader of the newspapers, many of which he subscribed to. While in exile, he even became a participant in the public debate. In a private letter to his daughter Leontine he explained what he meant by press policies:

> The current situation affords me the role of a pioneer for reason (I cannot find another expression that would correspond to my role), and from this results a fact which, I believe, is without parallel in the annals of England. For, the most important organs for what one calls public opinion and what influences it, put themselves at my disposal, and it suffices to read them in order to notice in the *Times* and especially in the *Morning Chronicle* a complete reversal of opinion regarding the most important questions. I sent you an issue of the *Quarterly Review,* the most important quarterly paper which deserves a place in every library. In it, you will find two articles, the one titled "Austria and Germany" was dictated by me, the other, covering the Italian affairs, was written under my influence. You will thus be able to convince yourself that the truth is beginning to affirm itself in this country. The *Spectateur* was an experiment which I launched into the public, which, however, did not last longer than a rocket, because a paper written in French is too expensive.[28]

It is no exaggeration to say that Metternich caused a stir in English public life: "My appearance in England immediately led to the conservative party gathering around me." His tools in this regard were the most influential press outlets. Although he thought he knew England very well from his previous visits, he was surprised by the many opportunities that opened up for him. His "opinions and feelings" found expression in the *Times,* the *Morning Chronicle,* and the *Quarterly Review,* where he was able to present his views at critical junctures during the battle for Italy and Hungary. Men like Disraeli adopted his arguments and presented them in Parliament, and the *Times* printed daily reports on the debates; thus, Metternich's views were spread further afield.[29]

Disraeli, in particular, noticed how Metternich built his network in the press after Metternich's own project, the *Spectateur de Londres,* failed.[30] Metternich had British partners who would carry his articles under aliases in various papers. One of them was Edward Cheney (1803–1894), who criticized Palmerston's policies as an obstacle to peace. In very modern fashion, Cheney carried out a whole series of interviews with Metternich and asked him questions we might like to ask him today. In the *Quarterly Review,* Travers Twiss (1809–1897) anonymously published a series of articles on the German states that had been written by Metternich. These articles explained in great detail the complex edifice of the Habsburg Monarchy, which the English found difficult to understand.

Disraeli offered panegyrics on Metternich that described him as his teacher. When on one occasion Disraeli told him that he had come down from London for only a couple of hours especially to see him, Metternich replied that this showed him that he was no longer a minister but "Professor Metternich." Disraeli admired the "divine talk" in which the "professor" then went on to give him a "masterly exposition of the present state of European affairs," containing a "greater number of wise & witty things that I ever recollected hearing from him": "He was indeed quite brilliant; & his eyes sometimes laughed with sunny sympathy with his shining thoughts."[31] After his return to Vienna, Metternich stayed in regular correspondence with all three, Cheney, Twiss, and Disraeli. Metternich's last, unfinished—and thus unsent—letter, of May 1859, was addressed to Travers Twiss.[32]

BRUSSELS 1849–1851: METTERNICH'S LOOK BACK AT A LIBERAL ECONOMIC POLICY THAT WAS NOT TO BE

Metternich left England with a heavy heart. It was "not the place to stay with a large family," he said, meaning that in the long term life in London was far too expensive for him.[33] He therefore moved to Brussels, where he stayed between October 11, 1849, and June 9, 1851. He had many fond memories of Belgium. We know how much his family had done for the country—first his father as the acting minister in Brussels, then Metternich himself, who together with Castlereagh had promoted the cause of an independent Netherlands during the battles against Napoleon. Following the July Revolution, Metternich had supported the formation of a separate Belgian state and helped Prince Leopold of Saxony-Coburg-Gotha to become Leopold I, king of Belgium. Leopold now respectfully welcomed the exile from London.

His stay in Brussels was a strange interlude in Metternich's life. He was, in fact, waiting for a signal from Vienna that they wanted him to return. But none arrived. Metternich was in limbo. It was also a mental limbo: the old Austria that, up until March 13, 1848, he had embodied, appeared to him to have vanished. The revolution ruled over Europe and over Metternich's life. At the same time, Metternich carefully observed how an answer to the German question and to the question of the Habsburg Monarchy's internal constitutional structure was gradually unfolding, even if both were as yet uncertain. On both, Metternich had some very clear predictions. In these nearly two years of exile in Brussels, Metternich was engaging in an incredibly intense exchange of ideas with the financial expert of the pre-1848 government, Karl (Baron) Kübeck, in which he reflected deeply and knowledgeably about these two central themes.

Following the death of Clam-Martinitz, Kübeck, who had been appointed president of the Court Chamber on November 25, 1840, had become Metternich's most important kindred spirit in political matters—so much so that Metternich even signed his letters "in steadfast friendship," which was rare in his correspondence with other statesmen.[34] Their correspondence served three important purposes. First, it helped Metternich to become clear in his own thoughts and to come to terms with his own situation.

Second, Metternich's concern for Austria's fate meant he could not simply remain passive in the face of the events of the day. He had to continue to offer advice and to intervene in political debates, just as he had done from London. Kübeck was a suitable addressee for this advice because he had been appointed by Emperor Franz Joseph I as one of four members of an interim commission for the period November 30, 1849, to September 30, 1850. Until a solution to the German question had been found, this commission was to take on Archduke Johann's role of imperial regent [*Reichsverweser*].[35] Kübeck was therefore at the heart of the discussions that were just beginning between Prussia and Austria regarding a new Constitution. On December 5, 1851, the emperor appointed Kübeck president of the newly formed imperial council. This was an exceptionally influential position, because this council served as an advisory body in addition to the ministerial council, and the emperor could choose to bypass the latter and simply accept the advice of the former. The monarch listened to Kübeck and accepted his suggestion to repeal the March Constitution step by step. Until his death on September 11, 1855, Kübeck therefore held a key position in domestic politics and was the ideal recipient for Metternich's advice.

Third, Metternich used their correspondence to justify his past policies and to attack talk of a "Metternich system." On March 13, 1848, he had been confronted by angry demonstrators who had assembled outside his palais, the state Chancellery, and loudly accused him of being "the cause of all 'obstacles to progress.'"[36] Metternich tried to refute such accusations by referring to the plans for economic and financial reform he had put forward before 1848. Nowhere else did Metternich explain himself as clearly on this topic as in his exchanges with the expert Kübeck.

Because historians are usually blinded by the conventional view of Metternich as a "doctrinal" character, his interest in social and economic questions has so far received little attention, and Srbik's judgment of the man has simply been parroted. Metternich, it is claimed, was *volksfremd*—out of touch with the people—and he was not prepared "to climb down from the loftiest spheres of high society and to convince himself of the needs and aspirations of the broad mass of people."[37] We have seen that this cannot possibly have been true: we have witnessed his personal involvement in the administration of his vineyards, his *Meierhöfe* [large manorial estates], and his ironworks. Metternich was also always one to insist that the revolutions after 1789 had had a social character. But faced with the prejudice now raised against him during the revolution of 1848, Metternich saw fit to reject these accusations completely.

He pointed to all the opportunities that had been missed because of Kolowrat's self-serving policies and the imperial bureaucracy. The Habsburg Monarchy did not have any top civil servants who would have reformed economic and financial policies in the way that Prussia had after 1806. Under Joseph II, Austria had been ahead of Prussia, but now it was living off its reserves and its political center was stagnating—there were no Steins, Hardenbergs, or Humboldts in sight; instead, Kolowrat, Eichhof, and Sedlnitzky held the reins. When considering Metternich's analysis, it is important to keep in mind that, as someone who had fled the revolution, he had to express himself carefully, cautiously, and indirectly. If he wanted to return to Vienna, he could not openly settle old scores with people who were still influential at court and among the civil servants. He never entered into personal polemics, not even against those who had harmed him considerably. That was, in any case, not his style; even in his most private writings, such as letters to his wife, Melanie, he did not make any derogatory remarks about his greatest opponents—Melanie, in contrast, did not mince her words in her diaries (which, as we have seen, led the court to censor them). Because of the sensitive nature of the ideas he communicated to Kübeck, Metternich marked his letters to him "For you alone," "Soli," or "Confidential," and wherever possible he had them delivered by people he trusted, such as his administrator. Metternich ended one letter with the words "Burn these lines."[38]

Metternich's central accusation was that there had been no genuine governance or action—merely administration.[39] With astonishing clarity he lays the failure at the door of the pre-1848 government. From his perspective two factors were important in assessing his political record: Looking back at the *Vormärz* period (as it was called even then), he rejected the insinuation that he was "all-powerful," that he usurped every position—that he was, therefore, solely responsible. He insisted that he had had neither responsibility nor authority when it came to domestic matters.[40] Following the death of Emperor Franz, Metternich said, the government had been paralyzed because of Kolowrat. From his perspective, if he had had responsibility, he would have had the power to govern and to push through his ideas. The decisive mistakes had been made by the financial administration—and he always had Kolowrat in mind when he said this. Metternich spoke of "sins of omission" that Emperor Franz and Kolowrat had committed regarding his proposals for reform.

Kübeck confirmed Metternich's view of economic matters—that is, "that the true source of prosperity, namely work, is the result of property and capital, and then the hope of acquiring both." He held that "without private credit there can be no substantial development in agriculture, or in the processing and commercial industries, and without state credit no lasting consolidation of power."[41] Instead, there had been the pursuit of self-interest, which had resulted in political stagnation. Recall the attempts by the Bohemian nobility, through Kolowrat, to prevent rises in the rate of land taxation. Metternich, in contrast, although he belonged to the same class, pointed out "the value of the assets of large-scale landowners," which needed to targeted for the "indispensable increase in the income of the empire."[42] It had been overlooked, according to Metternich, that "a truly liberal attitude would have found enough space to stimulate what needed to be stimulated."[43] If liberalism were understood rightly, Metternich had no reason whatsoever to reject it.

In Metternich's view, if the "deadly shortcomings" in Austria had not been fueled, then the country would have been spared the revolution. Kübeck reminded Metternich of their failures at the state conference, listing a whole catalogue of domestic policy measures that had not been implemented: the concentration of competencies in the central government; an appropriate organization of the administration across the country; a reform of the judiciary and of the armed forces; the harmonization of the representation of the estates; a fight against the "indifference and political parochialism of the large aristocratic landowners"; a end to the unacceptable living conditions faced by peasants. What really makes the reader of these letters sit up and take notice is the reference to a foiled intention to pass a law "which would have transformed the feudal relation into the simple relation of private law between debtor and creditor, and worker and employer, and which would have made any disputes arising a matter of the courts and no longer of political authorities, and finally which would have treated the discharge of obligations as a right of both parties, with claims to be settled by courts if necessary." Metternich himself had introduced such rights for his vine dressers at Johannisberg on his own initiative. The old president of the Court Chamber then added: "The proposals for this are filed in the registers of the toppled government without having been seriously considered, not to mention executed."[44]

Metternich agreed explicitly and unreservedly with this catalogue, and he confirmed that there had been solid proposals: "All this had been suggested many times, and was left undone due to the *vis inertiae* [force of inertia]." Metternich also came across an old presentation by Kübeck from 1834, which documented their agreement on the issue of the Customs Union. They had both endorsed Austria's accession to the union, even if it would have initially involved material sacrifices.[45] Kübeck referred specifically to the bundle of reforms Metternich had proposed in his memorandum of 1844 on the industrialization of Hungary. We have already seen that Metternich agreed, surprisingly, with the high priest of economic liberalism in Germany, Friedrich List. The main point Metternich lamented when looking at the past remained the crippling division at the political center between foreign and domestic politics. Metternich deconstructed the myth of the "Metternich system," at least for the time after the death of Emperor Franz:

> There is only one fitting answer to these questions, and it lies in the fact—unknown to the European public, and even to the Austrian public, and difficult to grasp—that following the death of Emperor Franz our empire was without a government. The coach of the state moved on, as vehicles do as a consequence of the impulses they have received, and they stop when a force confronts them. The role I played in this moving on was that of a pawn. . . . The old edifice therefore did not collapse out of inner feebleness, but out of a lack of caution in the use of power which had the duty to preserve it.[46]

Another of Metternich's judgments is even more surprising. Metternich considered the revolution a unique opportunity for reform, and the Austrian government in 1848 failed to take that opportunity. "The imperial government could have used the revolution in the interest of the necessary reforms, as the field was prepared for what was needed in terms of the new!" But the government did not know how to use "the freedom that the heavens had dropped on it."[47]

16

AT THE OBSERVATORY

Twilight Years in Vienna, 1851–1859

Politics in Transition: From the European Revolution to the Wars of National Formation

From November 1850 onward, Metternich was no longer the subject of the preposterous "fiscal investigation" we mentioned in Chapter 15. But it was only an order from the young emperor Franz Joseph that finally put an end to this farce, which had been driven by resentment and a petty desire for revenge on a disliked colleague. At the end of 1850 the aging state chancellor was finally granted a pension and the mortgages on his estates were canceled. Not even this, however, meant that Metternich was yet allowed to return to Vienna. He awaited an invitation—whether from the prime minister, Schwarzenberg, or from the young emperor. None arrived.

It is not possible to explain the reservations the Viennese court must have had solely on the basis of personal animosity toward Metternich. Between 1848 and 1851, the Habsburg Monarchy was in a difficult transitional period, during which the prediction made in the spring of 1848—that the empire might well disintegrate into three or four separate parts—began to look not at all unrealistic.[1] The experiments with different types of Constitution were also very risky, and it was never certain that they would not all end in civil war between the different nationalities. At times it seemed it was only the army, which was controlled by field marshals who had fought against Napoleon—Windischgrätz and Radetzky—that kept the state as a whole together. In response to the plans for a Constitution and the unification of Germany that were being developed in Frankfurt, the monarchy was threatening to divide up into German and non-German states. Against this background, the reappearance of as politically symbolic a figure as Metternich was too risky; it sent the wrong signal, especially because, from the summer of 1849 onward, Schwarzenberg started to pursue a neo-absolutist course with great determination. With the so-called New Year's Eve Patent of December 31, 1851, which abolished the March Constitution of 1849, this course was apparently achieving successes. It was also not clear whether, once back in Vienna, Metternich would really abstain from all political activity. Although he repeatedly insisted that he would not engage in any political activity, his numerous letters from London and his various initiatives and activities there suggested otherwise. Only after an explicit request from Metternich and with the support of the emperor's mother, Archduchess Sophie, was he rehabilitated by the emperor and assured that he would be allowed to return to Vienna. With this, his stay in hospitable Brussels ended; he left on June 9, 1851.

His first port of call was his sorely missed Johannisberg, which had apparently been occupied by the state of Nassau during the revolutionary turmoil. The Metternich family arrived there on June 11, 1851, and in the autumn of the same year they finally returned to Vienna. The fears that Metternich would be *persona non grata* turned out to be unfounded. On the contrary, he was invited to events and his advice was sought, and the young emperor also visited him frequently. Metternich could now continue the activities he had begun in London within more familiar surroundings. Among his posthumous papers there are heaps of newspapers and newspaper clippings from the 1850s. They document how the old politician, still sharp, kept up with all the great debates of the day, and how he still evaluated them in the fashion with which we are by now very familiar. He rejected the neo-absolutist reconstruction of the empire that was pushed by the new minister Alexander von Bach, who came from the bourgeois opposition. Metternich had regular exchanges with Kübeck, who, in his role as imperial council, was an *éminence gris* in the background.

Despite all the things Metternich had learned during his English exile, he remained fundamentally true to himself into old age. He continued to follow the conflict between the tsarist and Ottoman empires with great concern. The Crimean War demonstrated to him that the conference system of 1815 no longer worked. Russian policy was as expansionist as it had been in the 1820s. The preservation of the Ottoman Empire remained an existential necessity if peace was to be maintained in Europe. But although Metternich's thinking moved in an old groove, he remained eager to learn about everything new that happened—the building of the Suez Canal, for instance. The 1850s thus still afforded Metternich a rich spectrum of political pursuits. In this phase of his life, he lived "at an observatory," so to speak, from which he enjoyed a broad panorama of the political scene. Before, he had stood "on the ploughed-up ground for half a century" and, in the context of "the tough task of governing," he often could not be as conciliatory as he would have wished to be.[2] Now, in his state of perpetual contemplation, he kept up with the events of the day through extensive reading of the papers and his rich correspondence with individuals in all four corners of the Continent. The clarity and perspicacity with which he followed and commented on events right up until the last hours of his life is astonishing, and by itself would provide enough material for another book.

The eighty-year-old Metternich suffered yet another blow in his family life when his wife Melanie died on March 3, 1854, at age forty-nine. She, in particular, had supported Metternich throughout his years in exile. He received many heartfelt condolences—even from the Prussian king and Nesselrode. His temporary banishment and the reluctance many initially felt in talking about or associating with him were things of the past.[3]

The Austro-Italian War: The Final Test of Metternich's Political Convictions

One episode toward the end of his long life demonstrates particularly well the mental agility he still possessed in the 1850s, and it serves, too, to sum up the way he dealt with one of the most important questions of his life—namely, whether the conference and peace system created at the Congress of Vienna under his crucial leadership would come to an end even within his lifetime. During the last days of his life, the old state chancellor was forced to witness Austria stumble into a war because of a nonsensical ultimatum that, without even a thought for the risks involved, was put to Sardinia-Piedmont. On April 19, 1859, the Austrian government had handed an ultimatum to the kingdom of Sardinia in Turin, demanding the demobilization of its army and the withdrawal of troops from the border, on pain of Austrian military intervention. As might have been expected, the ultimatum was rejected, and ten days later, on April 29, Austrian troops marched into the Piedmont. This meant that the Habsburg Monarchy was also automatically at war with France (note the resemblances to the outbreak of the Great War), because the secret contract of Plombières of 1858 contained a clause stipulating that if Austrian troops attacked Sardinia, this would trigger French support.

Metternich saw that the fundamental principles of his own European policies were being completely ignored. Paradoxically, it was the French side that revived the principle of the "Concert of Europe," the very principle that constituted the substance of the Vienna order, which was now disowned by Austria itself. In the age of the telegraph, communications between Vienna and

Saint Petersburg, which previously would have taken two to three weeks, could now take place within hours—thankfully, it has to be said. The very same day the Austrian troops marched into the Piedmont (April 29, 1859), the French ambassador in Saint Petersburg, Louis Napoléon Lannes, Duc de Montebello, spoke with his Prussian counterpart, Otto von Bismarck. Bismarck summarized their conversation in a telegram, which he sent to Berlin on the same day. The wording of this message was strikingly reminiscent of the concerns Metternich had in 1824 that the Greek crisis might spark a major European war. With this telegram, Bismarck, or rather the Prussian government, acquired the role of European peacemaker that Metternich had filled so successfully after 1815. This text can in effect be read as a manifesto expressing Metternich's own political convictions at the end of his life—even if its fundamental idea came from a diplomat whose father had been one of Napoleon's closest friends and had died for him as a French marshal in the battle of Aspern in 1809. The telegram ran:

> The Duke of Montebello asks me, without formal instruction but on the basis of his familiarity with the views of Emperor Napoleon [Napoleon III], to ask whether we would be prepared to promise neutrality by way of an exchange of notes, if France promises to respect the federal borders, including within Austria, under all circumstances. He sees this as the only way, but also a reliable way, of keeping the war within harmless dimensions, and of guaranteeing Austria the security of its German provinces and peace from the Russian side. Without such an agreement, the expansion of the war, which he thinks has already broken out, across the whole of Europe, threatening all states, is in his view unavoidable. Russia and, according to the English envoy, England are inclined to think the same and would probably favor guaranteeing such an agreement, and thus here the decision is put into our hands.[4]

Montebello's evaluation of the danger to central Europe was perfectly correct. In Germany, national passions were already being stirred up by the prospect of war with France, and there were discussions about whether the German Confederation was required to enter into the conflict on the side of its ally; the confederation, the argument ran, had to support Austria if the federal borders were violated. That was not quite right: the Federal Act stipulated this only in the defensive case. But these were all just so many details—national honor was at stake, and "Germany" had to be defended "at the Po," as the slogan of the time had it.[5] What was needed was de-escalation. Bismarck acted like Metternich had before him: he kept a cool head, and fought for the neutrality of the German Confederation in this conflict.

Alexander von Hübner was at the Austrian embassy in Paris—and so at a crucial center of diplomatic activity during that time. He had been in the service of the state Chancellery since 1833, and he enjoyed Metternich's special trust.[6] Having trained Hübner, Metternich liked to use him as a diplomatic courier on special missions, and Hübner had been so successful that he was finally appointed to the post of ambassador in Paris. The outbreak of the war put him in the same position Metternich had been in in 1809. As an envoy, he asked for his passport and left Paris on May 4, 1859. On the evening of May 6 he arrived in Vienna, and he went to see the foreign minister, Buol, and then Emperor Franz Joseph. He then rushed to see Metternich at his Rennweg villa. Metternich invited him to his private rooms, and Hübner could still sense the excitement that had been provoked in the old state chancellor by a visit from the emperor that same morning. Metternich had taken the opportunity to give the emperor some lessons in history and diplomacy, touching upon his "uninterrupted efforts over many years to maintain harmony among the major powers, and whenever it was threatened, as he put it, to find a *centre d'entente*, whereby it was possible to secure the blessing of thirty-three years of peace for Europe."[7] This was the image Metternich had of himself. Hübner got the impression that all the fevered talk about the outbreak of war and the uncertainty over the course it might take had deprived Metternich, who was weak in any case, of his last reserves of energy. For Metternich, past and present again became peculiarly connected, because in Italy, past and present fought on the same battlefield. Field Marshal Heinrich Baron von Heß, who lost the Battle of Magenta in 1859, had fought at Aspern in 1809 and Wagram in 1813. Now, two of Metternich's sons, Richard and Paul, who had not even been born back then, were in the same theater of war in Italy, Richard as a diplomat and Paul with the army. And all the wars, past and present, were the result of mistaken policies.

On May 25, Hübner spent his last day with Metternich, accompanied him for a short walk in the Rennweg villa's beautiful garden, and engaged him in a lively and stimulating conversation that again revolved around questions of war and peace. Metternich repeatedly told his old employee: "I was a rock of order." Hübner's reflections on the moments after he had said farewell to Metternich, his friend, are moving, almost poetic. The image stayed with Hübner, and it deserves to be quoted at length here. A photograph of Metternich from the last years of his life seems to capture something of it.

> I had already closed the door behind me, but quietly opened it again in order to look at the great statesman one more time. He was sitting at his desk, quill in hand, looking pensively upward, with an upright body posture, distanced, proud, noble, as I had so often seen him at the state Chancellery when he was in the full glory of his power. The signs foreshadowing

death, which I thought I had noticed over the last few days, had disappeared from his face. A ray of sunlight illuminated the room, and the reflected light transfigured the noble features. After a while, he noticed me standing in the door, looked at me for a long time with intense benevolence, then turned away and murmured to himself: *un rocher d'ordre.*[8]

Metternich's Funeral: The "End of the Old Times"

On a Saturday afternoon, June 1, 1859, Prince Metternich "died peacefully and without pain," as the *Österreichische Zeitung* reported it.[9] He received the last rites. Present at his deathbed, in addition to his close relatives, were his personal physician Dr Jäger, Prince Paul Esterházy, Count Münch-Bellinghausen, and the former Transylvanian court chancellor, Baron Josika, who had supported him in his flight from Vienna in 1848. His sons Richard and Lothar had immediately set off from the headquarters at Verona and arrived on June 14 in the morning.

The funeral took place on June 15. It was "one of the most impressive that one has seen here for a long time," as a correspondent reported.[10] Now, finally, the Viennese aristocracy paid an overwhelming tribute to a statesman who had done so much to secure their survival. Almost the entire imperial court was present: the archdukes Franz Karl, Ludwig, Albrecht, Rainer, Sigismund, and Ludwig Victor all turned up.

The Lord Chamberlain [*Obersthofmeister*] Prince Carl Liechtenstein appeared with a division of the imperial guard and a division of the Arcièrengarde,[11] the latter as representatives of the Royal Hungarian Guards. In addition, there were privy councillors, chamberlains, and stewards [*Truchsessen*], all in their uniforms. The uniform of the Prussian chamberlains, the ceremonial garment of the pope's nuncio and the Greek popes, the attila of Hungarian magnates (a fur-trimmed overcoat), and the habits of Franciscans and Dominicans could all be spotted.

Beyond the inner circle of the court, there were the princes of Wasa and of Württemberg, the field marshals Windischgrätz and Count Wratislaw, Count Haugwitz, Count Thurn and Valsassina, and several other generals, the entire imperial cabinet, including the ministers Buol-Schauenstein, Rechberg, Bruck, Bach, Thun and Nádasdy, Ritter von Toggenburg and Baron Kempen. Then there was Governor Prince Lobkowitz, Count Münch-Bellinghausen, Baron Josika, the general of the cavalry, Count Wallmoden, municipal councillors, and other notables.

Among the groups attending were the entire diplomatic corps, including the apostolic nuncio, all the staff of the Foreign Ministry, the members of the

The last photograph of Metternich, from the late 1850s.

Oriental Academy, of the Haus-, Hof- und Staatsarchiv, and the civil servants from the Military Order of Maria Theresia, whose chancellor Metternich had been.

The hearse, drawn by six horses and surrounded by dignitaries and standard-bearers, was at the head of the procession. Accompanied by music and bells ringing, next came close relatives, with the two sons, Richard and Lothar, in the first line. Then followed the counts Sandor, Zichy, and Waldstein, Metternich's personal physician, and the servants of the Metternich household.

The European significance of the occasion, and of the deceased, was made visible by seven cushions, carried behind the coffin, on which were placed Metternich's official insignia. On the first cushion was the Golden Fleece, awarded by the emperor; the following six cushions carried forty-five further orders and nineteen grand crosses. With the exception of the English Order of the Garter, Metternich had been made a member of all important European orders.

The guards and court constables stood in line in front of the parish church of St. Karl, where the funeral service took place. It is one of the most important Baroque churches north of the Alps, and was built between 1716 and 1739, during the lifetime of Metternich's grandfather Johann Hugo Franz. The venue provided a dignified and traditional setting for the event. The square in front of Karlskirche was cordoned off by police on horseback; behind the cordon about 500 equipages were parked.

If the Congress of Vienna had been the last major celebration of old European court society, this was, perhaps, its last great memorial service. People paid their last respects not only to an important politician who had been a living connection to the time of the Holy Roman Empire but also, finally, to that old empire itself. It is astonishing that Srbik does not mention the funeral at all. The power of these sorts of symbolic ritual and the choreography around them should not be underestimated. In the case of Metternich the performance of this symbolic power was still tied to the life of one of the representatives of the old order. After him, this kind of event survived only in the form of the rituals performed at the funerals of members of the Habsburg dynasty. What was perishing was, in Metternich's own words, "the old historical order of things under the empire."[12] Metternich had thought that this old order had continued to exist in the form of the composite statehood of the Habsburg Monarchy. Because of his roots in the Holy Roman Empire, he had understood the peculiarity of the Austrian Monarchy better than anyone else in the nineteenth century.

The mourners and journalists got the same impression. One witness reporting on the funeral wrote: "The death of Prince Metternich is generally seen as the disappearance of the old times here, like a fatalistic conclusion. It was a time of forty years of peace;—new efforts will have to wring such peace from fate again. May this soon succeed!"[13]

Traditionally, Metternich is still seen as a politician not quite of his own time. But the present biography has shown that he had left the imperial tradition behind and stepped into nineteenth-century modernity. He knew how to analyze the problems of these new times, and he looked deeper than many of his contemporaries into the social transformations that were taking place and developed a new and original position from which to meet the challenges thrown up by the "laboratory of modernity." In contrast to his social peers, such as August von der Marwitz, he did not demonize market forces, industrialization, or technological progress. As he himself said, he was either born too early or too late: he stood between the ages, and he would have preferred to have been born in 1900, with the twentieth century ahead of him.[14]

Despite all his skepticism toward human nature and the "crooked timber" of which it is made, he did not fatalistically accept the crises of his times. To him, these did not spell final ruin; they were an intermediate stage. It was a "hateful time"[15]—"une période abominable"—which, however, would pass, so that in a more distant future it would again become possible to live in peace, to live according to his motto, "Strength in law." This biographer agrees with his analysis of the transitional times in which he lived. He was a postmodern character who emerged out of the eighteenth century into early modernity.

EPILOGUE

Metternich as a Postmodern Character in Early Modernity

The famous literary critic Marcel Reich-Ranicki used to end each of the seventy-seven editions of his *Literarische Quartett* with a modified quotation from Brecht: "And thus we see with consternation / The curtain's closed, and all questions open."[1] I assume that, after their long historical journey with Metternich, the readers of the present biography do not expect a succinct conclusion that summarizes what they can, as it were, "carry home in black and white."[2] Upon the death of our protagonist, the travel guide, however, does not take his leave in silence; although a book comes to an end, reflection on its content does not—at least not for those who find enough in it to want to further pursue some of the questions it raises. The appeal of a biography lies in the possibility of finding points in the life of another person with which one can identify, but it is not the task of the author to direct the readers' attention in this respect. This epilogue, therefore, instead attempts to ascertain the possible relevance that one of the most controversial politicians of the nineteenth century may still have today. In this endeavor, the terms "strategist" and "visionary" are two spotlights that may serve to illuminate a distant landscape in a novel way.

Let us first look at the foundation of political life, at states and their Constitutions, which fascinated, excited, and challenged Metternich throughout his life. He judged political Constitutions according to their suitability for the state in question. He therefore did not champion a particular type of Constitution per se, but was willing to consider any type as long as it guaranteed what the motto of his family's coat of arms demanded: "Strength in law." This formula expresses the elementary guarantees that any state should provide its citizens. The "law" here stands for an order that excludes arbitrariness and violence, and provides a protective space in which individuals can pursue their own well-being; this, for Metternich, included intellectual, economic, educational, and academic freedom, and the free development of the citizens of a state. This law had to be rooted in a tradition, because otherwise it would be arbitrary. The "strength" the formula mentions stands for everything that secures the state order. This can mean the executive power of police and military, but it may also mean the social ethos that exists within society, the self-assurance of the majority who know how to protect this order without having to resort to physical violence. This is what Metternich saw on the streets of London, where a healthy common sense offered broad protection against political and social extremism.

Against the background of the series of bloody wars that Metternich witnessed in 1794, 1814, and 1848–1849, the English Constitution as it had developed since Magna Carta could be seen as the ideal. He shared the values of the English gentry, who valued freedom more highly than equality. In England—where the "strength" of his motto ruled—he felt safe. He was not afraid of the press: indeed, he was an active journalist. The heated public and parliamentary debates invigorated him, and in his opinion they were proof that a political community had the strength to use conflict as a means for and a path toward mutually beneficial compromise. This model appeared ideal to him because he was against all forms of extremism; he was opposed to the fanaticism that sought universal happiness and, in achieving it, would conquer the world. For Metternich, the English model was the lived vision that he could imagine for the Continent only as a distant goal to be realized over a series of generations. For there all the necessary conditions were missing: capital, education, the will to make a fresh start, and—yes—even the will to take risks. He was fortunate that he could realize this ideal within the context of his own small state—his estates and possessions at the Rhine and in Bohemia and Vienna. Due to his mental agility and forward-thinking attitude, he was able to shake off the imperial tradition he had inherited, and yet to use the strength of patience and perseverance that was contained in it to follow his strategies. It may fly in the face of current methodological discussions about biographical writing to identify consistency where it has become customary to speak of what Pierre Bourdieu called a "biographical illusion." Metternich's life, shaken as it was by all kinds of catastrophe—revolution, war, terrorism, and an almost endless series of deaths in his own family—nevertheless expresses a degree of consistency that is, at first, irritating for a biographer. But it is intriguing: it awakens a curiosity about the inner compass that Metternich followed so unswervingly throughout his life.

"If I were not what I am, I would like to be an Englishman." This subjunctive confession tells us of that other Metternich—the Metternich he would have been under the conditions of British freedom. He always asked after the specific conditions that influence the particular Constitution of a particular state. These conditions might justify a republican, presidential Constitution, like the one in the United States. And the Hungarians lived under their "constitutionalism," with its particular traditions, and were part of the House of Habsburg. Metternich even learned to make his peace with the early Constitutions of the southern German states, although he remained suspicious about their radical intelligentsia, whose members experienced the rift between socioeconomic backwardness and constitutional progress (as opposed to the industrial awakening in Prussia), and had dreams of popular sovereignty despite large parts of the population still being illiterate.

The greatest problem for Metternich, though, was the state that he apparently directed over four decades, beginning with its foreign affairs but later as a kind of chief minister. But was he really the one who steered the Habsburg Monarchy? He was far too intelligent not to recognize the frailties of this state, which he called an irreparable "rotten building" that needed to be torn down and rebuilt from the ground up. Yet he drew a lesson from this state that he had also learned from its predecessor, the Holy Roman Empire. It was the lesson that a heterogeneous and composite state, as opposed to the central state of the French type, was much better able to protect the peace and security of many different nationalities and religions than the secular religion of a nation-state established through war. In declaring that nationality is a dangerous and objectionable force, as a building block or essential trait of a state, Metternich was ahead of his time. Today historians like Wolfgang Reinhard argue that it is time to say farewell to the fiction of the nation-state. We experience every day how modern states everywhere still use their national identity in order to legitimize new wars. Metternich was completely clear about the arbitrariness involved in defining a "nationality," and he knew that it was politically explosive to seek to destroy multinational orders such as the Habsburg Monarchy without being able to offer the nationalities within them what they hoped for: the prospect of peace within a sovereign state.

The great composite empire of the Habsburg Monarchy, however, was also not a forerunner of the European Union. Its peculiar form of rule was quite different from that of the EU, and it presented Metternich with a hopeless situation, one in which he would fail at whatever he decided to do. Metternich had more than enough ideas for how this empire might be led into a more prosperous future, in which the rule of law would be strengthened and political participation increased—carefully, however, through negotiation and compromise, through an evolutionary and not a violent or revolutionary path. Along this path, he did not exclude the possibility that his own class, the formerly ruling landed aristocracy, might have to make sacrifices—such as being prepared, together with other estates, to make sure that more revenue would flow into the state coffers, instead of rejecting reforms in the interests of protecting their privileges. We have seen the sorts of ideas he had for the development of the country. These may have surprised quite a few readers: they show him as a progressive conservative (a Whig like Edmund Burke) or as a conservative "liberal," although for him that term was tainted by his experience. But, in fact, such a liberal he was. He spoke out in favor of free trade, unregulated capital markets, and the reduction of trade and customs barriers, and he exchanged ideas with the model representative of economic liberalism, Friedrich List.

He rejected the idea of *the* nationality of *a* state, but promoted nationalities *within* a state, such as in the German Confederation, which was a home to numerous nationalities. For Metternich, the German question was the defining problem of central Europe. In his private and public life, he embodied the ambivalence that could be alleviated and contained only within a federal order of the sort the Swiss Confederation had managed to achieve, but which, in Metternich's lifetime, the German states had failed to achieve. Metternich himself is the best example of an individual with multiple identities, among which his German identity was only one of many. The Rhine flowed through his veins, as he put it, but he felt German not only when facing Napoleon, but also in his state Chancellery in Vienna, from where he directed a multinational state in which, he vowed, no nationality would have superiority over any other. It was this idea of equality between the nations, and of their equal worth, that led him to doubt whether the many peoples of this enormous Austrian empire could be represented in a single parliament—these doubts did not arise from some cleverly veiled absolutist conviction. And he was not the only one to harbor such doubts. After careful consideration, the British also decided against a central parliament in India. Metternich nevertheless thought absolutism and despotism fundamental evils, regardless of whether the rulers ruled "by the grace of God" or were modern-day Solons, like Napoleon—spreading war across all of Europe, from Portugal to Moscow, Palestine, and San Domingo, trying to bring about happiness with gunfire, promising the Poles, Italians, and Hungarians their own states, and leaving more than three million dead on the battlefields.

The memory of more than two decades of war remained firmly lodged in Metternich's mind. Like many other European politicians, he also had to deal with the consequences of these wars, and he was held responsible for the economic backwardness whose real cause was, by that time, on Saint Helena. But it would be a simplification to describe the problems of European society in the transitional period after 1815 as nothing but the collateral damage of Napoleon's imperialism. As one of the leading politicians of the Habsburg empire, Metternich observed how Austria's development was frustrated by the dynastic oligarchy that ruled over it and the powerful aristocracy in the provinces that was more interested in its own advantage than in the development of the monarchy as a whole. Even while Emperor Franz, whom Metternich revered, was still alive, Metternich discovered the limits of his power: his plans for a federal restructuring of the empire were foiled by the power politics of a dynastic family that treated the monarchy as its patrimony. The family's resistance to change meant that a talented politician and thinker like Metternich was not able to achieve what Cavour did for Italy or Bismarck did for Prussia. These two also had to overcome resistance from the aristocracy: in the case of Cavour, this resistance came not least from the Sicilians, and in the case of Bismarck from the *Juncker,* the landed nobility, east of the Elbe, of which he himself was actually a member. Metternich faced the toughest resistance in the 1830s and 1840s, when the economic interests of the estates and the interests of the dynastic family joined forces to oppose his policies to develop the monarchy. The responsibility for the economic backwardness or stagnation that resulted from this resistance was then mistakenly attributed to Metternich and his alleged "system."

The present biography should have demonstrated the absurdity of this view. In the alleged "police state" of Austria, which before 1849 did not even have a gendarmerie in its cities, towns, and rural communities, the state was not even capable of opposing the interests of particular groups or adopting the sorts of developmental policies that would have benefited it. Metternich was not fortunate enough to play the role of a Montgelas. Should he have forced himself into such a role on the back of the glory of having defeated Napoleon, as Srbik thinks? He would have had to take on not only his monarch but also the power of the entire Habsburg family. How could he have succeeded under such circumstances? His political acumen was such that he knew what he could achieve and what he could not. When his well-meaning friend Count Clam-Martinitz implored him in 1838–1839, at a pivotal point in the development of Austrian domestic politics, to strike against Kolowrat and at the same time publicize his move in order to make it a fait accompli, he shied away from it. He recognized that, in the face of the united archdukes alongside a scheming power politician, he had no chance of success. A strong Emperor Franz, receptive to new ideas, was what was needed at this point. Even his nephew Franz Joseph did not manage to escape the pressures of dynastic power politics.

The greatest problems in dealing with Metternich are still posed by his association with the police state, censorship, and the infamous Carlsbad Decrees. And yet this seems paradoxical: freedom and the rule of law were supreme goods for Metternich. We come here to a fundamental problem in the historian's methodology—the problem of values. Where does an observer of the past get his or her values? And given that the sources are always fragmentary, can a historian ever know enough about the time he or she evaluates? Might it be worthwhile, for once, not to look at the situation from the perspective of the fraternities or of those who attended the Hambacher Fest, and instead to look back, with Metternich, at a historical situation that the European politicians of the day perceived very differently from the way it is presented in today's textbooks: namely, as an outbreak of political violence against rulers, ministers, and other representatives of the state? How do governments today—democratic and autocratic ones alike—react when the very centers of their power are attacked? How does a state deal with the problem of having to protect its politicians? Is it only today that we permit, or even oblige, states to provide such protection? Was revolutionary violence 200 years ago an act of freedom? Is it permissible naively to demand absolutely no limits on the freedom of the press, as the journalists in the pre-1848 period did, even if anti-Semitism and incitement of the masses spread as a consequence? Should people be allowed to call for murder? And should the youth grow up singing songs that speak of nothing but blood and death, daggers and swords, of sacrifice, and of hatred of other peoples? Does every hero have to die? Who erects the barriers against all this? Today we know that an independent judiciary and a good criminal law are the best means of opposing these excesses.

Why—this question is meant seriously—is Metternich singled out as the embodiment of social repression? Why is it not taken into account that he acted in accordance with the wishes and the support of Prussia and most of the other German states, and that he acted no differently than the British, whose politicians welcomed the measures taken in Germany because, like him, they were thinking of Europe as a whole and remembered well how armies had swarmed out of France and all over Europe in pursuit of their noble aims? What did the situation look like from a contemporary and comparative European perspective if we recall that Napoleon, who was celebrated as progressive, practiced censorship and policing with a rigor that was second to none? There is nothing to suggest that he would have changed all this had his system of European satellite states survived Waterloo.

If there is one thing that our walk with Metternich through his life and times has taught us, it is that we should probe political ideals for their deeper, intentionally hidden motivations—we must disenchant them, so to speak. How should we evaluate the bourgeoisie's struggle for freedom and equality when we know that this was, at the same time, a struggle to enrich themselves? What are human rights, freedom, and revolutionary progress worth if aristocrats, the clergy, Girondins, and finally even Robespierre himself end up under the guillotine? What is the value of the democratic and republican Constitution of the United States if it needed slaves for its existence and deprived Native Americans of their rights? Metternich even asked the following question: How much do the English really value freedom and constitutionalism, given that they support them on the Continent but at the same time march into Ireland? How seriously can we take the German liberals' fight for freedom of the press when they celebrate the religiously and nationalistically motivated murder of a citizen, a murder in which the perpetrator—falsely cast as a victim—aimed to use a dagger to silence his, the only real, victim? If he sets an example for others, may anyone, at will, declare any other person a "traitor of the people" and execute him? When reading through Metternich's endless letters, especially those to people he trusted, these are the questions that come up. It would be wrong to think that they are now easier to answer just because all of this happened 200 years ago.

The writing of a biography is a good exercise for learning to avoid this mistake, because unlike other forms of historical writing, this genre forces the author to adopt a particular perspective. It looks, from the point of view of the past, toward a future that was unknown to the protagonist and his or her contemporaries. This leads to an almost irresolvable quandary. The historian possesses values, attitudes, perceptual horizons, and even ways of feeling and thinking that are peculiar to his or her own generation. No historian can shed this burden, and thus the author of the present biography should, in principle, confess that he also looks at the past from the perspective of his own times. The reader, however, will be spared such a confession, as an author should not draw too much attention to himself. At times the reader will, for all that, have sensed, from certain themes that run through the text, some of the coordinates the author has used to orient his account. It is enough that the author realizes that he cannot bring history back to life and create an image of "how it really was." That would be science fiction, not scholarship.

There is only one way to get out of this dilemma: the "veto of the sources," as Reinhart Koselleck called it. Historians must, as it were, listen to alien times, and systematically and eagerly look for evidence that contradicts their expectations and premature judgments. In the case of Metternich, that will yield a rich harvest because there is so much prejudice about him. A biographer of Metternich must pay attention, first, to the early modern period, then even more so to the eighteenth century, and must then look from these periods toward the later ones. The motto should not be: Let us find in the past what we consider valuable or harmful in the present. We should not look for "the West," for "freedom, equality, fraternity," for "unity and freedom" in the sense of the constitutional nation-state. If we liberate ourselves from this kind of historical approach, an unfamiliar perspective opens up for us. We no longer look at the historical mythology peddled by the committed propagandists of the pre-1848 period, who used the language at their disposal to present that mythology as a reality to their contemporaries and to posterity. They spoke of absolutism, selfless fighters for freedom and unity, the peoples and the fatherland, throne and altar, and so on. "Reactionary absolutists," "progressive democrats and liberals," "a united nation," "particularism and *Kleinstaaterei*"—these terms are all platitudes used by the agents of the past to impose their views on us. With Metternich, because he was something of an alien character to all parties, we may deconstruct what is otherwise taken for granted. If no national history, written from whatever perspective, determines our view, and there are thus no reliable values or pathways to guide us, Metternich is allowed to appear in a new light. I have been asked what attracts me in particular in Metternich. My answer is: the way he draws our attention—through his words and deeds—to the contradictions in human conduct; the way he allows us to participate in different times and experiences; the way he brings the problems of 200 years ago alive and how, via this detour through his experience, we may recognize their relevance for us today. To give an example: Do the holy warriors of 1789, 1813, and 1819 have something in common with those of today?

Readers will hopefully excuse this late excursion into methodological questions; it was necessary. From the perspective of Napoleon, not exactly an object of admiration in this book, one may put it like this: The commander must choose a different hill from which to survey the historical battle. The national perspective is not, or is no longer, suitable when the fight is a European and occasionally even a global one.

Let us consider some theses and questions that reveal how dealing with Metternich may at first be unsettling but may then afford us new insights as well as a deeper understanding of the man. Was the Holy Roman Empire really no more than a moribund edifice, an obsolete fancy-dress party, or was it perhaps a legal order that granted the less powerful a right to exist? The Holy Roman Empire had found its own solution for keeping a supranational order in balance, a quality that, according to Metternich, it was easier to destroy than to rebuild. There was a continuity between the Holy Roman Empire and the German Confederation. Following Metternich, we may put aside the traditional view of these associations as inefficient and irrational *Fleckenteppiche* [patchwork quilts], and remind ourselves, as he did, that both the Holy Roman Empire and the German Confederation were defensive federal orders, which were strong enough—the German Confederation at times had an army of 300,000 at its disposal—to defend themselves against bellicose neighbors. But they were also weak enough that they were not tempted to attack their peaceful neighbors. Perhaps, on a continent that the historian James Sheehan has branded the "continent of violence," this might be seen, for once, as embodying a good deal of political wisdom.[3]

And is it not this same political wisdom that led cosmopolitan politicians, chief among them Metternich himself, to meet at a large peace congress in Vienna in 1815 and found a new European order? That order had to come to terms, first of all, with the fact that all the old values and borders had been overthrown and violated in the space of a single generation. Do we not owe a little respect to the politicians who, in this situation, did not pursue the understandable desire for revenge and retribution, contrary to the expectations of the states of the Rhenish Confederation and France? These politicians did not calculate each party's damages, costs, and losses. Given that the category of nationality was not yet essential to the definition of states, was not even available to them, how can we accuse them of *Länderschacher* [haggling over countries]? And how should one have provided a new order of states, if not on the basis of populations, territories, and dynasties? Was it not certain that, in a Europe that in 1815 had only just become peaceful again, further wars would follow if borders were drawn along national lines? In 1848 the first glimmer of what would happen under nationalist conditions could be seen as German, Czech, and Croatian soldiers of the German Confederation, of Prussia, and of Habsburg marched against Danes, Poles, Czechs, Hungarians, and Italians. Is it not instructive to look at this ugly display, which Metternich had foreseen from his alternative perspective in exile in Britain?

The study of Metternich teaches us that monarchist ceremonies and rituals and the invocation of historical traditions do not automatically constitute threats to freedom. Every state that emerged from a revolution in the nineteenth century—thus every state emerging in Metternich's day—was given a king. That was the wish of the Greeks and the Belgians at the time of the July Revolution, and Metternich not only let it happen, he even supported it—even though it violated the Vienna order. Britain, Metternich's model state, showed that it was possible to have a Constitution based on freedom with a monarch at the top. It is commonly supposed that the reason modern states such as Belgium, the Netherlands, Denmark, Norway, Sweden, and even Luxembourg and Monaco still attach importance to their kings and queens is that it affords them additional prestige on the international stage. That was not Metternich's argument, but it shows that, in the long term, the monarchical form can turn into a costume. Through their symbolic force, "the emperor's old clothes," as

Barbara Stollberg-Rilinger has put it, have turned into new ones. For the rationally minded Metternich, the value of monarchy within the political system was not emotional but functional. That applied in particular to the question of how conflicts between constitutional bodies and the monarch were to be resolved. Who was to have the final say, as there were no constitutional courts yet? The monarchical principle provided a clear answer. Bismarck's four-year constitutional battle against the Prussian House of Representatives shows us what happened when the monarchical solution was rejected in the nineteenth century, and it was neither the democrats nor the liberals who emerged victorious from that conflict. For Metternich, the Habsburg Monarchy and its emperors provided the capstone to the multidimensional structure of the state, and in virtue of its own multidimensional and European character, it was the institution best suited to act as a final, neutral authority.

Metternich cared about this form of imperial rule right up until the end of his life. The way he tried to preserve it contributed to his controversial public persona. He was declared the originator of a "Metternich system," which was blamed for the failures of a whole generation. As a keen reader of the papers, he knew about this phrase, and he rejected it and the judgment it expressed. If we could ask him, he would probably not mind having the last word in this discussion of his life. Let us grant him that right. We may understand the following passage, in which Metternich even envisions his later biographers, as expressing what he himself might have understood by "strategist" and "visionary":

> We have never left the path shown to us by the good right. Unmoved by the errors of our time—errors which will always lead society to the abyss—we have had the satisfaction, in a time full of dangers, to serve the cause of peace and the welfare of nations, which never will be advanced by political revolutions. In the reports and lampoons of our epoch, a fixed significance has been attached to our name. We have not been able to recognise ourselves in these descriptions. It belongs to posterity alone to judge us according to our deeds; and in order to put it in a position to perform this important office, we have thought it proper to set the process underway on the right basis [with his Autobiographical Memorandum]. At the moment when we write these lines (1829) the historian is not yet born who will describe the numerous events of the first decades of the nineteenth century. Contemporaries cannot reasonably do more than collect materials for those who, at a subsequent period, will be called upon to write the true history of the past with that calmness and impartiality which are always wanting to those who have taken an active part in the events.[4]

ABBREVIATIONS

A. C.	"Acta Clementina" in NA Prag (Metternich's private posthumous papers)
ADB	*Allgemeine Deutsche Biographie*
AVA	Allgemeines Verwaltungsarchiv Vienna
DA	"Deutsche Akten" im HHStA Venna
GG	*Geschichte und Gesellschaft*
HHStA	Haus-, Hof- und Staatsarchiv Vienna
Krt.	Karton [box] (followed by the box number and, where applicable, the fascicle number, separated by a comma)
MKA	Minister Kolowrat-Akten in HHStA Vienna
MPM	Richard von Metternich, ed., *Memoirs of Prince Metternich,* 5 vols., trans. Alexander Napier (London: Richard Bentley & Son, 1880–1882)
NA	Nationalarchiv Prag (National Archive, Prague)
NP	Richard von Metternich, ed., *Aus Metternich's Nachgelassenen Papieren,* 8 vols. (Vienna, 1880–1884) (Metternich's published posthumous papers)
ÖNB	Österreichische Nationalbibliothek Vienna (National library of Austria, Vienna)
RAM	Rodinný Archiv Metternichů, Starý archiv (Metternich family archive)
StA	Staatsarchiv (state archive)
StK	Staatskanzlei (state chancellery)

NOTES

Introduction

1. See Externbrink, *"Generation Metternich,"* pp. 69–77; and Savoy, *Napoleon und Europa,* p. 155.

2. *Translator's note:* Hegel's phrase is often misquoted as "world-spirit on horseback" ("Weltgeist zu Pferde"). What Hegel actually wrote, in a letter from Jena to Friedrich Immanuel Niethammer (October 13, 1806), was: "den Kaiser—diese Weltseele—sah ich durch die Stadt zum Rekognoszieren hinausreiten" ("the emperor—this world soul—I saw as he rode through the city on reconnaissance").

3. Johann Gustav Droysen, *Outline of the Principles of History,* trans. E. Benjamin Andrews (New York: Fertig, 1893), p. 11.

4. Evans, "Nipperdeys Neunzehntes Jahrhundert," p. 137.

5. See MPM 1, p. 171–76; NP 1, pp. 138–42.

6. MPM 1, p. 35; NP1, p. 32.

7. MPM 1, p. 175 (trans. modified); NP 1, p. 142.

8. Metternich in a letter to his daughter Leontine, dated December 28, 1850; in NP 8, p. 239.

9. *Translator's note:* The "lesser German solution" refers to the unification of only the German states, without the German territories of the Habsburg Monarchy.

10. "Herr von Radowitz mein Biograph [Mr. Radowitz, my biographer] (1851)," in NP 8, p. 553.

11. See Metternich's letter of December 31, 1849, to the later president of the Austrian Reichsrat, Kübeck; in NP 8, p. 488.

12. Pertz, *Stein,* vol. 1.

13. Treitschke, *History of Germany in the Nineteenth Century,* vol. 2, p. 13; see esp. pp. 11–13.

14. *Translator's note: Deutschnational* indicates a supporter of the DNVP, the German National People's Party [Deutschnationale Volkspartei], a right-wing party of the Weimar Republic.

15. Bibl, *Metternich,* p. 27.

16. See Grunwald, *La vie de Metternich,* and—taking a similar stance—*Metternich et son temps* by Bertier de Sauvigny (born 1911).

17. Cecil, *Metternich,* p. 45.

18. See Palmer, *Metternich: Councillor of Europe;* Seward, *The First European;* Zorgbibe, *Le séducteur diplomate.*

19. Schroeder, *Transformation.*

20. Kissinger, *A World Restored.*

21. See Rumpler, *Österreichische Geschichte.*

22. Schmidt-Weissenfels, *Fürst Metternich.*

23. Beer, *Fürst Clemens Metternich.*

24. Malleson, *Life of Prince Metternich.*

25. Strobl von Ravelsberg, *Metternich und seine Zeit.*

26. Sandeman, *Metternich.*

27. Auernheimer, *Statesman and Lover.*

28. Missoffe, *Metternich.*

29. Vallotton, *Metternich.*

30. Béthouart, *Metternich et l'Europe.*

31. Hartau, *Metternich in Selbstzeugnissen.*

32. Herre, *Staatsmann des Friedens.*

33. Cartland, *The Passionate Diplomat.*

34. Fink, *Staatsmann, Spieler, Kavalier.*

35. Berglar, *Kutscher Europas.*

36. Schremmer, *Kavalier & Kanzler.*

37. See Just, *Wiener Kongress.*

38. See Botzenhart, *Botschafterzeit,* p. 262.

39. Srbik, *Metternich,* vol. 1, p. 117.

40. See Rauchensteiner, *Das Leben eines Geradlinigen,* p. 101 and p. 99 (note 1).

41. See Nipperdey, "Historismus und Historismuskritik," p. 65.

42. Srbik's only point of reference is an interview that Richard Cobden made with Metternich on July 10, 1847, in Vienna. The English text of this interview contains the word "race," which, however, has nothing to do with Srbik's biological concept of race. See Morley, *Cobden,* 1, p. 473 (Srbik erroneously gives p. 442 as the reference). In 1852, Metternich mentioned "race" once more, in NP 8, p. 521.

43. Koselleck, "Einleitung," p. xvii.

44. Srbik, *Geist und Geschichte*, vol. 2, p. 329.

45. Ibid., p. 349.

46. Ibid., p. 353.

47. Ibid., p. 248.

48. About Spengler, he says: "What a cult of power, what a glorification of violence, of the right of the stronger, of the victory of the blood! What a burning passion in this relentless battle, what a prize for success, what a biological naturalism in this prophecy!" Srbik, *Geist und Geschichte*, vol. 2, p. 322.

49. See Sked, *Metternich and Austria*.

50. Mascilli Migliorini, *L'artefice dell'Europa*.

1. Origins

1. Johann Gottfried Biedermann, *Geschlechts-Register Der Reichs Frey und unmittelbaren Ritterschafft Landes zu Francken* (Culmbach: Johann Albrecht Spindlern, 1751), Tabula CCLXV.

2. MPM 1, p. 270; NP 1, p. 276.

3. Just how little one should underestimate the aristocratic descent of the Metternichs and their embeddedness in the Holy Roman Empire is evident from recent research into the history of comparable aristocratic families of renown in the early modern period—such as, for instance, the House of Schönborn, a pillar of the Catholic imperial aristocracy of southern Germany. See Schraut, *Das Haus Schönborn*.

4. Of course, in late medieval times—from the eleventh to the fourteenth century—the transitions between the categories were more fluid, and only in the early modern German empire were the structures assumed here established more solidly. See Paravicini, *Die ritterlich-höfische Kultur*.

5. This was the "Ottohof" (later "Haus Velbrück"), which was passed on to the lineage of Otto II. The same "Metternich" was home to a second knightly residence, the "Burg Metternich," which was the ancestral seat of the Metternichs who bore a lion in their coat of arms. It still exists today, albeit as a ruin. See Broemser, *Zur Geschichte der Familien Metternich*, p. 2. This "Metternich" should not be confused with the part of Koblenz bearing the same name, as sometimes happens—e.g., in Palmer, *Metternich: Councillor of Europe*, p. 6.

6. See Broemser, *Zur Geschichte der Familien Metternich*, p. 7. On the basis of the available evidence, the oft-cited Arnold of Hemberg cannot be deemed the oldest ancestor.

7. "Darstellung des Rechtsverhältnisses des Hauses Metternich-Winneburg, bearbeitet nach den im Hausarchiv zu Plaß erliegenden Quellen im Monate Dezember 1882," NA Prague RAM Krt. 200, 1983.

8. See the maps in Broemser, *Zur Geschichte der Familien Metternich*, p. 33 and p. 52.

9. See "Pietro Nobile," Architektenlexikon, Wien 1770–1945, http://www.architektenlexikon .at/de/1196.htm.

10. *Translator's note:* An Appellationsrat is a legal councillor at a superior imperial court.

11. NA Prague RAM Krt. 74, 3614. The contract mentions imperial resolutions of April 4, 1627, July 19, 1629, and of March 28, 1630, as the basis of the agreement.

12. *Translator's note:* The election of the emperor of the Holy Roman Empire took place in two stages: at the royal election, a candidate was elected as the Roman king, and then he was crowned as emperor.

13. See Günther, *Die Habsburger-Liga 1625–1635,* p. 232.

14. *Translator's note: Freistift* was a medieval legal arrangement whereby a feudal lord could operate tenancy at will.

15. See the illustration in Rolf Toman (ed.), *Barock: Theatrum Mundi: Die Welt als Kunstwerk* (Potsdam, 2012), p. 227.

16. *Translator's note:* A *Meierhof* was a farm occupied by the administrator of a noble or ecclesiastical estate.

17. *Translator's note: Inkolat* was the term for the formal admission to the society of knights and landed gentry.

18. AVA Vienna, Adelsakten, Johann Reinhard von Metternich (draft).

19. For the exact sequence of events, see Paul Wagner: Philipp Christoph von Soetern, in *ADB* 26 (1888), 50–69.

20. Here, I follow the "*Succincta Facti Species zur Geschichte, wie Winneburg und Beilstein an die Metternichs kamen*" [A short summary of how Winneburg and Beilstein came into the hands of the Metternichs], NA Prague RAM Krt. 94, 3964.

21. NA Prague RAM Krt. 94, 3964.

22. AVA Vienna, Adelsakten, Johann Reinhard von Metternich Verleihung der Titel Winneburg und Beilstein, 28 März 1654 [Records on the nobility, Johann Reinhard von Metternich conferment of the titles of Winneburg and Beilstein, March 28, 1854].

23. Metternich in a letter to the former privy councillor of the Trier electorate, von Rieff, dated September 5, 1832; NA Prague RAM Krt. 172, 6195.

24. Von Rieff to Metternich, June 20, 1832, NA Prague RAM Krt. 172, 6195.

25. "Cochem, 14.10.1834," in *Didaskalie: Blätter für Geist, Gemüth und Publizität,* no. 305 (November 5, 1834).

26. Draft of the document: AVA Vienna, Adelsakten, Philipp Emmerich von Metternich Grafenstand, March 20, 1679 [Records on the nobility, Philipp Emmerich von Metternich Rank of Count, 3.20.1679]; fair copy: NA Prague RAM Krt. 58, 3231.

27. Franz Werner, *Der Dom zu Mainz und seine Denkmäler,* part 3, Mainz 1836, p. 69.

28. Peter Fuchs, "Metternich," *NDB* 17 (1994), 232–35.

29. Stiftsbrief [founding letter of the trust]; NA Prague RAM Krt. 61, 3286.

30. NA Prague RAM Krt. 62, 3344.

31. NA Prague RAM Krt. 62, 3324.

32. Decree of October 24, 1697, NA Prague RAM Krt. 62, 3336.

33. NA Prague RAM Krt. 6, 1774 and 1783.

34. NA Prague RAM Krt. 6, 1784 and 1785. Under Austrian law, the age of majority was reached at twenty-four; see Schwerin, *Rechtsgeschichte,* p. 15.

35. NA Prague RAM Krt. 62, 3340. Dated November 22, 1770 (copy).

36. Text of the document (copy): NA Prague RAM Krt. 59, 3240.

37. Srbik, *Metternich,* I, p. 55.

38. See Mathy, *Franz Georg von Metternich.*

39. Srbik, *Metternich,* I, p. 57.

40. Ibid.

41. NA Prague RAM Krt. 59, 3236.

42. Letter in Franz Georg's hand to the Emperor, May 26, 1803, NA Prague RAM Krt. 143, 5359.

43. Passage from the takeover record, Ochsenhausen, July 1, 1803, NA Prague RAM Krt. 59, 3242.

44. NA Prague RAM Krt. 143, 5359.

45. *Translator's note: Kurialstimme* was a vote shared by several members with a right to vote.

46. The original handwritten letter in NA Prague RAM Krt. 59, 3244. The announcement in *Wiener Zeitung,* no. 151, November 3, 1813, of which there is a copy in NA Prague RAM Krt. 59, 3245.

47. Tax notification of the president of the Imperial Chamber Ugarte, February 4, 1814, NA Prague RAM Krt. 59, 3246.

48. Metternich, February 1, 1814, HHStA Vienna StK Vorträge [presentations] Krt. 195.

49. Metternich to Emperor Franz, February 26, 1814, HHStA Vienna StK Vorträge [lectures] Krt. 195, Fol. 114. The design for the coat of arms in HHStA Vienna StK Interiora Personalia, Krt. 7, Fol. 14.

50. *Translator's note:* A literal translation of Ochsenhausen would be "oxhouse."

51. NP 7, p. 634.

52. MPM 3, pp. 394–95; NP 3, p. 348.

53. NP 8, p. 626.

2. Metternich's Generation

1. MPM 1, p. 3; NP 1, p. 7.

2. Metternich drafted a first sketch of his "Autobiographische Denkschrift" [autobiographical memoir] in 1826, recounting the "main moments of [my] life" in several increasingly detailed versions. NA Prague A. C. 8, Krt. 1, 1.

3. NA Prague RAM Krt. 1, 1714.

4. The process is documented in NA Prague RAM Krt. 126, 4767–4774.

5. *Translator's note:* Official confirmation of the correctness of all information given in documents, in particular genealogical tables.

6. This reference was made in connection with an application for another prebend, made in June 1789 to the cathedral chapter in Cologne; NA Prague RAM Krt. 126, 4772.

7. Maximilian Franz von Köln to Franz Georg, late in 1785, quoted in Mathy, "Die Entlassung des Franz Georg von Metternich," p. 95.

8. *Translator's note:* A *Hofmarschall* was a high-ranking court official overseeing the economic affairs of the imperial household.

9. "Hauptmomente meines Lebens" [Main moments of my life], NA Prague A. C. 8, Krt. 3, 21.

10. Franz Georg to Clemens, April 9, 1785, and November 2, 1787, NA Prague A. C. 14, Krt. 6, 95.

11. "Autobiographische Notizen," NA Prague A. C. 14, Krt. 13, 324.

12. Beatrix to Clemens, May 18, 1789, NA Prague A. C. 14, Krt. 6, 106.

13. Metternich to Dorothea von Lieven, December 1, 1818, in Mika, *Metternichs Briefe*, p. 60.

14. NA Prague RAM, Krt. 99, 1. On the events surrounding the election, see Hansen, *Quellen*, I, pp. 3–4.

15. *Translator's note:* Cameralism was a seventeenth- and eighteenth-century science of state administration focusing on increasing a nation's monetary wealth through the accumulation of bullion.

16. See Renaud, "Johann Friedrich Simon," pp. 449–500.

17. Hansen, *Quellen*, 1 (Introduction), p. 28*, p. 42*; p. 45, p. 50, p. 61, and p. 63.

18. Franz Georg to Clemens, December 30, 1790, MPM 1, pp. 382–83 [transl. amended in accordance with original letter quoted here]. Original letter at NA Prague A. C. 14, Krt. 6, 95.

19. The original of this hitherto unknown document, which is severely faded and only readable with the help of modern digital technology, can be found at NA Prague RAM Krt. 138, 5212.

20. See Renaud, "Johann Friedrich Simon," p. 468.

21. Johann Friedrich Simon to Pauline von Metternich, April 22, 1789, NA Prague A. C. 14, Krt. 13, 317.

22. Ibid.

23. Letter of May 7, 1789, from Johann Friedrich Simon to Metternich's sister Pauline: "L'expérience et la reflexion sont les seuls grands maîtres, qui forment l'esprit humain"; NA Prague A. C. 14, Krt. 13, 317. See Srbik, *Metternich,* I, p. 64.

24. MPM 1, p. 5 (transl. amended); NP 1, p. 9.

25. Note on cover page to the letters; NA Prague A. C. 14, Krt. 13, 317.

26. Ibid., p. 9; NP 1, p. 12.

27. Ibid., p. 10; NP 1, p. 14.

28. Ibid., p. 6; NP 1, p. 9.

29. Note on cover page to the letters; NA Prague A. C. 14, Krt. 13, 317.

30. "Bemerkungen als Zugabe und Erläuterung zu der Geschichte meines Lebens und Werkes, niedergeschrieben Dez. 1844" [Complementary and explanatory remarks on the history of my life and work, noted down in Dec. 1844]; NA Prague A. C. 8, Krt. 3, 22.

31. *Translator's note:* In full: The Order of Poor Clerics Regular of the Mother of God of the Pious Schools, the oldest Catholic educational order.

32. MPM 1, p. 9 (transl. amended); NP 1, p. 12.

33. Except for final sentence: ibid., pp. 415f (emphases by Metternich; transl. amended); NP 1, pp. 256–57. Original letter: NA Prague A. C. 13, Krt. 2, 37b.

34. Metternich to Dorothea von Lieven, December 1, 1818, in Mika, *Metternich's Briefe,* p. 59.

35. Srbik, *Metternich* I, p. 65, erroneously gives November 1788 as the date. The correct date is confirmed by the prebend and Metternich's own memory ("summer 1788") in "Bemerkungen als Zugabe und Erläuterung zu der Geschichte meines Lebens und Werkes, niedergeschrieben Dez. 1844" [Complementary and explanatory remarks on the history of my life and work, noted down in Dec. 1844]; NA Prague A. C. 8, Krt. 3, 22.

36. NA Prague RAM, Krt. 126, 4772. Contains the correspondence concerning the prebend.

37. Johann Friedrich Simon to Franz Georg, dated June 12 to November 7, 1789, NA Prague A. C. 14, Krt. 12, 271.

38. Abbé Bertrand to Franz Georg, May 13, 1789, NA Prague A. C. 14, Krt. 13, 313.

39. Franz Georg to Clemens, December 30, 1790, NA Prague A. C. 14, Krt. 6, 95.

40. Weis, *Montgelas,* I, p. 15.

41. Ibid., pp. 13–14.

42. MPM 1, p. 4; NP, I, p. 8.

43. Koch, *Gemählde der Revolutionen,* I, pp. 2–3.

44. Ibid., pp. 3–4.

45. Ibid., p. 5.

46. Ibid., II, p. 225.

47. The termini post and ante quem can be established from a letter of their mother, Beatrix, to Clemens, dated October 21, 1790 ("departed"), and her first letter to Mainz of October 23, 1790 (NA Prague A. C. 14, Krt. 6, 107), and from her letter of August 14, 1792, in which she expresses her wish that Clemens arrive in Brussels no later than September 10; NA Prague A. C. 14, Krt. 6, 109.

48. See Berg, *Niklas Vogt,* pp. 43–45.

49. Ibid., p. 45.

50. Ibid., p. 44.

51. See the table of contents in Vogt's *Die deutsche Nation.*

52. MPM 1, pp. 11–12 (transl. amended); NP 1, pp. 14–15.

53. Vogt, *Politisches Sistem,* p. 181.

54. "Ces trois puissances devroient former un repos ou une inaction. Mais comme, par le movement necessaire des choses, elles sont contraintes d'aller, elles seront forcées d'aller de concert." Montesquieu, *Esprit des Loix,* Liv. XI. Ch. VI. ["These three powers should naturally form a state of repose or inaction. But as there is a necessity for movement in the course of human affairs, they are forced to move, but still in concert." *On the Spirit of Laws,* Book XI, Ch. VI.]

55. Vogt, *Politisches Sistem,* p. 36.

56. See Weichlein, "Cosmopolitanism, Patriotism, Nationalism," p. 78.

57. Vogt, *Politisches Sistem,* p. 70.

58. See the quotations ibid., pp. 71–87.

59. Ibid., p. 95.

60. MPM 1, pp. 263–64; NP 1, p. 218.

61. See "Merkwürdiges Beispiel politischer Weissagung aus dem sechsten Buche der Geschichte des Polybius" [Remarkable example of political prophecy from the sixth book of Polybius's history], in Vogt, *Die deutsche Nation*, pp. 217–27.

62. See Karl Anton Schaab, *Geschichte der Stadt Mainz* (Mainz 1841), I, pp. xxvii f.; Karl Georg Bockenheimer, Nicolaus Vogt, in *ADB*, 40 (1896), pp. 189–92. Bockenheimer quotes the original text, which is reproduced here. Schaab erroneously writes "defender of the old *Empire*" (emph. W. S.). The correct wording can also be found in *Frankfurter Ober-Postamts-Zeitung*, Beilage No. 225, August 16, 1838.

63. MPM 1, p. 35; NP 1, p. 32.

64. Ibid., p. 36 (transl. amended); NP 1, p. 33.

65. Ibid., pp. 36–37 (transl. amended); NP 1, pp. 33–34.

66. Vogt, *Darstellung des europäischen Völkerbundes*, p. 248.

67. All quotations are taken from ibid., pp. 248–50.

68. See Burgdorf, *Ein Weltbild verliert seine Welt* [A world picture loses its world], pp. 11–16.

69. MPM 1, p. 137; NP 1, p. 113.

70. See also Siemann, *Metternich's Britain*.

3. A Double Crisis

1. Lang, *Memoiren*, I, p. 212.

2. See Stollberg-Rilinger, *Des Kaisers alte Kleider*, p. 8.

3. MPM 1, p. 7; NP I, p. 11.

4. Ibid., p. 8 (transl. amended); NP 1, p. 11.

5. I follow the *Vollständiges Diarium der Römisch-Königlichen Wahl* [Complete diary of the Roman-Royal elections], pp. 329–30.

6. The order of the ceremony can be found in ibid., pp. 316–30.

7. *Translator's note:* The Römer is the medieval city hall of Frankfurt.

8. *Translator's note:* The office of the Reichserbmarschall required the performance of a symbolic act at the coronation. The marshal had to ride on a horse into a pile of hay that had to reach at least to the animal's belly, symbolizing that the imperial stable was rich in provisions. The hay was then distributed among the population.

9. See for an overall account Hattenhauer, *Wahl und Krönung Franz II* [Election and coronation of Franz II].

10. *Vollständiges Diarium der Römisch-Königlichen Wahl* [Complete diary of the Roman-Royal elections], p. 331.

11. NA Prague A. C. 14, Krt. 6, 106.

12. *Kurtrierisches Intelligenzblatt*, August 28, 1789, in Hansen, *Quellen*, I, p. 428.

13. Beatrix to Clemens, August 14, 1789; NA Prague A. C. 14, Krt. 6, 106.

14. See Eimer, *Straßburg im Elsaß im Jahre 1789*, p. 101.

15. MPM 1, p. 8; NP I, pp. 11–12.

16. The following account is based on Eimer, *Straßburg im Elsaß im Jahre 1789*, pp. 66–101.

17. Ibid., p. 68.

18. Ibid., p. 73.

19. Ibid., p. 74.

20. "Bemerkungen als Zugabe und Erläuterung zu der Geschichte meines Lebens und Werkes, niedergeschrieben Dez. 1844" [Complementary and explanatory remarks on the history of my life and work, noted down in Dec. 1844"]; NA Prague A. C. 8, Krt. 3, 22.

21. Beatrix to Clemens, August 4, 1789; NA Prague A. C. 14, Krt. 6, 106.

22. "Bemerkungen als Zugabe und Erläuterung zu der Geschichte meines Lebens und Werkes, niedergeschrieben Dez. 1844"; NA Prague A. C. 8, Krt. 3, 22.

23. *La Constitution française, présentée au Roi par l'Assemblée Nationale le 3 Septembre 1791*, Paris 1791. The copy is still in the library at Königswart.

24. Renaud, "Johann Friedrich Simon," p. 474.

25. I follow ibid., pp. 449–500.

26. Ibid., p. 478.

27. "Bemerkungen als Zugabe und Erläuterung zu der Geschichte meines Lebens und Werkes, niedergeschrieben Dez. 1844"; NA Prague A. C. 8, Krt. 3, 22.

28. See Blanning, *Reform and Revolution in Mainz*, p. 300.

29. Renaud, "Johann Friedrich Simon," pp. 490–91.

30. MPM 1, pp. 5–6; NP I, p. 9.

31. "Bemerkungen als Zugabe und Erläuterung zu der Geschichte meines Lebens und Werkes, niedergeschrieben Dez. 1844"; NA Prague A. C. 8, Krt. 3, 22.

32. Metternich to Dorothea von Lieven, April 20, 1820; MPM 3, p. 369 (transl. amended); NP 3, p. 325.

33. MPM 1, p. 5 (transl. amended); NP 1, p. 9.

34. Ibid., p. 6; NP 1, p. 9.

35. Hansen, *Quellen*, I, p. 782. The election took place on March 6, 1791.

36. Quoted in Friese, *Vaterländische Geschichte*, 5, pp. 120–21.

37. MPM 1, p. 6; NP I, p. 9.

38. Metternich to Dorothea von Lieven, April 20, 1820; MPM 3, p. 369; NP 3, p. 325.

39. MPM 1, p. 11 (transl. modified); NP I, p. 14.

40. *Translator's note:* Pfaffe may denote any clergyman and was originally neutral, but it was used derogatively from the Reformation onward.

41. *Translator's note:* Hornvieh literally means "horned cattle," but used in the sense of "stupid cow" (though without prejudice as to gender).

42. See Dumont, *Mainzer Republik*, p. 48; Hansen, *Quellen*, 2, pp. 162–63; Kuhn and Schweigard, *Freiheit oder Tod!*, pp. 160–62.

43. Library Königswart, Mainzer Druckschriften 1791–1793 [Printed material: Mainz 1791–1793]. These were erroneously filed together with a collection of pamphlets from the period 1848–1849, and are still at that location, where all the documents referred to in the following can be found.

44. Srbik, *Metternich*, I, p. 96.

45. Hansen, *Quellen*, 2, p. 463.

46. Library Königswart, Printed material: Mainz 1791–1793.

47. *Anrede an die neu gebildete Gesellschaft der Freunde der Freiheit und Gleichheit in Mainz. Von A. J. Dorsch. Mainz im ersten Jahre der mainzer Freiheit und fränkischen Republik* [Address to the newly formed society of the friends of freedom and equality in Mainz. By A. J. Dorsch. Mainz in the first year of the freedom of Mainz and of the Franconian Republic]. Library Königswart, Flugschriftensammlung 1791–1793 [collection of pamphlets].

48. Hansen, *Quellen*, 1, pp. 660–61 and pp. 1035–40; Dumont, *Mainzer Republik*, pp. 47–48; Kuhn and Schweigard, *Freiheit oder Tod!*, pp. 159–60.

49. Custine, "Bekanntmachung an die Einwohner des Erzbisthums Mainz wie auch der Städte and Bißthümer Worms und Speyer," November 18, 1792, Library Königswart, Printed material: Mainz 1791–1793; see Hansen, *Quellen*, 2, p. 596.

50. Dumont, *Mainzer Republik*, p. 132.

51. Mathias Metternich, *Rede, worinn die Bedenklichkeiten*, p. 6 (Library Königswart).

52. Ibid., p. 12.

53. Library Königswart.

54. Library Königswart, Printed material: Mainz 1791–1793.

55. On this, see Lorenz, *Joseph II. und die Belgische Revolution*.

56. Kaunitz to Franz Georg, November 27, 1791, NA Prague RAM Krt. 227, 2017-4.

57. "Bemerkungen als Zugabe und Erläuterung zu der Geschichte meines Lebens und Werkes, niedergeschrieben Dez. 1844" [Complementary and explanatory remarks on the history of my life and work, noted down in Dec. 1844"]; NA Prague A. C. 8, Krt. 3, 22.

58. MPM 1, p. 10; NP I, p. 13.

59. See Zeißberg, *Zwei Jahre belgischer Geschichte*, 1, pp. 78–80.

60. Ibid., 2, p. 55.

61. See the detailed account of the prehistory in Zeißberg, *Zwei Jahre belgischer Geschichte*, 1, pp. 2–14, which is derived from the files in Vienna, but unfortunately leaves out the military development.

62. Ibid., 2, pp. 216–18.

63. Archduke Carl to Emperor Franz, December 23, 1792. See Zeißberg, *Zwei Jahre belgischer Geschichte*, 2, p. 237.

64. Ibid., 2, p. 239. Srbik's claim (*Metternich*, 1, p. 77) that Franz Georg had been "ignored in the awards" is therefore wrong.

65. Zeißberg, *Zwei Jahre belgischer Geschichte*, 2, p. 250.

66. Zeißberg, *Belgien unter der Generalstatthalterschaft Erzherzog Carls*, 1, p. 18.

67. Ibid., 2, p. 9.

68. Mathy, *Franz Georg von Metternich,* p. 176.

69. NA Prague RAM Krt. 142, 5344.

70. See Koll, *Die belgische Nation,* pp. 367–78.

71. See Zedinger, *Die Verwaltung der Österreichischen Niederlande,* p. 166.

72. NA Prague A. C. 14, Krt. 6, 109.

73. Aretin, *Vom Deutschen Reich zum Deutschen Bund,* p. 24.

74. Blanning, *The French Revolutionary Wars,* pp. 62–64.

75. Franz Georg to the Archbishop of Cologne, April 23, 1792, quoted after Mathy, *Franz Georg von Metternich,* p. 160.

76. Beatrix to Clemens, March 13, 1792, NA Prague A. C. 14, Krt. 6, 109.

77. Beatrix to Clemens, May 13, 1791, NA Prague A. C. 14, Krt. 6, 108.

78. MPM 1, p. 10; NP 1, p. 13.

79. "Bemerkungen als Zugabe und Erläuterung zu der Geschichte meines Lebens und Werkes, niedergeschrieben Dez. 1844" [Complementary and explanatory remarks on the history of my life and work, noted down in Dec. 1844"]; NA Prague A. C. 8, Krt. 3, 22.

80. MPM 1, p. 12; NP 1, p. 15.

81. Ibid.

82. "Bemerkungen als Zugabe und Erläuterung zu der Geschichte meines Lebens und Werkes, niedergeschrieben Dez. 1844" [Complementary and explanatory remarks on the history of my life and work, noted down in Dec. 1844"]; NA Prague A. C. 8, Krt. 3, 22.

83. MPM 1, p. 14; NP 1, p. 17.

84. Ibid., p. 13; NP 1, p. 16.

85. Beatrix to Clemens, September 1, 1789, NA Prague A. C. 14, Krt. 6, 106.

86. Beatrix to Clemens, September 4, 1789, NA Prague A. C. 14, Krt. 6, 106.

87. Beatrix to Clemens, June 14, 1789, NA Prague A. C. 14, Krt. 6, 108.

88. See Blisch, *Friedrich Carl Joseph von Erthal,* p. 207.

89. On the history of the origin of the manifesto, see Heigel, *Das Manifest des Herzogs von Braunschweig,* pp. 138–84.

90. MPM 1, p. 14; NP 1, p. 16.

91. Brunswick, "The Proclamation of the Duke of Brunswick" (trans. amended). German original, regest and commentary in Hansen, *Quellen,* 2, pp. 297–303.

92. Heigel, *Das Manifest des Herzogs von Braunschweig,* p. 146.

93. Blanning, *The French Revolutionary Wars,* p. 71.

94. MPM 1, p. 15; NP 1, p. 17.

95. Ibid., pp. 15–16; NP 1, p. 18.

96. Palmer, *Metternich: Councillor of Europe,* p. 23.

97. "Hauptmomente meines Lebens" [Main moments of my life], NA Prague A. C. 8, Krt. 3, 21.

98. Goethe, "The Campaign in France," p. 150.

99. MPM 1, p. 14 (transl. amended); NP 1, p. 17.

100. See Blanning, *The French Revolutionary Wars,* pp. 80–82.

101. Ibid., p. 88.

102. "Hauptmomente meines Lebens" [Main moments of my life], NA Prague A. C. 8, Krt. 3, 21.

103. Mathy, *Franz Georg von Metternich,* p. 169.

104. MPM 1, p. 14; NP 1, p. 17.

105. MPM 1, p. 15; NP 1 p. 17.

106. MPM 1, p. 9; NP 1, p. 12.

107. "Hauptmomente meines Lebens" [Main moments of my life], NA Prague A. C. 8, Krt. 3, 21.

108. Dumouriez, *Memoirs of General Dumouriez,* vol. 2, p. 202 (transl. modified).

109. MPM 1, p. 15 (transl. amended); NP 1, p. 18.

110. Hansen, *Quellen,* 2, p. 817.

111. MPM 1, p. 15 (transl. amended); NP 1, p. 18.

112. Büchner, *Danton's Death* (act 1, scene 5), p. 21. *Translator's note:* Vergniaud's reported words were: "Citoyens, il est à craindre que la révolution, comme Saturne, ne dévore successivement tous ses enfants et n'engendre enfin le despotisme avec les calamités qui l'accompagnent." M.-F. A. Mignet, *Histoire de la révolution française,* p. 221: "Citizens, it is to be feared that the revolution, like Saturn, may devour its own children, and engender, at length, despotism, with all its attendant calamities." After F. A. Mignet, *History of the French Revolution from 1789 to 1814,* p. 406.

113. Dumouriez, *Memoirs of General Dumouriez,* vol. 2, p. 226.

114. Ibid., p. 247.

115. "Hauptmomente meines Lebens" [Main moments of my life], NA Prague A. C. 8, Krt. 3, 21.

116. See Wagner, *Französische Gegenrevolution,* pp. 105–14; Schroeder, *Transformation,* pp. 125–32.

117. The text can be found in Grab, *Die Französische Revolution,* p. 126.

118. Wagner, *Französische Gegenrevolution,* p. 93.

119. Weis, *Durchbruch des Bürgertums,* pp. 187–88.

120. The protocol of the meeting can be found in Dohna, 1: *Feldzug der Preußen,* pp. 157–64.

121. Ludwig von Starhemberg to Baron von Thugut, April 12, 1793, in Vivenot and Zeißberg, *Quellen zur . . . Kaiserpolitik,* 3, 1, pp. 9–11.

122. Prokesch von Osten, "Der Feldzug in den Niederlanden," p. 203.

123. For a more detailed survey of the battles mentioned here, see John Rickard, "Siege of Valenciennes," January 14, 2009, http://www.historyofwar.org/articles/siege_valenciennes_1793.html.

124. MPM 1, p. 15; NP 1, p. 18.

125. MPM 1, p. 339 (transl. amended); NP 1, p. 339. Original with Metternich's later note commenting on the "youthful zeal" of his composition in NA Prague A. C. 8, Krt. 3, 24.

126. "Bemerkungen als Zugabe und Erläuterung zu der Geschichte meines Lebens und Werkes, niedergeschrieben Dez. 1844" [Complementary and explanatory remarks on the history of my life and work, noted down in Dec. 1844"]; NA Prague A. C. 8, Krt. 3, 22.

127. On the background and outcome, see Zeißberg, *Belgien unter der Generalstatthalter-schaft*, 3, pp. 56–71.

128. See Liedekerke Beaufort, *Souvenirs et Biographie*, pp. 1–4.

129. Metternich, *Journal de mon Voyage*, March 27, 1794.

130. Arnold-Baker, *The Companion to British History*, entry "Dagger Scene in the Commons," p. 393. *Translator's note:* The *History of Parliament* website has the following to say about the incident: "In a dramatic, yet slightly ludicrous episode in the debate on the aliens bill, 28 Dec., Burke threw to the floor a 'revolutionary' dagger manufactured in Birmingham, in protest against 'the introduction of French principles and French daggers.' To the consequent laughter and calls for a fork, Burke replied, 'When you smile, I see blood trickling down your face.' Fox, Burke, Sheridan (whose five-hour speech against Warren Hastings in 1787 had set the tone) and Pitt were the supreme exponents of the florid and prolix oratory that had become the fashion." See http://www.historyofparliamentonline.org/volume/1790-1820/parliament/1790.

131. MPM 1, p. 16; NP 1, p. 18.

132. Ibid.

133. Metternich, *Journal de mon Voyage*, April 3, 1794.

134. Ibid.

135. MPM 1, p. 16; NP 1, p. 18.

136. Ibid., p. 17; NP 1, p. 19.

137. Ibid.

138. Metternich, *Journal de mon Voyage*, April 8, 1794.

139. MPM 1, p. 16; NP 1, p. 19.

140. See Liedekerke Beaufort, *Voyage en Angleterre*, pp. 214–15.

141. See Wagner, *Französische Gegenrevolution*, p. 35.

142. Ibid., p. 61.

143. I follow the excellent analysis in ibid., pp. 42–65.

144. Ibid., p. 49.

145. Ibid., p. 48.

146. Ibid., p. 50.

147. Srbik, *Metternich*, I, p. 94.

148. MPM 1, p. 16; NP 1, p. 19.

149. Srbik, *Metternich*, I, p. 260.

150. The copy is held in the library in Königswart.

151. In the first edition of 1790, the passage runs from page 8, "When I see the spirit of liberty . . . till the liquor is cleared," to page 9: "Flattery corrupts both . . . which may be soon turned into complaints."

152. Gentz, *Betrachtungen*, p. 10 (edition of 1793) translates this misleadingly as *Ruhe und Ordnung* [law and order].

153. Beatrix to Clemens, September 1, 1789, NA Prague A. C. 14, Krt. 6, 106.

154. It begins on page 112 ("It is now sixteen or seventeen years . . .") and ends on page 114 (". . . to be subdued by manners").

155. NA Prague A. C. 11, Krt. 2, 49. The complete letter can be found in Edmund Burke, *The Works*, VII (London, 1826), pp. 345–72 ("Letter to William Elliot, occasioned by the account given in a newspaper of the speech made in the House of Lords by the **** [Duke] of ******* [Norfolk] in the Debate concerning Lord Fitzwilliam 1795").

156. See Ticknor, *Life, Letters, and Journals*, 2, p. 14.

157. Horace, *Carmina*, III 6, 5.

158. Metternich, *Journal de mon Voyage*, March 29, 1794; Liedekerke Beaufort, *Voyage en Angleterre*, p. 197.

159. Metternich, *Journal de mon Voyage*, April 2, 1794.

160. Liedekerke Beaufort, *Voyage en Angleterre*, p. 219.

161. Metternich, *Journal de mon Voyage*, April 1, 1794.

162. Ibid., April 4, 1794.

163. Liedekerke Beaufort, *Voyage en Angleterre*, p. 201.

164. Ibid., p. 198.

165. Metternich, *Journal de mon Voyage*, March 30, 1794.

166. Liedekerke Beaufort, *Voyage en Angleterre*, p. 200.

167. Metternich, *Journal de mon Voyage*, March 28, 1794; Liedekerke Beaufort, *Voyage en Angleterre*, p. 196.

168. Liedekerke Beaufort, *Voyage en Angleterre*, p. 223.

169. A description of the episode from Hofmann's perspective can be found in his "Rapport" of 1795: A. J. Hofmann, ". . . . Seine Sendung nach England in den Jahren 1793," *Nassauische Annalen* 29 (1897–1898), pp. 84–89.

170. Letter sent by Joseph Haydn from Eisenstadt to Metternich, September 27, 1802, NA Prague A. C. 7, Krt. 2, 111A.

171. Liedekerke Beaufort, *Voyage en Angleterre*, pp. 245–50.

172. MPM 1, p. 17; NP 1, p. 20.

173. Liedekerke Beaufort, *Voyage en Angleterre*, p. 228.

174. MPM 1, pp. 18–19; NP 1, p. 21.

175. Ibid.

176. Palmer, *Metternich: Councillor of Europe*, p. 24, also points out the chronological discrepancy.

177. A detailed description of the battle is given in "Umständlicher und genauer Bericht von der großen Seeschlacht am ersten Junius und dem Siege des Admiral Howe," *Politisches Journal* ([Hamburg] 1794), vol. 2, pp. 702–12.

178. Ibid., p. 766.

179. MPM 1, p. 20; NP 1, p. 22.

180. See Anderegg, *Die politischen Verhältnisse Englands*; Rohl, *Metternich und England*; Sadek, *Metternichs publizistische und pressepolitische Betätigung im Exil*.

181. All these judgments are taken from Anderegg, *Die politischen Verhältnisse Englands*.

182. Srbik, *Metternich*, 2, p. 446.

183. Metternich to Dorothea von Lieven, June 21, 1819, NA Prague A. C. 6, C19.4, Fols. 46–47 (emph. W. S.); shortened version in Corti, *Metternich*, 2, pp. 99–100.

184. Metternich to his daughter Leontine, April 22, 1848, NP 8, p. 148.

185. Letter sent by Metternich from Vienna to Benjamin Disraeli, October 23, 1858, NA Prague A. C. 13, Krt. 1, 25 (emph. W. S.).

186. See Ticknor, *Life, Letters, and Journals*, 2, p. 16.

187. By Palmer, *Metternich: Councillor of Europe*, p. 25.

188. *Politisches Journal (1794)*, vol. 2, p. 768.

189. See Schütz and Schulz, *Geschichte der Kriege*, part 3, pp. 245–46.

190. MPM 1, p. 20; NP 1, p. 22.

191. On the emperor's journey, see Zeißberg, *Belgien unter der Generalstatthalterschaft*, 3, pp. 1–27.

192. In June: Ypern (on the 18th), Charleroi (25th), Fleurus (26th). In July: Mons (1st), Brussels (9th), Leuven (14th), Mechelen (15th), Landrecies (16th), Namur (17th), Nieuwpoort (18th), Antwerp (24th), and Liege (27th). In August: Le Quesnoy (16th), Sluis (25th), and Valenciennes (28th). See the chronology compiled from standard sources of military historiography at http://cliomaps.de/timelines/1-koalitionskrieg/niederlande.

193. MPM 1, pp. 20–21; NP 1, p. 22.

194. Zeißberg, *Belgien unter der Generalstatthalterschaft*, and, following Zeißberg closely, Srbik, *Metternich*, Mathy, *Franz Georg von Metternich*, and Palmer, *Metternich: Councillor of Europe*, all of whom uncritically adopt Trauttmansdorff's statist and absolutist evaluation, representing Franz Georg as lazy, too lenient toward the estates, and not practical minded.

195. Zeißberg, *Belgien unter der Generalstatthalterschaft*, 2, pp. 124–8.

196. Franz Georg to Ferdinand von Trauttmansdorff, August 8, 1794, quoted in Zeißberg, *Belgien unter der Generalstatthalterschaft*, 3, pp. 164–65.

197. Zeißberg, *Belgien unter der Generalstatthalterschaft*, 3, p. 160.

198. Letter written in August 1794 from Franz Georg to the Archduke Carl, quoted after Zeißberg, *Belgien unter der Generalstatthalterschaft*, 3, p. 172.

199. In his "Hauptmomente meines Lebens" [Main moments of my life] (NA Prague A. C. 8, Krt. 3, 21), Metternich writes: "Return via Harwich to Helvoetsluys; journey through Holland to Benrath to which my father had fled with the government of Holland. Journey to the headquarters of the Duke of Coburg at Fouron le Comte." In a further note, he added "Aug." to the journey.

200. The pamphlet is reproduced, without the motto preceding it and with some editorial changes that deviate from the handwritten original, in MPM 1, pp. 340–47; NP 1, pp. 340–45. In the following, I quote exclusively from the original. *Translator's note:* The English follows the existing translation, except where it is incomplete or inaccurate.

201. As Srbik claims, *Metternich*, 1, pp. 76–77.

202. Hansen, *Quellen*, 3, pp. 168–71.

203. Ibid., 3, pp. 14–15.

204. Ibid., 3, p. 170.

205. Some examples can be found in ibid., 3, p. 170; there were many more.

206. NA Prague A. C. 8, Krt. 3, 24. *Translator's note:* Metternich's translation renders this as: "Blutige Spuren zeichnen die Straße, welche sie zogen. Sie verheerten oder zerstörten

alles in der Runde, ohne Unterschiede, heilige und weltliche Sachen. Kein Alter, kein Geschlecht, kein Rang blieb verschont. Was der Wut einer ersten Überschwemmung entfloh, fiel in der folgenden."

207. On the idea of total war, see Blanning, *The French Revolutionary Wars*, p. 101.

208. See Wagner, *Französische Gegenrevolution*, pp. 144–46.

209. William Robertson, *The History of the Reign of the Emperor Charles V* (Dublin: W. and W. Smith et. al., 1770), p. 9.

210. MPM 1, p. 341 (transl. modified); NP 1, p. 340.

211. MPM 1, p. 340; NP 1, p. 340.

212. See Blanning, *The French Revolutionary Wars*, pp. 116–20.

213. See ibid., p. 115.

214. On the context of the sociopolitical argument of the pamphlet, see Leonhard, *Bellizismus und Nation*, pp. 222–23.

215. See Wendland, *Versuche einer allgemeinen Volksbewaffnung*, pp. 140–41.

216. Ibid., p. 134.

217. Ibid., pp. 136–37, note 1.

218. *Magazin der Kunst und Literattur* (Vienna) 4, no. 3 (1796), pp. 212–14.

219. Quoted from the manuscript. NA Prague, A. C. 8, Krt. 3, 24. The printed version contains some idiosyncratic editorial interventions.

220. Letter sent by Beatrix from Benrath to Franz Georg, September 6, 1794, NA Prague, A. C. 14, Krt. 6, 110.

221. Letter sent by Beatrix from Benrath to Franz Georg, September 3, 1794, NA Prague, A. C. 14, Krt. 6, 110.

222. Letter sent by Beatrix from Rüdesheim to Franz Georg, October 11, 1794, NA Prague, A. C. 14, Krt. 6, 110.

223. "Biographische Andeutungen" [Biographical sketches], NA Prague, A. C. 8, Krt. 3, 21.

224. See the detailed account in Hansen, *Quellen*, 3, pp. 275–82.

225. NA Prague RAM Krt. 223, 2015-2.

226. For example, in the *Trierisches Wochenblatt* of December 13, 1795, which contains the announcement of an auction of farmland in Konz, Merzlich, and Matheis: NA Prague RAM Krt. 223, 2015-2.

227. Declaration signed in person by Metternich, dated Vienna, January 1, 1845, now an exhibit in the library at Königswart.

228. And not in February 1794, as Srbik—following Metternich's own account in NP 1, p. 23—erroneously claims; Srbik, *Metternich*, vol. 1, p. 79.

229. Details can be found in the correspondence of Eleonore von Liechtenstein, examined in Wolf, *Fürstin Eleonore Liechtenstein*, esp. pp. 242–50.

230. See, for example, Corti, *Metternich*, vol. 1, pp. 30–45; Srbik, *Metternich*, vol. 1, pp. 81–82; Wolf, *Fürstin Eleonore Liechtenstein*, pp. 242–50.

231. Asch, *Europäischer Adel*, p. 99.

232. See Kaunitz papers in the Metternich family archive, NA Prague RAM Krt. 391.

233. Quotations from the correspondence between Clemens and Eleonore, NA Prague RAM Krt. 391, 2576. The letters are not part of NP.

234. Undated letter from Eleonore von Kaunitz to Metternich, NA Prague RAM Krt. 391, 2576.

235. MPM 1, p. 22 (transl. modified); NP 1, p. 23.

236. See Wolf, *Fürstin Eleonore Liechtenstein*, pp. 244–45.

237. Metternich to Dorothea von Lieven, December 1, 1818, Mika, *Metternichs Briefe*, pp. 60–61.

238. The conversation is recorded in Röper's protocol, titled "Untertäniges Promemoria," March 29, 1795, NA Prague RAM Krt. 391, 2577.

239. This sum corresponds to 50,000–58,333 guilders in Austrian currency.

240. *Translator's note:* In German common law, *Nadelgeld* [pin money] was a regular sum paid by a husband to his wife, which she could use as she saw fit. *Morgengabe* [morning gift] was a one-off gift traditionally handed over the morning after the wedding; it could take the form of money or goods.

241. "Besitzungen und Vermögensstand des reichsgräflich Metternich-Winneburgischen Hauses in reinem Ertrag nach nach Abziehung aller Administrations-Unkosten" [Possessions and wealth of the House of the Imperial Counts Metternich Winneburg in terms of the pure yield after the deduction of all administrative costs], NA Prague RAM Krt. 390, 2574.

242. "Rubrizierter Überschlag des Ertrags und der Administrations-Kosten der gräflich Metternichschen böhmischen Herrschaften" [Categorized estimate of the yield and the administrative costs of the Bohemian dominions of the Count Metternichs], NA Prague RAM Krt. 390, 2574.

243. NA Prague Krt. 390, 2574.

244. The original is in NA Prague A. C. 12, Krt. 1, 1; a copy in NA Prague RAM Krt. 390, 2574.

245. "Beantwortung der gegen den vorgelegten Vermögensstand des gräflich Metternichschen Hauses gemachten Einwendungen" [Reply to the objections raised against the presentation of the assets of the House of the Counts Metternich], undated, NA Prague RAM Krt. 390, 2574.

246. *Translator's note:* Religionsfonds was a fund created by decree of February 27, 1782, that administered the capital generated from the sale of dissolved monasteries.

247. Franz Georg to Kaunitz, June 4, 1795, NA Prague RAM Krt. 390, 2574.

248. Undated memorandum from Franz Georg to Count von Rothenhan, NA Prague RAM Krt. 390, 2574.

249. NA Prague RAM Krt. 391, 2577.

250. NA Prague RAM Krt. 26, 2004.

251. Liechtenstern, *Geographie des Österreichischen Kaiserstaates*, 2, p. 1025.

252. This is what Kienmayer communicated to Clemens, NA Prague RAM Krt. 391, 2578.

253. Eleonore (with a note from Ernst von Kaunitz) to Clemens August 19, 1795, NA Prague RAM Krt. 391, 2576.

254. Wolf, *Fürstin Eleonore Liechtenstein*, pp. 248–50.

255. The wording of the "Short address according to the Viennese ritual," in NA Prague RAM Krt. 390, 2574.

256. Pauline Metternich, *Erinnerungen*, p. 45.

257. *Translator's note:* The Hof- und Kammerjuwelier was a jeweler appointed to the court.

258. Contract of the purchase, dated September 29, 1785, in NA Prague RAM Krt. 207, 2056.

259. Reference to this second wedding celebration is made in Corti, *Metternich*, vol. 1, p. 46.

260. MPM 1, p. 22 (transl. amended); NP I, p. 24.

261. MPM 1, p. 23; NP 1, 24.

262. See Kadletz-Schöffel, *Metternich und die Wissenschaften*.

263. Metternich to Wilhelmine Sagan, February 28, 1819, Mika, *Metternich's Briefe*, p. 204.

264. MPM 1, p. 21; NP I, p. 23.

265. MPM 1, p. 31; NP 1, p. 29.

266. MPM 1, pp. 32–33; NP 1, pp. 29–30.

267. MPM 1, p. 27; NP 1, p. 28. Srbik, *Metternich*, vol. 1, p. 87; Aretin, *Vom Deutschen Reich zum Deutschen Bund*, p. 80.

268. MPM 1, p. 24; NP 1, p. 26.

269. Ziegler, "Kaiser Franz II. (I.)," pp. 17–18.

270. Ibid., p. 14.

271. MPM 1, p. 49; NP I, p. 43.

272. See Srbik, *Metternich*, vol. 1, pp. 82–84; Mathy, "Ein berühmter Student der Mainzer Universität," p. 82.

273. Hansen, *Quellen*, 3, p. 163.

274. See Srbik, *Metternich*, vol. 1, pp. 82–83, who follows Hüffer, *Diplomatische Verhandlungen*, 2-1, pp. 41–42.

275. Hüffer, *Diplomatische Verhandlungen*, 2-2, p. 181.

276. Hansen, *Quellen*, 4, p. 274.

277. Hüffer, *Diplomatische Verhandlungen*, 2-1, p. 62.

278. Hansen, *Quellen*, 4, p. 592.

279. See Aretin, *Das Alte Reich*, 3, pp. 462–68.

280. Srbik, *Metternich*, vol. 1, p. 83.

281. Hüffer, *Diplomatische Verhandlungen*, 2-1, pp. 204–5, note.

282. Srbik, *Metternich*, vol. 1, p. 82.

283. Clemens to Franz Georg, February 8, 1798, NA Prague RAM Krt. 227, 2017-4.

284. See Aretin, *Das Alte Reich*, 3, p. 464. "Austria" was one of the ten imperial circles that existed from the mid-sixteenth century onward. They retained most of their importance as reference points of imperial politics right until the end of the empire.

285. Hüffer, *Diplomatische Verhandlungen*, 2-1, pp. 204–5, note.

286. MPM 1, p. 361. Clemens to Eleonore, January 6, 1798, NA Prague A. C. 12, Krt. 1, 2; incomplete version in NP 1, pp. 359–60.

287. MPM 1, p. 373. Clemens to Eleonore, May 4, 1798, NA Prague A. C. 12, Krt. 1, 2; incomplete version in NP 1, p. 371.

288. All letters to the congress in the years 1797–1798 asking for compensation in NA Prague RAM Krt. 362, 2403-1.

289. On the events, see Hüffer, *Diplomatische Verhandlungen*, 2-1, pp. 255–61.

290. Franz Georg von Metternich to Thugut, April 29, 1798. Draft in Clemens's handwriting, NA Prague RAM Krt. 362, 2403-2.

291. MPM 1, p. 363. Clemens to Eleonore, January 16, 1798, NA Prague A. C. 12, Krt. 1, 2; incomplete version in NP 1, p. 361.

292. Hüffer, *Diplomatische Verhandlungen*, 2-1, p. 93.

293. MPM 1, pp. 349–50. Clemens to Eleonore, December 5, 1797, NA Prague A. C. 12, Krt. 1, 2; incomplete version in NP 1, p. 349.

294. MPM 1, p. 368. Clemens to Eleonore, April 5, 1798, NA Prague A. C. 12, Krt. 1, 3; incomplete version in NP 1, p. 366.

295. See Blanning, *The French Revolutionary Wars*, pp. 158–61.

296. MPM 1, p. 350 (transl. amended). Clemens to Eleonore, December 7, 1797, NA Prague A. C. 12, Krt. 1, 2; incomplete version in NP 1, p. 349.

297. MPM 1, p. 351 (transl. modified). Clemens to Eleonore, December 9, 1797, NA Prague A. C. 12, Krt. 1, 2; incomplete version in NP 1, p. 351.

298. MPM 1, p. 358. Clemens to Eleonore, December 22, 1797, NA Prague A. C. 12, Krt. 1, 2; incomplete version in NP 1, p. 357.

299. MPM 1, p. 359 (transl. amended). Clemens to Eleonore, December 24, 1797, NA Prague A. C. 12, Krt. 1, 2; incomplete version in NP 1, p. 357.

300. MPM 1, p. 360 (transl. amended). Clemens to Eleonore, December 31, 1797, NA Prague A. C. 12, Krt. 1, 2; incomplete version in NP 1, p. 359; the printed version in NP gives "dans moins de soixante-dix ans"; the manuscript has "dans moins des 7 ans."

301. MPM 1, p. 361. Clemens to Eleonore, January 6, 1798, NA Prague A. C. 12, Krt. 1, 2; incomplete version in NP 1, pp. 359–60.

302. Hüffer, *Diplomatische Verhandlungen*, 1, p. 387.

303. Ibid., p. 387 and p. 450.

304. MPM 1, p. 24; NP 1, p. 26.

305. Hüffer, *Diplomatische Verhandlungen*, 2-2, pp. 297–98.

4. Between Peace and War

1. See Schroeder, *Transformation*, pp. 228–30.

2. MPM 1, p. 187; NP 1, p. 152.

3. Ludwig von Cobenzl's convoluted career, which oscillated between diplomatic and ministerial activities, is described in detail by Hermann Hüffer, "Cobenzl, Ludwig Graf," in *ADB* 4 (1876), pp. 355–63.

4. Cobenzl to Metternich, February 24, 1801, "Lettre particulière" [confidential letter] NA Prague RAM A. C. 2, 9-A.

5. MPM 1, p. 34; NP 1, p. 32.

6. MPM 1, p. 31; NP 1, p. 29.

7. Srbik, *Metternich*, 1, p. 80.

8. Aretin, *Das Alte Reich*, 3, pp. 461, 470, 472, 474, 477.

9. MPM 1, p. 34; NP 1, p. 32.

10. "Instruktion, nach welcher sich der hoch- und wohlgeborene Unser wirklicher Kämmerer und lieber getreuer des Heiligen Römischen Reichs Graf Clemens von Metternich-Winneburg zu benehmen hat, 2. November 1801" [Instructions to be followed by the highborn chamberlain and dear and faithful Count Clemens von Metternich-Winneburg of the Holy Roman Empire in his conduct, November 2, 1801]; HHStA Wien StK Instruktionen, Krt. 6, Fol. 56. Metternich had submitted the more detailed version, on which our account is based, on July 11, 1801 (Fols. 56–76); NP 2, pp. 3–17 presents only excerpts from the third part and contains numerous idiosyncratic editorial changes. The following interpretation is based on the original draft (Fols. 2–54). *Translator's note:* I follow the existing English translation where it corresponds to the "more detailed version"; all other translations are mine.

11. MPM 1, p. 46; NP, 1, p. 40.

12. Aretin, *Das Alte Reich*, 3, p. 490.

13. MPM 2, p. 15; NP 2, p. 14.

14. MPM 2, pp. 4–5; NP 2, pp. 4–5.

15. MPM 2, p. 5; NP 2, p. 5.

16. Ibid.

17. MPM 1, p. 7; NP 2, p. 6.

18. MPM 2, p. 7; NP 2, p. 7.

19. MPM 2, p. 9; NP 2, pp. 8–9.

20. On his contacts with the salons and with women, see Corti, *Metternich*, 1, pp. 68–78.

21. Marmont, *Mémoires*, vol. 6, p. 375.

22. MPM 1, pp. 40–41; NP, 1, p. 37.

23. MPM 1, p. 40; NP 1, p. 37.

24. MPM 1, p. 40; NP, 1, pp. 36–37.

25. MPM 1, p. 41; NP, 1, p. 38.

26. Gentz, *Fragments*, p. i, p. x, p. xx, p. xliii.

27. Ibid., pp. 58–59, p. 72 (transl. modified).

28. Gentz, *Tagebücher*, 1, p. 25.

29. MPM 1, p. 45; NP, 1, p. 39.

30. Ibid.

31. See Arndt, *Reichsgrafenkollegium*, pp. 141–45.

32. "Beschreibung der reichsgräflich Metternich-Winneburgschen Besitzungen auf dem linken Rheinufer nebst erläuternden Anmerkungen zu dem desfalsigen Rentenetat" [Account of the possession of the Imperial Counts Metternich-Winneburg on the left bank of the Rhine, with explanatory notes on the related rent], NA Prague RAM Krt. 141, 5298.

33. "Ueber Länderverlust und Zusage neuer Länder für die erblichen Regenten. Eine geographisch statistische Noth- und Hülfstafel zur richtigen Beurtheilung des Lüneviller Friedens vom 9. Februar 1801" [On lost territory and promised new territory for the hereditary rulers. A geographical and statistical emergency and ancillary table for the correct evaluation of the Peace of Lunéville of February 9, 1801], NA Prague RAM Krt. 294, 1, 2255; this document gives 46,000 fl. as the sum for the total income.

34. For example, "Generalliste des sämtlichen zur Entschädigung judizierten Revenueverlustes der katholischen Mitglieder des westphälischen Grafenkollegiums" [General list of all losses in revenue suffered by Catholic members of the Westphalian Association of Counts, presented for compensation], NA Prague RAM Krt. 329, 2321, 1.

35. All these communications at NA Prague RAM Krt. 263, 2194.

36. Talleyrand to Franz Georg von Metternich, 4 Germinal XI (March 25, 1803), NA Prague RAM Krt. 263, 2194.

37. MPM 1, p. 46; NP, 1, p. 40.

38. See Andreas, *Das Zeitalter Napoleons,* pp. 316–19.

39. Raumer and Botzenhart, *Deutschland um 1800,* p. 176.

40. HHStA Vienna StK Instruktionen, Krt. 6, "Instruktionen für den Kaiserl. Königl. Bevollmächtigten Minister am Berliner Hofe Herrn Grafen von Metternich, 5. Nov. 1803" [Instructions for the imperial and royal plenipotentiary minister at the Court in Berlin Mr. Count von Metternich], Fols. 1–16 (copy); in Fournier, *Gentz und Cobenzl,* pp. 203–333, but unfortunately with abridgments at the beginning and end. I therefore quote from the original.

41. Metternich to Colloredo, March 16, 1804, HHStA Wien Preußen Korrespondenz, Krt. 85, Fols. 108–111.

42. Metternich to Colloredo, September 24, 1804, MPM 2, pp. 23–28; here p. 27; NP, 2, pp. 20–25.

43. Comment in Metternich's hand in the margins of a tractate which Schulenburg had sent him in the winter of 1809–1810; NA Prague A. C. 8, Krt. 5, 34, 1.

44. MPM 2, p. 82; NP, 2, p. 72.

45. See Raumer and Botzenhart, *Deutschland um 1800,* p. 151.

46. Metternich to Colloredo, October 29 and October 31, 1805, MPM 2, pp. 79–84; NP 2, pp. 69–74.

47. MPM 2, p. 86; NP 2, p. 75.

48. MPM 2, p. 89; NP 2, p. 78.

49. MPM 2, p. 90 (transl. amended); NP 2, pp. 78–79.

50. Thus the judgment in Andreas, *Das Zeitalter Napoleons,* p. 330.

51. According to a supplement to a dispatch by Metternich (No. 99), NA Prague A. C. 8, Krt. 4, 28. This document is not part of NP.

52. "Quelques observations sur la situation actuelle des affaires relativement à la Prusse," NA Prague A. C. 8, Krt. 4, 28. In more detail: 193,000 Prussian troops; 25,000 Saxon troops; 16,000 Hessian troops; 8,000 from Darmstadt; 3,000 from Brunswick; 1,000 from Weimar; and 24,000 English and Hanoverian troops.

53. "Note sure la marche à suivre pour déterminer la Prusse à se joindre à la Russie." Dispatch no. 99, NA Prague A. C. 8 Krt. 4, 28 (not part of NP).

54. MPM 1, p. 58; NP 1, p. 50.

55. Schroeder, *Transformation*, p. 227.

56. Joint note from Metternich and Alopäus, the Russian ambassador in Berlin, to Hardenberg, December 13, 1805, NP 2, pp. 89–91. MPM 2, pp. 102–4; here: p. 103.

57. Metternich to Stadion, January 10, 1806, MPM 2, 110–15; NP 2, pp. 102–5.

58. MPM 2, pp. 118–19 (transl. modified); NP 2, p. 102.

59. MPM 2, p. 119; NP 2, p. 103.

60. The French version in Oer, *Der Friede von Preßburg*, p. 196 and pp. 271ff. German version: *Reg.Bl. für das Königreich Bayern* 1806, Nos. 7 and 8, pp. 49ff. and pp. 64ff.

61. A more detailed description of Hardenberg's plan of February 5, 1806, can be found in Angermeier, *Das Alte Reich*, p. 478.

62. Metternich to Stadion, March 7, 1806, MPM 2, pp. 130–34; here: p. 131. NP, 110–14.

63. See MPM 2, p. 134; NP 2, p. 114.

64. MPM 2, p. 138; NP 2, p. 117.

65. The "memoir" of April 12, 1806, in MPM 2, pp. 135–39; NP 2, pp. 114–18. The list of questions, with Hardenberg's answers, can be found in MPM 2, pp. 140–42; NP 2, pp. 118–20.

66. Transl. amended.

67. Transl. amended.

5. World War: Outset and Intensification, 1806–1812

1. Osterhammel, *The Transformation of the World*, p. xv.

2. Füssel, *Der Siebenjährige Krieg*.

3. Oncken, *Österreich und Preußen*, 1, p. 21.

4. Blanning, *The French Revolution in Germany*, p. 318.

5. Juhel, "1813—das Jahr eines Weltkriegs?" pp. 40–51.

6. Bayly, *The Birth of the Modern World*, p. 97.

7. Ibid., pp. 125–26.

8. MPM 1, p. 67; NP 1, p. 56.

9. Ibid.

10. See MPM 1, p. 253; NP 1, 209. Metternich's autographs, the copies and fair copies on which the memoirs of NP are based, are collected in NA Prague A. C. 8.

11. See Botzenhart, *Botschafterzeit*. Botzenhart's excellent study from the 1960s also draws on the Acta Clementina and the Metternich family archive in Prague, which was unusual at that time. It therefore serves to correct Srbik on certain essential points.

12. Ibid., p. 11.

13. Metternich to Gentz, January 21, 1806, Gentz, *Friedrich von Gentz*, 3-1, p. 44.

14. Vidal, *Caroline Bonaparte*, p. 257.

15. Napoleon to Talleyrand, March 26, 1806, Napoléon, *Correspondance*, 12, pp. 220–21. See Botzenhart, *Botschafterzeit*, p. 7.

16. Convincing and detailed reconstruction in Botzenhart, *Botschafterzeit*, pp. 9–13.

17. See ibid. p. 21.

18. MPM 1, p. 64; NP 1, p. 53.

19. HHStA Wien StK Frankreich Krt. 199; the following quotations from the instructions are taken from this file.

20. HHStA Wien StK Frankreich Krt. 199, Fol. 27.

21. The date of August 4 for the arrival (MPM 1, p. 67; NP 1, p. 55) is wrong; see Botzenhart, *Botschafterzeit*, p. 28, note 5.

22. See Bitterauf, *Geschichte des Rheinbundes*, p. 402.

23. Kraehe, *Metternich's German Policy*, 1, p. 52.

24. See Andreas, *Zeitalter Napoleons*, p. 341.

25. Stadion to Franz Georg von Metternich, April 3, 1806, NA Prague RAM Krt. 317, 2295, 3.

26. NA Prague RAM Krt. 317, 2295, 1.

27. Bassenheim to Franz Georg, July 3, 1806, NA Prague RAM Krt. 317, 2295, 1.

28. The exact wording in Pölitz, *Constitutionen*, 2, p. 85 (art. 24).

29. Jacob Chrétien to Franz Georg von Metternich, July 26, 1806, NA Prague RAM Krt. 317, 2295, 1.

30. Napoleon to Talleyrand, April 10, 1806, Napoléon, *Correspondance*, 12, p. 268.

31. Ibid., pp. 266–68.

32. See Botzenhart, *Botschafterzeit*, p. 19.

33. See Gollwitzer, *Die Standesherren*, p. 27.

34. Clemens von Metternich to Franz Georg, August 4, 1806, NA Prague A C. 12, Krt. 1, 5.

35. Clemens von Metternich to Franz Georg, September 16, 1806, NA Prague A C. 14, Krt. 10, 202.

36. See Endres, *Sauhirt in der Tükei*, pp. 837–56.

37. King Friedrich of Württemberg to Franz Georg, October 26, 1806, NA Prague RAM Krt. 317, 2296, 1.

38. Clemens von Metternich to Franz Georg, September 16, 1806, NA Prague A. C. 14, Krt. 10, 202.

39. See Gollwitzer, *Standesherren*, p. 17.

40. On Metternich's first audience with Napoleon, see Botzenhart, *Botschafterzeit*, pp. 38–40.

41. Stollberg-Rilinger, *Des Kaisers alte Kleider*, p. 134.

42. In MPM 1, pp. 269–87 (NP 1, 275–91), the essay is presented with some willful linguistic moderations introduced by the editor. I quote following the original with a title from Metternich's hand: "Portraits des hommes les plus marquants de l'époque pour servir materiaux à mes mémoires"; NA Prague A. C. 8, Krt. 1 (draft and fair copy). *Translator's*

note: the English translation at times differs significantly, both in terms of the expressions (and hence meaning), but also of the context between remarks. I follow the German text.

43. MPM 1, p. 270; NP 1, p. 276.

44. MPM 1, p. 280; NP 1, p. 285.

45. Ibid. (transl. modified).

46. MPM 1, pp. 274–75; NP 1, p. 280.

47. See Gottfried Eisermann, *Rolle und Maske* (Tübingen, 1991), esp. pp. 150–51.

48. See MPM 1, p. 270; NP 1, p. 276. The published version deviates from the original by toning "ignoble" down to "une tenue négligée" (in the English translation "negligent dress," better "sloppy dress").

49. See Günter Daniel Rey, *Methoden der Entwicklungspsychologie* (Norderstedt, 2012), p. 17.

50. MPM 1, p. 271; NP 1, p. 276.

51. MPM 1, pp. 270–71; NP 1, p. 276.

52. MPM 1, p. 287; NP 1, p. 291, note.

53. Tulard, *Napoleon,* p. 502.

54. Presser, *Napoleon,* p. 898.

55. MPM 1, p. 271; NP 1, p. 277.

56. Ibid.

57. Ibid.

58. MPM 1, p. 279; NP 1, p. 284.

59. MPM 1, pp. 283–84; NP 1, p. 288.

60. The image is Metternich's: MPM 1, p. 283; NP 1, p. 288.

61. See Helfert, *Maria Louise,* pp. 188–90; quotation: p. 190.

62. See MPM 1, p. 283; NP 1, p. 288.

63. Ibid.

64. Noialles, *Life and Memoirs of Count Molé,* p. 163.

65. MPM 1, p. 298 (transl. amended); NP 1, p. 300; the figures of the following paragraph are taken from *Memoirs,* 1, pp. 295–98; NP 1, 297–300.

66. MPM 1, p. 275; NP 1, pp. 280–81.

67. From the Dresden conversation with Metternich: MPM 1, p. 186; NP 1, pp. 151.

68. MPM 1, p. 275; NP 1, pp. 280–81.

69. MPM 1, p. 276 (transl. amended); NP 1, pp. 281.

70. MPM 1, p. 74; NP 1, pp. 61.

71. MPM 1, pp. 276–77 (transl. amended); NP 1, pp. 282.

72. MPM 1, pp. 274; NP 1, pp. 279.

73. MPM 1, p. 65; NP 1, p. 54.

74. MPM 1, p. 87; NP 1, p. 73.

75. MPM 1, p. 282; NP 1, p. 287.

76. MPM 1, p. 287, note (transl. amended); NP 1, p. 291, note.

77. MPM 1, p. 66; NP 1, pp. 54–55.

78. MPM 1, p. 66; NP 1, p. 54.

79. MPM 1, p. 284 (transl. amended); NP 1, pp. 288–89.

80. MPM 1, p. 281; NP 1, p. 286.

81. MPM 1, p. 286; NP 1, pp. 290–91.

82. MPM 1, p. 67; NP 1, p. 56.

83. Metternich to Friedrich Gentz, January 21, 1806 (Metternich's emphasis), Wittichen and Salzer, *Gentz*, 3-1, pp. 44–45.

84. Metternich to Franz Georg, September 16, 1806, NA Prague A. C. 14, Krt. 10, 202.

85. Metternich to Franz Georg, September 25, 1806, NA Prague A. C. 14, Krt. 10, 202.

86. MPM 1, p. 69; NP 1, p. 57.

87. Metternich to Stadion, July 26, 1807, MPM 2, pp. 143–44; NP 2, p. 121.

88. MPM 1, p. 70; NP 1, p. 58.

89. MPM 1, p. 69; NP 1, p. 57.

90. Talleyrand, *Memoirs*, 1, p. 238.

91. MPM 1, p. 69; NP 1, p. 57.

92. Metternich to Stadion (private letter), October 11, 1807, MPM 2, p. 146; NP 2, pp. 123–24.

93. Metternich to Stadion, October 12, 1807, MPM 2, pp. 146–54; here: p. 147; NP 2, pp. 124–30.

94. MPM 2, p. 151; NP 2, p. 128.

95. MPM 2, p. 152 (transl. amended); NP 2, p. 128.

96. MPM 2, p. 155; NP 2, p. 131.

97. On the Continental System, see Bayly, *The Birth of the Modern World*, pp. 96–100. The quotations are taken from p. 97.

98. See Tulard, *Napoleon*, pp. 231–37.

99. Metternich's report on the audience, which took place on August 2, 1807, in MPM 1, pp. 291–93; here: 292; NP 1, pp. 294–96; here: p. 295.

100. MPM 2, p. 157; NP 2, p. 133.

101. Metternich to Stadion, October 16, 1807, MPM 2, p. 158; NP 2, pp. 133.

102. See Tulard, *Napoleon*, p. 382; Fournier, *Napoleon*, 2, p. 432.

103. See Talleyrand, *Memoirs*, p. 291.

104. Dwyer and McPhee, *The French Revolution and Napoleon: A Sourcebook*, pp. 166–67 (transl. amended). *Translator's note:* The full text in the original French can be found at: http://www.histoire-empire.org/correspondance_de_napoleon/1807/novembre_02.htm.

105. MPM 1, p. 82; NP 1, p. 68.

106. Metternich to Stadion, August 26, 1808, MPM 2, p. 252; NP 2, p. 214.

107. MPM 2, p. 252 (transl. amended); NP 2, p. 215.

108. Metternich to Stadion, September 24, 1808, MPM 2, p. 278; NP 2, p. 237.

109. The circumstances are presented in four dispatches from Metternich to Stadion, all written prior to the congress; see MPM 2, pp. 261–74; NP 2, pp. 221–33.

110. MPM 2, pp. 264–65; NP 2, pp. 225.

111. Caulaincourt, *Mémoires*, 1, p. 252.

112. Talleyrand, *Memoirs*, p. 305.

113. Ibid., p. 307.

114. Ibid., pp. 302–3.

115. See Carl, "Erinnerungsbruch als Bedingung der Moderne?" p. 182.

116. See Beyer, *Neue Chronik.*

117. The text of the contract is given in Talleyrand, *Memoirs*, pp. 306–8; here: p. 306.

118. Ibid., pp. 307–8.

119. Ibid., p. 309.

120. See Caulaincourt, *Mémoires*, 1, pp. 249–53.

121. MPM 1, p. 75; NP 1, pp. 62–63.

122. MPM 1, p. 76; NP 1, p. 63.

123. MPM 1, p. 84; NP 1, p. 68.

124. Tallyerand, *Memoirs*, vol. 1, p. 227.

125. "On Talleyrand's position and the factions," in MPM 2, pp. 283–85 (transl. amended); here: p. 283; NP 2, pp. 240–43.

126. MPM 2, p. 284; NP 2, p. 241.

127. MPM 2, p. 284; NP 2, p. 242.

128. MPM 2, p. 283; NP 2, p. 240.

129. MPM 2, p. 285; NP 2, p. 243.

130. Metternich to Stadion, January 20, 1809, HHStA Wien StK Frankreich Krt. 205, Fol. 66.

131. See Dard, *Napoleon and Talleyrand*, pp. 199–200, which also gives further references.

132. See Willms, *Talleyrand*, p. 174.

133. For example, in Metternich's report of January 17, 1809, to Stadion ("réservé"; i.e., "top secret"), HHStA Wien StK Frankreich Krt. 205, Fol. 56.

134. Dard, *Napoleon and Talleyrand*, p. 203 (my translation, D. S.).

135. HHStA Wien StK Frankreich Krt. 201, Fol. 65.

136. HHStA Wien StK Frankreich Krt. 203, Fols. 101–110.

137. HHStA Wien StK Frankreich Krt. 203, Fol. 127.

138. Metternich to Stadion, July 26, 1808, HHStA Wien StK Frankreich Krt. 203, Fols. 200–203.

139. HHStA Wien StK Frankreich Krt. 203, Fols. 205–207.

140. HHStA Wien StK Frankreich Krt. 205, Fol. 98.

141. Metternich, February 27, 1809; HHStA Wien StK Frankreich Krt. 205, Fols. 111–128.

142. Metternich to Stadion, March 23, 1809, HHStA Wien StK Frankreich Krt. 205, Fols. 79–99.

143. Metternich to Stadion, August 26, 1808, MPM 2, p. 252; NP 2, p. 214.

144. Wolf, *Fürstin Eleonore Liechtenstein*, p. 318.

145. Srbik, *Metternich*, 1, p. 117.

146. See Botzenhart, *Botschafterzeit*, pp. 220, 262–63.

147. Metternich to Stadion, June 23, 1808, MPM 2, p. 215; NP 2, p. 183.

148. Metternich to Stadion, July 1, 1808, MPM 2, pp. 221–22 (transl. amended); NP 2, p. 189.

149. See Botzenhart, *Botschafterzeit*, pp. 229–30.

150. Metternich to Franz Georg, September 3, 1808, NA Prague, A. C. 12, Krt. 1, 5; see Botzenhart, *Botschafterzeit*, pp. 249–50.

151. October 10 as the date of arrival in Vienna (MPM 1, p. 76; NP 1, p. 63) must be corrected; see Botzenhart, *Botschafterzeit*, pp. 268–69.

152. MPM 1, p. 82; NP 1, p. 69.

153. First memorandum by Metternich, December 4, 1808, MPM 2, pp. 289–300; NP 2, pp. 246–57.

154. MPM 2, p. 299 (transl. amended); NP 2, p. 255.

155. This memorandum is not part of the published memoirs, but can be found in Beer, *Zehn Jahre österreichische Politik*, pp. 525–29.

156. Beer, *Zehn Jahre österreichische Politik*, p. 527.

157. See MPM 2, pp. 301–8; here: p. 305; NP 2, pp. 257–64; here: p. 261.

158. MPM 2, p. 308 (transl. amended); NP 2, p. 264.

159. MPM 2, p. 306; NP 2, p. 261.

160. Botzenhart, *Botschafterzeit*, p. 251.

161. "Historical Remarks on the Letter of General Grünne to Prince de Ligne, September 27 and 28"; MPM 1, pp. 389–90 (transl. amended); NP 1, pp. 228–29.

162. See Planert, *Der Mythos vom Befreiungskrieg*.

163. MPM 1, p. 98 (transl. amended); NP 1, p. 83.

164. See Raumer and Botzenhart, *Deutschland um 1800*, p. 508.

165. MPM 1, p. 83; NP 1, p. 70.

166. Ibid.

167. "Instruktion an Metternich: Remarques remises à Mr. l'ambassadeur Comte de Metternich lors de son retour à Paris, le 23 décembre 1808," in Beer, *Zehn Jahre österreichische Geschichte*, pp. 536–39.

168. MPM 2, p. 318; NP 2, p. 272.

169. MPM 2, p. 333; NP 2, pp. 284–85.

170. Metternich to Stadion, February 17, 1809, MPM 2, p. 329; NP 2, p. 281.

171. Metternich to Stadion, April 11, 1809, MPM 2, pp. 349–50; NP 2, p. 298.

172. MPM 2, pp. 355–56 (transl. amended); NP 2, pp. 303–4.

173. This perspective was developed by Metternich on April 24, 1809, while he was still in Paris; MPM 2, pp. 355–59; NP 2, pp. 303–6.

174. On the development of the war, see Gill, *Thunder on the Danube*.

175. Reproduced in Spies, *Die Erhebung gegen Napoleon*, pp. 117–18.

176. "Expédition du major Schill. 1809" and "Rapport confidentiel et détaillé sur les circonstances et négociations relatives au Projet d'Insurrection dans le Nord de l'Allemagne"; NA Prag A. C. 8, Krt. 5, 34, 1.

177. Metternich to Stadion, April 3, 1809, MPM 2, p. 344; NP 2, p. 293.

178. Quoted after Botzenhart, *Botschafterzeit*, p. 294. *Translator's note:* The German for "good-bye" is "Auf Wiedersehen," meaning "until we see each other again," giving the passage an ironic twist.

179. On May 25, 1809, Eleonore was given the passport depicted on p. 292 by Fouché in person. It allowed her to leave at any time. NA Prague A. C. 12, Krt. 1, 6.

180. Letter from Metternich to Stadion, sent from Paris, dated April 18, 1809, in MPM 2, pp. 351–55; NP 2, pp. 300–303.

181. MPM 1, p. 90; NP 1, p. 76.

182. MPM 1, p. 84; NP 1, p. 71. The departure date given in the memoirs (the 19) must be corrected on the basis of the report of the 18 in MPM 2, p. 351; NP 2, p. 300.

183. Abrantès, *Mémoires*, 12, p. 215.

184. MPM 1, p. 91 (transl. amended); NP 1, p. 77.

185. "Précis d'une conversation avec Mr. de Champagny le 6 Juin 1809," NA Prag, A. C. 8, Krt. 5, 34, 2; Corti, *Metternich*, vol. 1, p. 157, refers to parts of this report, but without referencing it, and omitting the political background of the "General Chasteler affair" altogether.

186. MPM 1, p. 92; NP 1, p. 78.

187. Ibid.

188. Letter of June 12, 1809, in Pelet, *Mémoires*, 3, pp. 452–53.

189. MPM 1, p. 93 (transl. amended); NP 1, p. 79.

190. "Précis d'une Conversation entre le Général Savary et l'Ambassadeur comte de Metternich à Grünberg le 15 Juin 1809"; NA Prag, RAM A. C. 8, Krt. 5, 34, 2. Corti oversimplifies when he calls this document "the basis for Metternich's remarkable later career"; see Corti, *Metternich*, vol. 1, p. 157. As this biography shows, Metternich's rise rests on a long prehistory.

191. MPM 1, p. 94; NP 1, p. 79. In his "Précis d'une Conversation" Metternich mentions the adjacent gardens, about which Savary must have known. On the basis of the "Précis," there is no reason for doubting, as Corti does, Metternich's account in the *Memoirs*, especially as Metternich explicitly emphasized his reservedness at the time; see Corti, *Metternich*, vol. 1, p. 159.

192. MPM 1, p. 97 (transl. amended); NP 1, p. 82.

193. Corti, in particular, has taken his cue from the suspicions at the court at the time and has spread this insinuation. See Corti, *Metternich*, 1, pp. 187–88.

194. See Srbik, *Metternich*, pp. 122–28.

195. MPM 1, p. 104; NP 1, p. 87.

196. See ibid.

197. Kaiserliche Resolution, Komorn, 31. 7. 1809, HHStA Wien StK Vorträge Krt. 182, Fol. 133.

198. MPM 1, pp. 103–4; NP 1, p. 85.

199. MPM 1, p. 104 (my transl., D. S.); NP 1, p. 87. *Translator's note:* the German for "more insight" is *einsichtsvollere,* a term that oscillates between "having a better understanding" and "with more knowledge of the facts."

200. MPM 1, p. 104; NP 1, p. 86. *Translator's note:* the German expression in square brackets is less clear-cut than the English translation. Literally "to end up on the wrong path," its meaning depends on the person from whose perspective the path is the wrong one. At least two interpretations are possible: the wrong path for Austria and the emperor (the option chosen by the existing translation), or the wrong path for Metternich if he wanted to reach his goals. Both possibilities would constitute a danger for the state, but one due to his ignorance, the other due to misapplied genius.

201. MPM 1, p. 104 (my transl., D. S.); NP 1, p. 86.

202. MPM 1, p. 106; NP 1, p. 88.

203. Ibid. (transl. amended).

204. See Corti, *Metternich*, 1, pp. 165–66.

205. MPM 1, p. 106; NP 1, p. 88.

206. Metternich's presentation to Emperor Franz, dated July 20, 1809, in NP 2, pp. 307–10, with numerous deleted passages and editorial interventions. Quotations follow the original at HHStA Wien StK Vorträge Krt. 182, Fols. 189–199. *Translator's note:* I follow the existing English translation where it is faithful to the German original.

207. MPM 2, p. 361; NP 2, p. 308.

208. Ibid.

209. MPM 2, p. 361–62; NP 2, pp. 308–9.

210. MPM 2, p. 362 (transl. modified); NP 2, p. 309.

211. Presentation by Metternich, July 20, 1809, HHStA Wien StK Vorträge Krt. 182, Fol. 194; deleted in NP.

212. See Šedivý, *Eastern Question,* pp. 437–74.

213. See MPM 2, p. 363; NP 2, p. 310.

214. Presentation by Metternich, HHStA Wien StK Vorträge Krt. 182, Fol. 194; deleted in NP.

215. MPM 2, p. 364; NP 2, p. 310.

216. Brecht, *Stories of Mr. Keuner,* p. 3.

217. Ibid.

218. See Srbik, *Metternich*, 1, p. 119.

219. Presentation by Metternich, dated August 10, 1809, in MPM 2, pp. 364–65 (transl. amended); NP 2, 311–12. The version in NP is partly distorted, even in the sentences containing the central message. I quote following the original in HHStA Wien StK Vorträge Krt. 182, Fols. 200–205.

220. HHStA Wien StK Vorträge Krt. 182, Fols. 200–205.

221. The exact details are described in Metternich's "Réflexions sur les Négotiations rélatives au traité de paix conclus 14 Octobre à Vienne l'an 1809," NA Prague RAM A. C. 8, Krt. 5, 34, 2.

222. MPM 1, p. 110; NP1, p. 91.

223. Imperial resolution of September 25, 1809, sent to Metternich; HHStA Wien StK Vorträge Krt. 182, Fol. 53–54.

224. MPM 1, p. 112; NP1, p. 93.

225. Metternich's presentation to Emperor Franz, dated September 30, 1809, HHStA Wien StK Vorträge Krt. 182, Fols. 45–47, 58.

226. Ibid., Fol. 61.

227. "Réflexions sur les Négotiations rélatives au traité de paix conclus 14 Octobre à Vienne l'an 1809," NA Prague RAM A. C. 8, Krt. 5, 34, 2.

228. Champagny, *Souvenirs*, p. 117.

229. MPM 1, pp. 114–15; NP1, pp. 95–96.

230. Protocol of the meeting in Totis on October 16, 1809, HHStA Wien StK Vorträge Krt. 182, Fols. 151–154.

231. The manuscript on which the memoirs published in NP are based contains a gap where material on the war of 1809 should be (*Memoirs of Metternich*, 1, p. 83; NP 1, p. 69), which is partly compensated for by Metternich's later discussion of a letter by the adjutant general and head of the chancellery of the generalissimo Archduke Karl, FML Count Philipp Grünne. In this letter, dated September 23, 1809, Grünne presents his take on the failure. Unfortunately, the beginning of this important text by Metternich, which explains the causes of the failure, is cut (*Memoirs of Metternich* 1, pp. 389–90; NP 1, pp. 228–29). The original, "Geschichtliche Bemerkungen zu dem Schreiben des Generals Grafen Grünne an den Prince de Ligne" [Historical remarks on the letter of General Grünne to Prince de Ligne, September 27 and 28] in NA Prague A. C. 8, Krt. 5, 34, 1.

232. Srbik, *Metternich*, 1, p. 123.

233. Metternich, "Geschichtliche Bemerkungen," NA Prag A. C. 8, Krt. 5, 34, 1.

234. The remark was made in the Dresden conversation; MPM 1, p. 187; NP 1, p. 152.

235. See MPM 1, p. 98; NP 1, p. 83.

236. See Gill, *Thunder on the Danube*, 1, XIIIf.

237. See Klueting, *Die Lehre von der Macht der Staaten.*

238. NA Prag RAM A. C. 8, Krt. 5, 34, 2. An entry for the losses in Croatia is missing, and hence the total sums are not correct. See *Der aufrichtige und wohlerfahrene Schweizer-Bote*, Aarau 6. Jg. (1809), p. 366.

239. See Raumer and Botzenhart, *Deutschland um 1800*, p. 514.

240. MPM 1, p. 116; NP 1, p. 96.

241. MPM 1, p. 117; NP 1, pp. 97–98.

242. Metternich to Eleonore in Paris, December 25, 1809, NA Prague A. C. 12, Krt. 1, 6. In NP this letter is erroneously inserted in the letter of November 28.

243. MPM 1, p. 116; NP 1, p. 97. *Translator's note*: all following quotations until the next note are from this page.

244. MPM 1, p. 282; NP 1, p. 287.

245. MPM 1, p. 117; NP 1, p. 97.

246. Ibid.

247. MPM 1, p. 115; NP 1, p. 96.

248. Imperial resolution of November 6, 1809, sent to Metternich; HHStA Wien StK Vorträge Krt. 139, Fol. 30.

249. See, for example, Lechner, *Gelehrte Kritik,* p. 56.

250. "Of the Necessity of a Censorship of the Press," Metternich to Stadion, June 23, 1808, MPM 2, pp. 225–27; here: p. 226; NP 2, pp. 191–93; here: p. 192.

251. See Lechner, *Gelehrte Kritik,* pp. 59–60.

252. Presentation by Metternich, dated November 19, 1809, HHStA Wien StK Vorträge Krt. 183, Fols. 100–104.

253. Ibid.

254. Imperial bill to all regional rulers (draft in Metternich's hand), October 3, 1809, HHStA Wien StK Vorträge Krt. 183, Fol. 3.

255. Imperial resolution addressed to Franz Georg, May 27, 1810, HHStA Wien StK Vorträge Krt. 185, Fol. 162.

256. Franz Georg, October 31, 1810, HHStA Wien StK Vorträge Krt. 186, Fols. 100–108.

257. Extensive file "Gründung und Einrichtung eines literarischen Bureaus 1810 bis 1811" [Foundation and establishment of a literary bureau 1810 to 1811], NA Prague RAM Krt. 212, 2008-1.

258. "Votum ad Imperatorem, das literarische Bureau betreffend," NA Prague RAM Krt. 215, 2009-4.

259. See Siemann, *Anfänge der politischen Polizei,* pp. 63–68.

260. Presentation by Metternich, November 19, 1809, HHStA Wien StK Vorträge Krt. 183, Fols. 96–99.

261. See imperial handwritten letter of January 18, 1811, to Mettenich, HHStA Wien StK Vorträge Krt. 188, Fol. 159.

262. Text in Pfaundler and Köfler, *Tiroler Freiheitskampf,* p. 73 (facsimile).

263. Ibid., p. 84.

264. Ibid., p. 127.

265. Ibid., p. 218 (facsimile).

266. Presentation by Metternich (no date); HHStA Wien StK Vorträge Krt. 182, Fol. 226. The date can be established from the location in which the text is filed.

267. Metternich to Emperor Franz, January 1, 1810, HHStA Wien StK Vorträge Krt. 184, Fol. 2.

268. Imperial resolution, February 12, 1810, HHStA Wien StK Vorträge Krt. 184, Fol. 144.

269. Imperial resolution, March 22, 1810, HHStA Wien StK Vorträge Krt. 184, Fol. 126.

270. Metternich to Emperor Franz, April 4, 1810, quoted after Corti, *Metternich,* 1, p. 265.

271. Talleyrand, *Memoirs,* vol. 2, pp. 5–6.

272. See Fournier, *Napoleon,* 2, p. 314.

273. MPM 1, p. 118; NP 1, p. 98.

274. Schwarzenberg to Metternich, December 4, 1809, Helfert, *Maria Louise,* pp. 349–50.

275. See Helfert, *Maria Louise,* pp. 79–80.

276. See Corti, *Metternich,* 1, p. 234.

277. Only extracts from the instructions are reproduced in MPM 1, pp. 370–72; NP 2, pp. 317–19. Helfert, *Maria Louise* (pp. 350–52), also quotes an abridged version. The introduc-

tory part, containing the basic considerations that justify the subsequent marriage policies, is missing. I quote following the complete version: NA Prague A. C. 8, Krt. 6, 36.

278. MPM 2, 370; NP 2, p. 317.

279. MPM 2, p. 371; NP 2, p. 318.

280. MPM 1, p. 118; NP 1, pp. 98–99.

281. "Bulletin de Paris de 22 Déc. 1809 jusqu'au 11 Janvier 1810," NA Prague A. C. 8, Krt. 6; the following account is mainly based on the Bulletin.

282. Eleonore to Clemens von Metternich, January 3, 1810, MPM 2, p. 374; NP 2, p. 321.

283. MPM 2, p. 373; NP 2, p. 320.

284. Ibid.

285. MPM 2, p. 373; NP 2, pp. 320–21.

286. MPM 2, p. 374; NP 2, pp. 321.

287. MPM 2, p. 374; NP 2, p. 321.

288. See the doubts expressed in Andreas, *Zeitalter Napoleons*, p. 427.

289. Metternich to Eleonore, January 27, 1810, MPM 2, p. 375; NP 2, p. 322. The original: NA Prague A. C. 12, Krt. 1, 6.

290. Ibid.

291. Metternich to Eleonore, February 14, 1810, NA Prague A. C. 12, Krt. 1, 6. Excerpts in Corti, *Metternich*, 1, p. 231.

292. Talleyrand, *Memoirs*, vol. 2, pp. 5–6.

293. Ibid., p. 6.

294. Ibid., p. 7.

295. Schwarzenberg to Metternich, February 14, 1810, Helfert, *Maria Louise*, p. 399.

296. Presentation by Metternich, March 13, 1810, HHStA Wien, StK Vorträge Krt. 184, Fols. 64–65 (draft).

297. Metternich to Eleonore in Paris, March 12, 1810, NA Prague A. C. 12, Krt. 1, 6.

298. A description can be found in *Allgemeine Ulmer Zeitung*, no. 85, March 26, 1810 (copy), NA Prague RAM Krt. 111, 4342.

299. Ibid.

300. Original protocol: "Proces verbal à Wesel sur le Rhin ce 12 Decembre 1792," NA Prague RAM Krt. 111, 4332.

301. Metternich filed the calculations for these; NA Prague A. C. 8, Krt. 6, 37. The handing-over ceremony, which today strikes us as odd, mirrored the one in the case of Marie Antoinette in 1770. It took place in a specially erected wooden construction with a canopy; the hall was divided into an Austrian and a French half; see Helfert, *Maria Louise*, pp. 116–20.

302. Presentation by Metternich, February 18, 1810, HHStA Wien StK Vorträge Krt. 184, Fols. 174–75.

303. Presentation by Metternich, March 14, 1810, HHStA Wien StK Vorträge Krt. 184, Fols. 68–71; MPM 1, pp. 129–30; NP 1, p. 106.

304. Presentation by Metternich, March 11, 1810, HHStA Wien StK Vorträge Krt. 184, Fol. 37.

305. Presentation by Metternich, March 14, 1810, HHStA Wien StK Vorträge Krt. 184, Fols. 68–71.

306. Paper clipping from "Journal de l'Empire," March 31, 1810, NA Prague A. C. 8, Krt. 6, 37.

307. Presentation by Metternich, March 21, 1810, HHStA Wien StK Vorträge Krt. 184, Fols. 261–62.

308. Presentation by Metternich, March 29, 1810, HHStA Wien StK Vorträge Krt. 184, Fol. 263.

309. Barante, *Souvenirs,* 1, pp. 316–18.

310. Helfert, *Maria Louise,* p. 142.

311. NA Prague A. C. 8, Krt. 6, 36.

312. Srbik, *Metternich,* 1, p. 132.

313. Talleyrand, *Memoirs,* vol. 2, p. 19.

314. Presentation by Metternich, September 5, 1810, NA Prague A. C. 8, Krt. 6, 35; MPM 2, pp. 460–62; here: p. 461; NP 2, 395–99; here: p. 396.

315. MPM 1, p. 191; NP 1, p. 156.

316. MPM 1, p. 130; NP 1, p. 107.

317. Ibid.

318. Presentation by Metternich, May 9, 1810, HHStA Wien StK Vorträge Krt. 185, Fols. 270f.

319. Presentation by Metternich, October 18, 1810, HHStA Wien StK Vorträge Krt. 186, Fols. 132–147, Zit. Fols. 134–35.

320. Ibid., Fol. 146.

321. Presentation by Metternich, May 9, 1810, HHStA Wien StK Vorträge Krt. 184, Fol. 271.

322. Helfert, *Maria Louise,* p. 161.

323. Presentation by Metternich, April 16, 1810, HHStA Wien StK Vorträge Krt. 184, Fols. 252–53.

324. "Convention sur la lévée des Séquestres 1810"; NA Prague A. C. 8, Krt. 6, 36.

325. "Convention de Paris, du 30. Août 1810, en exécution du Traité de Vienne du 14. Octobre 1809," in Meyer, *Staats-Acten,* pp. 149–51.

326. Presentation by Franz Georg von Metternich, September 17, 1810, HHStA StK Vorträge Krt. 186, Fol. 152.

327. MPM 1, p. 125 (transl. modified); NP 1, p. 102.

328. Presentation by Metternich, July 9, 1810 (emphasis in the original), HHStA Wien StK Vorträge Krt. 185, Fol. 73.

329. MPM 1, p. 130; NP 1, p. 106.

330. MPM 1, p. 131; NP 1, p. 107.

331. Ibid.

332. "Précis sommaire d'une conversation avec l'Empereur Napoléon après son lever à St. Cloud le 20 Septembre 1810," NA Prague A. C. 8, Krt. 6, 35 (draft); HHStA Wien StK

Vorträge Krt. 188, Fols. 136–157 (fair copy); unabridged translation in the *Memoirs:* MPM 1, p. 136 ("On September 20") to p. 139 ("what the Emperor Francis thinks on the matter"); NP 1, p. 112 ("Am 20. September") to p. 115 ("was der Kaiser Franz davon denkt").

333. MPM 1, p. 139; NP 1, p. 115.

334. MPM 1, p. 149; NP 1, p. 122.

335. MPM 1, p. 136; NP 1, p. 112.

336. MPM 1, p. 137; NP 1, p. 113.

337. MPM 1, p. 139; NP 1, p. 115.

338. MPM 1, p. 136 [transl. amended]; NP 1, p. 112.

339. Confidential letter, Laborde to Metternich, February 6, 1810. See Helfert, *Maria Louise,* p. 92.

340. MPM 1, p. 139 (transl. modified); NP 1, p. 115.

341. "Audience du 24. Septembre," HHStA StK Vorträge Krt. 188, 133 (fair copy); NA Prag A. C. 8, Krt. 6, 35 (draft); completely reworded in MPM 2, p. 466 ["It is more agreeable to me to have him on the throne of Austria than it would be to have any of my brothers there."]; NP 2, p. 400 ["Je le préfère de beaucoup à aucun de mes propres frères sur le trône de l'Autriche."].

342. Napoléon, *Correspondance,* 21, p. 222; see Corti, *Metternich,* 1, p. 278. The bust stood in Metternich's private study at the Chancellery; today, it is on display in Metternich's study in Königswart. Corti, *Metternich,* 1, p. 311.

343. *Wiener Zeitung,* no. 83, October 17, 1810, p. 1573.

344. "Original-Vortrag (Bericht) des Fürsten Metternich nach seiner Rückkehr aus Paris an Se. Majestät, d. d. Wien 17. Januar 1811" [Original presentation (report) by Prince Metternich after his return from Paris to His Majesty, dated Vienna January 17, 1811]; HHStA Wien StK Vorträge Krt. 188, Fols. 136–57; the version in MPM 2, pp. 474–91, NP 2, pp. 405–20, contains numerous redactions that affect the meaning, as well as omissions that are not indicated. I quote from the original. *Translator's note:* The English translation has been modified where necessary.

345. Article 97 of the proceedings of the Congress of Vienna aimed to redistribute this wealth to the restored states. The "monte napoleone" was a mortgage bank in the new Kingdom of Italy. It regulated the debts which derived from the former provinces out of which the kingdom had been formed, e.g., Monte di San Terese, San Ambrogio, Aque di Bologna, Beneditino, Modena, Ferrara, etc. It also collected the payments from the sale of state-owned property. See Johann Ernst Liebhold, *Comptoir-Handbuch zur Erklärung der Cours-Zettel,* 3 ed. (Frankfurt a. M., 1813), pp. 120–25.

346. MPM 2, pp. 486–87 (transl. modified); NP 2, p. 416.

347. MPM 2, pp. 487; NP 2, p. 417.

348. Presentation by Metternich, October 20, 1810, HHStA Wien StK Vorträge Krt. 186, Fols. 4–10; quotation in 4.

349. Presentation by Metternich, October 31, 1810, HHStA Wien StK Vorträge Krt. 186, Fols. 91–99; see MPM 2, pp. 469–73; NP 2, pp. 401–405.

350. MPM 2, p. 502; NP 2, p. 429.

351. Report, September 17, 1810, HHStA Wien StK Vorträge Krt. 186, Fols. 93ff.

352. See Srbik, *Metternich*, 1, pp. 129–30.

353. Presentation by Metternich, October 24, 1810, HHStA Wien StK Vorträge Krt. 186, Fols. 24–25.

354. Imperial resolution addressed to Metternich, November 28, 1810, HHStA Wien StK Vorträge Krt. 187, Fol. 151.

355. "Zustand der Armee im Oktober 1810," NA Prag A. C. 8, Krt. 6, 36.

356. Presentation by Metternich, November 28, 1811, HHStA Wien StK Vorträge Krt. 190, Fols. 154–67 (fair copy); Fols. 168–69 (draft). Fairly reliable version, with the exception of one omission, in MPM 2, pp. 499–511; NP 2, pp. 426–38.

357. MPM 2, p. 499 (transl. modified); NP 2, pp. 426–27.

358. MPM 2, p. 510; NP 2, pp. 436–37.

359. MPM 1, p. 154 (transl. amended); NP 1, p. 126.

360. MPM 2, p. 514 (transl. amended); NP 2, pp. 440.

361. Metternich's draft for a resolution, approved by the emperor, dated December 18, 1811, HHStA Wien StK Vorträge Krt. 190, Fol. 132.

362. Presentation by Metternich, January 15, 1812, HHStA Wien StK Vorträge Krt. 191. The complete presentation: Fols. 81–90; quotation in Fol. 81. In MPM 2, pp. 511–16; NP 2, pp. 438–42 the extensive exposition (up to Fol. 84), which is here elaborated on, is missing.

363. Presentation by Metternich, March 2, 1812, HHStA Wien StK Vorträge Krt. 191, Fols. 7–10.

364. Imperial resolution, written by Metternich and addressed to Zichy, March 2, 1812, HHStA Wien StK Vorträge Krt. 191, Fol. 5.

365. Presentation by Metternich, March 25, 1812, HHStA Wien StK Vorträge Krt. 191, Fol. 199.

366. See Clercq, *Recueil des traités de la France*, 2, pp. 355–56. The fact that it was a defensive and offensive alliance was, however, only contained in an additional secret article.

367. See Napoléon, *Correspondance*, p. 23.

368. According to the diary of Hudelist; NA Prag A. C. 8, Krt. 3, 22.

369. Presentation by Metternich, May 17, 1812, "Notizen über die bevorstehende Ankunft des Kaiser Napoleon in Dresden/Logement" [Notes on the imminent arrival of the Emperor Napoleon in Dresden/Lodgings]; HHStA Wien StK Vorträge Krt. 191, Fols. 7–8.

370. MPM 1, p. 150; NP 1, p. 122.

371. MPM 1, p. 154 (transl. amended); NP 1, p. 126.

372. MPM 1, p. 150 (transl. modified); NP 1, p. 122.

373. MPM 1, p. 152; NP 1, p. 124.

374. MPM 1, p. 155 (transl. amended); NP 1, p. 127.

375. MPM 1, p. 151 (transl. amended); NP 1, p. 123.

376. See Corti, *Metternich*, 1, p. 331–35.

377. Presentation by Metternich, June 28, 1812, HHStA Wien StK Vorträge Krt. 191, Fol. 137.

378. Presentation by Metternich, July 7, 1812, HHStA Wien StK Vorträge Krt. 192, Fol. 8.

379. *Translator's note:* A *Pfuhl* is a murky or muddy pool; figuratively also a cesspool of vice.

380. Presentation by Metternich, August 14, 1812, HHStA Wien StK Vorträge Krt. 192, Fol. 125.

381. Presentation by Metternich, September 8, 1812, HHStA Wien StK Vorträge Krt. 192, Fol. 46.

382. Presentation by Metternich, September 26, 1812, HHStA Wien StK Vorträge Krt. 192, Fol. 145.

383. "Neunzehntes Bulletin," Moscow, September 16, 1812, from *Leipziger Zeitung*, October 13, 1812, http://napoleonwiki.de/index.php?title=Neunzehntes_Bulletin_der_großen _Armee_(1812).

384. Presentation by Metternich, September 30, 1812, HHStA Wien StK Vorträge Krt. 192, Fol. 165; a copy of the French bulletin in Fols. 166–67.

385. "Zwanzigstes Bulletin," Moscow, September 17, 1812, from *Leipziger Zeitung*, no. 201, 13 October 1812, http://napoleonwiki.de/index.php?title=Zwanzigstes_Bulletin_der_großen _Armee_(1812).

386. Presentation by Metternich, October 4, 1812, HHStA Wien StK Vorträge Krt. 192, Fol. 30; a transcript of the 20 bulletin is appended.

387. Presentation by Metternich, December 17, 1812, HHStA Wien StK Vorträge Krt. 192, Fol. 173.

388. HHStA Wien, StK Vorträge Krt. 192, Fol. 211; contemporary archival note: "Handschrift des H. H. u. Staatskanzlers F. Metternich (Dec. 1813)" [Handwritten note by the Chancellor of the House, Court and State, F. Metternich (Dec. 1813)].

6. World War: Climax and Crisis, 1813

1. Zamoyski, *Rites of Peace*, p. 15.

2. Müchler, *1813*; the quotations are taken from pp. 158, 159, and 210.

3. See Platthaus, *1813*; also Thamer, *Völkerschlacht*, in which Metternich is not even mentioned in connection with the planning before and during the Battle of Leipzig.

4. Imperial resolution of January 24, 1813, addressed to Prince Schwarzenberg, HHStA Wien StK Vorträge Krt. 193, Fols. 65–66.

5. Presentation by Metternich, February 3, 1813, HHStA Wien StK Vorträge Krt. 193, Fol. 109; the pamphlet Fols. 111–116.

6. See Schroeder, *Transformation*, p. 462.

7. Krones, *Aus dem Tagebuche Erzherzog Johanns*, p. 73.

8. "Gewagte Bemerkungen über die gegenwärtige Lage Tirols" [Speculative remarks on the current situation in Tyrol], February 28, 1813, HHStA Wien Acta Secreta, Krt. 1, Fol. 15.

9. Metternich, January 7, 1811, HHStA Wien StK Vorträge Krt. 188, Fol. 32.

10. Krones, *Aus dem Tagebuche Erzherzog Johanns*, pp. 82–83.

11. HHStA Wien StK Acta Secreta Krt. 1.

12. HHStA Wien StK Acta Secreta Krt. 1, Fol. 151.

13. Metternich, March 10, 1813, HHStA Wien StK Vorträge Krt. 193, Fol. 83.

14. Metternich, March 3, 1813, HHStA Wien StK Vorträge Krt. 193, Fol. 12.

15. See Stahl, *Metternich und Wellington,* pp. 154–61.

16. Presentation by Metternich, March 4, 1813, and an imperial resolution formulated by him: HHStA Wien StK Vorträge Krt. 193, Fols. 41, 47.

17. Presentation by Metternich, March 14, 1813, including the draft of the resolution; HHStA Wien StK Vorträge Krt. 193, Fol. 113.

18. Presentation by Metternich, March 16, 1813, HHStA Wien, StK Vorträge Krt. 193, Fol. 117.

19. Presentation by Metternich, March 17, 1813, HHStA Wien StK Vorträge Krt. 193, Fol. 119.

20. Presentation by Metternich, April 10, 1813, HHStA Wien StK Vorträge Krt. 193, Fols. 32–33.

21. Published in *Allgemeine Handlungs-Zeitung,* no. 82, vol. 20, April 25, 1813, "K. K. Oesterreichische Verordnung die Ausfertigung von 45 Millionen Antizipations-Scheinen betreffend"; on the further history of this fund, see Raumer and Botzenhart, *Deutschland um 1800,* pp. 492–93.

22. Bubna to Metternich, May 16, 1813, Oncken, *Österreich und Preußen,* 2, p. 651.

23. Oncken, *Österreich und Preußen,* 1, pp. 439–45.

24. See ibid.

25. Presentation by Metternich, April 19, 1812, HHStA Wien StK Vorträge Krt. 191, Fol. 82.

26. Metternich to Hardenberg, October 5, 1812; see Oncken, *Österreich und Preußen,* 1, pp. 378–80.

27. Presentation by Metternich, April 21, 1813, HHStA Wien StK Vorträge Krt. 193, Fol. 83.

28. Report by Count Bubna from Dresden, May 16, 1813, Oncken, *Österreich und Preußen,* 1, p. 652.

29. See Aschmann, *Preußens Ruhm und Deutschlands Ehre,* p. 76.

30. See Hoffmann, *Hamburg im kalten Griff Napoleons.*

31. Metternich's instructions to Count von Stadion, Vienna, May 7, 1813, in Oncken, *Österreich und Preußen,* 2, pp. 640–44.

32. The following account of the war up to the Battle of Bautzen is based on Price, *Napoleon,* pp. 60–74.

33. See Zamoyski, *Rites of Peace,* p. 64.

34. Presentation by Metternich, May 27, 1813, HHStA Wien StK Vorträge Krt. 193, Fol. 130.

35. MPM 1, p. 172; NP 1, 139.

36. Metternich to the Emperor Franz, June 19, 1813, HHStA Wien StK Vorträge Krt. 194, Fol. 36.

37. Zamoyski, *Rites of Peace,* p. 132.

38. Metternich to Wilhelmine von Sagan; February 15, 1814, Ullrichová, *Metternich,* p. 207.

39. McGuigan, *Metternich,* pp. 54–76; McGuigan makes use of the family letters in NA Prague.

40. Schroeder, *Transformation,* p. 477.

41. MPM 1, p. 180; NP 1, p. 146.

42. Ibid.

43. MPM 1, pp. 215–16; NP 1, p. 178.

44. MPM 1, p. 216; NP 1, p. 178.

45. MPM 1, pp. 180–81 (transl. amended); NP 1, p. 146.

46. MPM 1, p. 181 (transl. amended); NP 1, p. 147.

47. Ibid.

48. See Oncken, *Österreich und Preußen*, 2, p. 356.

49. Ibid., p. 352.

50. Kronenbitter, *Friedrich Gentz*, p. 30; on his career and the role he played, see pp. 21–45.

51. Gentz's words on June 24, 1813, in MPM 1, p. 412 (transl. amended); NP 1, pp. 251–52. See also Gentz, *Friedrich von Gentz*, 3.1 pp. 109–13, cit. p. 111.

52. Presentation by Metternich (composed in Gitschin), June 24, 1813, HHStA Wien StK Vorträge Krt. 194, Fols. 11–12.

53. Müchler, *1813*, p. 229.

54. MPM 1, p. 191; NP 1, p. 156.

55. Metternich's description, in MPM 1, p. 183; NP 1, p. 149.

56. MPM 1, p. 194; NP 1, p. 158.

57. MPM 1, p. 188; NP 1, p. 153.

58. MPM 1, p. 189; NP 1, p. 154.

59. MPM 1, p. 188; NP 1, p. 153.

60. MPM 1, p. 192; NP 1, p. 157.

61. MPM 1, p. 194; NP 1, p. 158.

62. MPM 1, p. 194; NP 1, p. 159.

63. MPM 1, p. 197; NP 1, p. 161.

64. Oncken, *Österreich und Preußen*, 2, p. 652.

65. MPM 1, p. 186; NP 1, p. 151.

66. Ibid.

67. McGuigan, *Metternich*, p. 79.

68. Fain, *Manuscrit de mille huit cent treize*, 2, p. 39.

69. Ibid., pp. 40–42.

70. "Conversation de M. le Comte de Metternich avec l'empereur Napoléon, telle que S. M. me l'a rancontée," in Hanoteau, "Une nouvelle Relation"; see Price, *Napoleon*, pp. 75–76.

71. See Price, *Napoleon*, p. 84.

72. Talleyrand, *Memoirs*, 2, p. 113.

73. I here follow my own account, with some additions, in Siemann, *Metternich: Staatsmann*, pp. 47–48.

74. MPM 1, p. 189; NP 1, p. 154.

75. Ibid. (transl. amended).

76. MPM 1, p. 190 (transl. modified); NP 1, p. 155.

77. Ibid., footnote (transl. amended).

78. [Extrait du compte rendu par le C. de M. de son premier], "Entretien avec Napoléon à Dresde 28 Juin 1813," NA Prague A. C. 8, Krt. 1, 1. Metternich crossed out the initial title (here in square brackets). The second excerpt gives a fair copy from a different hand, together with notes in the margin from Metternich, and the softer expression "soucie peu" [cares little].

79. MPM 1, p. 191; NP 1 p. 156.

80. Bubna to Metternich, May 16, 1813, Oncken, *Österreich und Preußen*, 2, p. 649.

81. Metternich to Wilhelmine von Sagan, July 2, 1813, Ullrichová, *Metternich*, p. 28.

82. See Oncken, *Österreich und Preußen*, 2, pp. 397–99.

83. Ibid., p. 401.

84. Presentation by Metternich, July 12, 1813, HHStA Wien StK Vorträge Krt. 194, Fols. 67–71; also in Oncken, *Österreich und Preußen*, 2, pp. 402–5.

85. Presentation by Metternich, August 5, 1813, HHStA Wien StK Vorträge Krt. 194, Fol. 34.

86. See Price, *Napoleon*, pp. 89–94.

87. Oncken, *Österreich und Preußen*, 2, pp. 447–48.

88. MPM 1, p. 187 (transl. modified) and p. 191 (transl. modified); NP 1, p. 153 and p. 156.

89. Bubna to Metternich, August 9, 1813, Oncken, *Österreich und Preußen*, 2, pp. 684–87.

90. Metternich to Hudelist, August 18, 1813, Fournier, *Napoleon I*, 3, p. 419.

91. Metternich to Eleonore, August 10, 1813, NA Prague A. C. 12, Krt. 5, 33.

92. See Oncken, *Österreich und Preußen*, 2, p. 431; see also Sked, *Radetzky*.

93. As claimed by Thamer, *Völkerschlacht*, pp. 40–41.

94. Protocol of the "Kriegsplans von Trachtenberg" [Trachtenberg war plan] of July 12, 1813, in Oncken, *Österreich und Preußen*, 2, pp. 663–64.

95. Zeinar, *Geschichte des österreichischen Generalstabes*, p. 290.

96. Reliably reproduced in Spies, *Die Erhebung gegen Napoleon*, pp. 308–22.

97. Gentz to Metternich, September 4, 1813, Wittichen and Salzer, *Friedrich von Gentz*, 3-1, p. 139.

98. See Zeinar, *Geschichte des österreichischen Generalstabes*, p. 287.

99. Memorandum by Friedrich Gentz, November 11, 1813, MPM 1, p. 418; NP 1, p. 259.

100. Metternich to Hudelist, February 21, 1814, Fournier, *Congress von Châtillon*, p. 259.

101. On the overall situation and on Schwarzenberg and Radetzky, see Zeinar, *Geschichte des österreichischen Generalstabes*, pp. 288–90.

102. See Price, *Napoleon*, p. 129.

103. MPM 1, pp. 146–47; NP 1, p. 119.

104. Metternich to Wilhelmine von Sagan, August 27, 1813, Ullrichovà, *Metternich*, pp. 47–48.

105. Schwarzenberg to Emperor Franz, August 28, 1813, Fournier, *Napoleon*, 3, p. 428.

106. See Sked, *Radetzky*, p. 54.

107. See MPM 1, pp. 206–7; NP 1, pp. 169–70.

108. Memorandum, December 12, 1854, in NP 8, p. 371.

109. Ibid., p. 369.

110. See Zamoyski, *Rites of Peace*, pp. 98–100; the secret articles are ignored in this study.

111. The secret articles can be found in Martens, *Recueil de Traités*, 3, pp. 122–23.

112. See Oncken, *Zeitalter der Revolution*, 2, pp. 698–99; Oncken refers to the separate articles.

113. NA Prague A. C. 8, Krt. 7, 40 (Denkschriften 1813 [Memoranda 1813]).

114. See Schroeder, *Transformation*, pp. 477–78; for an extensive discussion of this thesis, see Zamoyski, *Rites of Peace*, pp. 106–29; here p. 106.

115. Castlereagh to Viscount Cathcart, July 5, 1813, Oncken, *Österreich und Preußen*, 2, pp. 702–5.

116. Metternich to his father Franz Georg, September 14, 1813, NA Prague, A. C. 12, Krt. 1, 5.

117. Metternich to Hudelist, September 1, 1813, Fournier, *Napoleon*, 3, p. 422.

118. Metternich to Hudelist, September 3, 1813, Fournier, *Napoleon*, 3, p. 422.

119. Metternich to Hudelist, September 28, 1813, Fournier, *Napoleon*, 3, p. 423.

120. Metternich to Eleonore, October 10, 1813, NA Prague A. C. 12 Krt. 5, 33.

121. HHStA Wien StK Vorträge Krt. 194, Fol. 30; reproduced in Schallaburg, *Napoleon*, p. 245.

122. MPM 1, p. 185 and p. 187; NP 1, pp. 151–52.

123. MPM 1, p. 208 (footnote); NP 1, pp. 171–72 (footnote).

124. Metternich, October 18, 1813, in Ullrichová, *Metternich*, pp. 81–82.

125. Metternich to Hudelist, October 19 (ten o'clock), 1813, Fournier, *Napoleon*, 3, p. 424.

126. Ibid.

127. Martens, *Recueil des traités*, 1, supplementary volume 5, p. 612; the full text of the treaty, including the secret articles containing the agreed territorial changes: pp. 610–14. The treaty guaranteed the extent of the territory, not its concrete borders, which made possible future territorial exchanges (as for instance in the case of Tyrol).

128. Srbik, *Metternich*, 1, p. 165.

129. Schwarzenberg to his wife Marie Anna, December 25, 1813, Novák, *Schwarzenberg*, p. 360.

130. Presentation by Metternich, October 13, 1813, HHStA Wien StK Vorträge Krt. 194, Fol. 29.

131. Metternich to Wilhelmine von Sagan, November 6, 1813, Ullrichová, *Metternich*, p. 100.

132. Metternich to Wilhelmine von Sagan, November 7, 1813, Ullrichová, *Metternich*, p. 101.

133. "Etablissement d'un système militaire général pour tout l'Allemagne," Martens, *Receuil des traités*, 1, supplementary volume 5, p. 624.

134. Schroeder, *Transformation*, p. 483.

135. Stein, *Briefe*, 4, pp. 242–48.

136. MPM 1, p. 200 (transl. amended); NP 1, p. 164.

137. See Oncken, "Aus den letzten Monaten," on the convention, pp. 19–20; on the general situation, pp. 1–40; Duchhardt, *Stein*, pp. 295–300.

138. MPM 1, p. 156, p. 209, and p. 252; NP 1, p. 128, p. 172, and p. 207.

139. MPM 2, p. 574 (transl. amended); NP 1, p. 492.

140. See the fitting characterization of the relationship between Stein and Metternich in Duchhardt, *Stein,* p. 295.

7. World War: Catastrophe and Resolution, 1814

1. See also Fournier, *Congress von Châtillon,* pp. 20–21.

2. "Propositions générales sur un plan d'opération contre la France (présenté à Francfort s. l. M. par le Feld-Maréchal prince de Schwarzenberg à S. M. L'Empereur de Russie)," in Bernhardi, *Denkwürdigkeiten,* vol. 4, part 2, pp. 390–92; see Fournier, *Congress von Châtillon,* pp. 17–19; Sked, *Radetzky,* pp. 56–57; Price, *Napoleon,* pp. 159–60.

3. MPM 1, p. 215 (transl. amended); NP 1, p. 177.

4. See Oncken, *Zeitalter der Revolution,* 2, pp. 713–14.

5. Schroeder, *Transformation,* p. 491.

6. See Oncken, *Zeitalter der Revolution,* 2, pp. 714–15.

7. Metternich to Hudelist, November 9, 1813, Fournier, *Congress von Châtillon,* p. 242.

8. Metternich to Hudelist, November 23, 1813, Fournier, *Congress von Châtillon,* p. 243.

9. Duchhardt, *Stein,* p. 299.

10. MPM 1, p. 214 (transl. modified); NP 1, p. 177.

11. Thus his marginal note in a letter from Hudelist, November 11, 1813, in Fournier, *Congress von Châtillon,* p. 25, note. 2.

12. MPM 1, p. 217; NP 1, p. 179.

13. Metternich to Hudelist, November 14, 1813, Fournier, *Congress von Châtillon,* p. 7, note 1.

14. Supplement "Keine Eroberungen" [No conquests], NA Prague A. C. 8, Krt. 3, 23; from the "Leitfaden" [Guidelines].

15. German text in Oncken, *Zeitalter der Revolution,* 2, p. 719; French version in Capefigue, *Le congrès de Vienne,* 1, pp. 78–79.

16. MPM 1, p. 214; NP 1, p. 177.

17. MPM 1, p. 215; NP 1, p. 178.

18. See Oncken, *Zeitalter der Revolution,* 2, p. 720.

19. Presentation by Metternich, December 15, 1813, HHStA Wien StK Vorträge Krt. 194, Fols. 195–197.

20. See Plotho, *Krieg in Deutschland und Frankreich,* part 3.

21. See Sked, *Radetzky;* on Schwarzenberg and Radetzky, based on new archival material, see Price, *Napoleon.*

22. Quoted after Oncken, *Lord Castlereagh,* p. 17.

23. Talleyrand, *Memoirs,* 2, p. 116.

24. Presentation by Metternich, January 27, 1814, HHStA Wien StK Vorträge Krt. 195, Fols. 40–47; a German version, part paraphrase, in Oncken, *Zeitalter der Revolution,* 2, pp. 62–66.

25. Reproduced in Fournier, *Congress von Châtillon,* pp. 306–8.

26. "L'Allemagne composée de princes souverains uni par un lien fédératif qui assure et garantisse l'indépendance de l'Allemagne," in Fournier *Congress von Châtillon,* p. 307; on Metternich's authorship, p. 73.

27. Oncken, *Zeitalter der Revolution,* 2, p. 764.

28. Fain, *Manuscrit de 1814,* pp. 94–95.

29. See Schroeder, *Transformation,* esp. p. 497 and pp. 504–5.

30. Metternich to Wilhelmine von Sagan, February 2, 1814, Ullrichová, *Metternich,* p. 198.

31. Metternich to Wilhelmine von Sagan, February 15, 1814, Ullrichová, *Metternich,* p. 207.

32. Schwarzenberg to his wife Marie Anna, February 11, 1814, Novák, *Schwarzenberg,* p. 374.

33. See Oncken, *Zeitalter der Revolution,* 2, p. 746.

34. Schwarzenberg to his wife Marie Anna, January 26, 1814, Novák, *Schwarzenberg,* p. 369.

35. Schwarzenberg to his wife Marie Anna, February 26, 1814, Novák, *Schwarzenberg,* p. 379.

36. MPM 1, p. 234; NP 1, p. 194.

37. See Forgues, *Baron de Vitrolles,* 1, 1814, p. 78; see also Oncken, *Zeitalter der Revolution,* 2, p. 779.

38. Metternich to Wilhelmine von Sagan, January 21, 1814, Ullrichová, *Metternich,* p. 183.

39. Letters from Metternich to Wilhelmine von Sagan, January 19 and 21, 1814, Ullrichová, *Metternich,* pp. 180, 183.

40. Presentation by Metternich, October 24, 1821, in MPM 3, p. 554; NP 3, p. 490.

41. From letters by Metternich, August 22 and 25, 1822, in MPM 3, pp. 591–92; NP 3, pp. 522–23. Castlereagh had slit his carotid artery with a letter opener. Contemporaries spoke of a nervous disease. Modern diagnoses suggest severe depression with psychotic symptoms; see Franklin, "Londonderry," pp. 20–23.

42. See Stahl, *Metternich und Wellington.*

43. The "Memorandum on the deliverance and security of Europe" had originally been written by William Pitt; see Hurd, *British Foreign Secretary,* pp. 23–25, and also Webster, *Castlereagh,* p. 125.

44. See Martens, *Recueil de traités 1808–1815,* pp. 155–65.

45. See Schroeder, *Transformation,* p. 504.

46. Ibid.

47. Metternich to Wilhelmine von Sagan, March 8, 1814, Ullrichová, *Metternich,* p. 227.

48. See Hardenberg, *Tagebücher,* p. 783.

49. Date given by Hardenberg, *Tagebücher,* p. 783; the full text can be found in Capefigue, *Congrès de Vienne,* 1, pp. 143–46; excerpts in Fournier, *Napoleon,* 3, p. 279.

50. See Talleyrand, *Memoirs,* 2, p. 114.

51. Metternich to Wilhelmine von Sagan, April 7, 1814 (one o'clock in the morning), Ullrichová, *Metternich,* p. 240.

52. Metternich to his daughter Marie, March 29, 1814 (one o'clock in the morning), NA Prague A. C. 12, Krt. 1, 7.

53. Metternich to Wilhelmine von Sagan, April 7, 1814 (one o' clock in the morning), in Ullrichová, *Metternich*, p. 242.

54. Hardenberg, *Tagebücher*, p. 785; on the business conducted in Dijon, see pp. 784–86.

55. See Fournier, *Napoleon*, 3, p. 285.

56. See Talleyrand, *Memoirs*, 2, p. 123.

57. See ibid., pp. 116–22.

58. "Traité dit de Fontainebleau, conclu à Paris," April 11, 1814, in Capefigue, *Congrès de Vienne*, 1, pp. 148–51.

59. MPM 1, p. 241; NP 1, p. 200.

60. Metternich to Wilhelmine von Sagan, April 13, 1814, Ullrichová, *Metternich*, p. 244.

61. Metternich to Wilhelmine von Sagan, April 19, 1814, Ullrichová, *Metternich*, p. 248.

62. MPM 1, pp. 249–50 (transl. modified); NP 1, p. 206.

63. The text of the treaty can be found in Capefigue, *Congrès de Vienne*, 1, p. 161.

64. As stipulated in article 27.

65. Presentation by Metternich, June 12, 1814, HHStA Wien StK Vorträge Krt. 196, Fols. 5–14.

66. Metternich to his wife Eleonore, June 12, 1814, NA Prague A. C. 12, Krt. 5, 34.

67. Presentation by Metternich, June 12, 1814, HHStA Wien StK Vorträge Krt. 196, Fols. 5–14.

68. Metternich to Eleonore, June 15, 1814, NA Prague A. C. Krt. 5, 34.

69. Presentation by Metternich, June 12, 1814, HHStA Wien StK Vorträge Krt. 196, Fols. 17–18.

70. Presentation by Metternich, June 25, 1814, HHStA Wien StK Vorträge Krt. 196, Fols. 43–44.

71. Presentation by Metternich, June 28, 1814, HHStA Wien StK Vorträge Krt. 196, Fols. 40–51.

72. Presentation by Metternich, June 3, 1814, HHStA Wien StK Vorträge Krt. 195, Fols. 173–74.

73. Presentation by Metternich, July 5, 1814, HHStA Wien StK Vorträge Krt. 196, Fols. 53–56.

74. Presentation by Metternich, June 28, 1814, HHStA Wien StK Vorträge Krt. 196, Fols. 49–51.

75. Presentation by Metternich, June 25, 1814, HHStA Wien StK Vorträge Krt. 196, Fol. 44.

76. Presentation by Metternich, July 7, 1814, HHStA Wien StK Vorträge Krt. 196, Fol. 59.

77. Presentation by Metternich, June 23, 1814, HHStA Wien StK Vorträge Krt. 196, Fols. 24f.

78. Presentation by Metternich, July 7, 1814, HHStA Wien StK Vorträge Krt. 196, Fol. 59.

79. Presentation by Metternich, June 25, 1814, HHStA Wien StK Vorträge Krt. 196, Fols. 47–48.

80. Presentation by Metternich, May 27, 1814, HHStA Wien StK Vorträge Krt. 195, Fols. 138–40.

81. Presentation by Metternich, June 3, 1814, HHStA Wien StK Vorträge Krt. 195, Fol. 168.

82. Metternich to his wife Eleonore, June 3, 1814, NA Prag A. C. 12, Krt. 5, 34.

83. See Zamoyski, *Rites of Peace,* on, for example, Metternich's judgment of the war, p. 108; on his vanity, p. 37 and p. 98; on his moderate intelligence, p. 38.

84. Ticknor, *Life, Letters, and Journals,* 2, pp. 14, 17, and 20.

85. Price, *Napoleon,* p. 87.

86. Metternich to Eleonore, June 28, 1813, NA Prag A. C. 12 Krt. 5, 33; partly reproduced in Price, *Napoleon,* p. 87. Zamoyski concludes from the letter that there was a visit to the theater in Dresden of which Metternich, however, says that it did not take place. At the same time, the picture of horror which Price discusses is ignored; see Zamoyski, *Rites of Peace,* p. 78.

87. Metternich to Wilhelmine von Sagan, September 1, 1813, Ullrichová, *Metternich,* p. 55.

88. Metternich to Wilhelmine von Sagan, October 23, 1813, Ullrichová, *Metternich,* p. 85.

89. Metternich to Wilhelmine von Sagan, October 20, 1813, Ullrichová, *Metternich,* p. 82.

90. Metternich to Wilhelmine von Sagan, November 2, 1813, Ullrichová, *Metternich,* p. 94.

91. Metternich to Wilhelmine von Sagan, November 5, 1813, Ullrichová, *Metternich,* p. 99.

92. Metternich to Wilhelmine von Sagan, December 13, 1813, Ullrichová, *Metternich,* p. 135.

93. Metternich to Wilhelmine von Sagan, February 25, 1814, Ullrichová, *Metternich,* p. 218.

94. See Price, *Napoleon,* pp. 198–99.

95. Metternich to Wilhelmine von Sagan, March 1, 1814, Ullrichová, *Metternich,* p. 221.

96. Metternich to Wilhelmine von Sagan, March 14, 1814, Ullrichová, *Metternich,* p. 231.

97. See Planert, *Der Mythos vom Befreiungskrieg,* pp. 116–20.

98. Metternich to Wilhelmine von Sagan, March 15, 1814, Ullrichová, *Metternich,* p. 232. ("C'est une vilaine chose que la guerre! Elle salit tout; jusqu'à l'imagination et je tiens beaucoup à ce que cela ne m'arrive pas.")

99. Metternich to his daughter Marie, September 4, 1813, NA Prag A. C. 12 Krt. 1, 7. An abbreviated version in Corti, *Metternich,* 1, p. 391.

100. Dorothea von Lieven to Metternich, September 24, 1820, NA Prag A. C. 6, C19.1–3.

101. Clausewitz, *On War* (book 1, section 24), p. 99.

102. See Schulz, *Normen und Praxis,* pp. 91–92.

103. Metternich to Dorothea von Lieven, November 28, 1824, NA Prag A. C. 6, C19.11. Nr. 151–162; an abbreviated version in Corti, *Metternich,* 2, pp. 253–54.

104. Kennan, *Around the Cragged Hill*, p. 80. The expression "great seminal catastrophe" in Kennan, *Decline of Bismarck's European Order*, p. 3.

105. Baumgart, *Akten zur Geschichte des Krimkriegs*, I, 3, p. 7.

106. Metternich to Gentz, June 21, 1824, MPM 4, pp. 108–9; NP 4, p. 101.

107. Metternich to Dorothea von Lieven, April 20, 1819, Mika, *Metternichs Briefe*, p. 265; the French original can be found in Hanoteau, *Lettres du Prince de Metternich*, p. 301. (The originals of the letters before May 1, 1819, are not in the Prague archive.)

108. Metternich to Apponyi, February 6, 1848, in NP 7, p. 559.

8. The End of an Era and a New Beginning for Europe

1. See Siemann, *Metternich. Staatsmann*, pp. 6–7.

2. Schroeder, *Transformation*, p. 486.

3. See Gruner, *Wiener Kongress*, p. 12.

4. MPM 1, p. 10; NP 1, p. 13.

5. Adam Krzemiński, "Der Griff nach der Weltmacht" [Grasping for world power], *Die Zeit*, no. 38, September 12, 2013, p. 22.

6. See Savoy, *Napoleon und Europa*, p. 155.

7. See Doering-Manteuffel, *Vom Wiener Kongreß*, pp. 13–14.

8. *Translator's note:* The term *Sattelzeit* is Reinhart Koselleck's, not to be confused with Karl Jaspers's *Achsenzeit* (axial age).

9. I follow Koselleck, "Einleitung," p. xv.

10. The following conceptual distinctions follow Münkler, *Empires*, pp. 9–17.

11. *Translator's note:* A reference to "Bella gerant alii, tu felix Austria nube" ("Let others wage war: thou, happy Austria, marry").

12. Note by Talleyrand, October 1, 1814, in Capefigue, *Le congrès de Vienne*, 2, pp. 1962–64.

13. See Stauber, *Wiener Kongress*, pp. 60–78; Mayr, "Aufbau und Arbeitsweise," pp. 64–127.

14. Stauber, *Wiener Kongress*, p. 57.

15. Gruner, *Wiener Kongress*, p. 7.

16. Duchhardt, *Wiener Kongress*, p. 14.

17. "Dixième Protocole de la séance du 12 mars 1815 des plénipotentiaires des huit Puissances signataires du Traité de Paris," in Capefigue, *Le congrès de Vienne*, 2, pp. 910–11.

18. MPM 2, p. 554; NP 2, p. 474.

19. See Stauber, *Wiener Kongress*, p. 59.

20. MPM 1, p. 36; NP 1, p. 33.

21. *Translator's note:* The German term for law and order is *Ruhe und Ordnung*, which has complex political connotations. Historically, it derives from Prussian law (Allgemeines Preußisches Landrecht of 1794, Part 2., 17. Titel, § 10): "Die nöthigen Anstalten zur Erhaltung der öffentlichen Ruhe, Sicherheit, und Ordnung und zu Abwendung der dem Publico,

oder einzelnen Mitgliedern desselben, bevorstehenden Gefahr zu treffen, ist das Amt der Po-lizey." [The necessary arrangements for the preservation of public peace, security, and order, and for the prevention of potential dangers to the public or individual members of it, are the responsibility of the police.] After the battle of Jena and Auerstedt, with French troops marching into Berlin, there was a famous Prussian slogan that *Ruhe* was now the prime virtue of the citizen. In other words, keep calm and carry on, as the English put it in 1939. In both instances, the intention was to stabilize the authority of the state and law in the face of external threats. However, more recently, the call for *Ruhe und Ordnung* has also taken on a conservative meaning—don't rock the boat—and is invoked in a wide range of political contexts.

22. This is the subtitle of a volume marking the 200 anniversary of the congress, see Just, Maderthaner, and Maimann, *Wiener Kongress.*

23. MPM 1, p. 253; NP 1, p. 208.

24. MPM 2, pp. 553–86 (the footnote giving Metternich's comments, handwritten on his draft copy of Gentz's report, is omitted in the English edition); NP 2, pp. 473–502; here: p. 473.

25. See for instance Rauchensteiner, "Das Leben eines Geradlinigen," p. 115.

26. Nesselrode to his father, April 25, 1806, Nesselrode, *Lettres et papiers,* 3, p. 132.

27. Krones, *Aus dem Tagebuche Erzherzog Johanns,* p. 166 (entry of July 24, 1814).

28. Memorandum by Castlereagh added to his report of October 24, 1814, in Müller, *Quellen,* pp. 221–22.

29. Metternich to Hardenberg, December 10, 1814, MPM 2, p. 586; NP 2, p. 503.

30. See Eynard, *Der tanzende Kongress,* p. 158.

31. Ibid., p. 67.

32. MPM 1, p. 327; NP 1, p. 326.

33. Metternich to Emperor Franz, October 24, 1814, Corti, *Metternich,* 1, p. 477.

34. MPM 2, p. 587; NP 2, p. 502.

35. See Mayr, "Aufbau und Arbeitsweise," p. 85.

36. Presentation by Metternich, December 2, 1814, HHStA Vienna StK Vorträge Krt. 196, Fol. 103.

37. See Duchhardt, *Wiener Kongress,* p. 86.

38. See Blank, *Sächsische Frage,* pp. 96–101.

39. Metternich uses the expression in a letter of December 31, 1849, which he sent from Brussels to the Austrian plenipotentiary in Frankfurt, Kübeck von Kübau, NP 8, p. 485 and p. 487.

40. On Alexander, see Oncken, *Österreich und Preußen,* 1, pp. 325–60; on Stein, see Hundt, *Die Mindermächtigen,* p. 32; Duchhardt, *Stein,* p. 294; on the imperial estates, see Hundt, *Die Mindermächtigen,* p. 43.

41. NA Prague A. C. 8, Krt. 3, 23.

42. Quoted from the (unpublished) part of the manuscript; NA Prague A. C. 8, Krt. 3, 23.

43. MPM 1, p. 161; NP 1, p. 132.

44. MPM 1, p. 166; NP 1, p. 136.

45. MPM 1, p. 161; NP 1, pp. 131–32.

46. MPM 1, p. 162; NP 1, p. 132.

47. MPM 1, p. 162; NP 1, p. 133.

48. "Die Deutsche Frage. Genesis, Verlauf und gegenwärtiger Stand derselben. Eine Denkschrift Metternich's an den Erzherzog Johann, deutschen Reichsverweser, ddo. London, August 1848" [The German question. Its genesis, development, and the present situation. A memorandum by Metternich for the Archduke Johann, German imperial regent, dated London, August 1848], in NP 8, pp. 443–53.

49. Memorandum by Metternich "Die deutsche Frage. Anfang des Jahres 1849" [The German question. Beginning of 1849], in NA Prag A. C. 8, Krt. 1, 10.

50. MPM 1, p. 263 [transl. amended; the existing English translation turns the meaning into its opposite]; NP 1, 216–17.

51. MPM 1, pp. 263–64 [transl. modified]; NP 1, p. 218; quoted after the original autograph of the "Leitfaden" [Guidelines], NA Prague A. C. 8, Krt. 3, 23.

52. See Schmidt, *Deutsche Geschichte*, pp. 55–81 and p. 233.

53. NA Prague RAM Krt. 220, 2013, 1; "Titulatur und Wapen [*sic*] Seiner Oesterreichisch-Kaiserlichen und Königlichen Apostolischen Majestät vom 6. Aug. 1806" [Title and coat of arms of his Austrian-imperial and royal apostolic majesty of August 6, 1806], Vienna 1806. [The title translates as: Francis I, by the Grace of God Emperor of Austria; King of Jerusalem, Hungary, Bohemia, Dalmatia, Croatia, Slavonia, Galicia and Lodomeria; Archduke of Austria; Duke of Lorraine, Salzburg, Würzburg and Franconia, Steyer, Corinthia and Krain; Grand Duke of Cracow; Grand Prince of Transsylvania; Margrave of Moravia; Duke of Sandomir, Massovien, Lublin, Upper and Lower Silesia, Auschwitz and Zator, Teschen and Friaul; Prince of Berchtesgaden and Mergentheim; Princely Count of Habsburg, Kyburg, Görz and Gradiska; Margrave of Upper and Lower Lausitz and in Istria; Lord of the lands of Volhynia, Podlochia and Brzesz, Triest, Freudenthal and Eulenberg, and the Windic March.]

54. *Translator's note:* The abbreviation "k. k." stands for *kaiserlich-königlich* ("imperial and royal").

55. Imperial Resolution of July 6, 1814, sent to Field Marshal Lieutenant Bellegarde, HHStA Vienna StK Vorträge Krt. 195, Fol. 50.

56. Stauber, *Wiener Kongress*, p. 161.

57. Imperial resolution (no date), sent to Metternich, HHStA Vienna StK Vorträge Krt. 195, Fol. 56.

58. Stauber, *Wiener Kongress*, p. 152.

59. On the policies regarding Italy in 1814–1815 in general, see Stauber, *Wiener Kongress*, pp. 151–60; the memorandum is reproduced in Müller, *Quellen*, pp. 496–98.

60. "Wielands Andenken in der Loge Amalia, gefeiert den 18. Februar 1813" [Celebration in memoriam Wieland at the Amalia Lodge on February 18, 1813], in *Goethes poetische Werke*, Part 2, vol. 8, 1: *Autobiographische Schriften*, ed. Liselotte Lohrer (Stuttgart, 1952), p. 1449.

61. MPM 1, p. 190; NP 1, p. 155. The French version of the original manuscript has "Vous oubliez, Sire, que vous parlez à un Allemand!" NA Prague A. C. 8, Krt. 1, 1.

62. Lang, *Memoiren,* 1, p. 212.

63. Jürgen Overhoff, "Ein Kaiser für Amerika. Nach Deutschland der Verfassung wegen: Wie der spätere US-Präsident Thomas Jefferson 1788 das Alte Reich erlebte" [An emperor for America—Traveling to Germany because of its Constitution: How the later American president Thomas Jefferson experienced the old empire], in *Die Zeit,* October 31, 2012, p. 20.

64. Montesquieu, *The Spirit of Laws,* Book IX, Chap. II: "That A confederate Government ought to be composed of States of the same Nature, especially of the republican Kind," p. 167.

65. Ibid., Book XII, Chap. IV: "The Same Subject Continued" [of Chap. III: "In What Liberty Consists"], p. 197.

66. See Montesquieu, *Meine Reisen,* pp. 19–35. *Translator's note:* the reference is to the part of the preface by the German editor. See Montesquieu, *Les Voyages des Montesquieu,* pp. 1–15 ("Voyage en Autriche"), and pp. 127–216 ("Voyage en Allemagne").

67. The following account of the confederation's prehistory is mainly based on Treichel's edition of sources, *Die Entstehung des Deutschen Bundes.*

68. See Treichel, *Die Entstehung des Deutschen Bundes,* 1–1, pp. xxxv–xliv.

69. Metternich to Hardenberg, October 5, 1812, Oncken, *Österreich und Preußen,* 1, p. 378.

70. Metternich to Schwarzenberg, March 28, 1813, Oncken, *Österreich und Preußen,* 1, pp. 439–45; here: p. 442.

71. Metternich's instructions for Stadion, May 7, 1813, Oncken, *Österreich und Preußen,* 2, pp. 640–44.

72. Treichel, *Die Entstehung des Deutschen Bundes,* 1–1, p. cxxx.

73. Ibid., p. xvii.

74. *Translator's note:* "Rational institutional state" is a translation of *Anstaltsstaat,* Max Weber's term for the modern nation state that exercises power through bureaucratized institutions.

75. *Translator's note:* The full article runs: "The sovereign princes and free cities of Germany, including Their Majesties the Emperor of Austria and the Kings of Prussia, Denmark, and the Netherlands; to wit, The Emperor of Austria and the King of Prussia, both acting on behalf of all their possessions formerly belonging to the German Empire, the King of Denmark on behalf of Holstein, the King of the Netherlands on behalf of the Grand Duchy of Luxemburg, unite in a perpetual union, which shall be called the German Confederation." German Federal Act, June 8, 1815, German History in Documents and Images website, http://ghdi.ghi-dc.org/sub_document.cfm?document_id=233.

76. *General Treaty,* art. 1, p. 4.

77. NA Prague A. C. 8, Krt. 1, 9.

78. Note from Schwarzenberg to Heinrich von Gagern, December 28, 1848, Huber, *Dokumente,* 1, p. 362.

79. All quotations from MPM 1, pp. 261–62; NP 1, p. 216.

80. On the idea of the Holy Alliance as a precursor of the League of Nations of 1920 and of the foundation of the UNO in 1945, see Koselleck in Bergeron, *Das Zeitalter,* pp. 218–19.

81. See Šedivý, *Eastern Question,* pp. 807–10.

82. See Fournier, "Julie von Krüdener"; Ter Meulen, *Gedanke der Internationalen Organisation,* pp. 157–68.

83. See for instance the most recent interpretation along these lines in Menger, *Die Heilige Allianz.*

84. See Hundt, *Die Mindermächtigen,* p. 315.

85. See Treichel, *Quellen zur Geschichte des Deutschen Bundes,* I, 1–2.

86. Königlich-Baierisches Regierungsblatt, March 28, 1807, pp. 466–67; see Kohler, *Die staatsrechtlichen Verhältnisse,* pp. 103–4.

87. Franz Georg, "Note verbale an den Minister der auswärtigen Angelegenheiten Fürsten von Metternich," Vienna, November 9, 1815, NA Prague, RAM 218, 2011–2.

88. Metternich to his father Franz Georg, June 8 [actually 9], 1815, one o'clock, NA Prague A. C. 12, Krt. 1, 5.

89. Franz Georg to Metternich, September 4 and 20, 1815, NA Prague A. C. 12, Krt. 1, 5.

90. Memorandum by Franz Georg, March 3, 1816, to the k.k. Staatsministerium, NA Prague RAM Krt. 218, 2011–2.

91. Morgenblatt für gebildete Stände, vol. 8 (1814), p. 828; see also Eduard Hanslick, *Geschichte des Concertwesens in Wien,* 1 (Vienna, 1869), p. 176.

92. MPM 1, p. 253, footnote; NP 1, p. 209, footnote.

93. See the timetable of the congress in Stauber, *Wiener Kongress,* pp. 255–60.

94. Imperial resolution of August 6, 1814, with map and presentation by von Trauttmansdorff, HHStA Wien StK Vorträge Krt. 195, Fols. 18–27.

95. The following account is based on *Feyerlichkeiten bei der Rückkehr* (see under "Printed Sources" in the Bibliography).

96. *Translator's note:* On the anticipatory fund, see Chapter 6.

97. *Feyerlichkeiten bei der Rückkehr,* p. 19. See Rauscher, "Staatsbankrott," p. 266.

98. See Mattl-Wurm, "Politisierende Frauen."

99. See Vick, *The Congress of Vienna,* which points out many new connections.

100. See the first study of this theme by McGuigan, *Metternich;* also King, *Vienna 1814;* Zamoyski, Keen, and Stölting, *1815;* recently the topic has been treated in the form of a novel: Ebert, *1815: Blutfrieden.*

101. Letter by Metternich sent from Paris, June 3, 1815, NA Prag A. C. 8, Krt. 7, 41 (original).

102. See the comments collected in Ouvrard, *Congrès de Vienne,* pp. 193–97.

103. See Albert Firmin-Didot, ed., *Souvenirs de Jean-Étienne Despréaux* (Issoudun, 1894).

104. Despréaux to Metternich, June 19, 1814, NA Prague A. C. 8, Krt. 7, 41; the program can be found in MPM 1, pp. 424–26; NP 1, pp. 266–68.

105. Despréaux to Metternich, June 18, 1814, NA Prague A. C. 8, Krt. 7, 41.

106. See Rauscher, "Staatsbankrott," p. 266.

107. See the detailed description of the ceremony in Chapter 5.

108. See Vick, "Der Kongress tanzt und arbeitet trotzdem," p. 281.

109. Eynard, *Der tanzende Kongress,* p. 52.

110. Talleyrand, *Correspondance,* p. 66; see Ouvrard, *Congrès de Vienne,* p. 197.

111. Imperial resolution, July 1, 1816, HHStA Wien StK Kleinere Betreffe, Johannisberg, Krt. 8.

112. *General Treaty, Signed in Congress at Vienna, June 9, 1815,* art. 51, p. 20.

113. See Struck, *Johannisberg,* pp. 295–308.

114. Hardenberg to Metternich, October 7, 1815, HHStA Wien StK Kleinere Betreffe, Johannisberg, Krt. 8.

115. I follow Struck, *Johannisberg,* pp. 311–12.

116. From 1842 onward, Metternich was allowed to pay this tenth in money, based on the total value of the annual wine yield, rather than in kind. This was granted, however, with the caveat that the permission could be revoked at any time. Each year, the payment in lieu required a new decree by the treasury—such as, for example, the one for the 1851 harvest, passed on January 27, 1852. See the letter sent from Frankfurt by Menßhengen to the office at the winery Johannisberg, February 21, 1852, HHStA Wien StK Kleinere Betreffe, Johannisberg, Krt. 10.

117. After Struck, *Johannisberg,* p. 312. Struck quotes from the presentation of May 11, 1816, and an 8-page submission, dated May 22, 1816.

118. Staab, Seeliger, and Schleicher, *Schloss Johannisberg,* 82; the French original of the letter in NA Prague A. C. 12, Krt. 2, 10.

119. Metternich to his daughter Leontine, August 22, 1857, NA Prague A. C. 14, Krt. 10, 193; also in NP 8, p. 276.

120. The second volume (1838–1857) and the commenced third volume are in the library at Königswart.

121. Metternich to Dorothea von Lieven, December 2, 1818, in Mika, *Metternichs Briefe,* p. 65. *Translator's note:* See Jean Paul Richter, "Impromtü's welche ich künftig," pp. 66–85; here: p. 80: "Die Erinnerung ist das einzige Paradies aus dem wir nicht getrieben werden können. Sogar die ersten Eltern waren nicht daraus zu bringen." [Remembrance is the only paradise from which we cannot be expelled. Not even the first parents could be removed from it.]

122. The portfolio is at Schloss Königswart.

123. Heine, *Die Bäder von Lukka* (Erste Fassung) [The baths of Lucca (first version)], in Heine, *Historisch-kritische Gesamtausgabe,* 7–1, p. 419.

124. Heine, *Lutetia,* p. 31.

125. *Poems of Heine,* trans. Edgar Alfred Bowring (London: George Bell and Sons, 1891), p. 179.

126. Ramberg's petition, dated April 9, 1822, and addressed to Metternich: NA Prague A. C. 7, Krt. 3, 150-A; the watercolor: A. C. 9, Krt. 2, 102. Ramberg's son had served as an officer in

the campaigns of 1813–1814 and was therefore well known. He had held positions at the headquarters and in 1815 even had been the link officer to Wellington's headquarters.

127. The following interpretation is indebted to explanations kindly provided by my Munich colleague from art history, Frank Büttner, who also helped me interpret the copper engraving of Franz Georg von Metternich in Belgium (1792). See also Frank Büttner, *Giovanni Battista Tiepolo: Die Fresken in der Residenz zu Würzburg* (Würzburg, 1980); on Ramberg: Alheidis von Rohr, "Ramberg, Johann Heinrich," in *Neue Deutsche Biographie* 21 (2003), pp. 128–29.

128. Eleonore to Metternich, January 13, 1822, NA Prague A. C. 14, Krt. 1, 15; see Corti, *Metternich,* 2, p. 192.

129. Most recently by Christian Staas in "Metternichs große Stunde," *Die Zeit,* no. 23, June 3, 2015, p. 18.

9. Connoisseur of Women and Head of the Entail

1. Srbik, *Metternich,* 1, p. 185.

2. Gentz to Wessenberg, April 9, 1815, Fournier, *Gentz und Wessenberg,* p. 86; see Erbe, *Dorothea Herzogin von Sagan,* pp. 27–29.

3. Corti, *Metternich,* is an indispensable source because of the wealth of new and reliably reproduced material from letters in the family archive in Prague. The typical clichés of his times that he employs, however, are less helpful.

4. See Mattl-Wurm, "Politisierende Frauen."

5. For instance, Schremmer, *Kavalier & Kanzler,* p. 277.

6. See Jørgensen, *Aufklärung, Sturm und Drang,* p. 157–58.

7. http://sammlungenonline.albertina.at/?query=record/objectnumber=%5b1362%5d&showtype=record#4f8eafe2-f71e-4135-823d-bd056a3cad6d.

8. I follow J. T. Herbert Baily, *Francesco Bartolozzi: A Biographical Essay* (London, 1907), p. x.

9. Metternich to Dorothea von Lieven, February 10, 1822, MPM 3, p. 570 (transl. modified); NP 3, p. 503.

10. Ullrichová, *Metternich,* p. 21, p. 35, p. 36.

11. Ullrichová, *Metternich,* pp. 38–38.

12. Metternich, letter of December 31, 1818, in Mika, *Metternichs Briefe,* p. 104.

13. As does Zamoyski, *Rites of Peace,* p. 79.

14. Vellusig, *Schriftliche Gespräche,* p. 61.

15. Reinlein, *Der Brief als Medium der Empfindsamkeit,* p. 53.

16. Metternich to Dorothea von Lieven, December 14, 1818, Mika, *Metternichs Briefe,* p. 74.

17. See Jørgensen, *Aufklärung, Sturm und Drang,* pp. 172–73.

18. Carl Friedrich Pockels, "Über die Verschiedenheit und Mischung der Charaktere," in Sauder, *Theorie der Empfindsamkeit,* p. 82.

19. Achim Krümmel, "Sophie von La Roche," Rheinische Geschicte website, http://www .rheinische-geschichte.lvr.de/persoenlichkeiten/L/Seiten/SophievonlaRoche.aspx; see Nenon, "Salongeselligkeit."

20. Daniel Jenisch, "Geist und Charakter des 18. Jahrhunderts," in Sauder, *Theorie der Empfindsamkeit,* pp. 135–36.

21. Metternich to Dorothea von Lieven, January 3, 1819, Mika, *Metternichs Briefe,* pp. 107–8.

22. Metternich to Dorothea von Lieven, December 1, 1818, Mika, *Metternichs Briefe,* p. 62.

23. Metternich to Dorothea von Lieven, December 20, 1818, Mika, *Metternichs Briefe,* p. 79.

24. Metternich to Dorothea von Lieven, February 2, 1819, Mika, *Metternichs Briefe,* p. 163.

25. Metternich to Dorothea von Lieven, February 3, 1819, Mika, *Metternichs Briefe,* p. 168.

26. See Nenon, "Salongeselligkeit," p. 285.

27. Metternich to Dorothea von Lieven, December 1, 1818, Mika, *Metternichs Briefe,* p. 58.

28. Metternich to Dorothea von Lieven, December 20, 1818, Mika, *Metternichs Briefe,* p. 79.

29. Metternich to Dorothea von Lieven, December 1, 1818, Mika, *Metternichs Briefe,* p. 64.

30. Nesselrode to his father, April 25, 1806, Nesselrode, *Lettres et papiers,* 3, p. 132.

31. Metternich to Wilhelmine von Sagan, January 15, 1814, Ullrichová, *Metternich,* p. 174.

32. Metternich to Dorothea von Lieven, December 1, 1818, Mika, *Metternichs Briefe,* p. 59.

33. Bouillé, *Souvenirs et Fragments,* pp. 44–46.

34. Metternich to Dorothea von Lieven, December 1, 1818, Mika, *Metternichs Briefe,* pp. 62–63.

35. Edouard-Marie Oettinger, *Moniteur des dates,* vol. 6 (Dresden, 1868), p. 32.

36. Varnhagen, *Denkwürdigkeiten,* 3, pp. 234–35.

37. Mika's edition of the letters follows the French edition by Jean Hanoteau, and thus ends on April 30, 1819. From that point onward, only partial excerpts from the letters at the Prague archive are reproduced in MPM / NP and in Corti. The present author is planning a complete edition.

38. Stella K. Hershan, *The Naked Angel* (London: Crowood Press, 1973). See also Corti, *Metternich,* 1, pp. 69–71; Corti confuses the father, Adam Kazimierz, with the son, Adam Jerzy Czartoryski.

39. Thürheim, *Mein Leben,* 2, pp. 100–101.

40. The dates given for the illegitimate Clementine's life diverge strongly, beginning with the birth, sometimes incorrectly given as 1802, see Corti, *Metternich,* 1, pp. 68–72; Thürheim, *Mein Leben,* 2, p. 100. The family archive does not contain any information. The most information about her can now be found in Peter Wulf, "Salzau—Paris—Salzau.

Die Hochzeit des Grafen Otto Blome mit der Prinzessin Clementine Bagration," *Jahrbuch für Regionalgeschichte* 25 (2007): pp. 71–85; on Metternich's paternity, see Metternich to Princess Bagration, April 18, 1825, see Corti, *Metternich*, 2, pp. 268–69; original in NA Prague A. C. 6, C12.

41. NP 8, p. 127.

42. Metternich in Vienna to his son Richard, June 5, 1857, NA Prague A. C. 12, Krt. 4, 32. Also in Corti, *Metternich*, 2, p. 460. The year of Princess Bagration's death is incorrectly given as 1856 in Mattl-Wurm, "Politisierende Frauen," p. 345.

43. The description of Saint Cloud follows Botzenhart, *Botschafterzeit*, p. 77.

44. P.[aul]-A.[rthur] Chéramy, ed., *Mémoires inédits de Mademoiselle George* (Paris, 1908), p. 160.

45. Vidal, *Caroline Bonaparte*, p. 65.

46. Vidal, *Caroline Bonaparte*, p. 75.

47. Bertier de Sauvigny, *Metternich et son temps*, p. 91.

48. MPM 1, p. 310 (transl. modified); NP 1, p. 311.

49. See Bertier de Sauvigny, *Metternich et son temps*, pp. 91–92.

50. Bertier de Sauvigny, *Metternich et son temps*, p. 92.

51. See Corti, *Metternich*, 1, pp. 215–19.

52. Metternich to Eleonore in Paris, December 14, 1810, NA Prague, A. C. 12, Krt. 1, 6; shortened version in Corti, *Metternich*, pp. 221–22; not included in MPM / NP.

53. Abrantès, *Mémoires*, vol. 23, p. 29.

54. Ibid., p. 27.

55. Ibid., p. 28.

56. See Missoffe, *Metternich*, pp. 125–26.

57. The whole affair is documented in NA Prague A. C. 2, Krt. 1, 002-A-Apponyi.

58. See the excellent essay by Erbe, "Wilhelmine von Sagan."

59. See Erbe, "Wilhelmine von Sagan," pp. 229–30.

60. The expression can be found in a letter to Alfred von Windisch-Graetz; see Erbe, "Wilhelmine von Sagan," p. 232.

61. Metternich to Wilhelmine, August 19, 1813, Ullrichová, *Metternich*, p. 41.

62. Wilhelmine to Metternich, August 27, 1813, Ullrichová, *Metternich*, p. 51.

63. "Good-bye, my friend, my dear Clemens, Good-bye—I do not know why I wrote to you in German, I have not been aware of it." Wilhelmine to Metternich, August 31, 1813, Ullrichová, *Metternich*, pp. 53–54.

64. Wilhelmine to Metternich, September 12, 1813, Ullrichová, *Metternich*, p. 60.

65. NA Prague RAM Krt. 404, 2812. The lock is still in an envelope among the correspondence.

66. Metternich to Wilhelmine, September 17, 1813, Ullrichová, *Metternich*, p. 64.

67. Metternich to Wilhelmine, November 7, 1813, Ullrichová, *Metternich*, p. 101.

68. Wilhelmine to Metternich, November 2, 1813, Ullrichová, *Metternich*, p. 97.

69. Metternich to Wilhelmine, January 13, 1814, Ullrichová, *Metternich*, pp. 165–66.

70. Wilhelmine to Metternich, January 20, 1814, Ullrichová, *Metternich,* p. 186.

71. Wilhelmine to Metternich, January 26, 1814, Ullrichová, *Metternich,* p. 194.

72. Wilhelmine to Metternich, March 1, 1814, Ullrichová, *Metternich,* pp. 223–24.

73. Private note, Gentz to Metternich, April 24, 1814, NA Prague A. C. 5, Krt. 1, 3.

74. Private note, Gentz to Metternich, April 5, 1814, NA Prague A. C. 5, Krt. 1, 3.

75. Private note, Gentz to Metternich, April 11, 1814, NA Prague A. C. 5, Krt. 1, 3.

76. Varnhagen, *Denkwürdigkeiten,* 3, pp. 235–36.

77. Metternich to Wilhelmine von Sagan, July 1814, Ullrichová, *Metternich,* p. 258.

78. See McGuigan, *Metternich,* pp. 311–13.

79. See ibid., pp. 189–90.

80. See ibid., pp. 368–72; here: p. 369.

81. Metternich in March 1815, in Ullrichová, *Metternich,* pp. 278–79.

82. Metternich to Dorothea von Lieven, January 5, 1819, Mika, *Metternichs Briefe,* pp. 114–15.

83. On her life in general, see Cromwell, *Dorothea Lieven.*

84. Temperley, *The Unpublished Diary and Political Sketches of Princess Lieven,* p. 40. *Translator's note:* "fashionable" is in English in the original.

85. Mika, *Metternichs Briefe,* p. 96.

86. Cromwell, *Dorothea Lieven,* p. 57; see the enthusiastic letter that Nesselrode sent Dorothea von Lieven on February 1, 1831, from Saint Petersburg, in Nesselrode, *Lettres et papiers,* vol. 7, pp. 171–76.

87. See the more detailed description in Cromwell, *Dorothea Lieven,* pp. 58–59.

88. Hanoteau, *Lettres du Prince de Metternich,* pp. 1–2. The translation into German in Mika, *Metternichs Briefe,* pp. 31–32, does not preserve the typical language of sensibility.

89. See Quennell, *The Private Letters of Princess Lieven to Prince Metternich.*

90. *Translator's note:* The Cato Street Conspiracy was a thwarted plot to assassinate British Cabinet ministers and the prime minister in 1820. The plotters met in Cato Street, London.

91. From the first, undated, letter of the collection in Hanoteau, *Lettres du Prince de Metternich,* p. 2.

92. Metternich to Dorothea von Lieven, January 3, 1819, Mika, *Metternichs Briefe,* p. 108.

93. Metternich to Dorothea von Lieven, January 17, 1819, Mika, *Metternichs Briefe,* pp. 136–37.

94. [Emph. W. S.].

95. Metternich to Dorothea von Lieven, January 30, 1819, Mika, *Metternichs Briefe,* pp. 155–56.

96. Metternich to Dorothea von Lieven, February 21, 1819, Mika, *Metternichs Briefe,* pp. 192–93.

97. Metternich to Wilhelmine von Sagan, November 29, 1813, Ullrichová, *Metternich,* pp. 129–31.

98. Metternich to Dorothea von Lieven, May 9, 1821, NA Prague A. C. 6, C19.7; excerpts in Corti, *Metternich,* 2, p. 173; omitted in MPM and NP.

99. See Corti, *Metternich*, 1, p. 323. *Translator's note:* The ironic use of *Feine* invokes an excessive subtlety, refinement, or sophistication that turns into weakness.

100. Metternich to Dorothea von Lieven, May 6, 1819, NA Prague A. C. 6, C19.4.

101. *Translator's note:* "Ich bin bei dir; du seist auch noch so ferne, / Du bist mir nah! / Die Sonne sinkt, bald leuchten mir die Sterne. / Oh, wärst du da!" From "Nähe des Geliebten." The title of this love poem is also used in the title for the section on Dorothea von Lieven, where, however, the male form has been changed into the female form ("Nähe der Geliebten").

102. I follow Reinlein, *Der Brief als Medium der Empfindsamkeit*, pp. 69–77; on Metternich's statements regarding his urge to write letters, see his letter to Dorothea von Lieven, January 21, 1819, Mika, *Metternichs Briefe*, p. 194.

103. Metternich to Dorothea von Lieven, February 2 and March 22, 1819, Mika, *Metternichs Briefe*, p. 161 and p. 231.

104. Heinrich von Kleist, "On the Gradual Formulation of Thoughts While Speaking," p. 255 (transl. modified).

105. *Translator's note:* Kleist's essay argues that it is not what the other person says that is important, but merely that person's presence as a neutral point for bouncing off one's own remarks. The title talks of "speaking," not of "having conversations."

106. Metternich to Dorothea von Lieven, January 3, 1819, Mika, *Metternichs Briefe*, p. 107.

107. Dorothea von Lieven to Metternich, May 16, 1826, Quennell, *The Private Letters of Princess Lieven*, p. 369 (transl. amended).

108. Ibid., p. 376 (transl. amended).

109. Metternich to Dorothea von Lieven, January 3, 1819, Mika, *Metternichs Briefe*, p. 107.

110. Pauline Metternich, *Erinnerungen*, p. 36; *The Days That Are No More*, p. 65.

111. Metternich to Dorothea von Lieven, November 15, 1818, Mika, *Metternichs Briefe*, p. 32.

112. Metternich to Dorothea von Lieven, December 14, 1818, Mika, *Metternichs Briefe*, pp. 73–74.

113. Metternich to Dorothea von Lieven, December 24, 1818, Mika, *Metternichs Briefe*, pp. 89–90.

114. Metternich to Dorothea von Lieven, November 15 and December 24, 1818, Mika, *Metternichs Briefe*, p. 32 and p. 90.

115. Metternich to Dorothea von Lieven, January 3, 1819, Mika, *Metternichs Briefe*, p. 109.

116. Metternich to Dorothea von Lieven, January 3, 1819, Mika, *Metternichs Briefe*, 107; Hanoteau, *Lettres du Prince de Metternich*, p. 102.

117. Metternich to Dorothea von Lieven, April 22, 1820, NA Prague A. C. 6, C19.5; excerpts (including the quotation) in MPM 3, p. 370 / NP 3, p. 326.

118. MPM 3, p. 364, p. 365 (transl. amended) and p. 371; NP 3, p. 320, p. 321 and p. 327; original letter from Metternich to Dorothea von Lieven, NA Prague A. C. 6, C19.5.

119. Metternich to Dorothea von Lieven, March 22, 1820, NA Prague A. C. 6, C19.5. Excerpts (including the quotation) in MPM 3, p. 364; NP 3, p. 321.

120. MPM 3, pp. 370–71 (transl. amended); NP 3, p. 326.

121. Metternich to Dorothea von Lieven, March 2, 1820, NA Prague A. C. 6, C19.5. Excerpt (including the quotation) in MPM 3, p. 370 (transl. amended); NP 3, p. 326.

122. Metternich to Dorothea von Lieven, May 5, 1820, NA Prague A. C. 6, C19.5. Excerpt (including the quotation) in MPM 3, p. 371; NP 3, p. 327.

123. Metternich to Dorothea von Lieven, May 16, 1820, NA Prague A. C. 6, C19.5. Excerpt (including the quotation) in MPM 3, p. 373; NP 3, p. 329. Metternich distinguished between his professional and his private and personal self *(moi même)*.

124. Metternich to Dorothea von Lieven, May 12, 1820, NA Prague A. C. 6, C19.5. Excerpt (including the quoted passage) in MPM 3, pp. 372–73 (transl. amended); NP 3, p. 328.

125. Metternich to Dorothea von Lieven, July 17, 1820, NA Prague A. C. 6, C19.6. Excerpt (including the quotation) in MPM 3, p. 385 (transl. amended); NP 3, pp. 339–40.

126. Metternich to Dorothea von Lieven, July 25, 1820, NA Prague A. C. 6, C19.6. Excerpt (including the quotation) in MPM 3, p. 387 (transl. amended); NP 3, p. 341.

127. Metternich to Dorothea von Lieven, January 28, 1819, in Mika, *Metternichs Briefe,* p. 150.

128. MPM 3, pp. 385–86; NP 3, p. 340.

129. Metternich writing from Weinzierl on July 17, and from Vienna on July 25, 1820. Excerpts (including the quotations) in MPM 3, p. 387; NP 3, pp. 340–41.

130. Metternich to Dorothea von Lieven, July 28, 1820, NA Prague A. C. 6, C19.6. Excerpt (including the quotation) in MPM 3, p. 389; NP 3, p. 343.

131. Metternich to Dorothea von Lieven, July 29, 1820, NA Prague A. C. 6, C19.6. Excerpt (including the quotation) in ibid.

132. Metternich to Dorothea von Lieven, July 28, 1820, NA Prague A. C. 6, C19.6. Excerpt (including the quotation) in MPM 3, pp. 388–89 (transl. amended); NP 3, p. 342.

133. Metternich to Dorothea von Lieven, May 17, 1823, NA Prague A. C. 6, C19.10. Excerpts (including the quotation) in MPM 4, p. 10; NP 4, p. 10.

134. Metternich to Dorothea von Lieven, May 27, 1823, NA Prague A. C. 6, C19.10. Excerpt (including the quotation) in MPM 4, p. 11; NP 4, p. 11; see Gen 2: 18: "It is not good that the man should be alone."

135. Metternich described the details of the situation to Dorothea von Lieven; NA Prague A. C. 6, C19.12; the following account is based on these letters. For reasons that are not entirely clear, the published posthumous papers keep the addressee of the letters secret and speak only of "Extracts from Metternich's private letters"; see MPM 4, pp. 154–65; NP 4, 147–157.

136. Metternich to Dorothea von Lieven, February 14, 1815, NA Prague A. C. 6, C 19.12; in MPM 4, p. 156 (transl. modified); NP 4, p. 149.

137. Eleonore to Metternich, January 28, 1825, NA Prague A. C. 14, Krt. 2, 18; in a liberal translation in Corti, *Metternich,* 2, pp. 257–58.

138. Metternich to Dorothea von Lieven, March 29, 1825, NA Prague A. C. 6, C 19.12, in MPM 4, p. 157; NP 4, pp. 149–50.

139. According to the marriage certificate, NA Prag RAM Krt. 8, 1795; Antonia von Leykam's birth certificate, dated August 10, 1806, Krt. 1, 1728.

140. See Corti, *Metternich,* 2, p. 289.

141. Decree of the Lord Chamberlain, December 21, 1827, NA Prague RAM Krt. 28.

142. Metternich to Victor, January 21, 1829, MPM 4, p. 562; NP 4, p. 532.

143. On Dorothea von Lieven's judgments, see Corti, *Metternich,* 2, pp. 292–93.

144. Metternich to Countess Molly Zichy-Ferraris, October 20, 1827, NA Prague A. C. 12, Krt. 4, 26; excerpts (including the quotations) in MPM 4, pp. 352–53; NP 4, p. 337.

145. Metternich to Countess Wrbna, October 16, 1827; original NA Prague A. C. 13, Krt. 5, 89b; MPM 4, p. 353.

146. Metternich to Molly Zichy-Ferraris, October 25, 1827, A. C. 12, Krt. 4, 26; MPM 4, pp. 353–54; NP 4, p. 338–39; the addressee is not given.

147. Metternich to Victor, January 17, 1829, NA Prague A. C. 12, Krt. 3, 18; excerpt (including the quotations) in MPM 4, pp. 351–52; NP 4, p. 530.

148. Metternich to Countess Molly Zichy, July 3, 1829; MPM 4, p. 581; NP 4, p. 551.

149. Metternich to Wilhelmine von Sagan, February 28, 1819, Mika, *Metternichs Briefe,* p. 204.

150. Birth certificate NA Prague RAM Krt. 1, 1729–1730.

151. Metternich to Victor, January 17, 1829, NA Prague A. C. 12, Krt. 3, 18; excerpts (including the quotation) in MPM 4, p. 560; NP 4, p. 530.

152. Metternich to Melanie Zichy-Ferraris, December 11, 1829, NA Prague A. C. 12, Krt.4, 27; MPM 4, p. 588; NP 4, 557–58.

153. Metternich to Melanie Zichy-Ferraris, October 2, 1830, NA Prague A. C. 12, Krt. 3, 19.

154. Metternich to Melanie Zichy-Ferraris, October 31, 1830, NA Prague A. C. 12, Krt. 3, 19.

155. Prokesch von Osten, *Tagebücher,* p. 84.

156. Diary entry for February 17, 1831, in MPM 5, p. 68; NP 5, pp. 91–92.

157. Prokesch von Osten, *Tagebücher,* p. 118.

158. MPM 5, p. 383; NP 5, p. 539.

159. MPM 5, p. 391, note; NP 5, p. 548, note. *Translator's note:* In the English edition of Metternich's papers, the sentence to which the quoted phrase belongs is omitted. The passage, with the omitted part in square brackets, runs: "If women exercise no influence on affairs—and that principle certainly holds good with us—it is attaching too much importance to a woman to assert that her enmity can have any weight as opposed to a Government. [A woman, just like a man, may have opinions, and those who have none place themselves below their sex.] The words enmity and Government seem to me, therefore, to stand too near together."

160. See the excellent reproduction in Kugler, *Staatskanzler Metternich und seine Gäste.*

161. "Leichenbefund des Hochgeborenen durchlauchtigsten Fürsten Clemens von Metternich" [Result of the autopsy of His Serene Highness Prince Clemens von Metternich], Vienna, July 5, 1833, NA Prague RAM Krt. 55, 3063.

162. Metternich to Victor, February 4, 1829, NA Prague A. C. 12, Krt. 3, 18; excerpt (including the quotation) in MPM 4, p. 566; NP 4, p. 536.

163. NA Prague RAM Krt. 55, 3049 (St. Margaretha), 3055 (St. Ursula).

164. Metternich to Dorothea von Lieven, June 29, 1820, NA Prague A. C. 6, C19.6; excerpt (including the quotation) in MPM 3, p. 381; NP 3, p. 336.

165. An image of the relic can be found in *Die Reliquien der heiligen Valentina in der fürstlich Metternichischen Gruftkirche zu Plaß* (Prague, 1829).

166. The events described here are documented in NA Prague RAM Krt. 132, 5022–5027.

167. Metternich to Dorothea von Lieven, June 29, 1820, NA Prague A. C. 6, C19.6; excerpt (including the quotation) in MPM 3, p. 381 (transl. amended); NP 3, p. 336.

10. The Construction of a New Beginning

1. Sellin, *Die geraubte Revolution*, p. 278.

2. See Haas, *Metternich, Reorganization and Nationality*.

3. Presentation by Metternich, December 29, 1815, HHStA Vienna StK Vorträge Krt. 200, Fols. 83–86.

4. Presentation by Metternich, January 21, 1816, HHStA Vienna StK Vorträge Krt. 201, Fols. 50–62.

5. Presentation by Metternich, October 12, 1819, HHStA Vienna StK Vorträge Krt. 219, Fols. 100–111; this presentation also contains a sketch for the reorganization of the academy of the arts and for the foundation of an academy of science.

6. Koselleck, *Zeitalter*, p. 227.

7. Metternich to Gentz, May 7, 1819, in Gentz, *Briefe*, vol. 3.1, p. 429; MPM 3, pp. 279–80; NP 3, p. 244; MPM and NP erroneously give "Pisan." Correct is "Pratoian"; see the original in NA Prague, RAM A. C. 08, Krt. 9, 46.

8. Presentation by Metternich, November 3, 1817, HHStA Vienna StK Vorträge Krt. 210, Fols. 468–470.

9. Presentation by Metternich, January 11, 1819, HHStA Vienna StK Vorträge Krt. 217, Fols. 85–87.

10. Presentation by Metternich, October 12, 1819, HHStA Vienna StK Vorträge Krt. 219, Fols. 119–122.

11. Presentation by Metternich, January 11, 1819, HHStA Vienna StK Vorträge Krt. 217, Fols. 85–87.

12. Presentation by Metternich, May 5, 1819, HHStA Vienna StK Vorträge Krt. 218, Fols. 50–58.

13. *Translator's note: Perlustrierung* is an old expression in Austrian German, in this context referring to the opening, copying, and resealing of correspondence. The copies were called *Interzepte*.

14. For example, NP 7, p. 910.

15. See Haas, *Metternich, Reorganization and Nationality*, p. 207; on the "Lega Italica," see pp. 65–66 and p. 207.

16. "Tableau de l'état moral de l'Italie depuis le rétablissement du Système politique actuel jusqu'au 31 Mai 1817" [Summary of the moral state of Italy from the reestablishment of

the present political system until May 31, 1817], HHStA Vienna StK Vorträge Krt. 210, Fols. 105–279.

17. "Bemerkungen über den inneren Stand von Italien," HHStA Vienna StK Vorträge Krt. 210, Fols. 41–74; excerpts in NP 3, pp. 75–91; "The Internal Condition of Italy," MPM 3, pp. 88–107.

18. All quotations MPM 3, p. 106; NP 3, p. 92.

19. MPM 3, p. 103; NP 3, p. 89. On the overall character of the policies as preserving continuity, see Mazohl-Wallnig, *Königreich Lombardo-Venetien.*

20. MPM 3, p. 103; NP 3, pp. 89–90.

21. Presentation by Metternich, November 3, 1817, HHStA Vienna StK Vorträge Krt. 210, Fols. 31–32; NP 3, pp. 90–91; MPM 3, p. 104. The text erroneously gives "entgegenzukommen" ("to conciliate") instead of "zu schmeicheln" ("to flatter").

22. See Haas, *Metternich, Reorganization and Nationality,* p. 95.

23. See Kuster, "Italienreise Kaiser Franz I," p. 323.

24. See Rosenstrauch, *Wahlverwandt und ebenbürtig.*

25. NA Prague A. C. 12, Krt. 1, 8.

26. The following account is based on letters held at NA Prague A. C. 12, Krt. 1, 9; they are partly reproduced in MPM 3, pp. 24–57; NP 3, pp. 22–50.

27. MPM 3, p. 25; NP 3, p. 23.

28. MPM 3, p. 27; NP 3, p. 25.

29. MPM 3, p. 28; NP 3, pp. 25–26.

30. MPM 3, p. 30; NP 3, p. 27.

31. Metternich to Dorothea von Lieven, April 5, 1819, in Mika, *Metternichs Briefe,* pp. 246–47.

32. Srbik, *Metternich,* 1, p. 254, and p. 126.

33. Metternich to Eleonore, June 28, 1817, MPM 3, p. 33; NP 3, p. 30.

34. Metternich to Dorothea von Lieven, April 7, 1819, in Mika, *Metternichs Briefe,* pp. 249–50.

35. *Translator's note:* In the sixth proposition of his *Idea for a Universal History with a Cosmopolitan Purpose,* Kant writes: "aus so krummem Holze, als woraus der Mensch gemacht ist, kann nichts ganz Gerades gezimmert werden" (Kant, *Werke,* VI, p. 41). This famous passage is most often referred to using Isaiah Berlin's rendering of the sentence: "Out of the crooked timber of humanity no straight thing was ever made" (see Isaiah Berlin, *The Crooked Timber of Humanity: Chapters in the History of Ideas* [London: Pimlico, 1959 / 2013], pp. xii–xiii).

36. See Siemann, "Kant. Aus so krummem Holz," pp. 240–44.

37. Metternich to Eleonore, August 29, 1817, NA Prague A. C. 12, Krt. 1, 9; edited version in MPM 3, p. 51; NP 3, p. 46.

38. Presentation by Metternich, March 24, 1818, HHStA Wien StK Vorträge Krt. 213, Fols. 156–164.

39. Nicosia, *Regioni e testimonianze d'Italia.*

40. On the process described here, see Knöbl, *Kontingenz der Moderne.*

41. Presentation by Metternich, October 27, 1817, HHStA Vienna StK Vorträge Krt. 209, Fols. 72–84.

42. See "Ueber die Ungarischen Zustände" [On conditions in Hungary], in NP 7, pp. 51–63.

43. See the interpretation in Haas, *Metternich, Reorganization and Nationality,* pp. 133–35.

44. Presentation by Metternich, May 24, 1816, HHStA Vienna Vorträge Krt. 209, Fol. 170; reproduced in Haas, *Metternich, Reorganization and Nationality,* p. 175.

45. See Hobsbawm and Ranger, *Invention of Tradition;* Anderson, *Imagined Communities.*

46. *Wiener Zeitung,* no. 295, December 24, 1817, reproduced in Haas, *Metternich, Reorganization and Nationality,* pp. 180–81.

47. Haas, *Metternich, Reorganization and Nationality,* p. 134.

48. Kaiserliche Resolution [imperial resolution] of November 6, 1816, HHStA Vienna StK Vorträge Krt. 205, Fol. 20.

49. See Bibl, *Metternich,* p. 8.

50. Berlinische Nachrichten von Staats- und gelehrten Sachen, January 29, 1818. 1/3 (January–March); report on "Wien, vom 9. Januar."

51. Presentation by Metternich, January 18, 1818, HHStA Vienna StK Vorträge Krt. 212, Fols. 60–82 (including supplements).

52. The memorandum is at HHStA Vienna StK Vorträge Krt. 212, Fols. 62–74.

53. Imperial resolution, February 14, 1818, HHStA Vienna StK Vorträge Krt. 213, Fol. 14.

54. "Protokoll der am 5ten März 1818 abgehaltenen Zusammentretung zur Beratung über das Allerhöchste Handschreiben v. 14. Hornung d. J. die zum teutschen Bunde gehörenden Provinzen und Teile der Österreichischen Monarchie betreffend" [Protocol of the meeting on March 5, 1818, in response to Her Majesty's personal note of February 14 the same year, regarding the provinces and parts of the Austrian monarchy that belong to the German Confederation], HHStA Vienna StK Vorträge Krt. 213, Fols. 13–28.

11. Defensive Security Policies

1. See Schulz, *Normen und Praxis,* p. 73.

2. See MPM 1, pp. 254–55; NP 1, pp. 209–10.

3. Napoleon had set foot on the Continent between Antibes and Cannes on March 1. The news reached Paris on March 5.

4. MPM 1, p. 255; NP 1, p. 210.

5. The text can be found in Capefigue, *Le congrès de Vienne,* vol. 2, pp. 971–73.

6. See Schroeder, *Transformation,* p. 552.

7. The text can be found in Capefigue, *Le congrès de Vienne,* vol. 4, pp. 1595–1601.

8. MPM 1, p. 258; NP 1, p. 213.

9. The text can be found in Capefigue, *Le congrès de Vienne,* vol. 4, pp. 1636–38.

10. *Translator's note:* The English text can be found at "Quadruple Alliance," Wikisource, https://en.wikisource.org/wiki/Quadruple_Alliance (transl. amended).

11. The signatories were Castlereagh (born 1769), Wellington (born 1769), Metternich (born 1773), Johann von Wessenberg (born 1773), Hardenberg (born 1750), Humboldt (born 1767), Rasumowski (born 1752), Capodistrias (born 1776); mentioned in the Preamble were Emperor Franz (born 1768), the British Prince Regent, from 1820 onward George IV (born 1762), Tsar Alexander (born 1777), and Friedrich Wilhelm III (born 1770).

12. "Friedrich Carl Fuldas Analyse der wirtschaftlichen Lage der Landwirtschaft zu Beginn der 1820er Jahre (1823)," in Steitz, *Quellen,* p. 80.

13. See Mieck, "Preußen," pp. 123–27 and p. 153.

14. Hamm, *Napoleon und Bayern,* p. 142.

15. Ullmann, *Steuerstaat,* pp. 36–37.

16. See Fischer, *Sozialgeschichtliches Arbeitsbuch,* p. 202 (marks have been translated into guilders, see p. 201).

17. See Rieck, *Friedrich Koenig,* p. 71.

18. See Behringer, *Tambora und das Jahr ohne Sommer.*

19. Wittmann, *Buchmarkt und Lektüre,* pp. 154–57.

20. See ibid., p. 162.

21. *Translator's note:* The Deutscher Bund was a secret association founded in 1810, headed by Friedrich Ludwig Jahn, with the purpose of liberating Germany from the French occupation. Not to be confused with the German Confederation.

22. *Translator's note:* The Jünglingsbund was a secret association that grew out of fraternities, founded in Brunswick.

23. On these themes and the functional role of backwardness, see Wehler, *Nationalismus,* p. 64.

24. Ibid., p. 25.

25. Ibid., p. 64.

26. Osterhammel, *The Transformation of the World,* p. 631.

27. Metternich to Wrede, February 26, 1833, quoted after Bibl, *Metternich in neuer Beleuchtung,* pp. 363–66; Siemann, *Anfänge der politischen Polizei,* p. 138.

28. *Translator's note:* On the attack on the prince regent, see Marjorie Bloy, "The Attack on the Prince Regent, 28 January 1817," Web of English History website, http://www.historyhome.co.uk/c-eight/constitu/regent.htm.

29. See Bock, *Terrorismus,* pp. 34–36.

30. Text No. 7, "Nationality," NA Prague A. C. 8, Krt. 1, 8.

31. Text No. 27, (untitled), NA Prague A. C. 8, Krt. 1, 8 [emph. W. S.].

32. Handwritten material for a press article; MPM 4, p. 633 (transl. modified); NP 4, p. 597.

33. See Siemann, "Zwietracht der Nationalitäten."

34. Grillparzer, *Werke,* vol. 1, p. 500.

35. Bayly, *The Birth of the Modern World,* p. 205.

36. *Translator's note: Kulturkampf* denotes Bismarck's attempts to subject the Roman Catholic Church to state control.

37. Reinhard, *Geschichte des modernen Staates,* p. 92.

38. See Langewiesche, *Reich, Nation, Föderation,* p. 53, p. 259, and p. 261; Langewiesche, *Nation, Nationalismus, Nationalstaat,* p. 45 and p. 49.

39. Thus Schulz, *Normen und Praxis,* p. 73.

40. Mieck, "Preußen," p. 112 and p. 189.

41. Temperley, *Canning,* p. 3.

42. Schulz, *Normen und Praxis,* p. 72.

43. Castlereagh to Lord William Bentinck, May 7, 1814, Castlereagh, *Correspondence,* vol. 10, p. 18.

44. According to Sir Henry Wellesley to Castlereagh, July 24, 1820, Castlereagh, *Correspondence,* vol. 12, p. 282. *Translator's note:* The Illuminati was a secret society founded by the philosopher and scholar of canon law Adam Weishaupt in 1776 and prohibited in 1784–1785. Its aims were enlightenment and liberation, with a strong emphasis on education as the only way to achieve these goals. A rich tradition of conspiracy theories claimed that the society continued to operate after its prohibition and that it was responsible for any number of political and social events.

45. William à Court to Castlereagh, July 6, 1820, Castlereagh, *Correspondence,* vol. 12, p. 279.

46. The following is based on "Extraits d'un discours de Mr. Canning en demandant des pouvoirs extraordinaires pour empêcher ou reprimer des casseurs elements séditieux en Fevrier 1817" [Extracts from a speech by Mr. Canning asking for extraordinary powers for preventing or repressing seditious elements], NA Prague A. C. 8, Krt. 8, 44.

47. See "Report of the Secret Committee of the House of Commons on the disturbed state of the country, 19. Feb. 1817," "The Habeas Corpus Suspension Act, 1817," "The Seditious Meetings Act, 1817," all in Aspinall, *Documents,* pp. 325–31; Canning's speech in Canning, *The Speeches,* vol. 3, pp. 439–55.

48. Ibid., p. 447.

49. Ibid., p. 449.

50. Ibid., p. 450.

51. Ibid., p. 451.

52. Ibid., p. 452.

53. Ibid.

54. Ibid., p. 455.

55. See Gash, *Aristocracy and People,* p. 91.

56. On the assassination attempt, see Stahl, *Metternich und Wellington,* pp. 178–79.

57. *Österreichischer Beobachter,* no. 134, May 14, 1819, pp. 663–64 (part 1 of the indictment); see also no. 136, May 16, 1819, pp. 673–75 (part 2).

58. *Österreichischer Beobachter,* no. 141, May 21, 1819, pp. 699–701 (part 3 of the indictment).

59. Metternich, February 22, 1818, HHStA Vienna StK Vorträge Krt. 212, Fol. 42.

60. See Mieck, "Preußen," p. 158.

61. *Lemberger Zeitung*, no. 249, December 14, 1818, p. 774.

62. *The Gentleman's Magazine for March, 1818*, p. 264.

63. See *Testament de Napoléon* (Brussels: Auguste Wahlen, 1824), p. 23; see also François G. de Coston, *Napoleon Bonaparte's erste Jahre, von der Geburt bis zur Ernennung als commandirender General von Italien*, part 2 (Leipzig, 1840), pp. 243–44. The passage is from the 4 codicil to the testament, Longwood, April 24, 1821, para. 5 ("Testament de Napoléon Ier," Rois et Présidents, http://www.roi-president.com/testament-de-napoleon-ier-1821/).

64. *Translator's note:* Luther's Ninety-five Theses against the selling of indulgences were appended to a letter to the archbishop of Mainz and Magdeburg. Whether he actually nailed them to the church's door is not clear.

65. See Kieser, *Wartburgsfest*.

66. Rödiger, "Rede."

67. Ibid., p. 124.

68. Ibid., p. 115.

69. "Almansor," in Heine, *Historisch-kritische Gesamtausgabe*, vol. 5, p. 16.

70. See Ascher, *Wartburgs-Feier*, p. 25.

71. Ibid., p. 31.

72. Ibid., p. 51.

73. *Österreichischer Beobachter*, no. 344, December 10, 1817, p. 1767.

74. *Österreichischer Beobachter*, nos. 359 and 360, December 25 and 26, 1817, p. 1846.

75. HHStA Vienna StK Vorträge Krt. 215, Fol. 135.

76. See Siemann, *Anfänge der politischen Polizei*, pp. 76–78.

77. Mattern, *Kotzebue's Allgewalt*, p. 209.

78. HHStA Vienna StK Vorträge Krt. 215, Fol. 139.

79. The following account is based on Cramer, *Acten-Auszüge Carl Ludwig Sand*, pp. 66ff.

80. See Hohnhorst, *Vollständige Übersicht*, vol. 1, p. 35.

81. Cramer, *Acten-Auszüge Carl Ludwig Sand*, p. 74.

82. The text is reproduced in Hohnhorst, *Vollständige Übersicht*, vol. 1, pp. 187–91.

83. Wehler, *Gesellschaftsgeschichte*, vol. 2, p. 332 and p. 337.

84. See Hohnhorst, *Vollständige Übersicht*, vol. 1, p. 105.

85. Ibid., p. 104.

86. Reproduced in Hohnhorst, *Vollständige Übersicht*, vol. 1, p. 191; all quotations here are from this source.

87. See Hohnhorst, *Vollständige Übersicht*, vol. 1, p. 113.

88. Ibid., pp. 118–19.

89. See Mattern, *Kotzebue's Allgewalt*, p. 209.

90. Hohnhorst, *Vollständige Übersicht*, vol. 1, p. 188.

91. See especially Büssem, *Karlsbader Beschlüsse;* the judgment in Schulz, *Normen und Praxis,* p. 74; the similar term *Friedhofsruhe* [peace of the graveyard] is used in Mieck, "Preußen," p. 189.

92. See MPM 1, p. 37; NP 1, p. 34: "'Do unto others as ye would they should do unto you.' This fundamental rule of every human fraternity, applied to the state, means in the political world reciprocity, and its effect is what in the language of diplomacy is called hons procédés, in other words, mutual consideration and honourable conduct."

93. Metternich to Dorothea von Lieven, April 20, 1819. French original in Hanoteau, *Lettres du Prince de Metternich,* p. 301; German translation in Mika, *Metternichs Briefe,* p. 265.

94. Metternich to Eleonore, April 10, 1819, NA Prague A. C. 12, Krt. 2, 11; in MPM 3, p. 224; NP 3, p. 194.

95. Metternich to his daughter Leontine, October 18, 1848, NA Prague, A. C. 12, Krt. 5, 46, 2, in NP 8, p. 190. Latour was murdered on October 6, 1848.

96. Metternich to Dorothea von Lieven, April 20, 1819. French original in Hanoteau, *Lettres du Prince de Metternich,* p. 301; German translation in Mika, *Metternichs Briefe,* p. 265.

97. Gentz to Metternich, April 14, 1819, Gentz, *Friedrich von Gentz,* 3.1, p. 396.

98. Metternich to Gentz, April 10, 1819, Gentz, *Friedrich von Gentz,* 3.1, p. 391. *Translator's note: Unbedingt* means "unconditional," that is, individuals who are free from the constraint of any conditions, who are independent and do not have to take the authority of others into consideration.

99. Metternich to Gentz, April 9, 1819, Gentz, *Friedrich von Gentz,* 3.1, p. 388.

100. Metternich to Eleonore, April 10, 1819, NA Prague A. C. 12, Krt. 2, 11, in MPM 3 (transl. amended), pp. 223–24; NP 3, p. 194.

101. See Hohnhorst, *Vollständige Übersicht;* also Feilchenfeldt, *Varnhagen von Ense,* 1, p. 383.

102. Metternich to Gentz, April 23, 1819, Gentz, *Friedrich von Gentz,* 3.1, p. 409.

103. NA Prague A. C. 5, Krt. 2, 5.

104. Huber, *Dokumente,* 1, p. 90.

105. See Siemann, "Zensur im Übergang," pp. 377–78.

106. See Hans-Heinrich Jescheck, ed., *Strafgesetzbuch* (Munich, 2002).

107. The following account is based on Metternich to Gentz, June 17, 1819, Gentz, *Friedrich von Gentz,* 3.1, pp. 464–70.

108. See Nipperdey, *Deutsche Geschichte,* 1, pp. 589–92.

109. Gentz to Metternich, April 14, 1819, Gentz, *Friedrich von Gentz,* 3.1, p. 396.

110. *Rheinische Blätter,* no. 54, April 5, 1819, p. 247, NA Prague A. C. 5, Krt. 2, 5.

111. Bruchmüller, *Karl Hases Rhein- und Lenzfahrt,* p. 160. In Heydemann, *Carl Ludwig Sand,* p. 126, the quotation was erroneously ascribed to Archduke Johann, a mistake that was then repeated by several other authors.

112. Doblinger, "Tagebucheintragungen des Erzherzogs Johann," p. 151.

113. See Nipperdey, *Deutsche Geschichte*, 1, p. 282.

114. See NA Prague A. C. 9, Krt. 1, 53; the article might have been a supplement to the *Aarauer Zeitung;* I was not able to find it in the regular editions of the paper.

115. Quoted after Rumpler, *Österreichische Geschichte*, p. 212.

116. Metternich to Gentz, June 17, 1819, Gentz, *Friedrich von Gentz*, 3.1, p. 465.

117. Wilhelm de Wette to Sand's mother, March 31, 1819, Cramer, *Acten-Auszüge Carl Ludwig Sand*, pp. 254–55.

118. Metternich to Gentz, June 17, 1819, Gentz, *Friedrich von Gentz*, 3.1, p. 465.

119. Gentz to Metternich, April 25, 1819, Gentz, *Friedrich von Gentz*, 3.1, pp. 415–16.

120. *Translator's note: Liebden* is a form of address used among princes and royalty.

121. Letter to Metternich, in Wittgenstein's own hand, June 28, 1819, HHStA Vienna StK Vorträge Krt. 218, Fols. 35–36.

122. *Translator's note:* At St. Peter's Field, 60,000 to 80,000 people demonstrated for a reform of parliamentary representation, following famines that were worsened by the introduction of the Corn Laws. Fifteen people were killed.

123. Presentation by Metternich, July 18, 1819, HHStA Vienna StK Vorträge Krt. 218, Fols. 83–88.

124. See Huber, *Dokumente*, 1, pp. 61–62.

125. "On the condition of the Prussian States (Enclosure No. 1)," enclosure in Metternich to Wittgenstein, November 14, 1818, MPM 3, pp. 199–204; here: pp. 200–201 (transl. modified); NP 3, pp. 171–78, here: p. 174.

126. MPM 3, pp. 201–2; NP 3, p. 175.

127. MPM 3, p. 202 (transl. modified): NP 3, p. 175.

128. Presentation by Metternich, July 25, 1819, HHStA Vienna StK Vorträge Krt. 218, Fols. 93–95.

129. Emphasis Metternich's.

130. Metternich to Dorothea von Lieven, July 27, 1819, NA Prague A. C. 6, C19.4; not part of the published posthumous papers.

131. MPM 3, 295–299; here: p. 295. Presentation by Metternich, July 30, 1819, HHStA Vienna StK Vorträge Krt. 218, Fols. 159–168. I quote from the original; the version in NP 3, pp. 258–61 omits essential passages.

132. MPM 3, p. 297; NP 3, p. 260.

133. *Translator's note:* Friedrich Ludwig Jahn (1778–1852) was an educator who, in 1811, founded his first *Turnplatz*, an open-air gymnasium, in Berlin. In 1848, he became a member of the Frankfurt Parliament. He is still widely known in Germany as "Turnvater Jahn," the father of gymnastics.

134. Presentation by Metternich, July 30, 1819, HHStA Vienna StK Vorträge Krt. 218, Fols. 159–168. I quote from the original.

135. Ibid.

136. MPM 3, p. 298; NP 3, p. 261.

137. Presentation by Metternich, August 1, 1819, HHStA Vienna StK Vorträge Krt. 219, Fols. 1–7.

138. MPM 3, p. 306; NP 3, p. 268; The NP erroneously gives "den deutschen Bund," rendered in MPM as "the German Bund," whereas Metternich actually wrote "Deutschland" (Germany).

139. MPM 3, p. 305; NP 3, p. 267.

140. Presentation by Metternich, August 31, 1819, HHStA Vienna StK Vorträge Krt. 218, Fols. 173f.

141. *Translator's note:* Carlsbad was a renowned spa.

142. Presentation by Metternich, September 1, 1819, HHStA Vienna StK Vorträge Krt. 219, Fols. 1–2.

143. MPM 3, p. 324; correctly reproduced in NP 3, p. 284; the original in NA Prague RAM Krt. 140, 5226 / 27.

144. "Presidential Proposition," MPM 3, pp. 309–23; here: p. 310. NP 3, pp. 271–84; here: p. 271.

145. Metternich to Dorothea von Lieven, September 25, 1819, NA Prague A. C. 6, C19.4; MPM 3, p. 335 (transl. modified); NP 3, p. 294 (transl. inaccurate).

146. MPM 3, p. 336 (transl. modified); NP 3, p. 294.

147. Huber, *Verfassungsgeschichte*, 1, p. 646.

148. Presentation by Metternich, November 18, 1819, HHStA Wien StK Vorträge Krt. 220, Fol. 104.

149. Metternich to Dorothea von Lieven, November 25, 1819, NA Prague A. C. 6, C19.4.

150. Metternich to Dorothea von Lieven, November 28, 1819, NA Prague A. C. 6, C19.4.

151. "Erster Vortrag" [first speech], HHStA Vienna StK Deutsche Akten Krt. 212, 138 " (emph. W. S.); this file contains all protocols.

152. "Übersicht der Beratungs-Gegenstände" [List of topics to be covered in the negotiations], HHStA Vienna StK Deutsche Akten Krt. 212, 138. "Kompetenz" [competencies] had its own commission, while "14. Artikel" [article 14] and "Kuriatstimmen" [collective votes] were covered by one commission.

153. MPM 3, pp. 410–12; here: p. 410 (transl. modified); NP 3, pp. 362–33; here: p. 362.

154. Metternich to Rechberg at the end of January 1820; MPM 3, p. 411; NP 3, p. 363.

155. "Grundzüge zur Interpretation des 13. Artikels der Bundes-Acte" [Fundamental principles for the interpretation of article 13], HHStA Vienna StK Deutsche Akten Krt. 212, 138.

156. See Langewiesche, *Monarchie*.

157. Metternich to Berstett, May 4, 1820, MPM 3, pp. 422–27; here: p. 424 (transl. amended); NP 3, pp. 372–77; here: p. 374.

158. Ibid.

159. Metternich to Dorothea von Lieven, April 8, 1820, NA Prague A. C. 6, C19.5; in MPM 3, p. 366; NP 3, p. 322.

160. Metternich to Canitz, February 10, 1847, NP 7, pp. 366–67.

161. MPM 3, p. 424; NP 3, p. 375.

162. See Späth, *Revolution in Europa*, pp. 440–45.

163. "Vortrag des Herrn Fürsten von Metternich über einige in Antrag gebrachte nähere Bestimmungen des 14. Artikel der Bundes-Acte" [Report of Prince Metternich regarding some proposed provisions for article 14 of the Federal Act], HHStA Vienna StK Deutsche Akten Krt. 212, 138.

164. Presentation by Metternich, February 12, 1819, HHStA Vienna StK Vorträge Krt. 221, Fols. 80–81.

165. See Landesmuseum Württemberg, ed., *Im Glanz der Zaren.*

166. *La Renommée*, no. 250, March 21, 1820, HHStA Vienna StK Vorträge Krt. 221, Fol. 142.

167. Presentation by Metternich, May 14, 1820, HHStA Vienna StK Vorträge Krt. 222, Fol. 72.

168. Nipperdey, *Deutsche Geschichte*, 1, p. 282.

169. Castlereagh to Christoph von Lieven, January 14, 1820, Castlereagh, *Correspondence*, vol. 12, pp. 179–80.

170. Metternich to the British Prince Regent, September 2, 1819, MPM 3, pp. 325–26; NP 3, pp. 285–86.

171. Castlereagh to Lord Stewart, January 14, 1820, Castlereagh, *Correspondence*, vol. 12, p. 189.

172. Castlereagh to Metternich, May 6, 1820, Castlereagh, *Correspondence*, vol. 12, p. 258.

173. Castlereagh ordered the ambassador in Vienna to convey these congratulatory words to Metternich. Castlereagh to Stewart, May 5, 1820, Webster, *Castlereagh*, vol. 2, p. 198.

174. Lamb to Castlereagh, May 28, 1820, Castlereagh, *Correspondence*, vol. 12, pp. 264–65.

175. See Koselleck, *Zeitalter*, pp. 221–22.

176. Diary of Melanie Metternich, 1820, pp. 67ff.; NA Prague.

177. Chateaubriand, *Memoirs*, vol. 4, p. 23; Chateaubriand, *Mémoires*, vol. 4, p. 63.

178. Chateaubriand, *Memoirs*, vol. 4, p. 46; Chateaubriand, *Mémoires*, vol. 4, p. 93.

179. Chateaubriand, *Memoirs*, vol. 4, p. 56; Chateaubriand, *Mémoires*, vol. 4, p. 105.

180. See Lions, *Duc de Berry*, pp. 58–61.

181. Presentation by Metternich, February 20, 1820, HHStA Vienna StK Vorträge Krt. 221, Fol. 47.

182. Metternich to Dorothea von Lieven, February 20, 1820, NA Prague A. C. 5, C19.5.

183. Metternich to Gentz, April 10, 1819, Gentz, *Friedrich von Gentz*, 3.1, pp. 391–92.

184. Prokesch von Osten, *Aus den Tagebüchern* [Excerpts from the diaries], p. 118; entry for December 6, 1831.

185. Presentation by Metternich, February 26, 1820, HHStA Vienna StK Vorträge Krt. 221, Fols. 93–94.

186. Presentation by Metternich, February 29, 1820, HHStA Vienna StK Vorträge Krt. 221, Fol. 101.

187. Presentation by Metternich, March 3, 1820, HHStA Vienna StK Vorträge Krt. 221, Fols. 77–78.

188. Dorothea von Lieven to Metternich, February 25, 1820, Quennell, *Vertrauliche Briefe der Fürstin Lieven,* pp. 34–36.

189. See Schulz, *Normen und Praxis,* p. 72.

190. Castlereagh to Lieven, January 14, 1820, Castlereagh, *Correspondence,* vol. 12, pp. 179–80.

191. Hafner, "Castlereagh," esp. pp. 71–75; on the long overdue reinterpretation of the scorned British foreign minister, see also Bew, *Castlereagh.*

192. Temperley, *Canning,* p. 4.

193. Castlereagh to Lord Liverpool, October 20, 1818, Castlereagh, *Correspondence,* vol. 12, pp. 54–55.

194. See Temperley, *Canning,* pp. 46–47.

195. Ibid., p. 20.

196. Stahl, *Metternich und Wellington,* pp. 254–65.

197. See Siemann, *Metternich's Britain,* pp. 23–24.

198. Anderegg, *Die politischen Verhältnisse Englands,* p. 33.

199. Metternich to his daughter Leontine, July 22, 1848, NP 8, p. 172.

200. Metternich to Count Buol, March 24, 1857, NP 8, p. 395; see also Anderegg, *Die politischen Verhältnisse Englands,* p. 41.

201. "La politique anglaise est devenu simplement utilitaire. C'est Lord Palmerston qui a été le représentant le plus avancé de cette politique douteuse," in NP 8, p. 322. Metternich to Buol, August 1, 1852.

202. Doering-Manteuffel, *Wiener Kongress,* p. 53; in my view, the argument recently made by Zamoyski in his programmatically titled *Phantom Terror* can be considered refuted on the basis of the available sources. J. L. Talmon's *The Origins of Totalitarian Democracy* deserves more attention for its healthy skepticism regarding simple division between "good" and "evil."

203. Doering-Manteuffel, *Wiener Kongress,* p. 55.

204. See Heydemann, *Konstitution,* p. 142, who does not so much as mention the French intervention when discussing the Congress of Verona, pp. 135–44.

205. See the most recent demonstration of this thesis in Šedivý, *Decline of the Congress System.*

206. On the following, see Daum, *Oszillationen,* pp. 55–63.

207. Ibid., pp. 56–57.

208. See Schroeder, *Transformation,* pp. 609–10.

209. The dates according to Metternich's correspondence with Dorothea von Lieven, NA Prague A. C. 6, C19.4.

210. Presentations by Metternich, November 3, 1820, HHStA Vienna StK Vorträge Krt. 224, Fols. 17–18.

211. "Principles of the Policy of Intervention" / "Grundsätze für die Interventionspolitik"; conceptual paper by Metternich, MPM 3, pp. 443–44; NP 3, p. 391.

212. In Droß, *Quellen zur Ära Metternich,* pp. 104–6.

213. MPM 3, pp. 402–3 (transl. modified). Metternich to Dorothea von Lieven, November 20, 1820, NA Prague A. C. 6, C19.6; excerpts in NP 3, 355–56.

214. MPM 3, pp. 403–4 (transl. amended); Metternich to Dorothea von Lieven, November 27, 1820, NA Prague A. C. 6, C19.6; excerpts in NP 3, p. 356.

215. "Circular Despatch of the Courts of Austria, Russia, and Prussia, to their Ambassadors and Agents at the German and Northern Courts, Troppau, December 8, 1820," MPM 3, pp. 444–47. "Zirkulardepesche der Höfe von Österreich, Russland und Preußen an ihre Gesandten und Geschäftsträger bei den deutschen und nordischen Höfen, Troppau, 8. Dezember 1820," NP 3, pp. 391–94.

216. Presentation by Metternich, December 19, 1820, HHStA Vienna StK Vorträge Krt. 224, Fol. 107.

217. Letter written in the emperor's own hand, May 25, 1821, HHStA Vienna StK Vorträge Krt. 226, Fol. 198.

218. MPM 3, p. 499. Metternich to Dorothea von Lieven, May 28, 1821, NA Prague A. C. 6, C19.8; excerpts in NP 3, pp. 441–42.

219. Ibid.

220. On the "Greek question" in general, see Šedivý, *Eastern Question,* pp. 59–337.

221. See Schroeder, *Transformation,* pp. 637–65.

222. Šedivý, *Eastern Question,* p. 126.

223. Ibid., p. 217.

224. Ibid., pp. 175–76; see also Temperley, *Canning,* p. 361.

12. The Economist

1. See Conze and Wienfort, *Adel und Moderne,* p. 1 and p. 7.

2. Quoted after Henning, *Quellen,* p. 43; see Frie, *von der Marwitz.*

3. *Translator's note:* The *Kudlichgesetz* refers to the *Grundentlastungspatent* of September 7, 1848, which removed the manorial system and with it the obligations of the peasants to the sovereign landowner and the latter's jurisdiction over his territory. The young parliamentarian Hans Kudlich, only twenty-five at the time, introduced the bill.

4. The family repeatedly received subventions from the imperial coffers. When Metternich took up his post as minister, he asked a civil servant of the Court Chamber to compile a list of the payments made to the family over the years. It contained reimbursements for traveling costs and exceptional expenses in connection with the imperial coronation in 1790 or the Congress of Rastatt, but not the secret payments made discreetly on the occasion, for instance, of the wedding of the young count or later during and after the wars against Napoleon. See Franz Weibel, "Die Herrn von Metternich, insoweit im k. k. Hofkammer-Archive Nachweisungen von Ihnen vorhanden sind" [The lordship of Metternich, insofar as the k. k. Hofkammer-archives contain entries on them]; library at Schloss Königswart.

5. The text of the judgment in NA Prague RAM Krt. 206, 2035-5.

6. "Eigenhändig niedergeschriebene Erklärung S. E. des Reichsgrafen Clemens W. L. Metternich über die Vermögens-Verhältnisse des Hauses zur Wissenschaft für die Nachkommenschaft, 23. Dezember 1810" [Declaration, written down by S. E. the imperial count Clemens W. L. Metternich, on the financial circumstances of the family for the knowledge of future generations, December 23, 1810], NA Prague RAM Krt. 63, 3353.

7. Ibid.

8. Vermögenserklärung [Declaration of assets], August 4, 1814, NA Prague RAM Krt. 64, 3398.

9. NA Prague RAM Krt. 63, 3358.

10. Verfügung des niederösterreichischen Landrechts [Order by the law of Lower Austria], Vienna, October 22, 1819, NA Prague RAM Krt. 192.

11. Declaration by Franz Georg, [no date], NA Prague RAM Krt. 64, 3410.

12. *Wiener Zeitung,* no. 282, October 8, 1816, Beilage Allgemeines Intelligenzblatt [Supplement containing official announcements], p. 707.

13. "Individueller Fürstlich-Metternichscher Passivstand mit Ende Dezember 1819" [Individual Liabilities of Count Metternich as of end of December 1819], NA Prague RAM Krt. 192.

14. Trial records and final judgment in NA Prague RAM Krt. 398.

15. Original of the contract at NA Prague RAM Krt. 192.

16. Letter to the Oberamt [central administration], February 13, 1826, Plaß, StA Pilsen Vs-Plasy, Krt. 111, 1826.

17. Bond, June 1, 1827, NA Prague RAM Krt. 200, 1996.

18. See Rieck, *Friedrich Koenig.*

19. Most of the statistical and topographical information on Plaß used in this chapter is taken from Anton Wiehl, "General-Karte von der hochfürstlich von Metternich'schen Herrschaft Plaß," in the Schloss Johannisberg archive; Wiehl was a princely [*hochfürstlich*] forester and charted k. k. surveyor. The chapter also draws on Sommer, *Das Königreich Böhmen,* vol. 6: Pilsener Kreis (including Plaß), vol. 15: Elbogner Kreis (including Königswart). *Translator's note:* The word *Meierhof* comes from Latin "maiores villae," a major farm or building that originally had been occupied by nobility or by their administrator—the *Meier* of a noble estate. They were now leased by Metternich to tenant farmers.

20. Order given by Metternich to the central administration in Plaß, June 24, 1835, StA Pilsen, Vs-Plasy, Krt. 125.

21. See Sommer, *Das Königreich Böhmen,* vol. 6, p. 322.

22. Joshua 1:17; the address in NA Prague RAM Krt. 141, 5294.

23. According to "Verzeichnis der Juden-Familien 1833" of the Elbogen district of the dominion Königswart, including Miltigau and Amonsgrün, StA Pilsen Vs-Kynžvart, K-174; the figures in Sommer, which relate to 1838 and 1847 (vol. 6 and vol. 15), differ slightly.

24. See Volkov, "Die Emanzipation der Juden."

25. See Sommer, *Das Königreich Böhmen,* vol. 6, p. 316.

26. Metternich to Handel in Frankfurt November 27, 1819, archive at Schloss Johannisberg.

27. See Bädeker, *Rheinreise,* pp. 169–70.

28. Ibid.

29. Metternich to the office of the administrator at Johannisberg, March 2, 1819, archive at Schloss Johannisberg.

30. Archive at Schloss Johannisberg, Akte 1836.

31. Archive at Schloss Johannisberg, Akte 1843.

32. On the events in 1848, see HHStA Vienna StK Kleinere Betreffe, Johannisberg, Krt. 8.

33. Report, HHStA Vienna StK Kleinere Betreffe, Johannisberg, Krt. 9.

34. Contract, December 20, 1850, HHStA Vienna StK Kleinere Betreffe, Johannisberg, Krt. 9.

35. Turnbull, *Austria,* vol. 1 *(Narrative of Travels),* p. 89.

36. Metternich to the central administration in Plaß, July 19, 1827, StA Pilsen Vs-Plasy Krt. 107.

37. *Translator's note:* A centner equals exactly 50 kilograms (about 110 pounds), and is thus close to, but not identical to, a hundredweight (50.8 kilograms or 112 pounds).

38. For the source of the data, see Anton Wiehl, "General-Karte von der hochfürstlich von Metternich'schen Herrschaft Plaß," in the Schloss Johannisberg archive.

39. NA Prague RAM Krt. 143, 5357.

40. Turnbull, *Austria,* vol. 1 *(Narrative of Travels),* p. 378.

41. "Ueber die Ungarischen Zustände" [On the condition of Hungary], NP 7, 51–63; the autograph is at NA Prague A. C. 8, 9a.

42. All five points in NP 7, pp. 58–59.

43. The publication of the memorandum was part of a series of articles on Hungary published by the conservative Vienna newspaper *Der Lloyd* from February 3, 1850, onward. NA Prague A. C. 8, Krt. 12, 73. Parts of the memorandum had also been published as an anonymous pamphlet: A. C. 8, Krt. 11, 71. The complete text was published in *Oesterreichische Zeitung* May 14, 1857, A. C. 8, Krt. 13, 80.

44. "Ueber die Ungarischen Zustände" [On the condition of Hungary], NP 7, p. 58.

45. Metternich to Kübeck, March 12, 1850, Beer, *Kübeck und Metternich,* pp. 94–95.

13. The Spring of Nations amid Poverty, 1830–1847

1. Metternich to Apponyi, June 5, 1830, MPM 5, p. 6; NP 5, p. 6.

2. Ibid.

3. Metternich to Emperor Franz, August 5, 1830, MPM 5, p. 18; NP 5, p. 17.

4. Metternich to Emperor Franz, August 5, 1830, MPM 5, p. 19; NP 5, p. 17.

5. Metternich to Emperor Franz, August 5, 1830, MPM 5, p. 18; NP 5, p. 17.

6. Metternich to Emperor Franz, undated, HHStA Vienna, StK Vorträge Krt. 263, Fols. 150ff.

7. See Wrede to Metternich, May 1831, Bibl, *Geheimer Briefwechsel,* pp. 223–24.

8. The event is described in Metternich to the envoy Fiquelmont, October 13, 1830, MPM 5, pp. 54–57; NP 5, pp. 63–69.

9. Metternich to Esterházy, October 21, 1830, MPM 5, pp. 39–41; NP 5, pp. 69–71.

10. HHStA Vienna StK Acta Secreta Krt. 4, Fols. 129–132.

11. Documented in HHStA Vienna StK Acta Secreta Krt. 6, No. 562, "Lola Montez betreffend" [Regarding Lola Montez].

12. MPM 5, p. 19 (footnote); NP 5, pp. 18–19 (footnote).

13. Schulz, *Normen und Praxis,* p. 104.

14. Ibid., p. 93.

15. "Louis Philipp, König der Franzosen" [Louis Philippe, King of the French], NA Prague A. C. 8, Krt. 1, 5 (autograph); in NP 5, pp. 84–88; MPM 5, p. 65. *Translator's note:* The character sketch was written after Louis Philippe's death and added to the German text on the French and the July revolutions. The English text only gives the character sketch, not the historical reflections.

16. The conversations and letters are documented in MPM 5, pp. 21–33; NP 5, pp. 18–34.

17. See Siemann, *Vom Staatenbund,* pp. 343–44.

18. Gervinus, *Introduction to the History of the Nineteenth Century,* pp. 129–30.

19. Ibid., p. 130.

20. Ibid.

21. Metternich to Nesselrode, September 1, 1830, MPM 5, p. 27; NP 5, p. 25.

22. See the excellent survey in the chapter "Die Büchse der Pandora" in Rumpler, *Österreichische Geschichte,* pp. 154–214; the quotations above: pp. 154–55.

23. See on this little-noticed socio-economic plurality Godsey, *Habsburgerreich,* pp. 29–35.

24. See Rumpler, *Habsburgermonarchie,* vol. 9: *Soziale Strukturen,* e.g., map no.161 "Soziale Strukturen nach der Stellung im Beruf" [Social structures according to professions].

25. Wehler, *Gesellschaftsgeschichte,* vol. 2, p. 366.

26. For a detailed account of the functioning, personnel, and connections of this institution, see Siemann, *Anfänge der politischen Polizei,* pp. 139–74; on the institution's work, see Hoefer, *Pressepolitik.*

27. HHStA Wien, Informationsbüro StK Mainzer Zentral-Polizei, Krt. 20.

28. *Translator's note:* The modern German spelling of *Policeystaat* is *Polizeistaat.*

29. The following account is based on Siemann, *Metternich: Staatsmann,* pp. 86–87.

30. See Šedivý, *Eastern Question,* pp. 777–838.

31. See Lutz, *Zwischen Habsburg und Preußen,* pp. 75–78; Godsey, "Habsburgerreich."

32. See Hahn, "Wirtschaftspolitische Offensive," p. 97.

33. Ticknor, *Life, Letters, and Journals,* vol. 2, p. 7 (June 26, 1836).

34. All quotations ibid.

35. Presentation by Metternich, June 24, 1833, NP 5, pp. 502–19; a faithful reproduction of the text. The original in HHStA Vienna StK Vorträge Krt. 271. *Translator's note:* The text is omitted from the English edition of this volume of Metternich's papers.

36. See Siemann, *Vom Staatenbund,* p. 339.

37. See Huber, *Dokumente,* 1, p. 90.

38. See Lutz, *Zwischen Habsburg und Preußen,* pp. 75–76.

39. Ibid., p. 76.

14. The Organization of Rule

1. See Vitzthum von Eckstädt, *Berlin und Wien,* p. 60; Srbik, *Metternich,* vol. 2, p. 262.

2. Kürnberger, "Die Poesie und die Freiheit," p. 45.

3. See Schüler, *Franz Anton Graf von Kolowrat-Liebsteinsky.*

4. Imperial resolution, August 20, 1817, HHStA Vienna StK Vorträge Krt. 208, Fol. 129.

5. See "Wer regiert in Österreich," in Rumpler, *Österreichische Geschichte,* pp. 69–77; here: p. 73.

6. NA Prague A. C. 8, Krt. 3, 23.

7. The following account is based on a report by the court councillor Hofrat Hudelist, February 2, 1810, HHStA Vienna StK Vorträge Krt. 184, Fols. 1–10; regarding the evacuation of the documents of the HHStA, the report confuses the point of departure (Pressburg) with the point of destination (Temesvar).

8. Emperor's comments on the presentation by Metternich, December 22, 1809, HHStA Vienna StK Vorträge Krt. 183, Fol. 73.

9. On the house at Ballhausplatz and its furnishings and facilities, see Mayr, *Österreichische Staatskanzlei,* p. 7.

10. NP 2, pp. 315–16; the original in HHStA Wien StK Vorträge Krt. 183, Fol. 55. *Translator's note:* The sketch for the reorganization is omitted from the English edition (MPM 2, p. 369) as being, in the eyes of the translator, "entirely without interest, as well as unintelligible to English readers."

11. Presentation by Metternich, May 19, 1816; imperial resolution and comments by the emperor, May 22, HHStA Wien StK Krt. 202, Fols. 96–119.

12. MPM 2, p. 522 (transl. modified); NP 2, pp. 444–53; the original draft concept in NA Prague A. C. 8, Krt. 7, 38.

13. MPM 2, pp. 527–28 (transl. modified); NP 2, pp. 452–53.

14. See Ziegler, "Franz I." and "Franz II."

15. Metternich to Dorothea von Lieven, December 20, 1818, Mika, *Metternichs Briefe,* p. 81.

16. These become apparent in a diary that the emperor wrote during his journey through Italy (February 10 to August 1, 1819); see Kuster, *Italienische Reisetagebuch Kaiser Franz' I,* pp. 65–402, and esp. pp. 407–8.

17. MPM 5, pp. 473–74; NP 5, p. 651.

18. MPM 5, p. 474; NP 5, p. 651. *Translator's note:* The English edition only gives the paragraph on Metternich.

19. See Mikoletzky, "Ferdinand I."

20. HHStA Vienna, Hausarchiv, Erzherzogin Marie Louise Krt. 3.

21. HHStA Wien, Hausarchiv. Familienkorrespondenz, K 30, Teil 1: "Tagebuch Kaiser Ferdinands I. über eine Reise nach Steiermark. 17. August–2. September 1847, und Reise nach Pressburg 11.-19. November 1847, Reise nach Olmütz 1. Okt. 1848." Teil 2: "Tagebuch Kaiser Ferdinands I über seine Reise nach Innsbruck 17. Mai–12. August 1848." These works would merit publication.

22. HHStA Vienna, Hausarchiv, Familienkorrespondenz, K 30, Teil 1 [family correspondence, K30, part 1].

23. See Ségur-Cabanac, *Kaiser Ferdinand*.

24. HHStA Vienna StK Informationbüro. Vorträge in Polizeisachen. Krt. 1–4.

25. As documented by the papers in HHStA Vienna StK Vorträge Krt. 278 (1836)–Krt. 296 (1848).

26. Metternich to Hartig, January 29, 1850, Hartig, *Metternich*, p. 43.

27. HHStA Vienna StK Acta Secreta Krt. 3–5.

28. HHStA Vienna StK Acta Secreta Krt. 5, Fol. 108.

29. NA Prague, Diary of Melanie von Metternich of 1851, entry for October 6, 1851: "Alors elle me dit: 'Ce que je reproche à votre mari, c'est d'avoir voulu une chose impossible que était celle de mener la Monarchie sans un Empereur, et avec un *Trottel*, représentant de la couronne.' 'Mais Madame, que était donc là pour remplacer celui-là? Elle doit bien savoir depuis les dernières années si un autre eût été plus fort.' Elle se mordit la langue et répondit—'oui, le reproche qu'il y a à faire, c'est que celui qui était né avec des qualités suffisantes pour régner, n'ait pas été élevé à cela et qu'on a perdu ces dispositions fort heureuses.'" Reproduced after the original diary in Schlitter, *Niederösterreich*, p. 122, where the pejorative expression, however, is redacted: "T . . . l."

30. NP 8, p. 114.

31. Quoted in Theodor Schiemann, *Geschichte Russlands unter Kaiser Nikolaus,* vol. 3 (Berlin, 1913.), p. 271.

32. See Srbik, *Metternich,* vol. 2, pp. 9–10.

33. See on the following Schlitter, *Niederösterreich,* vol. 4, pp. 40–41.

34. Reproduced in ibid., pp. 92–97.

35. Memorandum by Metternich, 1836, HHStA Vienna StK Interiora Personalia Krt. 7, Fols. 256–259.

36. *Hanauer Zeitung,* no. 310, November 9, 1836, title page, HHStA Vienna StK Interiora Personalia Krt. 7.

37. Details in Schüler, *Kolowrat.*

38. The following account, including the quotations from the diaries, are based on Srbik, *Metternich,* vol. 2, pp. 14–31.

39. See Srbik, *Metternich,* vol. 2, p. 15.

40. Ibid.

41. Reproduced in Schlitter, *Niederösterreich,* vol. 4, pp. 109–10.

42. Reproduced in ibid., p. 110.

43. *Journal du Commerce* (Paris), no. 332, November 27, 1836, title page, HHStA Vienna StK Interiora Personalia Krt. 7, 269.

44. *Journal du Commerce,* no. 280, October 6, 1835, HHStA Vienna StK Interiora Personalia Krt. 7, Fol. 267.

45. *Journal des Débats,* December 27, 1836, title page. The text is from *Allgemeine Zeitung.*

46. Kübeck, *Tagebücher,* vol. 1–2, p. 742.

47. NP 7, p. 629.

48. Grillparzer, *Erinnerungen aus dem Jahre 1848,* available at http://gutenberg.spiegel .de/buch/erinnerungen-aus-dem-jahre-1848-1519/1.

49. See Srbik, *Metternich,* vol. 2, p. 9.

50. The following account is based on Beidtel, *Staatsverwaltung,* pp. 228–31.

51. See ibid., p. 228, note 1.

52. Clam-Martinitz to Metternich, September 28, 1836, HHStA Vienna StK Interiora Personalia Krt. 7, Fols. 196–207.

53. Metternich to Archduke Ludwig, November 29, 1836, HHStA Vienna StK Interiora Personalia Krt. 7, Fols. 246–47.

54. Clam-Martinitz to Metternich, September 28, 1836, HHStA Wien StK Interiora Personalia Krt. 7, Fols. 196–207.

55. Metternich to Kübeck, February 25, 1843, Kübeck, *Metternich und Kübeck,* pp. 18–19.

56. See Rumpler, *Der Franziszeische Kataster,* esp. pp. 7–34.

57. NA Prague A. C. 2, Krt. 2, 8. Memorandum with covering letter by Clam-Martinitz, Vienna, January 10, 1838. Quotations follow the original.

58. NP 7, pp. 628–29.

59. Diary entry of March 29, 1839, NP 6, p. 301.

60. Diary entry of January 18, 1840, NP 6, p. 368.

61. Metternich to Kübeck, October 20 and December 10, 1841, NP 6, pp. 531–45.

62. On these events, see NP 6, pp. 539–40.

63. Metternich to Kübeck, May 1, 1843, Kübeck, *Metternich und Kübeck,* p. 20.

64. Metternich to Hartig, January 29, 1850, Hartig, *Metternich,* pp. 42–43.

65. NP 8, p. 625.

66. On the Ferdinand System, see Siemann, *Metternich: Staatsmann,* pp. 93–103.

67. NA Prague RAM Krt. 350, 1780. "Viertes Verzeichnis was des Heiligen Römischen Reichs Churfürsten, Fürsten und Stände an des Kaiserlichen und Reichs Kammer-Gerichts Unterhaltung . . . Wetzlar 1780."

68. Metternich to Hartig, October 10, 1847, NP 7, pp. 476–77.

69. Ticknor, *Life, Letters, and Journals,* 2, pp. 13–16; here: p. 13.

70. Ibid.

71. Ibid., p. 14.

72. All quotations, ibid.

73. Ibid., p. 15.

74. All quotations, ibid.

75. Ibid., p. 16.

76. Ibid.

77. Ibid., p. 17.

78. Ibid.

15. Revolution, Escape, Exile, 1848–1851

1. Gall, *1848*, p. 39 (contribution by Karin Schambach).

2. The following is based on Siemann, *Metternich: Staatsmann*, pp. 108–10; and Siemann, *1848*, pp. 13–52.

3. On the mobilization in the regions of the Habsburg Monarchy, see Langewiesche, *Europa, 1848*; and Rumpler, *Habsburgermonarchie*, vol. 7, 1–2: *Verfassung*; vol. 8, 1–2: *Öffentlichkeit*; and vol. 9, 1–2: *Soziale Strukturen*.

4. See Schlitter, *Niederösterreich*, vol. 4, p. 88.

5. See ibid., p. 41.

6. See Srbik, *Metternich*, vol. 2, p. 259.

7. See Schlitter, *Niederösterreich*, vol. 4, p. 37; Srbik, *Metternich*, vol. 2, p. 265.

8. Excerpts in NP 7, pp. 529–46, and in NP 8, pp. 3–141; the original diaries of the year 1848–1854 are in NA Prague.

9. NA Prague A. C. 9, Krt. 2, 82.

10. HHStA Vienna MKA 1848.

11. The following account is based on Srbik, *Metternich*, vol. 2, pp. 332–34.

12. Hormayr, *Kaiser Franz und Metternich*.

13. *Verhandlungen des österreichischen Reichstages* [Proceedings of the Austrian Diet], August 14, 1848, p. 532.

14. According to a report of the commission, September 22, 1850; quoted after Srbik, *Metternich*, vol. 2, p. 339.

15. Ibid., p. 335.

16. HHStA Vienna, MKA Krt. 103, Zl. 2230.

17. Based on Schüler, *Kolowrat*, pp. 286–90; on his dismissal, see p. 290.

18. The most important ones are in NA Prague A. C. 8, Krt. 1; on the Austrian question Fasc. 9, on the German question 1848–1849, Fasc. 10.

19. *Translator's note: Innere Reichsgründung* is a generic term for political and social developments within the German Reich from the end of the 1870s onward.

20. Metternich to Kübeck, February 24, 1850, Kübeck, *Metternich und Kübeck*, p. 75.

21. On the following, see Metternich to Kübeck ("Für Sie allein" [For you alone]), December 31, 1849, Kübeck, *Metternich und Kübeck*, pp. 48–52.

22. Metternich to Leontine, February 12, 1849, NP 8, p. 207.

23. Metternich to Leontine, December 20, 1848, NP 8, p. 199.

24. Metternich to Leontine, May 2, 1849, NP 8, pp. 217–18.

25. Metternich to Schwarzenberg, February 28, 1849, NP 8, p. 477.

26. Metternich to Leontine, September 7, 1848, NP 8, p. 180.

27. Metternich to Moritz II. von Dietrichstein, December 21, 1848, quoted after Anderegg, *Die politischen Verhältnisse Englands,* p. 22. Metternich develops the same idea in a later letter to Count Buol, August 1, 1852, NP 8, pp. 321–22.

28. Metternich to Leontine, December 17, 1849, NP 8, pp. 205–6.

29. Metternich to Kübeck ("Für Sie allein" [For you alone]), December 31, 1849, Kübeck, *Metternich und Kübeck,* p. 50.

30. This episode is examined in detail in Sadek, *Metternichs publizistische und pressepolitische Betätigung in Exil (1848–1852).*

31. Disraeli to Mary Anne Disraeli, January 7, 1849, Benjamin Disraeli, *Correspondence,* ed. M. G. Wiebe et al., vol. 5: 1848–1851 (Toronto, 1993), p. 127.

32. See NP 8, pp. 619–20. The correspondence with Twiss during the years 1849–1859 is at NA Prague A. C. 10, Krt. 13; the correspondence with Cheney at A. C. 10, Krt. 6 and A. C. 13, Krt. 2, 41. One could, and someone should, reconstruct the press network established by Metternich on the basis of the sources in Prague.

33. Metternich to Kübeck, December 31, 1849, Kübeck, *Metternich und Kübeck,* p. 51.

34. Beer, *Kübeck und Metternich,* p. 157.

35. See Huber, *Verfassungsgeschichte,* vol. 2, pp. 883–84; Beer, *Kübeck und Metternich,* pp. 9–13.

36. Kübeck, *Tagebücher,* vol. 2, p. 16.

37. Srbik, *Metternich,* vol. 2, p. 253.

38. Metternich to Kübeck, July 7, 1852, Beer, *Kübeck und Metternich,* p. 145.

39. Metternich to Kübeck, December 31, 1849, Beer, *Kübeck und Metternich,* p. 57.

40. Metternich to Kübeck, March 10, 1850, Beer, *Kübeck und Metternich,* pp. 94–95.

41. Kübeck to Metternich, March 9, 1850, Kübeck, *Metternich und Kübeck,* p. 86.

42. Metternich to Kübeck, February 20, 1850, Beer, *Kübeck und Metternich,* p. 77.

43. Metternich to Kübeck, February 24, 1850, Beer, *Kübeck und Metternich,* p. 84.

44. Kübeck to Metternich, undated, Beer, *Kübeck und Metternich,* pp. 90–91.

45. Metternich to Kübeck, July 15, 1852, Beer, *Kübeck und Metternich,* p. 146.

46. Metternich to Kübeck, March 12, 1850, Beer, *Kübeck und Metternich,* pp. 94–95.

47. Metternich to Kübeck, March 15, 1850, Beer, *Kübeck und Metternich,* p. 97.

16. At the Observatory

1. See Höbelt, *1848;* the prediction was made by, for example, Grillparzer (p. 89), *Allgemeine Österreichische Zeitung* (p. 100), the poet and journalist Count Anton von Auersperg (p. 111), and the ministry of Fiquelmont (p. 121).

2. The image of the "observatory" is Metternich's. He uses it in connection with Kübeck's position as president of the imperial council. See Metternich to Kübeck, February 23, 1850, Beer, *Kübeck und Metternich,* p. 83.

3. NA Prague RAM Krt. 48, 3 (death, notices), 48, 4 (estate), Krt. 141, 5278 (letters of condolence).

4. Otto Bismarck, *Die politischen Berichte des Fürsten Bismarck aus Petersburg und Paris (1859–1862),* ed. Ludwig Raschdau, vol. 1 (Berlin, 1920), p. 46.

5. See Siemann, *Gesellschaft im Aufbruch,* pp. 171–89.

6. The claim that Hübner was Metternich's illegitimate son, which is repeated every now and again, does not fit with the fact that Metternich did not tend to deny the existence of his illegitimate children—as, for instance, in the case of his daughter with Princess Bagration (Clementine). But the thesis should in any case be rejected; see Srbik, *Metternich,* vol. 2, p. 621.

7. NP 8, p. 623.

8. Ibid., p. 626.

9. *Österreichische Zeitung,* June 15, 1859.

10. The following account is based on descriptions given in an article of the *Österreichische Zeitung,* June 17, 1859, and in the *Fremden-Blatt,* June 16, 1859.

11. *Translator's note:* The Arcièrengarde was a personal guard of the Austrian emperor, made up of officers of higher rank who had distinguished themselves in battle.

12. NP 8, p. 621.

13. These are the words of the correspondent in Vienna of the *Klagenfurter Zeitung,* June 18, 1859, p. 546.

14. Metternich to Dorothea von Lieven, October 6, 1820, NA Prague A. C. 6, C19.6; in MPM 3, p. 395; NP 3, p. 348.

15. MPM 3, pp. 394–95; NP 3, p. 348.

Epilogue

1. *Translator's note:* From the epilogue of *The Good Person of Szechuan:* "Wir stehen selbst enttäuscht und sehn betroffen / Den Vorhang zu und alle Fragen offen" ("We're disappointed too. With consternation / We see the curtain closed, the plot unended"), p. 106. The lines have been translated in various ways, but the German literally says "and all questions open." *Das Literarische Quartett* was a long-running German television program in which Reich-Ranicki discussed newly published literature with three other critics. It has recently been revived with another host.

2. *Translator's note:* This is a reference to a scene in Goethe's *Faust,* Part 1, in which Mephistopheles impersonates Faust and talks to a student about a suitable subject. In the course of this conversation, the student says "Denn, was man Schwarz auf Weiß besitzt / Kann man getrost nach Hause tragen" ("You know where you are when you come away / With something down in black and white"), p. 66.

3. *Translator's note:* The German title of Sheehan's *Where Have All the Soldiers Gone? The Transformation of Modern Europe* is *Kontinent der Gewalt: Europas langer Weg zum Frieden* [Continent of violence: Europe's long path toward peace].

4. MPM 1, p. 175 (transl. amended); NP 1, p. 141. Kübeck was in possession of two letters from Metternich in which he spoke of the hope he placed in future historians. Kübeck's views on this were far more skeptical: "Alas, history is rarely more just in its judgments than the contemporary world which, after all, passes on the information to it. And even though the contemporaneous passions recede more into the background, and the causes and effects of actions can be better placed in their context, the perspectives of the various parties continue to resonate from the present into the future for a long time, and posterity is no less susceptible to invectives, slander, and insinuations, and it is no less gullible than the contemporary world. The appeal to posterity is therefore little consolation for the men who are presently subjected to slander and a hope in vain for those who are celebrated. One's own conscience, this divine court, stands above both the contemporary times and posterity." Diary entry, May 26, 1849, in Kübeck, *Tagebücher,* vol. 2, p. 46.

Acknowledgments

1. Clausewitz, *On War,* pp. 73–74.

BIBLIOGRAPHY

Unpublished Archival Sources

Preliminary Remark: The Metternich family archive, which contains sources from the medieval period up to 1945, is housed at the National Archive in Prague. It consists of 410 boxes, a substantial number of which contain Franz Georg von Metternich's files pertaining to the Holy Roman Empire. The family archive also contains documents such as birth and death certificates, and documents relating to elevations in rank, marriage, inheritance, purchase contracts, and so forth, covering the same period. In addition, there are the posthumous papers of Princess Melanie, which include correspondence from the time she spent in exile in London and all the documents relating to the finances of the House of Metternich, especially documents to do with loans and debt. In the 1960s an archivist tried to introduce a new order into the archive, and in the process upset the old system, in which the material had been ordered according to origin. There is therefore no inventory available at present.

There are also ninety-two boxes of the prince's private posthumous papers at the archive in Prague. These were organized by Metternich himself, and they mainly contain correspondence, newspaper clippings, and the material Metternich selected for the writing of his memoirs; the latter also contains copies of documents from the archive in Vienna. Documents relating to the administration of the Plaß and Königswart estates are kept separately at the Staatsarchiv Pilsen.

Nationalarchiv Prag (Státní ústřední archiv v Praze)

Rodinný archiv Metternichů, Starý archiv (Metternich family archive) Krt. 1–410

Vlastní rodinný archiv (Persönliches Familienarchiv) = Acta Clementina, Abteilungen [sections] 1–14 (Krt. 1–92)

RAM-FG mapy Krt. 1–8 (maps)

Diaries of Princess Melanie von Metternich 1819–1835, 1846–1853

Acta Richardiana (archive of Richard Metternich) Krt. 3, 4, 18, 19–29, 31–34, 400

Staatsarchiv Pilsen (Státní archiv v Plzni)

Fonds: Vs Plasy Krt. 110–131, 176–179
Fonds: Vs Kynžvart F-holdings F-156–157, 270
K-holdings 1–3, 16, 18, 20, 21, 137, 152, 173, 174

Schloss Königswart (Kynžvart)

Books, maps, drawings, archival documents (Sign. Ky)
Eva Stejskalová: Catalogue Zámecké Knihovny Kynžvart, 3 Bde. 1965–1967

Staatsarchiv Tetschen (Děčín)

Rodinný archiv Clary-Aldringenů (posthumous papers of Fiquelmont) Krt. 375, 376–378,
   382, 383, 385–389, 394, 398, 773

Haus-, Hof- und Staatsarchiv Wien

Staatskanzlei
   Interiora Krt. 1
   Acta Secreta Krt. 1–7
   Vorträge Krt. 180–296, 301, 304
   France Krt. 181, 199, 201, 203–206
   Prussia, correspondence Krt. 85
   Saxony Krt. 33
   Informationsbüro Vorträge Krt. 1–4
   Central Police Mainz (intelligence agency) Krt. 1–24
   Peace treaties Krt. 102, 103.1–2
   Instructions Krt. 6
   German files Krt. 210, 212, 278.1–2, 279–290
   Minor matter concerning Johannisberg Krt. 8–11
Minister Kolowrat-files Krt. 70, 73, 84, 90, 92, 93, 95, 101, 103, 105, 115, 122, 123, 127–129, 153,
   154, 173, 175, 177, 178, 180, 183, 184, 197, 218, 222, 225, 226
Posthumous papers Franz A. Kolowrat
Posthumous papers Gervay
Posthumous papers Kübeck Krt. 7, 8
Deposits Kübeck
Posthumous papers Schlitter
Political archive I Acta Secreta Krt. 451
Personalia Krt. 215
Archive of the Imperial House
   Kaiser Franz-files Krt. 13, 24, 83, 89

Erzherzogin Maria Luise Krt. 3

Family correspondence Krt. 30. 1–2

Große Korrespondenz [major correspondence] Krt. 481

Korrespondenz [correspondence] Krt. 71 Parts 1–2; Krt. 75 Part 2

Ministerrat [ministerial council] Krt. 1, 8, 9, 12, 14

Belgien Rot Krt. 1, 70 a, b, 114–116, 122, 123, 127, 129, 135, 141, 142

Allgemeines Verwaltungsarchiv Wien

Adelsakten [aristocratic records] Metternich

Schloss Johannisberg, Kellerei-Archiv Metternich

Fascicles for the years 1819–1859

Published Primary Sources

Abrantès, Laure Junot d'. 1831–1837. *Mémoires de Mme la Duchesse d'Abrantès, ou souvenirs historiques sur Napoléon, la revolution, le directoire, le consulat, l'empire et la restauration.* Vols. 1–25. Brussels.

Aktenstücke für die Deutschen, oder Sammlung aller officiellen Bekanntmachungen in dem Kriege von 1813. 1813. Dresden.

Anonym. 1848. *Metternich am Pranger und sein System vor dem Richterstuhle der Geschichte: Eine Warnungsstimme an das deutsche Volk.* Leipzig.

Ascher, Saul. 2011. *Flugschriften.* Ed. André Thiele. Mainz.

———. 1818. *Die Wartburgs-Feier: Mit Hinsicht auf Deutschlands religiöse und politische Stimmung.* Leipzig.

Aspinall, A., ed. 1959. *English Historical Documents, 1783–1832.* London.

Bädeker, Karl. (1849) 1983. *Rheinreise von Basel bis Düsseldorf.* Koblenz. Reprint, Dortmund.

Barante, Claude de. 1890. *Souvenirs du Baron de Barante: 1782–1866.* Vol. 1. Paris.

Baumgart, Winfried, ed. 1979. *Akten zur Geschichte des Krimkriegs.* Series 1, vol. 3: *Österreichische Akten.* Munich.

Beer, Adolf, ed. 1897. *Kübeck und Metternich: Denkschriften und Briefe.* Vienna.

Bernhardi, Theodor von, ed. 1866. *Denkwürdigkeiten aus dem Leben des [. . .] Carl Friedrich Grafen von Toll.* Vol. 4, part 2. Leipzig.

Beyer, Constantin. 1821. *Neue Chronik von Erfurt oder Erzählung alles dessen, was sich vom Jahre 1736 bis zum Jahre 1815 in Erfurt Denkwürdiges ereignete.* Erfurt.

Bibl, Viktor, ed. 1928. *Metternich in neuer Beleuchtung: Sein geheimer Briefwechsel mit dem bayerischen Staatsminister Wrede.* Vienna.

Bouillé, Marquies de. 1908. *Souvenirs et fragments pour servir aux mémoires de ma vie et de mon temps par le Marquis de Bouillé (Louis-Joseph-Amour).* Vol. 2: 1769–1812, ed. v. F.-L. Kermaingant. Paris.

Boyer d'Agen, [Augustin]. 1919. *Une dernière amitié de Metternich d'après une correspondance inédite du Prince de Metternich au Cardinal Viale Prela*. Paris.

Breycha-Vauthier, Arthur, ed. 1964. *Aus Diplomatie und Leben: Maximen des Fürsten Metternich*. Graz.

———. 1957. "Metternich à Bruxelles: Lettres inédites." *Revue Générale Belge*, 3–15.

———. 1965. "More Sources on Metternich." *Austrian Yearbook* 1: 38–44.

Bruchmüller, Wilhelm. 1966. "Karl Hases Rhein- und Lenzfahrt vom Jahre 1820." *Quellen und Darstellungen zur Geschichte der Burschenschaft* 8: 154–186.

Burckhardt, Carl J., ed. 1934. *Briefe des Staatskanzlers Fürsten Metternich-Winneburg an den österreichischen Minister . . . Grafen Buol-Schauenstein aus den Jahren 1852–1859*. Munich.

Burke, Edmund. 1790. *Reflections on the Revolution in France and on the Proceedings in Certain Societies in London*. London. (Original edition at Königswart library).

———. 2000. *The Writings and Speeches of Edmund Burke*. Vol. 7: *India: The Hastings Trial, 1789–1794*, ed. P. J. Marshall, Paul Langford, and William Todd. Oxford.

Canning, George. 1828. *The Speeches of the Right Honourable George Canning*. 6 vols. London.

Capefigue, M. [Comte d'Angeberg], ed. 1863–1864. *Le congrès de Vienne et les traités de 1815*. Vols. 1–4. Paris.

———. 1845. *The Diplomatists of Europe: From the French of M. Capefigue*. Ed. Major-General Monteith. London.

Castlereagh, Viscount. 1852–1853. *Correspondence, Despatches, and Other Papers*. Vols. 9–12. London.

Caulaincourt. 1933. *Mémoires du General de Caulaincourt, Duc de Vicence, grand écuyer de l'empereur*. Introduction and notes by Jean Hanoteau. 3 vols. Paris.

Champagny. 1846. *Souvenirs de M. de Champagny, duc de Cadore*. Paris.

Chateaubriand, François René. 1902. *The Memoirs of François René, Vicomte de Chateaubriand, Sometime Ambassador to England*. London.

Clercq, Alexandre Jehan Henry de. 1864. *Recueil des traités de la France*. 2 vols. Paris.

Confalonieri. 1910. *Carteggio del Conte Federico Confalonieri ed altri documenti spettanti alla sua biografia, pubblicato con annotazioni storiche a cura di Giuseppe Gallavresi*. Vol 1. Milan.

Cramer, Friedrich, ed. 1821. *Acten-Auszüge aus dem Untersuchungs-Proceß über Carl Ludwig Sand*. Altenburg.

Doblinger, Max. 1966. "Tagebucheintragungen des Erzherzogs Johann, des späteren Reichsverwesers, über Karl Ludwig Sand und die Karlsbader Beschlüsse." *Quellen und Darstellungen zur Geschichte der Burschenschaft* 8: 151–153.

Dohna, Albrecht zu. 1798. *Der Feldzug der Preußen gegen die Franzosen in den Niederlanden im Jahre 1793*. Vol. 1. Stendal.

Droß, Elisabeth, ed. 1999. *Quellen zur Ära Metternich*. Darmstadt.

Dumouriez. 1912. *Lebenserinnerungen des Generals Dumouriez*. Translated and with commentary by Karl Fritzsche. Voigtländers Quellenbücher, vol. 35. Leipzig.

———. 1794. *Mémoires du Général Dumouriez*. Vol. 2. Hamburg.

Eynard, Jean Gabriel. 1923. *Der tanzende Kongress: Tagebuch*. Berlin.

Fain, Baron de. 1823. *Manuscrit de 1814.* London.

———. 1824. *Manuscrit de mille huit cent treize, contenant le précis des événemens de cette année; pour servir à l'Histoire de l'Empereur Napoléon.* Vol. 2. Paris.

Feilchenfeldt, Konrad, Bernhard Fischer, and Dietmar Pravida, eds. 2006. *Varnhagen von Ense und Cotta: Briefwechsel, 1810–1848.* 2 vols. Stuttgart.

Feyerlichkeiten bey der Rückkehr Sr. Maj. des Kaisers von Österreich nach Wien im Jahre 1814. 1816. Vienna.

Fischer, Wolfram. 1982. *Sozialgeschichtliches Arbeitsbuch.* Vol. 1: *Materialien zur Geschichte des Deutschen Bundes, 1815–1817.* Munich.

Forgues, Eugène, ed. 1884. *Mémoires et relations politiques du Baron de Vitrolles.* Vol. 1: *1814.* Paris.

Fournier, August, ed. 1907. *Gentz und Wessenberg: Briefe des ersten an den zweiten.* Leipzig.

Franklin, Robert. 2007. "The Death of Lord Londonderry." *Historian* 96: 20–23.

Geisenhof, Georg. (1829) 1975. *Kurze Geschichte des vormaligen Reichsstifts Ochsenhausen in Schwaben.* Reprint, Ottobeuren.

General Treaty, Signed in Congress at Vienna, June 9th 1815. 1816. London.

Gentz, Friedrich von. 1793. *Betrachtungen über die französische Revolution.* Berlin.

———. 1913. *Briefe von und an Friedrich von Gentz.* Vol. 3, Parts 1–2. Ed. Friedrich Carl Wittichen and Ernst Saltzer. Munich.

———. 1806. *Fragmente aus der neusten Geschichte des Politischen Gleichgewichts in Europa.* Saint Petersburg.

———. 1806. *Fragments upon the Balance of Power in Europe.* London.

———. 1873–1874. *Aus dem Nachlaß Varnhagen's von Ense: Tagebücher von Friedrich von Gentz.* Ed. Ludmilla Assing. 4 vols. Leipzig.

———. 1920. *Tagebücher von Friedrich von Gentz (1829–1831).* Ed. August Fournier and Arnold Winkler. Zurich.

Gervinus, Georg Gottfried. (1853) 1866. *Introduction to the History of the Nineteenth Century.* London.

Grab, Walter, ed. 1973. *Die Französische Revolution: Eine Dokumentation.* Munich.

Grillparzer, Franz. [no year; 1892]. *Erinnerungen aus dem Jahre 1848.* In *Grillparzers sämmtliche Werke,* ed. August Sauer, vol. 20, 191–194. Stuttgart.

———. 1960. *Sämtliche Werke: Ausgewählte Briefe, Gespräche, Berichte.* Ed. Peter Frank and Karl Pörnbacher. 2 vols. Munich.

Günter, Heinrich. 1908. *Die Habsburger-Liga, 1625–1635: Briefe und Akten aus dem General-Archiv zu Simancas.* Berlin.

H. M. [Heinrich Herbatschek]. 1899. *Von Metternich bis Thun: 50 Jahre Oesterreich! 1848–1898.* Zurich.

Hanoteau, Jean, ed. 1909. *Lettres du Prince de Metternich à la comtesse de Lieven: 1818–1819.* Paris.

———, ed. 1933. "Une nouvelle relation de l'entrevue de Napoléon et de Metternich à Dresde." *Revue d'histoire diplomatique* 47: 421–440.

Hansen, Joseph, ed. 1931–1938. *Quellen zur Geschichte des Rheinlandes im Zeitalter der Französischen Revolution.* 4 vols. Bonn.

Hardenberg, Karl August von. 2000. *1750–1822: Tagebücher und autobiographische Aufzeichnungen.* Ed. Thomas Stamm-Kuhlmann. Munich.

Hartig, Franz, ed. 1923. *Metternich—Hartig: Ein Briefwechsel des Staatskanzlers aus dem Exil, 1848–1851.* Vienna.

Heidrich, Kurt. 1908. *Preußen im Kampfe gegen die Französische Revolution bis zur zweiten Teilung Polens.* Stuttgart.

Heine, Heinrich. 1975–1997. *Historisch-kritische Gesamtausgabe.* Ed. Manfred Windfuhr. 16 vols. Düsseldorfer Heine-Ausgabe. Hamburg.

———. 1893. *Lutetia: The Works of Heinrich Heine,* vol. 8. London.

Heller von Hellwald, Friedrich Jakob. 1858. *Der k.k. österreichische Feldmarschall Graf Radetzky: Eine biographische Skizze nach den eigenen Dictaten und der Correspondenz des Feldmarschalls von einem österreichischen Veteranen.* Stuttgart.

Hellinghaus, Otto, ed. 1914. *Napoleon auf St. Helena: Denkwürdigkeiten seiner Begleiter und Ärzte.* Freiburg i. Br.

Henning, Hansjoachim. 1977. *Quellen zur sozialgeschichtlichen Entwicklung in Deutschland von 1815–1860.* Paderborn.

Hohnhorst, Levin Karl v., ed. 1820. *Vollständige Übersicht der gegen Carl Ludwig Sand wegen Meuchelmordes verübt an dem K. russischen Staatsrath v. Kotzebue geführten Untersuchung aus den Originalakten.* 2 vols. Stuttgart.

Huber, Ernst Rudolf, ed. 1978. *Dokumente zur deutschen Verfassungsgeschichte.* Vol. 1. Stuttgart.

Huch, Ricarda. 1911. *Das Leben des Grafen Federigo Confalonieri.* Leipzig.

———. 1908. *Das Risorgimento.* Leipzig.

Jenak, Rudolf, ed. 2010. *"Mein Herr Bruder": Napoleon und Friedrich August I: Der Briefwechsel des Kaisers der Franzosen mit dem König von Sachsen, 1806–1813.* Beucha-Markkleeberg.

Kieser, D. G. 1818. *Das Wartburgsfest am 18. Oktober 1817: In seiner Entstehung, Ausführung und Folgen.* Jena.

Kircheisen, Friedrich Max, ed. 1909–1910. *Briefe Napoleons des Ersten: Auswahl aus der gesamten Korrespondenz des Kaisers.* 3 vols. Stuttgart.

Klein, Tim, ed. 1913. *Die Befreiung 1813, 1814, 1815: Urkunden, Berichte, Briefe.* Ebenhausen.

Kleßmann, Eckart, ed. 1976. *Deutschland unter Napoleon.* Munich.

Klüber, Johann Ludwig, ed. 1815–1818. *Acten des Wiener Congresses in den Jahren 1814 und 1815.* 8 vols. Vol. 9: 1835. Erlangen.

Krones, Franz von, ed. 1891. *Aus dem Tagebuche Erzherzog Johanns von Oesterreich, 1810–1815.* Innsbruck.

Kübeck, Max von, ed. 1910. *Metternich und Kübeck: Ein Briefwechsel.* Vienna.

———. 1960. *Aus dem Nachlass des Freiherrn Carl Friedrich Kübeck von Kübau: Tagebücher, Briefe, Aktenstücke (1841–1855).* Ed. Friedrich Walter. Graz.

————. 1909–1910. *Tagebücher des Carl Friedrich Freiherrn Kübeck von Kübau.* Ed. and with an introduction by Max Freiherrn von Kübeck. Vol. 1, parts 1–2, vols. 2–3. Vienna.

Kugler, Georg. 1991. *Staatskanzler Metternich und seine Gäste: Die wiedergefundenen Miniaturen von Moritz Michael Daffinger, Josef Kriehuber und anderen Meistern aus dem Gästealbum der Fürstin Melanie Metternich.* Graz.

Kuster, Thomas, ed. 2010. *Das italienische Reisetagebuch Kaiser Franz' I. von Österreich aus dem Jahre 1819: Eine kritische Edition.* Münster.

Lang, Karl Heinrich Ritter von. 1841–1842. *Memoiren.* 2 parts. Braunschweig.

Liedekerke Beaufort, Christian de. 1968. *Le Comte Hilarion: Souvenirs et Biographie du premier Comte de Liedekerke Beaufort: Histoire de sa famille.* Vol. 1. Paris.

————. 1968. "*Voyage en Angleterre* de M. le vicomte Desandrouin avec MM. les comtes de Metternich fils et M. le comte de Liedekerke Beaufort, son gendre." In Liedekerke Beaufort, *Comte Hilarion: Souvenirs et Biographie,* 190–252.

Lions, J., ed. 1820. *Histoire de S. A. R. Mgr. le Duc de Berry, assassiné dans la nuit du 13 février 1820.* Lyon.

Lothar, Rudolf. 1917. *Die Metternich-Pastete: Ein appetitliches Lustspiel in drei Gängen.* Reclams Universal-Bibliothek, no. 5983. Leipzig.

Malfatti von Monteregio, Johann. 1845. *Studien über Anarchie und Hierarchie des Wissens: Mit bes. Bez. auf die Medizin.* Leipzig. (Dedicated to Metternich as "protector and promoter of the sciences.")

Marmont. 1857. *Mémoires du Maréchal Marmont Duc de Raguse de 1792 à 1841.* 2nd ed. Vol. 6. Paris.

Martens, Friedrich, ed. 1876. *Recueil des traités et conventions conclus par la Russie avec les Puissance étrangères.* Vol. 3: *Traités avec l'Autriche, 1808–1815.* Saint Petersburg.

Metternich, Clemens von. [no date.] *Aphoristische Bemerkungen über die Ungarischen Zustände zu Ende des Jahres 1844, vom Fürsten von Metternich.* Printed by the Vienna k.k. Hof- u. Staatsdruckerei, 1857.

————. 1879. "'La coalition européenne en 1813 et 1814: Fragment tiré des Mémoires Inédits du Prince de Metternich." *Revue des Deux Mondes* (Dec. 1, 1879): 481–518.

————. 1921. *Denkwürdigkeiten.* Ed., with an introduction and annotations, by Otto H. Brandt. 2 vols. Munich.

————. 1882. *Documenti relativi ad alcune asserzioni del Principe di Metternich intorno al Re Carlo Felice ed a Carlo Alberto Principe di Carignano cos osservazioni di Nicomede Bianchi.* Rome.

————. 1875. *Fürst Metternich über Napoleon Bonaparte.* Translated from French into German by Dr. med. Hegewald. Vienna.

————. [no date.] *Journal de mon Voyage en Angleterre depuis le 25. Mars jusqu'au* [end date missing] *en l'année 1794.* Königswart, library.

————. 1906. "Noch nicht veröffentlichte Briefe Metternichs an Schwarzenberg aus dem Feldzuge 1814," ed. A. v. Janson. *Beiheft zum Militär-Wochenblatt* 3: 87–104.

———. 1891. *Relazione del Principe di Metternich a S. M. l'imperatore Francesco I sul suo colloquio col conte Federico Confaloniere (2 Febbraio 1824)*. Ed. Allessandro d'Ancona. Pisa.

Metternich, Melanie. [no date.] "Mon Voyage en Angeleterre l'année 1848." In Allgemeines Verwaltungsarchiv Wien: Kriegsarchiv, Nachlass Melanie Metternich [Tochter], Krt. B / 1449:2.

Metternich, Pauline. 1988. *Erinnerungen*. Ed. Lorentz Mikoletzky. Vienna.

———. 1921. *The Days That Are No More: Some Reminiscences*. London.

Metternich, Richard von, ed. 1880–1884. *Aus Metternich's Nachgelassenen Papieren*. 8 vols. Vienna.

Metternich, Richard von, ed. 1880–1882. *Memoirs of Prince Metternich*, 5 vols. Translated by Alexander Napier. London.

Meyer, Philipp Anton Guido, ed. 1833. *Staats-Acten für Geschichte und öffentliches Recht des Deutschen Bundes (Corpus Juris Confoederationis Germanicae)*. Frankfurt a. M.

Mika, Emil, ed. 1942. *Geist und Herz verbündet: Metternichs Briefe an die Gräfin Lieven*. Vienna.

Molé, Louis-Mathieu. 1923. *The Life and Memoirs of Count Molé, 1781–1855*. Ed. Marquis de Noialles. London.

Montesquieu, Charles-Louis de. 2014. *Meine Reisen in Deutschland, 1728–1729*. Ed. Jürgen Overhoff. Stuttgart.

Montesquieu, Charles Louis de Secondat. (1748) 1995. *De l'esprit des lois*. Paris. https://www.ecole-alsacienne.org/CDI/pdf/1400/14055_MONT.pdf.

———. (1748) 1777. *The Spirit of Laws*. London.

———. 1894. *Les Voyages de Montesquieu*. Bourdeaux.

Müller, Klaus, ed. 1986. *Quellen zur Geschichte des Wiener Kongresses, 1814 / 15*. Darmstadt.

Nabert, Thomas, ed. 2012. *Zeugen des Schreckens: Erlebnisberichte aus der Völkerschlachtzeit in und um Leipzig*. Leipzig.

Nachträgliche Aktenstücke der deutschen Bundes-Verhandlungen als Anhang zu den Protokollen der Bundesversammlung. 1817. Vol. 1. Frankfurt a. M.

Napoléon. 1858–1869. *Correspondance, publiée par ordre de l'Empereur Napoléon III*. 32 vols. Paris.

Nesselrode, Comte A. 1904–1911. *Lettres et papiers du chancelier Comte de Nesselrode: 1760–1850*. 10 vols. Paris.

Novák, Johann Friedrich, ed. 1913. *Briefe des Feldmarschalls Fürsten Schwarzenberg an seine Frau, 1799–1816*. Vienna.

Pelet, Jean-Jacques. 1825. *Mémoires sur la guerre de 1809 en Allemagne*. 4 vols. Paris.

Pfaundler, Wolfgang, and Werner Köfler, eds. 1984. *Der Tiroler Freiheitskampf 1809 unter Andreas Hofer: Zeitgenössische Bilder, Augenzeugenberichte und Dokumente*. Munich.

Pölitz, Karl Heinrich Ludwig, ed. 1817. *Die Constitutionen der europäischen Staaten seit den letzten 25 Jahren*. 2 vols. Leipzig.

Pozzo di Borgo, Charles André. 1890–1897. *Correspondance diplomatique du comte Pozzo di Borgo, 1814–1818*. Vols. 1–2. Paris.

Pribram, Albert Francis, ed. 1918. *Urkunden und Akten zur Geschichte der Juden in Wien.* Vol. 2. Vienna.

Prokesch von Osten, Anton von. 1842. "Der Feldzug in den Niederlanden 1793." In *Kleine Schriften.* Vol. 3. Stuttgart.

———. 1909. *Aus den Tagebüchern des Grafen Prokesch von Osten: 1830–1834.* Vienna.

Prudhomme, Marie-Louis. [no date.] *Histoire générale et impartiale des erreurs, des fautes et des crimes commis pendant la révolution française, à dater du 24 août 1789.* Vols. 1–6. Paris.

Quellen zur Geschichte des Deutschen Bundes. Ed. Eckhardt Treichel, section 1: 1815–1830, 2 vols. Munich 2000 / 2015. Ed. Ralf Zerback, section 2: 1830–1850, vol. 1, 2003. Ed. Jürgen Müller, section 3: 1850–1866, 4 vols 1996/1998/2012/2017.

Quennell, Peter. 1938. *The Private Letters of Princess Lieven to Prince Metternich.* New York.

———, ed. 1939. *Vertrauliche Briefe der Fürstin Lieven.* Berlin.

Radetzky von Radetz. 1858. *Denkschriften militärisch-politischen Inhalts aus dem handschriftlichen Nachlass.* Stuttgart.

Richter, Jean Paul. 1842. "Impromtü's welche ich künftig in Stammbücher schreiben werde." In *Sämmtliche Werke,* vol. 32. Berlin.

Riegel, Martin. 1838. *Der Buchhändler Johann Philipp Palm: Ein Lebensbild.* Hamburg. (Contains a complete reprint of "Deutschland in seiner tiefen Erniedrigung.")

Rödiger, L. 1818. "Rede, gehalten am Feuer auf dem Wartenberge, am Abend des 18. Oct. 1817." In Kieser, *Wartburgsfest,* 114–127.

Saint-Aulaire, Comte de. 1927. *Souvenirs (Vienne, 1832–1841).* Ed. Marcel Thiébaut. Paris.

Sassmann, Hanns. 1929. *Metternich: Historisches Schauspiel in fünf Akten.* Vienna.

Sauder, Gerhard, ed. 2003. *Theorie der Empfindsamkeit und des Sturm und Drang.* Stuttgart.

Servan de Sugny. 1831. *Épitre a. M. le Prince de Metternich.* Paris.

Sommer, Johann Gottfried. 1838, 1847. *Das Königreich Böhmen, statistisch-topographisch dargestellt.* Vol. 6: *Pilsner Kreis* [includes Plaß], 1838. Vol. 15: *Elbogner Kreis* [includes Königswart], 1847. Prague.

Spiel, Hilde, ed. 1978. *Der Wiener Kongreß in Augenzeugenberichten.* Munich.

Spies, Hans-Bernd, ed. 1981. *Die Erhebung gegen Napoleon. 1806–1814 / 15.* Darmstadt.

Stein, Freiherr vom. 1957–1974. *Briefe und amtliche Schriften.* Ed. Erich Botzenhart. Newly ed. Walther Hubatsch. 10 vols. Stuttgart.

Steitz, Walter, ed. 1980. *Quellen zur deutschen Wirtschafts- und Sozialgeschichte im 19. Jahrhundert bis zur Reichsgründung.* Darmstadt.

Stolberg-Wernigerode, Henrich Graf zu. 2004. *Tagebuch über meinen Aufenthalt in Wien zur Zeit des Congresses.* Ed. Boje Schmuhl. Halle.

Talleyrand, Charles-Maurice. 1881. *Correspondance inédite du Prince de Talleyrand et du Roi Louis XVIII pendant le Congrés de Vienne.* 2nd ed. M. G. Pallain. Paris.

———. 1891. *Memoirs of the Prince de Talleyrand,* 2 vols. London.

Temperley, H. W. V., ed. 1925. *The Unpublished Diary and Political Sketches of Princess Lieven.* London.

Theis, Anne, and Laurent Theis, eds. 2016. *Souvenirs et chronique de la Duchesse de Dino, niece aimée de Talleyrand.* Paris.

Thürheim, Lulu. 1913. *Mein Leben: Erinnerungen aus Österreichs großer Welt.* Ed. René van Rhyn. 2 vols. Munich.

Ticknor, George. 1876. *Life, Letters, and Journals.* 2 vols. Boston.

Translation of the General Treaty Signed in Congress at Vienna, June 9, 1815, with the Acts thereunto Annexed. Presented to both Houses of Parliament, by Command of his Royal Highness The Prince Regent. February 1816. 1816. London.

Turnbull, Peter Evan. 1840. *Austria.* Vol. 1: *Narrative of Travels.* London.

Ullrichová, Maria, ed. 1966. *Clemens Metternich—Wilhelmine von Sagan: Ein Briefwechsel, 1813–1815.* Graz.

Varnhagen von Ense, Karl August. 1843. *Denkwürdigkeiten des eignen Lebens.* Part 3. Leipzig.

———. 1865. *Aus dem Nachlaß Varnhagen's von Ense: Briefe von Stägemann, Metternich, Heine und Bettina von Arnim.* Leipzig.

Verhandlungen des österreichischen Reichstages nach der stenographischen Aufnahme. 1848. Vol 1. Vienna.

Vitzthum von Eckstädt and Carl Friedrich Graf. 1886. *Berlin und Wien in den Jahren 1845–1852: Politische Privatbriefe.* Stuttgart.

Vivenot, Alfred von, and Heinrich von Zeißberg, eds. 1882, 1885, 1890. *Quellen zur Geschichte der deutschen Kaiserpolitik Österreichs während der französischen Revolutionskriege, 1793–1797.* 3 vols. Vienna.

Vollständiges Diarium der Römisch-Königlichen Wahl und Kaiserlichen Krönung [. . .] Leopold des Zweiten. 1791. Frankfurt a. M.

Wildner-Maithstein, Ignaz v. 1848. *Wackere Mitbürger des großen herrlichen Oesterreichs!* March 14. Vienna.

Winkopp, Peter Adolph. 1808. *Die Rheinische Konföderations-Akte und das Staatsrecht des Rheinischen Bundes.* Frankfurt a. M.

Secondary Sources

Acemoglu, Daron, and James A. Robinson. 2012. *Why Nations Fail: The Origins of Power, Prosperity, and Poverty.* New York.

Alter, Peter. 1985. *Nationalismus.* Frankfurt a. M.

———. 2016. *Nationalismus: Ein Essay über Europa.* Stuttgart.

Amelunxen, Clemens. 1995. *Der Clan Napoleons: Eine Familie im Schatten des Imperators.* Berlin.

Anderegg, Paul. 1954. *Metternichs Urteil über die politischen Verhältnisse Englands.* Diss. Bern, Vienna.

Anderson, Benedict. 2003. *Imagined Communities: Reflections on the Origin and Spread of Nationalism.* London.

Andreas, Willi. 1955. *Das Zeitalter Napoleons und die Erhebung der Völker.* Heidelberg.

Angermeier, Heinz. 1991. *Das Alte Reich in der deutschen Geschichte: Studien über Kontinuitäten und Zäsuren.* Munich.

Anton, Annette C. 1995. *Authentizität als Fiktion: Briefkultur im 18. und 19. Jahrhundert.* Stuttgart.

Ara, Angelo. 2004. "Il problema delle nazionalità in Austria da Metternich al dualismo." *Rivista Storica Italiana* 116: 409–473.

Aretin, Karl Otmar von. 1993–2000. *Das Alte Reich, 1648–1806.* 4 vols. Stuttgart.

———. 1993. *Vom Deutschen Reich zum Deutschen Bund.* Göttingen.

———. 1967. *Heiliges Römisches Reich, 1776–1806: Reichsverfassung und Staatssouveränität.* 2 vols. Wiesbaden.

Arndt, Johannes. 1991. *Das niederrheinisch-westfälische Reichsgrafenkollegium und seine Mitglieder (1653–1806).* Mainz.

Arnold-Baker, Charles. 1996. *The Companion to British History.* Tunbridge Wells.

Asch, Ronald G. 2008. *Europäischer Adel in der Frühen Neuzeit.* Vienna.

Asche, Matthias, Thomas Nicklas, and Matthias Stickler, eds. 2011. *Was vom Alten Reiche blieb: Deutungen, Institutionen und Bilder des frühneuzeitlichen Heiligen Römischen Reiches Deutscher Nation im 19. u. 20. Jahrhundert.* Munich.

Aschmann, Birgit. 2013. *Preußens Ruhm und Deutschlands Ehre: Zum nationalen Ehrdiskurs im Vorfeld der preussisch-französischen Kriege des 19. Jahrhunderts.* Munich.

———, and Thomas Stamm-Kuhlmann, eds. 2015. *1813 im europäischen Kontext.* Stuttgart.

Auernheimer, Raoul. 1940. *Prince Metternich: Statesman and Lover.* New York. Translations: *Staatsmann und Kavalier,* 1947, Vienna; *Metternich: Staatsmann und Kavalier,* 1977, Munich.

Austensen, Roy A. 1977. "Felix Schwarzenberg: 'Realpolitiker' or Metternichian? The Evidence of the Dresden Conference." *Mitteilungen des Österreichischen Staatsarchivs* 30: 97–118.

Autin, Jean. 1991. *La duchesse d'Abrantès.* Paris.

Bauer, Franz J. 2004. *Das "lange" 19. Jahrhundert: Profil einer Epoche.* Stuttgart.

Bauer, Gerhard, Gorch Pieken, Matthias Rogg, and Militärhistor. Museum. 2013. *Blutige Romantik: 200 Jahre Befreiungskriege.* 2 vols. Dresden.

Baumgart, Winfried. 1999. *Europäisches Konzert und nationale Bewegung: Internationale Beziehungen, 1830–1878.* Handbuch der Geschichte der Internationalen Beziehungen, vol. 6. Paderborn.

Bayly, C. A. 2004. *The Birth of the Modern World, 1790–1913: Global Connections and Comparisons.* Oxford.

Beck, Ulrich, and Martin Mulsow, eds. 2014. *Vergangenheit und Zukunft der Moderne.* Berlin.

Beer, Adolf. 1877. *Fürst Clemens Metternich.* Leipzig. (= Rudolf Gottschall, *Der neue Plutarch,* Part 5, 255–397.)

———. 1893. "Metternich und die Entstehung des Zollvereins." *Zeitschrift für die gesamte Staatswissenschaft* 49, no. 2: 316–320.

———. 1877. *Zehn Jahre österreichischer Politik: 1801–1810.* Leipzig.

Behringer, Wolfgang. 2015. *Tambora und das Jahr ohne Sommer: Wie ein Vulkan die Welt in die Krise stürzte*. Munich.

Beidtel, Ignaz. 1898. *Geschichte der österreichischen Staatsverwaltung, 1740–1848*. Vol. 2: *1792–1848*. Innsbruck.

Beller, Steven. 2018. *The Habsburg Monarchy: 1815–1918*. Cambridge.

Benl, Rudolf, ed. 2008. *Der Erfurter Fürstenkongress 1808: Hintergründe, Ablauf, Wirkung*. Erfurt.

Berg, Ursula. 1992. *Niklas Vogt (1756–1836)*. Stuttgart.

Bergeron, Louis, François Furet, and Reinhart Koselleck, eds. 1969. *Das Zeitalter der europäischen Revolution, 1780–1848*. Fischer Weltgeschichte, vol. 26. Frankfurt a. M.

Berglar, Peter. 1973. *Metternich: "Kutscher Europas—Arzt der Revolutionen."* Göttingen.

Bertier de Sauvigny. 1959 / 1986. *Metternich et son temps*. Paris.

Béthouart, Antoine. 1979. *Metternich et l'Europe*. Paris.

Bettelheim, Anton. 1912. "Balzacs Begegnung mit Metternich: Ein biographisches Blatt." *Neue Freie Presse* (Vienna), 2 / 3 August.

Beutner, Eduard. 2001. "'Metternich und seine elende Umgebung': Strategien der Satire auf Exponenten des 'Systems' bei Franz Grillparzer im Vorfeld von 1848." In *Bewegung im Reich der Immobilität: Revolutionen in der Habsburgermonarchie, 1848–1849: Literarisch-publizistische Auseinandersetzungen*, ed. Hubert Lengauer and Primus Heinz Kucher, 67–75. Vienna.

Bew, John. 2011. *Castlereagh: The Biography of a Statesman*. London.

Bibl, Viktor. 1942. *Erzherzog Karl: Ein beharrlicher Kämpfer für Deutschlands Ehre*. Vienna.

———. 1938. *Kaiser Franz: Der letzte römisch-deutsche Kaiser*. Leipzig.

———. 1936. *Metternich: Der Dämon Österreichs*. Leipzig.

Billinger, Robert D. 1991. *Metternich and the German Question: States' Rights and Federal Duties, 1820–1934*. London.

———. 1990. "They Sing the Best Songs Badly: Metternich, Frederick William IV, and the German Confederation during the War Scare of 1840–41." In Helmut Rumpler, ed., *Deutscher Bund und deutsche Frage, 1815–1866: Europäische Ordnung, deutsche Politik und gesellschaftlicher Wandel im Zeitalter der bürgerlich-nationalen Emanzipation*, 94–113. Vienna.

Binder, Wilhelm. 1836 (3rd ed. 1845). *Fürst Clemens Metternich und sein Zeit-Alter: Eine geschichtlich-biographische Darstellung*. Ludwigsburg.

Bitterauf, Theodor. 1905. *Geschichte des Rheinbundes und der Untergang des alten Reiches*. Munich.

Blank, Isabella. 2013. *Der bestrafte König? Die Sächsische Frage, 1813–1815*. Diss. phil., Heidelberg.

Blanning, T. C. W. 2002. *The Culture of Power and the Power of Culture: Old Regime Europe, 1660–1789*. Oxford.

———. 1996. *The French Revolutionary Wars, 1787–1802*. London.

———. 1983. *The French Revolution in Germany: Occupation and Resistance in the Rhineland, 1792–1802*. Oxford.

———. 1974. *Reform and Revolution in Mainz, 1743–1803.* London.

———, and Hagen Schulze, eds. 2006. *Unity and Diversity in European Culture c. 1800.* Oxford.

Bleyer, Alexandra. 2013. *Auf gegen Napoleon! Mythos Volkskriege.* Darmstadt.

———. 2014. *Das System Metternich: Die Neuordnung Europas nach Napoleon.* Darmstadt.

Blisch, Bernd. 2005. *Friedrich Carl Joseph von Erthal (1774–1802): Erzbischof—Kurfürst—Erzkanzler.* Studien zur Kurmainzer Politik am Ausgang des Alten Reiches. Frankfurt a. M.

Bock, Andreas. 2009. *Terrorismus.* Paderborn.

Bödeker, Hans Erich, ed. 2003. *Biographie schreiben.* Göttingen.

Botzenhart, Manfred. 1967. *Metternichs Pariser Botschafterzeit.* Münster.

Bourke, Eoin, and Moritz Hartmann. 2003. "Bohemia and the Metternich System." In *Goethe im Vormärz,* ed. Detlev Kopp and Hans-Martin Kruckis, 353–371. Forum Vormärz Forschung, vol. 9. Bielefeld.

Brandt, Hartwig, ed. 1979. *Restauration und Frühliberalismus: 1814–1840.* Darmstadt.

Brecht, Bertolt. 1942. *The Good Person of Szechuan.* Digitized by RevSocialist, http://www.socialiststories.com/liberate/The%20Good%20Person%20of%20Szechuan.pdf.

———. (1965) 2001. *Stories of Mr. Keuner.* San Francisco.

Breitenstein, Hans. 1959. *Metternich und Consalvi: Das Bündnis von Thron und Altar (1815–1823).* Diss. (typescript), Vienna.

Broemser, Ferdinand. 1988. *Zur Geschichte der Familien Metternich mit den drei Muscheln und mit dem Löwenwappen bis zum Jahr 1700.* Andernach.

Broers, Michael. (1996) 2015. *Europe under Napoleon.* London.

Brühl, Clemens. 1941. *Die Sagan: Das Leben der Herzogin Wilhelmine von Sagan, Prinzessin von Kurland.* Berlin.

Brugger, Eveline, et al. 2006. *Geschichte der Juden in Österreich,* Österreichische Geschicte, vol. 15. Vienna.

Brunswick, Duke of. (1792) 1906. "The Proclamation of the Duke of Brunswick (July 25, 1792)." In *Readings in European History,* ed. J. H. Robinson, 2 vols., 2: 443–445. Boston.

Buchmann, Bertrand Michael. 1999. "Das Dilemma des Konservativismus in der beginnenden Moderne: Die Zeit des Neoabsolutismus." In Rill, *Konservatismus,* 89–108.

Budil, Ivo, and Miroslav Šedivý, eds. 2009. *Metternich & jeho doba.* Pilsen.

Burgdorf, Wolfgang. 2006. *Ein Weltbild verliert seine Welt: Der Untergang des Alten Reiches und die Generation 1806.* Munich.

Büsch, Otto, ed. 1992. *Handbuch der preußischen Geschichte,* Vol. 2: *Das 19. Jahrhundert und Große Themen der Geschichte Preußens.* Berlin.

Buschmann, Nikolaus, and Dieter Langewiesche, eds. 2003. *Der Krieg in den Gründungsmythen europäischer Nationen und der USA.* Frankfurt a. M.

Büssem, Eberhard. 1972. *Die Karlsbader Beschlüsse von 1819: Die endgültige Stabilisierung der restaurativen Politik im Deutschen Bund nach dem Wiener Kongress von 1814/15.* Munich.

Carl, Horst. 2008. "Erinnerungsbruch als Bedingung der Moderne? Tradition und bewusste Neuorientierung bei Hof und Zeremoniell nach 1806." In Klinger, *Das Jahr 1806,* 169–184.

Cartland, Barbara. 1964. *Metternich, the Passionate Diplomat.* London.

Castelot, André. 1980. *Talleyrand ou le cynisme.* Paris.

Cecil, Algernon. 1933 (3rd ed., 1947). *Metternich, 1773–1859: A Study of His Period and Personality.* London.

Cerman, Ivo, and Luboš Velek, eds. 2009. *Adel und Wirtschaft: Lebensunterhalt der Adeligen in der Moderne.* Munich.

———, eds. 2006. *Adelige Ausbildung: Die Herausforderung der Aufklärung und die Folgen.* Munich.

Cerman, Markus, and Hermann Zeitlhofer, eds. 2002. *Soziale Strukturen in Böhmen: Ein regionaler Vergleich von Wirtschaft und Gesellschaft in Gutsherrschaften, 16.–19. Jahrhundert.* Vienna.

Chvojka, Michal. 2010. *Josef Graf Sedlnitzky als Präsident der Polizei- und Zensurhofstelle in Wien (1817–1848): Ein Beitrag zur Geschichte der Staatspolizei in der Habsburgermonarchie.* Frankfurt a. M.

Clausewitz, Carl. 1993. *On War.* London.

Clewing, Konrad, and Oliver Jens Schmitt, eds. 2011. *Geschichte Südosteuropas vom frühen Mittelalter bis zur Gegenwart.* Regensburg.

Conrad, Sebastian, and Jürgen Osterhammel, eds. 2016. *1750–1870: Wege zur modernen Welt.* C. H. Beck / Harvard University Press. Geschichte der Welt, vol. 4. Munich.

Conze, Eckart, and Monika Wienfort, eds. 2004. *Adel und Moderne: Deutschland im europäischen Vergleich im 19. und 20. Jahrhundert.* Cologne.

Coons, Ronald E. 1977. "Metternich and the Lloyd Austriaco." *Mitteilungen des Österreichischen Staatsarchivs* 30: 49–66.

Corti, Egon Conte. 1948–1949. *Metternich und die Frauen.* 2 vols. Zurich.

Cromwell, Judith Lissauer. 2007. *Dorothea Lieven: A Russian Princess in London and Paris, 1785–1857.* Jefferson, NC.

Cwik, Christian. 2014. "Die amerikanische Dimension des Wiener Kongresses." In Just, *Wiener Kongress,* 120–145.

Dann, Otto, ed. 1994. *Die deutsche Nation: Geschichte, Probleme, Perspektiven.* Greifswald.

———. 2006. "The Invention of National Languages." In Blanning and Schulze, *Unity and Diversity,* 121–133.

Dard, Émile. 1933. "Les Mémoires de Caulaincourt." *Revue d'histoire diplomatique* 47: 368–453.

———. 1937. *Napoleon and Talleyrand.* Trans. C. R. Turner. New York.

Darwin, John. 2007. *After Tamerlane: The Rise and Fall of Global Empires, 1400–2000.* London.

———. 2012. *Unfinished Empire: The Global Expansion of Britain.* London.

Daum, Werner. 2005. *Oszillationen des Gemeingeistes: Öffentlichkeit, Buchhandel und Kommunikation in der Revolution des Königreichs beider Sizilien, 1820 / 21.* Cologne.

Demel, Walter, and Sylvia Schraut. 2014. *Der deutsche Adel: Lebensformen und Geschichte.* Munich.

Demelić, Vera von. 1907. "Fürst Metternich und der Uebertritt des Herzogs Karl II. von Lucca zum Protestantismus." *Deutsche Revue* 32, no. 4 (Dezember): 275–292.

Doering-Manteuffel, Anselm. 1993. *Die deutsche Frage und das europäische Staatensystem, 1815–1871.* Munich.

———. 1991. *Vom Wiener Kongreß bis zur Pariser Konferenz: England, die deutsche Frage und das europäische Mächtesystem, 1815–1856.* Göttingen.

Dortiguier, Pierre. 1997. "Metternich, le Taureau Blanc: De la philosophie politique du Prince-Chancelier." In *L'Autriche et l'idée d'Europe,* ed. Michel Reffet, 243–258. Dijon.

Dowe, Dieter, et al., eds. 1998. *Europa 1848: Revolution und Reform.* Bonn.

Droysen, Johann Gustav. 1974. *Historik. Vorlesungen über Enzyklopädie und Methodologie der Geschichte.* Ed. Rudolf Hübner. Darmstadt.

Duchhardt, Heinz. 2012. *Frieden im Europa der Vormoderne: Ausgewählte Aufsätze, 1979–2011.* Ed. Martin Espenhorst. Paderborn.

———. 2007. *Stein: Eine Biographie.* Münster.

———. 2013. *Der Wiener Kongress: Die Neugestaltung Europas, 1814/15.* Munich.

Duchkowitsch, Wolfgang. 2000. "Beschattet und gejagt vom Kanzler Metternich. Österreichische Publizisten im deutschen Exil." In *Deutsche Publizistik im Exil 1933 bis 1945: Personen—Positionen—Perspektiven,* ed. Markus Behmer, 31–45. Münster.

Dumont, Franz. 1982. *Die Mainzer Republik von 1792/93.* Alzey.

Dwyer, Philip. 2013. *Citizen Emperor: Napoleon in Power.* London.

———, and Peter McPhee, eds. 2002. *The French Revolution and Napoleon: A Sourcebook.* London.

Ebert, Sabine. 2015. *1815. Blutfrieden.* Munich.

Echternkamp, Jörg. 1998. *Der Aufstieg des deutschen Nationalismus (1770–1840).* Frankfurt a. M.

Eigenwill, Reinhardt. 2005. "Wiederherstellung des europäischen Gleichgewichts: Das Zusammentreffen Napoleons I. mit Metternich im Sommer 1813." *Dresdner Hefte* 23, no. 83: 45–50.

Eimer, Manfred. 1897. *Die politischen Verhältnisse und Bewegungen in Straßburg im Elsaß im Jahre 1789.* Strasbourg.

Endres, Rudolf. 2003. "Lieber Sauhirt in der Türkei als Standesherr in Württemberg." In *Alte Klöster–Neue Herren: Die Säkularisation im deutschen Südwesten, 1803,* vol. 2, 837–856. Sigmaringen.

Erbe, Günter. 2009. *Dorothea Herzogin von Sagan (1793–1862): Eine deutsch-französische Karriere.* Cologne.

———. 2007. "Wilhelmine von Sagan (1781–1839)." *Schlesische Lebensbilder* 9: 229–239.

Erbe, Michael. 2004. *Revolutionäre Erschütterung und erneuertes Gleichgewicht: Internationale Beziehungen, 1785–1830.* Handbuch der Geschichte der Internationalen Beziehungen, vol. 5. Paderborn.

Evans, Richard. 1994. "Nipperdeys Neunzehntes Jahrhundert." *Geschichte und Gesellschaft* 20: 119–139.

Externbrink, Sven. 2009. "Kulturtransfer, Internationale Beziehungen und die 'Generation Metternich' zwischen Französischer Revolution, Restauration und Revolution von 1848." In Pyta, *Das europäische Mächtekonzert,* 59–78.

Fahrmeir, Andreas. 2010. *Revolutionen und Reformen: Europa, 1789–1850*. Munich.

Fehrenbach, Elisabeth, ed. 1994. *Adel und Bürgertum in Deutschland: 1770–1848*. Munich.

Fink, Humbert. 1989. *Metternich: Staatsmann, Spieler, Kavalier*. Munich.

Fischer, Bernhard. 2014. *Johann Friedrich Cotta: Verleger—Entrepreneur—Politiker*. Göttingen.

Fischer, Wolfram, et al., eds. 1993. *Handbuch der europäischen Wirtschafts- und Sozialge-schichte*. Vol. 4. Stuttgart. (Contains "Alte Maße und Gewichte in Europa" [Old measures and weights of Europe].)

Förderverein "Historisches Torhaus zu Markkleeberg 1813," ed. 2013. *1813: Kampf für Europa. Die Österreicher in der Völkerschlacht bei Leipzig*. Markkleeberg.

Forgó, Hannelore. 1966. *Fürst Richard Metternich*. Diss. (typescript), Vienna. (Contains a genealogical map of Metternich's descendants.)

Forrest, Alan. 2011. *Napoleon*. London.

Fournier, August. 1900. *Der Congress von Châtillon: Die Politik im Kriege von 1814*. Vienna.

———. 1880. *Gentz und Cobenzl: Geschichte der österreichischen Diplomatie in den Jahren 1801–1805*. Vienna.

———. 1885. "Julie von Krüdener." In Fournier, *Historische Studien und Skizzen*, 331–348. Prague.

———. 1903. *Napoleon I: A Biography*. New York.

Frie, Ewald. 2001. *Friedrich August Ludwig von der Marwitz: 1777–1837: Biographien [sic] eines Preußen*. Paderborn.

Friese, Johannes. 1801. *Neue Vaterländische Geschichte der Stadt Straßburg*. Vol. 5. Strasbourg.

Frohmann, Inge. 1954. *Das Bild Metternichs in der deutschen Geschichtsliteratur mit beson-derer Berücksichtigung der Biographien*. Diss. (typescript), Graz.

Furlani, Silvio. 1960. "L'Austria e la questione Carignano alla vigilia del Congresso di Ve-rone." *Bollettino Storico-Bibliografico Subalpino* 58: 116–153.

Füssel, Marian. 2013. *Der Siebenjährige Krieg: Ein Weltkrieg im 18. Jahrhundert*. Munich.

Gall, Lothar, ed. 1998. *1848: Aufbruch zur Freiheit*. Berlin.

———. 1996. "Die Nationalisierung Europas seit der Französischen Revolution." In *Lothar Gall: Bürgertum, liberale Bewegung und Nation: Ausgewählte Aufsätze*, ed. Dieter Hein et al., 205–216. Munich.

———. 2011. *Wilhelm von Humboldt: Ein Preuße von Welt*. Berlin.

Gash, Norman. 1979. *Aristocracy and People: Britain, 1815–1866*. London.

Gehler, Michael, et al., eds. 1996. *Ungleiche Partner? Österreich und Deutschland im 19. und 20. Jahrhundert*. Stuttgart.

Geisthövel, Alexa. 2008. *Restauration und Vormärz: 1815–1847*. Paderborn.

Gersmann, Gudrun. 1993. "Der Schatten des toten Königs: Zur Debatte um die Régicides in der Restauration." In *Frankreich 1815–1830: Trauma oder Utopie? Die Gesellschaft der Res-tauration und das Erbe der Revolution*, ed. Gudrun Gersmann and Hubertus Kohle, 41–59. Stuttgart.

Giese, Ursula. 1964. "Studie zur Geschichte der Pressegesetzgebung, der Zensur und des Zeitungswesens im frühen Vormärz." *Archiv für Geschichte des Buchwesens* 6: 341–546.

Gill, John H. 2008–2010. *1809: Thunder on the Danube: Napoleon's Defeat of the Habsburgs.* 3 vols. London.

Godsey, William D. 2015. "Das Habsburgerreich während der Napoleonischen Kriege und des Wiener Kongresses." In Husslein-Arco, *Europa in Wien,* 29–35.

Goethe, Johann Wolfgang. (1908) 2011. "The Campaign in France." In *The Life and Works of Goethe: With Sketches of His Age and Contempories,* ed. George Henry Lewes, 140–153. Cambridge.

———. 2005. *Faust: Part I.* Trans. David Constantine. London.

Gollwitzer, Heinz. 1964. *Die Standesherren: Ein Beitrag zur deutschen Sozialgeschichte.* Göttingen.

Griewank, Karl. 1954. *Der Wiener Kongress und die europäische Restauration, 1814/15.* Leipzig.

Grobauer, Franz Josef. 1959. *Metternich, der Kutscher Europas.* Vienna. (2nd edition, 1961: *Ein Kämpfer für Europa.*)

Gruner, Wolf D. 2012. *Der Deutsche Bund: 1815–1866.* Munich.

———. 1985. *Die deutsche Frage: Ein Problem der europäischen Geschichte seit 1800.* Munich.

———. 2014. *Der Wiener Kongress, 1814/15.* Stuttgart.

Grunwald, Constantin de. 1938. *La vie de Metternich.* Paris.

Haas, Arthur G. 1963. *Metternich, Reorganization and Nationality, 1813–1818: A Story of Foresight and Frustration in the Rebuilding of the Austrian Empire.* Wiesbaden.

Hachtmann, Rüdiger. 2008. "Hinabgestiegen von den Barrikaden? Revolutionäre und gegenrevolutionäre Gewalt 1848/49." In *Gewalt im politischen Raum: Fallanalysen vom Spätmittelalter bis ins 20. Jahrhundert,* ed. Neithard Bulst et al., 134–163. Frankfurt a. M.

Haefs, Wilhelm, and York-Gothart Mix, eds. 2007. *Zensur im Jahrhundert der Aufklärung: Geschichte—Theorie—Praxis.* Göttingen.

Hafner, D. L. 1980. "Castlereagh, the Balance of Power, and 'Non-Intervention.'" *Australian Journal of Politics and History* 26: 71–84.

Hahn, Hans-Werner. 1996. "Wirtschaftspolitische Offensive mit deutschlandpolitischem Langzeiteffekt? Der Zollverein von 1834 in preußischer Perspektive." In Gehler, *Ungleiche Partner,* 95–111.

———, and Helmut Berding. 2010. *Reformen, Restauration und Revolution: 1806–1848/49.* Gebhardt Handbuch der deutschen Geschichte, vol. 14. Stuttgart.

Hamm, Margot, et al., eds. 2015. *Napoleon und Bayern: Katalog zur Bayerischen Landesausstellung, 2015.* Augsburg.

Hantsch, Hugo. 1966. "Metternich und das Nationalitätenproblem." *Der Donauraum: Zeitschrift des Institutes für den Donauraum und Mitteleuropa* 11: 51–63.

Hardtwig, Wolfgang. 1985. *Vormärz: Der monarchische Staat und das Bürgertum.* Munich.

Hartau, Friedrich. 1977. *Clemens Fürst von Metternich in Selbstzeugnissen und Bilddokumenten.* Reinbek.

Hartmann, Peter C., and Florian Schuller, eds. 2006. *Das Heilige Römische Reich und sein Ende, 1806: Zäsur in der deutschen und europäischen Geschichte.* Regensburg.

Hattenhauer, Christian. 1995. *Wahl und Krönung Franz II. AD 1792.* Frankfurt a. M.

Häusler, Wolfgang. 2013. "'Krieg ist das Losungswort! Sieg! Und so tönt es fort!': Deutsche und Österreicher für, mit und gegen Napoleon Bonaparte." In *Helden nach Maß,* ed. Stadtgeschichtliches Museum, 37–46. Leipzig.

———. 2001. "Politische und soziale Probleme des Vormärz in den Dichtungen Karl Becks." In *Bewegung im Reich der Immobilität. Revolutionen in der Habsbewegung im Reich der Immobilität. Revolutionen in der Habsburgermonarchie, 1848–1849: Literarisch-publizistische Auseinandersetzungen,* ed. Hubert Lengauer and Primus Heinz Kucher, 266–298. Vienna.

Heigel, Carl Theodor. 1872. *Ludwig I., König von Bayern.* Leipzig.

Heigel, Karl Theodor von. 1902. "Das Manifest des Herzogs von Braunschweig vom 25. Juli 1792." In Heigel, *Neue geschichtliche Essays,* 138–184. Munich.

Helfert, Joseph Alexander Freiherr von. 1867. *Kaiser Franz und die europäischen Befreiungskriege gegen Napoleon I.* Vienna.

———. 1873. *Maria Louise, Erzherzogin von Oesterreich, Kaiserin der Franzosen.* Vienna.

Herman, Arthur. 1932. *Metternich.* New York.

Herre, Franz. 1983. *Metternich: Staatsmann des Friedens.* Cologne.

Hershan, Stella K. 1973. *The Naked Angel.* London.

Heydemann, Günther. 1985. *Carl Ludwig Sand: Die Tat als Attentat.* Hof.

———. 1995. *Konstitution gegen Revolution: Die britische Deutschland- und Italienpolitik, 1815–1848.* Göttingen.

Heyden-Rynsch, Verena von der. 1992. *Europäische Salons: Höhepunkte einer versunkenen weiblichen Kultur.* Düsseldorf.

Hilbert, Wilfried. 1964. "Metternich était-il un Européen?" *Synthèses: Revue Internationale* 19: 432–441, Brussels.

Himmelein, Volker, and Hans Ulrich Rudolf, eds. 2003. *Alte Klöster, neue Herren: Die Säkularisation im deutschen Südwesten.* Vols 1 and 2, parts 1–2. Ostfildern.

Hirschfeld, [Gustav]. 1929. *Fürst Metternich und Herzog Ernst I. von Sachsen-Coburg und Gotha.* Coburg.

Höbelt, Lothar. 1999. "Die Konservativen Alt-Österreichs 1848 bis 1918: Parteien und Politik." In Rill, *Konservativismus,* 109–152.

———. 1998. *1848: Österreich und die deutsche Revolution.* Vienna.

Hobsbawm, Eric. 1990. *Nations and Nationalisms since 1780: Programme, Myth, Reality.* Cambridge.

———, and Terence Ranger, eds. (1984) 2005. *The Invention of Tradition.* Cambridge.

Hoefer, Frank Thomas. 1983. *Pressepolitik und Polizeistaat Metternichs: Die Überwachung von Presse und politischer Öffentlichkeit in Deutschland und den Nachbarstaaten durch das Mainzer Informationsbüro (1833–1848).* Munich.

Hoffmann, Gabriele. 2012. *Die Eisfestung: Hamburg im kalten Griff Napoleons.* Munich.

Hofschröer, Peter. 2013. *1813: Die Napoleonischen Befreiungskriege: Großgörschen (Lützen), Bautzen, Leipzig.* Königswinter. (Originally published in two parts in English as *Leipzig*

1813: The Battle of the Nations, Oxford 1993; and *Lützen & Bautzen 1813: The Turning Point,* Oxford 2011).

Hormayr, Josef von. 1848. *Kaiser Franz und Metternich.* Leipzig.

Huber, Ernst Rudolf. 1960–1963. *Deutsche Verfassungsgeschichte seit 1789.* Vols. 1–3. Stuttgart. (Reprinted 1975).

Hüffer, Hermann. 1868–1869. *Diplomatische Verhandlungen aus der Zeit der französischen Revolution.* Vol. 1 and supplementary volume, *Oestreich und Preußen gegenüber der französischen Revolution bis zum Abschluss des Friedens von Campo Formio.* Bonn.

———. 1878–1879. *Diplomatische Verhandlungen aus der Zeit der französischen Revolution.* Vol. 2, parts 1–2. *Der rastatter [sic] Congreß und die zweite Coalition.* Bonn.

Hundt, Michael. 1996. *Die Mindermächtigen deutschen Staaten auf dem Wiener Kongress.* Mainz.

Hunecke, Volker. 2011. *Napoleon: Das Scheitern eines guten Diktators.* Paderborn.

Hurd, Douglas. 2010. *Choose Your Weapons: The British Foreign Secretary.* London.

Husslein-Arco, Agnes, Sabine Grabner, and Werner Telesko, eds. 2015. *Europa in Wien: Der Wiener Kongress, 1814 / 15.* Vienna.

Jaeger, Friedrich, and Jörn Rüsen. 1992. *Geschichte des Historismus: Eine Einführung.* Munich.

Jansen, Christian. 2007. "'Revolution'—'Realismus'—'Realpolitik': Der nachrevolutionäre Paradigmenwechsel in den 1850er Jaharen im deutschen oppositionellen Diskurs und sein historischer Kontext." In *Weltanschauung, Philosophie und Naturwissenschaft im 19. Jahrhundert.* Vol. 1: *Der Materialismus-Streit,* ed. Kurt Bayertz et al., 223–259. Hamburg.

———. 2000. "Der schwierige Weg zur Realpolitik: Liberale und Demokraten zwischen Paulskirche und Erfurter Union." In *Die Erfurter Union und das Erfurter Unionsparlament, 1850,* ed. Gunther Mai, 341–368. Cologne.

Johnson, Paul. 1991. *The Birth of the Modern: World Society 1815–1830.* New York.

Jørgensen, Sven Aage, Klaus Bohnen, and Per Øhrgaard. 1990. *Aufklärung, Sturm und Drang, frühe Klassik: 1740–1789.* De Boor / Newald Geschichte der deutschen Literatur, vol. 4. Munich.

Judson, Pieter M. 2016. *The Habsburg Monarchy: A New History.* Cambridge, MA.

Judt, Tony, and Denis Lacorne, eds. 2004. *Language, Nation, and State: Identity Politics in a Multilingual Age.* New York.

Juhel, Pierre O. 2013. "1813—Das Jahr eines Weltkriegs?" In Bauer, *Blutige Romantik,* 40–51.

Jung, Willy, ed. 2015. *Napolén Bonaparte oder der entfesselte Prometheus: Napoléon Bonaparte ou Prométhee déchaîné.* Bonn.

Just, Thomas, Wolfgang Maderthaner, and Helene Maimann, eds. 2014. *Der Wiener Kongress: Die Erfindung Europas.* Vienna.

Kadletz-Schöffel, Hedwig. 1992. *Metternich und die Wissenschaften.* Vienna.

———, and Karl Kadletz. 2000. "Metternich (1773–1859) und die Geowissenschaften." *Geschichte der Erdwissenschaften in Österreich: Berichte der Geologischen Bundesanstalt* 51: 49–52.

Kaernbach, Andreas. 1991. *Bismarcks Konzepte zur Reform des Deutschen Bundes: Zur Kontinuität der Politik Bismarcks und Preußens in der deutschen Frage.* Göttingen.

Kaiser, Reinhard. 2016. *Der glückliche Kunsträuber: Das Leben des Vivant Denon.* Munich.

Kammerer, Frithjof. 1958. *Die Pressepolitik Metternichs: Versuch einer Gesamtdarstellung.* Diss. (typescript), Vienna.

Kann, Robert A. 1990. *Geschichte des Habsburgerreiches, 1526 bis 1918.* Vienna.

Kant, Immanuel. (1784) 1970. "Idea for a Universal History with a Cosmopolitan Purpose." In *Kant's Political Writings,* ed. Hans Reiss, 41–53. Cambridge.

———. (1784) 1964. "Idee zu einer allgemeinen Geschichte in weltbürgerlicher Absicht." In *Werke,* vol. 4, ed. Wilhelm Weischedel. Darmstadt.

Kennan, George F. 1993. *Around the Cragged Hill: A Personal and Political Philosophy.* New York.

———. 1979. *The Decline of Bismarck's European Order: Franco-Russian Relations, 1875–1890.* Princeton, NJ.

Kerchnawe, Hugo, and Alois Veltzé. 1913. *Feldmarschall Karl Fürst zu Schwarzenberg, der Führer der Verbündeten in den Befreiungskriegen.* Vienna.

King, David. 2008. *Vienna, 1814.* New York.

Kissinger, Henry Alfred. 1957. *A World Restored: Metternich, Castlereagh and the Problems of Peace, 1812–22.* London.

Kleist, Heinrich von. (1805) 2010. "On the Gradual Formulation of Thoughts while Speaking." In *Selected Prose of Heinrich von Kleist,* 255–263. Brooklyn.

Klinger, Andreas, Hans-Werner Hahn, and Georg Schmidt, eds. 2008. *Das Jahr 1806 im europäischen Kontext: Balance, Hegemonie und politische Kulturen.* Cologne.

Klueting, Harm. 1986. *Die Lehre von der Macht der Staaten: Das außerpolitische Machtproblem in der "politischen Wissenschaft" und in der praktischen Politik im 18. Jahrhundert.* Berlin.

Knöbl, Wolfgang. 2007. *Die Kontingenz der Moderne: Wege in Europa, Asien und Amerika.* Frankfurt a. M.

Koch, Christoph Wilhelm. 1807–1809. *Gemählde der Revolutionen in Europa: Seit dem Umsturze des Römischen Kaiserthums im Occident bis auf unsere Zeiten.* 3 vols. Berlin.

Kohler, J. C. 1844. *Die staatsrechtlichen Verhältnisse des mittelbar gewordenen vormals reichsständischen Adels in Deutschland.* Sulzbach.

Koll, Johannes. 2003. *"Die belgische Nation": Patriotismus und Nationalbewusstsein in den Südlichen Niederlanden im späten 18. Jahrhundert.* Münster.

Koselleck, Reinhart. 1972. "Einleitung." In *Geschichtliche Grundbegriffe,* vol. 1, xiii–xxvii. Stuttgart.

———. 1969. *Das Zeitalter der europäischen Revolution, 1780–1848,* ed. Louis Bergeron, François Furet, and Reinhart Koselleck, chaps. 7–10 [1815–1847]. Frankfurt a. M.

Kraehe, Enno Edward, ed. 1971. *The Metternich Controversy.* New York.

———. 1963 / 1983. *Metternich's German Policy.* 2 vols. Princeton, NJ.

Kraus, Hans-Christof. 1999. "Die politische Romantik in Wien: Friedrich Schlegel und Adam Müller." In Rill, *Konservativismus,* 35–70.

Kronenbitter, Günther. 1999. "Friedrich von Gentz und Metternich." In Rill, *Konservativismus,* 71–88.

————. 1994. *Wort und Macht: Friedrich Gentz als politischer Schriftsteller.* Berlin.

Kuhn, Axel, and Jörg Schweigard. 2005. *Freiheit oder Tod! Die deutsche Studentenbewegung zur Zeit der Französischen Revolution.* Cologne.

Kuster, Thomas. 2004. "Die Italienreise Kaiser Franz' I. von Österreich, 1819." *Römische Historische Mitteilungen* 46: 305–334.

Lachenicht, Susanne. 2004. *Information und Propaganda: Die Presse deutscher Jakobiner im Elsaß (1791–1800).* Munich.

Landesmuseum Württemberg. 2013. *Im Glanz der Zaren: Die Romanows, Württemberg und Europa.* Ulm.

Langewiesche, Dieter. 2014. "Kongress-Europa: Der Wiener Kongress und die internationale Ordnung im 19. Jahrhundert." In Just, *Wiener Kongress,* 14–35.

————. 2013. *Die Monarchie im Jahrhundert Europas: Selbstbehauptung durch Wandel im 19. Jahrhundert.* Heidelberg.

————. 2008. "Nation, nationale Bewegung, Nationalstaat in den europäischen Revolutionen von 1848: Demokratische Hoffnung und Kriegsgefahr." In Langewiesche, *Reich, Nation, Föderation,* 259–276.

————. 2000. *Nation, Nationalismus, Nationalstaat in Deutschland und Europa.* Munich.

————. 2008. *Reich, Nation, Föderation: Deutschland und Europa.* Munich.

————. 2012. "Zum Wandel sozialer Ordnungen durch Krieg und Revolution: Europa 1848—Wissenserzeugung durch Wissensvermittlung." In *Gewalträume: Soziale Ordnungen im Ausnahmezustand,* ed. Jörg Baberowski and Gabriele Metzler, 93–134. Frankfurt a. M.

Lauenberg, Diana Grazia. 1992. *Die Auswirkungen der Pariser Julirevolution von 1830 auf die Wiener Presse unter Berücksichtigung der absolutistischen Politik des Staatskanzlers Metternich.* Diss. (typescript), Vienna.

Lechner, Silvester. 1977. *Gelehrte Kritik und Restauration: Metternichs Wissenschafts- und Pressepolitik und die Wiener "Jahrbücher der Literatur" (1818–1849).* Tübingen.

Lefebvre, Georges. (1935) 2003. *Napoleon.* Ed. Peter Schöttler. Stuttgart.

Lentz, Thierry. 2013. *Le congrès de Vienne: Une refondation de l'Europe, 1814–1815.* Paris.

Leonhard, Jörn. 2008. *Bellizismus und Nation: Kriegsdeutung und Nationsbestimmung in Europa und den Vereinigten Staaten, 1750–1914.* Munich.

————, and Ulrike von Hirschhausen, eds. 2011. *Empires und Nationalstaaten im 19. Jahrhundert.* Göttingen.

Liechtenstern, Joseph Marx v. 1817–1818. *Handbuch der neuesten Geographie des Österreichischen Kaiserstaates.* 3 vols. Vienna.

Lieven, Dominic. 2009. *Russia against Napoleon: The Battle for Europe, 1807 to 1814.* London.

Linden, Marcel van der. 2014. "Zur Logik einer Nicht-Entscheidung: Der Wiener Kongress und der Sklavenhandel." In Just, *Wiener Kongress,* 354–373.

Lorenz, Ottokar. 1862. *Joseph II. und die Belgische Revolution: Nach den Papieren des General-Gouverneurs Grafen Murray, 1787.* Vienna.

Lutz, Heinrich. 1985. *Zwischen Habsburg und Preußen: Deutschland, 1815–1866.* Berlin.

Mader, Eric-Oliver. 2005. *Die letzten "Priester der Gerechtigkeit": Die Auseinandersetzung der letzten Generation von Richtern des Reichskammergerichts mit der Auflösung des Heiligen Römischen Reiches Deutscher Nation.* Berlin.

Magenschab, Hans. 2002. *Erzherzog Johann: Habsburgs grüner Rebell.* Munich.

Malleson, G[eorge] B[ruce]. 1888. *Life of Prince Metternich.* London.

Mascilli Migliorini, Luigi. 2014. *Metternich: L'artefice dell'Europa nata dal Congresso di Vienna.* Salerno.

Mathy, Helmut. 1968. "Ein berühmter Student der Mainzer Universität: Die diplomatischen Lehr- und Wanderjahre Metternichs." *Jahrbuch der Vereinigung "Freunde der Universität Mainz"* 17.

———. 1971. "Die Entlassung des österreichischen Gesandten Franz Georg von Metternich aus Mainz im Jahre 1785." *Mainzer Zeitschrift* 66: 73–95.

———. 1969. *Franz Georg von Metternich, der Vater des Staatskanzlers.* Meisenheim.

Mattern, Pierre. 2011. *"Kotzebue's Allgewalt": Literarische Fehde und politisches Attentat.* Würzburg.

Mattl-Wurm, Sylvia. 2014. "'La haute volaille de Vienne—Intelligänse und Elegänse': Politisierende Frauen und Frauen der Politik, 1814 / 15." In Just, *Wiener Kongress,* 338–351.

Mayr, Josef Karl. 1939. "Aufbau und Arbeitsweise des Wiener Kongresses." *Archivalische Zeitschrift* 45: 64–127.

———. 1935. *Geschichte der österreichischen Staatskanzlei im Zeitalter des Fürsten Metternich.* Inventare des Wiener Haus-, Hof- und Staatsarchivs V, 2. Vienna.

———. 1934. *Metternichs geheimer Briefdienst: Postlogen und Postkurse.* Inventare des Wiener Haus-, Hof- und Staatsarchivs V, 1. Vienna.

Mazohl, Brigitte. 2005. *Zeitenwende 1806: Das Heilige Römische Reich und die Geburt des modernen Europa.* Vienna.

Mazohl-Wallnig, Brigitte. 1993. *Österreichischer Verwaltungsstaat und administrative Eliten im Königreich Lombardo-Venetien, 1815–1859.* Mainz.

Mazower, Mark. 2013. *Governing the World: The History of an Idea.* London.

McGuigan, Dorothy Gies. 1975. *Metternich and the Duchess.* New York.

McLynn, Frank. 2002. *Napoleon: A Biography.* New York.

Meinecke, Friedrich. 1962. *Weltbürgertum und Nationalstaat.* Ed. Hans Herzfeld. Munich.

Melville, Ralph. 1998. *Adel und Revolution in Böhmen: Strukturwandel von Herrschaft und Gesellschaft in Österreich um die Mitte des 19. Jahrhunderts.* Mainz.

Menger, Philipp. 2014. *Die Heilige Allianz: Religion und Politik bei Alexander I. (1801–1825).* Stuttgart.

Meyer, Arnold Oskar. 1924. *Fürst Metternich.* Einzelschriften zur Politik und Geschichte 5. Berlin.

Mieck, Ilja. 1992. "Preußen von 1807 bis 1850: Reformen, Restauration und Revolution." In Büsch, *Handbuch,* 3–292.

Mignet, F. A. 1826. *History of the French Revolution from 1789 to 1814.* London.

Mikoletzky, Lorenz. 1990. "Ferdinand I. von Österreich: 1835–1848." In Schindling, *Kaiser der Neuzeit,* 329–339.

Milne, Andrew. 1975. *Metternich.* London.

Missoffe, Michel. 1959. *Metternich, 1773–1859.* Paris.

Mitterer, Karl Anton. 2013. *"Die Rolle Österreichs im Feldzug, 1813."* In Förderverein, ed., *Kampf für Europa,* 16–27.

Molden, Ernst. 1917. *Ein österreichischer Kanzler: Der Fürst von Metternich.* Österreichische Bibliothek, no. 27. Leipzig.

Möller, Frank. 2004. *Heinrich von Gagern: Eine Biographie.* Munich.

Moritz, Verena, and Hannes Leidinger. 2014. "Der Überwachungsstaat: Polizei, Geheimdienst und Zensur: Der Wiener Kongress und die Kontinuität staatlicher Kontrolle." In Just, *Wiener Kongress,* 162–179.

Morley, John. 1908. *The Life of Richard Cobden.* 2 vols. London.

Mraz, Gerda, and Gottfried Mraz. 1981. *Österreichische Profile.* Vienna.

Müchler, Günter. 2012. *1813: Napoleon, Metternich und das weltgeschichtliche Duell von Dresden.* Darmstadt.

Müller, Jürgen. 2006. *Der Deutsche Bund, 1815–1866.* Munich.

———. 1991. "Reichsstädtisches Selbstverständnis, traditionales Bürgerrecht und staatsbürgerliche Gleichstellung in Speyer vom Ancien Régime zur napoleonischen Zeit." In *Die Französische Revolution und die Oberrheinlande (1789–1798),* ed. Volker Rödel, 127–146. *Oberrheinische Studien* vol. 9. Sigmaringen.

Münkler, Herfried. 2007. *Empires.* Cambridge.

———. 2005. *The New Wars.* Cambridge.

———. 2011. *Über den Krieg: Stationen der Kriegsgeschichte im Spiegel ihrer theoretischen Reflexion.* Weilerswist.

Nenon, Monika. 2002. "Sophie von La Roches literarische Salongeselligkeit in Koblenz-Ehrenbreitstein, 1771–1780." *German Quarterly* 75, no. 3: 282–296.

Neuhaus, Helmut. 2004. "Das Reich als Mythos in der neueren Geschichte." In Helmut Altrichter et al., eds., *Mythen in der Geschichte,* 293–320. Freiburg.

Nicosia, Alessandro, ed. 2011. *1861–2011: Regioni e Testimonianze d'Italie.* Vol. 1: *I Luoghi: Le Testimonianze.* Vol. 2: *Le Regioni.* Rome.

Nipperdey, Thomas. 1983. *Deutsche Geschichte.* Vol. 1: *Bürgerwelt und starker Staat.* Munich.

———. 1976. "Historismus und Historismuskritik." In Nipperdey, *Gesellschaft, Kultur, Theorie: Gesammelte Aufsätze zur neueren Geschichte,* 59–73. Göttingen.

Oer, Rudolfine Freiin von. 1965. *Der Friede von Preßburg: Ein Beitrag zur Diplomatiegeschichte des napoleonischen Zeitalters.* Münster.

Okey, Robin. 2001. *The Habsburg Monarchy c. 1765–1918: From Enlightenment to Eclipse.* New York.

Oncken, Wilhelm. 1883. "Aus den letzten Monaten des Jahres 1813." In *Historisches Taschenbuch,* 1–40. Leipzig.

————. 1885. "Lord Castlereagh und die Ministerconferenz zu Langres am 29. Januar 1814." In *Historisches Taschenbuch*, 1–52. Leipzig.

————. 1876–1879. *Oesterreich und Preußen im Befreiungskriege: Urkundliche Aufschlüsse über die politische Geschichte des Jahres 1813*. 2 vols. Berlin.

————. 1884–1886. *Das Zeitalter der Revolution, des Kaiserreiches und der Befreiungskriege*. 2 vols. Berlin.

Opitz, Claudia, Ulrike Weckel, and Elke Kleinau, eds. 2000. *Tugend, Vernunft und Gefühl: Geschlechterdiskurse der Aufklärung und weibliche Lebenswelten*. Münster.

Osterhammel, Jürgen. 2014. *The Transformation of the World: A Global History of the Nineteenth Century*. Princeton, NJ.

Otto, Friedrich. 1897 / 1898. "A. J. Hofmann, Präsident des rheinisch-deutschen National-konvents zu Mainz: Seine Sendung nach England in den Jahren 1793, 1794, 1795 nebst einigen anderen Nachrichten über sein Leben." *Annalen des Vereins für Nassauische Altertumskunde* 29: 77–92. (Contains "Rapport: Observations que j'ai faites pendant mon séjour en Engleterre [*sic*]," 84–89.)

Ouvrard, Robert. 2014. *Le Congrès de Vienne (1814–1815): Carnet mondain et éphémérides*. Paris.

Paléologe, Georges Maurice. 1924. *Romantisme et diplomatie: Talleyrand, Metternich et Chateaubriand*. Paris.

Palmer, Alan. (1974) 2010. *Alexander I: The Tsar of War and Peace*. London.

————. 1972. *Metternich: Councillor of Europe*. London.

————. 1967. *Napoleon in Russia*. New York.

Paravicini, Werner. 1994. *Die ritterlich-höfische Kultur des Mittelalters*. Munich.

Pertz, Georg Heinrich. 1849–1855. *Das Leben des Ministers Freiherrn vom Stein*. 6 vols. Berlin.

Petschar, Hans. 2011. *Altösterreich: Menschen, Länder und Völker in der Habsburgermonarchie*. Vienna.

Planert, Ute. 2007. *Der Mythos vom Befreiungskrieg: Frankreichs Kriege und der deutsche Süden: Alltag, Wahrnehmung, Deutung, 1792–1841*. Paderborn.

————, ed. 2016. *Napoleon's Empire: European Politics in Global Perspective*. New York.

————. 2001. "Zwischen Alltag, Mentalität und Erinnerungskultur. Erfahrungsgeschichte an der Schwelle zum nationalen Zeitalter." In *Die Erfahrung des Krieges*, ed. Nikolaus Buschmann and Horst Carl, 51–66. Paderborn.

Platthaus, Andreas. 2013. *1813. Die Völkerschlacht und das Ende der Alten Welt*. Berlin.

Plischnack, Alfred. 2013. "'Sie sind alle verrückt und gehören ins Narrenhaus': Österreich und seine Alliierten im Kampf gegen Napoleon 1812 / 1814." In Bauer, *Blutige Romantik*, 184–191.

Plotho, Carl v. 1817. *Der Krieg in Deutschland und Frankreich in den Jahren 1813 und 1814*, Part 3. Berlin.

Poole, Steve. 2000. *The Politics of Regicide in England, 1760–1850: Troublesome Subjects*. Manchester.

Presser, Jacques. 1990. *Napoleon: Das Leben und die Legende*. Zurich.

Price, Munro. 2014. *Napoleon: The End of Glory*. Oxford.

Pyta, Wolfram, ed. 2009. *Das europäische Mächtekonzert: Friedens- und Sicherheitspolitik vom Wiener Kongress 1815 bis zum Krimkrieg 1853.* Cologne.

Quarg, Gunter. 1998. "Friedrich Gentz charakterisiert Metternich: Ein biographischer Vergleich aus dem Jahre 1830." *Mitteilungen des Instituts für Österreichische Geschichte* 106: 435–439.

Radvany, Egon. 1971. *Metternich's Projects for Reform in Austria.* The Hague.

Rauchensteiner, Manfred. 2014. "Clemens Lothar Fürst Metternich: Das Leben eines Geradlinigen." In Just, *Wiener Kongress,* 98–119.

Raumer, Kurt von, and Manfred Botzenhart. 1980. *Deutsche Geschichte im 19. Jahrhundert. Deutschland um 1800: Krise und Neugestaltung: Von 1789 bis 1815.* Wiesbaden.

Rauscher, Peter. 2014. "Staatsbankrott und Machtpolitik: Die österreichischen Finanzen und die Kosten des Wiener Kongresses." In Just, *Wiener Kongress,* 257–267.

Reden-Dohna, Armgard, and Ralph Melville, eds. 1988. *Der Adel an der Schwelle des bürgerlichen Zeitalters: 1780–1860.* Wiesbaden.

Reinhard, Wolfgang. 2007. *Geschichte des modernen Staates.* Munich.

Reinlein, Tanja. 2003. *Der Brief als Medium der Empfindsamkeit: Erschriebene Identitäten und Inszenierungspotentiale.* Würzburg.

Renaud, Theodor. 1908. "Johann Friedrich Simon, ein Strassburger Pädagog und Demagog (1751–1829)." *Zeitschrift für die Geschichte des Oberrheins* 62: 449–500.

Rieck, Eckhard. 2015. *Friedrich Koenig und die Erfindung der Schnellpresse: Wege eines Pioniers der modernen Unternehmensgeschichte.* Munich.

Rijn, Maaike van, and Matthias Ohm, eds. 2013. *Im Glanz der Zaren: Die Romanows, Württemberg und Europa.* Stuttgart.

Rill, Robert, and Ulrich E. Zellenberg, eds. 1999. *Konservatismus in Österreich: Strömungen, Ideen, Personen und Vereinigungen von den Anfängen bis heute.* Graz.

Riotte, Torsten. 2005. *Hannover in der britischen Politik (1792–1815): Dynastische Verbindung als Element außenpolitischer Entscheidungsprozesse.* Münster.

Ritzen, Renatus. 1927. *Der junge Sebastian Brunner in seinem Verhältnis zu Jean Paul, Anton Günther und Fürst Metternich.* Aichach.

Rodekamp, Volker, ed. 2013. *Helden nach Maß. 200 Jahre Völkerschlacht: Katalog.* Leipzig.

Rödel, Volker, ed. 1991. *Die Französische Revolution und die Oberrheinlande (1789–1798).* Oberrheinische Studien, vol. 9. Sigmaringen.

Rohl, Eva-Renate. 1967. *Metternich und England: Studien zum Urteil des Staatskanzlers über eine konstitutionelle Monarchie.* Diss. (typescript), Vienna.

Rosenstrauch, Hazel. 2014. *Congress mit Damen: Europa zu Gast in Wien, 1814/1815.* Vienna.

———. 2009. *Wahlverwandt und ebenbürtig: Caroline und Wilhelm von Humboldt.* Frankfurt a. M.

Rumpler, Helmut. 2013. *Der Franziszeische Kataster im Kronland Kärnten (1823–1844).* Klagenfurt.

———. 1997. *Österreichische Geschichte, 1804–1914: Eine Chance für Mitteleuropa: Bürgerliche Emanzipation und Staatsverfall in der Habsburgermonarchie.* Vienna.

————, and Peter Urbanitsch, eds. 1973–2018. *Die Habsburgermonarchie, 1848–1918.* 12 vols. Vienna. (Especially: vol. 7, parts 1–2: *Verfassung;* vol. 8, parts 1–2: *Öffentlichkeit;* vol. 9, parts 1–2: *Soziale Strukturen.*)

Rürup, Reinhard. 1984. *Deutschland im 19. Jahrhundert: 1815–1871.* Göttingen.

Sadek, Martin. 1968. *Metternichs publizistische und pressepolitische Betätigung im Exil (1848–1852).* Diss. (typescript), Vienna.

Sandeman, G[eorge] A[melius] C[rawshay]. 1911. *Metternich.* London.

Sapper, Theodor. 1973. *Metternich und das System aus anglo-amerikanischer Sicht.* Diss. (typescript), Vienna.

Sassen, Saskia. 2006. *Territory, Authority, Rights: From Medieval to Global Assemblages.* Princeton, NJ.

Savoy, Bénédicte, ed. 2011. *Napoleon und Europa: Traum und Trauma.* Munich.

Schaeffer, Franz B. 1933. *Metternich.* Monographien zur Weltgeschichte 35. Bielefeld.

Schallaburg Kulturbetriebsges. m.b.H. 2009. *Napoleon: Feldherr, Kaiser und Genie.* Schallaburg.

Schindling, Anton, and Walter Ziegler, eds. 1990. *Die Kaiser der Neuzeit, 1519–1918: Heiliges Römisches Reich, Österreich, Deutschland.* Munich.

Schininà, Giovanni. 2011. *La rivoluzione siciliana del 1848 nei documenti diplomatici austriaci.* Biblioteca siciliana vol. 8. Catania.

————. 2017. *Visioni asburgiche del Mediterraneo: La Sicilia nell'equilibrio metternichiano (1812–1824).* Rome.

Schlitter, Hanns. 1920. *Aus Österreichs Vormärz. I. Galizien and Krakau, II: Böhmen, III. Ungarn, IV: Niederösterreich.* Zurich.

Schmidt, Georg. 2009. *Wandel durch Vernunft: Deutsche Geschichte im 18. Jahrhundert.* Munich.

Schmidt-Brentano, Antonio. 1977. "Österreichs Weg zur Seemacht: Die Marinepolitik Österreichs in der Ära Erzherzog Ferdinand Maximilian (1854–1864)." *Mitteilungen des Österreichischen Staatsarchivs* 30: 119–152.

Schmidt-Weissenfels, Eduard. 1859–1860. *Fürst Metternich: Geschichte seines Lebens und seiner Zeit.* 2 vols. Prague.

Schneider, Günter. 2006. *1794: Die Franzosen auf dem Weg zum Rhein.* Aachen.

Scholz, Natalie. 2006. *Die imaginierte Restauration: Repräsentationen der Monarchie im Frankreich Ludwigs XVIII.* Darmstadt.

Schönpflug, Daniel. 2010. *Luise von Preußen: Königin der Herzen.* Munich.

————. 2002. *Der Weg in die Terreur: Radikalisierung und Konflikte im Straßburger Jakobinerclub (1790–1795).* Munich.

Schraut, Sylvia. 2005. *Das Haus Schönborn: Eine Familienbiographie: Katholischer Reichsadel, 1640–1840.* Paderborn.

Schremmer, Bernd. 1990. *Metternich: Kavalier & Kanzler.* Halle.

Schroeder, Paul W. 1962. *Metternich's Diplomacy at Its Zenith, 1820–1823.* Austin, TX.

————. 1994. *The Transformation of European Politics, 1763–1848*. Oxford.

Schüler, Isabella. 2016. *Franz Anton Graf von Kolowrat-Liebsteinsky (1778–1861): Der Prager Oberstburggraf und Wiener Staats- und Konferenzminister*. Munich.

Schulz, Gerhard. 1983, 2000. *Die deutsche Literatur zwischen Französischer Revolution und Restauration*. Vol. 1: 1789–1806 (1983); vol. 2: 1806–1830 (2000). De Boor / Newald, Geschichte der deutschen Literatur, vol. 7, parts 1–2. Munich.

Schulz, Matthias. 2009. *Normen und Praxis: Das Europäische Konzert der Großmächte als Sicherheitsrat, 1815–1860*. Munich.

Schulze, Hagen. 1994. *Staat und Nation in der europäischen Geschichte*. Munich.

Schumacher, Annemarie, ed. 1973. *Clemens Fürst von Metternich und seine Zeit: Aus den Beständen der Stadtbibliothek Koblenz*. Veröffentlichungen der Stadtbibliothek Koblenz, no. 10. Koblenz.

Schütz, Friedrich Wilhelm von, and Carl Gustav von Schulz. 1829. *Geschichte der Kriege in Europa seit dem Jahre 1792*. Part 3. Leipzig.

Schwarz, Henry F., ed. 1962. *Metternich the "Coachman of Europe": Statesman or Evil Genius?* Lexington, MA.

Schwerin, Claudius v. 1912. *Deutsche Rechtsgeschichte*. Leipzig.

Scoppola, Franceso, ed. 2007. *Il Palazzo d'Inverno di Villa Metternich a Vienna: Uno Scrigno Crisoelefantino*. Rome.

Šedivý, Miroslav. 2018. *The Decline of the Congress System: Metternich, Italy and European Diplomacy*. London.

————. 2008. "Metternich and the French Expedition to Algeria (1830)." *Archiv orientální* 76: 15–37.

————. 2013. *Metternich, the Great Powers and the Eastern Question*. Pilsen.

Ségur-Cabanac, Viktor Graf. 1912. *Kaiser Ferdinand als Regent und Mensch (Der Vormärz)*. Vienna.

Seibt, Gustav. 2008. *Goethe und Napoleon: Eine historische Begegnung*. Munich.

Sellin, Volker. 2001. *Die geraubte Revolution: Der Sturz Napoleons und die Restauration in Europa*. Göttingen.

Seward, Desmond. 1971. *Metternich: The First European*. New York.

Sheehan, James. 1988. *German History: 1770–1866*. Oxford.

————. 2008. *Where Have All the Soldiers Gone? The Transformation of Modern Europe*. Boston.

Sieben, Anton. 1924. *Die Stellung Österreichs zu den braunschweigisch-hannoverschen Angelegenheiten, 1822–1830*. Diss. (typescript), Vienna.

Siemann, Wolfram. 1994. "Die deutsche Revolution von 1848: Einheit der Nation und Zwietracht der Nationalitäten." In Dann, *Die deutsche Nation*, 24–34.

————. 1995. "*Deutschlands Ruhe, Sicherheit und Ordnung*": Die Anfänge der politischen Polizei, 1806–1871. Tübingen.

————. 1998. *The German Revolution of 1848–49*. London.

———. 1990. *Gesellschaft im Aufbruch: Deutschland, 1849–1871.* Frankfurt a. M.

———. 2000. "Immanuel Kant: 'Aus so krummem Holz, als woraus der Mensch gemacht ist, kann nichts ganz Gerades gezimmert werden.'" In *Ein solches Jahrhundert vergißt sich nicht mehr,* 240–244. Munich.

———. 2011. *Metternich's Britain.* London.

———. 2010. *Metternich: Staatsmann zwischen Restauration und Moderne.* Munich.

———. 1995. *Vom Staatenbund zum Nationalstaat: Deutschland, 1806–1871.* Munich.

———. 2007. "Zensur im Übergang zur Moderne: Die Bedeutung des 'langen 19. Jahrhunderts.'" In Haefs, *Zensur,* 357–388.

Simon, Christian, ed. *Basler Frieden, 1795: Revolution und Krieg in Europa.* Basel.

Sked, Alan. 2008. *Metternich and Austria: An Evaluation.* Basingstoke.

———. 2011. *Radetzky: Imperial Victor and Military Genius.* London.

Smith, E. A. 1999. *George IV.* New Haven, CT.

Späth, Jens. 2012. *Revolution in Europa, 1820–23: Verfassung und Verfassungskultur in den Königreichen Spanien, beider Sizilien und Sardinien-Piemont.* Cologne.

Srbik, Heinrich von. 1944. "Vom alten Metternich." *Archiv für österreichische Geschichte* 117: 1–35.

———. 1925. *Die Bedeutung der Naturwissenschaften für die Weltanschauung Metternichs.* Vienna.

———. 1950/1951. *Geist und Geschichte: Vom deutschen Humanismus bis zur Gegenwart.* 2 vols. Munich.

———. 1925. *Metternich: Der Staatsmann und der Mensch.* 2 vols. Munich. (Vols. 1 and 2 republished Munich 1956.) Vol. 3: *Quellenveröffentlichungen und Literatur: Eine Auswahlübersicht von 1925–1952,* Munich 1954.

Staab, Josef, Hans Reinhard Seeliger, and Wolfgang Schleicher, eds. 2001. *Schloss Johannisberg: Neun Jahrhunderte Weinkultur am Rhein.* Mainz.

Stahl, Andrea. 2013. *Metternich und Wellington: Eine Beziehungsgeschichte.* Munich.

Stauber, Reinhard. 2014. *Der Wiener Kongress.* Vienna.

———, Florian Kerschbaumer, and Marion Koschier, eds. 2014. *Mächtepolitik und Friedenssicherung: Zur politischen Kultur Europas im Zeichen des Wiener Kongresses.* Berlin.

Stern, Alfred. 1886. "L'idée d'une représentation centrale de l'Autriche." *Revue historique* 31: 1–14.

Stollberg-Rilinger, Barbara. 2006. *Das Heilige Römische Reich Deutscher Nation: Vom Ende des Mittelalters bis 1806.* Munich.

———. 2008. *Des Kaisers alte Kleider: Verfassungsgeschichte und Symbolsprache des Alten Reiches.* Munich.

Strobl von Ravelsberg, Ferdinand. 1906–1907. *Metternich und seine Zeit, 1773–1859.* 2 vols. Vienna.

Struck, Wolf-Heino. 1977. *Johannisberg im Rheingau: Eine Kloster-, Dorf-, Schloß- und Weinchronik.* Frankfurt a. M.

Sutermeister, Werner. 1895. *Metternich und die Schweiz.* Bern.

Talmon, J[acob] L. 1952. *The Origins of Totalitarian Democracy*. London.

Tausig, Paul. 1912. *Die Beziehungen des Staatskanzlers Metternich zu Baden*. [no place].

Taylor, Alan John Percivale. 1934. *The Italian Problem in European Diplomacy, 1847–1849*. Manchester.

Telesko, Werner. 2006. *Geschichtsraum Österreich: Die Habsburger und ihre Geschichte in der bildenden Kunst des 19. Jahrhunderts*. Vienna.

Temperley, Harold. 1966. *The Foreign Policy of Canning, 1822–1827: England, the Neo-Holy Alliance, and the New World*. London.

———, and Charles Webster. 1963. "The Congress of Vienna 1814–1815 and the Conference of Paris 1919." In *From Metternich to Hitler: Aspects of British and Foreign History, 1814–1939*, ed. W. N. Medlicott. London.

Ter Meulen, Jacob. 1968. *Der Gedanke der Internationalen Organisation in seiner Entwicklung*. The Hague.

Thamer, Hans-Ulrich. 2013. *Die Völkerschlacht bei Leipzig: Europas Kampf gegen Napoleon*. Munich.

Tischler, Ulrike. 2000. *Die habsburgische Politik gegenüber den Serben und Montenegrinern, 1791–1822: Förderung oder Vereinnahmung?* Munich.

Toussaint du Wast, Nicole. 1985. *Laure Junot, duchesse d'Abrantès*. Paris.

Treitschke, Heinrich von. 1927–1928. *Deutsche Geschichte im 19. Jahrhundert*. 5 vols. Leipzig. Berlin 1879–1894.

———. 1916. *Treitschke's History of Germany in the Nineteenth Century*. Vols. 1 and 2. New York.

Tritsch, Walther. 1934. *Metternich: Glanz und Versagen*. Berlin.

———. 1952. *Metternich und sein Monarch: Biographie eines seltsamen Doppelgestirns*. Darmstadt.

Tulard, Jean. 1984. *Napoleon: The Myth of the Saviour*. London.

———. 1978. *Napoleon oder der Mythos des Retters*. Tübingen.

Ullmann, Hans-Peter. 2005. *Der deutsche Steuerstaat: Geschichte der öffentlichen Finanzen vom 18. Jhd. bis heute*. Munich.

———. 2009. *Staat und Schulden: Öffentliche Finanzen in Deutschland seit dem 18. Jahrhundert*. Göttingen.

Ullrich, Volker. 2004. *Napoleon: Eine Biographie*. Hamburg.

Vallotton, Henry. 1965. *Metternich*. Paris.

Vellusig, Robert. 2000. *Schriftliche Gespräche: Briefkultur im 18. Jahrhundert*. Vienna.

Veltzé, Alois. 1909. "Napoleon und Erzherzog Karl 1809." *Österreichische Rundschau* 19: 215–224.

Venohr, Wolfgang. 1998. *Napoleon in Deutschland: Zwischen Imperialismus und Nationalismus. 1800–1813*. Munich.

Vick, Brian E. 2014. *The Congress of Vienna: Power and Politics after Napoleon*. Cambridge, MA.

———. 2014. "Der Kongress tanzt und arbeitet trotzdem. Festkultur und Kabinettspolitik." In Just, *Wiener Kongress*, 268–285.

Vidal, Florence. 2006. *Caroline Bonaparte: Soeur de Napoléon Ier*. Paris.

Vocelka, Karl. *Österreichische Geschichte, 1699–1815: Glanz und Untergang der höfischen Welt: Repräsentation, Reform und Reaktion im habsburgischen Vielvölkerstaat*. Vienna.

Vogt, Nicolaus. 1810. *Die deutsche Nation und ihre Schicksale*. Frankfurt a. M.

———. 1808. *Historische Darstellung des europäischen Völkerbundes. 1: Theil*. Frankfurt a. M.

———. 1787. *Ueber die Europäische Republik. 1: Politisches Sistem [sic]*. Frankfurt a. M.

Volkov, Shulamit. 2014. "Bitten und Streiten: Die Emanzipation der Juden auf dem Wiener Kongress." In Just, *Wiener Kongress*, 236–253.

Wachalla, J. W. 1872. *Der österreichische Reichskanzler [sic] Clemens Lothar Fürst v. Metternich: Historisch-politische Studie*. Vienna.

Wagner, Michael. 1994. *England und die Französische Gegenrevolution, 1789–1802*. Munich.

Webster, Charles. (1919) 1963. *The Congress of Vienna, 1814–1815*. London.

———. 1925. *The Foreign Policy of Castlereagh*. London. (31st ed. 1958–1963).

———. 1951. *The Foreign Policy of Palmerston*. 2 vols. London.

Wehler, Hans-Ulrich. 1987–2008. *Deutsche Gesellschaftsgeschichte*. 5 vols. Munich.

———. 2001. *Nationalismus: Geschichte, Formen, Folgen*. Munich.

Weichlein, Siegfried. 2006. "Cosmopolitanism, Patriotism, Nationalism." In Blanning, *Unity and Diversity*, 77–99.

Weikl, Katharina. 2006. *Krise ohne Alternative? Das Ende des Alten Reiches 1806 in der Wahrnehmung der süddeutschen Reichsfürsten*. Berlin.

Weis, Eberhard. 1982. *Der Durchbruch des Bürgertums, 1776–1847*. Frankfurt a. M.

———. (1971) 2005. *Montgelas*. 2 vols. Munich.

Weiß, Dieter J. 1999. "Die Reaktion auf Aufklärung und Französische Revolution." In Rill, *Konservatismus*, 11–34.

Weissensteiner, Friedrich. 2002. "Liebhaber von staatsmännischer Weltklasse: Clemens Wenzel Lothar Fürst Metternich." In Weissensteiner, *Liebe in fremden Betten: Große Persönlichkeiten und ihre Affären*, 139–175. Vienna.

Wendland, Wilhelm. 1901. *Versuche einer allgemeinen Volksbewaffnung in Süddeutschland während der Jahre 1791 bis 1794*. Berlin.

White, George W. 2000. *Nationalism and Territory: Constructing Group Identity in Southeastern Europe*. New York.

Widmann, Ernst. 1912. *Die religiösen Anschauungen des Fürsten Metternich*. Darmstadt.

Wilflinger, Gerhard. 2004. "Der aufgeklärte Reaktionär: Metternichs europäische Friedensordnung." In Claus Bussmann and Friedrich A. Uehlein, eds., *Wendepunkte: Interdisziplinäre Arbeiten zur Kulturgeschichte*, 249–268. Würzburg.

Willms, Johannes. 2005. *Napoleon: Eine Biographie*. Munich.

———. 2011. *Talleyrand: Virtuose der Macht, 1754–1838*. Munich.

Wimmer, Josef. 1910. *Beiträge und Bilder zur Geschichte Metternichs und seiner Zeit: Aus den Tagebüchern des Grafen Prokesch von Osten, 1830–1834. 14. Jahresbericht des k.k. Staats-Realgymnasiums in Gmunden*. Gmunden.

Winkelhofer, Martina. 2009. *Adel verpflichtet: Frauenschicksale in der k.u.k. Monarchie*. Vienna.

Winkler, Heinrich A., ed. 1982. *Nationalismus in der Welt von heute.* Göttingen.

Wittmann, Reinhard. 1982. *Buchmarkt und Lektüre im 18. und 19. Jahrhundert.* Tübingen.

Wolf, Adam. 1875. *Fürstin Eleonore Liechtenstein, 1745–1812: Nach Briefen und Memoiren ihrer Zeit.* Vienna.

Zamoyski, Adam. 2014. *Phantom Terror: The Threat of Revolution and the Repression of Liberty, 1789–1848.* London.

———. 2004. *1812: Napoleon's Fatal March on Moscow.* London.

———. 2007. *Rites of Peace: The Fall of Napoleon and the Congress of Vienna.* London.

Zedinger, Renate. 2000. *Die Verwaltung der Österreichischen Niederlande in Wien (1714–1795): Studien zu den Zentralisierungstendenzen des Wiener Hofes im Staatswerdungsprozess der Habsburgermonarchie.* Vienna.

Zeinar, Hubert. 2006. *Geschichte des österreichischen Generalstabes.* Vienna.

Zeißberg, Heinrich Ritter von. 1893–1894. *Belgien unter der Generalstatthalterschaft Erzherzog Carls.* 3 vols. Vienna.

———. 1891. *Zwei Jahre belgischer Geschichte.* 2 Parts. Vienna.

Ziegler, Walter. 1990. "Franz I. von Österreich, 1806–1835." In Schindling, *Kaiser der Neuzeit,* 309–328.

———. 1990. "Franz II, 1792–1806." In Schindling, *Kaiser der Neuzeit,* 290–306.

———. 1993. "Kaiser Franz II. (I.): Person und Wirkung." In *Heiliges Römisches Reich und moderne Staatlichkeit,* ed. Wilhelm Brauneder, 9–28. Frankfurt a. M.

Zimmermann, Harro. 2012. *Friedrich Gentz: Die Erfindung der Realpolitik.* Paderborn.

Zorgbibe, Charles. 2009. *Metternich: Le séducteur diplomate.* Paris.

———. 2012. *Talleyrand et l'invention de la diplomatie française.* Paris.

ACKNOWLEDGMENTS

"A biography is something for old age"—that is what historians are told when they discuss plans for future work. Having completed this book, I can confirm that this is good advice. In earlier years I would not have been able to write it. Experience is an invaluable asset that, indeed, only the maturity of years offers in abundance. *Erfahrung* [experience] is a nice word; it contains the image of traveling: *er-fahren;* and *fahren,* traveling, can take you through landscapes, through different times, and also into the life of another person. This is why I chose to frame this biography as a journey accompanied by a travel guide.

The path from the sources to the work requires endless debate, communication, and encouragement, because, although it contains happy discoveries, it is also strewn with doubts—doubts about whether the biographer attempting to convey the intellectual universe of his protagonist to his readers can be as impartial and just as our protagonist hoped "posterity" would be to him. The whole creative process is therefore supported by a host of people without whom the author could not have completed his work. This is why I should like to use this postscript to thank those who were involved in this project. That is easier said than done, though, because at this point I suddenly confront a network without fixed edges and with several nodal points. During my studies, and then in the course of working within the world of academia, different master weavers have contributed to this network. Anyone with whom I have had exchanges on the topics of revolution, the police, censorship, the German question, the Habsburgs and Germany, the period between the

French Revolution and the revolution of 1848–1849, anyone who, in university courses I taught, at conferences, or on excursions, talked with me about industrialization, rural societies, and the rise of the bourgeoisie, about "cosmopolitanism and the nation state," helped build that network and thus helped me to write this book, and therefore must be mentioned here, even if I cannot name every single one of these weavers individually. But the network has, as it were, a few load-bearing fibers without which it would not have kept its shape. And here some names must be mentioned.

The "opus magnum" program of the Thyssen Foundation and the Volkswagen Foundation, together with the German Research Foundation, allowed me to spend three terms exclusively on research by financing a deputy professorship and providing generous support in the form of equipment that enabled me to scan the archival sources. I had the unique opportunity of working for a whole year at the National Archive in Prague, sifting through the extensive unpublished papers of Prince Metternich and his family, something that had never been done before in such depth. The extraordinary support I received, whenever it was needed, at the archive—and the ideal working conditions of its reading room—make it a genuine pleasure to express my thanks to that institution and to all the staff there. I only regret that I cannot do it in the historically appropriate form: If it were up to me, I would award Jan Kahuda, who was looking after me, the highest Order of Civil Merit of the Habsburg monarchy, the Grand Cross of the Order of St. Stephen.

My thanks to the Haus-, Hof- und Staatsarchiv in Vienna are of the same magnitude, and I mention it second only for chronological reasons. Its director, Thomas Just, provided me with excellent working conditions, and were it not for his generosity in allowing me to make copies of the material, I could not have pursued my questions about Metternich's wide-ranging activities. Many members of the archival staff lent a helping hand moving boxes and bundles of papers. One of them, who was sitting in the office next to me, I must thank especially. Joachim Tepperberg went well above the call of duty in coming to my aid in my desperate search for the lost volumes of Princess Melanie von Metternich's diaries (covering some ten years), leading me through each and every floor of the archive.

An indispensable nodal point in the network was my German publisher, C. H. Beck. The support and encouragement I received from the owner, Wolfgang Beck, and the chief editor, Detlef Felken, were as much as any author could have hoped for. I am glad that the book was published by them.

On November 11, 2011, I delivered the annual lecture at the German Historical Institute in London on the topic "Metternich's Britain." It was a stroke of luck that the event was attended by Ian Malcolm, the senior executive editor at large (Europe) of Harvard University Press, who was intrigued enough to inquire about the biography after the talk. At that point it was still in the making, and during the many years in which I worked on it, I always dreamed of being able to present the book to the English-speaking world as well. I am delighted that this dream has now come true, and I would like to thank Ian Malcolm and Harvard University Press for making this possible.

I would also like to thank Geisteswissenschaften International—without their generous funding of the translation, it would not have been possible to publish this translation. Thank you also, again, to C. H. Beck, my German publisher, and its chief editor, Detlef Felken, who initiated the application to Geisteswissenschaften International.

Translation is, of course, more than the mere substitution of the words of one language for the words of another; it instead involves immersing oneself in two different worlds. My dialogue with Daniel Steuer, carried out over many months in comment boxes in the margins of the draft manuscript, were instructive, entertaining, and rich enough to make up a book in themselves. He involved me in the process of translation, and the points he raised led to many clarifications. As a result, readers now hold a better book in their hands. I am grateful that it was translated by such a talented and witty traveler between the worlds.

I have already mentioned the innumerable conversations that the creative process involves, conversations without which this book would not have come about in its present form. My main partner in this process was Anita, my wife. I cannot find better words to express how energetically she participated in this project than those of Marie von Clausewitz (born Countess Brühl), who played an equally instrumental role in the writing of her husband's book *On War*. In her preface to the posthumous publication of that work in 1832, one year after her husband's death, she wrote:

> Only as a sympathetic companion do I want to help its entry into the world. I may claim this role since I was granted a similar function in the creation and development of the work. Those who knew of our happy marriage and knew that we shared *everything,* not only joy and pain but also every occupation, every concern of daily life, will realize that a task of this kind could not occupy my beloved husband without at the same time becoming thoroughly familiar to me. For the same reason no one can testify as well as I do to the energy and love with which he dedicated himself to the task, the hopes he associated with it, and the manner and time of its creation.[1]

If someone were to ask me whether it was not the case that I succumbed to the temptations inherent in the writing of a biography by becoming too uncritical toward Metternich, I would point to my own "Countess Brühl." She also read every line, and she was an incorruptible critic, pointing out the sensitivity of the issue of Metternich's simultaneous relationships with multiple women, and pressing the question of whether someone could really justifiably claim supreme rights and privileges solely on the basis of his birth. Her excellent historical knowledge has left behind traces of social criticism in the work, as she reminded me, in ever changing variations, of the sentiment expressed in the old saying: "When Adam delved and Eve span, who was then the gentleman?"

ILLUSTRATION CREDITS

189: HHStA Wien Prussia, correspondence Krt. 85, Fol. 108

248: NA Prague A. C. 12 Krt. 1, 6

277: Presentation by Metternich, dated January 1, 1810, HHStA Wien StK Vorträge Krt 184, Fol. 2

287: NA Prague RAM Krt. 111, 4339

288: © bpk / Hermann Bunsch

294: akg-images / VISIOARS

296: NA Prague A. C. 8 Krt. 6, 36

316: © Stadtmuseum Pirna

343: © akg-images

349: NA Prague A. C. 8 Krt. 1, 1

350: NA Prague A. C. 8 Krt. 1, 1

365: Letter, dated October 10, 1813, sent by Metternich from Komotau to Eleonore, NA Prague A. C. 12 Krt 5, 33

366: HHStA Wien StK Vorträge Krt. 194, Fol. 30

398: NA Prague RAM Krt 117, 4495

403: Presentation by Metternich, dated May 27, 1814, HHStA Wien StK Vorträge Krt. 195, Fol. 140 (verso)

454: NA Prague A. C. 8 Krt. 7, 41

455: NA Prague A. C. 8 Krt. 7, 41

457: Königswart Castle

459: Königswart Castle

461: NA Prague RAM A. C. 9 Krt. 2, 102

465: Königswart Castle, Signatur Ky 78

468: Denkmalinstitut Pilsen, ed.: Schloss Kynžvart. Nymburk 2005

493: Letter, dated May 6, 1823, from Metternich to Dorothea von Lieven, RAM A. C. 6, C 19, 10, Nr. 138–150

499: ÖNB Österreichische Nationalbibliothek Wien (National Library of Austria, Vienna), 260.150-E. Fid.

500: ÖNB Österreichische Nationalbibliothek Wien (National Library of Austria, Vienna), 260.150-E. Fid.

502: © privately owned

513: Georg Kugler: Staatskanzler Metternich und seine Gäste. Graz u. a. 1991

514: © privately owned Siemann

515: NA Prague RAM Krt. 132, 5024 u. 5025

516: © privately owned Siemann

534: HHStA Wien StK Vorträge Krt. 209, Fol. 81

538: HHStA Wien, StK Vorträge, Krt. 205, Fol. 55

572: HHStA Wien StK Vorträge Krt. 215, Fol. 135

576: Levin Karl von Hohnhorst: Vollstaendige Uebersicht der gegen Carl Ludwig Sand wegen Meuchelmordes veruebt an dem k. russischen Staatsrath v. Kotzebue gefuehrten Untersuchung. Stuttgart 1820, vol. 1, frontispiece

589: NA Prague A. C. 9 Krt. 1, 53

601: NA Prague RAM Krt. 140, 5226

642: StA Pilsen Vs-Plasy, Krt. 125, 1833

643: StA Pilsen, Vs-Plasy, Krt. 125, 1834

646: Archive Johannisberg Castle

649: StA Pilsen, Vs-Plasy, Krt. 149

651: Anton Wiehl: General-Karte von der hochfürstlich von Metternich'schen Herrschaft Plaß (General map of the princely estate of the Metternich lordship), Archive Johannisberg Castle

653: StA Pilsen, Vs Plasy, Krt. 149

654: © privately owned Siemann

655: NA Prague RAM Krt. 143, 5357

662: HHStA Wien StK Acta Secreta Krt. 4, Fol. 129–132

669: HHStA Wien Informationsbüro StK Mainzer Zentral-Polizei (Central Police Mainz (intelligence agency), Krt. 16

670: HHStA Wien Informationsbüro StK Mainzer Zentral-Polizei (Central Police Mainz (intelligence agency), Krt. 20

684: Karl Vocelka, Österreichische Geschichte 1699–1815. Vienna 200, p. 359

694: HHStA Wien, Archive of the Imperial House, family correspondence, K 30, Teil 1

695: HHStA Wien, Archive of the Imperial House, family correspondence, K 30, Teil 1

698: NA Prague, Diary of Melanie von Metternich, volume 1851, October 6th, 1851

721: NA Prague A. C. 9 Krt. 2, 82

725: HHStA Wien Minister-Kolowrat-files Krt. 103, Zl. 2230

729: NA Prague, Diary of Princess Melanie v. Metternich, volume 1848

743: ÖNB Österreichische Nationalbibliothek Wien (National library of Austria, Vienna), Pf 159511B1

INDEX